Official
NBA GUIDE

1981-82 EDITION

Editor/NBA Guide
MATT WINICK

Contributing Editor
MIKE DOUCHANT

President-Chief Executive Officer
RICHARD WATERS

Editor
DICK KAEGEL

Director of Books and Periodicals
RON SMITH

NBA Statistics by Elias Sports Bureau

Published by

The Sporting News

1212 North Lindbergh Boulevard
P.O. Box 56 — St. Louis, Mo. 63166

Copyright © 1981
The Sporting News Publishing Company
a Times Mirror company

IMPORTANT NOTICE

The NBA Guide is protected by copyright. All information, in the form presented here, except playing statistics, was compiled by the publishers and proof is available.

Information from the NBA Guide must not be used elsewhere without special permission, and then only with full credit to the NBA Guide, published by THE SPORTING NEWS, St. Louis, Missouri.

ISBN 0-89204-079-3 ISSN 0071-7258

TABLE OF CONTENTS

1981-82 Season ... 3
- NBA Office Directory ... 4-5
- Team Directories, Scores ('80-81), Schedules ... 6-51
- Day-by-Day Schedule ... 52-61
- Referees, Divisional Alignment ... 61
- Team Rosters ... 62-70
- College Draft Review/List ... 71-79

1980-81 Season ... 81
- Regular-Season Review ... 83-94
- Championship Series Review, Box Scores ... 95-108
- Playoff Results ... 109
- Regular-Season Statistics, Team/Player ... 110-120
- Top Performances ... 121-123
- Playoff Statistics, Team/Player ... 124-128

All-Time and Career Records ... 129
- NBA Championship Teams ... 130
- Year-by-Year Statistical Leaders ... 130-132
- All-Time Statistical Leaders ... 133
- Top Career Scorers ... 134
- All-Time Top Performances ... 135-137
- Single-Game, Miscellaneous Records ... 138-143
- Post-Season Award Winners ... 144-145
- All-Rookie, All-Defensive, All-Star Teams ... 145-152
- Career Highs of Active Players ... 153-162
- Championship Series Records, Team/Player ... 163-193
- Top Scorers, Top Performances in Playoffs ... 194-196
- All-Time Playoff Leaders ... 197
- All-Time Records of NBA Teams ... 198-203
- Team Winning, Losing Streaks ... 203
- Enshrined Hall of Famers ... 204-205
- Wilt Chamberlain's 100-Point Game ... 206
- Continental Basketball Association ... 207
- ABA All-Star Teams, Award Winners ... 208-210
- Season-by-Season Statistics, 1946-80 ... 211-395
- Pepsi-Cola/NBA Hotshot Program ... 396

Official Rules for 1981-82 Season ... 397

◆◆◆◆◆◆◆◆

On the Cover: Boston's Cedric Maxwell set a fast pace for the Celtics in the 1981 Championship Series, lifting Boston past the upstart Houston Rockets while earning series MVP honors.

1981-82 INFORMATION

Including

NBA Office Directory

Team Directories

Team Schedules/1980-81 Results

Day-by-Day NBA Schedule

Team Rosters

NBA Draft Review/List

National Basketball Association

Founded June 6, 1946 as Basketball Association of America

OFFICE: Olympic Tower, 645 Fifth Avenue, New York, N. Y. 10022
TELEPHONE: (Area Code 212) 826-7000

COMMISSIONER: Lawrence F. O'Brien
DEPUTY COMMISSIONER: Simon P. Gourdine
EXECUTIVE VICE-PRESIDENT,
BUSINESS AND LEGAL AFFAIRS: David J. Stern
GENERAL COUNSEL: Russell T. Granik
VICE-PRESIDENT, OPERATIONS: Joseph A. Axelson
DIRECTOR OF SECURITY: John W. Joyce
CONTROLLER: Kenneth A. Bailey
ASSISTANT GENERAL COUNSEL: Gary B. Bettman
OPERATIONS COORDINATOR: Matt Winick
DIRECTOR OF INFORMATION: Alex Sachare
EXECUTIVE ASSISTANT TO THE COMMISSIONER: Janice E. Akerhielm
DIRECTOR OF BROADCASTING: Richard Dorfman
VICE-PRESIDENT OF MARKETING: Michael G. Suscavage
VICE-PRESIDENT OF TEAM SERVICES: Bob King
DIRECTOR OF MERCHANDISING: Bill Marshall
REFEREE DEVELOPMENT ADMINISTRATOR: Cecil K. Watkins
CHIEF OF OFFICIATING STAFF: Darell Garretson
ASSISTANT TO THE CONTROLLER: Connie Maroselli
PUBLIC RELATIONS ASSISTANT: Terry Lyons
STAFF: Gail Davey, Regina McDonald, Nat Broudy, Edythe Verdonck,
Nancy Progel, Madie Rouse, Rhea Williams, Noreen Reilly,
Liz Kupec, Barbara Ward, Susan Stein, Judy Gamm,
Marge Kellerman, Lizza Parrilla.

Simon P. Gourdine

David J. Stern

Russell T. Granik

NBA OFFICE

Joe Axelson

John W. Joyce

Kenneth A. Bailey

Gary B. Bettman

Matt Winick

Alex Sachare

Mike Suscavage

Janice E. Akerhielm

Richard Dorfman

Bob King

Bill Marshall

Cecil Watkins

ATLANTA HAWKS

Office: 100 Techwood Dr., N. W., Atlanta, Ga. 30303

Telephone: (Area Code 404) 681-3600

Board of Directors—R. E. (Ted) Turner,
M. B. (Bud) Seretean,
Bruce B. Wilson, J. Michael Gearon, Stan Kasten
President and Governor—J. Michael Gearon
Vice President and General Manager—Stan Kasten
Vice President and Business Manager—Steven Funk
Head Coach—Kevin Loughery
Assistant Coach—Michael Fratello
Assistant Coach—Brendan Suhr
Assistant Coach—Fred Carter
Trainer—Joe O'Toole
Director of Public Relations—Bill Needle
Director of Marketing—Lee Douglas
Director of Sales—Frank Timmerman
Director of Broadcasting—Wayne Long
Controller—Greg Clements
Voice of the Hawks—Skip Caray
Broadcaster—Chet Wright
Executive Assistant—Ann Leatherwood
Marketing Coordinator—Patty Hardiman
Ticket Coordinator—Katharine Herring
Public Relations Secretary—Lu Ann Cline
Accounting Secretary—Annie Rushin
Team/Marketing Secretary—Denise Dickson
Receptionist—Penny Wright
Sales Manager—Randy Smith
Sales—Gerald Alford, Rex Hussmann, Ron Johnson, Don Jones,
Chip Krauth, Dennis Pugh, John Reynolds, Art Ross
Public Relations Intern—Phil Stambaugh
Team Physician—Dr. David Apple
Team Dentist—Dr. Louis Freedman
Home Court—Omni (15,700)
Team Colors—Red, White and Gold
Radio—WSB (750), Skip Caray, Chet Wright
Television—WTBS (Channel 17), Skip Caray, Jim Washington
Game Times—7:35 p.m.
Ticket Prices—$15, $12.50, $10, $7.50, $5

Ted Turner

Stan Kasten

Kevin Loughery

1980-81 RESULTS, 1981-82 SCHEDULE

ATLANTA HAWKS

1980-81 Record (Won 31, Lost 51)

Date	Opponent	Score	Opp
Oct. 11	Chicago	101	93
14	Boston	122	116
17	New York	113	101
18	At Detroit	**125	123
21	Indiana	116	121—
24	At Indiana	97	104—
25	Philadelphia	100	113—
28	Kansas City	119	109
30	At New York	*115	116—
31	At Philadelphia	96	107—
Nov. 1	Milwaukee	93	99—
4	At Washington	98	122—
5	At Boston	87	104—
7	At Chicago	100	103—
8	At New Jersey	111	115—
11	Los Angeles	97	126—
13	At Cleveland	111	114—
15	Washington	88	100—
18	San Antonio	97	93
22	Utah	99	93
25	Portland	112	108
26	At Indiana	89	110—
28	At Milwaukee	*108	113—
29	Detroit	95	98—
Dec. 2	Philadelphia	*112	108
3	At Boston	101	106—
5	At Philadelphia	100	104—
6	Dallas	110	104
9	San Diego	114	87
10	At Detroit	100	92
13	Milwaukee	122	119
16	New Jersey	131	114
18	At Utah	109	97
19	At Seattle	92	95—
20	At Portland	*119	122—
23	Washington	100	83
26	At New Jersey	108	95
27	Boston	107	112—
30	Detroit	96	89
Jan. 2	Indiana	106	109—
3	At New York	95	131—
6	Phoenix	106	113—
8	At Milwaukee	95	98—
9	Cleveland	*107	135—
13	At Denver	132	135—
14	At San Diego	85	106—
16	At Golden State	111	110
18	At Phoenix	86	120—
21	At Los Angeles	106	116—
23	Cleveland	98	106—
24	Chicago	102	104—
27	Washington	104	105—
29	New York	111	114—
Feb. 3	Philadelphia	93	97—
6	At Dallas	100	98
7	At Houston	81	87—
10	At Golden State	116	108
12	At San Antonio	109	110—
13	At Kansas City	106	113—
15	At Philadelphia	98	116—
18	At Indiana	99	96
21	At Cleveland	118	105
22	At Chicago	121	116
24	New York	*117	120—
27	Boston	102	132—
Mar. 1	Seattle	108	102
3	At New York	100	93
5	At Milwaukee	91	107—
6	New Jersey	109	106
7	Houston	114	108
10	At Chicago	116	118—
11	At Detroit	97	100—
13	Denver	119	117
14	Cleveland	*110	112—
17	At Cleveland	107	122—
18	At Boston	108	97
20	At New Jersey	96	108—
22	At Washington	101	121—
24	Detroit	96	91
26	Indiana	107	115—
27	At Chicago	83	108—
29	Milwaukee	*128	132—

1981-82 SCHEDULE

Oct. Sat. 31	Philadelphia
Nov. Tue. 3	At Chicago
Wed. 4	At New Jersey
Fri. 6	At Philadelphia
Tue. 10	Milwaukee
Thu. 12	Washington
Sat. 14	Detroit
Wed. 18	Phoenix
Thu. 19	At New York
Sat. 21	Indiana
Tue. 24	Cleveland
Fri. 27	At Detroit
Sat. 28	Boston
Dec. Tue. 1	Philadelphia
Fri. 4	At Milwaukee
Sat. 5	Seattle
Tue. 8	New Jersey
Wed. 9	At Cleveland
Fri. 11	At Boston
Sat. 12	Boston
Tue. 15	New York
Thu. 17	At Denver
Sat. 19	At Golden State
Sun. 20	At Los Angeles
Tue. 22	At Indiana
Sat. 26	At San Antonio
Tue. 29	At Houston
Wed. 30	San Diego
Jan. Sat. 2	New Jersey
Tue. 5	Cleveland
Fri. 8	At Milwaukee
Sat. 9	New York
Tue. 12	Milwaukee
Wed. 13	At Boston
Fri. 15	At Philadelphia
Sun. 17	At Washington
Tue. 19	Portland
Thu. 21	At New York
Fri. 22	San Antonio
Sat. 23	At Cleveland
Tue. 26	Dallas
Wed. 27	At Detroit
Feb. Tue. 2	Detroit
Wed. 3	At New Jersey
Sat. 6	Cleveland
Tue. 9	Los Angeles
Wed. 10	At Chicago
Fri. 12	At Phoenix
Tue. 16	At San Diego
Wed. 17	At Utah
Fri. 19	At Seattle
Sun. 21	At Portland
Tue. 23	Kansas City
Fri. 26	Chicago
Sun. 28	Golden State
Mar. Wed. 3	Milwaukee
Fri. 5	At Philadelphia
Sat. 6	New Jersey
Tue. 9	Denver
Thu. 11	Utah
Sat. 13	Indiana
Sun. 14	At Washington
Wed. 17	At Boston
Thu. 18	Houston
Sat. 20	At New York
Sun. 21	Detroit
Tue. 23	Washington
Wed. 24	At Kansas City
Fri. 26	At Indiana
Sat. 27	At Dallas
Tue. 30	At Chicago
Apr. Thu. 1	At Milwaukee
Fri. 2	Boston
Sat. 3	Washington
Tue. 6	New York
Wed. 7	At Detroit
Fri. 9	At Philadelphia
Sun. 11	Chicago
Tue. 13	At Cleveland
Thu. 15	At Indiana
Fri. 16	Indiana
Sun. 18	At Washington

BOSTON CELTICS

Office: Boston Garden, North Station, Boston, Mass. 02114

Telephone: (Area Code 617) 523-6050

Chairman of the Board and Chief Executive Officer—
Harry T. Mangurian, Jr.
President and General Manager—Arnold "Red" Auerbach
Vice President, Assistant General Manager,
General Counsel—Jan Volk
Vice President-Finance—Stephen G. Mehallis
Executive Secretary, Office Manager—
Mary A. Faherty
Head Coach—Bill C. Fitch
Assistant Coach—K. C. Jones
Assistant Coach—Jim Rodgers
Team Historian—Howie McHugh
Treasurer and Controller—Herbert R. Green
Marketing Director—Michael J. Cole
Public Relations Director—Tod Rosensweig
Sales Director—Stephen Riley
Ticket Sales—Duane Johnson
Administrative Assistant—Robert Schron
Secretary—Mildred P. Duggan
Secretary—Susan Trodden Gramolini
Secretary—Patricia Chisholm
Bookkeeper—Annette Kaplan
Receptionist—Patricia Joyce
Trainer—Ray Melchiorre
Equipment Manager—Walter Randall
Team Physician—Thomas F. Silva, M.D., F.A.C.S.
Home Court—Boston Garden (15,320)
Team Colors—Green and White
Radio—WRKO (680 AM), Johnny Most
Television—WBZ (Channel 4), Gil Santos and Bob Cousy

Harry Mangurian

Red Auerbach

Bill Fitch

1980-81 RESULTS, 1981-82 SCHEDULE

BOSTON CELTICS

1980-81 Record (Won 62, Lost 20)

Date	Opponent	Pts	Opp
Oct. 10	Cleveland	130	103
Oct. 14	At Atlanta	116	122—
Oct. 16	At Milwaukee	110	103
Oct. 18	At Indiana	99	103—
Oct. 22	At New Jersey	108	104
Oct. 23	New York	*107	109—
Oct. 25	At Washington	103	87
Oct. 29	At Detroit	103	85
Oct. 31	Kansas City	115	110
Nov. 1	At Philadelphia	*113	117—
Nov. 5	Atlanta	104	87
Nov. 7	Milwaukee	101	102—
Nov. 9	Chicago	111	105
Nov. 12	Washington	93	86
Nov. 14	New Jersey	126	102
Nov. 18	At Chicago	113	112
Nov. 19	At Indiana	103	91
Nov. 21	Golden State	108	106
Nov. 22	At Cleveland	98	113—
Nov. 26	Portland	126	101
Nov. 28	New York	120	106
Nov. 30	At Milwaukee	105	107—
Dec. 2	At Detroit	94	85
Dec. 3	Atlanta	106	101
Dec. 5	Dallas	97	87
Dec. 7	Washington	103	113—
Dec. 9	Milwaukee	112	89
Dec. 10	At Washington	101	99
Dec. 12	New Jersey	119	104
Dec. 13	At Chicago	106	95
Dec. 17	Chicago	115	98
Dec. 19	Houston	133	119
Dec. 20	At Cleveland	107	102
Dec. 23	Denver	136	128
Dec. 25	At New York	117	108
Dec. 27	At Atlanta	112	107
Dec. 30	At Phoenix	116	97
Jan. 1	At San Diego	88	85
Jan. 2	At Golden State	106	121—
Jan. 4	At Portland	120	111
Jan. 7	Phoenix	108	90
Jan. 9	At New Jersey	*117	111
Jan. 10	At Chicago	117	115
Jan. 13	At New York	93	89
Jan. 14	Cleveland	120	113
Jan. 16	San Antonio	94	85
Jan. 18	Los Angeles	98	96
Jan. 19	Detroit	92	90
Jan. 21	Utah	117	87
Jan. 23	Indiana	104	103
Jan. 25	Seattle	115	106
Jan. 28	Philadelphia	104	101
Jan. 29	At Chicago	85	108—
Feb. 4	At Philadelphia	104	107—
Feb. 5	At Milwaukee	103	113—
Feb. 6	Indiana	111	98
Feb. 8	San Diego	123	107
Feb. 10	At Seattle	*107	108—
Feb. 11	At Los Angeles	105	91
Feb. 13	At Utah	89	104—
Feb. 15	At Denver	120	118
Feb. 17	At San Antonio	128	116
Feb. 18	At Kansas City	113	114—
Feb. 21	At Detroit	130	119
Feb. 25	Cleveland	124	103
Feb. 27	At Atlanta	132	102
Mar. 1	Philadelphia	114	107
Mar. 3	At Dallas	117	105
Mar. 4	At Houston	108	107
Mar. 6	At Indiana	104	110—
Mar. 8	New York	115	99
Mar. 11	Milwaukee	122	108
Mar. 13	Indiana	94	101—
Mar. 15	New Jersey	133	125
Mar. 17	At Washington	112	91
Mar. 18	At Atlanta	97	108—
Mar. 20	Washington	128	116
Mar. 22	At Philadelphia	94	126—
Mar. 24	At New York	118	116
Mar. 25	At New Jersey	111	105
Mar. 27	Detroit	90	115—
Mar. 29	Philadelphia	98	94

1981-82 SCHEDULE

Oct. Fri. 30	Washington
Sat. 31	At Milwaukee
Nov. Wed. 4	Chicago
Fri. 6	Indiana
Sat. 7	At Detroit
Tue. 10	At Washington
Wed. 11	Kansas City
Fri. 13	New Jersey at Hartford
Sat. 14	At Cleveland
Tue. 17	At Chicago
Wed. 18	Houston
Fri. 20	Milwaukee
Wed. 25	Golden State
Fri. 27	Washington
Sat. 28	At Atlanta
Dec. Tue. 1	At Indiana
Wed. 2	Detroit
Fri. 4	Philadelphia
Sat. 5	At New York
Wed. 9	New Jersey
Fri. 11	Atlanta at Hartford
Sat. 12	At Atlanta
Wed. 16	Dallas
Fri. 18	At Washington
Sat. 19	At Philadelphia
Tue. 22	Cleveland
Sat. 26	At Kansas City
Tue. 29	At Denver
Wed. 30	At Utah
Jan. Sat. 2	At Cleveland
Wed. 6	Chicago
Fri. 8	Philadelphia
Sun. 10	Detroit at Hartford
Mon. 11	At New Jersey
Wed. 13	At Atlanta
Fri. 15	At Milwaukee
Sat. 16	At Detroit
Tue. 19	At New York
Wed. 20	Indiana
Fri. 22	Seattle
Sun. 24	Portland
Wed. 27	New York
Thu. 28	At Cleveland
Feb. Tue. 2	At Indiana
Wed. 3	At Detroit
Fri. 5	Denver
Sun. 7	Los Angeles
Wed. 10	At Phoenix
Fri. 12	At San Diego
Sun. 14	At Los Angeles
Wed. 17	At Golden State
Fri. 19	At Portland
Sun. 21	At Seattle
Wed. 24	Utah
Fri. 26	San Diego
Sun. 28	Milwaukee
Mar. Tue. 2	At Dallas
Thu. 4	At San Antonio
Fri. 5	At Houston
Sun. 7	New York
Wed. 10	Indiana
Fri. 12	At New Jersey
Sun. 14	Phoenix
Tue. 16	At Washington
Wed. 17	Atlanta
Fri. 19	San Antonio
Sun. 21	At Philadelphia
Tue. 23	At Chicago
Wed. 24	Cleveland
Fri. 26	Detroit
Sun. 28	Philadelphia
Wed. 31	Washington
Apr. Fri. 2	At Atlanta
Sun. 4	Chicago
Tue. 6	At Milwaukee
Thu. 8	At New York
Fri. 9	New Jersey
Sun. 11	At Philadelphia
Tue. 13	At Chicago
Wed. 14	Milwaukee
Fri. 16	At New Jersey
Sun. 18	New York

CHICAGO BULLS

Office: 333 N. Michigan Ave., Suite 1325, Chicago, Ill. 60601
Telephone: (Area Code 312) 346-1122
Weekends: (Area Code 312) 346-0886

Directors—Lester Crown, Lamar Hunt, Jonathan Kovler, Philip M. Klutznik, Walter H. Shorenstein, George M. Steinbrenner III, Arthur M. Wirtz
Executive Committee—Philip M. Klutznik, Lester Crown, Arthur M. Wirtz, Jonathan Kovler
Managing Partner—Jonathan Kovler
NBA Governor—William W. Wirtz
General Manager—Rod Thorn
Head Coach—Jerry Sloan
Assistant Coach—Phil Johnson
Assistant Coach/Director of Scouting—Gene Tormohlen
Treasurer/Controller—Irwin Mandel
Director of Marketing/Media Information—Brian McIntyre
Trainer/Traveling Secretary—Mark Pfeil
Team Physician—Dr. Bates Noble
Ticket Manager—Joe O'Neil
Administrative Assistant—Tim Hallam
Accountant—Jan Angell
Executive Secretary—Janice Lichtenstein
Public Relations Secretary—Susan Parkin
Tickets/Receptionist—Linda Dwelle
Chief Statistician—Bob Rosenberg
Team Photographer—Bill Smith
West Coast Representative—Ron Weiss
Home Court—Chicago Stadium (17,374)
Team Colors—Red, White and Black
Game Times 7:30 p.m.
Ticket Prices—$11, $9, $7, $5, $4
Radio—WVON (1390 am), Jim Durham
Television—WGN-TV (Channel 9) John Kerr, Milo Hamilton

Jonathan Kovler

Rod Thorn

Jerry Sloan

CHICAGO BULLS

1980-81 RESULTS, 1981-82 SCHEDULE

1980-81 Record (Won 45, Lost 37)

Date	Opponent	Bulls	Opp
Oct. 11	At Atlanta	93	101–
15	At Indiana	108	97
17	Cleveland	98	79
18	At New Jersey	90	107–
21	At New York	97	105–
24	Washington	104	96
25	At Milwaukee	93	109–
28	Milwaukee	99	106–
29	At Philadelphia	102	115–
31	Indiana	114	121–
Nov. 1	Detroit	122	100
5	At New Jersey	120	105
7	Atlanta	103	100
8	Denver	**126	130–
9	At Boston	105	111–
11	Philadelphia	80	121–
14	At Detroit	99	106–
16	At Milwaukee	114	108
18	Boston	112	113–
21	New York	130	121
22	Washington	114	101
26	At San Antonio	122	125–
28	At Phoenix	101	102–
30	At Los Angeles	122	108
Dec. 2	At Denver	129	124
3	At Seattle	105	113–
5	At Portland	115	116–
9	Phoenix	108	123–
10	At Philadelphia	100	113–
12	Utah	118	98
13	Boston	95	106–
16	At Washington	96	94
17	At Boston	98	115–
19	Milwaukee	129	106
20	Houston	133	109
23	New York	117	114
26	At Cleveland	100	98
27	Detroit	104	97
30	New Jersey	121	110
Jan. 2	At Washington	92	82
3	San Antonio	111	119–
6	San Diego	108	93
9	At Boston	*111	117–
10	Philadelphia	102	117–
13	At Dallas	106	112–
14	At Houston	105	109–
16	Portland	112	113–
17	Cleveland	98	110–
20	Indiana	121	105
22	At Detroit	125	92
23	Dallas	106	98
24	At Atlanta	104	102
27	Golden State	118	101
29	Boston	108	85
Feb. 4	At Cleveland	109	96
6	New York	94	112–
7	Detroit	98	90
8	At Milwaukee	109	128–
10	Kansas City	116	115
11	At New Jersey	*133	135–
14	Seattle	134	117
15	At Indiana	107	113–
17	San Diego	95	128–
18	At Golden State	100	103–
20	At Utah	92	84
22	Atlanta	116	121–
24	Los Angeles	97	107–
27	Washington	112	100
28	At New York	101	97
Mar. 3	New Jersey	128	102
4	At Philadelphia	111	100
8	At Washington	99	103–
10	At Atlanta	118	116
13	At New York	117	127–
15	At Kansas City	97	87
17	Milwaukee	118	106
19	At Cleveland	116	111
20	Philadelphia	120	108
22	At Detroit	109	103
24	Cleveland	121	108
27	Atlanta	108	83
29	At Indiana	101	97

1981-82 SCHEDULE

Oct.	Fri.	30	At Indiana
	Sat.	31	Detroit
Nov.	Tue.	3	Atlanta
	Wed.	4	At Boston
	Fri.	6	San Diego
	Sat.	7	New Jersey
	Mon.	9	At Cleveland
	Tue.	10	Kansas City
	Wed.	11	At Philadelphia
	Sat.	14	At Washington
	Tue.	17	Boston
	Fri.	20	Utah
	Sat.	21	Washington
	Tue.	24	At San Diego
	Fri.	27	At Phoenix
	Sun.	29	At Portland
Dec.	Tue.	1	At Seattle
	Wed.	2	At Golden State
	Fri.	4	At Utah
	Tue.	8	Indiana
	Fri.	11	Houston
	Sat.	12	Philadelphia
	Tue.	15	Cleveland
	Wed.	16	At New Jersey
	Fri.	18	At New York
	Sat.	19	At Houston
	Tue.	22	Washington
	Sat.	26	At Detroit
	Sun.	27	At Milwaukee
	Tue.	29	New York
Jan.	Sat.	2	Milwaukee
	Tue.	5	Denver
	Wed.	6	At Boston
	Fri.	8	Los Angeles
	Tue.	12	Detroit
	Thu.	14	At New Jersey
	Fri.	15	At Washington
	Sun.	17	At Indiana
	Tue.	19	Indiana
	Fri.	22	Cleveland
	Sat.	23	At New York
	Tue.	26	At Washington
	Thu.	28	Golden State
Feb.	Tue.	2	New Jersey
	Wed.	3	At Milwaukee
	Fri.	5	Detroit
	Sun.	7	At Philadelphia
	Tue.	9	At Detroit
	Wed.	10	Atlanta
	Sat.	13	Milwaukee
	Tue.	16	Phoenix
	Wed.	17	At New Jersey
	Sun.	21	Dallas
	Tue.	23	Portland
	Fri.	26	At Atlanta
	Sun.	28	San Antonio
Mar.	Tue.	2	Philadelphia
	Thu.	4	At Detroit
	Fri.	5	New Jersey
	Sun.	7	At Kansas City
	Tue.	9	Seattle
	Wed.	10	At Milwaukee
	Fri.	12	At Los Angeles
	Sun.	14	At San Antonio
	Wed.	17	At Dallas
	Fri.	19	At Denver
	Sun.	21	At Cleveland
	Tue.	23	Boston
	Fri.	26	New York
	Sun.	28	At Indiana
	Tue.	30	Atlanta
	Wed.	31	At Philadelphia
Apr.	Fri.	2	Milwaukee
	Sun.	4	At Boston
	Tue.	6	Philadelphia
	Wed.	7	At Cleveland
	Fri.	9	Washington
	Sun.	11	At Atlanta
	Tue.	13	Boston
	Thu.	15	At New York
	Fri.	16	Cleveland
	Sun.	18	Indiana

CLEVELAND CAVALIERS

Office: The Coliseum, P.O. Box 355, Richfield, Ohio 44286
Telephone: (Area Code 216) 659-9100

President—Theodore J. Stepien
Vice President—Bill Musselman
Secretary—Kent Schneider
Board Members—Joseph DeGrandis, Bruce Fine, Kenneth H. Kirtz, Richard Miller, Augustine M. Pena, Arnold Pinkney, Tom Richey, Don Schneider, Peter J. Shimrak, Robert Shupala, M.D.
Public Relations Director—Joe Steranka
Director of Speakers' Bureau—Paul Porter
Director of Advertising—Tony Saranita
Director of Ticket Sales—Rich Rollins
Assistant Director of Ticket Sales—Rob Pike
Account Executives—Dawn DiSalvo, Mark Termini
Accounting—Leisa Caton
Executive Secretary—Denise Urbancik
Consumer Sales Secretary—Terri Naro
Public Relations Secretary—Jan House
Advertising Secretary—Debbee Zach-George
Box Office Manager—Bill Spetrino
Head Statistician—Chuck Broski
General Manager/Head Coach—Don Delaney
Assistant Coaches—Gerald Oliver, Bob Kloppenburg, Gus Johnson
Player Personnel Director—Paul Spicuzza
Team Orthopedists—Dr. Earl A. Brightman, Dr. William R. Bohl
Team Surgeon—Dr. Godofredo Domingo
Team Internist—Dr. William T. Wilder
Team Rehabilitator—Dr. Robert C. Grotz
Team Dentist—Dr. Stanley L. Brown
Home Court—Richfield Coliseum (19,548)
Team Colors—Wine and Gold
Game Times—Monday—Saturday (8:05 p.m.) Sunday (2/7 p.m.)
Ticket Prices $13.50 (Courtside), $9.50, $7.50, $5
Radio—WBBG (1260 AM) Paul Porter, Gus Johnson

Ted Stepien

Don Delaney

1980-81 RESULTS, 1981-82 SCHEDULE

CLEVELAND CAVALIERS

1980-81 Record (Won 28, Lost 54)

Date	Opponent	Cle	Opp
Oct. 10	At Boston	103	130–
11	New Jersey	96	99–
14	Detroit	99	91
16	Washington	90	88
17	At Chicago	79	98–
18	Milwaukee	105	107–
21	At Milwaukee	95	115–
22	At Washington	96	109–
24	At New Jersey	126	112
25	Indiana	118	100
28	Philadelphia	101	119–
31	At Los Angeles	98	107–
Nov. 2	At Portland	96	102–
3	At Seattle	83	118–
5	At Golden State	98	106–
6	At Utah	96	112–
8	At Kansas City	106	111–
11	Milwaukee	96	100–
13	Atlanta	114	111
15	At New York	95	100–
18	San Diego	104	94
20	Houston	114	117–
22	Boston	113	98
26	New York	*113	119–
28	Washington	126	105
29	At Indiana	101	117–
Dec. 2	At Dallas	109	102
3	At Houston	109	118–
4	At San Antonio	100	130–
6	Detroit	101	100
9	Philadelphia	83	96–
11	Indiana	100	103–
12	At Detroit	95	101–
13	Utah	110	103
17	At Philadelphia	79	103–
18	Denver	130	122
20	Boston	102	107–
23	Kansas City	100	102–
26	Chicago	98	100–
29	Dallas	112	100
Jan. 2	At New Jersey	111	105
3	Washington	132	112
9	At Atlanta	*108	107
10	New York	99	104–
13	Los Angeles	104	108–
14	At Boston	113	120–
16	At Philadelphia	119	137–
17	At Chicago	110	98
20	Portland	99	94
22	New Jersey	108	94
23	At Atlanta	106	98
24	At Detroit	94	117–
27	Indiana	114	109
29	Phoenix	115	111
Feb. 4	Chicago	96	109–
6	Milwaukee	99	103–
7	At Indiana	96	99–
11	At Philadelphia	*120	122–
12	New York	111	122–
14	Golden State	108	90
17	Detroit	109	108
18	At New Jersey	108	110–
19	San Antonio	118	104
21	Atlanta	105	118–
25	At Boston	103	124–
27	At Detroit	109	118–
Mar. 1	At Denver	127	137–
4	At Phoenix	106	126–
6	At San Diego	125	140–
9	At Milwaukee	100	118–
11	Seattle	95	101–
13	New Jersey	125	140–
14	At Atlanta	*112	110
15	At Washington	101	100
17	Atlanta	122	107
19	Chicago	111	116–
21	At New York	105	119–
22	At Indiana	101	107–
24	At Chicago	108	121–
26	At Milwaukee	109	137–
27	Philadelphia	117	138–
29	At Washington	103	138–

1981-82 SCHEDULE

	Date	Opponent
Oct.	Fri. 30	At Philadelphia
Nov.	Tue. 3	At Dallas
	Wed. 4	At San Antonio
	Sat. 7	At Houston
	Mon. 9	Chicago
	Tue. 10	At Indiana
	Thu. 12	At Detroit
	Sat. 14	Boston
	Sun. 15	At Milwaukee
	Wed. 18	Detroit
	Fri. 20	Philadelphia
	Tue. 24	At Atlanta
	Wed. 25	Indiana
	Fri. 27	New York
	Sat. 28	At New York
Dec.	Tue. 1	Milwaukee
	Wed. 2	At New Jersey
	Sat. 5	At Washington
	Wed. 9	At Atlanta
	Fri. 11	At Philadelphia
	Sat. 12	Denver
	Tue. 15	At Chicago
	Wed. 16	Washington
	Fri. 18	At Indiana
	Sat. 19	New Jersey
	Tue. 22	At Boston
	Wed. 23	Kansas City
	Sat. 26	Milwaukee
	Wed. 30	New York
Jan.	Sat. 2	Boston
	Tue. 5	At Atlanta
	Thu. 7	At Washington
	Fri. 8	At New Jersey
	Tue. 12	Los Angeles
	Wed. 13	At Kansas Ctiy
	Fri. 15	At San Diego
	Sat. 16	At Utah
	Tue. 19	Seattle
	Fri. 22	At Chicago
	Sat. 23	Atlanta
	Wed. 27	Golden State
	Thu. 28	Boston
Feb.	Tue. 2	At Washington
	Wed. 3	Indiana
	Sat. 6	At Atlanta
	Sun. 7	New Jersey
	Wed. 10	Portland
	Thu. 11	At Detroit
	Sat. 13	Indiana
	Sun. 14	Milwaukee
	Wed. 17	Houston
	Fri. 19	At Milwaukee
	Sat. 20	Dallas
	Wed. 24	At Phoenix
	Sun. 28	At Los Angeles
Mar.	Tue. 2	At Golden State
	Wed. 3	At Seattle
	Fri. 5	At Portland
	Sun. 7	At Denver
	Thu. 11	Phoenix
	Sat. 13	Utah
	Sun. 14	Detroit
	Wed. 17	San Diego
	Fri. 19	At Milwaukee
	Sat. 20	San Antonio
	Sun. 21	Chicago
	Tue. 23	At New York
	Wed. 24	At Boston
	Fri. 26	Philadelphia
	Sun. 28	Washington
	Wed. 31	At New Jersey
Apr.	Thu. 1	At New York
	Fri. 2	At Philadelphia
	Sun. 4	New Jersey
	Tue. 6	At Washington
	Wed. 7	At Chicago
	Fri. 9	At Indiana
	Sat. 10	New York
	Tue. 13	Atlanta
	Thu. 15	At Detroit
	Fri. 16	At Chicago
	Sun. 18	Detroit

DALLAS MAVERICKS

Office: Reunion Arena, 777 Sports Street, Dallas, Texas 75207
Telephone: (Area Code 214) 748-1808

Executive Committee—Donald J. Carter,
M. Douglas Adkins,
Norman A. Sonju
President—Donald Carter
Vice President/General Manager—Norm Sonju
Vice President/Council—Doug Adkins
Business Manager—Paul Phipps
Controller—Bob Wilson
Director of Player Personnel—Rick Sund
Head Coach—Dick Motta
Assistant Coach—Bob Weiss
Trainer—Doug Atkinson
Team Physician—J. Pat Evans, M. D.
Equipment Manager—Keith Grant
Director of Arena Operations/Ticket Sales—Greg Jamison
Director of Advertising and Sales Promotion—Russ Bookbinder
Director of Group Sales—Bob Cohen
Group Sales—Gil Sheehan
Director of Public Relations—Allen Stone
Public Relations Assistant—Kevin Sullivan
Broadcast Producer—Dave Burchett
Director of Ticket Administration—John Wright
Accountant—Susie Jaramillo
Executive Secretary—Diane Flack
Marketing Secretary—Bonnie Banker
Public Relations Secretary—Mary Wynne Wicker
Home Court—Reunion Arena (17,694)
Team Colors—Blue and Green
Game Times—7:35 p.m. except Sundays (1:35 p.m.), February 25 (7:10 p.m.)
Television—KXAS (Channel 5) play-by-play TBA, Rudy Davalos
Radio—WBAP (820 AM) Mark Holtz, Bob Cohen (home)
Ticket Prices—$15, $12, $8, $6, $4

Donald Carter

Norm Sonju

Dick Motta

1980-81 RESULTS, 1981-82 SCHEDULE

DALLAS MAVERICKS

1980-81 Record (Won 15, Lost 67)

Date	Opponent	DAL	OPP
Oct. 11	San Antonio	103	92
14	Seattle	83	85
15	At Denver	98	133
17	Kansas City	91	103
18	At San Antonio	96	110
21	At Phoenix	99	111
22	At Seattle	107	102
24	At Portland	105	120
25	At Golden State	79	86
28	Utah	96	104
29	At Houston	103	109
31	At Utah	122	144
Nov. 4	San Diego	102	116
6	At Washington	95	116
7	Los Angeles	102	126
8	At Detroit	73	101
11	Houston	94	105
14	Portland	113	106
16	At Los Angeles	102	110
18	Phoenix	91	102
21	Seattle	91	101
23	At Portland	96	116
25	Philadelphia	92	108
28	Denver	*117	119
29	At Houston	90	115
Dec. 2	Cleveland	102	109
5	At Boston	87	97
6	At Atlanta	104	110
9	Los Angeles	92	103
10	At Denver	107	116
12	San Diego	*112	109
13	At Kansas City	107	114
16	San Antonio	83	89
17	At Phoenix	102	115
18	At San Diego	92	102
20	Golden State	98	101
23	Utah	96	101
26	Denver	119	111
27	At Milwaukee	96	112
29	At Cleveland	100	112
30	At New York	98	100
Jan. 2	Houston	*120	124
5	At Seattle	89	103
7	At Golden State	111	109
8	At Utah	97	99
10	Washington	94	106
13	Chicago	112	106
16	New York	118	110
18	At San Diego	109	115
20	Kansas City	91	104
23	At Chicago	98	106
24	At Indiana	89	107
27	New Jersey	100	112
Feb. 3	Kansas City	100	121
4	At Houston	68	116
6	Atlanta	98	100
8	At San Antonio	98	102
10	Detroit	95	101
11	At Phoenix	97	119
14	San Antonio	99	107
15	At Los Angeles	99	107
17	Milwaukee	106	114
20	At Philadelphia	109	117
22	At New Jersey	132	109
24	Seattle	84	102
26	At Kansas City	102	105
28	Indiana	111	118
Mar. 1	San Diego	99	91
3	Boston	105	117
6	At Golden State	109	115
8	At San Antonio	108	133
10	Phoenix	107	103
12	Golden State	120	118
15	At Portland	110	135
17	Los Angeles	109	114
18	At Utah	113	120
20	Denver	126	125
21	Utah	105	95
24	Houston	*111	114
25	At Denver	126	115
27	Portland	109	123
29	At Kansas City	104	113

1981-82 SCHEDULE

Oct.	Fri. 30	At Utah
	Sat. 31	Kansas City
Nov.	Tue. 3	Cleveland
	Thu. 5	At Phoenix
	Fri. 6	New York
	Sun. 8	At Los Angeles
	Tue. 10	At Portland
	Wed. 11	At Seattle
	Sat. 14	Golden State
	Tue. 17	San Antonio
	Fri. 20	Seattle
	Sat. 21	Phoenix
	Tue. 24	Los Angeles
	Wed. 25	At Denver
	Sat. 28	New Jersey
Dec.	Wed. 2	At Utah
	Thu. 3	At San Diego
	Sat. 5	Denver
	Tue. 8	Utah
	Wed. 9	At Kansas City
	Fri. 11	San Antonio
	Sat. 12	At Houston
	Tue. 15	At Washington
	Wed. 16	At Boston
	Fri. 18	Houston
	Sat. 19	Portland
	Tue. 22	Detroit
	Sat. 26	Denver
	Tue. 29	Kansas City
Jan.	Sat. 2	At Golden State
	Wed. 6	At Seattle
	Thu. 7	At San Diego
	Sat. 9	Phoenix
	Tue. 12	At San Antonio
	Wed. 13	San Diego
	Fri. 15	At Denver
	Sat. 16	Portland
	Wed. 20	Milwaukee
	Thu. 21	At Kansas City
	Sat. 23	At Utah
	Tue. 26	At Atlanta
	Wed. 27	Philadelphia
Feb.	Tue. 2	At San Antonio
	Wed. 3	San Diego
	Fri. 5	At Milwaukee
	Sat. 6	At Indiana
	Wed. 10	At Washington
	Fri. 12	Seattle
	Sun. 14	At New Jersey
	Tue. 16	At New York
	Wed. 17	At Philadelphia
	Sat. 20	At Cleveland
	Sun. 21	At Chicago
	Tue. 23	At Houston
	Thu. 25	Golden State
	Sat. 27	Houston
Mar.	Tue. 2	Boston
	Thu. 4	At Golden State
	Fri. 5	At Seattle
	Sun. 7	Indiana
	Mon. 8	At San Antonio
	Wed. 10	Portland
	Sat. 13	At San Diego
	Sun. 14	At Los Angeles
	Wed. 17	Chicago
	Fri. 19	Los Angeles
	Sun. 21	At Portland
	Tue. 23	At Los Angeles
	Wed. 24	At Phoenix
	Fri. 26	Kansas City
	Sat. 27	Atlanta
	Tue. 30	At Houston
	Wed. 31	Denver
Apr.	Thu. 1	At Detroit
	Sat. 3	Golden State
	Tue. 6	At Utah
	Wed. 7	Utah
	Fri. 9	Phoenix
	Sun. 11	Houston
	Wed. 14	At Kansas City
	Fri. 16	San Antonio
	Sat. 17	At Denver

DENVER NUGGETS

Office: McNichols Sports Arena, 1635 Clay Street, Denver, Colorado 80204
Mailing Address: P. O. Box 4286, Denver, Colo. 80204
Telephone: (Area Code 303) 893-6700

Executive Committee—Fred Haynes (Chairman),
O. Wesley Box, Bob Cohen, Donald Egan, M. D.,
Edward Eisenman,
William Newland, Gerald Quiat, Carl Sheer
President and General Manager—Carl Scheer
Head Coach—Doug Moe
Vice-President/Assistant General Manager—
Paula Hanson
Corporate Secretary—Billye Tellinger
Corporate Treasurer/Business Manager—John Bostic
Director of Public Relations—Tom Hohensee
Ticket Manager—Nancy Strainic
Marketing Director—Susan Mirabella
Art Director—Debra Perito
Assistant Coaches—Donnie Walsh, John Nillen
Trainer/Traveling Secretary—Bob Travaglini
Team Assistant—Sharon Laidman
Accounting Assistant—Loretta Harmon
Public Relations Assistant—Barbara Knaster
Director of Promotional Sales—Don Johnson
Assistant Ticket Manager—Mark Koson
Promotions Coordinator—Terry Noonan
Marketing Assistant—Trisha Tracy
Sales Representatives—John Green, Jan Howard, Frank Rowe,
Tom Schaeffer, Ray Shaffer, Lisa Sloan, Mitzi Swentzell
Team Physicians—Dr. Irwin Vinnik, Dr. Dave Garland, Dr. Bruce Jafek,
Dr. Sheldon Roger, Dr. Francis Yamamoto, Dr. Arnold Heller,
Dr. Airell Nygaard
Team Dentist—Dr. Michael Dunn
Arena—William H. McNichols, Jr. Sports Arena (17,251)
Ticket Prices—$12, $10.50, $9.50, $8.50, $7, $6, $3.50
Starting Times—7:35 p.m., Monday-Saturday; 2:05 p.m. Sunday
Radio—KOA (850), Jeff Kingery, Bob Martin
Television—KWGN

Carl Scheer

Doug Moe

DENVER NUGGETS

1980-81 Record (Won 37, Lost 45)

Oct.	10—San Antonio	112	113—
	12—Utah	*121	125—
	15—Dallas	133	98
	17—At San Diego	129	116
	18—At Utah	115	117—
	21—Houston	117	119—
	24—Phoenix	94	117—
	25—At Kansas City	122	125—
	29—At Golden State	109	115—
Nov.	1—Seattle	123	118
	2—At Los Angeles	123	121
	5—At Seattle	125	117
	7—New York	115	124—
	8—At Chicago	**130	126
	11—At Washington	92	107—
	12—At New Jersey	111	118—
	15—Portland	125	123
	18—At Portland	103	122—
	21—Kansas City	134	121
	23—At Phoenix	113	131—
	25—At San Diego	94	108—
	26—San Diego	113	109
	28—At Dallas	*119	117
	29—Los Angeles	**123	124—
Dec.	2—Chicago	124	129—
	4—At Utah	118	122—
	5—Golden State	114	119—
	6—At Houston	108	111—
	10—Dallas	116	107
	13—At San Antonio	123	147—
	16—Kansas City	118	133—
	18—At Cleveland	122	130—
	20—At New York	114	120—
	23—At Boston	128	136—
	26—At Dallas	111	119—
	27—Philadelphia	125	121
	30—Indiana	127	110
Jan.	1—At Portland	119	122—
	2—Phoenix	132	133—
	3—At Houston	134	132
	7—Utah	117	121—
	9—At San Diego	130	116
	10—At Seattle	116	119—
	13—Atlanta	135	132
	14—At Phoenix	102	128—
	17—At Kansas City	123	122
	18—Houston	97	98—
	21—San Diego	116	125—
	23—At Los Angeles	105	110—
	24—San Antonio	129	115
	27—Detroit	143	123
	29—Milwaukee	131	118
Feb.	3—At Houston	*128	135—
	4—San Antonio	132	135—
	6—At Utah	120	116
	7—Golden State	135	125
	8—At Seattle	112	133—
	10—Washington	110	115—
	13—Portland	162	143
	15—Boston	118	120—
	19—Phoenix	127	126
	21—Kansas City	129	109
	22—At San Antonio	*129	133—
	24—New Jersey	140	123
	27—Golden State	137	130
Mar.	1—Cleveland	137	127
	4—Los Angeles	123	114
	6—At Philadelphia	112	131—
	7—At Detroit	121	109
	8—At Indiana	119	129—
	10—Portlad	137	142—
	12—At Milwaukee	113	131—
	13—At Atlanta	117	119—
	15—Houston	138	127
	17—Seattle	124	112
	18—At Kansas City	**126	124
	20—At Dallas	125	126—
	22—Utah	113	108
	24—At San Antonio	125	123
	25—Dallas	115	126—
	28—At Golden State	142	139
	29—At Los Angeles	*148	146

1981-82 SCHEDULE

Oct.	Fri.	30—Golden State
	Sat.	31—At San Antonio
Nov.	Wed.	4—Houston
	Fri.	6—At Seattle
	Sat.	7—At Golden State
	Sun.	8—At Portland
	Tue.	10—Phoenix
	Fri.	13—At Utah
	Wed.	18—San Diego
	Sat.	21—Kansas City
	Wed.	25—Dallas
	Fri.	27—At Kansas City
	Sat.	28—Utah
Dec.	Tue.	1—Portland
	Thu.	3—At Phoenix
	Fri.	4—Los Angeles
	Sat.	5—At Dallas
	Tue.	8—At New York
	Wed.	9—At Philadelphia
	Fri.	11—At New Jersey
	Sat.	12—At Cleveland
	Tue.	15—Seattle
	Thu.	17—Atlanta
	Sat.	19—San Antonio
	Tue.	22—At Houston
	Wed.	23—Detroit
	Sat.	26—At Dallas
	Tue.	29—Boston
	Wed.	30—At Kansas City
Jan.	Sat.	2—At San Antonio
	Sun.	3—At Milwaukee
	Tue.	5—At Chicago
	Wed.	6—San Diego
	Fri.	8—At Portland
	Sat.	9—Seattle
	Tue.	12—Kansas City
	Wed.	13—At Golden State
	Fri.	15—Dallas
	Sun.	17—At San Diego
	Tue.	19—Los Angeles
	Fri.	22—Milwaukee
	Sat.	23—At Houston
	Wed.	27—New Jersey
Feb.	Tue.	2—New York
	Thu.	4—At Indiana
	Fri.	5—At Boston
	Sun.	7—At Washington
	Wed.	10—Utah
	Sat.	13—San Diego
	Mon.	15—At Utah
	Tue.	16—Kansas City
	Fri.	19—San Antonio
	Sun.	21—Los Angeles
	Tue.	23—At Los Angeles
	Wed.	24—Houston
	Fri.	26—At Phoenix
	Sat.	27—Philadelphia
Mar.	Tue.	2—Indiana
	Fri.	5—Washington
	Sun.	7—Cleveland
	Tue.	9—At Atlanta
	Wed.	10—At Detroit
	Fri.	12—At Houston
	Sun.	14—Golden State
	Tue.	16—Utah
	Wed.	17—At Phoenix
	Fri.	19—Chicago
	Wed.	24—San Antonio
	Thu.	25—At San Diego
	Sat.	27—Phoenix
	Tue.	30—Seattle
	Wed.	31—At Dallas
Apr.	Fri.	2—Portland
	Sun.	4—At Seattle
	Tue.	6—At Portland
	Wed.	7—At Golden State
	Fri.	9—At Los Angeles
	Sat.	10—At Utah
	Tue.	13—At San Antonio
	Wed.	14—Houston
	Fri.	16—At Kansas City
	Sat.	17—Dallas

DETROIT PISTONS

Office: Pontiac Silverdome, 1200 Featherstone, Pontiac, Michigan 48057
Telephone: (Area Code 313) 338-4667

Managing Partner—William M. Davidson
Consulting Partner—Herbert Tyner
Legal Counsel—Oscar H. Feldman
Advisory Board—Warren J. Coville, Milt Dresner, Ted Ewald, Bud Gerson, Dorothy Gerson, David Mondry, Eugene Mondry, Ann Newman, Wilam M. Wetsman
Executive Director—Thomas S. Wilson
Director of Public Relations—Bill Kreifeldt
Director of Marketing—Harry E. Hutt
Director of Sales and Promotions—Dan Hauser
Director of Season Sales and Special Events—John Ciszewski
Account Representatives—Mark Cheklich, Jeff Corey
Controller—Doug Anthony
Administrative Assistant—John Kapral
Administrative Secretaries—Nancy Maas, Suzanne Nini, Nancy Purdo
Community Releations Director/Assistant to General Manager—Will Robinson
Statistician—Morris Moorawnick
General Manager—Jack McCloskey
Head Coach—Scotty Robertson
Assistant Coach—Don Chaney
Scouting Director—Stan Novak
Trainer—Mike Abdenour
Team Physician—Dr. Ben Paolucci
Team Dentist—Dr. Ron Berris
Team Podiatrist—Dr. Jerome Levine
Locker room Manager—Jerry Dziedzic
Home Court—Pontiac Silverdome (22,366)
Team Colors—Red, White and Blue
Game Times—8:05 p.m. (Monday-Saturday), 7:05 p.m. (Sunday)
Ticket Prices—$9, $8, $6, $3.50
Radio—WJR (760 AM)
Television—WKBD-TV (Channel 50)

William Davidson

Jack McCloskey

Scotty Robertson

DETROIT PISTONS

1980-81 Record (Won 21, Lost 61)

Date	Opponent	Det	Opp
Oct. 10	Washington	85	95
11	At Indiana	87	100
13	At New Jersey	92	108
14	At Cleveland	91	99
16	San Antonio	99	102
18	Atlanta	**123	125
22	Philadelphia	93	94
25	At Houston	112	109
29	Boston	85	103
31	Phoenix	*98	103
Nov. 1	At Chicago	100	122
4	At Milwaukee	98	96
5	At Philadelphia	103	107
7	At Washington	88	114
8	Dallas	101	73
11	At New York	118	149
12	Milwaukee	98	122
14	Chicago	106	99
16	At New Jersey	80	89
18	Indiana	97	102
20	San Diego	97	90
22	New Jersey	117	103
26	Utah	97	104
28	Kansas City	104	94
29	At Atlanta	98	95
Dec. 2	Boston	85	94
5	At Washington	92	103
6	At Cleveland	100	101
10	At Atlanta	92	100
12	Cleveland	101	95
13	At New York	94	100
17	New York	103	119
18	At Milwaukee	104	121
19	Indiana	109	106
21	At San Diego	97	117
23	At Phoenix	104	113
26	Houston	94	114
27	At Chicago	97	104
30	At Atlanta	89	96
Jan. 2	New York	102	100
6	At Portland	90	110
7	At Seattle	94	99
10	At Golden State	103	105
11	At Los Angeles	108	117
13	Milwaukee	96	119
14	At Indiana	99	101
15	Washington	89	106
17	New Jersey	104	116
19	At Boston	90	92
20	Philadelphia	83	75
22	Chicago	92	125
24	Cleveland	117	99
26	At Utah	99	102
27	At Denver	123	143
29	Golden State	112	117
Feb. 3	At San Antonio	99	102
4	At Kansas City	90	91
6	Los Angeles	102	111
7	At Chicago	90	98
8	Indiana	101	124
10	At Dallas	101	95
13	At New York	92	120
14	Washington	105	103
17	At Cleveland	108	109
18	At Philadelphia	97	111
19	Portland	106	115
21	Boston	119	130
27	Cleveland	118	109
Mar. 1	At New Jersey	117	104
3	At Milwaukee	98	115
5	New York	101	104
7	Denver	109	121
11	Atlanta	100	97
13	Seattle	100	102
14	At Indiana	101	94
18	New Jersey	118	115
20	Milwaukee	86	104
22	Chicago	103	109
24	At Atlanta	91	96
25	At Philadelphia	75	114
27	At Boston	115	90
28	At Washington	103	108

1981-82 SCHEDULE

Oct.	Fri.	30	Milwaukee
	Sat.	31	At Chicago
Nov.	Thu.	5	New Jersey
	Fri.	6	At Washington
	Sat.	7	Boston
	Tue.	10	Philadelphia
	Thu.	12	Cleveland
	Sat.	14	At Atlanta
	Wed.	18	At Cleveland
	Thu.	19	Washington
	Sat.	21	Utah
	Tue.	24	At Milwaukee
	Wed.	25	At Kansas City
	Fri.	27	Atlanta
	Sat.	28	At Philadelphia
Dec.	Tue.	1	At New York
	Wed.	2	At Boston
	Fri.	4	At Indiana
	Sat.	5	Milwaukee
	Thu.	10	New York
	Sat.	12	At Seattle
	Sun.	13	At Portland
	Tue.	15	At Golden State
	Thu.	17	Indiana
	Sat.	19	New York
	Tue.	22	At Dallas
	Wed.	23	At Denver
	Sat.	26	Chicago
	Tue.	29	At Washington
	Wed.	30	At New Jersey
Jan.	Sat.	2	At New York
	Tue.	5	Philadelphia
	Thu.	7	Phoenix
	Sat.	9	Los Angeles
	Sun.	10	At Boston
	Tue.	12	At Chicago
	Thu.	14	Washington
	Sat.	16	Boston
	Sun.	17	At Milwaukee
	Tue.	19	At Utah
	Thu.	21	At San Diego
	Fri.	22	At Los Angeles
	Sat.	23	At Phoenix
	Wed.	27	Atlanta
Feb.	Tue.	2	At Atlanta
	Wed.	3	Boston
	Fri.	5	At Chicago
	Sat.	6	New Jersey
	Tue.	9	Chicago
	Wed.	10	At New Jersey
	Thu.	11	Cleveland
	Sat.	13	Portland
	Tue.	16	Houston
	Wed.	17	At San Antonio
	Sat.	20	Indiana
	Thu.	25	San Antonio
	Sat.	27	Kansas City
	Sun.	28	At Indiana
Mar.	Tue.	2	At Milwaukee
	Thu.	4	Chicago
	Sat.	6	At New York
	Wed.	10	Denver
	Fri.	12	Golden State
	Sun.	14	At Cleveland
	Tue.	16	San Diego
	Thu.	18	Seattle
	Fri.	19	At Houston
	Sun.	21	At Atlanta
	Thu.	25	Philadelphia
	Fri.	26	At Boston
	Sat.	27	At New Jersey
	Tue.	30	At Washington
	Wed.	31	Indiana
Apr.	Thu.	1	Dallas
	Sat.	3	Indiana
	Wed.	7	Atlanta
	Fri.	9	Milwaukee
	Sun.	11	New York
	Wed.	14	At Philadelphia
	Thu.	15	Cleveland
	Sat.	17	New Jersey
	Sun.	18	At Cleveland

GOLDEN STATE WARRIORS

Office: Oakland Coliseum, Oakland, Calif. 94621
Telephone: (Area Code 415) 638-6300

Chairman of the Board and President—Franklin Mieuli
Executive Vice President and Chief Executive Officer—
P. K. Macker
Vice President and Head Coach—Al Attles
Director of Player Personnel—Gordon (Scotty) Stirling
Treasurer/Controller—Shirley Figgins
General Counsel—Luther J. Avery
Director of Communications/Broadcasting and
Marketing—Bob Bestor
Director of Media Services—Joe Dearborn
Promotions Director—Robin Braig
Director of Broadcasting—Mike Marquardt
Assistant to the President—Peter Mieuli
Office Manager—Anita Wood
Executive Secretary—Geri Verrett
Talent Consultant—Pete Newell
Ticket Manager—Lou Colla
Assistant Ticket Manager—Marie Stanfel
Production Manager—Louis King
Assistant Coach—John Bach
Trainer—Dick D'Oliva
Scout—Forddy Anderson
Team Physician—Dr. Robert Albo
Team Orthopedist—Dr. Thomas Schmitz
Physical Therapist Consultant—Dr. Steve Rocca
Receptionist—Sandria Frost
Media Secretary—Sandra Pace
Home Court—Oakland Coliseum Arena (13,237)
Ticket Prices—$13, $11, $9, $8, $7, $5
Radio—KNBR (68 KC) Bill King
Television—KBHK (Channel 44) San Francisco;
KRBK (Channel 31) Sacramento; KAME (Channel 29) Reno;
Star TV (Subscription TV) San Francisco, Bill King

Franklin Mieuli

Scotty Stirling

Al Attles

GOLDEN STATE WARRIORS

1980-81 Record (Won 39, Lost 43)

Date	Opponent	GS	Opp
Oct. 10	At Phoenix	101	121
11	San Diego	104	91
15	Portland	95	92
18	Houston	108	101
19	At Los Angeles	107	125
21	At Kansas City	116	111
23	At San Antonio	109	128
25	Dallas	86	79
28	At Seattle	102	119
29	Denver	115	109
31	At San Diego	104	120
Nov. 1	San Antonio	123	108
5	Cleveland	106	98
7	At Portland	113	122
8	Indiana	118	111
12	Kansas City	111	101
15	Phoenix	119	108
18	At Washington	103	97
19	At Philadelphia	101	110
21	At Boston	106	108
22	At New York	116	110
27	Los Angeles	119	128
29	Phoenix	108	113
30	At San Diego	100	120
Dec. 3	New Jersey	131	108
5	At Denver	119	114
6	Los Angeles	119	103
7	At Phoenix	88	106
10	Seattle	103	99
13	Houston	97	99
14	At Los Angeles	113	122
17	Portland	113	115
19	At San Antonio	111	126
20	At Dallas	101	98
23	At Houston	114	99
25	At Portland	114	115
26	At Utah	110	109
27	Seattle	104	98
30	At Kansas City	106	104
Jan. 2	Boston	121	106
3	Philadelphia	105	119
7	Dallas	109	111
10	Detroit	105	103
11	At Seattle	106	98
14	Utah	107	110
16	Atlanta	110	111
21	Milwaukee	98	105
23	At Utah	103	101
24	New York	117	110
27	At Chicago	101	118
28	At Indiana	102	108
29	At Detroit	117	112
Feb. 4	Portland	115	100
6	Washington	110	116
7	At Denver	125	135
8	Utah	107	101
10	At Atlanta	108	116
13	At Milwaukee	110	106
14	At Cleveland	90	108
15	At New Jersey	132	134
17	At Phoenix	109	118
18	Chicago	103	100
20	San Diego	114	115
22	Kansas City	104	96
24	At San Antonio	126	131
27	At Denver	130	137
28	At Kansas City	110	101
Mar. 4	Utah	107	105
6	Dallas	115	109
7	Seattle	106	103
8	At Portland	*112	120
11	At Houston	92	109
12	At Dallas	118	120
15	San Antonio	*112	114
18	Houston	118	117
19	At San Diego	113	139
21	Phoenix	114	105
22	San Diego	118	120
24	At Los Angeles	103	110
25	San Diego	120	114
28	Denver	139	142
29	At Seattle	92	96

1981-82 SCHEDULE

Day	Date	Opponent
Oct. Fri.	30	At Denver
Sat.	31	Utah
Nov. Wed.	4	Portland
Thu.	5	At Utah
Sat.	7	Denver
Tue.	10	Seattle
Fri.	13	At Houston
Sat.	14	At Dallas
Wed.	18	New Jersey
Thu.	19	At San Diego
Sat.	21	San Antonio
Tue.	24	At Washington
Wed.	25	At Boston
Fri.	27	At Milwaukee
Sun.	29	At Kansas City
Dec. Wed.	2	Chicago
Sat.	5	San Diego
Tue.	8	At Portland
Wed.	9	Phoenix
Sat.	12	Kansas City
Sun.	13	At Los Angeles
Tue.	15	Detroit
Thu.	17	At Los Angeles
Sat.	19	Atlanta
Wed.	23	At Phoenix
Sat.	26	Phoenix
Mon.	28	At Seattle
Tue.	29	At Philadelphia
Jan. Fri.	1	Kansas City
Sat.	2	Dallas
Tue.	5	Houston
Thu.	7	San Antonio
Sat.	9	Indiana
Tue.	12	Phoenix
Wed.	13	Denver
Fri.	15	New York
Sun.	17	At Seattle
Wed.	20	San Diego
Sat.	23	Milwaukee
Wed.	27	At Cleveland
Thu.	28	At Chicago
Feb. Tue.	2	Los Angeles
Wed.	3	At Phoenix
Fri.	5	Seattle
Sun.	7	San Antonio
Tue.	9	At Utah
Thu.	11	At New York
Fri.	12	At New Jersey
Sun.	14	At Kansas City
Wed.	17	Boston
Fri.	19	At Los Angeles
Sat.	20	Washington
Tue.	23	At San Antonio
Thu.	25	At Dallas
Fri.	26	At Houston
Sun.	28	At Atlanta
Mar. Tue.	2	Cleveland
Thu.	4	Dallas
Fri.	5	At San Diego
Sun.	7	Portland
Tue.	9	At Indiana
Wed.	10	At Philadelphia
Fri.	12	At Detroit
Sun.	14	At Denver
Wed.	17	At Kansas City
Thu.	18	At Portland
Sun.	21	Utah
Tue.	23	Phoenix
Thu.	25	At Utah
Fri.	26	Portland
Sun.	28	Houston
Tue.	30	At San Antonio
Apr. Thu.	1	At Houston
Sat.	3	At Dallas
Tue.	6	At San Diego
Wed.	7	Denver
Sat.	10	San Diego
Sun.	11	At Portland
Tue.	13	Los Angeles
Wed.	14	At Seattle
Fri.	16	At Los Angeles
Sat.	17	Seattle

HOUSTON ROCKETS

Office: The Summit, Ten Greenway Plaza East, Houston, Texas 77046
Telephone: (Area Code 713) 627-0600

President—Gavin P. Maloof
General Manager—Ray Patterson
Financial Officer—Bud Reynolds
Administrative Assistant—Cathy Bartley
Head Coach—Del Harris
Assistant Coach—Carroll Dawson
Trainer—Dick Vandervoort
Director of Public Relations—Jim Foley
Director of Broadcasting—Gene Peterson
Director of Marketing—Gary Loh
Controller—Bryan Windham
Ticket Assistant—Kathleen Reynolds
Receptionist/Secretary—Dianne McKinney
Equipment Manager—David Nordstrom
Photographer—Lou Witt
Physician—Charles Baker, M. D.
Dentist—William Worrell, D. D. S.
Home Court—The Summit (15,676)
Team Colors—Red and Gold
Ticket Prices—$12.50, $11.50, $9, $8, $7, $6
Radio—KPRC (950), Gene Peterson
Televison—KH-TV-39

Gavin Maloof

Ray Patterson

Del Harris

1980-81 RESULTS, 1981-82 SCHEDULE

HOUSTON ROCKETS

1980-81 Record (Won 40, Lost 42)

Oct.	10—At San Diego	104	120—
	12—At Los Angeles	103	114—
	15—Seattle	103	100
	17—At Portland	102	99
	18—At Golden State	101	108—
	21—At Denver	119	117
	23—Kansas City	96	105—
	25—Detroit	109	112—
	29—Dallas	109	103
Nov.	5—San Diego	104	111—
	8—Phoenix	115	116—
	11—At Dallas	105	94
	12—Los Angeles	107	104
	14—At Utah	115	117—
	15—At Seattle	*139	143—
	18—Seattle	138	118
	20—At Cleveland	117	114
	21—At New Jersey	116	108
	22—At Indiana	120	129—
	24—At New York	*110	113—
	26—Philadelphia	100	101—
	28—At San Antonio	124	115
	29—Dallas	115	90
	30—At Phoenix	114	117—
Dec.	3—Cleveland	118	109
	5—At Kansas City	100	108—
	6—Denver	111	108
	10—Los Angeles	108	109—
	12—At Portland	100	106—
	13—At Golden State	99	97
	17—San Antonio	107	113—
	19—At Boston	119	133—
	20—At Chicago	109	133—
	21—At Milwaukee	91	123—
	23—Golden State	99	114—
	26—At Detroit	114	94
	27—At Washington	97	115—
	30—San Diego	104	98
Jan.	1—Utah	117	103
	2—At Dallas	*124	120
	3—Denver	132	134—
	7—Kansas City	108	114—
	9—At Philadelphia	94	107—
	10—Portland	106	105
	14—Chicago	109	105
	16—At Phoenix	89	92—
	17—New York	98	99—
	18—At Denver	98	97
	21—Phoenix	106	100
	23—At Kansas City	107	113—
	24—Utah	106	91
	28—New Jersey	111	99
	29—At Utah	97	99—
Feb.	3—Denver	*135	128
	4—Dallas	116	68
	6—At Phoenix	99	112—
	7—Atlanta	87	81
	11—San Antonio	108	89
	13—Los Angeles	105	114—
	14—Milwaukee	112	117—
	19—At San Diego	99	116—
	20—At Los Angeles	110	107
	22—At Seattle	111	96
	23—At Utah	106	102
	25—Indiana	101	100
	27—Seattle	96	92
	28—San Diego	103	104—
Mar.	1—At San Antonio	86	102—
	4—Boston	101	108—
	6—Washington	104	105—
	7—At Atlanta	108	92
	11—At Golden State	109	92
	13—Portland	126	104
	14—At Denver	101	82
	15—At Denver	127	138—
	18—At Golden State	117	118—
	20—At Portland	103	107—
	22—At Kansas City	114	108
	24—At Dallas	*114	111
	25—San Antonio	117	111
	27—Kansas City	91	84
	29—At San Antonio	109	135—

1981-82 SCHEDULE

Oct.	Fri.	30—At Los Angeles
	Sat.	31—At San Diego
Nov.	Tue.	3—New York
	Wed.	4—At Denver
	Fri.	6—At Kansas City
	Sat.	7—Cleveland
	Wed.	11—Los Angeles
	Fri.	13—Golden State
	Sat.	14—Utah
	Tue.	17—Indiana
	Wed.	18—At Boston
	Fri.	20—At Washington
	Sat.	21—At Philadelphia
	Tue.	24—New Jersey
	Wed.	25—At Phoenix
	Fri.	27—At Seattle
	Sun.	29—At Los Angeles
Dec.	Tue.	1—Kansas City
	Sat.	5—Portland
	Tue.	8—Seattle
	Wed.	9—At Milwaukee
	Fri.	11—At Chicago
	Sat.	12—Dallas
	Tue.	15—Phoenix
	Fri.	18—At Dallas
	Sat.	29—Chicago
	Tue.	22—Denver
	Sat.	26—At Utah
	Tue.	29—Atlanta
	Wed.	30—At San Antonio
Jan.	Sat.	2—At San Diego
	Tue.	5—At Golden State
	Thu.	7—At Seattle
	Sun.	10—At Portland
	Tue.	12—San Diego
	Thu.	14—Portland
	Fri.	15—At San Antonio
	Sat.	16—San Antonio
	Tue.	19—Kansas City
	Fri.	22—Utah
	Sat.	23—Denver
	Tue.	26—Indiana
	Thu.	28—At Philadelphia
Feb.	Tue.	2—San Diego
	Fri.	5—Phoenix
	Sun.	7—At Kansas City
	Tue.	9—At San Diego
	Thu.	11—Seattle
	Sat.	13—Washington
	Tue.	16—At Detroit
	Wed.	17—At Cleveland
	Fri.	19—At New Jersey
	Sun.	21—At New York
	Tue.	23—Dallas
	Wed.	24—At Denver
	Fri.	26—Golden State
	Sat.	27—At Dallas
Mar.	Tue.	2—San Antonio
	Thu.	4—At Utah
	Fri.	5—Boston
	Sun.	7—At Phoenix
	Tue.	9—Milwaukee
	Fri.	12—Denver
	Sat.	13—Portland
	Tue.	16—Phoenix
	Thu.	18—At Atlanta
	Fri.	19—At Detroit
	Sun.	21—At Los Angeles
	Tue.	23—At Utah
	Thu.	25—At Portland
	Fri.	26—At Seattle
	Sun.	28—At Golden State
	Tue.	30—Dallas
Apr.	Thu.	1—Golden State
	Sun.	4—At San Antonio
	Tue.	6—Los Angeles
	Sat.	10—San Antonio
	Sun.	11—At Dallas
	Tue.	13—Kansas City
	Wed.	14—At Denver
	Fri.	16—Utah
	Sun.	18—At Kansas City

INDIANA PACERS

Office: Market Square Center, 151 North Delaware, Suite 60,
Indianapolis, Indiana 46204
Telephone: (Area Code 317) 263-0800

Chairman of the Board/NBA Governor—Sam Nassi
Alternate NBA Governor—David Licht
General Manager and Team Counsel—
Robert J. Salyers
Owner's Representative—Steve Waigand
Head Coach—Jack McKinney
Assistant Coach—George Irvine
Director of Player Personnel—Jerry Oliver
Athletic Trainer/Team Administrator—David Craig
Assistant General Manager—Bob Whitsitt
Controller—Douglas E. McKee, C.P.A.
Director of Media & Public Relations—Ed McKee
Director of Promotions—Greg McCollam
Accounting Secretary—Rosemary Fillmore
Administrative Secretary—Rhonda Wilson
Executive Secretary—Sandi Morrison
Media & Public Relations Secretary—Ginny Berg
Sales Secretary—Sherry Smith
Receptionist—Kim Jones
Community and Corporate Relations—Scott Edwards
Season Tickets and Group Sales—Bill Edwards, Larry Grider, Nick Hertz
Sales Staff—Dick Ebersold, Norm Epstein, Judy Harvey, Mike Henn, Dan
Rayner, Mike Walker, Fred Weidman, James White
Corporate Community Liaison—John T. Sutton
Team Physicians—F. Robert Brueckmann, M.D., Richard A. Hutson, M.D.
Team Dentist—Jack R. Leer, D.D.S.
Team Ophthalmologist—Robert W. Dyar, M.D.
Stat Crew Director—Bill York
Head Statistician—Gene Hemelgarn
Team Photographer—Frank McGrath
Home Court—Market Square Arena (17,092)
Team Colors—Blue and Gold
Radio—WIBC (1070 AM) Bob Lamey
Game Times—7:35 p.m. (Sundays—2, 4:05, 6:05 p.m.)
Ticket Prices—$20, $15, $10, $6, $4

INDIANA PACERS

Sam Nassi

Bob Salyers

Jack McKinney

1980-81 RESULTS, 1981-82 SCHEDULE
INDIANA PACERS

1980-81 Record (Won 44, Lost 38)

Oct.	10—At New Jersey	110	91
	11—Detroit	100	87
	15—Chicago	97	108—
	18—Boston	103	99
	21—At Atlanta	121	116
	22—Milwaukee	105	119—
	24—Atlanta	104	97
	25—At Cleveland	100	118—
	29—New York	102	95
	31—At Chicago	121	114
Nov.	1—New Jersey	113	100
	2—At Milwaukee	121	135—
	4—At Phoenix	108	109—
	8—At Golden State	111	118—
	10—At Utah	106	108—
	11—At San Antonio	119	113
	13—Philadelphia	103	130—
	14—Washington	118	108
	18—At Detroit	102	97
	19—Boston	91	103—
	21—At Philadelphia	88	97—
	22—Houston	129	120
	26—Atlanta	110	89
	27—At Washington	108	123—
	29—Cleveland	117	101
Dec.	2—At New York	113	96
	3—Washington	128	115
	5—At Milwaukee	100	102—
	6—Kansas City	107	88
	10—Phoenix	102	90
	11—At Cleveland	103	100
	13—At Washington	105	114—
	16—Philadelphia	107	109—
	19—At Detroit	106	109—
	20—At Kansas City	107	103
	23—New Jersey	125	109
	26—At Los Angeles	115	109—
	27—At San Diego	109	121—
	30—At Denver	110	127—
Jan.	2—At Atlanta	109	106
	3—San Diego	128	104
	4—At New Jersey	113	104
	7—New Jersey	112	103
	8—At New York	*116	115
	10—Milwaukee	106	102
	14—Detroit	101	99
	16—Seattle	94	95—
	18—Utah	110	89
	20—At Chicago	105	121—
	21—At Philadelphia	104	118—
	23—At Boston	103	104—
	24—Dallas	107	89
	27—At Cleveland	109	114—
	28—Golden State	108	102
Feb.	3—At Milwaukee	108	99
	4—Los Angeles	96	102—
	6—At Boston	98	111—
	7—Cleveland	99	96
	8—At Detroit	124	101
	11—Milwaukee	101	107—
	13—At New Jersey	100	103—
	15—Chicago	113	107
	18—Atlanta	96	99—
	20—San Antonio	109	106
	22—Portland	*109	113—
	25—At Houston	100	101—
	27—At Dallas	118	111
Mar.	3—At Portland	112	117—
	4—At Seattle	93	105—
	6—Boston	110	104
	8—Denver	129	119
	10—Philadelphia	102	103—
	12—At Washington	114	107
	13—At Boston	101	94
	14—Detroit	94	101—
	17—At New York	89	107—
	18—At Philadelphia	95	107—
	20—New York	107	110—
	22—Cleveland	107	101
	26—At Atlanta	115	107
	27—Washington	122	107
	29—Chicago	97	101—

1981-82 SCHEDULE

Oct.	Fri.	30—Chicago
	Sat.	31—At New York
Nov.	Wed.	4—At Philadelphia
	Fri.	6—At Boston
	Sun.	8—At New Jersey
	Tue.	10—Cleveland
	Thu.	12—At Phoenix
	Sat.	14—At San Diego
	Sun.	15—At Los Angeles
	Tue.	17—Houston
	Thu.	19—Kansas City
	Sat.	21—At Atlanta
	Tue.	24—New York
	Wed.	25—At Cleveland
	Fri.	27—Philadelphia
	Sat.	28—At Washington
Dec.	Tue.	1—Boston
	Fri.	4—Detroit
	Tue.	8—At Chicago
	Wed.	9—Utah
	Fri.	11—At Milwaukee
	Sat.	12—New Jersey
	Tue.	15—Milwaukee
	Thu.	17—At Detroit
	Fri.	18—Cleveland
	Tue.	22—Atlanta
	Fri.	25—At Washington
	Sat.	26—New York
	Mon.	28—At New Jersey
	Tue.	29—Milwaukee
Jan.	Sat.	2—Washington
	Tue.	5—Phoenix
	Fri.	8—At Utah
	Sat.	9—At Golden State
	Tue.	12—At Portland
	Wed.	13—At Seattle
	Fri.	15—Los Angeles
	Sun.	17—Chicago
	Tue.	19—At Chicago
	Wed.	20—At Boston
	Fri.	22—Philadelphia
	Sat.	23—At San Antonio
	Tue.	26—At Houston
Feb.	Tue.	2—Boston
	Wed.	3—At Cleveland
	Thu.	4—Denver
	Sat.	6—Dallas
	Tue.	9—Milwaukee
	Wed.	10—At Philadelphia
	Sat.	13—At Cleveland
	Sun.	14—Portland
	Wed.	17—At Milwaukee
	Thu.	18—San Diego
	Sat.	20—At Detroit
	Sun.	21—New Jersey
	Wed.	24—New York
	Fri.	26—San Antonio
	Sun.	28—Detroit
Mar.	Tue.	2—At Denver
	Wed.	3—At Kansas City
	Sun.	7—At Dallas
	Tue.	9—Golden State
	Wed.	10—At Boston
	Fri.	12—At Washington
	Sat.	13—At Atlanta
	Tue.	16—Seattle
	Fri.	19—At Philadelphia
	Sat.	20—New Jersey
	Wed.	24—Washington
	Fri.	26—Atlanta
	Sun.	28—Chicago
	Tue.	30—At New York
	Wed.	31—Detroit
Apr.	Sat.	3—At Detroit
	Sun.	4—At Milwaukee
	Wed.	7—At Washington
	Fri.	9—Cleveland
	Sat.	10—At New Jersey
	Tue.	13—At Philadelphia
	Thu.	15—Atlanta
	Fri.	16—At Atlanta
	Sun.	18—At Chicago

KANSAS CITY KINGS

**Office: 1800 Genessee, Suite 101, Kemper Arena,
Kansas City, Missouri 64102
Telephone: (Area Code 816) 421-3131**

President—H. Paul Rosenberg
Secretary-Treasurer/General Counsel—
Robert Margolin
Directors—H. Paul Rosenberg, Robert Margolin,
Tom Muir, Ray Evans, Leon Karosen, Truman Sloan,
Leonard Strauss, Dr. Clay Blair, Herbert Jacobson.
Executive Vice President/General Manager—
Jeffrey Cohen
Head Coach—Lowell "Cotton" Fitzsimmons
Assistant Coach—Frank Hamblen
Assistant Coach/Scout—Gary Fitzsimmons
Trainer—Bill Jones
Director of Public Relations—Craig Thompson
Assistant Director of Public Relations—Julie Fie
Director of Marketing—Lee Daniel
Controller—Dan Bedora
Director of Operations—Lanier Korsmeyer
Season Tickets—Elaine Grob
Suites/Tickets/Travel—Debbie Dunmire
Special Promotions Coordinator—Nancy Williams
Executive Secretary—Kelly Shannon
Accounting—Gayle Cancienne
Physician—Dr. Howard Ellfeldt
Statistician—Dave Herron
Home Court—Kemper Arena (16,642)
Team Colors—Red, White and Blue
Ticket Prices—$10.50, $9, $8, $7, $4
Radio—KCMO (810 AM), Neil Funk
Television—KBMA (Channel 41)

H. Paul Rosenberg

Jeff Cohen

Cotton Fitzsimmons

KANSAS CITY KINGS

1980-81 Record (Won 40, Lost 42)

Date	Opponent	KC	Opp
Oct. 11	Utah	98	91
12	At Phoenix	100	109–
14	At San Antonio	103	109–
15	Los Angeles	*107	112–
17	At Dallas	103	91
18	Seattle	122	127–
21	Golden State	111	116–
23	At Houston	105	96
25	Denver	125	122
28	At Atlanta	109	119–
29	Portland	115	98
31	At Boston	110	115–
Nov. 1	Phoenix	100	127–
4	At Utah	104	107–
5	New York	111	102
7	At Philadelphia	100	117–
8	Cleveland	111	106
11	At Portland	102	101
12	At Golden State	101	111–
14	At Seattle	125	127–
15	At San Diego	96	94
18	At Los Angeles	94	107–
21	At Denver	121	134–
26	New Jersey	118	100
28	At Detroit	94	104–
29	At San Antonio	104	106–
Dec. 2	At Washington	103	107–
3	Phoenix	103	100
5	Houston	108	100
6	At Indiana	88	107–
10	San Diego	112	100
11	At San Antonio	104	122–
13	Dallas	114	107
16	At Denver	133	118
17	At Seattle	94	101–
20	Indiana	103	107–
23	At Cleveland	102	100
26	Philadelphia	103	113–
27	At New York	99	100–
28	At New Jersey	102	99
30	Golden State	104	106–
Jan. 2	Utah	101	95
7	At Houston	114	108
8	Washington	136	118
10	At Utah	99	92
11	San Diego	105	115–
14	Portland	91	110–
16	At Milwaukee	*112	118–
17	Denver	122	123–
20	At Dallas	104	91
21	San Antonio	115	108
23	Houston	113	107
27	At San Diego	114	119–
29	At Los Angeles	104	118–
Feb. 3	At Dallas	121	100
4	Detroit	91	90
6	At Seattle	102	92
8	At Portland	*123	129–
10	At Chicago	115	116–
11	Utah	99	87
13	Atlanta	113	106
15	Seattle	107	105
18	Boston	114	113
20	Milwaukee	112	109
21	At Denver	109	129–
22	At Golden State	96	104–
26	Dallas	105	102
28	Golden State	101	110–
Mar. 3	Los Angeles	98	99–
4	At San Antonio	111	97
5	Portland	106	100
8	Phoenix	105	68
10	At San Diego	107	100
13	At Los Angeles	101	116–
15	Chicago	87	97–
18	At Denver	**124	126–
20	San Antonio	*111	114–
22	Houston	108	114–
24	At Utah	105	92
25	At Phoenix	110	101
27	At Houston	84	91–
29	Dallas	113	104

1981-82 SCHEDULE

Oct. Fri. 30—San Antonio
Sat. 31—At Dallas
Nov. Wed. 4—San Diego
Fri. 6—Houston
Tue. 10—At Chicago
Wed. 11—At Boston
Fri. 13—At Philadelphia
Sat. 14—At New Jersey
Tue. 17—At New York
Thu. 19—At Indiana
Sat. 21—At Denver
Wed. 25—Detroit
Fri. 27—Denver
Sun. 29—Golden State
Dec. Tue. 1—At Houston
Wed. 2—Portland
Fri. 4—Seattle
Sun. 6—At Los Angeles
Wed. 9—Dallas
Fri. 11—At Utah
Sat. 12—At Golden State
Wed. 16—Phoenix
Fri. 18—Utah
Sat. 19—At Phoenix
Tue. 22—At Milwaukee
Wed. 23—At Cleveland
Sat. 26—Boston
Tue. 29—At Dallas
Wed. 30—Denver
Jan. Fri. 1—At Golden State
Sun. 3—At Portland
Tue. 5—At San Diego
Thu. 7—New York
Sat. 9—At San Antonio
Tue. 12—At Denver
Wed. 13—Cleveland
Fri. 15—New Jersey
Sun. 17—Los Angeles
Tue. 19—At Houston
Thu. 21—Dallas
Sat. 23—At Washington
Wed. 27—Seattle
Thu. 28—At San Antonio
Feb. Tue. 2—At Portland
Wed. 3—At Seattle
Fri. 5—San Antonio
Sun. 7—Houston
Wed. 10—At Los Angeles
Fri. 12—Utah
Sun. 14—Golden State
Tue. 16—At Denver
Wed. 17—Phoenix
Fri. 19—San Diego
Sun. 21—Milwaukee
Tue. 23—At Atlanta
Wed. 24—Portland
Fri. 26—At Washington
Sat. 27—At Detroit
Mar. Tue. 2—At Utah
Wed. 3—Indiana
Fri. 5—At Phoenix
Sun. 7—Chicago
Tue. 9—At Los Angeles
Thu. 11—At San Diego
Sun. 14—Philadelphia
Wed. 17—At Golden State
Fri. 19—Seattle
Sun. 21—San Diego
Wed. 24—Atlanta
Fri. 26—At Dallas
Sun. 28—Los Angeles
Tue. 30—At Portland
Wed. 31—At Seattle
Apr. Fri. 2—At Utah
Sun. 4—At Phoenix
Wed. 7—At San Antonio
Fri. 9—Utah
Sun. 11—San Antonio
Tue. 13—At Houston
Wed. 14—Dallas
Fri. 16—Denver
Sun. 18—Houston

LOS ANGELES LAKERS

Office: 3900 West Manchester Blvd., P.O. Box 10,
The Forum, Inglewood, Calif. 90306
Telephone: (Area Code 213) 674-6000

Owner—Dr. Jerry Buss
President—Lou Baumeister
Treasurer—Frank Mariani
Vice-President—Dr. Dick Gold
Vice-President—Dr. Larry Noble
Vice-President, Advertising—Jim Harkins
Vice-President, Sales—Jim Hunkins
Vice-President, Booking and General Manager—
Claire Rothman
Director of Marketing—Steve Chase
Director of Broadcasting—Ed Desser
Director of Public Relations—Bob Steiner
Director of Promotions—Lon Rosen
Assistant General Manager—Gene Felling
Director of Advertising Sales—Steve Hohensee
Controller—Ross Cote
Ticket Manager—Vern Ausmus
Operations Manager—Rob Collins
Broadcast Coordinator—Keith Harris
General Manager—Bill Sharman
Head Coach—Paul Westhead
Assistant Coach—Pat Riley
Assistant Coach, Scouting—Mike Thibault
Special Consultant—Jerry West
Assistant General Manager—Chick Hearn
Trainer—Jack Curran
Public Relations Director—Bruce Jolesch
Team Physician—Dr. Robert Kerlan
Team Dentist—Dr. Larry Paben
Basketball Secretary—Mary Lou Liebich
Public Relations Secretary—Linda Hall
Home Court—The Forum (17,505)
Team Colors—Royal Purple and Gold
Radio/Television—KLAC (570); KHJ (9), Chick Hearn, Keith Erickson
Game Times—Weekdays, 7:30 p.m.; Sundays, 7 p.m.

Jerry Buss

Bill Sharman

Paul Westhead

LOS ANGELES LAKERS

1980-81 Record (Won 54, Lost 28)

Date	Opponent	Score	Opp
Oct. 10	At Seattle	99	98
12	Houston	114	103
15	At Kansas City	*112	107
17	Phoenix	116	109
19	Golden State	125	107
21	At Portland	103	107−
24	Seattle	104	98
25	At Utah	127	99
26	San Antonio	102	108−
28	At San Diego	131	101
31	Cleveland	107	98
Nov. 2	Denver	121	123−
4	Portland	119	118
7	At Dallas	126	102
8	At San Antonio	109	112−
11	At Atlanta	126	97
12	At Houston	104	107−
14	San Diego	113	100
16	Dallas	110	102
18	Kansas City	107	94
20	At Phoenix	99	102−
21	Phoenix	116	88
23	Milwaukee	94	110−
27	At Golden State	128	119
29	At Denver	**124	123
30	At Chicago	108	122−
Dec. 3	San Diego	114	120−
6	At Golden State	103	119−
7	At Utah	113	100
9	At Dallas	103	92
10	At Houston	109	108
12	At Seattle	113	107
14	Golden State	122	113
16	At San Diego	92	97−
19	Portland	106	110−
21	San Antonio	135	122
23	At Portland	102	108−
26	Indiana	116	115
27	At Phoenix	106	116−
28	Philadelphia	122	116
30	At Utah	100	110−
Jan. 2	At San Antonio	112	118−
6	Washington	107	98
9	Seattle	92	87
11	Detroit	117	108
13	At Cleveland	108	104
14	At Washington	104	114−
16	At New Jersey	113	111
18	At Boston	96	98−
21	Atlanta	116	106
23	Denver	110	105
26	Portland	124	112
27	At Utah	111	104
29	Kansas City	118	104
Feb. 4	At Indiana	102	96
6	At Detroit	111	102
8	At Philadelphia	99	102−
11	Boston	91	105−
13	At Houston	114	105
15	Dallas	107	99
17	New York	96	87
20	Houston	107	110−
22	At New York	96	93
24	At Chicago	107	97
25	At Milwaukee	108	126−
27	At New Jersey	107	103
Mar. 1	Phoenix	96	101−
3	At Kansas City	99	98
4	At Denver	114	123−
10	San Antonio	118	104
12	At San Diego	122	116
13	Kansas City	116	101
15	San Diego	118	122−
17	At Dallas	114	109
18	At Phoenix	114	126−
20	Seattle	133	119
21	At Portland	117	111
22	At Golden State	120	118
24	At Golden State	110	103
27	At Seattle	97	90
28	At Utah	*110	112−
29	Denver	*146	148−

1981-82 SCHEDULE

Oct. Fri. 30	At Houston
Nov. Tue. 3	At Portland
Wed. 4	At Seattle
Fri. 6	Phoenix
Sun. 8	Dallas
Tue. 10	At San Antonio
Wed. 11	At Houston
Fri. 13	Portland
Sat. 14	At Phoenix
Sun. 15	Indiana
Wed. 18	At Utah
Fri. 20	San Antonio
Sat. 21	At San Diego
Tue. 24	At Dallas
Wed. 25	At San Antonio
Fri. 27	At San Diego
Sun. 29	Houston
Dec. Tue. 1	Utah
Wed. 2	At Seattle
Fri. 4	At Denver
Sun. 6	Kansas City
Tue. 8	Washington
Fri. 11	Portland
Sun. 13	At Golden State
Thu. 17	At Golden State
Sat. 19	At San Diego
Sun. 20	Atlanta
Tue. 22	At Portland
Fri. 25	At Phoenix
Sun. 27	San Diego
Tue. 29	Utah
Jan. Sun. 3	Seattle
Fri. 8	At Chicago
Sat. 9	At Detroit
Sun. 10	At Milwaukee
Tue. 12	At Cleveland
Fri. 15	At Indiana
Sun. 17	At Kansas City
Tue. 19	At Denver
Wed. 20	New Jersey
Fri. 22	Detroit
Tue. 26	Milwaukee
Thu. 28	Phoenix
Feb. Tue. 2	At Golden State
Wed. 3	New York
Fri. 5	At Washington
Sun. 7	At Boston
Tue. 9	At Atlanta
Wed. 10	At Kansas City
Fri. 12	San Antonio
Sun. 14	Boston
Tue. 16	Seattle
Fri. 19	Golden State
Sun. 21	At Denver
Tue. 23	Denver
Thu. 25	At Seattle
Fri. 26	Philadelphia
Sun. 28	Cleveland
Mar. Wed. 3	At New Jersey
Thu. 4	At New York
Sun. 7	At Philadelphia
Tue. 9	Kansas City
Fri. 12	Chicago
Sun. 14	Dallas
Tue. 16	At Portland
Wed. 17	At Utah
Fri. 19	At Dallas
Sun. 21	Houston
Tue. 23	Dallas
Fri. 26	At San Antonio
Sun. 28	At Kansas City
Tue. 30	San Diego
Apr. Thu. 1	At San Diego
Fri. 2	Phoenix
Sun. 4	Portland
Tue. 6	At Houston
Fri. 9	Denver
Sun. 11	Seattle
Tue. 13	At Golden State
Wed. 14	At Utah
Fri. 16	Golden State
Sun. 18	At Phoenix

MILWAUKEE BUCKS

Office: 901 North Fourth Street, Milwaukee, Wisconsin 53203
Telephone: (Area Code 414) 272-6030

Chairman of the Board/President—James F. Fitzgerald
Vice President—William J. Blake
Vice President/Consultant—Wayne Embry
Secretary—Walter S. Davis
Treasurer—J.P. Cullen
Directors—William J. Blake, J.P. Cullen, Walter S. Davis,
Wayne Embry, John H. Figi, Jr.,
Daniel F. Finnane, James F. Fitzgerald,
Charles D. Jacobus, George J. Korkos, M.D., John C. Koss,
James Schelble, M.D., Robert J. Trecker,
William J. Ryan, Stuart Shadel
Director of Player Personnel/Head Coach—Don Nelson
Vice President-Business Operations—John Steinmiller
Assistant Coaches—John Killilea, Dave Wohl, Garry St. Jean
Trainer—Jeff Snedeker
Medical Staff—George Korkos, M.D., John Krebs, D.D.S., David Haskell,
M.D., Conrad Heinzelmann, M.D.
Publicity Director—Bill King II
Ticket Manager—Bea Westfahl
Controller—Chuck Reupert
Executive Secretary—Jean Schuler
Team Chaplin—Fr. Gene Jakubek, S.J.
Equipment Manager—Tom Hoffer
Staff—Vickie Bence, Judith Berger, Ethel Heywood, Carole Szczech,
Virginia Weber
Game Staff—Robert Wanek, Jim Manske, Andy Friedrich, Ted Herpel,
Frank Novara, David Schmitz, Dennis Sell, Jack Gallo
Home Court—Milwaukee Arena (11,052)
Colors—Forest Green, Red and White
Game Times—7:30 p.m. (Sunday-Thursday), 8 p.m. (Friday and Saturday)
Television—WVTV-18 Eddie Doucette and Jon McGlocklin
Radio—WTMJ (620 AM) Jim Irwin and Jon McGlocklin

James Fitzgerald

John Steinmiller

Don Nelson

MILWAUKEE BUCKS

1980-81 Record (Won 60, Lost 22)

Date	Opponent	Bucks	Opp
Oct. 10	At Philadelphia	106	103
11	At New York	109	114—
16	Boston	103	110
18	At Cleveland	107	105
19	New Jersey	105	93
21	Cleveland	115	95
22	At Indiana	119	105
25	Chicago	109	93
26	Washington	111	88
28	At Chicago	106	99
29	At New Jersey	132	116
Nov. 1	At Atlanta	99	93
2	Indiana	135	121
4	Detroit	96	98—
7	At Boston	102	101
9	Philadelphia	121	136—
11	At Cleveland	100	96
12	At Detroit	122	98
14	New York	125	106
16	Chicago	108	114—
18	At Utah	126	93
20	At Portland	97	93
23	At Los Angeles	110	94
28	Atlanta	*113	108
29	At Washington	89	98—
30	Boston	107	105
Dec. 2	At Utah	119	108
5	Indiana	102	100
6	At New York	94	104—
9	At Boston	89	112—
11	New York	119	107
13	At Atlanta	119	122—
14	San Antonio	115	98
17	At New Jersey	112	115—
18	Detroit	121	104
19	At Chicago	106	129—
21	Houston	123	91
27	Dallas	112	96
30	At Washington	115	94
Jan. 4	San Diego	128	95
6	New Jersey	102	86
8	At Atlanta	98	95
10	At Indiana	102	106—
11	Phoenix	123	109
13	At Detroit	119	96
15	Philadelphia	113	110
16	Kansas City	*118	112
18	Portland	110	103
21	At Golden State	105	98
23	At Phoenix	122	131—
24	At San Diego	121	117
28	At Seattle	119	110
29	At Denver	118	131—
Feb. 3	Indiana	99	108—
5	Boston	113	103
6	At Cleveland	103	99
8	Chicago	128	109
11	At Indiana	107	101
13	Golden State	106	110—
14	At Houston	117	112
15	At San Antonio	108	110—
17	At Dallas	114	106
20	At Kansas City	109	112—
22	At Washington	102	93
25	Los Angeles	126	108
Mar. 1	Washington	137	107
3	Detroit	115	98
5	Atlanta	107	91
6	At New York	122	111
8	At Philadelphia	100	123—
9	Cleveland	118	100
11	At Boston	108	122—
12	Denver	131	113
13	Philadelphia	120	104
15	Seattle	132	108
17	At Chicago	106	116—
18	New York	103	116—
20	At Detroit	104	86
22	At New Jersey	125	116
24	New Jersey	131	107
26	Cleveland	137	109
29	At Atlanta	*132	128

1981-82 SCHEDULE

Oct.	Fri.	30	At Detroit
	Sat.	31	Boston
Nov.	Thu.	5	Washington
	Sat.	7	San Diego
	Tue.	10	At Atlanta
	Wed.	11	At New Jersey
	Fri.	13	New York
	Sun.	15	Cleveland
	Tue.	17	At Washington
	Wed.	18	At Philadelphia
	Fri.	20	At Boston
	Sat.	21	At New York
	Tue.	24	Detroit
	Fri.	27	Golden State
	Sun.	29	San Antonio
Dec.	Tue.	1	At Cleveland
	Fri.	4	Atlanta
	Sat.	5	At Detroit
	Wed.	9	Houston
	Fri.	11	Dallas
	Sat.	12	At New York
	Sun.	13	Philadelphia
	Tue.	15	At Indiana
	Fri.	18	New Jersey
	Tue.	22	Kansas City
	Sat.	26	At Cleveland
	Sun.	27	Chicago
	Tue.	29	At Indiana
	Wed.	30	Washington
Jan.	Sat.	2	At Chicago
	Sun.	3	Denver
	Tue.	5	New York
	Wed.	6	At New Jersey
	Fri.	8	Atlanta
	Sun.	10	Los Angeles
	Tue.	12	At Atlanta
	Wed.	13	At Philadelphia
	Fri.	15	Boston
	Sun.	17	Detroit
	Wed.	20	At Dallas
	Fri.	22	At Denver
	Sat.	23	At Golden State
	Tue.	26	At Los Angeles
	Thu.	28	At Utah
Feb.	Wed.	3	Chicago
	Fri.	5	Dallas
	Sun.	7	Phoenix
	Tue.	9	At Indiana
	Thu.	11	Portland
	Sat.	13	At Chicago
	Sun.	14	At Cleveland
	Wed.	17	Indiana
	Fri.	19	Cleveland
	Sun.	21	At Kansas City
	Tue.	23	At New York
	Wed.	24	At New Jersey
	Sun.	28	At Boston
Mar.	Tue.	2	Detroit
	Wed.	3	At Atlanta
	Sat.	6	At San Antonio
	Tue.	9	At Houston
	Wed.	10	Chicago
	Fri.	12	Seattle
	Sun.	14	Utah
	Tue.	16	Philadelphia
	Fri.	19	Cleveland
	Sun.	21	New Jersey
	Tue.	23	At Portland
	Wed.	24	At Seattle
	Fri.	26	At Phoenix
	Sat.	27	At San Diego
	Tue.	30	At Philadelphia
Apr.	Thur.	1	Atlanta
	Fri.	2	At Chicago
	Sun.	4	Indiana
	Tue.	6	Boston
	Fri.	9	At Detroit
	Sat.	10	At Washington
	Wed.	14	At Boston
	Fri.	16	New York
	Sun.	18	At Philadelphia

NEW JERSEY NETS

Office: 185 East Union Ave., East Rutherford, N.J. 07073
Telephone: (Area Code 201) 935-8888

Chairman—Alan N. Cohen
President—Joseph A. Taub
General Manager—Bob MacKinnon
Vice President-Marketing—Phil Dundie
Controller—Ralph Leske
Head Coach—Larry Brown
Assistant Coaches—Bill Blair, Mike Schuler
Director of Player Personnel—Al Menendez
Trainer—Fritz Massmann
Director of Community Affairs—Larry Doby
Director of Promotions/Group Sales—Howard Freeman
Director of Public Relations—Ted Pase
Assistant Controller—Anne Erhard
Director of Sales—Jerry Dailey
Administrative Assistant—Kathy Fernandes
Ticket Supervisor—Ed Lyons
Season Tickets/Promotions/Group Sales—
Mitchell Kaufman
Season Tickets—Mark Appleman
Assistant to the Public Relations Director—
Kevin MacConnell
Bookkeeper—Dottie Moretto
Marketing Assistant—Tina Sohn
Receptionist—Minnie Bottiglia
Official Scorer—Herb Turetsky
Team Physician—Dr. Allan Levy
Team Dentist—Dr. Alan I. Levy
Podiatrist—Dr. John McNerny
Orthopedic Consultant—Dr. Kim Sloan
Radio—WWRL (1600 AM) Joe Tait and Mike DiTomasso
Television—WOR-TV (Channel 9) Steve Albert
Home Court—Brendan Byrne Arena (20,149)
Team Colors—Red, White and Blue

Joe Taub

Bob MacKinnon

Larry Brown

1980-81 RESULTS, 1981-82 SCHEDULE

NEW JERSEY NETS

1980-81 Record (Won 24, Lost 58)

Date	Opponent	NJ	Opp
Oct. 10	Indiana	91	110—
11	At Cleveland	99	96
13	Detroit	108	92
15	Philadelphia	111	119—
17	At Washington	114	112
18	At Chicago	107	90
19	At Milwaukee	93	105—
22	Boston	104	108—
24	Cleveland	112	126—
25	At New York	101	105—
29	Milwaukee	116	132—
31	Washington	100	98
Nov. 1	At Indiana	100	113—
5	Chicago	105	120—
8	Atlanta	115	111
12	Denver	118	111
14	At Boston	102	126—
15	At Philadelphia	108	115—
16	Detroit	89	80
19	San Antonio	*104	112—
21	Houston	108	116—
22	At Detroit	103	117—
26	At Kansas City	100	118—
28	Utah	122	95
30	At Seattle	89	113—
Dec. 2	At Portland	118	105
3	At Golden State	108	131—
5	At Phoenix	90	88
7	At San Diego	95	98—
10	New York	104	106—
12	At Boston	104	119—
14	Philadelphia	107	114—
16	At Atlanta	114	131—
17	Milwaukee	115	112
19	At Philadelphia	107	122—
23	At Indiana	109	125—
25	At Washington	94	109—
26	Atlanta	95	108—
28	Kansas City	99	102—
30	At Chicago	110	121—
Jan. 2	Cleveland	105	111—
4	Indiana	104	113—
6	At Milwaukee	86	102—
7	At Indiana	103	112—
9	Phoenix	95	112—
10	Boston	115	117—
14	At Philadelphia	105	110—
16	Los Angeles	111	113—
17	At Detroit	116	104
18	At Washington	99	110—
21	Seattle	*126	122
22	At Cleveland	94	108—
25	Washington	100	118—
27	At Dallas	112	100
28	At Houston	99	111—
29	At San Antonio	108	122—
Feb. 4	San Diego	102	110—
7	At New York	106	113—
8	New York	102	116—
11	Chicago	*135	133
13	Indiana	103	100
15	Golden State	134	93
18	Cleveland	110	132
20	Portland	*123	113
22	Dallas	109	132—
24	At Denver	123	140—
25	At Utah	106	132—
27	At Los Angeles	103	107—
Mar. 1	Detroit	104	117—
3	At Chicago	102	128—
6	At Atlanta	106	109—
11	Washington	109	104
13	At Cleveland	140	125
15	At Boston	125	133—
17	Philadelphia	*126	117—
18	At Detroit	115	118—
20	At Atlanta	108	96
22	Milwaukee	116	125—
24	At Milwaukee	107	131—
25	Boston	105	111—
28	New York	88	90—
29	At New York	95	103—

1981-82 SCHEDULE

Oct.	Fri.	30	—New York
Nov.	Wed.	4	—Atlanta
	Thu.	5	—At Detroit
	Sat.	7	—At Chicago
	Sun.	8	—Indiana
	Tue.	10	—At New York
	Wed.	11	—Milwaukee
	Fri.	13	—At Boston
	Sat.	14	—Kansas City
	Wed.	18	—At Golden State
	Fri.	20	—At Portland
	Sun.	22	—At Seattle
	Tue.	24	—At Houston
	Fri.	27	—At San Antonio
	Sat.	28	—At Dallas
Dec.	Wed.	2	—Cleveland
	Sat.	5	—Philadelphia
	Tue.	8	—At Atlanta
	Wed.	9	—At Boston
	Fri.	11	—Denver
	Sat.	12	—At Indiana
	Wed.	16	—Chicago
	Fri.	18	—At Milwaukee
	Sat.	19	—At Cleveland
	Wed.	23	—New York
	Fri.	25	—At New York
	Sat.	26	—Washington
	Mon.	28	—Indiana
	Wed.	30	—Detroit
Jan.	Sat.	2	—At Atlanta
	Tue.	5	—At Washington
	Wed.	6	—Milwaukee
	Fri.	8	—Cleveland
	Sat.	9	—At Philadelphia
	Mon.	11	—Boston
	Thu.	14	—Chicago
	Fri.	15	—At Kansas City
	Sun.	17	—Philadelphia
	Wed.	20	—At Los Angeles
	Fri.	22	—At Phoenix
	Sat.	23	—At San Diego
	Tue.	26	—At Utah
	Wed.	27	—At Denver
Feb.	Tue.	2	—At Chicago
	Wed.	3	—Atlanta
	Fri.	5	—At Philadelphia
	Sat.	6	—At Detroit
	Sun.	7	—At Cleveland
	Wed.	10	—Detroit
	Fri.	12	—Golden State
	Sun.	14	—Dallas
	Wed.	17	—Chicago
	Fri.	19	—Houston
	Sat.	20	—Utah
	Sun.	21	—At Indiana
	Wed.	24	—Milwaukee
	Fri.	26	—Portland
	Sun.	28	—San Diego
Mar.	Tue.	2	—At Washington
	Wed.	3	—Los Angeles
	Fri.	5	—At Chicago
	Sat.	6	—At Atlanta
	Wed.	10	—Phoenix
	Fri.	12	—Boston
	Sun.	14	—Seattle
	Wed.	17	—San Antonio
	Sat.	20	—At Indiana
	Sun.	21	—At Milwaukee
	Wed.	24	—At Philadelphia
	Fri.	26	—At Washington
	Sat.	27	—Detroit
	Sun.	28	—New York
	Wed.	31	—Cleveland
Apr.	Fri.	2	—Washington
	Sun.	4	—At Cleveland
	Wed.	7	—Philadelphia
	Fri.	9	—At Boston
	Sat.	10	—Indiana
	Tue.	13	—At New York
	Wed.	14	—Washington
	Fri.	16	—Boston
	Sat.	17	—At Detroit

NEW YORK KNICKERBOCKERS

Office: Madison Square Garden Center
Four Pennsylvania Plaza, New York, N.Y. 10001
Telephone: (Area Code 212) 563-8000

Honorary Chairman—Edward S. Irish
President—Michael Burke
General Manager—Edward J. Donovan
Controller—Mel Lowell
Head Coach—Red Holzman
Assistant Coaches—Harold Fischer,
Alfred (Butch) Beard
Director of Public Relations—Kevin Kennedy
Public Relations Assistant—Carl Martin
Business Manager—Frank Blauschild
Trainer—Michael Saunders
Chief Scout—Richard McGuire
Scout—Andrew Lavane
Season Subscriptions Director—George Graf
Group Sales Director—Marge Fearon
Team Physician—Dr. Norman Scott
Team Dentist—Dr. George L. Bergofin
Home Court—Madison Square Garden (19,591)
Team Colors—Red, White and Blue
Ticket Prices—$14, $11.50, $10, $6
Radio—WNEW (1130) Marv Albert, Richie Guerin
Television—WOR-TV (Channel 9) Marv Albert, Cal Ramsey

Michael Burke

Eddie Donovan

Red Holzman

NEW YORK KNICKERBOCKERS

1980-81 Record (Won 50, Lost 32)

Date	Opponent	NYK	Opp
Oct.	11–Milwaukee	114	109
	14–Philadelphia	113	93
	17–At Atlanta	101	113–
	21–At Chicago	105	97
	23–At Boston	*109	107
	25–New Jersey	105	101
	29–At Indiana	95	102–
	30–Atlanta	*116	115
Nov.	1–Washington	111	93
	5–At Kansas City	102	111–
	7–At Denver	124	115
	8–At Utah	109	102
	11–Detroit	149	118
	12–At Philadelphia	125	113
	14–At Milwaukee	106	125–
	15–Cleveland	100	95
	18–Philadelphia	99	113–
	21–At Chicago	121	130–
	22–At Golden State	110	116–
	24–Houston	*113	110
	26–At Cleveland	*119	113
	28–At Boston	106	120–
	29–Portland	111	110
Dec.	2–Indiana	96	113–
	3–At Philadelphia	98	104–
	6–Milwaukee	104	94
	9–Washington	107	104
	10–At New Jersey	106	104
	11–At Milwaukee	107	119–
	13–Detroit	100	94
	16–Utah	112	97
	17–At Detroit	119	103
	19–At Washington	102	96
	20–Denver	120	114
	23–At Chicago	114	117–
	25–Boston	108	117–
	27–Kansas City	100	99
	30–Dallas	100	98
Jan.	2–At Detroit	100	102–
	3–Atlanta	131	95
	6–San Antonio	108	113–
	8–Indiana	*115	116–
	10–At Cleveland	104	99
	13–At Boston	89	93–
	14–At San Antonio	105	116–
	16–At Dallas	110	118–
	17–At Houston	99	98
	20–Seattle	98	97
	22–At San Diego	100	93
	23–At Portland	90	117–
	24–At Golden State	110	117–
	26–Phoenix	94	99–
	29–At Atlanta	114	111
Feb.	3–San Diego	101	98
	6–At Chicago	112	94
	7–New Jersey	113	106
	8–At New Jersey	116	102
	12–At Cleveland	122	111
	13–Detroit	120	92
	15–At Phoenix	115	101
	17–At Los Angeles	87	96–
	18–At Seattle	105	103
	20–Washington	124	112
	22–Los Angeles	93	96–
	24–At Atlanta	*120	117
	25–At Washington	105	120–
	28–Chicago	97	101–
Mar.	3–Atlanta	93	100–
	5–At Detroit	104	101
	6–Milwaukee	111	122–
	8–At Boston	94	115–
	11–At Philadelphia	95	115–
	13–Chicago	127	117
	15–Philadelphia	120	109
	17–Indiana	114	89
	18–At Milwaukee	116	103
	20–At Indiana	110	107
	21–Cleveland	119	105
	24–Boston	116	118–
	25–At Washington	84	105–
	28–At New Jersey	90	88
	29–New Jersey	103	95

1981-82 SCHEDULE

Oct.	Fri.	30	At New Jersey
	Sat.	31	Indiana
Nov.	Tue.	3	At Houston
	Fri.	6	At Dallas
	Sat.	7	At San Antonio
	Tue.	10	New Jersey
	Fri.	13	At Milwaukee
	Sat.	14	Philadelphia
	Tue.	17	Kansas City
	Thu.	19	Atlanta
	Sat.	21	Milwaukee
	Tue.	24	At Indiana
	Fri.	27	At Cleveland
	Sat.	28	Cleveland
Dec.	Tue.	1	Detroit
	Thu.	3	Washington
	Sat.	5	Boston
	Tue.	8	Denver
	Thu.	10	At Detroit
	Sat.	12	Milwaukee
	Tue.	15	At Atlanta
	Wed.	16	At Philadelphia
	Fri.	18	Chicago
	Sat.	19	At Detroit
	Tue.	22	Philadelphia
	Wed.	23	At New Jersey
	Fri.	25	New Jersey
	Sat.	26	At Indiana
	Tue.	29	At Chicago
	Wed.	30	At Cleveland
Jan.	Sat.	2	Detroit
	Tue.	5	At Milwaukee
	Thu.	7	Kansas City
	Sat.	9	At Atlanta
	Sun.	10	Washington
	Tue.	12	At Utah
	Thu.	14	At Phoenix
	Fri.	15	At Golden State
	Tue.	19	Boston
	Thu.	21	Atlanta
	Sat.	23	Chicago
	Mon.	25	Seattle
	Wed.	27	At Boston
	Thu.	28	At Washington
Feb.	Tue.	2	At Denver
	Wed.	3	At Los Angeles
	Fri.	5	At San Diego
	Sun.	7	At Portland
	Tue.	9	At Seattle
	Thu.	11	Golden State
	Sat.	13	Philadelphia
	Sun.	14	At Philadelphia
	Tue.	16	Dallas
	Fri.	19	Phoenix
	Sun.	21	Houston
	Tue.	23	Milwaukee
	Wed.	24	At Indiana
	Sat.	27	Portland
	Sun.	28	At Washington
Mar.	Tue.	2	San Diego
	Thu.	4	Los Angeles
	Sat.	6	Detroit
	Sun.	7	At Boston
	Tue.	9	Utah
	Sat.	13	Washington
	Tue.	16	San Antonio
	Sat.	20	Atlanta
	Sun.	21	At Washington
	Tue.	23	Cleveland
	Fri.	26	At Chicago
	Sun.	28	At New Jersey
	Tue.	30	Indiana
Apr.	Thu.	1	Cleveland
	Sun.	4	At Philadelphia
	Tue.	6	At Atlanta
	Thu.	8	Boston
	Sat.	10	At Cleveland
	Sun.	11	At Detroit
	Tue.	13	New Jersey
	Thu.	15	Chicago
	Fri.	16	At Milwaukee
	Sun.	18	At Boston

PHILADELPHIA 76ers

Office: Veterans Stadium, P.O. Box 25040, Philadelphia, Pa. 19147-0240
Telephone: (Area Code 215) 339-7600

President—Harold Katz
General Counsel—S. Laurence Shaiman
Vice-President/General Manager—Pat Williams
Assistant General Manager/Business Manager—
John Nash
Head Coach—Billy Cunningham
Director of Player Personnel/Assistant Coach—
Jack McMahon
Assistant Coach—Chuck Daly
Director of Press Relations—Harvey Pollack
Director of Advertising Sales—Fred Liedman
Ticket Manager—Gerry Ryan
Group Sales Director—Jack Swope
Assistant Group Sales Director—
Clayton Sheldon
Director of Communications—Matt Guokas Jr.
Controller—Daniel P. Durso
Bookkeeper—Rosemary McCloskey
Public Relations Assistant—Mark Piazza
Administrative Assistant—Jeff Millman
Assistant Ticket Manager—Steve McKenna
Ticket Office Assistants—Sharon Chidester, Georgeanna Costello
Executive Secretary—Marlene Barnes
Receptionist—Debbie Davies
Trainer—Al Domenico
Team Physician—Dr. Michael Clancy
Consulting Physician—Dr. Stanley Lorber
Consulting Dentist—Dr. David Link
Consulting Podiatrist—Dr. David Berman
Team Photographer—Steve Toporov
Equipment Manager—Marc Cohen
Home Court—The Spectrum (18,276)
Team Colors—Red, White and Blue
Radio—WCAU (1210 AM)
Television—WKBS-TV (Channel 48) and PRISM (Cable)
Broadcasters—Matt Guokas, Andy Musser, Steve Frederichs, Jim Barniak
Game Times—Monday through Saturday 7:35 p.m., Sundays 1 p.m.
Ticket Prices—$11, $9, $8, $7, $5

Harold Katz

Pat Williams

Billy Cunningham

PHILADELPHIA 76ers

1980-81 Record (Won 62, Lost 20)

Oct.	10—Milwaukee		103	106—
	11—At Washington		**126	120
	14—At New York		93	113—
	15—At New Jersey		119	111
	18—Washington		117	101
	22—At Detroit		94	93
	25—At Atlanta		113	100
	28—At Cleveland		119	101
	29—Chicago		115	102
	31—At Atlanta		107	96
Nov.	1—Boston		*117	113
	5—Detroit		107	103
	7—Kansas City		117	100
	9—At Milwaukee		136	121
	11—At Chicago		121	80
	12—New York		113	125—
	13—At Indiana		130	103
	15—New Jersey		115	108
	18—At New York		113	99
	19—Golden State		110	101
	21—Indiana		97	88
	22—At San Antonio		108	101
	25—At Dallas		108	92
	26—At Houston		101	100
	28—Portland		116	103
	29—Utah		113	93
Dec.	2—At Atlanta		*108	112—
	3—New York		104	98
	5—Atlanta		104	100
	9—At Cleveland		96	83
	10—Chicago		113	100
	12—Washington		95	79
	14—At New Jersey		114	107
	16—At Indiana		109	107
	17—Cleveland		103	79
	19—New Jersey		122	107
	26—At Kansas City		113	103
	27—At Denver		121	125—
	28—At Los Angeles		116	122—
	30—At Portland		128	109—
Jan.	2—At Seattle		*120	117
	3—At Golden State		119	105
	7—San Diego		135	102
	9—Houston		107	94
	10—At Chicago		117	102
	14—New Jersey		110	105
	15—At Milwaukee		110	113—
	16—Cleveland		137	119
	18—Seattle		113	92
	20—At Detroit		75	83—
	21—Indiana		118	104
	22—At Washington		128	116
	25—Phoenix		98	93
	28—At Boston		101	104—
Feb.	3—At Atlanta		97	93
	4—Boston		107	104
	6—San Diego		129	113
	8—Los Angeles		102	99
	11—Cleveland		*122	120
	13—Washington		102	104—
	15—Atlanta		116	98
	18—Detroit		111	97
	19—At Washington		108	129—
	20—Dallas		117	109
	22—At Phoenix		110	116—
	25—At San Diego		107	95
	27—At Utah		87	83
Mar.	1—At Boston		107	114—
	4—Chicago		100	111—
	6—Denver		131	112
	8—Milwaukee		123	100
	10—At Indiana		103	102
	11—New York		115	95
	13—At Milwaukee		104	120—
	15—At New York		109	120—
	17—At New Jersey		*120	126—
	18—Indiana		107	95
	20—At Chicago		108	120—
	22—Boston		126	94
	25—Detroit		114	75
	27—At Cleveland		138	117
	29—At Boston		94	98—

1981-82 SCHEDULE

Oct.	Fri.	30—Cleveland
	Sat.	31—At Atlanta
Nov.	Tue.	3—At Washington
	Wed.	4—At Indiana
	Fri.	6—Atlanta
	Tue.	10—At Chicago
	Wed.	11—Chicago
	Fri.	13—Kansas City
	Sat.	14—At New York
	Wed.	18—Milwaukee
	Fri.	20—At Cleveland
	Sat.	21—Houston
	Fri.	27—At Indiana
	Sat.	28—Detroit
Dec.	Tue.	1—At Atlanta
	Wed.	2—San Antonio
	Fri.	4—At Boston
	Sat.	5—At New Jersey
	Wed.	9—Denver
	Fri.	11—Cleveland
	Sat.	12—At Chicago
	Sun.	13—At Milwaukee
	Wed.	16—New York
	Sat.	19—Boston
	Tue.	22—At New York
	Sun.	27—At Phoenix
	Tue.	29—At Golden State
	Wed.	30—At Seattle
Jan.	Fri.	1—At Portland
	Sat.	2—At Utah
	Tue.	5—At Detroit
	Wed.	6—Washington
	Fri.	8—At Boston
	Sat.	9—New Jersey
	Tue.	12—At Washington
	Wed.	13—Milwaukee
	Fri.	15—Atlanta
	Sun.	17—At New Jersey
	Wed.	20—Portland
	Fri.	22—At Indiana
	Sat.	23—Seattle
	Tue.	26—At San Antonio
	Wed.	27—At Dallas
	Thu.	28—At Houston
Feb.	Wed.	3—Washington
	Fri.	5—New Jersey
	Sun.	7—Chicago
	Wed.	10—Indiana
	Sat.	13—At New York
	Sun.	14—New York
	Wed.	17—Dallas
	Fri.	19—Utah
	Sun.	21—Phoenix
	Tue.	23—At San Diego
	Fri.	26—At Los Angeles
	Sat.	27—At Denver
Mar.	Tue.	2—At Chicago
	Wed.	3—San Diego
	Fri.	5—Atlanta
	Sun.	7—Los Angeles
	Wed.	10—Golden State
	Sun.	14—At Kansas City
	Tue.	16—At Milwaukee
	Wed.	17—Washington
	Fri.	19—Indiana
	Sun.	21—Boston
	Wed.	24—New Jersey
	Thu.	25—At Detroit
	Fri.	26—At Cleveland
	Sun.	28—At Boston
	Tue.	30—At Milwaukee
	Wed.	31—Chicago
Apr.	Fri.	2—Cleveland
	Sun.	4—New York
	Tue.	6—At Chicago
	Wed.	7—At New Jersey
	Fri.	9—At Atlanta
	Sun.	11—Boston
	Tue.	13—At Indiana
	Wed.	14—Detroit
	Fri.	16—At Washington
	Sun.	18—Milwaukee

PHOENIX SUNS

**Office: Office: Funk's Greyhound Building, 2910 N. Central,
Phoenix, Ariz. 85012-2779**

Telephone: (Area Code 602) 266-5753

President—Richard Bloch
Vice-President—Donald Diamond
Assistant Vice-President—Marvin Meyer
Secretary-Treasurer—Donald Pitt
Assistavt Secretary—Lawrence Kartiganer
General Manager—Jerry Colangelo
Head Coach—John MacLeod
Assistant Coaches—Al Bianchi, John Wetzel
Trainer—Joe Proski
Team Physician—Dr. Paul Steingard
Business Manager—Bob Machen
Accountant—Kel Hansen
Director of Public Relations—Tom Ambrose
Team Statistician—Barry Ringel
Director of Marketing—Harvey Shank
Season Ticket and Group Sales—Jay Abraham, Jeff Lind
Staff—Ruth Dryjanski, Connie Stewart, Val Hargis,
Cheryl Sydnor, Carolyn Cuddihy, Bargi Neary, Kenny Glenn
Team Photographers—Joey Beninato, Tut Curtis
Home Court—Arizona Veteran's Memorial Coliseum (12,660)
Team Colors—Purple, Orange and Copper
Ticket Prices—$12, $9.50, $7, $4.50
Game Times—Weekdays and Saturdays, 7:35 p.m.; Sundays, 7:05 p.m.
Radio—KTAR (620 AM) Al McCoy, Dick Van Arsdale
Television—KPNX-TV (Channel 12) Al McCoy, Dick Van Arsdale

Richard Bloch

Jerry Colangelo

John MacLeod

1980-81 RESULTS, 1981-82 SCHEDULE

PHOENIX SUNS

1980-81 Record (Won 57, Lost 25)

Date	Opponent	Sun	Opp
Oct. 10	Golden State	121	101
12	Kansas City	109	100
15	At Utah	107	93
17	At Los Angeles	109	116—
19	At San Diego	102	84
21	Dallas	111	99
24	At Denver	117	94
25	At Seattle	100	75
29	San Diego	105	89
31	At Detroit	*103	98
Nov. 1	At Kansas City	127	100
4	Indiana	109	108
5	At San Antonio	84	114—
8	At Houston	116	115
11	At San Diego	109	107
12	San Antonio	130	127
15	At Golden State	108	119—
16	Portland	119	107
18	At Dallas	102	91
20	Los Angeles	102	99
21	At Los Angeles	88	116—
23	Denver	131	113
26	Seattle	113	103
28	Chicago	102	101
29	At Golden State	113	108
30	Houston	117	114
Dec. 2	At San Antonio	122	107
3	At Kansas City	100	103—
5	New Jersey	88	90—
7	Golden State	106	88
9	At Chicago	123	108
10	At Indiana	90	102—
14	Portland	110	116—
17	Dallas	115	102
19	Utah	108	90
21	At Portland	111	100
22	At Seattle	109	98
23	Detroit	113	104
25	San Antonio	131	111
27	Los Angeles	116	106
30	At Boston	97	116—
Jan. 2	At Denver	133	132
6	At Atlanta	113	106
7	At Boston	90	108—
9	At New Jersey	112	95
11	At Milwaukee	109	123—
13	Seattle	104	99
14	Denver	128	102
16	Houston	92	89
18	Atlanta	120	86
20	At San Antonio	*112	119—
21	At Houston	100	106—
23	Milwaukee	131	122
25	At Philadelphia	93	98—
26	At New York	99	94
28	At Washington	98	108—
29	At Cleveland	111	115—
Feb. 4	Utah	114	89
6	Houston	112	99
8	Washington	*113	107
10	At San Diego	107	93
11	Dallas	119	97
13	San Diego	110	94
15	New York	101	115—
17	Golden State	118	109
19	At Denver	126	127—
20	At Seattle	111	112—
22	Philadelphia	116	110
27	At Portland	117	121—
Mar. 1	At Los Angeles	101	96
4	Cleveland	126	106
5	At Utah	112	100
6	Portland	128	107
8	At Kansas City	68	105—
10	At Dallas	103	107—
18	Los Angeles	126	114
21	At Golden State	105	114—
22	Seattle	107	91
24	At Portland	111	120—
25	Kansas City	101	110—
27	San Diego	124	100
29	Utah	105	90

1981-82 SCHEDULE

Oct.	Fri.	30	At Portland
	Sat.	31	At Seattle
Nov.	Tue.	3	San Antonio
	Thu.	5	Dallas
	Fri.	6	At Los Angeles
	Sat.	7	At Utah
	Tue.	10	At Denver
	Thu.	12	Indiana
	Sat.	14	Los Angeles
	Wed.	18	At Atlanta
	Sat.	21	At Dallas
	Wed.	25	Houston
	Fri.	27	Chicago
Dec.	Tue.	1	San Diego
	Thu.	3	Denver
	Sat.	5	Utah
	Tue.	8	At San Diego
	Wed.	9	At Golden State
	Thu.	10	Portland
	Sat.	12	Washington
	Tue.	15	At Houston
	Wed.	16	At Kansas City
	Fri.	18	At San Antonio
	Sat.	19	Kansas City
	Wed.	23	Golden State
	Fri.	25	Los Angeles
	Sat.	26	At Golden State
	Sun.	27	Philadelphia
	Wed.	30	Portland
Jan.	Sat.	2	Seattle
	Tue.	5	At Indiana
	Thu.	7	At Detroit
	Sat.	9	At Dallas
	Tue.	12	Golden State
	Thu.	14	New York
	Sat.	16	San Diego
	Tue.	19	San Antonio
	Fri.	22	New Jersey
	Sat.	23	Detroit
	Wed.	27	At San Diego
	Thu.	28	At Los Angeles
Feb.	Wed.	3	Golden State
	Thu.	4	At San Antonio
	Fri.	5	At Houston
	Sun.	7	At New Jersey
	Wed.	10	Boston
	Fri.	12	Atlanta
	Sat.	13	At Utah
	Tue.	16	At Chicago
	Wed.	17	At Kansas City
	Fri.	19	At New York
	Sun.	21	At Philadelphia
	Wed.	24	Cleveland
	Fri.	26	Denver
	Sun.	28	At Seattle
Mar.	Tue.	2	At Portland
	Wed.	3	Utah
	Fri.	5	Kansas City
	Sun.	7	Houston
	Tue.	9	At Washington
	Wed.	10	At New Jersey
	Thu.	11	At Cleveland
	Sun.	14	At Boston
	Tue.	16	At Houston
	Wed.	17	Denver
	Sun.	21	Seattle
	Tue.	23	At Golden State
	Wed.	24	Dallas
	Fri.	26	Milwaukee
	Sat.	27	At Denver
	Mon.	29	At Utah
	Wed.	31	San Diego
Apr.	Fri.	2	At Los Angeles
	Sun.	4	Kansas City
	Tue.	6	At Seattle
	Thu.	8	Portland
	Fri.	9	At Dallas
	Sat.	10	Seattle
	Tue.	13	At San Diego
	Wed.	14	San Antonio
	Fri.	16	At Portland
	Sun.	18	Los Angeles

PORTLAND TRAIL BLAZERS

Office: Suite 380 Lloyd Building, 700 N.E. Multnomah Street, Portland, Ore. 97232
Telephone: (Area Code 503) 234-9291

President—Lawrence Weinberg
Executive Vice-President—Harry Glickman
Vice-President, Administration—George Rickles
Treasurer—Herman Sarkowsky
Secretary—Moe Tonkon
Assistant Secretary-Treasurer—Morris J. Galen
General Manager/Director of Player Personnel—
Stuart K. Inman
Vice-President, Marketing—Jon Spoelstra
Head Coach—Jack Ramsay
Assistant Coach—Jimmy Lynam
Scout/Assistant Coach—Morris "Bucky" Buckwalter
Trainer—Ron Culp
Administrative Assistant—Sandy Chisholm
Marketing Manager—Berlyn Hodges
Publicity Director—John White
Publicity Assistant—Cheri White
Director of Promotions—Wally Scales
Coordinator of Communications—Art Johnson
Director of Television Productions—George Wasch
Broadcasting Producer—Steve Jones
Account Executive—Philippe Lavie
Media Broadcasting Manager—Sue Miller
Comptroller—Gail Miller
Ticket Coordinator—Mary Conchuratt
Ticket Secretary—Meredith Wayt
Accounting Department—Lori Ryan, Kathy Cereghino
Receptionist—Kim Riley
Team Physician—Dr. Robert D. Cook
Team Dentist—Dr. Larry Mudrick
Optometrist—Dr. Tim Noles
Colors—Scarlet, Black and White
Home Court—Memorial Coliseum (12,666)
Ticket Prices—Coliseum—$13.50, $10.50, $8, $6
Radio—KEX (1190 AM) Bill Schonely
Television—KPTV (Channel 12) Jimmy Jones
Game Times—Monday through Saturday, 7:30 p.m.; Sundays 7 p.m.

Lawrence Weinberg

Stu Inman

Jack Ramsay

1980-81 RESULTS, 1981-82 SCHEDULE

PORTLAND TRAIL BLAZERS

1980-81 Record (Won 45, Lost 37)

Oct.	10—At Utah	86	96—	
	12—Seattle	107	96	
	15—At Golden State	92	95—	
	17—Houston	99	102—	
	21—Los Angeles	107	103	
	24—Dallas	120	105	
	26—At Seattle	98	111—	
	28—At San Antonio	112	120—	
	29—At Kansas City	98	115—	
Nov.	1—Utah	87	95—	
	2—Cleveland	102	96	
	4—At Los Angeles	118	119—	
	7—Golden State	122	113	
	8—San Diego	*106	110—	
	11—Kansas City	101	102—	
	14—At Dallas	106	113—	
	15—At Denver	123	125—	
	16—At Phoenix	107	119—	
	18—Denver	122	103	
	20—Milwaukee	93	97—	
	23—Dallas	116	96	
	25—At Atlanta	108	112—	
	26—At Boston	101	126—	
	28—At Philadelphia	103	116—	
	29—At New York	110	111—	
Dec.	2—New Jersey	105	118—	
	4—At San Diego	103	100	
	5—Chicago	116	115	
	7—San Antonio	116	115	
	9—Seattle	111	98	
	12—Houston	106	100	
	14—At Phoenix	116	110	
	17—At Golden State	115	113	
	19—At Los Angeles	110	106	
	20—Atlanta	*122	119	
	21—Phoenix	100	111—	
	23—Los Angeles	108	102	
	25—Golden State	115	114	
	26—At Seattle	96	90	
	30—Philadelphia	109	108	
Jan.	1—Denver	122	119	
	3—At Utah	103	109—	
	4—Boston	111	120—	
	6—Detroit	110	90	
	9—At San Antonio	86	102—	
	10—At Houston	105	106—	
	14—At Kansas City	110	91	
	16—At Chicago	113	112	
	18—At Milwaukee	103	110—	
	20—At Cleveland	94	99—	
	23—New York	117	90	
	25—San Antonio	118	100	
	26—At Los Angeles	112	124—	
	29—At San Diego	108	106	
Feb.	3—Washington	*111	104	
	4—At Golden State	100	115—	
	6—At San Antonio	96	122—	
	8—Kansas City	*129	123	
	12—Seattle	109	112—	
	13—At Denver	143	162—	
	15—Utah	118	84	
	17—At Washington	124	104	
	19—At Detroit	115	106	
	20—At New Jersey	*113	123—	
	22—At Indiana	*113	109	
	24—San Diego	107	123—	
	27—Phoenix	121	117	
Mar.	1—Utah	108	97	
	3—Indiana	117	112	
	5—At Kansas City	100	106—	
	6—At Phoenix	107	128—	
	8—Golden State	*120	112	
	10—At Denver	142	137	
	13—At Houston	104	126—	
	15—Dallas	135	110	
	17—San Diego	127	112	
	20—Houston	107	103	
	21—Los Angeles	111	117—	
	24—Phoenix	120	111	
	25—Seattle	112	103	
	27—At Dallas	123	109	
	29—At San Diego	144	129	

1981-82 SCHEDULE

Oct.	Fri. 30—Phoenix	
Nov.	Sun. 1—Seattle	
	Tue. 3—Los Angeles	
	Wed. 4—At Golden State	
	Fri. 6—Utah	
	Sun. 8—Denver	
	Tue. 10—Dallas	
	Thu. 12—At San Antonio	
	Fri. 13—At Los Angeles	
	Sun. 15—San Antonio	
	Fri. 20—New Jersey	
	Wed. 25—At Seattle	
	Fri. 27—At Utah	
	Sun. 29—Chicago	
Dec.	Tue. 1—At Denver	
	Wed. 2—At Kansas City	
	Fri. 4—At San Antonio	
	Sat. 5—At Houston	
	Tue. 8—Golden State	
	Thu. 10—At Phoenix	
	Fri. 11—At Los Angeles	
	Sun. 13—Detroit	
	Tue. 15—San Diego	
	Sat. 19—At Dallas	
	Tue. 22—Los Angeles	
	Fri. 25—Seattle	
	Sat. 26—At San Diego	
	Wed. 30—At Phoenix	
Jan.	Fri. 1—Philadelphia	
	Sun. 3—Kansas City	
	Tue. 5—San Antonio	
	Fri. 8—Denver	
	Sun. 10—Houston	
	Tue. 12—Indiana	
	Thu. 14—At Houston	
	Sat. 16—At Dallas	
	Tue. 19—At Atlanta	
	Wed. 20—At Philadelphia	
	Fri. 22—At Washington	
	Sun. 24—At Boston	
	Thu. 28—San Diego	
Feb.	Tue. 2—Kansas City	
	Wed. 3—At Utah	
	Fri. 5—Utah	
	Sun. 7—New York	
	Wed. 10—At Cleveland	
	Thu. 11—At Milwaukee	
	Sat. 13—At Detroit	
	Sun. 14—At Indiana	
	Tue. 16—Washington	
	Fri. 19—Boston	
	Sun. 21—Atlanta	
	Tue. 23—At Chicago	
	Wed. 24—At Kansas City	
	Fri. 26—At New Jersey	
	Sat. 27—At New York	
Mar.	Tue. 2—Phoenix	
	Fri. 5—Cleveland	
	Sun. 7—At Golden State	
	Wed. 10—At Dallas	
	Fri. 12—At San Antonio	
	Sat. 13—At Houston	
	Tue. 16—Los Angeles	
	Thu. 18—Golden State	
	Fri. 19—At Utah	
	Sun. 21—Dallas	
	Tue. 23—Milwaukee	
	Thu. 25—Houston	
	Fri. 26—At Golden State	
	Sun. 28—At Seattle	
	Tue. 30—Kansas City	
Apr.	Thu. 1—San Antonio	
	Fri. 2—At Denver	
	Sun. 4—At Los Angeles	
	Tue. 6—Denver	
	Thu. 8—At Phoenix	
	Fri. 9—San Diego	
	Sun. 11—Golden State	
	Tue. 13—At Seattle	
	Thu. 15—At San Diego	
	Fri. 16—Phoenix	
	Sun. 18—Seattle	

SAN ANTONIO SPURS

Office: HemisFair Arena, P.O. Box 530, San Antonio, Texas 78292

Telephone: (Area Code 512) 224-4611

President/NBA Governor—Angelo Drossos
General Manager—Bob Bass
Secretary-Treasurer—Maury Holden
Head Coach—Stan Albeck
Assistant Coach—Morris McHone
Trainer—Bernie LaReau
Public Relations Director—Wayne Witt
Sales/Promotions—Jim Johnson
Communications Director—Lawrence Payne
Business Manager—Paula Oxendine
Concessions Manager—Chuck Ridge
Ticket Manager—LaWanda McCombs
Sales/Souvenirs—Jim Goodman
Financial Secretary—Debra Morgan
Secretaries—Myrna Rendon, Chris Cabrera
Ticket Office—Renee Neilson, Teresa Rehfeld
Physicians—Dr. Jack Henry, Dr. P. M. Kaihlanen
Dentist—Dr. Linton Weems
Home Court—HemisFair Arena (15,694)
Team Colors—Metallic Silver, Black
Ticket Prices—$15, $12, $11, $9, $8, $6, $4
Radio—WOAI (1200), Sam Smith
Television—UAC Cable, (Channel 19), Sam Smith
Game Times—7:30 p.m. (CST)
Chief Statistician—Bob Howen
Arena Announcer—Pat Tallman

Angelo Drossos

Bob Bass

Stan Albeck

1980-81 RESULTS, 1981-82 SCHEDULE

SAN ANTONIO SPURS

1980-81 Record (Won 52, Lost 30)

Oct.	10—At Denver	113	112
	11—At Dallas	92	103—
	14—Kansas City	109	103
	16—At Detroit	102	99
	18—Dallas	110	96
	21—San Diego	123	120
	23—Golden State	128	109
	25—At San Diego	116	98
	26—At Los Angeles	108	102
	28—Portland	120	112
	29—At Utah	96	109—
	31—At Seattle	112	96
Nov.	1—At Golden State	108	123—
	5—Phoenix	114	84
	8—Los Angeles	112	109
	11—Indiana	113	119—
	12—At Phoenix	127	130—
	13—At San Diego	113	107
	15—Utah	120	104
	18—At Atlanta	93	97—
	19—At New Jersey	*112	104
	22—Philadelphia	101	108—
	26—Chicago	125	122
	28—Houston	115	124—
	29—At Kansas City	106	104
Dec.	2—Phoenix	107	122—
	4—Cleveland	130	100
	7—At Portland	115	116—
	8—At Seattle	99	104—
	9—At Utah	115	90
	11—Kansas City	122	104
	13—Denver	147	123
	14—At Milwaukee	98	115—
	16—At Dallas	89	83
	17—At Houston	113	107
	19—Golden State	126	111
	21—At Los Angeles	122	135—
	25—At Phoenix	111	131—
	27—Utah	142	117
	30—Seattle	102	100
Jan.	2—Los Angeles	118	112
	3—At Chicago	119	111
	6—At New York	113	108
	7—At Philadelphia	102	135—
	9—Portland	102	86
	11—Washington	137	106
	14—New York	116	105
	16—At Boston	85	94—
	17—At Washington	93	103—
	20—Phoenix	*119	112
	21—At Kansas City	108	115—
	24—At Denver	115	129—
	25—At Portland	100	118—
	29—New Jersey	122	108
Feb.	3—Detroit	102	99
	4—At Denver	135	132
	6—Portland	122	96
	8—Dallas	102	98
	11—At Houston	89	108—
	12—Atlanta	110	109
	14—At Dallas	107	99
	15—Milwaukee	110	108
	17—Boston	116	128—
	19—At Cleveland	104	118—
	20—At Indiana	106	109—
	22—Denver	*133	129
	24—At Golden State	131	126
	26—Seattle	123	113
Mar.	1—Houston	102	86
	4—Kansas City	97	111—
	6—At Seattle	94	102—
	8—Dallas	133	108
	10—At Los Angeles	104	118—
	14—At San Diego	118	126—
	15—At Golden State	*114	112
	17—Utah	94	86
	20—At Kansas City	*114	111
	22—San Diego	107	99
	24—Denver	123	125—
	25—At Houston	111	117—
	26—At Utah	98	97
	29—Houston	135	109

1981-82 SCHEDULE

Oct.	Fri.	30—At Kansas City
	Sat.	31—Denver
Nov.	Tue.	3—At Phoenix
	Wed.	4—Cleveland
	Sat.	7—New York
	Tue.	10—Los Angeles
	Fri.	13—At Seattle
	Sun.	15—At Portland
	Tue.	17—At Dallas
	Wed.	18—Seattle
	Fri.	20—At Los Angeles
	Sat.	21—At Golden State
	Wed.	25—Los Angeles
	Fri.	27—New Jersey
	Sun.	29—At Milwaukee
Dec.	Tue.	1—At Washington
	Wed.	2—At Philadelphia
	Fri.	4—Portland
	Wed.	9—Seattle
	Fri.	11—At Dallas
	Sat.	12—Utah
	Tue.	15—At Utah
	Fri.	18—Phoenix
	Sat.	19—At Denver
	Wed.	23—At San Diego
	Sat.	26—Atlanta
	Tue.	29—San Diego
	Wed.	30—Houston
Jan.	Sat.	2—Denver
	Tue.	5—At Portland
	Wed.	6—At Utah
	Thu.	7—At Golden State
	Sat.	9—Kansas City
	Tue.	12—Dallas
	Fri.	15—Houston
	Sat.	16—At Houston
	Tue.	19—At Phoenix
	Thur.	21—Utah
	Fri.	22—At Atlanta
	Sat.	23—Indiana
	Tue.	26—Philadelphia
	Thu.	28—Kansas City
Feb.	Tue.	2—Dallas
	Thu.	4—Phoenix
	Fri.	5—At Kansas City
	Sun.	7—At Golden State
	Tue.	9—Washington
	Fri.	12—At Los Angeles
	Sun.	14—Seattle
	Wed.	17—Detroit
	Fri.	19—At Denver
	Sat.	20—San Diego
	Tue.	23—At Golden State
	Thu.	25—At Detroit
	Fri.	26—At Indiana
	Sun.	28—At Chicago
Mar.	Tue.	2—At Houston
	Thu.	4—Boston
	Sat.	6—Milwaukee
	Mon.	8—Dallas
	Tue.	9—At San Diego
	Fri.	12—Portland
	Sun.	14—Chicago
	Tue.	16—At New York
	Wed.	17—At New Jersey
	Fri.	19—At Boston
	Sat.	20—At Cleveland
	Tue.	23—San Diego
	Wed.	24—At Denver
	Fri.	26—Los Angeles
	Sat.	27—At Utah
	Tue.	30—Golden State
Apr.	Thu.	1—At Portland
	Fri.	2—At Seattle
	Sun.	4—Houston
	Wed.	7—Kansas City
	Sat.	10—At Houston
	Sun.	11—At Kansas City
	Tue.	13—Denver
	Wed.	14—At Phoenix
	Fri.	16—At Dallas
	Sun.	18—Utah

SAN DIEGO CLIPPERS

Office: San Diego International Sports Arena
3500 Sports Arena Boulevard, San Diego, California 92110
Telephone: (Area Code 714) 226-1275

President—Donald T. Sterling
Vice-President/General Manager—Ted Podleski
Vice President/Promotions-Director—Patricia Simmons
Head Coach—Paul Silas
Assistant Coach—Bill Westphal
Assistant Coach/Director of Scouting—Pete Babcock
Business Manager—Paul Mendes
Director of Public Relations—Dick Christman
Director of Marketing—Steve Lees
Trainer—Larry Roberts
Assistant Director of Marketing—Tom Seidel
Controller—Dee Rutledge
Executive Assistant/Office Manager—Jacqueline Wise
Accountant—Debbie Larkin
Ticket Sales—Carl Lahr
Marketing Secretary—Lynn Paul
Ticket Office Assistant—Karen Pieratt
Ticket Office Assistant—Lauri Deabler
Receptionist—Karen Ryan
Team Physician—Dr. Lee Rice
Home Arena—San Diego Sports Arena (13,841)
Radio—KOGO (600 AM)
Ticket Prices—$11, $9, $7, $5

Donald Sterling

Ted Podleski

Paul Silas

1980-81 RESULTS, 1981-82 SCHEDULE

SAN DIEGO CLIPPERS

1980-81 Record (Won 36, Lost 46)

Date	Opponent	Score	Opp
Oct. 10	Houston	120	104
11	At Golden State	91	104
17	Denver	116	129
19	Phoenix	84	102
21	At San Antonio	120	123
24	Utah	103	100
25	San Antonio	98	116
28	Los Angeles	101	131
29	At Phoenix	89	105
31	Golden State	120	104
Nov. 4	At Dallas	116	102
5	At Houston	111	104
7	At Seattle	94	113
8	At Portland	*110	106
11	Phoenix	107	109
13	San Antonio	107	113
14	At Los Angeles	110	113
15	Kansas City	94	96
18	At Cleveland	94	104
20	At Detroit	90	97
21	At Washington	90	102
23	Seattle	110	99
25	Denver	108	94
26	At Denver	109	113
28	At Seattle	93	92
30	Golden State	120	100
Dec. 3	At Los Angeles	120	114
4	Portland	100	103
7	New Jersey	98	95
9	At Atlanta	87	114
10	At Kansas City	100	112
12	At Dallas	*109	112
14	Seattle	91	81
16	Los Angeles	97	92
18	Dallas	102	92
20	At Utah	103	91
21	At Detroit	117	97
27	Indiana	121	109
30	At Houston	98	104
Jan. 1	Boston	85	88
3	At Indiana	104	128
4	At Milwaukee	95	128
6	At Chicago	93	108
9	Denver	116	130
11	At Kansas City	115	105
14	Atlanta	106	85
16	At Utah	109	112
18	Dallas	115	109
21	At Denver	125	116
22	New York	93	100
24	Milwaukee	117	121
27	Kansas City	119	114
29	Portland	106	108
Feb. 3	At New York	98	101
4	At New Jersey	110	102
6	At Philadelphia	113	129
8	At Boston	107	123
10	Phoenix	93	107
13	At Phoenix	94	110
17	Chicago	128	95
19	Houston	116	99
20	At Golden State	115	114
22	Utah	108	93
24	At Portland	121	107
25	Philadelphia	95	107
28	At Houston	104	103
Mar. 1	At Dallas	91	99
4	Washington	103	115
6	Cleveland	140	125
7	At Utah	94	97
8	At Seattle	103	92
10	Kansas City	100	107
12	Los Angeles	116	122
14	San Antonio	126	118
15	At Los Angeles	122	118
17	At Portland	112	127
19	Golden State	139	113
22	At San Antonio	99	107
24	Seattle	111	106
25	At Golden State	114	120
27	At Phoenix	100	124
29	Portland	129	144

1981-82 SCHEDULE

	Date	Opponent
Oct.	Sat. 31	Houston
Nov.	Wed. 4	At Kansas City
	Fri. 6	At Chicago
	Sat. 7	At Milwaukee
	Tue. 10	Utah
	Thu. 12	Portland
	Sat. 14	Indiana
	Wed. 18	At Denver
	Thu. 19	Golden State
	Sat. 21	Los Angeles
	Tue. 24	Chicago
	Wed. 25	At Utah
	Fri. 27	At Los Angeles
	Sat. 28	Seattle
Dec.	Tue. 1	At Phoenix
	Thu. 3	Dallas
	Sat. 5	At Golden State
	Tue. 8	Phoenix
	Fri. 11	Washington
	Sun. 13	At Seattle
	Tue. 15	At Portland
	Thu. 17	Seattle
	Sat. 19	Los Angeles
	Wed. 23	At San Antonio
	Sat. 26	Portland
	Sun. 27	At Los Angeles
	Tue. 29	At San Antonio
	Wed. 30	At Atlanta
Jan.	Sat. 2	Houston
	Tue. 5	Kansas City
	Wed. 6	At Denver
	Thu. 7	At Dallas
	Sat. 9	Utah
	Tue. 12	At Houston
	Wed. 13	At Dallas
	Fri. 15	Cleveland
	Sat. 16	At Phoenix
	Sun. 17	Denver
	Wed. 20	At Golden State
	Thu. 21	Detroit
	Sat. 23	New Jersey
	Wed. 27	Phoenix
	Thu. 28	At Portland
Feb.	Tue. 2	At Houston
	Wed. 3	At Dallas
	Fri. 5	New York
	Sun. 7	At Seattle
	Tue. 9	Houston
	Fri. 12	Boston
	Sat. 13	At Denver
	Tue. 16	Atlanta
	Thu. 18	At Indiana
	Fri. 19	At Kansas City
	Sat. 20	At San Antonio
	Tue. 23	Philadelphia
	Fri. 26	At Boston
	Sun. 28	At New Jersey
Mar.	Tue. 2	At New York
	Wed. 3	At Philadelphia
	Fri. 5	Golden State
	Sun. 7	At Seattle
	Tue. 9	San Antonio
	Thu. 11	Kansas City
	Sat. 13	Dallas
	Tue. 16	At Detroit
	Wed. 17	At Cleveland
	Fri. 19	At Washington
	Sun. 21	At Kansas City
	Tue. 23	At San Antonio
	Thu. 25	Denver
	Sat. 27	At Milwaukee
	Tue. 30	At Los Angeles
	Wed. 31	At Phoenix
Apr.	Thu. 1	Los Angeles
	Sat. 3	Utah
	Tue. 6	At Golden State
	Thu. 8	Seattle
	Fri. 9	At Portland
	Sat. 10	At Golden State
	Mon. 12	At Utah
	Tue. 13	Phoenix
	Thu. 15	Portland

SEATTLE SUPERSONICS

Office: 419 Occidental South, Seattle, Washington 98104
Telephone: (Area Code 206) 628-8400

Chairman of the Board—Samuel Schulman
President/General Manager—Zollie Volchok
Vice-President, Finance—Tony Tucker
Head Coach/Director of Player Personnel—
Lenny Wilkens
Assistant Coach—Les Habegger
Head Scout/Assistant Coach—Dave Harshman
Trainer—Frank Furtado
Director of Advertising and Marketing—Dave Watkins
Director of Broadcasting—Lloyd Cooney
Director of Public Relations—Nancy Welts
Director of Ticket Operations—Len Greenhalgh
Assistant to the Coaching Staff/Office Manager—Sarah Furtado
Sales and Promotions—Brian Caldirola
Assistant Director of Public Relations—Jim Bennett
Assistant Controller—Carmen Dino
Receptionist—Margaret Blanchett-Nelson
Secretaries—Louise Welle, Jean Fisken
Team Physician—Dr. Martin Kushner
Orthopedic Consultant—Dr. David Karges
Team Dentist—Dr. Jack Nichols
Team Optometrist—Dr. George Winston
Home Court—Kingdome (40,192)
Team Colors—Green and Gold
Game Times—Monday-Thursday, 7:30 p.m.; Friday and Saturday, 8 p.m.;
Sunday times vary
Ticket Prices—$12, $9, $7, $5, $2
Radio—KIRO (710) Bob Blackburn
Television—KIRO (Channel 7, CBS) Wayne Cody

Samuel Schulman

Zollie Volchok

Lenny Wilkens

SEATTLE SUPERSONICS

1980-81 Record (Won 34, Lost 48)

Date	Opponent	Sonics	Opp
Oct. 10	Los Angeles	98	99
12	At Portland	96	107
14	At Dallas	85	83
15	At Houston	100	103
18	At Kansas City	127	122
20	At Utah	98	92
22	Dallas	102	107
24	At Los Angeles	98	104
25	Phoenix	75	100
26	Portland	111	98
28	Golden State	119	102
31	San Antonio	96	112
Nov. 1	At Denver	118	123
3	Cleveland	118	83
5	Denver	117	125
7	San Diego	113	94
12	At Utah	106	114
14	Kansas City	127	125
15	Houston	*143	139
18	At Houston	118	138
21	At Dallas	101	91
23	At San Diego	99	110
26	At Phoenix	103	113
28	San Diego	92	93
30	New Jersey	113	89
Dec. 3	Chicago	113	105
6	At Utah	108	98
8	San Antonio	104	99
9	At Portland	98	111
10	At Golden State	108	103
12	Los Angeles	107	113
14	At San Diego	81	91
17	Kansas City	101	94
19	Atlanta	95	92
22	Phoenix	98	109
26	Portland	90	96
27	At Golden State	98	104
30	At San Antonio	102	—
Jan. 2	Philadelphia	*117	120
5	Dallas	103	89
7	Detroit	99	94
9	At Los Angeles	87	92
10	Denver	119	116
11	Golden State	98	106
13	At Phoenix	99	104
16	At Indiana	95	94
18	At Philadelphia	92	113
20	At New York	97	98
21	At New Jersey	*122	126
23	At Washington	91	103
25	At Boston	106	115
28	Milwaukee	110	119
Feb. 4	Washington	108	99
6	Kansas City	92	102
7	Utah	96	89
8	Denver	133	112
10	Boston	*108	107
12	At Portland	112	109
14	At Chicago	117	134
15	At Kansas City	105	107
17	At Utah	101	98
18	New York	103	105
20	Phoenix	112	111
22	Houston	96	111
24	At Dallas	102	84
26	At San Antonio	113	123
27	At Houston	92	96
Mar. 1	At Atlanta	102	108
4	Indiana	105	93
6	San Antonio	102	94
7	At Golden State	103	106
8	San Diego	92	103
11	At Cleveland	101	95
13	At Detroit	102	100
15	At Milwaukee	108	132
17	At Denver	112	124
20	At Los Angeles	119	133
22	At Phoenix	91	107
24	At San Diego	106	111
25	At Portland	103	112
27	Los Angeles	90	97
29	Golden State	96	92

1981-82 SCHEDULE

Oct.	Sat. 31	Phoenix
Nov.	Sun. 1	At Portland
	Wed. 4	Los Angeles
	Fri. 6	Denver
	Tue. 10	At Golden State
	Wed. 11	Dallas
	Fri. 13	San Antonio
	Wed. 18	At San Antonio
	Fri. 20	At Dallas
	Sun. 22	New Jersey
	Wed. 25	Portland
	Fri. 27	Houston
	Sat. 28	At San Diego
Dec.	Tue. 1	Chicago
	Wed. 2	Los Angeles
	Fri. 4	At Kansas City
	Sat. 5	At Atlanta
	Tue. 8	At Houston
	Wed. 9	At San Antonio
	Sat. 12	Detroit
	Sun. 13	San Diego
	Tue. 15	At Denver
	Thu. 17	At San Diego
	Sat. 19	At Utah
	Wed. 23	Utah
	Fri. 25	At Portland
	Mon. 28	Golden State
	Wed. 30	Philadelphia
Jan.	Sat. 2	At Phoenix
	Sun. 3	At Los Angeles
	Wed. 6	Dallas
	Thu. 7	Houston
	Sat. 9	At Denver
	Wed. 13	Indiana
	Fri. 15	Utah
	Sun. 17	Golden State
	Tue. 19	At Cleveland
	Wed. 20	At Washington
	Fri. 22	At Boston
	Sat. 23	At Philadelphia
	Mon. 25	At New York
	Wed. 27	At Kansas City
Feb.	Wed. 3	Kansas City
	Fri. 5	At Golden State
	Sat. 6	Utah
	Sun. 7	San Diego
	Tue. 9	New York
	Thu. 11	At Houston
	Fri. 12	At Dallas
	Sun. 14	At San Antonio
	Tue. 16	At Los Angeles
	Thu. 18	Washington
	Fri. 19	Atlanta
	Sun. 21	Boston
	Thu. 25	Los Angeles
	Fri. 26	At Utah
	Sun. 28	Phoenix
Mar.	Wed. 3	Cleveland
	Fri. 5	Dallas
	Sun. 7	San Diego
	Tue. 9	At Chicago
	Fri. 12	At Milwaukee
	Sun. 14	At New Jersey
	Tue. 16	At Indiana
	Thu. 18	At Detroit
	Fri. 19	At Kansas City
	Sun. 21	At Phoenix
	Wed. 24	Milwaukee
	Fri. 26	Houston
	Sun. 28	Portland
	Tue. 30	At Denver
	Wed. 31	Kansas City
Apr.	Fri. 2	San Antonio
	Sun. 4	Denver
	Tue. 6	Phoenix
	Thu. 8	At San Diego
	Sat. 10	At Phoenix
	Sun. 11	At Los Angeles
	Tue. 13	Portland
	Wed. 14	Golden State
	Sat. 17	At Golden State
	Sun. 18	At Portland

UTAH JAZZ

**Office: The Salt Palace, 100 South West Temple, Suite 206,
Salt Lake City, Utah 84101
Telephone: (Area Code 801) 355-5151**

Co-Owner and President—Sam D. Battistone
Co-Owner and Managing Partner—Larry Hatfield
General Manager—Frank Layden
Vice President/Business Operations—Dean Lindsay
Head Coach—Tom Nissalke
Assistant Coach/Director of Player Personnel—Bill Bertka
Assistant Coach—Gene Littles
Team Scout/Administrative Assistant—Scott Layden
Trainer/Traveling Secretary—Don Sparks
Director of Public Relations—David Fredman
Director of Marketing and Sales—Gary Totland
Ticket Manager—Maurine Rapp
Controller—Bob Weidauer
Sales Manager—Brian Hogan
Team Counsel—Tim Grandi
Administrative Staff—Laura Herlovich (Public Relations),
Sioux Roderick (Marketing), Tom Hicks and Steve Pearson (Sales),
Marianne Thalman (Tickets), Terri Locher
and Helen Daynes (Basketball), Patty Shy (Accounting)
and Leslie Rush (Receptionist)
Team Physicians—Dr. J. Ralph McDonald, Dr. Gordon Affleck, Dr. Lyle Mason, Dr. Robert Gordon
Team Dentist—John R. Conner, Jr., D.D.
Team Podiatrist—Michael Lowe
Team Physical Therapist—Marvin "Moe" Forsyth, R.P.
Team Photographer—Frank Jensen
Home Court—The Salt Palace (12,143)
Team Colors—Purple, Green and Gold
Ticket Prices—$12, $10, $9, $7 and $5
Game Times—7:30 p.m. and 8:30 p.m.
Radio—KSL (1160 AM) Rod Hundley
Television—KSL-TV (Channel 5)

Sam Battistone

Frank Layden

Tom Nissalke

1980-81 RESULTS, 1981-82 SCHEDULE

UTAH JAZZ

1980-81 Record (Won 28, Lost 54)

Oct.	10—Portland	96	86
	11—At Kansas City	91	98—
	12—At Denver	*125	121
	15—Phoenix	93	107—
	18—Denver	117	115
	20—Seattle	92	98—
	24—At San Diego	100	103—
	25—Los Angeles	99	127—
	28—At Dallas	104	96
	29—San Antonio	109	96
	31—Dallas	144	122
Nov.	1—At Portland	95	87
	4—Kansas City	107	104
	6—Cleveland	112	96
	8—New York	102	109—
	10—Indiana	108	106
	12—At Seattle	114	106
	14—Houston	117	115
	15—At San Antonio	104	120—
	18—Milwaukee	93	126—
	22—At Atlanta	93	99—
	26—At Detroit	104	97
	28—At New Jersey	95	122—
	29—At Philadelphia	93	113—
Dec.	2—At Milwaukee	108	119—
	4—Denver	122	118
	6—Seattle	98	108—
	7—At Los Angeles	100	113—
	9—San Antonio	90	115—
	12—At Chicago	98	118—
	13—At Cleveland	103	110—
	16—At New York	97	112—
	18—Atlanta	97	109—
	19—At Phoenix	90	108—
	20—San Diego	91	103—
	23—At Dallas	101	96
	26—Golden State	109	110—
	27—At San Antonio	117	142—
	30—Los Angeles	110	100
Jan.	1—At Houston	103	117—
	2—At Kansas City	95	101—
	3—Portland	109	103
	7—At Denver	121	117
	8—Dallas	99	97
	10—Kansas City	92	99—
	14—At Golden State	110	107
	16—San Diego	112	109
	18—At Indiana	89	110—
	20—At Washington	113	121—
	21—At Boston	87	117—
	23—Golden State	101	103—
	24—At Houston	91	106—
	26—Detroit	102	99
	27—At Los Angeles	104	111—
	29—Houston	99	97
Feb.	4—At Phoenix	89	114—
	6—Denver	116	120—
	7—At Seattle	89	96—
	8—At Golden State	101	107—
	11—At Kansas City	87	99—
	13—Boston	104	89
	15—At Portland	84	118—
	17—Seattle	98	101—
	20—Chicago	84	92—
	22—At San Diego	93	108—
	23—Houston	102	106—
	25—New Jersey	132	106
	27—Philadelphia	83	87—
Mar.	1—At Portland	97	108—
	3—Washington	93	112—
	4—At Golden State	105	107—
	5—Phoenix	100	112—
	7—San Diego	97	94
	14—At Houston	82	101—
	17—At San Antonio	86	94—
	18—Dallas	120	113
	21—At Dallas	95	105—
	22—At Denver	108	113—
	24—Kansas City	92	105—
	26—San Antonio	97	98—
	28—Los Angeles	*112	110
	29—At Phoenix	90	105—

1981-82 SCHEDULE

Oct.	Fri.	30—Dallas
	Sat.	31—At Golden State
Nov.	Thu.	5—Golden State
	Fri.	6—At Portland
	Sat.	7—Phoenix
	Tue.	10—At San Diego
	Fri.	13—Denver
	Sat.	14—At Houston
	Wed.	18—Los Angeles
	Fri.	20—At Chicago
	Sat.	21—At Detroit
	Wed.	25—San Diego
	Fri.	27—Portland
	Sat.	28—At Denver
Dec.	Tue.	1—At Los Angeles
	Wed.	2—Dallas
	Fri.	4—Chicago
	Sat.	5—At Phoenix
	Tue.	8—At Dallas
	Wed.	9—At Indiana
	Fri.	11—Kansas City
	Sat.	12—At San Antonio
	Tue.	15—San Antonio
	Fri.	18—At Kansas City
	Sat.	19—Seattle
	Wed.	23—At Seattle
	Sat.	26—Houston
	Tue.	29—At Los Angeles
	Wed.	30—Boston
Jan.	Sat.	2—Philadelphia
	Wed.	6—San Antonio
	Fri.	8—Indiana
	Sat.	9—At San Diego
	Tue.	12—New York
	Fri.	15—At Seattle
	Sat.	16—Cleveland
	Tue.	19—Detroit
	Thu.	21—At San Antonio
	Fri.	22—At Houston
	Sat.	23—At Dallas
	Tue.	26—New Jersey
	Thu.	28—Milwaukee
Feb.	Wed.	3—Portland
	Fri.	5—At Portland
	Sat.	6—At Seattle
	Tue.	9—At Golden State
	Wed.	10—At Denver
	Fri.	12—At Kansas City
	Sat.	13—Phoenix
	Mon.	15—Denver
	Wed.	17—Atlanta
	Fri.	19—At Philadelphia
	Sat.	20—At New Jersey
	Tue.	23—At Washington
	Wed.	24—At Boston
	Fri.	26—Seattle
Mar.	Tue.	2—Kansas City
	Wed.	3—At Phoenix
	Thu.	4—Houston
	Sat.	6—Washington
	Tue.	9—At New York
	Thu.	11—At Atlanta
	Sat.	13—At Cleveland
	Sun.	14—At Milwaukee
	Tue.	16—At Denver
	Wed.	17—Los Angeles
	Fri.	19—Portland
	Sun.	21—At Golden State
	Tue.	23—Houston
	Thu.	25—Golden State
	Sat.	27—At San Antonio
	Mon.	29—Phoenix
Apr.	Fri.	2—Kansas City
	Sat.	3—At San Diego
	Tue.	6—Dallas
	Wed.	7—At Dallas
	Fri.	9—At Kansas City
	Sat.	10—Denver
	Mon.	12—San Diego
	Wed.	14—At Los Angeles
	Fri.	16—At Houston
	Sun.	18—At San Antonio

WASHINGTON BULLETS

Office: One Harry S. Truman Drive, Landover, Maryland 20786

Telephone: (Area Code 301) 350-3400

President—Abe Pollin
Secretary/Legal Counsel—David Osnos
Executive Vice-President—Jerry Sachs
General Manager—Bob Ferry
Vice-President—Wes Unseld
General Manager's Secretary—Rosemary Donohue
Head Coach—Gene Shue
Assistant Coaches—Bernie Bickerstaff, Don Moran
Scout—Bill Gardiner
Trainer—John Lally
Director of Public Relations—Mark Pray
Public Relations Secretary—Judy Holland
Director of Marketing—Bob Zurfluh
Assistant Director of Marketing—Sam Oidick
Marketing Consultant—Greg TenEyck
Marketing Representative (Sales)—Tom Ward, Paul Moyer, Karlton Hart
Marketing Representative (Promotions)—Craig Estrain
Marketing Assistant—Doris Pileggi
Director of Season Subscriptions—Brenda Hillman
Director of Community Relations—Hyman Perlo
Controller—Ken Zuerlein
Assistant to the Controller—Lola Lopez
Box Office Director—Joe Wisnewski
Assistant Box Office Director—Ralph Beyer
Director of Television/Telescreen—Sheldon Shemer
Director of Clubhouse Operations—John "Chief" Gentry
Team Physicians—Dr. Herbert Singer, Dr. Carl MacCartee, Dr. Steve Haas
Team Podiatrist—Dr. Paul Taylor
Team Dentist—Dr. Howard Salob
Consulting Physical Therapist—Bill Neill
Arena—Capital Centre (19,035)
Ticket Prices—$11, $9, $5.50
Team Colors—Red, White and Blue
Television—WDCA (Channel 20) John Sterling, James Brown
Radio—WTOP (1500) Mel Proctor

Abe Pollin

Bob Ferry

Gene Shue

WASHINGTON BULLETS

1980-81 Record (Won 39, Lost 43)

Date	Opponent	WB	Opp
Oct.	10—At Detroit	95	85
	11—Philadelphia	**120	126—
	16—At Cleveland	88	90
	17—New Jersey	112	114—
	18—At Philadelphia	101	117—
	22—Cleveland	109	96
	24—At Chicago	96	104—
	25—Boston	87	103—
	26—At Milwaukee	88	111—
	31—At New Jersey	98	100—
Nov.	1—At New York	93	111—
	4—Atlanta	122	98
	6—Dallas	116	95
	7—Detroit	114	88
	11—Denver	107	92
	12—At Boston	86	93—
	14—At Indiana	108	118—
	15—At Atlanta	100	88
	18—Golden State	97	103—
	21—San Diego	102	90
	22—At Chicago	101	114—
	27—Indiana	123	108
	28—At Cleveland	105	126—
	29—Milwaukee	98	89
Dec.	2—Kansas City	107	103
	3—At Indiana	115	128—
	5—Detroit	103	92
	7—At Boston	113	103
	9—At New York	104	107—
	10—Boston	99	101—
	12—At Philadelphia	79	95—
	13—Indiana	114	105
	16—Chicago	94	96—
	19—New York	96	102—
	23—At Atlanta	83	100—
	25—New Jersey	109	94
	27—Houston	115	97
	30—Milwaukee	94	115—
Jan.	2—Chicago	82	92—
	3—At Cleveland	112	132—
	6—At Los Angeles	98	107—
	8—At Kansas City	118	136—
	10—At Dallas	106	94
	11—At San Antonio	106	137—
	14—Los Angeles	114	104
	15—At Detroit	106	89
	17—San Antonio	103	93
	18—New Jersey	110	99
	20—Utah	121	113
	22—Philadelphia	116	128—
	23—Seattle	103	91
	25—At New Jersey	118	100
	27—At Atlanta	105	104
	28—Phoenix	108	98
Feb.	3—At Portland	*104	111—
	4—At Seattle	99	108—
	6—At Golden State	116	110
	8—At Phoenix	*107	113—
	10—At Denver	115	110
	13—At Philadelphia	104	102
	14—At Detroit	103	105—
	17—Portland	104	124—
	19—Philadelphia	129	108
	20—At New York	112	124—
	22—Milwaukee	93	102—
	25—New York	120	105
	27—At Chicago	100	112—
Mar.	1—At Milwaukee	107	137—
	3—At Utah	112	93
	4—At San Diego	115	103
	6—At Houston	105	104
	8—Chicago	103	99
	11—At New Jersey	104	109—
	12—Indiana	107	114—
	15—Cleveland	100	101—
	17—Boston	91	112—
	20—At Boston	116	128—
	22—Atlanta	121	101
	25—New York	105	84
	27—At Indiana	107	122—
	28—Detroit	108	103
	29—Cleveland	138	103

1981-82 SCHEDULE

Oct.	Fri.	30—At Boston
Nov.	Tue.	3—Philadelphia
	Thu.	5—At Milwaukee
	Fri.	6—Detroit
	Tue.	10—Boston
	Thu.	12—At Atlanta
	Sat.	14—Chicago
	Tue.	17—Milwaukee
	Thu.	19—At Detroit
	Fri.	20—Houston
	Sat.	21—At Chicago
	Tue.	24—Golden State
	Fri.	27—At Boston
	Sat.	28—Indiana
Dec.	Tue.	1—San Antonio
	Thu.	3—At New York
	Sat.	5—Cleveland
	Tue.	8—At Los Angeles
	Fri.	11—At San Diego
	Sat.	12—At Phoenix
	Tue.	15—Dallas
	Wed.	16—At Cleveland
	Fri.	18—Boston
	Tue.	22—At Chicago
	Fri.	25—Indiana
	Sat.	26—At New Jersey
	Tue.	29—Detroit
	Wed.	30—At Milwaukee
Jan.	Sat.	2—At Indiana
	Tue.	5—New Jersey
	Wed.	6—At Philadelphia
	Thu.	7—At Cleveland
	Sun.	10—At New York
	Tue.	12—Philadelphia
	Thu.	14—At Detroit
	Fri.	15—Chicago
	Sun.	17—At Atlanta
	Wed.	20—Seattle
	Fri.	22—Portland
	Sat.	23—At Kansas City
	Tue.	26—Chicago
	Thu.	28—New York
Feb.	Tue.	2—Cleveland
	Wed.	3—At Philadelphia
	Fri.	5—Los Angeles
	Sun.	7—Denver
	Tue.	9—At San Antonio
	Wed.	10—At Dallas
	Sat.	13—At Houston
	Tue.	16—At Portland
	Thu.	18—At Seattle
	Sat.	20—At Golden State
	Tue.	23—Utah
	Fri.	26—Kansas City
	Sun.	28—New York
Mar.	Tue.	2—New Jersey
	Fri.	5—At Denver
	Sat.	6—At Utah
	Tue.	9—Phoenix
	Fri.	12—Indiana
	Sat.	13—At New York
	Sun.	14—Atlanta
	Tue.	16—Boston
	Wed.	17—At Philadelphia
	Fri.	19—San Diego
	Sun.	21—New York
	Tue.	23—At Atlanta
	Wed.	24—At Indiana
	Fri.	26—New Jersey
	Sun.	28—At Cleveland
	Tue.	30—Detroit
	Wed.	31—At Boston
Apr.	Fri.	2—At New Jersey
	Sat.	3—At Atlanta
	Tue.	6—Cleveland
	Wed.	7—At Indiana
	Fri.	9—At Chicago
	Sat.	10—Milwaukee
	Tue.	13—At Milwaukee
	Wed.	14—At New Jersey
	Fri.	16—Philadelphia
	Sun.	18—Atlanta

1981-82 NBA SCHEDULE

ALL TIMES SHOWN ARE LOCAL

FRIDAY, OCTOBER 30
Washington at Boston, 7:30
New York at New Jersey, 7:35
Cleveland at Philadelphia, 7:35
Milwaukee at Detroit, 8:05
Chicago at Indiana, 7:35
San Antonio at Kansas City, 7:35
Golden State at Denver, 7:35
Dallas at Utah, 7:30
Houston at Los Angeles, 8:30
Phoenix at Portland, 7:30

SATURDAY, OCTOBER 31
Indiana at New York, 8:05
Philadelphia at Atlanta, 7:35
Detroit at Chicago, 7:35
Boston at Milwaukee, 8:00
Kansas City at Dallas, 7:35
Denver at San Antonio, 7:30
Houston at San Diego, 7:35
Utah at Golden State, 8:05
Phoenix at Seattle, 8:00

SUNDAY, NOVEMBER 1
Seattle at Portland, 7:00

TUESDAY, NOVEMBER 3
Philadelphia at Washington, 8:05
Atlanta at Chicago, 7:35
Cleveland at Dallas, 7:35
New York at Houston, 8:05
San Antonio at Phoenix, 7:35
Los Angeles at Portland, 7:30

WEDNESDAY, NOVEMBER 4
Chicago at Boston, 7:30
Atlanta at New Jersey, 7:35
Indiana at Philadelphia, 7:35
Cleveland at San Antonio, 7:30
San Diego at Kansas City, 7:35
Houston at Denver, 7:35
Portland at Golden State, 7:35
Los Angeles at Seattle, 7:30

THURSDAY, NOVEMBER 5
New Jersey at Detroit, 8:10
Washington at Milwaukee, 7:10
Golden State at Utah, 7:30
Dallas at Phoenix, 8:30

FRIDAY, NOVEMBER 6
Indiana at Boston, 7:30
Atlanta at Philadelphia, 7:35
Detroit at Washington, 8:05
San Diego at Chicago, 7:35
New York at Dallas, 7:35
Houston at Kansas City, 7:35
Phoenix at Los Angeles, 7:30
Utah at Portland, 7:30
Denver at Seattle, 8:00

SATURDAY, NOVEMBER 7
Boston at Detroit, 8:05
New Jersey at Chicago, 7:35
San Diego at Milwaukee, 8:00
Cleveland at Houston, 7:35
New York at San Antonio, 7:30
Phoenix at Utah, 7:30
Denver at Golden State, 8:05

SUNDAY, NOVEMBER 8
Indiana at New Jersey, 7:35
Dallas at Los Angeles, 7:00
Denver at Portland, 7:00

MONDAY, NOVEMBER 9
Chicago at Cleveland, 8:05

TUESDAY, NOVEMBER 10
New Jersey at New York, 7:35
Boston at Washington, 8:05
Milwaukee at Atlanta, 7:35
Philadelphia at Detroit, 8:05
Cleveland at Indiana, 7:35
Kansas City at Chicago, 7:35
Los Angeles at San Antonio, 7:30
Phoenix at Denver, 7:35
Utah at San Diego, 7:35
Seattle at Golden State, 7:35
Dallas at Portland, 7:30

WEDNESDAY, NOVEMBER 11
Kansas City at Boston, 7:30
Milwaukee at New Jersey, 7:35
Chicago at Philadelphia, 7:35
Los Angeles at Houston, 8:05
Dallas at Seattle, 7:30

THURSDAY, NOVEMBER 12
Washington at Atlanta, 8:10
Cleveland at Detroit, 8:10
Indiana at Phoenix, 7:35
Portland at San Diego, 7:30

FRIDAY, NOVEMBER 13
New Jersey vs. Boston at Hartford, 7:30
Kansas City at Philadelphia, 7:35
New York at Milwaukee, 8:00
Golden State at Houston, 8:05
Denver at Utah, 7:30
Portland at Los Angeles, 7:30
San Antonio at Seattle, 8:00

SATURDAY, NOVEMBER 14
Kansas City at New Jersey, 7:35
Philadelphia at New York, 8:05
Chicago at Washington, 8:05
Detroit at Atlanta, 7:35
Boston at Cleveland, 8:05
Golden State at Dallas, 7:35
Utah at Houston, 7:35

NBA 1981-82 SCHEDULE

Los Angeles at Phoenix, 7:35
Indiana at San Diego, 7:35

SUNDAY, NOVEMBER 15
Cleveland at Milwaukee, 7:30
Indiana at Los Angeles, 7:00
San Antonio at Portland, 7:00

TUESDAY, NOVEMBER 17
Kansas City at New York, 7:35
Milwaukee at Washington, 8:05
Houston at Indiana, 7:35
Boston at Chicago, 7:35
San Antonio at Dallas, 7:35

WEDNESDAY, NOVEMBER 18
Houston at Boston, 7:30
Milwaukee at Philadelphia, 7:35
Phoenix at Atlanta, 7:35
Detroit at Cleveland, 8:05
Seattle at San Antonio, 7:30
San Diego at Denver, 7:35
Los Angeles at Utah, 7:30
New Jersey at Golden State, 7:35

THURSDAY, NOVEMBER 19
Atlanta at New York, 7:35
Washington at Detroit, 8:05
Kansas City at Indiana, 8:10
Golden State at San Diego, 7:30

FRIDAY, NOVEMBER 20
Milwaukee at Boston, 7:30
Houston at Washington, 8:05
Philadelphia at Cleveland, 8:05
Utah at Chicago, 7:35
Seattle at Dallas, 7:35
San Antonio at Los Angeles, 7:30
New Jersey at Portland, 7:30

SATURDAY, NOVEMBER 21
Milwaukee at New York, 8:05
Houston at Philadelphia, 7:35
Indiana at Atlanta, 7:35
Utah at Detroit, 8:05
Washington at Chicago, 7:35
Phoenix at Dallas, 7:35
Kansas City at Denver, 7:35
Los Angeles at San Diego, 7:35
San Antonio at Golden State, 8:05

SUNDAY, NOVEMBER 22
New Jersey at Seattle, 6:00

TUESDAY, NOVEMBER 24
Golden State at Washington, 8:05
Cleveland at Atlanta, 7:35
New York at Indiana, 7:35
Detroit at Milwaukee, 7:30
Los Angeles at Dallas, 7:35
New Jersey at Houston, 8:05
Chicago at San Diego, 7:35

WEDNESDAY, NOVEMBER 25
Golden State at Boston, 8:10
Indiana at Cleveland, 8:05
Los Angeles at San Antonio, 7:30
Detroit at Kansas City, 7:35
Dallas at Denver, 7:35
San Diego at Utah, 7:30

Houston at Phoenix, 7:35
Portland at Seattle, 7:30

FRIDAY, NOVEMBER 27
Washington at Boston, 7:30
New York at Cleveland, 8:05
Atlanta at Detroit, 8:05
Philadelphia at Indiana, 7:35
Golden State at Milwaukee, 8:00
New Jersey at San Antonio, 7:30
Denver at Kansas City, 7:35
Portland at Utah, 7:30
Chicago at Phoenix, 7:35
San Diego at Los Angeles, 7:30
Houston at Seattle, 8:00

SATURDAY, NOVEMBER 28
Cleveland at New York, 8:05
Detroit at Philadelphia, 7:35
Indiana at Washington, 8:05
Boston at Atlanta, 7:35
New Jersey at Dallas, 7:35
Utah at Denver, 7:35
Seattle at San Diego, 7:35

SUNDAY, NOVEMBER 29
San Antonio at Milwaukee, 7:30
Golden State at Kansas City, 2:05
Houston at Los Angeles, 7:00
Chicago at Portland, 7:00

TUESDAY, DECEMBER 1
Detroit at New York, 7:35
San Antonio at Washington, 8:05
Philadelphia at Atlanta, 7:35
Milwaukee at Cleveland, 8:05
Boston at Indiana, 7:35
Kansas City at Houston, 8:05
Portland at Denver, 7:35
San Diego at Phoenix, 7:35
Utah at Los Angeles, 7:30
Chicago at Seattle, 7:30

WEDNESDAY, DECEMBER 2
Detroit at Boston, 7:30
Cleveland at New Jersey, 7:35
San Antonio at Philadelphia, 7:35
Portland at Kansas City, 7:35
Dallas at Utah, 7:30
Chicago at Golden State, 7:35
Los Angeles at Seattle, 7:30

THURSDAY, DECEMBER 3
Washington at New York, 7:35
Denver at Phoenix, 8:10
Dallas at San Diego, 7:35

FRIDAY, DECEMBER 4
Philadelphia at Boston, 7:30
Detroit at Indiana, 7:35
Atlanta at Milwaukee, 8:00
Portland at San Antonio, 7:30
Seattle at Kansas City, 7:35
Los Angeles at Denver, 7:35
Chicago at Utah, 7:30

SATURDAY, DECEMBER 5
Philadelphia at New Jersey, 7:35
Boston at New York, 8:05
Cleveland at Washington, 8:05

NBA 1981-82 SCHEDULE

Seattle at Atlanta, 7:35
Milwaukee at Detroit, 8:05
Denver at Dallas, 7:35
Portland at Houston, 7:35
Utah at Phoenix, 7:35
San Diego at Golden State, 8:05

SUNDAY, DECEMBER 6
Kansas City at Los Angeles, 7:00

TUESDAY, DECEMBER 8
Denver at New York, 7:35
New Jersey at Atlanta, 7:35
Indiana at Chicago, 7:35
Utah at Dallas, 7:35
Seattle at Houston, 8:05
Phoenix at San Diego, 7:35
Washington at Los Angeles, 7:30
Golden State at Portland, 7:30

WEDNESDAY, DECEMBER 9
New Jersey at Boston, 7:30
Denver at Philadelphia, 7:35
Atlanta at Cleveland, 8:05
Utah at Indiana, 7:35
Houston at Milwaukee, 7:30
Seattle at San Antonio, 7:30
Dallas at Kansas City, 7:35
Phoenix at Golden State, 7:35

THURSDAY, DECEMBER 10
New York at Detroit, 8:10
Portland at Phoenix, 8:30

FRIDAY, DECEMBER 11
Atlanta vs. Boston at Hartford, 7:30
Denver at New Jersey, 7:35
Cleveland at Philadelphia, 7:35
Houston at Chicago, 7:35
Indiana at Milwaukee, 8:00
San Antonio at Dallas, 7:35
Kansas City at Utah, 7:30
Washington at San Diego, 7:35
Portland at Los Angeles, 7:30

SATURDAY, DECEMBER 12
Milwaukee at New York, 8:05
Boston at Atlanta, 7:35
Denver at Cleveland, 8:05
New Jersey at Indiana, 7:35
Philadelphia at Chicago, 7:35
Dallas at Houston, 7:35
Utah at San Antonio, 7:30
Washington at Phoenix, 7:35
Kansas City at Golden State, 8:05
Detroit at Seattle, 8:00

SUNDAY, DECEMBER 13
Philadelphia at Milwaukee, 7:30
Golden State at Los Angeles, 2:00
Detroit at Portland, 7:00
San Diego at Seattle, 6:00

TUESDAY, DECEMBER 15
Dallas at Washington, 8:05
New York at Atlanta, 7:35
Milwaukee at Indiana, 7:35
Cleveland at Chicago, 7:35
Phoenix at Houston, 8:05
Seattle at Denver, 7:35

San Antonio at Utah, 7:30
Detroit at Golden State, 7:35
San Diego at Portland, 7:30

WEDNESDAY, DECEMBER 16
Dallas at Boston, 7:30
Chicago at New Jersey, 7:35
New York at Philadelphia, 7:35
Washington at Cleveland, 8:05
Phoenix at Kansas City, 7:35

THURSDAY, DECEMBER 17
Indiana at Detroit, 8:10
Atlanta at Denver, 7:35
Seattle at San Diego, 7:35
Los Angeles at Golden State, 7:30

FRIDAY, DECEMBER 18
Chicago at New York, 7:35
Boston at Washington, 8:05
Cleveland at Indiana, 7:35
New Jersey at Milwaukee, 8:00
Houston at Dallas, 7:35
Phoenix at San Antonio, 7:30
Utah at Kansas City, 7:35

SATURDAY, DECEMBER 19
Boston at Philadelphia, 7:35
New Jersey at Cleveland, 8:05
New York at Detroit, 8:05
Portland at Dallas, 7:35
Chicago at Houston, 7:35
San Antonio at Denver, 7:35
Seattle at Utah, 8:30
Kansas City at Phoenix, 7:35
Los Angeles at San Diego, 7:35
Atlanta at Golden State, 8:05

SUNDAY, DECEMBER 20
Atlanta at Los Angeles, 7:00

TUESDAY, DECEMBER 22
Cleveland at Boston, 7:30
Philadelphia at New York, 7:35
Atlanta at Indiana, 7:35
Washington at Chicago, 7:35
Kansas City at Milwaukee, 7:30
Detroit at Dallas, 7:35
Denver at Houston, 8:05
Los Angeles at Portland, 7:30

WEDNESDAY, DECEMBER 23
New York at New Jersey, 7:35
Kansas City at Cleveland, 8:05
Detroit at Denver, 7:35
Golden State at Phoenix, 7:35
San Antonio at San Diego, 7:35
Utah at Seattle, 7:30

FRIDAY, DECEMBER 25
New Jersey at New York, 7:35
Indiana at Washington, 8:05
Los Angeles at Phoenix, 1:30
Seattle at Portland, 7:00

SATURDAY, DECEMBER 26
Washington at New Jersey, 7:35
Milwaukee at Cleveland, 8:05
Chicago at Detroit, 8:05
New York at Indiana, 7:35

NBA 1981-82 SCHEDULE

Denver at Dallas, 7:35
Atlanta at San Antonio, 7:30
Boston at Kansas City, 7:35
Houston at Utah, 7:30
Portland at San Diego, 7:35
Phoenix at Golden State, 8:05

SUNDAY, DECEMBER 27

Chicago at Milwaukee, 7:30
Philadelphia at Phoenix 7:10
San Diego at Los Angeles 7:00

MONDAY, DECEMBER 28

Indiana at New Jersey, 7:35
Golden State at Seattle, 7:30

TUESDAY, DECEMBER 29

Detroit at Washington, 8:05
Milwaukee at Indiana, 7:35
New York at Chicago, 7:35
Kansas City at Dallas, 7:35
Atlanta at Houston, 8:05
San Diego at San Antonio, 7:30
Boston at Denver, 7:35
Utah at Los Angeles, 7:30
Philadelphia at Golden State, 7:35

WEDNESDAY, DECEMBER 30

Detroit at New Jersey, 7:35
San Diego at Atlanta, 7:35
New York at Cleveland, 8:05
Washington at Milwaukee, 7:30
Houston at San Antonio, 7:30
Denver at Kansas City, 7:35
Boston at Utah, 7:30
Portland at Phoenix, 7:35
Philadelphia at Se'ttle, 7:30

FRIDAY, JANUARY 1

Kansas City at Golden State, 8:05
Philadelphia at Portland, 7:00

SATURDAY, JANUARY 2

Detroit at New York, 8:05
New Jersey at Atlanta, 7:35
Boston at Cleveland, 8:05
Washington at Indiana, 7:35
Milwaukee at Chicago, 7:35
Denver at San Antonio, 7:30
Philadelphia at Utah, 7:30
Seattle at Phoenix, 7:35
Houston at San Diego, 7:35
Dallas at Golden State, 8:05

SUNDAY, JANUARY 3

Denver at Milwaukee, 7:10
Seattle at Los Angeles, 7:00
Kansas City at Portland, 7:00

TUESDAY, JANUARY 5

New Jersey at Washington, 8:05
Cleveland at Atlanta, 7:35
Philadelphia at Detroit, 8:05
Phoenix at Indiana, 7:35
Denver at Chicago, 7:35
New York at Milwaukee, 7:30
Kansas City at San Diego, 7:35
Houston at Golden State, 7:35
San Antonio at Portland, 7:30

WEDNESDAY, JANUARY 6

Chicago at Boston, 7:30
Milwaukee at New Jersey, 7:35
Washington at Philadelphia, 7:35
San Diego at Denver, 7:35
San Antonio at Utah, 7:30
Dallas at Seattle, 7:30

THURSDAY, JANUARY 7

Washington at Cleveland, 8:10
Phoenix at Detroit, 8:05
New York at Kansas City, 7:35
Dallas at San Diego, 7:35
San Antonio at Golden State, 7:35
Houston at Seattle, 7:30

FRIDAY, JANUARY 8

Philadelphia at Boston, 7:30
Cleveland at New Jersey, 7:35
Los Angeles at Chicago, 7:35
Atlanta at Milwaukee, 8:00
Indiana at Utah, 7:30
Denver at Portland, 7:30

SATURDAY, JANUARY 9

New Jersey at Philadelphia, 7:35
New York at Atlanta, 7:35
Los Angeles at Detroit, 8:05
Phoenix at Dallas, 7:35
Kansas City at San Antonio, 7:30
Seattle at Denver, 7:35
Utah at San Diego, 7:35
Indiana at Golden State, 8:05

SUNDAY, JANUARY 10

Detroit vs. Boston at Hartford, 7:30
Washington at New York, 7:35
Los Angeles at Milwaukee, 7:30
Houston at Portland, 7:00

MONDAY, JANUARY 11

Boston at New Jersey, 7:35

TUESDAY, JANUARY 12

Philadelphia at Washington, 8:05
Milwaukee at Atlanta, 7:35
Los Angeles at Cleveland, 8:05
Detroit at Chicago, 7:35
San Diego at Houston, 8:05
Dallas at San Antonio, 7:30
Kansas City at Denver, 7:35
New York at Utah, 7:30
Golden State at Phoenix, 7:35
Indiana at Portland, 7:30

WEDNESDAY, JANUARY 13

Atlanta at Boston, 7:30
Milwaukee at Philadelphia, 7:35
San Diego at Dallas, 7:35
Cleveland at Kansas City, 7:35
Denver at Golden State, 7:35
Indiana at Seattle, 7:30

THURSDAY, JANUARY 14

Chicago at New Jersey, 7:35
Washington at Detroit, 8:05
Portland at Houston, 7:10
New York at Phoenix, 8:30

NBA 1981-82 SCHEDULE

FRIDAY, JANUARY 15
Atlanta at Philadelphia, 7:35
Chicago at Washington, 8:05
Los Angeles at Indiana, 7:35
Boston at Milwaukee, 8:00
Houston at San Antonio, 7:30
New Jersey at Kansas City, 7:35
Dallas at Denver, 7:35
Cleveland at San Diego, 7:35
New York at Golden State, 8:05
Utah at Seattle, 8:00

SATURDAY, JANUARY 16
Boston at Detroit, 8:05
Portland at Dallas, 7:35
San Antonio at Houston, 7:35
Cleveland at Utah, 7:30
San Diego at Phoenix, 7:35

SUNDAY, JANUARY 17
Philadelphia at NeK Jersey, 1:00
Atlanta at Washington, 1:05
Chicago at Indiana, 4:05
Detroit at Milwaukee, 7:30
Los Angeles at Kansas City, Noon
Denver at San Diego, 7:00
Golden State at Seattle, 3:00

TUESDAY, JANUARY 19
Boston at New York, 7:35
Portland at Atlanta, 7:35
Seattle at Cleveland, 8:05
Indiana at Chicago, 7:35
Kansas City at Houston, 8:05
Los Angeles at Denver, 7:35
Detroit at Utah, 7:30
San Antonio at Phoenix, 7:35

WEDNESDAY, JANUARY 20
Indiana at Boston, 7:30
Portland at Philadelphia, 7:35
Seattle at Washington, 8:05
Milwaukee at Dallas, 7:35
New Jersey at Los Angeles, 7:30
San Diego at Golden State, 7:35

THURSDAY, JANUARY 21
Atlanta at New York, 7:35
Utah at San Antonio, 7:10
Dallas at Kansas City, 7:35
Detroit at San Diego, 7:30

FRIDAY, JANUARY 22
Seattle at Boston, 7:30
Portland at Washington, 8:05
San Antonio at Atlanta, 7:35
Philadelphia at Indiana, 7:35
Cleveland at Chicago, 7:35
Utah at Houston, 8:05
Milwaukee at Denver, 7:35
New Jersey at Phoenix, 7:35
Detroit at Los Angeles, 7:30

SATURDAY, JANUARY 23
Chicago at New York, 8:05
Seattle at Philadelphia, 7:35
Atlanta at Cleveland, 8:05
Utah at Dallas, 7:35
Denver at Houston, 7:35

Indiana at San Antonio, 7:30
Washington at Kansas City, 7:35
Detroit at Phoenix, 7:35
New Jersey at San Diego, 7:35
Milwaukee at Golden State, 8:05

SUNDAY, JANUARY 24
Portland at Boston, Noon

MONDAY, JANUARY 25
Seattle at New York, 7:35

TUESDAY, JANUARY 26
Chicago at Washington, 8:05
Dallas at Atlanta, 7:35
Indiana at Houston, 8:05
Philadelphia at San Antonio, 7:30
New Jersey at Utah, 7:35
Milwaukee at Los Angeles, 7:30

WEDNESDAY, JANUARY 27
New York at Boston, 7:30
Golden State at Cleveland, 8:05
Atlanta at Drtroit, 8:05
Philadelphia at Dallas, 7:35
Seattle at Kansas City, 7:35
New Jersey at Denver, 7:35
Phoenix at San Diego, 7:35

THURSDAY, JANUARY 28
New York at Washington, 8:05
Boston at Cleveland, 8:05
Golden State at Chicago, 7:35
Philadelphia at Houston, 7:10
Kansas City at San Antonio, 7:30
Milwaukee at Utah, 7:30
Phoenix at Los Angeles, 7:30
San Diego at Portland, 7:30

SUNDAY, JANUARY 31
ALL-STAR GAME at THE MEADOWLANDS
EAST RUTHERFORD, N.J., 1:00

TUESDAY, FEBRUARY 2
Cleveland at Washington, 8:05
Detroit at Atlanta, 7:35
Boston at Indiana, 7:35
New Jersey at Chicago, 7:35
San Diego at Houston, 8:05
Dallas at San Antonio, 7:30
New York at Denver, 7:35
Los Angeles at Golden State, 7:35
Kansas City at Portland, 7:30

WEDNESDAY, FEBRUARY 3
Atlanta at New Jersey, 7:35
Washington at Philadelphia, 7:35
Indiana at Cleveland, 8:05
Boston at Detroit, 8:05
Chicago at Milwaukee, 7:30
San Diego at Dallas, 7:35
Portland at Utah, 7:30
Golden State at Phoenix, 7:35
New York at Los Angeles, 7:30
Kansas City at Seattle, 7:30

THURSDAY, FEBRUARY 4
Denver at Indiana, 7:35
Phoenix at San Antonio, 7:10

NBA 1981-82 SCHEDULE

FRIDAY, FEBRUARY 5
Denver at Boston, 7:30
New Jersey at Philadelphia, 7:35
Los Angeles at Washington, 8:05
Detroit at Chicago, 7:35
Dallas at Milwaukee, 8:00
Phoenix at Houston, 8:05
San Antonio at Kansas City, 7:35
New York at San Diego, 7:35
Seattle at Golden State, 8:05
Utah at Portland, 7:30

SATURDAY, FEBRUARY 6
Cleveland at Atlanta, 7:35
New Jersey at Detroit, 8:05
Dallas at Indiana, 7:35
Utah at Seattle, 8:00

SUNDAY, FEBRUARY 7
Los Angeles at Boston, TBA
Chicago at Philadelphia, TBA
Denver at Washington, 1:05
New Jersey at Cleveland, 7:30
Phoenix at Milwaukee, 1:30
Houston at Kansas City, 1:30
San Antonio at Golden State, 2:30
New York at Portland, 7:00
San Diego at Seattle, 6:00

TUESDAY, FEBRUARY 9
Los Angeles at Atlanta, 7:35
Chicago at Detroit, 8:05
Milwaukee at Indiana, 7:35
Washington at San Antonio, 7:30
Golden State at Utah, 7:30
Houston at San Diego, 7:35
New York at Seattle, 7:30

WEDNESDAY, FEBRUARY 10
Detroit at New Jersey, 7:35
Indiana at Philadelphia, 7:35
Portland at Cleveland, 8:05
Atlanta at Chicago, 7:35
Washington at Dallas, 7:35
Los Angeles at Kansas City, 7:35
Utah at Denver, 7:35
Boston at Phoenix, 7:35

THURSDAY, FEBRUARY 11
Golden State at New York, 7:35
Cleveland at Detroit, 8:05
Portland at Milwaukee, 7:10
Seattle at Houston, 8:05

FRIDAY, FEBRUARY 12
Golden State at New Jersey, 7:35
Seattle at Dallas, 7:35
Utah at Kansas City, 7:35
Atlanta at Phoenix, 7:35
Boston at San Diego, 7:35
San Antonio at Los Angeles, 7:30

SATURDAY, FEBRUARY 13
Philadelphia at New York, 8:05
Indiana at Cleveland, 8:05
Portland at Detroit, 8:05
Milwaukee at Chicago, 7:35
Washington at Houston, 7:35
San Diego at Denver, 7:35
Phoenix at Utah, 7:30

SUNDAY, FEBRUARY 14
Dallas at New Jersey, 4:00
New York at Philadelphia, TBA
Milwaukee at Cleveland, 7:30
Portland at Indiana, 6:05
Seattle at San Antonio, 2:45
Golden State at Kansas City, 2:45
Boston at Los Angeles, 12:45

MONDAY, FEBRUARY 15
Denver at Utah, 7:30

TUESDAY, FEBRUARY 16
Dallas at New York, 7:35
Houston at Detroit, 8:05
Phoenix at Chicago, 7:35
Kansas City at Denver, 7:35
Atlanta at San Diego, 7:35
Seattle at Los Angeles, 7:30
Washington at Portland, 7:30

WEDNESDAY, FEBRUARY 17
Chicago at New Jersey, 7:35
Dallas at Philadelphia, 7:35
Houston at Cleveland, 8:05
Indiana at Milwaukee, 7:30
Detroit at San Antonio, 7:30
Phoenix at Kansas City, 7:35
Atlanta at Utah, 7:30
Boston at Golden State, 7:35

THURSDAY, FEBRUARY 18
San Diego at Indiana, 8:10
Washington at Seattle, 7:30

FRIDAY, FEBRUARY 19
Houston at New Jersey, 7:35
Phoenix at New York, 7:35
Utah at Philadelphia, 7:35
Cleveland at Milwaukee, 8:00
San Diego at Kansas City, 7:35
San Antonio at Denver, 7:35
Golden State at Los Angeles, 7:30
Boston at Portland, 7:30
Atlanta at Seattle, 8:00

SATURDAY, FEBRUARY 20
Utah at New Jersey, 7:35
Dallas at Cleveland, 8:05
Indiana at Detroit, 8:05
San Diego at San Antonio, 7:30
Washington at Golden State, 8:05

SUNDAY, FEBRUARY 21
Houston at New York, 1:00
Phoenix at Philadelphia, 1:00
New Jersey at Indiana, 4:05
Dallas at Chicago, TBA
Milwaukee at Kansas City, Noon
Los Angeles at Denver, 2:05
Atlanta at Portland, 7:00
Boston at Seattle, 3:00

TUESDAY, FEBRUARY 23
Milwaukee at New York, 7:35
Utah at Washington, 8:05
Kansas City at Atlanta, 7:35
Portland at Chicago, 7:35
Dallas at Houston, 8:05

NBA 1981-82 SCHEDULE

Golden State at San Antonio, 7:30
Philadelphia at San Diego, 7:35
Denver at Los Angeles, 7:30

WEDNESDAY, FEBRUARY 24

Utah at Boston, 7:30
Milwaukee at New Jersey, 7:35
New York at Indiana, 7:35
Portland at Kansas City, 7:35
Houston at Denver, 7:35
Cleveland at Phoenix, 7:35

THURSDAY, FEBRUARY 25

San Antonio at Detroit, 8:05
Golden State at Dallas, 7:10
Los Angeles at Seattle, 7:30

FRIDAY, FEBRUARY 26

San Diego at Boston, 7:30
Portland at New Jersey, 7:35
Kansas City at Washington, 8:05
Chicago at Atlanta, 7:35
San Antonio at Indiana, 7:35
Golden State at Houston, 8:05
Seattle at Utah, 7:30
Denver at Phoenix, 7:35
Philadelphia at Los Angeles, 7:30

SATURDAY, FEBRUARY 27

Portland at New York, 8:05
Kansas City at Detroit, 8:05
Houston at Dallas, 7:35
Philadelphia at Denver, 7:35

SUNDAY, FEBRUARY 28

Milwaukee at Boston, TBA
San Diego at New Jersey, 4:00
New York at Washington, TBA
Golden State at Atlanta, 1:05
Detroit at Indiana, 6:05
San Antonio at Chicago, 1:15
Cleveland at Los Angeles, 2:00
Phoenix at Seattle, 3:00

TUESDAY, MARCH 2

San Antonio at New York, 7:35
New Jersey at Washington, 8:05
Philadelphia at Chicago, 7:35
Detroit at Milwaukee, 7:30
Boston at Dallas, 7:35
San Antonio at Houston, 8:05
Indiana at Denver, 7:35
Kansas City at Utah, 7:30
Cleveland at Golden State, 7:35
Phoenix at Portland, 7:30

WEDNESDAY, MARCH 3

Los Angeles at New Jersey, 7:35
San Diego at Philadelphia, 7:35
Milwaukee at Atlanta, 7:35
Indiana at Kansas City, 7:35
Utah at Phoenix, 7:35
Cleveland at Seattle, 7:30

THURSDAY, MARCH 4

Los Angeles at New York, 7:35
Chicago at Detroit, 8:05
Boston at San Antonio, 7:10
Houston at Utah, 8:30
Dallas at Golden State, 7:35

FRIDAY, MARCH 5

Atlanta at Philadelphia, 7:35
New Jersey at Chicago, 7:35
Boston at Houston, 8:05
Washington at Denver, 7:35
Kansas City at Phoenix, 7:35
Golden State at San Antonio, 7:35
Cleveland at Portland, 7:30
Dallas at Seattle, 8:00

SATURDAY, MARCH 6

Detroit at New York, 8:05
New Jersey at Atlanta, 7:35
Milwaukee at San Antonio, 7:30
Washington at Utah, 7:30

SUNDAY, MARCH 7

New York at Boston, 1:00
Los Angeles at Philadelphia, 1:00
Indiana at Dallas, 1:35
Chicago at Kansas City, 2:05
Cleveland at Denver, 2:05
Houston at Phoenix, 1:00
Portland at Golden State, 2:30
San Diego at Seattle, 3:00

MONDAY, MARCH 8

Dallas at San Antonio, 7:30

TUESDAY, MARCH 9

Utah at New York, 7:35
Phoenix at Washington, 8:05
Denver at Atlanta, 7:35
Golden State at Indiana, 7:35
Seattle at Chicago, 7:35
Milwaukee at Houston, 8:05
San Antonio at San Diego, 7:35
Kansas City at Los Angeles, 7:30

WEDNESDAY, MARCH 10

Indiana at Boston, 7:30
Phoenix at New Jersey, 7:35
Golden State at Philadelphia, 7:35
Denver at Detroit, 8:05
Chicago at Milwaukee, 7:30
Portland at Dallas, 7:35

THURSDAY, MARCH 11

Utah at Atlanta, 7:35
Phoenix at Cleveland, 8:10
Kansas City at San Diego, 7:30

FRIDAY, MARCH 12

Boston at New Jersey, 7:35
Indiana at Washington, 8:05
Golden State at Detroit, 8:05
Seattle at Milwaukee, 8:00
Denver at Houston, 8:05
Portland at San Antonio, 7:30
Chicago at Los Angeles, 7:30

SATURDAY, MARCH 13

Washington at New York, 8:05
Indiana at Atlanta, 7:35
Utah at Cleveland, 8:05
Portland at Houston, 7:35
Dallas at San Diego, 7:35

NBA 1981-82 SCHEDULE

SUNDAY, MARCH 14

Phoenix at Boston, TBA
Seattle at New Jersey, TBA
Atlanta at Washington, 1:05
Detroit at Cleveland, 7:30
Utah at Milwaukee, 2:30
Chicago at San Antonio, 2:30
Philadelphia at Kansas City, 2:05
Golden State at Denver, 2:05
Dallas at Los Angeles, 7:00

TUESDAY, MARCH 16

San Antonio at New York, 7:35
Boston at Washington, 8:05
San Diego at Detroit, 8:05
Seattle at Indiana, 7:35
Philadelphia at Milwaukee, 7:30
Phoenix at Houston, 8:05
Utah at Denver, 7:35
Los Angeles at Portland, 7:30

WEDNESDAY, MARCH 17

Atlanta at Boston, 7:30
San Antonio at New Jersey, 7:35
Washington at Philadelphia, 7:35
San Diego at Cleveland, 8:05
Chicago at Dallas, 7:35
Los Angeles at Utah, 7:30
Denver at Phoenix, 7:35
Kansas City at Golden State, 7:35

THURSDAY, MARCH 18

Houston at Atlanta, 8:10
Seattle at Detroit, 8:10
Golden State at Portland, 7:30

FRIDAY, MARCH 19

San Antonio at Boston, 7:30
Indiana at Philadelphia, 7:35
San Diego at Washington, 8:05
Cleveland at Milwaukee, 8:00
Los Angeles at Dallas, 7:35
Detroit at Houston, 8:05
Seattle at Kansas City, 7:35
Chicago at Denver, 7:35
Portland at Utah, 7:30

SATURDAY, MARCH 20

Atlanta at New York, 8:05
San Antonio at Cleveland, 8:05
New Jersey at Indiana, 7:35

SUNDAY, MARCH 21

Boston at Philadelphia, 1:05
New York at Washington, 1:05
Detroit at Atlanta, 7:05
Chicago at Cleveland, 7:30
New Jersey at Milwaukee, 1:30
San Antonio at Kansas City, 2:05
Seattle at Phoenix, 7:05
Houston at Los Angeles, 7:00
Utah at Golden State, 2:30
Dallas at Portland, 7:00

TUESDAY, MARCH 23

Cleveland at New York, 7:35
Washington at Atlanta, 7:35
Boston at Chicago, 7:35
San Diego at San Antonio, 7:30
Houston at Utah, 7:30
Dallas at Los Angeles, 7:30
Phoenix at Golden State, 7:35
Milwaukee at Portland, 7:30

WEDNESDAY, MARCH 24

Cleveland at Boston, 7:30
New Jersey at Philadelphia, 7:35
Washington at Indiana, 7:35
Atlanta at Kansas City, 7:35
San Antonio at Denver, 7:35
Dallas at Phoenix, 7:35
Milwaukee at Seattle, 7:30

THURSDAY, MARCH 25

Philadelphia at Detroit, 8:10
Golden State at Utah, 7:30
Denver at San Antonio, 7:35
Houston at Portland, 7:30

FRIDAY, MARCH 26

Detroit at Boston, 7:30
New Jersey at Washington, 8:05
Philadelphia at Cleveland, 8:05
Atlanta at Indiana, 7:35
New York at Chicago, 7:35
Kansas City at Dallas, 7:35
Los Angeles at San Antonio, 7:30
Milwaukee at Phoenix, 7:35
Portland at Golden State, 8:05
Houston at Seattle, 8:00

SATURDAY, MARCH 27

Detroit at New Jersey, 7:35
Atlanta at Dallas, 7:35
Phoenix at Denver, 7:35
San Antonio at Utah, 7:30
Milwaukee at San Diego, 7:35

SUNDAY, MARCH 28

Philadelphia at Boston, 2:00
New York at New Jersey, 2:00
Washington at Cleveland, 7:30
Chicago at Indiana, 2:00
Los Angeles at Kansas City, 1:00
Houston at Golden State, 2:30
Portland at Seattle, 3:00

MONDAY, MARCH 29

Phoenix at Utah, 7:30

TUESDAY, MARCH 30

Indiana at New York, 7:35
Detroit at Washington, 8:05
Atlanta at Chicago, 7:35
Philadelphia at Milwaukee, 7:30
Dallas at Houston, 8:05
Golden State at San Antonio, 7:30
Seattle at Denver, 7:35
San Diego at Los Angeles, 7:30
Kansas City at Portland, 7:30

WEDNESDAY, MARCH 31

Washington at Boston, 7:30
Cleveland at New Jersey, 7:35
Chicago at Philadelphia, 7:35
Detroit at Indiana, 7:35
Denver at Dallas, 7:35
San Diego at Phoenix, 7:35
Kansas City at Seattle, 7:30

NBA 1981-82 SCHEDULE

THURSDAY, APRIL 1
Cleveland at New York, 8:35
Dallas at Detroit, 8:05
Atlanta at Milwaukee, 7:30
Golden State at Houston, 7:10
Los Angeles at San Diego, 7:30
San Antonio at Portland, 7:30

FRIDAY, APRIL 2
Washington at New Jersey, 7:35
Cleveland at Philadelphia, 7:35
Boston at Atlanta, 7:35
Milwaukee at Chicago, 7:35
Portland at Denver, 7:35
Kansas City at Utah, 7:30
Phoenix at Los Angeles, 8:30
San Antonio at Seattle, 8:30

SATURDAY, APRIL 3
Washington at Atlanta, 7:35
Indiana at Detroit, 8:05
Golden State at Dallas, 7:35
Utah at San Diego, 7:35

SUNDAY, APRIL 4
Chicago at Boston, 1:00
New York at Philadelphia, 1:00
New Jersey at Cleveland, 2:00
Indiana at Milwaukee, Noon
Houston at San Antonio, 2:30
Kansas City at Phoenix, 1:30
Portland at Los Angeles, 12:30
Denver at Seattle, 12:30

TUESDAY, APRIL 6
Cleveland at Washington, 8:05
New York at Atlanta, 7:35
Philadelphia at Chicago, 7:35
Boston at Milwaukee, 7:30
Los Angeles at Houston, 8:05
Dallas at Utah, 7:30
Golden State at San Diego, 7:35
Denver at Portland, 7:30
Phoenix at Seattle, 7:30

WEDNESDAY, APRIL 7
Philadelphia at New Jersey, 7:35
Chicago at Cleveland, 8:05
Atlanta at Detroit, 8:05
Washington at Indiana, 7:35
Utah at Dallas, 7:35
Kansas City at San Antonio, 7:30
Denver at Golden State, 7:35

THURSDAY, APRIL 8
Boston at New York, 8:10
Portland at Phoenix, 7:35
Seattle at San Diego, 7:35

FRIDAY, APRIL 9
New Jersey at Boston, 7:30
Philadelphia at Atlanta, 7:35
Milwaukee at Detroit, 8:05
Cleveland at Indiana, 7:35
Washington at Chicago, 7:35
Phoenix at Dallas, 7:35
Utah at Kansas City, 7:35
Denver at Los Angeles, 7:30
San Diego at Portland, 7:30

SATURDAY, APRIL 10
Indiana at New Jersey, 7:35
Milwaukee at Washingto, 2:05
New York at Cleveland, 8:05
San Antonio at Houston, 7:35
Denver at Utah, 7:30
Seattle at Phoenix, 7:35
San Diego at Golden State, 8:05

SUNDAY, APRIL 11
Boston at Philadelphia, 1:00
Chicago at Atlanta, 1:00
New York at Detroit, 7:05
Houston at Dallas, 1:35
San Antonio at Kansas City, Noon
Seattle at Los Angeles, 7:00
Golden State at Portland, 7:00

MONDAY, APRIL 12
San Diego at Utah, 7:30

TUESDAY, APRIL 13
New Jersey at New York, 8:35
Atlanta at Cleveland, 8:05
Philadelphia at Indiana, 7:35
Boston at Chicago, 7:35
Washington at Milwaukee, 7:30
Kansas City at Houston, 8:05
Denver at San Antonio, 7:30
Phoenix at San Diego, 7:35
Los Angeles at Golden State, 7:35
Portland at Seattle, 7:30

WEDNESDAY, APRIL 14
Milwaukee at Boston, 7:30
Washington at New Jersey, 7:35
Detroit at Philadelphia, 7:35
Dallas at Kansas City, 7:35
Houston at Denver, 7:35
San Antonio at Phoenx, 7:35
Utah at Los Angeles, 7:30
Golden State at Seattle, 7:30

THURSDAY, APRIL 15
Chicago at New York, 8:35
Cleveland at Detroit, 8:10
Atlanta at Indiana, 7:35
Portland at San Diego, 7:35

FRIDAY, APRIL 16
Boston at New Jersey, 7:35
Philadelphia at Washington, 8:05
Indiana at Atlanta, 7:35
Cleveland at Chicago, 7:35
New York at Milwaukee, 8:00
San Antonio at Dallas, 7:35
Utah at Houston, 8:05
Denver at Kansas City, 7:35
Golden State at Los Angeles, 7:30
Phoenix at Portland, 7:30

SATURDAY, APRIL 17
New Jersey at Detroit, 8:05
Dallas at Denver, 7:35
Seattle at Golden State, 8:05

SUNDAY, APRIL 18
New York at Boston, 1:00
Milwaukee at Philadelphia, 1:00

Atlanta at Washington, 1:05
Detroit at Cleveland, 2:00
Indiana at Chicago, Noon
Utah at San Antonio, 2:30

Houston at Kansas City, Noon
Los Angeles at Phoenix, 1:30
Seattle at Portland, 12:30
TBA—To Be Announced

Referees for 1981-82

Darell Garretson

Chief of Staff—Darell Garretson
Referee Development Administrator—Cecil K. Watkins

- 4—Ed Rush
- 7—Joe Gushue
- 8—Lee Jones
- 9—John Vanak
- 10—Darell Garretson
- 11—Jake O'Donnell
- 12—Earl Strom
- 13—Mike Mathis
- 14—Jack Madden
- 15—Bob Rakel
- 16—Wally Rooney
- 17—Joe Crawford
- 18—Ed Middleton
- 19—Jim Capers
- 20—Jess Kersey
- 22—Paul Mihalak
- 24—Bill Saar
- 25—Hugh Evans
- 26—Bruce Alexander
- 27—Dick Bavetta
- 28—Tom Nunez
- 30—Jim Wishmier
- 31—Terry Durham
- 32—Bill Simmons
- 33—Jess Thompson
- 35—Jack Nies
- 37—Blane Reichelt
- 39—Barry Rogan
- 42—Hue Hollins

DIVISIONAL ALIGNMENT

EASTERN CONFERENCE

Atlantic Division

Boston Celtics
New Jersey Nets
New York Knicks
Philadelphia 76ers
Washington Bullets

Central Division

Atlanta Hawks
Chicago Bulls
Cleveland Cavaliers
Detroit Pistons
Indiana Pacers
Milwaukee Bucks

WESTERN CONFERENCE

Midwest Division

Dallas Mavericks
Denver Nuggets
Houston Rockets
Kansas City Kings
San Antonio Spurs
Utah Jazz

Pacific Division

Golden State Warriors
Los Angeles Lakers
Phoenix Suns
Portland Trail Blazers
San Diego Clippers
Seattle SuperSonics

ROSTERS OF NBA CLUBS

ATLANTA HAWKS
Coach—Kevin Loughery, St. John's '62

No.	Name	Pos.	Hgt.	Wgt.	Birthdate	Alma Mater
	Clyde Bradshaw	G	6-0	170	12-28-59	De Paul '81
16	Tom Burleson	C	7-3	228	2-24-52	No. Carolina St. '74
7	Art Collins	G	6-5	200	4-14-54	Biscayne (Fla.) '76
14	Charlie Criss	G	5-8	264	11- 6-49	New Mexico St. '70
	Marvin Delph	G	6-4	180	10-15-56	Arkansas '78
22	John Drew	F	6-6	205	9-30-54	Gardner-Webb '76
	Kevin Figaro	G	6-5	190	10-16-59	Southwestern La. '81
10	Steve Hawes	C-F	6-9	220	5-26-50	Washington '72
3	Eddie Johnson	G	6-2	175	2-24-55	Auburn '77
	Rudy Macklin	F	6-7	205	2-19-58	Louisiana St. '81
1	Wes Matthews	G	6-1	165	8-24-59	Wisconsin '81
33	James McElroy	G	6-3	190	10- 4-53	Central Mich. '75
54	Tom McMillen	F	6-11	215	5-26-52	Maryland '74
41	Sam Pellom	C	6-9	225	11- 2-51	Buffalo '78
30	Tree Rollins	C	7-1	235	6-16-55	Clemson '77
32	Dan Roundfield	F	6-8	205	5-26-53	Central Mich. '75
11	Craig Shelton	F	6-7	210	5- 1-57	Georgetown '80
	Rory Sparrow	G	6-2	195	6-12-58	Villanova '80
	Al Wood	F	6-6	193	6- 2-58	North Carolina '81

BOSTON CELTICS
Coach—Bill Fitch, Coe College (Iowa) '54

No.	Name	Pos.	Hgt.	Wgt.	Birthdate	Alma Mater
7	Nate Archibald	G	6-1	165	9- 2-48	Texas-El Paso '70
33	Larry Bird	F	6-9	220	12- 7-56	Indiana State '79
35	Charles Bradley	G	6-5	220	5-16-59	Wyoming '81
41	Jim Brandon	G	6-5	195	2-22-58	St. Peter's '80
30	M. L. Carr	G-F	6-6	205	1- 9-51	Guilford (N.C.) '73
	Terry Duerod	G	6-2	180	7-29-56	Detroit '79
45	Eric Fernsten	C-F	6-10	205	11- 1-53	San Francisco '75
42	Chris Ford	G	6-5	190	1-11-49	Villanova '72
12	Glenn Hagan	G	6-1	160	6-25-55	St. Bonaventure '78
43	Gerald Henderson	G	6-2	175	1-16-56	Va. Commonwealth '78
11	Tracy Jackson	F-G	6-6	205	4-21-59	Notre Dame '81
34	John Johnson	G	6-4	200	6- 1-59	Michigan '81
	Wayne Kreklow	G	6-4	185	1- 4-57	Drake '79
31	Cedric Maxwell	F	6-8	217	11-21-55	UNC-Charlotte '77
32	Kevin McHale	F-C	6-10	235	12-19-57	Minnesota '80
52	George Morrow	F	6-7	220	1- 5-59	Creighton '81
00	Robert Parish	C	7-1	230	8-30-53	Centenary '76
53	Rick Robey	C-F	6-10	235	1-30-56	Kentucky '78

CHICAGO BULLS
Coach—Jerry Sloan, Evansville '65

No.	Name	Pos.	Hgt.	Wgt.	Birthdate	Alma Mater
	Ray Blume	G	6-4	185	9-23-58	Oregon State '81
	Billy Bryant	G	6-5	190	10-12-57	Western Kentucky '79
	Roger Burkman	G	6-5	180	5-22-58	Louisville '81
26	Coby Dietrick	C-F	6-11	225	7-23-48	San Jose State '70
53	Artis Gilmore	C	7-2	240	9-21-49	Jacksonville '71

NBA TEAM ROSTERS

No.	Name	Pos.	Hgt.	Wgt.	Birthdate	Alma Mater
34	David Greenwood	F	6-9½	230	5-27-57	UCLA '79
	Tony Hall	F	6-3	184	11-14-55	Ohio State '80
	Steve Hayes	C	7-0	235	8- 2-55	Idaho '77
13	Dwight Jones	C-F	6-10	225	2-27-52	Houston '73
35	Larry Kenon	F	6-9	215	12-13-52	Memphis State '73
12	Ronnie Lester	G	6-2	175	7-30-59	Iowa '80
7	Scott May	F	6-7	215	3-19-54	Indiana '76
	Johnny Nash	F	6-6	185	12- 9-57	Arizona State '81
	Jackie Robinson	F	6-6	210	5-20-55	Nevada-Las Vegas '78
14	Ricky Sobers	G	6-3	195	1-15-53	Nevada-Las Vegas '75
24	Reggie Theus	G	6-7	205	10-13-57	Nevada-Las Vegas '79
32	James Wilkes	F	6-7	190	3-12-58	UCLA '80
	Orlando Woolridge	F	6-9	215	12-16-59	Notre Dame '81
31	Sam Worthen	G	6-6	195	1-17-58	Marquette '80

CLEVELAND CAVALIERS

Coach—Don Delaney, Kent State '60

No.	Name	Pos.	Hgt.	Wgt.	Birthdate	Alma Mater
	Boo Bowers	G	6-5	205	6- 8-58	American U. '81
23	Mike Bratz	G	6-2	185	10-17-55	Stanford '77
32	Kenny Carr	F	6-7	230	8-15-55	No. Carolina St. '78
40	James Edwards	C	7-1	230	11-22-55	Washington '77
35	Don Ford	F	6-9	215	12-31-52	Santa Barbara '75
20	Geoff Huston	G	6-2	175	11- 8-57	Texas Tech '79
44	Lee Johnson	F-C	6-11	220	6-16-57	East Texas St. '79
24	Walter Jordan	F	6-8	210	2-19-56	Purdue '78
41	Bill Laimbeer	C	6-11	245	5-19-57	Notre Dame '79
	Ethan Martin	G	6-0	170	6-20-59	Louisiana St. '81
30	Mike Mitchell	F	6-7	220	1- 1-56	Auburn '78
	Kenny Page	G	6-3	180	9-15-57	New Mexico '82
15	Roger Phegley	G	6-6	205	10-16-56	Bradley '78
13	James Silas	G	6-3	180	2-11-49	S. F. Austin '72
31	Richard Washington	F	6-11	225	7-15-55	UCLA '76
8	Scott Wedman	F	6-7	233	7-29-52	Colorado '74
33	Bob Wilkerson	G	6-7	200	8-15-54	Indiana '76
	Rich Yonakor	F	6-9	220	10- 3-58	North Carolina '80

DALLAS MAVERICKS

Coach—Dick Motta, Utah State '53

No.	Name	Pos.	Hgt.	Wgt.	Birthdate	Alma Mater
24	Mark Aguirre	F	6-5	220	12-10-59	DePaul '82
50	Karl Bankowski	F	6-7	210	1-31-59	Utah '81
22	Rolando Blackman	G	6-5	190	2-26-59	Kansas State '81
7	Scott Bosanko	G	6-4	180	10-27-59	Northern St. (S.D.) '81
42	Allan Bristow	F	6-7	210	8-23-51	Virginia Tech '73
45	Marty Byrnes	F	6-7	218	4-30-56	Syracuse '78
43	Wayne Cooper	C	6-10	220	11-16-56	New Orleans '78
15	Brad Davis	G	6-3	180	12-17-55	Maryland '78
35	Danny Davis	F	6-7	225	6-23-59	UNC-Wilmington '81
55	Art Housey	C	6-10	220	1-31-58	Kansas '81
53	Clarence Kea	F	6-7	225	2- 2-59	Lamar '80
10	David Kennedy	G	6-2	170	5-29-59	Cincinnati '81
21	Chad Kinch	G	6-4	190	5-22-58	UNC-Charlotte '80
25	Tom LaGarde	F	6-10	230	2-10-55	North Carolina '77
44	Scott Lloyd	C	6-10	230	12-19-52	Arizona State '76
17	Oliver Mack	G	6-3	195	6- 6-57	East Carolina '79
20	Eddie Moss	G	6-2	180	4-25-59	Syracuse '81
34	Jim Spanarkel	F-G	6-5	190	6-28-57	Duke '79
33	Elston Turner	G-F	6-5	200	6-10-59	Mississippi '81
31	Jay Vincent	F	6-7	220	6-10-59	Michigan State '81

DENVER NUGGETS
Coach—Doug Moe, North Carolina '61

No.	Name	Pos.	Hgt.	Wgt.	Birthdate	Alma Mater
23	T. R. Dunn	G	6-4	192	2-1-55	Alabama '77
2	Alex English	F	6-7	190	1-5-54	South Carolina '76
22	Glen Gondrezick	F	6-6	218	8-30-55	Nevada-Las Vegas '77
1	Ken Higgs	G	6-0	185	1-31-55	Louisiana State '78
34	Cedrick Hordges	F	6-8	220	1- 8-57	South Carolina '80
44	Dan Issel	C	6-9	240	10-25-48	Kentucky '70
5	Greg Manning	G	6-2	180	7-19-59	Maryland '81
7	Billy McKinney	G	6-0	165	6- 5-55	Northwestern '77
43	James Ray	F	6-9	215	7-27-57	Jacksonville '80
25	Dave Robisch	C	6-10	240	12-22-49	Kansas '71
10	John Roche	G	6-3	170	9-26-49	South Carolina '71
33	David Thompson	G	6-4	195	7-13-54	No. Carolina St. '75
42	Ron Valentine	F	6-7	210	11-27-57	Old Dominion '80
55	Kiki Vandeweghe	F	6-8	220	8- 1-58	UCLA '80

DETROIT PISTONS
Coach—Robert (Scotty) Robertson, La. Tech '51

No.	Name	Pos.	Hgt.	Wgt.	Birthdate	Alma Mater
54	Kent Benson	C-F	6-10	245	12-27-54	Indiana '77
43	Tony Fuller	G	6-3	185	9- 4-58	Pepperdine '80
33	Keith Herron	F-G	6-6	190	6-14-56	Villanova '78
35	Phil Hubbard	F	6-8	215	12-13-56	Michigan '79
52	Richard Johnson	C	7-1	260	5-17-56	LeMoyne-Owen '81
42	Edgar Jones	F-C	6-10	225	6-17-56	Nevada-Reno '79
32	Greg Kelser	F	6-8	200	9-17-57	Michigan State '79
10	Donnie Koonce	G	6-3	180	6-13-59	UNC-Charlotte '81
30	Ron Lee	G	6-4	204	11- 2-52	Oregon '76
25	John Long	G	6-5	190	8-28-56	Detroit '78
44	Paul Mokeski	C	7-0	250	1- 3-57	Kansas '79
40	Wayne Robinson	F	6-9	230	4-19-58	Virginia Tech '80
11	Isiah Thomas	G	6-1	185	4-30-61	Indiana '83
4	Kelly Tripucka	F	6-6	225	2-16-59	Notre Dame '81
41	Terry Tyler	F	6-7	215	10-30-56	Detroit '78
15	Larry Wright	G	6-1	160	11-23-54	Grambling '77
24	Carlos Zuniga	F	6-5	195	9- 8-56	Tulane '80

GOLDEN STATE WARRIORS
Coach—Al Attles, North Carolina A&T '60

No.	Name	Pos.	Hgt.	Wgt.	Birthdate	Alma Mater
23	Rickey Brown	F-C	6-10	235	8-29-58	Mississippi State '80
2	Joe Barry Carroll	C	7-0	245	7-24-58	Purdue '80
-	Phil Chenier	G	6-3	180	10-30-50	California '72
52	Greg Cornelius	G	6-9	220	2-15-56	East Carolina '79
21	Lloyd Free	G	6-3	185	12- 9-53	Guilford (N.C.) '76
12	Mike Gale	G	6-4	190	7-18-50	Eliz. City State '71
10	Joe Hassett	G	6-5	180	9-11-55	Providence '77
30	Bernard King	F	6-7	210	12- 4-56	Tennessee '77
32	Lewis Lloyd	F	6-6	220	2-22-59	Drake '81
4	John Lucas	G	6-3	175	10-31-53	Maryland '76
5	Mike Mendez	G	6-4	190	10- 9-59	San Jose State '81
35	Doug Murrey	G-F	6-5	218	10- 7-59	San Jose State '81
11	Carlton Neverson	G	6-5	190	3-16-58	Pittsburgh '81
22	Sonny Parker	F-G	6-7	200	3-22-55	Texas A&M '76
31	Billy Reid	G	6-5	195	9-10-57	San Francisco '80
18	Lorenzo Romar	G	6-1	180	11-13-58	Washington '80
45	Purvis Short	F-G	6-7	210	7- 2-57	Jackson State '78
13	Larry Smith	F	6-8	212	1-18-58	Alcorn State '80
33	Sam Williams	F	6-8	210	3- 7-59	Arizona State '81

HOUSTON ROCKETS
Coach—Del Harris, Milligan (Tenn.) '59

No.	Name	Pos.	Hgt.	Wgt.	Birthdate	Alma Mater
10	Mike Dunleavy	G	6-3	180	3-21-54	South Carolina '76
00	Calvin Garrett	F	6-7	195	7-11-56	Oral Roberts '80
44	Elvin Hayes	F	6-9	235	11-17-45	Houston '68
41	Jerome Henderson	F	6-10	200	10- 5-59	New Mexico '82
6	Tom Henderson	G	6-3	190	1-26-52	Hawaii '74
11	Major Jones	F	6-9	225	7- 9-53	Albany State (Ga.) '76
30	Allen Leavell	G	6-1	170	4-27-57	Oklahoma City '79
24	Moses Malone	C	6-10	235	3-23-55	Petersburg Va. HS '74
23	Calvin Murphy	G	5-10	165	5- 9-48	Niagara '70
51	Jawann Oldham	C	7-0	220	7- 4-57	Seattle '80
5	Billy Paultz	C	6-11	240	7-30-48	St. John's '70
50	Robert Reid	F	6-8	210	8-30-55	St. Mary's (Tex.) '77
35	Larry Spriggs	F	6-7	215	9- 8-59	Howard '81
42	John Stroud	F	6-7	215	10-29-57	Mississippi '80
45	Rudy Tomjanovich	F	6-8	220	11-24-48	Michigan '70
43	Ed Turner	G	6-7	220	11-20-57	Texas A&I '81
32	Bill Willoughby	F	6-8	205	5-20-57	Englewood N.J. HS '75

INDIANA PACERS
Coach—Jack McKinney, St. Joseph's (Pa.) '57

No.	Name	Pos.	Hgt.	Wgt.	Birthdate	Alma Mater
5	Tom Abernethy	F	6-7	220	5- 6-54	Indiana '76
42	Mike Bantom	F	6-9	220	12- 3-51	St. Joseph's '73
10	Don Buse	G	6-4	192	8-10-50	Evansville '72
43	Harry Davis	F	6-7	220	1-27-56	Florida State '78
16	Johnny Davis	G	6-2	170	10-21-55	Dayton '76
34	Bob Fronk	G	6-4	195	11- 1-58	Washington '81
45	Clemon Johnson	C-F	6-10	240	9-12-56	Florida A&M '78
24	George Johnson	F	6-7	225	12- 8-56	St. John's '78
25	Billy Knight	G-F	6-6	195	6- 9-52	Pittsburgh '74
22	Al Leslie	G	6-3	185	3-14-60	Bucknell '81
30	George McGinnis	F	6-8	235	8-12-50	Indiana '73
3	Mike Olliver	G	6-1	195	3-21-59	Lamar '81
55	Louis Orr	F	6-9	190	5- 7-58	Syracuse '80
26	Tom Owens	C	6-10	230	6-28-49	South Carolina '71
14	Jerry Sichting	G	6-1½	180	11-29-56	Purdue '79
32	Herb Williams	C-F	6-11	240	2-16-59	Ohio State '81

KANSAS CITY KINGS
Coach—Lowell (Cotton) Fitzsimmons, Midwestern State '56

No.	Name	Pos.	Hgt.	Wgt.	Birthdate	Alma Mater
31	Curtis Berry	F	6-8	205	6-16-59	Missouri '81
	B.B. Davis	F-C	6-8	220	2- 3-59	Lamar '81
9	Kenny Dennard	F	6-7	215	10-18-58	Duke '81
13	Leon Douglas	F-C	6-10	242	8-26-54	Alabama '76
22	Larry Drew	G	6-2	180	4- 2-58	Missouri '80
1	Phil Ford	G	6-2	183	2- 9-56	North Carolina '78
20	Ernie Grunfeld	G	6-6	222	4-24-55	Tennessee '77
8	Eddie Johnson	F	6-7	215	5- 1-59	Illinois '81
33	Steve Johnson	C	6-10	245	11- 3-57	Oregon State '81
51	Reggie King	F	6-6	244	2-14-57	Alabama '79
44	Sam Lacey	C	6-10	250	3- 8-48	New Mexico St. '70
24	John Lambert	F	6-10	225	1-14-53	USC '75
30	Kevin Loder	G-F	6-6	205	3-15-59	Alabama State '81
50	Joe C. Meriweather	F-C	6-10	220	10-26-53	Southern Illinois '75
21	Mike Perry	F	6-5	210	11-10-58	Richmond '81
	U.S. Reed	G	6-3	170	5-23-59	Arkansas '81

No.	Name	Pos.	Hgt.	Wgt.	Birthdate	Alma Mater
45	Cliff Robinson	F	6-9	220	3-13-60	USC '79
	Randy Smithson	G	6-3	185	10-24-57	Wichita State '81
14	Brian Walker	G	6-2	185	9-17-57	Purdue '81
	Clinton Wheeler	G	6-1	170		Wm. Paterson (N.J.) '81
43	Hawkeye Whitney	G-F	6-5	213	6-22-57	No. Carolina St. '80
	Mark Wilson	G	6-2	180	6-18-58	Ft. Hayes (Kan.) St. '81

LOS ANGELES LAKERS

Coach—Paul Westhead, St. Joseph's '61

No.	Name	Pos.	Hgt.	Wgt.	Birthdate	Alma Mater
33	Kareem Abdul-Jabbar	C	7-2	235	4-16-47	UCLA '69
	Darrell Allums	F	6-9	230	9-12-58	UCLA '80
8	Jim Brewer	F	6-9	220	12- 3-51	Minnesota '73
24	Butch Carter	G	6-5	200	6-11-58	Indiana '80
21	Mike Cooper	G-F	6-6	170	4-15-56	New Mexico '79
25	Alan Hardy	F	6-7	195	5-25-57	Michigan '78
34	Clay Johnson	G	6-4	185	7-18-56	Missouri '78
32	Earvin Johnson	G	6-9	215	8-14-59	Michigan State '79
15	Eddie Jordan	G	6-1	170	1-29-55	Rutgers '77
23	Harvey Knuckles	F	6-7	185	10- 3-58	Toledo '81
41	Mitch Kupchak	F	6-9	235	5-24-54	North Carolina '76
54	Mark Landsberger	F	6-8	225	5-21-55	Arizona State '78
40	Mike McGee	G-F	6-5	190	7-29-59	Michigan '81
30	Kevin McKenna	G	6-7	205	1- 8-59	Creighton '81
10	Norm Nixon	G	6-2	175	10-11-55	Duquesne '77
52	Jamaal Wilkes	F	6-6	190	5- 2-53	UCLA '74

MILWAUKEE BUCKS

Coach—Don Nelson, Iowa '62

No.	Name	Pos.	Hgt.	Wgt.	Birthdate	Alma Mater
2	Junior Bridgeman	G-F	6-5	210	9-17-53	Louisville '75
21	Quinn Buckner	G	6-3	205	8-20-54	Indiana '76
42	Harvey Catchings	C-F	6-10	220	9- 2-51	Hardin-Simmons '74
6	Pat Cummings	F	6-9½	235	7-11-56	Cincinnati '79
41	Len Elmore	F-C	6-9½	220	3-28-52	Maryland '74
5	Mike Evans	G	6-1	170	4-19-55	Kansas State '78
8	Marques Johnson	F	6-7	218	2- 8-56	UCLA '77
43	Mickey Johnson	F	6-10	200	8-31-52	Aurora (Il.) '74
16	Bob Lanier	C	6-10	265	9-10-48	St. Bonaventure '70
53	Alton Lister	C	6-11	240	10- 1-58	Arizona State '81
4	Sidney Moncrief	G	6-4	190	9-21-57	Arkansas '79
	Mark Smith	F	6-7	215	11- 5-59	Illinois '81
	Kelvin Troy	G-F	6-5	195	......	Rutgers '81
32	Brian Winters	G	6-4	185	3- 1-52	South Carolina '74

NEW JERSEY NETS

Coach—Larry Brown, North Carolina '63

No.	Name	Pos.	Hgt.	Wgt.	Birthdate	Alma Mater
40	Wayne Abrams	G	6-6	175	10- 9-58	Southern Illinois '80
	Marvin Barnes	F	6-9	225	7-27-52	Providence '74
10	Otis Birdsong	G	6-4	193	12- 9-55	Houston '77
21	David Burns	G	6-2	180	7- 3-58	St. Louis '81
12	Darwin Cook	G	6-3	184	8- 6-56	Portland '80
13	Joe Cooper	C	6-10	230	8- 1-57	Colorado '81
43	Mike Gminski	C	6-11	250	8- 3-59	Duke '80
33	Roy Hamilton	G	6-2	180	7-20-57	UCLA '79
55	Albert King	F	6-6	190	12-17-59	Maryland '81
20	Maurice Lucas	F-C	6-9	218	2-18-52	Marquette '74

NBA TEAM ROSTERS

No.	Name	Pos.	Hgt.	Wgt.	Birthdate	Alma Mater
11	Bob McAdoo	F-C	6-9	210	9-25-51	North Carolina '72
1	Lowes Moore	G	6-0	163	5- 5-57	West Virginia '80
31	Mike O'Koren	F	6-7	215	2- 7-78	North Carolina '80
15	Edmund Sherod	G	6-2	170	9-13-59	Va. Commonwealth '81
30	Ray Tolbert	F	6-9	225	9-10-58	Indiana '81
22	Jan van Breda Kolff	F-G	6-8	210	12-16-51	Vanderbilt '74
14	Foots Walker	G	5-11	172	5-21-51	West Georgia '74
52	Buck Williams	F	6-8	215	3- 8-60	Maryland '82
42	Mike Woodson	F	6-5	198	3-24-58	Indiana '80

NEW YORK KNICKERBOCKERS
Coach—William (Red) Holzman, CCNY '43

No.	Name	Pos.	Hgt.	Wgt.	Birthdate	Alma Mater
	Alex Bradley	F	6-7	225	10-30-59	Villanova '81
35	Reggie Carter	G	6-3	165	10- 6-57	St. John's '80
25	Bill Cartwright	C	7-1	237	7-30-57	San Francisco '79
	Greg Cook	F-C	6-9	230	12- 8-58	Louisiana State '81
45	Hollis Copeland	F	6-6	185	12-20-55	Rutgers '78
42	Larry Demic	F	6-9	225	6-27-57	Arizona '79
34	Mike Glenn	G	6-3	185	9-10-55	Southern Illinois '76
43	Toby Knight	F	6-9	210	5- 3-55	Notre Dame '77
	Wayne McKoy	F-C	6-8	235	3-26-58	St. John's '81
14	Mike Newlin	G	6-5	200	1- 2-49	Utah '71
20	Michael Ray Richardson	G	6-5	190	4-11-55	Montana '78
21	Campy Russell	F	6-8	215	1-12-52	Michigan '74
31	DeWayne Scales	F	6-9	210	12-28-58	Louisiana State '80
9	Randy Smith	G	6-3	180	12-14-48	Buffalo State '71
40	Marvin Webster	C	7-1	240	4-13-52	Morgan State '75
13	Ray Williams	G	6-2	188	10-14-54	Minnesota '77
33	Sly Williams	F	6-7	210	1-26-58	Rhode Island '80

PHILADELPHIA 76ERS
Coach—Billy Cunningham, North Carolina '65

No.	Name	Pos.	Hgt.	Wgt.	Birthdate	Alma Mater
10	Maurice Cheeks	G	6-1	181	9- 8-56	West Texas State '78
20	Doug Collins	G	6-7	180	7-28-51	Illinois State '73
23	Steve Craig	G	6-3	180	8-26-56	Brigham Young '81
7	John Crawford	F	6-7	178	6- 9-59	Kansas '81
25	Earl Cureton	F	6-9	215	9- 3-57	Detroit '80
53	Darryl Dawkins	C	6-11½	252	1-11-57	Orlando (Fla.) HS '75
14	Franklin Edwards	G	6-1	170	2- 2-59	Cleveland State '81
6	Julius Erving	F	6-6	210	2-22-50	Massachusetts '72
	Reggie Gaines	F	6-8	215	6-10-58	Winston-Salem St. '80
44	Frank Gilroy	F	6-6	220	3-18-58	St. John's '81
30	Ernest Graham	F	6-7	207	6-11-59	Maryland '81
9	Lionel Hollins	G	6-3	185	10-19-53	Arizona State '75
18	Ollie Johnson	F	6-6	200	5-11-49	Temple '49
24	Bobby Jones	F	6-9	205	12-18-51	North Carolina '74
11	Caldwell Jones	F-C	7-0	213	8- 4-50	Albany (Ga.) St. '73
50	Steve Mix	F	6-8	219	12-30-47	Toledo '69
40	Peter Mullenberg	F	6-8	210	9-10-59	Delaware '81
4	Clint Richardson	G	6-3	195	8- 7-56	Seattle '79
3	Vernon Smith	F	6-7	207	10-23-58	Texas A&M '81
21	Michael Thomas	F	6-1	175	3-24-59	North Park (Ill.) '81
22	Andrew Toney	G	6-3	190	11-23-57	Southwestern La. '80
33	Rynn Wright	F-G	6-6	210	1-12-59	Texas A&M '81

PHOENIX SUNS
Coach—John MacLeod, Bellarmine (Ky.) '59

No.	Name	Pos.	Hgt.	Wgt.	Birthdate	Alma Mater
33	Alvan Adams	C	6-9	212	7-19-54	Oklahoma '75
	Dudley Bradley	G	6-6	195	3-19-57	North Carolina '79
	Sam Clancy	F	6-7	241	5-29-58	Pittsburgh '81
45	Jeff Cook	F	6-10	215	10-21-56	Idaho State '78
6	Walter Davis	G	6-6	198	9- 9-54	North Carolina '77
	Craig Dykema	F	6-8	198	6-11-59	Long Beach St. '81
22	Johnny High	G	6-3	185	4-25-57	Nevada-Reno '79
24	Dennis Johnson	G	6-4	193	9-18-54	Pepperdine '76
53	Rich Kelley	C	7-0	240	3-23-53	Stanford '75
50	Joel Kramer	F	6-7	203	10-30-55	San Diego State '78
4	Kyle Macy	G	6-3	188	4- 9-57	Kentucky '80
	John McCullough	G	6-5	197	10- 5-56	Oklahoma '79
	Larry Nance	F	6-10	206	2-12-59	Clemson '81
21	Truck Robinson	F	6-7	239	10- 4-51	Tennessee State '74
14	Alvin Scott	F	6-7	206	9-14-55	Oral Roberts '77

PORTLAND TRAIL BLAZERS
Coach—Jack Ramsay, St. Joseph's '49

No.	Name	Pos.	Hgt.	Wgt.	Birthdate	Alma Mater
25	Herb Andrew	G	6-3	185	6-13-60	South Alabama '81
6	Tom Barker	C-F	6-11	230	3-11-55	Hawaii '76
12	Billy Ray Bates	G	6-4	210	5-31-56	Kentucky State '78
19	Geff Crompton	C	6-11	280	7- 4-55	North Carolina '78
30	Bob Gross	F	6-6	200	8- 3-53	Long Beach St. '75
40	Petur Gudmundsson	C	7-2	250	10-30-58	Washington '81
32	Mike Harper	C	6-10	215	12- 9-57	North Park (Ill.) '80
44	Kevin Kunnert	C	6-11	231	11-11-51	Iowa '73
3	Jeff Lamp	F	6-6	193	3- 9-59	Virginia '81
33	Calvin Natt	F	6-6	220	1- 8-57	NE Louisiana '79
4	Jim Paxson	F-G	6-6	200	7- 9-57	Dayton '79
14	Kelvin Ransey	G	6-2	180	5- 3-58	Ohio State '80
43	Mychal Thompson	C	6-10	226	1-30-55	Minnesota '78
13	Dave Twardzik	G	6-1	180	9-20-50	Old Dominion '72
41	Darnell Valentine	G	6-1	183	2- 3-59	Kansas '81
31	Peter Verhoeven	F	6-9	214	2-15-59	Fresno State '81
42	Kermit Washington	F	6-8	230	9-17-51	American U. '73
24	Julius Wayne	G	6-2	175	11- 8-59	Texas-El Paso '81

SAN ANTONIO SPURS
Coach—Stan Albeck, Bradley '55

No.	Name	Pos.	Hgt.	Wgt.	Birthdate	Alma Mater
	Gene Banks	F	6-7	215	5-15-59	Duke '81
10	Ron Brewer	G	6-4	180	9-16-55	Arkansas '78
40	Dave Corzine	C	6-11	265	4-25-56	DePaul '78
44	George Gervin	G	6-8	185	4-27-52	Eastern Michigan '72
30	Paul Griffin	F	6-9	220	1-20-54	Western Michigan '76
	Tony Jackson	G	6-0	170	1-17-58	Florida State '80
52	George Johnson	C	6-11	220	12-18-48	Dillard '70
32	Reggie Johnson	F	6-9	213	6-25-57	Tennessee '80
	Raymond Lewis	G	6-1	170	9- 3-53	Cal St. (L.A.) '73
00	Johnny Moore	G	6-3	175	3- 3-58	Texas '79
3	Kenny Natt	G	6-3	185	10- 6-58	NE Louisiana '80
53	Mark Olberding	F	6-9	230	4-21-56	Minnesota '75
	Ed Rains	F	6-7	196	12-24-59	South Alabama '81
31	Kevin Restani	F	6-10	230	12-26-51	San Francisco '74
	Willie Smith	G	6-2	166	10-26-53	Missouri '76
	Dean Uthoff	C	6-11	240	7- 7-58	Iowa State '80
33	Michael Wiley	F	6-9	202	10-16-57	Long Beach State '80

NBA TEAM ROSTERS

SAN DIEGO CLIPPERS

Coach—Paul Silas, Creighton '64

No.	Name	Pos.	Hgt.	Wgt.	Birthdate	Alma Mater
	Jim Brogan	G	6-6	180	2-24-58	W. Va. Wesleyan '80
7	Michael Brooks	F	6-7	210	8-17-58	La Salle '80
23	Joe Bryant	F	6-9	218	10-19-54	La Salle '76
	Tom Chambers	F-C	6-11	225	6-21-59	Utah '81
42	Ron Davis	F	6-7	205	5- 1-54	Washington State '76
13	John Douglas	G	6-3	185	6-12-56	Kansas '78
35	Kim Goetz	F	6-7	205	8-23-57	San Diego State '79
24	Garfield Heard	F	6-6	219	5- 3-48	Oklahoma '70
31	Swen Nater	C	6-11	250	1-14-50	UCLA '73
25	Lee Baker	G	6-5	195	3-13-59	Virginia '81
30	Jim Smith	F	6-9	228	4-12-58	Ohio State '81
11	Phil Smith	G	6-4	188	4-22-52	San Francisco '74
14	Brian Taylor	G	6-2	185	6- 9-51	Princeton '73
33	Jerome Whitehead	C	6-10	220	9-30-56	Marquette '78
20	Freeman Williams	G	6-4	195	5-15-56	Portland State '78

SEATTLE SUPERSONICS

Coach—Lenny Wilkens, Providence '60

No.	Name	Pos.	Hgt.	Wgt.	Birthdate	Alma Mater
25	Carl Bailey	C	7-0	205	4-23-58	Tuskegee Institute '80
20	James Bailey	F-C	6-9	220	5-21-57	Rutgers '79
32	Fred Brown	G	6-3	185	7- 7-48	Iowa '71
40	James Donaldson	C	7-2	270	8-16-57	Washington State '79
34	Jacky Dorsey	F	6-8	235	12-18-54	Georgia '78
31	Andra Griffin	F	6-7	210	12-29-59	Washington '81
22	Bill Hanzlik	G-F	6-7	200	12- 6-57	Notre Dame '80
24	Armond Hill	G	6-4	190	3-31-53	Princeton '76
27	John Johnson	F	6-7	200	10-18-47	Iowa '70
15	Vinnie Johnson	G	6-2	200	9- 1-56	Baylor '79
30	Mark Radford	G	6-4	190	7- 5-59	Oregon State '81
8	Lonnie Shelton	F	6-8	245	10-19-55	Oregon State '77
33	Tom Sienkiewicz	G	6-2	185	5- 2-59	Villanova '81
43	Jack Sikma	C-F	6-11	230	11-14-55	Illinois Wesleyan '77
23	Danny Vranes	F	6-7	210	10-29-58	Utah '81
42	Wally Walker	F	6-7	200	7-18-54	Virginia '76
44	Paul Westphal	G	6-4	205	11-30-50	USC '72
1	Gus Williams	G	6-2	175	10-10-53	USC '75

UTAH JAZZ

Coach—Tom Nissalke, Florida State '57

No.	Name	Pos.	Hgt.	Wgt.	Birthdate	Alma Mater
33	Mel Bennett	F	6-7	210	1- 4-55	Pittsburgh '78
	Bobby Cattage	F	6-9	250	8-17-58	Auburn '81
	Mike Clark	F	6-9	230	4- 7-59	Oregon '81
4	Adrian Dantley	F	6-5	205	2-28-56	Notre Dame '77
31	Paul Dawkins	F	6-5	190	6-10-57	Northern Illinois '79
18	John Duren	G	6-4	200	10-30-58	Georgetown '80
	Gus Gerard	F	6-8	210	7-27-53	Virginia '75
14	Rickey Green	G	6-0	170	8-18-54	Michigan '77
35	Darrell Griffith	G	6-4	190	6-16-58	Louisville '80
11	James Hardy	F	6-9	220	12- 1-56	San Francisco '79
5	Jeff Judkins	G-F	6-6	180	3-27-56	Utah '78
22	Carl Nicks	G	6-3	185	10- 6-58	Indiana State '80
	Ken Ollie	F	6-6	195	9-18-59	Wyoming '81

No.	Name	Pos.	Hgt.	Wgt.	Birthdate	Alma Mater
50	Ben Poquette	F-C	6-9	235	5- 7-55	Central Michigan '77
	Mike Robinson	F	6-9	245	7- 6-58	Central Michigan '81
52	Bill Robinzine	F	6-7	235	1-20-53	DePaul '75
	Dan Schayes	C	6-11	245	5-10-59	Syracuse '81
	George Torres	G	6-3	185	9-21-57	Beth. (Okla.) Naz. '81
45	Jeff Wilkins	C	6-10	240	3- 9-55	Illinois State '77
	Howard Wood	F	6-7	225	5-10-59	Tennessee '81

WASHINGTON BULLETS

Coach—Gene Shue, Maryland '54

No.	Name	Pos.	Hgt.	Wgt.	Birthdate	Alma Mater
42	Greg Ballard	F	6-7	215	1-29-55	Oregon '77
9	Jim Chones	F-C	6-11	220	11-30-49	Marquette '73
22	Don Collins	F-G	6-6	205	11-28-58	Washington State '80
10	Bob Dandridge	F	6-6	195	11-15-47	Norfolk (Va.) State '69
	Charles Davis	F	6-7	215	10- 5-58	Vanderbilt '81
	Mike Ferrara	G	6-3	190	9-25-58	Colgate '81
	Claude Gregory	F	6-8	215	12-26-58	Wisconsin '81
35	Kevin Grevey	G	6-5	210	5-12-53	Kentucky '75
14	Brad Holland	G	6-3	185	12- 6-56	UCLA '79
	Frank Johnson	G	6-2	185	11-23-58	Wake Forest '81
	Steve Lingenfelter	C-F	6-9	230	6-10-59	South Dakota State '81
44	Rick Mahorn	F-C	6-10	235	9-21-58	Hamp. (Va.) Inst. '80
33	Andre McCarter	G	6-3	190	8-25-53	UCLA '76
	Ed Odom	G	6-3	178	3-28-59	Oklahoma State '80
	Joe Pace	C	6-10	220	12-18-53	Coppin St. (Md.) '76
1	Kevin Porter	G	5-11	165	4-17-50	St. Francis (Pa.) '72
20	Anthony Roberts	F	6-5	185	4-15-55	Oral Roberts '77
	Jeff Ruland	C-F	6-11	240	12-16-58	Iona '81
12	Carlos Terry	G-F	6-5	220	6-22-59	Winston-Salem St. '78
	Garry Witts	G-F	6-7	190	7- 3-59	Holy Cross '81

NBA Commissioner Larry O'Brien (second from left) poses with the top selections in the 1981 draft, (left to right) top-pick Mark Aguirre, second-pick Isiah Thomas, fourth-pick Al Wood and third-pick Buck Williams.

The 1981 College Draft

By MIKE WEBER

NEW YORK—Will Mark Aguirre be "bad" or play it "straight?" Will Isiah and Kelly change the Pistons' losing ways? Will the Nets be caught off guard because they moved forward?

Only the 1981-82 season will tell whether the selections made in last June's NBA draft were propitious or poor. It would be stunning to discover that the teams picking 1-2-3 didn't help themselves simply because they need so much help. The Dallas Mavericks were 15-57 last season, the Detroit Pistons were 21-61 and the New Jersey Nets 24-58.

Mark Aguirre, the DePaul forward tabbed first by the Mavs, says he expects some "bumpy road." He should be an expert on the subject. Although an acknowledged star who averaged about 25 points per game over three seasons, his reputation is that of a sulker.

"There was no way I thought I was a bad actor," said Aguirre. "I've always been a straight shooter."

The Mavs hope so. Same goes for the Pistons and Isiah Thomas, the 6-1 Indiana guard who left school with two years of eligibility remaining. His brilliance will be complemented by Notre Dame forward Kelly Tripucka, giving Detroit cause for happy thoughts about the future.

New Jersey also is looking to the future, thanks to the acquisition via trade of All-Star guard Otis Birdsong, as well as the drafting of three first-round forwards—Maryland's 6-8 Buck Williams and 6-6 Albert King, plus Indiana's 6-9 Ray Tolbert.

"It was amazing," said new Nets Coach Larry Brown. "We never expected to be able to take Buck and Albert together. After watching the playoffs, I decided that you can't have too many forwards." The Nets might, since they already have veterans Maurice Lucas, Jan van Breda Kolff and Mike O'Koren. They still need a point guard to complement, then replace, 30-year-old Foots Walker.

It's hard to see what the Altanta Hawks need, save an injury-free season. Added to their strength on hand, they drafted North Carolina swingman Al Wood on the first round and guard Clyde Bradshaw of DePaul and forward Rudy Macklin of LSU later on.

The Seattle SuperSonics, also looking to rebound from a down year, finally signed reluctant free agent guard Gus Williams, then drafted Utah's 6-7 Danny Vranes with an eye to replacing 34-year-old John Johnson. Meanwhile, the Chicago Bulls, looking to shore up rather than replace, went for Notre Dame's 6-9 forward Orlando Woolridge, hoping he is the last piece in their playoff puzzle.

Speaking of puzzles, the Kansas City Kings were one last season. They'll continue to be one this season. They made it to the Western Conference finals without an injured Birdsong, who was lost to the Nets. They also lost Scott Wedman via free agency, but they drafted Oregon

Former DePaul star Mark Aguirre, the No. 1 choice in the NBA draft, holds the shirt he will be wearing as a member of the Dallas Mavericks.

State's 6-11 center, Steve Johnson, who'll learn under Sam Lacey before replacing him. Kevin Loder, 6-6 swingman from Alabama State, should get some of Wedman's time in the frontcourt.

San Diego Clippers' Coach Paul Silas had made no secret of his intention of drafting Utah's 6-10 Tom Chambers. Silas, who fancies himself a motivator of men, likes the challenge some feel he will have with Chambers.

Washington's Bullets have a challenge, one which they didn't meet last season. It's called rebuilding. Many observers feel the Bullets picked a strange place to begin when they selected Wake Forest guard Frank Johnson. The return from Europe of former Iona center Jeff Ruland should help.

Some felt former Syracuse center Danny Schayes should have followed Ruland's route to the NBA but the Utah Jazz don't want to wait for his development. Having Ben Poquette as your center can make you impatient. His best position is power forward.

Indiana, which lost center James Edwards to free agency, picked Ohio State's enigmatic center Herb Williams. Can he? Will he? Does he want to? It's up to Coach Jack McKinney to make sure he does.

The Portland Trail Blazers, still seeking to recapture past glory, drafted a gem in Virginia swingman Jeff Lamp. They also grabbed Kansas guard Darnell Valentine but there are those around the NBA who expected him to be dealt away. The Nets, for one, were hoping.

The Los Angeles Lakers, needing a forward, opted for a scoring swingman in Michigan's Mike McGee. He'll benefit from being brought along slowly and by the talent which will surround him. The Lakers could have taken 6-10 Larry Nance of Clemson but left him instead for the Phoenix Suns, who needed a rebounder.

Milwaukee tabbed Arizona State center Alton Lister, after failing to move up in the draft and obtain guard Mike Newlin from the Nets. Philadelphia, expected to take hometown hero Gene Banks of Duke, went instead for 6-1 guard Franklin Edwards of Cleveland State. Philly wanted an outside shooter and bid for Newlin, who eventually went to the Knicks in exchange for swingman Mike Woodson.

Boston (it wanted Newlin, too) settled on a possible successor to Chris Ford in Wyoming guard Charles Bradley. The Celts may have done better with their second pick—Brigham Young guard Danny Ainge. If he continues hitting as lightly as he has been with baseball's Toronto Blue Jays, he may give basketball a try.

Five teams had no first-round picks. New York acquired Newlin in a trade and drafted 6-9 LSU forward Greg Cook on the second round; San Antonio took Banks; Golden State, seeking a center or ballhandling guard, instead went for 6-8 forward Sam Williams, a backup, at best, to Larry Smith; Denver turned to Pan American forward Kenneth Green, one of only four NCAA Division I players to average 20 points and 10

Isiah Thomas will be trying to do for Detroit what he did for Indiana during the Hoosiers' 1980-81 NCAA championship season.

rebounds per game last season, and Cleveland, without a pick until the third round, took Mickey Dillard, a Florida State guard, and later added swingman Boo Bowers of American University.

Green finally signed with the Nuggets, while Dillard disappointed the Cavs by leaving their entry in the Southern California Summer Pro League.

OFFICIAL NBA COLLEGE DRAFT—JUNE 9, 1981

FIRST ROUND

TEAM	NAME	COLLEGE
1. Dallas	Mark Aguirre	DePaul
2. Detroit	Isiah Thomas	Indiana
3. New Jersey	Buck Williams	Maryland
4. Cleve. to Phila. to Port. to Chi. to Atl.	Al Wood	North Carolina
5. Utah to Seattle	Danny Vranes	Utah
6. Atlanta to Chicago	Orlando Woolridge	Notre Dame
7. Seattle to New York to Kansas City	Steve Johnson	Oregon State
8. San Diego	Tom Chambers	Utah
9. Denver to Dallas	Rolando Blackman	Kansas State
10. Golden St. to Port. to New Jersey	Albert King	Maryland
11. Washington	Frank Johnson	Wake Forest
12. Kan. City to Detroit	Kelly Tripucka	Notre Dame
13. Houston to Utah	Dan Schayes	Syracuse
14. Indiana	Herb Williams	Ohio State
15. Portland	Jeff Lamp	Virginia
16. Chicago to Portland	Darnell Valentine	Kansas
17. N.Y. to Cleveland to Kansas City	Kevin Loder	Alabama State
18. San Antonio to New Jersey	Ray Tolbert	Indiana
19. Los Angeles	Mike McGee	Michigan
20. Phoenix	Larry Nance	Clemson
21. Milwaukee	Alton Lister	Arizona State
22. Philadelphia	Franklin Edwards	Cleveland State
23. Boston	Charles Bradley	Wyoming

SECOND ROUND

TEAM	NAME	COLLEGE
24. Dallas	Jay Vincent	Michigan State
25. Detroit to Boston	Tracy Jackson	Notre Dame
26. New Jersey to Indiana to Portland	Brian Jackson	Utah State
27. Utah	Howard Wood	Tennessee
28. Cleve. to L.A. to Chi. to San Antonio	Gene Banks	Duke
29. Atl. to Utah to Atl. to Kansas City	Eddie Johnson	Illinois
30. Seattle to Chicago to San Antonio	Ed Rains	South Alabama
31. San Diego to Boston	Danny Ainge	Brigham Young
32. Denver to Chicago	Mike Olliver	Lamar
33. Washington to Golden State	Sam Williams	Arizona State
34. Golden State to Utah to Denver	Kenneth Green	Pan American
35. Houston to Wash.	Charles Davis	Vanderbilt
36. Kansas City to Cleve. to Indiana	Ray Blume	Oregon State
37. Indiana to Phoenix to Indiana	Al Leslie	Bucknell
38. Chicago to Atlanta	Clyde Bradshaw	DePaul

NBA 1981-82 DRAFT

SECOND ROUND

39. Portland to Detroit to Los Angeles	Harvey Knuckles	Toledo
40. New York	Greg Cook	LSU
41. San Antonio to Wash.	Claude Gregory	Wisconsin
42. Los Angeles	Elvis Rolle	Florida State
43. Phoenix to Dallas	Elston Turner	Mississippi
44. Milwaukee to K. C. to N. J. to Wash.	Steve Lingenfelter	South Dakota State
45. Boston to Houston	Ed Turner	Texas A&I
46. Philadelphia	Vernon Smith	Texas A&M

THIRD ROUND

TEAM	NAME	COLLEGE
47. Dallas	Art Housey	Kansas
48. Detroit to Wash.	Mike Ferrara	Colgate
49. New Jersey	David Burns	St. Louis
50. Cleveland to Portland	Derek Holcomb	Illinois
51. Utah to Los Angeles	Zam Fredrick	South Carolina
52. Atlanta	Rudy Macklin	LSU
53. Seattle	Mark Radford	Oregon State
54. San Diego	Jim Smith	Ohio State
55. Denver to Cleveland	Mickey Dillard	Florida State
56. Golden State	Carlton Neverson	Pittsburgh
57. Washington to N. Y.	Frank Brickowski	Penn State
58. Kansas City	Curtis Berry	Missouri
59. Houston to Cleveland	Russell Bowers	American U.
60. Indiana	Purvis Miller	USC
61. Portland	Petur Gudmundsson	Washington
62. Chicago to San Diego to Phoenix	Sam Clancy	Pittsburgh
63. New York	Wayne McKoy	St. John's (N.Y.)
64. San Antonio	Tom Baker	Eastern Kentucky
65. Los Angeles	Ron Cornelius	Pacific
66. Phoenix	Craig Dykema	Long Beach State
67. Milwaukee	Mark Smith	Illinois
68. Philadelphia	Ernest Graham	Maryland
69. Boston	John Johnson	Michigan

FOURTH ROUND

70. Dallas	Eddie Moss	Syracuse
71. Detroit	John May	South Alabama
72. New Jersey	Edmund Sherod	Virginia Commonwealth
73. Utah	George Torres	Bethany (Okla.) Nazarene
74. Cleveland	Ethan Martin	LSU
75. Atlanta	Kevin Figaro	Southwestern Louisiana
76. Seattle to Golden St.	Lewis Lloyd	Drake
77. San Diego	Lee Raker	Virginia
78. Denver to Kan. City	Kenny Dennard	Duke
79. Washington	Ron Davis	Arizona
80. Golden State	Terry Adolph	West Texas State
81. Houston	Larry Spriggs	Howard
82. Kansas City	B.B. Davis	Lamar
83. Indiana	Rolando Frazer	Briar Cliff (Iowa)
84. Chicago	Oliver Lee	Marquette
85. Portland	Pete Verhoeven	Fresno State
86. New York	Alex Bradley	Villanova
87. San Antonio	Earl Belcher	St. Bonaventure

NBA 1981-82 DRAFT

FOURTH ROUND

88. Los Angeles	Kevin McKenna	Creighton
89. Phoenix to Detroit	Donnie Koonce	UNC-Charlotte
90. Milwaukee	Kris Anderson	Florida State
91. Boston	Stanley Williams	La Salle
92. Philadelphia	Rynn Wright	Texas A&M

FIFTH ROUND

93. Dallas	Pete Budko	North Carolina
94. Detroit	George DeVone	UNC-Charlotte
95. New Jersey	Joe Cooper	Colorado
96. Cleveland	Kenny Page	New Mexico
97. Utah	Mike Clark	Oregon
98. Atlanta	Steve Krafcisin	Iowa
99. Seattle	Andra Griffin	Washington
100. San Diego	Dennis Isbell	Memphis State
101. Denver	Willie Sims	LSU
102. Golden State	Hank McDowell	Memphis State
103. Washington	Garry Witts	Holy Cross
104. Kansas City	U.S. Reed	Arkansas
105. Houston	Hasan Houston	Bradley
106. Indiana	George Peterson	Jersey City State
107. Portland	Herb Andrew	South Alabama
108. Chicago	Johnny Nash	Arizona State
109. New York	Jim Wright	Rhode Isand
110. San Antonio	Mike Rhodes	Vanderbilt
111. Los Angeles	Craig Watts	North Carolina State
112. Phoenix	Paul Heuerman	Michigan
133. Milwaukee	Kelvin Troy	Rutgers
114. Philadelphia	Steve Craig	Brigham Young
115. Boston	Glen Grunwald	Indiana

SIXTH ROUND

TEAM	NAME	COLLEGE
116. Dallas	Karl Bankowski	Utah
117. Detroit	Vince Brookins	Iowa
118. New Jersey	Kevin Lynam	La Salle
119. Utah	Kevin Sprewer	Loyola (Ill.)
120. Cleveland	Aaron Strayhorn	Hawaii
121. Atlanta	Darryl Warwick	Hampton (Va.) Institute
122. Seattle	Earl Banks	Auburn
123. San Diego	Mike Pepper	North Carolina
124. Denver	Alonzo Weatherly	Denver
125. Washington	Robert Williams	Grambling State
126. Golden State	Carter Scott	Ohio State
127. Houston	Fred Cowan	Kentucky
128. Kansas City	Brian Walker	Purdue
129. Indiana	Robert Fronk	Washington
130. Chicago	Roger Burkman	Louisville
131. Portland	Roshern Amie	Texas-El Paso
132. New York	John Blair	Monmouth (N.J.)
133. San Antonio	Northern Shavers	Jackson State
134. Los Angeles	Kevin Singleton	California
135. Phoenix	Pete Harris	Northeastern
136. Milwaukee	Jo Jo Hunter	Colorado
137. Boston	Steve Waite	Iowa
138. Philadelphia	Michael Thomas	North Park (Ill.)

NBA 1981-82 DRAFT

SEVENTH ROUND

#	Team	Player	School
139.	Dallas	Danny Davis	UNC-Wilmington
140.	Detroit	Greg Nance	West Virginia
141.	New Jersey	Rod Roberson	Northwestern
142.	Cleveland	Andre Smith	Nebraska
143.	Utah	Mike Robinson	Central Michigan
144.	Atlanta	Kevin Vesey	Iona
145.	Seattle	Tom Sienkiewicz	Villanova
146.	San Diego	Randy Johnson	Southern Colorado
147.	Denver	Greg Manning	Maryland
148.	Golden State	Robbie Dosty	Arizona
149.	Washington	Randy Martell	Houston Baptist
150.	Kansas City	Clinton Wheeler	William Paterson (N.J.)
151.	Houston	Joe Faine	Bowling Green State
152.	Indiana	Larry McKinney	Boise State
153.	Portland	Julius Wayne	Texas-El Paso
154.	Chicago	Scott Williams	South Alabama
155.	New York	Terry Cramer	Ripon (Wis.)
156.	San Antonio	Mark Mindeman	Northern Michigan
157.	Los Angeles	Larry Petty	Wisconsin
158.	Phoenix	David Williams	Southern (Baton Rouge)
159.	Milwaukee	Lewis Lattimore	Virginia
160.	Philadelphia	John Crawford	Kansas
161.	Boston	Tom Seaman	Holy Cross

EIGHTH ROUND

162.	Dallas	David Kennedy	Cincinnati
163.	Detroit	Joe Schoen	St. Francis (Pa.)
164.	New Jersey	Ken Webb	Fairleigh Dickinson
165.	Utah	Bobby Cattage	Auburn
166.	Cleveland	Glenn Marcus	Alabama-Birmingham
167.	Atlanta	Gilbert Salinas	Notre Dame
	Seattle	PASS	
168.	San Diego	Todd Haynes	Davidson
169.	Denver	Curtis Redding	St. John's (N.Y.)
170.	Washington	Mike Howard	Wofford (S.C.)
171.	Golden State	Yasutaka Okayama	U. of Osaka (Japan)
172.	Houston	Stanley Brewer	West Georgia
173.	Kansas City	Randy Smithson	Wichita State
174.	Indiana	Len Hatzenbeller	Drexel
175.	Chicago	Ben Mitchell	Alabama-Huntsville
176.	Portland	John Smith	Saint Joseph's (Pa.)
177.	New York	Brian O'Conner	Thomas More (Ky.)
178.	San Antonio	Bob Bartholomew	San Diego
179.	Los Angeles	Jay Triano	Simon Fraser (Canada)
180.	Phoenix	Steve Risley	Indiana
181.	Milwaukee	Mike Brkovich	Michigan State
182.	Boston	George Morrow	Creighton
183.	Philadelphia	Frank Gilroy	St. John's (N.Y.)

NINTH ROUND

#	Team	Player	School
184.	Dallas	John Hollinden	Indiana State-Evansville
185.	Detroit	Eddie Baker	Alcorn State
186.	New Jersey	Rudy Williams	Providence
187.	Cleveland	Paul Roba	Cleveland State
188.	Utah	Ken Ollie	Wyoming
189.	Atlanta	Howard Thompkins	Wagner
	Seattle	PASS	
190.	San Diego	Art Jones	North Carolina State

NINTH ROUND

191.	Denver	Andrew Burton	Austin Peay State
192.	Golden State	Doug Murrey	San Jose State
193.	Washington	Eddie Brown	Valdosta (Ga.) State
194.	Kansas City	Mike Perry	Richmond
	Houston	PASS	
195.	Indiana	Scott Whitley	William & Mary
196.	Portland	Sid Williams	San Jose State
197.	Chicago	Terry Martin	Lambuth (Tenn.)
198.	New York	Marty Headd	Syracuse
199.	San Antonio	Leonel Marquetti	Hampton (Va.) Institute
	Los Angeles	PASS	
200.	Phoenix	Brian Johnson	Colorado
201.	Milwaukee	Chip Rucker	Northeastern
202.	Philadelphia	Ron Wister	Temple
203.	Boston	Greg McCray	Va. Commonwealth

TENTH ROUND

204.	Dallas	Scott Bosanko	Northern State (S.D.)
205.	Detroit	Melvin Maxwell	Western Michigan
206.	New Jersey	Vic Sison	UCLA
207.	Utah	Joe Merten	Wisconsin-Eau Claire
208.	Cleveland	Greg Boone	Augsburg (Minn.)
209.	Atlanta	Mike Frazier	Georgetown
	Seattle	PASS	
210.	San Diego	Tony Gwynn	San Diego State
211.	Denver	Derrick Rowland	Potsdam State (N.Y.)
212.	Washington	Ralton Way	Houston Baptist
213.	Golden State	Barry Brooks	USC
	Houston	PASS	
214.	Kansas City	Mark Wilson	Ft. Hays (Kan.) State
215.	Indiana	Rodney Benson	Wright State
216.	Chicago	Kenny Easley	UCLA
217.	Portland	Steve Cochran	Lewis & Clark (Ore.)
218.	New York	Kevin Rogers	St. Peter's
219.	San Antonio	Alvin Brooks	Lamar
	Los Angeles	PASS	
220.	Phoenix	Felton Sealey	Oregon
221.	Milwaukee	Artie Green	Marquette
222.	Boston	Kenny Matthews	North Carolina State
223.	Philadelphia	Pete Mullenberg	Delaware

Pepsi-Cola, NBA Sponsor Awards

The National Basketball Association and the Pepsi-Cola Company again will sponsor awards for the NBA's top weekly and monthly performers.

These winners will receive a special gift from Pepsi-Cola. The monthly winners for the 1980-81 season were Earvin (Magic) Johnson of Los Angeles, Julius Erving of Philadelphia, Freeman Williams of San Diego, Bernard King of Golden State, Calvin Murphy of Houston and Kelvin Ransey of Portland.

Philadelphia's Julius Erving finally broke through and won the NBA's Most Valuable Player honors for the 1980-81 season.

1980-81 SEASON

Including

Review of the Regular Season

Review of the Championship Series

Championship Series Box Scores

Playoff Results

Regular-Season Statistics

Top Performances

Playoff Statistics

Calvin Murphy sat down on Houston's bench, but still found time to set an NBA consecutive free throw record.

The Year of the Bird
By STEVE HERSHEY

Finally, it was over. Larry Bird, slumped back in his chair, raised still another beer and said he was determined to stay up until the bus left for the airport at 7:30 in the morning.

It was dawn outside the Azalea Room of Stouffer's Hotel in Houston, just across the street from the arena where Bird and his Celtic teammates had defeated the Rockets to bring an unprecedented 14th world championship to Boston. Bird was the last survivor of the inevitable celebration that follows a championship series.

It was fitting that only Bird remained because, after the last shot had been fired, there was little doubt that the 1980-81 National Basketball Association season was The Year of the Bird.

Although he wasn't voted the most valuable player of the regular season, although he wasn't his team's top scorer in the championship series, although he was one of the team's two youngest players, everyone agreed he was the primary reason the Celtics were celebrating.

It was indeed, The Year of the Bird, but it also was a predicatably unpredictable year, a cross-country roller coaster ride that is the NBA. For instance: It was the year that Julius Erving finally won the MVP award, but still could not carry the frustrated 76ers to the championship.

It was the year that Rick Barry couldn't find a job, Dave Cowens didn't want one and Earl the Pearl's string snapped in New York.

It was the year Dick Motta walked away from a perennial playoff team in Washington and said he was happier in Dallas, where his expansion crew lost 67 games.

It was the year Gus Williams sat out, Bill Walton gave up and Kiki Vandeweghe refused to sign.

It was the year that George Gervin didn't win the scoring title and a 6-foot-5 forward who was triple-teamed all season did.

It was the year Dave Thompson returned and Rudy T sat down.

It was the year that Kevin Loughery quit a job he loved and Red Holzman said that 61 was too young to retire.

It was the year Wes Unseld had to give up the only job he ever had and became the best-known vice president in Washington.

It was a year that Larry Brown came back and Bill Musselman couldn't.

It was the year that Calvin Murphy became a part-time player, but still managed to sink 78 consecutive free throws, a record that could stay forever.

It was the year the new backcourt combination of Dennis Johnson and Walter Davis led Phoenix to 57 victories, then couldn't outplay Kansas City's makeshift duo of Ernie Grunfeld and Scott Wedman in the playoffs.

It was the year that John Lucas kept disappearing and Clifford Ray ended his 10-year career in his apartment.

It was the year of heart-warming comebacks by Bernard King and everybody's Coach of the Year, Jack McKinney.

It was the year that Donnie and Doug took turns putting excitement back in Denver and Stan Albeck talked Gervin out of the scoring title.

It was the year Paul Silas learned about losing and Jerry Sloan became a winner.

It was the year that Magic disappeared for much too long and Houston appeared out of nowhere to play in the championship series.

It was all this and much more.

While Boston was en route to its 14th championship, here's how the other clubs did:

ATLANTA (31-51)—Is the turmoil over for awhile? Can we sit back and relax? Can Ted Turner return to sailing again?

Injuries crippled this team and then Hubie Brown kicked the Hawks when they were down by applying for the Nets job in midseason.

The Hawks won 50 games and the Central Division title two years ago because Dan Roundfield, Tree Rollins and John Drew combined to miss just three games. Last season they sat out 78 and All-Star guard Eddie Johnson was sidelined for seven.

Drew still managed to lead the team in scoring for the seventh successive season while Johnson (19.1) and Roundfield (17.6) were selected to the All-Star Game. Kevin Loughery is the new coach and it will be interesting to see how he handles all this talent. He never had this luxury in New Jersey.

CHICAGO (45-37)—Winning the final eight games may have distorted the Bulls' record a little, but it should be an indication of things to come.

The season started on a sour note when top draft pick Ronnie Lester's knee gave way and Coach Jerry Sloan reluctantly rehired Ricky Sobers. However, the once moody guard responded to his second life by averaging 13.5 points a game and, more importantly, keeping his mouth shut.

Reggie Theus finally achieved the all-star status that he deserves after leading the team in scoring (18.9), assists and steals. Artis Gilmore made a mind-boggling 67 percent of his shots, finishing eighth in rebounding and sixth in blocks while averaging 17.9 points.

David Greenwood shook off several injuries to keep his string alive of never missing a pro game and contributed 14 points and nine rebounds a night. So where was the weakness? Well, Larry Kenon

Utah's Adrian Dantley survived triple-teaming tactics by the opposition to wrest the scoring title away from George Gervin.

started most of the year at small forward, but won't anymore.

CLEVELAND (28-54)—Eighteen players passed through Richfield and it is safe to assume that none of them was unhappy to leave.

The departure that seemed to please everyone was Coach Bill Musselman, who was relieved of his duties in the waning days of a disastrous season. Although his successor, Don Delaney, was popular with the players, most of them were disappointed that Owner Ted Stepien didn't even shop around.

Mike Mitchell's 24.5 scoring average gave the fans something to cheer about, Kenny Carr developed into one of the league's busiest rebounders (sixth at 10.3) and Mike Bratz provided some thrills with his prolific three-point shooting (a league-leading 169 attempts).

Still, this team has won more than 43 games just once in its 11-year history and it's going to take more than a couple of free agents to reverse that trend.

DALLAS (15-67)—Dick Motta said he was nothing but a caretaker when he nurse-maided the Bullets to the finals in '78 and '79 and he wanted to get back to coaching.

"I'm having more fun than I ever did in Washington," he insisted during the midst of one of his long losing streaks. But the most fun he had was on draft day when the Mavericks selected Mark Aguirre, Rolando Blackman and Jay Vincent.

This latest expansion team got off to a horrid start when top draft choice Kiki Vandeweghe decided he'd rather go back to UCLA than sign with the Mavericks. Then Athletes in Action star Ralph Drollinger was re-injured after signing a three-year contract. Surprisingly, the fans never lost interest, although the team set an expansion futility recored with 67 losses.

The biggest gains were made off the court as the Mavericks stockpiled 10 first-round draft choices in the next five years, mostly at Cleveland's expense. Motta, always a candid, revealing interview, became difficult to talk to, saying he couldn't stay on the phone too long because Cleveland might be calling again.

DENVER (37-45)—Let's see now. This year it's Donnie's turn to take the heat while Doug plays golf. Or is it Doug's turn in the hot seat while Donnie studies law. Oh well, all you have to know is that Moe and Walsh will be back as the two coaches and the team will give up more points than a tailender in a summer league.

It didn't take long for Moe to put his stamp on this team. His San Antonio Spurs used to lead the free world in scoring every season and that's exactly what the Nuggets did last year—by a whopping eight points a game over its nearest rival. As usual, his team also was last in defense.

The Nuggets became the first team since the 1971-72 Golden State Warriors to have three players average more than 20 points a game when David Thompson (25.5), Alex English (23.8) and Dan

Issel (21.9) finished in the top 12.

DETROIT (21-61)—Any team that finishes 39 games behind its division leader better have plenty of excuses. The Pistons are loaded in that department.

All losers moan about injuries and Coach Scotty Robertson certainly had his share with Bob McAdoo playing six games for his $525,000, Greg Kelser suiting up just 25 times and leading scorer Johnny Long (17.7) missing 23 games. Kent Benson also missed 23. The Pistons are counting on rookie Isiah Thomas and Kelly Tripucka to help turn their fortunes around.

The fact that this was the only team in the league that didn't average at least 100 points a game should tell you all you need to know about this wheel-spinning, rebuilding program. The auto industry wasn't the only one with labor problems in Detroit.

GOLDEN STATE (39-43)—The Warriors had the Comeback Player of the Year in Bernard King, but what they really needed was for John Lucas to come back, come back from wherever he was and show up at all the games.

Lucas started pouting when newly-acquired Lloyd Free was named captain and really got upset when the high-scoring guard (24.1) wanted the ball all the time. Finally, with a playoff berth in the balance, Lucas was gone for good and so were the Warriors' chances.

There were many bright spots, however, particularly the play of second-round draft choice Larry Smith, who finished third in the league in rebounding. Top pick Joe Barry Carroll stood out at center by averaging 18.9 points and 9.2 rebounds. If only Clifford Ray had stuck around for his final game, it would have been nicer.

HOUSTON (40-42)—Alfred Hitchcock couldn't have written a better script.

The Rockets muddled through a lackluster season before the overpowering performances of Moses Malone, who led the league in rebounding (14.8) and finished second in scoring (27.8), took them to the championship series.

Long-time favorite Calvin Murphy was relegated to reserve duty, but still managed to average 16.7 points and set an all-time record with 78 consecutive free throws. The remarkable 5-9 guard missed just nine of 215 foul shots for a record-shattering .958 percentage.

Meanwhile, much maligned Coach Del Harris was consistently shuffling his lineup while torn between making a drive for the playoffs or building for the future. Fortunately for the franchise, he settled on the former—and what surprises were in store.

INDIANA (44-38)—No wonder Jack McKinney was selected Coach of the Year. Check this roster and try to figure out how the Pacers ever won 44 games and qualified for the playoffs.

Bill Knight used his 30-point-one-night-and-four-the-next formula to compile his 17-point average. James Edwards, the 7-footer in the middle, managed to collect a mere seven rebounds a game and playmaker Johnny Davis fired up more than 900 shots, hitting at a 46 percent clip.

And what a collection of castoffs at forward, starting with Indiana favorite son George McGinnis and followed by George Johnson, Mike Bantom and Ted Abernethy.

The Pacers snuck up on a lot of people early and held on for awhile because McKinney insisted they play defense, but it's hard to imagine that trick working again.

KANSAS CITY (40-42)—The Kings had plenty of luck during the regular season and it was all bad. But in the playoffs, they reached the Conference Finals.

Scoring ace Otis Birdsong missed 11 games with injuries, then capitalized on free agency by originally signing with Cleveland before being traded to New Jersey where he will receive $1 million a year. Catalyst Phil Ford sat out 16 games and most of the playoffs with a bad knee and Coach Cotton Fitzsimmons needed a superlative effort from Ernie Grunfeld at point guard.

Fitzsimmons has been trying to ease 'ol Sam Lacey out of the pivot for years, but couldn't do it with backups like Leon Douglas, Joe C. Meriweather and John Lambert.

Scott Wedman enjoyed another fine season, but, alas, he bailed out, too, leaving Cotton to wonder if everything really is up to date in Kansas City.

LOS ANGELES (54-28)—That eerie jinx that has hovered over defending NBA champions ever since Bill Russell left the game 12 years ago took just 20 games to strike down the Lakers.

When Magic Johnson crumbled with a torn knee cartilage, so did his team's chances of winning the Pacific Division title. When he returned, resentment set in, egos were bruised and the team was a mere shell of itself as it slumbered through a mini-series loss to Houston.

Kareem Abdul-Jabbar showed no signs of slowing down at 34 as he finished fourth in scoring with a 26.2 average, Jamaal Wilkes was brilliant again with a 22.6 mark and Norm Nixon adjusted well to his ever-changing roles in the backcourt.

This team, however, has started to believe it can't go all the way unless Magic is doing his thing and the burden of that and a $25 million contract might prove to be too much for the effervescent youngster.

MILWAUKEE (60-22)—Even after the last drop of champagne had slid down Kevin McHale's throat, there were a few skeptics who secretly believed that Milwaukee was the best basketball team in the free world last season.

Marques Johnson was his usual consistent self in leading the Milwaukee Bucks to a 60-victory season.

A last-second, one-point loss at Philadelphia in the seventh game of the Eastern Conference semifinals eliminated the Bucks from further post-season honors, but not from consideration for future titles.

With Sidney Moncrief blossoming into another David Thompson, with Quinn Buckner developing a shooting touch that eliminated any double-teaming, with Junior Bridgeman continuing to lead all subs in scoring, with Bob Lanier making his presence felt in pressure situations and with Marques Johnson playing like, well, Marques Johnson, this team seemed to have everything.

By splitting six games with both Philadelphia and Boston in the regular season, by finishing second to Denver in team scoring and by winning a whopping 26 games on the road, the Bucks clearly established themselves among the elite.

NEW JERSEY (24-58)—With five rookies looking for stability, Coach Kevin Loughery walked out after 35 games and whatever hopes this young team had dissolved into a mass of uncertainty.

The daily rumors focused on the Browns, Hubie and Larry, as possible successor to lame-duck Coach Bob MacKinnon. Larry was named as soon as he concluded his business at UCLA and the first thing he did was bring in Bob McAdoo from Detroit, hardly a settling force.

Mike Newlin played hard throughout the year and was traded to New York for Mike Woodson. Young Cliff Robinson was second on the scoring chart behind Newlin with a 19.5 mark and subsequently traded to Kansas City.

First-round draft choices Mike Gminski and Mike O'Koren were impressive at times and third-round pick Lowes Moore was pressed into service when Foots Walker sat out 41 games with a groin pull. Things can only get better now that the club is leaving Piscataway.

NEW YORK (50-32)—Intelligent drafting in recent years paid off with a playoff berth for this once-crumbling franchise. Now the future seems bright.

In 1977, '78 and '79, the Knicks drafted Ray Williams, Michael Ray Richardson and Bill Cartwright and they were the three main reasons why the team improved its victory total by 11 games.

Cartwright averaged slightly more than 20 points a game for the second straight season, Williams posted a 19.7 mark and Richardson made the all-star team again, averaging 16.4 points while finishing fourth in the league in assists, second in steals and second on the team in rebounds.

If Toby Knight hadn't torn up a knee or somebody could have been found to help Cartwright rebound, the teams might have been even better.

PHILADELPHIA (62-20)—Once again, the only complaint the hard-to-please Philadelphia fans have with this club is its post-season collapses.

With the incomparable Julius Erving again setting the pace (24.6), the 76ers tied an NBA record by winning 37 of 41 home games. They outlasted talent-laden Milwaukee in the semifinals, then extended the champion Celtics to the closing minutes of the final game before bowing.

As usual, Darryl Dawkins did all the talking and Caldwell Jones most of the work around the basket. Bobby Jones remained the most versatile, valuable reserve in the league and Maurice Cheeks ran the high-powered offense at full throttle.

Coach Billy Cunningham keeps looking for a weakness, but can't find one.

PHOENIX (57-25)—Stop me if you've heard this before, but this is a team that won 50 games in the regular season and then folded in the playoffs.

The Suns have won 211 regular-season games in the last four years and never reached the NBA finals.

Despite the addition of Dennis Johnson, a nifty conversion to the backcourt by Walter Davis, another all-star performance by Truck Robinson and the eye-catching development of young guards Johnny High and Kyle Macy, few considered the Suns a threat in the playoffs.

PORTLAND (45-37)—A disappointing 105-95 loss at home in the decisive game of a mini-series with Kansas City took most of the enjoyment out of a seven-game improvement over the previous season.

Mychal Thompson recovered nicely from the broken leg that sidelined him for almost all of the 1979-80 season, averaging 17 points and 8.7 rebounds and, as usual, Kermit Washington did everything asked of him.

Coach Jack Ramsay developed another excellent young backcourt combo of Jim Paxson and rookie Kelvin Ransey and also picked up a steal with the development of Billy Ray Bates signed out of the Continental Basketball Association in 1980.

Now all Dr. Jack needs, besides a new pair of checkered pants, is a center who can stand up to Kareem, Jack Sikma and the rest of the giants in the Pacific Division.

SAN ANTONIO (52-30)—The incentive ran out too soon for this talented group.

Angelo Drossos thought it would be a good idea to pay his players extra for every victory they earned over 36. So George Gervin and his pals ran up 52 wins to win the Midwest Division by 12 lengths.

In the playoffs however, they allowed themselves to be lulled to sleep by Houston.

New Coach Stan Albeck did write the word D-E-F-E-N-S-E on

George Gervin relinquished his scoring title, but gave San Antonio a defensive lift.

the blackboard in training camp and in a few weeks everybody knew what it meant. The addition of centers Dave Corzine (10.5) and George Johnson gave the Spurs the bulk they needed and, as usual, the Iceman dazzled the Baseline Bums with his uncanny shooting. A good time was had by all—until April.

SAN DIEGO (36-46)—Gee, it seemed so easy to win in Boston and Seattle, Paul Silas must have thought while struggling through his first coaching assignment.

Well, the first thing he had to learn was not to count on Bill Walton, whose famous foot gave out in training camp. Also, it's wise not to reply too heavily on Sidney Wicks, either.

Freeman Williams and Brian Taylor had fun tossing up 256 three-pointers between them, Swen Nater always has fun and besides nobody in San Diego got very excited, even when the Clippers won.

SEATTLE (34-48)—Oh, how the mighty have fallen. The convenient villain here is an attorney named Howard Slusher, who convinced Gus Williams the best way to become independently wealthy was not to work.

Williams' absence wasn't the only reason the '79 world champs' victory total plunged from 56 to 34 in one year. There was THE TRADE.

Despite being named the MVP in the championship series of '79, Dennis Johnson was not one of Coach Lenny Wilkens' favorites, or even near favorites. So when the opportunity to swap him to Phoenix for Paul Westphal was presented, the coach jumped at it, never expecting his acquisition to sit out 46 games with foot and ankle injuries.

Lonnie Shelton, the valuable rebounding forward, played just 14 games before fracturing his wrist and Wilkens said that was the biggest blow of all.

What happened to this Sonic boom? Well, when you're counting on a backcourt of Gus Williams and Westphal and wind up using Armond Hill and rookie Bill Hanzlik it doesn't take a basketball genius to know you've got problems.

UTAH (28-54)—How could a team with the league's scoring champ and the Rookie of the Year manage to lose 54 games? That can happen when nobody else averages 10 points a game.

Adrian Dantley fought his way through triple-teaming to average 30.7 points and Darrell Griffith survived six different backcourt mates to post a 20.6 mark

WASHINGTON (39-43)—Just like the Democrats, the Bullets don't have much clout in Washington anymore.

It has been just two years since the team made its second straight appearance in the NBA finals and now only Greg Ballard and possible free agent Kevin Grevey remain.

The nucleus collapsed when Wes Unseld retired after the season and Elvin Hayes and Mitch Kupchak were traded away. Hayes struggled through his worst season (17.8) and was shipped home to Houston for a pair of second-round draft choices. Free agent Kupchak bounced back from back surgery (12.5) and was snatched away by the Lakers, who sent Jim Chones, Brad Holland and a future No. 1 pick and No. 2 pick in appreciation.

NBA Games on Television

CBS Sports will feature the Los Angeles Lakers in its first two telecasts of the 1981-82 National Basketball Association season.

The Houston Rockets will meet the Lakers in a season-opening game October 30 and then CBS will telecast the Lakers-Suns game in Phoenix on Christmas Day. CBS will begin its Sunday telecasts January 17 and continue through the conclusion of the regular season, adding two Friday night telecasts (April 2 and 16) to its card.

The USA Network will bring 41 regular-season games to its cable viewers beginning November 5. Most of those games will be telecast on Thursday nights and USA will show a minimum of 10 playoff games not carried by CBS.

The USA regular-season schedule:

November 5 (Thursday)—Washington at Milwaukee, Dallas at Phoenix.
November 12 (Thursday)—Cleveland at Detroit, Portland at San Diego.
November 19 (Thursday)—Kansas City at Indiana, Golden State at San Diego.
November 25 (Wednesday)—Golden State at Boston.
December 3 (Thursday)—Washington at New York, Denver at Phoenix.
December 10 (Thursday)—New York at Detroit, Portland at Phoenix.
December 17 (Thursday)—Indiana at Detroit, Los Angeles at Golden State.
December 27 (Sunday)—Philadelphia at Phoenix.
January 3 (Sunday)—Denver at Milwaukee.
January 7 (Thursday)—Washington at Cleveland, Houston at Seattle.
January 14 (Thursday)—Portland at Houston, New York at Phoenix.
January 21 (Thursday)—Utah at San Antonio, Detroit at San Diego.
January 28 (Thursday)—Philadelphia at Houston, Phoenix at Los Angeles.
February 4 (Thursday)—Phoenix at San Antonio.
February 11 (Thursday)—Portland at Milwaukee.
February 18 (Thursday)—San Diego at Indiana, Washington at Seattle.
February 25 (Thursday)—Golden State at Dallas, Los Angeles at Seattle.
March 4 (Thursday)—Boston at San Antonio, Houston at Utah.
March 11 (Thursday)—Phoenix at Cleveland, Kansas City at San Diego.
March 18 (Thursday)—Seattle at Detroit, Golden State at Portland.
March 25 (Thursday)—Philadelphia at Detroit, Houston at Portland.
April 1 (Thursday)—Golden State at Houston, Los Angeles at San Diego.
April 8 (Thursday)—Boston at New York.
April 15 (Thursday)—Cleveland at Detroit.

The Celtics Return

By GEORGE WHITE

And so, the Boston Celtics once again complete the cycle. For richer, for poorer, in sickness and in health, the saga of the Celtics so often seems to be the story of the NBA.

In the beginning, of course, there were Cousy and K. C., Sharman and Satch, Russell and Red, the long string of championships in the '50s. Then came a lull with the years B.C. (Before Cowens), and then another string of super teams with Cowens and Chaney and White and Havlicek.

The late '70s were the years of shame, the Celtics suffering through back-to-back 32-50 and 29-53 nightmares. Against such a miserable backdrop came the third renaissance, completed on Thursday night, May 14, 1981, in Houston, Tex.

On that evening, led by a man who personifies "Celtic" more than any other man in the NBA, Larry Bird and the Boston New Breed swept aside the Houston Rockets, 102-91, once again claiming for the Celtics a world championship, and possibly the start of dynasty No. 3.

It was a series with much more drama than anyone had reason to expect. In the beginning, this one had all the potential of a four-game snoozer.

Most of the basketball world figured the Celtics had played for the championship in the Eastern Conference finals, struggling out of a deep hole (down 3-1) to nip the Philadelphia 76ers in a seven-game matchup that some dubbed The Greatest Series Ever.

The Rockets were strictly beggars who crashed the party, a team which had bounced erratically up and down in the regular season to finish with a 40-42 record. Despite the fact that they jelled quickly in the playoffs, knocking off defending league champ Los Angeles, San Antonio and Kansas City, the basketball structure was singularly unimpressed when the Rockets showed up at the front door of the Boston Garden to begin the championship series. They were, after all, only the third team in NBA history to make it to that lofty height with an under-.500 record, and the first ever under the modern-day playoff format.

It would be, however, a series of surprises. From the opening game, when the Rockets leaped far ahead in the opening quarter, to the sixth and final confrontation when Bird finally snapped out of his two-week offensive slump to score 27 points with 13 rebounds, it was a series surprisingly worthy of the championship label.

A lot of observers feel the series' critical juncture came early—in the first game. Houston's best chance for a championship, most felt, would be to surprise the mentally weary Celtics early in Boston

Garden, perchance sneak away from town with two quick victories, then look at their more illustrious opponents on a bit more equal footing when they got home.

And late in the first quarter of game No. 1, look what was happening: The Rockets, led by the lightly regarded offense of Billy Paultz, were in command with a 22-8 lead.

The Rockets dominated, in fact, for most of three quarters. The Celtics were doing a superb defensive job on Moses Malone, the Rocket center eventually winding up with only four baskets in 17 shots, but Houston's Robert Reid was a particularly thorny problem. The young forward, who was to play exceptionally well defensively against Bird throughout the series, kept the Rockets in control of the evening with 27 points. And sure enough, as the fourth quarter began, the bedraggled Texans were refusing to wilt away, clinging to an 81-76 lead.

With four minutes left, however, the cream began to rise. Consecutive fast-break baskets by M. L. Carr and Cedric Maxwell gave the Celtics a 95-90 lead, and though the Rockets scrapped back to trail by just one point with 1:29 to go, Boston came up with five straight offensive rebounds in the final minute to choke the breath out of the Rockets.

"We were in trouble," said Maxwell, whose inspired play throughout the series would earn him Most Valuable Player honors.

"Houston was like a shark. We bled and they became aroused. We came back to win, but I hope we didn't arouse them enough to think they can win Game 2.

"It's obvious everyone thought we won the NBA championship when we beat Philadelphia. But Houston is here and is a very good team. We've got to put an ax to them if we want to win the championship."

The ax in Game No. 1 was offensive rebounding. With Bird, Maxwell and Robert Parish combining for 17 offensive caroms, the Celtics scored 32 points on second shots. That, in the end, was what pulled them over the hump on an evening in which they could hit only 43.2 percent of their shots.

Curiously, that victory was Boston's 14th in a row over the Rockets stretching back to 1978. The odds, as the dice players in Las Vegas stress, certainly were against any NBA team beating another 15 straight times. Sure enough, the odds, helped generously by an aroused Malone, were correct.

Game No. 2 was perhaps the most bizarre game in a bizarre series. The Celtics would hit 50 percent of their shots, outrebound Houston, 48-35, and still lose. To further compound the irony, the Rockets won on a night in which Reid, who the game before scored 27, couldn't score a single field goal.

The difference was twofold. No. 1, Malone rose up and scored 31

Cedric Maxwell's ups and downs were mostly the former en route to MVP honors in the championship series.

points. No. 2, the Celtics handled the ball as though it were a live hand grenade, committing 22 turnovers that resulted in 31 Houston points. The result was a 92-90 Houston victory.

It was a close game throughout, the Rockets playing their methodic power game to perfection. The Celtics, by far the more stylish of the two teams, got bogged down in the maddening slow tempo and destroyed themselves with turnovers.

Boston led late, 81-75, but the Rockets rallied behind, of all people, rookie Calvin Garrett and second-year pro Allen Leavell. Leavell made the game's most critical shot, a fallaway jumper in the final minute, putting the Rockets ahead by one with only five seconds remaining.

Like the after-shave commercial in which the gorgeous young thing slaps old beardie on the cheeks with a handful of smell-good, however, the Celtics were no in position to say, "Thanks, I needed that." "We got a slap in the face," said Carr. "And sometimes a slap in the face will wake you up. It better, because we can't go on playing like this and expect to win."

"The fans, the media and everyone else were taking Houston for granted," Chris Ford said afterward, "and I think some of that feeling dribbled into the locker room. Maybe some of the guys got a big head and felt they could just go through the motions and win. But you just can't go through the motions and win the NBA championships."

And so, the series moved to Houston tied at one win each. "The scary thing," reminded Maxwell, "is that they (the Rockets) could be going home ahead 2-0."

Scary, huh? The scary stuff was waiting just around the corner in Houston, where Maxwell was about to lead the Celtics off on a blowout of immense proportions. Maxwell hit nine of 16 shots, Ford was seven of 12 with a couple of three-pointers, and when the Rockets could only retaliate with a miserable 30 percent shooting night, Boston ran away with a 94-71 rout.

This was Celtic basketball at its best—six players scoring in double figures, the fast break sweeping upcourt like a storm surge before a hurricane and a strangling defense that forced the opponent into 22 turnovers.

"What really turned the tide was our strong pressure defense," said Ford. "We picked them up early and pressured them all over the court. That's how we beat the Rockets last year, with strong end-to-end pressure.

"The first two games we were very passive. We would let them make six or seven passes on every possession, get it to the good shooters every time. Today, each guy just committed himself to not letting his man catch the ball."

"It was good for us to get out of Boston Garden," said Bird. "It

Houston's Moses Malone was an awesome force during the championship series, but his words gave the Celtics the lift they needed.

was good for us to get away from the newspapers constantly reminding us that we ought to win this in four games. I felt some pressure at home, hearing all that stuff how there was no way we could lose. It was good for us to get in front of a hostile crowd again."

It would have been impossible for the Rockets to have not gotten the message. The message was that when the Celtics put their game together, they were indeed as awesome as their 62-20 regular-season record would suggest. That 23-point wipeout had to have dealt a thudding blow to the Rockets' swaggering confidence, even though the Rockets were to regroup in Game 4 and knot the series 2-2 with a 91-86 win.

Just to follow the whacky script, game No. 4 was another in a string of weird ones. Rocket Coach Del Harris, declaring that, "for the most part, substituting messes up a game," masterminded a win in a game in which he only used six players. Little guard Mike Dunleavy was the ultimate pest, prancing around to score 28 points, and Malone and Reid combined for 35 rebounds. For the Celtics, only Maxwell (25 points, 14 rebounds) played winning basketball.

"I don't know how they can win using only six guys," said the consistent Maxwell. "I never thought I'd see a championship team doing that. But you can't argue with the strategy. It worked."

It succeeded despite another horrible shooting day, the Rockets hitting just 35.9 percent of their shots. It worked, though, largely because of the excellence of Dunleavy, and because it was Boston's turn to handle the ball like it was covered with butter. On this day the Celtics committed 22 turnovers to only 10 for the Rockets, and that difference enabled Houston to launch 29 more shots than Boston.

What may be the most important event of the series took place that afternoon—not during the two-hour battle, but in the locker room afterward when Malone uttered the words that have become as widely quoted in Boston as "One if by land, two if by sea."

After it was over and the series tied after four games, Malone opined that, "I don't think Boston is all that good. They're a good team, but Philadelphia was better. People think they're that good because they get a lot of press. I could get four guys off the streets of Petersburg (Va., his hometown) and beat them. To my standpoint, they just aren't that good."

Prior to game No. 5, Celtic Coach Bill Fitch mimeographed copies of Malone's remarks and tacked them to the locker of each Celtic. Whether Malone can take credit for what happened next will never fully be known, but this much is in the record books for all interested parties to see: the Celtics came home to Boston not even a facsimile of the team that had fallen apart in Houston.

The Celtics were riled, miffed and tight-lipped as they went about the business of making a mockery of Malone's remarks. At the end of one quarter it was Boston 34-19. By halftime it was 59-37. By game's end it was a farce, Maxwell again taking command (28 points, 15 rebounds) as the Celtics won by 29 points, 109-80.

"Anytime anyone says stuff like that," said Rick Robey, referring to Malone's contention, "it makes you play harder." "None of us appreciated his comments," said Kevin McHale.

"We were upset after the loss in Houston," agreed Maxwell. "We were embarrassed; there was a lot of name-calling by them and we were determined to come out early and establish ourselves.

"These guys on this team have a lot of pride, and when somebody embarrasses us and says we don't have heart or character, well, that spurs you on. This team answered the challenge tonight."

It was as thorough a shellacking as was possible, the tidal wave beginning early when Boston outscored the Rockets, 19-1, over one stretch in the first quarter. "The way we played tonight, very few teams in the league could beat us," said Maxwell. "We have the best basketball team in the world right now."

To prove it, however, the Celtics had to win one more game. That came two nights later at Houston, on an evening when Bird stepped to the front in true championship fashion.

Reid had played superbly on defense against Bird for most of the series, so tightly, in fact, that in games 3, 4 and 5 Bird had hit just 29 percent of his shots (11 of 38). He was, everyone knew, a time bomb just waiting to explode.

And then it happened. In the sixth and final game, he reared up for 27 points, hitting 11 of 20 shots and contributing 13 rebounds. The 27 points weren't so damaging, however, as the time when he got them.

The Celtics had raced far ahead, leading by 17 points late in the third quarter. The gritty Rockets, however, came back kicking in the fourth quarter, eventually coming back to within three points of the lead at 86-83.

Bird retaliated with a pair of jumpers from 15 and 18 feet to momentarily defuse the rally, but the Rockets scrambled back into contention one more time, closing back to within 92-89 with 1:55 remaining.

Bird broke the back of that rally, however, with a three-point bomb from the corner, once again boosting Boston into a six-point advantage from which the Rockets could never recover.

"I have to say the man (Bird) is a helluva player," said Dunleavy after it was finally over. "He did all the things they had to do to get the championship.

"When he wasn't scoring, he rebounded, passed, provided leadership, did a lot of things to help them win. And tonight, when it came down to the big game, he was everywhere. He's the key to this Boston club, no question."

Bird remarked that, "The guys had carried me all the way through the series. I had a chance to carry them in this one, and I

Robert Reid's defensive job on Larry Bird kept Houston in the series, but Bird finally flew high in the decisive sixth game.

was glad to have it."

And about the 14th Celtic championship?

"The other 13 don't mean anything, because we did nothing to achieve those," he said. "The people who won those should be the ones to take the credit. We are a different team with different fans."

Reid, however, said the 1980-81 Celtics owed apologies to no one. "The whole Celtic team is a great champion. They're a great team. They can run around The Summit with their hands held up, because they are indeed No. 1.

"They have earned the right to call themselves the champions."

1981 NBA WORLD CHAMPIONSHIP SERIES

Game No. 1

At Boston, May 5, 1981

Houston	Pos.	Min.	FGM	FGA	FTM	FTA	Off.	Def.	Tot.	Ast.	PF	Stls.	Pts.
Paultz, Billy	F	37	7	16	0	0	3	4	7	4	2	3	14
Reid, Robert	F	48	12	22	3	4	5	3	8	3	2	4	27
Malone, Moses	C	45	4	17	5	6	8	7	15	3	1	3	13
Henderson, Tom	G	22	5	8	1	2	1	1	2	3	4	0	11
Dunleavy, Mike	G	37	2	9	2	2	0	2	2	7	3	0	6
Murphy, Calvin		24	8	15	0	0	0	2	2	0	5	2	16
Willoughby, Bill		13	1	4	0	0	1	3	4	0	2	2	2
Leavell, Allen		13	3	7	0	0	1	1	2	3	1	1	6
Tomjanovich, Rudy		1	0	1	0	0	0	0	0	0	0	0	0
Totals		240	42	99	11	14	19	23	42	23	20	15	95

FG Pct.: .424 FT Pct.: .786 Turnovers: Paultz 3, Reid 2, Malone 1, Dunleavy 1, Murphy 1, Willoughby 1, Leavell 1, Total—10 Team Rebounds: 12.

Boston	Pos.	Min.	FGM	FGA	FTM	FTA	Off.	Def.	Tot.	Ast.	PF	Stls.	Pts.
Maxwell, Cedric	F	34	4	12	2	2	5	4	9	5	4	0	10
Bird, Larry	F	44	9	17	0	0	7	14	21	9	1	1	18
Parish, Robert	C	34	8	16	0	0	5	5	10	1	4	3	16
Archibald, Nate	G	37	4	14	4	5	0	0	0	5	2	0	12
Ford, Chris	G	29	5	9	3	3	2	1	3	1	2	0	13
McHale, Kevin		11	1	7	2	2	4	0	4	0	2	0	4
Carr, M.L.		23	4	9	1	2	1	1	2	0	2	2	9
Henderson, Gerald		19	4	6	3	3	1	2	3	1	1	0	11
Robey, Rick		9	2	5	1	3	0	2	2	1	3	0	5
Totals		240	41	95	16	20	25	29	54	23	21	6	98

FG PCT.: .432 FT Pct.: .800 Turnovers: Maxwell 4, Bird 5, Parish 4, Archibald 4, Carr 1, Robey 1, Total—19 Team Rebounds: 10.

Score by Periods:	1st	2nd	3rd	4th	Totals
Houston	29	28	24	14	— 95
Boston	24	27	25	22	— 98

Blocked Shots: Malone 1, Paultz 1, Willoughby 1, Parish 2, Henderson 2, Maxwell 1. 3-Pt. Field Goals: Reid 0-1, Tomjanovich 0-1, Ford 0-1.
Officials: Darell Garretson and Jack Madden.
Attendance: 15,320.

1981 NBA WORLD CHAMPIONSHIP SERIES

Game No. 2

At Boston, May 7, 1981

Houston	Pos.	Min.	FGM	FGA	FTM	FTA	Off.	Def.	Tot.	Ast.	PF	Stls.	Pts.
Paultz, Billy	F	31	6	11	1	2	0	4	4	1	2	1	13
Reid, Robert	F	38	0	7	2	2	0	4	4	3	5	0	2
Malone, Moses	C	48	10	24	11	18	7	8	15	1	1	1	31
Henderson, Tom	G	34	2	8	2	2	1	0	1	3	2	2	6
Dunleavy, Mike	G	17	3	5	1	2	0	1	1	2	1	0	9
Garrett, Calvin		11	1	2	0	0	0	0	0	0	1	0	2
Murphy, Calvin		23	4	13	2	2	1	0	1	2	2	0	10
Willoughby, Bill		25	6	10	2	3	3	2	5	1	1	1	14
Leavell, Allen		13	2	5	1	1	1	3	4	3	2	1	5
Totals		240	34	85	22	32	13	22	35	16	17	6	92

FT Pct.: .400   FT Pct.: .688   Turnovers: Reid 3, Malone 2, Henderson 3, Dunleavy 1, Total—9   Team Rebounds: 19.

Boston	Pos.	Min.	FGM	FGA	FTM	FTA	Off.	Def.	Tot.	Ast.	PF	Stls.	Pts.
Maxwell, Cedric	F	37	3	8	0	0	2	2	4	2	4	0	6
Bird, Larry	F	45	8	18	3	3	4	17	21	3	3	5	19
Parish, Robert	C	14	4	7	1	2	1	1	2	0	6	0	9
Archibald, Nate	G	30	4	12	3	3	1	2	3	4	2	1	11
Ford, Chris	G	28	5	10	0	0	1	1	2	2	1	0	10
Robey, Rick		21	3	5	1	4	1	6	7	0	4	0	7
McHale, Kevin		26	6	8	0	0	2	3	5	2	5	0	12
Carr, M.L.		21	3	6	0	0	0	1	1	0	0	0	6
Henderson, Gerald		18	5	6	0	1	2	1	3	4	2	0	10
Totals		240	41	82	8	13	14	34	48	17	27	6	90

FG Pct.: .500   FT Pct.: .615   Turnovers: Maxwell 3, Bird 5, Parish 4, Archibald 2, Ford 2, Robey 1, McHale 3, Carr 1, Henderson 1, Total—22   Team Rebounds: 12.

Score by Periods:	1st	2nd	3rd	4th	Totals
Houston	22	23	23	24	92
Boston	26	23	19	22	90

Blocked Shots: Reid 2, Willoughby 2, Paultz 1, Malone 2, Leavell 1, Parish 3, McHale 3, Carr 1. 3-Pt. Field Goals: Dunleavy 2-2, Parish 0-1, Ford 0-2.

Officials: Joe Gushue and Jake O'Donnell.

Attendance: 15,320.

1980-81 CHAMPIONSHIP SERIES REVIEW

1981 NBA WORLD CHAMPIONSHIP SERIES

Game No. 3

At Houston, May 9, 1981

Boston	Pos.	Min.	FGM	FGA	FTM	FTA	Off.	Def.	Tot.	Ast.	PF	Stls.	Pts.
Bird, Larry	F	44	3	11	2	4	2	11	13	10	3	5	8
Maxwell, Cedric	F	36	9	16	1	2	9	1	10	0	4	0	19
Parish, Robert	C	13	5	10	1	1	0	6	6	1	5	1	11
Archibald, Nate	G	29	5	13	0	0	0	2	2	6	2	1	10
Ford, Chris	G	36	7	12	1	2	2	2	4	2	2	2	17
Robey, Rick		31	4	10	3	5	2	4	6	1	4	0	11
Henderson, Gerald		19	5	8	2	2	0	0	0	2	0	2	12
Carr, M.L.		14	1	5	0	0	1	0	1	0	3	0	2
McHale, Kevin		12	0	2	2	3	0	2	2	1	0	0	2
Fernsten, Eric		4	0	1	0	0	0	0	0	1	2	0	0
Duerod, Terry		2	1	1	0	0	0	0	0	0	0	1	2
Totals		240	40	89	12	19	16	28	44	24	25	12	94

FG Pct.: .449 FT Pct.: .632 Turnovers: Bird 3, Maxwell 4, Archibald 1, Ford 1, Henderson 1, McHale 1, Total—11 Team Rebounds: 13.

Houston	Pos.	Min.	FGM	FGA	FTM	FTA	Off.	Def.	Tot.	Ast.	PF	Stls.	Pts.
Paultz, Billy	F	34	2	10	2	4	2	6	8	0	1	1	6
Reid, Robert	F	26	2	11	0	0	1	4	5	2	3	0	4
Malone, Moses	C	40	7	13	9	12	6	9	15	2	1	0	23
Dunleavy, Mike	G	19	2	3	1	1	1	1	2	1	1	0	5
Henderson, Tom	G	26	3	5	0	0	2	1	3	1	1	2	6
Murphy, Calvin		29	3	10	3	4	0	0	0	1	3	1	9
Willoughby, Bill		31	2	12	8	9	3	4	7	0	3	2	12
Leavell, Allen		18	2	9	0	1	0	0	0	2	3	0	4
Garrett, Calvin		6	0	1	0	0	1	1	2	0	1	0	0
Jones, Major		4	1	2	0	0	1	2	3	1	2	0	2
Tomjanovich, Rudy		7	0	3	0	0	2	1	3	0	0	0	0
Totals		240	24	79	23	31	19	29	48	10	19	6	71

FG Pct.: .304 FT Pct.: .742 Turnovers: Paultz 5, Reid 1, Malone 1, Dunleavy 3, Henderson 2, Murphy 6, Willoughby 2, Tomjanovich 1, Total—21 Team Rebounds: 14.

Score by Periods:	1st	2nd	3rd	4th	Totals
Boston	21	20	24	29	— 94
Houston	17	13	18	23	— 71

Blocked Shots: Maxwell 2, Robey 1, Bird 2, Carr 1, Reid 2, Malone 4, Willoughby 1, Dunleavy 1, Paultz 1, Henderson 1. 3-Pt. Field Goals: Ford 2-3, Tomjanovich 0-1.

Officials: Earl Strom and John Vanak.

Attendance: 16,121.

1981 NBA WORLD CHAMPIONSHIP SERIES

Game No. 4

At Houston, May 10, 1981

Boston	Pos.	Min.	FGM	FGA	FTM	FTA	Off.	Def.	Tot.	Ast.	PF	Stls.	Pts.
Bird, Larry	F	43	3	11	2	2	0	12	12	7	3	2	8
Maxwell, Cedric	F	41	9	14	6	9	9	5	14	1	2	0	24
Parish, Robert	C	38	7	16	4	8	4	8	12	2	4	1	18
Archibald, Nate	G	36	3	5	4	5	0	1	1	3	1	0	10
Ford, Chris	G	21	2	5	0	0	1	1	2	3	3	0	4
Carl, M. L.		23	3	7	0	0	1	0	1	5	0	1	6
Robey, Rick		10	2	3	0	0	0	1	1	0	3	0	4
McHale, Kevin		11	2	5	0	0	1	0	1	0	4	0	4
Henderson, Gerald		15	4	7	0	0	1	1	2	1	2	1	8
Duerod, Terry		1	0	1	0	0	0	0	0	0	0	0	0
Fernsten, Eric		1	0	0	0	0	0	1	1	0	0	0	0
Totals		240	35	74	16	24	17	30	47	22	22	5	86

FG Pct.: .473 FT Pct.: .667 Turnovers: Bird 3, Maxwell 4, Robert 6, Archibald 3, Carr 1, Robey 3, Henderson 2, Total—22 Team Rebounds: 8.

Houston	Pos.	Min.	FGM	FGA	FTM	FTA	Off.	Def.	Tot.	Ast.	PF	Stls.	Pts.
Paultz, Billy	F	33	5	14	0	0	4	2	6	1	4	1	10
Reid, Robert	F	47	7	21	5	8	10	3	13	4	5	5	19
Malone, Moses	C	48	11	30	2	2	9	13	22	0	4	0	24
Dunleavy, Mike	G	45	11	22	5	6	3	1	4	6	4	2	28
Henderson, Tom	G	43	0	4	2	2	0	2	2	9	1	0	2
Willoughby, Bill		24	3	12	2	4	2	0	2	2	2	0	8
Totals		240	37	103	16	22	28	21	49	22	20	8	91

FG Pct.: .359 FT Pct.: .727 Turnovers: Reid 2, Malone 3, Dunleavy 3, Henderson 1, Willoughby 1, Total—10 Team Rebounds: 14.

Score by Periods:	1st	2nd	3rd	4th	Totals
Boston	26	24	17	19	— 86
Houston	26	24	25	16	— 91

Blocked Shots: Parish 5, Maxwell 1, Paultz 1, Willoughby 1. 3-Pt. Field Goals: Ford 0-1, Henderson 0-1, Duerod 0-1, Dunleavy 1-3.

Officials: Darell Garretson and Ed Rush.

Attendance: 16,121.

1981 NBA WORLD CHAMPIONSHIP SERIES

Game No. 5

At Boston, May 12, 1981

Houston	Pos.	Min.	FGM	FGA	FTM	FTA	Off.	Def.	Tot.	Ast.	PF	Stls.	Pts.
Paultz, Billy	F	31	5	12	0	0	1	4	5	1	4	1	10
Reid, Robert	F	38	3	11	3	4	4	3	7	3	4	2	9
Malone, Moses	C	41	7	14	6	10	6	5	11	0	2	0	20
Henderson, Tom	G	29	3	8	1	3	0	4	4	4	0	0	7
Dunleavy, Mike	G	14	1	5	3	4	0	2	2	2	6	0	5
Murphy, Calvin		12	2	5	0	0	0	1	1	0	0	1	4
Willoughby, Bill		17	1	7	2	4	3	2	5	0	3	1	4
Leavell, Allen		24	3	10	4	5	1	0	1	6	2	1	10
Garrett, Calvin		12	1	2	0	0	0	2	2	0	0	1	2
Jones, Major		13	3	6	1	3	0	2	2	0	2	1	7
Tomjanovich, Rudy		9	1	4	0	0	0	1	1	0	1	0	2
Totals		240	30	84	20	33	15	26	41	15	24	8	80

FG Pct.: .357 FT Pct.: .606 Turnovers: Paultz 1, Reid 2, Malone 4, Henderson 2, Dunleavy 2, Murphy 1, Willoughby 2, Leavell 3, Total—17 Team Rebounds: 17.

Boston	Pos.	Min.	FGM	FGA	FTM	FTA	Off.	Def.	Tot.	Ast.	PF	Stls.	Pts.
Maxwell, Cedric	F	39	10	13	8	10	7	8	15	3	3	1	28
Bird, Larry	F	38	5	16	2	2	1	11	12	8	3	0	12
Parish, Robert	C	36	6	14	6	8	4	6	10	2	4	1	18
Archibald, Nate	G	28	3	11	0	0	0	1	1	3	3	2	6
Ford, Chris	G	29	4	8	0	0	1	1	2	4	0	0	8
Robey, Rick		12	5	7	4	4	1	1	2	0	3	0	14
Henderson, Gerald		20	1	4	0	0	0	1	1	2	4	1	2
Carr, M. L.		17	3	6	5	6	1	2	3	1	2	0	11
McHale, Kevin		15	2	8	0	2	3	3	6	2	1	0	4
Fernsten, Eric		4	0	2	2	3	1	1	2	0	0	0	2
Duerod, Terry		2	2	5	0	0	0	0	0	0	0	0	4
Totals		240	41	94	27	35	19	35	54	25	23	5	109

FG Pct.: .436 FT Pct.: .771 Turnovers: Maxwell 1, Bird 2, Parish 3, Archibald 4, Ford 2, Robey 1, McHale 1, Total—14 Team Rebounds: 16.

Score by Periods:	1st	2nd	3rd	4th	Totals
Houston	19	18	18	25	— 80
Boston	34	25	18	32	— 109

Blocked Shots: Reid 1, Malone 4, Willoughby 1, Leavell 2, M. Jones 1, Maxwell 2, Bird 1, Parish 2, Carr 2, McHale 1. 3-Pt. Field Goals: Dunleavy 0-1, Archibald 0-2, Ford 0-1.

Officials: Earl Strom and Paul Mihalak.
Attendance: 15,320.

1981 NBA WORLD CHAMPIONSHIP SERIES

Game No. 6

At Houston, May 14, 1981

Boston	Pos.	Min.	FGM	FGA	FTM	FTA	Off.	Def.	Tot.	Ast.	PF	Stls.	Pts.
Bird, Larry	F	43	11	20	4	5	2	11	13	5	3	1	27
Maxwell, Cedric	F	40	7	11	5	6	2	3	5	6	2	0	19
Parish, Robert	C	32	9	14	0	0	2	4	6	0	4	1	18
Archibald, Nate	G	43	5	11	3	3	0	0	0	12	1	0	13
Ford, Chris	G	41	4	10	3	4	0	3	3	3	3	2	11
Robey, Rick		15	3	4	0	0	1	3	4	0	1	0	6
McHale, Kevin		8	1	1	0	0	0	2	2	0	1	0	2
Carr, M. L.		12	3	4	0	0	1	1	2	0	3	1	6
Henderson, Gerald		4	0	3	0	0	1	0	1	0	1	0	0
Duerod, Terry		1	0	0	0	0	0	0	0	0	0	0	0
Fernsten, Eric		1	0	0	0	0	0	1	1	0	0	1	0
Totals		240	43	78	15	18	9	28	37	26	21	6	102

FG Pct.: .551 FT Pct.: .833 Turnovers: Bird 1, Maxwell 3, Parish 2, Archibald 2, Ford 3, Robey 1, McHale 1, Total—13 Team Rebounds: 5.

Houston	Pos.	Min.	FGM	FGA	FTM	FTA	Off.	Def.	Tot.	Ast.	PF	Stls.	Pts.
Paultz, Billy	F	30	6	14	2	2	3	3	6	1	3	0	14
Reid, Robert	F	47	12	24	3	5	3	5	8	5	5	1	27
Malone, Moses	C	47	9	21	5	7	10	6	16	2	2	1	23
Dunleavy, Mike	G	33	3	9	0	0	0	3	3	1	3	0	6
Henderson, Tom	C	39	2	5	4	4	1	0	1	5	1	0	8
Willoughby, Bill		24	1	7	3	3	1	3	4	4	5	1	5
Garrett, Calvin		14	3	4	2	2	0	3	3	1	1	1	8
Leavell, Allen		5	0	2	0	0	0	0	0	3	1	0	0
Jones, Major		1	0	0	0	0	0	0	0	0	0	0	0
Total		240	36	86	19	23	18	23	41	22	21	4	91

FG Pct.: .419 FT Pct.: .826 Turnovers: Reid 2, Malone 1, Dunleavy 2, Henderson 3, Willoughby 2, Garrett 1, Leavell 1, Total—12 Team Rebounds: 9.

Score by Periods:	1st	2nd	3rd	4th	Totals
Boston	25	28	29	20	102
Houston	24	23	20	24	91

Blocked Shots: Malone 2. 3-Pt. Field Goals: Bird 1-2, Ford 0-2, Paultz 0-1, Dunleavy 0-1.
Officials: Jake O'Donnell and Jack Madden.
Attendance: 16,121.

1980-81 CHAMPIONSHIP SERIES REVIEW

1980-81 NBA PLAYOFF RESULTS
*—Overtime game

FIRST ROUND

EASTERN CONFERENCE

Chicago 2, New York 0

Mar. 31—Tue.—Chicago 90 at New York 80
Apr. 3—Fri.—New York 114 at Chicago *115

Philadelphia 2, Indiana 0

Mar. 31—Tue.—Indiana 108 at Philadelphia 124
Apr. 2—Thu.—Philadelphia 96 at Indiana 85

WESTERN CONFERENCE

Houston 2, Los Angeles 1

Apr. 1—Wed.—Houston 111 at Los Angeles 107
Apr. 3—Fri.—Los Angeles 111 at Houston 106
Apr. 5—Sun.—Houston 89 at Los Angeles 86

Kansas City 2, Portland 1

Apr. 1—Wed.—Kansas City 98 at Portland *97
Apr. 3—Fri.—Portland 124 at Kansas City *119
Apr. 5—Sun.—Kansas City 104 at Portland 95

CONFERENCE SEMI-FINALS SERIES

EASTERN CONFERENCE

Philadelphia 4, Milwaukee 3

Apr. 5—Sun.—Milwaukee 122 at Philadelphia 125
Apr. 7—Tue.—Milwaukee 109 at Philadelphia 99
Apr. 10—Fri.—Philadelphia 108 at Milwaukee 103
Apr. 12—Sun.—Philadelphia 98 at Milwaukee 109
Apr. 15—Wed.—Milwaukee 99 at Philadelphia 116
Apr. 17—Fri.—Philadelphia 86 at Milwaukee 109
Apr. 19—Sun.—Milwaukee 98 at Philadelphia 99

Boston 4, Chicago 0

Apr. 5—Sun.—Chicago 109 at Boston 121
Apr. 7—Tue.—Chicago 97 at Boston 106
Apr. 10—Fri.—Boston 113 at Chicago 107
Apr. 12—Sun.—Boston 109 at Chicago 103

WESTERN CONFERENCE

Kansas City 4, Phoenix 3

Apr. 7—Tue.—Kansas City 80 at Phoenix 102
Apr. 8—Wed.—Kansas City 88 at Phoenix 83
Apr. 10—Fri.—Phoenix 92 at Kansas City 93
Apr. 12—Sun.—Phoenix 95 at Kansas City 102
Apr. 15—Wed.—Kansas City 89 at Phoenix 101
Apr. 17—Fri.—Phoenix 81 at Kansas City 76
Apr. 19—Sun.—Kansas City 95 at Phoenix 88

Houston 4, San Antonio 3

Apr. 7—Tue.—Houston 107 at San Antonio 98
Apr. 8—Wed.—Houston 113 at San Antonio 125
Apr. 10—Fri.—San Antonio 99 at Houston 112
Apr. 12—Sun.—San Antonio 114 at Houston 112
Apr. 14—Tue.—Houston 123 at San Antonio 117
Apr. 15—Wed.—San Antonio 101 at Houston 96
Apr. 17—Fri.—Houston 105 at San Antonio 100

CONFERENCE FINALS

EASTERN CONFERENCE

Boston 4, Philadelphia 3

Apr. 21—Tue.—Philadelphia 105 at Boston 104
Apr. 22—Wed.—Philadelphia 99 at Boston 118
Apr. 24—Fri.—Boston 100 at Philadelphia 110
Apr. 26—Sun.—Boston 105 at Philadelphia 107
Apr. 29—Wed.—Philadelphia 109 at Boston 111
May   1—Fri.—Boston 100 at Philadelphia 98
May   3—Sun.—Philadelphia 90 at Boston 91

WESTERN CONFERENCE

Houston 4, Kansas City 1

Apr. 21—Tue.—Houston 97 at Kansas City 78
Apr. 22—Wed.—Houston 79 at Kansas City 88
Apr. 24—Fri.—Kansas City 88 at Houston 92
Apr. 26—Sun.—Kansas City 89 at Houston 100
Apr. 29—Wed.—Houston 97 at Kansas City 88

WORLD CHAMPIONSHIP SERIES

Boston 4, Houston 2

May   5—Tue.—Houston 95 at Boston 98
May   7—Thu.—Houston 92 at Boston 90
May   9—Sat.—Boston 94 at Houston 71
May 10—Sun.—Boston 86 at Houston 91
May 12—Tue.—Houston 80 at Boston 109
May 14—Thu.—Boston 102 at Houston 91

1980-81 Statistics

BOSTON CELTICS 1980-81 NBA WORLD CHAMPIONS

Front row (left to right): Chris Ford, Cedric Maxwell, President and General Manager Red Auerbach, Coach Bill Fitch, Chairman of the Board Harry T. Mangurian, Jr., Larry Bird, Nate Archibald. Back row: Assistant coach K. C. Jones, Wayne Kreklow, M. L. Carr, Rick Robey, Robert Parish, Kevin McHale, Eric Fernsten, Gerald Henderson, assistant coach Jimmy Rodgers, trainer Ray Melchiorre.

FINAL STANDINGS

ATLANTIC DIVISION

Team	Atl.	Bos.	Chi.	Clev.	Dall.	Den.	Det.	G.S.	Hou.	Ind.	K.C.	L.A.	Mil.	N.J.	N.Y.	Phil.	Pho.	Por.	S.A.	S.D.	Sea.	Utah	Wash.	W.	L.	Pct.	G.B.
Boston	4	..	5	4	2	2	4	1	2	3	1	2	3	6	5	3	2	2	2	2	1	1	5	62	20	.756	....
Philadelphia	5	3	4	6	2	1	4	2	2	6	2	1	2	5	5	3	..	1	1	2	2	2	4	62	20	.756	....
New York	4	1	3	5	1	2	5	..	2	2	1	..	3	6	..	3	1	1	..	2	2	2	4	50	32	.610	12
Washington	4	1	1	2	2	2	5	1	2	2	1	1	3	2	2	1	..	1	2	1	2	2	..	39	43	.476	23
New Jersey	2	..	2	3	1	1	3	1	..	1	..	..	1	..	..	1	1	2	..	1	1	1	3	24	58	.293	38

CENTRAL DIVISION

Milwaukee	5	3	3	6	2	1	5	1	2	4	1	2	..	5	3	3	1	2	1	2	2	2	4	60	22	.732	....
Chicago	4	1	..	5	1	1	5	1	1	3	2	1	3	3	3	2	..	..	1	1	2	5	45	37	.549	15	
Indiana	5	3	2	4	2	1	4	1	1	..	2	..	2	5	3	..	1	..	2	1	..	1	4	44	38	.537	16
Atlanta	..	2	2	1	2	1	4	2	1	1	1	..	1	3	2	1	..	1	1	1	1	2	1	31	51	.378	29
Cleveland	5	1	1	..	2	1	3	1	..	2	..	..	..	3	1	..	1	1	1	1	..	1	4	28	54	.341	32
Detroit	2	1	1	3	2	..	..	..	1	2	1	..	1	3	1	1	..	..	..	1	..	..	1	21	61	.256	39

MIDWEST DIVISION

San Antonio	1	..	2	1	5	4	2	4	3	..	4	3	1	2	2	..	2	3	..	4	3	5	1	52	30	.634	....
Kansas City	1	1	..	2	6	2	1	..	4	..	..	..	1	2	1	..	3	2	3	2	5	1	..	40	42	.488	12
Houston	1	..	1	2	6	4	1	2	..	1	2	2	..	2	..	..	1	3	3	1	4	4	..	40	42	.488	12
Denver	*1	..	1	1	3	..	2	3	2	1	4	3	1	1	..	1	1	2	2	3	3	2	..	37	45	.451	15
Utah	..	1	..	1	5	4	2	1	2	1	1	2	..	1	..	..	..	3	1	2	1	..	..	28	54	.341	24
Dallas	..	..	1	..	..	3	..	2	..	..	..	..	1	1	..	..	1	1	1	2	1	1	..	15	67	.183	37

PACIFIC DIVISION

Phoenix	2	..	2	1	4	4	2	4	4	1	2	4	1	1	1	..	3	3	6	5	5	1	..	57	25	.695	....
Los Angeles	2	..	1	2	5	2	2	5	3	2	5	..	..	2	2	1	2	3	2	3	6	3	1	54	28	.659	3
Portland	1	..	2	1	4	3	2	4	2	2	2	3	..	..	1	1	3	..	2	4	4	2	2	45	37	.549	12
Golden State	..	1	1	1	3	2	2	..	3	1	5	1	1	2	..	..	2	2	1	2	3	4	1	39	43	.476	18
San Diego	1	..	1	1	3	2	1	4	4	1	2	3	..	2	..	..	..	2	1	..	5	3	..	36	46	.439	21
Seattle	1	1	1	2	4	2	2	3	1	2	3	..	1	..	1	..	1	2	2	1	..	4	1	34	48	.415	23

TEAM STATISTICS—OFFENSE

Team	G.	FIELD GOALS Made	Att.	Pct.	FREE THROWS Made	Att.	Pct.	REBOUNDS Off.	Def.	Tot.	Ast.	PF	MISCELLANEOUS Dq.	Stl.	Turn Over	Blk. Sh.	SCORING Pts.	Avg.
Denver	82	3784	7960	.475	2388	3051	.783	1325	2497	3822	2030	2108	24	720	1444	380	9986	121.8
Milwaukee	82	3722	7472	.498	1802	2340	.770	1261	2408	3669	2319	2198	27	862	1581	530	9276	113.1
San Antonio	82	3571	7276	.491	2052	2668	.769	1304	2582	3886	2048	2114	25	685	1533	643	9209	112.3
Philadelphia	82	3636	7073	.514	1865	2427	.768	1091	2618	3709	2369	2061	21	857	1702	591	9156	111.7
Los Angeles	82	3780	7382	.512	1540	2113	.729	1165	2491	3656	2363	1955	17	808	1557	551	9117	111.2
Portland	82	3741	7535	.496	1573	2191	.718	1243	2388	3631	2244	2034	30	769	1518	480	9080	110.7
Phoenix	82	3587	7326	.490	1810	2430	.745	1234	2490	3724	2205	1996	13	876	1733	416	9019	110.0
Boston	82	3581	7099	.504	1781	2369	.752	1155	2424	3579	2202	1990	22	683	1577	594	9008	109.9
Golden State	82	3560	7284	.489	1826	2513	.727	1403	2366	3769	2026	2158	36	611	1547	301	9006	109.8
Chicago	82	3457	6903	.501	1985	2563	.774	1227	2475	3702	1925	2058	15	729	1672	514	8937	109.0
Houston	82	3573	7335	.487	1711	2223	.770	1216	2347	3563	2099	1901	8	705	1451	390	8878	108.3
New York	82	3505	7255	.483	1783	2386	.747	1137	2205	3342	1976	1917	12	861	1461	314	8849	107.9
Indiana	82	3491	7245	.482	1815	2540	.715	1325	2267	3592	2091	2006	26	833	1491	484	8827	107.6
Kansas City	82	3572	7151	.500	1576	2206	.714	1037	2450	3487	2271	2092	23	719	1448	385	8769	106.9
New Jersey	82	3477	7314	.475	1780	2371	.751	1092	2374	3466	2068	2204	35	750	1664	458	8768	106.9
San Diego	82	3477	7283	.477	1651	2246	.735	1169	2144	3313	2098	2078	21	764	1407	292	8737	106.5
Cleveland	82	3556	7609	.467	1486	1909	.778	1258	2243	3501	2007	1995	31	632	1396	322	8670	105.7
Washington	82	3549	7517	.472	1499	2072	.723	1155	2533	3688	2151	1895	21	641	1422	392	8662	105.6
Atlanta	82	3291	6866	.479	2012	2590	.777	1201	2224	3425	1846	2276	54	749	1605	469	8604	104.9
Seattle	82	3343	7145	.468	1813	2376	.763	1167	2434	3601	1945	1986	23	628	1524	438	8531	104.0
Dallas	82	3204	6928	.462	1868	2487	.751	1109	2177	3286	1984	2008	32	561	1494	214	8322	101.5
Utah	82	3332	6825	.488	1595	2080	.767	962	2325	3287	1948	2110	39	637	1423	386	8301	101.2
Detroit	82	3236	6986	.463	1689	2330	.725	1201	2111	3312	1819	2125	35	884	1759	492	8174	99.7

TEAM STATISTICS—DEFENSE

Team	FIELD GOALS Made	Att.	Pct.	FREE THROWS Made	Att.	Pct.	REBOUNDS Off.	Def.	Tot.	Ast.	PF	MISCELLANEOUS Dq.	Stl.	Turn Over	Blk. Sh.	SCORING Pts.	Avg.	Dif.
Philadelphia	3307	7337	.451	1850	2487	.744	1286	2287	3573	2033	2044	32	818	1642	379	8512	103.8	+ 7.9
Boston	3372	7296	.462	1752	2277	.769	1192	2174	3366	1890	2059	33	736	1473	351	8526	104.0	+ 5.9
Phoenix	3368	7221	.466	1762	2383	.739	1160	2284	3444	1970	2116	26	912	1752	401	8567	104.5	+ 5.5
Washington	3518	7491	.470	1588	2161	.735	1204	2638	3842	2060	1888	13	739	1410	469	8661	105.6	even
Seattle	3453	7421	.465	1718	2323	.740	1247	2357	3604	2044	2044	23	747	1348	387	8666	105.7	− 1.7
Milwaukee	3311	7220	.459	2023	2701	.749	1265	2209	3474	2033	2050	25	735	1670	400	8680	105.9	+ 7.2
Detroit	3499	6869	.509	1663	2217	.750	1090	2396	3486	2033	2095	20	793	1797	585	8692	106.0	− 6.3
Indiana	3457	7071	.489	1757	2290	.767	1246	2407	3653	2113	2064	27	695	1655	439	8712	106.2	+ 1.4
New York	3555	7092	.501	1563	2082	.751	1147	2457	3604	2088	1994	14	689	1660	452	8716	106.3	+ 1.6
Kansas City	3424	7117	.481	1889	2500	.736	1138	2510	3648	1857	2015	20	717	1520	383	8768	106.9	even
Chicago	3527	7209	.489	1669	2211	.755	1145	2096	3241	1950	2135	42	784	1502	441	8775	107.0	+ 2.0
Utah	3430	7018	.489	1879	2472	.760	1154	2440	3594	1985	1855	24	596	1303	406	8784	107.1	− 5.9
Los Angeles	3581	7701	.465	1598	2158	.741	1378	2274	3652	2280	1869	11	754	1473	357	8802	107.3	+ 3.9
Houston	3617	7341	.493	1568	2108	.744	1177	2367	3544	2191	1977	18	689	1430	367	8851	107.9	+ 0.4
Atlanta	3401	6867	.495	2024	2641	.766	1207	2318	3525	1935	2209	30	748	1685	555	8858	108.0	− 3.1
San Diego	3508	6951	.505	1818	2433	.747	1091	2377	3468	2097	2006	19	683	1553	392	8867	108.1	− 1.6
San Antonio	3581	7582	.472	1766	2387	.740	1214	2177	3391	2206	2198	37	700	1422	481	8973	109.4	+ 2.9
Portland	3584	7351	.488	1805	2377	.759	1249	2419	3668	2109	1932	30	802	1575	422	9007	109.8	+ 0.9
Dallas	3622	7060	.513	1731	2297	.754	1173	2498	3671	2098	2187	31	713	1433	480	9011	109.9	− 8.4
Cleveland	3608	7174	.503	1800	2395	.752	1158	2499	3657	2166	1956	21	681	1474	454	9068	110.6	− 4.9
Golden State	3631	7204	.504	1804	2411	.748	1137	2210	3347	2223	2093	19	714	1385	386	9103	111.0	− 1.2
New Jersey	3612	7159	.505	2010	2663	.755	1059	2499	3558	2144	2092	23	815	1637	502	9262	113.0	− 6.1
Denver	4059	8017	.506	1863	2507	.743	1320	2680	4000	2529	2387	52	704	1555	547	10025	122.3	− 0.5

DQ–Individual players disqualified (fouled out of game)

INDIVIDUAL LEADERS

SCORING

Minimum 70 games played or 1,400 points

	G.	FG	FT	Pts.	Avg.
Dantley, Utah	80	909	632	2452	30.7
Malone, Houston	80	806	609	2222	27.8
Gervin, San Antonio	82	850	512	2221	27.1
Abdul-Jabbar, L.A.	80	836	423	2095	26.2
Thompson, Denver	77	734	489	1967	25.5
Birdsong, K.C.	71	710	317	1747	24.6
Erving, Philadelphia	82	794	422	2014	24.6
Mitchell, Cleveland	82	853	302	2012	24.5
Free, Golden State	65	516	528	1565	24.1
English, Denver	81	768	390	1929	23.8
Wilkes, Los Angeles	81	786	254	1827	22.6
King, Golden State	81	731	307	1771	21.9
Issel, Denver	80	614	519	1749	21.9
Drew, Atlanta	67	500	454	1454	21.7
Newlin, New Jersey	79	632	414	1688	21.4
Bird, Boston	82	719	283	1741	21.2
Griffith, Utah	81	716	229	1671	20.6
Ma. Johnson, Mil	76	636	269	1541	20.3
Cartwright, N.Y.	82	619	408	1646	20.1
R. Williams, N.Y.	79	616	312	1560	19.7

1980-81 STATISTICS

FIELD GOAL PERCENTAGE
Minimum 300 FG Made

	FGM	FGA	Pct.
Gilmore, Chicago	547	816	.670
Dawkins, Philadelphia	423	697	.607
Maxwell, Boston	441	750	.588
King, Golden State	731	1244	.588
Abdul-Jabbar, Los Angeles	836	1457	.574
Washington, Portland	325	571	.569
Dantley, Utah	909	1627	.559
Cartwright, New York	619	1118	.554
Nater, San Diego	517	935	.553
Ma. Johnson, Milwaukee	636	1153	.552

FREE THROW PERCENTAGE
Minimum 125 FT Made

	FTM	FTA	Pct.
Murphy, Houston	206	215	.958
Sobers, Chicago	231	247	.935
Newlin, New Jersey	414	466	.888
Spanarkel, Dallas	375	423	.887
Bridgeman, Milwaukee	213	241	.884
Long, Detroit	160	184	.870
Criss, Atlanta	185	214	.864
Bird, Boston	283	328	.863
McKinney, Denver	162	188	.862
Bates, Portland	170	199	.854

REBOUNDS
Minimum 70 games or 800 rebounds

	G.	Off.	Def.	Tot.	Avg.
Malone, Houston	80	474	706	1180	14.8
Nater, San Diego	82	295	722	1017	12.4
Smith, Golden State	82	433	561	994	12.1
Bird, Boston	82	191	704	895	10.9
Sikma, Seattle	82	184	668	852	10.4
Carr, Cleveland	81	260	575	835	10.3
Abdul-Jabbar, L.A.	80	197	624	821	10.3
Gilmore, Chicago	82	220	608	828	10.1
C. Jones, Phila.	81	200	613	813	10.0
Hayes, Washington	81	235	554	789	9.7

BLOCKED SHOTS
Minimum 70 games or 100 blocked shots

	G.	No.	Avg.
G. Johnson, San Antonio	82	278	3.39
Rollins, Atlanta	40	117	2.93
Abdul-Jabbar, Los Angeles	80	228	2.85
Parish, Boston	82	214	2.61
Gilmore, Chicago	82	198	2.41
Catchings, Milwaukee	77	184	2.39
Tyler, Detroit	82	180	2.20
Thompson, Portland	79	170	2.15
Poquette, Utah	82	174	2.12
Hayes, Washington	81	171	2.11

ASSISTS
Minimum 70 games or 400 assists

	G.	No.	Avg.
Porter, Washington	81	734	9.1
Nixon, Los Angeles	79	696	8.8
Ford, Kansas City	66	580	8.8
Richardson, New York	79	627	7.9
Archibald, Boston	80	618	7.7
Lucas, Golden State	66	464	7.0
Ransey, Portland	80	555	6.9
Cheeks, Philadelphia	81	560	6.9
Davis, Indiana	76	480	6.3
Higgs, Denver	72	408	5.7

STEALS
Minimum 70 games or 125 steals

	G.	No.	Avg.
Johnson, Los Angeles	37	127	3.43
Richardson, New York	79	232	2.94
Buckner, Milwaukee	82	197	2.40
Cheeks, Philadelphia	81	193	2.38
R. Williams, New York	79	185	2.34
Bradley, Indiana	82	186	2.27
Erving, Philadelphia	82	173	2.11
Lee, Detroit	82	166	2.02
Reid, Houston	82	163	1.99
Bird, Boston	82	161	1.96

3-PT. FIELD GOALS
Minimum 25 made

	FGM	FGA	Pct.
Taylor, San Diego	44	115	.383
Williams, San Diego	48	141	.340
Hassett, Dall.-G.S.	53	156	.340
Bratz, Cleveland	57	169	.337
Bibby, San Diego	32	95	.337
Grevey, Washington	45	136	.331
Ford, Boston	36	109	.330
Wedman, Kansas City	25	77	.325

1980-81 REGULAR SEASON ATTENDANCE

1. Seattle 675,097
2. Boston 595,454
3. New York 544,641
4. Los Angeles 537,865
5. Portland 519,306
6. Phoenix 482,693
7. Philadelphia 469,355
8. Milwaukee 448,366
9. San Antonio 440,553
10. Denver 423,307
11. Golden State 413,480
12. Indiana 409,839
13. Chicago 389,718
14. Houston 385,354
15. Washington 375,360
16. Atlanta 362,702
17. Kansas City 336,585
18. Dallas 319,347
19. Utah 307,825
20. New Jersey 302,059
21. San Diego 257,597
22. Detroit 228,348
23. Cleveland 224,489

Total 9,449,340

TEAM BY TEAM STATISTICS

*Did not finish season with team.

ATLANTA

Player	G.	Min.	FGM	FGA	Pct.	FTM	FTA	Pct.	Off. Reb.	Def. Reb.	Tot. Reb.	Ast.	PF	Dsq.	Stl.	Blk. Sh.	Pts.	Avg.	Hi.
Drew	67	2075	500	1096	.456	454	577	.787	145	238	383	79	264	9	98	15	1454	21.7	47
Johnson	75	2693	573	1136	.504	279	356	.784	60	119	179	407	188	2	126	11	1431	19.1	40
Roundfield	63	2128	426	808	.527	256	355	.721	231	403	634	161	258	8	76	119	1108	17.6	29
Mat'ews (Tot.)	79	2266	385	779	.494	202	252	.802	46	93	139	411	242	2	107	17	977	12.4	26
Mat'ews (Atl.)	34	1105	161	330	.488	103	123	.837	16	56	72	212	122	1	61	7	425	12.5	26
Hawes	74	2309	333	637	.523	222	278	.799	165	396	561	168	289	13	73	32	889	12.0	32
Criss	66	1708	220	485	.454	185	214	.864	26	74	100	283	87	0	61	3	626	9.5	21
McMillen	79	1564	253	519	.487	80	108	.741	96	199	295	72	165	0	23	25	587	7.4	21
Rollins	40	1044	116	210	.552	46	57	.807	102	184	286	35	151	7	29	117	278	7.0	13
Pellom	77	1472	186	380	.489	81	116	.698	122	234	356	48	228	6	50	92	453	5.9	20
Shelton	55	586	100	219	.457	35	58	.603	59	79	138	27	128	1	18	5	235	4.3	22
McElroy	54	680	78	202	.386	48	59	.814	10	38	48	84	62	0	20	9	205	3.8	12
Burleson	31	363	41	99	.414	20	41	.488	44	50	94	12	73	2	8	19	102	3.3	12
A. Collins	29	395	35	99	.354	24	36	.667	19	22	41	25	35	0	11	1	94	3.2	15
*D. Collins	47	1184	230	530	.434	137	162	.846	96	91	187	115	166	5	69	11	597	12.7	25
*Hill	24	624	39	116	.336	42	50	.840	10	41	51	118	60	0	26	3	120	5.0	14

3Pt. FG: Atlanta 10-82 (.122) – Drew 0-7 (.000); Johnson 6-20 (.300); Roundfield 0-1 (.000); Matthews (Tot.) 5-21 (.238); Matthews (Atl.) 0-6 (.000); Hawes 1-4 (.250); Criss 1-21 (.048); McMillen 1-6 (.167); Rollins 0-1 (.000); Pellom 0-1 (.000); Shelton 0-1 (.000); McElroy 1-8 (.125); A. Collins 0-2 (.000); D. Collins 0-3 (.000); Hill 0-1 (.000). Opponents 32-152 (.211).

BOSTON

Player	G.	Min.	FGM	FGA	Pct.	FTM	FTA	Pct.	Off. Reb.	Def. Reb.	Tot. Reb.	Ast.	PF	Dsq.	Stl.	Blk. Sh.	Pts.	Avg.	Hi.
Bird	82	3239	719	1503	.478	283	328	.863	191	704	895	451	239	2	161	63	1741	21.2	36
Parish	82	2298	635	1166	.545	282	397	.710	245	532	777	144	310	9	81	214	1552	18.9	40
Maxwell	81	2730	441	750	.588	352	450	.782	222	303	525	219	256	5	79	68	1234	15.2	34
Archibald	80	2820	382	766	.499	342	419	.816	36	140	176	618	201	1	75	17	1106	13.8	26
McHale	82	1645	355	666	.533	108	159	.679	155	204	359	55	260	3	27	151	818	10.0	23
Robey	82	1569	298	547	.545	144	251	.574	132	258	390	126	204	0	38	19	740	9.0	24
Ford	82	2723	314	707	.444	64	87	.736	72	91	163	295	212	2	100	23	728	8.9	23
Henderson	82	1608	261	579	.451	113	157	.720	43	89	132	213	177	0	79	12	636	7.8	19
Carr	41	655	97	216	.449	53	67	.791	26	57	83	56	74	0	30	18	248	6.0	25
Duerod (Tot.)	50	451	104	234	.444	31	41	.756	17	27	44	36	27	0	17	4	247	4.9	22
Duerod (Bos.)	32	114	30	73	.411	13	14	.929	2	3	5	6	8	0	5	0	79	2.5	12
Fernsten	45	279	38	79	.481	20	30	.667	29	33	62	10	29	0	6	7	96	2.1	9
*Kreklow	25	100	11	47	.234	7	10	.700	2	10	12	9	20	0	2	1	30	1.2	4

3-Pt. FG: Boston 65-241 (.270) – Bird 20-74 (.270); Parish 0-1 (.000); Maxwell 0-1 (.000); Archibald 0-9 (.000); McHale 0-2 (.000); Robey 0-1 (.000); Ford 36-109 (.330); Henderson 1-16 (.063); Carr 1-14 (.071); Duerod (Tot.) 8-16 (.500), Duerod (Bos.) 6-10 (.600); Kreklow 1-4 (.250). Opponents 30-139 (.216).

CHICAGO

Player	G.	Min.	FGM	FGA	Pct.	FTM	FTA	Pct.	Off. Reb.	Def. Reb.	Tot. Reb.	Ast.	PF	Dsq.	Stl.	Blk. Sh.	Pts.	Avg.	Hi.
Theus	82	2820	543	1097	.495	445	550	.809	124	163	287	426	258	1	122	20	1549	18.9	32
Gilmore	82	2832	547	816	.670	375	532	.705	220	608	828	172	295	2	47	198	1469	17.9	31
Greenwood	82	2710	481	989	.486	217	290	.748	243	403	634	191	218	2	57	77	1179	14.4	28
Kenon	77	2161	454	946	.480	180	245	.735	179	219	398	120	160	2	75	18	1088	14.1	32
Sobers	71	1803	355	769	.462	231	247	.935	46	98	144	284	225	3	98	17	958	13.5	27
Wilkerson	80	2238	330	715	.462	137	163	.840	86	196	282	272	170	0	102	23	798	10.0	28
Jones	81	1574	245	507	.483	125	161	.776	127	274	401	99	200	1	40	36	615	7.6	29
May	63	815	165	338	.488	113	149	.758	62	93	155	63	83	0	35	7	443	7.0	20
Dietrich	82	1243	146	320	.456	77	111	.694	79	186	265	118	176	1	48	53	371	4.5	16
Wilkes	48	540	85	184	.462	29	46	.690	36	60	96	30	86	0	25	12	199	4.1	21
Lester	8	83	10	24	.417	0	11	.909	3	3	6	7	5	0	2	0	30	3.8	9
Worthen	64	945	95	192	.495	45	60	.750	22	93	115	115	115	0	57	6	235	3.7	18
*Mack	3	16	1	6	.167	1	2	.500	1	0	1	1	3	0	1	0	3	1.0	2

3-Pt. FG: Chicago 38-179 (.212) – Theus 18-90 (.200); Greenwood 0-2 (.000); Sobers 17-66 (.258); Wilkerson 1-10 (.100); Dietrick 2-6 (.333); Wilkes 0- (.000); Worthen 0-4 (.000). Opponents 52-223 (.233).

1980-81 STATISTICS

CLEVELAND

Player	G.	Min.	FGM	FGA	Pct.	FTM	FTA	Pct.	Off. Reb.	Def. Reb.	Tot. Reb.	Ast.	PF	Dsq.	Stl.	Blk. Sh.	Pts.	Avg.	Hi.
Mitchell	82	3194	853	1791	.476	302	385	.784	215	287	502	139	199	0	63	52	2012	24.5	42
Carr	81	2615	469	918	.511	292	409	.714	260	575	835	192	296	3	76	42	1230	15.2	31
Ra. Smith	82	2199	486	1043	.466	221	271	.815	46	147	193	357	132	0	113	14	1194	14.6	33
Phegley	82	2269	474	965	.491	224	267	.839	90	156	246	184	262	7	65	15	1180	14.4	30
H'ton (Tot.)	81	2434	461	942	.489	150	212	.708	45	93	138	394	148	1	58	7	1073	13.2	29
H'ton (Clev.)	25	542	76	153	.497	22	27	.815	12	27	39	117	35	0	13	1	174	7.0	19
Bratz	80	2595	319	817	.390	107	132	.811	66	132	198	452	194	1	136	17	802	10.0	24
Was'ton(Tot.)	80	1812	340	747	.455	119	159	.748	158	295	453	129	273	1	46	61	800	10.0	24
Was'ton(Clev)	69	1505	289	630	.459	102	136	.750	133	236	369	113	246	3	41	54	681	9.9	24
Laimbeer	81	2460	337	670	.503	117	153	.765	266	427	693	216	332	14	56	78	791	9.8	26
Ford	64	996	100	224	.446	22	24	.917	74	90	164	84	100	1	15	12	222	3.5	14
Calvin	21	128	13	39	.333	25	35	.714	2	10	12	28	13	0	5	0	52	2.5	6
Jordan	30	207	29	75	.387	10	17	.588	23	19	42	11	35	0	11	5	68	2.3	8
Hughes (Tot.)	53	490	27	70	.386	1	2	.500	48	79	127	35	106	2	28	35	55	1.0	6
H'hes (Clev.)	45	331	16	45	.356	0	0	.....	29	48	77	24	73	0	17	21	32	0.7	6
*Robisch	11	372	37	98	.378	29	36	.806	27	58	85	44	21	0	7	6	103	9.4	17
Ro. Smith	1	20	2	5	.400	4	4	1.000	1	2	3	3	6	1	0	0	8	8.0	8
*Robinzine	8	84	14	32	.438	5	8	.625	4	9	13	5	19	1	4	0	33	4.1	10
*W'h'd(Clev)	3	8	1	3	.333	0	0	.....	2	1	3	0	6	0	1	0	2	0.7	2
*Kinch	29	247	38	96	.396	4	5	.800	7	17	24	35	24	0	9	5	80	2.8	10
*Lambert	8	8	3	5	.600	0	0	.....	1	2	3	3	2	0	0	0	6	2.0	4

3-Pt. FG: Cleveland 72-249 (.289) — Mitchell 4-9 (.444); Carr 0-4 (.000); Ra. Smith 1-28 (.036); Phegley 8-28 (.286); Huston (Tot.) 1-5 (.200), Huston (Clev.) 0-1 (.000); Bratz 57-169 (.337); Washington (Clev.) 1-2 (.500); Ford 0-3 (.000); Calvin 1-5 (.200). Opponents 52-168 (.310).

DALLAS

Player	G.	Min.	FGM	FGA	Pct.	FTM	FTA	Pct.	Off. Reb.	Def. Reb.	Tot. Reb.	Ast.	PF	Dsq.	Stl.	Blk. Sh.	Pts.	Avg.	Hi.
Spanarkel	82	2317	404	866	.467	375	423	.887	142	155	297	232	230	3	117	20	1184	14.4	28
LaGarde	82	2670	417	888	.470	288	444	.649	177	488	665	237	293	6	35	45	1122	13.7	26
Rob'zine (Tot)	78	2016	392	826	.475	218	281	.776	168	365	533	118	275	6	75	9	1003	12.9	26
Rob'zine (Dal)	70	1932	378	794	.476	213	273	.780	164	356	520	113	256	5	71	9	970	13.9	26
B. Davis	56	1686	230	410	.561	163	204	.799	29	122	151	385	156	2	52	11	626	11.2	31
Mack (Tot)	65	1682	279	606	.460	80	125	.640	92	138	230	163	117	0	56	7	638	9.8	28
Mack (Dal)	62	1666	278	600	.463	79	123	.642	92	137	229	162	114	0	55	7	635	10.2	28
Lloyd	72	2186	245	547	.448	147	205	.717	161	293	454	159	269	8	34	25	637	8.8	28
Jeelani	66	1108	187	440	.425	179	220	.814	83	147	230	65	123	2	44	31	553	8.4	31
Byrnes	72	1360	216	451	.479	120	157	.764	74	103	177	113	126	0	29	17	561	7.8	25
Kea	28	226	37	81	.457	43	62	.694	28	39	67	5	44	2	6	1	117	7.3	22
P'tk'wicz(Tot)	42	461	57	138	.413	11	14	.786	13	29	42	77	28	0	15	2	144	3.4	10
P'tk'w'z (Dal)	36	431	55	133	.414	11	14	.786	13	28	41	75	26	0	15	2	140	3.9	10
Kinch (Tot)	41	353	52	141	.369	14	18	.778	7	26	33	45	33	0	11	6	118	2.9	10
Kinch (Dal)	12	106	14	45	.311	10	13	.769	0	9	9	10	9	0	2	1	38	3.2	7
*Huston	56	1892	385	789	.488	128	185	.692	33	66	99	277	113	1	45	6	899	16.1	29
*Washington	11	307	51	117	.436	17	23	.739	25	59	84	16	37	0	5	7	119	10.8	24
*Duerod	18	337	74	161	.460	18	27	.667	15	24	39	30	19	0	12	4	168	9.3	22
*Hassett	17	280	59	142	.415	10	13	.769	11	14	25	18	21	0	5	0	138	8.1	15
*Boynes	44	757	121	313	.387	45	55	.818	24	51	75	37	79	1	23	16	287	6.5	22
*Whitehead	7	118	16	38	.421	5	11	.455	8	20	28	2	16	0	4	1	37	5.3	14
*Allums	22	276	23	67	.343	13	22	.591	19	46	65	25	51	2	5	8	59	2.7	11
*Drollinger	6	67	7	14	.500	1	4	.250	5	14	19	14	16	0	1	2	15	2.5	8
*Carr	8	77	7	28	.250	2	4	.500	4	5	9	9	10	0	1	0	16	2.0	5
*M. D'is (Tot)	2	10	1	5	.200	1	5	.200	2	2	4	0	0	0	0	1	3	1.5	2
*M. D'is (Dal)	1	8	0	4	.000	1	5	.200	2	1	3	0	0	0	0	1	1	1.0	1

3-Pt. FG: Dallas 46-165 (.279) — Spanarkel 1-10 (.100); Robinzine 1-6 (.167); B. Davis 3-17 (.176); Mack 0-9 (.000); Lloyd 0-2 (.000); Jeelani 0-1 (.000); Byrnes 9-20 (.450); Kea 0-1 (.000); Pietkiewicz 19-48 (.396); Huston 1-4 (.250); Duerod 2-6 (.333); Hassett 10-40 (.250); Allums 0-1 (.000). Opponents 36-137 (.263).

DENVER

Player	G.	Min.	FGM	FGA	Pct.	FTM	FTA	Pct.	Off. Reb.	Def. Reb.	Tot. Reb.	Ast.	PF	Dsq.	Stl.	Blk. Sh.	Pts.	Avg.	Hi.
Thompson	77	2620	734	1451	.506	489	615	.795	107	180	287	231	231	3	53	60	1967	25.5	44
English	81	3093	768	1555	.494	390	459	.850	273	373	646	290	255	2	106	100	1929	23.8	42
Issel	80	2641	614	1220	.503	519	684	.759	229	447	676	158	249	6	83	53	1749	21.9	37
Vandeweghe	51	1376	229	537	.426	130	159	.818	86	184	270	94	116	0	29	24	588	11.5	30
Robisch (Tot)	84	2116	330	740	.446	200	247	.810	157	342	499	173	173	0	37	34	860	10.2	27
Robisch (Den)	73	1744	293	642	.456	171	211	.810	130	284	414	129	152	0	30	28	757	10.4	27
McKin'y (Tot)	84	2166	327	645	.507	162	188	.862	36	148	184	360	231	3	99	11	818	9.7	21

1980-81 STATISTICS

Player	G.	Min.	FGM	FGA	Pct.	FTM	FTA	Pct.	Off. Reb.	Def. Reb.	Tot. Reb.	Ast.	PF	Dsq.	Stl.	Blk. Sh.	Pts	Avg.	Hi.
McKin'y (Den)	49	1134	203	412	.493	118	140	.843	24	86	110	203	124	0	61	7	525	10.7	21
Roche	26	611	82	179	.458	58	77	.753	5	32	37	140	44	0	17	8	231	8.9	30
Hordges	68	1599	221	480	.460	130	186	.699	120	338	458	104	226	4	33	19	572	8.4	21
Higgs	72	1689	209	474	.441	140	172	.814	24	121	145	408	243	5	101	6	562	7.8	21
Gondrezick	73	1077	155	329	.471	112	137	.818	136	171	307	83	185	2	91	20	422	5.8	27
Dunn	82	1427	146	354	.412	79	121	.653	133	168	301	81	141	0	66	29	371	4.5	16
Valentine	24	123	37	98	.378	9	19	.474	10	20	30	7	23	0	7	4	84	3.5	9
Ray	18	148	15	49	.306	7	10	.700	13	24	37	11	31	0	4	4	37	2.1	7
*Nicks	27	493	65	149	.436	35	59	.593	13	36	49	80	52	0	28	2	165	6.1	17
*Hughes	8	159	11	25	.440	1	2	.500	19	31	50	11	33	2	11	14	23	2.9	6
*Oldham	4	21	2	6	.333	0	0	.....	3	2	5	0	3	0	0	2	4	1.0	2

3-Pt. FG: Denver 30-145 (.207)—Thompson 10-39 (.256); English 3-5 (.600); Issel 2-12 (.167); Vandeweghe 0-7 (.000); McKinney (Tot.) 2-12 (.167); McKinney (Den.) 1-10 (.100); Roche 9-27 (.333); Hordges 0-3 (.000); Higgs 4-34 (.118); Gondrezick 0-2 (.000); Dunn 0-2 (.000); Valentine 1-2 (.500); Ray 0-1 (.000); Nicks 0-1 (.000). Opponents 44-162 (.272).

DETROIT

Player	G.	Min.	FGM	FGA	Pct.	FTM	FTA	Pct.	Off. Reb.	Def. Reb.	Tot. Reb.	Ast.	PF	Dsq.	Stl.	Blk. Sh.	Pts.	Avg.	Hi.
Long	59	1750	441	957	.461	160	184	.870	95	102	197	106	164	3	95	22	1044	17.7	40
Benson	59	1956	364	770	.473	196	254	.772	124	276	400	172	184	1	72	67	924	15.7	27
Hubbard	80	2289	433	880	.492	294	426	.690	236	350	586	150	317	14	80	20	1161	14.5	29
Herron	80	2270	432	954	.453	228	267	.854	98	113	211	148	154	1	91	26	1094	13.7	29
Tyler	82	2549	476	895	.532	148	250	.592	198	369	567	136	215	2	112	180	1100	13.4	31
Kelser	25	654	120	285	.421	68	106	.642	53	67	120	45	89	0	34	29	308	12.3	33
Robinson	81	1592	234	509	.460	175	240	.729	117	177	294	112	186	2	46	24	643	7.9	19
Wright	45	997	140	303	.462	53	66	.803	26	62	88	153	114	1	42	9	335	7.4	19
Mokeski	80	1815	224	458	.489	120	200	.600	141	277	418	135	267	7	38	73	568	7.1	18
Drew	76	1581	197	484	.407	106	133	.797	24	96	120	249	125	0	88	7	504	6.6	23
Lee	82	1829	118	323	.350	113	156	.724	65	155	220	362	260	4	166	29	341	4.2	15
*McAdoo	6	168	30	82	.366	12	20	.600	9	32	41	20	16	0	8	7	72	12.0	16
*Fuller	15	248	24	66	.364	12	16	.750	13	29	42	28	25	0	10	1	60	4.0	9
*Lawrence	3	19	5	8	.625	2	4	.500	2	2	4	1	6	0	1	0	12	4.0	6
*Black	3	28	3	10	.300	2	8	.250	0	2	2	2	0	0	2	0	8	2.7	4
*J'son (Tot)	12	90	7	25	.280	0	0	.....	6	16	22	1	18	0	0	5	17	1.4	6
*J'son (Det)	2	10	0	2	.000	0	0	.....	2	2	4	0	0	0	0	0	0	0.0	0

3-Pt. FG: Detroit 13-84 (.155)—Long 2-11 (.182); Benson 0-4 (.000); Hubbard 1-3 (.333); Herron 2-11 (.182); Tyler 0-8 (.000); Kelser 0-2 (.000); Robinson 0-6 (.000); Wright 2-7 (.286); Mokeski 0-1 (.000); Drew 4-17 (.235); Lee 2-13 (.154); Fuller 0-1 (.000). Opponents 31-127 (.244).

GOLDEN STATE

Player	G.	Min.	FGM	FGA	Pct.	FTM	FTA	Pct.	Off. Reb.	Def. Reb.	Tot. Reb.	Ast.	PF	Dsq.	Stl.	Blk. Sh.	Pts.	Avg.	Hi.
Free	65	2370	516	1157	.446	528	649	.814	48	111	159	361	183	1	85	11	1565	24.1	39
King	81	2914	731	1244	.588	307	437	.703	178	373	551	287	304	5	72	34	1771	21.9	50
Carroll	82	2919	616	1254	.491	315	440	.716	274	485	759	117	313	10	50	121	1547	18.9	46
Short	79	2309	549	1157	.475	168	205	.820	151	240	391	249	244	3	78	19	1269	16.1	45
Smith	82	2578	304	594	.512	177	301	.588	433	561	994	93	316	10	70	63	785	9.6	23
Hassett (Tot)	41	714	143	340	.421	17	21	.810	24	44	68	74	65	0	13	2	356	8.7	23
Hassett (G.S.)	24	434	84	198	.424	7	8	.875	13	30	43	56	44	0	8	2	218	9.1	23
Parker	73	1317	191	388	.492	94	128	.734	101	93	194	106	112	0	67	13	476	6.5	18
Romar	53	726	87	211	.412	43	63	.683	10	46	56	136	64	0	27	3	219	4.1	14
Brown	45	580	83	162	.512	16	21	.762	52	114	166	21	103	4	9	14	182	4.0	15
Reid	59	597	84	185	.454	22	39	.564	27	33	60	71	111	0	33	5	190	3.2	14
Ray	66	838	64	152	.421	29	62	.468	73	144	217	52	194	2	24	13	157	2.4	15
Mayfield	7	54	8	18	.444	1	2	.500	7	2	9	1	8	0	0	1	17	2.4	6
Mengelt	2	11	0	4	.000	0	0	.....	0	0	0	2	0	0	0	0	0	0.0	0
*Lucas	66	1919	222	506	.439	107	145	.738	34	120	154	464	140	1	83	2	555	8.4	23
*White	4	43	9	18	.500	4	4	1.000	0	0	0	2	7	0	4	0	22	5.5	12
*Chenier	9	82	11	33	.333	6	6	1.000	1	7	8	7	10	0	0	0	29	3.2	6
*Abernethy	10	39	1	3	.333	2	3	.667	1	7	8	1	5	0	1	0	4	0.4	2

3-Pt. FG: Golden State 60-210 (.286)—Free 5-31 (.161); King 2-6 (.333); Carroll 0-2 (.000); Short 3-17 (.176); Hassett (Tot.) 53-156 (.340); Hassett (G.S.) 43-116 (.371); Romar 2-6 (.333); Reid 0-5 (.000); Lucas 4-24 (.167); Chenier 1-3 (.333) Opponents 37-160 (.231).

HOUSTON

Player	G.	Min.	FGM	FGA	Pct.	FTM	FTA	Pct.	Off. Reb.	Def. Reb.	Tot. Reb.	Ast.	PF	Dsq.	Stl.	Blk. Sh.	Pts.	Avg.	Hi.
Malone	80	3245	806	1545	.522	609	804	.757	474	706	1180	141	223	0	83	150	2222	27.8	51
Murphy	76	2014	528	1074	.492	206	215	.958	33	54	87	222	209	0	111	6	1266	16.7	42
Reid	82	2963	536	1113	.482	229	303	.756	164	419	583	344	325	4	163	66	1301	15.9	32
Tomjanovich	52	1264	263	563	.467	65	82	.793	78	130	208	81	121	0	19	6	603	11.6	25
Dunleavy	74	1609	310	632	.491	156	186	.839	28	90	118	268	165	1	64	2	777	10.5	48
Leavell	79	1686	258	548	.471	124	149	.832	30	104	134	384	160	1	97	15	642	8.1	24
Paultz	81	1659	262	517	.507	75	153	.490	111	280	391	105	182	1	28	72	599	7.4	20
Willoughby	55	1145	150	287	.523	49	64	.766	74	153	227	64	102	0	18	31	349	6.3	21
Garrett	70	1638	188	415	.453	50	62	.806	85	179	264	132	167	0	50	10	427	6.1	22
Henderson	66	1411	137	332	.413	78	95	.821	30	74	104	307	111	1	53	4	352	5.3	16
Jones	68	1003	117	252	.464	64	101	.634	96	138	234	41	112	0	18	23	298	4.4	18
Stroud	9	88	11	34	.324	3	4	.750	7	6	13	9	7	0	1	0	25	2.8	11
*Johnson	10	80	7	23	.304	3	5	.600	6	14	20	1	17	0	0	5	17	1.7	6

3-Pt. FG: Houston 21-118 (.178)—Malone 1-3 (.333); Murphy 4-17 (.235); Reid 0-4 (.000); Tomjanovich 12-51 (.235); Dunleavy 1-16 (.063); Leavell 2-17 (.118); Paultz 0-3 (.000); Garrett 1-3 (.333); Henderson 0-3 (.000); Jones 0-1 (.000). Opponents 49-171 (.287).

INDIANA

Player	G.	Min.	FGM	FGA	Pct.	FTM	FTA	Pct.	Off. Reb.	Def. Reb.	Tot. Reb.	Ast.	PF	Dsq.	Stl.	Blk. Sh.	Pts.	Avg.	Hi.
Knight	82	2385	546	1025	.533	341	410	.832	191	219	410	157	155	1	84	12	1436	17.5	52
Edwards	81	2375	511	1004	.509	244	347	.703	191	380	571	212	304	7	32	128	1266	15.6	39
Davis	76	2536	426	917	.465	238	299	.796	56	114	170	480	179	2	95	14	1094	14.4	30
Bantom	76	2375	431	882	.489	199	281	.708	150	277	427	240	284	9	80	85	1061	14.0	29
McGinnis	69	1845	348	768	.453	207	385	.538	164	364	528	210	242	3	99	28	903	13.1	27
G. Johnson	43	930	182	394	.462	93	122	.762	99	179	278	86	120	1	47	23	457	10.6	26
Orr	82	1787	348	709	.491	163	202	.807	172	189	361	132	153	0	55	25	859	10.5	22
Bradley	82	1887	265	559	.474	125	178	.702	70	123	193	188	236	2	186	37	657	8.0	24
C. Johnson	81	1643	235	466	.504	112	189	.593	173	295	468	144	185	1	44	119	582	7.2	17
Buse	58	1095	114	287	.397	50	65	.769	19	65	84	140	61	0	74	8	297	5.1	13
Sichting	47	450	34	95	.358	25	32	.781	11	32	43	70	38	0	23	1	93	2.0	12
Ab'ethy(Tot.)	39	298	25	59	.424	13	22	.591	20	28	48	19	34	0	7	3	63	1.6	6
Ab'ethy(Ind.)	29	259	24	56	.429	11	19	.579	19	21	40	18	29	0	6	3	59	2.0	6
*Natt	19	149	25	77	.325	7	11	.636	9	6	15	10	18	0	5	1	59	3.1	15
*Miller	5	34	2	6	.333	0	0		1	3	4	4	2	0	3	0	4	0.8	4

3-Pt. FG: Indiana 30-169 (.178)—Knight 3-19 (.158); Edwards 0-3 (.000); Davis 4-33 (.121); Bantom 0-6 (.000); McGinnis 0-7 (.000); G. Johnson 0-5 (.000); Orr 0-6 (.000); Bradley 2-16 (.125); C. Johnson 0-1 (.000); Buse 19-58 (.328); Sichting 0-5 (.000); Abernethy (Ind.) 0-1 (.000); Natt 2-8 (.250); Miller 0-1 (.000). Opponents 41-179 (.229).

KANSAS CITY

Player	G.	Min.	FGM	FGA	Pct.	FTM	FTA	Pct.	Off. Reb.	Def. Reb.	Tot. Reb.	Ast.	PF	Dsq.	Stl.	Blk. Sh.	Pts.	Avg.	Hi.
Birdsong	71	2593	710	1306	.544	317	455	.697	119	139	258	233	172	2	93	18	1747	24.6	42
Wedman	81	2902	685	1437	.477	140	204	.686	128	305	433	226	294	4	97	46	1535	19.0	41
Ford	66	2287	424	887	.478	294	354	.831	26	102	128	580	190	3	99	6	1153	17.5	38
King	81	2743	472	867	.544	264	386	.684	235	551	786	122	227	2	102	41	1208	14.9	33
Meriweather	74	1514	206	415	.496	148	213	.695	126	267	393	77	219	4	27	80	560	7.6	24
Grunfeld	79	1584	260	486	.535	75	101	.743	71	175	206	205	155	1	60	15	595	7.5	30
Whitney	47	782	149	306	.487	50	65	.769	29	77	106	68	98	0	47	6	350	7.4	24
Lacey	82	2228	237	536	.442	92	117	.786	131	453	584	399	302	5	95	120	567	6.9	16
Douglas	79	1356	185	323	.573	102	186	.548	150	234	384	69	251	2	38	42	472	6.0	17
Sanders	23	186	34	77	.442	20	22	.909	6	15	21	17	20	0	16	1	88	3.8	13
Walton	61	821	90	218	.413	26	33	.788	13	35	48	208	45	0	32	2	206	3.4	18
Lam'rt (Tot.)	46	483	68	165	.412	18	23	.783	28	65	93	27	76	0	12	5	154	3.3	12
Lam'rt (K.C.)	43	475	65	160	.406	18	23	.783	27	63	90	24	74	0	12	5	148	3.4	12
*White	13	236	36	82	.439	11	18	.611	3	18	21	37	21	0	11	1	83	6.4	12
*Gerard	16	123	19	51	.373	19	29	.655	13	16	29	6	34	0	5	0	57	3.6	12

3-Pt. FG: Kansas City 49-168 (.292)—Birdsong 10-35 (.286); Wedman 25-77 (.325); Ford 11-36 (.306); Whitney 2-6 (.333); Lacey 1-5 (.200); Douglas 0-3 (.000); Walton 0-1 (.000); Lambert (K.C.) 0-2 (.000); Gerard 0-3 (.000). Opponents 31-153 (.203).

1980-81 STATISTICS

LOS ANGELES

Player	G.	Min.	FGM	FGA	Pct.	FTM	FTA	Pct.	Off. Reb.	Def. Reb.	Tot. Reb.	Ast.	PF	Dsq.	Stl.	Blk. Sh.	Pts.	Avg.	Hi.
Abdul-Jabbar	80	2976	836	1457	.574	423	552	.766	197	624	821	272	244	4	59	228	2095	26.2	42
Wilkes	81	3028	786	1495	.526	254	335	.758	146	289	435	235	223	1	121	29	1827	22.6	34
Johnson	37	1371	312	587	.532	171	225	.760	101	219	320	317	100	0	127	27	798	21.6	41
Nixon	79	2962	576	1210	.476	196	252	.778	64	168	232	696	226	2	146	11	1350	17.1	30
Chones	82	2562	378	751	.503	126	193	.653	180	477	657	153	324	4	39	96	882	10.8	23
Cooper	81	2625	321	654	.491	117	149	.785	121	215	336	332	249	4	133	78	763	9.4	20
Landsberger	69	1086	164	327	.502	62	116	.534	152	225	377	27	135	0	19	6	390	5.7	22
Carter	54	672	114	247	.462	70	95	.737	34	31	65	52	99	0	23	1	301	5.6	16
Jordan (Tot.)	74	1226	150	352	.426	87	127	.685	30	68	98	241	165	0	98	8	393	5.3	18
Jordan (L.A.)	60	987	120	279	.430	63	95	.663	25	55	80	195	136	0	74	7	306	5.1	18
Holland	41	295	47	111	.423	35	49	.714	9	20	29	23	44	0	21	1	130	3.2	10
Brewer	78	1107	101	197	.513	15	40	.375	127	154	281	55	158	2	43	58	217	2.8	14
Hardy	22	111	22	59	.373	7	10	.700	8	11	19	3	13	0	1	9	51	2.3	8
*Patrick	3	9	2	5	.400	1	2	.500	1	1	2	1	3	0	0	0	5	1.7	3
*Jackson	2	14	1	3	.333	0	0	....	0	2	2	2	1	0	2	0	2	1.0	2

3-Pt. FG: Los Angeles 17-94 (.181)–Adbul-Jabbar 0-1 (.000); Wilkes 1-13 (.077); Johnson 3-17 (.176); Nixon 2-12 (.167); Chones 0-4 (.000); Cooper 4-19 (.211); Lansberger 0-1 (.000); Carter 3-10 (.300); Jordan (Tot.) 6-22 (.273); Jordan (L.A.) 3-12 (.250); Holland 1-3 (.333); Brewer 0-2 (.000). Opponents 42-184 (.228).

MILWAUKEE

Player	G.	Min.	FGM	FGA	Pct.	FTM	FTA	Pct.	Off. Reb.	Def. Reb.	Tot. Reb.	Ast.	PF	Dsq.	Stl.	Blk. Sh.	Pts.	Avg.	Hi.
Ma. Johnson	76	2542	636	1153	.552	269	381	.706	225	293	518	346	196	1	115	41	1541	20.3	40
Bridgeman	77	2215	537	1102	.487	213	241	.884	78	211	289	234	182	2	88	28	1290	16.8	34
Lanier	67	1753	376	716	.525	208	277	.751	128	285	413	179	184	0	73	81	961	14.3	29
Moncrief	80	2417	400	739	.541	320	398	.804	186	220	406	264	156	1	90	37	1122	14.0	27
Buckner	82	2384	471	956	.493	149	203	.734	88	210	298	384	271	3	197	3	1092	13.3	31
Mi. Johnson	82	2118	379	846	.448	262	332	.789	183	362	545	286	256	4	94	71	1023	12.5	23
Winters	69	1771	331	697	.475	119	137	.869	32	108	140	229	185	2	70	10	799	11.6	26
Cummings	74	1084	248	460	.539	99	140	.707	97	195	292	62	192	4	31	19	595	8.0	30
Evans	71	911	134	291	.460	50	64	.781	22	65	87	167	114	0	34	4	320	4.5	16
Catchings	77	1635	134	300	.447	59	92	.641	154	319	473	99	284	7	33	184	327	4.2	14
Elmore	72	925	76	212	.358	54	75	.720	68	140	208	69	178	3	37	52	206	2.9	12

3-Pt. FG: Milwaukee 30-131 (.229)–Ma. Johnson 0-9 (.000); Bridgeman 3-21 (.143); Lanier 1-1 (1.000); Moncrief 2-9 (.222); Buckner 1-6 (.167); Mi. Johnson 3-18 (.167); Winters 18-51 (.353); Cummings 0-2 (.000); Evans 2-14 (143). Opponents 35-199 (.176).

NEW JERSEY

Player	G.	Min.	FGM	FGA	Pct.	FTM	FTA	Pct.	Off. Reb.	Def. Reb.	Tot. Reb.	Ast.	PF	Dsq.	Stl.	Blk. Sh.	Pts.	Avg.	Hi.
Newlin	79	2911	632	1272	.497	414	466	.888	78	141	219	299	237	2	87	9	1688	21.4	43
Robinson	63	1822	525	1070	.491	178	248	.718	120	361	481	105	216	6	58	52	1229	19.5	38
Lucas	68	2162	404	835	.484	191	254	.752	153	422	575	173	260	3	57	59	999	14.7	39
Gminski	56	1579	291	688	.423	155	202	.767	137	282	419	72	127	1	54	100	737	13.2	31
Cook	81	1980	383	819	.468	132	180	.733	96	140	236	297	197	4	141	36	904	11.2	35
O'Koren	79	2473	365	751	.486	155	212	.637	179	299	478	252	243	8	86	27	870	11.0	28
McAdoo (Tot.)	16	321	68	157	.433	29	41	.707	17	50	69	30	38	0	17	13	165	10.3	17
McAdoo	10	153	38	75	.507	17	21	.810	8	18	26	16	22	0	9	6	93	9.3	17
Jones	60	950	189	357	.529	146	218	.670	92	171	263	43	185	4	36	81	524	8.7	27
Elliott	73	1320	214	419	.511	121	202	.599	104	157	261	129	175	3	34	16	550	7.5	22
Moore	71	1406	212	478	.444	69	92	.750	43	125	168	228	179	1	61	17	497	7.0	19
Walker	41	172	72	169	.426	88	111	.793	22	80	102	253	105	0	52	1	234	5.7	25
van B. Kolff	78	1426	100	245	.408	98	117	.838	48	154	202	129	214	3	38	50	300	3.8	11
Sparrow	15	212	22	63	.349	12	16	.750	7	11	18	32	15	0	13	3	56	3.7	14
*Jordan	14	239	30	73	.411	24	32	.750	5	13	18	46	29	0	24	1	87	6.2	14

3-Pt. FG: New Jersey 34-138 (.246)–Newlin 10-30 (.333); Robinson 1-1 (1.000); Lucas 0-2 (.000); Gminski 0-1 (.000); Cook 6-25 (240); O'Koren 5-18 (.278); McAdoo 0-1 (.000); Jones 0-4 (.000); Elliott 1-2 (.500); Moore 4-27 (.148); Walker 2-9 (.222); van Breda Kolff 2-8 (.250); Jordan 3-10 (.300). Opponents 28-130 (.215).

1980-81 STATISTICS

NEW YORK

Player	G.	Min.	FGM	FGA	Pct.	FTM	FTA	Pct.	Off. Reb.	Def. Reb.	Tot. Reb.	Ast.	PF	Dsq.	Stl.	Blk. Sh.	Pts.	Avg.	Hi.
Cartwright	82	2925	619	1118	.554	408	518	.788	161	452	613	111	259	2	48	83	1646	20.1	33
R. Williams	79	2742	616	1335	.461	312	382	.817	122	199	321	432	270	4	185	37	1560	19.7	42
Richardson	79	3175	523	1116	.469	224	338	.663	173	372	545	627	258	2	232	35	1293	16.4	28
Russell	79	2865	508	1095	.464	268	343	.781	109	244	353	257	248	2	99	8	1292	16.4	36
S. Williams	67	1976	349	708	.493	185	268	.690	159	257	416	180	199	0	116	18	885	13.2	27
Glenn	82	1506	285	511	.558	98	110	.891	27	61	88	108	126	0	72	5	672	8.2	29
Webster	82	1708	159	341	.466	104	163	.638	162	303	465	72	187	2	27	97	423	5.2	16
Scales	44	484	94	225	.418	26	39	.667	47	85	132	10	54	0	12	4	215	4.9	20
Woodson	81	949	165	373	.442	49	64	.766	33	64	97	75	95	0	36	12	380	4.7	25
Demic	76	964	128	254	.504	58	92	.630	114	129	243	28	153	0	12	13	314	4.1	17
Carter	60	536	59	179	.330	51	69	.739	30	39	69	76	68	0	22	2	169	2.8	11

3-Pt. FG: New York 56-236 (.237)—Cartwright 0-1 (.000); R. Williams 16-68 (.235); Richardson 23-102 (.225); Russell 8-26 (.308); S. Williams 2-8 (.250); Glenn 4-11 (.364); Webster 1-4 (.250); Scales 1-6 (.167); Woodson 1-5 (.200); Demic 0-2 (.000); Carter 0-3 (.000). Opponents 43-172 (.250).

PHILADELPHIA

Player	G.	Min.	FGM	FGA	Pct.	FTM	FTA	Pct.	Off. Reb.	Def. Reb.	Tot. Reb.	Ast.	PF	Dsq.	Stl.	Blk. Sh.	Pts.	Avg.	Hi.
Erving	82	2874	794	1524	.521	422	536	.787	244	413	657	364	233	0	173	147	2014	24.6	45
Dawkins	76	2088	423	697	.607	219	304	.720	106	439	545	109	316	9	38	112	1065	14.0	26
B. Jones	81	2046	407	755	.539	282	347	.813	142	293	435	226	226	2	95	74	1096	13.5	26
Toney	75	1768	399	806	.495	161	226	.712	32	111	143	273	234	5	59	10	968	12.9	35
Collins	12	329	62	126	.492	24	29	.828	6	23	29	42	23	0	7	4	148	12.3	19
Mix	72	1327	288	575	.501	200	240	.833	105	159	264	114	107	0	59	18	776	10.8	28
Hollins	82	2154	327	696	.470	125	171	.731	47	144	191	352	205	2	104	18	781	9.5	23
Cheeks	81	2415	310	581	.534	140	178	.787	67	178	245	560	231	1	193	39	763	9.4	27
C. Jones	81	2639	218	485	.449	148	193	.767	200	613	813	122	271	2	53	134	584	7.2	15
Richardson	77	1313	227	464	.489	84	108	.778	83	93	176	152	102	0	36	10	538	7.0	19
Johnson	40	372	87	158	.551	27	31	.871	8	47	55	30	45	0	20	2	202	5.1	20
Cureton	52	528	93	205	.454	33	64	.516	51	104	155	25	68	0	20	23	219	4.2	16
*Davis	1	2	1	1	1.000	0	0		0	1	1	0	0	0	0	0	2	2.0	2

3-Pt. FG: Philadelphia 19-84 (.226)—Erving 4-18 (.222); B. Jones 0-3 (.000); Toney 9-29 (.310); Mix 0-3 (.000); Hollins 2-15 (.133); Cheeks 3-8 (.375); Richardson 0-1 (.000); Johnson 1-6 (.167); Cureton 0-1 (.000). Opponents 48-200 (.240).

PHOENIX

Player	G.	Min.	FGM	FGA	Pct.	FTM	FTA	Pct.	Off. Reb.	Def. Reb.	Tot. Reb.	Ast.	PF	Dsq.	Stl.	Blk. Sh.	Pts.	Avg.	Hi.
Robinson	82	3088	647	1280	.505	249	396	.629	216	573	789	206	220	1	68	38	1543	18.8	40
Johnson	79	2615	532	1220	.436	411	501	.820	160	203	363	291	244	2	136	61	1486	18.8	39
Davis	78	2182	593	1101	.539	209	250	.836	6	137	200	302	192	3	97	12	1402	18.0	32
Adams	75	2054	458	870	.526	199	259	.768	157	389	546	344	226	2	106	69	1115	14.9	31
Cook	79	2192	286	616	.464	100	155	.645	170	297	467	201	236	3	82	54	672	8.5	16
High	81	1750	246	576	.427	183	264	.693	89	139	228	202	251	2	129	26	677	8.4	20
Macy	82	1469	272	532	.511	107	119	.899	44	88	132	160	120	0	76	5	663	8.1	21
Kelley	81	1686	196	387	.506	175	231	.758	131	310	441	282	210	0	79	63	567	7.0	17
Scott	82	1423	173	348	.497	97	127	.764	101	167	268	114	124	0	60	70	444	5.4	14
Kramer	82	1065	136	258	.527	63	91	.692	77	155	232	88	132	0	35	17	335	4.1	17
Niles	44	231	48	138	.348	17	37	.459	26	32	58	15	41	0	8	1	115	2.6	10

3-Pt. FG: Phoenix 35-161 (.217)—Johnson 11-51 (.216); Davis 7-17 (.412); Cook 0-5 (.000); High 2-24 (.083); Macy 12-51 (.235); Kelley 0-2 (.000); Scott 1-6 (.167); Kramer 0-1 (.000); Niles 2-4 (.500). Opponents 69-209 (.330).

PORTLAND

Player	G.	Min.	FGM	FGA	Pct.	FTM	FTA	Pct.	Off. Reb.	Def. Reb.	Tot. Reb.	Ast.	PF	Dsq.	Stl.	Blk. Sh.	Pts.	Avg.	Hi.
Paxson	79	2701	585	1092	.536	182	248	.734	74	137	211	299	172	1	140	9	1354	17.1	32
Thompson	79	2790	569	1151	.494	207	323	.641	223	463	686	284	260	5	62	170	1345	17.0	33
Ransey	80	2431	525	1162	.452	164	219	.749	42	153	195	555	201	1	88	9	1217	15.2	35
Bates	77	1560	439	902	.487	170	199	.854	71	86	157	196	120	0	82	6	1062	13.8	40
Natt	74	2111	395	794	.497	200	283	.707	149	282	431	159	188	2	73	18	994	13.4	29
Washington	73	2120	325	571	.569	181	288	.628	236	450	686	149	258	5	85	86	831	11.4	27
Owens	79	1843	322	630	.511	191	250	.764	165	291	456	140	273	10	36	47	835	10.6	27
Gross	82	1934	253	479	.528	135	159	.849	126	202	328	251	238	5	90	67	641	7.8	17
Gale (Tot.)	77	1112	157	309	.508	55	68	.809	16	83	99	169	117	0	94	7	371	4.8	19
Gale (Port.)	42	476	71	145	.490	36	42	.857	9	38	47	70	61	0	39	5	179	4.3	19
Kunnert	55	842	101	216	.468	42	54	.778	98	189	287	67	143	1	17	32	244	4.4	19
Harper	55	461	56	136	.412	37	85	.435	28	65	93	17	73	0	23	20	149	2.7	12
Crompton	6	33	4	8	.500	1	5	.200	7	11	18	2	4	0	0	4	9	1.5	6
*Brewer	29	548	95	246	.386	26	34	.765	13	20	33	55	42	0	34	9	217	7.5	26
*Hamilton	1	5	1	3	.333	2	2	.500	2	1	3	0	1	0	0	0	3	3.0	3

SAN ANTONIO

Player	G.	Min.	FGM	FGA	Pct.	FTM	FTA	Pct.	Off. Reb.	Def. Reb.	Tot. Reb.	Ast.	PF	Dsq.	Stl.	Blk. Sh.	Pts.	Avg.	Hi.
Gervin	82	2765	850	1729	.492	512	620	.826	126	293	419	260	212	4	94	56	2221	27.1	49
Silas	75	2055	476	997	.477	374	440	.850	44	187	231	285	129	0	51	12	1326	17.7	34
Olberding	82	2408	348	685	.508	315	380	.829	146	325	471	277	307	6	75	31	1012	12.3	28
Corzine	82	1960	366	747	.490	125	175	.714	228	408	636	117	212	0	42	99	857	10.5	24
R. Johnson	79	1716	340	682	.499	128	193	.663	132	226	358	78	283	8	45	48	808	10.2	27
Brewer (Tot.)	75	1452	275	631	.436	91	114	.798	34	52	86	148	95	0	61	34	642	8.6	26
Brewer (S.A.)	46	904	180	385	.468	65	80	.813	21	32	53	93	53	0	27	25	425	9.2	20
Moore	82	1578	249	520	.479	105	172	.610	58	138	196	373	178	0	120	22	604	7.4	22
Restani	64	999	192	369	.520	62	88	.705	71	103	174	81	103	0	16	14	449	7.0	22
Griffin	82	1930	166	325	.511	170	253	.672	184	321	505	249	207	3	77	38	502	6.1	12
Wiley	33	271	76	138	.551	36	48	.750	22	42	64	11	38	1	8	6	188	5.7	17
Restani																			
G. Johnson	82	1935	164	347	.473	80	109	.734	215	387	602	92	273	3	47	278	408	5.0	15
*Shumate	22	519	56	128	.438	53	73	.726	33	54	87	24	46	0	21	9	165	7.5	15
*Gale	35	636	86	164	.524	19	26	.731	7	45	52	99	56	0	55	2	192	5.5	15
*Gerard (Tot.)	27	252	41	111	.369	27	40	.675	30	37	67	15	41	0	10	9	109	4.0	12
*Gerard (S.A.)	11	129	22	60	.367	8	11	.727	17	21	38	9	17	0	7	3	52	4.7	12

3-Pt. FG: San Antonio 15-85 (.176)—Gervin 9-35 (.257); Silas 0-2 (.000); Olberding 1-7 (.143); Corzine 0-3 (.000); R. Johnson 0-1 (.000); Brewer (Tot.) 1-7 (.143); Brewer (S.A.) 0-4 (.000); Moore 1-19 (.053); Restani 3-8 (.375); Wiley 0-2 (.000); Gale 1-3 (.333); Gerard (Tot.) 0-3 (.000); Gerard (S.A.) 0-1 (.000). Opponents 45-168 (.268).

SAN DIEGO

Player	G.	Min.	FGM	FGA	Pct.	FTM	FTA	Pct.	Off. Reb.	Def. Reb.	Tot. Reb.	Ast.	PF	Dsq.	Stl.	Blk. Sh.	Pts.	Avg.	Hi.
Williams	82	1976	642	1381	.465	253	297	.852	75	54	129	164	157	0	91	5	1585	19.3	41
Smith	76	2378	519	1057	.491	237	313	.757	49	107	156	372	231	1	84	18	1279	16.8	35
Nater	82	2809	517	935	.553	244	307	.795	295	722	1017	199	295	8	49	46	1278	15.6	30
Brooks	82	2479	488	1018	.479	226	320	.706	210	232	442	208	234	2	99	31	1202	14.7	35
Bryant	82	2359	379	791	.479	193	244	.791	146	294	440	189	264	4	72	34	953	11.6	34
Taylor	80	2312	310	591	.525	146	185	.789	58	93	151	440	212	0	118	23	810	10.1	31
Davis	64	817	139	314	.443	94	158	.595	47	72	119	47	98	0	36	11	374	5.8	18
Heard	78	1631	149	396	.376	79	101	.782	120	228	348	122	196	0	104	72	377	4.8	16
Bibby	73	1112	118	306	.386	67	98	.684	25	49	74	200	85	0	47	2	335	4.6	16
W'head (Tot.)	48	688	83	180	.461	28	56	.500	58	156	214	26	122	2	20	9	194	4.0	16
W'head (S.D.)	38	562	66	139	.475	23	45	.511	48	135	183	24	100	2	15	8	155	4.1	16
Rank	25	153	21	57	.368	13	28	.464	17	13	30	17	33	1	7	1	55	2.2	6
*Pietkiewicz	6	30	2	5	.400	0	0		0	1	1	2	2	0	0	0	4	0.7	2
*Wicks	49	1083	125	286	.437	76	150	.507	79	144	223	111	168	3	40	40	326	6.7	18
*Price	5	29	2	7	.286	0	0		0	3	3	0	3	0	2	1	4	0.8	2

3-Pt. FG: San Diego 132-407 (.324)—Williams 48-141 (.340); Smith 4-18 (.222); Brooks 0-6 (.000); Bryant 2-15 (.133); Taylor 44-115 (.383); Davis 2-8 (.250); Heard 0-7 (.000); Bibby 32-95 (.337); Whitehead (S.D.) 0-1 (.000); Wicks 0-1 (.000). Opponents 33-153 (.216).

SEATTLE

Player	G.	Min.	FGM	FGA	Pct.	FTM	FTA	Pct.	Off. Reb.	Def. Reb.	Tot. Reb.	Ast.	PF	Dsq.	Stl.	Blk. Sh.	Pts.	Avg.	Hi.
Sikma	82	2920	595	1311	.454	340	413	.823	184	668	852	248	282	5	78	93	1530	18.7	38
Westphal	36	1078	221	500	.442	153	184	.832	11	57	68	148	70	0	46	14	601	16.7	32
Brown	78	1986	505	1035	.488	173	208	.832	53	122	175	233	141	0	88	13	1206	15.5	28
Bailey	82	2539	444	889	.499	256	361	.709	192	415	607	98	332	0	74	143	1145	14.0	27
V. Johnson	81	2311	419	785	.534	214	270	.793	193	173	366	341	198	0	78	20	1053	13.0	30
Shelton	14	440	73	174	.420	36	55	.655	31	47	78	35	48	0	22	3	182	13.0	30
J. Johnson	80	2324	373	866	.431	173	214	.808	135	227	362	312	202	2	57	25	919	11.5	26
Walker	82	1796	290	626	.463	109	169	.645	105	210	315	122	168	1	53	15	689	8.4	21
Hanzlik	74	1259	138	289	.478	119	150	.793	67	86	153	111	168	1	58	20	396	5.4	21
Donaldson	68	980	129	238	.542	101	170	.594	107	202	309	42	79	0	8	74	359	5.3	20
Hill (Tot.)	75	1738	117	335	.349	141	172	.820	41	118	159	292	207	3	66	11	375	5.0	17
Hill (Sea.)	51	1114	78	219	.356	99	122	.811	31	77	108	174	147	3	40	8	255	5.0	17
Awtrey	47	607	44	93	.473	14	20	.700	33	75	108	14	108	0	9	1	102	2.2	8
Dorsey	29	253	20	70	.286	13	25	.520	23	65	88	9	47	0	9	1	53	1.8	8
*White (Tot.)	16	208	23	65	.354	15	16	.938	1	10	11	4	28	0	5	1	61	3.8	13
*White (Sea.)	12	165	14	47	.298	11	12	.917	1	10	11	18	16	0	5	1	39	3.3	13
*Shu'te (Tot)	24	527	56	131	.427	55	76	.724	34	54	88	24	49	0	21	9	167	7.0	15
*Shu'te (Sea.)	14	289	3	9	.000	2	3	.667	1	0	1	0	3	0	0	0	2	1.0	2

3-Pt. FG: Seattle 32-117 (.274)—Sikma 0-5 (.000); Westphal 6-25 (.240); Brown 23-64 (.359); Bailey 1-2 (.500); V. Johnson 1-5 (.200); J. Johnson 0-1 (.000); Walker 0-3 (.000); Hanzlik 1-5 (.200); Hill (Tot.) 0-7 (.000); Hill (Sea.) 0-6 (.000); White 0-1 (.000); Opponents 42-157 (.268).

UTAH

Player	G.	Min.	FGM	FGA	Pct.	FTM	FTA	Pct.	Off. Reb.	Def. Reb.	Tot. Reb.	Ast.	PF	Dsq.	Stl.	Blk. Sh.	Pts.	Avg.	Hi.
Dantley	80	3417	909	1627	.559	632	784	.806	192	317	509	322	245	1	109	18	2452	30.7	55
Griffith	81	2867	716	1544	.464	229	320	.716	79	209	288	194	219	0	106	50	1671	20.6	38
Poquette	82	2808	324	614	.528	126	162	.778	160	469	629	161	342	18	67	174	777	9.5	25
Green	47	1307	176	366	.481	70	97	.722	30	86	116	235	123	2	75	1	422	9.0	20
Bristow	82	2001	271	611	.444	166	198	.838	103	327	430	383	190	1	63	3	713	8.7	18
Cooper	71	1420	213	471	.452	62	90	.689	166	274	440	52	219	8	18	51	489	6.9	22
Nicks (Tot)	67	1109	172	359	.479	71	126	.563	37	73	110	149	141	0	60	3	415	6.2	24
Nicks (Utah)	40	616	107	210	.510	36	67	.537	24	37	61	69	89	0	32	1	250	6.3	24
Wilkins	56	1058	117	260	.450	27	40	.675	62	212	274	40	169	3	32	46	261	4.7	22
Judkins	62	666	92	216	.426	45	51	.882	29	64	93	59	84	0	16	2	238	3.8	13
Bennett	28	313	26	60	.433	53	81	.654	33	60	93	15	56	0	3	11	105	3.8	12
Duren	40	458	33	101	.327	5	9	.556	8	27	35	54	54	0	18	2	71	1.8	10
*McKinney	35	1032	124	233	.532	44	48	.917	12	62	74	157	107	3	38	4	293	8.4	21
*Boone	52	1146	160	371	.431	75	94	.798	17	67	84	161	126	0	33	8	406	7.8	18
*Hardy	23	509	52	111	.468	11	20	.550	39	94	133	36	58	2	21	20	115	5.0	13
*Vroman	11	93	10	27	.370	14	19	.737	7	18	25	9	26	1	5	5	34	3.1	9
*Miller (Tot)	8	53	4	9	.444	0	0		2	5	7	5	5	0	4	0	8	1.0	4
*Miller (Utah)	5	19	2	3	.667	0	0		1	2	3	2	3	1	3	0	4	1.3	4

3-Pt. FG: Utah 42-163 (.258)—Dantley 2-7 (.286); Griffith 10-52 (.192); Poquette 3-6 (.500); Green 0-1 (.000); Bristow 5-18 (.278); Cooper 1-3 (.333); Nicks (Tot) 0-4 (.000); Nicks (Utah) 0-3 (.000); Judkins 9-28 (.321); Bennett 0-2 (.000); Duren 0-1 (.000); McKinney 1-2 (.500); Boone 11-39 (.282); Vroman 0-1 (.000); Miller (Tot) 0-1 (.000). Opponents 45-147 (.306).

WASHINGTON

Player	G.	Min.	FGM	FGA	Pct.	FTM	FTA	Pct.	Off. Reb.	Def. Reb.	Tot. Reb.	Ast.	PF	Dsq.	Stl.	Blk. Sh.	Pts.	Avg.	Hi.
Hayes	81	2931	584	1296	.451	271	439	.617	235	554	789	98	300	6	68	171	1439	17.8	34
Grevey	75	2616	500	1103	.453	244	290	.841	67	152	219	300	161	1	68	17	1289	17.2	36
Ballard	82	2610	549	1186	.463	166	196	.847	167	413	580	195	194	1	118	39	1271	15.5	28
Porter	81	2577	446	859	.519	191	247	.773	35	89	124	734	257	4	110	10	1086	13.4	31
Kupchak	82	1934	392	747	.525	240	340	.706	198	371	569	62	195	1	36	26	1024	12.5	30
Dandridge	23	545	101	237	.426	28	39	.718	19	64	83	60	54	1	16	9	230	10.0	20
Collins (Tot)	81	1845	360	811	.444	211	272	.776	129	139	268	190	259	6	104	25	931	11.5	27
C'lins (Wash)	34	661	130	281	.463	74	110	.673	33	48	81	75	93	1	35	14	334	9.8	27
Unseld	63	2032	225	429	.524	55	86	.640	207	466	673	170	171	1	52	36	507	8.0	22
Terry	26	504	80	160	.500	28	42	.667	43	73	116	70	68	1	27	13	188	7.2	16
Roberts	26	350	54	144	.375	19	29	.655	18	50	68	20	52	0	11	0	127	4.9	18
Mahorn	52	696	111	219	.507	27	40	.675	67	148	215	25	134	3	21	44	249	4.8	28
Carr (Tot)	47	657	87	234	.372	34	54	.630	22	39	61	58	53	0	15	2	208	4.4	17
Carr (Wash)	39	580	80	206	.388	32	50	.640	18	34	52	49	43	0	14	2	192	4.9	17
McCarter	43	448	51	135	.378	18	24	.750	16	23	39	73	36	0	14	0	122	2.8	14
*Matthews	45	1161	224	449	.499	99	129	.767	30	37	67	199	120	1	46	10	552	12.3	24
*Williamson	9	112	18	56	.321	5	6	.833	0	7	7	17	13	0	4	1	42	4.7	12
*Britton	2	9	2	3	.667	0	0		0	2	2	3	2	0	1	0	4	2.0	4
*McCord	2	9	2	4	.500	0	0		1	1	2	1	0	0	0	0	4	2.0	2
*Brown	2	5	0	3	.000	2	5	.400	1	1	2	0	2	0	0	0	2	1.0	2

3-Pt. FG: Washington 65-241 (.270)—Hayes 0-10 (.000); Grevey 45-136 (.331); Ballard 7-32 (.219); Porter 3-12 (.250); Kupchak 0-1 (.000); Dandridge 0-1 (.000); Collins (Tot) 0-6 (.000); Collins (Wash) 0-3 (.000); Unseld 2-4 (.500); Carlos 0-6 (.000); Carr 0-7 (.000); McCarter 2-8 (.250); Matthews 5-15 (.333); Williamson 1-6 (.167). Opponents 37-176 (.210).

HOME-ROAD RECORDS OF NBA TEAMS

EASTERN CONFERENCE

Atlantic Division	Home	Road
Boston	35-6	27-14
New Jersey	16-25	8-33
New York	28-13	22-19
Philadelphia	37-4	25-16
Washington	26-15	13-28

Central Division	Home	Road
Atlanta	20-21	11-30
Chicago	26-15	19-22
Cleveland	20-21	8-33
Detroit	14-27	7-34
Indiana	27-14	17-24
Milwaukee	34-7	26-15

WESTERN CONFERENCE

Midwest Division	Home	Road
Dallas	11-30	4-37
Denver	23-18	14-27
Houston	25-16	15-26
Kansas City	24-17	16-25
San Antonio	34-7	18-23
Utah	20-21	8-33

Pacific Division	Home	Road
Golden State	26-15	13-28
Los Angeles	30-11	24-17
Phoenix	36-5	21-20
Portland	30-11	15-26
San Diego	22-19	14-27
Seattle	22-19	12-29

TOP 1980-81 PERFORMANCES

MOST POINTS SCORED IN A GAME

	FG.	FT.	Pts.
Adrian Dantley, Utah vs. Denver, February 6, 1981	24	7	55
Billy Knight, Indiana at San Antonio, November 11, 1980	19	14	52
Adrian Dantley, Utah at Denver, January 7, 1981	20	11	51
Moses Malone, Houston vs. Golden State, March 11, 1981	20	11	51
Adrian Dantley, Utah vs. Dallas, October 31, 1980	12	26	50
Bernard King, Golden State vs. Philadelphia, January 3, 1981	20	10	50
George Gervin, San Antonio vs. Boston, February 17, 1981	17	15	49
Mike Dunleavy, Houston vs. Denver, December 6, 1980	19	10	48
Adrian Dantley, Utah vs. Dallas, March 18, 1981	17	14	48
John Drew, Atlanta vs. Boston, December 27, 1980	18	11	47
Joe Barry Carroll, Golden State vs. San Diego, February 20, 1981	17	12	46
Julius Erving, Philadelphia vs. Boston, November 1, 1980	*16	13	45
Adrian Dantley, Utah at Golden State, January 14, 1981	15	15	45
Purvis Short, Golden State at Dallas, March 12, 1981	18	7	45
David Thompson, Denver vs. Cleveland, March 1, 1981	18	8	44
David Thompson, Denver vs. Seattle, November 1, 1980	17	9	43
Adrian Dantley, Utah vs. Houston, November 14, 1980	16	11	43
Mike Newlin, New Jersey vs. San Diego, February 4, 1981	13	16	43
David Thompson, Denver at Los Angeles, March 29, 1981	*17	9	43
Adrian Dantley, Utah vs. Denver, October 18, 1980	16	9	42
George Gervin, San Antonio at Golden State, November 1, 1980	16	10	42
Otis Birdsong, Kansas City vs. Houston, December 5, 1980	19	4	42
Ray Williams, New York vs. Washington, December 9, 1980	16	9	42
Kareem Abdul-Jabbar, Los Angeles vs. San Antonio, December 21, 1980	15	12	42
Calvin Murphy, Houston vs. Denver, January 3, 1981	16	10	42
Mike Mitchell, Cleveland at New Jersey, February 18, 1981	19	4	42
Bernard King, Golden State vs. San Antonio, February 24, 1981	17	7	42
Alex English, Denver at Kansas City, March 18, 1981	**17	8	42
Moses Malone, Houston at Denver, October 21, 1980	12	17	41
Moses Malone, Houston at Seattle, November 15, 1980	*15	11	41
George Gervin, San Antonio at Portland, December 7, 1980	17	7	41
Freeman Williams, San Diego at Kansas City, December 10, 1980	15	10	41
Moses Malone, Houston vs. Chicago, January 14, 1981	17	7	41
Mike Mitchell, Cleveland vs. Detroit, February 17, 1981	19	3	41
Earvin Johnson, Los Angeles at Utah, March 18, 1981	*17	7	41
Scott Wedman, Kansas City vs. Denver, March 18, 1981	**18	4	41
Marques Johnson, Milwaukee vs. Indiana, November 2, 1980	17	6	40
David Thompson, Denver at Phoenix, November 23, 1980	15	10	40
Kareem Abdul-Jabbar, Los Angeles at Golden State, November 27, 1980	15	10	40
Moses Malone, Houston at San Antonio, November 28, 1980	14	12	40
Adrian Dantley, Utah vs. Denver, December 4, 1980	14	12	40
Len Robinson, Phoenix at Chicago, December 9, 1980	18	4	40
Eddie Johnson, Atlanta at Portland, December 20, 1980	*16	8	40
Moses Malone, Houston at Dallas, January 2, 1981	*13	14	40
Adrian Dantley, Utah vs. Dallas, January 8, 1981	17	6	40
John Long, Detroit at San Antonio, February 3, 1981	17	5	40
Robert Parish, Boston at San Antonio, February 17, 1981	15	10	40
Adrian Dantley, Utah vs. New Jersey, February 25, 1981	12	16	40
Billy Ray Bates, Portland at San Diego, March 29, 1981	16	6	40

MOST FIELD GOALS IN A GAME

	FGA	FGM
Adrian Dantley, Utah vs. Denver, February 6, 1981	36	24
Bernard King, Golden State vs. Philadelphia, January 3, 1981	25	20
Adrian Dantley, Utah at Denver, January 7, 1981	25	20
Moses Malone, Houston vs. Golden State, March 11, 1981	28	20
Billy Knight, Indiana vs. San Antonio, November 11, 1980	30	19
Otis Birdsong, Kansas City vs. Houston, December 5, 1980	25	19
Mike Dunleavy, Houston vs. Denver, December 6, 1980	30	19
Mike Mitchell, Cleveland vs. Detroit, February 17, 1981	23	19
Mike Mitchell, Cleveland at New Jersey, February 18, 1981	36	19
Otis Birdsong, Kansas City at San Antonio, March 4, 1981	25	19
Len Robinson, Phoenix at Chicago, December 9, 1980	25	18
John Drew, Atlanta vs. Boston, December 27, 1980	32	18
Bernard King, Golden State vs. Detroit, January 10, 1981	24	18
David Thompson, Denver vs. Cleveland, March 1, 1981	28	18
Purvis Short, Golden State at Dallas, March 12, 1981	30	18
Scott Wedman, Kansas City vs. Denver, March 18, 1981	*27	18

MOST FREE THROWS IN A GAME

	FTA.	FTM.
Adrian Dantley, Utah vs. Dallas, October 31, 1980	29	26
Jack Sikma, Seattle vs. Kansas City, November 14, 1980	23	21
Lloyd Free, Golden State at Milwaukee, February 13, 1981	20	18
David Thompson, Denver at Philadelphia, March 6, 1981	19	18
Moses Malone, Houston at Denver, October 21, 1980	21	17
Foots Walker, New Jersey at New York, October 25, 1980	18	17
John Drew, Atlanta at Cleveland, November 13, 1980	21	17
Lloyd Free, Golden State vs. Utah, January 14, 1981	18	17
Adrian Dantley, Utah at Denver, October 12, 1980	*18	16
John Drew, Atlanta vs. New Jersey, December 16, 1980	18	16
Mike Newlin, New Jersey vs. San Diego, February 4, 1981	17	16
Adrian Dantley, Utah vs. New Jersey, February 25, 1981	22	16
Reggie Theus, Chicago at Philadelphia, March 4, 1981	18	16
Earvin Johnson, Los Angeles vs. Seattle, March 20, 1981	21	16
Steve Hawes, Atlanta vs. Milwaukee, March 29, 1981	*17	16

MOST REBOUNDS IN A GAME

	Off.	Def.	Tot.
Larry Smith, Golden State vs. Denver, March 28, 1981	14	17	31
Moses Malone, Houston at Denver, October 21, 1980	8	18	26
Moses Malone, Houston vs. Kansas City, October 23, 1980	10	16	26
Moses Malone, Houston vs. Denver, February 3, 1981	*8	18	26
Larry Smith, Golden State vs. Portland, February 4, 1981	13	12	25
Caldwell Jones, Philadelphia vs. Cleveland, February 11, 1981	*7	18	25
Larry Smith, Golden State vs. Los Angeles, March 22, 1981	9	15	24
Larry Smith, Golden State vs. San Diego, March 25, 1981	13	11	24
Sidney Wicks, San Diego vs. Houston, October 10, 1980	6	17	23
Larry Smith, Golden State at Portland, March 8, 1981	*10	13	23
Moses Malone, Houston vs. Denver, March 15, 1981	13	10	23
Larry Smith, Golden State vs. Denver, October 29, 1980	8	14	22
Larry Smith, Golden State vs. Indiana, November 8, 1980	10	12	22
Larry Smith, Golden State at Denver, February 7, 1981	6	16	22
Bill Laimbeer, Cleveland vs. San Antonio, February 19, 1981	7	15	22
Moses Malone, Houston at Dallas, March 24, 1981	*9	13	22
Moses Malone, Houston vs. Dallas, October 29, 1980	9	12	21
Larry Bird, Boston at Philadelphia, November 1, 1980	*8	13	21
Artis Gilmore, Chicago vs. Denver, November 8, 1980	**9	12	21
James Bailey, Seattle vs. Los Angeles, December 12, 1980	7	14	21
Moses Malone, Houston vs. Denver, December 30, 1980	8	13	21
Dan Issel, Denver vs. San Antonio, January 24, 1981	12	9	21
Robert Parish, Boston at Seattle, February 10, 1981	*6	15	21
Larry Bird, Boston at Los Angeles, February 11, 1981	5	16	21
Moses Malone, Houston at Los Angeles, February 20, 1981	7	14	21
Phil Hubbard, Detroit vs. Cleveland, February 27, 1981	3	18	21
Joe Barry Carroll, Golden State vs. San Antonio, March 15, 1981	*12	9	21
Jack Sikma, Seattle vs. Phoenix, October 25, 1980	7	13	20
Dan Roundfield, Atlanta vs. Milwaukee, November 1, 1980	7	13	20
Mike Gminski, New Jersey vs. Atlanta, November 8, 1980	5	15	20
Wes Unseld, Washington vs. Denver, November 11, 1980	7	13	20
Kareem Abdul-Jabbar, Los Angeles vs. Phoenix, November 21, 1980	9	11	20
Swen Nater, San Diego vs. Denver, November 25, 1980	4	16	20
Kenny Carr, Cleveland vs. Washington, November 28, 1980	3	17	20
Swen Nater, San Diego at Seattle, November 28, 1980	4	16	20
Larry Smith, Golden State at Denver, December 5, 1980	8	12	20
Artis Gilmore, Chicago vs. Utah, December 12, 1980	8	12	20
Larry Bird, Boston at Chicago, December 13, 1980	2	18	20
Larry Bird, Boston at Cleveland, December 20, 1980	6	14	20
Larry Bird, Boston at New York, December, 25, 1980	3	17	20
Swen Nater, San Diego vs. Atlanta, January 14, 1981	4	16	20
Caldwell Jones, Philadelphia vs. Boston, February 4, 1981	7	13	20
Kenny Carr, Cleveland vs. New York, February 12, 1981	11	9	20
Swen Nater, San Diego at Portland, February 24, 1981	4	16	20
Caldwell Jones, Philadelphia at Milwaukee, March 8, 1981	10	10	20
Reggie King, Kansas City vs. Phoenix, March 8, 1981	3	17	20
Swen Nater, San Diego at Seattle, March 8, 1981	6	14	20
Mitch Kupchak, Washington vs. New York, March 25, 1981	7	13	20

MOST ASSISTS IN A GAME

	Ast.
John Lucas, Golden State at Denver, February 27, 1981	22
Johnny Moore, San Antonio vs. Washington, January 11, 1981	19
John Lucas, Golden State at New Jersey, February 15, 1981	19
Kevin Porter, Washington vs. New York, February 25, 1981	19
Michael Ray Richardson, New York vs. Cleveland, March 21, 1981	19
Ray Williams, New York at Milwaukee, November 14, 1980	18
Norm Nixon, Los Angeles vs. Portland, January 26, 1981	18
Kevin Porter, Washington at Golden State, February 6, 1981	18
Wes Matthews, Atlanta vs. Seattle, March 1, 1981	18
Kevin Porter, Washington vs. Cleveland, March 29, 1981	18
Kevin Porter, Washington at New Jersey, January 25, 1981	17
Kevin Porter, Washington at Phoenix, February 8, 1981	*17
Kevin Porter, Washington at Denver, February 10, 1981	17
Kevin Porter, Washington vs. New York, March 25, 1981	17
Earvin Johnson, Los Angeles vs. Denver, March 29, 1981	*17
Ray Williams, New York at Philadelphia, November 12, 1980	16
Foots Walker, New Jersey vs. Utah, November 28, 1980	16
Phil Ford, Kansas City vs. Houston, December 5, 1980	16
Phil Ford, Kansas City at Denver, December 16, 1980	16
Phil Ford, Kansas City at Cleveland, December 23, 1980	16
Kevin Porter, Washington at Portland, February 3, 1981	*16
Brad Davis, Dallas at Kansas City, February 26, 1981	16
Brad Davis, Dallas vs. Los Angeles, March 17, 1981	16
Kevin Porter, Washington vs. Detroit, March 28, 1981	16
Ken Higgs, Denver at Los Angeles, March 29, 1981	*16
Norm Nixon, Los Angeles at San Antonio, November 8, 1980	15
Norm Nixon, Los Angeles at San Antonio, January 2, 1981	15
John Lucas, Golden State vs. Detroit, January 10, 1981	15
Kevin Porter, Washington vs. Los Angeles, January 14, 1981	15
Kevin Porter, Washington at Detroit, January 15, 1981	15
Darwin Cook, New Jersey vs. Chicago, February 11, 1981	*15
Kevin Porter, Washington vs. Philadelphia, February 19, 1981	15
Kevin Porter, Washington at New York, February 20, 1981	15
Kevin Porter, Washington at San Diego, March 4, 1981	15
Wes Matthews, Atlanta vs. Chicago, March 10, 1981	15
Phil Smith, San Diego vs. Golden State, March 19, 1981	15
Kevin Porter, Washington at Boston, March 20, 1981	15
Norm Nixon, Los Angeles at Portland, March 21, 1981	15
Norm Nixon, Los Angeles at Golden State, March 22, 1981	15
Wes Matthews, Atlanta vs. Milwaukee, March 29, 1981	*15

MOST STEALS IN A GAME

	Stl.
Dudley Bradley, Indiana at Utah, November 10, 1980	9
Dudley Bradley, Indiana vs. Cleveland, November 29, 1980	9
Michael Ray Richardson, New York at Chicago, December 23, 1980	9
Johnny High, Phoenix at Washington, January 28, 1981	9
Randy Smith, Cleveland vs. Detroit, October 14, 1980	8
Earvin Johnson, Los Angeles at Dallas, November 7, 1980	8
John Drew, Atlanta at Philadelphia, December 5, 1980	8
Michael Ray Richardson, New York vs. San Antonio, January 6, 1981	8
Robert Reid, Houston at Phoenix, January 16, 1981	8
Jim Spanarkel, Dallas vs. Phoenix, March 10, 1981	8

MOST BLOCKED SHOTS IN A GAME

	Blk.
George Johnson, San Antonio vs. Golden State, February 24, 1981	13
Ben Poquette, Utah at Chicago, December 12, 1980	10
Artis Gilmore, Chicago vs. Detroit, December 7, 1980	9
Mychal Thompson, Portland at New Jersey, February 20, 1981	*9
Artis Gilmore, Chicago vs. Atlanta, March 27, 1981	9
Wayne Rollins, Atlanta vs. Detroit, November 29, 1980	8
Elvin Hayes, Washington vs. Detroit, December 5, 1980	8
Wayne Rollins, Atlanta vs. Indiana, January 2, 1981	8
Mike Gminski, New Jersey at Milwaukee, January 8, 1981	8
Kareem Abdul-Jabbar, Los Angeles vs. Denver, January 23, 1981	8
George Johnson, San Antonio vs. Denver, March 24, 1981	8

NBA WORLD CHAMPIONSHIP SERIES

BOSTON VS. HOUSTON

Player	G.	Min.	FGM	FGA	Pct.	FTM	FTA	Pct.	Off. Reb.	Def. Reb.	Tot. Reb.	Ast.	PF	Dsq.	Stl.	Blk. Sh.	Pts.	Avg.	Hi.
Maxwell	6	227	42	74	.568	22	29	.759	34	23	57	17	21	0	1	6	106	17.7	28
Bird	6	257	39	93	.419	13	16	.813	16	76	92	42	16	0	14	3	92	15.3	27
Parish	6	167	39	77	.506	12	19	.632	16	30	46	6	27	1	7	12	90	15.0	18
Ford	6	184	27	54	.500	7	9	.778	7	9	16	15	11	0	4	0	63	10.5	17
Archibald	6	203	24	66	.364	14	16	.875	1	6	7	33	11	0	4	0	62	10.3	13
Robey	6	98	19	34	.559	9	16	.563	5	17	22	2	18	0	0	1	47	7.8	14
Henderson	6	95	19	36	.528	5	6	.833	5	5	10	10	10	0	4	2	43	7.2	12
Carr	6	110	17	37	.459	6	8	.750	5	5	10	6	10	0	4	4	40	6.7	11
McHale	6	83	12	31	.387	4	7	.571	10	10	20	5	13	0	0	4	28	4.7	12
Duerod	4	6	3	7	.429	0	0	.....	0	0	0	0	0	0	1	0	6	1.5	4
Fernsten	4	10	0	3	.000	2	3	.667	1	3	4	1	2	0	1	0	2	0.5	2

3-Pt. FG: Boston 3-17 (.176) – Bird 1-3 (.333); Ford 2-10 (.200); Archibald 0-2 (.000); Henderson 0-1 (.000); Duerod 0-1 (.000).

HOUSTON VS. BOSTON

Player	G.	Min.	FGM	FGA	Pct.	FTM	FTA	Pct.	Off. Reb.	Def. Reb.	Tot. Reb.	Ast.	PF	Dsq.	Stl.	Blk. Sh.	Pts.	Avg.	Hi.
Malone	6	269	48	119	.403	38	55	.691	46	48	94	8	11	0	5	13	134	22.3	31
Reid	6	244	36	96	.375	16	23	.696	23	22	45	19	24	0	12	5	88	14.7	27
Paultz	6	196	31	77	.403	5	8	.625	13	23	36	8	16	0	7	4	67	11.2	14
Dunleavy	6	165	22	53	.415	12	15	.800	4	10	14	19	18	1	2	1	59	9.8	28
Murphy	4	88	17	43	.395	5	6	.833	1	3	4	3	10	0	4	0	39	9.8	16
Willoughby	6	134	14	52	.269	17	23	.739	13	14	27	7	16	0	7	6	45	7.5	14
Henderson	6	193	15	38	.395	10	13	.769	5	8	13	25	9	0	4	1	40	6.7	11
Leavell	5	73	10	33	.303	5	7	.714	3	4	7	17	9	0	3	3	25	5.0	10
Garrett	4	43	5	9	.556	2	2	1.000	1	6	7	1	3	0	2	0	12	3.0	8
Jones	3	18	4	8	.500	1	3	.333	1	4	5	1	4	0	1	1	9	3.0	7
Tomjanovich	3	17	1	8	.125	0	0	.....	2	2	4	0	4	0	0	0	2	0.7	2

3-Pt. FG: Houston 3-11 (.273) – Reid 0-1 (.000); Paultz 0-1 (.000); Dunleavy 3-7 (.429); Tomjanovich 0-2 (.000).

Player	G.	Min.	FGM	FGA	Pct.	FTM	FTA	Pct.	Off. Reb.	Def. Reb.	Tot. Reb.	Ast.	PF	Dsq.	Stl.	Blk. Sh.	Pts.	Avg.	Hi.
BOSTON	6	1440	241	512	.471	94	129	.729	100	184	284	137	139	1	40	32	579	96.5	109
HOUSTON	6	1440	203	536	.379	111	155	.716	112	144	256	108	121	1	47	34	520	86.7	95

FINAL NBA PLAYOFF STATISTICS

TEAM STATISTICS—OFFENSE

Team	G.	FIELD GOALS Made	Att.	Pct.	FREE THROWS Made	Att.	Pct.	REBOUNDS Off.	Def.	Tot.	Ast.	MISCELLANEOUS PF	Dq.	Stl.	Turn Over	Blk. Sh.	SCORING Pts.	Avg.
San Antonio	7	298	608	.490	156	206	.746	100	196	296	180	173	6	41	107	47	754	107.7
Milwaukee	7	292	611	.478	162	212	.764	124	179	303	189	195	2	71	119	37	749	107.0
Portland	3	134	276	.486	47	70	.671	42	96	138	65	61	0	31	53	16	316	105.3
Philadelphia	16	637	1309	.487	394	510	.773	205	449	654	389	420	4	131	293	137	1669	104.3
Chicago	6	248	529	.469	122	160	.763	99	168	267	125	150	1	47	99	30	621	103.5
Boston	17	700	1457	.481	347	460	.754	246	509	755	388	420	3	127	277	112	1757	103.4
Los Angeles	3	118	255	.463	68	99	.687	43	110	153	72	69	1	21	43	17	304	101.3
Houston	21	819	1796	.456	413	550	.751	309	547	856	474	466	4	174	296	113	2059	98.0
New York	2	79	171	.439	43	63	.683	31	52	83	37	57	1	20	42	4	194	97.0
Indiana	2	75	182	.412	41	57	.719	37	56	93	46	51	0	22	39	5	193	96.5
Phoenix	7	252	561	.449	132	192	.688	99	218	317	133	167	1	50	115	26	642	91.7
Kansas City	15	554	1190	.466	254	354	.718	178	415	593	353	349	6	132	252	64	1375	91.7

TEAM STATISTICS—DEFENSE

Team	FIELD GOALS Made	Att.	Pct.	FREE THROWS Made	Att.	Pct.	REBOUNDS Off.	Def.	Tot.	Ast.	MISCELLANEOUS PF	Dq.	Stl.	Turn Over	Blk. Sh.	SCORING Pts.	Avg.	Dif.
Phoenix	236	554	.426	146	206	.709	95	192	287	146	172	3	62	112	34	623	89.0	+ 2.7
Kansas City	580	1226	.473	255	366	.697	204	453	657	307	326	1	133	248	65	1423	94.9	– 3.2
Boston	645	1471	.438	357	473	.755	261	457	718	356	412	2	122	261	103	1654	97.3	+ 6.1
Houston	835	1743	.479	389	534	.728	293	616	909	508	490	9	148	341	117	2068	98.5	– 0.5
Los Angeles	122	285	.428	61	77	.792	55	93	148	79	73	1	21	36	19	306	102.0	– 0.7
New York	79	166	.476	47	56	.839	31	66	97	39	52	1	19	47	17	205	102.5	– 5.5
Milwaukee	272	564	.482	187	239	.782	100	169	269	171	175	3	62	133	62	731	104.4	+ 2.6
Philadelphia	646	1413	.457	373	497	.751	265	440	705	388	434	4	147	263	93	1671	104.4	– 0.1
Portland	140	268	.522	37	51	.725	33	97	130	88	68	2	24	51	9	321	107.0	– 1.7

1980-81 PLAYOFF STATISTICS

Team	FIELD GOALS Made	Att.	Pct.	FREE THROWS Made	Att.	Pct.	REBOUNDS Off.	Def.	Tot.	Ast.	MISCELLANEOUS PF	Dq.	Stl.	Turn Over	Blk. Sh.	SCORING Pts.	Avg.	Dif.
Chicago	255	496	.514	126	166	.759	73	172	245	135	150	1	53	112	33	643	107.2	– 3.7
San Antonio	300	586	.512	165	214	.771	79	171	250	178	174	2	54	98	37	768	109.7	– 2.0
Indiana	92	173	.532	36	57	.632	24	69	93	56	52	0	22	40	19	220	110.0	– 13.5

BOSTON

Player	G.	Min.	FGM	FGA	Pct.	FTM	FTA	Pct.	Off. Reb.	Def. Reb.	Tot. Reb.	Ast.	PF	Dsq.	Stl.	Blk. Sh.	Pts.	Avg.	Hi.
Bird	17	750	147	313	.470	76	85	.894	49	189	238	103	53	0	39	17	373	21.9	35
Maxwell	17	598	101	174	.580	72	88	.818	61	64	125	46	53	0	12	16	274	16.1	28
Archibald	17	630	95	211	.450	76	94	.809	6	22	28	107	39	0	13	0	266	15.6	27
Parish	17	492	108	219	.493	39	58	.672	50	96	146	19	74	2	21	39	255	15.0	27
Ford	17	507	66	146	.452	15	25	.600	13	32	45	46	47	0	14	1	154	9.1	17
McHale	17	296	61	113	.540	23	36	.639	29	30	59	14	51	0	4	25	145	8.5	21
Carr	17	288	42	101	.416	18	24	.750	8	17	25	14	32	0	10	6	102	6.0	11
Henderson	16	228	41	86	.477	10	12	.833	10	15	25	26	24	0	10	3	92	5.8	12
Robey	17	265	35	81	.432	16	35	.457	19	41	60	12	44	0	2	5	86	5.1	14
Duerod	10	12	4	10	.400	0	0	....	0	0	0	0	0	0	1	0	8	0.8	4
Fernsten	8	14	0	3	.000	2	3	.667	1	3	4	1	3	0	1	0	2	0.3	2

3-Pt. FG: Boston 10-45 (.222) – Bird 3-8 (.375); Archibald 0-5 (.000); Ford 7-25 (.280); Carr 0-4 (.000); Henderson 0-1 (.000); Duerod 0-2 (.000). Opponents 7-38 (.184).

CHICAGO

Player	G.	Min.	FGM	FGA	Pct.	FTM	FTA	Pct.	Off. Reb.	Def. Reb.	Tot. Reb.	Ast.	PF	Dsq.	Stl.	Blk. Sh.	Pts.	Avg.	Hi.
Theus	6	232	40	90	.444	37	43	.860	7	14	21	38	22	0	15	0	119	19.8	37
Gilmore	6	247	35	60	.583	38	55	.691	24	43	67	12	15	0	6	17	108	18.0	25
Greenwood	6	212	51	87	.586	5	12	.417	16	28	44	11	26	0	9	5	107	17.8	24
Sobers	6	162	35	81	.432	8	9	.889	3	8	11	22	26	1	4	0	79	13.2	18
Jones	6	217	29	61	.475	17	17	1.000	18	41	59	11	21	0	5	3	75	12.5	19
Wilkerson	6	152	25	59	.424	5	5	1.000	6	10	16	14	13	0	5	1	55	9.2	14
Kenon	6	114	18	46	.391	4	8	.500	17	10	27	8	4	0	4	1	40	6.7	10
Lester	5	42	7	18	.389	5	7	.714	5	1	6	4	4	0	2	0	19	3.8	10
Dietrick	6	81	8	26	.308	3	4	.750	3	12	15	4	19	0	2	3	19	3.2	8
Wilkes	2	5	0	1	.000	0	0	....	0	1	1	0	0	0	1	0	0	0.0	0
Worthen	1	1	0	0	....	0	0	....	0	0	0	0	0	0	0	0	0	0.0	0

3-Pt. FG: Chicago 3-23 (.130) – Theus 2-9 (.222); Greenwood 0-2 (.000); Sobers 1-6 (.167); Wilkerson 0-1 (.000); Kenon 0-1 (.000); Lester 0-1 (.000); Dietrick 0-3 (.000). Opponents 7-24 (.292).

HOUSTON

Player	G.	Min.	FGM	FGA	Pct.	FTM	FTA	Pct.	Off. Reb.	Def. Reb.	Tot. Reb.	Ast.	PF	Dsq.	Stl.	Blk. Sh.	Pts.	Avg.	Hi.
Malone	21	955	207	432	.479	148	208	.711	125	180	305	35	54	0	13	34	562	26.8	42
Murphy	19	540	142	287	.495	58	60	.967	7	17	24	57	69	0	26	0	344	18.1	42
Reid	21	868	139	303	.459	61	92	.663	56	86	142	98	80	2	50	24	339	16.1	33
Paultz	21	720	111	246	.451	32	48	.667	53	94	147	35	69	1	13	27	254	12.1	20
Dunleavy	20	472	69	152	.454	33	38	.868	9	33	42	68	59	1	15	1	177	8.9	28
Henderson	21	615	59	132	.447	23	28	.821	14	41	55	104	39	0	17	1	141	6.7	13
Willoughby	19	417	42	116	.362	30	40	.750	28	57	85	22	42	0	14	19	114	6.0	14
Leavell	17	217	30	77	.390	15	17	.882	5	12	17	44	26	0	18	4	75	4.4	10
Garrett	13	117	9	21	.429	7	8	.875	3	12	15	6	10	0	5	1	25	1.9	8
Jones	12	88	10	21	.476	2	5	.400	7	11	18	5	15	0	3	2	22	1.8	7
Tomjanovich	8	31	1	9	.111	4	6	.667	2	4	6	2	4	0	0	0	6	0.8	2

3-Pt. FG: Houston 8-32 (.250) – Malone 0-2 (.000); Murphy 2-7 (.286); Reid 0-2 (.000); Paultz 0-1 (.000); Dunleavy 6-15 (.400); Henderson 0-1 (.000); Willoughby 0-1 (.000); Tomjanovich 0-3 (.000). Opponents 9-54 (.167).

INDIANA

Player	G.	Min.	FGM	FGA	Pct.	FTM	FTA	Pct.	Off. Reb.	Def. Reb.	Tot. Reb.	Ast.	PF	Dsq.	Stl.	Blk. Sh.	Pts.	Avg.	Hi.
Davis	2	74	14	35	.400	12	13	.923	2	6	8	11	6	0	2	0	40	20.0	21
Knight	2	71	16	30	.533	5	8	.625	6	6	12	5	5	0	1	0	37	18.5	25
Bantom	2	51	12	16	.750	5	7	.714	5	3	8	1	10	0	1	1	29	14.5	19
Orr	2	56	9	25	.360	6	7	.857	6	4	10	4	4	0	5	1	24	12.0	16
C. Johnson	2	55	5	12	.417	5	10	.500	10	10	20	3	3	0	4	2	15	7.5	10
Edwards	2	56	7	24	.292	0	0	....	4	10	14	5	8	0	1	1	14	7.0	14
G. Johnson	2	23	5	8	.625	0	0	....	1	3	4	1	1	0	0	0	10	5.0	8
McGinnis	2	39	3	15	.200	4	8	.500	2	8	10	7	6	0	2	0	10	5.0	7
Bradley	2	19	3	9	.333	2	2	1.000	1	1	2	2	4	0	2	0	9	4.5	7
Buse	2	35	1	8	.125	2	2	1.000	0	5	5	7	4	0	3	0	5	2.5	5
Sichting	1	1	0	0	....	0	0	....	0	0	0	0	0	0	1	0	0	0.0	0

3-Pt. FG: Indiana 2-6 (.333) – Davis 0-1 (.000); Bradley 1-1 (1.000); Buse 1-4 (.250). Opponents 0-3 (.000).

1980-81 PLAYOFF STATISTICS

KANSAS CITY

Player	G.	Min.	FGM	FGA	Pct.	FTM	FTA	Pct.	Off. Reb.	Def. Reb.	Tot. Reb.	Ast.	PF	Dsq.	Stl.	Blk. Sh.	Pts.	Avg.	Hi.
King	15	620	122	248	.492	75	102	.735	56	93	149	25	49	0	18	10	319	21.3	31
Wedman	15	657	129	297	.434	40	56	.714	16	71	87	58	51	0	18	8	307	20.5	31
Grunfeld	15	633	98	201	.488	54	67	.806	11	52	63	88	51	1	30	9	252	16.8	27
Birdsong	8	234	56	98	.571	11	18	.611	8	13	21	27	13	1	12	0	124	15.5	30
Lacey	15	533	60	143	.420	30	35	.857	30	90	120	80	63	2	28	23	150	10.0	18
Ford	5	158	15	35	.429	9	13	.692	1	7	8	29	9	0	5	0	39	7.8	17
Meriweather	10	199	24	49	.490	8	14	.571	12	19	31	5	31	1	5	7	56	5.6	13
Lambert	15	175	22	54	.407	5	6	.833	19	18	37	9	21	0	5	4	49	3.3	16
Douglas	15	318	15	32	.469	15	35	.429	18	47	65	11	47	1	4	3	45	3.0	11
Sanders	9	50	9	18	.500	4	4	1.000	4	1	5	2	8	0	3	0	23	2.6	13
Walton	8	73	4	15	.267	3	4	.750	3	4	7	19	6	0	4	0	11	1.4	6

3-Pt. FG: Kansas City 13-48 (.271)—King 0-1 (.000); Wedman 9-32 (.281); Grunfeld 2-4 (.500); Birdsong 1-1 (1.000); Lacey 0-3 (.000); Ford 0-1 (.000); Lambert 0-3 (.000); Sanders 1-2 (.500); Walton 0-1 (.000). Opponents 8-27 (.296).

LOS ANGELES

Player	G.	Min.	FGM	FGA	Pct.	FTM	FTA	Pct.	Off. Reb.	Def. Reb.	Tot. Reb.	Ast.	PF	Dsq.	Stl.	Blk. Sh.	Pts.	Avg.	Hi.
Abdul-Jabbar	3	134	30	65	.462	20	28	.714	13	37	50	12	14	0	3	8	80	26.7	32
Nixon	3	133	25	49	.510	8	10	.800	1	10	11	26	9	0	1	1	58	19.3	22
Wilkes	3	113	21	48	.438	12	18	.667	4	4	8	4	10	0	1	1	54	18.0	22
Johnson	3	127	19	49	.388	13	20	.650	8	33	41	21	14	1	8	3	51	17.0	26
Cooper	3	102	11	20	.550	10	14	.714	2	8	10	7	7	0	6	0	32	10.7	17
Chones	3	67	10	17	.588	4	8	.400	6	11	17	1	9	0	1	4	24	8.0	12
Landsberger	3	32	2	7	.286	1	1	1.000	9	6	15	0	5	0	1	0	5	1.7	3
Brewer	3	7	0	0	....	0	0	....	0	1	1	0	1	0	0	0	0	0.0	0
Holland	1	1	0	0	....	0	0	....	0	0	0	0	0	0	0	0	0	0.0	0
Jordan	2	4	0	0	....	0	0	....	0	0	0	1	0	0	0	0	0	0.0	0

3-Pt. FG: Los Angeles 0-4 (.000)—Wilkes 0-1 (.000); Cooper 0-3 (.000). Opponents 1-4 (.250).

MILWAUKEE

Player	G.	Min.	FGM	FGA	Pct.	FTM	FTA	Pct.	Off. Reb.	Def. Reb.	Tot. Reb.	Ast.	PF	Dsq.	Stl.	Blk. Sh.	Pts.	Avg.	Hi.
Ma. Johnson	7	266	75	135	.556	23	32	.719	41	25	66	34	14	0	10	7	173	24.7	36
Lanier	7	236	50	85	.588	23	32	.719	12	40	52	28	18	0	12	8	123	17.6	24
Bridgeman	7	183	42	91	.462	13	16	.813	6	9	15	23	27	0	6	0	98	14.0	32
Moncrief	7	277	30	69	.435	38	51	.745	19	28	47	20	24	0	12	3	98	14.0	20
Mi. Johnson	7	170	26	65	.400	30	35	.857	24	23	47	13	25	0	9	6	82	11.4	22
Winters	7	181	28	61	.459	12	16	.750	4	19	23	22	22	1	10	1	70	10.0	18
Buckner	7	183	26	60	.433	11	16	.688	5	15	20	35	26	1	11	0	63	9.0	16
Evans	4	38	9	17	.529	7	8	.875	0	1	1	6	9	0	0	1	25	6.3	13
Cummings	5	25	3	11	.273	3	4	.750	3	3	6	0	2	0	1	0	9	1.8	7
Catchings	7	109	3	16	.188	2	2	1.000	10	16	26	8	24	0	0	11	8	1.1	4
Elmore	4	12	0	1	.000	0	0	....	0	0	0	1	4	0	0	0	0	0.0	0

3-Pt. FG: Milwaukee 3-11 (.273)—Ma. Johnson 0-1 (.000); Bridgeman 1-1 (1.000); Mi. Johnson 0-1 (.000); Winters 2-6 (.333); Evans 0-2 (.000) Opponents 0-9 (.000).

NEW YORK

Player	G.	Min.	FGM	FGA	Pct.	FTM	FTA	Pct.	Off. Reb.	Def. Reb.	Tot. Reb.	Ast.	PF	Dsq.	Stl.	Blk. Sh.	Pts.	Avg.	Hi.
Russell	2	89	15	34	.441	16	17	.941	1	8	9	9	9	0	4	1	46	23.0	29
R. Williams	2	84	18	41	.439	6	11	.545	3	5	8	9	10	1	4	0	43	21.5	24
S. Williams	2	56	13	18	.722	0	0	....	4	5	9	5	7	0	3	0	26	13.0	18
Richardson	2	86	8	33	.242	7	12	.583	6	13	19	5	7	0	8	0	23	11.5	14
Cartwright	2	49	6	17	.353	8	12	.667	4	9	13	1	7	0	1	1	20	10.0	11
Webster	2	63	6	12	.500	0	4	.000	4	6	10	1	6	0	0	1	12	6.0	6
Glenn	2	26	4	7	.571	3	3	1.000	1	3	4	1	0	0	1	0	11	5.5	6
Demic	2	37	4	5	.800	1	2	.500	5	2	7	0	3	0	0	1	9	4.5	5
Woodson	2	8	1	3	.333	2	2	1.000	2	0	2	0	3	0	0	0	4	2.0	4
Carter	1	7	0	1	.000	0	0	....	1	1	2	0	4	0	0	0	0	0.0	0

3-Pt. FG: New York 1-10 (.100)—Russell 0-2 (.000); R. Williams 1-3 (.333); Richardson 0-4 (.000); Glenn 0-1 (.000) Opponents 0-0 (....).

1980-81 PLAYOFF STATISTICS

PHILADELPHIA

Player	G.	Min.	FGM	FGA	Pct.	FTM	FTA	Pct.	Off. Reb.	Def. Reb.	Tot. Reb.	Ast.	PF	Dsq.	Stl.	Blk. Sh.	Pts.	Avg.	Hi.
Erving	16	592	143	301	.475	81	107	.757	52	62	114	54	54	0	22	41	367	22.9	38
B. Jones	16	443	81	160	.506	73	88	.830	35	53	88	33	60	1	18	21	235	14.7	22
Dawkins	16	421	86	153	.562	49	68	.721	28	70	98	14	71	2	3	16	221	13.8	24
Toney	16	356	77	180	.428	66	81	.815	10	27	37	54	50	0	11	7	221	13.8	35
Cheeks	16	513	68	125	.544	32	42	.762	4	47	51	116	55	1	40	12	168	10.5	22
Hollins	16	490	67	152	.441	29	37	.784	8	26	34	65	42	0	17	1	163	10.2	23
C. Jones	16	580	54	95	.568	31	42	.738	37	118	155	27	53	0	7	31	139	8.7	16
Mix	16	206	32	77	.416	24	26	.923	19	23	42	10	16	0	4	2	88	5.5	17
Richardson	13	181	20	38	.526	9	17	.529	9	12	21	12	15	0	6	3	49	3.8	8
Cureton	9	36	6	18	.333	0	2	.000	1	8	9	2	3	0	1	2	12	1.3	4
Johnson	8	22	3	10	.300	0	0	.....	2	3	5	2	1	0	2	1	6	0.8	2

3-Pt. FG: Philadelphia 1-16 (.063)—Erving 0-1 (.000); Toney 1-9 (.111); Cheeks 0-3 (.000); Hollins 0-1 (.000); Mix 0-1 (.000); Johnson 0-1 (.000) Opponents 6-31 (.194).

PHOENIX

Player	G.	Min.	FGM	FGA	Pct.	FTM	FTA	Pct.	Off. Reb.	Def. Reb.	Tot. Reb.	Ast.	PF	Dsq.	Stl.	Blk. Sh.	Pts.	Avg.	Hi.
Johnson	7	267	52	110	.473	32	42	.762	7	26	33	20	18	0	9	9	137	19.6	31
Davis	7	199	51	106	.481	10	17	.588	7	12	19	22	17	0	7	1	112	16.0	20
Adams	7	218	27	60	.450	20	28	.714	11	30	41	26	20	0	4	1	74	10.6	19
Robinson	7	233	27	77	.351	20	34	.588	23	52	75	13	15	0	5	2	74	10.6	23
Cook	7	206	25	54	.463	14	19	.737	17	30	47	11	29	1	1	0	65	9.3	16
Macy	7	102	19	36	.528	7	7	1.000	2	11	13	11	8	0	5	0	49	7.0	17
Scott	7	120	14	30	.467	10	15	.667	8	11	19	7	6	0	4	6	38	5.4	10
High	7	117	14	33	.424	9	14	.643	9	10	19	6	24	0	6	3	37	5.3	11
Kelley	7	113	10	25	.400	9	14	.643	13	22	35	13	12	0	6	3	29	4.1	7
Kramer	7	101	13	25	.520	1	2	.500	2	14	16	4	18	0	2	2	27	3.9	8
Niles	2	4	0	5	.000	0	0	.....	0	0	0	0	1	0	0	0	0	0.0	0

3-Pt. FG: Phoenix 6-16 (.375)—Johnson 1-5 (.200); Davis 0-1 (.000); Cook 1-1 (1.000); Macy 4-8 (.500); Kelley 0-1 (.000). Opponents 5-19 (.263).

PORTLAND

Player	G.	Min.	FGM	FGA	Pct.	FTM	FTA	Pct.	Off. Reb.	Def. Reb.	Tot. Reb.	Ast.	PF	Dsq.	Stl.	Blk. Sh.	Pts.	Avg.	Hi.
Bates	3	115	35	62	.565	14	17	.824	3	4	7	13	11	0	5	1	85	28.3	34
Thompson	3	132	31	51	.608	13	18	.722	5	18	23	4	10	0	3	9	75	25.0	40
Ransey	3	131	23	65	.354	3	6	.500	5	7	12	25	8	0	6	1	49	16.3	26
Natt	3	95	14	31	.452	4	8	.500	6	14	20	1	4	0	1	1	32	10.7	17
Gross	3	60	9	14	.643	9	14	.643	5	3	8	5	9	0	2	2	27	9.0	11
Washington	3	128	12	23	.522	2	2	1.000	14	38	52	7	9	0	3	6	26	8.7	10
Kunnert	3	43	5	10	.500	1	4	.250	2	7	9	1	7	0	1	0	11	3.7	5
Harper	1	6	1	1	1.000	1	1	1.000	0	1	1	0	0	0	0	0	3	3.0	3
Gale	3	51	4	16	.250	0	0	.....	2	3	5	9	2	0	5	0	8	2.7	4
Owens	1	5	0	0	.....	0	0	.....	0	1	1	0	1	0	0	0	0	0.0	0
Paxson	1	4	0	3	.000	0	0	.....	0	0	0	0	0	0	0	0	0	0.0	0

3-Pt. FG: Portland 1-4 (.250)—Bates 1-1 (1.000); Ransey 0-1 (.000); Washington 0-1 (.000); Kunnert 0-1 (.000). Opponents 4-8 (.500).

SAN ANTONIO

Player	G.	Min.	FGM	FGA	Pct.	FTM	FTA	Pct.	Off. Reb.	Def. Reb.	Tot. Reb.	Ast.	PF	Dsq.	Stl.	Blk. Sh.	Pts.	Avg.	Hi.
Gervin	7	274	77	154	.500	36	45	.800	9	26	35	24	19	1	5	4	190	27.1	33
Olberding	7	254	58	105	.552	21	25	.840	11	30	41	30	31	1	4	0	138	19.7	34
R. Johnson	7	224	35	73	.479	19	25	.760	15	19	34	16	27	2	4	5	89	12.7	25
Brewer	7	118	29	61	.475	21	29	.724	0	5	5	13	6	0	1	6	80	11.4	21
Silas	7	161	27	69	.391	26	32	.813	5	10	15	19	9	0	4	1	80	11.4	21
Corzine	7	161	27	55	.491	9	13	.692	12	36	48	16	15	0	4	8	63	9.0	18
Moore	7	124	18	37	.486	6	8	.750	8	5	13	27	14	0	10	1	42	6.0	11
Griffin	7	183	14	24	.583	9	20	.450	16	24	40	29	28	2	6	5	37	5.3	12
G. Johnson	7	165	12	26	.462	7	10	.700	24	39	63	6	20	0	3	16	31	4.4	6
Restani	3	11	1	3	.333	0	0	.....	0	2	2	0	2	0	0	1	2	0.7	2
Wiley	3	5	0	1	.000	2	2	1.000	0	0	0	0	2	0	0	0	2	0.7	2

3 Pt. FG: San Antonio 2-12 (.167)—Gervin 0-3 (.000); Olberding 1-3 (.333); Brewer 1-3 (.333); Moore 0-3 (.000) Opponents 3-10 (.300).

1981 PLAYOFF HIGHS

SCORING

Player	Points	Opponents	Date
1. Calvin Murphy	42	San Antonio	April 17
Moses Malone	42	San Antonio	April 26
3. Moses Malone	41	San Antonio	April 10
4. Mychal Thompson	40	Kansas City	April 3
5. Moses Malone	38	Los Angeles	April 1
Julius Erving	38	Milwaukee	April 5

REBOUNDS

Player	Rebounds	Opponents	Date
1. Moses Malone	23	Los Angeles	April 1
Moses Malone	23	Kansas City	April 26
3. Moses Malone	22	Boston	May 10
4. Larry Bird	21	Houston	May 5
Larry Bird	21	Houston	May 7

ASSISTS

Player	Assists	Opponents	Date
1. Nate Archibald	14	Philadelphia	April 26
2. Nate Archibald	12	Houston	May 14
3. Andrew Toney	11	Indiana	March 31
Reggie Theus	11	New York	April 3
Norm Nixon	11	Houston	April 3
Maurice Cheeks	11	Milwaukee	April 19

INDIVIDUAL HIGHS

Most Points, Game .... 42, Murphy, Hou. at S.A. 4/17
42, Malone, Hou. vs. K.C. 4/26
Most Field Goals, Game .... 19, Murphy, Hou. at S.A. 4/17
Most Free Throws, Game .... 18, Malone, Hou. at S.A. 4/14
Most Rebounds, Game .... 23, Malone, Hou. at L.A. 4/1
23, Malone, Hou. vs. K.C. 4/26
Most Offensive Rebounds, Game .... 11, Malone, Hou. vs. L.A. 4/1
Most Defensive Rebounds, Game .... 15, by three players
Most Assists, Game .... 14, Archibald, Bos. at Phil. 4/26
Most Blocked Shots, Game .... 7, Gilmore, Chi. at N.Y. 3/31
Most Steals, Game .... 6, by five players

TEAM HIGHS & LOWS

Most Points, Game .... 125, Phil. vs. Mil. 4/5
125, S.A. vs. Hou. 4/8
Fewest Points, Game .... 71, Hou. vs. Bos. 5/9
Most Points, Half .... 67, Phil. vs. Ind. 3/31
67, Bos. vs. Chi. 4/5
Fewest Points, Half .... 30, Hou. vs. Bos. 5/9
Most Points, Quarter .... 40, Bos. vs. Chi. 4/5
Fewest Points, Quarter .... 11, K.C. vs. Hou. 4/29
Most Field Goals, Game .... 51, K.C. vs. Port. 4/3
Fewest Field Goals, Game .... 24, Hou. vs. Bos. 5/9
Most Free Throws, Game .... 45, Mil. at Phil. 4/7
Fewest Free Throws, Game .... 4, K.C. at Port. 4/1
Most Rebounds, Game .... 56, Port. vs. K.C. 4/1
Fewest Rebounds, Game .... 29, Phil. at Mil. 4/17
29, K.C. at Hou. 4/24

ALL-TIME AND CAREER RECORDS

Including

NBA Championship Teams

Career Statistical Leaders

Top Performances

All-Time Records

Award Winners

Career Highs of Active Players

Championship Series Statistics/Records

Playoff Statistics/Records

Yearly Records of NBA Teams

Team Winning, Losing Streaks

Enshrined Hall of Famers

Chamberlain's "100-Point" Box Score

ABA Award Winners

Season-by-Season Statistics, 1946-1980

NBA CHAMPIONS OVER THE YEARS

Season	Champion	Eastern Division	W.	L.	Western Division	W.	L.	Top Scorer	Pts.
1946-47	Philadelphia	Washington	49	11	Chicago	39	22	Joe Fulks, (Phil.)	1389
1947-48	Baltimore	Philadelphia	27	21	St. Louis	29	19	Max Zaslofsky (Chi.)	1007
1948-49	Minneapolis	Washington	38	22	Rochester	45	15	George Mikan (Mpls.)	1698
1949-50	Minneapolis	Syracuse	51	13	Indianapolis*	39	25	George Mikan (Mpls.)	1865
1950-51	Rochester	Philadelphia	40	26	Minneapolis	44	24	George Mikan (Mpls.)	1932
1951-52	Minneapolis	Syracuse	40	26	Rochester	41	25	Paul Arizin (Phil.)	1674
1952-53	Minneapolis	New York	47	23	Minneapolis	48	22	Neil Johnston (Phil.)	1564
1953-54	Minneapolis	New York	44	28	Minneapolis	46	26	Neil Johnston (Phil.)	1759
1954-55	Syracuse	Syracuse	43	29	Ft. Wayne	43	29	Neil Johnston (Phil.)	1631
1955-56	Philadelphia	Philadelphia	45	27	Ft. Wayne	37	35	Bob Pettit (St. Louis)	1849
1956-57	Boston	Boston	44	28	StL-Mpl-FtW	34	38	Paul Arizin (Phil.)	1817
1957-58	St. Louis	Boston	49	23	St. Louis	41	31	George Yardley (Det.)	2001
1958-59	Boston	Boston	52	20	St. Louis	49	23	Bob Pettit (St. Louis)	2105
1959-60	Boston	Boston	59	16	St. Louis	46	29	Wilt Chamberlain (Phil.)	2707
1960-61	Boston	Boston	57	22	St. Louis	51	28	Wilt Chamberlain (Phil.)	3033
1961-62	Boston	Boston	60	20	Los Angeles	54	26	Wilt Chamberlain (Phil.)	4029
1962-63	Boston	Boston	58	22	Los Angeles	53	27	Wilt Chamberlain (S.F.)	3586
1963-64	Boston	Boston	59	21	San Fran.	48	32	Wilt Chamberlain (S.F.)	2948
1964-65	Boston	Boston	62	18	Los Angeles	49	31	W. Cha'lain (S.F.-Phil.)	2534
1965-66	Boston	Philadelphia	55	25	Los Angeles	45	35	Wilt Chamberlain (Phil.)	2649
1966-67	Philadelphia	Philadelphia	68	13	San Fran.	44	37	Rick Barry (San Fran.)	2775
1967-68	Boston	Philadelphia	62	20	St. Louis	56	26	Dave Bing (Detroit)	2142
1968-69	Boston	Baltimore	57	25	Los Angeles	55	27	Elvin Hayes (San Diego)	2327
1969-70	New York	New York	60	22	Atlanta	48	34	Jerry West (L.A.)	†31.2
1970-71	Milwaukee	Baltimore	42	40	Milwaukee	66	16	Lew Alcindor (Milw.)	†31.7
1971-72	Los Angeles	New York	48	34	Los Angeles	69	13	K. Abdul-Jabbar (Mil.)	†34.8
1972-73	New York	New York	57	25	Los Angeles	60	22	Nate Archibald (KC-O)	†34.0
1973-74	Boston	Boston	56	26	Milwaukee	59	23	Bob McAdoo (Buffalo)	†30.6
1974-75	Golden State	Washington	60	22	Golden State	48	34	Bob McAdoo (Buffalo)	†34.5
1975-76	Boston	Boston	54	28	Phoenix	42	40	Bob McAdoo (Buffalo)	†31.1
1976-77	Portland	Philadelphia	50	32	Portland	49	33	Pete Maravich (N.O)	†31.1
1977-78	Washington	Washington	44	38	Seattle	47	35	George Gervin (S.A.)	†27.2
1978-79	Seattle	Washington	54	28	Seattle	52	30	George Gervin (S.A.)	†29.6
1979-80	Los Angeles	Philadelphia	59	23	Los Angeles	60	22	George Gervin (S.A.)	†33.1
1980-81	Boston	Boston	62	20	Houston	40	42	Adrian Dantley (Utah)	†30.7

*1949-50 Central Division Champ: Minneapolis and Rochester tied 51-17.
†Scoring champion based on average.

Year-by-Year Statistical Leaders

Season	FG Pct. Leaders	FT Pct. Leaders	Top Rebounders	
1946-47	.401 Bob Feerick (Wash.)	.811 Fred Scolari (Wash.)		
1947-48	.340 Bob Feerick (Wash.)	.788 Bob Feerick (Wash.)		
1948-49	.423 Arnie Risen (Roch.)	.859 Bob Feerick (Wash.)		
1949-50	.478 Alex Groza (Indpls.)	.843 Max Zaslofsky (Chi.)		
1950-51	.470 Alex Groza (Indpls.)	.855 Joe Fulks (Phil.)	1080	Dolph Schayes (Syr.)
1951-52	.448 Paul Arizin (Phil.)	.904 Bob Wanzer (Roch.)	880	{Larry Foust (Ft.W.) / Mel Hutchins (Milw.)}
1952-53	.452 Neil Johnston (Phil.)	.850 Bill Sharman (Bos.)	1007	George Mikan (Mpls.)
1953-54	.486 Ed Macauley (Boston)	.844 Bill Sharman (Bos.)	1098	Harry Gallatin (N.Y.)
1954-55	.487 Larry Foust (Ft. W.)	.897 Bill Sharman (Bos.)	1085	Neil Johnston (Phil.)
1955-56	.457 Neil Johnston (Phil.)	.867 Bill Sharman (Bos.)	1164	Bob Pettit (St. Louis)
1956-57	.447 Neil Johnston (Phil.)	.905 Bill Sharman (Bos.)	1256	Maurice Stokes (Roch.)
1957-58	.452 Jack Twyman (Cinn.)	.904 Dolph Schayes (Syr.)	1564	Bill Russell (Boston)
1958-59	.490 Ken Sears (N. Y.)	.932 Bill Sharman (Bos.)	1612	Bill Russell (Boston)
1959-60	.477 Ken Sears (N. Y.)	.892 Dolph Schayes (Syr.)	1941	W. Chamberlain (Phil.)
1960-61	.509 Wilt Chamberlain (Phil.)	.921 Bill Sharman (Bos.)	2149	W. Chamberlain (Phil.)
1961-62	.519 Walt Bellamy (Chi.)	.896 Dolph Schayes (Syr.)	2052	W. Chamberlain (Phil.)
1962-63	.528 Wilt Chamberlain (S.F.)	.881 Larry Costello (Syr.)	1946	W. Chamberlain (S. F.)
1963-64	.527 Jerry Lucas (Cinn.)	.853 Oscar Robertson (Cin.)	1930	Bill Russell (Boston)
1964-65	.510 Wilt Cham'ain (S.F.-Phil.)	.877 Larry Costello (Phil.)	1878	Bill Russell (Boston)
1965-66	.540 Wilt Chamberlain (Phil.)	.881 Larry Siegfried (Bos.)	1943	W. Chamberlain (Phil.)
1966-67	.683 Wilt Chamberlain (Phil.)	.903 Adrian Smith (Cin.)	1957	W. Chamberlain (Phil.)
1967-68	.595 Wilt Chamberlain (Phil.)	.873 Oscar Robertson (Cin.)	1952	W. Chamberlain (Phil.)
1968-69	.583 Wilt Chamberlain (L.A.)	.864 Larry Siegfried (Bos.)	1712	W. Chamberlain (L.A.)
1969-70	.559 Johnny Green (Cinn.)	.898 Flynn Robinson (Mil.)	16.9*	Elvin Hayes (S.D.)
1970-71	.587 Johnny Green (Cinn.)	.859 Chet Walker (Chi.)	18.2*	W. Chamberlain (L.A.)
1971-72	.649 Wilt Chamberlain (L.A.)	.894 Jack Marin (Balt.)	19.2*	W. Chamberlain (L.A.)
1972-73	.727 Wilt Chamberlain (L.A.)	.902 Rick Barry (G.S.)	18.6*	W. Chamberlain (L.A.)
1973-74	.547 Bob McAdoo (Buffalo)	.902 Ernie DiGregorio (Buff.)	18.1*	Elvin Hayes (Capital)
1974-75	.539 Don Nelson (Boston)	.904 Rick Barry (Golden State)	14.8*	Wes Unseld (Washington)
1975-76	.561 Wes Unseld (Wash.)	.923 Rick Barry (Golden State)	16.9*	K. Abdul-Jabbar (L.A.)
1976-77	.579 K. Abdul-Jabbar (L.A.)	.945 Ernie DiGregorio (Buff.)	14.4*	Bill Walton (Port.)
1977-78	.578 Bobby Jones (Den.)	.924 Rick Barry (Golden State)	15.7*	Len Robinson (N.O.)

ALL-TIME NBA STATISTICS

Season	FG Pct. Leaders		Ft Pct. Leaders		Top Rebounders	
1978-79	.584	Cedric Maxwell (Bos.)	.947	Rick Barry (Hou.)	17.6*	Moses Malone (Hou.)
1979-80	.609	Cedric Maxwell (Bos.)	.935	Rick Barry (Hou.)	15.0*	Swen Nater (S.D.)
1980-81	.670	Artis Gilmore (Chi.)	.958	Calvin Murphy (Hou.)	14.8*	Moses Malone (Hou.)

*Based on highest average per game.

Most Assists

Season	No.	
1946-47	202	Ernie Calverly (Prov.)
1947-48	120	Howie Dallmar (Phil.)
1948-49	321	Bob Davies (Roch.)
1949-50	386	Dick McGuire (N. Y.)
1950-51	414	Andy Phillip (Phil.)
1951-52	539	Andy Phillip (Phil.)
1952-53	547	Bob Cousy (Boston)
1953-54	578	Bob Cousy (Boston)
1954-55	557	Bob Cousy (Boston)
1955-56	642	Bob Cousy (Boston)
1956-57	478	Bob Cousy (Boston)
1957-58	463	Bob Cousy (Boston)
1958-59	557	Bob Cousy (Boston)
1959-60	715	Bob Cousy (Boston)
1960-61	690	Oscar Robertson (Cinn.)
1961-62	899	Oscar Robertson (Cinn.)
1962-63	825	Guy Rodgers (S.F.)
1963-64	868	Oscar Robertson (Cinn.)
1964-65	861	Oscar Robertson (Cinn.)
1965-66	847	Oscar Robertson (Cinn.)
1966-67	908	Guy Rodgers (Chi.)
1967-68	702	Wilt Chamberlain (Phil.)
1968-69	772	Oscar Robertson (Cinn.)
1969-70	9.1*	Len Wilkens (Sea.)
1970-71	10.1*	Norm Van Lier (Cinn.)
1971-72	9.7*	Jerry West (L.A.)
1972-73	11.4*	Nate Archibald (KC-O)
1973-74	8.2*	Ernie DiGregorio (Buff.)
1974-75	8.0*	Kevin Porter (Wash.)
1975-76	8.1*	Don Watts (Seattle)
1976-77	8.5*	Don Buse (Indiana)
1977-78	10.2*	Kevin Porter (Det.-N.J.)
1978-79	13.4*	Kevin Porter (Det.)
1979-80	10.1*	Michael Richardson (N.Y.)
1980-81	9.1*	Kevin Porter (Wash.)

Most Minutes

No.	
2939	Paul Arizin (Phil.)
3166	Neil Johnston (Phil.)
3296	Neil Johnston (Phil.)
2953	Paul Arizin (Phil.)
2838	Slater Martin (Mpls.)
2851	Dolph Schayes (Syr.)
2918	Dolph Schayes (Syr.)
2979	Bill Russell (Boston)
3338	W. Chamberlain (Phil.) / Gene Shue (Detroit)
3773	W. Chamberlain (Phil.)
3882	W. Chamberlain (Phil.)
3806	W. Chamberlain (S.F.)
3689	W. Chamberlain (S.F.)
3466	Bill Russell (Boston)
3737	W. Chamberlain (Phil.)
3682	W. Chamberlain (Phil.)
3836	W. Chamberlain (Phil.)
3695	Elvin Hayes (S.D.)
3665	Elvin Hayes (S.D.)
3678	John Havlicek (Bos.)
3698	John Havlicek (Bos.)
3681	Nate Archibald (KC-O)
3602	Elvin Hayes (Capital)
3539	Bob McAdoo (Buff.)
3379	K. Abdul-Jabbar (L.A.)
3364	Elvin Hayes (Wash.)
3638	Len Robinson (N.O.)
3390	Moses Malone (Hou.)
3226	Norm Nixon (L.A.)
3417	Adrian Dantley (Utah)

Most Personals

No.	
208	Stan Miasek (Detroit)
231	Charles Gilmur (Chi.)
273	Ed Sadowski (Phil.)
297	George Mikan (Mpls.)
308	George Mikan (Mpls.)
286	George Mikan (Mpls.)
334	Don Meineke (Ft. W.)
303	Earl Lloyd (Syracuse)
319	Vern Mikkelsen (Mpls.)
319	Vern Mikkelsen (Mpls.)
312	Vern Mikkelsen (Mpls.)
311	Walt Dukes (Detroit)
332	Walt Dukes (Detroit)
311	Tom Gola (Phil.)
335	Paul Arizin (Phil.)
330	Tom Meschery (Phil.)
312	Zelmo Beaty (St. Louis)
325	Wayne Embry (Cinn.)
345	Bailey Howell (Balt.)
344	Zelmo Beaty (St. Louis)
344	Joe Strawder (Detroit)
366	Bill Bridges (St. Louis)
329	Billy Cunningham (Phil.)
335	Jim Davis (Atlanta)
350	Dave Cowens (Boston)
314	Dave Cowens (Boston)
323	Neal Walk (Phoenix)
319	Kevin Porter (Capital)
330	Bob Dandridge (Mil.) / Phil Jackson (N.Y.)
356	Charlie Scott (Boston)
363	Lonnie Shelton (Knicks)
350	Lonnie Shelton (N.Y.)
367	Bill Robinzine (K.C.)
328	Darryl Dawkins (Phil.)
342	Ben Poquette (Utah)

Most Disqualifications

Season	No.	
1946-47	—	
1947-48	—	
1948-49	—	
1949-50	—	
1950-51	19	Cal Christensen (Tri-City)
1951-52	18	Don Boven (Milwaukee)
1952-53	26	Don Meineke (Ft. Wayne)
1953-54	12	Earl Lloyd (Syracuse)
1954-55	17	Charley Share (Milwaukee)
1955-56	17	Vern Mikkelsen (Minneapolis) / Arnie Risen (Boston)
1956-57	18	Vern Mikkelsen (Minneapolis)
1957-58	20	Vern Mikkelsen (Minneapolis)
1958-59	22	Walt Dukes (Detroit)
1959-60	20	Walt Dukes (Detroit)
1960-61	16	Walt Dukes (Detroit)
1961-62	20	Walt Dukes (Detroit)
1962-63	13	Frank Ramsey (Boston)
1963-64	11	Zelmo Beaty (St. Louis) / Gus Johnson (Baltimore)
1964-65	15	Tom Sanders (Boston)
1965-66	19	Tom Sanders (Boston)
1966-67	19	Joe Strawder (Detroit)
1967-68	18	John Tresvant (Det.-Cinn.) / Joe Strawder (Detroit)
1968-69	14	Art Harris (Seattle)
1969-70	18	Norm Van Lier (Cincinnati)
1970-71	16	John Trapp (San Diego)
1971-72	14	Curtis Perry (Hous.-Milw.)
1972-73	16	Elmore Smith (Buffalo)
1973-74	15	Mike Bantom (Phoenix)
1974-75	12	Kevin Porter (Washington)
1975-76	15	Bill Robinzine (Kansas City)
1976-77	21	Joe Meriweather (Atlanta)
1977-78	20	George Johnson (New Jersey)
1978-79	19	John Drew (Atlanta) / Wayne Rollins (Atlanta)
1979-80	12	Wayne Rollins (Atlanta) / James Edwards (Indiana) / George McGinnis (Indiana)
1980-81	18	Ben Poquette (Utah)

Fred Brown performs from the outer limits of the Kingdome with his accurate three-point bombs.

Most Steals

Season	No.	
1973-74	2.68*	Larry Steele (Portland)
1974-75	2.85*	Rick Barry (Golden State)
1975-76	3.18*	Don Watts (Seattle)
1976-77	3.47*	Don Buse (Indiana)
1977-78	2.74*	Ron Lee (Phoenix)
1978-79	2.46*	M. L. Carr (Detroit)
1979-80	3.23*	Michael Richardson (New York)
1980-81	3.43*	Magic Johnson (L.A.)

Three-Point FG Pct. Leaders

Season	Pct.	
1979-80	.443	Fred Brown (Seattle)
1980-81	.383	Brian Taylor (San Diego)

*Based on highest average per game.

Most Blocked Shots

No.	
4.85*	Elmore Smith (Los Angeles)
3.26*	K. Abdul-Jabbar (Milwaukee)
4.12*	K. Abdul-Jabbar (Los Angeles)
3.25*	Bill Walton (Portland)
3.38*	George Johnson (New Jersey)
3.95*	K. Abdul-Jabbar (Los Angeles)
3.41*	K. Abdul-Jabbar (Los Angeles)
3.39*	George Johnson (San Antonio)

ALL-TIME STATISTICAL LEADERS

Most Games Played
John Havlicek	1,270
Paul Silas	1,254
Hal Greer	1,122
Lenny Wilkens	1,077
Elvin Hayes	1,059
Dolph Schayes	1,059
Johnny Green	1,057
Don Nelson	1,053
Leroy Ellis	1,048
Wilt Chamberlain	1,045

Most Field Goals Made
Wilt Chamberlain	12,681
Kareem Abdul-Jabbar	10,815
John Havlicek	10,513
Elvin Hayes	9,875
Oscar Robertson	9,508
Jerry West	9,016
Elgin Baylor	8,693
Hal Greer	8,504
Walt Bellamy	7,914
Gail Goodrich	7,431

Most Field Goals Attempted
John Havlicek	23,900
Wilt Chamberlain	23,497
Elvin Hayes	21,893
Elgin Baylor	20,171
Oscar Robertson	19,620
Kareem Abdul-Jabbar	19,440
Jerry West	19,032
Hal Greer	18,811
Bob Pettit	16,872
Bob Cousy	16,468

Highest Scoring Average
(400 Games or 10,000 Points Minimum)

	G.	FGM	FTM	Pts.	Avg.
Wilt Chamberlain	1045	12681	6057	31419	30.1
Kareem Abdul-Jabbar	935	10815	4640	26270	28.1
George Gervin	404	4411	2435	11298	28.0
Elgin Baylor	846	8693	5763	23149	27.4
Jerry West	932	9016	7160	25192	27.0
Bob McAdoo	599	6225	3339	15792	26.4
Bob Pettit	792	7349	6182	20880	26.4
Oscar Robertson	1040	9508	7694	26710	25.7
Pete Maravich	658	6187	3564	15948	24.2
Elvin Hayes	1059	9875	4794	24547	23.2

Most Minutes Played
Wilt Chamberlain	47,859
John Havlicek	46,471
Oscar Robertson	43,886
Elvin Hayes	43,672
Bill Russell	40,726
Hal Greer	39,788
Walt Bellamy	38,940
Lenny Wilkens	38,064
Kareem Abdul-Jabbar	37,890
Jerry West	36,571

Highest Field Goal Percentage
(2000 FGM Minimum)

	FGA	FGM	Pct.
Artis Gilmore	4990	2879	.577
Kareem Abdul-Jabbar	19440	10815	.556
Bobby Jones	3847	2124	.552
Walter Davis	5123	2800	.547
Marques Johnson	5115	2773	.542
Adrian Dantley	5801	3135	.540
Wilt Chamberlain	23497	12681	.540
Swen Nater	4080	2201	.539
George Gervin	8364	4411	.527
Bernard King	4405	2310	.524

Highest Free Throw Percentage
(1200 FTM Minimum)

	FTA	FTM	Pct.
Rick Barry	4243	3818	.900
Calvin Murphy	3604	3207	.890
Bill Sharman	3557	3143	.884
Mike Newlin	3309	2879	.870
Fred Brown	1924	1650	.858
Ricky Sobers	1705	1460	.856
Larry Siegfried	1945	1662	.854
Flynn Robinson	1881	1597	.849
Brian Winters	1472	1247	.847
Dolph Schayes	8273	6979	.844

Most Free Throws Made
Oscar Robertson	7,694
Jerry West	7,160
Dolph Schayes	6,979
Bob Pettit	6,182
Wilt Chamberlain	6,057
Elgin Baylor	5,763
Lenny Wilkens	5,394
John Havlicek	5,369
Walt Bellamy	5,113
Chet Walker	5,079

Most Free Throws Attempted
Wilt Chamberlain	11,862
Oscar Robertson	9,185
Jerry West	8,801
Dolph Schayes	8,273
Bob Pettit	8,119
Walt Bellamy	8,088
Elgin Baylor	7,391
Elvin Hayes	7,158
Lenny Wilkens	6,973
John Havlicek	6,589

Most Rebounds
Wilt Chamberlain	23,924
Bill Russell	21,620
Elvin Hayes	14,656
Nate Thurmond	14,464
Walt Bellamy	14,241
Wes Unseld	13,769
Kareem Abdul-Jabbar	13,167
Jerry Lucas	12,942
Bob Pettit	12,849
Paul Silas	12,357

Most Assists
Oscar Robertson	9,887
Lenny Wilkens	7,211
Bob Cousy	6,955
Guy Rodgers	6,917
Jerry West	6,238
John Havlicek	6,114
Dave Bing	5,397
Nate Archibald	5,366
Kevin Porter	5,268
Norm Van Lier	5,217

Most Personal Fouls
Hal Greer	3,855
Dolph Schayes	3,664
Elvin Hayes	3,551
Walt Bellamy	3,536
Bailey Howell	3,498
Bill Bridges	3,375
Lenny Wilkens	3,285
John Havlicek	3,281
Sam Lacey	3,125
Paul Silas	3,105

Most Disqualifications
Vern Mikkelsen	127
Walter Dukes	121
Charlie Share	105
Paul Arizin	104
Tom Gola	94
Tom Sanders	94
Bailey Howell	90
Dolph Schayes	90
Tom Meschery	89
Frank Ramsey	87

TOP CAREER SCORERS

Figures from National Basketball League are included below; NBL did not record field goal attempts, however, so all field goal percentages listed here are based only on field goals and attempts in NBA competition. Minutes played not compiled prior to 1952; rebounds not compiled prior to 1951.

Player	Yrs.	G.	Min.	FGM	FGA	Pct.	FTM	FTA	Pct.	Reb.	Ast.	PF	Pts.	Avg.	Career
Wilt Chamberlain	14	1045	47859	12681	23497	.540	6057	11862	.511	23924	4643	2075	31419	30.1	60-73
Oscar Robertson	14	1040	43886	9508	19620	.485	7694	9185	.838	7804	9887	2931	26710	25.7	61-74
John Havlicek	16	1270	46471	10513	23930	.439	5369	6589	.815	8007	6114	3281	26395	20.8	63-78
K. Abdul-Jabbar	12	935	37890	10815	19440	.556	4640	6486	.715	13167	4083	2859	26270	28.1	70-81
Jerry West	14	932	36571	9016	19032	.474	7160	8801	.814	5376	6238	2435	25192	27.0	61-74
Elvin Hayes	13	1059	43672	9875	21893	.451	4794	7158	.670	14656	2025	3551	24547	23.2	69-81
Elgin Baylor	14	846	33863	8693	20171	.431	5763	7391	.780	11463	3650	2596	23149	27.4	59-72
Hal Greer	15	1122	39788	8504	18811	.452	4578	5717	.801	5665	4540	3855	21586	19.2	59-73
Walt Bellamy	14	1043	38940	7914	15340	.516	5113	8088	.632	14241	2544	3536	20941	20.1	62-75
Bob Pettit	11	792	36994	7349	16872	.436	6182	8119	.761	12849	2369	2529	20880	26.4	55-65
Dolph Schayes	16	1059	29800	6135	15427	.380	6979	8273	.844	11256	3072	3664	19249	18.2	49-64
Gail Goodrich	14	1031	33527	7431	16300	.456	4319	5354	.807	3279	4805	2775	19181	18.6	66-79
Chet Walker	13	1032	33433	6876	14628	.470	5079	6384	.796	7314	2126	2727	18831	18.2	63-75
Rick Barry	10	794	28825	7252	16163	.449	3818	4243	.900	5168	4017	2264	18395	23.2	66-80
Dave Bing	12	901	32769	6962	15769	.441	4403	5683	.775	3420	5397	2615	18327	20.3	67-78
Lou Hudson	13	890	29794	7392	15129	.489	3156	3960	.797	3926	2432	2439	17940	20.2	67-79
Len Wilkens	15	1077	38064	6189	14327	.432	5394	6973	.774	5030	7211	3285	17772	16.5	61-75
Bailey Howell	12	950	30627	6515	13585	.480	4740	6224	.762	9383	1853	3498	17770	18.7	60-71
Earl Monroe	13	926	29636	6906	14898	.464	3642	4513	.807	2796	3594	2416	17454	18.8	68-80
Bob Cousy	14	924	30165	6168	16468	.375	4624	5756	.803	4786	6955	2242	16960	18.4	51-70
Bob Lanier	11	774	27132	6799	13246	.509	3257	4209	.774	8655	2497	2484	16857	21.8	71-81
Calvin Murphy	11	874	27980	6633	13628	.487	3207	3604	.890	1968	4081	2945	16478	18.9	71-81
Paul Arizin	10	713	24897	5628	13356	.421	5010	6189	.810	6129	1665	2764	16266	22.8	51-62
Pete Maravich	10	658	24316	6187	14025	.441	3564	4344	.820	2747	3563	1865	15948	24.2	71-80
Jack Twyman	11	823	26147	6237	13873	.450	3366	4525	.778	5424	1861	2782	15840	19.2	56-66
Bob McAdoo	9	599	23243	6225	12314	.506	3339	4433	.753	6955	1704	2048	15792	26.4	73-81
Walt Frazier	13	825	30965	6130	12516	.490	3321	4226	.786	4830	5040	2180	15581	18.9	68-80
Bob Dandridge	12	828	29328	6424	13262	.484	2628	3365	.781	5698	2833	2915	15478	18.7	70-81
Sam Jones	12	871	24285	6271	13745	.456	2869	3572	.803	4305	2209	1735	15411	17.7	58-69
Dick Barnett	14	971	28937	6034	13227	.456	3290	4324	.761	2812	2729	2514	15358	15.8	60-74
Dick Van Arsdale	12	921	31771	5413	11661	.464	4253	5385	.790	3807	3060	2575	15079	16.4	66-77
Randy Smith	10	814	28005	6055	12905	.469	2657	3423	.776	3346	4026	2218	14778	18.2	72-81
Richie Guerin	13	848	27449	5174	12451	.416	4328	5549	.780	4278	4211	2769	14676	17.3	57-70
Nate Archibald	12	696	26143	5220	11144	.468	4144	5047	.821	1763	5366	1683	14588	21.0	71-81
Bill Russell	13	963	40726	5687	12930	.440	3148	5614	.561	21620	4100	2592	14522	15.1	57-69
Nate Thurmond	14	964	35875	5521	13105	.421	3395	5089	.667	14464	2575	2624	14437	15.0	64-77
Jo Jo White	12	837	29941	6169	13884	.444	2060	2471	.834	3345	4095	2056	14399	17.2	70-81
Tom Van Arsdale	12	929	28682	5505	12763	.431	3222	4426	.762	3942	2085	2922	14232	15.3	66-77
Dave DeBusschere	12	875	31202	5722	13296	.432	2609	3730	.699	9618	2497	2801	14053	16.1	63-74
Jerry Lucas	11	829	32131	5709	11441	.499	2635	3365	.783	12942	2730	2389	14053	17.0	64-74
Bob Love	11	789	25120	5447	12688	.429	3001	3728	.805	4653	1123	2130	13895	17.6	66-77
Billy Cunningham	9	654	22406	5116	11467	.446	3394	4717	.720	6638	2625	2431	13626	20.8	66-76
Cliff Hagan	10	745	21733	5239	11630	.450	2969	3722	.798	5116	2242	2388	13447	18.0	57-66
Rudy Tomjanovich	11	768	25714	5630	11240	.501	2089	2666	.784	6198	1573	1937	13383	17.4	71-81
Spencer Haywood	10	646	22739	5270	11306	.466	2729	3419	.798	6433	1257	1824	13270	20.5	71-80
Dave Cowens	10	726	28551	5608	12198	.460	1975	2527	.782	10170	2828	2783	13192	18.2	71-80
Jeff Mullins	12	802	24574	5383	11631	.463	2251	2764	.814	3427	3023	2165	13017	16.2	65-76
Bob Boozer	11	874	25449	4961	10738	.462	3042	3998	.761	7119	1237	2519	12964	14.8	61-71
Sidney Wicks	10	760	25762	5046	11002	.459	2711	3955	.685	6620	2437	2524	12803	16.8	72-81
Bill Sharman	11	711	21793	4761	11168	.426	3143	3559	.883	2779	2101	1925	12665	17.8	51-61
Jack Marin	11	849	24590	5068	10890	.465	2405	2922	.843	4405	1813	2416	12541	14.8	67-77
John Kerr	12	905	27784	4909	11751	.418	2662	3682	.723	10092	2004	2287	12480	13.8	55-66
Cazzie Russell	12	817	22213	5172	11154	.464	2033	2459	.827	3068	1838	1693	12377	15.1	67-78
Johnny Green	14	1057	24624	4973	10091	.493	2335	4226	.553	9083	1449	2856	12281	11.6	60-73
Tom Heinsohn	9	654	19254	4773	11787	.405	2648	3531	.750	5749	1318	2454	12194	18.6	57-65
Willis Reed	10	650	23073	4859	10202	.476	2465	3298	.747	8414	1186	2411	12183	18.7	65-74
Clyde Lovellette	11	704	19075	4784	10795	.443	2379	3141	.757	6663	1097	2289	11947	17.0	54-64
Archie Clark	10	725	23581	4693	9784	.480	2433	3163	.769	2427	3498	1806	11819	16.3	67-76
Mike Newlin	10	761	23067	4434	9518	.466	2879	3309	.870	2403	3194	2348	11802	15.5	72-81
Paul Silas	16	1254	34989	4293	9949	.432	3196	4748	.673	12357	2572	3105	11782	9.4	65-80
George Mikan	9	520	8350	4097	8783	.404	3570	4588	.778	4167	1245	2162	11764	22.6	47-56
Dick Snyder	13	946	25676	4890	10019	.488	1975	2398	.824	2732	2767	2453	11755	12.2	67-79
Fred Brown	10	730	20076	4984	10485	.475	1650	1924	.858	2308	2486	1644	11680	16.0	72-81
Jimmy Walker	9	698	23590	4624	10039	.461	2407	2903	.829	1860	2429	1735	11655	16.7	68-76
Kevin Loughery	11	755	22208	4477	10829	.413	2621	3262	.803	2254	2803	2543	11575	15.3	63-73
Don Ohl	10	727	22413	4685	10806	.434	2179	2975	.732	2163	2243	2014	11549	15.9	61-70
Rudy LaRusso	10	736	24477	4102	9521	.431	3303	4308	.767	6936	1556	2553	11507	15.6	60-69
Harold Hairston	11	776	24330	4240	8872	.478	3025	4080	.741	8019	1268	2334	11505	14.8	65-75

ALL-TIME TOP PERFORMANCES
(IN REGULAR SEASON PLAY)

*Denotes each overtime period played.

MOST POINTS SCORED IN ONE GAME

	FG	FT	Pts.
Wilt Chamberlain, Philadelphia vs. New York at Hershey, Pa., March 2, 1962	36	28	100
Wilt Chamberlain, Philadelphia vs. Los Angeles at Philadelphia, December 8, 1961	***31	16	78
Wilt Chamberlain, Philadelphia vs. Chicago at Philadelphia, January 13, 1962	29	15	73
Wilt Chamberlain, San Francisco at New York, November 16, 1962	29	15	73
David Thompson, Denver at Detroit, April 9, 1978	28	17	73
Wilt Chamberlain, San Francisco at Los Angeles, November 3, 1962	29	14	72
Elgin Baylor, Los Angeles at New York, November 15, 1960	28	15	71
Wilt Chamberlain, San Francisco at Syracuse, March 10, 1963	27	16	70
Wilt Chamberlain, Philadelphia at Chicago, December 16, 1967	30	8	68
Pete Maravich, New Orleans vs. Knicks, February 25, 1977	26	16	68
Wilt Chamberlain, Philadelphia vs. New York at Philadelphia, March 9, 1961	27	13	67
Wilt Chamberlain, Philadelphia at St. Louis, February 17, 1962	26	15	67
Wilt Chamberlain, Philadelphia vs. New York at Philadelphia, February 25, 1962	25	17	67
Wilt Chamberlain, San Francisco vs. Los Angeles at San Francisco, January 17, 1963	28	11	67
Wilt Chamberlain, Los Angeles at Phoenix, February 9, 1969	29	8	66
Wilt Chamberlain, Philadelphia at Cincinnati, February 13, 1962	24	17	65
Wilt Chamberlain, Philadelphia at St. Louis, February 27, 1962	25	15	65
Wilt Chamberlain, Philadelphia vs. Los Angeles at Philadelphia, February 7, 1966	28	9	65
Elgin Baylor, Minneapolis vs. Boston at Minneapolis, November 8, 1959	25	14	64
Rick Barry, Golden State vs. Portland at Oakland, March 26, 1974	30	4	64
Joe Fulks, Philadelphia vs. Indianapolis at Philadelphia, February 10, 1949	27	9	63
Elgin Baylor, Los Angeles at Philadelphia, December 8, 1961	***23	17	63
Jerry West, Los Angeles vs. New York at Los Angeles, January 17, 1962	22	19	63
Wilt Chamberlain, San Francisco vs. Los Angeles at San Francisco, December 14, 1962	24	15	63
Wilt Chamberlain, San Francisco at Philadelphia, November 26, 1964	27	9	63
George Gervin, San Antonio at New Orleans, April 9, 1978	23	17	63
Wilt Chamberlain, Philadelphia at Boston, January 14, 1962	27	8	62
Wilt Chamberlain, Philadelphia vs. St. Louis at Detroit, January 17, 1962	*24	14	62
Wilt Chamberlain, Philadelphia vs. Syracuse at Utica, New York, January 21, 1962	*25	12	62
Wilt Chamberlain, San Francisco at New York, January 29, 1963	27	8	62
Wilt Chamberlain, San Francisco at Cincinnati, November 15, 1964	26	10	62
Wilt Chamberlain, Philadelphia vs. San Francisco at Philadelphia, March 3, 1966	26	10	62
George Mikan, Minneapolis vs. Rochester at Minneapolis, January 20, 1952	**22	17	61
Wilt Chamberlain, Philadelphia vs. Chicago at Philadelphia, December 9, 1961	28	5	61
Wilt Chamberlain, Philadelphia vs. St. Louis at Philadelphia, February 22, 1962	21	19	61
Wilt Chamberlain, Philadelphia vs. Chicago, February 28, 1962	24	13	61
Wilt Chamberlain, San Francisco vs. Cincinnati at San Francisco, November 21, 1962	27	7	61
Wilt Chamberlain, San Francisco vs. Syracuse at San Francisco, December 11, 1962	27	7	61
Wilt Chamberlain, San Francisco vs. St. Louis at San Francisco, December 18, 1962	26	9	61
Wilt Chamberlain, Philadelphia at Los Angeles, December 1, 1961	22	16	60
Wilt Chamberlain, Philadelphia vs. Los Angeles at Hershey, Pa., December 29, 1961	24	12	60
Wilt Chamberlain, Los Angeles vs. Cincinnati at Cleveland, January 26, 1969	22	16	60

MOST FIELD GOALS SCORED IN ONE GAME

	FGA	FGM
Wilt Chamberlain, Philadelphia vs. New York at Hershey, Pa., March 2, 1962	63	36
Wilt Chamberlain, Philadelphia vs. Los Angeles at Philadelphia, December 8, 1961	***62	31
Wilt Chamberlain, Philadelphia at Chicago, December 16, 1967	40	30
Rick Barry, Golden State vs. Portland at Oakland, March 26, 1974	45	30
Wilt Chamberlain, Los Angeles at Phoenix, February 9, 1969	35	29
Wilt Chamberlain, Philadelphia vs. Chicago at Philadelphia, January 13, 1962	48	29
Wilt Chamberlain, San Francisco at Los Angeles, November 3, 1962	48	29
Wilt Chamberlain, San Francisco at New York, November 16, 1962	43	29
Elgin Baylor, Los Angeles at New York, November 15, 1960	48	28
Wilt Chamberlain, Philadelphia vs. Chicago at Philadelphia, December 9, 1961	48	28
Wilt Chamberlain, San Francisco vs. Los Angeles at San Francisco, January 11, 1963	47	28
Wilt Chamberlain, Philadelphia vs. Los Angeles at Philadelphia, February 7, 1966	43	28
David Thompson, Denver at Detroit, April 9, 1978	38	28
Joe Fulks, Philadelphia vs. Indianapolis at Philadelphia, February 10, 1949	56	27
Wilt Chamberlain, Philadelphia vs. New York at Philadelphia, March 9, 1961	37	27
Wilt Chamberlain, Philadelphia at Boston, January 14, 1962	45	27
Wilt Chamberlain, San Francisco vs. Cincinnati at San Francisco, November 21, 1962	52	27
Wilt Chamberlain, San Francisco vs. Syracuse at San Francisco, December 11, 1962	57	27
Wilt Chamberlain, San Francisco at New York, January 29, 1963	44	27
Wilt Chamberlain, San Francisco at Syracuse, March 10, 1963	38	27
Wilt Chamberlain, San Francisco at Philadelphia, November 26, 1964	58	27
Wilt Chamberlain, Philadelphia at New York, February 21, 1960	47	26
Wilt Chamberlain, Philadelphia at St. Louis, February 17, 1962	44	26
Wilt Chamberlain, San Francisco vs. St. Louis at San Francisco, December 18, 1962	53	26
Wilt Chamberlain, San Francisco vs. Los Angeles at San Francisco, February 16, 1963	**47	26
Wilt Chamberlain, San Francisco at Cincinnati, November 15, 1964	44	26
Wilt Chamberlain, Philadelphia vs. San Francisco at Philadelphia, March 3, 1966	39	26

	FGA	FGM
Wilt Chamberlain, Philadelphia vs. Cincinnati at Philadelphia, February 13, 1967	34	26
Pete Maravich, New Orleans vs. Knicks at New Orleans, February 25, 1977	43	26

MOST FREE THROWS MADE IN ONE GAME

	FTA	FTM
Wilt Chamberlain, Philadelphia vs. New York at Hershey, Pa., March 2, 1962	32	28
Adrian Dantley, Utah vs. Dallas at Utah, October 31, 1980	29	26
Frank Selvy, Milwaukee vs. Minnnapolis at Ft. Wayne, December 2, 1954	26	24
Dolph Schayes, Syracuse vs. Minneapolis at Syracuse, January 17, 1952	***27	23
Nate Archibald, Cincinnati vs. Detroit at Cincinnati, February 5, 1972	*24	23
Nate Archibald, K.C.-Omaha vs. Portland at Kansas City, January 21, 1975	25	23
Pete Maravich, New Orleans vs. New York, October 26, 1975	**26	23
Larry Foust, Minneapolis vs. St. Louis at Minneapolis, November 30, 1957	26	23
Richie Guerin, New York at Boston, February 11, 1961	26	22
Oscar Robertson, Cincinnati vs. Los Angeles at Cincinnati, December 18, 1964	23	22
Oscar Robertson, Cincinnati vs. Baltimore, December 27, 1964	26	22
Oscar Robertson, Cincinnati vs. Baltimore at Cincinnati, November 20, 1966	23	22
John Williamson, New Jersey vs. San Diego at New Jersey, December 9, 1978	24	22
Lloyd Free, San Diego at Atlanta, January 13, 1979	29	22
Dolph Schayes, Syracuse vs. New York at Syracuse, February 15, 1953	25	21
Richie Guerin, New York vs. Syracuse at New York, December 11, 1959	26	21
Rick Barry, San Francisco at New York, December 14, 1965	22	21
Rick Barry, San Francisco vs. Baltimore at Cincinnati, November 6, 1966	25	21
Flynn Robertson, Milwaukee vs. Atlanta at Baltimore, February 17, 1969	22	21
Lenny Wilkens, Seattle at Philadelphia, November 8, 1969	25	21
Connie Hawkins, Phoenix vs. Seattle, January 17, 1970	25	21
Spencer Haywood, Seattle vs. K.C.-Omaha at Seattle, January 3, 1973	27	21
John Drew, Atlanta at Phoenix, April 5, 1977	28	21
Rich Kelley, New Orleans vs. New Jersey at New Orleans, March 21, 1978	25	21
Moses Malone, Houston vs. Washington, February 17, 1980	23	21
Jack Sikma, Seattle vs. Kansas City at Seattle, November 14, 1980	23	21

MOST REBOUNDS IN ONE GAME

	Reb.
Wilt Chamberlain, Philadelphia vs. Boston at Philadelphia, November 24, 1960	55
Bill Russell, Boston vs. Syracuse at Boston, February 5, 1960	51
Bill Russell, Boston vs. Philadelphia at Boston, November 16, 1957	49
Bill Russell, Boston vs. Detroit at Providence, March 11, 1965	49
Wilt Chamberlain, Philadelphia vs. Syracuse at Philadelphia, February 6, 1960	45
Wilt Chamberlain, Philadelphia vs. Los Angeles at Philadelphia, January 21, 1961	45
Wilt Chamberlain, Philadelphia vs. New York at Philadelphia, November 10, 1959	45
Wilt Chamberlain, Philadelphia vs. Los Angeles at Philadelphia, December 8, 1961	***43
Bill Russell, Boston vs. Los Angeles at Boston, January 20, 1963	43
Wilt Chamberlain, Philadelphia vs. Boston at Philadelphia, March 6, 1965	43
Wilt Chamberlain, Philadelphia vs. Boston at Philadelphia, January 15, 1960	42
Wilt Chamberlain, Philadelphia vs. Detroit at Bethlehem, Pa., January 25, 1960	42
Nate Thurmond, San Francisco vs. Detroit at San Francisco, November 9, 1965	42
Wilt Chamberlain, Philadelphia vs. Boston at Philadelphia, January 14, 1966	42
Wilt Chamberlain, Los Angeles vs. Boston at Boston, March 7, 1969	42
Bill Russell, Boston vs. Syracuse at Boston, February 12, 1958	41
Wilt Chamberlain, San Francisco vs. Detroit at San Francisco, October 26, 1962	41
Bill Russell, Boston vs. San Francisco at Boston, March 14, 1965	*41
Bill Russell, Boston vs. Cincinnati at Boston, December 12, 1958	41
Wilt Chamberlain, Philadelphia vs. Syracuse at Philadelphia, November 4, 1959	*40
Bill Russell, Boston vs. Philadelphia at Boston, February 12, 1961	40
Jerry Lucas, Cincinnati at Philadelphia, February 29, 1964	40
Wilt Chamberlain, San Francisco vs. Detroit at San Francisco, November 22, 1964	40
Wilt Chamberlain, Philadelphia vs. Boston at Philadelphia, December 28, 1965	40

MOST ASSISTS IN ONE GAME

	Ast.
Kevin Porter, New Jersey vs. Houston at New Jersey, February 24, 1978	29
Bob Cousy, Boston-Minneapolis at Boston, February 27, 1959	28
Guy Rodgers, San Francisco vs. St. Louis at San Francisco, March 14, 1963	28
Ernie DiGregorio, Buffalo vs. Portland, January 1, 1974	25
Kevin Porter, Detroit vs. Boston at Detroit, March 9, 1979	25
Kevin Porter, Detroit at Phoenix, April 1, 1979	25
Guy Rodgers, Chicago vs. New York at Chicago, December 21, 1966	24
Kevin Porter, Washington vs. Detroit, March 23, 1980	24
Jerry West, Los Angeles vs. Philadelphia at Los Angeles, February 1, 1967	23
Kevin Porter, Detroit vs. Houston at Detroit, December 27, 1978	23
Kevin Porter, Detroit at Los Angeles, March 30, 1979	23
Oscar Robertson, Cincinnati vs. Syracuse at Cincinnati, October 29, 1961	22
Oscar Robertson, Cincinnati vs. New York at Cincinnati, March 5, 1966	*22
Art Williams, San Diego at Phoenix, December 28, 1968	22
Art Williams, San Diego vs. San Francisco, February 14, 1970	22
Kevin Porter, Washington vs. Atlanta at Washington, March 5, 1975	22
Kevin Porter, Detroit vs. San Antonio at Detroit, December 23, 1978	22
Phil Ford, Kansas City vs. Milwaukee at Kansas City, February 21, 1979	22
Kevin Porter, Detroit at Chicago, February 27, 1979	22
John Lucas, Golden State at Denver, February 27, 1981	22
Clem Haskins, Chicago vs. Boston, December 6, 1969	*21
Richie Guerin, New York vs. St. Louis at New York, December 12, 1958	21

ALL-TIME NBA STATISTICS

	Ast.
Bob Cousy, Boston vs. St. Louis at Boston, December 21, 1960	21
Oscar Robertson, Cincinnati vs. New York at Cincinnati, February 14, 1964	21
Guy Rodgers, Chicago vs. San Francisco at Chicago, October 18, 1966	21
Wilt Chamberlain, Philadelphia vs. Detroit, February 2, 1968	21
Guy Rodgers, Milwaukee vs. Detroit, October 31, 1968	21
Larry Siegfried, San Diego at Portland, November 16, 1970	21
Nate Archibald, K.C.-Omaha vs. Detroit at Omaha, December 15, 1972	*21
Kevin Porter, Washington vs. Los Angeles at Washington, March 2, 1975	21
Kevin Porter, Detroit at Houston, February 6, 1979	21
Phil Ford, Kansas City vs. Phoenix at Kansas City, February 23, 1979	21

MOST STEALS IN ONE GAME

	Stl.
Larry Kenon, San Antonio at Kansas City, December 26, 1976	11
Jerry West, Los Angeles vs. Seattle at Los Angeles, December 7, 1973	10
Larry Steele, Portland vs. Los Angeles at Portland, November 16, 1974	10
Fred Brown, Seattle at Philadelphia, December 3, 1976	10
Gus Williams, Seattle at New Jersey, February 22, 1978	10
Eddie Jordan, New Jersey at Philadelphia, March 23, 1979	10
Calvin Murphy, Houston vs. Boston at Houston, December 14, 1973	9
Larry Steele, Portland vs. Los Angeles at Portland, March 5, 1974	9
Rick Barry, Golden State vs. Buffalo at Oakland, October 29, 1974	9
Don Watts, Seattle vs. Philadelphia at Seattle, February 23, 1975	9
Larry Steele, Portland vs. Phoenix at Portland, March 7, 1975	9
Larry Steele, Portland vs. Detroit at Portland, March 14, 1976	9
Quinn Buckner, Milwaukee vs. Indiana at Milwaukee, January 2, 1977	9
Don Watts, Seattle vs. Phoenix at Seattle, March 27, 1977	9
Earl Tatum, Detroit at Los Angeles, November 28, 1978	9
Gus Williams, Seattle at Washington, January 23, 1979	9
Ron Lee, Detroit vs. Houston, March 16, 1980	9
Dudley Bradley, Indiana at Utah, November 10, 1980	9
Dudley Bradley, Indiana vs. Cleveland at Indiana, November 29, 1980	9
Michael Ray Richardson, New York at Chicago, December 23, 1980	9
Johnny High, Phoenix at Washington, January 28, 1981	9

MOST BLOCKED SHOTS IN ONE GAME

	Blk.
Elmore Smith, Los Angeles vs. Portland at Los Angeles, October 28, 1973	17
Elmore Smith, Los Angeles vs. Detroit at Los Angeles, October 26, 1973	14
Elmore Smith, Los Angeles vs. Houston at Los Angeles, November 4, 1973	14
George Johnson, San Antonio vs. Golden State at San Antonio, February 24, 1981	13
Nate Thurmond, Chicago vs. Atlanta at Chicago, October 18, 1974	12
George Johnson, New Jersey at New Orleans, April 21, 1978	12
Wayne Rollins, Atlanta vs. Portland at Atlanta, February 21, 1979	12
Elmore Smith, Los Angeles vs. Golden State at Los Angeles, March 15, 1974	11
Kareem Abdul-Jabbar, Los Angeles at Detroit, December 3, 1975	11
George Johnson, Golden State at Chicago, March 30, 1976	11
Artis Gilmore, Chicago vs. Atlanta at Chicago, December 20, 1977	11
Elvin Hayes, Washington at Detroit, March 3, 1978	11
Robert Parish, Golden State vs. Cleveland, October 29, 1978	11
Kareem Abdul-Jabbar, Los Angeles vs. Detroit at Los Angeles, November 28, 1978	11
Kareem Abdul-Jabbar, Los Angeles vs. Kansas City, November 25, 1979	11
Elmore Smith, Los Angeles at Houston, October 23, 1973	10
Kareem Abdul-Jabbar, Milwaukee vs. Detroit at Milwaukee, November 3, 1973	*10
Elmore Smith, Los Angeles vs. K.C.-Omaha, November 30, 1973	10
Elmore Smith, Los Angeles at Cleveland, December 11, 1973	10
Elmore Smith, Los Angeles vs. Golden State at Los Angeles, March 16, 1975	*10
Harvey Catchings, Philadelphia vs. Atlanta at Philadelphia, March 21, 1975	10
Kareem Abdul-Jabbar, Los Angeles vs. Atlanta at Los Angeles, November 2, 1975	*10
George Johnson, Golden State vs. Seattle at Oakland, April 3, 1976	10
George Johnson, New Jersey vs. Atlanta at New Jersey, October 26, 1977	*10
Joe C. Meriweather, New Orleans vs. Phoenix at New Orleans, October 28, 1977	10
Joe C. Meriweather, New York at Atlanta, December 12, 1979	10
Kareem Abdul-Jabbar, Los Angeles vs. Atlanta, January 18, 1980	10
George Johnson, New Jersey vs. Indiana, March 4, 1980	10
Wayne Rollins, Atlanta vs. Boston, March 14, 1980	10
Ben Poquette, Utah at Chicago, December 12, 1980	10

ALL-TIME SINGLE GAME RECORDS

*Denotes each overtime period played.

PLAYER

FULL GAME

Most Points—100 by Wilt Chamberlain, Phila. vs. N.Y. at Hershey, Pa. 3- 2-62
Most FGA—63 by Wilt Chamberlain, Phila. vs. N. Y. at Hershey, Pa. 3- 2-62
Most FGM—36 by Wilt Chamberlain, Phila. vs. N. Y. at Hershey, Pa. 3- 2-62
Consecutive FGM—18 by Wilt Chamberlain, S. F. vs. N. Y. at Bos. 11-27-63
          18 by Wilt Chamberlain, Phil. vs. Balt. at Pitt. 2-24-67
Most FTA—34 by Wilt Chamberlain, Phila. vs. St. Louis at Phila............... 2-22-62
Most FTM—28 by Wilt Chamberlain, Phila. vs. N.Y. at Hershey, Pa. 3- 2-62
Most Rebounds—55 by Wilt Chamberlain, Phila. vs. Bos. at Phila..............11-24-60
Most Assists—29 by Kevin Porter, New Jersey vs. Houston at N.J.............. 2-24-78
Most Personals—8 on Don Otten, Tri-Cities at Sheboygan..........................11-24-49

ONE HALF

Most Points—59 by Wilt Chamberlain, Phila. vs. N.Y. at Hershey, Pa. 3- 2-62
Most FGA—37 by Wilt Chamberlain, Phila. vs. N.Y. at Hershey, Pa. 3- 2-62
Most FGM—22 by Wilt Chamberlain, Phila. vs. N.Y. at Hershey, Pa. 3- 2-62
Most FTA—22 by Oscar Robertson, Cincinnati at Baltimore......................12-27-64
Most FTM—19 by Oscar Robertson, Cincinnati at Baltimore 12-27-64
Most Rebounds—32 by Bill Russell, Boston vs. Philadelphia at Boston 11-16-57
Most Assists—19 by Bob Cousy, Boston vs. Minneapolis at Boston.............. 2-27-59
Most Personals—6 on many players.
          Last: Bobby Jones, Philadelphia at Chicago..................... 3-20-81

ONE QUARTER

Most Points—33 by George Gervin, San Antonio at New Orleans 4- 9-78
     (overtime period) 13 by Earl Monroe, Balt. vs. Detroit.......... 2- 6-70
     13 by Joe Caldwell, Atlanta vs.
                      Cincinnati at Memphis..................... 2-18-70
Most FGA—21 by Wilt Chamberlain, Phila. vs. N.Y. at Hershey, Pa. 3- 2-62
Most FGM—13 by David Thompson, Denver at Detroit................................ 4- 9-78
Most FTA—16 by Oscar Robertson, Cincinnati at Baltimore......................12-27-64
          16 by Stan McKenzie, Phoenix at Philadelphia......................... 2-15-70
          16 by Pete Maravich, Atlanta at Chicago 1- 2-73
Most FTM—14 by Rick Barry, San Francisco at New York......................12- 6-66
Most Rebounds—18 by Nate Thurmond, San Francisco at Baltimore 2-28-65
Most Assists—12 by Bob Cousy, Boston vs. Minneapolis at Boston.............. 2-27-59
          12 by John Lucas, Houston vs. Milwaukee at Houston..........10-27-77
Most Personals—6 on Connie Dierking, Syracuse vs. Cincinnati at N.Y. ...11-17-59
          6 on Henry Akin, Seattle vs. Philadelphia..........12-20-67
          6 on Bud Ogden, Philadelphia vs. Phoenix at Phila. 2-15-70
          6 on Don Smith, Houston vs. Cleveland at Houston......... 2- 8-74
          6 on Roger Brown, Detroit vs. Golden State at Detroit.... 3-25-77
          6 on Paul Mokeski, Detroit vs. Chicago at Detroit 1-22-81

ONE TEAM

FULL GAME

Most Points—173 by Boston vs. Minneapolis at Boston 2-27-59
Most FGA—153 by Philadelphia vs. Los Angeles at Philadelphia ***12- 8-61
          150 by Boston vs. Philadelphia at Boston..................................... 3- 2-60

Most FGM—72 by Boston vs. Minneapolis at Boston 2-27-59
Most FTA—86 by Syracuse vs. Anderson at Syracuse *****11-24-49
Most FTA—71 by Chicago vs. Phoenix at Chicago......................... 1- 8-70
Most FTM—59 by Syracuse vs. Anderson.............................*****11-24-49
Most Rebounds—112 by Philadelphia vs. Cincinnati at Philadelphia..........11- 8-59
              112 by Boston vs. Detroit at Boston 12-24-60
Most Personals—66 by Anderson at Syracuse.................................*****11-24-49
Most Assists—53 by Milwaukee vs. Detroit at Milwaukee...........................12-26-78
           60 by Syracuse vs. Baltimore at Syracuse...........................*11-15-52
           55 by Milwaukee at Baltimore...*11-12-52
Most Disqualifications—8 from Syracuse vs. Baltimore at Syracuse.........*11-15-52

ONE HALF

Most Points—97 by Atlanta vs. San Diego at San Diego................................ 2-11-70
Most FGA—83 by Philadelphia vs. Syracuse at Philadelphia.....................11- 4-59
          83 by Boston at Philadelphia......................................12-27-60
Most FGM—40 by Boston vs. Minneapolis at Boston 2-27-59
          40 by Syracuse vs. Detroit at Syracuse 1-13-63
          40 by Atlanta at San Antonio 11-27-79
Most FTA—48 by Chicago vs. Phoenix at Chicago... 1- 8-70
Most FTM—36 by Chicago vs. Phoenix at Chicago... 1- 8-70
Most Rebounds—62 by Boston vs. Philadelphia at Boston 11-16-57
          62 by New York at Philadelphia...11-19-60
          62 by Philadelphia vs. Syracuse at Philadelphia..............11- 9-61
Most Assists—30 by Milwaukee vs. Detroit at Milwaukee...........................12-26-78
Most Personals—30 on Rochester at Syracuse... 1-15-53
Most Disqualifications—6 from Rochester at Syracuse............... 12-26-50
Most Disqualifications—6 from Syracuse at Boston 12-26-50
          6 from Syracuse vs. Baltimore at Syracuse.........*11-15-52

ONE QUARTER

Most Points—58 by Buffalo at Boston...10-20-72
          (overtime period)—22 by Detroit at Cleveland 3-28-73
Most FGA—47 by Boston vs. Minneapolis at Boston 2-27-59
Most FGM—23 by Boston vs. Minneapolis at Boston 2-27-59
          23 by Buffalo at Boston 10-20-72
Most FTA—30 by Boston at Chicago... 1- 9-63
Most FTM—24 by St. Louis vs. Syracuse at Detroit.................................12-21-57
          24 by Cincinnati at Baltimore...12-27-64
Most Rebounds—40 by Philadelphia vs. Syracuse at Philadelphia 11- 9-61
Most Assists—19 by Milwaukee vs. Detroit at Milwaukee...........................12-26-78
Most Personals—18 on Portland at Atlanta 1-16-77
Most Disqualifications—5 from Syracuse at Boston 12-26-50
          5 from Syracuse vs. Baltimore at Syracuse.........*11-15-52

TWO TEAMS

FULL GAME

Most Points—316 (Philadelphia 169, N. Y. 147) at Hershey, Pa................... 3- 2-62
          316 (Cincinnati 165, San Diego 151) at Cincinnati 3-12-70
Most FGA—291 (Philadelphia 153, Los Ang. 138) at Philadelphia..........***12- 8-61
          274 (Boston 149, Detroit 125) at Boston.....................................1-27-61
Most FGM—134 (Cincinnati 67, San Diego 67) at Cincinnati 3-12-70

Most FTA—160 (Syracuse 86, Anderson 74) at Syracuse *****11-24-49
           136 (Baltimore 70, Syracuse 66) at Syracuse *11-15-52
           127 (Fort Wayne 67, Minneapolis 60) 12-31-54
Most FTM—116 (Syracuse 59, Anderson 57) at Syracuse ****11-24-49
Most Rebounds—215 (Philadelphia 110, Los Ang. 105) at Phila. ***12 8-61
           196 (Boston 106, Detroit 90) at Boston 1-27-61
Most Assists—89 (Detroit 48, Cleveland 41) at Cleveland .... * 3-28-73
           88 (Phoenix 47, San Diego 41) at Tucson 3-15-69
Most Personals—122 (Anderson 66 at Syracuse 56) *****11-24-49
           114 (Syracuse 60 vs. Baltimore 54) at Syracuse *11-15-52
           97 (Syracuse 50 vs. N. Y. 47) at Syracuse 2-15-53
Most Disqualifications—13 (Syracuse 8, Baltimore 5) at Syracuse *11-15-52
           11 (Syracuse 6, Boston 5) at Boston 12-26-50

ONE HALF

Most Points—170 (Philadelphia 90, Cincinnati 80) at Philadelphia 3-19-71
Most FGA—153 (Boston 80, Minneapolis 73) at Boston 2-27-59
Most FGM—70 (Boston 40, Minneapolis 30) at Boston 2-27-59
Most FTA—76 (New York 40, St. Louis 36) at St. Louis 12-14-57
Most FTM—54 (Boston 32, Syracuse 22) at Boston 12-26-50
      54 (Boston 31, Rochester 23) at Boston 2- 1-53
      54 (Minneapolis 32, Philadelphia 22) at Camden, N. J. 2-15-57
Most Rebounds—109 (Philadelphia 60, Syracuse 49) at Philadelphia 11- 4-59
           109 (Boston 59, Philadelphia 50) at Philadelphia 12-27-60
Most Assists—47 (Atlanta 24, Portland 23) at Portland 11-18-70
Most Personals—51 (Syracuse 28, Boston 23) at Boston 12-26-50
Most Disqualifications—8 (Rochester 5, Philadelphia 3) at Phila. 12-11-52
         9 (Syracuse 6, Baltimore 3) at Syracuse *11-15-52

ONE QUARTER

Most Points—96 (Boston 52, Minneapolis 44) at Boston 2-27-59
         96 (Detroit 53, Cincinnati 43) at Detroit 1- 7-72
         (overtime period) 37 (Los Ang. 21, Balt. 16) at Balt. 10-21-69
Most FGA—86 (Boston 47, Minneapolis 39) at Boston 2-27-59
Most FGM—40 (Boston 23, Minneapolis 17) at Boston 2-27-59
Most FTA—50 (New York 26 at St. Louis 24) 12-14-57
      50 (Cincinnati 29, Baltimore 21) at Baltimore 12-27-64
Most FTM—39 (Cincinnati 24, Baltimore 15) at Baltimore 12-27-64
      39 (Chicago 22, Denver 17) at Chicago 12-29-78
Most Rebounds—64 (Boston 30, Syracuse 34) at Boston 3-11-61
Most Assists—26 (Philadelphia 14, Los Angeles 12) at Philadelphia 10-21-70
      26 (Milwaukee 19, Detroit 7) at Milwaukee 12-26-78
      26 (San Antonio 17, Boston 9) at San Antonio 2-14-79
      26 (Philadelphia 14, Denver 12) at Denver 2-25-79
      26 (San Antonio 17, Golden State 9) at San Antonio 2-24-81
      26 (Los Angeles 14, Denver 12) at Los Angeles 3-29-81
Most Personals—28 (Portland 18, Atlanta 10) at Atlanta 1-16-77
Most Disqualifications—7 (Syracuse 5, Baltimore 2) at Syracuse *11-15-52
         7 (Syracuse 4, Boston 3) at Boston 12-26-50
         7 (Portland 4, Atlanta 3) at Atlanta 1-16-77

ALL-TIME NBA STATISTICS
MISCELLANEOUS RECORDS

*Overtime.

Most games won—69 by Los Angeles 1971-72
Most games lost—73 by Philadelphia 1972-73
Highest winning percentage—.841 by Los Angeles (69-13) 1971-72
Lowest winning percentage—.110 by Philadelphia (9-73) 1972-73
Most games won at home—37 by Los Angeles..1976-77, 79-80
                                 37 by Philadelphia....................................... 1977-78, 80-81
Most games lost at home—33 by San Diego...1967-68
Most games won on road—32 by Boston ....1972-73 and 1974-75
Most games lost on road—38 by New Orleans..1974-75
                                 38 by Detroit 1979-80
Longest game—6 overtime periods—Indianapolis (75) at Rochester (73) 1- 6-51
Longest winning streak—33 by Los Angeles.............................11- 5-71 to 1- 7-72
Longest winning streak at start of season—15 by Wash............11- 3-48 to 12- 4-48
Longest winning streak at home—36 by Philadelphia ....1-14-66 thru 1-20-67
Longest losing streak—20 by Philadelphia .... 1- 9-73 thru 2-11-73
Longest losing streak at start of season—15 by Denver.........10-29-49 thru 12-25-49
                                 15 by Cleveland.......10-14-70 to 11-10-70
                                 15 by Phila ....10-10-72 thru 11-10-72
Longest winning streak in playoffs—7 by Los Angeles................ 4- 5-70 to 4-19-70
Most points scored in season— 10,143 by Philadelphia 1966-67
Most points scored against— 10,261 on Seattle 1967-68
Highest average points per game —125.4 by Philadelphia 1961-62
Highest average points against— 125.1 vs. Seattle 1967-68
Highest average per game, at home—128.6 by Boston 1959-60
Highest average per game, away —122.4 by Boston......................................1959-60
Most FGA—9,295 by Boston 1960-61
Most FGM—3,972 by Milwaukee 1970-71
Highest FG Pct.—.529 by Los Angeles 1979-80
Highest FT Pct.—.821 by K.C.-Omaha 1974-75
Most FTA—3,411 by Philadelphia..1966-67
Most FTM—2,434 by Phoenix 1969-70
Most rebounds—6,131 by Boston 1960-61
Most assists—2,562 by Milwaukee 1978-79
Most games, 100 points—81 by Los Angeles 1971-72
Most consecutive 100-point games—77 by New York....................................1966-67
Most players scoring 1000 points —6 by Syracuse...1960-61
Most points scored in one game— 173 by Boston vs. Minneapolis 2-27-59
Most points scored in losing game—151 by San Diego at Cincinnati 3-12-70
Most consecutive points in game— 24 by Philadelphia at Baltimore.............3-20-66
Most consecutive points in game—
    15 by Wilt Chamberlain, Philadelphia at Baltimore 3-20-66
Widest margin between teams— 63 (Los Angeles 162, Golden State 99) 3-19-72
Most points scored in season—4,029 by Wilt Chamberlain, Philadelphia 1961-62
Most seasons scoring 1,000 or more points—16 by John Havlicek, Bos........1963-78
Highest scoring average—50.4 by Wilt Chamberlain, Philadelphia..............1961-62
Highest scoring average (in playoffs)—40.6 by Jerry West, L. A 1964-65
Most games 50 or more points— 45 by Wilt Chamberlain, Philadelphia.......1961-62
Most consecutive points, without missing—32 (13-6-32) by Larry Costello...12-8-61
Most points in playoffs—562 by Jerry West, Los Angeles....................................1970
                       562 by Moses Malone, Houston.....................................1981
Most career points in playoffs—4,457 by Jerry West, Los Angeles 1961-74
Highest career scoring average in playoffs—
                30.4 by Kareem Abdul-Jabbar, Milwaukee, L.A..........1969-80
Most FGA—3,159 by Wilt Chamberlain, Philadelphia 1961-62

Most FGM—1,597 by Wilt Chamberlain, Philadelphia 1961-62
Most Consecutive FGM—35 by Wilt Chamberlain, 4 games.....2-17-67 thru 2-28-67
Highest FG Percentage—.727 by Wilt Chamberlain, Los Angeles 1972-73
Most FTA—1,363 by Wilt Chamberlain, Philadelphia 1961-62
Most FTM—840 by Jerry West, Los Angeles 1965-66
Most FTM in playoffs—170 by Jerry West, Los Angeles 1970
Highest FT%—.958 by Calvin Murphy, Houston (206-215)..............................1980-81
Most FTM in game without a miss—19 by Bob Pettit, St. Louis at Bos.......11-22-61
Most FT missed—578 by Wilt Chamberlain, Philadelphia 1967-68
Most FT missed in one game—22 by W. Chamberlain, Phila. vs Seattle.....12- 1-67
Most FT missed in playoff game—17 by W. Chamberlain, Phila. vs. Bos......4-12-66
Most FT missed in a half—12 by Wilt Chamberlain, Phila. vs. Syra 11-17-60
Most FT missed in half, playoff game—
           12 by Wilt Chamberlain, Philadelphia vs. Boston 4-12-66
Most Rebounds—2,149 by Wilt Chamberlain, Philadelphia 1960-61
Most Assists—1,099 by Kevin Porter, Detroit...1978-79
Most Assists by center—702 by Wilt Chamberlain, Philadelphia 1967-68
Highest Assist Average—13.4 by Kevin Porter, Detroit....................................1978-79
Most Personals—367 by Bill Robinzine, Kansas City 1978-79
Most Disqualifications—26 by Don Meineke, Ft. Wayne 1952-53
Most Steals—281 by Don Buse, Indiana..1976-77
Most Blocked Shots—393 by Elmore Smith, Los Angeles.................................1973-74
Most consecutive free throws made—
   78 by Calvin Murphy, Houston ....12-27-80 thru 2-28-81
   56 by Bill Sharman, Boston (playoffs) .... 3-18-59 thru 4- 9-59
Most consecutive games played—844 by John Kerr................10-31-54 thru 11- 4-65
Most consecutive games, no disqualifications (on personals)—
   1,045 by Wilt Chamberlain.......................10-24-59 thru 3-28-73
Most minutes played in one season—3882 by Wilt Chamberlain 1961-62
Most minutes per game, average—48.5 by Wilt Chamberlain 1961-62
Most consecutive minutes played—2193 by Wilt Chamberlain 1960-61
Most consecutive complete games—47 by Wilt Chamberlain 1961-62
Most complete games in season—79 by Wilt Chamberlain 1961-62

MAJOR-LEAGUE ALL-TIME TOP TEN
(ABA INCLUDED)

Most Field Goals Made

Wilt Chamberlain	12,681
Kareem Abdul-Jabbar	10,815
John Havlicek	10,513
Elvin Hayes	9,875
*Rick Barry	9,695
Oscar Robertson	9,508
Jerry West	9,016
Elgin Baylor	8,693
Hal Greer	8,504
*Julius Erving	8,224

Most Field Goals Attempted

John Havlicek	23,900
Wilt Chamberlain	23,497
Elvin Hayes	21,893
*Rick Barry	21,285
Elgin Baylor	20,171
Oscar Robertson	19,620
Kareem Abdul-Jabbar	19,440
Jerry West	19,032
Hal Greer	18,811
Bob Pettit	16,872

HIGHEST SCORING AVERAGE
(400 games or 10,000 Points Minimum)

	G.	FGM	FTM	Pts.	Avg.
Wilt Chamberlain	1045	12681	6057	31419	30.1
Kareem Abdul-Jabbar	935	10815	4640	26270	28.1
Elgin Baylor	846	8693	5763	23149	27.4
Jerry West	932	9016	7160	25192	27.0
Bob McAdoo	599	6225	3339	15792	26.4
Bob Pettit	792	7349	6182	20880	26.4
*Julius Erving	801	8224	4333	20877	26.1
Oscar Robertson	1040	9508	7694	26710	25.7
*George Gervin	673	6734	3631	17185	25.5
*David Thompson	437	4173	2720	11086	25.4

Highest Field Goal Percentage
(2000 FGM Minimum)

	FGA	FGM	Pct.
*Artis Gilmore	11571	6550	.566
*Bobby Jones	5601	3163	.565
Kareem Abdul-Jabbar	19440	10815	.556
Walter Davis	5123	2800	.547
Marques Johnson	5115	2773	.542
Adrian Dantley	5801	3135	.540
Wilt Chamberlain	23497	12681	.540
*Swen Nater	6491	3483	.537
Bernard King	4405	2310	.524
Clifford Ray	2333	4450	.524

Highest Free Throw Percentage
(1200 FTM Minimum)

	FTA	FTM	Pct.
*Rick Barry	6397	5713	.893
Calvin Murphy	3604	3207	.890
Bill Sharman	3557	3143	.884
Mike Newlin	3309	2879	.870
*Mack Calvin	4801	4144	.863
Fred Brown	1924	1650	.858
Ricky Sobers	1705	1460	.856
*James Silas	3424	2926	.855
Larry Siegfried	1945	1662	.854
*Darel Carrier	2024	1723	.851

Most Free Throws Made

Oscar Robertson	7,694
Jerry West	7,160
Dolph Schayes	6,979
Bob Pettit	6,182
Wilt Chamberlain	6,057
Elgin Baylor	5,763
*Rick Barry	5,713
Lenny Wilkens	5,394
John Havlicek	5,369
Walt Bellamy	5,113

Most Minutes Played

Wilt Chamberlain	47,859
John Havlicek	46,471
Oscar Robertson	43,886
Elvin Hayes	43,672
Bill Russell	40,726
Hal Greer	39,788
Walt Bellamy	38,940
*Rick Barry	38,153
Lenny Wilkens	38,064
Kareem Abdul-Jabbar	37,890

*Includes statistics compiled in the ABA

MAJOR-LEAGUE ALL-TIME TOP SCORERS
(ABA included)

Player	Yrs.	G.	Pts.	Avg.
Wilt Chamberlain	14	1045	31419	30.1
Oscar Robertson	14	1040	26710	25.7
John Havlicek	16	1270	26395	20,8
Kareem Abdul-Jabbar	12	935	26270	28.1
*Rick Barry	14	1020	25279	24.8
Jerry West	14	932	25192	27.0
Elvin Hayes	13	1059	24547	23.2
Elgin Baylor	14	846	23149	27.4
Hal Greer	15	1122	21586	19.2
*Dan Issel	11	904	21414	23.7
Walt Bellamy	14	1043	20941	20.1
Bob Pettit	11	792	20880	26.4
*Julius Erving	10	801	20877	26.1
Dolph Schayes	16	1059	19249	18.2
Gail Goodrich	14	1031	19181	18.6
Chet Walker	13	1032	18831	18.2
Dave Bing	12	901	18327	20.3
Lou Hudson	13	890	17940	20.2
Lenny Wilkens	15	1077	17772	16.5
Bailey Howell	12	950	17770	18.7
Earl Monroe	13	926	17454	18.8
*Ron Boone	13	1041	17437	16.8
*George Gervin	9	673	17185	25.5
*Artis Gilmore	10	796	17032	21.4
Bob Cousy	14	924	16960	18.4

*Includes points scored in the ABA

POST-SEASON AWARDS
MOST VALUABLE PLAYER
(Maurice Podoloff Trophy)

1955-56—Bob Pettit, St. Louis
1956-57—Bob Cousy, Boston
1957-58—Bill Russell, Boston
1958-59—Bob Pettit, St. Louis
1959-60—Wilt Chamberlain, Phila.
1960-61—Bill Russell, Boston
1961-62—Bill Russell, Boston
1962-63—Bill Russell, Boston
1963-64—Oscar Robertson, Cincinnati
1964-65—Bill Russell, Boston
1965-66—Wilt Chamberlain, Phila.
1966-67—Wilt Chamberlain, Phila.
1967-68—Wilt Chamberlain, Phila.
1968-69—Wes Unseld, Baltimore
1969-70—Willis Reed, New York
1970-71—Lew Alcindor, Milwaukee
1971-72—Kareem Abdul-Jabbar, Milw.
1972-73—Dave Cowens, Boston
1973-74—Kareem Abdul-Jabbar, Milw.
1974-75—Bob McAdoo, Buffalo
1975-76—Kareem Abdul-Jabbar, L.A.
1976-77—Kareem Abdul-Jabbar, L.A.
1977-78—Bill Walton, Portland
1978-79—Moses Malone, Houston
1979-80—Kareem Abdul-Jabbar, L.A.
1980-81—Julius Erving, Philadelphia

EXECUTIVE OF THE YEAR
Selected by THE SPORTING NEWS

1972-73—Joe Axelson, Kansas City-Omaha
1973-74—Eddie Donovan, Buffalo
1974-75—Dick Vertlieb, Golden State
1975-76—Jerry Colangelo, Phoenix
1976-77—Ray Patterson, Houston
1977-78—Angelo Drossos, San Antonio
1978-79—Bob Ferry, Washington
1979-80—Red Auerbach, Boston
1980-81—Jerry Colangelo, Phoenix

COACH OF THE YEAR
Selected by Writers and Broadcasters

1962-63—Harry Gallatin, St. Louis
1963-64—Alex Hannum, San Francisco
1964-65—Red Auerbach, Boston
1965-66—Dolph Schayes, Philadelphia
1966-67—Johnny Kerr, Chicago
1967-68—Richie Guerin, St. Louis
1968-69—Gene Shue, Baltimore
1969-70—Red Holzman, New York
1970-71—Dick Motta, Chicago
1971-72—Bill Sharman, Los Angeles
1972-73—Tom Heinsohn, Boston
1973-74—Ray Scott, Detroit
1974-75—Phil Johnson, Kansas City-Omaha
1975-76—Bill Fitch, Cleveland
1976-77—Tom Nissalke, Houston
1977-78—Hubie Brown, Atlanta
1978-79—Cotton Fitzsimmons, Kansas City
1979-80—Bill Fitch, Boston
1980-81—Jack McKinney, Indiana

ROOKIE OF THE YEAR
(Eddie Gottlieb Trophy)
Selected by Writers and Broadcasters

1952-53—Don Meineke, Fort Wayne
1953-54—Ray Felix, Baltimore
1954-55—Bob Pettit, Milwaukee
1955-56—Maurice Stokes, Rochester
1956-57—Tom Heinsohn, Boston
1957-58—Woody Sauldsberry, Phila.
1958-59—Elgin Baylor, Minneapolis
1959-60—Wilt Chamberlain, Phila.
1960-61—Oscar Robertson, Cincinnati
1961-62—Walt Bellamy, Chicago
1962-63—Terry Dischinger, Chicago
1963-64—Jerry Lucas, Cincinnati
1964-65—Willis Reed, New York
1965-66—Rick Barry, San Francisco

1966-67 – Dave Bing, Detroit
1967-68 – Earl Monroe, Baltimore
1968-69 – Wes Unseld, Baltimore
1969-70 – Lew Alcindor, Milwaukee
1970-71 – Dave Cowens, Boston, and
 Geoff Petrie, Portland
1971-72 – Sidney Wicks, Portland
1972-73 – Bob McAdoo, Buffalo

1973-74 – Ernie DiGregorio, Buffalo
1974-75 – Keith Wilkes, Golden State
1975-76 – Alvan Adams, Phoenix
1976-77 – Adrian Dantley, Buffalo
1977-78 – Walter Davis, Phoenix
1978-79 – Phil Ford, Kansas City
1979-80 – Larry Bird, Boston
1980-81 – Darrell Griffith, Utah

ALL-ROOKIE TEAMS
Selected by NBA Coaches

1963-64
Jerry Lucas, Cincinnati
Gus Johnson, Baltimore
Nate Thurmond, San Francisco
Art Heyman, New York
Rod Thorn, Baltimore

1964-65
Willis Reed, New York
Jim Barnes, New York
Howard Komives, New York
Lucious Jackson, Philadelphia
Wally Jones, Baltimore
Joe Caldwell, Detroit

1965-66
Rick Barry, San Francisco
Bill Cunningham, Philadelphia
Tom Van Arsdale, Detroit
Dick Van Arsdale, New York
Fred Hetzel, San Francisco

1966-67
Lou Hudson, St. Louis
Jack Marin, Baltimore
Erwin Mueller, Chicago
Cazzie Russell, New York
Dave Bing, Detroit

1967-68
Earl Monroe, Baltimore
Bob Rule, Seattle
Walt Frazier, New York
Al Tucker, Seattle
Phil Jackson, New York

1968-69
Wes Unseld, Baltimore
Elvin Hayes, San Diego
Bill Hewitt, Los Angeles
Art Harris, Seattle
Gary Gregor, Phoenix

1969-70
Lew Alcindor, Milwaukee
Bob Dandridge, Milwaukee
Jo Jo White, Boston
Mike Davis, Baltimore
Dick Garrett, Los Angeles

1970-71
Geoff Petrie, Portland
Dave Cowens, Boston
Pete Maravich, Atlanta
Calvin Murphy, San Diego
Bob Lanier, Detroit

1971-72
Elmore Smith, Buffalo
Sidney Wicks, Portland
Austin Carr, Cleveland
Phil Chenier, Baltimore
Clifford Ray, Chicago

1972-73
Bob McAdoo, Buffalo
Lloyd Neal, Portland
Fred Boyd, Philadelphia
Dwight Davis, Cleveland
Jim Price, Los Angeles

1973-74
Ernie DiGregorio, Buffalo
Ron Behagen, Kansas City-Omaha
Mike Bantom, Phoenix
John Brown, Atlanta
Nick Weatherspoon, Capital

1974-75
Keith Wilkes, Golden State
John Drew, Atlanta
Scott Wedman, Kan. City-Omaha
Tom Burleson, Seattle
Brian Winters, Los Angeles

1975-76
Alvan Adams, Phoenix
Gus Williams, Golden State
Joe Meriweather, Houston
John Shumate, Phoenix-Buffalo
Lionel Hollins, Portland

1976-77
Adrian Dantley, Buffalo
Scott May, Chicago
Mitch Kupchak, Washington
John Lucas, Houston
Ron Lee, Phoenix

1977-78
Walter Davis, Phoenix
Marques Johnson, Milwaukee
Bernard King, New Jersey
Jack Sikma, Seattle
Norm Nixon, Los Angeles

1978-79
Phil Ford, Kansas City
Mychal Thompson, Portland
Ron Brewer, Portland
Reggie Theus, Chicago
Terry Tyler, Detroit

1979-80
Larry Bird, Boston
Earvin Johnson, Los Angeles
Bill Cartwright, New York
Calvin Natt, Portland
David Greenwood, Chicago

1980-81
Joe Barry Carroll, Golden State
Darrell Griffith, Utah
Larry Smith, Golden State
Kevin McHale, Boston
Kelvin Ransey, Portland

ALL-DEFENSIVE TEAMS
Selected by NBA Coaches

FIRST	1968-69	SECOND
Dave DeBusschere, New York		Rudy LaRusso, San Francisco
Nate Thurmond, San Francisco		Tom Sanders, Boston
Bill Russell, Boston		John Havlicek, Boston
Walt Frazier, New York		Jerry West, Los Angeles
Jerry Sloan, Chicago		Bill Bridges, Atlanta

FIRST	1969-70	SECOND
Dave DeBusschere, New York		John Havlicek, Boston
Gus Johnson, Baltimore		Bill Bridges, Atlanta
Willis Reed, New York		Lew Alcindor, Milwaukee
Walt Frazier, New York		Joe Caldwell, Atlanta
Jerry West, Los Angeles		Jerry Sloan, Chicago

FIRST	1970-71	SECOND
Dave DeBusschere, New York		John Havlicek, Boston
Gus Johnson, Baltimore		Paul Silas, Phoenix
Nate Thurmond, San Francisco		Lew Alcindor, Milwaukee
Walt Frazier, New York		Jerry Sloan, Chicago
Jerry West, Los Angeles		Norm Van Lier, Cincinnati

FIRST	1971-72	SECOND
Dave DeBusschere, New York		Paul Silas, Phoenix
John Havlicek, Boston		Bob Love, Chicago
Wilt Chamberlain, Los Angeles		Nate Thurmond, Golden State
Jerry West, Los Angeles		Norm Van Lier, Chicago
Walt Frazier, New York, tie		Don Chaney, Boston
Jerry Sloan, Chicago, tie		

FIRST	1972-73	SECOND
Dave DeBusschere, New York		Paul Silas, Boston
John Havlicek, Boston		Mike Riordan, Baltimore
Wilt Chamberlain, Los Angeles		Nate Thurmond, Golden State
Jerry West, Los Angeles		Norm Van Lier, Chicago
Walt Frazier, New York		Don Chaney, Boston

NBA AWARD WINNERS

FIRST	1973-74	SECOND
Dave DeBusschere, New York		Elvin Hayes, Capital
John Havlicek, Boston		Bob Love, Chicago
Kareem Abdul-Jabbar, Milwaukee		Nate Thurmond, Golden State
Norm Van Lier, Chicago		Don Chaney, Boston
Walt Frazier, New York, tie		Dick Van Arsdale, Phoenix, tie
Jerry Sloan, Chicago, tie		Jim Price, Los Angeles, tie

FIRST	1974-75	SECOND
John Havlicek, Boston		Elvin Hayes, Washington
Paul Silas, Boston		Bob Love, Chicago
Kareem Abdul-Jabbar, Milwaukee		Dave Cowens, Boston
Jerry Sloan, Chicago		Norm Van Lier, Chicago
Walt Frazier, New York		Don Chaney, Boston

FIRST	1975-76	SECOND
Paul Silas, Boston		Jim Brewer, Cleveland
John Havlicek, Boston		Jamaal Wilkes, Golden State
Dave Cowens, Boston		Kareem Abdul-Jabbar, L.A.
Norm Van Lier, Chicago		Jim Cleamons, Cleveland
Don Watts, Seattle		Phil Smith, Golden State

FIRST	1976-77	SECOND
Bobby Jones, Denver		Jim Brewer, Cleveland
E. C. Coleman, New Orleans		Jamaal Wilkes, Golden State
Bill Walton, Portland		Kareem Abdul-Jabbar, L.A.
Don Buse, Indiana		Brian Taylor, Kansas City
Norm Van Lier, Chicago		Don Chaney, Los Angeles

FIRST	1977-78	SECOND
Bobby Jones, Denver		E. C. Coleman, Golden State
Maurice Lucas, Portland		Bob Gross, Portland
Bill Walton, Portland		Kareem Abdul-Jabbar, Los Angeles, tie
		Artis Gilmore, Chicago, tie
Lionel Hollins, Portland		Norm Van Lier, Chicago
Don Buse, Phoenix		Quinn Buckner, Milwaukee

FIRST	1978-79	SECOND
Bobby Jones, Philadelphia		Maurice Lucas, Portland
Bobby Dandridge, Washington		M. L. Carr, Detroit
Kareem Abdul-Jabbar, Los Angeles		Moses Malone, Houston
Dennis Johnson, Seattle		Lionel Hollins, Portland
Don Buse, Phoenix		Eddie Johnson, Atlanta

FIRST	1979-80	SECOND
Bobby Jones, Philadelphia		Scott Wedman, Kansas City
Dan Roundfield, Atlanta		Kermit Washington, Portland
Kareem Abdul-Jabbar, Los Angeles		Dave Cowens, Boston
Dennis Johnson, Seattle		Quinn Buckner, Milwaukee
Don Buse, Phoenix, tie		Eddie Johnson, Atlanta
Michael Ray Richardson, New York, tie		

FIRST	1980-81	SECOND
Bobby Jones, Philadelphia		Dan Roundfield, Atlanta
Caldwell Jones, Philadelphia		Kermit Washington, Portland
Kareem Abdul-Jabbar, Los Angeles		George Johnson, San Antonio
Dennis Johnson, Phoenix		Quinn Buckner, Milwaukee
Michael Ray Richardson, New York		Dudley Bradley, Indiana, tie
		Michael Cooper, Los Angeles, tie

ALL-STAR TEAMS
Selected by Writers and Broadcasters

FIRST	1946-47	SECOND
Joe Fulks (Philadelphia)		Ernie Calverley (Providence)
Bob Feerick (Washington)		Frank Baumholtz (Cleveland)
Stan Miasek (Detroit)		John Logan (St. Louis)
Bones McKinney (Washington)		Chuck Halbert (Chicago)
Max Zaslofsky (Chicago)		Fred Scolari (Washington)

FIRST	1947-48	SECOND
Joe Fulks (Philadelphia)		John Logan (St. Louis)
Max Zaslofsky (Chicago)		Carl Braun (New York)
Ed Sadowski (Boston)		Stan Miasek (Chicago)
Howie Dallmar (Philadelphia)		Fred Scolari (Washington)
Bob Feerick (Washington)		Buddy Jeannette (Baltimore)

FIRST	1948-49	SECOND
George Mikan (Minneapolis)		Arnie Risen (Rochester)
Joe Fulks (Philadelphia)		Bob Feerick (Washington)
Bob Davies (Rochester)		Bones McKinney (Washington)
Max Zaslofsky (Chicago)		Ken Sailors (Providence)
Jim Pollard (Minneapolis)		John Logan (St. Louis)

FIRST	1949-50	SECOND
George Mikan (Minneapolis)		Frank Brian (Anderson)
Jim Pollard (Minneapolis)		Fred Schaus (Fort Wayne)
Alex Groza (Indianapolis)		Dolph Schayes (Syracuse)
Bob Davies (Rochester)		Al Cervi (Syracuse)
Max Zaslofsky (Chicago)		Ralph Beard (Indianapolis)

FIRST	1950-51	SECOND
George Mikan (Minneapolis)		Dolph Schayes (Syracuse)
Alex Groza (Indianapolis)		Frank Brian (Tri-Cities)
Ed Macauley (Boston)		Vern Mikkelsen (Minneapolis)
Bob Davies (Rochester)		Joe Fulks (Philadelphia)
Ralph Beard (Indianapolis)		Dick McGuire (New York)

FIRST	1951-52	SECOND
George Mikan (Minneapolis)		Larry Foust (Fort Wayne)
Ed Macauley (Boston)		Vern Mikkelsen (Minneapolis)
Paul Arizin (Philadelphia)		Jim Pollard (Minneapolis)
Bob Cousy (Boston)		Bob Wanzer (Rochester)
{Bob Davies (Rochester) / Dolph Schayes (Syracuse)}		Andy Phillip (Philadelphia)

FIRST	1952-53	SECOND
George Mikan (Minneapolis)		Bill Sharman (Boston)
Bob Cousy (Boston)		Vern Mikkelsen (Minneapolis)
Neil Johnston (Philadelphia)		Bob Wanzer (Rochester)
Ed Macauley (Boston)		Bob Davies (Rochester)
Dolph Schayes (Syracuse)		Andy Phillip (Philadelphia)

FIRST	1953-54	SECOND
Bob Cousy (Boston)		Ed Macauley (Boston)
Neil Johnston (Philadelphia)		Jim Pollard (Minneapolis)
George Mikan (Minneapolis)		Carl Braun (New York)
Dolph Schayes (Syracuse)		Bob Wanzer (Rochester)
Harry Gallatin (New York)		Paul Seymour (Syracuse)

NBA AWARD WINNERS

FIRST	1954-55	SECOND
Neil Johnston (Philadelphia)		Vern Mikkelsen (Minneapolis)
Bob Cousy (Boston)		Harry Gallatin (New York)
Dolph Schayes (Syracuse)		Paul Seymour (Syracuse)
Bob Pettit (Milwaukee)		Slater Martin (Minneapolis)
Larry Foust (Fort Wayne)		Bill Sharman (Boston)

FIRST	1955-56	SECOND
Bob Pettit (St. Louis)		Dolph Schayes (Syracuse)
Paul Arizin (Philadelphia)		Maurice Stokes (Rochester)
Neil Johnston (Philadelphia)		Clyde Lovellette (Minneapolis)
Bob Cousy (Boston)		Slater Martin (Minneapolis)
Bill Sharman (Boston)		Jack George (Philadelphia)

FIRST	1956-57	SECOND
Paul Arizin (Philadelphia)		George Yardley (Fort Wayne)
Dolph Schayes (Syracuse)		Maurice Stokes (Rochester)
Bob Pettit (St. Louis)		Neil Johnston (Philadelphia)
Bob Cousy (Boston)		Dick Garmaker (Minneapolis)
Bill Sharman (Boston)		Slater Martin (St. Louis)

FIRST	1957-58	SECOND
Dolph Schayes (Syracuse)		Cliff Hagan (St. Louis)
George Yardley (Detroit)		Maurice Stokes (Cincinnati)
Bob Pettit (St. Louis)		Bill Russell (Boston)
Bob Cousy (Boston)		Tom Gola (Philadelphia)
Bill Sharman (Boston)		Slater Martin (St. Louis)

FIRST	1958-59	SECOND
Bob Pettit (St. Louis)		Paul Arizin (Philadelphia)
Elgin Baylor (Minneapolis)		Cliff Hagan (St. Louis)
Bill Russell (Boston)		Dolph Schayes (Syracuse)
Bob Cousy (Boston)		Slater Martin (St. Louis)
Bill Sharman (Boston)		Richie Guerin (New York)

FIRST	1959-60	SECOND
Bob Pettit (St. Louis)		Jack Twyman (Cincinnati)
Elgin Baylor (Minneapolis)		Dolph Schayes (Syracuse)
Wilt Chamberlain (Philadelphia)		Bill Russell (Boston)
Bob Cousy (Boston)		Richie Guerin (New York)
Gene Shue (Detroit)		Bill Sharman (Boston)

FIRST	1960-61	SECOND
Elgin Baylor (Los Angeles)		Dolph Schayes (Syracuse)
Bob Pettit (St. Louis)		Tom Heinsohn (Boston)
Wilt Chamberlain (Philadelphia)		Bill Russell (Boston)
Bob Cousy (Boston)		Larry Costello (Syracuse)
Oscar Robertson (Cincinnati)		Gene Shue (Detroit)

FIRST	1961-62	SECOND
Bob Pettit (St. Louis)		Tom Heinsohn (Boston)
Elgin Baylor (Los Angeles)		Jack Twyman (Cincinnati)
Wilt Chamberlain (Philadelphia)		Bill Russell (Boston)
Jerry West (Los Angeles)		Richie Guerin (New York)
Oscar Robertson (Cincinnati)		Bob Cousy (Boston)

FIRST	1962-63	SECOND
Elgin Baylor (Los Angeles)		Tom Heinsohn (Boston)
Bob Pettit (St. Louis)		Bailey Howell (Detroit)
Bill Russell (Boston)		Wilt Chamberlain (San Francisco)
Oscar Robertson (Cincinnati)		Bob Cousy (Boston)
Jerry West (Los Angeles)		Hal Greer (Syracuse)

NBA AWARD WINNERS

1963-64

FIRST
- Bob Pettit (St. Louis)
- Elgin Baylor (Los Angeles)
- Wilt Chamberlain (San Francisco)
- Oscar Robertson (Cincinnati)
- Jerry West (Los Angeles)

SECOND
- Tom Heinsohn (Boston)
- Jerry Lucas (Cincinnati)
- Bill Russell (Boston)
- John Havlicek (Boston)
- Hal Greer (Philadelphia)

1964-65

FIRST
- Elgin Baylor (Los Angeles)
- Jerry Lucas (Cincinnati)
- Bill Russell (Boston)
- Oscar Robertson (Cincinnati)
- Jerry West (Los Angeles)

SECOND
- Bob Pettit (St. Louis)
- Gus Johnson (Baltimore)
- Wilt Chamberlain (S. F.-Phila.)
- Sam Jones (Boston)
- Hal Greer (Philadelphia)

1965-66

FIRST
- Rick Barry (San Francisco)
- Jerry Lucas (Cincinnati)
- Wilt Chamberlain (Philadelphia)
- Oscar Robertson (Cincinnati)
- Jerry West (Los Angeles)

SECOND
- John Havlicek (Boston)
- Gus Johnson (Baltimore)
- Bill Russell (Boston)
- Sam Jones (Boston)
- Hal Greer (Philadelphia)

1966-67

FIRST
- Rick Barry (San Francisco)
- Elgin Baylor (Los Angeles)
- Wilt Chamberlain (Philadelphia)
- Jerry West (Los Angeles)
- Oscar Robertson (Cincinnati)

SECOND
- Willis Reed (New York)
- Jerry Lucas (Cincinnati)
- Bill Russell (Boston)
- Hal Greer (Philadelphia)
- Sam Jones (Boston)

1967-68

FIRST
- Elgin Baylor (Los Angeles)
- Jerry Lucas (Cincinnati)
- Wilt Chamberlain (Philadelphia)
- Dave Bing (Detroit)
- Oscar Robertson (Cincinnati)

SECOND
- Willis Reed (New York)
- John Havlicek (Boston)
- Bill Russell (Boston)
- Hal Greer (Philadelphia)
- Jerry West (Los Angeles)

1968-69

FIRST
- Billy Cunningham (Philadelphia)
- Elgin Baylor (Los Angeles)
- Wes Unseld (Baltimore)
- Earl Monroe (Baltimore)
- Oscar Robertson (Cincinnati)

SECOND
- John Havlicek (Boston)
- Dave DeBusschere (Detroit-New York)
- Willis Reed (New York)
- Hal Greer (Philadelphia)
- Jerry West (Los Angeles)

1969-70

FIRST
- Billy Cunningham (Philadelphia)
- Connie Hawkins (Phoenix)
- Willis Reed (New York)
- Jerry West (Los Angeles)
- Walt Frazier (New York)

SECOND
- John Havlicek (Boston)
- Gus Johnson (Baltimore)
- Lew Alcindor (Milwaukee)
- Lou Hudson (Atlanta)
- Oscar Robertson (Cincinnati)

1970-71

FIRST
- John Havlicek (Boston)
- Billy Cunningham (Philadelphia)
- Lew Alcindor (Milwaukee)
- Jerry West (Los Angeles)
- Dave Bing (Detroit)

SECOND
- Gus Johnson (Baltimore)
- Bob Love (Chicago)
- Willis Reed (New York)
- Walt Frazier (New York)
- Oscar Robertson (Milwaukee)

1971-72

FIRST
- John Havlicek (Boston)
- Spencer Haywood (Seattle)
- Kareem Abdul-Jabbar (Milwaukee)
- Jerry West (Los Angeles)
- Walt Frazier (New York)

SECOND
- Bob Love (Chicago)
- Billy Cunningham (Philadelphia)
- Wilt Chamberlain (Los Angeles)
- Nate Archibald (Cincinnati)
- Archie Clark (Phila.-Balt.)

NBA AWARD WINNERS

FIRST	1972-73	SECOND
John Havlicek (Boston)		Elvin Hayes (Baltimore)
Spencer Haywood (Seattle)		Rick Barry (Golden State)
Kareem Abdul-Jabbar (Milwaukee)		Dave Cowens (Boston)
Nate Archibald (Kansas City-Omaha)		Walt Frazier (New York)
Jerry West (Los Angeles)		Pete Maravich (Atlanta)

FIRST	1973-74	SECOND
John Havlicek (Boston)		Elvin Hayes (Capital)
Rick Barry (Golden State)		Spencer Haywood (Seattle)
Kareem Abdul-Jabbar (Milwaukee)		Bob McAdoo (Buffalo)
Walt Frazier (New York)		Dave Bing (Detroit)
Gail Goodrich (Los Angeles)		Norm Van Lier (Chicago)

FIRST	1974-75	SECOND
Rick Barry (Golden State)		John Havlicek (Boston)
Elvin Hayes (Washington)		Spencer Haywood (Seattle)
Bob McAdoo (Buffalo)		Dave Cowens (Boston)
Nate Archibald (Kansas City-Omaha)		Phil Chenier (Washington)
Walt Frazier (New York)		Jo Jo White (Boston)

FIRST	1975-76	SECOND
Rick Barry (Golden State)		Elvin Hayes (Washington)
George McGinnis (Philadelphia)		John Havlicek (Boston)
Kareem Abdul-Jabbar (Los Angeles)		Dave Cowens (Boston)
Nate Archibald (Kansas City)		Randy Smith (Buffalo)
Pete Maravich (New Orleans)		Phil Smith (Golden State)

FIRST	1976-77	SECOND
Elvin Hayes (Washington)		Julius Erving (Philadelphia)
David Thompson (Denver)		George McGinnis (Philadelphia)
Kareem Abdul-Jabbar (L. Ang.)		Bill Walton (Portland)
Pete Maravich (New Orleans)		George Gervin (San Antonio)
Paul Westphal (Phoenix)		Jo Jo White (Boston)

FIRST	1977-78	SECOND
Leonard Robinson (New Orleans)		Walter Davis (Phoenix)
Julius Erving (Philadelphia)		Maurice Lucas (Portland)
Bill Walton (Portland)		Kareem Abdul-Jabbar (Los Angeles)
George Gervin (San Antonio)		Paul Westphal (Phoenix)
David Thompson (Denver)		Pete Maravich (New Orleans)

FIRST	1978-79	SECOND
Marques Johnson (Milwaukee)		Walter Davis (Phoenix)
Elvin Hayes (Washington)		Bobby Dandridge (Washington)
Moses Malone (Houston)		Kareem Abdul-Jabbar (Los Angeles)
George Gervin (San Antonio)		Lloyd Free (San Diego)
Paul Westphal (Phoenix)		Phil Ford (Kansas City)

FIRST	1979-80	SECOND
Julius Erving (Philadelphia)		Dan Roundfield (Atlanta)
Larry Bird (Boston)		Marques Johnson (Milwaukee)
Kareem Abdul-Jabbar (Los Angeles)		Moses Malone (Houston)
George Gervin (San Antonio)		Dennis Johnson (Seattle)
Paul Westphal (Phoenix)		Gus Williams (Seattle)

NBA AWARD WINNERS

FIRST	1980-81	SECOND
Julius Erving, Philadelphia		Marques Johnson, Milwaukee
Larry Bird, Boston		Adrian Dantley, Utah
Kareem Abdul-Jabbar, Los Angeles		Moses Malone, Houston
George Gervin, San Antonio		Otis Birdsong, Kansas City
Dennis Johnson, Phoenix		Nate Archibald, Boston

PLAYERS WHO HAVE MADE NBA ALL-STAR TEAMS
(Official All-Star Teams at End of Season; Active 1980-81 Players in CAPS)

	1st Team	2nd
Bob Cousy	10	2
Jerry West	10	2
Bob Pettit	10	1
Elgin Baylor	10	0
Oscar Robertson	9	2
KAREEM ABDUL-JABBAR	8	3
Wilt Chamberlain	7	3
George Mikan	6	0
Dolph Schayes	6	6
RICK BARRY	5	1
John Havlicek	4	7
Bill Sharman	4	3
Walt Frazier	4	2
NATE ARCHIBALD	4	1
Bob Davies	4	1
GEORGE GERVIN	4	1
Neil Johnston	4	1
Max Zaslofsky	4	0
Bill Russell	3	8
ELVIN HAYES	3	3
Jerry Lucas	3	2
Paul Arizin	3	1
Billy Cunningham	3	1
JULIUS ERVING	3	1
Joe Fulks	3	1
Ed Macauley	3	1
PAUL WESTPHAL	3	1
Spencer Haywood	2	2
Pete Maravich	2	2
Jim Pollard	2	1
Dave Bing	2	1
Bob Feerick	2	1
LARRY BIRD	2	0
Alex Groza	2	0
DAVID THOMPSON	2	0
Willis Reed	1	4
MARQUES JOHNSON	1	2
MOSES MALONE	1	2
Ralph Beard	1	1
Larry Foust	1	1
Harry Gallatin	1	1
DENNIS JOHNSON	1	1
BOB McADOO	1	1
GEORGE McGINNIS	1	1
Bones McKinney	1	1
Stan Miasek	1	1
Gene Shue	1	1
Bill Walton	1	1
George Yardley	1	1
Howard Dallmar	1	0
Gail Goodrich	1	0
Connie Hawkins	1	0
Earl Monroe	1	0
LEONARD ROBINSON	1	0
WES UNSELD	1	0
Hal Greer	0	7
Slater Martin	0	5
Tom Heinsohn	0	4
Gus Johnson	0	4
Vern Mikkelsen	0	4
Dave Cowens	0	3
Richie Guerin	0	3
Sam Jones	0	3
John Logan	0	3
Maurice Stokes	0	3
Bob Wanzer	0	3
Carl Braun	0	2
Frank Brian	0	2
Cliff Hagan	0	2
WALTER DAVIS	0	2
Bob Love	0	2
Andy Phillip	0	2
Fred Scolari	0	2
Paul Seymour	0	2
Jack Twyman	0	2
JO JO WHITE	0	2
Frank Baumholtz	0	1
OTIS BIRDSONG	0	1
Ernie Calverley	0	1
Al Cervi	0	1
PHIL CHENIER	0	1
Archie Clark	0	1
Larry Costello	0	1
BOBBY DANDRIDGE	0	1
ADRIAN DANTLEY	0	1
Dave DeBusschere	0	1
PHIL FORD	0	1
LLOYD FREE	0	1
Dick Garmaker	0	1
Jack George	0	1
Tom Gola	0	1
Chuck Halbert	0	1
Bailey Howell	0	1
Lou Hudson	0	1
Buddy Jeannette	0	1
Clyde Lovellette	0	1
MAURICE LUCAS	0	1
Dick McGuire	0	1
Arnie Risen	0	1
DAN ROUNDFIELD	0	1
Ken Sailors	0	1
Fred Schaus	0	1
PHIL SMITH	0	1
RANDY SMITH	0	1
Norm Van Lier	0	1
Gus Williams	0	1

INDIVIDUAL CAREER HIGHS
REGULAR SEASON

Player	FGM	FGA	FTM	FTA	Reb.	Ast.	Pts.
Kareem Abdul-Jabbar	24	39	20	25	34	14	55
Tom Abernethy	11	17	8	11	12	6	24
Alvan Adams	18	31	14	17	19	12	47
Darrell Allums	4	8	3	5	8	4	11
Nate Archibald	22	39	23	25	9	21	55
Dennis Awtrey	10	20	9	10	21	9	24
James Bailey	12	19	11	14	21	5	27
Greg Ballard	16	27	9	11	18	7	38
Mike Bantom	16	27	12	15	19	11	38
Billy Ray Bates	16	25	10	11	9	10	40
Mel Bennett	6	11	11	14	14	5	19
Kent Benson	12	23	10	13	16	8	28
Henry Bibby	12	24	14	16	11	15	28
Larry Bird	19	32	12	13	21	12	45
Otis Birdsong	20	30	12	17	11	11	49
Norman Black	2	5	2	8	1	1	4
Ron Boone	16	28	13	15	9	11	43
Winford Boynes	12	21	8	10	9	6	32
Dudley Bradley	11	16	10	13	8	10	22
Mike Bratz	10	18	9	11	8	12	22
Jim Brewer	12	22	7	10	21	9	26
Ron Brewer	14	28	9	11	9	8	33
Junior Bridgeman	16	25	11	12	12	10	41
Allan Bristow	12	20	9	10	13	14	31
David Britton	1	2	0	0	1	2	2
Michael Brooks	16	24	9	13	14	10	35
Fred Brown	24	37	13	15	14	15	58
Lewis Brown	0	3	2	5	2	0	2
Ricky Brown	7	13	3	3	15	2	15
Joe Bryant	14	23	14	17	14	7	34
Quinn Buckner	19	25	8	10	10	18	40
Tom Burleson	15	25	11	17	20	8	35
Don Buse	10	15	8	10	12	17	21
Marty Byrnes	10	17	8	10	10	5	25
Mack Calvin	8	21	14	15	8	10	26
Austin Carr	18	32	14	15	13	11	42
Kenny Carr	15	20	12	16	20	6	32
M. L. Carr	15	24	11	13	18	9	36
Joe Barry Carroll	17	31	12	17	21	7	46
Butch Carter	8	14	6	8	5	4	16
Reggie Carter	5	12	4	5	5	7	11
Bill Cartwright	16	23	13	17	18	5	37
Harvey Catchings	7	13	7	8	19	7	16
Maurice Cheeks	11	16	7	9	10	15	27
Phil Chenier	22	33	12	16	12	11	53
Jim Chones	14	26	9	14	21	7	31
Art Collins	5	8	5	6	4	4	15
Don Collins	10	18	11	17	9	8	27
Doug Collins	15	25	14	16	12	14	39
Darwin Cook	13	21	9	10	13	15	35
Jeff Cook	8	15	9	10	15	6	16

ACTIVE PLAYERS CAREER HIGHS

Player	FGM	FGA	FTM	FTA	Reb.	Ast.	Pts.
Mike Cooper	9	19	7	8	13	11	20
Wayne Cooper	11	19	12	14	19	4	30
Dave Corzine	11	18	8	10	17	7	24
Charlie Criss	11	23	12	13	6	11	30
Geff Crompton	3	7	2	3	7	2	6
Pat Cummings	13	17	10	11	12	4	30
Earl Cureton	7	17	4	6	15	3	16
Bob Dandridge	18	33	13	16	18	12	40
Adrian Dantley	24	36	26	29	19	10	55
Brad Davis	11	15	8	9	7	16	31
Johnny Davis	14	26	13	14	8	14	35
Monti Davis	1	4	0	0	3	0	2
Ron Davis	8	14	7	10	6	3	18
Walter Davis	17	33	19	21	13	10	42
Darryl Dawkins	14	25	11	19	18	7	34
Larry Demic	9	16	7	9	15	4	19
Coby Dietrick	11	18	9	13	13	9	24
James Donaldson	8	13	6	10	14	3	20
Jacky Dorsey	3	9	3	6	10	3	9
Leon Douglas	13	22	11	14	24	6	30
John Drew	21	34	21	28	25	8	50
Larry Drew	11	17	8	11	7	9	23
Ralph Drollinger	4	5	1	4	7	5	8
Terry Duerod	13	28	5	8	8	7	28
Mike Dunleavy	19	30	12	15	7	16	48
T. R. Dunn	10	18	8	12	14	7	23
John Duren	5	11	1	2	4	6	10
James Edwards	16	25	11	16	17	7	39
Bob Elliott	8	14	12	14	11	7	22
Len Elmore	7	15	9	9	15	6	23
Alex English	17	29	12	14	20	9	40
Julius Erving	19	32	19	20	18	12	45
Mike Evans	9	16	6	7	6	9	21
Eric Fernsten	5	11	5	7	9	4	11
Chris Ford	17	28	15	16	14	15	34
Don Ford	10	20	7	8	15	8	25
Phil Ford	15	28	18	22	7	22	38
Lloyd Free	21	33	22	29	11	13	49
Tony Fuller	4	10	3	4	12	5	9
Mike Gale	10	16	8	8	10	14	24
Calvin Garrett	9	18	4	7	13	7	22
Gus Gerard	10	17	9	11	9	6	25
George Gervin	24	49	18	21	13	11	63
Artis Gilmore	15	26	20	25	28	9	42
Mike Glenn	13	17	9	9	6	8	31
Mike Gminski	12	23	15	16	20	6	31
Glen Gondrezick	9	16	9	10	16	6	27
Ricky Green	10	17	7	11	8	10	22
David Greenwood	14	26	12	13	18	8	31
Kevin Grevey	15	26	13	15	10	10	43
Paul Griffin	9	14	9	13	25	10	20
Darrell Griffith	15	28	10	12	8	8	38
Bob Gross	13	20	12	12	17	11	27
Ernie Grunfeld	12	18	9	13	13	12	30
Roy Hamilton	7	15	7	9	6	9	17

ACTIVE PLAYERS CAREER HIGHS

Player	FGM	FGA	FTM	FTA	Reb.	Ast.	Pts.
Bill Hanzlik	8	11	6	8	7	7	21
Alan Hardy	4	9	3	4	3	1	8
James Hardy	9	15	5	6	16	8	22
Mike Harper	5	9	6	12	7	2	12
Joey Hassett	11	21	5	6	6	7	23
Steve Hawes	11	23	16	17	21	10	32
Elvin Hayes	20	45	17	23	35	11	54
Garfield Heard	17	27	11	14	25	9	36
Gerald Henderson	9	20	9	10	6	10	19
Tom Henderson	14	27	12	16	12	17	33
Keith Herron	14	23	10	11	7	4	29
Ken Higgs	9	13	9	12	6	16	21
Johnny High	9	15	7	9	9	8	20
Armond Hill	11	20	13	17	8	18	26
Brad Holland	5	11	5	7	4	4	12
Lionel Hollins	20	31	12	14	10	12	43
Cedrick Hordges	7	15	8	10	17	4	21
Phil Hubbard	11	22	14	19	21	7	30
Kim Hughes	7	13	3	6	18	7	14
Geoff Huston	13	25	8	11	6	11	29
Dan Issel	17	29	19	23	21	10	47
Tony Jackson	1	2	0	0	2	2	2
Abdul Jeelani	12	20	13	14	11	5	31
Clemon Johnson	9	14	7	9	17	7	22
Dennis Johnson	14	29	16	18	12	11	39
Earvin Johnson	17	26	15	21	18	17	41
Eddie Johnson	16	30	11	14	9	13	40
George Johnson	12	21	8	12	16	7	30
George T. Johnson	11	20	7	10	30	7	25
John Johnson	17	27	17	20	16	16	40
Lee Johnson	2	5	2	3	6	1	6
Marques Johnson	17	32	14	18	18	11	40
Mickey Johnson	16	33	17	21	22	15	41
Ollie Johnson	12	19	11	16	14	8	24
Reggie Johnson	11	19	8	11	13	4	27
Vinnie Johnson	13	20	11	12	11	12	31
Bobby Jones	12	21	13	14	18	9	33
Caldwell Jones	10	18	11	13	27	7	22
Dwight Jones	14	23	9	11	22	8	33
Edgar Jones	10	18	10	13	13	3	27
Major Jones	9	19	5	11	10	6	18
Eddie Jordan	13	26	11	13	13	15	30
Walter Jordan	4	7	2	3	5	3	8
Jeff Judkins	13	18	7	10	7	6	29
Clarence Kea	7	11	11	15	13	2	22
Rich Kelley	12	28	21	25	25	12	33
Greg Kelser	14	26	12	15	17	6	34
Larry Kenon	23	33	14	16	21	11	51
Chad Kinch	5	13	4	4	5	4	10
Bernard King	20	34	13	18	18	11	50
Reggie King	13	21	12	18	20	5	33
Billy Knight	20	32	15	18	16	9	52
Toby Knight	19	30	11	12	16	5	43
Joel Kramer	8	11	8	11	12	6	18
Wayne Kreklow	2	6	3	4	3	2	4

ACTIVE PLAYERS CAREER HIGHS

Player	FGM	FGA	FTM	FTA	Reb.	Ast.	Pts.
Kevin Kunnert	14	23	7	9	23	7	31
Mitch Kupchak	13	21	14	19	20	6	32
Sam Lacey	13	27	10	14	26	14	28
Tom LaGarde	14	20	9	13	17	9	32
Bill Laimbeer	11	18	8	9	22	8	26
John Lambert	9	14	7	8	22	5	18
Mark Landsberger	12	26	7	12	29	5	25
Bob Lanier	20	41	16	24	33	12	48
Edmund Lawrence	3	4	2	4	3	1	6
Allen Leavell	11	18	8	9	7	17	24
Ron Lee	14	25	8	10	15	15	33
Ronnie Lester	4	6	4	4	3	3	9
Scott Lloyd	11	19	8	11	16	10	28
John Long	18	31	11	13	13	12	40
John Lucas	15	26	11	15	10	22	35
Maurice Lucas	19	32	15	19	26	10	46
Oliver Mack	13	23	6	7	10	7	28
Kyle Macy	9	14	6	7	6	6	21
Ricky Mahorn	10	13	8	9	16	4	28
Moses Malone	20	33	21	26	37	6	51
Wes Matthews	11	18	12	13	7	18	26
Cedric Maxwell	13	20	19	22	19	9	35
Scott May	11	21	10	11	14	8	27
William Mayfield	3	6	1	2	4	1	6
Bob McAdoo	22	37	18	22	29	10	52
Andre McCarter	11	16	4	6	8	10	22
Keith McCord	1	3	0	0	2	1	2
James McElroy	16	26	12	16	8	16	40
George McGinnis	16	32	15	23	25	12	43
Kevin McHale	10	17	8	9	11	3	23
Billy McKinney	14	16	11	12	7	11	30
Tom McMillen	14	22	9	10	19	6	31
John Mengelt	14	22	13	16	11	12	33
Joe C. Meriweather	14	27	11	15	20	6	29
Dick Miller	2	3	0	0	3	2	4
Mike Mitchell	20	36	11	13	19	6	46
Steve Mix	15	23	12	14	24	8	38
Paul Mokeski	8	16	6	9	13	6	18
Sidney Moncrief	12	19	13	14	14	8	27
Johnny Moore	10	18	7	11	7	19	22
Lowes Moore	9	20	5	6	9	10	19
Calvin Murphy	24	40	13	16	8	16	57
Swen Nater	15	26	12	15	33	10	35
Calvin Natt	15	25	16	22	19	6	39
Kenny Natt	5	15	4	4	2	3	15
Mike Newlin	19	33	18	19	12	15	52
Carl Nicks	11	21	7	9	8	8	24
Mike Niles	5	8	3	4	5	4	10
Norm Nixon	14	24	9	12	9	19	30
Mike O'Koren	12	18	11	14	16	10	28
Mark Olberding	11	20	13	15	16	12	28
Jawann Oldham	1	4	0	0	3	0	2
Louie Orr	11	18	11	12	12	5	22
Tom Owens	15	23	16	19	20	9	37
Robert Parish	16	31	11	15	32	7	40

ACTIVE PLAYERS CAREER HIGHS

Player	FGM	FGA	FTM	FTA	Reb.	Ast.	Pts.
Sonny Parker	16	24	10	14	12	9	36
Myles Patrick	1	3	1	2	1	1	3
Billy Paultz	14	22	11	16	19	8	31
Jim Paxson	15	23	7	10	8	9	32
Sam Pellom	10	17	5	7	14	3	20
Roger Phegley	12	23	13	14	9	7	35
Stan Pietkiewicz	9	13	6	7	6	8	20
Ben Poquette	12	19	9	11	17	6	28
Kevin Porter	16	28	9	12	7	29	40
Tony Price	1	3	0	0	0	3	2
Wally Rank	2	6	2	7	4	3	6
Kelvin Ransey	16	30	7	10	9	14	35
Clifford Ray	11	20	8	16	24	10	24
James Ray	3	9	2	2	6	3	7
Billy Reid	7	13	3	4	6	6	14
Robert Reid	15	26	9	13	16	11	32
Kevin Restani	11	18	7	7	18	9	24
Clint Richardson	11	17	7	8	9	7	24
Michael Ray Richardson	12	22	11	16	16	19	28
Anthony Roberts	10	19	9	11	14	6	27
Rick Robey	13	27	11	13	21	7	28
Cliff Robinson	19	29	9	11	16	6	45
Leonard Robinson	20	33	14	18	27	8	51
Wayne Robinson	8	16	10	12	11	5	19
Bill Robinzine	15	22	12	15	18	7	32
Dave Robisch	15	27	11	13	21	8	36
John Roche	14	24	8	9	5	13	33
Wayne Rollins	11	20	8	9	23	5	24
Lorenzo Romar	7	11	7	8	4	9	14
Dan Roundfield	15	28	14	21	26	9	38
Campy Russell	16	29	15	21	16	12	41
Frankie Sanders	8	18	7	7	11	5	16
DeWayne Scales	9	18	3	5	12	1	20
Alvin Scott	7	11	7	10	12	6	18
Craig Shelton	9	11	6	8	10	3	22
Lonnie Shelton	15	32	11	13	19	7	41
Purvis Short	18	30	13	13	13	12	45
John Shumate	12	19	17	23	22	8	31
Jerry Sichting	4	6	5	7	7	7	12
Jack Sikma	14	25	21	23	23	10	38
James Silas	15	24	17	19	8	12	35
Elmore Smith	17	31	14	21	26	8	40
Larry Smith	10	19	8	10	31	5	23
Phil Smith	20	30	15	20	12	15	51
Randy Smith	18	35	15	18	14	14	41
Robert Smith	7	12	11	12	11	9	19
Ricky Sobers	14	25	14	15	12	16	34
Jim Spanarkel	10	20	12	13	10	10	28
Rory Sparrow	6	11	4	5	4	5	14
Larry Steele	13	21	11	13	11	13	30
John Stroud	5	13	2	2	6	4	11
Brian Taylor	17	24	12	13	2	12	38
Carlos Terry	7	14	14	5	10	6	16
Reggie Theus	14	26	16	18	17	15	33
David Thompson	28	38	20	22	11	12	73

ACTIVE PLAYERS CAREER HIGHS

Player	FGM	FGA	FTM	FTA	Reb.	Ast.	Pts.
Mychal Thompson	14	28	11	14	22	8	37
Rudy Tomjanovich	19	36	12	17	24	10	42
Andrew Toney	14	21	14	17	8	11	35
Dave Twardzik	9	14	16	17	8	11	28
Terry Tyler	14	25	7	10	18	8	32
Wes Unseld	12	24	13	17	32	13	30
Ron Valentine	4	13	2	3	4	2	9
Jan van Breda Kolff	10	16	12	14	16	9	25
Kiki Vandeweghe	9	18	12	13	12	7	30
Brett Vroman	4	6	3	5	5	2	9
Foots Walker	9	17	17	18	12	18	26
Wally Walker	9	17	6	10	13	7	21
Bill Walton	17	31	12	17	26	14	36
Lloyd Walton	9	17	6	8	6	14	20
Kermit Washington	13	20	11	15	21	7	29
Richard Washington	12	22	10	14	21	5	30
Marvin Webster	11	18	11	15	29	8	26
Scott Wedman	19	31	11	16	18	11	45
Paul Westphal	20	35	13	15	10	14	49
Jo Jo White	18	35	12	14	12	15	41
Rudy White	7	14	6	7	5	4	14
Jerome Whitehead	8	13	4	6	14	3	16
Hawkeye Whitney	9	13	5	8	6	6	20
Sidney Wicks	15	33	15	19	27	14	38
Michael Wiley	8	9	7	8	7	2	17
Jeff Wilkins	10	16	3	5	16	3	22
Bob Wilkerson	13	27	8	11	16	14	31
Jamaal Wilkes	16	28	14	17	19	10	34
James Wilkes	10	14	4	5	9	4	21
Freeman Williams	22	34	11	12	8	8	51
Gus Williams	16	35	13	13	9	10	41
Ray Williams	18	32	16	20	12	18	42
Sly Williams	13	19	10	13	15	8	27
John Williamson	19	35	22	24	10	12	50
Bill Willoughby	9	16	8	11	18	5	21
Brian Winters	20	32	15	18	10	18	43
Mike Woodson	11	17	8	9	6	5	25
Sam Worthen	7	9	4	6	7	6	18
Larry Wright	18	21	8	11	10	12	43

PLAYOFFS

Player	FGM	FGA	FTM	FTA	Reb.	Ast.	Pts.
Kareem Abdul-Jabbar	20	37	13	18	31	11	46
Tom Abernethy	7	11	7	8	6	5	16
Alvan Adams	14	27	7	9	20	12	33
Nate Archibald	11	26	12	14	7	14	28
Dennis Awtrey	6	10	4	6	15	8	15
James Bailey	6	11	5	7	7	1	13
Greg Ballard	8	15	7	11	15	6	19
Mike Bantom	9	12	4	6	6	3	19
Billy Ray Bates	16	28	8	8	5	6	34
Kent Benson	3	7	4	4	5	1	6

ACTIVE PLAYERS CAREER HIGHS

Player	FGM	FGA	FTM	FTA	Reb.	Ast.	Pts.
Henry Bibby	9	19	7	9	7	11	22
Larry Bird	15	30	10	10	21	10	35
Otis Birdsong	14	24	7	12	9	7	30
Ron Boone	10	16	5	5	3	4	24
Dudley Bradley	3	7	2	2	2	2	7
Mike Bratz	9	17	8	8	5	6	25
Jim Brewer	7	13	5	7	16	6	15
Ron Brewer	11	24	6	8	7	5	27
Junior Bridgeman	12	19	8	9	7	8	32
Allan Bristow	5	8	4	6	8	7	13
Fred Brown	19	35	11	14	7	6	45
Joe Bryant	5	12	4	5	8	3	13
Quinn Buckner	8	17	5	7	6	10	19
Tom Burleson	12	22	11	13	20	4	33
Don Buse	8	12	8	8	9	9	17
Marty Byrnes	1	2	0	0	1	1	2
Austin Carr	13	23	8	8	6	5	27
Kenny Carr	5	11	2	3	5	2	12
M. L. Carr	8	18	6	7	10	5	23
Reggie Carter	0	1	0	0	2	0	0
Bill Cartwright	3	9	5	8	8	1	11
Harvey Catchings	4	6	2	3	12	3	8
Maurice Cheeks	12	19	9	12	8	13	33
Phil Chenier	14	29	13	15	14	11	39
Jim Chones	11	23	5	6	12	4	23
Doug Collins	15	27	8	11	10	8	36
Jeff Cook	7	12	5	6	12	4	17
Michael Cooper	6	13	8	9	6	10	17
Dave Corzine	6	11	4	6	11	7	18
Charlie Criss	8	16	5	7	3	6	18
Pat Cummings	3	9	3	3	6	1	9
Earl Cureton	2	5	0	2	3	2	4
Bob Dandridge	16	31	10	12	16	9	37
Adrian Dantley	10	14	8	12	10	6	26
Johnny Davis	11	20	7	8	6	8	25
Walter Davis	12	27	11	13	10	8	31
Darryl Dawkins	14	25	14	17	16	6	30
Larry Demic	2	3	1	2	5	0	5
Coby Dietrick	8	14	2	4	8	3	17
John Drew	11	26	11	14	13	4	29
Terry Duerod	2	5	0	0	0	0	4
Leon Douglas	3	8	5	11	8	4	11
Mike Dunleavy	11	22	6	6	4	10	28
T. R. Dunn	2	6	2	2	4	4	6
James Edwards	7	18	0	0	8	3	14
Len Elmore	2	6	1	2	5	1	4
Alex English	10	14	6	8	10	5	26
Julius Erving	17	29	12	16	15	10	40
Mike Evans	3	8	7	8	2	3	13
Eric Fernsten	2	5	2	3	3	1	4
Chris Ford	10	17	5	5	8	9	22
Don Ford	6	13	6	8	14	6	14
Phil Ford	7	17	5	8	6	13	20
Lloyd Free	10	27	11	13	6	6	29
Mike Gale	8	13	2	5	7	9	18

ACTIVE PLAYERS CAREER HIGHS

Player	FGM	FGA	FTM	FTA	Reb.	Ast.	Pts.
Calvin Garrett	3	5	4	4	3	3	8
Gus Gerard	3	5	2	2	6	1	6
George Gervin	19	32	13	17	12	9	46
Artis Gilmore	9	19	9	13	16	3	27
Mike Glenn	3	4	3	3	2	1	6
Glen Gondrezick	4	5	2	4	5	3	8
David Greenwood	11	18	2	5	12	3	24
Kevin Grevey	15	24	11	13	7	6	41
Paul Griffin	4	7	4	7	8	7	12
Bob Gross	12	17	11	12	14	7	26
Ernie Grunfeld	11	19	11	12	8	8	27
Mike Harper	1	1	1	1	1	0	3
Joey Hassett	3	5	0	0	1	1	6
Steve Hawes	9	16	7	8	14	7	20
Elvin Hayes	19	34	12	16	23	6	46
Garfield Heard	11	20	9	11	20	5	24
Gerald Henderson	5	11	3	5	3	6	12
Tom Henderson	11	22	9	13	5	12	31
Johnny High	4	9	5	6	9	6	11
Armond Hill	7	13	4	4	3	9	16
Brad Holland	3	4	2	2	3	1	8
Lionel Hollins	15	28	9	13	9	13	55
Kim Hughes	1	2	1	2	6	0	2
Dan Issel	13	23	14	15	18	6	36
Clemon Johnson	3	7	4	7	13	2	10
Dennis Johnson	12	23	13	17	11	9	33
Earvin Johnson	14	23	14	14	18	16	42
Eddie Johnson	12	22	7	8	6	8	26
George L. Johnson	4	6	0	0	2	1	8
George T. Johnson	8	11	5	7	15	5	18
John Johnson	10	16	9	12	11	13	22
Marques Johnson	16	25	11	11	17	9	36
Mickey Johnson	13	25	14	14	15	5	34
Ollie Johnson	8	14	5	5	6	2	19
Reggie Johnson	10	15	5	7	9	5	25
Vinnie Johnson	1	3	0	0	1	2	2
Bobby Jones	10	20	11	14	11	7	25
Caldwell Jones	8	14	8	11	26	5	24
Dwight Jones	8	15	6	6	14	4	19
Major Jones	5	7	3	3	9	3	11
Eddie Jordan	9	25	4	5	10	9	22
Jeff Judkins	1	2	0	0	2	0	3
Rich Kelley	6	8	3	4	10	7	14
Larry Kenon	15	26	7	7	21	6	37
Bernard King	11	22	5	14	7	5	27
Reggie King	13	24	10	13	16	6	31
Billy Knight	10	18	5	7	7	4	25
Toby Knight	3	8	2	4	9	1	8
Joel Kramer	8	10	5	7	11	5	19
Kevin Kunnert	10	15	4	6	17	5	21
Mitch Kupchak	14	18	8	10	16	6	32
Sam Lacey	7	14	10	12	20	10	18
Tom LaGarde	4	12	4	4	8	6	10
John Lambert	7	12	2	3	6	2	16
Bob Lanier	16	28	11	14	19	9	38

ACTIVE PLAYERS CAREER HIGHS

Player	FGM	FGA	FTM	FTA	Reb.	Ast.	Pts.
Mark Landsberger	5	11	4	4	10	1	10
Allan Leavell	5	10	6	6	4	8	10
Ron Lee	3	6	0	0	3	0	6
Ronnie Lester	4	8	2	3	3	1	10
John Lucas	10	20	7	12	6	14	24
Maurice Lucas	14	24	10	14	16	9	29
Kyle Macy	7	8	4	4	5	3	17
Moses Malone	16	34	18	20	26	5	42
Cedric Maxwell	10	16	8	10	15	6	28
Scott May	4	11	7	8	6	2	15
Bob McAdoo	21	40	12	14	22	6	50
James McElroy	4	6	2	3	2	1	8
George McGinnis	16	24	11	16	16	9	34
Kevin McHale	10	15	5	7	6	2	21
Billy McKinney	5	9	2	2	5	7	10
Tom McMillen	7	14	5	7	14	2	19
John Mengelt	10	17	8	9	5	6	28
Joe C. Meriweather	6	12	4	8	8	2	13
Steve Mix	9	16	7	8	10	7	22
Sidney Moncrief	9	15	11	12	10	4	20
Johnny Moore	4	8	3	5	5	10	11
Calvin Murphy	19	29	12	13	4	13	42
Calvin Natt	11	19	5	8	11	2	27
Mike Newlin	12	21	10	11	9	11	31
Mike Niles	0	4	0	0	0	0	0
Norm Nixon	12	20	6	9	7	19	26
Mark Olberding	14	20	7	9	13	8	34
Louis Orr	7	17	4	4	5	3	16
Tom Owens	12	21	7	10	16	8	31
Robert Parish	12	22	11	15	18	3	27
Sonny Parker	4	8	2	2	6	3	10
Billy Paultz	10	16	8	11	14	6	20
Jim Paxson	4	6	6	6	2	3	8
Sam Pellom	0	3	0	0	0	1	1
Kevin Porter	10	20	8	10	4	13	24
Kelvin Ransey	12	26	2	4	7	10	26
Clifford Ray	12	19	6	10	20	7	25
Robert Reid	12	24	11	14	14	10	33
Kevin Restani	6	12	3	5	8	2	15
Clint Richardson	4	6	2	6	4	3	8
Michael Ray Richardson	4	17	6	10	13	6	14
Anthony Roberts	9	20	10	12	11	6	23
Rick Robey	7	14	4	5	10	4	14
Dave Robisch	8	13	2	3	6	2	16
Leonard Robinson	9	20	10	13	20	4	23
Bill Robinzine	6	14	4	6	10	1	16
Wayne Rollins	6	14	6	10	17	3	18
Dan Roundfield	10	20	10	13	18	7	24
Campy Russell	13	25	13	14	11	6	32
Frankie Sanders	5	10	2	2	3	1	13
Alvin Scott	4	11	6	7	7	4	10
Lonnie Shelton	10	17	11	14	15	6	25
John Shumate	10	16	8	13	16	5	23
Jerry Sichting	0	0	0	0	0	0	0
Jack Sikma	11	18	13	15	17	8	33

ACTIVE PLAYERS CAREER HIGHS

Player	FGM	FGA	FTM	FTA	Reb.	Ast.	Pts.
James Silas	14	25	12	14	8	8	32
Elmore Smith	13	21	8	10	17	2	30
Phil Smith	17	27	9	12	9	8	37
Randy Smith	13	23	10	12	14	13	29
Robert Smith	4	6	2	3	2	4	10
Ricky Sobers	11	22	7	8	8	8	25
Jim Spanarkel	0	1	2	2	1	1	2
Larry Steele	6	15	8	8	6	4	17
Reggie Theus	10	18	17	18	8	11	37
David Thompson	16	30	12	14	8	7	40
Mychal Thompson	15	23	10	12	17	3	40
Rudy Tomjanovich	13	23	10	14	12	5	30
Andrew Toney	11	23	13	14	7	11	35
Dave Twardzik	7	12	8	13	4	5	19
Wes Unseld	12	22	7	12	34	10	26
Jan van Breda Kolff	4	10	3	4	13	5	11
Foots Walker	8	13	4	7	5	11	20
Wally Walker	5	9	6	8	7	2	11
Bill Walton	12	22	6	7	24	10	28
Lloyd Walton	4	8	5	6	2	11	11
Kermit Washington	7	13	3	4	17	6	15
Richard Washington	10	14	2	2	7	2	21
Marvin Webster	11	19	12	17	23	7	28
Scott Wedman	14	25	7	9	11	9	32
Paul Westphal	16	30	10	15	6	10	39
Jo Jo White	16	31	11	12	8	11	40
Rudy White	1	3	0	0	1	0	2
Sidney Wicks	7	15	9	10	13	3	21
Michael Wiley	0	1	2	2	0	0	2
Bob Wilkerson	8	17	4	6	12	10	17
Jamaal Wilkes	16	30	10	13	18	7	37
James Wilkes	0	1	0	0	1	1	0
Gus Williams	17	33	12	16	8	11	38
Ray Williams	10	21	8	11	5	10	24
Sly Williams	9	11	0	0	6	3	18
John Williamson	14	34	10	12	4	5	38
Bill Willoughby	6	12	8	9	9	4	14
Brian Winters	16	24	7	8	7	11	33
Mike Woodson	1	2	2	2	1	0	4
Sam Worthen	0	0	0	0	0	0	0
Larry Wright	12	18	6	6	5	8	26

NOTE

The following pages contain statistics that reflect extensive research on the NBA World Championship Series. Keep in mind that rebounds were not kept as official statistics before 1951, minutes before 1952, offensive rebounds, defensive rebounds, steals and blocked shots before 1974, team turnovers before 1971 and player turnovers before 1978.

NBA WORLD CHAMPIONSHIP SERIES

Year	Dates	Winner (Coach)	Loser (Coach)	Games
1947	Apr. 16-Apr. 22	Philadelphia (Gottlieb)	Chicago (Olsen)	4-1
1948	Apr. 10-Apr. 21	Baltimore (Jeannette)	Philadelphia (Gottlieb)	4-2
1949	Apr. 4-Apr. 13	Minneapolis (Kundla)	Washington (Auerbach)	4-2
1950	Apr. 8-Apr. 23	Minneapolis (Kundla)	*Syracuse (Cervi)	4-2
1951	Apr. 7-Apr. 21	Rochester (Harrison)	New York (Lapchick)	4-3
1952	Apr. 12-Apr. 25	Minneapolis (Kundla)	New York (Lapchick)	4-3
1953	Apr. 4-Apr. 10	*Minneapolis (Kundla)	New York (Lapchick)	4-1
1954	Mar. 31-Apr. 12	*Minneapolis (Kundla)	Syracuse (Cervi)	4-3
1955	Mar. 31-Apr. 10	*Syracuse (Cervi)	*Ft. Wayne (Eckman)	4-3
1956	Mar. 31-Apr. 7	*Philadelphia (Senesky)	Ft. Wayne (Eckman)	4-1
1957	Mar. 30-Apr. 13	*Boston (Auerbach)	St. Louis (Hannum)	4-3
1958	Mar. 29-Apr. 12	St. Louis (Hannum)	*Boston (Auerbach)	4-2
1959	Apr. 4-Apr. 9	*Boston (Auerbach)	Minneapolis (Kundla)	4-0
1960	Mar. 27-Apr. 9	*Boston (Auerbach)	St. Louis (Macauley)	4-3
1961	Apr. 2-Apr. 11	*Boston (Auerbach)	St. Louis (Seymour)	4-1
1962	Apr. 7-Apr. 18	*Boston (Auerbach)	Los Angeles (Schaus)	4-3
1963	Apr. 14-Apr. 24	*Boston (Auerbach)	Los Angeles (Schaus)	4-2
1964	Apr. 18-Apr. 26	*Boston (Auerbach)	San Francisco (Hannum)	4-1
1965	Apr. 18-Apr. 25	*Boston (Auerbach)	Los Angeles (Schaus)	4-1
1966	Apr. 17-Apr. 28	Boston (Auerbach)	Los Angeles (Schaus)	4-3
1967	Apr. 14-Apr. 24	*Philadelphia (Hannum)	San Francisco (Sharman)	4-2
1968	Apr. 21-May 2	Boston (Russell)	Los Ang. (van Breda Kolff)	4-2
1969	Apr. 23-May 5	Boston (Russell)	Los Ang. (van Breda Kolff)	4-3
1970	Apr. 24-May 8	*New York (Holzman)	Los Angeles (Mullaney)	4-3
1971	Apr. 21-Apr. 30	*Milwaukee (Costello)	Baltimore (Shue)	4-0
1972	Apr. 26-May 7	*Los Angeles (Sharman)	New York (Holzman)	4-1
1973	May 1-May 10	New York (Holzman)	Los Angeles (Sharman)	4-1
1974	Apr. 28-May 12	Boston (Heinsohn)	*Milwaukee (Costello)	4-3
1975	May 18-May 25	Golden State (Attles)	*Washington (Jones)	4-0
1976	May 23-June 6	Boston (Heinsohn)	Phoenix (MacLeod)	4-2
1977	May 22-June 5	Portland (Ramsay)	Philadelphia (Shue)	4-2
1978	May 21-June 7	Washington (Motta)	Seattle (Wilkens)	4-3
1979	May 20-June 1	Seattle (Wilkens)	*Washington (Motta)	4-1
1980	May 4-May 16	Los Angeles (Westhead)	Philadelphia (Cunningham)	4-2
1981	May 5-May 14	*Boston (Fitch)	Houston (Harris)	4-2

*Had best record (or tied for best record) during regular season.

Individuals (Series)

MOST POINTS

4 Games
118—Rick Barry, G.S. 1975
108—Lew Alcindor, Milw. 1971
97—Tom Heinsohn, Bos. 1959

5 Games
169—Jerry West, L.A. 1965
147—Cliff Hagan, St.L. 1961
146—Wilt Chamberlain, S.F. 1964

6 Games
245—Rick Barry, S.F. 1967
203—Elgin Baylor, L.A. 1963
193—George Mikan, Minn. 1950

7 Games
284—Elgin Baylor, L.A. 1962
265—Jerry West, L.A. 1969
237—Jerry West, L.A. 1966

MOST MINUTES PLAYED

4 Games
186—Bob Cousy, Bos. 1959
　　　Bill Russell, Bos. 1959
173—Phil Chenier, Wash. 1975
172—Rick Barry, G.S. 1975
　　　Wes Unseld, Wash. 1975

5 Games
240—Wilt Chamberlain, L.A. 1973
236—Wilt Chamberlain, L.A. 1972
233—Bill Russell, Bos. 1961

6 Games
292—Bill Russell, Bos. 1968
291—John Havlicek, Bos. 1968
287—Bill Russell, Bos. 1963
　　　Wilt Chamberlain, Phila. 1967

7 Games
345—K. Abdul-Jabbar, Milw. 1974
338—Bill Russell, Bos. 1962
337—Oscar Robertson, Milw. 1974

Highest Field Goal Percentage
(minimum: 4 FG per game)

4 Games
.739—Derrek Dickey, G.S. 1975
.605—Lew Alcindor, Milw. 1971
.558—Kevin Porter, Wash. 1975

5 Games
.702—Bill Russell, Bos. 1965
.600—Wilt Chamberlain, L.A. 1972
.585—Walt Frazier, N.Y. 1972

6 Games
.667—Bob Gross, Port. 1977
.589—Don Nelson, Bos. 1968
.577—Maurice Cheeks, Phila. 1980

7 Games
.625—Wilt Chamberlain, L.A. 1970
.545—Mickey Davis, Milw. 1974
.543—Bill Russell, Bos. 1962

MOST FIELD GOALS

4 Games
46—Lew Alcindor, Milw. 1971
44—Rick Barry, G.S. 1975
38—Tom Heinsohn, Bos. 1959

5 Games
62—Wilt Chamberlain, S.F. 1964
59—Jerry West, L.A. 1965
56—Gus Williams, Sea. 1979

6 Games
94—Rick Barry, S.F. 1967
76—Elgin Baylor, L.A. 1963
　　Jerry West, L.A. 1963
73—K. Abdul-Jabbar, L.A. 1980

7 Games
101—Elgin Baylor, L.A. 1962
 97—K. Abdul-Jabbar, Milw. 1974
 96—Jerry West, L.A. 1969

MOST FIELD GOAL ATTEMPTS

4 Games
102—Elgin Baylor, Minn. 1959
 99—Rick Barry, G.S. 1975
 80—Tom Heinsohn, Bos. 1959

5 Games
139—Jerry West, L.A. 1965
129—Paul Arizin, Phila. 1956
120—Wilt Chamberlain, S.F. 1964

6 Games
235—Rick Barry, S.F. 1967
163—Elgin Baylor, L.A. 1963
155—Jerry West, L.A. 1963

7 Games
235—Elgin Baylor, L.A. 1962
196—Jerry West, L.A. 1969
185—K. Abdul-Jabbar, Milw. 1974

CHAMPIONSHIP SERIES STATISTICS

HIGHEST FREE THROW PERCENTAGE
(minimum: 2 FTM per game)

4 Games
.944—Phil Chenier, Wash. 1975
.941—Bill Sharman, Bos. 1959
.938—Rick Barry, G.S. 1975

5 Games
.957—Jim McMillian, L.A. 1972
.950—Vern Mikkelsen, Minn. 1953
.929—Bill Bradley, N.Y. 1973

6 Games
.968—Bill Sharman, Bos. 1958
.944—Al Cervi, Syr. 1950
.929—Lionel Hollins, Phila. 1980

7 Games
.959—Bill Sharman, Bos. 1957
.947—Don Meineke, Ft.W. 1955
.944—Dick Garrett, L.A. 1970

MOST FREE THROWS MADE

4 Games
34—Phil Chenier, Wash. 1975
30—Rick Barry, G.S. 1975
26—Frank Ramsey, Bos. 1959
　　Oscar Robertson, Milw. 1971

5 Games
51—Jerry West, L.A. 1965
48—Bob Pettit, St.L. 1961
44—George Mikan, Minn. 1953

6 Games
67—George Mikan, Minn. 1950
61—Joe Fulks, Phila. 1948
60—Bob Pettit, St.L. 1958

7 Games
82—Elgin Baylor, L.A. 1962
75—Jerry West, L.A. 1970
73—Bob Pettit, St.L. 1957
　　Jerry West, L.A. 1969

MOST FREE THROW ATTEMPTS

4 Games
36—Phil Chenier, Wash. 1975
35—Elgin Baylor, Minn. 1959
32—Oscar Robertson, Milw. 1971
　　Rick Barry, G.S. 1975

5 Games
60—Bob Pettit, St.L. 1961
59—Jerry West, L.A. 1965
58—George Mikan, Minn. 1953

6 Games
86—George Mikan, Minn. 1950
79—Bob Pettit, St.L. 1958
72—Rick Barry, S.F. 1967
　　Wilt Chamberlain, Phila. 1967

7 Games
99—Elgin Baylor, L.A. 1962
97—Bob Pettit, St.L. 1957
90—Jerry West, L.A. 1970

MOST REBOUNDS

4 Games
118—Bill Russell, Bos. 1959
76—Wes Unseld, Balt. 1971
74—Lew Alcindor, Milw. 1971

5 Games
144—Bill Russell, Bos. 1961
138—Wilt Chamberlain, S.F. 1964
126—Bill Russell, Bos. 1964

6 Games
171—Wilt Chamberlain, Phila. 1967
160—Nate Thurmond, S.F. 1967
156—Bill Russell, Bos. 1963

7 Games
189—Bill Russell, Bos. 1962
175—Wilt Chamberlain, L.A. 1969
174—Bill Russell, Bos. 1960

MOST OFFENSIVE REBOUNDS

4 Games
16—George Johnson, G.S. 1975
15—Clifford Ray, G.S. 1975
14—Wes Unseld, Wash. 1975

5 Games
21—Elvin Hayes, Wash. 1979
20—Wes Unseld, Wash. 1979
13—Bob Dandridge, Wash. 1979
  John Johnson, Sea. 1979
  Lonnie Shelton, Sea. 1979

6 Games
46—Moses Malone, Hou. 1981
34—Cedric Maxwell, Bos. 1981
27—Paul Silas, Bos. 1976

7 Games
33—Elvin Hayes, Wash. 1978
  Marvin Webster, Sea. 1978
25—Wes Unseld, Wash. 1978
22—K. Abdul-Jabbar, Milw. 1974

MOST DEFENSIVE REBOUNDS

4 Games
53—Wes Unseld, Wash. 1975
30—Elvin Hayes, Wash. 1975
26—Keith Wilkes, G.S. 1975

5 Games
62—Jack Sikma, Sea. 1979
38—Elvin Hayes, Wash. 1979
37—Wes Unseld, Wash. 1979

6 Games
91—Bill Walton, Port. 1977
76—Larry Bird, Bos. 1981
72—Dave Cowens, Bos. 1976

7 Games
64—Marvin Webster, Sea. 1978
63—K. Abdul-Jabbar, Milw. 1974
57—Wes Unseld, Wash. 1978

MOST ASSISTS

4 Games
51—Bob Cousy, Bos. 1959
38—Oscar Robertson, Milw. 1971
36—Bob Leonard, Minn. 1959

5 Games
53—Bob Cousy, Bos. 1961
44—Jerry West, L.A. 1972
40—Walt Frazier, N.Y. 1972

6 Games
53—Lionel Hollins, Phila. 1980
52—Magic Johnson, L.A. 1980
51—Bob Cousy, Bos. 1963

7 Games
73—Walt Frazier, N.Y. 1970
70—Bob Cousy, Bos. 1960
65—Bob Cousy, Bos. 1962

MOST PERSONAL FOULS

4 Games
19—Kevin Porter, Wash. 1975
18—Elgin Baylor, Minn. 1959
  John Tresvant, Balt. 1971
17—Frank Ramsey, Bos. 1959

5 Games
27—George Mikan, Minn. 1953
25—Lonnie Shelton, Sea. 1979
24—Connie Simmons, N.Y. 1953
  Tom Sanders, Bos. 1964
  Elvin Hayes, Wash. 1979

6 Games
35—Charlie Scott, Bos. 1976
33—Tom Heinsohn, Bos. 1958
  Tom Meschery, S.F. 1967
32—Vern Mikkelsen, Minn. 1950
  Frank Ramsey, Bos. 1958
  Tom Sanders, Bos. 1963

7 Games
37—Arnie Risen, Bos. 1957
36—Vern Mikkelsen, Minn. 1952
  Jack McMahon, St.L. 1957
35—Arnie Johnson, Roch. 1951
  Jack Sikma, Sea. 1978

MOST DISQUALIFICATIONS

4 Games

1—John Tresvant, Balt. 1971
   Elvin Hayes, Wash. 1975
   George Johnson, G.S. 1975
   Kevin Porter, Wash. 1975

5 Games

5—Art Hillhouse, Phila. 1947
4—Chuck Gilmur, Chi. 1947
3—George Mikan, Minn. 1953
   Tom Sanders, Bos. 1964

6 Games

5—Charlie Scott, Bos. 1976
3—By eight players

7 Games

5—Arnie Risen, Bos. 1957
3—Mel Hutchins, Ft.W. 1955
   Jack McMahon, St.L. 1957
2—By many players

MOST STEALS

4 Games

14—Rick Barry, G.S. 1975
10—Phil Chenier, Wash. 1975
 8—Butch Beard, G.S. 1975

5 Games

9—Dennis Johnson, Sea. 1979
7—Lonnie Shelton, Sea. 1979
6—John Johnson, Sea. 1979
   Jack Sikma, Sea. 1979
   Wes Unseld, Wash. 1979

6 Games

16—Julius Erving, Phila. 1977
    Magic Johnson, L.A. 1980
15—Maurice Cheeks, Phila. 1980
14—Larry Bird, Bos. 1981

7 Games

14—Don Chaney, Bos. 1974
13—John Havlicek, Bos. 1974
11—Jo Jo White, Bos. 1974

MOST BLOCKED SHOTS

4 Games

11—Elvin Hayes, Wash. 1975
    George Johnson, G.S. 1975
 6—Clifford Ray, G.S. 1975
 5—Phil Smith, G.S. 1975

5 Games

16—Jack Sikma, Sea. 1979
11—Dennis Johnson, Sea. 1979
10—Elvin Hayes, Wash. 1979

6 Games

23—K. Abdul-Jabbar, L.A. 1980
22—Bill Walton, Port. 1977
16—Caldwell Jones, Phila. 1980

7 Games

18—Marvin Webster, Sea. 1978
17—Dennis Johnson, Sea. 1978
15—K. Abdul-Jabbar, Milw. 1974

MOST TURNOVERS

5 Games

18—Bob Dandridge, Wash. 1979
15—Elvin Hayes, Wash. 1979
    Dennis Johnson, Sea. 1979
    Gus Williams, Sea. 1979
14—John Johnson, Sea. 1979

6 Games

30—Magic Johnson, L.A. 1980
22—Norm Nixon, L.A. 1980
21—K. Abdul-Jabbar, L.A. 1980

7 Games

26—Gus Williams, Sea. 1978
25—Marvin Webster, Sea. 1978
23—Bob Dandridge, Wash. 1978

Teams (Series)

MOST POINTS

4 Games
487—Bos. vs. Minn. 1959
446—Minn. vs. Bos. 1959
425—Milw. vs. Balt. 1971

5 Games
617—Bos. vs. L.A. 1965
605—Bos. vs. St.L. 1961
554—L.A. vs. Bos. 1965

6 Games
747—Phila. vs. S.F. 1967
707—S.F. vs. Phila. 1967
696—Bos. vs. L.A. 1968

7 Games
827—Bos. vs. L.A. 1966
824—Bos. vs. L.A. 1962
806—Bos. vs. St.L. 1957

FEWEST POINTS

4 Games
376—Balt. vs. Milw. 1971
382—Wash. vs. G.S. 1975
398—G.S. vs. Wash. 1975

5 Games
467—Ft.W. vs. Phila. 1956
481—Wash. vs. Sea. 1979
484—L.A. vs. N.Y. 1973

6 Games
520—Hou. vs. Bos. 1981
579—Bos. vs. Hou. 1981
597—Phoe. vs. Bos. 1976

7 Games
636—Syr. vs. Ft.W. 1955
640—Ft.W. vs. Syr. 1955
644—Milw. vs. Bos. 1974

HIGHEST FIELD GOAL PERCENTAGE

4 Games
.504—Milw. vs. Balt. 1971
.447—G.S. vs. Wash. 1975
.434—Wash. vs. G.S. 1975

5 Games
.470—N.Y. vs. L.A. 1972
.465—Sea. vs. Wash. 1979
.459—N.Y. vs. L.A. 1973

6 Games
.489—L.A. vs. Phila. 1980
.487—Phila. vs. L.A. 1980
.479—Port. vs. Phila. 1977

7 Games
.494—L.A. vs. N.Y. 1970
.465—Milw. vs. Bos. 1974
.460—N.Y. vs. L.A. 1970

LOWEST FIELD GOAL PERCENTAGE

4 Games
.384—Balt. vs. Milw. 1971
.388—Minn. vs. Bos. 1959
.406—Bos. vs. Minn. 1959

5 Games
.365—Ft.W. vs. Phila. 1956
.372—St.L. vs. Bos. 1961
.389—Phila. vs. Ft.W. 1956

6 Games
.355—Bos. vs. St.L. 1958
.379—Hou. vs. Bos. 1981
.386—S.F. vs. Phila. 1967

7 Games
.339—Syr. vs. Ft.W. 1955
.369—Bos. vs. St.L. 1957
.376—St.L. vs. Bos. 1957

MOST FIELD GOALS

4 Games
188—Bos. vs. Minn. 1959
180—Minn. vs. Bos. 1959
171—Milw. vs. Balt. 1971

5 Games
243—Bos. vs. L.A. 1965
238—Bos. vs. St.L. 1961
216—N.Y. vs. L.A. 1972

6 Games
287—Phila. vs. S.F. 1967
    S.F. vs. Phila. 1967
272—L.A. vs. Bos. 1968
270—L.A. vs. Phila. 1980

7 Games
332—N.Y. vs. L.A. 1970
324—Bos. vs. L.A. 1962
314—Bos. vs. St.L. 1960

CHAMPIONSHIP SERIES STATISTICS

FEWEST FIELD GOALS

4 Games
147—Wash. vs. G.S. 1975
162—Balt. vs. Milw. 1971
163—G.S. vs. Wash. 1975

5 Games
163—Ft.W. vs. Phila. 1956
182—Phila. vs. Ft.W. 1956
187—L.A. vs. N.Y. 1973

6 Games
203—Hou. vs. Bos. 1981
211—St.L. vs. Bos. 1958
216—Bos. vs. St.L. 1958

7 Games
207—Syr. vs. Ft.W. 1955
217—Ft.W. vs. Syr. 1955
263—St.L. vs. Bos. 1957

MOST FIELD GOAL ATTEMPTS

4 Games
464—Minn. vs. Bos. 1959
463—Bos. vs. Minn. 1959
422—Balt. vs. Milw. 1971

5 Games
568—Bos. vs. L.A. 1965
555—Bos. vs. St.L. 1961
546—St.L. vs. Bos. 1961

6 Games
743—S.F. vs. Phila. 1967
640—Bos. vs. L.A. 1963
639—Phila. vs. S.F. 1967

7 Games
799—Bos. vs. St.L. 1957
769—Bos. vs. St.L. 1960
740—Bos. vs. L.A. 1962

FEWEST FIELD GOAL ATTEMPTS

4 Games
339—Milw. vs. Balt. 1971
  Wash. vs. G.S. 1975
365—G.S. vs. Wash. 1975
422—Balt. vs. Milw. 1971

5 Games
434—L.A. vs. N.Y. 1973
446—Ft.W. vs. Phila. 1956
460—N.Y. vs. L.A. 1972

6 Games
512—Hou. vs. Bos. 1981
529—Phila. vs. Port. 1977
530—Phila. vs. L.A. 1980

7 Games
558—Ft.W. vs. Syr. 1955
585—Milw. vs. Bos. 1974
610—Syr. vs. Ft.W. 1955

HIGHEST FREE THROW PERCENTAGE

4 Games
.769—Milw. vs. Balt. 1971
.746—Wash. vs. G.S. 1975
.735—Minn. vs. Bos. 1959

5 Games
.774—L.A. vs. N.Y. 1972
.765—St.L. vs. Bos. 1961
.760—N.Y. vs. L.A. 1973

6 Games
.821—Bos. vs. Phoe. 1976
.813—L.A. vs. Phila. 1980
.786—L.A. vs. Bos. 1963

7 Games
.827—Bos. vs. L.A. 1966
.805—L.A. vs. Bos. 1962
.791—Bos. vs. L.A. 1969

LOWEST FREE THROW PERCENTAGE

4 Games
.675—Balt. vs. Milw. 1971
.698—Bos. vs. Minn. 1959
.706—G.S. vs. Wash. 1975

5 Games
.616—S.F. vs. Bos. 1964
.647—L.A. vs. N.Y. 1973
.664—Sea. vs. Wash. 1979

6 Games
.613—Phila. vs. S.F. 1967
.700—S.F. vs. Phila. 1967
.701—L.A. vs. Bos. 1968

7 Games
.641—L.A. vs. Bos. 1969
.688—L.A. vs. N.Y. 1970
.692—Wash. vs. Sea. 1978

MOST FREE THROWS MADE

4 Games
111—Bos. vs. Minn. 1959
88—Wash. vs. G.S. 1975
86—Minn. vs. Bos. 1959

5 Games
146—L.A. vs. Bos. 1965
145—N.Y. vs. Minn. 1953
141—Ft.W. vs. Phila. 1956

6 Games
232—Bos. vs. St.L. 1958
215—St.L. vs. Bos. 1958
173—Phila. vs. Balt. 1948
　　　L.A. vs. Bos. 1963
　　　Phila. vs. S.F. 1967

7 Games
244—St.L. vs. Bos. 1957
239—L.A. vs. Bos. 1962
222—Syr. vs. Ft.W. 1955

FEWEST FREE THROWS MADE

4 Games
52—Balt. vs. Milw. 1971
72—G.S. vs. Wash. 1975
83—Milw. vs. Balt. 1971

5 Games
73—N.Y. vs. L.A. 1973
81—N.Y. vs. L.A. 1972
89—Sea. vs. Wash. 1979

6 Games
94—Bos. vs. Hou. 1981
108—Phila. vs. L.A. 1980
111—Hou. vs. Bos. 1981

7 Games
100—Milw. vs. Bos. 1974
117—Bos. vs. Milw. 1974
122—N.Y. vs. L.A. 1970

MOST FREE THROW ATTEMPTS

4 Games
159—Bos. vs. Minn. 1959
118—Wash. vs. G.S. 1975
117—Minn. vs. Bos. 1959

5 Games
211—S.F. vs. Bos. 1964
199—N.Y. vs. Minn. 1953
　　　L.A. vs. Bos. 1965
190—Bos. vs. St.L. 1961

6 Games
298—Bos. vs. St.L. 1958
292—St.L. vs. Bos. 1958
282—Phila. vs. S.F. 1967

7 Games
341—St.L. vs. Bos. 1957
299—Bos. vs. St.L. 1957
297—L.A. vs. Bos. 1962

FEWEST FREE THROW ATTEMPTS

4 Games
77—Balt. vs. Milw. 1971
102—G.S. vs. Wash. 1975
108—Milw. vs. Balt. 1975

5 Games
96—N.Y. vs. L.A. 1973
117—N.Y. vs. L.A. 1972
134—Sea. vs. Wash. 1979
　　　Wash. vs. Sea. 1979

6 Games
129—Bos. vs. Hou. 1981
144—L.A. vs. Phila. 1980
　　　Phila. vs. L.A. 1980
155—Hou. vs. Bos. 1981

7 Games
137—Milw. vs. Bos. 1974
151—Bos. vs. Milw. 1974
160—N.Y. vs. L.A. 1970

HIGHEST REBOUND PERCENTAGE

4 Games
.557—G.S. vs. Wash. 1975
.533—Milw. vs. Balt. 1971
.524—Bos. vs. Minn. 1959

5 Games
.548—Bos. vs. St.L. 1961
.542—L.A. vs. N.Y. 1972
.532—L.A. vs. N.Y. 1973

6 Games
.580—L.A. vs. Phila. 1980
.570—Bos. vs. Phoe. 1976
.543—Port. vs. Phila. 1977

7 Games
.541—Roch. vs. N.Y. 1951
.538—Bos. vs. L.A. 1966
.533—Bos. vs. St.L. 1957

MOST REBOUNDS

4 Games
295—Bos. vs. Minn. 1959
268—Minn. vs. Bos. 1959
218—Milw. vs. Balt. 1971

5 Games
369—Bos. vs. St.L. 1961
316—Bos. vs. L.A. 1965
309—S.F. vs. Bos. 1964

6 Games
435—S.F. vs. Phila. 1967
425—Phila. vs. S.F. 1967
393—Bos. vs. St.L. 1958

7 Games
487—Bos. vs. St.L. 1957
448—Bos. vs. St.L. 1960
431—Bos. vs. L.A. 1962

FEWEST REBOUNDS

4 Games
171—Wash. vs. G.S. 1975
191—Balt. vs. Milw. 1971
215—G.S. vs. Wash. 1975

5 Games
228—Sea. vs. Wash. 1979
232—N.Y. vs. L.A. 1973
233—Wash. vs. Sea. 1979

6 Games
223—Phila. vs. L.A. 1980
254—Phoe. vs. Bos. 1976
256—Hou. vs. Bos. 1981

7 Games
297—Bos. vs. Milw. 1974
306—Milw. vs. Bos. 1974
342—Ft. W. vs. Syr. 1955
    N.Y. vs. L.A. 1970

HIGHEST OFFENSIVE REBOUND PERCENTAGE

4 Games
.375—G.S. vs. Wash. 1975
.263—Wash. vs. G.S. 1975

5 Games
.336—Wash. vs. Sea. 1979
.304—Sea. vs. Wash. 1979

6 Games
.410—Bos. vs. Hou. 1981
.383—L.A. vs. Phila. 1980
.378—Hou. vs. Bos. 1981

7 Games
.366—Sea. vs. Wash. 1978
.355—Wash. vs. Sea. 1978
.293—Milw. vs. Bos. 1974

MOST OFFENSIVE REBOUNDS

4 Games
72—G.S. vs. Wash. 1975
51—Wash. vs. G.S. 1975

5 Games
82—Wash. vs. Sea. 1979
66—Sea. vs. Wash. 1979

6 Games
112—Hou. vs. Bos. 1981
103—L.A. vs. Phila. 1980

7 Games
127—Sea. vs. Wash. 1978
123—Wash. vs. Sea. 1978

FEWEST OFFENSIVE REBOUNDS

4 Games
51—Wash. vs. G.S. 1975
72—G.S. vs. Wash. 1975

5 Games
66—Sea. vs. Wash. 1979
82—Wash. vs. Sea. 1979

6 Games
57—Phila. vs. L.A. 1980
72—Phoe. vs. Bos. 1976
    Phila. vs. Port. 1977

7 Games
86—Milw. vs. Bos. 1974
89—Bos. vs. Milw. 1974

HIGHEST DEFENSIVE REBOUND PERCENTAGE

4 Games
.737—Wash. vs. G.S. 1975
.625—G.S. vs. Wash. 1975

5 Games
.696—Sea. vs. Wash. 1979
.664—Wash. vs. Sea. 1979

6 Games
.782—L.A. vs. Phila. 1980
.769—Bos. vs. Phoe. 1976
.760—Port. vs. Phila. 1977

7 Games
.712—Milw. vs. Bos. 1974
.707—Bos. vs. Milw. 1974

MOST DEFENSIVE REBOUNDS

4 Games
143—G.S. vs. Wash. 1975
120—Wash. vs. G.S. 1975

5 Games
162—Sea. vs. Wash. 1979
151—Wash. vs. Sea. 1979

6 Games
240—Bos. vs. Phoe. 1976
228—Port. vs. Phila. 1977
205—L.A. vs. Phila. 1980

7 Games
223—Sea. vs. Wash. 1978
220—Milw. vs. Bos. 1974
     Wash. vs. Sea. 1978

FEWEST DEFENSIVE REBOUNDS

4 Games
120—Wash. vs. G.S. 1975
143—G.S. vs. Wash. 1975

5 Games
151—Wash. vs. Sea. 1979
162—Sea. vs. Wash. 1979

6 Games
144—Hou. vs. Bos. 1981
166—Phila. vs. L.A. 1980
182—Phoe. vs. Bos. 1976

7 Games
208—Bos. vs. Milw. 1974
220—Milw. vs. Bos. 1974
     Wash. vs. Sea. 1978

MOST ASSISTS

4 Games
114—Bos. vs. Minn. 1959
100—Minn. vs. Bos. 1959
 93—Milw. vs. Balt. 1971

5 Games
130—Bos. vs. St.L. 1961
127—N.Y. vs. L.A. 1972
124—Phila. vs. Ft.W. 1956

6 Games
173—Phila. vs. S.F. 1967
168—Port. vs. Phila. 1977
147—L.A. vs. Phila. 1980

7 Games
192—N.Y. vs. L.A. 1970
190—Bos. vs. L.A. 1962
187—Ft.W. vs. Syr. 1955

FEWEST ASSISTS

4 Games
78—Balt. vs. Milw. 1971
82—G.S. vs. Wash. 1975
84—Wash. vs. G.S. 1975

5 Games
88—S.F. vs. Bos. 1964
    L.A. vs. N.Y. 1973
97—L.A. vs. N.Y. 1972
99—L.A. vs. Bos. 1965

6 Games
105—L.A. vs. Bos. 1963
108—Hou. vs. Bos. 1981
110—Bos. vs. St.L. 1958

7 Games
121—Sea. vs. Wash. 1978
135—L.A. vs. Bos. 1962
     Bos. vs. L.A. 1969
144—Bos. vs. St.L. 1960

MOST PERSONAL FOULS

4 Games
116—G.S. vs. Wash. 1975
108—Minn. vs. Bos. 1959
101—Wash. vs. G.S. 1975

5 Games
146—Bos. vs. S.F. 1964
144—Minn. vs. N.Y. 1953
139—N.Y. vs. Minn. 1953

6 Games
194—Bos. vs. St.L. 1958
   St.L. vs. Bos. 1958
182—S.F. vs. Phila. 1967
   Port. vs. Phila. 1977
179—Minn. vs. Syr. 1950

7 Games
221—Bos. vs. St.L. 1957
210—Bos. vs. L.A. 1962
209—St.L. vs. Bos. 1957
   Bos. vs. L.A. 1969

FEWEST PERSONAL FOULS

4 Games
84—Milw. vs. Balt. 1971
90—Bos. vs. Minn. 1959
91—Balt. vs. Milw. 1971

5 Games
106—L.A. vs. N.Y. 1972
113—Ft.W. vs. Phila. 1956
115—L.A. vs. N.Y. 1973

6 Games
121—Hou. vs. Bos. 1981
135—Phila. vs. L.A. 1980
139—Bos. vs. Hou. 1981

7 Games
150—L.A. vs. N.Y. 1970
153—Bos. vs. Milw. 1974
154—Milw. vs. Bos. 1974

MOST DISQUALIFICATIONS

4 Games
2—Wash. vs. G.S. 1975
1—Balt. vs. Milw. 1971
   G.S. vs. Wash. 1975

5 Games
9—Chi. vs. Phila. 1947
8—Phila. vs. Chi. 1947
6—Minn. vs. N.Y. 1953
   N.Y. vs. Minn. 1953
   S.F. vs. Bos. 1964

6 Games
11—Bos. vs. St.L. 1958
9—Minn. vs. Syr. 1950
8—Bos. vs. Phoe. 1976

7 Games
10—Bos. vs. St.L. 1957
9—Minn. vs. N.Y. 1952
   St.L. vs. Bos. 1957
   Bos. vs. L.A. 1962
8—N.Y. vs. Roch. 1951

FEWEST DISQUALIFICATIONS

4 Games
0—Bos. vs. Minn. 1959
   Minn. vs. Bos. 1959
   Milw. vs. Balt. 1971

5 Games
0—L.A. vs. N.Y. 1972
1—N.Y. vs. L.A. 1972
2—By four teams

6 Games
0—L.A. vs. Phila. 1980
1—Bos. vs. Hou. 1981
   Hou. vs. Bos. 1981

7 Games
0—St.L. vs. Bos. 1960
1—L.A. vs. Bos. 1969
   L.A. vs. N.Y. 1970

MOST STEALS

4 Games
55—G.S. vs. Wash. 1975
45—Wash. vs. G.S. 1975

5 Games
38—Sea. vs. Wash. 1979
29—Wash. vs. Sea. 1979

6 Games
71—Phila. vs. Port. 1977
64—Port. vs. Phila. 1977

7 Games
58—Bos. vs. Milw. 1974
54—Wash. vs. Sea. 1978

FEWEST STEALS

4 Games
45—Wash. vs. G.S. 1975
55—G.S. vs. Wash. 1975

5 Games
29—Wash. vs. Sea. 1979
38—Sea. vs. Wash. 1979

6 Games
40—Bos. vs. Hou. 1981
41—Bos. vs. Phoe. 1976
47—Hou. vs. Bos. 1981

7 Games
21—Milw. vs. Bos. 1974
40—Sea. vs. Wash. 1978
54—Wash. vs. Sea. 1978

MOST BLOCKED SHOTS

4 Games
32—G.S. vs. Wash. 1975
20—Wash. vs. G.S. 1975

5 Games
39—Sea. vs. Wash. 1979
23—Wash. vs. Sea. 1979

6 Games
60—Phila. vs. L.A. 1980
37—Port. vs. Phila. 1977
    L.A. vs. Phila. 1980
34—Hou. vs. Bos. 1981

7 Games
49—Sea. vs. Wash. 1978
32—Wash. vs. Sea. 1978
28—Milw. vs. Bos. 1974

FEWEST BLOCKED SHOTS

4 Games
20—Wash. vs. G.S. 1975
32—G.S. vs. Wash. 1975

5 Games
23—Wash. vs. Sea. 1979
39—Sea. vs. Wash. 1979

6 Games
10—Bos. vs. Milw. 1974
21—Milw. vs. Bos. 1974
30—Phila. vs. Port. 1977

7 Games
7—Bos. vs. Milw. 1974
28—Milw. vs. Bos. 1974
32—Wash. vs. Sea. 1978

MOST TURNOVERS

4 Games
94—G.S. vs. Wash. 1975
92—Milw. vs. Balt. 1971
89—Wash. vs. G.S. 1975

5 Games
104—L.A. vs. N.Y. 1973
88—N.Y. vs. L.A. 1972
80—Wash. vs. Sea. 1979

6 Games
149—Port. vs. Phila. 1977
144—Bos. vs. Phoe. 1976
132—Phila. vs. Port. 1977

7 Games
142—Milw. vs. Bos. 1974
126—Sea. vs. Wash. 1978
107—Bos. vs. Milw. 1974

FEWEST TURNOVERS

4 Games
67—Balt. vs. Milw. 1971
89—Wash. vs. G.S. 1975
92—Milw. vs. Balt. 1971

5 Games
74—N.Y. vs. L.A. 1973
77—Sea. vs. Wash. 1979
78—L.A. vs. N.Y. 1972

6 Games
82—Hou. vs. Bos. 1981
92—Phila. vs. L.A. 1980
102—Bos. vs. Hou. 1981

7 Games
105—Wash. vs. Sea. 1978
107—Bos. vs. Milw. 1974
126—Sea. vs. Wash. 1978

CHAMPIONSHIP SERIES STATISTICS 175

INDIVIDUAL RECORDS

MINUTES

Most Minutes, Game
- 61—Garfield Heard, Phoenix at Boston, June 4, 1976 (3 ot)
- 60—Jo Jo White, Boston vs. Phoenix, June 4, 1976 (3 ot)
- 58—Bob Cousy, Boston vs. St. Louis, Apr. 13, 1957 (2 ot)
    - Kareem Abdul-Jabbar, Milwaukee at Boston, May 10, 1974 (2 ot)
    - John Havlicek, Boston vs. Milwaukee, May 10, 1974 (2 ot)
    - Oscar Robertson, Milwaukee at Boston, May 10, 1974 (2 ot)
    - John Havlicek, Boston vs. Phoenix, June 4, 1976 (3 ot)

Most Minutes per Game, One Championship Series
- 49.3—Kareem Abdul-Jabbar, Milwaukee vs. Boston, 1974 (345/7)
- 48.7—Bill Russell, Boston vs. Los Angeles, 1968 (292/6)
- 48.5—John Havlicek, Boston vs. Los Angeles, 1968 (291/6)

SCORING

Most Points, Game
- 61—Elgin Baylor, Los Angeles at Boston, Apr. 14, 1962
- 55—Rick Barry, San Francisco vs. Philadelphia, Apr. 18, 1967
- 53—Jerry West, Los Angeles vs. Boston, Apr. 23, 1969

Most Points, Rookie, Game
- 42—Magic Johnson, Los Angeles at Philadelphia, May 16, 1980
- 37—Joe Fulks, Philadelphia vs. Chicago, Apr. 16, 1947
    - Tom Heinsohn, Boston vs. St. Louis, Apr. 13, 1957 (2 ot)
- 34—Joe Fulks, Philadelphia vs. Chicago, Apr. 22, 1947
    - Elgin Baylor, Minneapolis at Boston, Apr. 4, 1959

Highest Scoring Average, One Championship Series
- 40.8—Rick Barry, San Francisco vs. Philadelphia, 1967 (245/6)
- 40.6—Elgin Baylor, Los Angeles vs. Boston, 1962 (284/7)
- 37.9—Jerry West, Los Angeles vs. Boston, 1969 (265/7)

Highest Scoring Average, Rookie, One Championship Series
- 26.2—Joe Fulks, Philadelphia vs. Chicago, 1947 (131/5)
- 24.0—Tom Heinsohn, Boston vs. St. Louis, 1957 (168/7)
- 23.0—Alvan Adams, Phoenix vs. Boston, 1976 (138/6)

Most Consecutive Games, 20+ Points
- 25—Jerry West, Los Angeles, Apr. 20, 1966—May 8, 1970
- 16—Kareem Abdul-Jabbar, Milwaukee-Los Angeles, Apr. 21, 1971—May 14, 1980 (current)
- 15—Elgin Baylor, Minneapolis-Los Angeles, Apr. 9, 1959—Apr. 17, 1966

Most Consecutive Games, 30+ Points
- 13—Elgin Baylor, Minneapolis-Los Angeles, Apr. 9, 1959—Apr. 21, 1963
- 6—Rick Barry, San Francisco, Apr. 16, 1967—Apr. 24, 1967
    - John Havlicek, Boston, Apr. 30, 1968—Apr. 26, 1969
    - Jerry West, Los Angeles, May 5, 1969—May 1, 1970
- 5—Bob Pettit, St. Louis, Apr. 7, 1957—Mar. 29, 1958
    - Jerry West, Los Angeles, Apr. 20, 1966—Apr. 28, 1966

Most Consecutive Games, 40+ Points
   2—Jerry West, Los Angeles, Apr. 19-21, 1965
      Rick Barry, San Francisco, Apr. 18-20, 1967
      Jerry West, Los Angeles, Apr. 23-25, 1969

Scoring 30+ Points in All Games in Championship Series
   Elgin Baylor, Los Angeles vs. Boston, 1962 (7-game series)
   Rick Barry, San Francisco vs. Philadelphia, 1967 (6-game series)

Scoring 20+ Points in All Games of 7-Game Championship Series
   Bob Pettit, St. Louis vs. Boston, 1960
   Elgin Baylor, Los Angeles vs. Boston, 1962
   Jerry West, Los Angeles vs. Boston, 1962
   Jerry West, Los Angeles vs. Boston, 1969
   Jerry West, Los Angeles vs. New York, 1970
   Kareem Abdul-Jabbar, Milwaukee vs. Boston, 1974

FIELD GOALS

Highest Field Goal Percentage, Game (minimum: 8 field goals)
   .917—Bill Bradley, New York at Los Angeles, Apr. 26, 1972 (11/12)
   .909—Bill Russell, Boston vs. Los Angeles, Apr. 19, 1965 (10/11)
   .900—Wilt Chamberlain, Los Angeles at New York, May 3, 1972 (9/10)
   .846—Maurice Cheeks, Philadelphia at Los Angeles, May 7, 1980 (11/13)
   .818—Dick Garrett, Los Angeles vs. New York, May 6, 1970 (9/11)

Most Field Goals, Game
   22—Elgin Baylor, Los Angeles at Boston, Apr. 14, 1962
      Rick Barry, San Francisco vs. Philadelphia, Apr. 18, 1967
   20—Wilt Chamberlain, Los Angeles vs. New York, May 6, 1970
   19—Bob Pettit, St. Louis vs. Boston, Apr. 12, 1958
      Jerry West, Los Angeles vs. Boston, Apr. 22, 1966
      Kareem Abdul-Jabbar, Los Angeles vs. Philadelphia, May 7, 1980

Most Field Goal Attempts, Game
   48—Rick Barry, San Francisco vs. Philadelphia, Apr. 18, 1967
   46—Elgin Baylor, Los Angeles at Boston, Apr. 14, 1962
   43—Rick Barry, San Francisco at Philadelphia, Apr. 14, 1967 (ot)

FREE THROWS

Most Free Throws Made, None Missed, Game
   14—Magic Johnson, Los Angeles at Philadelphia, May 16, 1980
   12—Jack George, Philadelphia at Ft. Wayne, Apr. 5, 1956
      Bob Pettit, St. Louis vs. Boston, Apr. 9, 1961
      John Havlicek, Boston at Los Angeles, May 2, 1968
      Walt Frazier, New York vs. Los Angeles, May 8, 1970
   11—Dick Barnett, Los Angeles at Boston, Apr. 14, 1963

Most Free Throws Made, Game
   19—Bob Pettit, St. Louis at Boston, Apr. 9, 1958
   17—Cliff Hagan, St. Louis at Boston, Mar. 30, 1958
      Elgin Baylor, Los Angeles at Boston, Apr. 14, 1962
      Jerry West, Los Angeles vs. Boston, Apr. 21, 1965
      Jerry West, Los Angeles vs. Boston, Apr. 25, 1969
   16—Bob Pettit, St. Louis vs. Boston, Apr. 11, 1957

CHAMPIONSHIP SERIES STATISTICS

Most Free Throw Attempts, Game
- 24—Bob Pettit, St. Louis at Boston, Apr. 9, 1958
- 22—Bob Pettit, St. Louis vs. Boston, Apr. 11, 1957
- 21—Elgin Baylor, Los Angeles at Boston, Apr. 18, 1962 (ot)

REBOUNDS

Most Rebounds, Game
- 40—Bill Russell, Boston vs. St. Louis, Mar. 29, 1960
  Bill Russell, Boston vs. Los Angeles, Apr. 18, 1962 (ot)
- 38—Bill Russell, Boston vs. St. Louis, Apr. 11, 1961
  Bill Russell, Boston vs. Los Angeles, Apr. 16, 1963
  Wilt Chamberlain, San Franscisco vs. Boston, Apr. 24, 1964
  Wilt Chamberlain, Philadelphia vs. San Francisco, Apr. 16, 1967
- 35—Bill Russell, Boston vs. St. Louis, Apr. 9, 1960

Most Rebounds, Rookie, Game
- 32—Bill Russell, Boston vs. St. Louis, Apr. 13, 1957 (2 ot)
- 25—Bill Russell, Boston vs. St. Louis, Mar. 31, 1957
- 23—Bill Russell, Boston vs. St. Louis, Apr. 9, 1957
  Bill Russell, Boston at St. Louis, Apr. 11, 1957
  Tom Heinsohn, Boston vs. St. Louis, Apr. 13, 1957 (2 ot)

Highest Average, Rebounds per Game, One Championship Series
- 29.5—Bill Russell, Boston vs. Minneapolis, 1959 (118/4)
- 28.8—Bill Russell, Boston vs. St. Louis, 1961 (144/5)
- 28.5—Wilt Chamberlain, Philadelphia vs. San Francisco, 1967 (171/6)

Highest Average, Rebounds per Game, Rookie, One Championship Series
- 22.9—Bill Russell, Boston vs. St. Louis, 1957 (160/7)
- 13.0—Nate Thurmond, San Francisco vs. Boston, 1964 (65/5)
- 12.6—Tom Heinsohn, Boston vs. St. Louis, 1957 (88/7)

Most Consecutive Games, 20+ Rebounds
- 15—Bill Russell, Boston, Apr. 9, 1960—Apr. 16, 1963
- 12—Wilt Chamberlain, San Francisco—Philadelphia—Los Angeles, Apr. 18, 1964—Apr. 23, 1969
- 6—Bill Russell, Boston vs. St. Louis, Apr. 7, 1957—Mar. 30, 1958
  Nate Thurmond, San Francisco vs. Philadelphia, Apr. 14, 1967—Apr. 24, 1967
  Wilt Chamberlain, Los Angeles vs. New York, Apr. 30, 1972—May 3, 1973

Most Consecutive Games, 30+ Rebounds
- 3—Bill Russell, Boston, Apr. 5, 1959—Apr. 9, 1959
- 2—Bill Russell, Boston, Apr. 9, 1960—Apr. 2, 1961
  Wilt Chamberlain, Philadelphia, Apr. 14, 1967—Apr. 16, 1967
  Wilt Chamberlain, Los Angeles, Apr. 29, 1969—May 1, 1969

20+ Rebounds in All Championship Series Games
- Bill Russell, Boston vs. Minneapolis, 1959 (4-game series)
- Bill Russell, Boston vs. St. Louis, 1961 (5-game series)
- Bill Russell, Boston vs. Los Angeles, 1962 (7-game series)
- Wilt Chamberlain, San Francisco vs. Boston, 1964 (5-game series)
- Wilt Chamberlain, Philadelphia vs. San Francisco, 1967 (6-game series)
- Nate Thurmond, San Francisco vs. Philadelphia, 1967 (6-game series)

Most Offensive Rebounds, Game
- 11—Elvin Hayes, Washington at Seattle, May 27, 1979
- 10—Marvin Webster, Seattle vs. Washington, June 7, 1978
  - Robert Reid, Houston vs. Boston, May 10, 1981
  - Moses Malone, Houston vs. Boston, May 14, 1981
- 9—Elvin Hayes, Washington vs. Seattle, May 28, 1978
  - Cedric Maxwell, Boston at Houston, May 9, 1981
  - Moses Malone, Houston vs. Boston, May 10, 1981
  - Cedric Maxwell, Boston at Houston, May 10, 1981

Most Defensive Rebounds, Game
- 20—Bill Walton, Portland at Philadelphia, June 3, 1977
  - Bill Walton, Portland vs. Philadelphia, June 5, 1977
- 18—Dave Cowens, Boston vs. Phoenix, May 23, 1976
- 17—Bill Walton, Portland at Philadelphia, May 22, 1977
  - Larry Bird, Boston vs. Houston, May 7, 1981

ASSISTS

Most Assists, Game
- 19—Bob Cousy, Boston vs. St. Louis, Apr. 9, 1957
  - Bob Cousy, Boston at Minneapolis, Apr. 7, 1959
  - Walt Frazier, New York vs. Los Angeles, May 8, 1970
- 18—Jerry West, Los Angeles vs. New York, May 1, 1970 (ot)
- 15—Bob Cousy, Boston vs. Minneapolis, Apr. 5, 1959

Highest Average, Assists per Game, One Championship Series
- 12.8—Bob Cousy, Boston vs. Minneapolis, 1959 (51/4)
- 10.6—Bob Cousy, Boston vs. St. Louis, 1961 (53/5)
- 10.4—Walt Frazier, New York vs. Los Angeles, 1970 (73/7)

Most Assists, Rookie, Game
- 11—Magic Johnson, Los Angeles vs. Philadelphia, May 7, 1980
- 10—Tom Gola, Philadelphia vs. Ft. Wayne, Mar. 31, 1956
  - Walt Hazzard, Los Angeles at Boston, Apr. 25, 1965
  - Magic Johnson, Los Angeles vs. Philadelphia, May 4, 1980
  - Magic Johnson, Los Angeles vs. Philadelphia, May 14, 1980
- 9—Magic Johnson, Los Angeles at Philadelphia, May 11, 1980

Highest Average, Assists per Game, Rookie, One Championship Series
- 8.7—Magic Johnson, Los Angeles vs. Philadelphia, 1980 (52/6)
- 6.0—Tom Gola, Philadelphia vs. Ft. Wayne, 1956 (30/5)
- 5.2—Walt Hazzard, Los Angeles vs. Boston, 1965 (26/5)

Most Consecutive Games, 10+ Assists
- 4—Bob Cousy, Boston, Apr. 5, 1959—Mar. 27, 1960
- 2—By many players. Most recent:
  - Lionel Hollins, Philadelphia, May 11, 1980—May 14, 1980

PERSONAL FOULS

Most Minutes Played, No Personal Fouls, Game
- 50—Jo Jo White, Boston at Milwaukee, Apr. 30, 1974 (ot)
- 48—Bill Russell, Boston at St. Louis, Apr. 3, 1960
  - Bill Russell, Boston at Los Angeles, Apr. 17, 1963
  - Wilt Chamberlain, Los Angeles vs. Boston, May 1, 1969
- 46—Bob Cousy, Boston vs. Minneapolis, Apr. 4, 1959
  - Oscar Robertson, Milwaukee vs. Boston, Apr. 28, 1974

DISQUALIFICATIONS

Most Consecutive Games Disqualified
>5—Art Hillhouse, Philadelphia, 1947
>>Charlie Scott, Boston, 1976
>
>4—Arnie Risen, Boston, 1957
>3—Howie Dallmar, Philadelphia, 1948

Fewest Minutes Played, Disqualified Player, Game
>9—Bob Harrison, Minneapolis vs. New York, Apr. 13, 1952
>10—Bob Harrison, Minneapolis vs. New York, Apr. 4, 1953
>11—Jim Loscutoff, Boston vs. St. Louis, Apr. 18, 1962 (ot)

STEALS

Most Steals, Game
>6—John Havlicek, Boston vs. Milwaukee, May 3, 1974
>>Steve Mix, Philadelphia vs. Portland, May 22, 1977
>>Maurice Cheeks, Philadelphia at Los Angeles, May 7, 1980
>
>5—Accomplished 10 times. Most recent:
>>Robert Reid, Houston vs. Boston, May 10, 1981

BLOCKED SHOTS

Most Blocked Shots, Game
>8—Bill Walton, Portland vs. Philadelphia, June 5, 1977
>7—Dennis Johnson, Seattle at Washington, May 28, 1978
>6—Kareem Abdul-Jabbar, Los Angeles vs. Philadelphia, May 4, 1980

TURNOVERS

Most Turnovers, Game
>10—Magic Johnson, Los Angeles vs. Philadelphia, May 14, 1980
>8—Gus Williams, Seattle at Washington, May 24, 1979
>7—Bob Dandridge, Washington vs. Seattle, May 20, 1979

Most Minutes Played, No Turnovers, Game
>47—Wes Unseld, Washington at Seattle, May 27, 1979
>42—Jack Sikma, Seattle at Washington, May 28, 1978
>>Elvin Hayes, Washington vs. Seattle, May 28, 1978
>>Wes Unseld, Washington at Seattle, June 2, 1978
>
>41—Tom Henderson, Washington at Seattle, June 7, 1978

TEAM RECORDS

WON-LOST

Most Consecutive Games Won, All Championship Series
>5—Minneapolis, 1953-54
>>Boston, 1959-60
>>Los Angeles, 1972-73
>
>4—Accomplished eight times.

Most Consecutive Games Won, One Championship Series
>4—Minneapolis vs. New York, 1953 (5-game series)
>>Boston vs. Minneapolis, 1959 (4-game series)
>>Milwaukee vs. Baltimore, 1971 (4-game series)
>>Los Angeles vs. New York, 1972 (5-game series)

New York vs. Los Angeles, 1973 (5-game series)
Golden State vs. Washington, 1975 (4-game series)
Portland vs. Philadelphia, 1977 (6-game series)
Seattle vs. Washington, 1979 (5-game series)

Most Consecutive Games Won at Home, All Championship Series
7—Minneapolis, 1949-52
6—Boston, 1960-62
  Boston, 1964-65
  Syracuse/Philadelphia, 1955-67
5—Philadelphia/San Francisco, 1948-64
  Boston, 1968-73

Most Consecutive Games Won at Home, One Championship Series
4—Syracuse vs. Ft. Wayne, 1955 (7-game series)

Most Consecutive Games Won on Road, All Championship Series
4—Minneapolis, 1953-54
3—Boston, 1959-60
  Boston, 1965-66
  San Francisco/Golden State, 1967-75

Most Consecutive Games Won on Road, One Championship Series
3—Minneapolis vs. New York, 1953 (5-game series)

Most Consecutive Games Lost, All Championship Series
9—Baltimore/Washington, 1971-78
5—Minneapolis/Los Angeles, 1959-62
  New York, 1972-73
  Philadelphia, 1977-80

Most Consecutive Games Lost at Home, All Championship Series
4—Baltimore/Washington, 1971-75
3—New York, 1953
  Los Angeles, 1965-66

Most Consecutive Games Lost on Road, All Championship Series
7—Ft. Wayne, 1955-56
5—Philadelphia, 1947-56
  St. Louis, 1960-61
  Syracuse/Philadelphia, 1954-67
  Los Angeles, 1968-70
  Baltimore/Washington, 1972-78
4—Philadelphia, 1977-80

SCORING

Most Points, Game
142—Boston vs. Los Angeles (110), Apr. 18, 1965
141—Philadelphia vs. San Francisco (135), Apr. 14, 1967 (ot)
140—Boston vs. St. Louis (122), Mar. 27, 1960

Fewest Points, Game
71—Syracuse vs. Ft. Wayne (74) at Indianapolis, Apr. 7, 1955
  Houston vs. Boston (94), May 9, 1981
74—Ft. Wayne vs. Syracuse (71) at Indianapolis, Apr. 7, 1955
80—Phoenix vs. Boston (87), June 6, 1976

CHAMPIONSHIP SERIES STATISTICS

Most Points, Both Teams, Game

276—Philadelphia (141) vs. San Francisco (135), Apr. 14, 1967 (ot)
262—Boston (140) vs. St. Louis (122), Mar. 27, 1960
   Los Angeles (133) at Boston (129), Apr. 17, 1966 (ot)
254—San Francisco (130) vs. Philadelphia (124), Apr. 18, 1967
   Boston (128) vs. Phoenix (126), June 4, 1976 (3 ot)

Fewest Points, Both Teams, Game

145—Syracuse (71) vs. Ft. Wayne (74) at Indianapolis, Apr. 7, 1955
165—Houston (71) vs. Boston (94), May 9, 1981
167—Philadelphia (83) at Ft. Wayne (84), Apr. 1, 1956
   Phoenix (80) vs. Boston (87), June 6, 1976

Largest Margin of Victory, Game

35—Washington vs. Seattle, June 4, 1978 (117-82)
34—Boston vs. St. Louis, Apr. 2, 1961 (129-95)
33—Boston vs. Los Angeles, Apr. 25, 1965 (129-96)
32—Boston vs. Los Angeles, Apr. 18, 1965 (142-110)
   Portland vs. Philadelphia, May 31, 1977 (130-98)

BY HALF

Most Points, First Half

76—Boston vs. St. Louis, Mar. 27, 1960
73—Los Angeles at Boston, Apr. 8, 1962
   Philadelphia vs. San Francisco, Apr. 14, 1967
72—Boston vs. Minneapolis, Apr. 5, 1959
   San Francisco vs. Philadelphia, Apr. 24, 1967

Fewest Points, First Half

30—Houston vs. Boston, May 9, 1981
31—Syracuse vs. Ft. Wayne at Indianapolis, Apr. 7, 1955
33—Phoenix vs. Boston, June 6, 1976

Most Points, Both Teams, First Half

140—San Francisco (72) vs. Philadelphia (68), Apr. 24, 1967
138—Philadelphia (73) vs. San Francisco (65), Apr. 14, 1967
134—Boston (68) vs. Los Angeles (66), Apr. 14, 1962

Fewest Points, Both Teams, First Half

69—Syracuse (31) vs. Ft. Wayne (38) at Indianapolis, Apr. 7, 1955
71—Phoenix (33) vs. Boston (38), June 6, 1976
   Houston (30) vs. Boston (41), May 9, 1981
82—Seattle (35) at Washington (47), June 4, 1978

Largest Lead at Halftime

27—New York vs. Los Angeles, May 8, 1970 (led 69-42; won 113-99)
25—Boston vs. St. Louis, Mar. 27, 1960 (led 76-51; won 140-122)
24—Boston vs. Minneapolis, Apr. 5, 1959 (led 72-48; won 128-108)
   San Francisco vs. Boston, Apr. 22, 1964 (led 67-43; won 115-91)
   Boston vs. Los Angeles, Apr. 19, 1966 (led 71-47; won 129-109)

Largest Deficit at Halftime, Overcome to Win Game

21—Baltimore at Philadelphia, Apr. 13, 1948 (trailed 41-20; won 66-63)
14—New York at Los Angeles, Apr. 29, 1970 (trailed 42-56; won 111-108)
   Golden State at Washington, May 18, 1975 (trailed 40-54; won 101-95)
13—Boston vs. Los Angeles, Apr. 21, 1968 (trailed 48-61; won 107-101)
   New York vs. Los Angeles, May 4, 1970 (trailed 40-53; won 107-100)

Most Points, Second Half
>   78—Boston vs. Los Angeles, Apr. 18, 1965
>   73—Boston vs. St. Louis, Apr. 2, 1961
>   Portland vs. Philadelphia, May 31, 1977
>   72—Boston vs. Los Angeles, Apr. 25, 1965

Fewest Points, Second Half
>   30—Washington vs. Seattle, May 24, 1979
>   31—St. Louis vs. Boston, Apr. 2, 1960
>   34—Boston vs. Phoenix, June 4, 1976

Most Points, Both Teams, Second Half
>   139—Boston (78) vs. Los Angeles (61), Apr. 18, 1965
>   138—Los Angeles (71) at Boston (67), Apr. 21, 1963
>   130—Boston (67) vs. Los Angeles (63), Apr. 19, 1965

Fewest Points, Both Teams, Second Half
>   73—Washington (30) vs. Seattle (43), May 24, 1979
>   76—Ft. Wayne (38) at Syracuse (38), Mar. 31, 1955
>   Ft. Wayne (36) vs. Syracuse (40) at Indianapolis, Apr. 7, 1955
>   77—Boston (36) at Houston (41), May 10, 1981

BY QUARTER, OVERTIME PERIOD

Most Points, First Quarter
>   43—Philadelphia vs. San Francisco, Apr. 14, 1967
>   Philadelphia at San Francisco, Apr. 24, 1967
>   41—San Francisco vs. Philadelphia, Apr. 24, 1967
>   40—San Francisco vs. Boston, Apr. 22, 1964

Fewest Points, First Quarter
>   13—Syracuse vs. Ft. Wayne, Apr. 2, 1955
>   Milwaukee at Boston, May 3, 1974
>   15—Los Angeles at Boston, Apr. 29, 1969
>   Milwaukee vs. Boston, May 7, 1974
>   Philadelphia vs. Portland, June 3, 1977
>   16—By many teams

Most Points, Both Teams, First Quarter
>   84—Philadelphia (43) at San Francisco (41), Apr. 24, 1967
>   73—Philadelphia (43) vs. San Francisco (30), Apr. 14, 1967
>   72—St. Louis (39) at Boston (33), Apr. 11, 1961

Fewest Points, Both Teams, First Quarter
>   31—Los Angeles (15) at Boston (16), Apr. 29, 1969
>   33—Ft. Wayne (13) at Syracuse (20), Apr. 2, 1955
>   35—Milwaukee (15) vs. Boston (20), May 7, 1974

Largest Lead at End of First Quarter
>   20—Los Angeles vs. New York, May 6, 1970 (led 36-16; won 135-113)
>   19—San Francisco vs. Boston, Apr. 22, 1964 (led 40-21; won 115-91)
>   Boston vs. Milwaukee, May 3, 1974 (led 32-13; won 95-83)
>   18—Los Angeles vs. Boston, Apr. 21, 1965 (led 35-17; won 126-105)
>   Boston vs. Phoenix, June 4, 1976 (led 36-18; won 128-126)

CHAMPIONSHIP SERIES STATISTICS

Largest Deficit at End of First Quarter, Overcome to Win
    14—Los Angeles at Boston, Apr. 17, 1966 (trailed 20-34; won 133-129)
    11—Seattle at Washington, June 1, 1979 (trailed 19-30; won 97-93)
    10—Syracuse vs. Ft. Wayne, Apr. 10, 1955 (trailed 21-31; won 92-91)
        New York vs. Los Angeles, May 4, 1970 (trailed 20-30; won 107-100)
        Golden State at Washington, May 18, 1975 (trailed 17-27; won 101-95)
        Golden State at Washington, May 25, 1975 (trailed 20-30; won 96-95)

Most Points, Second Quarter
    46—Boston vs. St. Louis, Mar. 27, 1960
    43—Los Angeles at Boston, Apr. 8, 1962
    42—St. Louis at Boston, Mar. 29, 1958

Fewest Points, Second Quarter
    12—Boston vs. Milwaukee, May 5, 1974
    13—Syracuse vs. Ft. Wayne at Indianapolis, Apr. 7, 1955
        Phoenix vs. Boston, June 6, 1976
        Houston vs. Boston, May 9, 1981
    14—Seattle at Washington, June 4, 1978

Most Points, Both Teams, Second Quarter
    73—St. Louis (38) vs. Boston (35), Apr. 8, 1961
        Boston (38) vs. Los Angeles (35), Apr. 14, 1962
    72—St. Louis (42) at Boston (30), Mar. 29, 1958
Boston (46) vs. St. Louis (26), Mar. 27, 1960
    71—Boston (40) vs. Minneapolis (31), Apr. 5, 1959

Fewest Points, Both Teams, Second Quarter
    29—Syracuse (13) vs. Ft. Wayne (16) at Indianapolis, Apr. 7, 1955
    31—Phoenix (13) vs. Boston (18), June 6, 1976
    33—Boston (12) vs. Milwaukee (21), May 5, 1974
        Houston (13) vs. Boston (20), May 9, 1981

Most Points, Third Quarter
    41—Portland vs. Philadelphia, May 31, 1977
    40—Boston vs. Los Angeles, Apr. 21, 1963
        Portland at Philadelphia, June 3, 1977
    39—Boston at St. Louis, Apr. 9, 1961
        Boston vs. Los Angeles, Apr. 18, 1965

Fewest Points, Third Quarter
    11—New York at Los Angeles, Apr. 30, 1972
    12—Boston at St. Louis, Apr. 7, 1960
    13—Los Angeles at New York, May 6, 1973

Most Points, Both Teams, Third Quarter
    75—Boston (40) vs. Los Angeles (35), Apr. 21, 1963
    73—Boston (39) vs. Los Angeles (34), Aprl 18, 1965
    72—Boston (38) vs. St. Louis (34), Mar. 27, 1960

Fewest Points, Both Teams, Third Quarter
    33—Washington (14) vs. Seattle (19), May 24, 1979
    34—Syracuse (14) vs. Ft. Wayne (20) at Indianapolis, Apr. 7, 1955
    36—Boston (17) at Milwaukee (19), Apr. 28, 1974
        Boston (18) vs. Houston (18), May 12, 1981

Largest Lead at End of Third Quarter
- 31—Portland vs. Philadelphia, May 31, 1977 (led 98-67; won 130-98)
- 30—Boston vs. San Francisco, Apr. 20, 1964 (led 98-68; won 124-101)
- 29—Boston vs. St. Louis, Mar. 27, 1960 (led 114-85; won 140-122)

Largest Deficit at End of Third Quarter, Overcome to Win
- 12—San Francisco at Philadelphia, Apr. 23, 1967 (trailed 84-96; won 117-109)
- 11—Seattle vs. Washington, May 21, 1978 (trailed 73-84; won 106-102)
- 9—Washington at Seattle, May 30, 1978 (trailed 78-87; won 120-116)

Most Points, Fourth Quarter
- 42—Boston vs. Los Angeles, Apr. 25, 1965
  - Portland vs. Philadelphia, May 29, 1977
- 41—Philadelphia vs. San Francisco, Apr. 16, 1967
- 39—Boston vs. Los Angeles, Apr. 18, 1965

Fewest Points, Fourth Quarter
- 13—Philadelphia vs. San Francisco, Apr. 23, 1967
  - Milwaukee vs. Boston, Apr. 30, 1974
- 14—Boston at St. Louis, Apr. 11, 1957
  - St. Louis vs. Boston, Apr. 2, 1960
  - Houston at Boston, May 5, 1981
- 15—St. Louis vs. Boston, Apr. 7, 1960

Most Points, Both Teams, Fourth Quarter
- 72—Los Angeles (38) vs. Boston (34), Apr. 23, 1969
- 69—Los Angeles (36) vs. New York (33), May 6, 1970
- 68—Los Angeles (36) at Boston (32), Apr. 16, 1963)
  - Los Angeles (38) vs. Boston (30), Apr. 28, 1968

Fewest Points, Both Teams, Fourth Quarter
- 33—Boston (14) at St. Louis (19), Apr. 11, 1957
- 35—Ft. Wayne (17) at Syracuse (18), Apr. 10, 1955
  - Houston (16) vs. Boston (19), May 10, 1981
- 36—Houston (14) at Boston (22), May 5, 1981.

Most Points, Overtime Period
- 22—Los Angeles vs. New York, May 1, 1970
- 16—New York at Los Angeles, May 1, 1970
  - Boston vs. Phoenix, June 4, 1976
- 15—Los Angeles at New York, May 5, 1972
  - Milwaukee vs. Boston, Apr. 30, 1974

Fewest Points, Overtime Period
- 4—Boston vs. Milwaukee, May 10, 1974
  - Milwaukee at Boston, May 10, 1974
- 6—Los Angeles vs. New York, Apr. 29, 1970
  - Boston at Milwaukee, Apr. 30, 1974
  - Boston vs. Phoenix, June 4, 1976
  - Phoenix at Boston, June 4, 1976
- 7—Los Angeles at Boston, Apr. 18, 1962
  - San Francisco at Philadelphia, Apr. 14, 1967

Most Points, Both Teams, Overtime Period
- 38—Los Angeles (22), vs. New York (16), May 1, 1970
- 30—Boston (16) vs. Phoenix (14), June 4, 1976
- 25—Los Angeles (15) vs. New York (10), May 5, 1972

Fewest Points, Both Teams, Overtime Period
    8—Boston (4) vs. Milwaukee (4), May 10, 1974
   12—Boston (6) vs. Phoenix (6), June 4, 1976
   15—Los Angeles (6) vs. New York (9), Apr. 29, 1970

100-POINT GAMES

Most Consecutive Games, 100+ Points, All Championship Series
   20—Minneapolis/Los Angeles, 1959-65
   17—Boston, 1960-63
   14—Boston, 1957-60

Most Consecutive Games Scoring Fewer Than 100 Points, All Championship Series
   6—Houston, 1981 (current)
   5—Boston, 1974
      Seattle, 1978-79
      Boston, 1976-81
   4—Ft. Wayne, 1955-56
      Los Angeles, 1973

PLAYERS SCORING

Most Players, 30+ Points, Game
   2—Accomplished 21 times. Most recent:
      Los Angeles at Philadelphia, May 16, 1980.

Most Players, 30+ Points, Both Teams, Game
   3—Los Angeles (2) vs. Boston (1), Apr. 16, 1962
      Los Angeles (2) at Boston (1), Apr. 18, 1962 (ot)
      Los Angeles (2) vs. Boston (1), Apr. 17, 1963
      Los Angeles (2) at Boston (1), Apr. 21, 1963
      Los Angeles (2) at Boston (1), Apr. 24, 1966
      Philadelphia (2) vs. San Francisco (1), Apr. 14, 1967 (ot)
      Philadelphia (2) at San Francisco (1), Apr. 20, 1967
      Los Angeles (2) vs. Boston (1), Apr. 25, 1969

Most Players, 20+ Points, Game
   5—Boston vs. Los Angeles, Apr. 19, 1965
   4—By many teams.

Most Players, 20+ Points, Both Teams, Game
   8—Boston (4) at Los Angeles (4), Apr. 26, 1966
   7—Boston (5) vs. Los Angeles (2), Apr. 19, 1965
      Philadelphia (4) vs. San Francisco (3), Apr. 14, 1967 (ot)
      Boston (4) vs. Los Angeles (3), Apr. 30, 1968 (ot)

   6—In many games.

Most Players, 10+ Points, Game
   7—Accomplished 12 times. Most recent:
      Washington at Seattle, May 30, 1978 (ot)

Most Players, 10+ Points, Both Teams, Game
   14—Boston (7) vs. St. Louis (7), Mar. 27, 1960
   13—Los Angeles (7) at Boston (6), Apr. 19, 1966
   12—In many games

Fewest Players, 10+ Points, Game

2—Ft. Wayne vs. Philadelphia, Apr. 1, 1956
   St. Louis at Boston, Mar. 29, 1958
   St. Louis vs. Boston, Apr. 12, 1958
   Los Angeles at Boston, Apr. 29, 1969
3—By many teams.

Fewest Players, 10+ Points, Both Teams, Game

5—Ft. Wayne (2) vs. Philadelphia (3), Apr. 1, 1956
   Los Angeles (2) at Boston (3), Apr. 29, 1969
6—Boston (3) vs. Los Angeles (3), Apr. 18, 1962 (ot)
   Boston (3) vs. Los Angeles (3), Apr. 25, 1969
   Baltimore (3) at Milwaukee (3), Apr. 21, 1971
   Golden State (3) vs. Washington (3), May 20, 1975
7—In many games.

FIELD GOAL PERCENTAGE

Highest Field Goal Percentage, Game

.606—Los Angeles vs. New York, May 6, 1970 (57-94)
.563—Portland vs. Philadelphia, May 31, 1977 (54-96)
.561—Milwaukee at Baltimore, Apr. 30, 1971 (46-82)
.551—Boston at Houston, May 14, 1981 (43-78)
.539—Los Angeles vs. Philadelphia, May 4, 1980 (48-89)

Lowest Field Goal Percentage, Game

.275—Syracuse vs. Ft. Wayne at Indianapolis, Apr. 7, 1955 (25-91)
.280—Ft. Wayne vs. Syracuse at Indianapolis, Apr. 7, 1955 (23-82)
.293—Boston at St. Louis, Apr. 6, 1957 (29-99)
.295—San Francisco at Philadelphia, Apr. 16, 1967 (38-129)
.302—Boston vs. St. Louis, Apr. 9, 1958 (32-106)

Highest Field Goal Percentage, Both Teams, Game

.548—Los Angeles (.606) vs. New York (.495), May 6, 1970 (109-199)
.509—Portland (.563) vs. Philadelphia (.440), May 31, 1977 (87-171)
.508—Philadelphia (.528) vs. Los Angeles (.489), May 16, 1980 (92-181)

Lowest Field Goal Percentage, Both Teams, Game

.277—Syracuse (.275) vs. Ft. Wayne (.280) at Indianapolis, Apr. 7, 1955 (48-173)
.312—Boston (.304) at St. Louis (.320), Apr. 11, 1957 (68-218)
.325—Boston (.293) at St. Louis (.356), Apr. 6, 1957 (65-200)

FIELD GOALS

Most Field Goals, Game

61—Boston vs. St. Louis, Mar. 27, 1960
57—Philadelphia vs. San Francisco, Apr. 14, 1967 (ot)
   Los Angeles vs. New York, May 6, 1970
55—Boston vs. St. Louis, Apr. 5, 1960
   Boston vs. Los Angeles, Apr. 25, 1965
   San Francisco at Philadelphia, Apr. 14, 1967 (ot)
   Philadelphia vs. San Francisco, Apr. 16, 1967

Fewest Field Goals, Game

23—Ft. Wayne vs. Syracuse at Indianapolis, Apr. 7, 1955
25—Syracuse vs. Ft. Wayne at Indianapolis, Apr. 7, 1955
26—Syracuse vs. Ft. Wayne at Indianapolis, Apr. 3, 1955
   Syracuse vs. Ft. Wayne, Apr. 10, 1955

CHAMPIONSHIP SERIES STATISTICS 187

Most Field Goals, Both Teams, Game

    112—Philadelphia (57) vs. San Francisco (55), Apr. 14, 1967 (ot)
    110—Boston (61) vs. St. Louis (49), Mar. 27, 1960
    109—Los Angeles (57) vs. New York (52), May 6, 1970

Fewest Field Goals, Both Teams, Game

    48—Ft. Wayne (23) vs. Syracuse (25) at Indianapolis, Apr. 7, 1955
    57—Syracuse (26) vs. Ft. Wayne (31) at Indianapolis, Apr. 3, 1955
    58—Ft. Wayne (28) at Syracuse (30), Mar. 31, 1955

FIELD GOAL ATTEMPTS

Most Field Goal Attempts, Game

    140—San Francisco at Philadelphia, Apr. 14, 1967 (ot)
    133—Boston vs. St. Louis, Mar. 27, 1960
    130—Boston vs. Minneapolis, Apr. 4, 1959

Fewest Field Goal Attempts, Game

    66—Los Angeles at New York, May 4, 1970
    71—Ft. Wayne at Syracuse, Mar. 31, 1955
    74—Los Angeles at Boston, May 3, 1969
        Boston at Houston, May 10, 1981

Most Field Goal Attempts, Both Teams, Game

    256—San Francisco (140) at Philadelphia (114), Apr. 14, 1967 (ot)
    250—Boston (130) vs. Minneapolis (120), Apr. 4, 1959
    247—San Francisco (129) at Philadelphia (116), Apr. 16, 1967

Fewest Field Goal Attempts, Both Teams, Game

    156—Ft. Wayne (71) at Syracuse (85), Mar. 31, 1955
    157—Ft. Wayne (77) vs. Syracuse (80) at Indianapolis, Apr. 3, 1955
    160—Phoenix (77) vs. Boston (83), June 6, 1976

FREE THROW PERCENTAGE

Highest Free Throw Percentage, Game

    .943—Los Angeles at Philadelphia, May 16, 1980 (33-35)
    .933—Ft. Wayne at Philadelphia, Mar. 31, 1956 (28-30)
    .926—Boston vs. Los Angeles, Apr. 14, 1962 (25-27)
    .923—Golden State vs. Washington, May 20, 1975 (12-13)
    .920—Boston vs. Los Angeles, May 3, 1969 (23-25)

Lowest Free Throw Percentage, Game

    .444—Philadelphia vs. San Francisco, Apr. 16, 1967 (16-36)
        Golden State at Washington, May 25, 1975 (8-18)
    .476—Baltimore at Milwaukee, Apr. 21, 1971 (10-21)
    .478—San Francisco at Boston, Apr. 18, 1964 (22-46)
        Seattle at Washington, May 20, 1979 (11-23)
    .500—Los Angeles vs. Boston, May 2, 1968 (13-26)

Highest Free Throw Percentage, Both Teams, Game

    .903—Boston (.926) vs. Los Angeles (.889), Apr. 14, 1962 (65-72)
    .881—Los Angeles (.903) vs. Boston (.857), Apr. 20, 1966 (52-59)
    .875—Boston (.893) at Los Angeles (.861), Apr. 17, 1963 (56-64)

Lowest Free Throw Percentage, Both Teams, Game

    .538—Philadelphia (.444) vs. San Francisco (.655), Apr. 16, 1967 (35-65)
    .541—San Francisco (.478) at Boston (.615), Apr. 18, 1964 (46-85)
    .600—Los Angeles (.600) vs. New York (.600), May 10, 1973 (33-55)

FREE THROWS MADE

Most Free Throws Made, Game
- 45—St. Louis at Boston, Apr. 13, 1957 (2 ot)
- 44—St. Louis at Boston, Apr. 9, 1958
- 43—Boston at St. Louis, Apr. 12, 1958
  Los Angeles vs. Boston, Apr. 10, 1962
  Boston at Los Angeles, Apr. 26, 1966

Fewest Free Throws Made, Game
- 8—Los Angeles vs. Philadelphia, May 7, 1980
  Boston vs. Houston, May 7, 1981
- 9—New York at Los Angeles, May 6, 1970
  Milwaukee vs. Boston, Apr. 28, 1974
  Milwaukee at Boston, May 3, 1974
- 10—Baltimore at Milwaukee, Apr. 21, 1971
  Boston at Milwaukee, Apr. 30, 1974 (ot)
  Philadelphia vs. Los Angeles, May 10, 1980

Most Free Throws Made, Both Teams, Game
- 80—St. Louis (44) at Boston (36), Apr. 9, 1958
- 77—Syracuse (39) vs. Ft. Wayne (38), Apr. 9, 1955
  Boston (43) at St. Louis (34), Apr. 12, 1958
- 76—St. Louis (45) at Boston (31), Apr. 13, 1957 (2 ot)
  Boston (40) vs. St. Louis (36), Mar. 30, 1958

Fewest Free Throws Made, Both Teams, Game
- 23—Milwaukee (9) vs. Boston (14), Apr. 28, 1974
- 25—Baltimore (11) vs. Milwaukee (14), Apr. 25, 1971
  Golden State (8) at Washington (17), May 25, 1975
- 26—Seattle (11) at Washington (15), May 20, 1979

FREE THROW ATTEMPTS

Most Free Throw Attempts, Game
- 64—Philadelphia at San Francisco, Apr. 24, 1967
- 62—St. Louis at Boston, Apr. 13, 1957 (2 ot)
- 60—Boston at St. Louis, Apr. 2, 1958

Fewest Free Throw Attempts, Game
- 12—Los Angeles vs. Philadelphia, May 7, 1980
- 13—Milwaukee vs. Boston, Apr. 28, 1974
  Milwaukee at Boston, May 3, 1974
  Golden State vs. Washington, May 20, 1975
  Boston vs. Houston, May 7, 1981
- 16—Houston at Boston, May 5, 1981

Most Free Throw Attempts, Both Teams, Game
- 116—St. Louis (62) at Boston (54), Apr. 13, 1957 (2 ot)
- 107—Boston (60) at St. Louis (47), Apr. 2, 1958
  St. Louis (57) at Boston (50), Apr. 9, 1958
- 105—St. Louis (54) vs. Boston (51), Apr. 7, 1957

Fewest Free Throw Attempts, Both Teams, Game
- 31—Milwaukee (13) vs. Boston (18), Apr. 28, 1974
- 33—Milwaukee (16) at Baltimore (17), Apr. 25, 1971
- 34—Houston (14) at Boston (20), May 5, 1981

CHAMPIONSHIP SERIES STATISTICS

TOTAL REBOUNDS

Highest Rebound Percentage, Game
.667—Boston vs. St. Louis, Apr. 9, 1960 (78-117)
.632—Los Angeles vs. New York, May 7, 1972 (67-106)
.631—Boston vs. St. Louis, Mar. 30, 1958 (77-122)
.622—Los Angeles vs. Boston, Apr. 21, 1965 (79-127)
.612—Boston vs. St. Louis, Apr. 2, 1961 (85-139)

Most Rebounds, Game
93—Philadelphia vs. San Francisco, Apr. 16, 1967
86—Boston vs. Minneapolis, Apr. 4, 1959
85—Boston vs. St. Louis, Apr. 2, 1961

Fewest Rebounds, Game
34—Phoenix vs. Boston, June 2, 1976
   Philadelphia at Los Angeles, May 7, 1980
   Philadelphia vs. Los Angeles, May 11, 1980
35—Houston at Boston, May 7, 1981
36—Philadelphia vs. Los Angeles, May 16, 1980

Most Rebounds, Both Teams, Game
169—Philadelphia (93) vs. San Francisco (76), Apr. 16, 1967
159—San Francisco (80) at Philadelphia (79), Apr. 14, 1967 (ot)
152—Boston (81) vs. St. Louis (71), Apr. 13, 1957 (2 ot)
   Boston (82) vs. Minneapolis (70), Apr. 5, 1959

Fewest Rebounds, Both Teams, Game
77—Philadelphia (38) at Ft. Wayne (39), Apr. 5, 1956
78—Boston (37) at Houston (41), May 14, 1981
79—Syracuse (39) vs. Ft. Wayne (40), Apr. 9, 1955

OFFENSIVE REBOUNDS

Highest Offensive Rebound Percentage, Game
.529—Seattle vs. Washington, June 7, 1978 (27-51)
.521—Boston vs. Houston, May 5, 1981 (25-48)
.483—Houston vs. Boston, May 10, 1981 (28-58)
.478—Los Angeles at Philadelphia, May 10, 1980 (22-46)
.474—Portland at Philadelphia, May 22, 1977 (18-38)

Most Offensive Rebounds, Game
28—Houston vs. Boston, May 10, 1981
27—Seattle vs. Washington, June 7, 1978
26—Washington vs. Seattle, May 28, 1978

Fewest Offensive Rebounds, Game
5—Philadelphia at Los Angeles, May 7, 1980
   Philadelphia vs. Los Angeles, May 11, 1980
6—Philadelphia vs. Portland, May 26, 1977
7—Milwaukee at Boston, May 10, 1974 (2 ot)

Most Offensive Rebounds, Both Teams, Game
45—Houston (28) vs. Boston (17), May 10, 1981
44—Seattle (27) vs. Washington (17), June 7, 1978
   Boston (25) vs. Houston (19), May 5, 1981
43—Washington (25) vs. Seattle (18), June 4, 1978

Fewest Offensive Rebounds, Both Teams, Game
- 19—Milwaukee (9) vs. Boston (10), Apr. 28, 1974
- 20—Milwaukee (9) at Boston (11), May 5, 1974
  - Philadelphia (5) at Los Angeles (15), May 7, 1980
- 21—Seattle (8) at Washington (13), May 24, 1979

DEFENSIVE REBOUNDS

Highest Defensive Rebound Percentage, Game
- .881—Los Angeles vs. Philadelphia, May 7, 1980 (37-42)
- .861—Los Angeles at Philadelphia, May 11, 1980 (31-36)
- .857—Portland at Philadelphia, May 26, 1977 (36-42)
- .833—Los Angeles at Philadelphia, May 16, 1980 (35-42)
- .822—Boston at Phoenix, June 6, 1976 (37-45)
  - Washington vs. Seattle, May 24, 1979 (37-45)

Most Defensive Rebounds, Game
- 48—Portland at Philadelphia, June 3, 1977
- 46—Philadelphia vs. Portland, May 26, 1977
- 44—Boston vs. Phoenix, May 27, 1976
  - Washington vs. Seattle, June 4, 1978

Fewest Defensive Rebounds, Game
- 20—Philadelphia vs. Portland, May 22, 1977
- 21—Houston vs. Boston, May 10, 1981
- 22—Washington at Seattle, May 27, 1979
  - Houston at Boston, May 7, 1981

Most Defensive Rebounds, Both Teams, Game
- 84—Portland (48) at Philadelphia (36), June 3, 1977
- 82—Philadelpha (46) vs. Portland (36), May 26, 1977
- 79—Golden State (43) vs. Washington (36), May 20, 1975
  - Boston (42) vs. Phoenix (37), June 4, 1976 (3 ot)

Fewest Defensive Rebounds, Both Teams, Game
- 50—Philadelphia (20) vs. Portland (30), May 22, 1977
  - Washington (24) at Seattle (26), June 7, 1978
- 51—Houston (21) vs. Boston (30), May 10, 1981
- 52—Milwaukee (25) vs. Boston (27), May 7, 1974
  - Houston (23) at Boston (29), May 5, 1981

ASSISTS

Most Assists, Game
- 44—Los Angeles vs. New York, May 6, 1970
- 38—Los Angeles vs. New York, May 1, 1970 (ot)
- 37—Portland vs. Philadelphia, May 31, 1977

Fewest Assists, Game
- 5—Boston at St. Louis, Apr. 3, 1960
- 9—Los Angeles at Boston, Apr. 28, 1966
- 10—Los Angeles at Boston, Apr. 29, 1969
  - Los Angeles at Boston, May 3, 1969
  - Houston vs. Boston, May 9, 1981

Most Assists, Both Teams, Game
   73—Los Angeles (44) vs. New York (29), May 6, 1970
   66—Los Angeles (38) vs. New York (28), May 1, 1970 (ot)
      Philadelphia (34) at Los Angeles (32), May 7, 1980
   62—Boston (33) vs. Phoenix (29), June 4, 1976 (3 ot)

Fewest Assists, Both Teams, Game
   21—Los Angeles (10) at Boston (11), Apr. 29, 1969
   24—Los Angeles (10) at Boston (14), May 3, 1969
   26—Boston (5) at St. Louis (21), Apr. 3, 1960

PERSONAL FOULS

Most Personal Fouls, Game
   42—Minneapolis vs. Syracuse, Apr. 23, 1950
   40—Portland vs. Philadelphia, May 31, 1977
   39—Minneapolis at New York, Apr. 18, 1952 (ot)
      New York vs. Minneapolis, Apr. 10, 1953

Fewest Personal Fouls, Game
   17—Baltimore vs. Milwaukee, Apr. 25, 1971
      Boston at Milwaukee, Apr. 28, 1974
      Boston vs. Milwaukee, May 3, 1974
      Philadelphia at Los Angeles, May 4, 1980
      Houston at Boston, May 7, 1981
   18—Ft. Wayne at Philadelphia, Mar. 31, 1956
      Boston vs. St. Louis, Mar. 29, 1960
      St. Louis at Boston, Apr. 5, 1960
      Los Angeles at New York, May 6, 1973
      Milwaukee vs. Boston, Apr. 28, 1974
      Boston at Milwaukee, May 7, 1974
   19—By many teams

Most Personal Fouls, Both Teams, Game
   77—Minneapolis (42) vs. Syracuse (35), Apr. 23, 1950
   76—Minneapolis (39) at New York (37), Apr. 18, 1952 (ot)
   74—Boston (37) vs. St. Louis (37), Apr. 13, 1957 (2 ot)
      Portland (40) vs. Philadelphia (34), May 31, 1977

Fewest Personal Fouls, Both Teams, Game
   35—Boston (17) at Milwaukee (18), Apr. 28, 1974
   36—Baltimore (17) vs. Milwaukee (19), Apr. 25, 1971
   37—Boston (17) vs. Milwaukee (20), May 3, 1974

DISQUALIFICATIONS

Most Disqualifications, Game
   4—Minneapolis vs. Syracuse, Apr. 23, 1950
     Minneapolis vs. New York, Apr. 4, 1953
     New York vs. Minneapolis, Apr. 10, 1953
     St. Louis at Boston, Apr. 13, 1957 (2 ot)
     Boston vs. Los Angeles, Apr. 18, 1962 (ot)
   3—By many teams. Most recent:
     Washington at Seattle, May 29, 1979 (ot)

Most Disqualifications, Both Teams, Game
   7—Boston (4) vs. Los Angeles (3), Apr. 18, 1962 (ot)
   6—St. Louis (4) at Boston (2), Apr. 13, 1957 (2 ot)
   5—Minneapolis (4) vs. Syracuse (1), Apr. 23, 1950
      Boston (3) vs. Phoenix (2), June 4, 1976 (3 ot)
      Seattle (3) vs. Washington (2), May 30, 1978 (ot)

STEALS

Most Steals, Game
   17—Golden State vs. Washington, May 23, 1975
   16—Philadelphia vs. Portland, May 22, 1977
   15—Golden State at Washington, May 25, 1975
      Philadelphia vs. Portland, May 26, 1977
      Houston at Boston, May 5, 1981

Fewest Steals, Game
   1—Milwaukee at Boston, May 10, 1974 (2 ot)
     Boston vs. Phoenix, May 23, 1976
   2—Milwaukee at Boston, May 3, 1974
     Milwaukee at Boston, May 5, 1974
     Milwaukee vs. Boston, May 12, 1974
   3—Milwaukee vs. Boston, Apr. 30, 1974 (ot)

Most Steals, Both Teams, Game
   31—Golden State (17) vs. Washington (14), May 23, 1975
   28—Golden State (15) at Washington (13), May 25, 1975
   26—Philadelphia (14) at Los Angeles (12), May 7, 1980

Fewest Steals, Both Teams, Game
   8—Milwaukee (2) at Boston (6), May 5, 1974
     Milwaukee (1) at Boston (7), May 10, 1974 (2 ot)
     Seattle (4) vs. Washington (4), June 2, 1978
     Seattle (4) vs. Washington (4), May 29, 1979 (ot)
   10—Boston (4) at Milwaukee (6), May 7, 1974
      Seattle (4) vs. Washington (6), May 21, 1978
      Houston (4) vs. Boston (6), May 14, 1981
   11—Washington (5) at Seattle (6), May 27, 1979

BLOCKED SHOTS

Most Blocked Shots, Game
   13—Seattle at Washington, May 28, 1978
      Philadelphia at Los Angeles, May 4, 1980
   12—Golden State vs. Washington, May 20, 1975
   11—Seattle at Washington, May 20, 1979
      Seattle vs. Washington, May 29, 1979 (ot)
      Philadelphia at Los Angeles, May 7, 1980
      Philadelphia vs. Los Angeles, May 16, 1980

Fewest Blocked Shots, Game
   0—Boston vs. Milwaukee, May 5, 1974
     Boston vs. Milwaukee, May 10, 1974 (2 ot)
     Boston vs. Phoenix, June 4, 1976 (3 ot)
     Philadelphia vs. Portland, May 22, 1977
     Washington at Seattle, May 21, 1978
     Boston at Houston, May 14, 1981
   1—By many teams

CHAMPIONSHIP SERIES STATISTICS

Most Blocked Shots, Both Teams, Game
- 22—Philadelphia (13) at Los Angeles (9), May 4, 1980
- 19—Washington (10) vs. Seattle (9), June 4, 1978
- 18— Philadelphia (11) at Los Angeles (7), May 7, 1980

Fewest Blocked Shots, Both Teams, Game
- 2—Boston (0) at Houston (2), May 14, 1981
- 3—Boston (0) vs. Milwaukee (3), May 5, 1974
  Boston (0) vs. Milwaukee (3), May 10, 1974 (2 ot)
  Boston (1) vs. Phoenix (2), June 4, 1976 (3 ot)
- 4—In many games

TURNOVERS

Most Turnovers, Game
- 34—Portland at Philadelphia, May 22, 1977
- 31—Golden State at Washington, May 25, 1975
- 30—Philadelphia at Portland, May 31, 1977

Fewest Turnovers, Game
- 9—New York at Los Angeles, May 3, 1973
- 10—Washington at Seattle, May 29, 1979
  Houston at Boston, May 5, 1981
  Houston at Boston, May 7, 1981
- 11—Seattle at Washington, May 20, 1979
  Washington at Seattle, May 27, 1979
  Boston at Houston, May 9, 1981

Most Turnovers, Both Teams, Game
- 60—Golden State (31) at Washington (29), May 25, 1975
- 54—Phoenix (29) at Boston (25), June 4, 1976 (3 ot)
  Portland (34) at Philadelphia (20), May 22, 1977
- 52—Portland (29) at Philadelphia (23), May 26, 1977

Fewest Turnovers, Both Teams, Game
- 25—Washington (10) at Seattle (15), May 29, 1979 (ot)
  Houston (12) vs. Boston (13), May 14, 1981
- 26—Los Angeles (12) vs. New York (14), Apr. 26, 1972
  Los Angeles (12) at New York (14), May 5, 1972 (ot)
- 28—New York (9) at Los Angeles (19), May 3, 1973
  Boston (12) at Milwaukee (16), May 12, 1974
  Washington (12) at Seattle (16), June 7, 1978

PLAYOFF MVP AWARD

1969—Jerry West, Los Angeles
1970—Willis Reed, New York
1971—Lew Alcindor, Milwaukee
1972—Wilt Chamberlain, Los Angeles
1973—Willis Reed, New York
1974—John Havlicek, Boston
1975—Rick Barry, Golden State

1976—Jo Jo White, Boston
1977—Bill Walton, Portland
1978—West Unseld, Washington
1979—Dennis Johnson, Seattle
1980—Earvin Johnson, Los Angeles
1981—Cedric Maxwell, Boston

TOP SCORERS IN PLAYOFF HISTORY

Figures from National Basketball League are included below; NBL did not record field goal attempts, however, so all field goal percentages listed here are based only on field goals and attempts in NBA competition. Minutes played not compiled prior to 1952; rebounds not compiled prior to 1951.

Player	Yrs.	G.	Min.	FGM	FGA	Pct.	FTM	FTA	Pct.	Reb.	Ast.	PF	Pts.	Avg.
Jerry West	13	153	6321	1622	3463	.469	1213	1507	.805	855	970	541	4457	29.1
John Havlicek	13	172	6860	1451	3329	.436	874	1046	.836	1186	825	517	3776	22.0
Elgin Baylor	12	134	5510	1388	3161	.439	847	1101	.769	1725	541	445	3623	27.0
Wilt Chamberlain	13	160	7559	1425	2728	.522	757	1627	.465	3913	673	412	3607	22.5
Kareem Abdul-Jabbar	10	97	4276	1214	2276	.533	513	706	.727	1524	379	319	2941	30.3
Sam Jones	12	154	4654	1149	2571	.447	611	753	.811	718	358	391	2909	18.9
Bill Russell	13	165	7497	1003	2335	.430	667	1106	.603	4104	770	546	2673	16.2
Bob Pettit	9	88	3545	766	1834	.418	708	915	.744	1304	241	277	2240	25.5
Elvin Hayes	9	93	4036	866	1851	.468	420	641	.655	1214	182	366	2152	23.1
George Mikan	9	91	1500	723	1394	.404	695	906	.767	665	155	390	2141	23.5
Tom Heinsohn	9	104	3203	818	2035	.402	422	568	.743	954	215	417	2058	19.8
Bob Cousy	13	109	4140	689	2016	.342	640	799	.801	546	937	314	2018	18.5
Dolph Schayes	15	103	2687	609	1491	.390	755	918	.822	1051	257	397	1973	19.2
Bob Dandridge	8	93	3882	823	1716	.480	321	422	.761	754	365	377	1967	20.1
Walt Frazier	8	82	2715	567	1292	.439	337	426	.791	266	264	216	1471	17.9
Chet Walker	13	105	3688	687	1531	.449	542	689	.787	737	212	286	1916	18.2
Oscar Robertson	10	86	3673	675	1466	.460	560	655	.855	578	769	267	1910	22.2
Hal Greer	13	92	3642	705	1657	.425	466	574	.812	505	393	357	1876	20.4
Cliff Hagan	9	88	2965	701	1544	.454	432	540	.800	744	305	320	1834	20.4
Rick Barry	7	74	2723	719	1688	.426	392	448	.875	418	340	232	1833	24.8
Julius Erving	5	72	2774	689	1381	.499	500	392	.784	539	311	207	1772	24.6
Jo Jo White	6	80	3428	732	1629	.449	256	309	.828	348	452	241	1720	21.5
Dave Cowens	7	89	3268	733	1627	.451	218	293	.744	1285	333	398	1684	18.9
Don Nelson	11	150	3209	585	1175	.498	407	498	.817	719	210	399	1577	10.5
Dick Barnett	11	102	3027	603	1317	.458	333	445	.748	273	247	282	1539	15.1
Dave DeBusschere	8	96	3682	634	1253	.416	268	384	.698	1155	253	327	1536	16.0
Earl Monroe	8	82	2715	567	1292	.439	337	426	.791	266	264	216	1471	17.9
Gail Goodrich	8	80	2622	542	1227	.442	366	447	.819	250	333	219	1450	18.1
Bill Sharman	10	78	2573	538	1262	.426	370	406	.911	285	201	220	1446	18.5
Bailey Howell	11	86	2712	542	1165	.465	317	433	.732	697	130	376	1401	16.3
Willis Reed	7	78	2641	570	1203	.474	218	285	.765	801	149	275	1385	17.4
Gus Williams	5	75	2236	555	1163	.477	261	361	.723	245	286	202	1372	18.3
Rudy LaRusso	9	93	3188	467	1152	.405	410	546	.751	779	194	366	1344	14.5
Frank Ramsey	9	98	2396	469	1105	.424	393	476	.826	494	151	362	1331	13.6
Lou Hudson	9	61	2199	519	1164	.446	262	326	.804	318	164	196	1300	21.3
Wes Unseld	12	119	4889	513	1040	.493	234	385	.608	1777	453	371	1260	10.6
Bill Bradley	8	95	3161	510	1165	.438	202	251	.805	333	263	313	1222	12.9
Jim McMillian	7	72	2722	497	1101	.451	200	253	.791	377	137	169	1194	16.6
Paul Westphal	7	84	2071	501	1019	.492	187	240	.779	137	282	205	1190	14.2
Paul Arizin	8	49	1815	411	1001	.411	364	439	.829	404	128	177	1186	24.2

ALL-TIME PLAYOFF STATISTICS

Player	Yrs.	G.	Min.	FGM	FGA	Pct.	FTM	FTA	Pct.	Reb.	Ast.	PF	Pts.	Avg.
Bill Bridges	12	113	3521	475	1135	.419	235	349	.673	1305	219	408	1185	10.5
Jamaal Wilkes	7	70	2479	500	1105	.452	178	240	.742	532	149	205	1178	16.8
Tom Sanders	11	130	3039	465	1066	.436	212	296	.716	763	127	508	1142	8.8
Vern Mikkelsen	9	85	2102	396	999	.396	349	446	.783	585	152	377	1141	13.5
Archie Clark	10	71	2387	444	977	.454	237	307	.772	229	297	197	1125	15.8
Paul Silas	14	163	4619	396	998	.397	332	480	.692	1527	335	469	1124	6.9
Dennis Johnson	4	61	2367	409	950	.431	280	372	.753	302	218	192	1104	18.1
Jim Pollard	8	82	1724	397	1029	.339	306	413	.741	407	259	234	1100	13.4
Phil Chenier	7	60	2088	438	974	.450	212	251	.845	230	131	152	1088	18.1
Jeff Mullins	10	83	2255	462	1030	.449	160	213	.751	304	259	217	1084	13.1
Bob Love	6	47	2061	441	1023	.431	194	250	.776	352	87	144	1076	22.9
Zelmo Beaty	7	63	2345	399	857	.466	273	380	.718	696	98	267	1071	17.0
Fred Brown	5	68	1624	434	937	.463	169	204	.828	171	160	132	1047	15.4
Lenny Wilkens	7	64	2403	359	899	.399	313	407	.769	373	372	258	1031	16.1
Moses Malone	4	42	1826	380	773	.492	257	360	.714	646	51	119	1017	24.2
Arnie Risen	12	73	1023	320	684	.385	325	747	.686	561	86	300	985	13.5
Nate Thurmond	9	81	2875	379	912	.416	208	335	.621	1101	227	266	966	11.9
Clyde Lovellette	10	69	1642	371	892	.416	221	323	.684	557	89	232	963	14.0
George Gervin	5	32	1198	369	709	.520	201	250	.804	182	93	110	939	29.3
George Yardley	7	46	1693	324	767	.442	285	349	.817	457	112	143	933	20.3
John Kerr	12	76	2275	370	759	.386	193	281	.687	827	152	173	933	12.3
Calvin Murphy	5	48	1603	383	795	.482	158	169	.935	75	209	190	928	19.3
Slater Martin	11	92	2876	304	867	.351	316	442	.715	270	354	342	924	10.0
Bob Davies	10	67	571	311	508	.341	282	371	.760	78	162	193	904	13.5
Larry Foust	10	73	1920	301	763	.394	300	384	.781	707	94	255	902	12.4
Max Zaslofsky	8	63	732	306	850	.360	287	372	.772	121	101	174	899	14.3
Jerry Lucas	8	72	2370	367	786	.467	162	206	.786	717	214	197	896	12.4
Keith Erickson	7	87	2393	364	806	.452	144	189	.762	386	216	286	872	10.0
Darryl Dawkins	5	71	1794	345	645	.535	181	272	.665	472	86	268	871	12.3
Lionel Hollins	5	62	2079	346	821	.421	168	229	.734	189	301	194	860	13.9
Larry Siegfried	6	79	1826	301	753	.400	256	307	.834	199	209	249	859	10.9
Cazzie Russell	8	72	1566	359	781	.460	134	154	.870	222	97	151	852	11.8
Walt Bellamy	7	46	1939	323	686	.471	204	318	.642	680	136	160	850	18.5
Bob McAdoo	4	28	1242	338	716	.472	171	237	.722	362	71	110	847	30.3
Connie Simmons	7	62	879	278	728	.382	286	391	.731	317	96	256	842	13.6
Wali Jones	9	70	1761	333	821	.406	167	215	.777	166	202	234	833	11.9
Harold Hairston	9	69	2020	307	690	.445	187	255	.733	559	121	185	801	11.6

TOP PERFORMANCES IN PLAYOFFS

*Denotes each overtime period played.

MOST POINTS SCORED IN ONE GAME

	FG.	FT.	Pts.
Elgin Baylor, Los Angeles at Boston, April 14, 1962	22	17	61
Wilt Chamberlain, Philadelphia vs. Syracuse at Philadelphia, March 22, 1962	22	12	56
Rick Barry, San Francisco vs. Philadelphia at San Francisco, April 18, 1967	22	11	55
John Havlicek, Boston vs. Atlanta at Boston, April 1, 1973	24	6	54
Wilt Chamberlain, Philadelphia vs. Syracuse at Philadelphia, March 14, 1960	24	5	53
Jerry West, Los Angeles vs. Boston, April 23, 1969	21	11	53
Jerry West, Los Angeles vs. Baltimore at Los Angeles, April 5, 1965	16	20	52
Sam Jones, Boston at New York, March 30, 1967	19	13	51
Bob Cousy, Boston vs. Syracuse at Boston, March 21, 1953	****10	30	50
Bob Pettit, St. Louis vs. Boston at St. Louis, April 12, 1958	19	12	50
Wilt Chamberlain, Philadelphia vs. Boston at Boston, March 22, 1960	22	6	50
Billy Cunningham, Philadelphia vs. Milwaukee at Philadelphia, April 1, 1970	20	10	50
Wilt Chamberlain, San Francisco vs. St. Louis at San Francisco, April 10, 1964	22	6	50
Bob McAdoo, Buffalo vs. Washington at Buffalo, April 18, 1975	20	10	50
Elgin Baylor, Los Angeles vs. Detroit at Los Angeles, March 15, 1961	17	15	49
Jerry West, Los Angeles vs. Baltimore at Los Angeles, April 3, 1965	15	19	49
Jerry West, Los Angeles vs. Baltimore at Baltimore, April 9, 1965	20	8	48
George Mikan, Minneapolis at Rochester, March 29, 1952	15	17	47
Elgin Baylor, Los Angeles at Detroit, March 18, 1961	17	13	47
Elgin Baylor, Los Angeles at St. Louis, March 27, 1961	17	13	47
Sam Jones, Boston vs. Cincinnati at Boston, April 10, 1963	18	11	47
Rick Barry, San Francisco vs. St. Louis at San Francisco, April 1, 1967	17	13	47
Wilt Chamberlain, Philadelphia vs. Syracuse at Philadelphia, March 14, 1961	19	8	46
Wilt Chamberlain, San Francisco at St. Louis, April 5, 1964	19	8	46
Wilt Chamberlain, Philadelphia vs. Boston at Philadelphia, April 12, 1966	19	8	46
Lew Alcindor, Milwaukee vs. Philadelphia at Madison, Wisc., April 3, 1970	18	10	46
Elvin Hayes, Washington vs. Buffalo at Washington, April 20, 1975	18	10	46
George Gervin, San Antonio vs. Washington at San Antonio, April 18, 1978	17	12	46

MOST FIELD GOALS SCORED IN ONE GAME

	FGA	FGM
Wilt Chamberlain, Philadelphia vs. Syracuse at Philadelphia, March 14, 1960	42	24
John Havlicek, Boston vs. Atlanta at Boston, April 1, 1973	36	24
Wilt Chamberlain, Philadelphia vs. Boston at Boston, March 22, 1960	42	22
Elgin Baylor, Los Angeles at Boston, April 14, 1962	46	22
Wilt Chamberlain, San Francisco vs. St. Louis at San Francisco, April 10, 1964	32	22
Rick Barry, San Francisco vs. Philadelphia at San Francisco, April 18, 1967	48	22
Billy Cunningham, Philadelphia vs. Milwaukee at Philadelphia, April 1, 1970	39	22
Jerry West, Los Angeles vs. Boston, April 23, 1969	41	21
Bob McAdoo, Buffalo vs. Boston at Buffalo, April 6, 1974	40	21
Jerry West, Los Angeles at Baltimore, April 9, 1965	43	20
Wilt Chamberlain, Los Angeles vs. New York at Los Angeles, May 6, 1970	27	20
Kareem Abdul-Jabbar, Milwaukee at Chicago, April 18, 1974	29	20
Bob McAdoo, Buffalo vs. Washington at Buffalo, April 18, 1975	32	20
Wilt Chamberlain, San Francisco at St. Louis, April 5, 1964	36	19
Wilt Chamberlain, San Francisco vs. St. Louis at San Francisco, April 16, 1964	29	19
Wilt Chamberlain, Philadelphia vs. Boston at Philadelphia, April 12, 1966	34	19
Jerry West, Los Angeles vs. Boston at Los Angeles, April 22, 1966	31	19
Wilt Chamberlain, Philadelphia vs. Cincinnati at Philadelphia, March 21, 1967	30	19
Sam Jones, Boston at New York, March 30, 1967	30	19
Gail Goodrich, Los Angeles vs. Golden State at Los Angeles, April 25, 1973	26	19
Elvin Hayes, Capital at New York, March 29, 1974	29	19
Elvin Hayes, Washington vs. Buffalo at Washington, April 20, 1975	26	19
George Gervin, San Antonio vs. Washington at San Antonio, May 11, 1979	31	19
George Gervin, San Antonio vs. Houston, April 4, 1980	29	19
Kareem Abdul-Jabbar, Los Angeles vs. Philadelphia, May 7, 1980	31	19
Calvin Murphy, Houston at San Antonio, April 17, 1981	28	19

MOST FREE THROWS SCORED IN ONE GAME

	FTA.	FTM.
Bob Cousy, Boston vs. Syracuse at Boston, March 21, 1953	****32	30
Oscar Robertson, Cincinnati at Philadelphia, April 10, 1963	22	21
Bob Cousy, Boston vs. Syracuse at Boston, March 17, 1954	*25	20
Jerry West, Los Angeles at Detroit, April 3, 1962	23	20
Jerry West, Los Angeles vs. Baltimore at Los Angeles, April 5, 1965	21	20
Bob Pettit, St. Louis at Boston, April 9, 1958	24	19
Jerry West, Los Angeles vs. Baltimore at Los Angeles, April 3, 1965	21	19

MOST REBOUNDS IN ONE GAME

	Reb.
Wilt Chamberlain, Philadelphia vs. Boston at Philadelphia, April 5, 1967	41
Bill Russell, Boston vs. Philadelphia at Boston, March 23, 1958	40
Bill Russell, Boston vs. St. Louis at Boston, March 29, 1960	40
Bill Russell, Boston vs. Los Angeles at Boston, April 18, 1962	*40
Bill Russell, Boston vs. Philadelphia at Boston, March 19, 1960	39
Bill Russell, Boston vs. Syracuse at Boston, March 23, 1961	39
Wilt Chamberlain, Philadelphia vs. Boston at Philadelphia, April 6, 1965	39
Bill Russell, Boston vs. St. Louis at Boston, April 11, 1961	38
Wilt Chamberlain, San Francisco vs. Boston at San Francisco, April 24, 1964	38
Wilt Chamberlain, Philadelphia vs. San Francisco at Philadelphia, April 16, 1967	38

MOST ASSISTS IN ONE GAME

	Ast.
Bob Cousy, Boston vs. St. Louis at Boston, April 9, 1957	19
Bob Cousy, Boston at Minneapolis, April 7, 1959	19
Wilt Chamberlain, Philadelphia vs. Cincinnati at Philadelphia, March 24, 1967	19
Walt Frazier, New York vs. Los Angeles at New York, May 8, 1970	19
Jerry West, Los Angeles vs. Chicago at Los Angeles, April 1, 1973	19
Norm Nixon, Los Angeles vs. Seattle at Los Angeles, April 22, 1979	19
Bob Cousy, Boston vs. Syracuse at Boston, March 18, 1959	18
Oscar Robertson, Cincinnati at Philadelphia, March 29, 1964	18
Jerry West, Los Angeles vs. New York at Los Angeles, May 1, 1970	18
Walt Frazier, New York at Baltimore, March 30, 1969	17
Bob Cousy, Boston vs. Cincinnati at Boston, April 10, 1963	16
Oscar Robertson, Cincinnati vs. Philadelphia at Cincinnati, March 22, 1964	16
Oscar Robertson, Milwaukee at Los Angeles, April 2, 1974	16
Norm Nixon, Los Angeles vs. Denver at Los Angeles, April 13, 1979	16
Earvin (Magic) Johnson, Los Angeles vs. Phoenix, April 8, 1980	16

Pro-Am Leagues Formed

The National Basketball Association, in conjunction with Converse and Champion Knitwear, has set up Pro-Am leagues throughout various NBA cities for the second straight year.

The purpose of the leagues are to develop a referee training program. Last year's program included leagues in six cities and eventually will expand to every NBA city.

ALL-TIME PLAYOFF LEADERS

Most Games Played

John Havlicek	172
Bill Russell	165
Paul Silas	163
Wilt Chamberlain	160
Sam Jones	154
Jerry West	153
Don Nelson	150
Elgin Baylor	134
Tom Sanders	130
Wes Unseld	119

Most Field Goals Attempted

Jerry West	3460
John Havlicek	3329
Elgin Baylor	3161
Wilt Chamberlain	2728
Sam Jones	2571
Bill Russell	2335
Kareem Abdul-Jabbar	2276
Tom Heinsohn	2035
Bob Cousy	2016
Elvin Hayes	1851

Most Field Goals Made

Jerry West	1622
John Havlicek	1451
Wilt Chamberlain	1425
Elgin Baylor	1388
Kareem Abdul-Jabbar	1214
Sam Jones	1149
Bill Russell	1003
Elvin Hayes	866
Bob Dandridge	823
Tom Heinsohn	818

Highest Scoring Average
(25 games or 625 Points Minimum)

	G.	FGM	FTM	Pts.	Avg.
Kareem Abdul-Jabbar	97	1214	513	2941	30.3
Bob McAdoo	28	338	171	847	30.3
George Gervin	32	369	201	939	29.3
Jerry West	153	1622	1213	4457	29.1
Elgin Baylor	134	1388	847	3623	27.0
Bob Pettit	88	766	708	2240	25.5
Rick Barry	74	719	392	1833	24.8
Julius Erving	72	689	392	1772	24.6
Moses Malone	42	380	257	1017	24.2
Paul Arizin	49	411	364	1186	24.2

Most Minutes Played

Wilt Chamberlain	7559
Bill Russell	7497
John Havlicek	6860
Jerry West	6321
Elgin Baylor	5510
Wes Unseld	4889
Sam Jones	4654
Paul Silas	4619
Kareem Abdul-Jabbar	4276
Bob Cousy	4140

Highest Field Goal Percentage
(150 FGM Minimum)

	FGA	FGM	Pct.
Cedric Maxwell	267	160	.599
Bob Lanier	615	334	.543
Clifford Ray	385	207	.538
Darryl Dawkins	645	345	.535
Kareem Abdul-Jabbar	2276	1214	.533
Maurice Cheeks	420	223	.531
Bobby Jones	599	316	.528
Doug Collins	536	282	.526
Wilt Chamberlain	2728	1425	.522
George Gervin	709	369	.520

Highest Free Throw Percentage
(100 FTM Minimum)

	FTA	FTM	Pct.
Calvin Murphy	169	158	.935
Bill Sharman	406	370	.911
Vince Boryla	135	120	.889
Rick Barry	448	392	.875
Bobby Wanzer	270	236	.874
Cazzie Russell	154	134	.870
Steve Mix	167	145	.868
Oscar Robertson	655	560	.855
Larry Costello	230	196	.852
Phil Chenier	251	212	.845

Most Free Throws Made

Jerry West	1213
John Havlicek	874
Elgin Baylor	847
Wilt Chamberlain	757
Dolph Schayes	755
Bob Pettit	708
George Mikan	695
Bill Russell	667
Bob Cousy	640
Sam Jones	611

Most Free Throws Attempted

Wilt Chamberlain	1627
Jerry West	1507
Bill Russell	1106
Elgin Baylor	1101
John Havlicek	1046
Dolph Schayes	918
Bob Pettit	915
George Mikan	906
Bob Cousy	799
Sam Jones	753

Most Rebounds

Bill Russell	4104
Wilt Chamberlain	3913
Wes Unseld	1777
Elgin Baylor	1725
Paul Silas	1527
Kareem Abdul-Jabbar	1524
Bill Bridges	1305
Bob Pettit	1304
Dave Cowens	1285
Elvin Hayes	1214

Most Assists

Jerry West	970
Bob Cousy	937
John Havlicek	825
Bill Russell	770
Oscar Robertson	769
Wilt Chamberlain	673
Walt Frazier	599
Elgin Baylor	541
Wes Unseld	453
Jo Jo White	452

Most Personal Fouls

Bill Russell	546
John Havlicek	517
Tom Sanders	508
Paul Silas	469
Jerry West	451
Elgin Baylor	445
Tom Heinsohn	417
Wilt Chamberlain	412
Bill Bridges	408
Don Nelson	399

Most Disqualifications

Tom Sanders	26
Vern Mikkelsen	24
Bailey Howell	21
Gene Shue	17
Dave Cowens	15
Alex Hannum	15
Walter Dukes	14
Tom Heinsohn	14
Frank Ramsey	14
Charlie Scott	14
Sam Jones	12
John Kerr	12
Arnie Risen	12
Paul Seymour	12
Wes Unseld	12

Most Series Played

Bill Russell	13
Chet Walker	13
Jerry West	13
Elgin Baylor	12
Bill Bridges	12
Dolph Schayes	15
Paul Silas	14
Wilt Chamberlain	13
Bob Cousy	13
Hal Greer	13
John Havlicek	13

ALL-TIME RECORD OF NBA TEAMS

ANDERSON PACKERS

Season	Coach	Reg. Sea'n W.	L.	Playoffs W.	L.
1949-50	Howard Schultz, 21-14	..	..	..	..
	Ike Duffey, 1-2	..	..	..	..
	Doxie Moore, 15-11	37	27	4	4

ATLANTA HAWKS

Season	Coach	Reg. Sea'n W.	L.	Playoffs W.	L.
1949-50	Roger Potter, 1-6	..	..	..	..
	Arnold A'rbach, 28-29	29	35	1	2
1950-51	Dave McMillan, 9-14	..	..	..	..
	John Logan 2-1	..	..	..	..
	Marko Todorovich, 14-28	25	43	..	..
1951-52*	Doxie Moore	17	49	..	..
1952-53	Andrew Levane	27	44	..	..
1953-54	Andrew Levane, 11-35	..	..	..	..
	Red Holzman, 10-16	21	51	..	..
1954-55	Red Holzman	26	46	..	..
1955-56†	Red Holzman	33	39	4	4
1956-57	Red Holzman, 14-19	..	..	..	..
	Slater Martin, 5-3	..	..	..	..
	Alex Hannum, 15-16	34	38	6	4
1957-58	Alex Hannum	41	31	8	3
1958-59	Andy Phillip, 6-4	..	..	..	..
	Ed Macauley, 43-19	49	23	2	4
1959-60	Ed Macauley	46	29	7	7
1960-61	Paul Seymour	51	28	5	7
1961-62	Paul Seymour, 5-9	..	..	..	..
	Andrew Levane, 20-40	..	..	..	..
	Bob Pettit, 4-2	29	51	..	..
1962-63	Harry Gallatin	48	32	6	5
1963-64	Harry Gallatin	46	34	6	6
1964-65	Harry Gallatin, 17-16	..	..	..	..
	Richie Guerin, 28-19	45	35	1	3
1965-66	Richie Guerin	36	44	6	4
1966-67	Richie Guerin	39	42	5	4
1967-68	Richie Guerin	56	26	2	4
1968-69‡	Richie Guerin	48	34	5	6
1969-70	Richie Guerin	48	34	4	5
1970-71	Richie Guerin	36	46	1	4
1971-72	Richie Guerin	36	46	2	4
1972-73	Cotton Fitzsimmons	46	36	2	4
1973-74	Cotton Fitzsimmons	35	47	..	..
1974-75	Cotton Fitzsimmons	31	51	..	..
1975-76	Cotton Fitzsimmons, 28-46	..	..	..	..
	Gene Tormohlen, 1-7	29	53	..	..
1976-77	Hubie Brown	31	51	..	..
1977-78	Hubie Brown	41	41	0	2
1978-79	Hubie Brown	46	36	5	4
1979-80	Hubie Brown	50	32	1	4
1980-81	Hubie Brown, 31-48	..	..	..	..
	Michael Fratello, 0-3	31	51	..	..
Totals		1206	1278	79	90

*Team moved from Tri-Cities to Milwaukee.
†Team moved from Milwaukee to St. Louis.
‡Team moved from St. Louis to Atlanta.

BALTIMORE BULLETS

Season	Coach	Reg. Sea'n W.	L.	Playoffs W.	L.
1947-48	Buddy Jeannette	28	20	8	3
1948-49	Buddy Jeannette	29	31	1	2
1949-50	Buddy Jeannette	25	43	..	..
1950-51	Buddy Jeannette, 14-23	..	..	..	..
	Walter Budko, 10-19	24	42	..	..
1951-52	Fred Scolari, 12-27	..	..	..	..
	John Reiser, 8-19	20	46	..	..
1952-53	John Reiser, 0-3	..	..	..	..
	Clair Bee, 16-51	16	54	0	2
1953-54	Clair Bee	16	56	..	..
1954-55	Clair Bee, 2-9	..	..	..	..
	*Al Barthelme, 1-2	3	11	..	..
Totals		161	303	9	7

*Team disbanded November 27.

BOSTON CELTICS

Season	Coach	Reg. Sea'n W.	L.	Playoffs W.	L.
1946-47	John Russell	22	38	..	..
1947-48	John Russell	20	28	1	2
1948-49	Alvin Julian	25	35	..	..
1949-50	Alvin Julian	22	46	..	..
1950-51	Arnold Auerbach	39	30	0	2
1951-52	Arnold Auerbach	39	27	1	2
1952-53	Arnold Auerbach	46	25	3	3
1953-54	Arnold Auerbach	42	30	2	4
1954-55	Arnold Auerbach	36	36	3	4
1955-56	Arnold Auerbach	39	33	1	2
1956-57	Arnold Auerbach	44	28	7	3
1957-58	Arnold Auerbach	49	23	6	5
1958-59	Arnold Auerbach	52	20	8	3
1959-60	Arnold Auerbach	59	16	8	5
1960-61	Arnold Auerbach	57	22	8	2
1961-62	Arnold Auerbach	60	20	8	6
1962-63	Arnold Auerbach	58	22	8	5
1963-64	Arnold Auerbach	59	21	8	2
1964-65	Arnold Auerbach	62	18	8	4
1965-66	Arnold Auerbach	54	26	11	6
1966-67	Bill Russell	60	21	4	5
1967-68	Bill Russell	54	28	12	7
1968-69	Bill Russell	48	34	12	6
1969-70	Tom Heinsohn	34	48	..	..
1970-71	Tom Heinsohn	44	38	..	..
1971-72	Tom Heinsohn	56	26	5	6
1972-73	Tom Heinsohn	68	14	7	6
1973-74	Tom Heinsohn	56	26	12	6
1974-75	Tom Heinsohn	60	22	6	5
1975-76	Tom Heinsohn	54	28	12	6
1976-77	Tom Heinsohn	44	38	5	4
1977-78	Tom Heinsohn, 11-23	..	..	..	..
	Tom Sanders, 21-27	32	50	..	..
1978-79	Tom Sanders, 2-12	..	..	..	..
	Dave Cowens, 27-41	29	53	..	..
1979-80	Bill Fitch	61	21	5	4
1980-81	Bill Fitch	62	20	12	5
Totals		1646	1011	183	120

CHICAGO BULLS

Season	Coach	Reg. Sea'n W.	L.	Playoffs W.	L.
1966-67	John Kerr	33	48	0	3
1967-68	John Kerr	29	53	1	4
1968-69	Dick Motta	33	49	..	..
1969-70	Dick Motta	39	43	1	4
1970-71	Dick Motta	51	31	3	4
1971-72	Dick Motta	57	25	0	4
1972-73	Dick Motta	51	31	3	4
1973-74	Dick Motta	54	28	4	4
1974-75	Dick Motta	47	35	7	6
1975-76	Dick Motta	24	58	..	..
1976-77	Ed Badger	44	38	1	2
1977-78	Ed Badger	40	42	..	..
1978-79	Larry Costello, 20-36	..	..	..	..
	Scotty Robertson, 11-15	31	51	..	..
1979-80	Jerry Sloan	30	52	..	..
1980-81	Jerry Sloan	45	37	2	4
Totals		608	621	22	42

ALL TIME NBA TEAM RECORDS

CHICAGO STAGS

Season	Coach	Reg. Sea'n W. L.	Playoffs W. L.
1946-47	Harold Olsen	39 22	5 6
1947-48	Harold Olsen	28 20	2 3
1948-49	Harold Olsen, 28-21	38 22	0 2
	*Philip Brownstein, 10-1		
1949-50	Philip Brownstein	40 28	0 2
Totals		145 92	7 13

*Substituted during Olsen's illness.

CLEVELAND CAVALIERS

Season	Coach	Reg. Sea'n W. L.	Playoffs W. L.
1970-71	Bill Fitch	15 67	.. ..
1971-72	Bill Fitch	23 59	.. ..
1972-73	Bill Fitch	32 50	.. ..
1973-74	Bill Fitch	29 53	.. ..
1974-75	Bill Fitch	40 42	.. ..
1975-76	Bill Fitch	49 33	6 7
1976-77	Bill Fitch	43 39	1 2
1977-78	Bill Fitch	43 39	0 2
1978-79	Bill Fitch	30 52	.. ..
1979-80	Stan Albeck	37 45	.. ..
1980-81	Bill Musselman, 25-46	.. ..	.. ..
	Don Delaney, 3-8	28 54	.. ..
Totals		369 533	7 11

CLEVELAND REBELS

Season	Coach	Reg. Sea'n W. L.	Playoffs W. L.
1946-47	Dutch Dehnert, 17-20	.. ..	.. ..
	Roy Clifford, 13-10	30 30	1 2

DALLAS MAVERICKS

Season	Coach	Reg. Sea'n W. L.	Playoffs W. L.
1980-81	Dick Motta	15 67	.. ..

DENVER NUGGETS

Season	Coach	Reg. Sea'n W. L.	Playoffs W. L.
1949-50	James Darden	11 51	.. ..

DENVER NUGGETS

Season	Coach	Reg. Sea'n W. L.	Playoffs W. L.
1976-77	Larry Brown	50 32	2 4
1977-78	Larry Brown	48 34	6 7
1978-79	Larry Brown, 28-25		
	Donnie Walsh, 19-10	47 35	1 2
1979-80	Donnie Walsh	30 52	.. ..
1980-81	Donnie Walsh, 11-20	.. ..	.. ..
	Doug Moe, 26-25	37 45	.. ..
Totals		212 198	9 13

DETROIT FALCONS

Season	Coach	Reg. Sea'n W. L.	Playoffs W. L.
1946-47	Glenn Curtis, 12-22	.. ..	.. ..
	Philip Sachs, 8-18	20 40	.. ..

DETROIT PISTONS

Season	Coach	Reg. Sea'n W. L.	Playoffs W. L.
1948-49	Carl Bennett, 0-6	.. ..	.. ..
	Paul Armstrong, 22-32	22 38	.. ..
1949-50	Murray Mendenhall	40 28	2 2
1950-51	Murray Mendenhall	32 36	1 2
1951-52	Paul Birch	29 37	0 2
1952-53	Paul Birch	36 33	4 4
1953-54	Paul Birch	40 32	0 4
1954-55	Charles Eckman	43 29	6 5
1955-56	Charles Eckman	37 35	4 6
1956-57	Charles Eckman	34 38	0 2
1957-58	Charles Eckman, 9-16		
	Ephraim Rocha, 24-23	33 39	3 4
1958-59	Ephraim Rocha	28 44	1 2
1959-60	Ephraim Rocha, 13-21		
	Dick McGuire, 17-24	30 45	0 2
1960-61	Dick McGuire	34 45	2 3
1961-62	Dick McGuire	37 43	5 5
1962-63	Dick McGuire	34 46	1 3
1963-64	Charles Wolf	23 57	.. ..
1964-65	Charles Wolf, 2-9		
	D. DeBusschere, 29-40	31 49	.. ..
1965-66	Dave DeBusschere	22 58	.. ..
1966-67	D. DeBusschere, 28-45		
	Donnis Butcher, 2-6	30 51	.. ..
1967-68	Donnis Butcher	40 42	2 4
1968-69	D. Butcher, 10-12		
	Paul Seymour, 22-38	32 50	.. ..
1969-70	Bill van Breda Kolff	31 51	.. ..
1970-71	Bill van Breda Kolff	45 37	.. ..
1971-72	B. van Breda Kolff, 6-6		
	Earl Lloyd, 20-50	26 56	.. ..
1972-73	Earl Lloyd, 2-5		
	Ray Scott, 38-37	40 42	.. ..
1973-74	Ray Scott	52 30	3 4
1974-75	Ray Scott	40 42	1 2
1975-76	Ray Scott, 17-25		
	Herb Brown, 19-21	36 46	4 5
1976-77	Herb Brown	44 38	1 2
1977-78	Herb Brown, 9-15		
	Bob Kauffman, 29-29	38 44	.. ..
1978-79	Dick Vitale	30 52	.. ..
1979-80	Dick Vitale, 4-8		
	Richie Adubato, 12-58	16 66	.. ..
1980-81	Scotty Robertson	21 61	.. ..
Totals		1106 1440	40 63

*Team moved from Ft. Wayne to Detroit.

GOLDEN STATE WARRIORS

Season	Coach	Reg. Sea'n W. L.	Playoffs W. L.
1946-47	Edward Gottlieb	35 25	8 2
1947-48	Edward Gottlieb	27 21	6 7
1948-49	Edward Gottlieb	28 32	0 2
1949-50	Edward Gottlieb	26 42	0 2
1950-51	Edward Gottlieb	40 26	0 2
1951-52	Edward Gottlieb	33 33	1 2
1952-53	Edward Gottlieb	12 57	.. ..
1953-54	Edward Gottlieb	29 43	.. ..
1954-55	Edward Gottlieb	33 39	.. ..
1955-56	George Senesky	45 27	7 3
1956-57	George Senesky	37 35	0 2
1957-58	George Senesky	37 35	3 5
1958-59	Al Cervi	32 40	.. ..
1959-60	Neil Johnston	49 26	4 5
1960-61	Neil Johnston	46 33	0 3
1961-62	Frank McGuire	49 31	6 6
1962-63	*Bob Feerick	31 49	.. ..
1963-64	Alex Hannum	48 32	5 7
1964-65	Alex Hannum	17 63	.. ..
1965-66	Alex Hannum	35 45	.. ..
1966-67	Bill Sharman	44 37	9 6
1967-68	Bill Sharman	43 39	4 6
1968-69	George Lee	41 41	2 4
1969-70	George Lee, 22-30		
	Al Attles, 8-22	30 52	.. ..
1970-71	Al Attles	41 41	1 4
1971-72	Al Attles	51 31	1 4
1972-73	Al Attles	47 35	5 6

ALL TIME NBA TEAM RECORDS

Season	Coach	Reg. Sea'n W. L.	Playoffs W. L.
1973-74	Al Attles	44 38	.. ..
1974-75	Al Attles	48 34	12 5
1975-76	Al Attles	59 23	7 6
1976-77	Al Attles	46 36	5 5
1977-78	Al Attles	43 39	.. ..
1978-79	Al Attles	38 44	.. ..
1979-80	Al Attles, 18-43		
	John Bach, 6-15	24 58	.. ..
1980-81	Al Attles	39 43	.. ..
Totals		1327 1325	86 94

*Team moved from Philadelphia to San Francisco.

HOUSTON ROCKETS

Season	Coach	Reg. Sea'n W. L.	Playoffs W. L.
Season	Coach	Reg. Sea'n W. L.	Playoffs W. L.
1967-68	Jack McMahon	15 67	.. ..
1968-69	Jack McMahon	37 45	2 4
1969-70	Jack McMahon, 9-17	.. ..	
	Alex Hannum, 18-38	27 55	.. ..
1970-71	Alex Hannum	40 42	.. ..
1971-72	*Tex Winter	34 48	.. ..
1972-73	Tex Winter, 17-30		
	John Egan, 16-19	33 49	.. ..
1973-74	John Egan	32 50	.. ..
1974-75	John Egan	41 41	3 5
1975-76	John Egan	40 42	.. ..
1976-77	Tom Nissalke	49 33	6 6
1977-78	Tom Nissalke	28 54	.. ..
1978-79	Tom Nissalke	47 35	0 2
1979-80	Del Harris	41 41	2 5
1980-81	Del Harris	40 42	12 9
Totals		504 644	25 31

*Team moved from San Diego to Houston.

INDIANA PACERS

Season	Coach	Reg. Sea'n W. L.	Playoffs W. L.
1976-77	Bob Leonard	36 46	.. ..
1977-78	Bob Leonard	31 51	.. ..
1978-79	Bob Leonard	38 44	.. ..
1979-80	Bob Leonard	37 45	.. ..
1980-81	Jack McKinney	44 38	0 2
Totals		186 224	0 2

INDIANAPOLIS JETS

Season	Coach	Reg. Sea'n W. L.	Playoffs W. L.
1948-49	Bruce Hale, 4-13	.. ..	
	Burl Friddle, 14-29	18 42	.. ..

INDIANAPOLIS OLYMPIANS

Season	Coach	Reg. Sea'n W. L.	Playoffs W. L.
1949-50	Clifford Barker	39 25	3 3
1950-51	Clifford Barker	24 32	.. ..
	Wallace Jones	7 5	1 2
1951-52	Herman Schaefer	34 32	0 2
1952-53	Herman Schaefer	28 43	0 2
Totals		132 137	4 9

KANSAS CITY KINGS

Season	Coach	Reg. Sea'n W. L.	Playoffs W. L.
1948-49	Les Harrison	45 15	2 2
1949-50	Les Harrison	51 17	0 2
1950-51	Les Harrison	41 27	9 5
1951-52	Les Harrison	41 25	3 3
1952-53	Les Harrison	44 26	1 2
1953-54	Les Harrison	44 28	3 3
1954-55	Les Harrison	29 43	1 2
1955-56	Bob Wanzer	31 41	.. ..
1956-57	Bob Wanzer	31 41	.. ..
1957-58	*Bob Wanzer	33 39	0 2
1958-59	Bob Wanzer, 3-15	.. ..	
	Tom Marshall, 16-38	19 53	.. ..
1959-60	Tom Marshall	19 56	.. ..
1960-61	Charles Wolf	33 46	.. ..
1961-62	Charles Wolf	43 37	1 3
1962-63	Charles Wolf	42 38	6 6
1963-64	Jack McMahon	55 25	4 6
1964-65	Jack McMahon	48 32	1 3
1965-66	Jack McMahon	45 35	2 3
1966-67	Jack McMahon	39 42	1 3
1967-68	Ed Jucker	39 43	.. ..
1968-69	Ed Jucker	41 41	.. ..
1969-70	Bob Cousy	36 46	.. ..
1970-71	Bob Cousy	33 49	.. ..
1971-72	Bob Cousy	30 52	.. ..
1972-73	†Bob Cousy	36 46	.. ..
1973-74	Bob Cousy, 6-16		
	Draff Young, 0-3		
	Phil Johnson, 27-30	33 49	.. ..
1974-75	Phil Johnson	44 38	2 4
1975-76	Phil Johnson	31 51	.. ..
1976-77	Phil Johnson	40 42	.. ..
1977-78	Phil Johnson, 13-24		
	Larry Staverman, 18-27	31 51	.. ..
1978-79	Cotton Fitzsimmons	48 34	1 4
1979-80	Cotton Fitzsimmons	47 35	1 2
1980-81	Cotton Fitzsimmons	40 42	7 8
Totals		1262 1285	45 63

*Team moved from Rochester to Cincinnati.
†Team moved from Cincinnati to Kansas City-Omaha.

LOS ANGELES LAKERS

Season	Coach	Reg. Sea'n W. L.	Playoffs W. L.
1948-49	John Kundla	44 16	8 2
1949-50	John Kundla	51 17	10 2
1950-51	John Kundla	44 24	3 4
1951-52	John Kundla	40 26	9 4
1952-53	John Kundla	48 22	9 3
1953-54	John Kundla	46 26	9 4
1954-55	John Kundla	40 32	3 4
1955-56	John Kundla	33 39	1 2
1956-57	John Kundla	34 38	2 3
1957-58	George Mikan, 9-30	.. ..	
	John Kundla, 10-23	19 53	.. ..
1958-59	John Kundla	33 39	6 7
1959-60	John Castellani, 11-25	.. ..	
	Jim Pollard, 14-25	25 50	5 4
1960-61	*Fred Schaus	36 43	6 6
1961-62	Fred Schaus	54 26	7 6
1962-63	Fred Schaus	53 27	6 7
1963-64	Fred Schaus	42 38	2 3
1964-65	Fred Schaus	49 31	5 6
1965-66	Fred Schaus	45 35	7 7
1966-67	Fred Schaus	36 45	0 3
1967-68	Bill van Breda Kolff	52 30	10 5
1968-69	Bill van Breda Kolff	55 27	11 7
1969-70	Joe Mullaney	46 36	11 7
1970-71	Joe Mullaney	48 34	5 7
1971-72	Bill Sharman	69 13	12 3
1972-73	Bill Sharman	60 22	9 8
1973-74	Bill Sharman	47 35	1 4
1974-75	Bill Sharman	30 52	.. ..
1975-76	Bill Sharman	40 42	.. ..
1976-77	Jerry West	53 29	4 7
1977-78	Jerry West	45 37	1 2

ALL TIME NBA TEAM RECORDS

Season	Coach	Reg. Sea'n W.	Reg. Sea'n L.	Playoffs W.	Playoffs L.
1978-79	Jerry West	47	35	3	5
1979-80	Jack McKinney, 10-4				
	Paul Westhead, 50-18	60	22	12	4
1980-81	Paul Westhead	54	28	1	2
Totals		1478	1069	178	138

*Team moved from Minneapolis to Los Angeles.

MILWAUKEE BUCKS

Season	Coach	Reg. Sea'n W.	Reg. Sea'n L.	Playoffs W.	Playoffs L.
1968-69	Larry Costello	27	55		
1969-70	Larry Costello	56	26	5	5
1970-71	Larry Costello	66	16	12	2
1971-72	Larry Costello	)63	19	6	5
1972-73	Larry Costello	60	22	2	4
1973-74	Larry Costello	59	23	11	5
1974-75	Larry Costello	38	44		
1975-76	Larry Costello	38	44	1	2
1976-77	Larry Costello, 3-15				
	Don Nelson, 27-37	30	52		
1977-78	Don Nelson	44	38	5	4
1978-79	Don Nelson	38	44		
1979-80	Don Nelson	49	33	3	4
1980-81	Don Nelson	60	22	3	4
Totals		628	438	48	35

NEW JERSEY NETS

Season	Coach	Reg. Sea'n W.	Reg. Sea'n L.	Playoffs W.	Playoffs L.
1976-77	Kevin Loughery	22	60		
1977-78*	Kevin Loughery	24	58		
1978-79	Kevin Loughery	37	45	0	2
1979-80	Kevin Loughery	34	48		
1980-81	Kevin Loughery, 12-23				
	Bob MacKinnon, 12-35	24	58		
Totals		141	269	0	2

*Team moved from New York to New Jersey.

NEW YORK KNICKERBOCKERS

Season	Coach	Reg. Sea'n W.	Reg. Sea'n L.	Playoffs W.	Playoffs L.
1946-47	Neil Cohalan	33	27	2	3
1947-48	Joe Lapchick	26	22	1	2
1948-49	Joe Lapchick	32	28	3	3
1949-50	Joe Lapchick	40	28	3	2
1950-51	Joe Lapchick	36	30	8	6
1951-52	Joe Lapchick	37	29	8	6
1952-53	Joe Lapchick	47	23	6	5
1953-54	Joe Lapchick	44	28	0	4
1954-55	Joe Lapchick	38	34	1	2
1955-56	Joe Lapchick, 26-25				
	Vince Boryla, 9-12	35	37		
1956-57	Vince Boryla	36	36		
1597-58	Vince Boryla	35	37		
1958-59	Andrew Levane	40	32	0	2
1959-60	Andrew Levane, 8-19				
	Carl Braun, 19-29	27	48		
1960-61	Carl Braun	21	58		
1961-62	Eddie Donovan	29	51		
1962-63	Eddie Donovan	22	58		
1963-64	Eddie Donovan	22	58		
1964-65	Eddie Donovan, 12-26				
	Harry Gallatin, 19-23	31	49		
1965-66	Harry Gallatin, 6-15				
	Dick McGuire, 24-35	30	50		
1966-67	Dick McGuire	36	45	1	3
1967-68	Dick McGuire, 15-22				
	Red Holzman, 28-17	43	39	2	4
1968-69	Red Holzman	54	28	6	4
1969-70	Red Holzman	60	22	12	7
1970-71	Red Holzman	52	30	7	5
1971-72	Red Holzman	48	34	9	7
1972-73	Red Holzman	57	25	12	5
1973-74	Red Holzman	49	33	5	7
1974-75	Red Holzman	40	42	1	2
1975-76	Red Holzman	38	44		
1976-77	Red Holzman	40	42		
1977-78	Willis Reed	43	39	2	4
1978-79	Willis Reed, 6-8				
	Red Holzman, 25-43	31	51		
1979-80	Red Holzman	39	43		
1980-81	Red Holzman	50	32	0	2
Totals		1340	1313	89	85

PHILADELPHIA 76ERS

Season	Coach	Reg. Sea'n W.	Reg. Sea'n L.	Playoffs W.	Playoffs L.
1949-50	Al Cervi	51	13	6	5
1950-51	Al Cervi	32	34	4	3
1951-52	Al Cervi	40	26	3	4
1952-53	Al Cervi	47	24	0	2
1953-54	Al Cervi	42	30	9	4
1954-55	Al Cervi	43	29	7	4
1955-56	Al Cervi	35	37	4	4
1956-57	Al Cervi, 4-8				
	Paul Seymour, 34-26	38	34	2	3
1957-58	Paul Seymour	41	31	1	2
1958-59	Paul Seymour	35	37	5	4
1959-60	Paul Seymour	45	30	1	2
1960-61	Alex Hannum	38	41	4	4
1961-62	Alex Hannum	41	39	2	3
1962-63	Alex Hannum	48	32	2	3
1963-64*	Dolph Schayes	34	46	2	3
1964-65	Dolph Schayes	40	40	6	5
1965-66	Dolph Schayes	55	25	1	4
1966-67	Alex Hannum	68	13	11	4
1967-68	Alex Hannum	62	20	7	6
1968-69	Jack Ramsay	55	27	1	4
1969-70	Jack Ramsay	42	40	1	4
1970-71	Jack Ramsay	47	35	3	4
1971-72	Jack Ramsay	30	52		
1972-73	Roy Rubin, 4-47				
	Kevin Loughery, 5-26	9	73		
1973-74	Gene Shue	25	57		
1974-75	Gene Shue	34	48		
1975-76	Gene Shue	46	36	1	2
1976-77	Gene Shue	50	32	10	9
1977-78	Gene Shue, 2-4				
	Billy Cunningham, 53-23	55	27	6	4
1978-79	Billy Cunningham	47	35	5	4
1979-80	Billy Cunningham	59	23	12	6
1980-81	Billy Cunningham	62	20	9	7
Totals		1396	1086	125	113

*Team moved from Syracuse to Philadelphia.

PHOENIX SUNS

Season	Coach	Reg. Sea'n W.	Reg. Sea'n L.	Playoffs W.	Playoffs L.
1968-69	Johnny Kerr	16	66		
1969-70	Johnny Kerr, 15-23				
	Jerry Colangelo 24-20	39	43	3	4
1970-71	Cotton Fitzsimmons	48	34		
1971-72	Cotton Fitzsimmons	49	33		
1972-73	B. van Breda Kolff, 3-5				
	Jerry Colangelo, 35-39	38	44		
1973-74	John MacLeod	30	52		
1974-75	John MacLeod	32	50		
1975-76	John MacLeod	42	40	10	9
1976-77	John MacLeod	34	48		
1977-78	John MacLeod	49	33	0	2
1978-79	John MacLeod	50	32	9	6
1979-80	John MacLeod	55	27	3	5
1980-81	John MacLeod	57	25	3	4
Totals		539	527	28	30

ALL TIME NBA TEAM RECORDS

PITTSBURGH IRONMEN

Season	Coach	Reg. Sea'n W.	L.	Playoffs W.	L.
1946-47	Paul Birch	15	45	..	..

PORTLAND TRAIL BLAZERS

Season	Coach	Reg. Sea'n W.	L.	Playoffs W.	L.
1970-71	Rolland Todd	29	53	..	..
1971-72	Rolland Todd, 12-44				
	Stu Inman, 6-20	18	64	..	..
1972-73	Jack McCloskey	21	61	..	..
1973-74	Jack McCloskey	27	55	..	..
1974-75	Len Wilkens	38	44	..	..
1975-76	Len Wilkens	37	45	..	..
1976-77	Jack Ramsay	49	33	14	5
1977-78	Jack Ramsay	58	24	2	4
1978-79	Jack Ramsay	45	37	1	2
1979-80	Jack Ramsay	38	44	1	2
1980-81	Jack Ramsay	45	37	1	2
Totals		405	497	19	15

PROVIDENCE STEAMROLLERS

Season	Coach	Reg. Sea'n W.	L.	Playoffs W.	L.
1946-47	Robert Morris	28	32	..	..
1947-48	Albert Soar, 2-17				
	Nat Hickey, 4-25	6	42	..	..
1948-49	Ken Loeffler	12	48	..	..
Totals		46	122	..	..

ST. LOUIS BOMBERS

Season	Coach	Reg. Sea'n W.	L.	Playoffs W.	L.
1946-47	Ken Loeffler	38	23	1	2
1947-48	Ken Loeffler	29	19	3	4
1948-49	Grady Lewis	29	31	0	2
1949-50	Grady Lewis	26	42	..	..
Totals		122	115	4	8

SAN ANTONIO SPURS

Season	Coach	Reg. Sea'n W.	L.	Playoffs W.	L.
1976-77	Doug Moe	44	38	0	2
1977-78	Doug Moe	52	30	2	4
1978-79	Doug Moe	48	34	7	7
1979-80	Doug Moe, 33-33				
	Bob Bass, 8-8	41	41	1	2
1980-81	Stan Albeck	52	30	3	4
Totals		237	173	13	19

SAN DIEGO CLIPPERS

Season	Coach	Reg. Sea'n W.	L.	Playoffs W.	L.
1970-71	Dolph Schayes	22	60	..	..
1971-72	Dolph Schayes, 0-1				
	John McCarthy, 22-59	22	60	..	..
1972-73	Jack Ramsay	21	61	..	..
1973-74	Jack Ramsay	42	40	2	4
1974-75	Jack Ramsay	49	33	3	4
1975-76	Jack Ramsay	46	36	4	5
1976-77	Tates Locke, 16-30				
	Bob MacKinnon, 3-4				
	Joe Mullaney, 11-18	30	52	..	..
1977-78	Cotton Fitzsimmons	27	55	..	..
1978-79*	Gene Shue	43	39	..	..
1979-80	Gene Shue	35	47	..	..
1980-81	Paul Silas	36	46	..	..
Totals		376	526	9	13

*Team moved from Buffalo to San Diego

SEATTLE SUPERSONICS

Season	Coach	Reg. Sea'n W.	L.	Playoffs W.	L.
1967-68	Al Bianchi	23	59	..	..
1968-69	Al Bianchi	30	52	..	..
1969-70	Len Wilkens	36	46	..	..
1970-71	Len Wilkens	38	44	..	..
1971-72	Len Wilkens	47	35	..	..
1972-73	Tom Nissalke, 13-32				
	B. Buckwalter, 13-24	26	56	..	..
1973-74	Bill Russell	36	46	..	..
1974-75	Bill Russell	43	39	4	5
1975-76	Bill Russell	43	39	2	4
1976-77	Bill Russell	40	42	..	..
1977-78	Bob Hopkins, 5-17				
	Lenny Wilkens, 42-18	47	35	13	9
1978-79	Lenny Wilkens	52	30	12	5
1979-80	Lenny Wilkens	56	26	7	8
1980-81	Lenny Wilkens	34	48	..	..
Totals		551	597	38	31

SHEBOYGAN REDSKINS

Season	Coach	Reg. Sea'n W.	L.	Playoffs W.	L.
1949-50	Ken Suesens	22	40	1	2

TORONTO HUSKIES

Season	Coach	Reg. Sea'n W.	L.	Playoffs W.	L.
1946-47	Ed Sadowski, 3-9				
	Lew Hayman, 0-1				
	Dick Fitzgerald, 2-1				
	Robert Rolfe, 17-27	22	38	..	..

UTAH JAZZ

Season	Coach	Reg. Sea'n W.	L.	Playoffs W.	L.
1974-75	Scotty Robertson, 1-14				
	Elgin Baylor, 0-1				
	B. van Breda Kolff, 22-44	23	59	..	..
1975-76	B. van Breda Kolff	38	44	..	..
1976-77	B. van Breda Kolff, 14-12				
	Elgin Baylor, 21-35	35	47	..	..
1977-78	Elgin Baylor	39	43	..	..
1978-79	Elgin Baylor	26	56	..	..
1979-80*	Tom Nissalke	24	58	..	..
1980-81	Tom Nissalke	28	54	..	..
Totals		213	361	..	..

*Team moved from New Orleans to Utah.

WASHINGTON BULLETS

Season	Coach	Reg. Sea'n W.	L.	Playoffs W.	L.
1961-62*	Jim Pollard	18	62	..	..
1962-63‡	Jack McMahon, 12-26				
	Bob Leonard, 13-29	25	55	..	..
1963-64‡	Bob Leonard	31	49	..	..
1964-65	Buddy Jeannette	37	43	5	5
1965-66	Paul Seymour	38	42	0	3
1966-67	Mike Farmer, 1-8				
	Buddy Jeannette, 3-13				
	Gene Shue, 16-40	20	61	..	..
1967-68	Gene Shue	36	46	..	..
1968-69	Gene Shue	57	25	0	4
1969-70	Gene Shue	50	32	3	4
1970-71	Gene Shue	42	40	8	10
1971-72	Gene Shue	38	44	2	4
1972-73	Gene Shue	52	30	1	4
1973-74	K. C. Jones	47	35	3	4
1974-75	K. C. Jones	60	22	8	9
1975-76	K. C. Jones	48	34	3	4
1976-77	Dick Motta	48	34	4	5
1977-78	Dick Motta	44	38	14	7

ALL TIME NBA TEAM RECORDS

		Reg. Sea'n		Playoffs	
Season	Coach	W.	L.	W.	L.
1978-79	Dick Motta	54	28	9	10
1979-80	Dick Motta	39	43	0	2
1980-81	Gene Shue	39	43	..	..
Totals		823	806	60	75

*Known as Chicago Packers.
†Name changed to Chicago Zephyrs.
‡Moved to Baltimore; new name Bullets.
*Known as Capital Bullets.

WASHINGTON CAPITOLS

		Reg. Sea'n		Playoffs	
Season	Coach	W.	L.	W.	L.
1946-47	Arnold Auerbach	49	11	2	4
1947-48	Arnold Auerbach	28	20	..	..
1948-49	Arnold Auerbach	38	22	6	5
1949-50	Robert Feerick	32	36	0	2
1950-51*	Horace McKinney	10	25	..	..
Totals		157	114	8	11

*Team disbanded January 9.

WATERLOO HAWKS

		Reg. Sea'n		Playoffs	
Season	Coach	W.	L.	W.	L.
1949-50	Charles Shipp	8	27	..	..
	Jack Smiley	11	16	..	..
Totals		19	43		

ALL-TIME TEAM WINNING, LOSING STREAKS

Team	Winning Streak	Losing Streak
Atlanta	(12) .... 12- 8-68 to 1- 3-69	(16) .... 3-11-76 to 4- 9-76
Boston	(17) .... 11-28-59 to 12-30-59	(10) .... 1- 7-49 to 1-25-49
Chicago	(12) .... 10-13-73 to 11-11-73	(13) .... 10-29-76 to 12- 3-76
Cleveland	(8) .... 2- 6-76 to 2-22-76	(15) .... 10-14-70 to 11-10-70
	10-22-76 to 11- 6-76	
	3- 7-80 to 3-22-80	
Dallas	(2) .... 1-13-81 to 1-16-81	(15) .... 1-18-81 to 2-20-81
	3-10-81 to 3-12-81	
	3-20-81 to 3-21-81	
Denver	(10) .... 12-26-77 to 1-17-78	(7) .... 10-13-79 to 10-24-79
		1- 6-80 to 1-16-80
Detroit	(9) .... 10-14-70 to 10-28-70	(14) .... 3- 7-80 to 3-30-80
Golden State	(11) .... 12-29-71 to 1-22-72	(17) .... 12-20-64 to 1-26-65
Houston	(9) .... 3- 2-77 to 3-17-77	(17)• .... 1-18-68 to 2-16-68
		(13) .... 2-27-78 to 3-22-78
Indiana	(7) .... 1- 2-81 to 1-28-81	(9) .... 1-24-78 to 2-10-78
Kansas City	(15)† .... 2-17-50 to 3-19-50	(14)†† .... 1-16-60 to 2-10-60
	(8) .... 12- 2-79 to 12-19-79	(14)†† .... 12-12-71 to 1- 9-72
		(11) .... 11-16-73 to 12- 1-73
		(11) .... 12-13-75 to 1- 3-76
Los Angeles	(33) .... 11- 5-71 to 1- 7-72	(11)‡ .... 1- 1-59 to 1-20-59
		(6) .... 1-28-64 to 2- 4-64
		(6) .... 2-16-75 to 2-26-75
		(6) .... 1- 4-78 to 1-14-78
Milwaukee	(20) .... 2- 6-71 to 3- 8-71	(11) .... 10-25-74 to 11-16-74
New Jersey	(5) .... 10-24-78 to 11- 1-78	(16) .... 1- 5-78 to 2- 3-78
	2-11-81 to 2-20-81	
New York	(18) .... 10-24-69 to 11-28-69	(11) .... 2-18-60 to 3- 5-60
Philadelphia	(12)•• .... 11-12-49 to 12- 8-49	(20) .... 1- 9-73 to 2-11-73
	(12) .... 10-15-80 to 11-13-80	
Phoenix	(9) .... 2- 4-72 to 2-20-72	(12) .... 11-14-68 to 12- 3-68
	12-11-79 to 12-28-79	2-19-77 to 3-13-77
Portland	(9) .... 10-12-79 to 10-26-79	(13) .... 2-12-72 to 3- 4-72
	12- 4-80 to 12-20-80	
San Antonio	(8) .... 1-17-78 to 2- 2-78	(8) .... 2-22-80 to 3- 9-80
	12-13-78 to 12-26-78	
	10-14-80 to 10-28-80	
San Diego	(11)••• .... 11- 3-74 to 11-23-74	(12)••• .... 12-15-71 to 1- 7-72
	(8) .... 2-15-79 to 3- 2-79	(7) .... 3-16-80 to 3-30-80
		11-11-80 to 11-21-80
Seattle	(8) .... 2-11-76 to 2-25-76	(10) .... 12-12-68 to 12-29-68
	1- 9-80 to 1-23-80	1-16-76 to 2- 8-76
	1-31-80 to 2-17-80	
Utah	(10)• .... 1-14-78 to 2- 1-78	(14) .... 10-27-79 to 11-27-79
	(6) .... 10-28-80 to 11- 6-80	
Washington	(9)•• .... 12- 4-68 to 12-25-68	(13)•• .... 12-17-66 to 1- 8-67
	(9) .... 11-14-78 to 12- 1-78	

•Club located in San Diego.
†Club located in Rochester.
††Club located in Cincinnati.
‡Club located in Minneapolis.
••Club located in Syracuse.
•••Club located in Buffalo.
●Club located in New Orleans.
●●Club located in Baltimore.

Enshrined Hall of Famers

CONTRIBUTORS

Name	Year Elected
*Allen, Dr. Forrest C. (Phog)	1959
BEE, CLAIR F.	**1967**
***BROWN, WALTER A.**	**1965**
Bunn, John W.	1964
*Douglas, Robert L. (Bob)	1971
*Fisher, Harry A.	1973
***GOTTLIEB, EDWARD**	**1971**
*Gulick, Dr. Luther H.	1959
HARRISON, LESTER	**1979**
*Hepp, Ferenc	1980
*Hickox, Edward J.	1959
Hinkle, Paul D. (Tony)	1965
IRISH, NED	**1964**
Jones, R. William	1964
***KENNEDY, J. WALTER**	**1980**
*Liston, Emil S.	1974
McLendon, John B.	1978
***MOKRAY, WM. G. (BILL)**	**1965**
*Morgan, Ralph	1959
*Morgenweck, Frank	1962
*Naismith, Dr. James	1959
NEWELL, PETER F.	**1978**
*O'Brien, John J.	1961
***OLSEN, HAROLD G.**	**1959**
PODOLOFF, MAURICE	**1973**
*Porter, H. V.	1960
*Reid, William A.	1963
Ripley, Elmer	1972
*St. John, Lynn W.	1962
*Saperstein, Abe	1970
*Schabinger, Arthur A.	1961
*Stagg, Amos Alonzo	1959
*Taylor, Charles H. (Chuck)	1968
*Tower, Oswald	1959
*Trester, Arthur L.	1961
*Wells, Clifford	1971

PLAYERS

Name	Year Elected
ARIZIN, PAUL J.	**1977**
Barlow, Thomas B.	1980
BAYLOR, ELGIN	**1976**
*Beckman, John	1972
*Borgmann, Bennie	1961
Brennan, Joseph	1974
CHAMBERLAIN, WILT	**1978**
*Cooper, Charles (Tarzan)	1976
COUSY, ROBERT J.	**1970**
DAVIES, ROBERT E. (BOB)	**1969**
*DeBernardi, Forrest S.	1961
***DEHNERT, H. G. (DUTCH)**	**1968**
Endacott, Paul	1971
Foster, Harold (Bud)	1964
Friedman, Max (Marty)	1971
***FULKS, JOSEPH F. (JOE)**	**1977**
Gale, Lauren (Laddie)	1976
GOLA, TOM	**1975**
*Gruenig, Robert (Ace)	1963
HAGAN, CLIFFORD O	**1977**
Hanson, Victor	1960

HALL OF FAMERS

Name	Year Elected
Holman, Nat	1964
*Hyatt, Charles (Chuck)	1959
*Johnson, William C.	1976
Krause, Edward (Moose)	1975
Kurland, Robert (Bob)	1961
*LAPCHICK, JOE	**1966**
LUCAS, JERRY	**1979**
Luisetti, Angelo (Hank)	1959
*McCracken, Branch	1960
*McCracken, Jack	1962
MACAULEY, C. EDWARD	**1960**
MIKAN, GEORGE L.	**1959**
Murphy, Charles (Stretch)	1960
*Page, H. O. (Pat)	1962
PETTIT, ROBERT L.	**1970**
PHILLIP, ANDY	**1961**
POLLARD, JAMES C. (JIM)	**1977**
ROBERTSON, OSCAR	**1979**
Roosma, Col. John S.	1961
*RUSSELL, JOHN (HONEY)	**1964**
RUSSELL, WILLIAM (BILL)	**1974**
SCHAYES, ADOLPH	**1972**
Schmidt, Ernest J.	1973
*Schommer, John J.	1959
*Sedran, Barney	1962
SHARMAN, BILL	**1975**
*Steinmetz, Christian	1961
Thompson, John A. (Cat)	1962
Vandivier, Robert (Fuzzy)	1974
*Wachter, Edward A.	1961
WEST, JERRY	**1979**
Wooden, John R.	1960

TEAMS

First Team	1959
Original Celtics	1959
Buffalo Germans	1961
Renaissance	1963

Men associated with the NBA in bold face type.

*Deceased.

Individuals Elected—126.

Teams Elected—4.

COACHES

Name	Year Elected
AUERBACH, A. J. (RED)	**1968**
*Barry, Sam	1978
*Blood, Ernest A.	1960
Cann, Howard G.	1967
*Carlson, Dr. H. Clifford	1959
Carnevale, Ben	1969
Dean, Everett S.	1966
*Diddle, Edgar A.	1971
Drake, Bruce	1972
*Gill, Amory T. (Slats)	1967
*Hickey, Edgar S.	1978
Hobson, Howard A.	1965
Iba, Henry P. (Hank)	1968
*JULIAN, ALVIN F. (DOGGIE)	**1967**
*Keaney, Frank W.	1960
*Keogan, George E.	1961
*Lambert, Ward L.	1960
Litwack, Harry	1975
*LOEFFLER, KENNETH D.	**1964**
Lonborg, A. C. (Dutch)	1972
McCutchan, Arad A.	1980
McGUIRE, FRANK	**1976**
*Meanwell, Dr. Walter E.	1959
Meyer, Raymond J.	1978
*Rupp, Adolph F.	1968
*Sachs, Leonard D.	1961
*Shelton, Everett F.	1979
Wooden, John R.	1972

REFEREES

Enright, James E.	1978
*Hepbron, George T.	1960
*Hoyt, George	1961
*KENNEDY, MATTHEW P.	**1959**
NUCATOLA, JOHN P.	**1977**
*Quigley, Ernest C.	1961
Shirley, J. Dallas	1979
Tobey, David	1961
*Walsh, David H.	1961

WILT CHAMBERLAIN'S 100-POINT GAME

This historic game was played March 2, 1962, at Hershey, Pa. With 46 seconds left in the game, Wilt Chamberlain reached 100 points on a layup off a pass from Paul Arizin.

PHILADELPHIA WARRIORS (169)

Player	Pos.	Min.	FGA	FGM	FTA	FTM	Reb.	Ast.	PF	Pts.
Paul Arizin	F	31	18	7	2	2	5	4	0	16
Ed Conlin		14	4	0	0	0	4	1	1	0
Joe Ruklick		8	1	0	2	0	2	1	2	0
Tom Meschery	F	40	12	7	2	2	7	3	4	16
Ted Luckenbill		3	0	0	0	0	1	0	2	0
Wilt Chamberlain	C	48	63	36	32	28	25	2	2	100
Guy Rodgers	G	48	4	1	12	9	7	20	5	11
Al Attles	G	34	8	8	1	1	5	6	4	17
York Larese		14	5	4	1	1	1	2	5	9
Totals		240	115	63	52	43	60	39	25	169

Team Rebounds—3.

NEW YORK KNICKS (147)

Player	Pos.	Min.	FGA	FGM	FTA	FTM	Reb.	Ast.	PF	Pts.
Willie Naulls	F	43	22	9	15	13	7	2	5	31
Johnny Green	F	21	7	3	0	0	7	1	5	6
Cleveland Buckner		33	26	16	1	1	8	0	4	33
Darrall Imhoff	C	20	7	3	1	1	6	0	6	7
Dave Budd		27	8	6	1	1	10	1	1	13
Richie Guerin	G	46	29	13	17	13	8	6	5	39
Al Butler	G	32	13	4	0	0	7	3	1	8
Donnie Butcher		18	6	3	6	4	3	4	5	10
Totals		240	118	57	41	33	60	17	32	147

Team Rebounds—4.

Score by Periods:	1st	2nd	3rd	4th	Totals
Philadelphia	42	37	46	44	— 169
New York	26	42	38	41	— 147

CHAMBERLAIN'S SCORING BY PERIODS:

	Pos.	Min.	FGA	FGM	FTA	FTM	Reb.	Ast.	PF	Pts.
First Quarter		12	14	7	9	9	10	0	0	23
Second Quarter		12	12	7	5	4	4	1	1	18
Third Quarter		12	16	10	8	8	6	1	0	28
Fourth Quarter		12	21	12	10	7	5	0	1	31
Totals		48	63	36	32	28	25	2	2	100

Referees—Willie Smith and Pete D'Ambrosio. Attendance—4,124.

CBA Adopts Point System

The Continental Basketball Association, emerging as a minor league for the National Basketball Association, will begin its 37th season with a new system for determining division winners.

Ignoring the traditional won-loss percentage for determining division winners, the CBA will use a points system awarding three points for each victory and a single point for every quarter in which the team outscores its opponent.

Last season, the CBA acted as a proving ground for referees, rules changes and the pressure-release safety rims that have been installed throughout the NBA for the 1981-82 season.

The league also placed 22 players on NBA Rosters throughout the course of the 1980-81 season, up from nine the year before. Four years ago, the league placed just one player on an NBA roster.

The final standings, playoff results, award winners and statistical leaders of the 1980-81 CBA season are listed below.

1980-81 CONTINENTAL BASKETBALL ASSOCIATION FINAL STANDINGS

Eastern Division

	W	L	Pct.	GB
Rochester Zeniths	34	6	.850	....
Atlantic City Hi Rollers	22	18	.550	12
Philadelphia Kings	17	23	.425	27
Lehigh Valley Jets	16	24	.400	18
Maine Lumberjacks	16	24	.400	18
Scranton Aces	13	27	.325	21

Western Division

	W	L	Pct.	GB
Montana Golden Nuggets	27	15	.643	....
Anchorage No. Knights	25	17	.595	2
Billings Volcanos	23	19	.548	4
Alberta Dusters	11	31	.262	16

CBA CHAMPIONSHIP SERIES
Rochester defeated Montana, 4-0

CBA STATISTICAL LEADERS
Scoring: Jacky Dorsey, (Maine)–31.2
Rebounding: Jacky Dorsey, (Ma.)–16.6
Assists: Greg Jackson, (Lehigh Val.)–11.2
Blocked Shots: Lee Johnson, (Roch.)–3.6
Steals: Glenn Hagan, (Roch.)–3.5

CBA ALL-STAR TEAM
FIRST TEAM
Lee Johnson (Rochester)
Larry Fogle (Rochester)
Jacky Dorsey (Maine)
Willie Smith (Montana)
Glenn Hagan (Rochester)

WILLIE SMITH
Mont. Golden Nuggets
Most Valuable Player

LEE JOHNSON
Rochester Zeniths
Rookie-of-the-Year
Playoff MVP

GEORGE KARL
Mont. Golden Nuggets
Coach-of-the-Year

ABA All-League Teams

1976

FIRST	Pts.	SECOND	Pts.
Julius Erving, New York	F	David Thompson, Denver	F
Billy Knight, Indiana	F	Bobby Jones, Denver	F
Artis Gilmore, Kentucky	C	Dan Issel, Denver	C
James Silas, San Antonio	G	Don Buse, Indiana	G
Ralph Simpson, Denver	G	George Gervin, San Antonio	G

1975

FIRST	Pts.	SECOND	Pts.
Julius Erving, New York	F	Marvin Barnes, St. Louis	F
George McGinnis, Indiana	F	George Gervin, San Antonio	F
Artis Gilmore, Kentucky	C	Swen Nater, San Antonio	C
Mack Calvin, Denver	G	Brian Taylor, New York	G
Ron Boone, Utah	G	James Silas, San Antonio	G

1974

FIRST	Pts.	SECOND	Pts.
Julius Erving, New York	F	Dan Issel, Kentucky	F
George McGinnis, Indiana	F	Willie Wise, Utah	F
Artis Gilmore, Kentucky	C	Swen Nater, San Antonio	C
James Jones, Utah	G	Ron Boone, Utah	G
Mack Calvin, Carolina	G	Louie Dampier, Kentucky	G

1973

FIRST	Pts.	SECOND	Pts.
Billy Cunningham, Carolina	F	George McGinnis, Indiana	F
Julius Erving, Virginia	F	Dan Issel, Kentucky	F
Artis Gilmore, Kentucky	C	Mel Daniels, Indiana	C
James Jones, Utah	G	Ralph Simpson, Denver	G
Warren Jabali, Denver	G	Mack Calvin, Carolina	G

1972

FIRST	Pts.	SECOND	Pts.
Dan Issel, Kentucky	F	Willie Wise, Utah	F
Rick Barry, New York	F	Julius Erving, Virginia	F
Artis Gilmore, Kentucky	C	Zelmo Beaty, Utah	C
Don Freeman, Dallas	G	Ralph Simpson, Denver	G
Bill Melchionni, New York	G	Charlie Scott, Virginia	G

1971

FIRST	Pts.	SECOND	Pts.
Roger Brown, Indiana	F	John Brisker, Pittsburgh	F
Rick Barry, New York	F	Joe Caldwell, Carolina	F
Mel Daniels, Indiana	C	Zelmo Beaty, Utah (tie)	C
Mack Calvin, Floridians	G	Dan Issel, Kentucky (tie)	C
Charlie Scott, Virginia	G	Don Freeman, Texas	G
		Larry Cannon, Denver	G

1970

FIRST	Pts.	SECOND	Pts.
Rick Barry, Washington	F	Roger Brown, Indiana	F
Spencer Haywood, Denver	F	Bob Netolicky, Indiana	F
Mel Daniels, Indiana	C	Red Robbins, New Orleans	C
Bob Verga, Carolina	G	Louie Dampier, Kentucky	G
Larry Jones, Denver	G	Don Freeman, Miami	G

1969

FIRST	Pts.	SECOND	Pts.
Connie Hawkins, Minnesota	F	John Beasley, Dallas	F
Rick Barry, Oakland	F	Doug Moe, Oakland	F
Mel Daniels, Indiana	C	Red Robbins, New Orleans	C
James Jones, New Orleans	G	Don Freeman, Miami	G
Larry Jones, Denver	G	Louie Dampier, Kentucky	G

1968

FIRST	Pts.	SECOND	Pts.
Connie Hawkins, Pittsburgh	F	Roger Brown, Indiana	F
Doug Moe, New Orleans	F	Cincy Powell, Dallas	F
Mel Daniels, Minnesota	C	John Beasley, Dallas	C
Larry Jones, Denver	G	Larry Brown, New Orleans	G
Charlie Williams, Pittsburgh	G	Louie Dampier, Kentucky	G

Players Who Made All-ABA Teams

	1st Team	2nd
Marvin Barnes	0	1
Rick Barry	4	0
John Beasley	0	2
Zelmo Beaty	0	2
Ron Boone	1	1
John Brisker	0	1
Larry Brown	0	1
Roger Brown	1	2
Don Buse	0	1
Joe Caldwell	0	1
Mack Calvin	3	1
Larry Cannon	0	1
Billy Cunningham	1	0
Louie Dampier	0	4
Mel Daniels	4	1
Julius Erving	4	1
Don Freeman	1	3
George Gervin	0	2
Artis Gilmore	5	0
Connie Hawkins	2	0
Spencer Haywood	1	0

	1st Team	2nd
Dan Issel	1	4
Warren Jabali	1	0
Bobby Jones	0	1
James Jones	3	0
Larry Jones	3	0
Billy Knight	1	0
George McGinnis	2	1
Bill Melchionni	1	0
Doug Moe	1	1
Swen Nater	0	2
Bob Netolicky	0	1
Cincy Powell	0	1
Red Robbins	0	2
Charlie Scott	1	1
James Silas	1	1
Ralph Simpson	1	2
Brian Taylor	0	1
David Thompson	0	1
Bob Verga	1	0
Charlie Williams	1	0
Willie Wise	0	2

ABA Most Valuable Players

1976—Julius Erving, New York
1975—Julius Erving, New York
    George McGinnis, Indiana (tie)
1974—Julius Erving, New York
1973—Billy Cunningham, Carolina
1972—Artis Gilmore, Kentucky
1971—Mel Daniels, Indiana
1970—Spencer Haywood, Denver
1969—Mel Daniels, Indiana
1968—Connie Hawkins, Pittsburgh

ABA Rookies of the Year

1976—David Thompson, Denver
1975—Marvin Barnes, St. Louis
1974—Swen Nater, San Antonio
1973—Brian Taylor, New York
1972—Artis Gilmore, Kentucky
1971—Charlie Scott, Virginia
    Dan Issel, Kentucky (tie)
1970—Spencer Haywood, Denver
1969—Warren Armstrong, Oakland
1968—Mel Daniels, Minnesota

ABA Coaches of the Year

1976—Larry Brown, Denver
1975—Larry Brown, Denver
1974—Babe McCarthy, Kentucky
    Joe Mullaney, Utah (tie)
1973—Larry Brown, Carolina
1972—Tom Nissalke, Dallas
1971—Al Bianchi, Virginia
1970—Bill Sharman, Los Angeles
    Joe Belmont, Denver (tie)
1969—Alex Hannum, Oakland
1968—Vince Cazetta, Pittsburgh

ABA All-Rookie Teams

1976
David Thompson .... Denver
Mark Olberding .... San Antonio
Kim Hughes .... New York
M.L. Carr .... St. Louis
Tickey Burden .... Virginia

1975
Bobby Jones .... Denver
Marvin Barnes .... St. Louis
Moses Malone .... Utah
Billy Knight .... Indiana
Gus Gerard .... St. Louis

1974
Larry Kenon .... New York
Mike Green .... Denver
Swen Nater .... San Antonio
Dwight Lamar .... San Antonio
John Williamson .... New York

1973
George Gervin
Virginia .... Dennis Wuycik
Carolina .... Jim Chones
New York .... Brian Taylor
New York .... Jim Silas
Dallas

1972
Julius Erving .... Virginia
George McGinnis .... Indiana
Artis Gilmore .... Kentucky
John Roche .... New York
John Neumann .... Memphis

1971
Wendell Ladner .... Memphis
Sam Robinson .... Floridians
Dan Issel .... Kentucky
Charlie Scott .... Virginia
Joe Hamilton .... Texas

1970
Willie Wise .... Los Angeles
John Brisker .... Pittsburgh
Spencer Haywood .... Denver
Mike Barrett .... Washington
Mack Calvin .... Los Angeles

1969
Larry Miller .... Los Angeles
Walt Piatkowski .... Denver
Gene Moore .... Kentucky
Warren Armstrong .... Oakland
Ron Boone .... Dallas

1968
Tom Washington .... Pittsburgh
Bob Netolicky .... Indiana
Mel Daniels .... Minnesota
Louie Dampier .... Kentucky
James Jones .... New Orleans

ABA All-Defensive Teams

1976
Bobby Jones, Denver .... F
Julius Erving, New York .... F
Artis Gilmore, Kentucky C
Don Buse, Indiana .... G
Brian Taylor, New York .... G

1975
Bobby Jones, Denver .... F
Wil Jones, Kentucky .... F
Artis Gilmore, Kentucky C
Brian Taylor, New York .... G
Don Buse, Indiana .... G

1974
Willie Wise, Utah .... F
Julius Keye, Denver .... F
Artis Gilmore, Kentucky C
Ted McClain, Carolina .... G
Roland Taylor, Virginia .... G
Mike Gale, New York .... (tie) G

1973
Willie Wise, Utah .... F
Joe Caldwell, Carolina .... F
Julius Keye, Denver .... (tie) F
Artis Gilmore, Kentucky C
Roland Taylor, Virginia .... G
Mike Gale, Kentucky .... G

1979-80 STATISTICS

LOS ANGELES LAKERS 1979-80 NBA WORLD CHAMPIONS
Back Row (left to right): Head Coach Paul Westhead, Butch Lee, Brad Holland, Mark Landsberger, Marty Byrnes, Michael Cooper, Norm Nixon, Trainer Jack Curran, Assistant Coach Pat Riley. Seated: Chairman of the Board Dr. Jerry Buss, Spencer Haywood, Jamaal Wilkes, Kareem Abdul-Jabbar, Earvin Johnson, Jim Chones, General Manager Bill Sharman.

FINAL STANDINGS
ATLANTIC DIVISION

Team	Atl.	Bos.	Chi.	Cle.	Den.	Det.	G.S.	Hou.	Ind.	K.C.	L.A.	Mil.	N.J.	N.Y.	Phi.	Pho.	Por.	S.A.	S.D.	Sea.	Utah	Was.	W.	L.	Pct.	G.B.
Boston	4	..	2	4	2	6	2	6	4	1	..	2	5	5	3	1	2	4	2	..	2	4	61	21	.744	....
Philadelphia	2	3	1	5	2	5	2	4	5	1	1	2	5	6	..	1	2	4	1	1	1	5	59	23	.720	2
Washington	3	2	2	3	1	4	2	4	2	..	1	1	3	3	1	..	1	2	1	1	2	..	39	43	.476	22
New York	2	1	2	3	1	4	2	3	2	1	..	1	4	..	..	2	2	4	1	..	1	3	39	43	.476	22
New Jersey	2	1	1	3	1	4	..	3	4	1	..	1	..	2	1	1	..	3	1	1	1	3	34	48	.415	27

CENTRAL DIVISION

Team	Atl.	Bos.	Chi.	Cle.	Den.	Det.	G.S.	Hou.	Ind.	K.C.	L.A.	Mil.	N.J.	N.Y.	Phi.	Pho.	Por.	S.A.	S.D.	Sea.	Utah	Was.	W.	L.	Pct.	G.B.
Atlanta	..	2	1	4	2	6	2	2	4	..	1	1	4	4	4	1	2	5	1	..	2	3	50	32	.610	....
Houston	4	..	1	4	1	5	1	..	4	..	..	1	3	3	2	1	1	3	2	1	2	2	41	41	.500	9
San Antonio	1	2	2	2	1	4	2	3	4	1	..	2	3	2	2	1	1	..	2	1	1	4	41	41	.500	9
Indiana	2	2	2	4	1	5	1	2	..	1	..	..	2	4	1	..	2	2	1	..	1	4	37	45	.451	13
Cleveland	2	2	..	..	1	6	2	2	2	1	..	..	3	3	1	1	..	4	1	..	1	3	37	45	.451	13
Detroit	..	..	1	..	1	..	1	1	1	..	..	1	2	2	1	..	..	2	..	..	1	2	16	66	.195	34

MIDWEST DIVISION

Team	Atl.	Bos.	Chi.	Cle.	Den.	Det.	G.S.	Hou.	Ind.	K.C.	L.A.	Mil.	N.J.	N.Y.	Phi.	Pho.	Por.	S.A.	S.D.	Sea.	Utah	Was.	W.	L.	Pct.	G.B.
Milwaukee	1	..	5	2	3	1	6	1	2	3	3	..	1	1	..	4	5	..	4	2	4	1	49	33	.598	....
Kansas City	2	1	3	..	6	2	3	2	1	..	2	3	1	1	1	1	1	5	3	6	2	2	47	35	.573	2
Denver	1	..	4	1	..	1	3	1	1	3	1	1	..	1	2	1	3	3	1	3	1	1	30	52	.366	19
Chicago	1	..	..	2	2	1	4	1	..	3	1	1	1	..	1	1	3	..	4	2	2	..	30	52	.366	19
Utah	..	..	4	1	3	1	3	..	1	..	..	2	1	1	..	3	1	1	..	1	..	1	24	58	.293	25

PACIFIC DIVISION

Team	Atl.	Bos.	Chi.	Cle.	Den.	Det.	G.S.	Hou.	Ind.	K.C.	L.A.	Mil.	N.J.	N.Y.	Phi.	Pho.	Por.	S.A.	S.D.	Sea.	Utah	Was.	W.	L.	Pct.	G.B.
Los Angeles	1	2	5	1	5	2	5	2	2	4	..	3	2	2	1	3	2	2	5	4	6	1	60	22	.732	....
Seattle	2	2	4	2	5	2	6	1	2	3	2	4	1	2	1	2	5	1	3	..	5	1	56	26	.683	4
Phoenix	1	1	5	1	5	2	4	1	2	5	3	2	1	..	1	..	6	1	2	4	6	2	55	27	.671	5
Portland	..	..	3	2	4	2	4	1	..	5	4	1	2	..	..	..	..	1	4	1	3	1	38	44	.463	22
San Diego	1	..	2	1	3	2	3	..	1	1	1	2	1	1	1	4	2	..	..	3	5	1	35	47	.427	25
Golden State	..	..	2	..	3	1	..	1	1	3	1	..	2	..	..	2	2	..	3	..	3	..	24	58	.293	36

TEAM STATISTICS—OFFENSE

Team	G.	FIELD GOALS Made	Att.	Pct.	FREE THROWS Made	Att.	Pct.	REBOUNDS Off.	Def.	Tot.	MISCELLANEOUS Ast.	PF	Dq.	Stl.	Turn Over	Blk. Sh.	SCORING Pts.	Avg.
San Antonio	82	3856	7738	.498	2024	2528	.801	1153	2515	3668	2326	2103	29	771	1589	333	9788	119.4
Los Angeles	82	3898	7368	.529	1622	2092	.775	1085	2653	3738	2413	1784	15	774	1639	546	9438	115.1
Cleveland	82	3811	8041	.474	1702	2205	.772	1307	2381	3688	2108	1934	18	764	1370	342	9360	114.1
New York	82	3802	7672	.496	1698	2274	.747	1236	2303	3539	2265	2168	33	881	1613	457	9344	114.0
Boston	82	3617	7387	.490	1907	2449	.779	1227	2457	3684	2198	1974	19	809	1539	308	9303	113.5
Indiana	82	3639	7689	.473	1753	2333	.751	1398	2326	3724	2148	1973	37	900	1517	530	9119	111.2
Phoenix	82	3570	7235	.493	1906	2466	.773	1071	2458	3529	2283	1853	9	908	1629	344	9114	111.1
Houston	82	3599	7496	.480	1782	2326	.766	1394	2217	3611	2149	1927	11	782	1565	373	9084	110.8
Milwaukee	82	3685	7553	.488	1605	2102	.764	1245	2396	3641	2277	1937	12	778	1496	510	9025	110.1
Philadelphia	82	3523	7156	.492	1876	2431	.772	1187	2635	3822	2226	1860	17	792	1708	652	8949	109.1
Detroit	82	3643	7596	.480	1590	2149	.740	1226	2415	3641	1950	2069	47	783	1742	562	8933	108.9
Seattle	82	3554	7565	.470	1730	2253	.768	1380	2550	3930	2043	1865	27	750	1496	428	8897	108.5
New Jersey	82	3456	7504	.461	1882	2406	.782	1229	2535	3764	2094	2181	38	869	1702	581	8879	108.3
Denver	82	3462	7470	.463	1871	2539	.737	1311	2524	3835	2079	1917	24	746	1533	404	8878	108.3
Kansas City	82	3582	7489	.478	1671	2250	.743	1187	2429	3616	2123	2135	20	863	1439	356	8860	108.0
San Diego	82	3524	7494	.470	1595	2167	.736	1294	2308	3602	1688	1896	24	664	1443	288	8820	107.6
Chicago	82	3362	6943	.484	2019	2592	.779	1115	2465	3580	2152	2144	26	704	1684	392	8813	107.5
Washington	82	3574	7796	.458	1552	2048	.758	1334	2723	4057	2201	1893	24	530	1380	443	8773	107.0
Atlanta	82	3261	7027	.464	2038	2645	.771	1369	2406	3775	1913	2293	46	782	1495	539	8573	104.5
Golden State	82	3527	7318	.482	1412	1914	.738	1155	2437	3592	2028	2082	28	779	1492	339	8493	103.6
Portland	82	3408	7167	.476	1560	2100	.743	1295	2408	3703	1898	1956	23	708	1552	472	8402	102.5
Utah	82	3382	6817	.496	1571	1943	.809	967	2359	3326	2005	2006	33	656	1543	362	8394	102.4

TEAM STATISTICS—DEFENSE

Team	FIELD GOALS Made	Att.	Pct.	FREE THROWS Made	Att.	Pct.	REBOUNDS Off.	Def.	Tot.	MISCELLANEOUS Ast.	PF	Dq.	Stl.	Turn Over	Blk. Sh.	SCORING Pts.	Avg.	Dif.
Atlanta	3144	6872	.458	2000	2616	.765	1261	2339	3600	1758	2171	35	682	1660	554	8334	101.6	+ 2.9
Portland	3349	7008	.478	1716	2281	.752	1138	2358	3496	2008	1880	23	756	1450	395	8469	103.3	− 0.8
Seattle	3408	7424	.459	1640	2147	.764	1203	2409	3612	2016	1997	24	728	1519	393	8515	103.8	+ 4.7
Kansas City	3328	6992	.476	1906	2497	.763	1140	2644	3784	1778	2072	17	695	1762	425	8603	104.9	+ 3.1
Philadelphia	3444	7561	.455	1640	2145	.765	1318	2352	3670	2089	2100	39	876	1561	388	8603	104.9	+ 4.2
Boston	3439	7313	.470	1712	2222	.770	1168	2294	3462	1867	2059	34	686	1635	419	8664	105.7	+ 7.8
Milwaukee	3456	7487	.462	1714	2275	.753	1360	2293	3653	2154	1912	15	717	1638	358	8702	106.1	+ 4.0
Phoenix	3563	7480	.476	1593	2119	.752	1216	2447	3663	2026	2051	32	882	1663	389	8819	107.5	+ 3.6
Golden State	3438	6975	.493	1905	2544	.749	1056	2564	3620	2091	1785	14	720	1486	361	8853	108.0	− 4.4
Utah	3559	7182	.496	1702	2205	.772	1159	2288	3447	1997	1782	15	710	1274	398	8887	108.4	− 6.0
Los Angeles	3723	7921	.470	1430	1884	.759	1312	2242	3554	2324	1860	27	797	1420	382	8954	109.2	+ 5.9
New Jersey	3480	7427	.469	1957	2572	.761	1285	2594	3879	2189	2042	27	849	1692	514	8975	109.5	− 1.2
Washington	3615	7771	.465	1696	2184	.777	1197	2672	3869	2120	1901	24	734	1222	519	8982	109.5	− 2.5
Chicago	3585	7222	.496	1811	2358	.768	1159	2345	3504	2109	2203	38	846	1543	498	9035	110.2	− 2.7
Houston	3658	7382	.496	1696	2153	.788	1290	2317	3607	2223	2049	29	778	1597	428	9070	110.6	+ 0.2
San Diego	3752	7508	.500	1613	2086	.773	1222	2487	3709	2012	1889	16	764	1391	408	9160	111.7	− 4.1
Indiana	3693	7545	.489	1734	2295	.756	1394	2552	3946	2323	2028	26	738	1758	470	9176	111.9	− 0.7
Denver	3736	7591	.492	1698	2235	.760	1197	2587	3784	2289	2033	22	812	1438	455	9240	112.7	− 4.4
Cleveland	3811	7610	.501	1645	2150	.765	1230	2638	3868	2208	2033	30	708	1667	490	9332	113.8	+ 0.3
New York	3707	7492	.495	1969	2556	.770	1293	2432	3725	2143	2042	31	813	1694	390	9439	115.1	− 1.1
Detroit	3847	7761	.496	1858	2405	.773	1319	2572	3891	2306	1871	14	874	1583	470	9609	117.2	− 8.3
San Antonio	4000	7997	.500	1731	2283	.758	1248	2472	3720	2537	2192	28	828	1513	457	9819	119.7	− 0.3

DQ—Individual players disqualified (fouled out of game).

INDIVIDUAL SCORING LEADERS
Minimum 70 games played or 1400 points

	G.	FG	FT	Pts.	Avg.		G.	FG	FT	Pts.	Avg.
Gervin, San Antonio	78	1024	505	2585	33.1	Williams, Seattle	82	739	331	1816	22.1
Free, San Diego	68	737	572	2055	30.2	Westphal, Phoenix	82	692	382	1792	21.9
Dantley, Utah	68	730	443	1903	28.0	Cartwright, New York	82	665	451	1781	21.7
Erving, Philadelphia	78	838	420	2100	26.9	Johnson, Milwaukee	77	689	291	1671	21.7
Malone, Houston	82	778	563	2119	25.8	Davis, Phoenix	75	657	299	1613	21.5
Abdul-Jabbar, L. A.	82	835	364	2034	24.8	Bird, Boston	82	693	301	1745	21.3
Issel, Denver	82	715	517	1951	23.8	Newlin, New Jersey	78	611	367	1634	20.9
Hayes, Washington	81	761	334	1859	23.0	R. Williams, New York	82	687	333	1714	20.9
Birdsong, Kansas City	82	781	286	1858	22.7	Theus, Chicago	82	566	500	1660	20.2
Mitchell, Cleveland	82	775	270	1820	22.2	Kenon, San Antonio	78	647	270	1565	20.1

1979-80 STATISTICS

FIELD GOAL LEADERS
Minimum 300 FG Made

	FGM	FGA	Pct.
Maxwell, Boston	457	750	.609
Abdul-Jabbar, Los Angeles	835	1383	.604
Gilmore, Chicago	305	513	.595
Dantley, Utah	730	1267	.576
Boswell, Utah	346	613	.564
Davis, Phoenix	657	1166	.563
Nater, San Diego	443	799	.554
Washington, Portland	421	761	.553
Cartwright, New York	665	1215	.547
Johnson, Milwaukee	689	1267	.544

FREE THROW LEADERS
Minimum 125 FT Made

	FTM	FTA	Pct.
Barry, Houston	143	153	.935
Murphy, Houston	271	302	.897
Boone, Utah	175	196	.893
Silas, San Antonio	339	382	.887
Newlin, New Jersey	367	415	.884
Furlow, Utah	171	196	.872
Phegley, New Jersey	177	203	.872
Bratz, Phoenix	141	162	.870
Grevey, Washington	216	249	.867
Roche, Denver	175	202	.866

REBOUND LEADERS
Minimum 70 games or 800 rebounds

	G.	Off.	Def.	Tot.	Avg.
Nater, San Diego	81	352	864	1216	15.0
Malone, Houston	82	573	617	1190	14.5
Unseld, Washington	82	334	760	1094	13.3
C. Jones, Philadelphia	80	219	731	950	11.9
Sikma, Seattle	82	198	710	908	11.1
Hayes, Washington	81	269	627	896	11.1
Parish, Golden State	72	247	536	783	10.9
Abdul-Jabbar, L. A.	82	190	696	886	10.8
Washington, Portland	80	325	517	842	10.5
Bird, Boston	82	216	636	852	10.4

BLOCKED SHOTS LEADERS
Minimum 70 games or 100 blocked shots

	G.	No.	Avg.
Abdul-Jabbar, Los Angeles	82	280	3.41
Johnson, New Jersey	81	258	3.19
Rollins, Atlanta	82	244	2.98
Tyler, Detroit	82	220	2.68
Hayes, Washington	81	189	2.33
Catchings, Milwaukee	72	162	2.25
C. Jones, Philadelphia	80	162	2.03
Poquette, Utah	82	162	1.98
Meriweather, New York	65	120	1.85
Erving, Philadelphia	78	140	1.79

ASSISTS LEADERS
Minimum 70 games or 400 assists

	G.	No.	Avg.
Richardson, New York	82	832	10.1
Archibald, Boston	80	671	8.4
Walker, Cleveland	76	607	8.0
Nixon, Los Angeles	82	642	7.8
Lucas, Golden State	80	602	7.5
Ford, Kansas City	82	610	7.4
Johnson, Los Angeles	77	563	7.3
Cheeks, Philadelphia	79	556	7.0
Jordan, New Jersey	82	557	6.8
Porter, Washington	70	457	6.5

STEALS LEADERS
Minimum 70 games or 125 steals

	G.	No.	Avg.
Richardson, New York	82	265	3.23
Jordan, New Jersey	82	223	2.72
Bradley, Indiana	82	211	2.57
Williams, Seattle	82	200	2.44
Johnson, Los Angeles	77	187	2.43
Cheeks, Philadelphia	79	183	2.32
Erving, Philadelphia	78	170	2.18
Parker, Golden State	82	173	2.11
Walker, Cleveland	76	155	2.04
R. Williams, New York	82	167	2.04

3 PT. FG LEADERS
Minimum 25 Made

	FGM	FGA	Pct.
Brown, Seattle	39	88	.443
Ford, Boston	70	164	.427
Bird, Boston	58	143	.406
Roche, Denver	49	129	.380
Taylor, San Diego	90	239	.377
Winters, Milwaukee	38	102	.373
Grevey, Washington	34	92	.370
Hassett, Indiana	69	198	.348
Barry, Houston	73	221	.330
Williams, San Diego	42	128	.328

1979-80 STATISTICS

INDIVIDUAL STATISTICS

ATLANTA

Player	G.	Min.	FGM	FGA	Pct.	FTM	FTA	Pct.	Off. Reb.	Def. Reb.	Tot. Reb.	Ast.	PF	Dsq.	Stl.	Blk. Sh.	Pts.	Avg.	Hi.
Drew	80	2306	535	1182	.453	489	646	.757	203	268	471	101	313	10	91	23	1559	19.5	40
Johnson	79	2622	590	1212	.487	280	338	.828	95	105	200	370	216	2	120	24	1465	18.5	36
Roundfield	81	2588	502	1007	.499	330	465	.710	293	544	837	184	317	6	101	139	1334	16.5	31
Hawes	82	1885	304	605	.502	150	182	.824	148	348	496	144	205	4	74	29	761	9.3	24
Rollins	82	2123	287	514	.558	157	220	.714	283	491	774	76	322	12	54	244	731	8.9	20
McElroy (Tot)	67	1528	228	527	.433	132	172	.767	32	67	99	227	123	2	46	19	593	8.9	33
McElroy (Atl)	31	516	66	171	.386	37	53	.698	20	29	49	65	45	1	21	5	171	5.5	20
McMillen	53	1071	191	382	.500	81	107	.757	70	150	220	62	126	2	36	14	463	8.7	24
Furlow	21	404	66	161	.410	44	51	.863	23	19	42	72	19	0	19	9	177	8.4	22
Criss	81	1794	249	578	.431	172	212	.811	27	89	116	246	133	0	74	4	671	8.3	26
Hill	79	2092	177	431	.411	124	146	.849	31	107	138	424	261	7	107	8	479	6.1	17
Givens	82	1254	182	473	.385	106	128	.828	114	128	242	59	132	1	51	19	470	5.7	20
Brown (Tot)	32	385	37	105	.352	38	48	.792	26	45	71	18	70	0	3	4	112	3.5	12
Brown (Atl)	28	361	37	98	.378	34	44	.773	21	41	62	14	66	0	3	4	108	3.9	12
Pellom	44	373	44	108	.407	21	30	.700	28	64	92	18	70	0	12	12	109	2.5	10
Lee	30	364	29	91	.319	9	17	.529	11	22	33	67	65	1	15	4	67	2.2	8
Wilson	5	59	2	14	.143	4	6	.667	2	1	3	11	3	0	4	1	8	1.6	3

3-Pt. FG: Atlanta 13-75 (.173)—Drew 0-7 (.000); Johnson 5-13 (.385); Roundfield 0-4 (.000); Hawes 3-8 (.375); McElroy (Tot) 5-21 (.238); (Atl) 2-7 (.286); McMillen 0-1 (.000); Furlow 1-9 (.111); Criss 1-17 (.059); Hill 1-4 (.250); Givens 0-2 (.000); Lee 0-3 (.000). Opponents 46-183 (.251).

BOSTON

Player	G.	Min.	FGM	FGA	Pct.	FTM	FTA	Pct.	Off. Reb.	Def. Reb.	Tot. Reb.	Ast.	PF	Dsq.	Stl.	Blk. Sh.	Pts.	Avg.	Hi.
Bird	82	2955	693	1463	.474	301	360	.836	216	636	852	370	279	4	143	53	1745	21.3	45
Maxwell	80	2744	457	750	.609	436	554	.787	284	420	704	199	266	6	76	61	1350	16.9	29
Cowens	66	2159	422	932	.453	95	122	.779	126	408	534	206	216	2	69	61	940	14.2	32
Archibald	80	2864	383	794	.482	361	435	.830	59	138	197	671	218	2	106	10	1131	14.1	29
Marav'h (Tot)	43	964	244	543	.449	91	105	.867	17	61	78	83	79	1	24	6	589	13.7	31
Marav'h (Bos)	26	442	123	249	.494	50	55	.909	10	28	38	29	49	1	9	2	299	11.5	31
Robey	82	1918	379	727	.521	184	269	.684	209	321	530	92	244	2	53	15	942	11.5	27
Ford	73	2115	330	709	.465	86	114	.754	77	104	181	215	178	0	111	27	816	11.2	27
Carr	82	1994	362	763	.474	178	241	.739	106	224	330	156	214	1	120	36	914	11.1	25
Henderson	76	1061	191	382	.500	89	129	.690	37	46	83	147	96	0	45	15	473	6.2	17
Judkins	65	674	139	276	.504	62	76	.816	32	34	66	47	91	0	29	5	351	5.4	17
Fernsten	56	431	71	153	.464	33	52	.635	40	56	96	28	43	0	17	12	175	3.1	11
Chaney	60	523	67	189	.354	32	42	.762	31	42	73	38	80	1	31	11	167	2.8	8

3-Pt. FG: Boston 162-422 (.384)—Bird 58-143 (.406); Cowens 1-12 (.083); Archibald 4-18 (.222); Maravich (Tot) 10-15 (.667), (Bos) 3-4 (.750); Robey 0-1 (.000); Ford 70-164 (.427); Carr 12-41 (.293); Henderson 2-6 (.333); Judkins 11-27 (.407); Chaney 1-6 (.167). Opponents 74-259 (.286).

CHICAGO

Player	G.	Min.	FGM	FGA	Pct.	FTM	FTA	Pct.	Off. Reb.	Def. Reb.	Tot. Reb.	Ast.	PF	Dsq.	Stl.	Blk. Sh.	Pts.	Avg.	Hi.
Theus	82	3029	566	1172	.483	500	597	.838	143	186	329	515	262	4	114	20	1660	20.2	33
Gilmore	48	1568	305	513	.595	245	344	.712	108	324	432	133	167	5	29	59	855	17.8	32
Greenwood	82	2791	498	1051	.474	337	416	.810	223	550	773	182	313	8	60	129	1334	16.3	31
Sobers	82	2673	470	1002	.469	200	239	.837	75	167	242	426	294	4	136	17	1161	14.2	33
May	54	1298	264	587	.450	144	172	.837	78	140	218	104	126	2	45	5	672	12.4	26
Jones (Tot)	44	1248	257	506	.508	146	201	.726	114	254	368	101	207	0	28	42	660	8.9	24
Jones (Chi)	53	1170	207	387	.535	119	165	.721	83	213	296	90	159	0	24	37	533	10.1	24
Smith	30	496	97	230	.422	57	63	.905	22	32	54	42	54	0	25	7	259	8.6	22
Landsberger	54	1136	183	346	.529	87	166	.524	157	293	450	32	113	1	23	17	453	8.4	25
Johnson	79	1535	262	527	.497	82	93	.882	50	113	163	161	165	0	59	24	607	7.7	21
Dietrick	79	1830	227	500	.454	90	118	.763	101	262	363	216	230	2	89	51	545	6.9	19
Mengelt	36	387	90	166	.542	39	49	.796	3	20	23	38	54	0	10	0	219	6.1	21
Mack (Tot)	50	681	98	199	.492	38	51	.745	32	39	71	53	50	0	24	3	234	4.7	18
Mack (Chi)	23	526	77	149	.517	29	33	.879	25	24	49	33	34	0	20	3	183	8.0	18
Beshore	68	869	88	250	.352	58	87	.667	16	47	63	139	105	0	58	5	244	3.6	15
Awtrey	26	560	27	60	.450	32	50	.640	29	86	115	40	66	0	12	15	86	3.3	9
Brown	4	37	1	3	.333	0	0	.000	2	8	10	1	4	0	0	3	2	0.5	2

3-Pt. FG: Chicago 70-275 (.255)—Theus 28-105 (.267); Greenwood 1-7 (.143); Sobers 21-68 (.309); May 0-4 (.000); Smith 8-35 (.229); Johnson 1-11 (.091); Dietrick 1-9 (.111); Mengelt 0-6 (.000); Mack (Tot) 0-5 (.000); (Chi) 0-4 (.000); Beshore 10-26 (.385). Opponents 54-199 (.271).

1979-80 STATISTICS

CLEVELAND

Player	G.	Min.	FGM	FGA	Pct.	FTM	FTA	Pct.	Off. Reb.	Def. Reb.	Tot. Reb.	Ast.	PF	Dsq.	Stl.	Blk. Sh.	Pts.	Avg.	Hi.
Mitchell	82	2802	775	1482	.523	270	343	.787	206	385	591	93	259	4	70	77	1820	22.2	46
Russell	41	1331	284	630	.451	178	239	.745	76	149	225	173	113	1	72	20	747	18.2	33
R. Smith	82	2677	599	1326	.452	233	283	.823	93	163	256	363	190	1	125	7	1441	17.6	36
Robisch	82	2670	489	940	.520	277	329	.842	225	433	658	192	211	2	53	53	1255	15.3	36
A. Carr	77	1549	390	839	.465	127	172	.738	81	84	165	150	120	0	39	3	909	11.8	32
K. Carr (Tot)	79	1838	378	768	.492	173	263	.658	199	389	588	77	246	3	66	52	929	11.8	32
K. Carr (Clev)	74	1781	371	752	.493	171	261	.655	194	377	571	76	240	3	64	51	913	12.3	32
Walker	76	2422	258	568	.454	195	243	.802	78	209	287	607	202	2	155	12	712	9.4	23
B. Smith	8	135	33	72	.458	7	8	.875	2	12	14	7	21	0	3	2	74	9.3	17
Willoughby	78	1447	219	457	.479	96	127	.756	122	207	329	72	189	0	32	62	535	6.9	20
Lambert	74	1324	165	400	.413	73	101	.723	138	214	352	56	203	4	47	42	403	5.4	18
W. Smith	62	1051	121	315	.384	40	52	.769	56	65	121	259	110	1	75	1	299	4.8	14
Ford (Tot)	73	999	131	274	.478	45	53	.849	44	141	185	65	131	0	22	21	308	4.2	17
Ford (Clev)	21	419	65	144	.451	22	25	.880	21	66	87	29	45	0	11	6	153	7.3	17
Frazier	3	27	4	11	.364	2	2	1.000	1	2	3	8	2	0	2	1	10	3.3	6
Tatum	33	225	36	94	.383	11	19	.579	1	*15	26	20	29	0	16	5	85	2.6	11
Lee	3	24	2	11	.182	0	1	.000	3	0	3	0	0	0	0	0	4	1.3	2

3-Pt. FG: Cleveland 36-255 (.193)—Mitchell 0-6 (.000); Russell 1-9 (.111); R. Smith 10-53 (.189); Robisch 0-3 (.000); A. Carr 2-6 (.333); K. Carr (Clev.) 0-4 (.000); Walker 1-9 (.111); B. Smith 1-5 (.200); Willoughby 1-9 (.111); Lambert 0-3 (.000); W. Smith 17-71 (.239); Ford (Tot) 1-3 (.333), Ford (Clev) 1-2 (.500); Frazier 0-1 (.000); Tatum 2-6 (.333). Opponents 65-223 (.291).

DENVER

Player	G.	Min.	FGM	FGA	Pct.	FTM	FTA	Pct.	Off. Reb.	Def. Reb.	Tot. Reb.	Ast.	PF	Dsq.	Stl.	Blk. Sh.	Pts.	Avg.	Hi.
Issel	82	2938	715	1416	.505	517	667	.775	236	483	719	198	190	1	88	54	1951	23.8	47
Thompson	39	1239	289	617	.468	254	335	.758	56	118	174	124	106	0	39	38	839	21.5	38
English(Tot)	78	2401	553	1113	.497	210	266	.789	269	336	605	224	206	0	73	62	1318	16.9	40
English(Den)	24	875	207	427	.485	96	126	.762	102	123	225	82	78	0	28	29	512	21.3	40
McGinnis	45	1424	268	584	.459	166	307	.541	134	328	462	221	187	8	69	17	703	15.6	43
Wilkerson	75	2381	430	1030	.417	166	222	.748	85	231	316	243	194	1	93	27	1033	13.8	31
Roche	82	2286	354	741	.478	175	202	.866	24	91	115	405	139	0	82	12	932	11.4	33
Boswell	18	522	72	135	.533	58	70	.829	40	74	114	46	56	1	5	8	203	11.3	24
Johnson	75	1938	309	649	.476	148	189	.783	190	394	584	157	260	4	84	67	768	10.2	30
Scott	69	1860	276	688	.401	85	118	.720	51	115	166	250	197	3	47	23	639	9.3	30
Roberts	23	486	69	181	.381	39	60	.650	54	55	109	20	52	1	13	3	177	7.7	18
Gondrezick	59	1020	148	286	.517	92	121	.760	107	152	259	81	119	0	68	16	390	6.6	20
Garland	78	1106	155	356	.435	18	26	.692	50	88	138	145	80	1	54	4	334	4.3	17
Ellis	48	502	61	136	.449	40	53	.755	51	65	116	30	67	1	10	24	162	3.4	12
Hughes	70	1208	102	202	.505	15	41	.366	125	201	326	74	184	3	66	77	219	3.1	14
Kramer	8	45	7	22	.318	2	2	1.000	6	6	12	3	8	0	0	5	16	2.0	10

3-Pt. FG: Denver 83-255 (.325)—Issel 4-12 (.333); Thompson 7-19 (.368); English (Tot.) 2-6 (.333), English (Den.) 2-3 (.667); McGinnis 1-7 (.143); Wilkerson 7-34 (.206); Roche 49-129 (.380); Boswell 1-2 (.500); Johnson 2-9 (.222); Scott 2-11 (.182); Roberts 0-1 (.000); Gondrezick 2-6 (.333); Garland 6-19 (.316); Ellis 0-3 (.000). Opponents 70-214 (.327).

DETROIT

Player	G.	Min.	FGM	FGA	Pct.	FTM	FTA	Pct.	Off. Reb.	Def. Reb.	Tot. Reb.	Ast.	PF	Dsq.	Stl.	Blk. Sh.	Pts.	Avg.	Hi.
Lanier	37	1392	319	584	.546	164	210	.781	108	265	373	122	130	2	38	60	802	21.7	34
McAdoo	58	2097	492	1025	.480	235	322	.730	100	367	467	200	178	3	73	65	1222	21.7	37
Long	69	2364	588	1164	.505	160	194	.825	152	185	337	206	221	4	129	26	1337	19.4	38
Kelser	50	1233	280	593	.472	146	203	.719	124	152	276	108	176	5	60	34	709	14.2	34
Tyler	82	2670	430	925	.465	143	187	.765	228	399	627	129	237	3	107	220	1005	12.3	29
McElroy	36	1012	162	356	.455	95	119	.798	12	38	50	162	78	1	25	14	422	11.7	33
Money(Tot)	61	1549	273	546	.500	83	106	.783	31	73	104	254	146	3	53	11	629	10.3	26
Money(Det)	55	1467	259	510	.508	81	104	.779	28	69	97	238	135	3	53	10	599	10.9	26
Shumate	0	228	35	65	.538	17	25	.680	-18	52	70	9	16	0	9	5	87	9.7	20
Benson(Tot)	73	1891	299	618	.484	99	141	.702	126	327	453	178	246	4	73	92	698	9.6	25
Benson(Det)	17	502	86	187	.460	33	44	.750	30	90	120	51	68	3	19	18	206	12.1	26
Duerod	67	1331	282	598	.472	45	66	.682	29	69	98	117	102	0	41	11	624	9.3	28
Hubbard	64	1189	210	451	.466	165	220	.750	114	206	320	70	202	9	48	10	585	9.1	30
Douglas	70	1782	221	455	.486	125	185	.676	171	330	501	121	249	10	30	62	567	8.1	23
Lee(Tot)	61	1167	113	305	.370	44	70	.629	40	83	123	241	172	5	99	17	292	4.8	23
Lee(Det)	31	803	84	214	.393	35	53	.660	29	61	90	174	107	4	84	13	225	7.3	23
Hamilton	72	1116	115	287	.401	103	150	.687	45	62	107	192	82	0	48	5	333	4.6	17
Evans	36	381	63	140	.450	24	42	.571	26	49	75	37	64	0	14	1	157	4.4	16
Robinson	7	51	9	17	.529	9	11	.818	3	2	5	0	8	0	3	2	27	3.9	10
Malovic(Tot)	39	445	31	67	.463	18	27	.667	36	50	86	26	51	0	8	6	80	2.1	9
Malovic(Det)	10	162	8	25	.320	10	14	.714	9	19	28	14	16	0	2	5	26	2.6	9

3-Pt. FG: Detroit 57-219 (.260)—Lanier (Tot.) 0-5 (.000); (Det.) 0-5 (.000); McAdoo 3-24 (.125); Long 1-12 (.083); Kelser 3-15 (.200); Tyler 2-12 (.167); McElroy 3-14 (.214); Benson (Tot.) 1-5 (.200); (Det.) 1-4 (.250); Duerod 15-53 (.283); Hubbard 0-2 (.000); Douglas 0-1 (.000); Lee (Tot.) 22-59 (.373); (Det.) 22-56 (.393); Hamilton 0-2 (.000); Evans 7-18 (.389); Robinson 0-1 (.000). Opponents 57-206 (.277).

1979-80 STATISTICS

GOLDEN STATE

Player	G.	Min.	FGM	FGA	Pct.	FTM	FTA	Pct.	Off. Reb.	Def. Reb.	Tot. Reb.	Ast.	PF	Dsq.	Stl.	Blk. Sh.	Pts.	Avg.	Hi.
Short	62	1636	461	916	.503	134	165	.812	119	197	316	123	186	4	63	9	1056	17.0	37
Parish	72	2119	510	1006	.507	203	284	.715	247	536	783	122	248	6	58	115	1223	17.0	29
Smith	51	1552	325	685	.474	135	171	.789	28	118	146	187	154	1	62	15	792	15.5	29
Parker	82	2849	483	988	.489	237	302	.785	166	298	464	254	195	2	173	32	1203	14.7	36
Lucas	80	2763	388	830	.467	222	289	.768	61	159	220	602	196	2	138	3	1010	12.6	27
Cooper	79	1781	367	750	.489	136	181	.751	202	305	507	42	246	5	20	79	871	11.0	30
White	78	2052	336	706	.476	97	114	.851	42	139	181	239	186	0	88	13	770	9.9	21
Ray	81	1683	203	383	.530	84	149	.564	122	344	466	183	266	6	51	32	490	6.0	19
Townsend	75	1159	171	421	.406	60	84	.714	33	56	89	116	113	0	60	4	406	5.4	17
Abernethy	67	1222	153	318	.481	56	82	.683	62	129	191	87	118	0	35	12	362	5.4	20
Hillman	49	708	82	179	.458	34	68	.500	59	121	180	47	128	2	21	24	198	4.0	19
Johnson	9	53	12	30	.400	3	5	.600	6	8	14	2	11	0	1	0	27	3.0	6
Coughran	24	160	29	81	.358	8	14	.571	2	17	19	12	24	0	7	1	68	2.8	11
Wilson	16	143	7	25	.280	3	6	.500	6	10	16	12	11	0	2	0	17	1.1	4

3-Pt. FG: Golden State 27-121 (.223)—Short 0-6 (.000); Parish 0-1 (.000); Smith 7-22 (.318); Parker 0-2 (.000); Lucas 12-42 (.286); Cooper 1-4 (.250); White 1-6 (.167); Ray 0-2 (.000); Townsend 4-26 (.154); Abernethy 0-1 (.000); Coughran 2-9 (.222). Opponents 72-219 (.329).

HOUSTON

Player	G.	Min.	FGM	FGA	Pct.	FTM	FTA	Pct.	Off. Reb.	Def. Reb.	Tot. Reb.	Ast.	PF	Dsq.	Stl.	Blk. Sh.	Pts.	Avg.	Hi.
Malone	82	3140	778	1549	.502	563	783	.719	573	617	1190	147	210	0	80	107	2119	25.8	45
Murphy	76	2676	624	1267	.493	271	302	.897	68	82	150	299	269	3	143	9	1520	20.0	38
Tomjanovich	62	1834	370	778	.476	118	147	.803	132	226	358	109	161	2	32	10	880	14.2	27
Reid	76	2304	419	861	.487	153	208	.736	140	301	441	244	281	2	132	57	991	13.0	31
Barry	72	1816	325	771	.422	143	153	.935	53	183	236	268	182	0	80	28	866	12.0	30
Leavell	77	2123	330	656	.503	180	221	.814	57	127	184	417	197	1	127	28	843	10.9	22
Paultz(Tot)	84	2193	327	673	.486	109	182	.599	187	399	586	188	213	3	69	84	764	9.1	28
Paultz(Hou)	38	980	138	292	.473	43	82	.524	92	173	265	70	86	0	22	39	319	8.6	28
Dunleavy	51	1036	148	319	.464	111	134	.828	26	74	100	210	120	2	40	4	410	8.0	31
D.Jones	21	278	50	119	.420	27	36	.750	31	41	72	11	48	0	4	5	127	6.0	23
Henderson	66	1551	154	323	.477	56	77	.727	34	77	111	274	107	1	55	4	364	5.5	19
M. Jones	82	1545	188	392	.480	61	108	.565	147	234	381	67	186	0	50	67	438	5.3	17
Shumate	29	332	34	64	.531	33	44	.750	25	54	79	23	39	0	8	9	101	3.5	12
White	9	106	13	24	.542	10	13	.769	0	9	9	5	8	0	5	0	36	4.0	11
Mokeski	12	113	11	33	.333	7	9	.778	14	15	29	2	24	0	1	6	29	2.4	6
Bradley	22	94	17	48	.354	9	9	.667	2	4	6	3	9	0	3	0	43	1.9	8

3-Pt. FG: Houston 104-379 (.274)—Malone 0-6 (.000); Murphy 1-25 (.040); Tomjanovich 22-79 (.278); Reid 0-3 (.000); Barry 73-221 (.330); Leavell 3-19 (.158); Dunleavy 3-20 (.150); Henderson 0-2 (.000); M. Jones 1-3 (.333); Bradley 1-1 (1.000). Opponents 58-215 (.270).

INDIANA

Player	G.	Min.	FGM	FGA	Pct.	FTM	FTA	Pct.	Off. Reb.	Def. Reb.	Tot. Reb.	Ast.	PF	Dsq.	Stl.	Blk. Sh.	Pts.	Avg.	Hi.
M. Johnson	82	2647	588	1271	.463	385	482	.799	258	423	681	344	291	11	153	112	1566	19.1	41
J. Davis	82	2912	496	1159	.428	304	352	.864	102	124	226	440	178	0	110	23	1300	15.9	32
Edwards	82	2314	528	1032	.512	231	339	.681	179	399	578	127	324	12	55	104	1287	15.7	35
English	54	1526	346	686	.504	114	140	.814	167	213	380	142	128	0	45	33	806	14.9	37
McG'nis (Tot)	73	2208	400	886	.451	270	488	.553	222	477	699	333	303	12	101	23	1072	14.7	43
McG'nis (Ind)	28	784	132	302	.437	104	181	.575	68	149	237	112	116	4	32	6	369	13.2	31
Knight	75	1910	385	722	.533	212	262	.809	136	225	361	155	96	0	82	9	986	13.1	44
Bantom	77	2330	384	760	.505	139	209	.665	192	264	456	279	268	7	85	49	908	11.8	27
Bradley	82	2027	275	609	.452	136	174	.782	69	154	223	252	194	1	211	48	688	8.4	22
Chenier (Tot)	43	673	136	349	.390	49	67	.731	19	59	78	89	55	0	33	15	326	7.6	22
Chenier (Ind)	23	380	52	135	.385	18	26	.692	9	26	35	47	29	0	15	10	124	5.4	14
Hassett	74	1135	215	509	.422	24	29	.828	35	59	94	104	85	0	46	8	523	7.1	23
C. Johnson	79	1541	199	396	.503	74	117	.632	145	249	394	115	211	2	48	121	472	6.0	22
Carter	13	117	15	37	.405	2	7	.286	5	14	19	9	19	0	2	3	32	2.5	6
Zeno	8	59	6	21	.286	2	2	1.000	3	11	14	1	13	0	4	3	14	1.8	4
B. Davis	5	43	2	7	.286	3	4	.750	0	2	2	5	7	0	3	0	7	1.4	5
Kuester	24	100	12	34	.353	5	7	.714	3	11	14	16	8	0	7	1	29	1.2	6
Calhoun	7	30	4	9	.444	0	2	.000	7	3	10	0	6	0	2	0	8	1.1	2

3-Pt. FG: Indiana 88-314 (.280)—M. Johnson 5-32 (.156); J. Davis 4-42 (.095); Edwards 0-1 (.000); English 0-3 (.000); McGinnis (Tot.) 2-15 (.133); (Ind.) 1-8 (.125); Knight 4-15 (.267); Bantom 1-3 (.333); Bradley 2-5 (.400); Chenier (Tot.) 5-12 (.417); (Ind.) 2-6 (.333); Hassett 69-198 (.348); Kuester 0-1 (.000). Opponents 56-228 (.246).

KANSAS CITY

Player	G.	Min.	FGM	FGA	Pct.	FTM	FTA	Pct.	Off. Reb.	Def. Reb.	Tot Reb.	Ast.	PF	Dsq.	Stl.	Blk. Sh.	Pts.	Avg.	Hi.
Birdsong	82	2885	781	1546	.505	286	412	.694	170	161	331	202	226	2	136	22	1858	22.7	49
Wedman	68	2347	569	1112	.512	145	181	.801	114	272	386	145	230	1	84	45	1290	19.0	45
Ford	82	2621	489	1058	.462	346	423	.818	29	143	172	610	208	0	136	4	1328	16.2	35
Robinzine	81	1917	362	723	.501	200	274	.730	184	342	526	62	311	5	106	23	925	11.4	28
Lacey	81	2412	303	677	.448	137	185	.741	172	473	645	460	307	8	111	109	743	9.2	24
King	82	2052	257	499	.515	159	219	.726	184	382	566	106	230	2	69	31	673	8.2	21
Green	21	459	69	159	.434	24	42	.571	35	78	113	28	55	0	13	21	162	7.7	21
McKinney	76	1333	206	459	.449	107	133	.805	20	66	86	248	87	0	58	5	520	6.8	26
Grunfeld	80	1397	186	420	.443	101	131	.771	87	145	232	109	151	1	56	9	474	5.9	18
Redmond	24	298	59	138	.428	24	34	.706	18	34	52	19	27	0	4	9	142	5.9	19
Gerard	73	869	159	348	.457	66	100	.660	77	100	177	43	96	1	41	26	385	5.3	25
Elmore	58	915	104	242	.430	51	74	.689	74	183	257	64	154	0	41	39	259	4.5	23
Burleson	37	272	36	104	.346	23	40	.575	23	49	72	20	49	0	8	13	95	2.6	12
Crosby	4	28	2	4	.500	2	2	1.000	0	1	1	7	4	0	0	0	6	1.5	4

3-Pt. FG: Kansas City 25-114 (.219)—Birdsong 10-36 (.278); Wedman 7-22 (.318); Ford 4-23 (.174); Robinzine 1-2 (.500); Lacey 0-1 (.000); King 0-1 (.000); Green 0-2 (.000); McKinney 1-10 (.100); Grunfeld 1-2 (.500); Redmond 0-9 (.000); Gerard 1-3 (.333); Burleson 0-3 (.000). Opponents 41-172 (.238).

LOS ANGELES

Player	G.	Min.	FGM	FGA	Pct.	FTM	FTA	Pct.	Off. Reb.	Def. Reb.	Tot Reb.	Ast.	PF	Dsq.	Stl.	Blk. Sh.	Pts.	Avg.	Hi.
Abdul-Jabbar	82	3143	835	1383	.604	364	476	.765	190	696	886	371	216	2	81	280	2034	24.8	42
Wilkes	82	3111	726	1358	.535	189	234	.808	176	349	525	250	220	1	129	28	1644	20.0	30
Johnson	77	2795	503	949	.530	374	462	.810	166	430	596	563	218	1	187	41	1387	18.0	31
Nixon	82	3226	624	1209	.516	197	253	.779	52	177	229	642	241	1	147	14	1446	17.6	30
Chones	82	2394	372	760	.489	125	169	.740	143	421	564	151	271	5	56	65	869	10.6	23
Haywood	76	1544	288	591	.487	159	206	.772	132	214	346	93	197	2	35	57	736	9.7	25
Cooper	82	1973	303	578	.524	111	143	.776	101	128	229	221	215	3	86	38	722	8.8	20
Lands'r (Tot)	77	1510	249	483	.516	116	222	.523	226	387	613	46	140	1	33	22	614	8.0	25
Landsb'r (LA)	23	374	66	137	.482	29	56	.518	69	94	163	14	27	0	10	5	161	7.0	14
Boone	6	106	14	40	.350	6	7	.857	4	7	11	7	13	0	5	0	34	5.7	10
Carr	5	57	7	16	.438	2	2	1.000	5	12	17	1	6	0	2	1	16	3.2	6
Ford	52	580	66	130	.508	23	28	.821	23	75	98	36	86	0	11	15	155	3.0	15
Holland	38	197	44	104	.423	15	16	.938	4	13	17	22	24	0	15	1	106	2.8	12
Byrnes	32	194	25	50	.500	13	15	.867	9	18	27	13	32	0	5	1	63	2.0	11
Mack	27	155	21	50	.420	9	18	.500	7	15	22	20	16	0	4	0	51	1.9	10
Lee (Tot)	14	55	6	24	.250	6	8	.750	7	4	11	12	2	0	1	0	18	1.3	4
Lee (LA)	11	31	4	13	.308	6	7	.857	4	4	8	9	2	0	1	0	14	1.3	4

3-Pt. FG: Los Angeles 20-100 (.200)—Abdul-Jabbar 0-1 (.000); Wilkes 3-17 (.176); Johnson 7-31 (.226); Nixon 1-8 (.125); Chones 0-2 (.000); Haywood 1-4 (.250); Cooper 5-20 (.250); Ford 0-1 (.000); Holland 3-15 (.200); Mack 0-1 (.000). Opponents 78-274 (.285).

MILWAUKEE

Player	G.	Min.	FGM	FGA	Pct.	FTM	FTA	Pct.	Off. Reb.	Def. Reb.	Tot Reb.	Ast.	PF	Dsq.	Stl.	Blk. Sh.	Pts.	Avg.	Hi.
Johnson	77	2686	689	1267	.544	291	368	.791	217	349	566	273	173	0	100	70	1671	21.7	37
Lanier (Tot)	63	2131	466	867	.537	277	354	.782	152	400	552	184	200	3	74	89	1210	19.2	34
Lanier (Mil)	26	739	147	283	.519	113	144	.785	44	135	179	62	70	1	36	29	408	15.7	32
Bridgeman	81	2316	594	1243	.478	230	266	.865	104	197	301	237	216	3	94	20	1423	17.6	35
Winters	80	2623	535	1116	.479	184	214	.860	48	175	223	362	208	0	101	24	1292	16.2	34
Meyers	79	2204	399	830	.481	156	246	.634	140	308	448	225	218	3	72	40	955	12.1	28
Buckner	77	1690	306	655	.467	105	143	.734	69	169	238	383	202	1	135	4	719	10.7	40
Benson	56	1389	213	431	.494	66	97	.680	96	237	333	127	178	1	54	74	492	8.8	19
Moncrief	77	1557	211	451	.468	232	292	.795	154	184	338	133	106	0	72	16	654	8.5	23
Cummings	71	900	187	370	.505	94	123	.764	81	157	238	53	141	0	22	17	468	6.6	30
Washington	75	1092	197	421	.468	46	76	.605	95	181	276	55	166	2	26	48	440	5.9	20
Walton	76	1243	110	242	.455	49	71	.690	33	58	91	285	68	0	43	2	270	3.6	18
Catchings	72	1366	97	244	.398	39	62	.629	164	246	410	82	191	1	23	162	233	3.2	12

3-Pt. FG: Milwaukee 50-155 (.323)—Johnson 2-9 (.222); Lanier (Tot.) 1-6 (.167); (Mil.) 1-1 (1.000); Bridgeman 5-27 (.185); Winters 38-102 (.373); Meyers 1-5 (.200); Buckner 2-5 (.400); Benson 0-1 (.000); Moncrief 0-1 (.000); Walton 1-3 (.333); Catchings 0-1 (.000). Opponents 76-305 (.249).

1979-80 STATISTICS

NEW JERSEY

Player	G.	Min.	FGM	FGA	Pct.	FTM	FTA	Pct.	Off. Reb.	Def. Reb.	Tot. Reb.	Ast.	PF	Dsq.	Stl.	Blk. Sh.	Pts.	Avg.	Hi.
Newlin	78	2510	611	1329	.460	367	415	.884	101	163	264	314	195	1	115	4	1634	20.9	52
Natt	53	2046	421	879	.479	199	280	.711	173	340	513	112	148	1	78	22	1042	19.7	33
Williamson	28	771	206	461	.447	76	88	3864	24	30	54	87	71	1	26	9	496	17.7	32
Lucas(Tot)	63	1884	371	813	.456	179	239	.749	143	394	537	208	223	2	42	62	923	14.7	32
Lucas(NJ)	22	708	128	261	.490	79	102	.775	58	154	212	83	82	1	19	27	335	25.2	32
Robinson	70	1661	391	833	.469	168	242	.694	174	332	506	98	178	1	61	34	951	13.6	45
Jordan	82	2657	437	1017	.430	201	258	.779	62	208	270	557	238	7	223	27	1087	13.3	28
Phegley(Tot)	78	1512	350	733	.477	177	203	.872	75	110	185	102	158	1	34	7	881	11.3	35
Phegley(NJ)	28	541	126	260	.485	73	83	.880	26	44	70	32	52	0	15	4	327	11.7	26
Kelley	57	1466	186	399	.466	197	250	.788	156	241	397	128	215	5	50	79	569	10.0	26
Boynes	64	1102	221	467	.473	104	136	.765	51	82	133	95	132	1	59	14	546	8.5	32
Johnson	81	2119	248	543	.457	89	126	.706	192	410	602	173	312	7	53	258	585	7.2	22
van B. Kolff	82	2399	212	458	.463	130	155	.839	103	326	429	247	307	11	100	76	564	6.8	18
Elliott	54	722	228	.443	104	152	.684		67	118	185	53	97	0	29	14	307	5.7	18
Simpson	8	81	18	47	.383	5	10	.500	6	5	11	14	3	0	9	0	41	5.1	12
Smith(Tot)	65	809	118	269	.439	80	92	.870	20	59	79	92	105	1	26	4	324	5.0	17
Smith(NJ)	59	736	113	254	.445	75	87	.862	17	59	76	85	102	1	22	4	309	5.2	17
Jackson	16	194	29	46	.630	7	10	.700	12	12	24	12	35	1	5	4	65	4.1	14
Bassett	7	92	8	22	.364	8	12	.667	7	11	18	4	14	0	5	0	24	3.4	11

3-Pt. FG: 85-298 (.285)—Newlin 45-152 (.296); Natt 1-5 (.200); Williamson 8-19 (.421); Lucas (Tot.) 2-9 (.222), (NJ) 0-4 (.000); Robinson 1-4 (.250); Jordan 12-48 (.250); Phegley (Tot.) 1-4 .9 (.444), (NJ) 2-4 (.500); Kelley 0-3 (.000); Boynes 0-4 (.000); Johnson 0-1 (.000); van Breda Kolff 7-20 (.350); Elliott 1-4 (.250); Simpson 0-2 (.000); Smith (Tot.) 8-26 (.308), (NJ) 8-26 (.308); Jackson 0-2 (.000). Opponents 58-208 (.279).

NEW YORK

Player	G.	Min.	FGM	FGA	Pct.	FTM	FTA	Pct.	Off. Reb.	Def. Reb.	Tot. Reb.	Ast.	PF	Dsq.	Stl.	Blk. Sh.	Pts.	Avg.	Hi.
Cartwright	82	3150	665	1215	.547	451	566	.797	194	532	726	165	279	2	48	101	1781	21.7	37
R. Williams	82	2582	687	1384	.496	333	423	.787	149	263	412	512	295	5	167	24	1714	20.9	39
Knight	81	2945	669	1265	.529	211	261	.808	201	292	493	150	302	4	117	86	1549	19.1	34
Richardson	82	3060	502	1063	.472	223	338	.660	151	388	539	832	260	3	265	35	1254	15.3	28
Meriweather	65	1565	252	477	78	121	.645		122	228	350	66	239	8	37	120	582	9.0	24
Monroe	51	633	161	352	.457	56	64	.875	16	20	36	67	46	0	21	3	378	7.4	25
Demic	82	1872	230	528	.436	110	183	.601	195	288	483	64	306	10	56	30	570	7.0	19
Glenn	75	800	188	364	.516	63	73	.863	21	45	66	85	79	0	35	7	441	5.9	19
Copeland	75	1142	182	368	.495	63	86	.733	70	86	156	80	154	0	61	25	427	5.7	19
S. Williams	57	556	104	267	.390	58	90	.644	65	56	121	36	73	0	19	8	266	4.7	21
Webster	20	298	38	79	.481	12	16	.750	28	52	80	9	39	1	3	11	88	4.4	13
Cleamons	22	254	30	69	.435	12	15	.800	10	9	19	40	13	0	13	2	75	3.4	13
Huston	71	923	94	241	.390	28	38	.737	14	44	58	159	83	0	39	5	219	3.1	14

3-Pt. FG: New York 42-191 (.220); R. Williams 7-37 (.189); Knight 0-2 (.000); Richardson 27-110 (.245); Meriweather 0-1 (.000); Glenn 2-10 (.200); Copeland 0-2 (.000); S. Williams 0-4 (.000); Cleamons 3-8 (.375); Huston 3-17 (.176). Opponents 55-198 (.278).

PHILADELPHIA

Player	G.	Min.	FGM	FGA	Pct.	FTM	FTA	Pct.	Off. Reb.	Def. Reb.	Tot. Reb.	Ast.	PF	Dsq.	Stl.	Blk. Sh.	Pts.	Avg.	Hi.
Erving	78	2812	838	1614	.5194	20	534	.787	215	361	576	355	208	0	170	140	2100	26.9	44
Dawkins	80	2541	494	946	.522	190	291	.653	197	496	693	149	238	8	49	142	1178	14.7	34
Collins	36	963	191	410	.466	113	124	.911	29	65	94	100	76	0	30	7	495	13.8	33
B. Jones	81	2125	398	748	.532	257	329	.781	152	298	450	146	223	3	102	118	1053	13.0	26
Mix	81	1543	363	703	.516	207	249	.831	114	176	290	149	114	0	67	9	937	11.6	25
Cheeks	79	2623	357	661	.540	180	231	.779	75	199	274	556	197	1	183	32	898	11.4	27
Hollins(Tot)	47	1209	212	526	.403	101	140	.721	29	60	89	162	103	0	76	10	528	11.2	26
Hollins(Phil)	27	796	130	313	.415	67	87	.770	24	45	69	112	68	0	46	9	329	12.2	26
Bibby	82	2035	226	526	.401	226	286	.790	65	143	208	307	161	0	62	6	739	9.0	21
C. Jones	80	2771	232	532	.426	124	178	.697	219	731	950	164	298	5	43	162	588	7.4	20
Richardson	52	988	159	348	.457	28	45	.622	55	68	123	107	97	0	24	15	347	6.7	24
Spanarkel	40	442	72	153	.471	54	65	.831	27	27	54	51	58	0	12	6	198	5.0	19
Money	6	82	14	36	.389	2	2	1.000	3	4	7	16	11	0	0	1	30	5.0	10
Toone	23	124	23	64	.359	8	10	.800	12	22	34	12	20	0	4	5	55	2.4	8
Skinner	2	10	1	2	.500	0	0	.000	0	0	0	2	1	0	0	0	2	1.0	2

3-Pt. FG: Philadelphia 27-125 (.216); Erving 4-20 (.200); Dawkins 0-6 (.000); Collins 0-1 (.000); B. Jones 0-3 (.000); Mix 4-10 (.400); Cheeks (.444); Hollins (Tot.) 3-20 (.150); (Phil.) 2-10).200); Bibby 11-52 (.212); C. Jones 0-2 (.000); Richardson 1-3 (.333); Spanarkel 0-2 (.000); Toone 1-7 (.143). Opponents 75-277 (.271).

1979-80 STATISTICS

PHOENIX

Player	G.	Min	FGM	FGA	Pct.	FTM	FTA	Pct.	Off. Reb.	Def. Reb.	Tot. Reb.	Ast.	PF	Dsq.	Stl.	Blk. Sh.	Pts.	Avg.	Hi.
Westphal	82	2665	692	1317	.525	382	443	.862	46	141	187	416	162	0	119	35	1792	21.9	49
Davis	75	2309	657	1166	.563	299	365	.819	75	197	272	337	202	2	114	19	1613	21.5	40
Robinson	82	2710	545	1064	.512	325	487	.667	213	557	770	142	262	2	58	59	1415	17.3	34
Adams	75	2168	468	875	.531	188	236	.797	158	451	609	322	237	4	108	55	1118	14.9	32
Kelley(Tot)	80	1839	229	484	.473	244	310	.787	200	315	515	178	273	5	78	96	702	8.8	26
Kelley(Phoe)	23	373	43	85	.506	47	60	.783	44	74	118	50	58	0	28	17	133	5.8	10
Bratz	82	1589	269	687	.392	141	162	.870	50	117	167	223	165	0	93	9	700	8.5	21
Buse	81	2499	261	589	.443	85	128	.664	70	163	233	320	111	0	132	10	626	7.7	17
Cook	66	904	129	275	.469	104	129	.806	90	151	241	84	102	0	28	18	362	5.5	16
High	82	1121	144	323	.446	120	178	.674	69	104	173	119	172	1	71	15	409	5.0	18
Heard	82	1403	171	410	.417	64	86	.744	118	262	380	97	177	0	84	49	406	5.0	18
Scott	79	1303	127	301	.422	95	122	.779	89	139	228	98	101	0	47	53	350	4.4	10
Kramer	54	711	67	143	.469	56	70	.800	49	102	151	75	104	0	26	5	190	3.5	13

3-Pt. FG: Phoenix 68-280 (.243); Westphal 26-93 (.280); Davis 0-4 (.000); Adams 0-2 (.000); Kelley (Tot.) 0-3 (.000); Phoe. 0-0 (.000); Bratz 21-86 (.244); Buse 19-79 (.241); Cook 0-3 (.000); High 1-7 (.143); Heard 0-2 (.000); Scott 1-3 (.333); Kramer 0-1 (.000). Opponents 100-297 (.337).

PORTLAND

Player	G.	Min.	FGM	FGA	Pct.	FTM	FTA	Pct.	Off. Reb.	Def. Reb.	Tot. Reb.	Ast.	PF	Dsq.	Stl.	Blk. Sh.	Pts.	Avg.	Hi.
Natt (Tot)	78	2857	622	1298	.479	306	419	.730	239	452	691	169	205	2	102	34	1553	19.9	39
Natt (Port)	25	811	201	419	.480	107	139	.770	66	142	208	57	57	0	24	12	511	20.4	39
Owens	76	2337	518	1008	.514	213	283	.753	189	384	573	194	270	5	45	53	1250	16.4	32
R. Brewer	82	2815	548	1182	.464	184	219	.840	54	160	214	216	154	0	98	48	1286	15.7	33
Lucas	41	1176	243	552	.440	100	137	.730	85	240	325	125	141	1	23	35	588	14.3	30
Washington	80	2657	421	761	.553	231	360	.642	325	517	842	167	307	8	73	131	1073	13.4	27
Bates	16	235	72	146	.493	28	39	.718	13	16	29	31	26	0	14	2	180	11.3	26
Hollins	20	413	82	213	.385	34	53	.642	5	15	20	50	35	0	30	1	199	10.0	24
Jeelani	77	1286	288	565	.510	161	204	.789	114	156	270	95	155	0	40	40	737	9.6	28
Steele	16	446	62	146	.425	22	27	.815	13	32	45	67	53	0	25	1	146	9.1	18
Gross	62	1581	221	472	.468	95	114	.833	84	165	249	228	179	3	60	47	538	8.7	22
Twardzik	67	1594	183	394	.464	197	252	.782	52	104	156	273	149	2	77	1	567	8.5	23
Kunnert	18	302	50	114	.439	26	43	.605	37	75	112	29	59	1	7	22	126	7.0	16
Dunn	82	1841	240	551	.436	84	111	.757	132	192	324	147	145	1	102	31	564	6.9	23
Paxson	72	1270	189	460	.411	64	90	.711	25	84	109	144	97	0	48	5	443	6.2	21
J. Brewer	67	1016	90	184	.489	14	29	.483	101	156	257	75	129	2	42	43	194	2.9	17

3-Pt. FG: Portland 26-132 (.197)—Natt (Tot) 3-9) (.333); (Port) 2-4 (.500); Owens 1-2 (.500); R. Brewer 6-32 (.188); Washington 0-3 (.000); Bates 8-19 (.421); Jeelani 0-6 (.000); Steele 0-4 (.000); Gross 1-10 (.100); Twardzik 4-7 (.571); Dunn 0-3 (.000); Paxson 1-22 (.045); J. Brewer 0-5 (.000); Lucas 2-5 (.400); Hollins 1-10 (.100). Opponents 55-186 (.296).

SAN ANTONIO

Player	G.	Min.	FGM	FGA	Pct.	FTM	FTA	Pct.	Off. Reb.	Def. Reb.	Tot. Reb.	Ast.	PF	Dsq.	Stl.	Blk. Sh.	Pts.	Avg.	Hi.
Gervin	78	2934	1024	1940	.528	505	593	.852	154	249	403	202	208	0	110	79	2585	33.1	55
Kenon	78	2798	647	1333	.485	270	345	.783	258	517	775	231	192	0	111	18	1565	20.1	51
Silas	77	2293	513	999	.514	339	382	.887	45	122	167	347	206	2	61	14	1365	17.7	35
Restani	82	1966	369	727	.508	131	161	.814	142	244	386	189	186	0	54	12	874	10.7	24
Olberding	75	2111	291	609	.478	210	264	.795	83	335	418	327	274	7	67	22	792	10.6	22
Paultz	47	1213	189	381	.496	66	100	.660	95	226	321	118	127	3	47	45	444	9.4	26
S'mate (Tot)	65	1337	207	392	.528	165	216	.764	108	255	363	84	126	1	40	45	579	8.9	29
Shumate (SA)	27	777	138	263	.525	115	147	.782	65	149	214	52	71	1	23	31	391	14.5	29
Gale	67	1474	171	377	.454	97	120	.808	34	118	152	312	134	2	123	13	441	6.6	22
Griffin	82	1812	173	313	.553	174	240	.725	154	284	438	250	306	9	81	53	520	6.3	18
Evans	79	1246	208	464	.448	58	85	.682	29	78	107	230	194	2	60	9	486	6.2	21
Peck	52	628	73	169	.432	34	55	.618	66	117	183	33	100	2	17	23	180	3.5	13
Davis	4	30	6	12	.500	1	2	.500	2	4	6	0	8	0	1	0	13	3.3	9
Kiffin	26	212	32	96	.333	18	25	.720	12	28	40	19	43	0	10	2	82	3.2	12
Bassett (Tot)	12	164	12	34	.353	10	15	.667	11	22	33	14	27	0	8	0	34	2.8	11
Bassett (SA)	5	72	4	12	.333	2	4	.500	4	11	15	10	13	0	3	0	10	2.0	4
Norris	17	189	18	43	.419	4	6	.667	10	33	43	6	41	1	3	12	40	2.4	8

3-Pt. FG: San Antonio 52-206 (.252)—Gervin 32-102 (.314); Kenon 1-9 (.111); Silas 0-4 (.000); Restani 5-29 (.172); Olberding 0-3 (.000); Paultz 0-1 (.000); Shumate (Tot) 0-1 (.000); (SA) 0-1 (.000); Gale 2-13 (.154); Evans 12-42 (.286); Peck 0-2 (.000). Opponents 88-288 (.306).

1979-80 STATISTICS

SAN DIEGO

Player	G.	Min.	FGM	FGA	Pct.	FTM	FTA	Pct.	Off. Reb.	Def. Reb.	Tot. Reb.	Ast.	PF	Dsq.	Stl.	Blk. Sh.	Pts.	Avg.	Hi.
Free	68	2585	737	1556	.474	572	760	.753	129	169	298	283	195	0	81	32	2055	30.2	49
Williams	82	2118	645	1343	.480	194	238	.815	103	89	192	166	145	0	72	9	1526	18.6	51
Walton	14	337	81	161	.503	32	54	.593	28	98	126	34	37	0	8	38	194	13.9	23
Taylor	78	2754	418	895	.467	130	162	.802	76	112	188	335	246	6	147	25	1056	13.5	28
Nater	81	2860	443	799	.554	196	273	.718	352	864	1216	233	259	3	45	37	1082	13.4	28
Smith (Tot)	78	2123	385	891	.432	100	115	.870	94	165	259	100	209	4	62	17	893	11.4	23
Smith (SD)	70	1988	352	819	.430	93	107	.869	92	153	245	93	188	4	59	15	819	11.7	23
Bryant	82	2328	294	682	.431	161	217	.742	171	345	516	144	258	4	102	39	754	9.3	23
Wicks	71	2146	210	496	.423	83	152	.546	138	271	409	213	241	5	76	52	503	7.1	17
Weatherspoon	57	1124	164	378	.434	63	91	.692	83	125	208	54	136	1	34	17	391	6.9	23
Pietkiewicz	50	577	91	179	.508	37	46	.804	26	19	45	94	52	1	25	4	228	4.6	20
Carrington	10	134	15	37	.405	6	8	.750	6	7	13	3	18	0	4	1	36	3.6	9
Whitehead	18	225	27	45	.600	5	8	.278	29	41	70	6	32	0	1	6	59	3.3	11
Barnes	20	287	24	60	.400	16	32	.500	34	43	77	18	52	0	5	12	64	3.2	8
Malovic	28	277	23	42	.548	7	9	.778	27	31	58	12	35	0	5	1	53	1.9	6
Olive	1	15	0	2	.000	0	0	—	0	1	1	0	2	0	0	0	0	0.0	0

3-Pt. FG: San Diego 177-543 (.326)—Free 9-25 (.360); Williams 42-128 (.328); Taylor 90-239 (.377); Nater 0-2 (.000); Smith (Tot) 23-81 (.284); (SD) 22-76 (.289); Bryant 5-34 (.147); Wicks 0-1 (.000); Pietkiewicz 9-36 (.250); Carrington 0-2 (.000). Opponents 43-187 (.230).

SEATTLE

Player	G.	Min.	FGM	FGA	Pct.	FTM	FTA	Pct.	Off. Reb.	Def. Reb.	Tot. Reb.	Ast.	PF	Dsq.	Stl.	Blk. Sh.	Pts.	Avg.	Hi.
Williams	82	2969	739	1533	.482	331	420	.788	127	148	275	397	160	1	200	37	1816	22.1	41
D. Johnson	81	2937	574	1361	.422	380	487	.780	173	241	414	332	267	6	144	82	1540	19.0	36
Sikma	82	2793	470	989	.475	235	292	.805	198	710	908	279	232	5	68	77	1175	14.3	32
Shelton	76	2243	425	802	.530	184	241	.763	199	383	582	145	292	11	92	79	1035	13.6	30
Brown	80	1701	404	843	.479	113	135	.837	35	120	155	174	117	0	65	17	960	12.0	27
J. Johnson	81	2533	377	772	.488	161	201	.801	163	263	426	424	213	1	76	35	915	11.3	22
LaGarde	82	1164	146	306	.477	90	137	.657	127	185	312	91	206	2	19	34	382	4.7	14
Walker	70	844	139	274	.507	48	64	.750	64	106	170	53	102	0	21	4	326	4.7	23
Bailey	67	726	122	271	.450	68	101	.673	71	126	197	28	116	1	21	54	312	4.7	14
Silas	82	1595	113	299	.378	89	136	.654	204	232	436	66	120	0	25	5	315	3.8	14
V. Johnson	38	325	45	115	.391	31	39	.795	19	36	55	54	40	0	19	4	121	3.2	12

3-Pt. FG: Seattle 59-189 (.312)—Williams 7-36 (.194); D. Johnson 12-58 (.207); Sikma 0-1 (.000); Shelton 1-5 (.200); Brown 39-88 (.443) V. Johnson 0-1 (.000). Opponents 59-240 (246).

UTAH

Player	G.	Min.	FGM	FGA	Pct.	FTM	FTA	Pct.	Off. Reb.	Def. Reb.	Tot. Reb.	Ast.	PF	Dsq.	Stl.	Blk. Sh.	Pts.	Avg.	Hi.
Dantley	68	2674	730	1267	.576	443	526	.842	183	333	516	191	211	2	96	14	1903	28.0	50
Maravich	17	522	121	294	.412	41	50	.820	7	33	40	54	30	0	15	4	290	17.1	31
Furlow (Tot)	76	2122	430	926	.464	171	196	.872	70	124	194	293	98	0	73	23	1055	13.9	37
Furlow (Utah)	55	1718	364	765	.476	127	145	.876	47	105	152	221	79	0	54	14	878	16.0	37
Boone (Tot)	81	2392	405	915	.443	175	196	.893	54	173	227	309	232	3	97	3	1004	12.4	35
Boone (Utah)	75	2286	391	875	.447	169	189	.894	50	166	216	302	219	3	92	3	970	12.9	35
Bristow	82	2304	377	785	.480	197	243	.811	170	342	512	341	211	2	88	6	953	11.6	31
Boswell (Tot)	79	2077	346	613	.564	206	273	.755	146	296	442	161	270	9	29	37	903	11.4	25
Boswell (Ut)	61	1555	274	478	.573	148	203	.729	106	222	328	115	214	8	24	29	700	11.5	25
King	19	419	71	137	.518	34	63	.540	24	64	88	52	66	3	7	4	176	9.3	24
Poquette	82	2349	296	566	.523	139	167	.832	124	436	560	131	283	8	45	162	731	8.9	27
Williams	77	1794	232	519	.447	42	60	.700	21	85	106	183	166	0	100	11	506	6.6	22
Calvin	48	772	100	227	.440	105	117	.897	13	71	84	134	72	0	27	0	306	6.4	17
Hardy	76	1600	184	363	.507	51	66	.773	124	275	399	104	207	4	47	87	420	5.5	22
Dawkins	57	776	141	300	.470	33	48	.688	42	83	125	77	112	0	33	9	316	5.5	30
Davis (Tot)	18	268	35	63	.556	13	16	.813	4	13	17	50	28	0	13	1	83	4.6	17
Davis (Utah)	13	225	33	56	.586	10	12	.833	4	11	15	45	21	0	10	1	76	5.8	17
Gianelli	17	285	23	66	.348	9	16	.563	14	48	62	17	26	0	6	7	55	3.2	10
W'head (Tot)	50	553	58	114	.509	10	35	.286	56	111	167	24	97	3	8	17	126	2.5	11
W'head (Ut)	32	328	31	69	.449	5	17	.294	27	70	97	18	65	3	7	11	67	2.1	8
Smith	6	73	5	15	.333	5	5	1.000	3	0	3	7	3	0	4	0	15	2.5	5
Wakefield	8	47	6	15	.400	3	3	1.000	0	4	4	3	13	0	1	0	15	1.9	5
Kilpatrick	2	6	1	2	.500	1	2	.500	1	3	4	0	1	0	0	0	3	1.5	3
Deane	7	48	2	11	.182	5	7	.714	2	4	6	3	0	0	0	0	10	1.4	3
Brown	4	24	0	7	.000	4	4	1.000	5	4	9	4	4	0	0	0	4	1.0	2

3 Pt. FG: Utah 59-185 (.319)—Dantley 0-2 (.000); Maravich 7-11 (.636); Furlow (Tot.) 24-82 (.293) (Utah) 23-73 (.315); Boone (Utah) 19-50 (.380); Bristow 2-7 (.286); Boswell 5-10 (.500); Poquette 0-2 (.000); Williams 0-12 (.000); Calvin 1-11 (.091) Hardy 1-2 (.500); Dawkins 1-5 (.200); Davis (Utah) 0-1 (.000); Deans 1-1 (1.000). Opponents 59-185 (.319).

WASHINGTON

Player	G.	Min.	FGM	FGA	Pct.	FTM	FTA	Pct.	Off. Reb.	Def. Reb.	Tot. Reb.	Ast.	PF	Dsq.	Blk. Sh.	Stl.	Pts.	Avg.	Hi.
Hayes	81	3183	761	1677	.454	334	478	.699	269	627	896	129	309	9	62	189	1859	23.0	43
Dandridge	45	1457	329	729	.451	123	152	.809	63	183	246	178	112	1	29	36	783	17.4	31
Ballard	82	2438	545	1101	.495	171	227	.753	240	398	638	159	197	2	90	36	1277	15.6	32
W'mson (Tot)	58	1374	359	817	.439	116	138	.841	38	61	99	126	137	1	36	19	845	14.6	32
W'mson (Wa)	30	603	153	356	.430	40	50	.800	14	31	45	39	66	0	10	10	349	11.6	24
Grevey	65	1818	331	804	.412	216	249	.867	80	107	187	177	158	0	56	16	912	14.0	32
Phegley	50	971	224	473	.474	104	120	.867	49	66	115	70	106	1	19	3	554	11.1	35
Chenier	20	470	84	214	.393	31	41	.756	10	33	43	42	26	0	18	5	202	10.1	22
Unseld	82	2973	327	637	.513	139	209	.665	334	760	1094	366	249	5	65	61	794	9.7	24
Wright	76	1286	229	500	.458	96	108	.889	40	82	122	222	144	3	49	18	558	7.3	25
Porter	70	1494	201	438	.459	110	137	.803	25	57	82	457	180	1	59	11	512	7.3	24
Cl'mons (Tot)	79	1789	214	450	.476	84	113	.743	53	99	152	288	133	0	57	11	519	6.6	20
Cl'mons (Wa)	57	1535	184	381	.483	72	98	.735	43	90	133	248	120	0	44	9	444	7.8	20
Kupchak	40	451	67	160	.419	52	75	.693	32	73	105	16	49	1	8	8	186	4.7	20
Boston	13	125	24	52	.462	8	13	.615	19	20	39	2	25	0	4	2	56	4.3	15
Behagen	6	64	9	23	.391	5	6	.833	6	8	14	7	14	0	0	4	23	3.8	9
Corzine	78	826	90	216	.417	45	68	.662	104	166	270	63	120	1	9	31	225	2.9	13
Bailey	20	180	16	35	.457	5	13	.385	6	22	28	26	18	0	7	4	38	1.9	6
Malovic		1	6	0	0	...	1	4	.250	0	0	0	0	0	0	1	0	1	1.0	1

3-Pt. FG: Washington 73-238 (.307)—Hayes 3-13 (.231); Dandridge 2-11 (.182); Ballard 16-47 (.340); Williamson (Tot) 11-35 (.314); Williamson (Wash) 3-16 (.188); Grevey 34-92 (.370); Phegley 2-5 (.400); Chenier 3-6 (.500); Unseld 1-2 (.500); Wright 4-16 (.250); Porter 0-4 (.000); Cleamons (Tot) 7-31 (.226), Cleamons (Wash) 4-23 (.174); Kupchak 0-2 (.000); Bailey 1-1 (1.000). Opponents 56-214 (.262).

INDIVIDUAL HIGHS

Most Minutes Played, Season	3226, Nixon, Los Angeles
Most Points, Game	55, Gervin, San Antonio at Indiana 1/23
Most Field Goals, Game	23, Gervin, San Antonio vs. Denver 1/8
	23, Kenon, San Antonio vs. Detroit 3/30
Most Free Throws, Game	21, Malone, Houston vs. Washington 2/27
Most Rebounds, Game	32, Nater, San Diego vs. Denver 12/14
Most Offensive Rebounds, Game	16, Malone, Houston vs. Indiana 10/17
Most Defensive Rebounds, Game	25, Nater, San Diego vs. Denver 12/14
Most Offensive Rebounds, Season	573, Malone, Houston
Most Defensive Rebounds, Season	864, Nater, San Diego
Most Assists, Game	24, Porter, Washington vs. Detroit 3/23
Most Blocked Shots, Game	11, Abdul-Jabbar, Los Angeles vs. Kansas City 11/25
Most Steals, Game	9, Ron Lee, Detroit vs. Houston 3/16
Most Personal Fouls, Season	328, Dawkins, Philadelphia
Most Game Disqualified, Season	12, Rollins, Atlanta, Edwards and McGinnis, Indiana

TEAM HIGHS AND LOWS

Longest Winning Streak	10, Milwaukee (10/13–11/3)
Longest Losing Streak	14, Utah (10/27–11/27)
	14, Detroit (3/7–3/30)
Most Points, Game	154, Cleveland vs. Los Angeles 1/29
Fewest Points, Game	72, Kansas City vs. Milwaukee 2/24
Most Points, Half	87, Atlanta at San Antonio 11/27
Fewest Points, Half	30, Golden State at Portland 10/21
Most Points, Quarter	50, Detroit at Chicago 1/22
Fewest Points, Quarter	10, Houston at Utah 2/22
	10, Golden State vs. Milwaukee 3/8
Most Field Goals, Game	65, Los Angeles vs. Cleveland 1/11
	65, Cleveland vs. Los Angeles 1/29
Fewest Field Goals, Game	25, Chicago at Kansas City 1/10
	25, Utah vs. Atlanta 2/7
Most Free Throws, Game	46, Boston vs. Chicago 1/16
Fewest Free Throws, Game	2, Los Angeles vs. San Diego 3/28
Most Rebounds, Game	71, Phoenix vs. Chicago 12/1
Fewest Rebounds, Game	25, Atlanta at New York 12/18
	25, Milwaukee vs. Denver 1/18
	25, Houston at San Diego 3/25
Most Assists, Game	47, San Antonio vs. Detroit 3/30
Most Steals, Game	21, Philadelphia vs. Phoenix 12/8
	21, Phoenix vs. Portland 3/28
Most Personal Fouls, Game	43, New Jersey at Detroit 2/29
Fewest Personal Fouls, Game	10, Milwaukee at Los Angeles 12/2
Most Blocked Shots, Game	19, Indiana at Washington 11/30

1979-80 PLAYOFF RESULTS

FIRST ROUND

EASTERN CONFERENCE

Philadelphia 2, Washington 0

Apr. 2—Wed.—Washington 96 at Philadelphia......111
Apr. 4—Fri.—Philadelphia 112 at Washington......104

Houston 2, San Antonio 1

Apr. 2—Wed.—San Antonio 85 at Houston............ 95
Apr. 4—Fri.—Houston 101 at San Antonio............106
Apr. 6—Sun.—San Antonio 120 at Houston............141

WESTERN CONFERENCE

Phoenix 2, Kansas City 1

Apr. 2—Wed.—Kansas City 93 at Phoenix............. 96
Apr. 4—Fri.—Phoenix 96 at Kansas City............106
Apr. 6—Sun.—Kansas City 99 at Phoenix............114

Seattle 2, Portland 1

Apr. 2—Wed.—Portland 110 at Seattle 120
Apro. 4—Fri.—Seattle 95 at Portland 105
Apr. 6—Sun.—Portland 86 at Seattle................103

CONFERENCE SEMI-FINALS SERIES

EASTERN CONFERENCE

Boston 4, Houston 0

Apr. 9—Wed.—Houston 101 at Boston....................119
Apr. 11—Fri.—Houston 75 at Boston 95
Apr. 13—Sun.—Boston 100 at Houston.................... 81
Apr. 14—Mon.—Boston 138 at Houston 121

Philadelphia 4, Atlanta 1

Apr. 6—Sun.—Atlanta 104 at Philadelphia 107
Apr. 9—Wed.—Atlanta 92 at Philadelphia 99
Apr. 10—Thu.—Philadelphia 93 at Atlanta 105
Apr. 13—Sun.—Philadelphia 107 at Atlanta 83
Apr. 15—Tue.—Atlanta 100 at Philadelphia 105

WESTERN CONFERENCE

Los Angeles 4, Phoenix 1

Apr. 8—Tue.—Phoenix 110 at Los Angeles..............119
Apr. 9—Wed.—Phoenix 128 at Los Angeles..............131
Apr. 11—Fri.—Los Angeles 108 at Phoenix 105
Apr. 13—Sun.—Los Angeles 101 at Phoenix 127
Apr. 15—Tue.—Phoenix 101 at Los Angeles 126

Seattle 4, Milwaukee 3

Apr. 8—Tue.—Milwaukee 113 at Seattle................114
Apr. 9—Wed.—Milwaukee 114 at Seattle................112
Apr. 11—Fri.—Seattle 91 at Milwaukee.................. 95
Apr. 13—Sun.—Seattle 112 at Milwaukee................107
Apr. 15—Tue.—Milwaukee 108 at Seattle................ 97
Apr. 18—Fri.—Seattle 86 at Milwaukee.................. 85
Apr. 20—Sun.—Milwaukee 94 at Seattle................. 98

CONFERENCE FINALS

EASTERN CONFERENCE

Philadelphia 4, Boston 1

Apr. 18—Fri.—Philadelphia 96 at Boston................. 93
Apr. 20—Sun.—Philadelphia 90 at Boston 96
Apr. 23—Wed.—Boston 97 at Philadelphia................. 99
Apr. 24—Thu.—Boston 90 at Philadelphia 102
Apr. 27—Sun.—Philadelphia 105 at Boston 94

WESTERN CONFERENCE

Los Angeles 4, Seattle 1

Apr. 22—Tue.—Seattle 108 at Los Angeles 107
Apr. 23—Wed.—Seattle 99 at Los Angeles............108
Apr. 25—Fri.—Los Angeles 104 at Seattle 100
Apr. 27—Sun.—Los Angeles 98 at Seattle............... 93
Apr. 30—Wed.—Seattle 105 at Los Angeles 111

WORLD CHAMPIONSHIP SERIES

Los Angeles 4, Philadelphia 2

May 4—Sun.—Philadelphia 102 at Los Angeles......................109
May 7—Wed.—Philadelphia 107 at Los Angeles 104
May 10—Sat.—Los Angeles 111 at Philadelphia 101
May 11—Sun.—Los Angeles 102 at Philadelphia 105
May 14—Wed.—Philadelphia 103 at Los Angeles 108
May 16—Fri.—Los Angeles 123 at Philadelphia........................107

1978-79 STATISTICS

SEATTLE SUPERSONICS 1978-79 NBA WORLD CHAMPIONS

Front row (left to right): Trainer Frank Furtardo, Dick Snyder, Jackie Robinson, Fred Brown, Joe Hassett, Dennis Johnson, Gus Williams. Second row: Coach Lenny Wilkens, Dennis Awtrey, Tom LaGarde, John Johnson, Lonnie Shelton, Paul Silas, Scout Mike Uporsky, Assistant Coach Les Habegger. Back row: Jack Sikma, General Manager Zollie Volchok. Missing from photo: Wally Walker.

FINAL STANDINGS

ATLANTIC DIVISION

Team	Atl.	Bos.	Chi.	Cle.	Den.	Det.	G.S.	Hou.	Ind.	K.C.	L.A.	Mil.	N.J.	N.O.	N.Y.	Phi.	Pho.	Por.	S.A.	S.D.	Sea.	Was.	W.	L.	Pct.	G.B.
Washington	2	4	3	4	3	3	2	2	3	..	2	3	3	4	3	1	3	1	3	3	2	..	54	28	.659	..
Philadelphia	2	2	3	2	3	3	1	4	2	2	3	2	2	2	2	..	1	1	3	3	1	3	47	35	.573	7
New Jersey	2	3	2	1	..	4	3	1	2	1	2	2	..	3	1	2	3	2	..	2	..	1	37	45	.451	17
New York	2	1	1	2	1	3	1	..	2	1	..	3	3	2	..	2	..	1	1	2	2	1	31	51	.378	23
Boston	2	..	1	2	1	2	2	1	3	1	1	1	1	2	3	2	..	1	..	1	2	..	29	53	.354	25
CENTRAL DIVISION																										
San Antonio	1	4	3	4	1	3	3	1	1	3	2	3	4	2	3	1	1	1	..	4	2	1	48	34	.585	..
Houston	1	3	2	2	3	2	2	..	..	3	2	2	3	4	4	..	2	3	3	2	2	2	47	35	.573	1
Atlanta	..	2	3	3	3	3	1	3	1	2	1	3	2	2	2	2	2	2	3	3	1	2	46	36	.561	2
Cleveland	1	2	3	..	..	1	1	2	2	1	1	2	1	3	2	2	2	..	..	2	2	..	30	52	.366	18
Detroit	1	2	2	3	2	..	1	2	2	2	2	2	2	..	2	1	1	..	1	1	2	..	30	52	.366	18
New Orleans	2	2	2	2	1	2	1	..	1	1	2	1	1	..	..	2	2	1	1	2	..	..	26	56	.317	22
MIDWEST DIVISION																										
Kansas City	2	3	4	3	3	2	2	1	3	..	2	2	3	3	2	2	2	1	1	2	2	3	48	34	.585	..
Denver	1	3	2	2	..	2	4	1	3	1	3	2	4	3	3	..	3	1	3	2	3	1	47	35	.573	1
Indiana	3	1	2	3	1	2	2	4	..	1	..	2	1	2	2	2	2	3	3	1	..	1	38	44	.463	10
Milwaukee	..	3	3	3	2	1	2	2	2	2	1	..	2	3	1	2	2	2	2	1	1	1	38	44	.463	10
Chicago	1	2	..	1	2	2	3	2	2	..	1	1	2	2	3	1	1	4	..	..	..	1	31	51	.378	17
PACIFIC DIVISION																										
Seattle	3	2	4	2	1	3	1	2	4	2	2	2	4	3	2	3	3	3	2	2	..	2	52	30	.634	..
Phoenix	1	4	3	4	1	4	3	2	2	2	2	..	..	3	4	3	..	3	3	2	1	..	50	32	.610	2
Los Angeles	3	3	3	2	1	2	3	1	4	2	..	3	2	2	3	1	2	2	2	2	2	2	47	35	.573	5
Portland	2	3	..	4	3	3	2	1	3	2	2	2	3	3	2	1	..	2	2	1	3	..	45	37	.549	7
San Diego	1	3	4	2	2	2	3	1	3	2	2	3	2	4	2	1	2	2	..	..	2	..	43	39	.524	9
Golden State	3	1	1	1	..	3	..	2	2	1	2	1	3	3	3	1	2	1	3	2	..	..	38	44	.463	14

TEAM STATISTICS—OFFENSE

Team	G.	FIELD GOALS Att.	Made	Pct.	FREE THROWS Made	Att.	Pct.	REBOUNDS Off.	Def.	Tot.	Ast.	PF	MISCELLANEOUS Dq.	Stl.	Turn Over	Blk. Sh.	SCORING Pts.	Avg.
S.A.	82	3927	7760	.506	1926	2423	.795	1096	2619	3715	2313	2071	25	829	1652	509	9780	119.3
Phoe.	82	3847	7516	.512	1765	2299	.768	1083	2379	3462	2500	1944	19	915	1760	337	9459	115.4
Wash.	82	3819	7873	.485	1785	2428	.735	1309	2768	4077	2169	1804	18	614	1420	401	9423	114.9
Mil.	82	3906	7773	.503	1541	2021	.762	1157	2370	3527	2562	2106	25	862	1574	435	9353	114.1
Hou.	82	3726	7498	.497	1845	2330	.792	1256	2504	3760	2302	2001	19	632	1510	286	9297	113.4
S.D.	82	3721	7706	.483	1836	2471	.743	1392	2413	3805	1539	2127	43	703	1623	392	9278	113.1
K.C.	82	3764	7644	.492	1746	2392	.730	1191	2404	3595	2239	2419	53	825	1631	390	9274	113.1
L.A.	82	3827	7397	.517	1606	2088	.769	949	2557	3506	2338	1851	16	793	1569	500	9260	112.9
Den.	82	3584	7338	.488	1607	2242	.717	1303	2380	3683	2092	2141	37	847	1599	550	9203	110.0
Det.	82	3708	7802	.475	1815	2411	.753	1149	2712	3861	2253	2072	26	779	1771	599	8983	109.5
Phila.	82	3584	7338	.488	1681	2341	.722	1381	2722	3722	1938	2424	72	801	1523	596	8950	109.1
Atl.	82	3505	7410	.473	1940	2534	.766	1225	2530	3755	2005	2093	41	687	1536	416	8909	108.6
Ind.	82	3575	7525	.475	1759	2317	.759	1256	2435	3691	1946	2187	49	776	1658	512	8888	108.4
Port.	82	3541	7338	.483	1806	2362	.765	1256	2435	3691	1946	2187	49	776	1658	512	8888	108.4
N.O.	82	3517	7511	.468	1848	2409	.767	1234	2676	3910	2079	1940	27	760	1764	559	8882	108.3
Bos.	82	3527	7347	.480	1820	2321	.784	1119	2396	3515	1995	1977	33	710	1713	283	8874	108.2
N.J.	82	3464	7523	.460	1904	2613	.729	1241	2370	3611	1907	2329	43	853	1861	619	8832	107.7
N.Y.	82	3676	7554	.487	1478	2111	.700	1200	2430	3630	2121	2154	34	699	1605	397	8830	107.7
Sea.	82	3504	7484	.468	1732	2298	.754	1310	2591	3901	1973	1914	23	690	1586	398	8740	106.6
Clev.	82	3556	7602	.468	1620	2103	.770	1229	2256	3485	1796	2027	21	688	1376	334	8732	106.5
G.S.	82	3627	7453	.487	1367	1872	.730	1169	2513	3682	2064	2023	25	774	1500	420	8621	105.1
Chi.	82	3478	7108	.489	1632	2184	.747	1224	2544	3768	2169	1970	30	576	1813	324	8588	104.7

TEAM STATISTICS—DEFENSE

Team	Made	FIELD GOALS Att.	Pct.	FREE THROWS Made	Att.	Pct.	REBOUNDS Off.	Def.	Tot.	Ast.	PF	MISCELLANEOUS Dq.	Stl.	Turn Over	Blk. Sh.	SCORING Pts.	Avg.	Dif.
Sea.	3475	7509	.463	1567	2108	.743	1156	2453	3609	1910	2057	27	755	1493	407	8517	103.9	+ 2.7
G.S.	3493	7255	.481	1604	2155	.744	1147	2533	3680	2094	1854	20	637	1580	362	8590	104.8	+ 0.3
Atl.	3367	6886	.489	2045	2727	.750	1176	2440	3616	1928	2135	45	646	1799	559	8779	107.1	− 2.0
Port.	3448	7059	.488	1889	2501	.755	1080	2350	3430	1963	2206	48	797	1650	422	8785	107.1	+ 1.3
Phila.	3542	7626	.464	1747	2331	.749	1252	2506	3758	2094	2128	35	795	1627	353	8831	107.7	+ 1.8
Chi.	3682	7408	.497	1549	2029	.763	1095	2377	3472	2146	2093	38	844	1468	503	8913	108.7	− 4.0
Den.	3631	7616	.477	1713	2277	.752	1218	2429	3647	2173	2262	56	738	1529	471	8975	109.5	+ 1.2
L.A.	3797	7848	.484	1415	1391	.733	1288	2486	3774	2234	1958	28	737	1542	359	9009	109.9	+ 3.0
Wash.	3804	8011	.475	1406	1897	.741	1178	2541	3719	2180	2144	37	726	1338	434	9014	109.9	+ 5.0
Clev.	3600	7150	.503	1837	2423	.758	1123	2587	3710	2062	2001	21	658	1557	503	9037	110.2	− 3.7
K.C.	3434	7061	.486	2170	2897	.749	1156	2547	3703	1776	2223	41	678	1879	435	9038	110.2	+ 3.1
Ind.	3586	7499	.478	1868	2416	.773	1299	2605	3904	2178	2091	30	677	1618	437	9040	110.2	− 1.6
N.Y.	3600	7457	.483	1907	2506	.761	1225	2489	3714	2114	1961	29	751	1558	378	9107	111.1	− 3.4
Phoe.	3775	7626	.495	1606	2127	.755	1238	2424	3662	2091	2144	33	890	1841	402	9156	111.7	+ 3.7
Mil.	3676	7505	.490	1819	2415	.753	1229	2437	3666	2301	1928	17	763	1748	462	9171	111.8	+ 2.3
N.J.	3507	7306	.480	2160	2861	.755	1234	2667	3901	2185	2208	37	861	1919	492	9174	111.9	− 4.2
Hou.	3795	7625	.498	1627	2211	.736	1186	2315	3501	2278	2055	43	660	1400	431	9217	112.4	+ 1.0
Det.	3755	7623	.493	1732	2295	.755	1301	2628	3929	2197	1914	21	666	1744	504	9242	112.7	− 2.7
Bos.	3855	7593	.508	1578	2079	.759	1122	2453	3575	2170	2075	27	717	1603	438	9288	113.3	− 5.1
S.A.	3798	7970	.477	1759	2343	.751	1297	2531	3828	2232	2168	41	788	1700	405	9355	114.1	+ 5.2
N.O.	3864	8039	.481	1666	2246	.742	1486	2664	4150	2264	2061	28	955	1600	566	9394	114.6	− 6.3
S.D.	3832	7801	.491	1760	2295	.767	1294	2322	3616	1896	2064	30	747	1517	350	9424	114.9	− 1.8

DQ—Individual players disqualified (fouled out of game).

INDIVIDUAL SCORING LEADERS

Minimum 70 games played or 1400 points

	G.	FG	FT	Pts.	Avg.
Gervin, S.A.	80	947	471	2365	29.6
Free, S.D.	78	795	654	2244	28.8
M. Johnson, Mil	77	820	332	1972	25.6
McAdoo, N.Y.-Bos	60	596	295	1487	24.8
Malone, Hou.	82	716	599	2031	24.8
Thompson, Den.	76	693	439	1825	24.0
Westphal, Phoe.	81	801	339	1941	24.0
Abdul-Jabbar, L.A.	80	777	349	1903	23.8
Gilmore, Chi.	82	753	434	1940	23.7
Davis, Phoe.	79	764	340	1868	23.6
Erving, Phil.	78	715	373	1803	23.1
Drew, Atl.	79	650	495	1795	22.7
McGinnis, Den.	76	603	509	1715	22.6
Williamson, N.J.	74	635	373	1643	22.2
Kenon, S.A.	81	748	295	1791	22.1
Russell, Clev.	74	603	417	1623	21.9
Hayes, Wash.	82	720	349	1789	21.8
Birdsong, K.C.	82	741	296	1778	21.7
King, N.J.	82	710	349	1769	21.6
Robinson, N.O.-Phoe.	69	566	324	1456	21.1

1978-79 STATISTICS

FIELD GOAL LEADERS
Minimum 300 FG Made

	FGM	FGA	Pct.
Maxwell, Boston	472	808	.584
Abdul-Jabbar, Los Angeles	777	1347	.577
Unseld, Washington	346	600	.577
Gilmore, Chicago	753	1310	.575
Nater, San Diego	357	627	.569
Washington, San Diego	350	623	.562
Davis, Phoenix	764	1362	.561
M. Johnson, Milwaukee	820	1491	.550
Robinzine, Kansas City	459	837	.548
Owens, Portland	600	1095	.548

FREE THROW LEADERS
Minimum 125 FT Made

	FTM	FTA	Pct.
Barry, Houston	160	169	.947
Murphy, Houston	246	265	.928
Brown, Seattle	183	206	.888
Smith, Denver	159	180	.883
Sobers, Indiana	298	338	.882
White, Boston-Golden State	139	158	.880
Twardzik, Portland	261	299	.873
Newlin, Houston	212	243	.872
Dunleavy, Houston	159	184	.864
Winters, Milwaukee	237	277	.856

REBOUND LEADERS
Minimum 70 games or 800 rebounds

	G.	Off.	Def.	Tot.	Avg.
Malone, Hou.	82	587	857	1444	17.6
Kelley, N.O.	80	303	723	1026	12.8
Abdul-Jabbar, L.A.	80	207	818	1025	12.8
Gilmore, Chi.	82	293	750	1043	12.7
Sikma, Sea.	82	232	781	1013	12.4
Hayes, Wash.	82	312	682	994	12.1
Parish, G.S.	76	265	651	916	12.1
Robinson, Phoe.	69	195	607	802	11.6
McGinnis, Den.	76	256	608	864	11.4
Roundfield, Atl.	80	326	539	865	10.8

BLOCKED SHOTS LEADERS
Minimum 70 games or 100 blocked shots

	G.	No.	Avg.
Abdul-Jabbar, Los Angeles	80	316	3.95
Johnson, New Jersey	78	253	3.24
Rollins, Atlanta	81	254	3.14
Parish, Golden State	76	217	2.86
Tyler, Detroit	82	201	2.45
Hayes, Washington	82	190	2.32
Roundfield, Atlanta	80	176	2.20
Kelley, New Orleans	80	166	2.08
C. Jones, Philadelphia	78	157	2.01
Gilmore, Chicago	82	156	1.90

ASSISTS LEADERS
Minimum 70 games or 400 assists

	G.	No.	Avg.
Porter, Detroit	82	1099	13.4
Lucas, Golden State	82	762	9.3
Nixon, Los Angeles	82	737	9.0
Ford, Kansas City	79	681	8.6
Westphal, Phoenix	81	529	6.5
Barry, Houston	80	502	6.3
Williams, New York	81	504	6.2
Henderson, Washington	70	419	6.0
Hill, Atlanta	82	480	5.9
Buckner, Milwaukee	81	468	5.8

STEALS LEADERS
Minimum 70 games or 125 steals

	G.	No.	Avg.
Carr, Detroit	80	197	2.46
Jordan, New Jersey	82	201	2.45
Nixon, Los Angeles	82	201	2.45
Walker, Cleveland	55	130	2.36
Ford, Kansas City	79	174	2.20
Smith, San Diego	82	177	2.16
Cheeks, Philadelphia	82	174	2.12
Williams, Seattle	76	158	2.08
Porter, Detroit	82	158	1.93
Buckner, Milwaukee	81	156	1.93

RECORDS OF TEAMS BY MONTHS

Team	Oct. W-L	Nov. W-L	Dec. W-L	Jan. W-L	Feb. W-L	Mar. W-L	Apr. W-L	Total W-L
Atlanta	4-4	8-5	7-9	9-7	6-4	8-7	4-0	46-36
Boston	1-6	4-10	8-5	5-10	7-5	3-12	1-5	29-53
Chicago	1-8	5-8	9-5	3-11	5-8	6-10	2-1	31-51
Cleveland	4-4	3-11	7-6	6-8	6-8	3-11	1-4	30-52
Denver	6-3	4-10	7-6	11-6	7-6	9-2	3-2	47-35
Detroit	2-7	6-7	4-10	6-8	5-7	6-9	1-4	30-52
Golden State	5-4	7-6	6-8	7-10	3-8	7-7	3-1	38-44
Houston	5-3	5-7	9-5	8-7	7-6	9-5	4-2	47-35
Indiana	4-3	4-10	3-11	9-6	6-8	10-5	2-1	38-44
Kansas City	4-5	8-3	8-6	10-6	10-4	5-10	3-0	48-34
Los Angeles	4-4	11-3	8-7	9-6	7-4	5-8	3-3	47-35
Milwaukee	4-6	5-10	6-8	7-7	5-6	10-4	1-3	38-44
New Jersey	6-4	7-6	4-6	6-7	8-6	5-11	1-5	37-45
New Orleans	4-5	6-9	2-11	5-10	4-9	4-10	1-2	26-56
New York	4-5	8-7	7-7	4-11	4-9	4-9	0-3	31-51
Philadelphia	5-1	8-5	9-5	6-7	6-8	10-8	3-1	47-35
Phoenix	7-3	10-4	7-7	7-6	6-6	10-4	3-2	50-32
Portland	4-4	9-6	5-6	5-9	8-5	12-4	2-3	45-37
San Antonio	5-4	5-7	12-4	9-5	7-5	6-8	4-1	48-34
San Diego	5-6	6-9	7-6	8-6	8-4	7-6	2-2	43-39
Seattle	7-1	9-4	6-7	10-4	6-9	11-3	3-2	52-30
Washington	4-5	11-2	9-5	10-3	8-4	9-6	3-3	54-28

1978-79 STATISTICS

ATLANTA HAWKS

Player	G.	Min.	FGM	FGA	Pct.	FTM	FTA	Pct.	Off. Reb.	Def. Reb.	Tot. Reb.	Ast.	PF	Dsq.	Stl.	Blk. Sh.	Pts.	Avg.	Hi.
Drew	79	2410	650	1375	.473	495	677	.731	225	297	522	119	332	19	128	16	1795	22.7	50
Johnson	78	2413	501	982	.510	243	292	.832	65	105	170	360	241	6	121	11	1245	16.0	30
Roundfield	80	2539	462	916	.504	300	420	.714	326	539	865	131	358	16	87	176	1224	15.3	38
Furlow (Tot)	78	1686	388	804	.483	163	195	.836	76	91	167	184	122	1	58	30	939	12.0	30
Furlow (Atl)	29	576	111	235	.481	60	70	.857	32	39	71	81	42	0	18	13	286	9.9	30
Hawes	81	2205	372	756	.492	108	132	.818	190	401	591	184	264	1	79	47	852	10.5	27
Hill	82	2527	296	682	.434	246	288	.854	41	123	164	480	292	8	102	16	838	10.2	26
Rollins	81	1900	297	555	.535	89	141	.631	219	369	588	49	328	19	46	254	683	8.4	24
Givens	74	1347	234	564	.415	102	135	.756	98	116	214	83	121	0	72	17	570	7.7	22
Lee	49	997	144	313	.460	88	117	.752	11	48	59	169	88	0	56	1	376	7.7	21
McMillen	82	1392	232	498	.466	106	119	.891	131	201	332	69	211	2	15	32	570	7.0	22
Criss	54	879	109	289	.377	67	86	.779	19	41	60	138	70	0	41	3	285	5.3	17
Wilson	61	589	81	197	.411	24	44	.545	20	56	76	72	66	1	30	8	186	3.0	10
Herron	14	81	14	48	.292	12	13	.923	4	6	10	3	11	0	6	2	40	2.9	7

BOSTON CELTICS

Player	G.	Min.	FGM	FGA	Pct.	FTM	FTA	Pct.	Off. Reb.	Def. Reb.	Tot. Reb.	Ast.	PF	Dsq.	Stl.	Blk. Sh.	Pts.	Avg.	Hi.
McAdoo (Tot)	60	2231	596	1127	.529	295	450	.656	130	390	520	168	189	3	74	67	1487	24.8	45
McAdoo (Bos)	20	637	167	334	.500	77	115	.670	36	105	141	40	55	1	12	20	411	20.6	42
Maxwell	80	2969	472	808	.584	574	716	.802	272	519	791	228	266	4	98	74	1518	19.0	35
Cowens	68	2517	488	1010	.483	151	187	.807	152	500	652	242	263	16	76	51	1127	16.6	32
Ford (Tot)	81	2737	538	1142	.471	172	227	.758	124	150	274	374	209	3	115	25	1248	15.4	34
Ford (Bos)	78	2629	525	1107	.474	165	219	.753	115	141	256	369	200	2	114	24	1215	15.6	34
Knight	40	1119	219	436	.502	118	146	.808	41	132	173	66	86	1	31	3	556	13.9	37
White	47	1455	255	596	.428	79	89	.888	22	106	128	214	100	1	54	4	589	12.5	28
Archibald	69	1662	259	573	.452	242	307	.788	25	78	103	324	132	2	55	6	760	11.0	25
Robey (Tot)	79	1763	322	673	.478	174	224	.777	168	345	513	132	232	4	48	15	818	10.4	28
Robey (Bos)	36	914	182	378	.481	84	103	.816	88	171	259	79	121	3	23	3	448	12.4	27
Judkins	81	1521	295	587	.503	119	146	.815	70	121	191	145	184	1	81	12	709	8.8	29
Barnes	38	796	133	271	.491	43	66	.652	57	120	177	53	144	3	38	39	309	8.1	29
Rowe	53	1222	151	346	.436	52	75	.693	79	163	242	69	105	2	15	13	354	6.7	21
Tatum	3	38	8	20	.400	4	5	.800	1	3	4	1	7	0	0	1	20	6.7	11
Williams	20	273	54	123	.439	14	24	.583	41	64	105	12	41	0	12	9	122	6.1	17
Chaney	65	1074	174	414	.420	36	42	.857	63	78	141	75	167	3	72	11	384	5.9	20
Sanders (Tot)	46	479	105	246	.427	54	68	.794	35	75	110	52	69	1	21	6	264	5.7	16
Sanders (Bos)	24	216	55	119	.462	22	27	.815	22	29	51	17	25	0	7	3	132	5.5	14
Stacom (Tot)	68	831	128	342	.374	44	60	.733	20	55	85	112	47	0	29	1	300	4.4	16
Stacom (Bos)	24	260	52	133	.391	13	19	.684	10	14	24	35	18	0	15	0	117	4.9	15
Barker	14	131	21	48	.438	11	15	.733	12	18	30	6	26	0	4	4	53	4.4	14
Awtrey	23	247	17	44	.386	16	20	.800	13	34	47	20	37	0	3	6	50	2.2	7

CHICAGO BULLS

Player	G.	Min.	FGM	FGA	Pct.	FTM	FTA	Pct.	Off. Reb.	Def. Reb.	Tot. Reb.	Ast.	PF	Dsq.	Stl.	Blk. Sh.	Pts.	Avg.	Hi.
Gilmore	82	3265	753	1310	.575	434	587	.739	293	750	1043	274	280	2	50	156	1940	23.7	41
Theus	82	2753	537	1119	.480	264	347	.761	92	136	228	429	270	2	93	18	1338	16.3	30
M. Johnson	82	2594	496	1105	.449	273	329	.830	193	434	627	380	286	9	88	59	1265	15.4	33
Holland	82	2483	445	940	.473	141	176	.801	78	176	254	330	240	9	122	12	1031	12.6	32
Mengelt	75	1705	338	689	.491	150	182	.824	25	93	118	187	148	1	46	4	826	11.0	26
O. Johnson	71	1734	281	540	.520	88	110	.800	58	169	227	163	182	2	54	33	650	9.2	24
Landsberger	80	1959	278	585	.475	91	194	.469	292	450	742	68	125	0	27	22	647	8.1	21
Brown	77	1265	152	317	.479	84	98	.857	83	155	238	104	180	5	18	10	388	5.0	14
May	37	403	59	136	.434	30	40	.750	14	50	64	39	51	0	22	1	148	4.0	15
Dudley	43	684	45	125	.360	28	42	.667	25	61	86	116	82	0	32	1	118	2.7	14
Sheppard	22	203	24	51	.471	12	19	.632	16	12	28	15	16	0	5	0	60	2.7	11
Armstrong	26	259	28	70	.400	10	13	.769	7	13	20	21	31	0	10	0	66	2.5	8
Lloyd (Tot)	72	496	42	122	.344	27	47	.574	49	47	96	32	92	0	10	8	111	1.5	11
Lloyd (Chi)	67	465	42	120	.350	27	47	.574	48	45	93	32	86	0	9	8	111	1.7	11
Wakefield	2	8	0	1	.000	0	0	.....	0	0	0	1	2	0	0	0	0	0.0	0

1978-79 STATISTICS

CLEVELAND CAVALIERS

Player	G.	Min.	FGM	FGA	Pct.	FTM	FTA	Pct.	Off. Reb.	Def. Reb.	Tot. Reb.	Ast.	PF	Dsq.	Stl.	Blk. Sh.	Pts.	Avg.	Hi.
Russell	74	2859	603	1268	.476	417	523	.797	147	356	503	348	222	2	98	25	1623	21.9	41
Carr	82	2714	551	1161	.475	292	358	.861	155	135	290	217	210	1	77	14	1394	17.0	30
Chones	82	2850	472	1073	.440	158	215	.735	260	582	842	181	278	4	47	102	1102	13.4	28
Furlow	49	1110	275	569	.483	103	125	.824	44	52	96	103	80	1	40	17	653	13.3	25
B. Smith	72	1650	361	784	.460	83	106	.783	77	129	206	121	188	2	43	7	805	11.2	23
Frazier	12	279	54	122	.443	21	27	.778	7	13	20	32	22	0	13	2	129	10.8	18
Mitchell	80	1576	362	706	.513	131	178	.736	127	202	329	60	215	6	51	29	855	10.7	32
Walker	55	1753	208	448	.464	137	175	.783	59	139	198	321	153	0	130	18	553	10.1	26
Lee (Tot)	82	1779	290	634	.457	175	230	.761	33	93	126	295	146	0	86	1	755	9.2	22
Lee (Clev)	33	782	146	321	.455	87	113	.770	22	45	67	126	58	0	30	0	379	11.5	22
E. Smith	24	332	69	130	.531	18	26	.692	45	61	106	13	60	0	7	16	156	6.5	16
Higgs	68	1050	127	279	.455	85	111	.766	18	84	102	141	176	2	66	11	339	5.0	21
Lambert	70	1030	148	329	.450	35	55	.636	116	174	290	43	163	0	25	29	331	4.7	16
Brewer	55	1301	114	259	.440	23	48	.479	125	245	370	74	136	2	48	56	251	4.6	14
Davis	40	394	66	153	.431	30	43	.698	27	39	66	16	66	1	13	8	162	4.1	12

DENVER NUGGETS

Player	G.	Min.	FGM	FGA	Pct.	FTM	FTA	Pct.	Off. Reb.	Def. Reb.	Tot. Reb.	Ast.	PF	Dsq.	Stl.	Blk. Sh.	Pts.	Avg.	Hi.
Thompson	76	2670	693	1353	.512	439	583	.753	109	165	274	225	180	2	70	82	1825	24.0	44
McGinnis	76	2552	603	1273	.474	509	765	.665	256	608	864	283	321	16	129	52	1715	22.6	41
Issel	81	2742	532	1030	.517	316	419	.754	240	498	738	255	233	6	61	46	1380	17.0	29
Scott	79	2617	393	854	.460	161	215	.749	54	156	210	428	284	12	78	30	947	12.0	28
Wilkerson	80	2425	396	869	.456	119	173	.688	100	314	414	284	190	0	118	21	911	11.4	26
Boswell	79	2201	321	603	.532	198	284	.697	248	290	538	242	263	4	50	51	840	10.6	22
Roberts	63	1236	211	498	.424	76	110	.691	106	152	258	107	142	2	20	2	498	7.9	18
Smith	82	1479	184	436	.422	159	180	.883	41	105	146	208	165	1	58	13	527	6.4	19
Ellis	42	268	42	92	.457	29	36	.806	17	45	62	10	45	0	10	13	113	2.7	10
Hughes	81	1086	98	182	.538	18	45	.400	112	223	335	74	215	2	56	102	214	2.6	14
Hicks	20	128	18	43	.419	3	5	.600	13	15	28	8	20	0	5	0	39	2.0	15
Kuester	33	212	16	52	.308	13	14	.929	5	8	13	37	29		18	1	45	1.4	8
Crompton	20	88	10	26	.385	6	12	.500	6	17	23	5	19	0	0	3	26	1.3	6

DETROIT PISTONS

Player	G.	Min.	FGM	FGA	Pct.	FTM	FTA	Pct.	Off. Reb.	Def. Reb.	Tot. Reb.	Ast.	PF	Dsq.	Stl.	Blk. Sh.	Pts.	Avg.	Hi.
Lanier	53	1835	489	950	.515	275	367	.749	164	330	494	140	181	5	50	75	1253	23.6	38
Carr	80	3207	587	1143	.514	323	435	.743	219	370	589	262	279	2	197	46	1497	18.7	36
Long	82	2498	581	1240	.469	157	190	.826	127	139	266	121	224	1	102	19	1319	16.1	29
Porter	82	2804	534	1110	.481	192	266	.722	62	147	209	1099	302	5	158	5	1260	15.4	32
Tyler	82	2560	456	946	.482	144	219	.658	211	437	648	89	254	3	104	201	1056	12.9	24
Douglas	78	2215	342	698	.490	208	328	.634	248	416	664	74	319	13	39	55	892	11.4	24
Ford	3	108	13	35	.371	7	8	.875	9	9	18	5	9	1	1	1	33	11.0	22
Tatum (Tot)	79	1233	280	627	.447	52	71	.732	41	84	125	73	165	3	78	34	612	7.7	20
Tatum (Det)	76	1195	272	607	.448	48	66	.727	40	81	121	72	158	3	78	33	592	7.8	20
Poquette	76	1337	198	464	.427	111	142	.782	99	237	336	57	198	4	38	98	507	6.7	28
Green	27	431	67	177	.379	45	67	.672	15	25	40	63	37	0	25	1	179	6.6	17
Hawkins	4	28	6	16	.375	6	6	1.000	3	3	6	4	7	0	5	0	18	4.5	10
Howard (Tot)	14	113	24	56	.429	11	23	.478	18	23	41	5	24	0	2	2	59	4.2	16
Howard (Det)	11	91	19	45	.422	11	23	.478	13	21	34	4	16	0	2	2	49	4.5	16
Brewer (Tot)	80	1611	141	319	.442	26	63	.413	159	316	475	87	174	2	61	66	308	3.9	14
Brewer (Det)	25	310	27	60	.450	3	5	.200	34	71	105	13	38	0	13	10	57	2.3	7
Hollis	25	154	30	75	.400	9	12	.750	21	24	45	6	28	0	11	1	69	2.8	10
McNeill	11	46	9	20	.450	11	12	.917	3	7	10	3	7	0	0	0	29	2.6	19
Wakef'd (Tot)	73	586	62	177	.350	48	69	.696	25	51	76	70	70	0	19	2	172	2.4	17
Wakef'd (Det)	71	578	62	176	.352	48	69	.696	25	51	76	69	68	0	19	2	172	2.4	17
Shepp'd (Tot)	42	279	36	76	.474	20	34	.588	25	22	47	19	26	0	8	1	92	2.2	15
Shepp'd (Det)	20	76	12	25	.480	8	15	.533	9	10	19	4	10	0	3	1	32	1.6	15
Gerard	2	6	1	3	.333	1	2	.500	1	0	1	0	0	0	2	0	3	1.5	3
Boyd	5	40	3	12	.250	0	0	.....	0	2	2	7	5	0	0	0	6	1.2	2
Behagen	1	1	0	0	.....	0	0	.....	0	0	0	0	1	0	0	0	0	0.0	0

1978-79 STATISTICS

GOLDEN STATE WARRIORS

Player	G.	Min.	FGM	FGA	Pct.	FTM	FTA	Pct.	Off. Reb.	Def. Reb.	Tot. Reb.	Ast.	PF	Dsq.	Stl.	Blk. Sh.	Pts.	Avg.	Hi.
Smith	59	2288	489	977	.501	194	255	.761	48	164	212	261	159	3	101	23	1172	19.9	37
Parish	76	2411	554	1110	.499	196	281	.698	265	651	916	115	303	10	100	217	1304	17.2	33
Lucas	82	3095	530	1146	.462	264	321	.822	65	182	247	762	229	1	152	9	1324	16.1	35
Parker	79	2893	512	1019	.502	175	222	.788	164	280	444	291	187	0	144	33	1199	15.2	28
White (Tot)	76	2338	404	910	.444	139	158	.880	42	158	200	347	173	1	80	7	947	12.5	30
White (GS)	29	883	149	314	.475	60	69	.870	20	52	72	133	73	0	26	3	358	12.3	30
Short	75	1703	369	771	.479	57	85	.671	127	220	347	97	233	6	54	12	795	10.6	27
Williams	81	1299	284	567	.501	102	117	.872	68	139	207	61	169	0	55	5	670	8.3	27
Ray	82	1917	231	439	.526	106	190	.558	213	395	608	136	264	4	47	50	568	6.9	21
Abernethy	70	1219	176	342	.515	70	94	.745	74	142	216	79	133	1	39	13	422	6.0	21
Cox	31	360	53	123	.431	40	92	.435	18	45	63	11	68	0	13	5	146	4.7	16
Townsend	65	771	127	289	.439	50	68	.735	11	44	55	91	70	0	27	6	304	4.7	24
Cooper	65	795	128	293	.437	41	61	.672	90	190	280	21	118	0	7	44	297	4.6	22
Robertson	12	74	15	40	.375	6	9	.667	6	4	10	4	10	0	8	0	36	3.0	8
Epps	13	72	10	23	.435	6	8	.750	0	5	5	2	7	0	1	0	26	2.0	10

HOUSTON ROCKETS

Player	G.	Min.	FGM	FGA	Pct.	FTM	FTA	Pct.	Off. Reb.	Def. Reb.	Tot. Reb.	Ast.	PF	Dsq.	Stl.	Blk. Sh.	Pts.	Avg.	Hi.
Malone	82	3390	716	1325	.540	599	811	.739	587	857	1444	147	223	0	79	119	2031	24.8	45
Murphy	82	2941	707	1424	.496	246	265	.928	17	95	173	351	288	5	117	6	1660	20.2	38
Tomjanovich	74	2641	620	1200	.517	168	221	.760	170	402	572	137	186	0	44	18	1408	19.0	33
Barry	80	2566	461	1000	.461	160	169	.947	40	237	277	502	195	0	95	38	1082	13.5	38
Reid	82	2259	382	777	.492	131	186	.704	129	354	483	230	302	7	75	48	895	10.9	21
Newlin	76	1828	283	581	.487	212	243	.872	51	119	170	291	218	3	51	79	778	10.2	24
Dunleavy	74	1486	215	425	.506	159	184	.864	28	100	128	324	168	2	56	5	589	8.0	24
Jones	81	1215	181	395	.458	96	132	.727	110	218	328	57	204	1	34	26	458	5.7	16
Watts	61	1046	92	227	.405	41	67	.612	35	68	103	243	143	1	73	14	225	3.7	16
Dorsey	20	108	24	43	.558	8	16	.500	12	11	23	2	25	0	1	2	56	2.8	8
Bradley	34	245	37	88	.420	22	33	.667	13	33	46	17	33	0	5	1	96	2.8	17
Coleman	6	39	5	7	.714	1	1	1.000	1	6	7	1	11	0	2	0	11	1.8	9
Barker	5	16	3	6	.500	2	2	1.000	2	4	6	0	5	0	0	0	8	1.6	4

INDIANA PACERS

Player	G.	Min.	FGM	FGA	Pct.	FTM	FTA	Pct.	Off. Reb.	Def. Reb.	Tot. Reb.	Ast.	PF	Dsq.	Stl.	Blk. Sh.	Pts.	Avg.	Hi.
J. Davis	79	2971	565	1240	.456	314	396	.793	70	121	191	453	177	1	95	22	1444	18.3	34
Sobers	81	2825	553	1194	.463	298	338	.882	118	183	301	450	315	8	138	23	1404	17.3	34
Edwards	82	2546	534	1065	.501	298	441	.676	179	514	693	92	363	16	60	109	1366	16.7	36
English	81	2696	563	1102	.511	173	230	.752	253	402	655	271	214	3	70	78	1299	16.0	32
Bantom	82	2828	482	1036	.465	227	338	.672	225	425	650	223	316	8	99	62	1191	14.7	29
Knight (Tot)	79	2095	441	835	.528	249	296	.841	94	253	347	152	160	1	63	8	1131	14.3	37
Knight (Ind)	39	976	222	399	.556	131	150	.873	53	121	174	86	74	0	32	5	575	14.7	37
Robey	43	849	140	295	.475	90	121	.744	80	174	254	53	111	1	25	12	370	8.6	28
Calhoun	81	1332	153	335	.457	72	86	.837	64	174	238	104	189	1	37	19	378	4.7	19
Elmore	80	1264	139	342	.406	56	78	.718	115	287	402	75	183	3	62	79	334	4.2	17
Stacom	44	571	76	209	.364	31	41	.756	20	41	61	77	29	0	14	1	183	4.2	16
Radford	52	649	83	175	.474	36	45	.800	25	43	68	57	61	0	30	1	202	3.9	15
B. Davis(Tot)	27	298	31	55	.564	16	23	.696	1	16	17	52	32	0	16	2	78	2.9	11
B. Davis (Ind)	22	233	23	44	.523	13	19	.684	1	15	16	43	22	0	14	2	59	2.7	11
Green	39	265	42	89	.472	20	34	.588	22	30	52	21	39	0	11	3	104	2.7	13

KANSAS CITY KINGS

Player	G.	Min.	FGM	FGA	Pct.	FTM	FTA	Pct.	Off. Reb.	Def. Reb.	Tot. Reb.	Ast.	PF	Dsq.	Stl.	Blk. Sh.	Pts.	Avg.	Hi.
Birdsong	82	2839	741	1456	.509	296	408	.725	176	178	354	281	255	2	125	17	1778	21.7	39
Wedman	73	2498	561	1050	.534	216	271	.797	135	251	386	144	239	4	76	30	1338	18.3	35
Ford	79	2723	467	1004	.465	326	401	.813	33	149	182	681	245	3	174	6	1260	15.9	33
Robinzine	82	2179	459	837	.548	180	246	.732	218	420	638	104	367	16	105	15	1098	13.4	32
Lacey	82	2827	350	697	.502	167	226	.739	179	523	702	430	309	11	106	141	867	10.6	26
McKinney	78	1242	240	477	.503	129	162	.796	20	65	85	253	121	0	58	3	609	7.8	30
Burleson	56	927	157	342	.459	121	169	.716	84	197	281	50	183	3	26	58	435	7.8	18
Redmond	49	736	162	375	.432	31	50	.620	57	51	108	57	93	2	28	16	355	7.2	18
Hillman	78	1618	211	428	.493	125	224	.558	138	293	431	91	228	11	50	66	547	7.0	16
Nash	82	1307	227	522	.435	69	86	.802	76	130	206	71	135	0	29	15	523	6.4	24
Allen	31	413	69	174	.397	19	33	.576	14	32	46	44	52	0	21	6	157	5.1	16
Behagen (Tot)	15	165	28	62	.452	10	13	.769	13	29	42	7	36	0	4	1	66	4.4	12
Behagen (KC)	9	126	23	50	.460	8	11	.727	11	20	31	5	27	0	2	1	54	6.0	12
Gerard (Tot)	58	465	84	194	.433	50	91	.549	40	58	98	21	74	14	20	13	218	3.8	11
Gerard (KC)	56	459	83	191	.435	49	89	.551	39	58	97	21	74	1	18	13	215	3.8	11
Washington	18	161	14	41	.341	10	16	.625	11	37	48	7	31	0	7	3	38	2.1	12

1978-79 STATISTICS

LOS ANGELES LAKERS

Player	G.	Min.	FGM	FGA	Pct	FTM	FTA	Pct.	Off. Reb.	Def. Reb.	Tot. Reb.	Ast.	PF	Dsq.	Stl.	Blk. Sh.	Pts.	Avg.	Hi.
Abdul-Jabbar	80	3157	777	1347	.577	349	474	.736	207	818	1025	431	230	3	76	316	1903	23.8	40
Wilkes	82	2915	626	1242	.504	272	362	.751	164	445	609	227	275	2	134	27	1524	18.6	31
Dantley	60	1775	374	733	.510	292	342	.854	131	211	342	138	162	0	63	12	1040	17.3	40
Nixon	82	3145	623	1149	.542	158	204	.775	48	183	231	737	250	6	201	17	1404	17.1	29
Hudson	78	1686	329	636	.517	110	124	.887	64	76	140	141	133	5	28	17	768	9.8	23
Boone	82	1583	259	569	.455	90	104	.865	53	92	145	154	171	1	66	11	608	7.4	18
Carr	72	1149	225	450	.500	83	137	.606	70	222	292	60	152	0	38	31	533	7.4	17
Ford	79	1540	228	450	.507	72	89	.809	83	185	268	101	177	2	51	25	528	6.7	22
Price	75	1207	171	344	.497	55	79	.696	26	97	123	218	128	0	66	12	397	5.3	19
Robisch	80	1219	150	336	.446	86	115	.748	82	203	285	97	108	0	20	25	386	4.8	15
Davis	5	65	8	11	.727	3	4	.750	0	1	1	9	10	0	2	0	19	3.8	9
Carter	46	332	54	124	.435	36	54	.667	21	24	45	25	54	1	17	7	144	3.1	14
Cooper	3	7	3	6	.500	0	0	....	0	0	0	1	0	1	0	6	2.0	4

MILWAUKEE BUCKS

Player	G.	Min.	FGM	FGA	Pct	FTM	FTA	Pct.	Off. Reb.	Def. Reb.	Tot. Reb.	Ast.	PF	Dsq.	Stl.	Blk. Sh.	Pts.	Avg.	Hi.
M. Johnson	77	2779	820	1491	.550	332	437	.760	212	374	586	234	186	1	116	89	1972	25.6	40
Winters	79	2575	662	1343	.493	237	277	.856	48	129	177	383	243	1	83	40	1561	19.8	37
Bridgeman	82	1963	540	1067	.506	189	228	.829	113	184	297	163	184	2	88	41	1269	15.5	37
Benson	82	2132	413	798	.518	180	245	.735	187	397	584	204	280	4	89	81	1006	12.3	28
Grunfeld	82	1778	326	661	.493	191	251	.761	124	236	360	216	220	3	58	15	843	10.3	27
Buckner	81	1757	251	553	.454	79	125	.632	57	153	210	468	224	1	156	17	581	7.2	19
Gianelli	82	2057	256	527	.486	72	102	.706	122	286	408	160	196	4	44	67	584	7.1	16
Restani	81	1598	262	529	.495	51	73	.699	141	244	385	122	155	0	30	27	575	7.1	22
G. Johnson	67	1157	165	342	.482	84	117	.718	106	254	360	81	187	5	75	49	414	6.2	20
Walton	75	1381	157	327	.480	61	90	.678	34	70	104	356	103	0	72	9	375	5.0	20
Smith	16	125	19	47	.404	18	24	.750	0	9	9	16	12	0	8	1	56	3.5	10
Howard	3	22	5	11	.455	0	0	.000	5	2	7	1	8	0	0	0	10	3.3	6
Van Lier	38	555	30	77	.390	47	52	.904	8	32	40	158	108	4	43	3	107	2.8	16
Beshore	1	1	0	0	.000	0	0	.000	0	0	0	0	0	0	0	0	0	0.0	0

NEW JERSEY NETS

Player	G.	Min.	FGM	FGA	Pct.	FTM	FTA	Pct.	Off. Reb.	Def. Reb.	Tot. Reb.	Ast.	PF	Dsq.	Stl.	Blk. Sh.	Pts.	Avg.	Hi.
Williamson	74	2451	635	1367	.465	373	437	.854	53	143	196	255	215	3	89	12	1643	22.2	48
King	82	2859	710	1359	.522	349	619	.564	251	418	669	295	326	10	118	39	1769	21.6	41
Money	47	1434	325	676	.481	136	183	.743	55	70	125	249	132	0	74	10	786	16.7	40
Jordan	82	2260	401	960	.418	213	274	.777	74	141	215	365	209	0	201	40	1015	12.4	29
Boynes	69	1176	256	595	.430	133	169	.787	60	95	155	75	117	1	43	7	645	9.3	29
Elliott	14	282	41	73	.562	41	56	.732	16	40	56	22	34	2	6	4	123	8.8	16
Washington	62	1139	218	434	.502	66	104	.635	88	206	294	47	186	5	31	67	502	8.1	26
Skinner	23	334	55	125	.440	72	82	.878	12	30	42	49	53	0	22	2	182	7.9	19
van B Kolff	80	1998	196	423	.463	146	183	.798	108	274	382	180	235	4	85	74	538	6.7	25
Johnson	78	2058	206	483	.427	105	138	.761	201	415	616	88	315	8	68	253	517	6.6	25
Jackson	59	1070	144	303	.475	86	105	.819	59	119	178	85	168	7	45	22	374	6.3	20
Simpson (Tot)	68	979	174	433	.402	76	111	.685	35	61	96	126	57	0	37	5	424	6.2	20
Simpson (NJ)	32	527	87	237	.367	48	71	.676	19	42	61	68	30	0	12	4	222	6.9	17
Cat'ngs (Tot)	56	948	102	243	.420	60	78	.769	101	201	302	48	132	3	23	91	264	4.7	16
Cat'ngs (NJ)	32	659	74	175	.423	47	61	.770	71	133	204	30	90	2	15	56	195	6.1	16
Bassett	82	1508	116	313	.371	89	131	.679	174	244	418	99	219	1	44	29	321	3.9	16

NEW ORLEANS JAZZ

Player	G.	Min.	FGM	FGA	Pct.	FTM	FTA	Pct.	Off. Reb.	Def. Reb.	Tot. Reb.	Ast.	PF	Dsq.	Stl.	Blk. Sh.	Pts.	Avg.	Hi.
Robinson	43	1781	397	819	.485	245	339	.723	139	438	577	84	130	1	29	63	1039	24.2	51
Maravich	49	1824	436	1035	.421	233	277	.841	33	88	121	243	104	2	60	18	1105	22.6	41
Haywood(Tot)	68	2361	595	1205	.494	231	292	.791	172	361	533	127	236	8	40	82	1421	20.9	46
Haywood(NO)	34	1338	346	696	.497	124	146	.849	106	221	327	71	128	6	30	53	816	24.0	33
McElroy	79	2698	539	1097	.491	259	340	.762	61	154	215	453	183	1	148	49	1337	16.9	40
Kelley	80	2705	440	870	.506	373	458	.814	303	723	1026	285	309	8	126	166	1253	15.7	30
Goodrich	74	2130	382	850	.449	174	204	.853	68	115	183	357	177	1	90	13	938	12.7	26
James	73	1417	311	630	.494	105	140	.750	97	151	248	78	202	1	28	21	727	10.0	29
Lee (Tot)	60	1346	218	507	.430	98	141	.695	63	105	168	205	182	3	107	6	534	8.9	24
Lee (N.O.)	17	398	45	124	.363	24	37	.649	21	34	55	73	44	1	38	2	114	6.7	14
Hardy	68	1456	196	426	.460	61	88	.693	121	189	310	65	133	1	52	61	453	6.7	19
Byrnes(Tot)	79	1264	187	389	.481	106	154	.688	90	101	191	104	111	0	27	10	480	6.1	16
Byrnes(N.O.)	36	530	78	166	.470	33	54	.611	41	53	94	43	42	0	12	8	189	5.3	16
Meriweather	36	640	84	187	.449	51	78	.654	62	122	184	31	105	2	17	41	219	6.1	24

Player	G.	Min.	FGM	FGA	Pct.	FTM	FTA	Pct.	Off. Reb.	Def. Reb.	Tot. Reb.	Ast.	PF	Dsq.	Stl.	Blk. Sh.	Pts.	Avg.	Hi.
Terrell	31	572	63	144	.438	27	38	.711	34	75	109	26	73	0	15	22	153	4.9	12
Green	59	809	92	237	.388	48	63	.762	20	48	68	140	111	0	61	6	232	3.9	9
Griffin	77	1398	106	223	.475	91	147	.619	126	265	391	138	198	3	54	36	303	3.9	14
Bailey	2	9	2	7	.286	0	0	.000	2	0	2	2	1	0	0	0	4	2.0	2

NEW YORK KNICKS

Player	G.	Min.	FGM	FGA	Pct.	FTM	FTA	Pct.	Off. Reb.	Def. Reb.	Tot. Reb.	Ast.	PF	Dsq.	Stl.	Blk. Sh.	Pts.	Avg.	Hi.
McAdoo	40	1594	429	793	.541	218	335	.651	94	285	379	128	134	2	62	47	1076	26.9	45
Haywood	34	1023	249	509	.489	107	146	.733	66	140	206	56	108	2	10	29	605	17.8	46
Williams	81	2370	575	1257	.457	251	313	.802	104	187	291	504	274	4	128	19	1401	17.3	37
Knight	82	2667	609	1174	.519	145	206	.704	201	347	548	124	309	7	61	60	1363	16.6	43
Monroe	64	1393	329	699	.471	129	154	.838	26	48	74	189	123	0	48	6	787	12.3	34
Webster	60	2027	264	558	.473	150	262	.573	198	457	655	172	183	6	24	112	678	11.3	23
Cleamons	79	2390	311	657	.473	130	171	.760	65	160	225	376	174	1	73	11	752	9.5	24
Meriw'ther(T)	77	1693	242	500	.484	126	187	.674	143	266	409	79	283	10	40	94	610	7.9	24
Meriw'r(NY)	45	1063	158	313	.505	75	109	.688	81	144	225	48	178	8	23	53	391	9.5	22
Glenn	75	1171	263	486	.541	57	63	.905	28	54	82	136	113	0	37	6	583	7.8	31
Richardson	72	1218	200	483	.414	69	128	.539	78	155	233	213	188	2	100	18	469	6.5	19
Gondrezick	75	1602	161	326	.494	55	97	.567	147	277	424	106	226	1	98	18	377	5.0	16
Barker (Tot)	39	476	68	156	.436	27	37	.730	45	74	119	15	76	0	11	11	163	4.2	14
Barker (NY)	22	329	44	102	.431	14	20	.700	31	52	83	9	45	0	6	7	102	4.6	13
Rudd	58	723	59	133	.444	66	93	.710	69	98	167	35	95	1	17	8	184	3.2	17
Beard	7	85	11	26	.423	0	0	....	1	9	10	19	13	0	7	0	22	3.1	6
Behagen	5	38	5	12	.417	2	2	1.000	2	9	11	2	8	0	2	0	12	2.4	6
Bunch	12	97	9	26	.346	10	12	.833	9	8	17	4	10	0	3	3	28	2.3	7

PHILADELPHIA 76ERS

Player	G.	Min.	FGM	FGA	Pct.	FTM	FTA	Pct.	Off. Reb.	Def. Reb.	Tot. Reb.	Ast.	PF	Dsq.	Stl.	Blk. Sh.	Pts.	Avg.	Hi.
Erving	78	2802	715	1455	.491	373	501	.745	198	366	564	357	207	0	133	100	1803	23.1	37
Collins	47	1595	358	717	.499	201	247	.814	36	87	123	191	139	1	52	20	917	19.5	32
Money (Tot)	69	1979	444	893	.497	170	237	.717	70	92	162	331	202	2	87	12	1058	15.3	40
Money (Phil)	23	545	119	217	.548	34	54	.630	15	22	37	82	70	2	13	2	272	11.8	21
Dawkins	78	2035	430	831	.517	158	235	.672	123	508	631	128	295	5	32	143	1018	13.1	30
Bibby	82	2538	368	869	.423	266	335	.794	72	172	244	371	199	0	72	7	1002	12.2	27
B. Jones	80	2304	378	704	.537	209	277	.755	199	332	531	201	245	2	107	96	965	12.1	33
Mix	74	1269	265	493	.538	161	201	.801	109	184	293	121	112	0	57	16	691	9.3	34
C. Jones	78	2171	302	637	.474	121	162	.747	177	570	747	151	303	10	39	157	725	9.3	27
Cheeks	82	2409	292	572	.510	101	140	.721	63	191	254	431	198	2	174	12	685	8.4	27
Bryant	70	1064	205	478	.429	123	170	.724	96	163	259	103	171	1	49	9	533	7.6	27
Redm'd(Tot)	53	759	163	387	.421	31	50	.620	57	52	109	58	96	2	28	16	357	6.7	18
Redm'd(Phil)	4	23	1	12	.083	0	0	....	0	1	1	3	0	0	0	2	0.5	2
Skinner(Tot)	45	643	91	214	.425	99	114	.868	27	59	86	89	114	2	40	3	281	6.2	22
Skinner(Phil)	22	309	36	89	.404	27	32	.844	15	29	44	40	61	2	18	1	99	4.5	22
Simpson	37	452	87	196	.444	28	40	.700	16	19	35	58	27	8	25	1	202	5.5	20
Catchings	25	289	28	68	.412	13	17	.765	30	68	98	18	42	1	8	35	69	2.8	12

PHOENIX SUNS

Player	G.	Min.	FGM	FGA	Pct.	FTM	FTA	Pct.	Off. Reb.	Def. Reb.	Tot. Reb.	Ast.	PF	Dsq.	Stl.	Blk. Sh.	Pts.	Avg.	Hi.
Westphal	81	2641	801	1496	.535	339	405	.837	35	124	159	529	159	1	111	26	1941	24.0	43
Davis	79	2437	764	1362	.561	340	409	.831	111	262	373	339	250	50	147	26	1868	23.6	42
R'son (Tot)	69	2537	566	1152	.491	324	462	.701	195	607	802	113	206	2	46	75	1456	21.1	51
R'son (Phoe)	26	756	169	333	.508	79	123	.642	56	169	225	39	76	1	17	12	417	16.0	28
Adams	77	2364	569	1073	.530	231	289	.799	220	485	705	360	246	4	110	63	1369	17.8	33
Lee	43	948	173	383	.452	74	104	.712	42	71	113	132	138	2	69	4	420	9.8	24
Bratz	77	1297	242	533	.454	139	170	.818	55	86	141	179	151	0	64	7	623	8.1	20
Buse	82	2544	285	576	.495	70	91	.769	44	173	217	356	149	0	156	18	640	7.8	21
Byrnes	43	734	109	223	.489	73	100	.730	49	48	97	61	69	0	15	2	291	6.8	16
Scott	81	1737	212	396	.535	120	168	.714	104	256	360	126	139	2	80	62	544	6.7	18
Heard	63	1213	162	367	.441	71	103	.689	98	253	351	60	141	1	53	57	395	6.3	18
Kramer	82	1401	181	370	.489	125	176	.710	134	203	337	92	224	2	45	23	487	5.9	18
McClain	36	465	62	132	.470	42	46	.913	25	44	69	60	51	0	19	0	166	4.6	16
Forrest	75	1243	118	272	.434	62	115	.539	110	205	315	167	151	1	29	37	298	4.0	15

1978-79 STATISTICS

PORTLAND TRAIL BLAZERS

Player	G.	Min.	FGM	FGA	Pct.	FTM	FTA	Pct.	Off. Reb.	Def. Reb.	Tot. Reb.	Ast.	PF	Dsq.	Stl.	Blk. Sh.	Pts.	Avg.	Hi.
Lucas	69	2462	568	1208	.470	270	345	.783	192	524	716	215	254	3	66	81	1406	20.4	46
Owens	82	2791	600	1095	.548	320	403	.794	263	477	740	301	329	15	59	58	1520	18.5	37
Hollins	64	1967	402	886	.454	172	221	.778	32	117	149	325	199	3	114	24	976	15.3	33
Thompson	73	2144	460	938	.490	154	209	.737	252	198	406	604	176	270	10	67	134	1074	14.7	37
Brewer	81	2454	434	878	.494	210	256	.820	88	141	229	165	181	3	102	79	1078	13.3	30
Twardzik	64	1570	203	381	.533	261	299	.873	39	80	119	176	185	5	84	4	667	10.4	23
Gross	53	1441	209	443	.472	96	119	.807	106	144	250	184	161	4	70	47	514	9.7	19
Dunn	80	1828	246	549	.448	122	158	.772	145	199	344	103	166	1	86	23	614	7.7	18
Steele	72	1488	203	483	.420	112	136	.824	58	113	171	142	208	4	74	10	518	7.2	29
Terrell (Tot)	49	732	93	198	.470	35	53	.660	44	102	146	41	100	0	22	28	221	4.5	12
Terrell (Port)	18	160	30	54	.556	8	15	.533	10	27	37	15	27	0	7	6	68	3.8	11
Smith	13	131	23	44	.523	12	17	.706	7	6	13	17	19	0	10	1	58	4.5	14
McMillian	23	278	33	74	.446	17	21	.810	16	23	39	33	18	0	10	3	83	3.6	12
Johnson	74	794	102	217	.470	36	74	.486	83	143	226	78	121	1	23	36	240	3.2	8
Anderson	21	224	24	77	.312	15	28	.536	17	28	45	15	42	0	4	5	63	3.0	10
Neal	4	48	4	11	.364	1	1	1.000	2	7	9	1	7	0	1	0	9	2.3	5

SAN ANTONIO SPURS

Player	G.	Min.	FGM	FGA	Pct.	FTM	FTA	Pct.	Off. Reb.	Def. Reb.	Tot. Reb.	Ast.	PF	Dsq.	Stl.	Blk. Sh.	Pts.	Avg.	Hi.
Gervin	80	2888	947	1749	.541	471	570	.826	142	258	400	219	275	5	137	91	2365	29.6	52
Kenon	81	2947	748	1484	.504	295	349	.845	260	530	790	335	192	1	154	19	1791	22.1	39
Silas	79	2171	466	922	.505	334	402	.831	35	148	183	273	215	1	76	20	1266	16.0	31
Paultz	79	2122	399	758	.526	114	194	.588	169	456	625	178	204	4	35	125	912	11.5	28
Olberding	80	1885	261	551	.474	233	290	.803	96	333	429	211	282	2	53	18	755	9.4	25
Gale	82	2121	284	612	.464	91	108	.843	40	146	186	374	192	1	152	40	659	8.0	19
Green	76	1641	235	477	.493	101	144	.701	131	223	354	116	230	3	37	122	571	7.5	21
Dietrick	76	1487	209	400	.523	79	99	.798	88	227	315	198	206	7	72	38	497	6.5	16
Bristow	74	1324	174	354	.492	124	149	.832	80	167	247	231	154	0	56	15	472	6.4	19
Sanders	22	263	50	127	.394	32	41	.780	13	46	59	35	44	1	14	3	132	6.0	16
Dampier	70	760	123	251	.490	29	39	.744	15	48	63	124	42	0	35	8	275	3.9	18
Mosley	26	221	31	75	.413	23	38	.605	27	37	64	19	35	0	8	10	85	3.3	11

SAN DIEGO CLIPPERS

Player	G.	Min.	FGM	FGA	Pct.	FTM	FTA	Pct.	Off. Reb.	Def. Reb.	Tot. Reb.	Ast.	PF	Dsq.	Stl.	Blk. Sh.	Pts.	Avg.	Hi.
Free	78	2954	795	1653	.481	654	865	.756	127	174	301	340	253	8	111	35	2244	28.8	49
Smith	82	3111	693	1523	.455	292	359	.813	102	193	295	395	177	1	177	5	1678	20.5	37
Weatherspoon	82	2642	479	998	.480	176	238	.739	179	275	454	135	287	6	80	37	1134	13.8	38
Washington	82	2764	350	623	.562	227	330	.688	296	504	800	125	317	11	85	121	927	11.3	29
Nater	79	2006	357	627	.569	132	165	.800	218	483	701	140	244	6	38	29	846	10.7	22
Williams	72	1195	335	683	.490	76	98	.776	48	50	98	83	88	0	42	2	746	10.4	26
Wicks	79	2022	312	676	.462	147	226	.650	159	246	405	126	274	4	70	36	771	9.8	22
Norman	22	323	71	165	.430	19	23	.826	13	19	32	24	35	0	10	3	161	7.3	21
Kunnert	81	1684	234	501	.467	56	85	.659	202	367	569	113	309	7	45	118	524	6.5	16
Taylor	20	212	30	83	.361	16	18	.889	13	13	26	20	34	0	24	0	76	3.8	13
Bigelow	29	413	36	90	.400	13	21	.619	15	31	46	25	37	0	12	2	85	2.9	11
Olive	34	189	13	40	.325	18	23	.783	3	16	19	3	32	0	4	0	44	1.3	7
Whitehead	31	152	15	34	.441	8	18	.444	16	34	50	7	29	0	3	4	38	1.2	6
Pietkiewicz	4	32	1	8	.125	2	2	1.000	0	6	6	3	5	0	1	0	4	1.0	2
Lloyd	5	31	0	2	.....	0	0	.000	7	6	13	0	6	0	1	0	0	0.0	0

SEATTLE SUPERSONICS

Player	G.	Min.	FGM	FGA	Pct.	FTM	FTA	Pct.	Off. Reb.	Def. Reb.	Tot. Reb.	Ast.	PF	Dsq.	Stl.	Blk. Sh.	Pts.	Avg.	Hi.
Williams	76	2266	606	1224	.495	245	316	.775	111	134	245	307	162	3	158	29	1457	19.2	38
D. Johnson	80	2717	482	1110	.434	306	392	.781	146	228	374	280	209	2	100	97	1270	15.9	30
Sikma	82	2958	476	1034	.460	329	404	.814	232	787	1013	261	295	4	82	67	1281	15.6	30
Brown	77	1961	446	951	.469	183	206	.888	38	134	172	260	142	0	119	23	1075	14.0	28
Shelton	76	2158	446	859	.519	131	189	.693	182	286	468	110	266	7	76	75	1023	13.5	28
J. Johnson	82	2386	356	821	.434	190	250	.760	127	285	412	358	245	2	59	25	902	11.0	21
LaGarde	23	575	98	181	.541	57	95	.600	61	129	190	32	75	2	6	18	253	11.0	32
Walker	60	969	167	343	.490	58	96	.604	66	111	177	69	127	0	12	26	394	6.6	19
Silas	82	1957	170	402	.423	116	194	.598	259	316	575	115	177	3	31	19	456	5.6	16
Hansen	15	205	29	57	.509	18	31	.581	22	37	59	14	28	0	1	1	76	5.1	19
Hassett	55	463	100	211	.474	23	23	1.000	13	32	45	42	58	0	14	4	223	4.1	18
Robinson	12	105	19	41	.463	8	15	.533	9	10	19	13	9	0	5	1	46	3.8	10
Snyder	23	536	81	187	.433	43	51	.843	15	33	48	63	52	0	14	6	205	3.7	16
Awtrey (Tot)	63	746	44	107	.411	41	56	.732	42	109	151	69	106	0	16	13	129	2.0	8
Awtrey (Sea)	40	499	27	63	.429	25	36	.694	29	75	104	49	69	0	13	7	79	2.0	8

WASHINGTON BULLETS

Player	G.	Min.	FGM	FGA	Pct.	FTM	FTA	Pct.	Off. Reb.	Def. Reb.	Tot. Reb.	Ast.	PF	Dsq.	Stl.	Blk. Sh.	Pts.	Avg.	Hi.
Hayes	82	3105	720	1477	.487	349	534	.654	312	682	994	143	308	5	75	190	1789	21.8	36
Dandridge	78	2629	629	1260	.499	331	401	.825	109	338	447	365	259	4	71	57	1589	20.4	38
Grevey	65	1856	418	922	.453	173	224	.772	90	142	232	153	159	1	46	14	1009	15.5	28
Kupchak	66	1604	369	685	.539	223	300	.743	152	278	430	88	141	0	23	23	961	14.6	32
Unseld	77	2406	346	600	.577	151	235	.643	274	556	830	315	204	2	71	37	843	10.9	28
Henderson	70	2081	299	641	.466	156	195	.800	51	112	163	419	123	0	87	10	754	10.8	24
Wright	73	1658	276	589	.469	125	168	.744	48	92	140	298	166	3	69	13	677	9.3	30
Johnson	82	1819	342	786	.435	67	79	.848	70	132	202	177	161	0	95	6	751	9.2	28
Ballard	82	1552	260	559	.465	119	172	.692	143	307	450	116	167	3	58	30	639	7.8	24
Chenier	27	385	69	158	.437	18	28	.643	3	17	20	31	28	0	4	5	156	5.8	20
Corzine	59	532	63	118	.534	49	63	.778	52	95	147	49	67	0	10	14	175	3.0	15
Phegley	29	153	28	78	.359	24	29	.828	5	17	22	15	21	0	5	2	80	2.8	14

INDIVIDUAL HIGHS

Most Minutes Played, Season .... 3390, Malone, Houston
Most Points, Game .... 52, Gervin, San Antonio vs. San Diego, 1/11
Most Field Goals, Game .... 24, Gervin, San Antonio vs. San Diego, 1/11
Most Free Throws, Game .... 22, Williamson, New Jersey vs. San Diego, 12/9
                                                                                       22, Free, San Diego at Atlanta, 1/13
Most Rebounds, Game .... 37, Malone, Houston at New Orleans, 2/9
Most Offensive Rebounds, Game .... 19, Malone, Houston at New Orleans, 2/9
Most Defensive Rebounds, Game .... 25, Gilmore, Chicago vs. San Antonio, 12/22
                                                                                       25, Parish, Golden State vs. New York, 3/30
Most Offensive Rebounds, Season .... 587, Malone, Houston
Most Defensive Rebounds, Season .... 857, Malone, Houston
Most Assists, Game .... 25, Porter, Detroit vs. Boston, 3/9, vs. Phoenix, 4/1
Most Blocked Shots, Game .... 12, Rollins, Atlanta vs. Portland, 2/21
Most Steals, Game .... 10, Jordan, New Jersey at Philadelphia, 3/23
Most Personal Fouls, Season .... 367, Robinzine, Kansas City
Most Games Disqualified, Season .... 19, Drew and Rollins, Atlanta
Most Turnovers, Season .... 346, McGinnis, Denver

TEAM HIGHS AND LOWS

Longest Winning Streak .... 14, Los Angeles (10/27-11/22)
Longest Losing Streak .... 9, Chicago (10/17-11/3)
Most Points, Game .... 163, San Antonio vs. San Diego, 11/8
Fewest Points, Game .... 76, Denver at Portland, 1/30
Most Points, Half .... 88, Los Angeles vs. San Diego, 3/23
Fewest Points, Half .... 27, Portland at New York, 12/2
                                                                                       27, Phoenix at Atlanta, 2/24
Most Points, Quarter .... 49, San Antonio vs. Detroit 10/28
Fewest Points, Quarter .... 9, Golden State vs. Portland, 4/6
Most Field Goals, Game .... 69, Detroit vs. Boston, 3/9
                                                                                       69, Milwaukee vs. New Orleans, 3/14
Fewest Field Goals, Game .... 29, Seattle vs. Milwaukee, 10/27
                                                                                       29, Portland at New York, 12/2
Most Free Throws, Game .... 44, Atlanta vs. Denver, 10/21
Fewest Free Throws, Game .... 4, Houston at Philadelphia, 12/15
                                                                                       4, Detroit at Milwaukee, 12/26
Most Rebounds, Game .... 74, Washington vs. Milwaukee, 3/16
Fewest Rebounds, Game .... 26, Phoenix vs. Denver, 11/10
Most Assists, Game .... 53, Milwaukee vs. Detroit, 12/26
Most Steals, Game .... 24, Philadelphia vs. Detroit, 11/11
Most Personal Fouls, Game .... 41, by four teams
Fewest Personal Fouls, Game .... 10, Phoenix vs. New York, 1/26
Most Blocked Shots, Game .... 19, Detroit vs. Chicago, 11/10
                                                                                       19, New Orleans vs. Indiana, 3/27
Most Turnovers, Game .... 38, Chicago vs. Phoenix, 10/27
                                                                                       38, Philadelphia vs. Phoenix, 3/4
Fewest Turnovers, Game .... 8, by seven teams

1978-79 PLAYOFF RESULTS

FIRST ROUND

EASTERN CONFERENCE

Philadelphia 2, New Jersey 0

Apr. 11—Wed.—New Jersey 114 at Philadelphia 122
Apr. 13—Fri.—Philadelphia 111 at New Jersey 101

Atlanta 2, Houston 0

Apr. 11—Wed.—Atlanta 109 at Houston...................106
Apr. 13—Fri.—Houston 91 at Atlanta.......................100

WESTERN CONFERENCE

Phoenix 2, Portland 1

Apr. 10—Tue.—Portland 103 at Phoenix 107
Apr. 13—Fri.—Phoenix 92 at Portland 96
Apr. 15—Sun.—Portland 91 at Phoenix.....................101

Los Angeles 2, Denver 1

Apr. 10—Tue.—Los Angeles 105 at Denver 110
Apr. 13—Fri.—Denver 109 at Los Angeles................121
Apr. 15—Sun.—Los Angeles 112 at Denver 111

CONFERENCE SEMI-FINAL SERIES

EASTERN CONFERENCE

Washington 4, Atlanta 3

Apr. 15—Sun.—Atlanta 89 at Washington 103
Apr. 17—Tue.—Atlanta 107 at Washington................99
Apr. 20—Fri.—Washington 89 at Atlanta...................77
Apr. 22—Sun.—Washington 120 at Atlanta (ot) 118
Apr. 24—Tue.—Atlanta 107 at Washington..............103
Apr. 26—Thu.—Washington 86 at Atlanta................104
Apr. 29—Sun.—Atlanta 94 at Washington 100

San Antonio 4, Philadelphia 3

Apr. 15—Sun.—Philadelphia 106 at San Antonio 119
Apr. 17—Tue.—Philadelphia 120 at San Antonio.....121
Apr. 20—Fri.—San Antonio 115 at Philadelphia......123
Apr. 22—Sun.—San Antonio 115 at Philadelphia....112
Apr. 26—Thu.—Philadelphia 120 at San Antonio 97
Apr. 29—Sun.—San Antonio 90 at Philadelphia 92
May 2—Wed.—Philadelphia 108 at San Antonio ...111

WESTERN CONFERENCE

Seattle 4, Los Angeles 1

Apr. 17—Tue.—Los Angeles 101 at Seattle 112
Apr. 18—Wed.—Los Angeles 103 at Seattle (ot) 108
Apr. 20—Fri.—Seattle 112 at Los Angeles (ot) 118
Apr. 22—Sun.—Seattle 117 at Los Angeles...............115
Apr. 25—Wed.—Los Angeles 100 at Seattle 106

Phoenix 4, Kansas City 1

Apr. 17—Tue.—Kansas City 99 at Phoenix 102
Apr. 20—Fri.—Phoenix 91 at Kansas City 111
Apr. 22—Sun.—Kansas City 93 at Phoenix 108
Apr. 25—Wed.—Phoenix 108 at Kansas City 94
Apr. 27—Fri.—Kansas City 99 at Phoenix 120

CONFERENCE FINALS

EASTERN CONFERENCE

Washington 4, San Antonio 3

May 4—Fri.—San Antonio 118 at Washington....... 97
May 6—Sun.—San Antonio 95 at Washington.......115
May 9—Wed.—Washington 114 at San Antonio 116
May 11—Fri.—Washington 102 at San Antonio......118
May 13—Sun.—San Antonio 103 at Washington 107
May 16—Wed.—Washington 108 at San Antonio ...100
May 18—Fri.—San Antonio 105 at Washington......107

WESTERN CONFERENCE

Seattle 4, Phoenix 3

May 1—Tue.—Phoenix 93 at Seattle 108
May 4—Fri.—Phoenix 91 at Seattle........................103
May 6—Sun.—Seattle 103 at Phoenix 113
May 8—Tue.—Seattle 91 at Phoenix 100
May 11—Fri.—Phoenix 99 at Seattle......................... 93
May 13—Sun.—Seattle 106 at Phoenix 105
May 17—Thu.—Phoenix 110 at Seattle 114

WORLD CHAMPIONSHIP SERIES

Seattle 4, Washington 1

May 20—Sun.—Seattle 97 at Washington 99
May 24—Thu.—Seattle 92 at Washington 82
May 27—Sun.—Washington 95 at Seattle 105
May 29—Tue.—Washington 112 at Seattle (ot) 114
June 1—Fri.—Seattle 97 at Washington................. 93

1977-78 STATISTICS

WASHINGTON BULLETS—1977-78 NBA CHAMPIONS

Seated (Left to Right): General Manager Bob Ferry, Coach Dick Motta, Larry Wright, Phil Chenier, Tom Henderson, Phil Walker, Owner Abe Pollin, Vice President Jerry Sachs. Standing: Assistant Coach Bernie Bickerstaff, Kevin Grevey, Greg Ballard, Elvin Hayes, Wes Unseld, Mitch Kupchak, Joe Pace, Bob Dandridge, Trainer John Lally. Inset: Charles Johnson.

FINAL STANDINGS AND TEAM FIGURES

ATLANTIC DIVISION

Team	Atl.	Bos.	Buf.	Chi.	Cle.	Den.	Det.	G.S.	Hou.	Ind.	K.C.	L.A.	Mil.	N.J.	N.O.	N.Y.	Phi.	Pho.	Por.	S.A.	Sea.	Was.	W.	L.	Pct.	G.B.
Philadelphia	2	4	3	1	3	3	4	3	2	2	3	2	2	4	2	3	-	2	2	3	3	2	55	27	.671	--
New York	2	2	1	3	1	3	3	2	2	3	4	1	1	3	3	-	1	1	1	2	2	2	43	39	.524	12
Boston	2	-	3	1	1	1	1	2	2	2	2	1	3	3	2	2	-	2	1	-	-	1	32	50	.390	23
Buffalo	1	1	-	3	1	1	1	-	3	1	1	1	1	2	2	3	1	-	1	1	1	1	27	55	.329	28
New Jersey	1	1	2	2	1	1	1	1	1	2	2	-	1	-	1	-	2	-	-	2	2	2	24	58	.293	31

CENTRAL DIVISION

San Antonio	3	4	3	2	4	1	2	1	3	3	4	2	2	4	3	2	1	2	2	-	2	2	52	30	.634	--
Washington	3	3	3	1	2	1	2	2	3	1	2	2	1	2	4	2	2	2	1	2	3	-	44	38	.537	8
Cleveland	3	3	3	1	-	3	2	2	2	2	2	2	3	3	2	3	1	1	-	-	3	2	43	39	.524	9
Atlanta	-	2	3	1	1	1	2	1	3	3	2	3	2	3	2	2	2	3	1	1	2	1	41	41	.500	11
New Orleans	2	2	2	2	2	1	1	4	3	2	2	1	1	4	-	1	2	1	3	1	2	-	39	43	.476	13
Houston	1	2	1	1	2	-	1	1	-	3	2	1	1	2	1	2	2	1	2	1	-	1	28	54	.341	24

MIDWEST DIVISION

Denver	3	3	3	2	1	-	2	2	3	2	2	3	3	3	3	1	1	2	3	2	1	3	48	34	.585	--
Milwaukee	2	1	3	3	1	2	2	3	4	4	1	-	3	2	3	1	1	1	2	1	3	2	44	38	.537	4
Chicago	3	3	1	-	3	2	2	1	3	3	-	2	1	1	2	1	3	2	1	2	2	2	40	42	.488	8
Detroit	2	3	3	2	2	2	-	2	3	1	2	2	3	3	-	-	2	1	1	1	1	3	38	44	.463	10
Indiana	1	1	3	1	1	2	3	1	2	-	2	1	-	2	2	2	1	2	1	1	1	1	31	51	.378	17
Kansas City	1	2	2	4	2	2	3	1	2	2	-	2	-	2	-	2	-	1	-	-	-	1	.2	31	51	.378	17

PACIFIC DIVISION

Portland	3	3	3	3	4	1	3	3	2	3	4	4	3	3	1	3	2	3	-	2	3	2	58	24	.707	--
Phoenix	1	2	4	2	2	2	2	2	3	3	4	3	2	3	3	1	-	1	2	2	2	2	49	33	.598	9
Seattle	1	4	3	2	1	3	3	2	4	3	3	3	2	1	1	2	1	2	-	2	1	-	47	35	.573	11
Los Angeles	1	2	3	2	2	1	2	4	3	3	2	-	3	4	2	3	2	1	-	2	1	2	45	37	.549	13
Golden State	3	2	3	3	2	2	2	-	2	3	3	-	2	3	-	2	1	2	1	3	2	2	43	39	.524	15

TEAM STATISTICS—OFFENSE

Team	G.	FIELD GOALS Made	Att.	Pct.	FREE THROWS Made	Att.	Pct.	REBOUNDS Off.	Def.	Tot.	MISCELLANEOUS Ast.	PF	Stl.	Blk. Sh.	Turn Over	Dq.	SCORING Pts.	Avg.
Phil.	82	3628	7471	.486	2153	2863	.752	1299	2694	3993	2220	2188	80	548	1752	20	9409	114.7
S.A.	82	3794	7594	.500	1797	2234	.804	1030	2594	3624	2240	1871	797	553	1665	16	9385	114.5
N.Y.	82	3815	7822	.488	1670	2225	.751	1180	2689	3869	2338	2193	818	442	1764	26	9300	113.4
Mil.	82	3801	7883	.482	1612	2220	.726	1239	2480	3719	2306	2038	867	472	1680	23	9214	112.4
Phoe.	82	3731	7836	.476	1749	2329	.751	1166	2579	3745	2338	1956	1059	372	1766	14	9211	112.3
Den.	82	3548	7441	.477	2068	2705	.765	1177	2736	3913	2187	2116	824	422	1748	20	9164	111.8
Wash.	82	3580	7772	.461	1887	2655	.711	1349	2815	4164	1948	1879	668	386	1613	25	9047	110.3
L.A.	82	3734	7672	.487	1576	2095	.752	1136	2647	3783	2229	1964	802	409	1548	18	9044	110.3
K.C.	82	3601	7731	.466	1775	2262	.785	1208	2632	3840	1992	2228	794	370	1690	37	8977	109.5
Det.	82	3552	7424	.478	1832	2490	.736	1229	2601	3830	1840	1980	866	330	1858	29	8936	109.0
Ind.	82	3500	7783	.450	1904	2564	.743	1386	2624	4010	1982	2230	808	456	1642	53	8904	108.6
Port.	82	3556	7367	.483	1717	2259	.760	1187	2686	3873	2067	2068	798	390	1625	30	8829	107.7
N.O.	82	3568	7717	.462	1690	2331	.725	1309	2907	4216	2079	1938	662	514	1694	35	8826	107.6
N.J.	82	3547	8004	.443	1652	2304	.717	1306	2595	3901	1879	2312	857	631	1774	72	8746	106.7
G.S.	82	3574	7654	.467	1550	2081	.745	1183	2629	3812	2097	2113	873	405	1518	29	8698	106.1
Bos.	82	3494	7635	.458	1682	2159	.779	1235	2850	4085	1969	2033	643	295	1652	32	8670	105.7
Buff.	82	3413	7323	.466	1808	2314	.781	1205	2538	3621	1975	2017	650	327	1575	31	8634	105.3
Sea.	82	3445	7715	.447	1675	2352	.712	1456	2601	4057	1799	2008	782	429	1636	24	8565	104.5
Clev.	82	3496	7707	.454	1569	2116	.741	1187	2676	3863	1740	1832	692	455	1382	15	8561	104.4
Chi.	82	3330	7041	.473	1863	2471	.754	1248	2577	3825	2119	1930	665	322	1667	30	8523	103.9
Hou.	82	3523	7691	.458	1467	1896	.774	1301	2421	3722	1942	2025	683	319	1376	32	8513	103.8
Atl.	82	3335	7253	.460	1836	2316	.793	1160	2359	3519	1901	2470	916	408	1592	80	8506	103.7

TEAM STATISTICS—DEFENSE

Team	FIELD GOALS Made	Att.	Pct.	FREE THROWS Made	Att.	Pct.	REBOUNDS Off.	Def.	Tot.	MISCELLANEOUS Ast.	PF	Stl.	Blk. Sh.	Turn Over	Dq.	SCORING Pts.	Avg.	Dif.
Port.	3289	7418	.449	1747	2282	.766	1187	2523	3710	2018	2093	748	390	1624	36	8325	101.5	+ 6.2
Sea.	3384	7377	.459	1670	2203	.758	1121	2600	3721	1956	2067	735	410	1646	26	8438	102.9	+ 1.6
Atl.	3162	6671	.474	2193	2930	.748	1160	2606	3766	1774	2122	750	484	1980	36	8517	103.9	– 0.2
Clev.	3474	7620	.456	1574	2113	.745	1214	2779	3993	1915	1952	690	446	1475	16	8522	103.9	+ 0.4
Chi.	3565	7273	.490	1466	1980	.740	1065	2367	3432	2074	2199	777	451	1479	46	8596	104.8	– 0.9
G.S.	3425	7368	.465	1820	2408	.756	1185	2794	3979	2037	1975	728	408	1738	21	8670	105.7	– 0.4
L.A.	3648	7880	.463	1529	2050	.746	1365	2599	3964	2073	1919	756	379	1570	33	8825	107.6	+ 2.7
Bos.	3539	7761	.456	1752	2258	.769	1142	2575	3717	1981	1871	763	374	1412	24	8830	107.7	– 2.0
Hou.	3571	7404	.482	1699	2238	.759	1195	2525	3720	1990	1752	605	360	1410	18	8841	107.8	– 4.0
Phoe.	3578	7622	.469	1749	2319	.754	1202	2743	3945	1988	2178	937	372	1969	41	8905	108.6	+ 3.7
Buff.	3623	7609	.476	1695	2250	.753	1178	2587	3765	2137	2003	722	375	1476	25	8941	109.0	– 3.7
Wash.	3767	8065	.467	1437	1895	.758	1166	2683	3849	2144	2312	779	427	1437	50	8971	109.4	+ 0.9
N.O.	3659	7938	.461	1661	2213	.751	1273	2747	4020	2084	2062	851	476	1511	28	8979	109.5	– 1.9
Phil.	3592	7788	.461	1803	2435	.740	1363	2473	3836	2095	2287	823	346	1709	50	8993	109.6	+ 5.1
Det.	3688	7706	.479	1662	2177	.763	1244	2494	3738	2105	2088	902	395	1719	27	9038	110.2	– 1.2
Den.	3678	7799	.472	1740	2365	.736	1267	2126	25463813	2248	2220	877	524	1620	49	9096	110.9	+ 0.9
Ind.	3634	7663	.474	1841	2455	.750	1350	2793	4143	2259	2135	727	466	1762	39	9109	111.1	– 2.5
S.A.	3808	8063	.472	1494	1996	.748	1345	2576	3921	2145	2059	837	379	1662	25	9110	111.1	+ 3.4
K.C.	3564	7521	.474	2004	2635	.761	1232	2684	3916	1928	2088	796	408	1694	18	9132	111.4	– 1.9
N.J.	3544	7620	.465	2135	2830	.754	1312	2996	4308	2073	1999	852	560	1864	29	9223	112.5	– 5.8
Mil.	3715	7728	.481	1832	2404	.762	1234	2617	3851	2248	2019	790	468	1783	28	9262	113.0	– 0.6
N.Y.	3658	7742	.472	2029	2785	.729	1254	2623	3877	2113	1989	879	357	1677	31	9345	114.0	– 0.6

DQ—Individual players disqualified (fouled out of game)

INDIVIDUAL SCORING LEADERS

(Minimum 70 games played) or 1400 points

	G.	FG	FT	Pts.	Avg.		G.	FG	FT	Pts.	Avg.
Gervin, S.A.	82	864	504	2232	27.22	Williamson, Ind.-N.J.	75	723	331	1777	23.7
Thompson, Den.	80	826	520	2172	27.15	Drew, Atl.	70	593	437	1623	23.2
McAdoo, N.Y.	79	814	469	2097	26.5	Barry, G.S.	82	760	378	1898	23.1
Abdul-Jabbar, L.A.	62	663	274	1600	25.8	Gilmore, Chi.	82	704	471	1879	22.9
Murphy, Hou.	76	852	245	1949	25.6	Robinson, N.O.	82	748	366	1862	22.7
Westphal, Phoe.	80	809	396	2014	25.2	Dantley, L.A.	79	578	541	1697	21.5
Smith, Buff.	82	789	443	2021	24.6	Issel, Den.	82	659	428	1746	21.3
Lanier, Det.	63	622	298	1542	24.5	Erving, Phila.	74	611	306	1528	20.6
Davis, Phoe.	81	786	387	1959	24.2	Kenon, S.A.	81	698	276	1672	20.6
King, N.J.	79	798	313	1909	24.2	McGinnis, Phil.	78	588	411	1587	20.3

FIELD GOAL LEADERS
(Minimum 300 FG Made)

	FGM	FGA	Pct.
Jones, Den.	440	761	.578
Dawkins, Phil.	332	577	.575
Gilmore, Chi.	704	1260	.559
Abdul-Jabbar, L.A.	663	1205	.550
English, Mil.	343	633	.542
Lanier, Det.	622	1159	.537
Gervin, S.A.	864	1611	.536
Gross, Port.	381	720	.529
Paultz, S.A.	518	979	.529
Davis, Phoe.	786	1494	.526

FREE THROW LEADERS
(Minimum 125 FT Made)

	FTM	FTA	Pct.
Barry, G.S.	378	409	.924
Murphy, Hou.	245	267	.918
Brown, Sea.	176	196	.898
Newlin, Hou.	152	174	.874
Wedman, K.C.	221	254	.870
Maravich, N.O.	240	276	.870
Havlicek, Bos.	230	269	.855
Kenon, S.A.	276	323	.854
Boone, K.C.	322	377	.854
Frazier, Clev.	153	180	.850

REBOUND LEADERS
Minimum 70 games or 800 rebounds

	G.	Off.	Def.	Tot.	Avg.
Robinson, N.O.	82	298	990	1288	15.7
Malone, Hou.	59	380	506	886	15.0
Cowens, Bos.	77	248	830	1078	14.0
Hayes, Wash.	81	335	740	1075	13.3
Nater, Buff.	78	278	751	1029	13.2
Gilmore, Chi.	82	318	753	1071	13.1
Abdul-Jabbar, L.A.	62	186	615	801	12.9
McAdoo, N.Y.	79	236	774	1010	12.8
Webster, Sea.	82	361	674	1035	12.6
Unseld, Wash.	80	286	669	955	11.9

BLOCKED SHOTS LEADERS
Minimum 70 games or 100 blocked shots

	G.	No.	Avg.
Johnson, N.J.	81	274	3.38
Abdul-Jabbar, L.A.	62	185	2.98
Rollins, Atl.	80	218	2.73
Walton, Port.	58	146	2.52
Paultz, S.A.	80	194	2.43
Gilmore, Chi.	82	181	2.21
Meriweather, N.O.	54	118	2.19
E. Smith, Clev.	81	176	2.17
Webster, Sea.	82	162	1.98
Hayes, Wash.	81	159	1.96

ASSISTS LEADERS
Minimum 70 games or 400 assists

	G.	No.	Avg.
K. Porter, Det.-N.J.	82	837	10.2
Lucas, Hou.	82	768	9.4
Sobers, Ind.	79	584	7.4
Nixon, L.A.	81	553	6.8
Van Lier, Chi.	78	531	6.8
Bibby, Phil.	82	464	5.7
Walker, Clev.	81	453	5.6
Smith, Buff.	82	458	5.6
Buckner, Mil.	82	456	5.6
Westphal, Phoe.	80	437	5.5

STEALS LEADERS
Minimum 70 games or 125 steals

	G.	No.	Avg
Lee, Phoe.	82	225	2.74
Williams, Sea.	79	185	2.34
Buckner, Mil.	82	188	2.29
Gale, S.A.	70	159	2.27
Buse, Phoe.	82	185	2.26
Walker, Clev.	81	176	2.17
Sobers, Ind.	79	170	2.15
Smith, Buff.	82	172	2.10
Ford, Det.	82	166	2.02
Holland, Chi.	82	164	2.00

RECORDS OF TEAMS BY MONTHS

Team	Oct. W-L	Nov. W-L	Dec. W-L	Jan. W-L	Feb. W-L	Mar. W-L	Apr. W-L	Total W-L
Atlanta	3-1	8-6	6-11	6-9	6-6	8-7	4-1	41-41
Boston	1-5	6-7	4-11	4-7	7-5	8-10	2-5	32-50
Buffalo	2-4	8-6	3-10	3-9	3-10	7-10	1-6	27-55
Chicago	4-2	6-7	10-5	7-8	5-10	6-8	2-2	40-42
Cleveland	3-3	10-2	5-10	4-9	8-7	8-8	5-0	43-39
Denver	4-2	10-6	7-5	10-4	8-6	5-9	4-2	48-34
Detroit	4-3	4-8	7-7	7-7	6-7	8-8	2-4	38-44
Golden State	5-2	5-9	5-9	9-5	5-7	11-5	3-2	43-39
Houston	3-2	4-10	6-8	3-11	8-7	1-13	3-3	28-54
Indiana	3-2	4-11	7-4	5-11	3-11	7-10	2-2	31-51
Kansas City	3-4	4-9	6-8	3-13	8-4	7-8	0-5	31-51
Los Angeles	2-5	6-8	8-5	7-7	9-4	10-6	3-2	45-37
Milwaukee	3-2	8-8	9-7	6-8	7-4	8-7	3-2	44-38
New Jersey	1-4	2-13	5-9	1-14	5-7	9-7	1-4	24-58
New Orleans	4-1	7-9	3-10	11-4	4-9	7-9	3-1	39-43
New York	3-2	8-7	8-6	7-8	6-5	7-10	4-1	43-39
Philadelphia	2-3	14-2	6-6	10-3	9-5	12-3	2-5	55-27
Phoenix	3-3	8-4	10-6	12-2	5-8	9-7	2-3	49-33
Portland	4-1	12-2	11-2	12-3	11-2	6-11	2-3	58-24
San Antonio	4-3	8-7	7-6	11-2	7-5	12-5	3-2	52-30
Seattle	1-6	5-11	11-3	10-2	7-5	9-7	4-1	47-35
Washington	1-3	9-4	10-6	6-8	5-8	10-7	3-2	44-38

INDIVIDUAL STATISTICS

ATLANTA

Player	G.	Min.	FGM	FGA	Pct.	FTM	FTA	Pct.	Off. Reb.	Def. Reb.	Tot. Reb.	Ast.	PF	Dsq.	Stl.	Blk. Sh.	Pts.	Avg.	Hi.
Drew	70	2203	593	1236	.480	437	575	.760	213	298	511	141	247	8	119	27	1623	23.2	48
Hawes	75	2325	387	854	.453	175	214	.818	180	510	690	190	230	4	78	57	949	12.7	27
Criss	77	1935	319	751	.425	236	296	.797	24	97	121	294	143	0	108	5	874	11.4	30
Behagen	26	571	117	249	.470	51	70	.729	53	120	173	34	97	3	30	12	285	11.0	22
E. Johnson	79	1875	332	686	.484	164	201	.816	51	102	153	235	232	4	100	4	828	10.5	29
McMillen	68	1683	280	568	.493	116	145	.800	151	265	416	84	233	8	33	16	676	9.9	23
Hill	82	2530	304	732	.415	189	223	.848	59	172	231	427	302	15	151	15	797	9.7	21
Charles	21	520	73	184	.397	42	50	.840	6	18	24	82	53	0	25	5	188	9.0	17
O. Johnson	82	1704	292	619	.472	111	130	.854	89	171	260	120	180	2	80	36	695	8.5	22
Rollins	80	1795	253	520	.487	104	148	.703	179	373	552	79	326	16	57	218	610	7.6	21
Brown	75	1594	192	405	.474	165	200	.825	137	166	303	105	280	18	55	8	549	7.3	27
Robertson	63	929	168	381	.441	37	53	.698	15	55	70	103	133	2	74	5	373	5.9	18
Terry	27	166	25	68	.368	9	11	.818	3	12	15	7	14	0	6	0	59	2.2	6

BOSTON

Player	G.	Min.	FGM	FGA	Pct.	FTM	FTA	Pct.	Off. Reb.	Def. Reb.	Tot. Reb.	Ast.	PF	Dsq.	Stl.	Blk. Sh.	Pts.	Avg.	Hi.
Cowens	77	3215	598	1220	.490	239	284	.842	248	830	1078	351	297	5	102	67	1435	18.6	36
Scott	31	1080	210	485	.433	84	118	.712	24	77	101	143	97	2	51	6	504	16.3	30
Havlicek	82	2797	546	1217	.449	230	269	.855	93	239	332	328	185	2	90	22	1322	16.1	32
White	46	1641	289	690	.419	103	120	.858	53	127	180	209	109	2	49	7	681	14.8	27
Bing	80	2256	422	940	.449	244	296	.824	76	136	212	300	247	2	79	18	1088	13.6	30
Wicks	81	2413	433	927	.467	217	329	.660	223	450	673	171	318	9	67	46	1083	13.4	35
Wash'n (Tot)	57	1617	247	507	.487	170	246	.691	215	399	614	72	188	3	47	64	664	11.6	22
Wash'n (Bs)	32	866	137	263	.521	102	136	.750	105	230	335	42	114	2	28	40	376	11.8	18
Stacom	55	1006	206	484	.426	54	71	.761	26	80	106	111	60	0	28	3	466	8.5	22
Maxwell	72	1213	170	316	.538	188	250	.752	138	241	379	68	151	2	53	48	528	7.3	21
Boswell	65	1149	185	357	.518	93	123	.756	117	171	288	71	204	5	25	14	463	7.1	22
Rowe	51	911	123	273	.451	66	89	.742	74	129	203	45	94	1	14	8	312	6.1	20
Chaney (Tot)	51	835	104	269	.387	38	45	.844	40	76	116	66	107	0	44	13	246	4.8	17
Chaney (Bs)	42	702	91	233	.391	33	39	.846	36	69	105	49	93	0	36	10	215	5.1	17
Abdul-Aziz	2	24	3	13	.231	2	3	.667	6	9	15	3	4	0	1	1	8	4.0	6
DiGi'o (Tot)	52	606	88	209	.421	28	33	.848	7	43	50	137	44	0	18	1	204	3.9	24
DiGi'o (Bos)	27	247	47	109	.431	12	13	.923	2	25	27	66	22	0	12	1	106	3.9	24
Saunders	26	243	30	91	.330	14	17	.824	11	26	37	11	34	0	7	4	74	2.8	12
Bi'low (Tot)	5	24	4	13	.308	0	0	....	3	6	9	0	3	0	0	0	8	1.6	4
Bi'low (Bos)	4	17	3	12	.250	0	0	....	1	3	4	0	1	0	0	0	6	1.5	4
Ard	1	9	0	1	.000	1	2	.500	1	3	4	1	1	0	0	0	1	1.0	1
Kuberski	3	14	1	4	.250	0	0	....	1	5	6	0	2	0	1	0	2	0.7	2

BUFFALO

Player	G.	Min.	FGM	FGA	Pct.	FTM	FTA	Pct.	Off. Reb.	Def. Reb.	Tot. Reb.	Ast.	PF	Dsq.	Stl.	Blk. Sh.	Pts.	Avg.	Hi.
Smith	82	3314	789	1697	.465	443	554	.800	110	200	310	458	224	2	172	11	2021	24.6	40
Knight	53	2155	457	926	.494	301	372	.809	126	257	383	161	137	0	82	13	1215	22.9	41
Nater	78	2778	501	994	.504	208	272	.765	278	751	1029	216	274	3	40	47	1210	15.5	35
Shumate	18	590	75	151	.497	74	99	.747	32	96	128	58	58	1	14	9	224	12.4	26
Barnes (Tot)	60	1646	279	661	.422	128	182	.703	135	304	439	136	241	9	64	83	686	11.4	27
Barnes (Bf)	48	1377	226	543	.416	114	153	.745	107	241	348	117	198	7	57	72	566	11.8	27
McN'l (Tot)	46	940	162	356	.455	145	175	.829	80	122	202	47	114	1	18	11	469	10.2	31
McN'l (Buff)	37	873	156	338	.462	130	156	.833	78	110	188	45	100	1	18	10	442	11.9	31
Av'itt (Tot)	55	1085	198	484	.409	100	141	.709	17	66	83	196	123	3	39	9	496	9.0	32
Av'itt (Buff)	34	676	129	296	.436	64	96	.667	10	40	50	128	86	2	22	8	322	9.5	24
Glenn	56	947	195	370	.527	51	65	.785	14	65	79	78	98	0	35	5	441	7.9	25
Williams	73	2002	208	436	.477	114	138	.826	29	108	137	317	137	0	48	4	530	7.3	22
Jones	79	1711	226	514	.440	84	119	.706	106	228	334	116	255	7	70	43	536	6.8	18
Willoughby	56	1079	156	363	.430	64	80	.800	76	143	219	38	131	2	24	47	376	6.7	20
McDaniels	42	694	100	234	.427	36	42	.857	46	135	181	44	112	3	4	37	236	5.6	26
McClain	41	727	81	184	.440	50	63	.794	11	64	75	123	88	2	42	2	212	5.2	17
Gerard	10	85	16	40	.400	11	15	.733	6	8	14	9	13	0	2	3	43	4.3	13
Brokaw	13	130	18	43	.419	18	24	.750	3	9	12	20	11	0	3	5	54	4.2	16
Lloyd (Tot)	29	267	39	80	.487	26	36	.721	52	93	145	44	105	1	14	14	209	3.0	10
Lloyd (Buff)	56	566	68	160	.425	43	58	.741	45	74	119	35	83	1	11	9	179	3.2	10
Owens	8	63	9	21	.429	3	6	.500	5	5	10	5	9	0	1	0	21	2.6	8
Johnson	4	38	3	13	.231	0	2	.000	4	5	7	3	0	5	2	6	1.5	6

1977-78 STATISTICS

CHICAGO

Player	G.	Min.	FGM	FGA	Pct.	FTM	FTA	Pct.	Off. Reb.	Def. Reb.	Tot. Reb.	Ast.	PF	Dsq.	Stl.	Blk. Sh.	Pts.	Avg.	Hi.
Gilmore	82	3067	704	1260	.559	471	669	.704	318	753	1071	263	261	4	42	81	1879	22.9	38
Johnson	81	2870	561	1215	.462	362	446	.812	218	520	738	267	317	8	92	68	1484	18.3	39
Holland	82	2884	569	1285	.443	223	279	.799	105	189	294	313	258	4	164	14	1361	16.6	36
May	55	1802	280	617	.454	175	216	.810	118	214	332	114	170	4	50	6	735	13.4	27
Mengelt	81	1767	325	675	.481	184	238	.773	41	88	129	232	169	0	51	4	834	10.3	27
Russell	36	789	133	304	.438	49	57	.860	31	52	83	61	63	1	19	4	315	8.8	24
Van Lier	78	2524	200	477	.419	172	229	.751	86	198	284	531	279	9	144	5	572	7.3	23
Landsberger	62	926	127	251	.506	91	157	.580	110	191	301	41	78	0	21	6	345	5.6	25
Wea'spoon	41	611	86	194	.443	37	42	.881	57	68	125	32	74	0	19	10	209	5.1	17
Sheppard	64	698	119	262	.454	37	56	.661	67	64	131	43	72	0	14	3	275	4.3	22
Armstrong	66	716	131	280	.468	22	27	.815	24	44	68	74	42	0	23	0	284	4.3	22
Dickey (Tot)	47	493	87	198	.439	30	36	.833	36	61	97	21	56	0	14	4	204	4.3	18
Dickey (Chi)	25	220	27	68	.397	14	19	.737	15	33	48	10	27	0	4	2	68	2.7	11
Boerwinkle	22	227	23	50	.460	10	13	.769	14	45	59	44	36	0	3	4	56	2.5	10
Pondexter	64	534	37	85	.435	14	20	.700	36	94	130	87	66	0	19	15	88	2.0	14
Ard (Tot)	15	125	8	17	.471	3	5	.600	9	27	36	8	19	0	0	0	19	1.3	4
Ard (Chi)	14	116	8	16	.500	2	3	.667	8	24	32	7	18	0	0	0	18	1.3	4
Hansen	2	4	0	2	.000	0	0	......	0	0	0	0	0	0	0	0	0	0.0	0

CLEVELAND

Player	G.	Min.	FGM	FGA	Pct.	FTM	FTA	Pct.	Off. Reb.	Def. Reb.	Tot. Reb.	Ast.	PF	Dsq.	Stl.	Blk. Sh.	Pts.	Avg.	Hi.
Russell	72	2520	523	1168	.448	352	469	.751	154	304	458	278	193	3	88	12	1398	19.4	38
Frazier	51	1664	336	714	.471	153	180	.850	54	155	209	209	124	1	77	13	825	16.2	29
Chones	82	2906	525	1113	.472	180	250	.720	219	625	844	131	235	4	52	58	1230	15.0	31
E. Smith	81	1996	402	809	.497	205	309	.663	178	500	678	57	241	4	50	176	1009	12.5	32
Carr	82	2186	414	945	.438	183	225	.813	76	111	187	225	168	1	68	19	1011	12.3	30
B. Smith	82	1581	369	840	.439	108	135	.800	65	142	207	91	155	1	38	21	846	10.3	30
Walker	81	2496	287	641	.448	159	221	.719	76	218	294	453	218	0	176	24	733	9.0	20
Furlow	53	827	192	443	.433	88	99	.889	47	60	107	72	67	0	21	14	472	8.9	23
Brewer	80	1798	175	390	.449	46	100	.460	182	313	495	98	178	1	60	48	396	5.0	20
Snyder	58	660	112	252	.444	56	64	.875	9	40	49	56	74	0	23	19	280	4.8	17
Lambert	76	1075	142	336	.423	27	48	.563	125	199	324	38	169	0	27	50	311	4.1	16
Jordan	22	171	19	56	.339	12	16	.750	2	9	11	32	10	0	12	1	50	2.3	11

DENVER

Player	G.	Min.	FGM	FGA	Pct.	FTM	FTA	Pct.	Off. Reb.	Def. Reb.	Tot. Reb.	Ast.	PF	Dsq.	Stl.	Blk. Sh.	Pts.	Avg.	Hi.
Thompson	80	3025	826	1584	.521	520	668	.778	156	234	390	362	213	1	92	99	2172	27.2	73
Issel	82	2851	659	1287	.512	428	547	.782	253	577	830	304	279	5	100	41	1746	21.3	40
Jones	75	2440	440	761	.578	208	277	.751	164	472	636	252	221	2	137	126	1088	14.5	29
Taylor	39	1222	182	403	.452	88	115	.765	30	68	98	132	120	1	71	9	452	11.6	23
Wilkerson	81	2780	382	936	.408	157	210	.748	98	376	474	439	275	3	126	21	921	11.4	24
Hill'n (Tot)	78	1966	340	710	.479	167	286	.584	199	378	577	102	290	11	63	81	847	10.9	28
Hill'n (Den)	33	746	104	209	.498	49	81	.605	73	166	239	53	130	4	14	37	257	7.8	16
Roberts	82	1598	311	736	.423	153	212	.722	135	216	351	105	212	1	40	7	775	9.5	27
S'son (Tot)	64	1323	216	576	.375	85	104	.817	53	104	157	159	90	1	75	7	517	8.1	23
S'son (Den)	32	584	73	230	.317	31	40	.775	26	49	75	72	42	0	43	4	177	5.5	21
Price	49	1090	141	293	.481	51	66	.773	30	129	159	158	118	0	69	4	333	6.8	22
Calvin	77	988	147	333	.441	173	206	.840	11	73	84	148	87	0	46	5	467	6.1	20
Ellis	78	1213	133	320	.416	72	104	.692	114	190	304	73	208	2	49	47	338	4.3	13
LaGarde	77	868	96	237	.405	114	150	.760	75	139	214	47	146	1	17	17	306	4.0	14
Smith	45	378	50	97	.515	21	24	.875	6	30	36	39	52	0	18	3	121	2.7	10
Dorsey	7	37	3	12	.250	3	5	.600	5	15	20	2	9	0	2	2	9	1.3	3
Cook	2	10	1	3	.333	0	0	......	1	2	3	1	4	0	0	0	2	1.0	2

1977-78 STATISTICS

DETROIT

Player	G.	Min.	FGM	FGA	Pct.	FTM	FTA	Pct.	Off. Reb.	Def. Reb.	Tot. Reb.	Ast.	PF	Dsq.	Stl.	Blk. Sh.	Pts.	Avg.	Hi.
Lanier	63	2311	622	1159	.537	298	386	.772	197	518	715	216	185	2	82	93	1542	24.5	41
Money	76	2557	600	1200	.500	214	298	.718	90	119	209	356	237	5	123	12	1414	18.6	39
Shu'te (Tot)	80	2760	391	773	.506	400	508	.787	157	525	682	180	200	2	90	52	1182	14.8	31
Shu'te (Det)	62	2170	316	622	.508	326	409	.797	125	429	554	122	142	1	76	43	958	15.5	31
Carr	79	2556	390	857	.455	200	271	.738	202	355	557	185	243	4	147	27	980	12.4	28
Douglas	79	1993	321	667	.481	221	345	.641	181	401	582	112	295	6	57	48	863	10.9	28
Simpson	32	739	143	346	.413	54	64	.844	27	55	82	87	48	1	32	3	340	10.6	23
Ford	82	2582	374	777	.481	113	154	.734	117	151	268	381	182	2	166	17	861	10.5	25
Barnes	12	269	53	118	.449	14	29	.483	28	63	91	19	43	2	7	11	120	10.0	15
Price (Tot)	83	1929	294	656	.448	135	169	.799	57	203	260	260	200	0	114	9	723	8.7	26
Price (Det)	34	839	153	363	.421	84	103	.816	27	74	101	102	82	0	45	5	390	11.5	26
Sk'ner (Tot)	77	1551	222	488	.455	162	203	.798	67	157	224	146	242	6	65	20	606	7.9	28
Sk'ner (Det)	69	1274	181	387	.468	123	159	.774	53	119	172	113	208	4	52	15	485	7.0	27
Gerard (Tot)	57	890	170	395	.430	75	108	.694	55	105	160	53	109	1	36	25	415	7.3	20
Gerard (Det)	47	805	154	355	.434	64	93	.688	49	97	146	44	96	1	34	22	372	7.9	20
Bostic	4	48	12	22	.545	2	5	.400	8	8	16	3	5	0	0	0	26	6.5	12
Norwood	16	260	34	82	.415	20	29	.690	27	27	54	14	45	0	13	3	88	5.5	13
Eberhard	37	576	71	160	.444	41	61	.672	37	65	102	26	64	0	13	4	183	4.9	20
K. Porter	8	127	14	31	.452	9	13	.692	5	10	15	36	18	0	5	0	37	4.6	14
Poquette	52	626	95	225	.422	42	60	.700	50	95	145	20	69	1	10	22	232	4.5	18
H. Porter	8	107	16	43	.372	4	7	.571	5	12	17	2	15	0	3	5	36	4.5	11
Britt	7	16	3	10	.300	3	4	.750	1	3	4	2	3	0	1	0	9	1.3	4

GOLDEN STATE

Player	G.	Min.	FGM	FGA	Pct.	FTM	FTA	Pct.	Off. Reb.	Def. Reb.	Tot. Reb.	Ast.	PF	Dsq.	Stl.	Blk. Sh.	Pts.	Avg.	Hi.
Barry	82	3024	760	1686	.451	378	409	.924	75	374	449	446	188	1	158	45	1898	23.1	55
Smith	82	2940	648	1373	.472	316	389	.812	100	200	300	393	219	2	108	27	1612	19.7	33
Parish	82	1969	430	911	.472	165	264	.625	211	469	680	95	291	10	79	123	1025	12.5	28
Parker	82	2069	406	783	.519	122	173	.705	167	222	389	155	186	0	135	36	934	11.4	26
Wil'ms (Tot)	73	1249	312	724	.431	101	121	.835	65	139	204	74	181	3	57	34	725	9.9	27
Wil'ms (GS)	46	815	222	510	.435	70	84	.833	38	76	114	40	120	2	36	22	514	11.2	27
Ray	79	2268	272	476	.571	148	243	.609	236	522	758	147	291	9	74	90	692	8.8	21
Coleman	72	1801	212	446	.475	40	55	.727	117	259	376	100	253	4	66	23	464	6.4	18
Johnson	32	492	96	235	.409	7	10	.700	23	29	52	48	53	0	31	4	199	6.2	23
Dickey	22	273	60	130	.462	16	17	.941	21	28	49	11	29	0	10	2	136	6.2	18
Dudley	78	1660	127	249	.510	138	195	.708	86	201	287	409	181	0	68	2	392	5.0	14
Cox	43	453	69	173	.399	58	100	.580	42	101	143	12	82	1	21	10	196	4.6	23
Marsh	60	851	123	289	.426	23	33	.697	16	59	75	90	111	0	29	19	269	4.5	23
Green	76	1098	143	375	.381	54	90	.600	49	67	116	149	95	0	58	5	340	4.5	22
McNeill	9	67	6	18	.333	15	19	.789	2	12	14	2	14	0	0	1	27	3.0	6

HOUSTON

Player	G.	Min.	FGM	FGA	Pct.	FTM	FTA	Pct.	Off. Reb.	Def. Reb.	Tot. Reb.	Ast.	PF	Dsq.	Stl.	Blk. Sh.	Pts.	Avg.	Hi.
Murphy	76	2900	852	1737	.491	245	267	.918	57	107	164	259	241	4	112	3	1949	25.6	57
Tomjanovich	23	849	217	447	.485	61	81	.753	40	98	138	32	63	0	15	5	495	21.5	35
Malone	59	2107	413	828	.499	318	443	.718	380	506	886	31	179	3	48	76	1144	19.4	39
Newlin	45	1181	216	495	.436	152	174	.874	36	84	120	203	128	1	52	9	584	13.0	27
Lucas	82	2933	412	947	.435	193	250	.772	51	204	255	768	208	1	160	9	1017	12.4	28
D.Jones	82	2476	346	777	.445	181	233	.777	215	426	641	109	265	2	77	39	873	10.6	22
Kunnert	80	2152	368	842	.437	93	135	.689	262	431	693	97	315	13	44	90	829	10.4	27
Reid	80	1849	261	574	.455	63	96	.656	111	248	359	121	277	8	67	51	585	7.3	29
Bradley	43	798	130	304	.428	43	59	.729	24	75	99	54	83	1	16	6	303	7.0	20
Behagen	3	33	7	11	.636	0	1	1.000	2	5	7	2	6	0	0	0	14	4.7	8
Ratleff	68	1163	130	310	.419	39	47	.830	56	106	162	153	109	0	60	22	299	4.4	16
Johnson	1	11	1	4	.250	2	3	.667	2	1	3	1	3	0	0	0	4	4.0	4
Kupec	49	626	84	197	.426	27	33	.818	27	64	91	50	54	0	10	3	195	4.0	14
Ab.-Aziz (T)	16	158	23	60	.383	17	23	.739	19	31	50	10	29	0	3	3	63	3.9	8
Ab.-Aziz (H)	14	134	20	47	.426	15	20	.750	13	22	35	7	25	0	2	2	55	3.9	8
White	21	219	31	85	.365	14	18	.778	8	13	21	22	24	0	8	0	76	3.6	10
D'leavy (Tot)	15	119	20	50	.400	13	18	.722	1	9	10	28	12	0	9	1	53	3.5	9
D'leavy (H)	11	102	17	43	.395	11	16	.688	1	8	9	22	12	0	8	1	45	4.1	9
R. Jones	12	66	11	20	.550	4	10	.400	5	9	14	2	16	0	1	1	26	2.2	6
Moffett	20	110	5	17	.294	6	10	.600	10	11	21	7	16	0	2	2	16	0.8	6
Bond	7	21	2	6	.333	0	......	......	1	3	4	2	1	0	1	0	4	0.6	2

INDIANA

Player	G.	Min.	FGM	FGA	Pct.	FTM	FTA	Pct.	Off. Reb.	Def. Reb.	Tot. Reb.	Ast.	PF	Dsq.	Stl.	Blk. Sh.	Pts.	Avg.	Hi.
Dantley	23	948	201	403	.499	207	263	.787	94	122	216	65	76	1	48	17	609	26.5	37
Williamson....	42	1449	335	795	.421	134	161	.832	34	86	120	132	131	4	47	0	804	19.1	43
Sobers...........	79	3019	553	1221	.453	330	400	.825	92	235	327	584	308	10	170	23	1436	18.2	31
Bantom	82	2775	502	1047	.479	254	342	.743	184	426	610	238	333	13	100	50	1258	15.3	38
Edw'ds (Tot)	83	2405	495	1093	.453	272	421	.646	197	418	615	85	322	12	53	78	1262	15.2	33
Edw'ds (Ind)	58	1682	350	777	.450	192	296	.649	153	282	435	56	233	9	36	50	892	15.4	33
Tatum (Tot)..	82	2522	510	1087	.469	153	196	.781	79	216	295	296	257	5	140	40	1173	14.3	25
Tatum (Ind)	57	1859	357	773	.462	108	137	.788	56	149	205	226	172	4	103	30	822	14.4	25
Roundfield	79	2423	421	861	.489	218	300	.727	275	527	802	196	297	4	81	149	1060	13.4	36
B'agen (Tot)	80	1735	346	804	.430	179	247	.725	201	312	513	101	263	4	62	31	871	10.9	24
B'agen (Ind)	51	1131	222	544	.408	128	176	.727	146	187	333	65	160	1	32	19	572	11.2	24
Car'ton (Tot)	72	1653	253	589	.430	130	171	.760	70	104	174	117	205	6	65	23	636	8.8	28
Car'ton (Ind)	35	621	96	197	.487	58	74	.784	28	34	62	62	73	1	22	11	250	7.1	17
Robisch	23	598	73	181	.403	50	64	.781	47	126	173	49	59	1	20	15	196	8.5	16
Elmore	69	1327	142	386	.368	88	132	.667	139	281	420	80	174	4	74	71	372	5.4	19
Flynn	71	955	120	267	.449	55	97	.567	47	70	117	142	52	0	41	10	295	4.2	14
Neumann	20	216	35	86	.407	13	18	.722	5	9	14	27	24	0	6	1	83	4.2	15
Green	44	449	56	128	.438	39	56	.696	31	40	71	30	67	0	14	2	151	3.4	13
Wilson	12	86	14	36	.389	2	3	.667	6	6	12	8	16	0	2	1	30	2.5	12
Bennett	31	285	23	81	.284	28	45	.622	49	44	93	22	54	1	11	7	74	2.4	8
Smith	1	7	0	0	......	0	0	......	0	0	0	1	1	0	0	0	0	0.0	...

KANSAS CITY

Player	G.	Min.	FGM	FGA	Pct.	FTM	FTA	Pct.	Off. Reb.	Def. Reb.	Tot. Reb.	Ast.	PF	Dsq.	Stl.	Blk. Sh.	Pts.	Avg.	Hi.
Wedman........	81	2961	607	1192	.509	221	254	.870	144	319	463	201	242	2	99	22	1435	17.7	35
Boone	82	2653	563	1271	.443	322	377	.854	112	157	269	311	233	3	105	11	1448	17.7	40
Birdsong	73	1878	470	955	.492	216	310	.697	70	105	175	174	179	1	74	12	1156	15.8	37
Washington ..	78	2231	425	891	.477	150	199	.754	188	466	654	118	324	12	74	73	1000	12.8	29
Allen.............	77	2147	373	846	.441	174	220	.791	66	163	229	360	180	0	93	28	920	11.9	30
Robinzine......	82	1748	305	677	.451	206	271	.760	173	366	539	72	281	5	74	11	816	10.0	28
Lacey	77	2131	265	590	.449	134	187	.717	155	487	642	300	264	7	120	108	664	8.6	24
Burleson........	76	1525	228	525	.434	197	248	.794	170	312	482	131	259	6	62	81	653	8.6	20
Nash	66	800	157	304	.516	50	69	.725	75	94	169	46	75	0	27	18	364	5.5	33
Kuester..........	78	1215	145	359	.455	87	105	.829	19	95	114	252	143	1	58	1	377	4.8	21
Restani (Tot)	54	547	72	167	.431	9	13	.692	36	72	108	30	41	0	5	5	153	2.8	10
Restani (KC)	46	463	59	139	.424	9	11	.818	32	62	94	21	37	0	5	4	127	2.8	10
Bigelow	1	7	1	1	1.000	0	0	......	2	3	5	0	2	0	0	0	2	2.0	2
Nelson	8	53	3	14	.214	9	11	.818	1	2	3	5	5	0	2	1	15	1.9	4
McCarter	1	9	0	2	.000	0	0	......	0	1	1	0	1	0	0	0	0	0.0	...
Hansen (Tot)	5	13	0	7	.000	0	0	......	1	0	1	1	3	0	1	0	0	0.0	...
Hansen (KC)	3	9	0	5	.000	0	0	......	1	0	1	1	3	0	1	0	0	0.0	...

LOS ANGELES

Player	G.	Min.	FGM	FGA	Pct.	FTM	FTA	Pct.	Off. Reb.	Def. Reb.	Tot. Reb.	Ast.	PF	Dsq.	Stl.	Blk. Sh.	Pts.	Avg.	Hi.
Ab-Jabbar	62	2265	663	1205	.550	274	350	.783	186	615	801	269	182	1	103	185	1600	25.8	43
D'tley (Tot) ..	79	2933	578	1128	.512	541	680	.796	265	355	620	253	233	2	118	24	1697	21.5	37
D'tley (LA) ..	56	1985	377	725	.520	334	417	.801	171	233	404	188	157	1	70	7	1088	19.4	37
Edwards	25	723	145	316	.459	80	125	.640	44	136	180	29	89	3	16	28	370	14.8	32
Tatum	25	663	153	314	.487	45	59	.763	23	67	90	70	85	1	37	10	351	14.0	25
Hudson..........	82	2283	493	992	.497	137	177	.774	80	108	188	193	196	0	94	14	1123	13.7	30
Nixon	81	2779	496	998	.497	115	161	.714	41	198	239	553	259	3	138	7	1107	13.7	28
Scott (Tot) ...	79	2473	435	994	.438	194	260	.746	62	187	249	378	252	6	110	17	1064	13.5	30
Scott (LA) ...	48	1393	225	509	.442	110	142	.775	38	110	148	235	155	4	59	11	560	11.7	24
Wilkes	51	1490	277	630	.440	106	148	.716	113	267	380	182	162	1	77	22	660	12.9	29
Washington ..	25	751	110	244	.451	68	110	.618	110	169	279	30	74	1	19	24	288	11.5	22
Ford	79	1945	272	576	.472	68	90	.756	64	287	353	142	210	1	68	46	612	7.7	22
Abernethy	73	1317	201	404	.498	91	111	.820	105	160	265	101	122	1	55	22	493	6.8	24
Carr	73	1277	134	302	.444	55	85	.647	53	155	208	26	127	0	18	14	323	6.2	15
R'isch (Tot) ..	78	1277	177	430	.412	100	129	.775	100	252	352	88	130	1	39	29	454	5.8	16
R'isch (LA) ..	55	679	104	249	.418	50	65	.769	53	126	179	40	71	0	19	14	258	4.7	16
DiGregorio	25	332	41	100	.410	16	20	.800	5	18	23	71	22	0	6	0	98	3.9	11
Chaney	9	133	13	36	.361	5	6	.833	4	7	11	17	14	0	8	3	31	3.4	11
Davis	33	334	30	72	.417	22	29	.759	4	31	35	83	39	1	15	2	82	2.5	10

1977-78 STATISTICS

MILWAUKEE

Player	G.	Min.	FGM	FGA	Pct.	FTM	FTA	Pct.	Off. Reb.	Def. Reb.	Tot. Reb.	Ast.	PF	Dsq.	Stl.	Blk. Sh.	Pts.	Avg.	Hi.
Winters	80	2751	674	1457	.463	246	293	.840	87	163	250	393	239	4	124	27	1594	19.9	37
Johnson	80	2765	628	1204	.522	301	409	.736	292	555	847	190	221	3	92	103	1557	19.5	32
Meyers	80	2416	432	938	.461	314	435	.722	144	393	537	241	240	2	86	46	1178	14.7	34
Bridgeman	82	1876	476	947	.503	166	205	.810	114	176	290	175	202	1	72	30	1118	13.6	35
English	82	1552	343	633	.542	104	143	.727	144	251	395	129	178	1	41	55	790	9.6	21
Buckner	82	2072	314	671	.468	131	203	.645	78	169	247	456	287	6	188	19	759	9.3	27
Gianelli	82	2327	307	629	.488	79	123	.642	166	343	509	192	189	4	54	92	693	8.5	21
Benson	69	1288	220	473	.465	92	141	.652	89	206	295	99	177	1	69	54	532	7.7	21
Grunfeld	73	1261	204	461	.443	94	143	.657	70	124	194	145	150	1	54	19	502	6.9	22
Walton	76	1264	154	344	.448	54	83	.651	26	50	76	253	94	0	77	13	362	4.8	14
Eakins (Tot)	33	406	44	86	.512	50	60	.833	29	46	75	29	71	0	7	17	138	4.2	10
Eakins (Mil)	17	155	14	34	.411	21	26	.808	12	17	29	12	25	0	4	7	49	2.9	9
Restani	8	84	13	28	.464	0	2	.000	4	10	14	9	4	0	0	1	26	3.3	8
Laurel	10	57	10	31	.323	4	4	1.000	6	4	10	3	10	0	3	1	24	2.4	8
Lloyd	14	112	12	33	.364	6	10	.600	7	19	26	9	22	0	3	5	30	2.1	5

NEW JERSEY

Player	G.	Min.	FGM	FGA	Pct.	FTM	FTA	Pct.	Off. Reb.	Def. Reb.	Tot. Reb.	Ast.	PF	Dsq.	Stl.	Blk. Sh.	Pts.	Avg.	Hi.
King	79	3092	798	1665	.479	313	462	.677	265	486	751	193	302	5	122	36	1909	24.2	44
Wil'son (Tot)	75	2731	723	1649	.438	331	391	.847	66	161	227	214	236	6	94	10	1777	23.7	50
Wil'son (NJ)	33	1282	388	854	.454	197	230	.857	32	75	107	82	105	2	47	1	973	29.5	50
Skinner	8	277	41	101	.406	39	44	.886	14	38	52	33	34	2	13	5	121	15.1	28
K. P'tr (Tot)	82	2813	495	1055	.469	244	320	.763	53	161	214	837	283	6	123	15	1234	15.0	40
K. P'ter (NJ)	74	2686	481	1024	.470	235	307	.765	48	151	199	801	265	6	118	15	1197	16.2	40
Hillman	45	1220	236	501	.471	118	205	.576	126	212	338	49	160	7	49	44	590	13.1	28
H. P'tr (Tot)	63	1323	309	635	.487	124	155	.800	100	179	279	42	134	0	29	38	742	11.8	29
H. P'ter (NJ)	55	1216	293	592	.495	120	148	.811	95	167	262	40	119	0	26	33	706	12.8	29
Hawkins	15	343	69	150	.460	25	29	.862	21	29	50	37	51	1	22	13	163	10.9	25
Carrington	37	1032	157	392	.401	72	97	.742	42	70	112	55	132	5	43	12	386	10.4	28
Johnson	81	2411	285	721	.395	133	185	.719	245	534	779	111	339	20	78	274	703	8.7	24
Averitt	21	409	69	188	.367	36	45	.800	7	26	33	68	37	1	17	1	174	8.3	32
Jordan (Tot)	73	1213	215	538	.400	131	167	.784	35	84	119	177	94	0	126	19	561	7.7	30
Jordan (NJ)	51	1042	196	482	.407	119	151	.788	33	75	108	145	84	0	114	18	511	10.0	30
Nelson (Tot)	33	406	85	211	.403	57	84	.679	13	39	52	34	33	0	22	7	227	6.9	22
Nelson (NJ)	25	353	82	197	.416	48	73	.658	12	37	49	29	28	0	20	6	212	8.5	22
Wash'n (Tot)	38	561	100	206	.485	29	53	.547	50	106	156	10	75	2	18	37	229	6.0	19
Wash'n (NJ)	24	523	92	187	.492	26	47	.553	48	94	142	9	72	2	17	35	210	8.8	19
Crow	15	154	35	80	.438	14	20	.700	14	13	27	8	24	0	5	1	84	5.6	16
Bassett	65	1474	149	384	.388	50	97	.515	142	262	404	63	181	5	62	33	348	5.4	17
van B Kolff	68	1419	107	292	.366	87	123	.707	66	178	244	105	192	7	52	46	301	4.4	13
Wohl	10	118	12	34	.353	11	12	.917	1	3	4	13	24	0	3	0	35	3.5	17
Hughes	56	854	57	160	.356	9	29	.310	95	145	240	38	163	9	49	49	123	2.2	13

NEW ORLEANS

Player	G.	Min.	FGM	FGA	Pct.	FTM	FTA	Pct.	Off. Reb.	Def. Reb.	Tot. Reb.	Ast.	PF	Dsq.	Stl.	Blk. Sh.	Pts.	Avg.	Hi.
Maravich	50	2041	556	1253	.444	240	276	.870	49	129	178	335	116	1	101	8	1352	27.0	42
Robinson	82	3638	748	1683	.444	366	572	.640	298	990	1288	171	265	5	73	79	1862	22.7	39
Goodrich	81	2553	520	1050	.495	264	332	.795	75	102	177	388	186	0	82	22	1304	16.1	38
James	80	2118	428	861	.497	117	157	.745	163	258	421	112	254	5	36	22	973	12.2	30
Kelley	82	2119	304	602	.505	225	289	.779	249	510	759	233	293	6	89	129	833	10.2	33
McElroy	74	1760	287	607	.473	123	167	.737	44	104	148	292	110	0	58	34	697	9.4	27
Meriweather	54	1277	194	411	.472	87	133	.654	135	237	372	58	188	8	18	118	475	8.8	21
Williams	27	434	90	214	.421	31	37	.838	27	63	90	34	61	1	21	12	211	7.8	23
Watts (Tot)	71	1584	219	558	.392	92	156	.590	60	119	179	294	184	1	108	31	530	7.5	26
Watts (NO)	39	775	109	286	.381	62	103	.602	39	59	98	161	96	0	55	17	280	7.2	26
Griffin	82	1853	160	358	.447	112	157	.713	157	353	510	172	228	6	88	45	432	5.3	15
Boyd	21	363	44	110	.400	14	22	.636	2	17	19	48	23	0	9	3	102	4.9	14
S'nders (Tot)	56	643	99	234	.423	26	36	.722	38	73	111	46	106	3	21	14	224	4.0	18
S'nders (NO)	30	400	69	143	.483	12	19	.632	27	47	74	35	72	3	14	10	150	5.0	18
Bailey	48	449	59	139	.424	37	67	.552	44	38	82	40	46	0	18	15	155	3.2	20

NEW YORK

Player	G.	Min.	FGM	FGA	Pct.	FTM	FTA	Pct.	Off. Reb.	Def. Reb.	Tot. Reb.	Ast.	PF	Dsq.	Stl.	Blk. Sh.	Pts.	Avg.	Hi.
McAdoo	79	3182	814	1564	.520	469	645	.727	236	774	1010	298	297	6	105	126	2097	26.5	40
Monroe	76	2369	556	1123	.495	242	291	.832	47	135	182	361	189	0	60	19	1354	17.8	37
Shelton	82	2319	508	988	.514	203	276	.736	204	376	580	195	350	11	109	112	1219	14.9	41
Haywood	67	1765	412	852	.484	96	135	.711	141	301	442	126	188	1	37	72	920	13.7	37
Beard	79	1979	308	614	.502	129	160	.806	76	188	264	339	201	2	117	3	745	9.4	32
Williams	81	1550	305	689	.443	146	207	.705	85	124	209	363	211	4	108	15	756	9.3	29
McMillian	81	1977	288	623	.462	115	134	.858	80	209	289	205	116	0	76	17	691	8.5	24
Cleamons	79	2009	215	448	.480	81	103	.786	69	143	212	283	142	1	68	17	511	6.5	18
Knight	80	1169	222	465	.477	63	97	.649	121	200	321	38	211	1	50	28	507	6.3	22
Gondrezick	72	1017	131	339	.386	83	121	.686	92	158	250	83	181	0	56	18	345	4.8	17
Jackson	63	654	55	115	.478	43	56	.768	29	81	110	46	106	0	31	15	153	2.4	16
Burden	2	15	1	2	.500	0	0	......	0	0	0	1	1	0	1	0	2	1.0	2

PHILADELPHIA

Player	G.	Min.	FGM	FGA	Pct.	FTM	FTA	Pct.	Off. Reb.	Def. Reb.	Tot. Reb.	Ast.	PF	Dsq.	Stl.	Blk. Sh.	Pts.	Avg.	Hi.
Erving	74	2429	611	1217	.502	306	362	.845	179	302	481	279	207	0	135	97	1528	20.6	43
McGinnis	78	2533	588	1270	.463	411	574	.716	282	528	810	294	287	6	137	27	1587	20.3	37
Collins	79	2770	643	1223	.526	267	329	.812	87	143	230	320	228	2	128	25	1553	19.7	37
Free	76	2050	390	857	.455	411	562	.731	92	120	212	306	199	0	68	41	1191	15.7	29
Dawkins	70	1722	332	577	.575	156	220	.709	117	438	555	85	268	5	34	125	820	11.7	23
Mix	82	1819	291	560	.520	175	220	.795	96	201	297	174	158	1	87	3	757	9.2	27
Bibby	82	2518	286	659	.434	171	219	.781	62	189	251	464	207	0	91	6	743	9.1	22
Bryant	81	1236	190	436	.436	111	144	.771	103	177	280	129	185	1	56	24	491	6.1	28
Jones	81	1636	169	359	.471	96	153	.627	165	405	570	92	281	4	26	127	434	5.4	18
McCl'n (Tot)	70	1020	123	280	.439	57	73	.781	20	92	112	157	124	2	58	6	303	4.3	17
McC'n (Phil)	29	293	42	96	.438	7	10	.700	9	28	37	34	36	0	16	4	97	3.1	16
Catchings	61	748	70	178	.393	34	55	.618	105	145	250	34	124	1	20	67	174	2.9	10
Mosley	6	21	5	13	.385	3	7	.429	0	5	5	2	5	0	0	0	13	2.2	6
Dunleavy	4	17	3	7	.429	2	2	1.000	0	1	1	6	0	0	1	0	8	2.0	4
Washington	14	38	8	19	.421	3	6	.500	2	12	14	1	3	0	1	2	19	1.4	4

PHOENIX

Player	G.	Min.	FGM	FGA	Pct.	FTM	FTA	Pct.	Off. Reb.	Def. Reb.	Tot. Reb.	Ast.	PF	Dsq.	Stl.	Blk. Sh.	Pts.	Avg.	Hi.
Westphal	80	2481	809	1568	.516	396	487	.813	41	123	164	437	162	0	138	31	2014	25.2	48
Davis	81	2590	786	1494	.526	387	466	.830	158	326	484	273	242	2	113	20	1959	24.2	40
Adams	70	1914	434	895	.485	214	293	.730	158	407	565	225	242	8	86	63	1082	15.5	35
Lee	82	1928	417	950	.439	170	228	.746	95	159	254	305	257	3	225	17	1004	12.2	30
Buse	82	2547	287	626	.458	112	136	.824	59	190	249	391	144	0	185	14	686	8.4	19
Heard	80	2099	265	625	.424	90	147	.612	166	486	652	132	213	0	129	101	620	7.8	24
Scott	81	1538	180	369	.488	132	191	.691	135	222	357	88	158	0	52	40	492	6.1	16
Perry	45	818	110	243	.453	51	65	.785	87	163	250	48	120	2	34	22	271	6.0	18
Bratz	80	933	159	395	.403	56	68	.824	42	73	115	123	104	1	39	5	374	4.7	16
Forrest	64	887	111	238	.466	49	103	.476	84	166	250	129	105	0	23	34	271	4.2	23
Griffin	36	422	61	169	.361	23	36	.639	44	59	103	24	56	0	16	0	145	4.0	15
Awtrey	81	1623	112	264	.424	69	109	.633	97	205	302	163	153	0	19	25	293	3.6	15

PORTLAND

Player	G.	Min.	FGM	FGA	Pct.	FTM	FTA	Pct.	Off. Reb.	Def. Reb.	Tot. Reb.	Ast.	PF	Dsq.	Stl.	Blk. Sh.	Pts.	Avg.	Hi.
Walton	58	1929	460	882	.522	177	246	.720	118	648	766	291	145	3	60	146	1097	18.9	34
Lucas	68	2119	453	989	.458	207	270	.767	186	435	621	173	221	3	61	56	1113	16.4	35
Hollins	81	2741	531	1202	.442	223	300	.743	81	196	277	380	268	4	157	29	1285	15.9	38
Gross	72	2163	381	720	.529	152	190	.800	180	220	400	254	234	5	100	52	914	12.7	27
Neal	61	1174	272	540	.504	127	177	.718	116	257	373	81	128	0	29	21	671	11.0	35
Davis	82	2188	343	756	.454	188	227	.828	65	108	173	217	173	0	81	14	874	10.7	23
Owens	82	1714	313	639	.490	206	278	.741	195	346	541	160	263	7	33	37	832	10.1	27
Twardzik	75	1820	242	409	.592	183	234	.782	36	98	134	244	186	2	107	4	667	8.9	22
Steele	65	1132	210	447	.470	100	122	.820	34	79	113	87	138	2	59	5	520	8.0	21
Norw'd (Tot)	35	611	74	181	.409	50	75	.667	49	70	119	33	101	1	31	3	198	5.7	14
Norw'd (Po)	19	351	40	99	.404	30	46	.652	22	43	65	19	56	1	18	0	110	5.8	14
Calhoun	79	1370	175	365	.479	66	76	.868	73	142	215	87	141	3	42	15	416	5.3	24
Walker	9	101	19	41	.463	5	8	.625	7	10	17	8	13	0	2	0	43	4.8	12
Dunn	23	768	100	240	.417	37	56	.661	63	84	147	45	74	0	46	8	237	3.8	13
Dorsey (Tot)	11	88	12	31	.387	10	16	.625	11	19	30	5	17	0	2	3	34	3.1	9
Dorsey (Po)	4	51	9	19	.474	7	11	.636	6	4	10	3	8	0	0	1	25	6.3	9
Schlueter	10	109	8	19	.421	9	18	.500	5	16	21	18	20	0	3	2	25	2.5	10

SAN ANTONIO

Player	G.	Min.	FGM	FGA	Pct.	FTM	FTA	Pct.	Off. Reb.	Def. Reb.	Tot. Reb.	Ast.	PF	Dsq.	Stl.	Blk. Sh.	Pts.	Avg.	Hi.
Gervin	82	2857	864	1611	.536	504	607	.830	118	302	420	302	255	3	136	110	2232	27.2	63
Kenon	81	2869	698	1426	.489	276	323	.854	245	528	773	268	209	2	115	24	1672	20.6	42
Paultz	80	2479	518	979	.529	230	306	.752	172	503	675	213	222	3	42	194	1266	15.8	29
Dampier	82	2037	336	660	.509	76	101	.752	24	98	122	285	84	0	87	13	748	9.1	21
Gale	70	2091	275	581	.473	87	100	.870	57	166	223	376	170	2	159	25	637	9.1	22
Olberding	79	1773	231	480	.481	184	227	.811	104	269	373	131	235	1	45	26	646	8.2	22
Bristow	82	1481	257	538	.478	152	208	.731	99	158	257	194	150	0	69	4	666	8.1	27
Green (Tot)	72	1382	238	514	.463	107	142	.754	130	229	359	76	193	1	30	100	583	8.1	18
Green (S.A.)	63	1132	195	427	.457	86	111	.775	108	196	304	66	167	1	24	87	476	7.6	20
Dietrick	79	1876	250	543	.460	89	114	.781	73	285	358	217	231	4	81	55	589	7.5	18
Eakins	16	251	30	52	.577	29	34	.853	17	29	46	17	46	0	3	10	89	5.6	10
Layton	41	498	85	168	.506	12	13	.923	4	28	32	108	51	0	21	4	182	4.4	14
Silas	37	311	43	97	.443	60	73	.822	4	19	23	38	29	0	11	1	146	3.9	15
Sims	12	95	10	26	.385	10	15	.667	5	8	13	20	16	0	3	0	30	2.5	11
Karl	4	30	2	6	.333	2	2	1.000	0	5	5	5	6	0	1	0	6	1.5	4

SEATTLE

Player	G.	Min.	FGM	FGA	Pct.	FTM	FTA	Pct.	Off. Reb.	Def. Reb.	Tot. Reb.	Ast.	PF	Dsq.	Stl.	Blk. Sh.	Pts.	Avg.	Hi.
Williams	79	2572	602	1335	.451	227	278	.817	83	173	256	294	198	2	185	41	1431	18.1	37
Brown	72	1965	508	1042	.488	176	196	.898	61	127	188	240	145	0	110	25	1192	16.6	37
Webster	82	2910	427	851	.502	290	461	.629	361	674	1035	203	262	8	48	162	1144	14.0	26
D. Johnson	81	2209	367	881	.417	297	406	.732	152	142	294	230	213	2	118	51	1031	12.7	27
Green	9	250	43	87	.494	21	31	.677	22	33	55	10	26	0	6	13	107	11.9	20
Sikma	82	2238	342	752	.455	192	247	.777	196	482	678	134	300	6	68	40	876	10.7	28
J. J'son (Tot)	77	1823	342	824	.415	133	177	.751	102	208	310	211	197	0	43	19	817	10.6	26
J. J'son (Sea)	76	1812	341	820	.416	131	174	.753	100	207	307	210	194	0	43	19	813	10.7	26
Seals	73	1322	230	551	.417	111	175	.634	62	164	226	81	210	4	41	33	571	7.8	28
Watts	32	809	110	272	.404	30	53	.566	21	60	81	133	88	1	53	14	250	7.8	18
Walker (Tot)	77	1104	204	461	.443	75	120	.625	87	132	219	77	138	1	26	10	483	6.3	18
Walker (Sea)	68	1003	185	420	.440	70	112	.625	80	122	202	69	125	1	24	10	440	6.5	18
Silas	82	2172	187	464	.397	109	186	.586	289	377	666	145	182	0	65	16	477	5.8	17
Hassett	48	404	91	205	.444	10	12	.833	14	22	36	41	45	0	21	0	192	4.0	14
Fleming	20	97	15	31	.484	10	17	.588	13	17	30	7	16	0	0	5	40	2.0	8
Wise	2	10	0	3	.000	1	4	.250	2	1	3	0	2	0	0	0	1	0.5	1
Tolson	1	7	0	1	.000	0	0		0	0	0	2	2	0	0	0	0	0.0	0

WASHINGTON

Player	G.	Min.	FGM	FGA	Pct.	FTM	FTA	Pct.	Off. Reb.	Def. Reb.	Tot. Reb.	Ast.	PF	Dsq.	Stl.	Blk. Sh.	Pts.	Avg.	Hi.
Hayes	81	3246	636	1409	.451	326	514	.634	335	740	1075	149	313	7	96	159	1598	19.7	37
Dandridge	75	2777	560	1190	.471	330	419	.788	137	305	442	287	262	6	101	44	1450	19.3	37
Kupchak	67	1759	393	768	.512	280	402	.697	162	298	460	71	196	1	28	42	1066	15.9	32
Grevey	81	2121	505	1128	.448	243	308	.789	124	166	290	155	203	4	61	17	1253	15.5	43
Chenier	36	937	200	451	.443	109	138	.790	15	87	102	73	54	0	36	9	509	14.1	28
Henderson	75	2315	339	784	.432	179	240	.746	66	127	193	406	131	0	93	15	857	11.4	24
Wright	70	1466	283	570	.496	76	107	.710	31	71	102	260	195	3	68	15	642	9.2	43
Unseld	80	2644	257	491	.523	93	173	.538	286	669	955	326	234	2	98	45	607	7.6	25
J'son (Tot)	71	1299	237	581	.408	49	61	.803	43	112	155	130	129	0	62	5	523	7.4	29
J'son (Wsh)	39	807	141	346	.408	42	51	.824	20	73	93	82	76	0	31	1	324	8.3	29
Ballard	76	936	142	334	.425	88	114	.772	102	164	266	62	90	1	30	13	372	4.9	19
Walker	40	384	57	161	.354	64	96	.667	21	31	52	54	39	0	14	5	178	4.5	23
Pace	49	438	67	140	.479	57	93	.613	50	84	134	23	86	1	12	21	191	3.9	18

FINAL 1977-78 NBA HOME AND ROAD RECORDS

	Home	Road		Home	Road
Atlanta	29-12	12-29	Milwaukee	28-13	16-25
Boston	24-17	8-33	New Jersey	18-23	6-35
Buffalo	20-21	7-34	New Orleans	27-14	12-29
Chicago	29-12	11-30	New York	29-12	14-27
Cleveland	27-14	16-25	Philadelphia	37-4	18-23
Denver	33-8	15-26	Phoenix	34-7	15-26
Detroit	24-17	14-27	Portland	36-5	22-19
Golden State	30-11	13-28	San Antonio	32-9	20-21
Houston	21-20	7-34	Seattle	31-10	16-25
Indiana	21-20	10-31	Washington	29-12	15-26
Kansas City	22-19	9-32	Totals	610-292	292-610
Los Angeles	29-12	16-25	Pct.	.676	.324

1977-78 PLAYOFF RESULTS

FIRST ROUND

EASTERN CONFERENCE

New York 2, Cleveland 0

Apr. 12—Wed.—New York 132 at Cleveland..............114
Apr. 14—Fri.—Cleveland 107 at New York................109

Washington 2, Atlanta 0

Apr. 12—Wed.—Atlanta 94 at Washington................103
Apr. 14—Fri.—Washington 107 at Atlanta.........103 (ot)

WESTERN CONFERENCE

Milwaukee 2, Phoenix 0

Apr. 11—Tue.—Milwaukee 111 at Phoenix.................103
Apr. 14—Fri.—Phoenix 90 at Milwaukee....................94

Seattle 2, Los Angeles 1

Apr. 12—Wed.—Los Angeles 90 at Seattle..................102
Apr. 14—Fri.—Seattle 99 at Los Angeles 105
Apr. 16—Sun.—Los Angeles 102 at Seattle................111

CONFERENCE SEMI-FINAL SERIES

EASTERN CONFERENCE

Philadelphia 4, New York 0

Apr. 16—Sun.—New York 90 at Philadelphia............130
Apr. 18—Tue.—New York 100 at Philadelphia..........119
Apr. 20—Thu.—Philadelphia 137 at New York 126
Apr. 23—Sun.—Philadelphia 112 at New York..........107

Washington 4, San Antonio 2

Apr. 16—Sun.—Washington 103 at San Antonio.......114
Apr. 18—Tue.—Washington 121 at San Antonio.......117
Apr. 21—Fri.—San Antonio 105 at Washington........118
Apr. 23—Sun.—San Antonio 95 at Washington..........98
Apr. 25—Tue.—Washington 105 at San Antonio.......116
Apr. 28—Fri.—San Antonio 100 at Washington........103

WESTERN CONFERENCE

Seattle 4, Portland 2

Apr. 18—Tue.—Seattle 104 at Portland.............................95
Apr. 21—Fri.—Seattle 93 at Portland..............................96
Apr. 23—Sun.—Portland 84 at Seattle.............................99
Apr. 26—Wed.—Portland 98 at Seattle..........................100
Apr. 30—Sun.—Seattle 89 at Portland..........................113
May 1—Mon.—Portland 94 at Seattle..........................105

Denver 4, Milwaukee 3

Apr. 18—Tue.—Milwaukee 103 at Denver......................119
Apr. 21—Fri.—Milwaukee 111 at Denver......................127
Apr. 23—Sun.—Denver 112 at Milwaukee 143
Apr. 25—Tue.—Denver 118 at Milwaukee 104
Apr. 28—Fri.—Milwaukee 117 at Denver......................112
Apr. 30—Sun.—Denver 91 at Milwaukee 119
May 3—Wed.—Milwaukee 110 at Denver...................116

CONFERENCE FINALS

EASTERN CONFERENCE

Washington 4, Philadelphia 2

Apr. 30—Sun.—Washington 122 at Philadelphia......117
May 3—Wed.—Washington 104 at Philadelphia 110
May 5—Fri.—Philadelphia 108 at Washington........123
May 7—Sun.—Philadelphia 105 at Washington......121
May 10—Wed.—Washington 94 at Philadelphia.......107
May 12—Fri.—Philadelphia 99 at Washington 101

WESTERN CONFERENCE

Seattle 4, Denver 2

May 5—Fri.—Seattle 107 at Denver............................116
May 7—Sun.—Seattle 121 at Denver 111
May 10—Wed.—Denver 91 at Seattle 105
May 12—Fri.—Denver 94 at Seattle............................100
May 14—Sun.—Seattle 114 at Denver 123
May 17—Wed.—Denver 108 at Seattle 123

WORLD CHAMPIONSHIP SERIES

Washington 4, Seattle 3

May 21—Sun.—Washington 102 at Seattle................106
May 25—Thur.—Seattle 98 at Washington................106
May 28—Sun.—Seattle 93 at Washington..................92
May 30—Tue.—Washington 120 at Seattle ....116 (ot)
June 2—Fri.—Washington 94 at Seattle 98
June 4—Sun.—Seattle 82 at Washington 117
June 7—Wed.—Washington 105 at Seattle................99

1976-77 STATISTICS

PORTLAND TRAIL BLAZERS—1976-77 NBA CHAMPIONS

Seated (Left to Right): President Larry Weinberg, General Manager Harry Glickman, Herm Gilliam, Dave Twardzik, Johnny Davis, Lionel Hollins, Coach Jack Ramsay, Assistant Coach Jack McKinney. Second row: Lloyd Neal, Larry Steele, Corky Calhoun, Bill Walton, Maurice Lucas, Wally Walker, Robin Jones, Bob Gross. Back row: Bill Schonlan, radio announcer; Dr. Robert Cook, team physician; Ron Culp, trainer; Wallace Scales, promotions director; Dr. Larry Mudrick, team dentist; George Rickles, business manager; Berlyn Hodges, administrative assistant.

FINAL STANDINGS AND TEAM FIGURES

ATLANTIC DIVISION

Team	Atl.	Bos.	Buf.	Chi.	Cle.	Den.	Det.	G.S.	Hou.	Ind.	K.C.	L.A.	Mil.	N.O.	NYK.	NYN.	Phi.	Pho.	Por.	S.A.	Sea.	Was.	W.	L.	Pct.	G.B.
Philadelphia	3	3	2	2	3	3	2	1	3	2	3	2	2	4	3	3	..	1	2	1	2	3	50	32	.610	....
Boston	4	..	3	2	1	3	2	1	2	1	3	2	3	2	2	3	1	2	1	4	2	..	44	38	.537	6
N.Y. Knicks	3	2	3	2	2	2	2	3	2	2	..	3	3	1	..	2	1	2	1	1	1	2	40	42	.488	10
Buffalo	..	1	..	1	2	2	3	..	1	1	..	1	3	3	1	2	2	3	1	..	3	..	30	52	.366	20
N.Y. Nets	1	1	2	1	1	1	1	1	2	..	..	..	1	2	2	..	1	2	..	1	1	1	22	60	.268	28

CENTRAL DIVISION

Team	Atl.	Bos.	Buf.	Chi.	Cle.	Den.	Det.	G.S.	Hou.	Ind.	K.C.	L.A.	Mil.	N.O.	NYK.	NYN.	Phi.	Pho.	Por.	S.A.	Sea.	Was.	W.	L.	Pct.	G.B.
Houston	3	2	3	3	3	..	2	1	..	4	2	3	2	2	2	3	1	3	3	2	3	3	49	33	.598	....
Washington	3	4	4	2	3	2	3	1	1	4	2	..	3	2	2	3	1	3	2	2	1	..	48	34	.585	1
San Antonio	..	..	4	1	2	2	2	2	2	2	3	1	1	3	3	3	3	3	2	..	..	3	2	44	38	.537	5
Cleveland	2	3	2	1	..	2	1	2	1	2	3	2	4	2	2	3	1	2	2	2	3	1	43	39	.524	6
New Orleans	3	2	1	..	2	1	1	3	2	2	2	..	2	..	3	2	..	3	2	1	1	2	35	47	.427	14
Atlanta	..	..	4	2	2	2	..	..	1	..	1	2	2	1	1	3	1	..	3	4	1	1	31	51	.378	18

MIDWEST DIVISION

Team	Atl.	Bos.	Buf.	Chi.	Cle.	Den.	Det.	G.S.	Hou.	Ind.	K.C.	L.A.	Mil.	N.O.	NYK.	NYN.	Phi.	Pho.	Por.	S.A.	Sea.	Was.	W.	L.	Pct.	G.B.
Denver	2	1	2	3	2	..	3	2	3	3	3	3	2	3	2	3	1	3	2	1	4	2	50	32	.610	....
Detroit	4	2	1	2	3	1	..	3	2	2	4	1	3	3	1	3	2	2	2	1	1	1	44	38	.537	6
Chicago	2	2	3	..	3	1	2	1	2	1	2	3	4	2	2	2	..	3	2	..	3	2	44	38	.537	6
Kansas City	2	1	3	2	1	1	..	3	2	2	..	1	2	2	4	4	1	3	2	1	1	2	40	42	.488	10
Indiana	4	2	3	2	1	1	2	..	..	..	2	1	2	2	4	2	2	..	2	2	..	1	36	46	.439	14
Milwaukee	2	1	1	1	..	1	1	3	1	2	2	1	..	1	1	3	1	1	2	3	1	1	30	52	.366	20

PACIFIC DIVISION

Team	Atl.	Bos.	Buf.	Chi.	Cle.	Den.	Det.	G.S.	Hou.	Ind.	K.C.	L.A.	Mil.	N.O.	NYK.	NYN.	Phi.	Pho.	Por.	S.A.	Sea.	Was.	W.	L.	Pct.	G.B.
Los Angeles	2	1	3	1	2	3	2	2	2	3	3	..	3	3	1	4	2	3	3	3	3	4	53	29	.646	....
Portland	1	3	3	4	2	2	2	3	1	4	2	1	2	2	3	3	2	3	..	2	3	1	49	33	.598	4
Golden State	4	3	3	2	2	1	..	2	4	1	2	1	1	1	3	3	4	1	2	1	3	46	36	.561	7
Seattle	2	2	1	2	1	..	3	3	1	2	3	1	3	3	2	3	2	1	1	1	..	3	40	42	.488	13
Phoenix	4	2	1	2	1	2	..	1	2	1	3	1	2	2	..	1	1	3	1	34	48	.415	19

TEAM STATISTICS—OFFENSE

Team	G.	FIELD GOALS Made	Att.	Pct.	FREE THROWS Made	Att.	Pct.	REBOUNDS Off.	Def.	Tot.	MISCELLANEOUS Ast.	PF	Stl.	Blk. Sh.	Turn Over	Dq.	SCORING Pts.	Avg.
S.A.	82	3711	7657	.485	2010	2522	.797	1110	2550	3660	2115	1966	857	499	1770	35	9432	115.0
Den.	82	3590	7471	.481	2053	2783	.738	1288	2700	3988	2262	2142	953	471	2011	29	9233	112.6
Port.	82	3623	7537	.481	1917	2515	.762	1260	2703	3963	1990	2220	868	492	1757	38	9163	111.7
G.S.	82	3724	7832	.475	1649	2172	.759	1300	2639	3939	2120	2058	904	432	1624	24	9097	110.9
Phil.	82	3511	7322	.480	2012	2732	.736	1293	2752	4045	1966	2074	814	561	1915	18	9034	110.2
Det.	82	3764	7792	.483	1442	1960	.736	1169	2495	3664	2004	2200	877	459	1718	39	8970	109.4
Knicks	82	3659	7530	.486	1587	2078	.764	974	2680	3654	1596	2007	714	304	1680	16	8905	108.6
Mil.	82	3668	7840	.468	1553	2072	.750	1220	2519	3739	1970	2094	790	342	1648	27	8889	108.4
K.C.	82	3561	7733	.460	1706	2140	.797	1222	2593	3815	1982	2173	849	386	1576	36	8828	107.7
L.A.	82	3663	7657	.478	1437	1941	.740	1177	2628	3805	2057	1867	801	445	1538	14	8763	106.9
Ind.	82	3522	7840	.449	1714	2297	.746	1409	2584	3993	2009	2030	924	458	1609	37	8758	106.8
Hou.	82	3535	7325	.483	1656	2103	.787	1254	2632	3886	1913	2132	616	411	1600	35	8726	106.4
Wash.	82	3514	7479	.470	1622	2264	.716	1185	2758	3943	1935	1940	642	433	1677	19	8650	105.5
Buff.	82	3366	7475	.450	1880	2492	.754	1213	2623	3836	1883	1842	683	392	1699	15	8612	105.0
Phoe.	82	3406	7249	.470	1791	2345	.764	1059	2493	3552	2100	2089	750	346	1830	24	8603	104.9
N.O.	82	3443	7602	.453	1688	2183	.773	1249	2828	4077	1854	2099	613	357	1706	32	8574	104.6
Bos.	82	3462	7775	.445	1648	2181	.756	1241	2966	4207	2010	2039	506	263	1673	49	8572	104.5
Sea.	82	3439	7639	.450	1646	2386	.690	1355	2433	3788	1772	2198	932	503	1759	23	8524	104.0
Atl.	82	3279	7176	.457	1836	2451	.749	1244	2512	3756	1882	2302	733	330	1779	71	8394	102.4
Clev.	82	3451	7688	.450	1468	1993	.737	1312	2563	3875	1845	1951	579	472	1356	24	8370	102.1
Chi.	82	3249	7186	.452	1613	2159	.747	1292	2705	3997	1989	1871	699	364	1552	26	8111	98.9
Nets	82	3096	7222	.429	1673	2274	.736	1157	2547	3704	1422	2178	802	435	1630	43	7865	95.9

TEAM STATISTICS—DEFENSE

Team	FIELD GOALS Made	Att.	Pct.	FREE THROWS Made	Att.	Pct.	REBOUNDS Off.	Def.	Tot.	MISCELLANEOUS Ast.	PF	Stl.	Blk. Sh.	Turn Over	Dq.	SCORING Pts.	Avg.	Dif.
Chi.	3306	7095	.466	1425	1907	.747	1055	2559	3614	1917	2166	723	460	1598	51	8037	98.0	+ 0.9
Clev.	3265	7268	.449	1748	2325	.752	1202	2711	3913	1736	1908	660	389	1542	23	8278	101.0	+ 1.1
Nets	3279	7074	.464	1863	2488	.749	1149	2937	4086	1910	1970	778	512	1735	21	8421	102.7	− 6.8
L.A.	3515	7781	.452	1510	1990	.759	1348	2625	3973	1900	1816	763	362	1599	21	8540	104.1	+ 2.8
Phoe.	3320	7192	.462	1903	2525	.754	1180	2594	3774	1856	2325	897	440	1835	39	8543	104.2	+ 0.7
Wash.	3552	7751	.458	1462	1943	.752	1167	2565	3732	1893	2088	815	348	1506	31	8566	104.5	+ 1.0
Hou.	3424	7356	.465	1746	2252	.775	1121	2232	3353	1883	1978	547	350	1395	27	8594	104.8	+ 1.6
Sea.	3394	7339	.462	1863	2474	.753	1257	2651	3908	2046	2104	726	476	1905	24	8651	105.5	− 1.5
Port.	3408	7404	.460	1889	2514	.751	1197	2510	3707	1817	2242	840	478	1765	37	8705	106.2	+ 5.5
Phil.	3575	7920	.451	1561	2074	.753	1416	2448	3864	2012	2232	823	371	1769	44	8711	106.2	+ 4.0
Atl.	3409	7137	.478	1909	2527	.755	1121	2533	3654	2020	2174	803	442	1692	44	8727	106.4	− 4.0
Bos.	3559	7904	.450	1616	2180	.741	1110	2753	3863	1918	1954	699	349	1369	24	8734	106.5	− 2.0
K.C.	3422	7244	.472	1912	2513	.761	1097	2739	3836	1744	2030	722	392	1755	35	8756	106.8	+ 0.9
Den.	3585	7743	.463	1635	2231	.733	1269	2481	3750	2082	2285	941	470	1944	41	8805	107.4	+ 5.2
N.O.	3486	7712	.452	1833	2448	.749	1318	2781	4099	1748	2125	835	361	1615	35	8805	107.4	− 2.8
G.S.	3567	7584	.470	1699	2282	.745	1256	2640	3896	2114	1939	757	420	1778	27	8833	107.7	+ 3.2
Ind.	3599	7629	.472	1705	2252	.757	1378	2770	4148	2097	2043	715	466	1792	23	8903	108.6	− 1.8
Knicks	3577	7610	.470	1752	2327	.753	1163	2716	3879	1847	2008	793	412	1612	20	8906	108.6	Even
Buff.	3786	7917	.478	1404	1859	.755	1268	2721	3989	2192	2129	729	446	1607	31	8976	109.5	− 4.5
Det.	3561	7539	.472	1933	2543	.760	1317	2637	3954	1952	1827	793	381	1828	15	9055	110.4	− 1.0
Mil.	3712	7753	.478	1721	2330	.739	1265	2613	3878	2193	1940	736	410	1644	22	9145	111.5	− 3.1
S.A.	3935	8075	.487	1512	2059	.734	1329	2687	4016	2159	2189	811	420	1822	40	9382	114.4	+ 0.6

DQ—Individual players disqualified (fouled out of game).

INDIVIDUAL SCORING LEADERS

(Minimum 70 games played) or 1400 points

	G.	FG	FT	Pts.	Avg.
Maravich, N.O.	73	886	501	2273	31.1
Knight, Ind.	78	831	413	2075	26.6
Abdul-Jabbar, L.A.	82	888	376	2152	26.2
Thompson, Den.	82	824	477	2125	25.9
McAdoo, Buff.-Knicks	72	740	381	1861	25.8
Lanier, Det.	64	678	260	1616	25.3
Drew, Atl.	74	689	412	1790	24.2
Hayes, Wash.	82	760	422	1942	23.7
Gervin, S.A.	82	726	443	1895	23.1
Issel, Den.	79	660	445	1765	22.3
Boone, K.C.	82	747	324	1818	22.2
Kenon, S.A.	78	706	293	1705	21.9
Barry, G.S.	79	682	359	1723	21.8
Erving, Phil.	82	685	400	1770	21.6
Tomjanovich, Hou.	81	733	287	1753	21.6
McGinnis, Phil.	79	659	372	1690	21.4
Westphal, Phoe.	81	682	362	1726	21.3
Williamson, Nets-Ind.	72	618	259	1495	20.8
Dandridge, Mil.	70	585	283	1453	20.8
Smith, Buff.	82	702	294	1698	20.7

1976-77 STATISTICS

FIELD GOAL LEADERS
(Minimum 300 FG Made)

	FGM	FGA	Pct.
Abdul-Jabbar, L.A.	888	1533	.579
Kupchak, Wash.	341	596	.572
Jones, Den.	501	879	.570
Gervin, S.A.	726	1335	.544
Lanier, Det.	678	1269	.534
Gross, Port.	376	711	.529
Nater, Mil.	383	725	.528
Walton, Port.	491	930	.528
Meriweather, Atl.	319	607	.526
Gilmore, Chi.	570	1091	.522

FREE THROW LEADERS
(Minimum 125 FT Made)

	FTM	FTA	Pct.
DiGregorio, Buff.	138	146	.945
Barry, G.S.	359	392	.916
Murphy, Hou.	272	307	.886
Newlin, Hou.	269	304	.885
Brown, Sea.	168	190	.884
D. Van Arsdale, Phoe.	145	166	.873
White, Bos.	333	383	.869
Bridgeman, Mil.	197	228	.864
Russell, L.A.	188	219	.858
van Breda Kolff, Nets.	195	228	.855

REBOUND LEADERS
Minimum 70 games or 800 rebounds

	G.	Off.	Def.	Tot.	Avg.
Walton, Port.	65	211	723	934	14.4
Abdul-Jabbar, L.A.	82	266	824	1090	13.3
Malone, Buff.-Hou.	82	437	635	1072	13.1
Gilmore, Chi.	82	313	757	1070	13.0
McAdoo, Buff.-Knicks	72	199	727	926	12.9
Hayes, Wash.	82	289	740	1029	12.5
Nater, Mil.	72	266	599	865	12.0
McGinnis, Phil.	79	324	587	911	11.5
Lucas, Port.	79	271	628	899	11.4
Kenon, S.A.	78	282	597	879	11.3

BLOCKED SHOTS LEADERS
Minimum 70 games or 100 blocked shots

	G.	No.	Avg.
Walton, Port.	65	211	3.25
Abdul-Jabbar, L.A.	82	261	3.18
Hayes, Wash.	82	220	2.68
Gilmore, Chi.	82	203	2.48
Jones, Phil.	82	200	2.44
Johnson, G.S.-Buff.	78	177	2.27
Malone, Buff.-Hou.	82	181	2.21
Roundfield, Ind.	61	131	2.15
Paultz, S.A.	82	173	2.11
E. Smith, Mil.-Clev.	70	144	2.06

ASSISTS LEADERS
Minimum 70 games or 400 assists

	G.	No.	Avg.
Buse, Ind.	81	685	8.5
Watts, Sea.	79	630	8.0
Van Lier, Chi.	82	636	7.8
K. Porter, Det.	81	592	7.3
Henderson, Atl.-Wash.	87	598	6.9
Barry, G.S.	79	475	6.0
White, Bos.	82	492	6.0
Gale, S.A.	82	473	5.8
Westphal, Phoe.	81	459	5.7
Lucas, Hou.	82	463	5.6

STEALS LEADERS
Minimum 70 games or 125 steals

	G.	No.	Avg.
Buse, Ind.	81	281	3.47
Taylor, K.C.	72	199	2.76
Watts, Sea.	79	214	2.71
Buckner, Mil.	79	192	2.43
Gale, S.A.	82	191	2.33
Jones, Den.	82	186	2.27
Hollins, Port.	76	166	2.18
Ford, Det.	82	179	2.18
Barry, G.S.	79	172	2.18
Smith, Buff.	82	176	2.15

RECORDS OF TEAMS BY MONTHS

Team	Oct. W-L	Nov. W-L	Dec. W-L	Jan. W-L	Feb. W-L	Mar. W-L	Apr. W-L	Total W-L
Atlanta	2-4	5-9	5-12	6-7	7-5	5-10	1-4	31-51
Boston	4-0	6-8	7-7	6-11	8-4	9-6	4-2	44-38
Buffalo	2-3	7-9	5-8	3-10	6-7	5-11	2-4	30-52
Chicago	2-3	0-10	9-5	9-10	7-6	12-3	5-1	44-38
Cleveland	5-0	10-4	5-9	6-7	5-7	9-8	3-4	43-39
Denver	4-0	9-5	10-5	9-5	8-5	7-9	3-3	50-32
Detroit	2-4	9-6	9-5	8-6	9-4	5-9	2-4	44-38
Golden State	2-2	7-8	7-5	10-6	8-7	9-6	3-2	46-36
Houston	3-1	8-4	8-6	7-9	7-6	13-5	3-2	49-33
Indiana	3-3	6-8	7-9	6-7	5-7	5-11	4-1	36-46
Kansas City	2-3	9-7	5-10	9-5	5-6	10-5	0-6	40-42
Los Angeles	3-3	8-5	10-5	11-3	6-6	11-5	4-2	53-29
Milwaukee	1-5	3-13	5-8	6-11	6-7	6-6	3-2	30-52
New Orleans	3-2	8-6	7-9	4-10	4-7	8-8	1-5	35-47
Knicks	3-2	6-9	8-4	4-10	7-8	7-8	5-1	40-42
Nets	2-4	7-7	3-9	1-14	6-8	2-13	1-5	22-60
Philadelphia	3-2	8-6	7-6	11-3	7-5	11-6	3-4	50-32
Phoenix	1-4	5-8	8-7	8-9	4-9	4-12	4-2	34-48
Portland	3-1	9-5	11-6	11-5	3-8	7-8	5-0	49-33
San Antonio	2-4	9-5	7-7	7-7	8-5	10-6	1-4	44-38
Seattle	3-2	9-7	6-10	8-5	5-8	7-7	2-3	40-42
Washington	1-4	6-8	8-5	12-2	9-5	8-8	4-2	48-34
Totals	56	154	157	162	140	170	63	902

INDIVIDUAL STATISTICS

ATLANTA

Player	G.	Min.	FGM	FGA	Pct.	FTM	FTA	Pct.	Off. Reb.	Def. Reb.	Tot. Reb.	Ast.	PF	Dsq.	Stl.	Blk. Sh.	Pts.	Avg.	Hi.
Drew	74	2688	689	1416	.487	412	577	.714	280	395	675	133	275	9	102	29	1790	24.2	42
Rob'son (Tot)	77	2777	574	1200	.478	314	430	.730	252	576	828	142	253	3	66	38	1462	19.0	34
Rob'son (Atl)	36	1449	310	648	.478	186	241	.772	133	329	462	97	130	3	38	20	806	22.4	34
Hudson	58	1745	413	905	.456	142	169	.840	48	81	129	155	160	2	67	19	968	16.7	39
Henderson	46	1568	196	453	.433	126	168	.750	18	106	124	386	74	0	79	8	518	11.3	27
Charles	82	2487	354	855	.414	205	256	.801	41	127	168	295	240	4	141	45	913	11.1	27
Meriweather	74	2068	319	607	.526	182	255	.714	216	380	596	82	324	21	41	82	820	11.1	27
Hawes	44	945	147	305	.480	67	88	.761	78	183	261	63	141	4	36	24	361	8.2	19
Barker	59	1354	182	436	.417	112	164	.683	111	290	401	60	223	11	33	41	476	8.1	21
Hill	81	1825	175	439	.399	139	174	.799	39	104	143	403	245	8	85	6	489	6.0	26
Brown	77	1405	160	350	.457	121	150	.807	75	161	236	103	217	7	46	7	441	5.7	20
Denton	45	700	103	256	.402	33	47	.702	81	137	218	33	100	1	14	16	239	5.3	25
Terry (Tot)	45	545	96	191	.503	36	44	.818	12	34	46	58	48	0	20	1	228	5.1	22
Terry (Atl)	12	241	47	87	.540	18	21	.857	8	10	18	25	21	0	9	1	112	9.3	22
Willoughby	39	549	75	169	.444	43	63	.683	65	105	170	13	64	1	19	23	193	4.9	16
Sojourner	51	551	95	203	.468	41	57	.719	49	97	146	21	66	0	15	9	231	4.5	18
Davis	7	67	8	35	.229	4	13	.308	2	5	7	2	9	0	7	0	20	2.9	6
Dickerson	6	63	6	12	.500	8	8	.625	0	2	2	11	13	0	1	0	17	2.8	6

BOSTON

Player	G.	Min.	FGM	FGA	Pct.	FTM	FTA	Pct.	Off. Reb.	Def. Reb.	Tot. Reb.	Ast.	PF	Dsq.	Stl.	Blk. Sh.	Pts.	Avg.	Hi.
White	82	3333	638	1488	.429	333	383	.869	87	296	383	492	193	5	118	22	1609	19.6	41
Scott	43	1581	326	734	.444	129	173	.746	52	139	191	196	153	3	60	12	781	18.2	31
Havlicek	79	2913	580	1283	.452	235	288	.816	109	273	382	400	208	4	84	18	1395	17.7	33
Cowens	50	1888	328	756	.434	162	198	.818	147	550	697	248	181	7	64	49	818	16.4	33
Wicks	82	2642	464	1012	.458	310	464	.668	268	556	824	169	331	14	64	61	1238	15.1	25
Rowe	79	2190	315	632	.489	170	240	.708	188	375	563	107	215	3	24	47	800	10.1	22
Boswell	70	1083	175	340	.515	96	135	.711	111	195	306	85	237	9	27	8	446	6.4	22
Saunders	68	1051	184	395	.466	35	53	.660	73	150	223	85	191	3	26	7	403	5.9	21
Stacom	79	1051	179	438	.409	46	58	.793	40	57	97	117	65	0	19	3	404	5.1	16
Kuberski	76	860	131	312	.420	63	83	.759	76	133	209	39	89	0	7	5	325	4.3	16
Ard	63	969	96	254	.378	49	76	.645	77	219	296	53	128	1	18	28	241	3.8	14
Cook	25	138	27	72	.375	9	17	.529	10	17	27	5	27	0	10	3	63	2.5	10
Wilson	25	131	19	59	.322	11	13	.846	3	6	9	14	19	0	3	0	49	2.0	10

BUFFALO

Player	G.	Min.	FGM	FGA	Pct.	FTM	FTA	Pct.	Off. Reb.	Def. Reb.	Tot. Reb.	Ast.	PF	Dsq.	Stl.	Blk. Sh.	Pts.	Avg.	Hi.
McAdoo	20	767	182	400	.455	110	158	.696	66	198	264	65	74	1	16	34	474	23.7	42
Smith	82	3094	702	1504	.467	294	386	.762	134	323	457	441	264	2	176	8	1698	20.7	41
Dantley	77	2816	544	1046	.520	476	582	.818	251	336	587	144	215	2	91	15	1564	20.3	39
Shumate	74	2601	407	810	.502	302	450	.671	163	538	701	159	197	1	90	84	1116	15.1	26
DiGregorio	81	2267	365	875	.417	138	146	.945	52	132	184	378	150	1	57	3	868	10.7	36
Neumann	4	49	15	34	.441	5	6	.833	5	4	9	4	7	0	3	2	35	8.8	21
G'nelli (Tot)	76	1913	257	579	.444	90	125	.720	154	321	475	83	171	0	35	98	604	7.9	19
G'nelli (Buf)	57	1283	171	397	.431	55	77	.714	94	203	297	57	117	0	21	70	397	7.0	16
Averitt	75	1136	234	619	.378	121	169	.716	20	58	78	134	127	2	30	5	589	7.9	26
Gerard (Tot)	65	1048	201	454	.443	78	117	.667	89	128	217	92	164	1	64	42	480	7.4	21
Gerard (Buf)	41	592	100	244	.410	40	61	.656	51	66	117	43	91	0	23	32	240	5.9	18
Adams	77	1710	216	526	.411	129	173	.746	130	241	371	150	201	0	74	16	561	7.3	28
J'nson (Tot)	78	1652	198	429	.462	71	98	.724	204	407	611	104	246	8	37	177	467	6.0	16
J'nson (Buf)	39	1055	125	279	.448	46	67	.687	117	283	400	78	141	5	22	104	296	7.6	16
Price (Tot)	26	444	65	145	.448	24	29	.828	9	38	47	53	66	0	32	6	154	5.9	20
Price (Buf)	20	333	44	104	.423	17	20	.850	5	29	34	38	52	0	25	5	105	5.3	17
McMillen	20	270	45	92	.489	26	36	.722	29	43	72	16	29	0	1	2	116	5.8	19
Foster	59	689	99	247	.401	30	44	.682	33	43	76	48	92	0	16	0	228	3.9	14
Abdul-Aziz	22	195	25	74	.338	33	43	.767	41	49	90	7	21	0	3	9	83	3.8	16
Terry	33	304	49	104	.471	18	23	.783	4	24	28	33	27	0	11	0	116	3.5	14
Wil'ms (Tot)	65	867	78	210	.371	68	87	.782	26	75	101	132	60	0	32	5	224	3.4	14
Wil'ms (Buf)	44	556	43	117	.368	38	48	.792	18	49	67	88	34	0	24	3	124	2.8	8
Mayes (Tot)	4	28	3	10	.300	3	7	.429	4	6	10	3	7	0	0	2	9	2.3	4
Mayes (Buf)	2	7	0	3	.000	2	3	.667	0	3	3	0	2	0	0	0	2	1.0	2
Malone	2	6	0	0	....	0	0	....	0	1	1	0	1	0	0	0	0	0.0	0

CHICAGO

Player	G.	Min.	FGM	FGA	Pct.	FTM	FTA	Pct.	Off. Reb.	Def. Reb.	Tot. Reb.	Ast.	PF	Dsq.	Stl.	Blk. Sh.	Pts.	Avg.	Hi.
Gilmore	82	2877	570	1091	.522	387	586	.660	313	757	1070	199	266	4	44	203	1527	18.6	42
Johnson	81	2847	538	1205	.446	324	407	.796	297	531	828	195	315	10	103	64	1400	17.3	37
Holland	79	2453	509	1120	.454	158	192	.823	78	175	253	201	3	169	16	1176	14.9	30	
May	72	2369	431	955	.451	188	227	.828	141	296	437	145	185	2	78	17	1050	14.6	25
Love	14	496	68	201	.338	35	46	.761	38	35	73	23	47	1	8	2	171	12.2	22
Van Lier	82	3097	300	729	.412	238	306	.778	108	262	370	636	268	3	129	16	838	10.2	27
Mengelt	61	1178	209	458	.456	89	113	.788	29	81	110	114	102	2	37	4	507	8.3	26
Marin	54	869	167	359	.465	31	39	.795	27	64	91	62	85	0	13	6	365	6.8	18
McCracken	9	119	18	47	.383	11	18	.611	6	10	16	14	17	0	6	0	47	5.2	13
Laskowski	47	562	75	212	.354	27	30	.900	16	47	63	44	22	0	32	2	177	3.8	15
Boerwinkle	82	1070	134	273	.491	34	63	.540	101	211	312	189	147	0	19	19	302	3.7	19
Kropp	53	480	73	152	.480	28	41	.683	21	26	47	39	77	1	18	1	174	3.3	18
Pondexter	78	996	107	257	.416	42	65	.646	77	159	236	41	82	0	34	11	256	3.3	12
Fernsten	5	61	3	15	.200	8	11	.727	9	7	16	6	9	0	1	3	14	2.8	5
Hicks (Tot)	37	262	41	89	.461	11	13	.846	26	40	66	24	37	0	8	0	93	2.5	12
Hicks (Chi)	35	255	41	87	.471	11	13	.846	25	40	65	23	36	0	7	0	93	2.7	12
Starr	17	65	6	24	.250	2	2	1.000	6	4	10	6	11	0	1	0	14	0.8	4
Smith	2	11	0	1	.000	0	0	......	0	0	0	0	1	0	0	0	0	0.0	0

DQ—Individual players disqualified (fouled out of game).

CLEVELAND

Player	G.	Min.	FGM	FGA	Pct.	FTM	FTA	Pct.	Off. Reb.	Def. Reb.	Tot. Reb.	Ast.	PF	Dsq.	Stl.	Blk. Sh.	Pts.	Avg.	Hi.
Russell	70	2109	435	1003	.434	288	370	.778	144	275	419	189	196	3	70	24	1158	16.5	36
Carr	82	2409	558	1221	.457	213	268	.795	120	120	240	220	221	3	57	10	1329	16.2	42
B. Smith	81	2135	513	1149	.446	148	181	.818	92	225	317	152	211	3	61	30	1174	14.5	34
Chones	82	2378	450	972	.463	155	212	.731	208	480	688	104	258	3	32	77	1055	12.9	24
Cleamons	60	2045	257	592	.434	112	148	.757	99	174	273	308	126	0	66	23	626	10.4	25
Snyder	82	1685	316	693	.456	127	149	.852	47	102	149	160	177	2	45	30	759	9.3	18
E.Smith(Tot)	70	1464	241	507	.475	117	213	.549	114	325	439	43	207	4	35	144	599	8.6	30
E.Smith(Cle)	36	675	128	254	.504	56	108	.519	62	169	231	13	98	2	16	75	312	8.7	30
Brewer	81	2672	296	657	.451	97	178	.545	275	487	762	195	214	3	94	82	689	8.5	20
Brokaw (Tot)	80	1487	242	564	.429	163	219	.744	22	101	123	228	164	2	36	36	647	8.1	27
Brokaw (Clev)	39	596	112	240	.467	58	82	.707	12	47	59	117	79	2	14	13	282	7.2	21
Walker	62	1216	157	349	.450	89	115	.774	55	105	160	254	124	1	83	4	403	6.5	23
Thurmond	49	997	100	246	.407	68	106	.642	121	253	374	83	128	2	16	81	268	5.5	13
Garrett	29	215	40	93	.430	18	22	.818	10	30	40	7	30	0	7	3	98	3.4	12
Lambert	63	555	67	157	.427	25	36	.694	62	92	154	31	75	0	16	18	159	2.5	11
Howard	9	28	8	15	.533	5	6	.833	2	3	5	5	7	0	1	2	21	2.3	8
Williams	22	65	14	47	.298	9	12	.750	3	1	4	7	7	0	1	0	37	1.7	6

DENVER

Player	G.	Min.	FGM	FGA	Pct.	FTM	FTA	Pct.	Off. Reb.	Def. Reb.	Tot. Reb.	Ast.	PF	Dsq.	Stl.	Blk. Sh.	Pts.	Avg.	Hi.
Thompson	82	3001	824	1626	.507	477	623	.766	138	196	334	337	236	1	114	53	2125	25.9	44
Issel	79	2507	660	1282	.515	445	558	.797	211	485	696	177	246	7	91	29	1765	22.3	40
Jones	82	2419	501	879	.570	236	329	.717	174	504	678	264	238	3	186	162	1238	15.1	27
Gerard	24	456	101	210	.481	38	56	.679	38	62	100	49	73	1	21	30	240	10.0	21
Calvin (Tot)	76	1438	220	544	.404	287	338	.849	36	60	96	240	127	0	61	3	727	9.6	22
Calvin (Den)	29	625	100	225	.444	123	144	.854	19	30	49	115	53	0	27	1	323	11.1	22
Wise	75	1403	237	513	.462	142	218	.651	76	177	253	142	180	2	60	18	616	8.2	20
McClain	72	2002	245	551	.445	99	133	.744	52	177	229	324	255	9	106	13	589	8.2	18
Price (Tot)	81	1828	253	567	.446	83	103	.806	50	181	231	261	247	3	128	20	589	7.3	20
Price (Den)	55	1384	188	422	.445	59	74	.797	41	143	184	208	181	3	96	14	435	7.9	20
Silas	81	1959	206	572	.360	170	255	.667	236	370	606	132	183	0	58	23	582	7.2	20
Webster	80	1276	198	400	.495	143	220	.650	152	332	484	62	149	2	23	118	539	6.7	17
Williams	21	311	35	93	.376	30	39	.769	8	26	34	44	26	0	8	0	100	4.8	14
Beck	53	480	107	246	.435	36	44	.818	45	51	96	53	59	1	15	1	250	4.7	16
Taylor	79	1548	132	314	.420	37	65	.569	90	121	211	288	202	0	132	9	301	3.8	11
Towe	51	409	56	138	.406	18	25	.720	8	26	34	87	26	0	16	0	130	2.5	8

1976-77 STATISTICS

DETROIT

Player	G.	Min.	FGM	FGA	Pct.	FTM	FTA	Pct.	Off. Reb.	Def. Reb.	Tot. Reb.	Ast.	PF	Dsq.	Stl.	Blk. Sh.	Pts.	Avg.	Hi.
Lanier	64	2446	678	1269	.534	260	318	.818	200	545	745	214	174	0	70	126	1616	25.3	40
Carr	82	2643	443	931	.476	205	279	.735	211	420	631	181	287	8	165	58	1091	13.3	29
H. Porter	78	2200	465	962	.483	103	120	.858	155	303	458	53	202	0	50	73	1033	13.2	27
Ford	82	2539	437	918	.476	131	170	.771	96	174	270	337	192	1	179	26	1005	12.3	33
Simpson	77	1597	356	834	.427	138	195	.708	48	133	181	180	100	0	68	5	850	11.0	25
Money	73	1586	329	631	.521	90	114	.789	43	81	124	243	199	3	91	14	748	10.2	32
Barnes	53	989	202	452	.447	106	156	.679	69	184	253	45	139	1	38	33	510	9.6	33
K. Porter	81	2117	310	605	.512	97	133	.729	28	70	98	592	271	8	88	8	717	8.9	28
Douglas	82	1626	245	512	.479	127	229	.555	181	345	526	68	294	10	44	81	617	7.5	30
Eberhard	68	1219	181	380	.476	109	138	.790	76	145	221	50	197	4	45	15	471	6.9	24
Trapp	6	68	15	29	.517	3	4	.750	4	6	10	3	13	0	0	1	33	5.5	15
Sellers	44	329	73	190	.384	52	72	.722	19	22	41	25	56	0	22	0	198	4.5	17
Cash	6	49	9	23	.391	3	6	.500	8	8	16	1	8	0	2	1	21	3.5	11
Brown	43	322	21	56	.375	18	26	.692	31	59	90	12	68	4	15	18	60	1.4	10

GOLDEN STATE

Player	G.	Min.	FGM	FGA	Pct.	FTM	FTA	Pct.	Off. Reb.	Def. Reb.	Tot. Reb.	Ast.	PF	Dsq.	Stl.	Blk. Sh.	Pts.	Avg.	Hi.
Barry	79	2904	682	1551	.440	359	392	.916	73	349	422	475	194	2	172	58	1723	21.8	42
Smith	82	2880	631	1318	.479	295	376	.785	101	231	332	328	227	0	98	29	1557	19.0	51
Wilkes	76	2579	548	1147	.478	247	310	.797	155	423	578	211	222	1	127	16	1343	17.7	32
Williams	82	1930	325	701	.464	112	150	.747	72	161	233	292	154	3	74	19	762	9.3	26
Parish	77	1384	288	573	.503	121	171	.708	201	342	543	74	224	7	55	94	697	9.1	30
Ray	77	2018	263	450	.584	105	199	.528	199	416	615	112	242	5	74	81	631	8.2	23
Dickey	49	856	158	345	.458	45	61	.738	100	140	240	63	101	1	20	11	361	7.4	20
Dudley	79	1682	220	421	.523	129	203	.635	119	177	296	347	169	0	67	6	569	7.2	19
C. Johnson	79	1196	255	583	.437	49	69	.710	50	91	141	91	134	1	77	7	559	7.1	22
McNeill (Tot)	24	230	47	112	.420	52	61	.852	28	47	75	6	32	1	10	2	146	6.1	23
McNeill (G.S.)	16	137	29	61	.475	28	31	.903	18	31	49	3	19	0	6	1	86	5.4	17
Parker	65	889	154	292	.527	71	92	.772	85	88	173	59	77	0	53	26	379	5.8	20
Davis	33	552	55	124	.444	49	72	.681	34	61	95	59	93	1	11	8	159	4.8	12
G. Johnson	39	597	73	150	.487	25	31	.806	87	124	211	26	105	2	15	73	171	4.4	13
Rogers	26	176	43	116	.371	14	15	.933	6	5	11	10	33	0	8	3	100	3.8	10

HOUSTON

Player	G.	Min.	FGM	FGA	Pct.	FTM	FTA	Pct.	Off. Reb.	Def. Reb.	Tot. Reb.	Ast.	PF	Dsq.	Stl.	Blk. Sh.	Pts.	Avg.	Hi.
Tomjanovich	81	3130	733	1437	.510	287	342	.839	172	512	684	172	198	1	57	27	1753	21.6	40
Murphy	82	2764	596	1216	.490	272	307	.886	54	118	172	386	281	6	144	3	1464	17.9	34
Malone (Tot)	82	2506	389	810	.480	305	440	.693	437	635	1072	89	275	3	67	181	1083	13.2	26
Malone (Hou)	80	2500	389	810	.480	305	440	.693	437	634	1071	89	274	3	67	181	1083	13.5	26
Newlin	82	2119	387	850	.455	269	304	.885	52	132	184	320	226	2	60	3	1043	12.7	38
Lucas	82	2531	388	814	.477	135	171	.789	55	164	219	463	174	0	125	19	911	11.1	25
Kunnert	81	2050	333	685	.486	93	126	.738	210	459	669	154	361	17	35	105	759	9.4	31
Johnson	79	1738	319	696	.458	94	132	.712	75	191	266	163	199	1	47	24	732	9.3	30
Jones	74	1239	167	338	.494	101	126	.802	98	186	284	48	175	1	38	19	435	5.9	18
Ratleff	37	533	70	161	.435	26	42	.619	24	53	77	43	45	0	20	6	166	4.5	12
Owens	46	462	68	135	.504	52	76	.684	47	95	142	18	96	2	4	13	188	4.1	13
White	46	368	47	106	.443	15	25	.600	13	28	41	35	39	0	11	1	109	2.4	14
Kennedy	32	277	31	58	.534	3	8	.375	14	37	51	6	45	1	7	5	65	2.0	10
Wohl	14	62	7	17	.412	4	4	1.000	1	4	5	15	18	1	0	0	18	1.3	4
Hicks	2	7	0	2	.000	0	0	......	1	0	1	1	0	1	0	0	0	0.0	0

INDIANA

Player	G.	Min.	FGM	FGA	Pct.	FTM	FTA	Pct.	Off. Reb.	Def. Reb.	Tot. Reb.	Ast.	PF	Dsq.	Stl.	Blk. Sh.	Pts.	Avg.	Hi.
Knight	78	3117	832	1687	.493	413	506	.816	223	359	582	260	197	0	117	19	2075	26.6	43
Wil'son (Tot.)	72	2481	318	1347	.459	259	329	.787	42	151	193	201	246	4	107	13	1495	20.8	37
Wil'son (Ind.)	30	1055	261	544	.480	98	125	.784	18	56	74	111	103	1	48	7	620	20.7	33
Roundfield	61	1645	342	734	.466	164	239	.686	179	339	518	69	243	8	61	131	848	13.9	33
Jones	80	2709	438	1019	.430	160	215	.744	218	386	604	189	305	10	102	80	1042	13.0	29
Robisch	80	1900	369	811	.455	213	256	.832	171	383	554	158	169	1	55	37	951	11.9	30
Hillman	82	2302	359	811	.443	161	244	.660	228	465	693	166	353	15	95	106	879	10.7	27
Flynn	73	1324	250	573	.436	101	142	.711	76	111	187	179	106	0	57	6	601	8.2	24
Buse	81	2947	266	639	.416	114	145	.786	66	204	270	685	129	0	281	16	646	8.0	19
Lewis	32	552	81	199	.407	62	77	.805	17	30	47	56	58	0	18	2	224	7.0	20

1976-77 STATISTICS

Player	G.	Min.	FGM	FGA	Pct.	FTM	FTA	Pct.	Off. Reb.	Def. Reb.	Tot. Reb.	Ast.	PF	Dsq.	Stl.	Blk. Sh.	Pts.	Avg.	Hi.
Green	70	918	183	424	.432	84	113	.743	79	98	177	46	157	2	46	12	450	6.4	24
Bennett	67	911	101	294	.344	112	187	.599	110	127	237	70	155	0	37	33	314	4.7	19
Mayes	2	21	3	7	.429	1	4	.250	4	3	7	3	5	0	0	2	7	3.5	4
Elmore	6	46	7	17	.412	4	5	.800	7	8	15	2	11	0	0	4	18	3.0	7
Anderson	27	164	26	59	.441	14	20	.700	9	3	12	10	26	0	6	2	66	2.4	14
Hackett (Tot.)	6	46	3	10	.300	8	14	.571	4	9	13	3	8	0	0	1	14	2.3	3
Hackett (Ind.)	5	38	3	8	.375	6	9	.667	3	7	10	3	7	0	0	1	12	2.4	3
Elston	5	40	2	14	.143	1	2	.500	1	5	6	2	6	0	1	0	5	1.0	5

KANSAS CITY

Player	G.	Min.	FGM	FGA	Pct.	FTM	FTA	Pct.	Off. Reb.	Def. Reb.	Tot. Reb.	Ast.	PF	Dsq.	Stl.	Blk. Sh.	Pts.	Avg.	Hi.
Boone	82	3021	747	1577	.474	324	384	.844	128	193	321	338	258	1	119	19	1818	22.2	43
Taylor	72	2488	501	995	.504	225	275	.818	88	150	238	320	206	1	199	16	1227	17.0	38
Wedman	81	2743	521	1133	.460	206	241	.855	187	319	506	227	226	3	100	23	1248	15.4	38
Washington	82	2265	446	1034	.431	177	254	.697	201	497	698	85	324	13	63	90	1069	13.0	30
Lacey	82	2595	327	774	.422	215	282	.762	189	545	734	386	292	9	119	133	869	10.6	28
Robinzine	75	1594	307	677	.453	159	216	.736	164	310	474	95	283	7	86	13	773	10.3	27
Johnson	81	1386	218	446	.489	101	115	.878	68	144	212	105	169	1	43	21	537	6.6	18
Eakins	82	1338	151	336	.449	188	222	.847	112	249	361	119	195	1	29	49	490	6.0	23
McCarter	59	725	119	257	.463	32	45	.711	16	39	55	99	63	0	23	0	270	4.6	22
Barr	73	1224	122	279	.437	41	57	.719	33	97	130	175	96	0	52	18	285	3.9	14
Hansen	41	289	67	155	.432	23	32	.719	28	31	59	25	44	0	13	3	157	3.8	13
Bigelow	29	162	35	70	.500	15	17	.882	8	19	27	8	17	0	3	1	85	2.9	11

LOS ANGELES

Player	G.	Min.	FGM	FGA	Pct.	FTM	FTA	Pct.	Off. Reb.	Def. Reb.	Tot. Reb.	Ast.	PF	Dsq.	Stl.	Blk. Sh.	Pts.	Avg.	Hi.
Abdul-Jabbar	82	3016	888	1533	.579	376	536	.701	266	824	1090	319	262	4	101	261	2152	26.2	40
Russell	82	2583	578	1179	.490	188	219	.858	86	208	294	210	163	1	86	7	1344	16.4	35
Allen	78	2482	472	1035	.456	195	252	.774	58	193	251	405	183	0	116	19	1139	14.6	30
Washington	53	1342	191	380	.503	132	187	.706	182	310	492	48	183	1	43	52	514	9.7	20
Tatum	68	1249	283	607	.466	72	100	.720	83	153	236	118	168	1	85	22	638	9.4	23
Calvin	12	207	27	82	.329	41	48	.854	6	10	16	21	16	0	11	1	95	7.9	20
Ford	82	1782	262	570	.460	73	102	.716	105	248	353	133	170	0	60	21	597	7.3	19
Lamar	71	1165	228	561	.406	46	68	.676	30	62	92	177	73	0	59	3	502	7.1	22
Abernethy	70	1378	169	349	.484	101	134	.754	113	178	291	98	118	1	49	10	439	6.3	19
Chaney	81	2408	213	522	.408	70	94	.745	120	210	330	308	224	4	140	33	496	6.1	16
Neum'n (Tot).	63	937	161	397	.406	59	87	.678	24	48	72	141	134	2	31	10	381	6.0	24
Neum'n (LA)	59	868	146	363	.402	54	81	.667	19	44	63	137	127	2	28	8	346	5.9	24
Kupec	82	908	153	342	.447	78	101	.772	76	123	199	53	113	0	18	4	384	4.7	14
Warner	14	170	25	53	.472	4	6	.667	21	48	69	11	28	0	1	2	54	3.9	10
Murphy	2	18	1	5	.200	3	7	.429	3	1	4	0	5	0	0	0	5	2.5	3
Roberts	28	209	27	76	.355	4	6	.667	9	16	25	19	34	0	4	2	58	2.1	12

MILWAUKEE

Player	G.	Min.	FGM	FGA	Pct.	FTM	FTA	Pct.	Off. Reb.	Def. Reb.	Tot. Reb.	Ast.	PF	Dsq.	Stl.	Blk. Sh.	Pts.	Avg.	Hi.
Dandridge	70	2501	585	1253	.467	283	367	.771	146	294	440	268	222	1	95	28	1453	20.8	37
Winters	78	2717	652	1308	.498	205	242	.847	64	167	231	337	228	1	114	29	1509	19.3	43
Bridgeman	82	2410	491	1094	.449	197	228	.864	129	287	416	205	221	3	82	26	1179	14.4	41
Nater	72	1960	383	725	.528	152	228	.754	266	599	865	108	214	6	54	51	938	13.0	30
Meyers	50	1262	179	383	.467	127	192	.661	122	219	341	86	152	4	42	32	485	9.7	31
Brokaw	41	891	130	324	.401	105	137	.766	10	54	64	111	85	0	22	23	365	8.9	27
Buckner	79	2095	299	689	.434	83	154	.539	91	173	264	372	291	5	192	25	681	8.6	21
E. Smith	34	789	123	253	.447	61	105	.581	52	156	208	30	109	2	19	69	287	8.4	21
Price	6	111	21	41	.512	7	9	.778	4	9	13	15	14	0	7	1	49	8.2	20
Carter (Tot)	61	1112	209	500	.418	68	96	.708	55	62	117	125	125	0	39	9	486	8.0	27
Carter (Mil)	47	875	166	399	.416	58	77	.753	45	48	93	104	96	0	28	7	390	8.3	27
Lloyd	69	1025	153	324	.472	95	126	.754	81	129	210	33	158	5	21	13	401	5.8	22
Restani	64	1116	173	334	.518	12	24	.500	81	181	262	88	102	0	33	11	358	5.6	22
English	60	648	132	277	.477	46	60	.767	68	100	168	25	78	0	17	18	310	5.2	21
Walton	53	678	88	188	.468	53	65	.815	15	36	51	141	52	0	40	2	229	4.3	13
Davis	19	165	29	68	.426	23	25	.920	11	18	29	20	11	0	6	4	81	4.3	9
Garrett (Tot)	62	598	106	239	.444	41	51	.804	37	75	112	27	80	0	21	10	253	4.1	12
Garrett (Mil)	33	383	66	146	.452	23	29	.739	27	45	72	20	50	0	14	7	155	4.7	12
McDonald	9	79	8	34	.235	3	4	.750	8	4	12	7	11	0	4	0	19	2.1	12

NEW ORLEANS

Player	G.	Min.	FGM	FGA	Pct.	FTM	FTA	Pct.	Off. Reb.	Def. Reb.	Tot. Reb.	Ast.	PF	Dsq.	Stl.	Blk. Sh.	Pts.	Avg.	Hi.
Maravich	73	3041	886	2047	.433	501	600	.835	90	284	374	392	191	1	84	22	2273	31.1	68
Goodrich	27	609	136	305	.446	68	85	.800	25	36	61	74	43	0	22	2	340	12.6	28
Williams	79	1776	414	917	.451	146	194	.753	107	199	306	92	200	0	76	16	974	12.3	41
James	52	1059	238	486	.490	89	114	.781	56	130	186	55	127	1	20	5	565	10.9	36
McElroy	73	2029	301	640	.470	169	217	.779	55	128	183	260	119	0	60	8	771	10.6	37
Boyd	47	1212	194	406	.478	79	98	.806	19	71	90	147	78	0	44	6	467	9.9	24
Behagen	60	1170	213	509	.418	90	126	.714	144	287	431	83	166	1	41	19	516	8.6	24
Coleman	77	2369	290	628	.462	82	112	.732	149	399	548	103	280	9	62	32	662	8.2	22
Kelley	76	1505	184	386	.477	156	197	.792	210	377	587	208	244	7	45	63	524	6.9	21
Stallworth	40	526	126	272	.463	17	29	.586	19	52	71	23	76	1	19	11	269	6.7	26
Moore	81	2084	193	477	.405	91	134	.679	170	466	636	181	231	3	54	117	477	5.9	17
Griffin	81	1645	140	256	.547	145	201	.721	167	328	495	167	241	6	50	43	425	5.2	20
Howard (Tot)	32	345	64	132	.485	24	35	.686	17	22	39	42	51	0	17	8	152	4.8	17
How'd (N.O.)	23	317	56	117	.479	19	29	.655	15	19	34	37	44	0	16	6	131	5.7	17
Walker	40	438	72	156	.462	36	47	.766	23	52	75	32	59	0	20	7	180	4.5	17

N.Y. KNICKS

Player	G.	Min.	FGM	FGA	Pct.	FTM	FTA	Pct.	Off. Reb.	Def. Reb.	Tot. Reb.	Ast.	PF	Dsq.	Stl.	Blk. Sh.	Pts.	Avg.	Hi.
McAdoo (Tot)	72	2798	740	1445	.512	381	516	.738	199	727	926	205	262	3	77	99	1861	25.8	43
McAdoo (Ks)	52	2031	558	1045	.534	271	358	.757	133	529	662	140	188	2	61	65	1387	26.7	43
Monroe	77	2656	613	1185	.517	307	366	.839	45	178	223	366	197	0	91	23	1533	19.9	37
Frazier	76	2687	532	1089	.489	259	336	.771	52	241	293	403	194	0	132	9	1323	17.4	41
Haywood	31	1021	202	449	.450	109	131	.832	77	203	280	50	72	0	14	29	513	16.5	35
Shelton	82	2104	398	836	.476	159	225	.707	220	413	633	149	363	10	125	98	955	11.6	31
Gianelli	19	630	86	182	.473	35	48	.729	60	118	178	26	54	0	14	8	207	10.9	19
McMillian	29	642	464	67	.464	67	86	.779	66	241	307	139	103	0	63	5	663	9.9	25
McM'len (Tot)	76	1492	274	563	.487	96	123	.780	114	275	389	67	163	0	11	6	644	8.5	31
McM'len (Ks)	56	1222	229	471	.486	70	87	.805	85	232	317	51	134	0	10	4	528	9.4	31
Layton	56	765	134	277	.484	58	73	.795	11	36	47	154	87	0	21	6	326	5.8	24
Burden	61	608	148	293	.505	75	109	.688	50	113	163	144	137	0	57	5	371	5.3	18
Walk	11	135	28	57	.491	6	7	.857	2	22	27	6	22	0	4	3	62	5.6	17
Beard	70	1082	148	293	.505	75	109	.688	50	113	163	144	137	0	57	5	371	5.3	18
Davis	22	342	41	110	.373	22	31	.710	30	70	100	24	45	0	9	1	104	4.7	13
Bradley	67	1027	127	274	.464	34	42	.810	27	76	103	128	122	0	25	8	288	4.3	20
Jackson	76	1033	102	232	.440	51	71	.718	75	154	229	85	184	4	33	18	255	3.4	19
Meminger	32	254	15	36	.417	13	23	.565	12	14	26	29	17	0	8	1	43	1.3	10

N.Y. NETS

Player	G.	Min.	FGM	FGA	Pct.	FTM	FTA	Pct.	Off. Reb.	Def. Reb.	Tot. Reb.	Ast.	PF	Dsq.	Stl.	Blk. Sh.	Pts.	Avg.	Hi.
Williamson	42	1426	357	803	.445	161	204	.789	24	95	119	90	143	3	59	6	875	20.8	37
Archibald	34	1277	250	560	.446	197	251	.785	22	58	80	254	77	1	59	11	697	20.5	34
Hawkins	52	1485	406	909	.447	194	282	.688	67	87	154	93	163	2	77	26	1006	19.3	44
Skinner	79	2256	382	887	.431	231	292	.791	112	251	363	289	279	7	103	53	995	12.6	24
Bantom (Tot)	77	1909	361	705	.478	224	310	.723	184	287	471	102	233	7	63	49	946	12.3	32
Bantom (Nts)	33	1114	224	474	.473	166	226	.735	101	184	285	50	120	4	28	28	614	18.6	32
Love (Tot)	27	724	117	307	.381	68	85	.800	53	58	111	27	70	1	9	4	302	11.2	22
Love (Nets)	13	228	49	106	.462	33	39	.846	15	23	38	4	23	0	1	2	131	10.1	22
Jones	34	877	134	348	.385	92	121	.760	48	146	194	46	109	2	38	11	360	10.6	20
van B. Kolff	72	2398	271	609	.445	195	228	.855	156	304	460	117	205	2	74	68	737	10.2	24
Bassett	76	2442	293	739	.396	101	177	.571	175	466	641	109	246	10	95	53	687	9.0	24
McNeill	8	93	18	51	.353	24	30	.800	10	16	26	3	13	1	4	1	60	7.5	23
Davis (Tot)	56	1094	168	464	.362	64	91	.703	98	-195	293	71	130	0	31	5	400	7.1	25
Davis (Nets)	34	752	127	354	.359	42	60	.700	68	125	193	47	85	0	22	4	296	8.7	25
Fox	71	1165	184	398	.462	95	114	.833	100	229	329	49	158	1	20	25	463	6.5	21
Wohl (Tot)	51	986	116	290	.400	61	89	.685	16	65	81	142	115	2	39	6	293	5.7	22
Wohl (Nets)	37	924	109	273	.399	57	85	.671	15	61	76	127	97	1	39	6	275	7.4	22
Terry	61	1075	128	318	.403	48	62	.774	43	100	143	39	120	0	58	10	304	5.0	19
Hughes	81	2081	151	354	.427	19	69	.275	189	375	564	98	308	9	122	119	321	4.0	14
Daniels	11	126	13	35	.371	13	23	.565	10	24	34	6	29	0	3	11	39	3.5	7
Williams	1	7	0	2	.000	3	6	.500	1	1	2	1	2	0	0	1	3	3.0	3
Hackett	1	8	0	2	.000	2	5	.400	1	2	3	0	1	0	0	0	2	2.0	2

1976-77 STATISTICS

PHILADELPHIA

Player	G.	Min.	FGM	FGA	Pct.	FTM	FTA	Pct.	Off. Reb.	Def. Reb.	Tot. Reb.	Ast.	PF	Dsq.	Stl.	Blk. Sh.	Pts.	Avg.	Hi.
Erving	82	2940	685	1373	.499	400	515	.777	192	503	695	306	251	1	159	113	1770	21.6	40
McGinnis	79	2769	659	1439	.458	372	546	.681	324	587	911	302	299	4	163	37	1690	21.4	37
Collins	58	2037	426	823	.518	210	250	.840	64	131	195	271	174	2	70	15	1062	18.3	33
Free	78	2253	467	1022	.457	334	464	.720	97	140	237	266	207	2	75	25	1268	16.3	39
Mix	75	1958	288	551	.523	215	263	.817	127	249	376	152	167	0	90	20	791	10.5	37
Bibby	81	2639	302	702	.430	221	282	.784	86	187	273	356	200	2	108	5	825	10.2	28
Carter	14	237	43	101	.426	10	19	.526	10	14	24	21	29	0	11	2	96	6.9	19
Jones	82	2023	215	424	.507	64	116	.552	190	476	666	92	301	3	43	200	494	6.0	16
Dawkins	59	684	135	215	.628	40	79	.506	59	171	230	24	129	1	12	49	310	5.3	20
Dunleavy	32	359	60	145	.414	34	45	.756	10	24	34	56	64	1	13	2	154	4.8	32
Bryant	61	612	107	240	.446	53	70	.757	45	72	117	48	84	1	36	13	267	4.4	22
Barnett	16	231	28	64	.438	10	18	.556	7	7	14	23	28	0	4	0	66	4.1	10
Catchings	53	864	62	123	.504	33	47	.702	64	170	234	30	130	1	23	78	157	3.0	16
Furlow	32	174	34	100	.340	16	18	.889	18	21	39	19	11	0	7	2	84	2.6	13

PHOENIX

Player	G.	Min.	FGM	FGA	Pct.	FTM	FTA	Pct.	Off. Reb.	Def. Reb.	Tot. Reb.	Ast.	PF	Dsq.	Stl.	Blk. Sh.	Pts.	Avg.	Hi.
Westphal	81	2600	682	1317	.518	362	439	.825	57	133	190	459	171	1	134	21	1726	21.3	40
Adams	72	2278	522	1102	.474	252	334	.754	180	472	652	322	260	4	95	87	1296	18.0	47
Sobers	79	2005	414	834	.496	243	289	.841	82	152	234	238	258	3	93	14	1071	13.6	32
Perry	44	1391	179	414	.432	112	142	.789	149	246	395	79	163	3	49	28	472	10.7	20
Lee	82	1849	347	786	.441	142	210	.676	99	200	299	263	276	10	156	33	836	10.2	33
Heard	46	1363	173	457	.379	100	138	.725	120	320	440	89	139	2	55	55	446	9.7	28
Terrell	78	1751	277	545	.508	111	176	.631	99	288	387	103	165	0	41	47	665	8.5	22
D. V. A'dale	78	1535	227	498	.456	145	166	.873	31	86	117	120	94	0	35	5	599	7.7	19
Erickson	50	949	142	294	.483	37	50	.740	36	108	144	104	122	0	30	7	321	6.4	19
T. V. A'dale	77	1425	171	395	.433	102	145	.703	47	137	184	67	163	0	20	3	444	5.8	20
Awtrey	72	1760	160	373	.429	91	126	.722	111	245	356	182	170	1	23	31	411	5.7	17
Feher	48	487	86	162	.531	76	99	.768	18	56	74	36	46	0	11	7	248	5.2	23
Schlueter	39	337	26	72	.361	18	31	.581	30	50	80	38	62	0	8	8	70	1.8	7

PORTLAND

Player	G.	Min.	FGM	FGA	Pct.	FTM	FTA	Pct.	Off. Reb.	Def. Reb.	Tot. Reb.	Ast.	PF	Dsq.	Stl.	Blk. Sh.	Pts.	Avg.	Hi.
Lucas	79	2863	632	1357	.466	335	438	.765	271	628	899	229	294	6	83	56	1599	20.2	41
Walton	65	2264	491	930	.528	228	327	.697	211	723	934	245	174	5	66	211	1210	18.6	30
Hollins	76	2224	452	1046	.432	215	287	.749	52	158	210	313	265	5	166	38	1119	14.7	43
Gross	82	2232	376	711	.529	183	215	.851	173	221	394	242	255	7	107	57	935	11.4	25
Twardzik	74	1937	263	430	.612	239	284	.842	75	127	202	247	228	6	128	15	765	10.3	28
Steele	81	1680	326	652	.500	183	227	.806	71	117	188	172	216	3	118	13	835	10.3	28
Gilliam	80	1665	326	744	.438	92	120	.767	64	137	201	170	168	1	76	6	744	9.3	23
Davis	79	1451	234	531	.441	166	209	.794	62	64	126	148	128	1	41	11	634	8.0	25
Neal	58	955	160	340	.471	77	114	.675	87	168	255	58	148	0	8	35	397	6.8	20
Jones	63	1065	139	299	.465	66	109	.606	103	193	296	80	124	3	37	38	344	5.5	21
Walker	66	627	137	305	.449	67	100	.670	45	63	108	51	92	0	14	2	341	5.2	19
Calhoun	70	743	85	183	.464	66	85	.776	40	104	144	35	123	1	24	8	236	3.4	16
Mayes (Tot)	9	52	5	19	.263	3	7	.429	10	6	16	3	12	0	0	4	13	1.4	4
Mayes (Port.)	5	24	2	9	.222	0	0	......	6	6	12	0	5	0	0	2	4	0.4	2

SAN ANTONIO

Player	G.	Min.	FGM	FGA	Pct.	FTM	FTA	Pct.	Off. Reb.	Def. Reb.	Tot. Reb.	Ast.	PF	Dsq.	Stl.	Blk. Sh.	Pts.	Avg.	Hi.
Gervin	82	2705	726	1335	.544	443	532	.833	134	320	454	238	286	12	105	104	1895	23.1	42
Kenon	78	2936	706	1435	.492	293	356	.823	282	597	879	229	190	0	167	60	1705	21.9	43
Paultz	82	2694	521	1102	.473	238	320	.744	192	495	687	223	262	5	55	173	1280	15.6	31
Bristow	82	2017	365	747	.489	206	258	.798	119	229	348	240	195	1	89	7	936	11.4	25
Olberding	82	1949	301	598	.503	251	316	.794	162	287	449	119	277	6	59	29	853	10.4	23
Gale	82	2598	353	754	.468	137	167	.820	54	219	273	473	224	3	191	50	843	10.3	24
Silas	22	356	61	142	.430	87	107	.813	7	25	32	50	36	0	13	3	209	9.5	28
Galvin	35	606	93	237	.392	123	146	.842	11	20	31	104	58	0	23	1	309	8.8	24
Dietrick	82	1772	285	620	.460	119	166	.717	111	261	372	148	267	8	88	57	689	8.4	24
Dampier	80	1634	233	507	.460	64	86	.744	22	54	76	234	93	0	49	15	530	6.6	21
Nelson	4	57	7	14	.500	4	7	.571	2	5	7	3	9	0	2	0	18	4.5	7
Ward	27	171	34	90	.378	15	17	.882	10	23	33	6	30	0	6	5	83	3.1	16
Karl	29	251	25	73	.342	29	42	.690	4	13	17	46	36	0	10	0	79	2.7	9
D'Antoni	2	9	1	3	.333	1	2	.500	2	2	2	3	0	0	0	0	3	1.5	2

SEATTLE

Player	G.	Min.	FGM	FGA	Pct.	FTM	FTA	Pct.	Off. Reb.	Def. Reb.	Tot. Reb.	Ast.	PF	Dsq.	Stl.	Blk. Sh.	Pts.	Avg.	Hi.
Brown	72	2098	534	1114	.479	168	190	.884	68	164	232	176	140	1	124	19	1236	17.2	42
Watts	79	2627	428	1015	.422	172	293	.587	81	226	307	630	256	5	214	25	1028	13.0	37
Gray	25	643	114	262	.435	59	78	.756	23	84	107	55	84	1	27	13	287	11.5	23
W'spoon (T)	62	1657	310	690	.449	91	144	.632	120	308	428	53	168	1	52	28	711	11.5	25
W'spoon (S)	51	1505	283	614	.461	86	136	.632	109	295	404	51	149	1	49	23	652	12.8	25
Seals	81	1977	378	851	.444	138	195	.708	118	236	354	93	262	6	45	129	746	9.8	31
Green	76	1928	290	658	.441	166	235	.706	191	312	503	120	201	1	45	129	746	9.8	31
Burleson	82	1803	288	652	.442	220	301	.731	184	367	551	93	259	1	74	117	796	9.7	26
Johnson	81	1667	285	566	.504	179	287	.624	161	141	302	123	221	3	123	57	749	9.2	24
Norwood	76	1647	216	461	.469	151	206	.733	127	165	292	99	191	1	62	6	583	7.7	21
Bantom	44	795	137	281	.488	58	84	.690	83	103	186	52	113	3	35	21	332	7.5	18
Love (Tot)	59	1174	162	428	.379	109	132	.826	79	119	198	48	120	1	22	6	433	7.3	22
Love (Sea.)	32	450	45	121	.372	41	47	.872	26	61	87	21	50	0	13	2	131	4.1	14
Wilkerson	78	1552	221	573	.386	84	122	.689	96	162	258	171	136	0	72	8	526	6.7	20
Tolson	60	587	137	242	.566	85	159	.535	73	84	157	27	83	0	32	21	359	6.0	19
Oleynick	50	516	81	223	.363	39	53	.736	13	32	45	60	48	0	13	4	201	4.0	19
Barnhill	4	10	2	6	.333	0	0		2	1	3	1	5	0	0	0	4	1.0	2

WASHINGTON

Player	G.	Min.	FGM	FGA	Pct.	FTM	FTA	Pct.	Off. Reb.	Def. Reb.	Tot. Reb.	Ast.	PF	Dsq.	Stl.	Blk. Sh.	Pts.	Avg.	Hi.
Hayes	82	3364	760	1516	.501	422	614	.687	289	740	1029	158	312	1	87	220	1942	23.7	47
Chenier	78	2842	654	1472	.444	270	321	.841	56	243	299	294	166	0	120	39	1578	20.2	38
Robinson	41	1328	264	522	.478	128	189	.677	119	247	366	45	123	0	28	18	656	16.0	33
H'son (Tot)	87	2791	371	826	.449	233	313	.744	43	196	239	598	148	0	138	17	975	11.2	27
H'son (Wash.)	41	1223	175	373	.469	107	145	.738	25	90	115	212	74	0	59	9	457	11.1	23
Bing	64	1516	271	597	.454	136	176	.772	54	89	143	275	150	1	61	5	678	10.6	32
Kupchak	82	1513	341	596	.572	170	246	.691	183	311	494	62	204	3	22	34	852	10.4	26
Wright	78	1421	262	595	.440	88	115	.765	32	66	98	232	170	0	55	5	612	7.8	27
Unseld	82	2860	270	551	.490	100	166	.602	243	634	877	363	253	5	87	45	640	7.8	18
Gray (Tot)	83	1639	258	592	.436	118	158	.747	84	209	293	124	273	9	58	31	634	7.6	23
Gray (Wash.)	58	996	144	330	.436	59	80	.738	61	125	186	69	189	8	31	18	347	6.0	18
Grevey	76	1306	224	530	.423	79	119	.664	73	105	178	68	148	1	29	9	527	6.9	22
W'spoon	11	152	27	76	.355	5	8	.625	11	13	24	2	19	0	3	5	59	5.4	14
Weiss	62	768	62	133	.466	29	37	.784	15	54	69	130	66	0	53	7	153	2.5	10
Pace	30	119	24	55	.436	16	29	.552	16	18	34	4	29	0	2	17	64	2.1	12
Jones	3	33	2	9	.222	2	4	.500	1	3	4	1	4	0	2	0	6	2.0	4
Riordan	49	289	34	94	.362	11	15	.733	7	20	27	20	33	0	3	2	79	1.6	8

OVER/UNDER 100 POINTS

	OFFENSE			DEFENSE		
	Held Below 100	High Game	Low Game	Opp. Below 100	Opp. High Game	Opp. Low Game
Atlanta	35	125	83	23	132	81
Boston	29	133	76	21	134	84
Buffalo	25	135	84	18	142	86
Chicago	40	120	74	49	125	76
Cleveland	35	130	78	37	133	75
Denver	11	145	83	19	139	78
Detroit	16	140	88	17	144	83
Golden State	15	150	85	21	136	84
Houston	24	137	80	23	126	79
Indiana	18	135	79	24	150	73
Kansas City	18	132	82	25	139	83
Los Angeles	21	136	81	30	145	81
Milwaukee	19	139	83	11	140	74
New Orleans	28	139	76	25	135	85
Knicks	17	144	85	20	135	80
Nets	53	127	73	33	139	73
Philadelphia	15	143	88	22	146	76
Phoenix	27	133	73	30	139	79
Portland	16	150	84	23	133	79
San Antonio	11	142	89	6	150	87
Seattle	30	131	83	29	138	76
Washington	30	135	84	27	143	87
Totals	533	150	73	533	150	73

1976-77 PLAYOFF RESULTS
FIRST ROUND

EASTERN CONFERENCE

Boston 2, San Antonio 0

Apr. 12–Tue.–San Antonio 94 at Boston................104
Apr. 15–Fri.–Boston 113 at San Antonio................109

Washington 2, Cleveland 1

Apr. 13–Wed.–Cleveland 100 at Washington........109
Apr. 15–Fri.–Washington 83 at Cleveland.............91
Apr. 17–Sun.–Cleveland 98 at Washington..........104

WESTERN CONFERENCE

Golden State 2, Detroit 1

Apr. 12–Tue.–Detroit 95 at Golden State................90
Apr. 14–Thur.–Golden State 138 at Detroit...........108
Apr. 17–Sun.–Detroit 101 at Golden State............109

Portland 2, Chicago 1

Apr. 12–Tue.–Chicago 83 at Portland......................96
Apr. 15–Fri.–Portland 104 at Chicago....................107
Apr. 17–Sun.–Chicago 98 at Portland....................106

CONFERENCE SEMI-FINAL SERIES

EASTERN CONFERENCE

Philadelphia 4, Boston 3

Apr. 17–Sun.–Boston 113 at Philadelphia.............111
Apr. 20–Wed.–Boston 101 at Philadelphia............113
Apr. 22–Fri.–Philadelphia 109 at Boston...............100
Apr. 24–Sun.–Philadelphia 119 at Boston.............124
Apr. 27–Wed.–Boston 91 at Philadelphia..............110
Apr. 29–Fri.–Philadelphia 108 at Boston...............113
May 1–Sun.–Boston 77 at Philadelphia.................83

Houston 4, Washington 2

Apr. 19–Tue.–Washington 111 at Houston............101
Apr. 21–Thur.–Washington 118 at Houston ..124 (ot)
Apr. 24–Sun.–Houston 90 at Washington...............93
Apr. 26–Tue.–Houston 107 at Washington............103
Apr. 29–Fri.–Washington 115 at Houston.............123
May 1–Sun.–Houston 108 at Washington............103

WESTERN CONFERENCE

Los Angeles 4, Golden State 3

Apr. 20–Wed.–Golden State 106 at Los Angeles ..115
Apr. 22–Fri.–Golden State 86 at Los Angeles........95
Apr. 24–Sun.–Los Angeles 105 at Golden State....109
Apr. 26–Tue.–Los Angeles 103 at Golden State....114
Apr. 29–Fri.–Golden State 105 at Los Angeles 112
May 1–Sun.–Los Angeles 106 at Golden State....115
May 4–Wed.–Golden State 84 at Los Angeles......97

Portland 4, Denver 2

Apr. 20–Wed.–Portland 101 at Denver..................100
Apr. 22–Fri.–Portland 110 at Denver.....................121
Apr. 24–Sun.–Denver 106 at Portland...................110
Apr. 26–Tue.–Denver 96 at Portland.....................105
May 1–Sun.–Portland 105 at Denver.............114 (ot)
May 2–Mon.–Denver 92 at Portland....................108

CONFERENCE FINALS

EASTERN CONFERENCE

Philadelphia 4, Houston 2

May 5–Thur.–Houston 117 at Philadelphia........128
May 8–Sun.–Houston 97 at Philadelphia............106
May 11–Wed.–Philadelphia 94 at Houston..........118
May 13–Fri.–Philadelphia 107 at Houston.............95
May 15–Sun.–Houston 118 at Philadelphia.........115
May 17–Tue.–Philadelphia 112 at Houston.........109

WESTERN CONFERENCE

Portland 4, Los Angeles 0

May 6–Fri.–Portland 121 at Los Angeles............109
May 8–Sun.–Portland 99 at Los Angeles..............97
May 10–Tue.–Los Angeles 97 at Portland............102
May 13–Fri.–Los Angeles 101 at Portland............105

WORLD CHAMPIONSHIP SERIES

Portland 4, Philadelphia 2

May 22–Sun.–Portland 101 at Philadelphia..........107
May 26–Thur.–Portland 89 at Philadelphia..........107
May 29–Sun.–Philadelphia 107 at Portland..........129
May 31–Tue.–Philadelphia 98 at Portland............130
June 3–Fri.–Portland 110 at Philadelphia 104
June 5–Sun.–Philadelphia 107 at Portland..........109

1975-76 STATISTICS

BOSTON CELTICS—1975-76 NBA CHAMPIONS

Seated (Left to Right): Charlie Scott, Paul Silas, Dave Cowens, Irving Levin, Chairman of the Board; Coach Tom Heinsohn, President Arnold (Red) Auerbach, Captain John Havlicek, Jo Jo White, Don Nelson. Standing (Left to Right): Dr. Tom Silva, Mark Volk, assistant trainer; Kevin Stacom, Glenn McDonald, Tom Boswell, Jim Ard, Steve Kuberski, Jerome Anderson, Frank Challant, trainer; Dr. Sam Kane. Inset: John Killilea, assistant coach and chief scout.

FINAL STANDINGS AND TEAM FIGURES

ATLANTIC DIVISION

Team	Atl.	Bos.	Buf.	Chi.	Cle.	Det.	G.S.	Hou.	KC	L.A.	Mil.	N.O.	N.Y.	Phi.	Pho.	Por.	Sea.	Was.	W.	L.	Pct.	G.B.
Boston	3	..	4	2	3	4	2	4	2	4	2	4	5	4	4	2	2	3	54	28	.659	..
Buffalo	3	3	..	3	3	1	1	3	4	2	3	4	4	3	3	2	2	2	46	36	.561	8
Philadelphia	3	3	4	4	2	3	1	2	3	2	2	4	2	..	3	4	2	2	46	36	.561	8
New York	2	2	3	4	2	1	..	2	3	1	2	3	..	5	2	3	..	3	38	44	.463	16

CENTRAL DIVISION

Cleveland	5	2	2	4	..	2	1	2	1	2	4	4	3	3	3	4	3	4	49	33	.598	..
Washington	5	2	3	4	2	2	1	4	3	3	2	3	2	3	4	2	3	..	48	34	.585	1
Houston	5	1	2	3	4	2	2	..	2	1	2	2	3	3	..	3	2	3	40	42	.488	9
New Orleans	4	1	1	2	3	3	2	4	3	1	2	..	2	1	1	3	1	4	38	44	.463	11
Atlanta	..	2	2	2	2	1	2	2	2	1	2	2	3	2	..	2	1	1	29	53	.354	20

MIDWEST DIVISION

Milwaukee	2	2	1	4	..	4	..	2	5	3	..	2	2	2	3	2	2	2	38	44	.463	..
Detroit	3	0	3	4	2	..	0	0	2	5	1	3	1	3	1	1	2	3	2	36	46	.439	2
Kansas City	2	2	..	6	3	2	1	2	..	2	2	2	1	1	3	..	2	1	31	51	.378	7
Chicago	2	2	1	..	..	3	1	1	1	3	3	2	..	..	2	1	2	..	24	58	.293	14

PACIFIC DIVISION

Golden State	2	2	3	4	3	5	..	2	4	5	5	2	4	3	4	4	4	3	59	23	.720	..
Seattle	3	2	2	3	1	2	3	2	3	3	3	3	4	2	3	3	..	1	43	39	.524	16
Phoenix	4	..	1	3	1	4	2	4	2	4	2	3	2	1	..	5	4	..	42	40	.512	17
Los Angeles	3	..	2	2	2	4	2	3	..	2	3	3	2	2	3	3	1	..	40	42	.488	19
Portland	2	2	2	4	..	3	2	1	5	4	3	1	1	..	2	..	3	2	37	45	.451	22

1975-76 STATISTICS
TEAM STATISTICS—OFFENSE

Team	G.	FIELD GOALS Made	Att.	Pct.	FREE THROWS Made	Att.	Pct.	REBOUNDS Off.	Def.	Tot.	MISCELLANEOUS Ast.	PF	Stl.	Blk. Sh.	Turn Over	Dq.	SCORING Pts.	Avg.
G.S.	82	3691	7982	.462	1620	2158	.751	1349	2912	4261	2041	2022	928	416	1613	13	9002	109.8
Buff.	82	3481	7307	.476	1833	2368	.774	1002	2719	3721	2112	2017	720	366	1743	22	8795	107.3
L.A.	82	3547	7622	.465	1670	2164	.772	1132	2870	4002	1939	2025	674	528	1612	24	8764	106.9
Phil.	82	3462	7752	.447	1811	2469	.733	1385	2684	4069	1658	2187	809	367	1729	35	8735	106.5
Sea.	82	3542	7730	.458	1642	2309	.711	1217	2498	3715	1935	2133	866	355	1615	38	8726	106.4
Bos.	82	3527	7901	.446	1654	2120	.780	1369	2972	4341	1980	2002	561	260	1609	37	8708	106.2
Hou.	82	3546	7304	.485	1616	2046	.790	1059	2644	3703	2213	2045	656	359	1665	36	8708	106.2
Phoe.	82	3420	7251	.472	1780	2337	.762	1108	2558	3666	2083	2018	853	349	1852	31	8620	105.1
Det.	82	3524	7598	.464	1557	2049	.760	1205	2545	3750	1751	2086	786	332	1619	26	8605	104.9
N.O.	82	3352	7491	.447	1831	2415	.758	1189	2779	3968	1765	2175	750	343	1659	30	8535	104.1
Port.	82	3417	7292	.469	1699	2350	.723	1116	2843	3959	2094	2091	776	408	1867	35	8533	104.1
K.C.	82	3341	7379	.453	1792	2335	.767	1133	2668	3801	1864	2056	751	324	1607	44	8474	103.3
Wash.	82	3416	7234	.472	1595	2215	.720	1019	2812	3831	1823	1921	696	485	1672	20	8427	102.8
N.Y.	82	3443	7555	.456	1532	1985	.772	1022	2723	3745	1660	2006	575	259	1403	14	8418	102.7
Atl.	82	3301	7338	.450	1809	2467	.733	1225	2540	3765	1666	1983	790	277	1553	39	8411	102.6
Mil.	82	3456	7435	.465	1437	1952	.736	1094	2688	3782	1817	2041	715	468	1624	30	8349	101.8
Clev.	82	3497	7709	.454	1346	1827	.737	1192	2588	3780	1844	1871	638	397	1330	10	8340	101.7
Chi.	82	3106	7499	.414	1651	2197	.751	1375	2726	4101	1704	1977	627	255	1413	37	7863	95.9

TEAM STATISTICS—DEFENSE

Team	FIELD GOALS Made	Att.	Pct.	FREE THROWS Made	Att.	Pct.	REBOUNDS Off.	Def.	Tot.	MISCELLANEOUS Ast.	PF	Stl.	Blk. Sh.	Turn Over	Dq.	SCORING Pts.	Avg.	Dif.
Chi.	3246	6946	.467	1609	2137	.753	930	2809	3739	1669	2081	615	461	1485	31	8101	98.8	− 2.9
Clev.	3262	7188	.454	1610	2152	.748	1134	2792	3926	1728	1860	610	325	1579	17	8134	99.2	+ 2.5
Wash.	3377	7636	.442	1482	1992	.744	1145	2687	3832	1705	1988	810	338	1510	33	8236	100.4	+ 2.4
G.S.	3437	7742	.444	1583	2150	.736	1288	2730	4018	2006	1946	743	395	1761	22	8457	103.1	+ 6.7
Mil.	3402	7624	.446	1664	2182	.763	1229	2604	3833	1897	1828	683	325	1503	21	8468	103.3	− 1.5
Bos.	3489	7772	.449	1538	2074	.742	1037	2659	3696	1835	1895	650	334	1422	25	8516	103.9	+ 2.3
N.Y.	3407	7426	.459	1705	2274	.750	1068	2891	3959	1812	1954	608	335	1453	31	8519	103.9	− 1.2
Phoe.	3444	7357	.468	1682	2265	.743	1143	2513	3656	1979	2163	912	336	1746	41	8570	104.5	+ 0.6
N.O.	3396	7413	.458	1816	2464	.737	1182	2846	4028	1684	2162	777	405	1748	40	8608	105.0	− 0.9
Port.	3405	7531	.452	1825	2333	.782	1121	2657	3778	1920	2128	917	386	1613	29	8635	105.3	− 1.2
Atl.	3529	7357	.480	1592	2102	.757	1186	2728	3914	1778	2177	779	427	1663	30	8650	105.5	− 2.9
Det.	3492	7479	.467	1707	2211	.772	1218	2690	3908	2014	1994	724	437	1671	21	8691	106.0	− 1.1
K.C.	3477	7454	.466	1753	2310	.759	1153	2778	3931	1825	2124	680	321	1639	26	8707	106.2	− 2.9
Phil.	3467	7337	.448	1780	2334	.763	1435	2717	4152	1849	2151	730	342	1794	37	8714	106.3	+ 0.2
Buff.	3558	7722	.461	1611	2156	.747	1183	2645	3828	2079	2137	729	319	1660	38	8727	106.4	+ 0.9
Sea.	3486	7464	.467	1777	2407	.738	1239	2713	3952	2109	2115	745	388	1852	34	8749	106.7	− 0.3
L.A.	3592	7980	.450	1573	2148	.732	1384	2837	4221	2032	1987	775	363	1564	22	8757	106.8	+ 0.1
Hou.	3603	7551	.477	1568	2072	.757	1116	2473	3589	2028	2050	684	311	1522	23	8774	107.0	− 0.8

DQ—Individual players disqualified (fouled out of game).

INDIVIDUAL SCORING LEADERS
Minimum: 70 games played or 1400 points

	G.	FG	FT	Pts.	Avg.		G.	FG	FT	Pts.	Avg.
McAdoo, Buff.	78	934	559	2427	31.1	Murphy, Hou.	82	675	372	1722	21.0
Abdul-Jabbar, L.A.	82	914	447	2275	27.7	Collins, Phil.	77	614	372	1600	20.8
Maravich, N.O.	62	604	396	1604	25.9	Monroe, N.Y.	76	647	280	1574	20.7
Archibald, K.C.	78	717	501	1935	24.8	Westphal, Phoe.	82	657	365	1679	20.5
F. Brown, Sea.	76	742	273	1757	23.1	P. Smith, G.S.	82	659	323	1641	20.0
McGinnis, Phil.	77	647	475	1769	23.0	Chenier, Wash.	80	654	282	1590	19.9
R. Smith, Buff.	82	702	383	1787	21.8	Haywood, N.Y.	78	605	339	1549	19.9
Drew, Atl.	77	586	488	1660	21.6	Hayes, Wash.	80	649	287	1585	19.8
Dandridge, Mil.	73	650	271	1571	21.5	Goodrich, L.A.	75	583	293	1459	19.5
Barry, G.S.	81	707	287	1701	21.0	Love, Chi.	76	543	362	1448	19.1

FIELD GOAL LEADERS
Minimum: 300 FG Made

	FGM	FGA	Pct.
Unseld, Wash.	318	567	.560
Shumate, Phoe.-Buff.	332	592	.560
McMillian, Buff.	492	918	.536
Lanier, Det.	541	1017	.532
Abdul-Jabbar, L.A.	914	1728	.529
E. Smith, Mil.	498	962	.518
Tomjanovich, Hou.	622	1202	.517
Collins, Phil.	614	1196	.513
O. Johnson, K.C.	348	678	.513
Newlin, Hou.	569	1123	.507

FREE THROW LEADERS
Minimum: 125 FTM

	FTM	FTA	Pct.
Barry, G.S.	287	311	.923
Murphy, Hou.	372	410	.907
C. Russell, L.A.	132	148	.892
Bradley, N.Y.	130	148	.878
F. Brown, Sea.	273	314	.869
Newlin, Hou.	385	445	.865
J. Walker, K.C.	231	267	.865
McMillian, Buff.	188	219	.858
Marin, Buff.-Chi.	161	188	.856
Erickson, Phoe.	134	157	.854

REBOUND LEADERS
Minimum: 70 games or 800 rebounds

	G.	Off.	Def.	Tot.	Avg.
Abdul-Jabbar, L.A.	82	272	1111	1383	16.9
Cowens, Bos.	78	335	911	1246	16.0
Unseld, Wash.	78	271	765	1036	13.3
Silas, Bos.	81	365	660	1025	12.7
Lacey, K.C.	81	218	806	1024	12.6
McGinnis, Phil.	77	260	707	967	12.6
McAdoo, Buff.	78	241	724	965	12.4
E. Smith, Mil.	78	201	692	893	11.4
Haywood, N.Y.	78	234	644	878	11.3
Hayes, Wash.	80	210	668	878	11.0

BLOCKED SHOTS LEADERS
Minimum: 70 games or 100 blocked shots

	G.	No.	Avg.
Abdul-Jabbar, L.A.	82	338	4.12
E. Smith, Mil.	78	238	3.05
Hayes, Wash.	80	202	2.53
Catchings, Phil.	75	164	2.19
G. Johnson, G.S.	82	174	2.12
McAdoo, Buff.	78	160	2.05
Burleson, Sea.	82	150	1.83
Moore, N.O.	81	136	1.68
Lacey, K.C.	81	134	1.65
Neal, Port.	68	107	1.57

ASSISTS LEADERS
Minimum: 70 games or 400 assists

	G.	No.	Avg.
Watts, Sea.	82	661	8.1
Archibald, K.C.	78	615	7.9
Murphy, Hou.	82	596	7.3
Van Lier, Chi.	76	500	6.6
Barry, G.S.	81	496	6.1
Bing, Wash.	82	492	6.0
R. Smith, Buff.	82	484	5.9
A. Adams, Phoe.	80	450	5.6
Goodrich, L.A.	75	421	5.6
Newlin, Hou.	82	457	5.6

STEALS LEADERS
Minimum: 70 games or 125 steals

	G.	No.	Avg.
Watts, Sea.	82	261	3.18
McGinnis, Phil.	77	198	2.57
Westphal, Phoe.	82	210	2.56
Barry, G.S.	81	202	2.49
C. Ford, Det.	82	178	2.17
Steele, Port.	81	170	2.10
Chenier, Wash.	80	158	1.98
Van Lier, Chi.	76	150	1.97
Mix, Phil.	81	158	1.95
F. Brown, Sea.	76	143	1.88

Records of Teams by Months

Team	Oct. W-L	Nov. W-L	Dec. W-L	Jan. W-L	Feb. W-L	Mar. W-L	Apr. W-L	Total W-L
Atlanta	1-1	9-6	7-6	6-12	3-10	2-12	1-6	29-53
Boston	3-0	6-6	12-3	12-4	7-5	11-6	3-4	54-28
Buffalo	3-0	6-9	10-6	11-5	5-6	7-9	4-1	46-36
Chicago	2-2	2-10	4-12	6-9	4-8	4-13	2-4	24-58
Cleveland	1-2	6-9	11-4	9-6	9-3	9-6	4-3	49-33
Detroit	3-1	7-4	3-12	5-10	6-8	8-8	4-3	36-46
Golden State	2-2	10-3	11-3	12-4	8-5	13-4	3-2	59-23
Houston	0-3	8-5	7-7	8-8	7-8	8-7	2-4	40-42
Kansas City	0-3	7-5	3-14	8-9	4-8	7-8	2-4	31-51
Los Angeles	3-2	11-5	7-8	3-10	7-6	7-9	2-2	40-42
Milwaukee	0-3	7-8	6-7	7-10	6-6	8-8	4-2	38-44
New Orleans	4-1	3-9	5-9	9-5	6-9	8-8	3-3	38-44
New York	2-3	5-11	9-6	8-7	6-5	4-10	4-2	38-44
Philadelphia	2-1	10-5	9-5	8-8	6-8	7-7	4-2	46-36
Phoenix	1-1	6-6	8-7	4-13	8-5	12-5	3-3	42-40
Portland	0-4	8-7	4-10	9-6	6-8	7-7	3-3	37-45
Seattle	3-2	7-8	8-7	5-9	8-5	8-5	4-3	43-39
Washington	1-0	6-8	9-7	11-6	11-4	8-6	2-3	48-34
Totals	31	124	133	141	117	138	54	738

INTER-CLUB RECORDS—HOME AND AWAY

	Home	Away	Total
Atlanta	20-21	9-32	29-53
Boston	31-10	23-18	54-28
Buffalo	28-13	18-23	46-36
Chicago	15-26	9-32	24-58
Cleveland	29-12	20-21	49-33
Detroit	24-17	12-29	36-46
Golden State	36-5	23-18	59-23
Houston	28-13	12-29	40-42
Kansas City	25-16	6-35	31-51
Los Angeles	31-10	9-32	40-42
Milwaukee	22-19	16-25	38-44
New Orleans	22-19	16-25	38-44
New York	24-17	14-27	38-44
Philadelphia	34-7	12-29	46-36
Phoenix	27-14	15-26	42-40
Portland	26-15	11-30	37-45
Seattle	31-10	12-29	43-39
Washington	31-10	17-24	48-34

1975-76 STATISTICS
INDIVIDUAL STATISTICS

ATLANTA

Player	G.	Min.	FGM	FGA	Pct.	FTM	FTA	Pct.	Off. Reb.	Def. Reb.	Tot. Reb.	Ast.	PF	Dsq.	Stl.	Blk. Sh.	Pts.	Avg.	Hi.
Drew	77	2351	586	1168	.502	488	656	.744	286	374	660	150	261	11	138	30	1660	21.6	42
Hudson	81	2558	569	1205	.472	237	291	.814	104	196	300	214	241	3	124	17	1375	17.0	42
Henderson	81	2900	469	1136	.413	216	305	.708	58	207	265	374	195	1	137	10	1154	14.2	33
T. V. Arsdale	75	2026	346	785	.441	126	166	.759	35	151	186	146	202	5	57	7	818	10.9	26
D. Jones	66	1762	251	542	.463	163	219	.744	171	353	524	83	214	8	52	61	665	10.1	24
Sojourner	67	1602	248	524	.473	80	119	.672	126	323	449	58	174	2	38	40	576	8.6	22
C. Hawkins	74	1907	237	530	.447	136	191	.712	102	343	445	212	172	2	80	46	610	8.2	22
J. Brown	75	1758	215	486	.442	162	209	.775	146	257	403	126	235	7	45	16	592	7.9	22
Meminger	68	1418	155	379	.409	100	152	.658	65	86	151	222	116	0	54	8	410	6.0	27
Holland	33	351	85	213	.399	22	34	.647	15	26	41	26	48	0	20	2	192	5.8	21
Willoughby	62	870	113	284	.398	66	100	.660	103	185	288	31	87	0	37	29	292	4.7	20
DuVal	13	130	15	43	.349	6	9	.667	1	7	8	20	15	0	6	2	36	2.8	10
Creighton	32	172	12	43	.279	7	16	.438	13	32	45	4	23	0	2	9	31	1.0	5

BOSTON

Player	G.	Min.	FGM	FGA	Pct.	FTM	FTA	Pct.	Off. Reb.	Def. Reb.	Tot. Reb.	Ast.	PF	Dsq.	Stl.	Blk. Sh.	Pts.	Avg.	Hi.
Cowens	78	3101	611	1305	.468	257	340	.756	335	911	1246	325	314	10	94	71	1479	19.0	39
J. White	82	3257	670	1492	.449	212	253	.838	61	252	313	445	183	2	107	20	1552	18.9	34
Scott	82	2913	588	1309	.449	267	335	.797	106	252	358	341	356	17	103	24	1443	17.6	32
Havlicek	76	2598	504	1121	.450	281	333	.844	116	198	314	278	204	1	97	29	1289	17.0	38
Silas	81	2662	315	740	.426	236	333	.709	365	660	1025	203	227	3	56	33	866	10.7	19
D. Nelson	75	943	175	379	.462	127	161	.789	56	126	182	77	115	0	14	7	477	6.4	27
McDonald	75	1019	191	456	.419	40	56	.714	56	79	135	68	123	0	39	20	422	5.6	18
Stacom	77	1114	170	387	.439	68	91	.747	62	99	161	128	117	0	23	5	408	5.3	16
Ku'ski (Tot)	70	967	135	291	.464	71	79	.899	90	169	259	47	133	1	12	13	341	4.9	20
Ku'ski (Bos)	60	882	128	274	.467	68	76	.895	86	148	234	44	123	1	11	11	324	5.4	20
Ard	81	853	107	294	.364	71	100	.710	96	193	289	48	141	2	12	36	285	3.5	18
J. Anderson	22	126	25	45	.556	11	16	.688	4	9	13	6	25	0	3	3	61	2.8	8
Boswell	35	275	41	93	.441	14	24	.583	26	45	71	16	70	1	2	1	96	2.7	9
Searcy	4	12	2	6	.333	2	2	1.000	0	0	0	1	4	0	0	0	6	1.5	2

BUFFALO

Player	G.	Min.	FGM	FGA	Pct.	FTM	FTA	Pct.	Off. Reb.	Def. Reb.	Tot. Reb.	Ast.	PF	Dsq.	Stl.	Blk. Sh.	Pts.	Avg.	Hi.
McAdoo	78	3328	934	1918	.487	559	734	.762	241	724	965	315	298	5	93	160	2427	31.1	52
R. Smith	82	3167	702	1422	.494	383	469	.817	104	313	417	484	274	5	153	4	1787	21.8	35
McMillian	74	2610	492	918	.536	188	219	.858	134	256	390	205	141	0	88	14	1172	15.8	35
S'mate (Tot)	75	1976	332	592	.561	212	326	.650	143	411	554	127	159	2	82	34	876	11.7	28
S'mate (Buf)	32	1046	146	254	.575	97	143	.678	82	232	314	65	83	1	38	18	389	12.2	25
Charles	81	2247	328	719	.456	161	205	.785	58	161	219	204	257	5	123	48	817	10.1	29
Heard	50	1527	207	492	.421	82	135	.607	138	373	511	126	183	0	66	55	496	9.9	20
Marin	12	278	41	94	.436	27	33	.818	10	30	40	23	30	0	7	6	109	9.1	23
DiGregorio	67	1364	182	474	.384	86	94	.915	15	97	112	265	158	1	37	1	450	6.7	22
McMillen	50	708	96	222	.432	41	54	.759	64	122	186	69	87	1	7	6	233	4.7	18
Gibbs	72	866	129	301	.429	77	93	.828	42	64	106	49	133	2	16	14	335	4.7	19
Weiss	66	995	89	183	.486	35	48	.729	13	53	66	150	94	0	48	14	213	3.2	17
D. Adams	56	704	67	170	.394	40	57	.702	38	107	145	73	128	1	30	7	174	3.1	20
Schlueter	71	773	61	122	.500	54	81	.667	58	166	224	80	141	1	13	17	176	2.5	9
Kuberski	10	85	7	17	.412	3	3	1.000	4	21	25	3	10	0	1	2	17	1.7	5
J. Wash'ton	1	7	0	1	.000	0	0	.000	1	0	1	1	0	0	0	0	0	0.0	0

CHICAGO

Player	G.	Min.	FGM	FGA	Pct.	FTM	FTA	Pct.	Off. Reb.	Def. Reb.	Tot. Reb.	Ast.	PF	Dsq.	Stl.	Blk. Sh.	Pts.	Avg.	Hi.
Love	76	2823	543	1391	.390	362	452	.801	191	319	510	145	233	3	63	10	1448	19.0	40
M. Johnson	81	2390	478	1033	.463	283	360	.786	279	479	758	130	292	8	93	66	1239	15.3	30
Van Lier	76	3026	361	987	.366	235	319	.737	138	272	410	500	298	9	150	26	957	12.6	28
Marin (Tot)	79	1909	343	812	.422	161	188	.856	69	183	252	141	164	0	45	11	847	10.7	34
Marin (Chi)	67	1631	302	718	.421	134	155	.865	59	153	212	118	134	0	38	5	738	11.0	34
Garrett	14	324	57	131	.435	38	44	.864	27	48	75	7	32	0	8	4	152	10.9	22
Sloan	22	617	84	210	.400	55	78	.705	40	76	116	22	77	1	27	5	223	10.1	21
Laskowski	71	1570	284	690	.412	87	120	.725	52	167	219	55	90	0	56	10	655	9.2	29
Boerwinkle	74	2045	265	530	.500	118	177	.667	263	529	792	283	263	9	47	52	648	8.8	31
Wilson	58	856	197	489	.403	43	58	.741	32	62	94	52	96	1	25	2	437	7.5	28
Benbow	76	1586	219	551	.397	105	140	.750	65	111	176	158	186	1	62	11	543	7.1	19
Pondexter	75	1326	156	380	.411	122	182	.670	113	268	381	90	134	4	28	26	434	5.8	22
Guokas	18	278	36	74	.486	9	11	.818	4	12	16	28	23	0	5	0	81	4.5	12

1975-76 STATISTICS

Player	G.	Min.	FGM	FGA	Pct.	FTM	FTA	Pct.	Off. Reb.	Def. Reb.	Tot. Reb.	Ast.	PF	Dsq.	Stl.	Blk. Sh.	Pts.	Avg.	Hi.
Thurmond	13	260	20	45	.444	8	18	.444	14	57	71	26	15	0	4	12	48	3.7	8
Pat'son (Tot)	66	918	84	220	.382	34	54	.630	80	148	228	80	93	1	16	16	202	3.1	13
Pat'son (Chi)	52	672	69	182	.379	26	44	.591	73	127	200	71	82	1	13	11	164	3.2	13
F'sten (Tot)	37	268	33	86	.384	26	37	.703	25	45	70	19	21	0	7	14	92	2.5	8
F'sten (Chi)	33	259	33	84	.393	26	37	.703	25	44	69	19	20	0	7	14	92	2.8	8
Block	2	7	2	4	.500	0	2	.000	0	2	2	0	2	0	1	0	4	2.0	4

CLEVELAND

Player	G.	Min.	FGM	FGA	Pct.	FTM	FTA	Pct.	Off. Reb.	Def. Reb.	Tot. Reb.	Ast.	PF	Dsq.	Stl.	Blk. Sh.	Pts.	Avg.	Hi.
Chones	82	2741	563	1258	.448	172	260	.662	197	542	739	163	241	2	42	93	1298	15.8	29
M. Russell	82	1961	483	1003	.482	266	344	.773	134	211	345	107	231	5	69	10	1232	15.0	35
B. Smith	81	2338	495	1121	.442	111	136	.816	83	258	341	155	231	0	58	36	1101	13.6	30
Snyder	82	2274	441	881	.501	155	188	.824	50	148	198	220	215	0	59	33	1037	12.6	36
Cleamons	82	2835	413	887	.466	174	218	.798	124	230	354	428	214	2	124	20	1000	12.2	29
Brewer	82	2913	400	874	.458	140	214	.654	298	593	891	209	214	0	94	89	940	11.5	25
Carr	65	1282	276	625	.442	106	134	.791	67	65	132	122	92	0	37	2	658	10.1	27
Beard	15	255	35	90	.389	27	37	.730	14	29	43	45	36	0	10	2	97	6.5	16
Gar't (Tot)	55	540	108	258	.419	53	65	.815	45	72	117	17	68	0	25	7	269	4.9	22
Gar't (Clev)	41	216	51	127	.402	15	21	.714	18	24	42	10	36	0	17	3	117	2.9	15
C. Walker	81	1280	143	369	.388	84	108	.778	53	129	182	288	136	0	98	5	370	4.6	17
T'mond (Tot)	78	1393	142	337	.421	62	123	.504	115	300	415	94	160	1	22	98	346	4.4	15
T'mond (Clev)	65	1133	122	292	.418	54	105	.514	101	243	344	68	145	1	18	86	298	4.6	15
Patterson	14	136	15	38	.395	8	10	.800	7	21	28	9	11	0	3	5	38	2.7	8
Lambert	54	333	49	110	.445	25	37	.676	37	65	102	16	54	0	8	12	123	2.3	10
Witte	22	99	11	32	.344	9	15	.600	9	29	38	4	14	0	1	1	31	1.4	6
Fernsten	4	9	0	2	.000	0	0	.000	0	1	1	0	1	0	0	0	0	0.0	0

DETROIT

Player	G.	Min.	FGM	FGA	Pct.	FTM	FTA	Pct.	Off. Reb.	Def. Reb.	Tot. Reb.	Ast.	PF	Dsq.	Stl.	Blk. Sh.	Pts.	Avg.	Hi.
Lanier	64	2363	541	1017	.532	284	370	.768	217	529	746	217	203	2	79	86	1366	21.3	41
Rowe	80	2998	514	1098	.468	252	342	.737	231	466	697	183	209	3	47	45	1280	16.0	29+
Money	80	2267	449	947	.474	145	180	.806	77	130	207	338	243	4	137	11	1043	13.0	26
K. Porter	19	687	99	235	.421	42	56	.750	14	30	44	193	83	2	35	3	240	12.6	23
Mengelt	67	1105	264	540	.489	192	237	.810	27	88	115	108	138	1	40	5	720	10.7	32
Eberhard	81	2066	283	683	.414	191	229	.834	139	251	390	83	250	5	87	15	757	9.3	30
H. Porter	75	1482	298	635	.469	73	97	.753	81	214	295	25	133	0	31	36	669	8.9	28
C. Ford	82	2198	301	707	.426	83	115	.722	80	211	291	272	222	0	178	24	685	8.4	24
Trapp	76	1091	278	602	.462	63	88	.716	79	150	229	50	167	3	33	23	619	8.1	27
W. Jones	1	19	4	11	.364	0	0	.000	0	0	0	2	2	0	2	0	8	8.0	8
Clark	79	1589	250	577	.433	100	116	.862	27	110	137	218	157	0	62	4	600	7.6	18
Hairston	47	651	104	228	.456	65	112	.580	65	114	179	21	84	2	21	32	273	5.8	25
E. Williams	46	562	73	152	.480	22	44	.500	103	148	251	18	81	0	22	20	168	3.7	13
Thomas	28	136	28	65	.431	21	29	.724	15	21	36	3	21	1	4	2	77	2.8	18
R. Brown	29	454	29	72	.403	14	18	.778	47	83	130	12	76	1	6	25	72	2.5	11
Dickerson	17	112	9	29	.310	10	16	.625	3	0	3	8	17	1	2	1	28	1.6	11

GOLDEN STATE

Player	G.	Min.	FGM	FGA	Pct.	FTM	FTA	Pct.	Off. Reb.	Def. Reb.	Tot. Reb.	Ast.	PF	Dsq.	Stl.	Blk. Sh.	Pts.	Avg.	Hi.
Barry	81	3122	707	1624	.435	287	311	.923	74	422	496	496	215	1	202	27	1701	21.0	41
P. Smith	82	2793	659	1383	.477	323	410	.788	133	243	376	362	223	0	108	18	1641	20.0	51
Wilkes	82	2716	617	1334	.463	227	294	.772	193	527	720	167	222	0	102	31	1461	17.8	34
G. Williams	77	1728	365	853	.428	173	233	.742	62	97	159	240	143	2	140	26	903	11.7	27
C. Johnson	81	1549	342	732	.467	60	79	.759	77	125	202	122	178	1	100	7	744	9.2	26
Ray	82	2184	212	404	.525	140	230	.609	270	506	776	149	247	2	78	83	564	6.9	20
Dickey	79	1207	220	473	.465	62	79	.785	114	235	349	83	141	1	26	11	502	6.4	20
Dudley	82	1456	182	345	.528	157	245	.641	112	157	269	239	170	0	77	2	521	6.4	18
G. Johnson	82	1745	165	341	.484	70	104	.673	200	427	627	82	275	6	51	174	400	4.9	16
Mullins	29	311	58	120	.483	23	29	.793	12	20	32	39	36	0	14	1	139	4.8	18
D. Davis	72	866	111	269	.413	78	113	.690	86	139	225	46	141	0	20	28	300	4.2	12
R. Hawkins	32	153	53	104	.510	20	31	.645	16	14	30	16	31	0	10	8	126	3.9	15

1975-76 STATISTICS

HOUSTON

Player	G.	Min.	FGM	FGA	Pct.	FTM	FTA	Pct.	Off. Reb.	Def. Reb.	Tot. Reb.	Ast.	PF	Dsq.	Stl.	Blk. Sh.	Pts.	Avg.	Hi.
Murphy	82	2995	675	1369	.493	372	410	.907	52	157	209	596	294	3	151	6	1722	21.0	40
Newlin	82	3065	569	1123	.507	385	445	.865	72	264	336	457	263	5	106	15	1523	18.6	34
Tomjanovich	79	2912	622	1202	.517	221	288	.767	167	499	666	188	206	1	42	19	1465	18.5	32
Kunnert	80	2335	465	954	.487	102	156	.654	267	520	787	155	315	14	57	105	1032	12.9	29
Ratleff	72	2401	314	647	.485	168	206	.816	107	272	379	260	234	4	114	37	796	11.1	33
Meriweather	81	2042	338	684	.494	154	239	.644	163	353	516	82	219	4	36	120	830	10.2	29
J. J'son (Tot)	76	1697	316	697	.453	120	155	.774	94	238	332	217	194	1	57	36	752	9.9	23
J. J'son (Hou)	67	1485	275	609	.452	97	128	.758	81	211	292	197	163	0	50	28	647	9.7	23
Meely	14	174	32	81	.395	9	16	.563	12	40	52	10	31	1	9	4	73	5.2	15
R. Riley	65	1049	115	280	.411	38	56	.679	91	213	304	75	137	1	32	21	268	4.1	21
Wohl	50	700	66	163	.405	38	49	.776	9	47	56	112	112	2	26	1	170	3.4	10
R. White	32	284	42	102	.412	18	25	.720	13	25	38	30	32	0	19	5	102	3.2	14
Bailey	30	262	28	77	.364	14	28	.500	20	30	50	41	33	1	14	8	70	2.3	10
Hawes	6	51	5	13	.385	0	0	.000	5	13	18	10	6	0	0	0	10	1.7	8

KANSAS CITY

Player	G.	Min.	FGM	FGA	Pct.	FTM	FTA	Pct.	Off. Reb.	Def. Reb.	Tot. Reb.	Ast.	PF	Dsq.	Stl.	Blk. Sh.	Pts.	Avg.	Hi.
Archibald	78	3184	717	1583	.453	501	625	.802	67	146	213	615	169	0	126	15	1935	24.8	39
J. Walker	73	2490	459	950	.483	231	267	.865	49	128	177	176	186	2	87	14	1149	15.7	32
Wedman	82	2968	538	1181	.456	191	245	.780	199	407	606	199	280	8	103	36	1267	15.5	28
Lacey	81	3083	409	1019	.401	217	286	.759	218	806	1024	378	286	7	132	134	1035	12.8	26
O. Johnson	81	2150	348	678	.513	125	149	.839	116	241	357	146	217	4	67	42	821	10.1	23
McNeill	82	1613	295	610	.484	207	273	.758	157	353	510	72	244	2	51	32	797	9.7	25
Robinzine	75	1327	229	499	.459	145	198	.732	128	227	355	60	290	19	80	8	603	8.0	21
Hansen	66	1145	173	420	.412	85	117	.726	77	110	187	67	144	1	47	13	431	6.5	26
Winfield	22	214	32	66	.485	9	14	.643	8	16	24	19	14	0	10	6	73	3.3	14
Guokas (Tot)	56	793	73	173	.422	18	27	.667	22	41	63	70	76	0	18	3	164	2.9	12
Guokas (KC)	38	515	37	99	.374	9	16	.563	18	29	47	42	53	0	13	2	83	2.2	9
Roberson	74	709	73	180	.406	42	103	.408	74	159	233	53	126	1	18	17	188	2.5	13
Kosmalski	9	93	8	20	.400	4	7	.571	9	16	25	12	11	0	3	4	20	2.2	11
Bigelow	31	163	16	47	.340	24	33	.727	9	20	29	9	18	0	4	1	56	1.8	8
D'Antoni	9	101	7	27	.259	2	2	1.000	4	10	14	16	18	0	10	0	16	1.8	6

LOS ANGELES

Player	G.	Min.	FGM	FGA	Pct.	FTM	FTA	Pct.	Off. Reb.	Def. Reb.	Tot. Reb.	Ast.	PF	Dsq.	Stl.	Blk. Sh.	Pts.	Avg.	Hi.
Abdul-Jabbar	82	3379	914	1728	.529	447	636	.703	272	1111	1383	413	292	6	119	338	2275	27.7	48
Goodrich	75	2646	583	1321	.441	293	346	.847	94	120	214	421	238	3	123	17	1459	19.5	37
Allen	76	2388	461	1004	.459	197	254	.776	64	150	214	357	241	2	101	20	1119	14.7	28
C. Russell	74	1625	371	802	.463	132	148	.892	50	133	183	122	122	0	53	3	874	11.8	33
Freeman	64	1480	263	606	.434	163	199	.819	72	108	180	171	160	1	57	11	689	10.8	25
D. Ford	76	1838	311	710	.438	104	139	.748	118	215	333	111	186	3	50	14	726	9.6	25
Warner	81	2512	251	524	.479	89	128	.695	223	499	722	106	283	3	55	46	591	7.3	24
P. Riley	2	23	5	13	.385	1	3	.333	1	2	3	0	5	0	1	1	11	5.5	9
Calhoun	76	1816	172	368	.467	65	83	.783	117	224	341	85	216	4	62	35	409	5.4	15
R. Williams	9	158	17	43	.395	10	13	.769	2	17	19	21	15	0	3	0	44	4.9	12
Lantz	53	853	85	204	.417	80	89	.899	28	71	99	76	105	1	27	3	250	4.7	19
Meely (Tot)	34	313	52	132	.394	33	48	.688	22	75	97	19	61	1	14	8	137	4.0	15
Meely (LA)	20	139	20	51	.392	24	32	.750	10	35	45	9	30	0	5	4	64	3.2	11
Wesley	1	7	1	2	.500	2	4	.500	0	1	1	1	2	0	0	0	4	4.0	4
Washington	36	492	39	90	.433	45	66	.682	51	114	165	20	76	0	11	26	123	3.4	14
McDaniels	35	242	41	102	.402	9	9	1.000	26	48	74	15	40	1	4	10	91	2.6	12
Kupec	16	55	10	40	.250	7	11	.636	4	19	23	5	7	0	3	0	27	1.7	6
Roche	15	52	3	14	.214	2	4	.500	0	3	3	6	7	0	0	0	8	0.5	4

MILWAUKEE

Player	G.	Min.	FGM	FGA	Pct.	FTM	FTA	Pct.	Off. Reb.	Def. Reb.	Tot. Reb.	Ast.	PF	Dsq.	Stl.	Blk. Sh.	Pts.	Avg.	Hi.
Dandridge	73	2735	650	1296	.502	271	329	.824	171	369	540	206	263	5	111	38	1571	21.5	40
Winters	78	2795	618	1333	.464	180	217	.829	66	183	249	366	240	0	124	25	1416	18.2	34
E. Smith	78	2809	498	962	.518	222	351	.632	201	692	893	97	268	7	78	238	1218	15.6	31
Price	80	2525	398	958	.415	141	166	.849	74	187	261	395	264	3	148	32	937	11.7	26
Bridgeman	81	1646	286	651	.439	128	161	.795	113	181	294	157	235	3	52	21	700	8.6	28
Brokaw	75	1468	237	519	.457	159	227	.700	26	99	125	246	138	1	37	17	633	8.4	28
Meyers	72	1589	198	472	.419	135	210	.643	121	324	445	100	145	0	72	25	531	7.4	28
Restani	82	1650	234	493	.475	24	42	.571	115	261	376	96	151	3	36	12	492	6.0	18
Mayes	65	948	114	248	.460	56	97	.577	97	166	263	37	154	7	9	42	284	4.4	19
McGlocklin	33	336	63	148	.426	9	10	.900	3	14	17	38	18	0	8	0	135	4.1	12
Fox	70	918	105	203	.517	62	79	.785	82	153	235	42	129	1	27	16	272	3.9	21
Mi. Davis	45	411	55	152	.362	50	63	.794	25	59	84	37	36	0	13	2	160	3.6	12

NEW ORLEANS

Player	G.	Min.	FGM	FGA	Pct.	FTM	FTA	Pct.	Off. Reb.	Def. Reb.	Tot. Reb.	Ast.	PF	Dsq.	Stl.	Blk. Sh.	Pts.	Avg.	Hi.
Maravich	62	2373	604	1316	.459	396	488	.811	46	254	300	332	197	3	87	23	1604	25.9	49
N. Williams	81	1935	421	948	.444	197	239	.824	135	225	360	107	253	6	109	17	1039	12.8	33
L. Nelson	66	2030	327	755	.433	169	230	.735	81	121	202	169	147	1	82	6	823	12.5	27
Behagen	66	1733	308	691	.446	144	179	.804	190	363	553	139	222	6	67	26	760	11.5	27
Bibby	79	1772	266	622	.428	200	251	.797	58	121	179	225	165	0	62	3	732	9.3	24
Stallworth	56	1051	211	483	.437	85	124	.685	42	103	145	53	135	1	30	17	507	9.1	22
James	75	1346	262	594	.441	153	204	.750	93	156	249	59	172	1	33	6	677	9.0	24
Moore	81	2407	293	672	.436	144	226	.637	162	631	793	216	250	3	85	136	730	9.0	20
McElroy	51	1134	151	296	.510	81	110	.736	34	76	110	107	70	0	44	4	383	7.5	20
Coleman	67	1850	216	479	.451	59	89	.663	124	295	419	87	227	2	56	30	491	7.3	20
Kelley	75	1346	184	379	.485	159	205	.776	193	335	528	155	209	5	52	60	527	7.0	20
Boyd (Tot)	36	617	74	171	.433	29	51	.569	4	28	32	80	59	0	28	7	177	4.9	18
Boyd (NO)	30	584	72	165	.436	28	49	.571	4	26	30	78	54	0	27	7	172	5.7	18
Counts	30	319	37	91	.407	16	21	.762	27	73	100	38	74	1	16	8	90	3.0	16

NEW YORK

Player	G.	Min.	FGM	FGA	Pct.	FTM	FTA	Pct.	Off. Reb.	Def. Reb.	Tot. Reb.	Ast.	PF	Dsq.	Stl.	Blk. Sh.	Pts.	Avg.	Hi.
Monroe	76	2889	647	1354	.478	280	356	.787	48	225	273	304	209	1	111	22	1574	20.7	37
Haywood	78	2892	605	1360	.445	339	448	.757	234	644	878	92	255	5	53	80	1549	19.9	35
Frazier	59	2427	470	969	.485	186	226	.823	79	321	400	351	163	1	106	9	1126	19.1	38
Bradley	82	2709	392	906	.433	130	148	.878	47	187	234	247	256	2	68	18	914	11.1	25
Gianelli	82	2332	325	687	.473	114	160	.713	187	365	552	115	194	1	25	62	764	9.3	24
Beard (Tot)	75	1704	228	496	.460	144	192	.750	103	207	310	218	216	2	81	8	600	8.0	21
Beard (N.Y.)	60	1449	193	406	.475	117	155	.755	89	178	267	173	180	2	71	6	503	8.4	21
Walk	82	1340	262	607	.432	79	99	.798	98	291	389	119	209	3	26	22	603	7.4	21
Jackson	80	1461	185	387	.478	110	150	.733	80	263	343	105	275	3	41	20	480	6.0	17
Barnett	71	1026	164	371	.442	90	114	.789	48	40	88	90	86	0	24	3	418	5.9	18
Mel Davis	42	408	76	193	.394	22	29	.759	43	105	148	31	56	0	16	5	174	4.1	20
Wingo	57	533	72	163	.442	40	60	.667	46	61	107	18	59	0	19	8	184	3.2	13
Mayfield	13	64	17	46	.370	3	3	1.000	1	7	8	4	18	0	0	0	37	2.8	8
Short (Tot)	34	222	32	91	.352	20	32	.625	19	29	48	10	36	0	8	3	84	2.5	10
Short (N.Y.)	27	185	26	80	.325	19	30	.633	17	24	41	8	31	0	8	3	71	2.6	10
Bell	10	76	8	21	.381	3	7	.429	4	10	14	3	11	0	6	1	19	1.9	8
Fogle	2	14	0	1	5	.200	0	0	.000	1	2	3	0	4	0	1	0	2	1.0	2

PHILADELPHIA

Player	G.	Min.	FGM	FGA	Pct.	FTM	FTA	Pct.	Off. Reb.	Def. Reb.	Tot. Reb.	Ast.	PF	Dsq.	Stl.	Blk. Sh.	Pts.	Avg.	Hi.
McGinnis	77	2946	647	1552	.417	475	642	.740	260	707	967	359	334	13	198	41	1769	23.0	39
Collins	77	2995	614	1196	.513	372	445	.836	126	181	307	191	249	2	110	24	1600	20.8	38
Carter	82	2992	665	1594	.417	219	312	.702	113	186	299	372	286	5	137	13	1549	18.9	35
Mix	81	3039	421	844	.499	287	351	.818	215	447	662	216	288	6	158	29	1129	13.9	33
Cunningham	20	640	103	251	.410	68	88	.773	29	118	147	107	57	1	24	10	274	13.7	26
Free	71	1121	239	533	.448	112	186	.602	64	61	125	104	107	0	37	6	590	8.3	29
Bryant	75	1203	233	552	.422	92	147	.626	97	181	278	61	165	0	44	23	558	7.4	25
Norman	65	818	183	422	.434	20	24	.833	51	50	101	66	87	1	28	7	386	5.9	20
Ellis	29	489	61	132	.462	17	28	.607	47	75	122	21	62	0	16	9	139	4.8	14
Lee	79	1421	123	282	.436	63	95	.663	164	289	453	59	188	0	23	27	309	3.9	14
Catchings	75	1731	103	242	.426	58	96	.604	191	329	520	63	262	6	21	164	264	3.5	13
W.Jones(Tot)	17	176	23	49	.469	9	13	.692	0	9	9	33	27	0	6	0	55	3.2	10
W.Jones(Phil)	16	157	19	38	.500	9	13	.692	0	9	9	31	25	0	4	0	47	2.9	10
Dawkins	37	165	41	82	.500	8	24	.333	15	34	49	3	40	1	2	9	90	2.4	12
Baskerville	21	105	8	26	.308	10	16	.625	13	15	28	3	32	0	6	5	26	1.2	4
Boyd	6	33	2	6	.333	1	2	.500	0	2	2	8	5	0	1	0	5	0.8	2

PHOENIX

Player	G.	Min.	FGM	FGA	Pct.	FTM	FTA	Pct.	Off. Reb.	Def. Reb.	Tot. Reb.	Ast.	PF	Dsq.	Stl.	Blk. Sh.	Pts.	Avg.	Hi.
Westphal	82	2904	657	1329	.494	365	440	.830	74	185	259	440	218	3	210	38	1679	20.5	39
A. Adams	80	2656	629	1341	.469	261	355	.735	215	512	727	450	274	6	121	116	1519	19.0	35
Perry	71	2353	386	776	.497	175	239	.732	197	487	684	182	269	5	84	66	947	13.3	27
D. V'Arsdale	58	1870	276	570	.484	195	235	.830	39	98	137	140	113	2	92	11	747	12.9	26
Shumate	43	930	186	338	.550	115	183	.628	61	179	240	62	76	1	44	16	487	11.3	28
Heard (Tot)	86	2747	392	901	.435	158	248	.637	247	622	869	190	303	2	117	96	942	11.0	27
Heard (Phoe)	36	1220	185	452	.452	76	113	.673	109	249	358	64	120	2	51	41	446	12.4	27
Erickson	74	1850	305	649	.470	134	157	.854	106	226	332	185	196	4	79	6	744	10.1	26
Sobers	78	1898	280	623	.449	158	192	.823	80	179	259	215	253	6	106	7	718	9.2	27
Hawthorne	79	1144	182	423	.430	115	170	.676	86	123	209	46	147	0	33	15	479	6.1	25
Awtrey	74	1376	142	304	.467	75	109	.688	93	200	293	159	153	1	21	22	359	4.9	12

1975-76 STATISTICS

Player	G.	Min.	FGM	FGA	Pct.	FTM	FTA	Pct.	Off. Reb.	Def. Reb.	Tot. Reb.	Ast.	PF	Dsq.	Stl.	Blk. Sh.	Pts.	Avg.	Hi.
Riley (Tot)	62	813	117	301	.389	55	77	.714	16	34	50	57	112	0	22	6	289	4.7	16
Riley (Phoe)	60	790	112	288	.389	54	74	.730	15	32	47	57	107	0	21	5	278	4.6	16
Saunders	17	146	28	64	.438	6	11	.545	11	26	37	13	23	0	5	1	62	3.6	12
Bantom	7	68	8	26	.308	5	5	1.000	7	16	23	3	13	1	2	2	21	3.0	9
Lumpkin	34	370	22	65	.338	26	30	.867	7	16	23	48	26	0	15	0	70	2.1	10
Wetzel	37	249	22	46	.478	20	24	.833	8	30	38	19	30	0	9	3	64	1.7	6

PORTLAND

Player	G.	Min.	FGM	FGA	Pct.	FTM	FTA	Pct.	Off. Reb.	Def. Reb.	Tot. Reb.	Ast.	PF	Dsq.	Stl.	Blk. Sh.	Pts.	Avg.	Hi.
Wicks	79	3044	580	1201	.483	345	512	.674	245	467	712	244	250	5	77	53	1505	19.1	35
Petrie	72	2557	543	1177	.461	277	334	.829	38	130	168	330	194	0	82	5	1363	18.9	34
Walton	51	1687	345	732	.471	133	228	.583	132	549	681	220	144	3	49	82	823	16.1	36
Neal	68	2320	435	904	.481	186	268	.694	145	440	585	118	254	4	53	107	1056	15.5	31
J. Johnson	9	212	41	88	.466	23	27	.852	13	27	40	20	31	1	7	8	105	11.7	21
Hollins	74	1891	311	738	.421	178	247	.721	39	136	175	306	235	5	131	28	800	10.8	25
Steele	81	2382	322	651	.495	154	203	.759	77	215	292	324	289	8	170	19	798	9.9	30
Gross	76	1474	209	400	.523	97	142	.683	138	169	307	163	186	3	91	43	515	6.8	24
Hawes (Tot)	72	1411	199	403	.494	87	120	.725	171	326	497	115	169	5	44	25	485	6.7	23
Hawes (Port)	66	1360	194	390	.497	87	120	.725	166	313	479	105	163	5	44	25	475	7.2	23
S. Jones	64	819	168	380	.442	78	94	.830	13	62	75	63	96	0	17	6	414	6.5	23
D. Anderson	52	614	88	181	.486	51	61	.836	15	47	62	85	58	0	20	2	227	4.4	17
Martin	63	889	109	302	.361	57	77	.740	68	243	311	72	126	1	6	23	275	4.4	18
Clemens	49	443	70	143	.490	31	35	.886	27	43	70	33	57	0	27	7	171	3.5	20
G. Lee	5	35	2	4	.500	2	2	1.000	0	2	2	11	6	0	2	0	6	1.2	4
G. Smith	1	3	0	1	.000	0	0	.000	0	0	0	0	2	0	0	0	0	0.0	0

SEATTLE

Player	G.	Min.	FGM	FGA	Pct.	FTM	FTA	Pct.	Off. Reb.	Def. Reb.	Tot. Reb.	Ast.	PF	Dsq.	Stl.	Blk. Sh.	Pts.	Avg.	Hi.
F. Brown	76	2516	742	1522	.488	273	314	.869	111	206	317	207	186	0	143	18	1757	23.1	41
Burleson	82	2647	496	1032	.481	291	388	.750	258	484	742	180	273	1	70	150	1283	15.6	35
Gray	66	2139	394	831	.474	126	169	.746	109	289	398	203	260	10	75	36	914	13.8	32
Watts	82	2776	433	1015	.427	199	344	.578	112	253	365	661	270	3	261	16	1065	13.0	26
Seals	81	2435	388	889	.436	181	267	.678	157	350	507	119	314	11	64	44	957	11.8	29
Gilliam	81	1644	299	676	.442	90	116	.776	56	164	220	202	139	0	82	12	688	8.5	24
Bantom (Tot)	73	1571	220	476	.462	136	199	.683	140	251	391	105	221	4	28	28	576	7.9	21
Bantom (Sea)	66	1503	212	450	.471	131	194	.675	133	235	368	102	208	3	26	26	555	8.4	21
Norwood	64	1004	146	301	.485	152	203	.749	91	138	229	59	139	3	42	4	444	6.9	24
Oleynick	52	650	127	316	.402	53	77	.688	10	35	45	53	62	0	21	6	307	5.9	22
Skinner	72	1224	132	285	.463	49	80	.613	89	175	264	67	116	1	50	7	313	4.3	26
Derline	49	339	73	181	.403	45	56	.804	8	19	27	26	22	0	11	1	191	3.9	16
Abdul-Aziz	27	223	35	75	.467	16	29	.552	30	46	76	16	29	0	8	15	86	3.2	11
Hummer	29	364	32	67	.478	17	41	.415	21	56	77	25	71	5	6	9	81	2.8	14
Carlson	28	279	27	79	.342	18	29	.621	30	43	73	13	39	1	7	11	72	2.6	7
Short	7	37	6	11	.545	1	2	.500	2	5	7	2	5	0	0	0	13	1.9	6

WASHINGTON

Player	G.	Min.	FGM	FGA	Pct.	FTM	FTA	Pct.	Off. Reb.	Def. Reb.	Tot. Reb.	Ast.	PF	Dsq.	Stl.	Blk. Sh.	Pts.	Avg.	Hi.
Chenier	80	2952	654	1355	.483	282	341	.827	84	236	320	255	186	2	158	45	1590	19.9	44
Hayes	80	2975	649	1381	.470	287	457	.628	210	668	878	121	293	5	104	202	1585	19.8	37
Bing	82	2945	497	1113	.447	332	422	.787	94	143	237	492	262	0	118	23	1326	16.2	34
Robinson	82	2055	354	779	.454	211	314	.672	139	418	557	113	239	3	42	107	919	11.2	29
Unseld	78	2922	318	567	.561	114	195	.585	271	765	1036	404	203	3	84	59	750	9.6	25
Riordan	78	1943	291	662	.440	71	96	.740	44	143	187	122	201	2	54	13	653	8.4	22
Weatherspoon	44	1083	218	458	.476	96	137	.701	85	189	274	55	172	2	46	16	532	8.3	31
Haskins	55	737	148	269	.550	54	65	.831	12	42	54	73	79	2	23	8	350	6.4	25
J. Jones	44	1133	153	308	.497	72	94	.766	32	99	131	120	127	1	35	5	378	5.9	16
Grevey	56	504	79	213	.371	52	58	.897	24	36	60	27	65	0	13	3	210	3.8	19
Kozelko	67	584	48	99	.485	19	30	.633	19	63	82	33	74	0	19	4	115	1.7	15
Kropp	25	72	7	30	.233	5	6	.833	5	10	15	8	20	0	2	0	19	0.8	5

1975-76 PLAYOFF RESULTS

CONFERENCE QUALIFYING ROUND

EASTERN CONFERENCE
Buffalo 2, Philadelphia 1

Apr. 15—Thu.—Buffalo 95 at Philadelphia 89
Apr. 16—Fri.—Philadelphia 131 at Buffalo...............106
Apr. 18—Sun.—Buffalo 124 at Philadelphia ....123 (ot)

WESTERN CONFERENCE
Detroit 2, Milwaukee 1

Apr. 13—Tue.—Detroit 107 at Milwaukee 110
Apr. 15—Thu.—Milwaukee 123 at Detroit................126
Apr. 18—Sun.—Detroit 107 at Milwaukee 104

CONFERENCE SEMI-FINAL SERIES

EASTERN CONFERENCE
Boston 4, Buffalo 2

Apr. 21—Wed.—Buffalo 98 at Boston 107
Apr. 23—Fri.—Buffalo 96 at Boston 101
Apr. 25—Sun.—Boston 93 at Buffalo 98
Apr. 28—Wed.—Boston 122 at Buffalo 124
Apr. 30—Fri.—Buffalo 88 at Boston 99
May 2—Sun.—Boston 104 at Buffalo 100

WESTERN CONFERENCE
Golden State 4, Detroit 2

Apr. 20—Tue.—Detroit 103 at Golden State 127
Apr. 22—Thu.—Detroit 123 at Golden State 111
Apr. 24—Sat.—Golden State 113 at Detroit 96
Apr. 26—Mon.—Golden State 102 at Detroit...........106
Apr. 28—Wed.—Detroit 109 at Golden State............128
Apr. 30—Fri.—Golden State 118 at Detroit ......116 (ot)

Cleveland 4, Washington 3

Apr. 13—Tue.—Washington 100 at Cleveland 95
Apr. 15—Thu.—Cleveland 80 at Washington 79
Apr. 17—Sat.—Washington 76 at Cleveland.............88
Apr. 21—Wed.—Cleveland 98 at Washington 109
Apr. 22—Thu.—Wash. 91 at Cleveland 92
Apr. 26—Mon.—Cleveland 98 at Washington ..102 (ot)
Apr. 29—Thu.—Washington 85 at Cleveland 87

Phoenix 4, Seattle 2

Apr. 13—Tue.—Phoenix 99 at Seattle 102
Apr. 15—Thu.—Phoenix 116 at Seattle 111
Apr. 18—Sun.—Seattle 91 at Phoenix 103
Apr. 20—Tue.—Seattle 114 at Phoenix 130
Apr. 25—Sun.—Phoenix 108 at Seattle 114
Apr. 27—Tue.—Seattle 112 at Phoenix 123

CONFERENCE FINALS

EASTERN CONFERENCE FINALS
Boston 4, Cleveland 2

May 6—Thu.—Cleveland 99 at Boston....................111
May 9—Sun.—Cleveland 89 at Boston......................94
May 11—Tue.—Boston 78 at Cleveland 83
May 14—Fri.—Boston 87 at Cleveland 106
May 16—Sun.—Cleveland 94 at Boston.....................99
May 18—Tue.—Boston 94 at Cleveland.....................87

WESTERN CONFERENCE FINALS
Phoenix 4, Golden State 3

May 2—Sun.—Phoenix 103 at Golden State 128
May 5—Wed.—Phoenix 108 at Golden State.........101
May 7—Fri.—Golden State 99 at Phoenix...............91
May 9—Sun.—Golden State 129 at Phoenix 133 (2 ot)
May 12—Wed.—Phoenix 95 at Golden State............111
May 14—Fri.—Golden State 104 at Phoenix 105
May 16—Sun.—Phoenix 94 at Golden State 86

CHAMPIONSHIP SERIES
Boston 4, Phoenix 2

May 23—Sun.—Phoenix 87 at Boston.........................98
May 27—Thu.—Phoenix 90 at Boston 105
May 30—Sun.—Boston 98 at Phoenix......................105
June 2—Wed.—Boston 107 at Phoenix....................109
June 4—Fri.—Phoenix 126 at Boston..........128 (3 o.t.)
June 6—Sun.—Boston 87 at Phoenix........................80

1974-75 STATISTICS

GOLDEN STATE WARRIORS—1974-75 NBA CHAMPIONS

Back Row (Left to Right): Hal Childs, Assistant General Manager; Charles Dudley; Bill Bridges; Clifford Ray; George Johnson; Derrek Dickey; Keith Wilkes; Steve Bracey; Bob Feerick, Director of Player Personnel; Dick Vertlieb, General Manager. Front Row (Left to Right): Charles Johnson; Jeff Mullins; Joe Roberts, Assistant Coach; Al Attles, Head Coach; Franklin Mieuli, Owner; Rick Barry, Captain; Butch Beard; Phil Smith; Dick D'Oliva, Trainer.

FINAL STANDINGS

ATLANTIC DIVISION

Team	Atl.	Bos.	Buf.	Chi.	Cle.	Det.	G.S.	Hou.	KC-O.	L.A.	Mil.	N.O.	N.Y.	Phi.	Pho.	Por.	Sea.	Was.	W.	L.	Pct.	G.B.
Boston	4	..	5	3	3	3	1	4	2	4	4	4	7	5	3	4	2	2	60	22	.732	....
Buffalo	3	4	..	1	3	2	3	2	1	4	1	4	5	6	3	2	3	2	49	33	.598	11
New York	4	2	3	1	3	2	1	3	2	4	1	2	..	4	3	2	2	1	40	42	.488	20
Philadelphia	2	3	3	2	1	1	1	2	3	1	1	2	5	..	2	2	2	1	34	48	.415	26

CENTRAL DIVISION

Team	Atl.	Bos.	Buf.	Chi.	Cle.	Det.	G.S.	Hou.	KC-O.	L.A.	Mil.	N.O.	N.Y.	Phi.	Pho.	Por.	Sea.	Was.	W.	L.	Pct.	G.B.
Washington	5	2	2	3	5	3	3	5	3	3	4	7	3	3	3	3	3	..	60	22	.732	....
Houston	5	..	2	2	4	2	2	..	4	2	3	5	1	2	2	2	1	2	41	41	.500	19
Cleveland	4	1	1	2	..	2	2	4	2	2	1	6	1	3	2	2	3	2	40	42	.488	20
Atlanta	..	..	1	..	3	2	1	2	2	2	2	3	..	2	4	1	3	3	31	51	.378	29
New Orleans	5	..	..	..	1	..	2	3	2	1	1	..	2	2	1	2	1	..	23	59	.280	37

MIDWEST DIVISION

Team	Atl.	Bos.	Buf.	Chi.	Cle.	Det.	G.S.	Hou.	KC-O.	L.A.	Mil.	N.O.	N.Y.	Phi.	Pho.	Por.	Sea.	Was.	W.	L.	Pct.	G.B.
Chicago	4	1	3	..	2	4	3	2	4	3	3	4	4	3	2	2	2	4	47	35	.573	....
KC-Omaha	2	2	3	5	2	6	2	..	..	3	6	2	2	1	3	3	1	1	44	38	.537	3
Detroit	2	1	2	5	2	..	1	2	2	3	3	3	4	2	3	2	3	2	40	42	.488	7
Milwaukee	2	..	..	3	5	3	6	1	1	3	..	..	3	3	3	2	2	1	38	44	.463	9

PACIFIC DIVISION

Team	Atl.	Bos.	Buf.	Chi.	Cle.	Det.	G.S.	Hou.	KC-O.	L.A.	Mil.	N.O.	N.Y.	Phi.	Pho.	Por.	Sea.	Was.	W.	L.	Pct.	G.B.
Golden State	3	3	1	1	2	3	..	2	2	5	3	2	3	3	5	5	4	1	48	34	.585	....
Seattle	1	2	1	..	2	2	3	3	3	6	3	3	2	2	3	6	..	1	43	39	.524	5
Portland	3	..	2	2	2	1	3	2	1	5	2	2	2	2	6	..	2	1	38	44	.463	10
Phoenix	..	1	1	2	2	2	3	2	1	4	2	3	1	2	..	1	4	1	32	50	.390	16
Los Angeles	2	..	..	1	2	1	2	2	1	..	4	3	..	3	4	2	2	1	30	52	.366	18

1974-75 STATISTICS

TEAM STATISTICS—OFFENSE

Team	G.	FIELD GOALS Made	Att.	Pct.	FREE THROWS Made	Att.	Pct.	REBOUNDS Off.	Def.	Tot.	Ast.	PF	MISCELLANEOUS Stl.	Blk. Sh.	Turn Over	Dq.	SCORING Pts.	Avg.
Golden State	82	3714	7981	.465	1470	1915	.768	1416	2854	4270	2076	2109	972	365	1716	22	8898	108.5
Buffalo	82	3552	7469	.476	1735	2224	.780	1108	2735	3843	2063	1879	718	456	1710	18	8839	107.8
Boston	82	3587	7825	.458	1560	1971	.791	1315	2949	4264	2159	1913	662	288	1625	23	8734	106.5
Atlanta	82	3424	7824	.438	1772	2435	.728	1441	2653	4094	1878	1964	744	227	1550	33	8620	105.1
Washington	82	3555	7697	.462	1475	1962	.752	1133	2764	3897	2005	1961	929	409	1594	26	8585	104.7
Houston	82	3448	7231	.477	1625	2034	.799	1177	2495	3672	2155	2068	746	351	1759	30	8521	103.9
Portland	82	3414	7113	.480	1680	2265	.742	1049	2758	3807	2209	2055	755	399	1853	29	8508	103.8
Los Angeles	82	3409	7577	.450	1641	2182	.752	1312	2763	4075	2091	2079	755	423	1785	23	8459	103.2
Seattle	82	3488	7653	.456	1475	1970	.749	1142	2579	3721	1997	1977	837	378	1610	27	8451	103.1
New Orleans	82	3301	7509	.440	1717	2247	.764	1144	2616	3760	1818	2222	725	256	1802	34	8319	101.5
KC-Omaha	82	3257	7258	.449	1797	2190	.821	991	2745	3736	1853	1968	724	347	1542	19	8311	101.4
Phoenix	82	3381	7561	.447	1535	2082	.737	1349	2684	4033	1879	2090	664	317	1760	45	8297	101.2
Milwaukee	82	3450	7367	.468	1354	1746	.775	1021	2766	3787	1932	1949	596	400	1540	30	8254	100.7
New York	82	3464	7469	.450	1518	1967	.772	981	2652	3633	1675	2001	652	300	1374	22	8236	100.4
Philadelphia	82	3325	7476	.445	1530	2043	.749	1200	2706	3906	1709	1974	576	263	1591	34	8180	99.8
Cleveland	82	3408	7371	.462	1301	1753	.742	1058	2502	3560	1903	1881	600	348	1462	16	8117	99.0
Detroit	82	3289	7053	.466	1533	1975	.776	1002	2515	3517	1916	1866	679	380	1557	13	8111	98.9
Chicago	82	3167	7085	.447	1711	2203	.777	1107	2786	3893	1840	1952	668	379	1482	23	8045	98.1

TEAM STATISTICS—DEFENSE

Team	FIELD GOALS Made	Att.	Pct.	FREE THROWS Made	Att.	Pct.	REBOUNDS Off.	Def.	Tot.	Ast.	PF	MISCELLANEOUS Stl.	Blk. Sh.	Turn Over	Dq.	SCORING Pts.	Avg.	Dif.
Chicago	3167	7070	.448	1457	1900	.767	1008	2647	3655	1686	2168	625	404	1580	37	7791	95.0	− 3.1
Washington	3249	7415	.438	1499	1967	.762	1184	2819	4003	1811	2004	710	259	1842	25	7997	97.5	+ 7.2
Cleveland	3263	7243	.451	1621	2102	.771	1235	2694	3929	1746	1932	711	277	1618	26	8147	99.4	− 0.4
Detroit	3409	7257	.470	1410	1793	.786	1104	2550	3654	2012	1875	663	306	1523	24	8228	100.3	− 1.4
Milwaukee	3371	7600	.444	1495	1910	.783	1153	2645	3798	1960	1704	660	298	1379	11	8237	100.5	+ 0.2
Boston	3432	7726	.444	1401	1882	.744	1060	2622	3682	1833	1869	599	283	1475	24	8265	100.8	+ 5.7
KC-Omaha	3410	7400	.461	1515	1972	.768	1060	2812	3872	1840	2029	606	312	1605	25	8335	101.6	− 0.2
New York	3361	7357	.457	1615	2082	.776	1070	2856	3926	1668	1912	572	369	1493	15	8337	101.7	− 1.3
Philadelphia	3445	7466	.461	1541	1979	.779	1167	2748	3915	1959	2036	742	343	1577	26	8431	102.8	− 3.0
Houston	3429	7127	.481	1576	2127	.741	1036	2380	3416	2024	2003	704	308	1685	37	8434	102.9	+ 1.0
Portland	3379	7502	.450	1714	2178	.787	1207	2572	3779	2090	2085	927	383	1607	34	8472	103.3	+ 0.5
Phoenix	3356	7323	.458	1780	2350	.757	1112	2564	3676	2062	1992	870	412	1586	20	8492	103.6	− 2.4
Seattle	3490	7606	.459	1560	2090	.746	1286	2754	4040	2188	1948	692	349	1755	24	8540	104.1	− 1.0
Golden State	3481	7628	.456	1666	2209	.754	1185	2658	3843	2084	1855	794	387	1644	17	8628	105.2	+ 3.3
Buffalo	3575	7943	.450	1513	1943	.779	1295	2619	3914	2151	2030	730	383	1670	31	8663	105.6	+ 2.2
Atlanta	3563	7504	.475	1606	2098	.765	1169	2851	4020	1914	2265	744	422	1723	33	8732	106.5	− 1.4
Los Angeles	3595	7914	.454	1603	2117	.757	1422	2807	4229	2239	2015	822	442	1606	25	8793	107.2	− 4.0
New Orleans	3553	7433	.478	1857	2465	.753	1193	2924	4117	1891	2126	783	349	1924	33	8963	109.3	− 7.8

DQ—Individual players disqualified (fouled out of game).

INDIVIDUAL SCORING LEADERS

Minimum: 70 games played or 1400 points

	G.	FG	FT	Pts.	Avg.		G.	FG	FT	Pts.	Avg.
McAdoo, Buff.	82	1095	641	2831	34.5	Chenier, Wash.	77	690	301	1681	21.8
Barry, G.S.	80	1028	394	2450	30.6	Wicks, Port.	82	692	394	1778	21.7
Abdul-Jabbar, Mil.	65	812	325	1949	30.0	Maravich, N.O.	79	655	390	1700	21.5
Archibald, KC-O.	82	759	652	2170	26.5	Frazier, N.Y.	78	672	331	1675	21.5
Scott, Phoe.	69	703	274	1680	24.3	F. Brown, Sea.	81	737	226	1700	21.0
Lanier, Det.	76	731	361	1823	24.0	Monroe, N.Y.	78	668	297	1633	20.9
Hayes, Wash.	82	739	409	1887	23.0	Tomjanovich, Hou.	81	694	289	1677	20.7
Goodrich, L.A.	72	656	318	1630	22.6	Dandridge, Mil.	80	691	211	1593	19.9
Haywood, Sea.	68	608	309	1525	22.4	Cunningham, Phil.	80	609	345	1563	19.5
Carter, Phil.	77	715	256	1686	21.9	Ch. Walker, Chi.	76	524	413	1461	19.2

FIELD GOAL LEADERS
Minimum: 300 FGM

	FGM	FGA	Pct.
D. Nelson, Bos.	423	785	.539
Beard, G.S.	408	773	.528
Tomjanovich, Hou.	694	1323	.525
Abdul-Jabbar, Mil.	812	1584	.513
McAdoo, Buff.	1095	2138	.512
Kunnert, Hou.	346	676	.512
Westphal, Bos.	342	670	.510
Lanier, Det.	731	1433	.510
Snyder, Clev.	498	988	.504
McMillian, Buff.	347	695	.499

FREE THROW LEADERS
Minimum: 125 FTM

	FTM	FTA	Pct.
Barry, G.S.	394	436	.904
Murphy, Hou.	341	386	.883
Bradley, N.Y.	144	165	.873
Archibald, KC-O.	652	748	.872
Price, L.A.-Mil.	169	194	.871
Havlicek, Bos.	289	332	.870
Marin, Buff.	193	222	.869
Newlin, Hou.	265	305	.869
Ch. Walker, Chi.	413	480	.860
J. Walker, KC-O.	247	289	.855

1974-75 STATISTICS

REBOUND LEADERS
Minimum: 70 games or 800 rebounds

	G.	Off.	Def.	Tot.	Avg.
Unseld, Wash.	73	318	759	1077	14.8
Cowens, Bos.	65	229	729	958	14.7
Lacey, KC-O.	81	228	921	1149	14.2
McAdoo, Buff.	82	307	848	1155	14.1
Abdul-Jabbar, Mil.	65	194	718	912	14.0
Hairston, L.A.	74	304	642	946	12.8
Silas, Bos.	82	348	677	1025	12.5
Hayes, Wash.	82	221	783	1004	12.2
Lanier, Det.	76	225	689	914	12.0
Perry, Phoe.	79	347	593	940	11.9

BLOCKED SHOTS LEADERS
Minimum: 70 games or 100 blocked shots

	G.	No.	Avg.
Abdul-Jabbar, Mil.	65	212	3.26
E. Smith, L.A.	74	216	2.92
Thurmond, Chi.	80	195	2.44
Hayes, Wash.	82	187	2.28
Lanier, Det.	76	172	2.26
McAdoo, Buff.	82	174	2.12
Lacey, KC-O.	81	168	2.07
Burleson, Sea.	82	153	1.87
Heard, Buff.	67	120	1.79
Chones, Clev.	72	120	1.67

ASSISTS LEADERS
Minimum: 70 games or 400 assists

	G.	No.	Avg.
K. Porter, Wash.	81	650	8.0
Bing, Det.	79	610	7.7
Archibald, KC-O.	82	557	6.8
R. Smith, Buff.	82	534	6.5
Maravich, N.O.	79	488	6.2
Barry, G.S.	80	492	6.2
Watts, Sea.	82	499	6.1
Frazier, N.Y.	78	474	6.1
Goodrich, L.A.	72	420	5.8
Van Lier, Chi.	70	403	5.8

STEALS LEADERS
Minimum: 70 games or 125 steals

	G.	No.	Avg.
Barry, G.S.	80	228	2.85
Frazier, N.Y.	78	190	2.44
Steele, Port.	76	183	2.41
Watts, Sea.	82	190	2.32
F. Brown, Sea.	81	187	2.31
Chenier, Wash.	77	176	2.29
Sloan, Chi.	78	171	2.19
Allen, Mil.-L.A.	66	136	2.06
Van Lier, Chi.	70	139	1.99
Hayes, Wash.	82	158	1.93

RECORDS OF TEAMS BY MONTHS

Team	Oct. W-L	Nov. W-L	Dec. W-L	Jan. W-L	Feb. W-L	Mar. W-L	Apr. W-L	Total W-L
Atlanta	3-4	6-8	6-9	6-11	3-9	7-8	0-2	31-51
Boston	3-4	8-6	10-3	13-1	10-4	13-4	3-0	60-22
Buffalo	4-2	12-4	6-7	11-4	7-7	8-6	1-3	49-33
Chicago	3-5	7-6	7-6	11-4	11-2	5-11	3-1	47-35
Cleveland	4-4	7-4	7-6	4-12	10-6	7-9	1-1	40-42
Detroit	3-4	8-6	8-7	11-4	3-12	6-7	1-2	40-42
Golden State	4-2	11-4	8-6	7-7	6-8	11-6	1-1	48-34
Houston	4-3	7-7	8-5	5-10	9-6	7-9	1-1	41-41
K.C.-Omaha	5-1	7-9	8-8	5-8	10-2	8-8	1-2	44-38
Los Angeles	3-3	5-9	7-9	4-8	3-11	8-8	0-4	30-52
Milwaukee	1-5	5-9	8-5	10-5	4-10	7-9	3-1	38-44
New Orleans	0-7	2-13	1-10	2-12	10-5	8-9	0-3	23-59
New York	4-3	9-5	6-7	7-8	4-10	8-7	2-2	40-42
Philadelphia	3-3	4-10	7-8	6-9	7-7	7-8	0-3	34-48
Phoenix	3-3	6-9	6-6	5-9	8-6	3-15	1-2	32-50
Portland	3-4	9-6	3-9	7-8	4-10	9-7	3-0	38-44
Seattle	4-3	7-9	5-7	9-7	7-7	9-5	4-0	43-39
Washington	7-1	9-5	10-3	10-4	11-4	9-4	4-1	60-22
Totals	61	129	121	131	127	140	29	738

INTER-CLUB RECORDS—HOME AND AWAY

	Home	Away	Total
Atlanta	22-19	9-32	31-51
Boston	28-13	32-9	60-22
Buffalo	30-11	19-22	49-33
Chicago	29-12	18-23	47-35
Cleveland	29-12	11-30	40-42
Detroit	26-15	14-27	40-42
Golden State	31-10	17-24	48-34
Houston	29-12	12-29	41-41
K.C.-Omaha	29-12	15-26	44-38
Los Angeles	21-20	9-32	30-52
Milwaukee	25-16	13-28	38-44
New Orleans	20-21	3-38	23-59
New York	23-18	17-24	40-42
Philadelphia	20-21	14-27	34-48
Phoenix	22-19	10-31	32-50
Portland	28-13	10-31	38-44
Seattle	24-17	19-22	43-39
Washington	36-5	24-17	60-22

1974-75 STATISTICS
INDIVIDUAL STATISTICS
ATLANTA

Player	G.	Min.	FGM	FGA	Pct.	FTM	FTA	Pct.	Off. Reb.	Def. Reb.	Tot. Reb.	Ast.	PF	Dsq.	Stl.	Blk. Sh.	Pts.	Avg.	Hi.
Hudson	11	380	97	225	.431	48	57	.842	14	33	47	40	33	1	13	2	242	22.0	36
Drew	78	2289	527	1230	.428	388	544	.713	357	479	836	138	274	4	119	39	1442	18.5	44
T.V'dale (Tot)	82	2843	593	1385	.428	322	424	.759	77	201	278	223	257	5	91	3	1508	18.1	35
T. V'dale (Atl)	73	2570	544	1269	.429	294	383	.768	70	179	249	207	231	5	78	3	1382	18.9	35
Gilliam	60	1393	314	736	.427	94	113	.832	76	128	204	170	124	1	77	13	722	12.0	26
Sojourner	73	2129	378	775	.488	95	146	.651	196	446	642	93	217	10	35	57	851	11.7	29
Henderson	79	2131	367	893	.411	168	241	.697	51	161	212	314	149	0	105	7	902	11.4	32
J. Brown	73	1986	315	684	.461	185	250	.740	180	254	434	133	228	7	54	15	815	11.2	28
D. Jones	75	2086	323	752	.430	132	183	.721	236	461	697	152	226	1	51	51	778	10.4	24
Meninger	80	2177	233	500	.466	168	263	.639	84	130	214	397	160	0	118	11	634	7.9	26
J. Washington	38	905	114	259	.440	41	55	.745	52	141	193	68	86	2	23	13	269	7.1	19
Lee	9	177	12	36	.333	32	39	.821	24	46	70	8	25	0	1	4	56	6.2	16
Kauffman	73	797	113	261	.433	59	84	.702	67	115	182	81	103	1	19	4	285	3.9	17
Wetzel	63	785	87	204	.426	68	77	.883	34	80	114	77	108	1	51	8	242	3.8	14

BOSTON

Player	G.	Min.	FGM	FGA	Pct.	FTM	FTA	Pct.	Off. Reb.	Def. Reb.	Tot. Reb.	Ast.	PF	Dsq.	Stl.	Blk. Sh.	Pts.	Avg.	Hi.
Cowens	65	2632	569	1199	.475	191	244	.783	229	729	958	296	243	7	87	73	1329	20.4	38
Havlicek	82	3132	642	1411	.455	289	332	.870	154	330	484	432	231	2	110	15	1573	19.2	40
White	82	3220	658	1440	.457	186	223	.834	84	227	311	458	207	1	128	17	1502	18.3	33
D. Nelson	79	2052	423	785	.539	263	318	.827	127	342	469	181	239	2	32	15	1109	14.0	35
Silas	82	2661	312	749	.417	244	344	.709	348	677	1025	224	229	3	60	22	868	10.6	22
Westphal	82	1581	342	670	.510	119	156	.763	44	119	163	235	192	0	78	33	803	9.8	27
Chaney	82	2208	321	750	.428	133	165	.806	171	199	370	181	244	5	122	66	775	9.5	28
Hankinson	3	24	6	11	.545	0	0	.000	1	6	7	2	3	0	1	0	12	4.0	6
Ard	59	719	89	266	.335	48	65	.738	59	140	199	40	96	2	13	32	226	3.8	19
Stacom	61	447	72	159	.453	29	33	.879	30	25	55	49	65	0	11	3	173	2.8	10
Clyde	25	157	31	72	.431	7	9	.778	15	26	41	5	34	1	5	3	69	2.8	16
McDonald	62	395	70	182	.385	28	37	.757	20	48	68	24	58	0	8	5	168	2.7	14
Finkel	62	518	52	129	.403	23	43	.535	33	79	112	32	72	0	7	3	127	2.0	10
Downing	3	9	0	2	.000	0	0	.000	0	2	2	0	0	0	0	0	0	0.0	-

BUFFALO

Player	G.	Min.	FGM	FGA	Pct.	FTM	FTA	Pct.	Off. Reb.	Def. Reb.	Tot. Reb.	Ast.	PF	Dsq.	Stl.	Blk. Sh.	Pts.	Avg.	Hi.
McAdoo	82	3539	1095	2138	.512	641	796	.805	307	848	1155	179	278	3	92	174	2831	34.5	51
R. Smith	82	3001	610	1261	.484	236	295	.800	95	249	344	534	247	2	137	3	1456	17.8	35
McMillian	62	2132	347	695	.499	194	231	.840	127	258	385	156	129	0	69	15	888	14.3	28
Marin	81	2147	380	836	.455	193	222	.869	104	259	363	133	238	7	51	16	953	11.8	26
Heard	67	2148	318	819	.388	106	188	.564	185	481	666	190	242	2	106	120	742	11.1	24
DiGregorio	31	712	103	234	.440	35	45	.778	6	39	45	151	62	0	19	0	241	7.8	33
Charles	79	1690	240	515	.466	120	146	.822	68	96	164	171	165	1	87	20	600	7.6	19
J. W'ton (Tot)	80	1579	191	421	.454	62	93	.667	110	280	390	111	167	5	34	26	444	5.6	19
J. W'ton (Buf)	42	674	77	162	.475	21	38	.553	58	139	197	43	81	3	11	13	175	4.2	16
Winfield	68	1259	164	312	.526	49	68	.721	48	81	126	134	106	1	43	30	377	5.5	16
Schlueter	76	962	92	178	.517	84	121	.694	78	186	264	104	163	0	18	42	268	3.5	13
Weiss	76	1338	120	261	.391	54	67	.806	21	83	104	260	146	0	82	19	258	3.4	14
Ruffner	22	103	22	47	.468	1	5	.200	12	10	22	7	22	0	3	3	45	2.0	8
Harris	11	25	2	11	.182	1	2	.500	2	6	8	1	0	0	0	1	5	0.5	2

CHICAGO

Player	G.	Min.	FGM	FGA	Pct.	FTM	FTA	Pct.	Off. Reb.	Def. Reb.	Tot. Reb.	Ast.	PF	Dsq.	Stl.	Blk. Sh.	Pts.	Avg.	Hi.
B. Love	61	2401	539	1256	.429	264	318	.830	99	286	385	102	209	3	63	12	1342	22.0	39
Ch. Walker	76	2452	524	1076	.487	413	480	.860	114	318	432	169	181	0	49	6	1461	19.2	39
VanLier	70	2590	407	970	.420	236	298	.792	86	242	328	403	246	5	139	14	1050	15.0	42
Sloan	78	2577	380	865	.439	193	258	.748	177	361	538	161	265	5	171	17	953	12.2	27
Adelman	12	340	43	104	.413	28	39	.718	6	20	26	35	31	0	16	1	114	9.5	16
Block (Tot)	54	939	159	346	.460	114	144	.792	69	163	232	51	121	0	42	32	432	8.0	29
Block (Chi)	50	882	150	317	.473	105	134	.784	63	151	214	44	110	0	38	31	405	8.1	29
Thurmond	80	2756	250	686	.364	132	224	.589	259	645	904	328	271	6	46	195	632	7.9	25
Garrett	70	1183	228	474	.481	77	97	.794	80	167	247	43	124	0	24	13	533	7.6	21
Guokas	82	2089	255	500	.510	78	103	.757	24	115	139	178	154	1	45	17	588	7.2	20
Hewitt	18	467	56	129	.434	14	23	.609	30	86	116	24	46	1	9	10	126	7.0	17
Wilson	48	425	115	225	.511	46	58	.793	18	34	52	36	54	1	22	1	276	5.8	20
Boerwinkle	80	1175	132	271	.487	73	95	.768	105	275	380	272	163	0	25	45	337	4.2	17
W. Johnson	38	291	53	118	.449	37	58	.638	32	62	94	20	57	1	0	11	143	3.8	16
Benbow	39	252	35	94	.372	15	18	.833	14	24	38	25	41	0	11	6	85	2.2	8

1974-75 STATISTICS

CLEVELAND

Player	G.	Min.	FGM	FGA	Pct.	FTM	FTA	Pct.	Off. Reb.	Def. Reb.	Tot. Reb.	Ast.	PF	Dsq.	Stl.	Blk. Sh.	Pts.	Avg.	Hi.
R. Smith	82	2636	585	1212	.483	132	160	.825	108	299	407	229	227	1	80	26	1302	15.9	41
Chones	72	2427	446	916	.487	152	224	.679	156	521	677	132	247	5	49	120	1044	14.5	28
Carr	41	1081	252	538	.468	89	106	.840	51	56	107	154	57	0	48	2	593	14.5	34
Snyder	82	2590	498	988	.504	165	195	.846	37	201	238	281	226	3	69	43	1161	14.2	30
Cleamons	74	2691	369	768	.480	144	181	.796	97	232	329	381	194	0	84	21	882	11.9	29
D. Davis	78	1964	295	666	.443	176	245	.718	108	356	464	150	254	3	45	39	766	9.8	24
Brewer	82	1991	291	639	.455	103	159	.648	205	304	509	128	150	2	77	43	685	8.4	26
Foster	73	1136	217	521	.417	124	165	.752	43	109	152	45	100	0	21	3	424	6.2	18
M. Russell	68	754	150	365	.411	124	165	.752	43	109	152	45	100	0	21	3	424	6.2	18
Patterson	81	1269	161	387	.416	48	73	.658	112	217	329	93	128	1	21	20	370	4.6	23
Cl. Walker	72	1070	111	275	.404	80	117	.684	47	99	146	192	126	0	80	7	302	4.2	18
Witte	39	271	33	96	.344	19	31	.613	38	54	92	15	42	0	4	22	85	2.2	9

DETROIT

Player	G.	Min.	FGM	FGA	Pct.	FTM	FTA	Pct.	Off. Reb.	Def. Reb.	Tot. Reb.	Ast.	PF	Dsq.	Stl.	Blk. Sh.	Pts.	Avg.	Hi.
Lanier	76	2987	731	1433	.510	361	450	.802	225	689	914	350	237	1	75	172	1823	24.0	45
Bing	79	3222	578	1333	.434	343	424	.809	86	200	286	610	222	3	116	26	1499	19.0	32
Rowe	82	2787	422	874	.483	171	227	.753	174	411	585	121	190	0	50	44	1015	12.4	26
Mengelt	80	1995	336	701	.479	211	248	.851	38	153	191	201	198	2	72	4	883	11.0	33
Trapp	78	1472	288	652	.442	99	131	.756	71	205	276	63	210	1	37	14	675	8.7	24
Porter (Tot)	58	1163	201	412	.488	66	79	.835	79	175	254	19	93	0	23	26	468	8.1	22
Porter (Det)	41	1030	188	376	.500	59	70	.843	66	150	216	17	76	0	20	25	435	10.6	22
Norwood	24	347	64	123	.520	31	42	.738	31	57	88	16	51	0	23	0	159	6.6	18
Ford	80	1962	206	435	.474	63	95	.663	93	176	269	230	187	0	113	26	475	5.9	18
Adams	51	1376	127	315	.403	45	78	.577	63	181	244	75	179	1	69	20	299	5.9	19
Money	66	889	144	319	.451	31	45	.689	27	61	88	101	121	3	33	2	319	4.8	21
J. Davis	79	1078	118	260	.454	85	117	.726	96	189	285	90	129	2	50	36	321	4.1	21
Ligon	38	272	55	143	.385	16	25	.640	14	12	26	25	31	0	8	9	126	3.3	15
Eberhard	34	277	31	85	.365	17	21	.810	18	29	47	16	33	0	13	1	79	2.3	11
Moore	2	11	1	4	.250	1	2	.500	0	2	2	1	2	0	1	3	3	1.5	3

GOLDEN STATE

Player	G.	Min.	FGM	FGA	Pct.	FTM	FTA	Pct.	Off. Reb.	Def. Reb.	Tot. Reb.	Ast.	PF	Dsq.	Stl.	Blk. Sh.	Pts.	Avg.	Hi.
Barry	80	3235	1028	2217	.464	394	436	.904	92	364	456	492	225	0	228	33	2450	30.6	55
Wilkes	82	2515	502	1135	.442	160	218	.734	203	468	671	183	222	0	107	72	1164	14.2	31
Beard	82	2521	408	773	.528	232	279	.832	116	200	316	345	297	9	132	11	1048	12.8	29
C. Johnson	79	2171	394	957	.412	75	102	.735	134	177	311	233	204	2	138	4	863	10.9	25
Ray	82	2519	299	573	.522	171	284	.602	259	611	870	178	305	9	95	116	769	9.4	20
Mullins	86	1141	234	514	.455	71	87	.816	46	77	123	153	123	0	57	14	539	8.2	24
P. Smith	74	1055	221	464	.476	127	158	.804	51	89	140	135	141	0	62	0	569	7.7	26
Dickey	80	1859	274	569	.482	66	99	.667	190	360	550	125	199	0	52	19	614	7.7	20
G. Johnson	82	1439	152	319	.476	60	91	.659	217	357	574	67	206	1	82	136	364	4.4	16
Dudley	67	756	102	217	.470	70	97	.722	61	84	145	103	105	1	40	2	274	4.1	15
Kendrick	24	121	31	77	.403	18	22	.818	19	17	36	6	22	0	11	3	80	3.3	10
Bracey	42	340	54	130	.415	25	38	.658	10	28	38	52	41	0	14	1	133	3.2	13
Bridges (Tot)	32	415	35	93	.376	17	34	.500	64	70	134	31	65	1	11	5	87	2.7	15
Bridges (G.S.)	15	108	15	36	.417	1	4	.250	18	20	38	4	19	0	4	0	31	2.1	8

HOUSTON

Player	G.	Min.	FGM	FGA	Pct.	FTM	FTA	Pct.	Off. Reb.	Def. Reb.	Tot. Reb.	Ast.	PF	Dsq.	Stl.	Blk. Sh.	Pts.	Avg.	Hi.
Tomjanovich	81	3134	694	1323	.525	289	366	.790	184	429	613	236	230	1	76	24	1677	20.7	41
Murphy	78	2513	557	1152	.484	341	386	.883	52	121	173	381	281	8	128	4	1455	18.7	45
Newlin	79	2709	436	905	.482	265	305	.869	55	205	260	403	288	4	111	7	1137	14.4	37
Ratleff	80	2563	392	851	.461	157	190	.826	185	274	459	259	231	5	146	51	941	11.8	31
Kunnert	75	1801	346	676	.512	116	169	.686	214	417	631	108	223	2	34	84	808	10.8	27
Abdul-Aziz	65	1450	235	538	.437	159	203	.783	154	334	488	84	128	1	37	74	629	9.7	26
Meely	48	753	156	349	.447	68	94	.723	55	109	164	45	117	4	21	21	380	7.9	21
Wohl	75	1722	203	462	.439	79	106	.745	26	86	112	340	184	1	75	9	485	6.5	29
R. Riley	77	1578	196	470	.417	71	97	.732	137	243	380	130	197	3	56	22	463	6.0	19
Hawes	55	897	140	279	.502	45	55	.818	80	195	275	88	99	1	36	36	325	5.9	20
Wells	33	214	42	100	.420	15	22	.682	12	23	35	22	38	0	9	3	99	3.0	12
Bailey	47	446	51	126	.405	20	41	.488	23	59	82	59	52	0	17	16	122	2.6	14

K.C.-OMAHA

Player	G.	Min.	FGM	FGA	Pct.	FTM	FTA	Pct.	Off. Reb.	Def. Reb.	Tot. Reb.	Ast.	PF	Dsq.	Stl.	Blk. Sh.	Pts.	Avg.	Hi.
Archibald	82	3244	759	1664	.456	652	748	.872	48	174	222	557	187	0	119	7	2170	26.5	41
J. Walker	81	3122	553	1164	.475	247	289	.855	51	188	239	226	222	2	85	13	1353	16.7	32

1974-75 STATISTICS

Player	G.	Min.	FGM	FGA	Pct.	FTM	FTA	Pct.	Off. Reb.	Def. Reb.	Tot. Reb.	Ast.	PF	Dsq.	Stl.	Blk. Sh.	Pts.	Avg.	Hi.
N. Williams	50	1131	265	584	.454	97	118	.822	58	121	179	78	152	2	53	24	627	12.5	27
Lacey	81	3378	392	917	.427	144	191	.754	228	921	1149	428	274	4	139	168	928	11.5	23
Wedman	80	2554	375	806	.465	139	170	.818	202	288	490	129	270	2	81	27	889	11.1	26
Behagen	81	2205	333	834	.399	199	264	.754	146	446	592	153	301	8	60	42	865	10.7	23
McNeill	80	1749	296	645	.459	189	241	.784	149	348	497	73	229	1	69	27	781	9.8	26
O. J'son (Tot)	73	1667	203	429	.473	95	114	.833	87	156	243	110	172	5	59	33	501	6.9	20
O.J'on(KC-O)	30	508	64	130	.492	33	37	.892	27	39	66	30	69	0	17	13	161	5.4	15
Ad'man (Tot)	58	1074	123	291	.423	73	103	.709	25	70	95	112	101	1	70	8	319	5.5	16
Ad'n (KC-O)	18	121	13	28	.464	4	5	.800	6	8	14	8	12	0	7	1	30	1.7	9
Kojis	21	232	46	98	.469	20	30	.667	14	25	39	10	31	0	12	1	112	5.3	18
Durrett	21	175	32	78	.410	11	20	.550	14	26	40	8	30	0	5	4	75	3.6	9
D'Antoni	67	759	69	173	.399	28	36	.778	13	64	77	107	106	0	67	12	166	2.5	14
May	29	139	27	54	.500	10	12	.833	4	9	13	5	21	0	4	2	64	2.2	12
Kosmalski	67	413	33	83	.398	24	29	.828	31	88	119	41	64	0	6	6	90	1.3	7

LOS ANGELES

Player	G.	Min.	FGM	FGA	Pct.	FTM	FTA	Pct.	Off. Reb.	Def. Reb.	Tot. Reb.	Ast.	PF	Dsq.	Stl.	Blk. Sh.	Pts.	Avg.	Hi.
Goodrich	72	2668	656	1429	.459	318	378	.841	96	123	219	420	214	1	102	6	1630	22.6	53
Price	9	339	75	167	.449	41	45	.911	17	26	43	63	36	1	21	3	191	21.2	27
Allen (Tot)	66	2353	511	1170	.437	238	306	.778	90	188	278	372	217	4	136	29	1260	19.1	39
Allen (L.A.)	56	2011	443	1006	.440	207	269	.770	81	166	247	319	194	4	122	28	1093	19.5	39
C. Russell	40	1055	264	580	.455	101	113	.894	34	81	115	109	56	0	27	2	629	15.7	30
Winters	68	1536	359	810	.443	76	92	.826	39	99	138	195	168	1	74	18	794	11.7	30
P. Riley	46	1016	219	523	.419	69	93	.742	25	60	85	121	128	0	36	4	507	11.0	38
E. Smith	74	2341	346	702	.493	112	231	.485	210	600	810	145	255	6	84	216	804	10.9	30
Hairston	74	2283	271	536	.506	217	271	.801	304	642	946	173	218	2	52	11	759	10.3	21
Lantz (Tot)	75	1783	228	561	.406	192	229	.838	88	106	194	188	162	1	56	12	648	8.6	26
Lantz (L.A.)	56	1430	189	446	.424	145	176	.824	81	89	170	158	134	1	44	10	523	9.3	26
Hawkins	43	1026	139	324	.429	68	99	.687	54	144	198	120	116	1	51	23	346	8.0	24
S. Love	30	431	85	194	.438	47	66	.712	31	66	97	26	69	1	16	13	217	7.2	18
Beaty	69	1213	136	310	.439	108	135	.800	93	234	327	74	130	1	45	29	380	5.5	19
Calhoun (Tot)	70	1378	132	318	.415	58	77	.753	109	160	269	79	180	1	55	25	322	4.6	13
Calhoun (LA)	57	1270	120	286	.420	46	62	.710	95	141	236	75	160	1	49	23	284	5.0	13
K. Wash'ton	55	949	87	207	.420	72	122	.590	106	244	350	66	155	2	25	32	246	4.5	12
Bridges	17	307	20	57	.351	16	30	.533	46	48	94	27	46	1	7	5	56	3.3	15

MILWAUKEE

Player	G.	Min.	FGM	FGA	Pct.	FTM	FTA	Pct.	Off. Reb.	Def. Reb.	Tot. Reb.	Ast.	PF	Dsq.	Stl.	Blk. Sh.	Pts.	Avg.	Hi.
Abdul-Jabbar	65	2747	812	1584	.513	325	426	.763	194	718	912	264	205	2	65	212	1949	30.0	52
Dandridge	80	3031	691	1460	.473	211	262	.805	142	409	551	243	330	7	122	48	1593	19.9	33
Allen	10	342	68	164	.415	31	37	.838	9	22	31	53	23	0	14	1	167	16.7	23
Price (Tot)	50	1870	317	717	.442	169	194	.871	62	136	198	286	182	1	111	24	803	16.1	43
Price (Mil)	41	1531	242	550	.440	128	149	.859	45	110	155	223	146	0	90	21	612	14.9	43
Thompson	73	1983	306	691	.443	168	214	.785	50	131	181	225	203	5	66	6	780	10.7	24
McGlocklin	79	1853	323	651	.496	63	72	.875	25	94	119	255	142	2	51	6	709	9.0	24
Brokaw	73	1639	234	514	.455	126	184	.685	36	111	147	221	176	3	31	18	594	8.1	24
Warner	79	2519	248	541	.458	106	155	.684	238	574	812	127	267	8	49	54	602	7.6	19
Mi. Davis	76	1755	188	427	.440	35	49	.714	131	272	403	119	172	1	36	19	411	5.4	18
Restani	46	526	62	165	.376	24	29	.828	10	33	43	71	70	2	23	2	148	3.2	15
R. Williams	54	544	57	159	.390	44	56	.786	52	71	123	35	59	0	11	3	168	2.8	10
Kuberski	59	567	62	159	.390	44	56	.786	52	71	123	35	59	0	11	3	168	2.8	10
Wesley (Tot)	45	247	42	93	.452	16	27	.593	18	45	63	12	51	0	7	5	100	2.2	10
Wesley (Mil)	41	214	37	84	.440	14	23	.609	14	41	55	11	43	0	7	5	88	2.1	10
Driscoll	11	52	3	13	.231	1	2	.500	2	5	7	3	7	0	1	0	7	0.6	3
D. Cun'gham	2	8	0	1	.000	0	0	.000	0	2	2	1	1	0	0	0	0	0.0	0
Rule	1	11	0	1	.000	0	0	.000	0	0	0	2	2	0	0	0	0	0.0	0

NEW ORLEANS

Player	G.	Min.	FGM	FGA	Pct.	FTM	FTA	Pct.	Off. Reb.	Def. Reb.	Tot. Reb.	Ast.	PF	Dsq.	Stl.	Blk. Sh.	Pts.	Avg.	Hi.
Maravich	79	2853	655	1562	.419	390	481	.811	93	329	422	488	227	4	120	18	1700	21.5	47
N. W'ms (Tot)	85	1945	474	988	.480	181	220	.823	102	235	337	145	251	3	97	30	1129	13.3	28
N. W'ms (N.O.)	35	814	209	404	.517	84	102	.824	44	114	158	67	99	1	44	6	502	14.3	28
Barnett	45	1238	215	480	.448	156	188	.830	45	83	128	128	137	1	35	16	586	13.0	30
James	76	1731	370	776	.477	147	189	.778	140	226	366	66	217	4	41	15	887	11.7	34
L. Nelson	72	1898	307	679	.452	192	250	.768	75	121	196	179	186	1	65	6	806	11.2	29
B. Stallw'th	73	1668	298	710	.420	125	182	.687	78	168	246	46	208	4	59	11	721	9.9	24
Walk	37	851	151	358	.422	64	80	.800	73	189	262	101	122	3	30	20	366	9.9	23
Bibby	75	1400	270	619	.436	137	189	.725	47	90	137	181	157	0	54	5	677	9.0	27
Bibby (N.O.)	28	524	91	219	.416	49	67	.731	18	32	50	76	61	0	25	0	250	8.9	20

1974-75 STATISTICS

Player	G.	Min.	FGM	FGA	Pct.	FTM	FTA	Pct.	Off. Reb.	Def. Reb.	Tot. Reb.	Ast.	PF	Dsq.	Stl.	Blk. Sh.	Pts.	Avg.	Hi.
Coleman	77	2176	253	568	.445	116	166	.699	189	360	549	105	277	10	82	37	622	8.1	23
O. Johnson	43	1159	139	299	.465	62	77	.805	60	117	177	80	103	1	42	20	340	7.9	20
Roberson	16	339	48	108	.444	23	40	.575	39	79	118	23	49	0	7	8	119	7.4	20
Counts	75	1421	217	495	.438	86	113	.761	102	339	441	182	196	0	49	43	520	6.9	20
Block	4	57	9	29	.310	9	10	.900	6	12	18	7	11	0	4	1	27	6.8	12
Moore (Tot)	42	1066	118	262	.450	46	69	.667	92	238	330	83	148	3	21	40	282	6.7	16
Moore (N.O.)	40	1055	117	258	.453	45	67	.672	92	236	328	82	146	3	21	39	279	7.0	16
Kimball	3	90	7	23	.304	6	7	.857	8	18	26	4	12	0	2	0	20	6.7	8
Lantz	19	353	39	115	.339	47	53	.887	7	17	24	30	28	0	12	2	125	6.6	22
Adelman	28	613	67	159	.421	41	·59	.695	13	42	55	69	58	1	47	6	175	6.3	16
Bellamy	1	14	2	2	1.000	2	2	1.000	0	5	5	0	2	0	0	0	6	6.0	6
R. Lee	15	139	29	76	.382	7	14	.500	15	16	31	7	17	1	1	1	65	4.3	17
Fryer	31	432	47	106	.443	33	43	.767	16	30	46	52	54	0	22	0	127	4.1	17
Green	15	280	24	70	.343	9	20	.450	28	81	109	16	38	0	4	5	57	3.8	10
K. Boyd	6	25	7	13	.538	5	11	.455	3	2	5	2	2	0	3	0	19	3.2	7

NEW YORK

Player	G.	Min.	FGM	FGA	Pct.	FTM	FTA	Pct.	Off. Reb.	Def. Reb.	Tot. Reb.	Ast.	PF	Dsq.	Stl.	Blk. Sh.	Pts.	Avg.	Hi.
Frazier	78	3204	672	1391	.483	331	400	.828	90	375	465	474	205	2	190	14	1675	21.5	43
Monroe	78	2814	668	1462	.457	297	359	.827	56	271	327	270	200	0	108	29	1633	20.9	38
Bradley	79	2787	452	1036	.436	144	165	.873	65	186	251	247	283	5	74	18	1048	13.3	32
P. Jackson	78	2285	324	712	.455	193	253	.763	137	463	600	136	330	10	84	53	841	10.8	29
Barnett (Tot)	73	1776	285	652	.437	199	238	.836	60	119	179	176	160	1	47	16	769	10.5	30
Barnett (N.Y.)	28	538	70	172	.407	43	50	.860	15	36	51	39	51	0	12	0	183	6.5	22
Gianelli	80	2777	343	726	.472	135	195	.692	214	475	689	163	263	3	38	118	821	10.3	23
Bibby	47	876	179	400	.448	69	96	.719	29	58	87	105	96	0	29	3	427	9.1	27
Wingo	82	1686	233	506	.460	141	187	.754	163	293	456	84	215	2	48	35	607	7.4	19
Walk (Tot)	67	1125	198	473	.419	86	105	.819	91	248	339	123	177	3	37	23	482	7.2	23
Walk (N.Y.)	30	274	47	115	.409	22	25	.880	18	59	77	22	55	0	7	3	116	3.9	12
Mel Davis	62	903	154	395	.390	48	70	.686	70	251	321	54	105	0	16	8	356	5.7	24
Dark	47	401	74	157	.471	22	40	.550	15	22	37	30	48	0	3	1	170	3.6	13
Bell	52	465	68	181	.376	20	36	.556	48	57	105	25	54	0	22	9	156	3.0	20
Riker	51	483	53	147	.361	46	82	.561	40	67	107	19	64	0	15	5	152	3.0	12
H. Porter	17	133	13	36	.361	7	9	.778	13	25	38	2	17	0	3	1	33	1.9	7
G. Jackson	5	27	4	10	.400	0	0	.000	0	2	3	5	3	0	0	0	8	1.6	6
D. Stallw'th	7	57	5	18	.278	0	0	.000	6	14	20	2	10	0	3	0	10	1.4	6

PHILADELPHIA

Player	G.	Min.	FGM	FGA	Pct.	FTM	FTA	Pct.	Off. Reb.	Def. Reb.	Tot. Reb.	Ast.	PF	Dsq.	Stl.	Blk. Sh.	Pts.	Avg.	Hi.
Carter	77	3046	715	1598	.447	256	347	.738	73	267	340	336	257	5	82	20	1686	21.9	37
Cunningham	80	2859	609	1423	.428	345	444	.777	130	596	726	442	270	4	91	35	1563	19.5	38
Collins	81	2820	561	1150	.488	331	392	.844	104	211	315	213	291	6	108	17	1453	17.9	39
Mix	46	1748	280	582	.481	159	205	.776	155	345	500	99	175	6	79	21	719	15.6	36
T.V.A'dale	9	273	49	116	.422	28	41	.683	7	22	29	16	26	0	13	0	126	14.0	21
Ellis	82	2183	287	623	.461	72	99	.727	195	387	582	117	178	1	44	55	646	7.9	27
F. Boyd	66	1362	205	495	.414	55	115	.478	16	73	89	161	134	0	43	4	465	7.0	35
Bristow	72	1101	163	393	.415	121	153	.791	111	143	254	99	101	0	25	2	447	6.2	23
Lee (Tot)	80	2456	176	427	.412	119	177	.672	288	469	757	105	285	9	30	20	471	5.9	19
Lee (Phil)	71	2279	164	391	.419	87	138	.630	264	423	687	97	260	9	29	16	415	5.8	19
D. Smith	54	538	131	321	.408	21	21	1.000	14	16	30	47	45	0	20	3	283	5.2	19
Norman	12	72	23	44	.523	2	3	.667	3	9	12	4	9	0	3	1	48	4.0	10
Durrett (Tot)	48	445	67	166	.404	31	52	.596	35	67	102	18	72	0	9	8	165	3.4	9
Durrett (Phil)	27	270	35	88	.398	20	32	.625	21	41	62	10	42	0	4	4	90	3.3	9
Tschogl	39	623	53	148	.358	13	22	.591	52	59	111	30	80	2	25	25	119	3.1	13
Wesley	4	33	5	9	.556	2	4	.500	4	4	8	1	8	0	0	0	12	3.0	10
Catchings	37	528	41	74	.554	16	25	.640	49	104	153	21	82	1	10	60	98	2.6	8
Warbington	5	70	4	21	.190	2	2	1.000	2	6	8	16	16	0	0	0	10	2.0	4

PHOENIX

Player	G.	Min.	FGM	FGA	Pct.	FTM	FTA	Pct.	Off. Reb.	Def. Reb.	Tot. Reb.	Ast.	PF	Dsq.	Stl.	Blk. Sh.	Pts.	Avg.	Hi.
Scott	69	2592	703	1594	.441	274	351	.781	72	201	273	311	296	11	111	24	1680	24.3	47
D. VArsdale	70	2419	421	895	.470	282	339	.832	52	137	189	195	177	2	81	11	1124	16.1	46
Perry	79	2688	437	917	.476	247	284	.870	57	129	186	288	10	108	78	1058	13.4	26	
Bantom	82	2239	418	907	.461	185	259	.714	211	342	553	159	273	8	62	47	1021	12.5	29
Erickson	49	1469	237	557	.425	130	156	.833	70	173	243	170	153	0	52	12	604	12.3	29
Awtrey	82	2837	339	722	.470	132	195	.677	242	462	704	342	227	2	60	52	810	9.9	24
Melchionni	68	1529	232	539	.430	114	141	.809	45	142	187	156	116	1	48	12	578	8.5	23
Saunders	69	1059	176	406	.433	66	95	.695	82	171	253	80	151	3	41	15	418	6.1	21

1974-75 STATISTICS

Player	G.	Min.	FGM	FGA	Pct.	FTM	FTA	Pct.	Off. Reb.	Def. Reb.	Tot. Reb.	Ast.	PF	Dsq.	Stl.	Blk. Sh.	Pts.	Avg.	Hi
Hawthorne	50	618	118	287	.411	61	94	.649	34	58	92	39	94	0	30	21	297	5.9	20
E. Williams	79	1040	163	394	.414	45	103	.437	156	300	456	95	146	0	28	32	371	4.7	22
G. J'on (Tot)	49	802	73	176	.415	36	62	.581	19	50	69	96	130	5	23	9	182	3.7	18
G. J'on (Pho)	44	775	69	166	.416	36	62	.581	17	50	67	93	125	5	23	9	174	4.0	18
Owens	41	432	56	145	.386	12	16	.750	7	36	43	49	27	0	16	2	124	3.0	12
Calhoun	13	108	12	32	.375	14	15	.933	14	19	33	4	20	0	6	2	38	2.9	13

PORTLAND

Player	G.	Min.	FGM	FGA	Pct.	FTM	FTA	Pct.	Off. Reb.	Def. Reb.	Tot. Reb.	Ast.	PF	Dsq.	Stl.	Blk. Sh.	Pts.	Avg.	Hi
Wicks	82	3162	692	1391	.497	394	558	.706	231	646	877	287	289	5	108	80	1778	21.7	36
Petrie	80	3109	602	1319	.456	261	311	.839	38	171	209	424	215	1	81	13	1465	18.3	37
J. Johnson	80	2540	527	1082	.487	236	301	.784	162	339	501	240	249	3	75	39	1290	16.1	35
Walton	35	1153	177	345	.513	94	137	.686	92	349	441	167	115	4	29	94	448	12.8	25
Neal	82	2278	409	869	.471	189	295	.641	186	501	687	139	239	2	43	87	1007	12.3	29
Steele	76	2389	265	484	.548	122	146	.836	86	140	226	287	254	6	183	16	652	8.6	23
Martin	81	1372	236	522	.452	99	142	.697	136	272	408	69	239	5	33	49	571	7.0	22
Wilkens	65	1161	134	305	.439	152	198	.768	38	82	120	235	96	1	77	9	420	6.5	20
Clemens	77	952	168	355	.473	45	60	.750	33	128	161	76	139	0	68	2	381	4.9	24
Lumpkin	48	792	86	190	.453	30	39	.769	10	49	59	177	80	1	20	3	202	4.2	14
G. Smith	55	519	71	146	.486	32	48	.667	29	60	89	27	96	1	22	6	174	3.2	16
Anderson	43	453	47	105	.448	26	30	.867	8	21	29	81	44	0	16	1	120	2.8	10

SEATTLE

Player	G.	Min.	FGM	FGA	Pct.	FTM	FTA	Pct.	Off. Reb.	Def. Reb.	Tot. Reb.	Ast.	PF	Dsq.	Stl.	Blk. Sh.	Pts.	Avg.	Hi
Haywood	68	2529	608	1325	.459	309	381	.811	198	432	630	137	173	1	54	108	1525	22.4	40
F. Brown	81	2669	737	1537	.480	226	272	.831	113	230	343	284	227	2	187	14	1700	21.0	40
Clark	77	2481	455	919	.495	161	193	.834	59	176	235	433	188	4	110	5	1071	13.9	31
Gray	75	2280	378	773	.489	104	144	.722	133	345	478	163	292	9	63	24	860	11.5	33
Burleson	82	1888	322	772	.417	182	265	.687	155	417	572	115	221	1	64	153	826	10.1	29
Fox	75	1766	253	540	.469	170	212	.802	128	363	491	59	168	1	48	17	676	9.0	28
Brisker	21	276	60	141	.426	42	49	.857	15	18	33	19	33	0	7	3	162	7.7	28
Watts	82	2056	232	551	.421	93	153	.608	95	167	262	499	254	7	190	12	557	6.8	23
Derline	58	666	142	332	.428	43	56	.768	12	47	59	45	47	0	23	4	327	5.6	20
Skinner	73	1574	142	347	.409	63	97	.649	135	209	344	85	161	0	49	17	347	4.8	22
W. Jackson	56	939	96	242	.397	51	71	.718	53	80	133	30	126	2	26	5	243	4.3	23
McIntosh	6	101	6	29	.207	6	9	.667	6	9	15	5	7	12	0	4	3	18	3.0	6
Tolson	19	87	16	37	.432	11	17	.647	12	10	22	5	12	0	4	6	43	2.3	14
Hummer	43	568	41	108	.380	14	51	.275	28	76	104	38	63	0	8	7	96	2.2	13

WASHINGTON

Player	G.	Min.	FGM	FGA	Pct.	FTM	FTA	Pct.	Off. Reb.	Def. Reb.	Tot. Reb.	Ast.	PF	Dsq.	Stl.	Blk. Sh.	Pts.	Avg.	Hi
Hayes	82	3465	739	1668	.443	409	534	.766	221	783	1004	206	238	0	15K	187	1887	23.0	39
Chenier	77	2869	690	1533	.450	301	365	.825	74	218	292	248	158	3	176	58	1681	21.8	38
Riordan	74	2191	520	1057	.492	98	117	.838	90	194	284	198	238	4	72	0	1138	15.4	39
K. Porter	81	2589	406	827	.491	131	186	.704	55	97	152	650	320	12	152	11	943	11.6	29
Unseld	73	2904	273	544	.502	126	184	.685	318	759	1077	297	180	2	65	21	615	7.5	24
Weatherspoon	82	1347	256	562	.456	103	138	.746	132	214	346	51	212	2	65	21	615	7.5	24
J. Jones	73	1424	207	400	.518	103	142	.725	36	101	137	162	190	0	76	10	517	7.1	24
Robinson	76	995	191	393	.486	60	115	.522	94	207	301	40	132	0	36	32	442	5.8	18
Haskins	70	702	115	290	.397	53	63	.841	29	51	80	79	73	0	23	6	283	4.0	18
Gibbs	59	424	74	190	.389	48	64	.750	26	35	61	19	60	0	12	3	196	3.3	13
Kozelko	73	754	60	167	.359	31	36	.861	50	90	140	41	125	4	28	5	151	2.1	14
DuVal	37	137	24	65	.369	12	18	.667	8	15	23	14	34	0	16	2	60	1.6	5
S. Wash'ton	1	4	0	1	.000	0	0	.000	0	0	0	0	1	0	0	0	0	0.0	0

N.W.T.—Not With Team
DQ—Individual Players Disqualified (Fouled out of Game)

1974-75 PLAYOFF RESULTS

CONFERENCE QUALIFYING ROUNDS

EASTERN CONFERENCE

Houston 2, New York 1
Apr. 8–Tue.–New York 84 at Houston 99
Apr. 10–Thu.–Houston 96 at New York 106
Apr. 12–Sat.–New York 86 at Houston 118

WESTERN CONFERENCE

Seattle 2, Detroit 1
Apr. 8–Tue.–Detroit 77 at Seattle 90
Apr. 10–Thu.–Seattle 106 at Detroit 122
Apr. 12–Sat.–Detroit 93 at Seattle........................100

CONFERENCE SEMI-FINALS SERIES

EASTERN CONFERENCE

Boston 4, Houston 1
Apr. 14–Mon.–Houston 106 at Boston....................123
Apr. 16–Wed.–Houston 100 at Boston 112
Apr. 19–Sat.–Boston 102 at Houston 117
Apr. 22–Tue.–Boston 122 at Houston 117
Apr. 24–Thu.–Houston 115 at Boston 128

Washington 4, Buffalo 3
Apr. 10–Thu.–Buffalo 113 at Washington 102
Apr. 12–Sat.–Washington 120 at Buffalo 106
Apr. 16–Wed.–Buffalo 96 at Washington 111
Apr. 18–Fri.–Washington 102 at Buffalo 108
Apr. 20–Sun.–Buffalo 93 at Washington 97
Apr. 23–Wed.–Washington 96 at Buffalo 102
Apr. 25–Fri.–Buffalo 96 at Washington 115

WESTERN CONFERENCE

Golden State 4, Seattle 2
Apr. 14–Mon.–Seattle 96 at Golden State 123
Apr. 16–Wed.–Seattle 100 at Golden State........... 99
Apr. 17–Thu.–Golden State 105 at Seattle 96
Apr. 19–Sat.–Golden State 94 at Seattle................111
Apr. 22–Tue.–Seattle 100 at Golden State 124
Apr. 24–Thu.–Golden State 105 at Seattle 96

Chicago 4, K.C.-Omaha 2
Apr. 9–Wed–K.C.-Omaha 89 at Chicago 95
Apr. 13–Sun.–Chicago 95 at K.C.-Omaha 102
Apr. 16–Wed.–K.C.-Omaha 90 at Chicago 93
Apr. 18–Fri.–Chicago 100 at K.C.-Omaha ......104(ot)
Apr. 20–Sun.–K.C.-Omaha 77 at Chicago 104
Apr. 23–Wed.–Chicago 101 at K.C.-Omaha 89

CONFERENCE FINALS

EASTERN CONFERENCE FINALS

Washington 4, Boston 2
Apr. 27–Sun.–Washington 100 at Boston 95
Apr. 30–Wed.–Boston 92 at Washington 117
May 3–Sat.–Washington 90 at Boston 101
May 7–Wed.–Boston 108 at Washington 119
May 9–Fri.–Washington 99 at Boston 103
May 11–Sun.–Boston 92 at Washington 98

WESTERN CONFERENCE FINALS

Golden State 4, Chicago 3
Apr. 27–Sun.–Chicago 89 at Golden State 107
Apr. 30–Wed.–Golden State 89 at Chicago........... 90
May 4–Sun.–Golden State 101 at Chicago 108
May 6–Tue.–Chicago 106 at Golden State 111
May 8–Thu.–Chicago 89 at Golden State 79
May 11–Sun.–Golden State 86 at Chicago 72
May 14–Wed.–Chicago 79 at Golden State........... 83

CHAMPIONSHIP SERIES

Golden State 4, Washington 0
May 18–Sun.–Golden State 101 at Washington.... 95
May 20–Tue.–Washington 91 at Golden State...... 92
May 23–Fri.–Washington 101 at Golden State 109
May 25–Sun.–Golden State 96 at Washington...... 95

1973-74 STATISTICS

BOSTON CELTICS—1973-74 NBA CHAMPIONS

Seated from left, Jo Jo White, Don Chaney, John Havlicek, President and General Manager Arnold "Red" Auerbach, Chairman of the Board Robert Schmertz, Coach Tom Heinsohn, Dave Cowens, Paul Silas and Assistant Coach John Killilea. Standing from left, Assistant Trainer Mark Volk, Team Dentist Dr. Samuel Kane, Paul Westphal, Phil Hankinson, Steve Downing, Don Nelson, Hank Finkel, Steve Kuberski, Art Williams, Team Physician Dr. Thomas Silva and Trainer Frank Challant.

FINAL STANDINGS

ATLANTIC DIVISION

Team	Atl.	Bos.	Buf.	Cap.	Chi.	Clv.	Det.	G.S.	Hou.	KC-O.	L.A.	Mil.	N.Y.	Phil.	Pho.	Prt.	Sea.	W.	L.	Pct.	G.B.
Boston	5	..	5	2	2	4	3	3	4	3	2	2	5	7	3	4	2	56	26	.683	....
New York	5	2	4	3	2	5	3	3	2	3	2	2	..	4	3	2	4	49	33	.598	7
Buffalo	4	2	..	3	1	5	1	1	4	2	0	1	4	6	3	3	2	42	40	.512	14
Philadelphia	3	1	1	2	1	1	2	1	2	3	0	0	3	..	3	2	0	25	57	.305	31

CENTRAL DIVISION

Capital	4	4	3	..	1	6	2	3	4	3	2	1	3	4	2	3	2	47	35	.573	....
Atlanta	..	1	2	4	1	4	0	1	5	1	4	1	1	3	1	2	4	35	47	.427	12
Houston	2	2	2	3	0	4	1	0	..	2	2	0	4	4	2	3	1	32	50	.390	15
Cleveland	3	2	1	1	0	..	2	0	4	0	3	0	1	5	1	4	2	29	53	.354	18

MIDWEST DIVISION

Milwaukee	3	2	3	3	3	4	4	3	4	7	2	..	2	4	5	6	4	59	23	.720	....
Chicago	3	2	3	3	..	4	5	4	4	5	1	3	2	3	4	4	4	54	28	.659	5
Detroit	4	1	3	2	2	2	..	5	3	4	4	3	1	2	6	5	5	52	30	.634	7
K.C.-Omaha	3	1	2	1	2	4	2	3	2	..	1	0	1	4	4	2	33	49	.402	26	

PACIFIC DIVISION

Los Angeles	0	2	4	2	5	1	2	2	2	5	..	4	2	4	4	4	4	47	35	.573	....
Golden State	3	1	3	1	2	4	1	..	4	3	4	3	1	3	5	3	3	44	38	.537	3
Seattle	0	2	2	2	2	2	1	3	3	4	3	2	0	4	3	3	..	36	46	.439	11
Phoenix	3	1	1	2	2	3	0	2	2	2	2	1	1	1	..	3	4	30	52	.366	17
Portland	2	0	1	1	2	0	1	4	1	2	3	0	2	2	3	..	3	27	55	.329	20

TEAM STATISTICS—OFFENSE

Team	G.	FIELD GOALS Made	Att.	Pct.	FREE THROWS Made	Att.	Pct.	REBOUNDS Off.	Def.	Tot.	MISCELLANEOUS Ast.	PF	Stl.	Blk. Sh.	Turn Over	Dq.	SCORING Pts.	Avg.
Buffalo	82	3728	7763	.480	1699	2221	.765	1150	2830	3980	2165	1875	786	600	1828	17	9155	111.6
Golden State	82	3721	8020	.464	1569	2018	.778	1379	3035	4414	1989	1893	668	450	1667	33	9011	109.9
Los Angeles	82	3536	7803	.453	1879	2443	.769	1365	2970	4335	2179	2032	794	653	1913	26	8951	109.2
Boston	82	3630	7969	.456	1677	2097	.800	1378	3074	4452	2187	1868	561	305	1796	22	8937	109.0
Atlanta	82	3602	7744	.465	1703	2264	.752	1240	2712	3952	1993	2073	758	332	1823	33	8907	108.6
Phoenix	82	3555	7726	.460	1737	2235	.777	1090	2723	3813	2052	2123	658	305	1666	46	8847	107.9
Houston	82	3564	7426	.480	1682	2071	.812	1063	2588	3651	2212	2104	727	407	1681	36	8810	107.4
Milwaukee	82	3726	7571	.492	1328	1741	.763	1133	2881	4014	2225	1864	726	519	1694	26	8780	107.1
Seattle	82	3584	8056	.445	1606	2095	.767	1323	2706	4029	2106	2074	689	294	1622	31	8774	107.0
Portland	82	3585	7684	.467	1591	2112	.753	1254	2598	3852	2106	2050	797	341	1823	23	8761	106.8
Detroit	82	3453	7515	.459	1654	2164	.764	1200	2681	3881	1956	1930	793	419	1763	19	8560	104.4
Chicago	82	3292	7378	.446	1784	2314	.771	1143	2616	3759	1868	1874	764	316	1690	17	8368	102.0
KC-Omaha	82	3369	7342	.459	1628	2104	.774	1112	2554	3666	1744	1916	796	384	1791	22	8366	102.0
Capital	82	3480	7886	.441	1393	1869	.745	1286	2887	4173	1770	1746	703	441	1568	24	8353	101.9
New York	82	3478	7483	.465	1350	1738	.777	959	2725	3684	1937	1884	554	277	1463	14	8306	101.3
Philadelphia	82	3331	7702	.432	1633	2118	.771	1182	2626	3808	1799	1964	756	220	1665	25	8295	101.2
Cleveland	82	3420	7787	.439	1381	1788	.772	1275	2492	3767	2048	1925	598	293	1545	22	8221	100.3

TEAM STATISTICS—DEFENSE

Team	FIELD GOALS Made	Att.	Pct.	FREE THROWS Made	Att.	Pct.	REBOUNDS Off.	Def.	Tot.	MISCELLANEOUS Ast.	PF	Stl.	Blk. Sh.	Turn Over	Dq.	SCORING Pts.	Avg.	Dif.
New York	3292	7377	.446	1496	1974	.758	1042	2790	3832	1580	1792	479	248	1555	13	8080	98.5	+ 2.8
Chicago	3336	7246	.460	1425	1847	.772	1136	2734	3870	1830	2200	614	406	1880	34	8097	98.7	+ 3.3
Milwaukee	3311	7799	.425	1499	1969	.761	1269	2487	3756	1909	1707	719	312	1554	12	8121	99.0	+ 8.1
Detroit	3376	7499	.450	1475	1932	.763	1173	2632	3805	1980	1996	772	410	1822	30	8227	100.3	+ 4.1
Capital	3496	7760	.451	1239	1639	.756	1206	2915	4121	1900	1840	651	350	1651	9	8231	100.4	+ 1.5
Cleveland	3440	7342	.469	1696	2163	.784	1137	2802	3939	2120	1853	630	343	1654	27	8576	104.6	- 4.3
Boston	3561	8047	.443	1494	1936	.772	1131	2604	3735	1934	1858	540	309	1599	29	8616	105.1	+ 3.9
KC-Omaha	3580	7514	.476	1512	1950	.775	1210	2650	3860	1916	1907	723	373	1765	22	8672	105.8	- 3.8
Golden State	3619	7995	.453	1563	2054	.761	1227	2702	3929	2027	1826	714	465	1477	15	8801	107.3	+ 2.6
Philadelphia	3600	7685	.468	1617	2066	.783	1311	3107	4418	1930	1991	755	446	1830	23	8817	107.5	- 6.3
Houston	3551	7434	.478	1719	2337	.736	1162	2619	3781	2122	1994	707	355	1796	34	8819	107.5	- 0.2
Los Angeles	3667	8364	.438	1546	2044	.756	1525	2786	4311	2061	2135	797	430	1719	37	8880	108.3	+ 0.9
Seattle	3554	7675	.463	1875	2427	.773	1173	2932	4105	2255	2012	730	355	1796	34	8983	109.5	- 2.5
Atlanta	3573	7628	.468	1878	2386	.787	1142	2754	3896	2028	2128	823	388	1846	40	9024	110.0	- 1.4
Phoenix	3648	7809	.467	1843	2356	.782	1220	2773	3993	2180	2003	810	396	1637	25	9139	111.5	- 3.6
Portland	3664	7571	.484	1825	2299	.794	1197	2678	3875	2308	1961	866	415	1713	29	9153	111.6	- 4.8
Buffalo	3786	8106	.467	1592	2013	.791	1271	2733	4004	2256	1992	798	435	1763	37	9164	111.8	- 0.2

DQ = Individual players disqualified (fouled out of game).

INDIVIDUAL SCORING LEADERS
(Minimum 70 Games Played)

	G.	FG	FT	Pts.	Avg.		G.	FG	FT	Pts.	Avg.
McAdoo, Buff	74	901	459	2261	30.6	Lanier, Det	81	748	326	1822	22.5
Maravich, Atl	76	819	469	2107	27.7	Wicks, Port	75	685	314	1684	22.5
Abdul-Jabbar, Mil	81	948	295	2191	27.0	Chenier, Cap	76	697	274	1668	21.9
*Hudson, Atl	65	678	295	1651	25.4	Carr, Clev	81	748	279	1775	21.9
Goodrich, L.A.	82	784	508	2076	25.3	B. Love, Chi.	82	731	323	1785	21.8
Barry, G.S.	80	796	417	2009	25.1	Hayes, Cap	81	689	357	1735	21.4
Tomjanovich, Hou	80	788	385	1961	24.5	Carter, Phil	78	706	254	1666	21.4
Petrie, Port	73	740	291	1771	24.3	Frazier, N.Y.	80	674	295	1643	20.5
Haywood, Sea	75	694	373	1761	23.5	Russell, G.S.	82	738	208	1684	20.5
Havlicek, Bos	76	685	346	1716	22.6	Murphy, Hou	81	671	310	1652	20.4
						T. Van Arsdale, Phil.	78	614	298	1526	19.6

FIELD GOAL LEADERS
(Minimum 560 Attempts)

	FGM	FGA	Pct.
McAdoo, Buff	901	1647	.547
Abdul-Jabbar, Mil	948	1759	.539
Tomjanovich, Hou	788	1470	.536
Murphy, Hou	671	1285	.522
Beard, G.S.	316	617	.512
Ray, Chi	313	612	.511
D. Nelson, Bos	364	717	.508
Hairston, L.A.	385	759	.507
Lanier, Det. §	748	1483	.504
Dandridge, Mil	583	1158	.503

FREE THROW LEADERS
(Minimum 160 Attempts)

	FTM	FTA	Pct.
DiGregorio, Buff	174	193	.902
Barry, G.S.	417	464	.899
Mullins, G.S.	168	192	.875
C. Walker, Chi.	439	502	.875
Bradley, N.Y.	146	167	.874
Murphy, Hou	310	357	.868
Snyder, Sea	194	224	.866
Goodrich, L.A.	508	588	.864
F. Brown, Sea	195	226	.863
McMillian, Buff	325	379	.858

REBOUND LEADERS
(Minimum 70 games)

	G.	Off.	Def.	Tot.	Avg.
Hayes, Cap.	81	354	1109	1463	18.1
Cowens, Bos.	80	264	993	1257	15.7
McAdoo, Buff.	74	281	836	1117	15.1
Abdul-Jabbar, Mil.	81	287	891	1178	14.5
*Thurmond, G.S.	62	249	629	878	14.2
Hairston, L.A.	77	335	705	1040	13.5
Haywood, Sea.	75	318	689	1007	13.4
Lacey, KC-O	79	293	762	1055	13.4
Lanier, Det.	81	269	805	1074	13.3
Ray, Chi.	80	285	692	977	12.2
Heard, Buff.	81	270	677	947	11.7
D. Smith, Hou.	79	259	664	923	11.7

BLOCKED SHOTS LEADERS
(Minimum 70 games)

	G.	No.	Avg.
E. Smith, L.A.	81	393	4.85
Abdul-Jabbar, Mil.	81	283	3.49
McAdoo, Buff.	74	246	3.32
Lanier, Det.	81	247	3.04
Hayes, Cap.	81	240	2.96
*Thurmond, G.S.	62	179	2.89
Heard, Buff.	81	230	2.84
Lacey, KC-O	79	184	2.33
Ray, Chi.	80	173	2.16
*G.T. Johnson, G.S.	66	124	1.88
Haywood, Sea.	75	106	1.41
D. Smith, Hou.	79	104	1.32

ASSISTS LEADERS
(Minimum 70 games)

	G.	No.	Avg.
DiGregorio, Buff.	81	663	8.2
Murphy, Hou.	81	603	7.4
Wilkens, Clev.	74	522	7.1
Frazier, N.Y.	80	551	6.9
Bing, Det.	81	555	6.9
Van Lier, Chi.	80	548	6.9
Robertson, Mil.	70	446	6.4
Barry, G.S.	80	484	6.1
Havlicek, Bos.	76	447	5.9
K. Porter, Cap.	81	469	5.8

STEALS LEADERS
(Minimum 70 games)

	G.	No.	Avg.
Steele, Port.	81	217	2.68
Mix, Phil.	82	212	2.59
R. Smith, Buff.	82	203	2.48
*Hudson, Atl.	65	160	2.46
Sloan, Chi.	77	183	2.38
*Gilliam, Atl.	62	134	2.16
Barry, G.S.	80	169	2.11
Chenier, Cap.	76	155	2.04
Van Lier, Chi.	80	162	2.03
Frazier, N.Y.	80	161	2.01
Murphy, Hou.	81	157	1.94
Price, L.A.	82	157	1.91

*Does not qualify but would still rank among leaders if missing games were added.

RECORDS OF TEAMS BY MONTHS

Team	Oct. W-L	Nov. W-L	Dec. W-L	Jan. W-L	Feb. W-L	Mar. W-L	Total W-L
Atlanta	6-4	6-7	7-7	4-13	5-9	7-7	35-47
Boston	5-3	11-1	13-2	7-6	9-6	11-8	56-26
Buffalo	6-4	4-11	6-7	10-7	10-5	6-6	42-40
Capital	3-5	8-4	9-6	7-8	11-6	9-6	47-35
Chicago	7-2	11-4	10-6	8-6	11-4	7-6	54-28
Cleveland	2-7	7-9	5-11	5-9	4-11	6-6	29-53
Detroit	7-4	5-7	12-5	10-3	10-6	8-5	52-30
Golden State	4-3	9-4	4-10	10-5	10-5	7-11	44-38
Houston	4-7	4-8	4-12	6-10	8-4	6-9	32-50
K.C.-Omaha	4-6	2-14	8-7	7-8	6-8	6-6	33-49
Los Angeles	7-3	9-4	6-11	7-4	8-8	10-5	47-35
Milwaukee	9-1	12-3	9-4	10-3	9-7	10-5	59-23
New York	5-4	7-8	11-4	9-5	9-5	8-7	49-33
Philadelphia	2-7	6-8	3-12	4-8	5-11	5-11	25-57
Phoenix	2-8	5-8	8-8	6-7	4-12	5-9	30-52
Portland	5-4	5-9	7-8	2-11	2-14	6-9	27-55
Seattle	3-9	6-8	8-10	7-6	6-6	6-7	36-46
Totals	81	117	130	119	127	123	697

INTER-CLUB RECORDS—HOME, AWAY AND NEUTRAL COURT

	Home	Away	Neutral	Total
Atlanta	23-18	12-25	0-4	35-47
Boston	26-6	21-18	9-2	56-26
Buffalo	19-13	17-21	6-6	42-40
Capital	31-10	15-25	1-0	47-35
Chicago	32-9	21-19	1-0	54-28
Cleveland	18-23	11-28	0-2	29-53
Detroit	29-12	23-17	0-1	52-30
Golden State	23-18	20-20	1-0	44-38
Houston	18-23	13-25	1-2	32-50
K.C.-Omaha	20-21	13-28	0-0	33-49
Los Angeles	30-11	17-24	0-0	47-35
Milwaukee	31-7	24-16	4-0	59-23
New York	28-13	21-19	0-1	49-33
Philadelphia	14-23	9-30	2-4	25-57
Phoenix	24-17	6-34	0-1	30-52
Portland	22-19	5-34	0-2	27-55
Seattle	22-19	14-27	0-0	36-46

1973-74 STATISTICS

INDIVIDUAL STATISTICS

ATLANTA

Player	G.	Min.	FGM	FGA	Pct	FTM	FTA	Pct.	Off. Reb.	Def. Reb.	Tot. Reb.	Ast.	PF	Dsq.	Stl.	Blk. Sh.	Pts.	Avg.	Hi.
Maravich	76	2903	819	1791	.457	469	568	.826	98	276	374	396	261	4	111	13	2107	27.7	42
Hudson	65	2588	678	1356	.500	295	353	.836	126	224	350	213	205	3	160	29	1651	25.4	44
Gilliam	62	2003	384	846	.454	106	134	.791	61	206	267	355	190	5	134	18	874	14.1	35
Bellamy	77	2440	389	801	.486	233	383	.608	264	476	740	189	232	2	52	48	1011	13.1	34
J. Washington	73	2519	297	612	.485	134	196	.684	207	528	735	156	249	5	49	74	728	10.0	23
J. Brown	77	1715	277	632	.438	163	217	.751	177	264	441	114	239	10	29	16	717	9.3	25
D. Jones	74	1448	238	502	.474	116	156	.744	145	309	454	86	197	3	29	64	592	8.0	33
Bracey	75	1463	241	520	.463	69	96	.719	26	120	146	231	157	0	60	5	551	7.3	25
Wetzel	70	1232	107	252	.425	41	57	.719	39	131	170	138	147	1	73	19	255	3.6	17
Schlueter	57	547	63	135	.467	38	50	.760	54	101	155	45	84	0	25	22	164	2.9	12
Ingelsby	48	398	50	131	.382	29	37	.784	10	34	44	37	43	0	19	4	129	2.7	10
Tschogl	64	499	59	166	.355	10	17	.588	33	43	76	33	69	0	17	20	128	2.0	14

BOSTON

Player	G.	Min.	FGM	FGA	Pct	FTM	FTA	Pct.	Off. Reb.	Def. Reb.	Tot. Reb.	Ast.	PF	Dsq.	Stl.	Blk. Sh.	Pts.	Avg.	Hi.
Havlicek	76	3091	685	1502	.456	346	416	.832	138	349	487	447	196	1	95	32	1716	22.6	34
Cowens	80	3352	645	1475	.437	228	274	.832	264	993	1257	354	294	7	95	101	1518	19.0	35
White	82	3238	649	1445	.449	190	227	.837	100	251	351	448	185	1	105	5	1488	18.1	37
Silas	82	2599	340	772	.440	264	337	.783	334	581	915	186	246	3	63	20	944	11.5	31
D. Nelson	82	1748	364	717	.508	215	273	.788	90	255	345	162	189	1	19	16	943	11.5	29
Chaney	81	2258	348	750	.464	149	180	.828	210	168	378	176	247	7	83	62	845	10.4	26
Westphal	82	1165	238	475	.501	112	153	.732	49	94	143	171	173	1	39	34	588	7.2	28
Kuberski	78	985	157	368	.427	86	111	.775	96	141	237	38	125	0	7	7	400	5.1	21
Hankinson	28	163	50	103	.485	10	13	.769	22	28	50	4	18	0	3	1	110	3.9	13
Downing	24	137	21	64	.328	22	38	.579	14	25	39	11	33	0	5	0	64	2.7	4
A. Williams	67	617	73	168	.435	27	32	.844	20	95	115	163	100	0	44	3	173	2.6	14
Finkel	60	427	60	130	.462	28	43	.651	41	94	135	27	62	1	3	7	148	2.5	14

BUFFALO

Player	G.	Min.	FGM	FGA	Pct	FTM	FTA	Pct.	Off. Reb.	Def. Reb.	Tot. Reb.	Ast.	PF	Dsq.	Stl.	Blk. Sh.	Pts.	Avg.	Hi.
McAdoo	74	3185	901	1647	.547	459	579	.793	281	836	1117	170	252	3	88	246	2261	30.6	52
McMillian	82	3322	600	1214	.494	325	379	.858	216	394	610	256	186	0	129	26	1525	18.6	48
R. Smith	82	2745	531	1079	.492	205	288	.712	87	228	315	383	261	4	203	4	1267	15.5	32
Heard	81	2889	524	1205	.435	191	294	.650	270	677	947	180	300	3	136	230	1239	15.3	36
DiGregorio	31	2910	530	1260	.421	174	193	.902	48	171	219	663	242	2	59	9	1234	15.2	32
Marin (Tot.)	74	1782	355	709	.501	153	179	.855	59	109	168	227	167	213	5	46	26	863	11.7	26
Marin (Buff.)	29	680	145	266	.545	71	81	.877	30	92	122	46	93	3	23	18	361	13.4	24
Kauffman	74	1304	171	366	.467	107	150	.713	97	229	326	142	155	0	37	18	449	6.1	16
Guokas (Tot.)	75	1871	195	396	.492	39	60	.650	31	90	121	238	150	3	54	21	429	5.7	23
G'kas (Buff.)	27	549	61	110	.555	10	20	.500	12	28	40	69	56	1	19	6	132	4.9	23
Wohl	41	606	60	150	.400	42	60	.700	7	22	29	127	72	1	33	1	162	4.0	16
Charles	59	693	88	185	.476	53	79	.671	25	40	65	54	91	0	31	10	229	3.9	16
Winfield	36	433	37	105	.352	33	52	.635	19	24	43	47	42	0	15	5	107	3.0	9
Kunnert	39	340	49	101	.485	11	16	.688	43	63	106	25	83	0	5	25	109	2.8	9
Macaluso	30	112	19	44	.432	10	17	.588	10	15	25	3	31	0	7	1	48	1.6	8
Ruffner	20	51	11	27	.407	8	13	.615	4	7	11	0	10	0	1	1	30	1.5	7
Garvin	6	11	1	4	.250	0	0	.000	1	4	5	0	1	0	0	0	2	0.3	2

CAPITAL

Player	G.	Min.	FGM	FGA	Pct	FTM	FTA	Pct.	Off. Reb.	Def. Reb.	Tot. Reb.	Ast.	PF	Dsq.	Stl.	Blk. Sh.	Pts.	Avg.	Hi.
Chenier	76	2942	697	1607	.434	274	334	.820	114	274	388	239	135	0	155	67	1668	21.9	38
Hayes	81	3602	689	1627	.423	357	495	.721	354	1109	1463	163	252	1	86	240	1735	21.4	43
Riordan	81	3230	577	1223	.472	136	174	.782	120	260	380	264	237	2	102	14	1290	15.9	33
K. Porter	81	2339	477	997	.478	180	249	.723	79	100	179	469	319	14	95	9	1134	14.0	28
Clark	56	1786	315	675	.467	103	131	.786	44	97	141	285	122	0	59	6	733	13.1	28
Weath'spoon	65	1216	199	483	.412	96	139	.691	133	264	397	38	179	1	48	16	494	7.6	19
Unseld	56	1727	146	333	.438	36	55	.655	152	365	517	159	121	1	56	16	328	5.9	14
L. Nelson	49	556	93	215	.433	53	73	.726	26	44	70	52	62	0	31	2	239	4.9	17
D. St'lworth	45	458	75	187	.401	47	55	.855	52	73	125	25	61	0	28	4	197	4.4	19
Wesley	39	400	71	151	.470	26	43	.605	63	73	136	14	74	1	9	20	168	4.3	20
Leaks	53	845	79	232	.341	58	83	.699	94	150	244	25	95	1	10	39	216	4.1	19
Kozelko	49	573	59	133	.444	23	32	.719	52	72	124	25	82	3	21	7	141	2.9	15
Rinaldi	7	63	8	22	.136	3	4	.750	2	5	7	10	7	0	3	1	9	1.3	3
T. Patterson	2	8	0	1	.000	1	2	.500	1	1	2	2	0	0	0	0	1	0.5	1

1973-74 STATISTICS

CHICAGO

Player	G.	Min.	FGM	FGA	Pct.	FTM	FTA	Pct.	Off. Reb.	Def. Reb.	Tot. Reb.	Ast.	PF	Dsq.	Stl.	Blk. Sh.	Pts.	Avg.	Hi.
B. Love	82	3292	731	1752	.417	323	395	.818	183	309	492	130	221	1	84	28	1785	21.8	43
C. Walker	82	2661	572	1178	.486	439	502	.875	131	275	406	200	201	1	68	4	1583	19.3	39
Van Lier	80	2863	427	1051	.406	288	370	.778	114	263	377	548	282	4	162	7	1142	14.3	30
Sloan	77	2860	412	921	.447	194	273	.711	150	406	556	149	273	3	183	10	1018	13.2	25
H. Porter	73	1229	296	658	.450	92	115	.800	86	199	285	32	116	0	23	39	684	9.4	25
Ray	80	2632	313	612	.511	121	199	.608	285	692	977	246	281	5	58	173	747	9.3	24
Weiss	79	1708	263	564	.466	142	170	.835	32	71	103	303	156	0	104	12	668	8.5	24
R. Garrett	41	373	68	184	.370	21	32	.656	11	39	70	11	43	0	5	9	157	3.8	16
Boerwinkle	46	602	58	119	.487	42	60	.700	53	160	213	94	80	0	16	18	158	3.4	16
Adelman	55	618	64	170	.376	54	76	.711	16	53	69	56	63	0	36	1	182	3.3	12
Hummer	18	186	23	46	.500	14	28	.500	13	24	37	13	30	0	3	1	60	3.3	12
Awtrey	68	756	65	123	.528	54	94	.574	49	125	174	86	128	3	22	14	184	2.7	10

CLEVELAND

Player	G.	Min.	FGM	FGA	Pct.	FTM	FTA	Pct.	Off. Reb.	Def. Reb.	Tot. Reb.	Ast.	PF	Dsq.	Stl.	Blk. Sh.	Pts.	Avg.	Hi.
Carr	81	3100	748	1682	.445	279	326	.856	139	150	289	305	189	2	92	14	1775	21.9	39
Wilkens	74	2483	462	994	.465	289	361	.801	80	197	277	522	165	2	97	17	1213	16.4	34
B. Smith	82	2612	536	1179	.455	139	169	.822	134	301	435	198	242	4	89	30	1211	14.8	34
D. Davis	76	2477	376	862	.436	197	274	.719	174	470	644	186	291	6	63	74	949	12.5	25
S. Patterson	76	1910	262	599	.437	69	112	.616	223	396	619	165	193	3	48	58	593	7.8	22
Rule	26	540	76	192	.396	34	46	.739	43	60	103	47	71	0	12	10	186	7.2	22
Cleamons	81	1642	236	545	.433	93	133	.699	63	167	230	227	152	1	61	17	565	7.0	21
Brewer	82	1862	210	548	.383	80	123	.650	207	317	524	149	192	1	46	35	500	6.1	18
Clemens	71	913	163	346	.471	62	73	.849	42	124	166	80	136	2	36	2	388	5.5	18
Foster	58	649	112	288	.389	54	64	.844	43	65	108	62	79	0	19	6	278	4.8	21
Witte	57	728	105	243	.432	46	62	.742	80	147	227	41	91	0	8	22	256	4.5	17
Warren	69	790	132	291	.454	35	41	.854	42	86	128	62	117	1	27	6	299	4.3	24
Warner	5	49	2	13	.154	4	4	1.000	5	12	17	4	7	0	0	2	8	1.6	4

DETROIT

Player	G.	Min.	FGM	FGA	Pct.	FTM	FTA	Pct.	Off. Reb.	Def. Reb.	Tot. Reb.	Ast.	PF	Dsq.	Stl.	Blk. Sh.	Pts.	Avg.	Hi.
Lanier	81	3047	748	1483	.504	326	409	.797	269	805	1074	343	273	7	110	247	1822	22.5	45
Bing	81	3124	582	1336	.436	356	438	.813	108	173	281	555	216	1	109	17	1520	18.8	33
Rowe	82	2499	380	769	.494	118	169	.698	167	348	515	136	177	1	49	36	878	10.7	28
Adams	74	2249	303	742	.408	153	201	.761	133	315	448	141	242	2	110	12	759	10.3	25
Trapp	82	1489	333	693	.481	99	134	.739	97	216	313	81	226	2	47	33	765	9.3	22
Lantz	50	980	154	361	.427	139	164	.848	34	79	113	97	79	0	38	3	447	8.9	24
Mengelt	77	1555	249	558	.446	182	229	.795	40	166	206	148	164	2	68	7	680	8.8	30
Norwood	74	1178	247	484	.510	95	143	.664	95	134	229	58	156	2	60	9	589	8.0	29
Ford	82	2059	264	595	.444	57	77	.740	109	195	304	279	159	1	148	14	585	7.1	24
J. Davis	78	947	117	283	.413	90	139	.647	102	191	293	86	158	1	39	30	324	4.2	15
Nash	35	281	41	115	.357	24	39	.615	31	43	74	14	35	0	3	10	106	3.0	16
Kelso	46	298	35	96	.365	15	22	.682	15	16	31	18	45	0	12	1	85	1.8	8

GOLDEN STATE

Player	G.	Min.	FGM	FGA	Pct.	FTM	FTA	Pct.	Off. Reb.	Def. Reb.	Tot. Reb.	Ast.	PF	Dsq.	Stl.	Blk. Sh.	Pts.	Avg.	Hi.
Barry	80	2918	796	1746	.456	417	464	.899	103	437	540	484	265	4	169	40	2009	25.1	64
Russell	82	2574	738	1531	.482	208	249	.835	142	211	353	192	194	1	54	19	1684	20.5	49
Mullins	77	2498	541	1144	.473	168	192	.875	86	190	276	305	214	2	69	22	1250	16.2	32
Thurmond	62	2463	308	694	.444	191	287	.666	249	629	878	165	179	4	41	179	807	13.0	31
J. Barnett	77	1689	350	755	.464	184	226	.814	76	146	222	209	146	1	56	11	884	11.5	30
Beard	79	2134	316	617	.512	173	234	.739	136	253	389	300	241	11	105	9	805	10.2	30
C. Johnson	59	1051	194	468	.415	38	55	.691	49	126	175	102	111	1	62	7	426	7.2	20
G.T. Johnson	66	1291	173	358	.483	59	107	.551	190	332	522	73	176	3	35	124	405	6.1	23
C. Lee	54	1642	129	284	.454	62	107	.579	188	410	598	68	179	3	27	17	320	5.9	14
Dickey	66	930	115	233	.494	51	66	.773	123	216	339	54	112	1	17	15	281	4.3	17
J. Ellis	50	515	61	190	.321	18	31	.581	37	85	122	37	76	2	33	9	140	2.8	17

HOUSTON

Player	G.	Min.	FGM	FGA	Pct.	FTM	FTA	Pct.	Off. Reb.	Def. Reb.	Tot. Reb.	Ast.	PF	Dsq.	Stl.	Blk. Sh.	Pts.	Avg.	Hi.
Tomjanovich	80	3227	788	1470	.536	385	454	.848	230	487	717	250	230	0	89	66	1961	24.5	42
Murphy	81	2922	671	1285	.522	310	357	.868	51	137	188	603	310	8	157	4	1652	20.4	39
Newlin	76	2591	510	1139	.448	380	444	.856	77	185	262	363	259	5	87	9	1400	18.4	36
D. Smith	79	2459	336	732	.459	193	240	.804	259	664	923	166	227	3	80	104	865	10.9	27
Marin	47	1102	210	443	.474	82	98	.837	29	77	106	121	120	2	23	8	502	10.7	26

1973-74 STATISTICS

Player	G.	Min.	FGM	FGA	Pct.	FTM	FTA	Pct.	Off. Reb.	Def. Reb.	Tot. Reb.	Ast.	PF	Dsq.	Stl.	Blk. Sh.	Pts.	Avg.	Hi.
Meely	77	1754	330	773	.427	90	140	.643	103	336	439	124	234	5	53	77	750	9.7	22
Ratleff	81	1773	254	585	.434	103	129	.798	93	193	286	181	182	2	90	27	611	7.5	18
Guokas	39	1007	93	203	.458	21	28	.750	17	43	60	133	73	1	27	14	207	5.3	14
Coleman	58	1075	128	250	.512	47	74	.635	81	171	252	76	162	4	37	20	303	5.2	19
Moore	13	313	32	69	.464	4	8	.500	20	64	84	18	37	2	10	18	68	5.2	14
Wohl (Tot.)	67	1055	121	277	.437	75	102	.735	11	35	46	236	136	3	76	2	317	4.7	18
Wohl (Hou.)	26	449	61	127	.480	33	42	.786	4	13	17	109	64	2	43	1	155	6.0	18
J. Walker	3	38	7	12	.583	0	1	.000	0	2	2	4	4	0	0	0	14	4.7	6
R.Riley(Tot.)	48	591	81	202	.401	24	38	.632	48	129	177	37	95	0	18	24	186	3.9	15
R.Riley(Hou.)	36	421	57	145	.393	10	14	.714	35	86	121	29	68	0	15	22	124	3.4	13
Kunnert(Tot.)	64	701	105	215	.488	21	33	.636	83	134	217	43	151	1	10	54	231	3.6	12
K'nert (Hou.)	25	361	56	114	.491	10	17	.588	40	71	111	18	68	1	5	29	122	4.9	12
G.E. Johnson	26	238	23	51	.451	8	17	.471	20	41	61	9	46	1	8	8	54	2.1	8
McKenzie	11	112	7	24	.292	6	8	.750	3	13	16	6	17	0	3	0	20	1.8	9
McCracken	4	13	1	4	.250	0	0	.000	1	5	6	2	3	0	0	0	2	0.5	2

K. C.-OMAHA

Player	G.	Min.	FGM	FGA	Pct.	FTM	FTA	Pct.	Off. Reb.	Def. Reb.	Tot. Reb.	Ast.	PF	Dsq.	Stl.	Blk. Sh.	Pts.	Avg.	Hi.
J.W'ker (Tot.)	75	2958	582	1240	.469	273	333	.820	39	165	204	307	170	0	81	9	1437	19.2	38
J.W'er(KC-O)	72	2920	575	1228	.468	273	332	.822	39	163	202	303	166	0	81	9	1423	19.8	38
Archibald	35	1272	222	492	.451	173	211	.820	21	64	85	266	76	0	56	7	617	17.6	42
N. Williams	82	2513	538	1165	.462	193	236	.818	118	226	344	182	290	5	149	34	1269	15.5	30
Lacey	79	3107	467	982	.476	185	247	.749	293	762	1055	299	254	3	126	184	1119	14.2	26
Kojis	77	2091	400	836	.478	210	272	.772	126	257	383	110	157	2	77	15	1010	13.1	30
Behagen	80	2059	357	827	.432	162	212	.764	188	379	567	134	291	9	56	37	876	11.0	27
Guokas	9	315	41	83	.494	8	12	.667	2	19	21	36	21	1	8	1	90	10.0	18
Block	82	1777	275	634	.434	164	206	.796	129	260	389	94	229	2	68	35	714	8.7	27
McNeill	54	516	106	220	.482	99	140	.707	60	86	146	24	76	0	35	6	311	5.8	21
R. Riley	12	170	24	57	.421	14	24	.583	13	43	56	8	27	0	3	2	62	5.2	15
D'Antoni	52	989	107	266	.402	33	47	.702	24	69	93	123	112	0	75	15	247	4.8	15
Durrett	45	462	86	176	.489	42	69	.609	28	50	78	19	68	0	13	5	214	4.8	24
Komives	44	830	78	192	.406	33	38	.868	10	33	43	97	83	0	32	3	189	4.3	18
Moore (Tot.)	78	946	120	240	.500	39	62	.629	80	204	284	65	99	2	26	49	279	3.6	15
Mo're (KC-O)	65	633	88	171	.515	35	54	.648	60	140	200	47	62	0	16	31	211	3.2	15
Manakas	5	45	4	10	.400	4	4	1.000	0	3	3	2	4	0	1	0	12	2.4	4
Thigpen	1	2	1	3	.333	0	0	.000	1	0	1	0	0	0	0	0	2	2.0	2
Ratliff	2	4	0	0	.000	0	0	.000	0	0	0	0	0	0	0	0	0	0.0	0

LOS ANGELES

Player	G.	Min.	FGM	FGA	Pct.	FTM	FTA	Pct.	Off. Reb.	Def. Reb.	Tot. Reb.	Ast.	PF	Dsq.	Stl.	Blk. Sh.	Pts.	Avg.	Hi.
Goodrich	82	3061	784	1574	.442	508	588	.864	95	155	250	427	227	3	126	12	2076	25.3	49
West	31	967	232	519	.447	165	198	.833	30	86	116	206	80	0	81	23	629	20.3	35
Price	82	2628	538	1197	.449	187	234	.799	120	258	378	369	229	2	157	29	1263	15.4	31
Hairston	77	2634	385	759	.507	343	445	.771	335	705	1040	208	264	2	64	17	1113	14.5	29
H'kins (Tot.)	79	2761	404	807	.501	191	251	.761	176	389	565	407	223	4	113	81	999	12.6	26
H'kins (L.A.)	71	2538	368	733	.502	173	224	.772	162	360	522	379	203	1	105	78	909	12.8	26
E. Smith	81	2922	434	949	.457	147	249	.590	204	702	906	150	309	8	71	393	1015	12.5	37
P. Riley	72	1361	287	667	.430	110	144	.764	38	90	128	148	173	1	54	3	684	9.5	22
Bridges	65	1812	216	513	.421	116	164	.707	193	306	499	148	219	3	58	31	548	8.4	28
S. Love	45	698	119	278	.428	49	64	.766	54	116	170	48	132	3	28	20	287	5.6	21
K. Wash'ton	45	400	73	151	.483	26	49	.531	62	85	147	19	77	0	21	18	172	3.8	18
Counts	45	499	61	167	.365	24	33	.727	56	90	146	54	85	2	20	23	146	3.2	16
Hawthorne	33	229	38	93	.409	30	48	.625	16	16	32	23	33	1	9	6	106	3.2	13
Grant	3	6	1	4	.250	1	3	.333	0	1	1	0	1	0	0	0	3	1.0	3

MILWAUKEE

Player	G.	Min.	FGM	FGA	Pct.	FTM	FTA	Pct.	Off. Reb.	Def. Reb.	Tot. Reb.	Ast.	PF	Dsq.	Stl.	Blk. Sh.	Pts.	Avg.	Hi.
Abd.-Jabbar	81	3548	948	1759	.539	295	420	.702	287	891	1178	386	238	2	112	283	2191	27.0	44
Dandridge	71	2521	583	1158	.503	175	214	.818	117	362	479	201	271	4	111	41	1341	18.9	32
Allen	72	2388	526	1062	.495	216	274	.788	89	202	291	374	215	2	137	22	1268	17.6	39
Robertson	70	2477	338	772	.438	212	254	.835	71	208	279	446	132	0	77	4	888	12.7	24
McGlocklin	79	1910	329	693	.475	72	80	.900	33	106	139	241	128	1	43	7	730	9.2	29
Perry	81	2386	325	729	.446	78	134	.582	242	461	703	183	301	8	104	97	728	9.0	23
R. Will'ms	71	1130	192	393	.489	60	68	.882	19	50	69	153	114	1	49	2	444	6.3	21
W'ner (Tot.)	72	1405	174	349	.499	85	114	.746	106	291	397	71	204	8	27	42	433	6.0	21
W'ner (Mil.)	67	1356	172	336	.512	81	110	.736	101	279	380	67	197	8	27	40	425	6.3	21
Mick Davis	73	1012	169	335	.504	93	112	.830	78	146	224	87	94	0	27	5	431	5.9	22
Driscoll	64	697	88	187	.471	30	46	.652	73	126	199	54	121	0	21	16	206	3.2	15

Player	G.	Min.	FGM	FGA	Pct.	FTM	FTA	Pct.	Off. Reb.	Def. Reb.	Tot. Reb.	Ast.	PF	Dsq.	Stl.	Blk. Sh.	Pts.	Avg.	Hi.
D. Gar't (Tot.)	40	326	43	126	.341	15	19	.789	15	25	40	23	56	0	10	1	101	2.5	14
D. Gar't (Mil.)	15	87	11	35	.314	5	6	.833	9	5	14	9	15	0	3	0	27	1.8	8
R. Lee	36	166	38	94	.404	11	16	.688	16	24	40	20	29	0	11	0	87	2.4	10
Terry	7	32	4	12	.333	0	0	.000	1	2	3	4	4	0	2	0	8	1.1	4
Cunningham	8	45	3	6	.500	0	7	.000	1	15	16	0	5	0	2	2	6	0.8	4

NEW YORK

Player	G.	Min.	FGM	FGA	Pct.	FTM	FTA	Pct.	Off. Reb.	Def. Reb.	Tot. Reb.	Ast.	PF	Dsq.	Stl.	Blk. Sh.	Pts.	Avg.	Hi.
Frazier	80	3338	674	1429	.472	295	352	.838	120	416	536	551	212	2	161	15	1643	20.5	44
DeBusschere	71	2699	559	1212	.461	164	217	.756	134	623	757	253	222	2	67	39	1282	18.1	41
Bradley	82	2813	502	1112	.451	146	167	.874	59	194	253	242	278	2	42	15	1150	14.0	31
Monroe	41	1194	240	513	.468	93	113	.823	22	99	121	110	97	0	34	19	573	14.0	29
Jackson	82	2050	361	757	.477	191	246	.776	123	355	478	134	277	7	42	67	913	11.1	30
Reed	19	500	84	184	.457	42	53	.792	47	94	141	30	49	0	12	21	210	11.1	25
Meminger	78	2079	274	539	.508	103	160	.644	125	156	281	162	161	0	62	8	651	8.3	27
Bibby	66	986	210	465	.452	73	88	.830	48	85	133	91	123	0	65	2	493	7.5	22
Gianelli	70	1423	208	434	.479	92	121	.760	110	233	343	77	159	1	23	42	508	7.3	25
Lucas	73	1627	194	420	.462	67	96	.698	62	312	374	230	134	0	28	24	455	6.2	17
D. Barnett	5	58	10	26	.385	2	3	.667	1	3	4	6	2	0	1	0	22	4.4	10
Wingo	60	536	82	172	.477	48	76	.632	72	94	166	25	85	0	7	14	212	3.5	14
D. Garrett	25	239	32	91	.352	10	13	.769	0	16	26	14	41	0	7	1	74	3.0	14
Mel Davis	30	167	33	95	.347	12	16	.750	17	37	54	8	36	0	3	4	78	2.6	12
Riker	17	57	13	29	.448	12	17	.706	9	6	15	3	6	0	0	0	38	2.2	11
McGuire	2	10	2	4	.500	0	0	.000	0	2	2	1	2	0	0	0	4	2.0	2
Bell	1	4	0	1	.000	0	0	.000	0	0	0	0	0	0	0	0	0	0.0	0

PHILADELPHIA

Player	G.	Min.	FGM	FGA	Pct.	FTM	FTA	Pct.	Off. Reb.	Def. Reb.	Tot. Reb.	Ast.	PF	Dsq.	Stl.	Blk. Sh.	Pts.	Avg.	Hi.
Carter	78	3044	706	1641	.430	254	358	.709	82	289	371	443	276	4	113	23	1666	21.4	35
T. V'Arsdale	78	3041	614	1433	.428	298	350	.851	88	305	393	202	300	6	62	3	1526	19.6	35
Mix	82	2969	495	1042	.475	228	288	.792	305	559	864	152	305	9	212	37	1218	14.9	38
L. Jones	72	1876	263	622	.423	197	235	.838	71	113	184	230	116	0	85	18	723	10.0	22
L. Ellis	81	2831	326	722	.452	147	196	.750	292	598	890	189	224	2	86	87	799	9.9	24
Boyd	75	1818	286	712	.402	141	195	.723	16	77	93	249	173	1	60	9	713	9.5	24
Collins	25	436	72	194	.371	55	72	.764	7	39	46	40	65	1	13	2	199	8.0	17
Kimball	75	1592	216	456	.474	127	185	.686	185	367	552	73	199	1	49	23	559	7.5	22
May	56	812	152	367	.414	89	102	.873	25	111	136	63	137	0	25	8	393	7.0	28
Cannon	19	335	49	127	.386	19	28	.679	16	20	36	52	48	0	7	4	117	6.2	17
Bristow	55	643	108	270	.400	42	57	.737	68	99	167	92	68	1	29	1	258	4.7	20
Freeman	35	265	39	103	.379	28	41	.683	22	32	54	14	42	0	12	1	106	3.0	11
Rackley	9	68	5	13	.385	8	11	.727	5	17	22	0	11	0	3	4	18	2.0	5

PHOENIX

Player	G.	Min.	FGM	FGA	Pct.	FTM	FTA	Pct.	Off. Reb.	Def. Reb.	Tot. Reb.	Ast.	PF	Dsq.	Stl.	Blk. Sh.	Pts.	Avg.	Hi.
Scott	52	2003	538	1171	.459	246	315	.781	64	158	222	271	194	6	99	22	1322	25.4	44
D.VanArsdale	78	2832	514	1028	.500	361	423	.853	66	155	221	324	241	2	96	17	1389	17.8	37
Walk	82	2549	573	1245	.460	235	297	.791	235	602	837	331	255	9	73	57	1381	16.8	32
Erickson	66	2033	393	824	.477	177	221	.801	94	320	414	205	193	3	63	20	963	14.6	40
Hawkins	8	223	36	74	.486	18	27	.667	14	29	43	28	20	0	8	3	90	11.3	21
Haskins	81	1882	364	792	.460	171	203	.842	78	144	222	259	166	1	81	16	899	11.1	36
Bantom	76	1982	314	787	.399	141	213	.662	172	347	519	163	289	15	50	47	769	10.1	26
Calhoun	77	2207	268	581	.461	98	129	.760	115	292	407	135	253	4	71	30	634	8.2	25
Melchionni	69	1251	202	439	.460	92	107	.860	46	96	142	142	85	1	41	9	496	7.2	23
Chamberlain	28	367	57	130	.438	39	56	.696	33	47	80	37	74	2	20	12	153	5.5	19
Christian	81	1244	140	288	.486	106	151	.702	85	254	339	98	191	3	19	32	386	4.8	21
Green	72	1103	129	317	.407	38	68	.559	85	265	350	43	150	1	32	18	296	4.1	14
Owens	17	101	21	39	.538	11	14	.786	1	8	9	15	6	0	5	0	53	3.1	10
Reaves	7	38	6	11	.545	4	11	.364	2	6	8	1	6	0	0	2	16	2.3	4

PORTLAND

Player	G.	Min.	FGM	FGA	Pct.	FTM	FTA	Pct.	Off. Reb.	Def. Reb.	Tot. Reb.	Ast.	PF	Dsq.	Stl.	Blk. Sh.	Pts.	Avg.	Hi.
Petrie	73	2800	740	1537	.481	291	341	.853	64	144	208	315	199	2	84	15	1771	24.3	43
Wicks	75	2853	685	1492	.459	314	412	.762	194	488	684	326	214	2	90	63	1684	22.5	38
J. Johnson	69	2287	459	990	.464	212	261	.812	160	355	515	284	221	1	69	29	1130	16.4	32
Roberson	69	2060	364	797	.457	205	316	.649	251	450	701	133	252	4	65	55	933	13.5	37
Steele	81	2648	325	680	.478	135	171	.789	89	221	310	323	295	10	217	32	785	9.7	28
Neal	80	1517	246	502	.490	117	168	.696	150	344	494	89	190	0	45	73	609	7.6	22
Fryer	80	1674	226	491	.460	107	135	.793	60	99	159	279	187	1	92	10	559	7.0	27
O. Johnson	79	1718	209	434	.482	77	94	.819	116	208	324	167	179	2	60	30	495	6.3	23

The hustle and board play of Dave Cowens helped lift the Boston Celtics to the top of the NBA in 1973-74.

Player	G.	Min.	FGM	FGA	Pct.	FTM	FTA	Pct.	Off. Reb.	Def. Reb.	Tot. Reb.	Ast.	PF	Dsq.	Stl.	Blk. Sh.	Pts.	Avg.	Hi.
Layton	22	327	55	112	.491	14	26	.538	7	26	33	51	45	0	9	1	124	5.6	19
Verga	21	216	42	93	.452	20	32	.625	11	7	18	17	22	0	12	0	104	5.0	22
Martin	50	538	101	232	.435	42	66	.636	74	107	181	20	90	0	7	26	244	4.9	17
C. Davis	8	90	14	40	.350	3	4	.750	2	9	11	11	7	0	2	0	31	3.9	11
G. Smith	67	878	99	228	.434	48	79	.608	65	124	189	78	126	1	41	6	246	3.7	12
Sibley	28	124	20	56	.357	6	7	.857	9	16	25	13	23	0	4	1	46	1.6	8

SEATTLE

Player	G.	Min.	FGM	FGA	Pct.	FTM	FTA	Pct.	Off. Reb.	Def. Reb.	Tot. Reb.	Ast.	PF	Dsq.	Stl.	Blk. Sh.	Pts.	Avg.	Hi.
Haywood	75	3039	694	1520	.457	373	458	.814	318	689	1007	240	198	2	65	106	1761	23.5	37
Snyder	74	2670	572	1189	.481	194	224	.866	90	216	306	265	257	4	90	26	1338	18.1	41
F. Brown	82	2501	578	1226	.471	195	226	.863	114	287	401	414	276	6	136	18	1351	16.5	58
Brisker	35	717	178	396	.449	82	100	.820	59	87	146	56	70	0	28	6	438	12.5	47
Fox	78	2179	322	673	.478	241	293	.823	244	470	714	227	247	5	56	21	885	11.3	29
Gibbs	71	1528	302	700	.431	162	201	.806	91	132	223	79	195	1	39	18	766	10.8	30
Watts	62	1424	198	510	.388	100	155	.645	72	110	182	351	207	8	115	13	496	8.0	24
McIntosh	69	2056	223	573	.389	65	107	.607	111	250	361	94	178	4	52	29	511	7.4	22
Hum'r (Tot.)	53	1119	144	305	.472	59	124	.476	84	199	283	107	119	0	28	22	347	6.5	16
Hum'r (Sea.)	35	933	121	259	.467	45	96	.469	71	175	246	94	89	0	25	21	287	8.2	16
B. St'lworth	67	1019	188	479	.392	48	77	.623	51	123	174	33	129	0	21	12	424	6.3	23
McDaniels	27	439	63	173	.364	23	43	.535	51	77	128	24	48	0	7	15	149	5.5	29
Abd.-Rahman	49	571	76	180	.422	34	45	.756	18	39	57	122	78	0	26	6	186	3.8	24
M. Williams	53	505	62	149	.416	41	63	.651	19	28	47	103	82	1	25	0	165	3.1	22
Marshall	13	174	7	29	.241	3	7	.429	14	23	37	4	20	0	4	3	17	1.3	5

NWT—Not With Team.
Dsq.—Individual Players Disqualified (Fouled Out of Game).

1973-74 PLAYOFF RESULTS

CONFERENCE SEMI-FINAL SERIES

EASTERN CONFERENCE

Boston Defeated Buffalo, 4-2
Mar. 30—Buffalo 97 at Boston 107
Apr. 2—Boston 105 at Buffalo 115
Apr. 3—Buffalo 107 at Boston 120
Apr. 6—Boston 102 at Buffalo 104
Apr. 9—Buffalo 97 at Boston 100
Apr. 12—Boston 106 at Buffalo 104

New York Defeated Capital, 4-3
Mar. 29—Capital 91 at New York 102
Mar. 31—New York 87 at Capital 99
Apr. 2—Capital 88 at New York 79
Apr. 5—New York 101 at Capital ....93 (ot)
Apr. 7—Capital 105 at New York 106
Apr. 10—New York 92 at Capital 109
Apr. 12—Capital 81 at New York 91

WESTERN CONFERENCE

Milwaukee Defeated Los Angeles, 4-1
Mar. 29—Los Angeles 95 at Milwaukee 99
Mar. 31—Los Angeles 90 at Milwaukee 109
Apr. 2—Milwaukee 96 at Los Angeles 98
Apr. 4—Milwaukee 112 at Los Angeles 90
Apr. 7—Los Angeles 92 at Milwaukee 114

Chicago Defeated Detroit, 4-3
Mar. 30—Detroit 97 at Chicago 88
Apr. 1—Chicago 108 at Detroit 103
Apr. 5—Detroit 83 at Chicago 84
Apr. 7—Chicago 87 at Detroit 102
Apr. 9—Detroit 94 at Chicago 98
Apr. 11—Chicago 88 at Detroit 92
Apr. 13—Detroit 94 at Chicago 96

CONFERENCE FINAL SERIES

EASTERN CONFERENCE FINALS

Boston Defeated New York, 4-1
Apr. 14—New York 88 at Boston 113
Apr. 16—Boston 111 at New York 99
Apr. 19—New York 103 at Boston 100
Apr. 21—Boston 98 at New York 91
Apr. 24—New York 94 at Boston 105

WESTERN CONFERENCE FINALS

Milwaukee Defeated Chicago, 4-0
Apr. 16—Chicago 85 at Milwaukee 101
Apr. 18—Milwaukee 113 at Chicago 111
Apr. 20—Chicago 90 at Milwaukee 113
Apr. 22—Milwaukee 115 at Chicago 99

CHAMPIONSHIP SERIES

Boston Defeated Milwaukee, 4-3
Apr. 28—Boston 98 at Milwaukee 83
Apr. 30—Boston 96 at Milwaukee ....105 (ot)
May 3—Milwaukee 83 at Boston 95
May 5—Milwaukee 97 at Boston 89
May 7—Boston 96 at Milwaukee 87
May 10—Milwaukee 102 at Boston ....101 (2 ot)
May 12—Boston 102 at Milwaukee 87

1972-73 STATISTICS

1972-73 NBA CHAMPION NEW YORK KNICKERBOCKERS

Seated from left: Henry Bibby, Walt Frazier, President Ned Irish, Chairman of the Board Irving Mitchell Felt, General Manager and Coach Red Holzman, Earl Monroe, Dick Barnett. Standing: Bill Bradley, Phil Jackson, John Gianelli, Dave DeBusschere, Willis Reed, Jerry Lucas, Tom Riker, Dean Meminger, Trainer Danny Whalen, Harthorne Wingo (inset).

FINAL STANDINGS AND TEAM FIGURES

Team	Atl.	Balt.	Bos.	Buf.	Chi.	Clv.	Det.	G.S.	Hou.	KC-O.	L.A.	Mil.	N.Y.	Phil.	Pho.	Prt.	Sea.	W.	L.	Pct.	G.B.
ATLANTIC DIVISION																					
Boston	5	5	..	7	3	5	3	3	5	3	4	2	4	7	4	4	4	68	14	.829	....
New York	3	3	4	6	1	6	3	2	5	4	2	2	..	6	3	3	4	57	25	.695	11
Buffalo	1	1	..	..	2	1	1	..	1	1	..	1	7	1	2	2	2	21	61	.256	47
Philadelphia	..	1	..	1	..	..	1	1	1	..	1	1	..	..	1	1	1	9	73	.110	59
CENTRAL DIVISION																					
Baltimore	4	..	1	5	..	8	2	3	5	3	1	2	3	5	2	4	4	52	30	.634	....
Atlanta	..	3	1	5	2	3	2	1	4	2	3	1	3	6	3	4	3	46	36	.561	6
Houston	4	2	1	5	..	3	3	1	..	..	1	1	1	5	2	2	2	33	49	.402	19
Cleveland	4	..	1	5	1	..	1	1	4	2	1	1	..	6	1	1	3	32	50	.390	20
MIDWEST DIVISION																					
Milwaukee	3	2	2	4	4	3	5	5	3	6	3	..	2	3	5	5	5	60	22	.732	....
Chicago	2	4	1	2	..	3	3	3	4	5	1	2	3	4	4	5	5	51	31	.622	9
Detroit	2	2	1	3	4	3	..	2	1	3	1	2	1	3	4	6	2	40	42	.488	20
KC-Omaha	2	1	1	3	2	2	3	2	4	..	..	1	1	3	3	4	4	36	46	.439	24
PACIFIC DIVISION																					
Los Angeles	1	3	..	4	5	3	5	4	3	5	..	3	2	4	6	6	6	60	22	.732	....
Golden State	3	1	1	4	3	3	4	..	3	4	3	1	2	4	2	5	4	47	35	.573	13
Phoenix	1	2	..	3	2	4	2	4	2	3	1	1	1	4	..	5	4	38	44	.463	22
Seattle	1	..	..	2	1	1	4	3	2	2	..	1	..	3	2	4	..	26	56	.317	34
Portland	..	..	..	2	1	3	..	1	2	2	..	1	1	3	2	..	3	21	61	.256	39

1972-73 STATISTICS

TEAM STATISTICS—OFFENSE

	G.	FIELD GOALS Made	Att.	Pct.	FREE THROWS Made	Att.	Pct.	MISCELLANEOUS Rbds.	Ast.	PF.	Dis.*	SCORING Pts.	Avg.	Pt. Dif.
Houston	82	3772	8249	.457	1706	2152	.793	4060	1939	1949	25	9250	112.8	- 1.7
Boston	82	3811	8511	.448	1616	2073	.780	4802	2320	1805	19	9238	112.7	+ 8.2
Atlanta	82	3700	8033	.461	1819	2482	.733	4174	2074	1916	30	9219	112.4	+ 0.1
Los Angeles	82	3740	7819	.478	1679	2264	.742	4562	2302	1636	9	9159	111.7	+ 8.5
Phoenix	82	3612	7942	.455	1931	2437	.792	4003	1944	2012	40	9155	111.6	- 1.3
Detroit	82	3666	7916	.463	1710	2294	.745	4105	1882	1812	10	9042	110.3	+ 0.3
Golden State	82	3715	8163	.455	1493	1871	.798	4405	1985	1693	15	8923	108.8	+ 3.1
K.C.-Omaha	82	3621	7581	.478	1580	2036	.776	3628	2118	2054	33	8822	107.6	- 2.9
Milwaukee	82	3759	7808	.481	1271	1687	.753	4245	2226	1763	13	8789	107.2	+ 8.2
Portland	82	3588	7842	.458	1531	2129	.719	3928	2102	1970	33	8707	106.2	- 6.2
New York	82	3627	7764	.467	1356	1739	.780	3882	2187	1775	10	8610	105.0	+ 6.8
Baltimore	82	3656	7883	.464	1294	1742	.743	4205	2051	1672	14	8606	105.0	+ 3.4
Philadelphia	82	3471	8264	.420	1598	2130	.750	4174	1688	1984	28	8540	104.1	- 12.1
Chicago	82	3480	7835	.444	1574	2073	.759	4000	2023	1881	26	8534	104.1	+ 3.5
Seattle	82	3447	7681	.449	1606	2080	.772	4161	1958	1877	24	8500	103.7	- 5.9
Buffalo	82	3536	7877	.449	1399	1966	.712	4158	2218	2034	40	8471	103.3	- 9.2
Cleveland	82	3431	7884	.435	1556	2084	.747	4063	2106	1941	21	8418	102.7	- 2.6

TEAM STATISTICS—DEFENSE

Allowed By	G.	FIELD GOALS Made	Att.	Pct.	FREE THROWS Made	Att.	Pct.	MISCELLANEOUS Rbds.	Ast.	PF.	Dis.*	SCORING Pts.	Avg.
New York	82	3291	7561	.435	1471	1961	.750	4100	1714	1781	18	8053	98.2
Milwaukee	82	3385	8028	.422	1345	1783	.754	3916	1906	1601	13	8115	99.0
Chicago	82	3343	7098	.471	1562	2080	.751	3915	1910	2002	38	8248	100.6
Baltimore	82	3531	8010	.441	1269	1702	.746	4226	1852	1682	11	8331	101.6
Los Angeles	82	3646	8409	.434	1167	1583	.737	4101	1963	1941	27	8459	103.2
Boston	82	3513	8095	.434	1540	2032	.758	3958	1957	1821	23	8566	104.5
Cleveland	82	3465	7673	.452	1707	2230	.765	4115	2311	1932	25	8637	105.3
Golden State	82	3603	8163	.441	1463	1891	.774	4265	2034	1766	14	8669	105.7
Seattle	82	3678	8093	.454	1628	2156	.755	4158	2145	1875	25	8984	109.6
Detroit	82	3803	8064	.472	1418	1862	.762	4019	2263	1891	22	9024	110.0
K.C.-Omaha	82	3698	7640	.484	1665	2174	.766	3961	1885	1816	9	9061	110.5
Atlanta	82	3758	8152	.461	1696	2193	.773	4147	2020	2104	35	9212	112.3
Portland	82	3709	7780	.477	1800	2327	.774	4236	2271	1885	18	9218	112.4
Buffalo	82	3745	7947	.471	1733	2299	.754	4278	2383	1822	23	9223	112.5
Phoenix	82	3758	8005	.469	1744	2318	.752	4139	2166	2068	46	9260	112.9
Houston	82	3824	8119	.471	1744	2290	.762	4338	2104	1902	22	9302	114.5
Philadelphia	82	3882	8215	.473	1767	2358	.749	4683	2239	1885	21	9531	116.2

INDIVIDUAL SCORING LEADERS

(Minimum 70 Games Played)

	G.	FG	FT	Pts.	Avg.		G.	FG	FT	Pts.	Avg.
Archibald, KC-O.	80	1028	663	2719	34.9	B. Love, Chicago	82	774	347	1895	23.1
Abdul-Jabbar, Mil.	76	982	328	2292	30.2	Bing, Detroit	82	692	456	1840	22.4
Haywood, Seattle	77	889	473	2251	29.2	Barry, G. S.	82	737	358	1832	22.3
Hudson, Atlanta	75	816	397	2029	27.1	Hayes, Baltimore	81	713	291	1717	21.2
Maravich, Atlanta	79	789	485	2063	26.1	Frazier, N. Y.	78	681	286	1648	21.1
Scott, Phoenix	81	806	436	2048	25.3	Carr, Cleveland	82	702	281	1685	20.5
Petrie, Portland	79	836	298	1970	24.9	Cowens, Boston	82	740	204	1684	20.5
Goodrich, L. A.	76	750	314	1814	23.9	Wilkens, Cleveland	75	572	394	1538	20.5
Wicks, Portland	80	761	384	1906	23.8	Dandridge, Mil.	73	638	198	1474	20.2
Lanier, Detroit	81	810	307	1927	23.8	Walk, Phoenix	81	678	279	1635	20.2
Havlicek, Boston	80	766	370	1902	23.8						

FIELD GOALS
(Minimum 560 Attempts)

	FGM	FGA	Pct.
Chamberlain, Los Angeles	426	586	.727
Guokas, KC-O.	322	565	.570
Abdul-Jabbar, Mil.	982	1772	.554
Rowe, Detroit	547	1053	.519
J. Fox, Seattle	316	613	.515
Lucas, New York	312	608	.513
Riordan, Baltimore	652	1278	.510
Clark, Baltimore	302	596	.507
Kauffman, Buffalo	535	1059	.505
Bellamy, Atlanta	455	901	.505

FREE THROWS
(Minimum 160 Attempts)

	FTM	FTA	Pct.
Barry, Golden State	358	397	.902
Murphy, Houston	239	269	.888
Newlin, Houston	327	369	.886
J. Walker, Houston	244	276	.884
Bradley, New York	169	194	.871
C. Russell, Golden State	172	199	.864
Snyder, Seattle	186	216	.861
D. Van Arsdale, Phoenix	426	496	.859
Havlicek, Boston	370	431	.858
Marin, Houston	248	292	.849

REBOUNDS
(Minimum 70 Games)

	G.	No.	Avg.
Chamberlain, Los Angeles	82	1526	18.6
Thurmond, Golden State	79	1349	17.1
Cowens, Boston	82	1329	16.2
Abdul-Jabbar, Milwaukee	76	1224	16.1
Unseld, Baltimore	79	1260	15.9
Lanier, Detroit	81	1205	14.9
Hayes, Baltimore	81	1177	14.5
Bellamy, Atlanta	74	964	13.0
Silas, Boston	80	1039	13.0
Haywood, Seattle	77	995	12.9

ASSISTS
(Minimum 70 Games)

	G.	No.	Avg.
Archibald, Kansas City-Omaha	80	910	11.4
Wilkens, Cleveland	75	628	8.4
Bing, Detroit	82	637	7.8
Robertson, Milwaukee	73	551	7.5
Van Lier, Chicago	80	567	7.1
Maravich, Atlanta	79	546	6.9
Havlicek, Boston	80	529	6.6
Gilliam, Atlanta	76	482	6.3
Scott, Phoenix	81	495	6.1
White, Boston	82	498	6.1

RECORDS OF TEAMS BY MONTHS

Team	Oct. W-L	Nov. W-L	Dec. W-L	Jan. W-L	Feb. W-L	Mar. W-L	Total W-L
Atlanta	4-6	6-7	12-4	7-9	8-4	9-6	46-36
Baltimore	4-5	7-7	10-4	12-2	9-6	10-6	52-30
Boston	9-0	9-3	11-3	12-3	12-4	15-1	68-14
Buffalo	2-7	2-12	6-8	7-8	2-12	2-14	21-61
Chicago	7-3	7-4	10-6	7-7	12-3	8-8	51-31
Cleveland	3-8	5-8	2-12	9-5	5-9	8-8	32-50
Detroit	3-6	6-7	7-8	6-10	9-4	9-7	40-42
Golden State	6-2	9-5	8-5	10-8	7-7	7-8	47-35
Houston	5-3	5-9	6-7	5-13	6-8	6-9	33-49
K.C.-Omaha	3-6	11-4	6-12	5-9	8-8	3-7	36-46
Los Angeles	7-3	12-0	10-4	11-4	9-7	11-4	60-22
Milwaukee	8-1	8-5	12-5	9-4	10-7	13-0	60-22
New York	8-1	12-3	11-6	12-3	8-5	6-7	57-25
Philadelphia	0-9	2-13	1-13	1-16	5-9	0-13	9-73
Phoenix	3-4	7-9	9-6	6-8	7-9	6-8	38-44
Portland	1-8	5-8	3-14	4-10	3-11	5-10	21-61
Seattle	4-5	4-13	4-11	5-9	4-11	5-7	26-56
Totals	77	117	128	128	124	123	697

INTER-CLUB RECORDS—HOME, AWAY AND NEUTRAL COURT

	Home	Away	Neutral	Total
Atlanta	28-13	17-23	1-0	46-36
Baltimore	24-9	21-17	7-4	52-30
Boston	33-6	32-8	3-0	68-14
Buffalo	14-27	6-31	1-3	21-61
Chicago	29-12	20-19	2-0	51-31
Cleveland	20-21	10-27	2-2	32-50
Detroit	26-15	13-25	1-2	40-42
Golden State	27-14	18-20	2-1	47-35
Houston	14-14	10-28	9-7	33-49
K.C.-Omaha	24-17	12-29	0-0	36-46
Los Angeles	30-11	28-11	2-0	60-22
Milwaukee	33-5	25-15	2-2	60-22
New York	35-6	21-18	1-1	57-25
Philadelphia	5-26	2-36	2-11	9-73
Phoenix	22-19	15-25	1-0	38-44
Portland	13-28	8-32	0-1	21-61
Seattle	16-25	10-29	0-2	28-56

INDIVIDUAL PLAYER STATISTICS
ATLANTA

Player	G.	Min.	FGM	FGA	Pct.	FTM	FTA	Pct.	Reb.	Ast.	PF	Disq.	Tot. Pts.	Avg. Pts.
Lou Hudson	75	3027	816	1710	.477	397	481	.825	467	258	197	1	2029	27.1
Pete Maravich	79	3089	789	1788	.441	485	606	.800	346	546	245	1	2063	26.1
Walt Bellamy	74	2802	455	901	.505	283	526	.538	964	179	244	1	1193	16.1
Herm Gilliam	76	2741	471	1007	.468	123	150	.820	399	482	257	8	1065	14.0
George Trapp	77	1853	359	824	.436	150	194	.773	455	127	274	11	868	11.3
Jim Washington	75	2833	308	713	.432	163	224	.728	801	174	252	5	779	10.4
Steve Bracey	70	1050	192	395	.486	73	110	.664	107	125	125	0	457	6.5
Don Adams*	4	76	8	38	.211	7	8	.875	22	5	11	0	23	5.8
Jeff Halliburton*	24	238	50	116	.431	21	22	.955	26	28	29	0	121	5.0
Don May*	32	317	61	134	.455	22	31	.710	67	21	55	0	144	4.5
Bob Christian	55	759	85	155	.548	60	79	.759	305	47	111	2	230	4.2
John Wetzel	28	504	42	94	.447	14	17	.824	58	39	41	1	98	3.5
John Tschogl	10	94	14	40	.350	2	4	.500	21	6	25	0	30	3.0
Eddie Mast	42	447	50	118	.424	19	30	.633	136	37	50	0	119	2.8

1972-73 STATISTICS

BALTIMORE

Player	G.	Min.	FGM	FGA	Pct.	FTM	FTA	Pct.	Reb.	Ast.	PF	Disq.	Tot. Pts.	Avg. Pts.
Elvin Hayes	81	3347	713	1607	.444	291	434	.671	1177	127	232	3	1717	21.2
Phil Chenier	71	2776	602	1332	.452	194	244	.795	288	301	160	0	1398	19.7
Archie Clark	39	1477	302	596	.507	111	137	.810	129	275	111	1	715	18.3
Mike Riordan	82	3466	652	1278	.510	179	218	.821	404	426	216	0	1483	18.1
Wes Unseld	79	3085	421	854	.493	149	212	.703	1260	347	168	0	991	12.5
Mike Davis	13	283	50	118	.424	23	25	.920	35	19	45	4	123	9.5
Rich Rinaldi	33	646	116	284	.408	48	64	.750	68	48	40	0	280	8.5
Flynn Robinson***	44	630	133	288	.462	32	39	.821	62	85	71	0	298	6.8
Flynn Robinson**	38	583	119	260	.458	26	31	.839	55	77	60	0	264	6.9
Kevin Porter	71	1217	205	451	.455	62	101	.614	72	237	206	5	472	6.6
Stan Love	72	995	190	436	.436	79	100	.790	300	46	175	0	459	6.4
Dave Stallworth	73	1217	180	435	.414	78	101	.772	236	112	139	1	438	6.0
John Tresvant	55	541	85	182	.467	41	59	.695	156	33	101	0	211	3.8
Tom Patterson	23	92	21	49	.429	13	16	.813	22	3	18	0	55	2.4
Terry Driscoll*	1	5	0	1	.000	0	0	.000	3	0	1	0	0	0.0

BOSTON

Player	G.	Min.	FGM	FGA	Pct.	FTM	FTA	Pct.	Reb.	Ast.	PF	Disq.	Tot. Pts.	Avg. Pts.
John Havlicek	80	3367	766	1704	.450	370	431	.858	567	529	195	1	1902	23.8
Dave Cowens	82	3425	740	1637	.452	204	262	.779	1329	333	311	7	1684	20.5
Jo Jo White	82	3250	717	1655	.431	178	228	.781	414	498	185	2	1612	19.7
Paul Silas	80	2618	400	851	.470	266	380	.700	1039	251	197	1	1066	13.3
Don Chaney	79	2488	414	859	.482	210	267	.787	449	221	276	6	1038	13.1
Don Nelson	72	1425	309	649	.476	159	188	.846	315	102	155	0	777	10.8
Steve Kuberski	78	762	140	347	.403	65	84	.774	197	26	92	0	345	4.4
Paul Westphal	60	482	89	212	.420	67	86	.779	67	69	88	0	245	4.1
Art Williams	81	974	110	261	.421	43	56	.768	182	236	136	1	263	3.2
Hank Finkel	76	496	78	173	.451	28	52	.538	151	26	83	0	184	2.4
Tom Sanders	59	423	47	149	.315	23	35	.657	88	27	82	0	117	2.0
Mark Minor	4	20	1	4	.250	3	4	.750	4	2	5	0	5	1.3

BUFFALO

Player	G.	Min.	FGM	FGA	Pct.	FTM	FTA	Pct.	Reb.	Ast.	PF	Disq.	Tot. Pts.	Avg. Pts.
Elmore Smith	76	2829	600	1244	.482	188	337	.558	946	192	295	16	1388	18.3
Bob McAdoo	80	2562	585	1293	.452	271	350	.774	728	139	256	6	1441	18.0
Bob Kauffman	77	3049	535	1059	.505	280	359	.780	855	396	211	1	1350	17.5
Randy Smith	82	2603	511	1154	.443	192	264	.727	391	422	247	1	1214	14.8
Dick Garrett	78	1805	341	813	.419	96	110	.873	209	217	217	4	778	10.0
John Hummer	66	1546	206	464	.444	115	205	.561	323	138	185	5	527	8.0
Dave Wohl***	78	1933	254	568	.447	103	133	.774	109	326	227	3	611	7.8
Dave Wohl**	56	1540	207	454	.456	79	100	.790	89	258	182	3	493	8.8
Fred Hilton	59	731	191	494	.387	41	53	.774	98	74	100	0	423	7.2
Howard Komives	67	1468	163	429	.380	85	98	.867	118	239	155	1	411	6.1
M. Abdul-Rahman*	9	134	25	60	.417	3	6	.500	10	17	19	0	53	5.9
Bill Hewitt	73	1332	152	364	.418	41	74	.554	368	110	154	3	345	4.7
Cornell Warner*	4	47	8	17	.471	1	2	.500	15	6	6	0	17	4.3
Harold Fox	10	84	12	32	.375	7	8	.875	8	10	7	0	31	3.1

CHICAGO

Player	G.	Min.	FGM	FGA	Pct.	FTM	FTA	Pct.	Reb.	Ast.	PF	Disq.	Tot. Pts.	Avg. Pts.
Bob Love	82	3033	774	1794	.431	347	421	.824	532	119	240	1	1895	23.1
Chet Walker	79	2455	597	1248	.478	376	452	.832	395	179	166	1	1570	19.9
Norm Van Lier	80	2882	474	1064	.445	166	211	.787	438	567	269	5	1114	13.9
Garfield Heard***	81	1552	350	824	.425	116	178	.652	453	60	171	1	816	10.1
Garfield Heard**	78	1535	346	815	.425	115	177	.650	447	58	167	1	807	10.3
Jerry Sloan	69	2412	301	733	.411	94	133	.707	475	151	235	5	696	10.1
Bob Weiss	82	2086	279	655	.426	159	189	.841	148	295	151	1	717	8.7
Clifford Ray	73	2009	254	516	.492	117	189	.619	797	271	232	5	625	8.6
Kennedy McIntosh*	3	33	8	13	.615	0	2	.000	9	1	4	0	16	5.3
Howard Porter	43	407	98	217	.452	22	29	.759	118	16	52	1	218	5.1
Dennis Awtrey***	82	1687	146	305	.479	86	153	.562	447	224	234	6	378	4.6
Dennis Awtrey**	79	1650	143	298	.480	85	149	.570	433	222	226	6	371	4.7
Jim King	65	785	116	263	.441	44	52	.846	76	81	76	0	276	4.2
Tom Boerwinkle	8	176	9	24	.375	12	20	.600	54	40	22	0	30	3.8
Rowland Garret	35	211	52	118	.441	21	31	.677	61	8	29	0	125	3.6
Frank Russell	23	131	29	77	.377	16	18	.889	17	15	12	0	74	3.2

1972-73 STATISTICS

CLEVELAND

Player	G.	Min.	FGM	FGA	Pct.	FTM	FTA	Pct.	Reb.	Ast.	PF	Disq.	Tot. Pts.	Avg. Pts.
Austin Carr	82	3097	702	1575	.446	281	342	.822	369	279	185	1	1685	20.5
Lenny Wilkens	75	2973	572	1275	.449	394	476	.828	346	628	221	2	1538	20.5
John Johnson	82	2815	492	1143	.430	199	271	.734	552	309	246	3	1183	14.4
Rick Roberson	62	2127	307	709	.433	167	290	.576	693	134	249	5	781	12.6
Dwight Davis	81	2151	293	748	.392	176	222	.793	563	118	297	5	762	9.4
Bobby Smith	73	1068	268	603	.444	64	81	.790	199	108	80	0	600	8.2
Charlie Davis*	6	86	20	41	.488	4	7	.571	5	10	20	1	44	7.3
Barry Clemens	72	1119	209	405	.516	53	68	.779	211	115	136	0	471	6.5
Jim Cleamons	80	1392	192	423	.454	75	101	.743	167	205	108	0	459	5.7
Cornell Warner***	72	1370	174	421	.413	59	90	.656	522	72	178	3	407	5.7
Cornell Warner**	68	1323	166	404	.411	58	88	.659	507	66	172	3	390	5.7
John Warren	40	290	54	111	.486	18	19	.947	42	34	45	0	126	3.2
Walt Wesley*	12	110	14	47	.298	8	12	.667	38	7	21	0	36	3.0
Steve Patterson	62	710	71	198	.359	34	65	.523	228	51	79	1	176	2.8
Bob Rule***	52	452	60	158	.380	20	31	.645	108	38	68	0	140	2.7
Bob Rule**	49	440	60	157	.382	20	31	.645	106	37	66	0	140	2.9
Dave Sorenson*	10	129	11	45	.244	5	11	.455	37	5	16	0	27	2.7

DETROIT

Player	G.	Min.	FGM	FGA	Pct.	FTM	FTA	Pct.	Reb.	Ast.	PF	Disq.	Tot. Pts.	Avg. Pts.
Bob Lanier	81	3075	810	1654	.490	307	397	.773	1205	260	278	4	1927	23.8
Dave Bing	82	3361	692	1545	.448	456	560	.814	298	637	229	1	1840	22.4
Curtis Rowe	81	3009	547	1053	.519	210	327	.642	760	172	191	0	1304	16.1
John Mengelt***	79	1647	320	651	.492	127	160	.794	181	153	148	0	767	9.7
John Mengelt**	67	1435	294	583	.504	116	141	.823	159	128	124	0	704	10.5
Stu Lantz	51	1603	185	455	.407	120	150	.800	172	138	117	0	490	9.6
Don Adams***	74	1874	265	678	.391	145	184	.788	441	117	231	2	675	9.1
Don Adams**	70	1798	257	640	.402	138	176	.784	419	112	220	2	652	9.3
Fred Foster	63	1460	243	627	.388	61	87	.701	183	94	150	0	547	8.7
Willie Norwood	79	1282	249	504	.494	154	225	.684	324	56	182	0	652	8.3
Chris Ford	74	1537	208	434	.479	60	93	.645	266	194	133	1	476	6.4
Jim Davis	73	771	131	257	.510	72	114	.632	261	56	126	2	334	4.6
Justus Thigpen	18	99	23	57	.404	0	0	.000	9	8	18	0	46	2.6
Bob Nash	36	169	16	72	.222	11	17	.647	34	16	30	0	43	1.2
Erwin Mueller	21	80	9	31	.290	5	7	.714	14	7	13	0	23	1.1
Harvey Marlatt	7	26	2	4	.500	0	0	.000	1	4	1	0	4	0.6

GOLDEN STATE

Player	G.	Min.	FGM	FGA	Pct.	FTM	FTA	Pct.	Reb.	Ast.	PF	Disq.	Tot. Pts.	Avg. Pts.
Rick Barry	82	3075	737	1630	.452	358	397	.902	728	399	245	2	1832	22.3
Jeff Mullins	81	3005	651	1321	.493	143	172	.831	363	337	201	2	1445	17.8
Nate Thurmond	79	3419	517	1159	.446	315	439	.718	1349	280	240	2	1349	17.1
Cazzie Russell	80	2429	541	1182	.458	172	199	.864	350	187	171	0	1254	15.7
Jim Barnett	82	2215	394	844	.467	183	217	.843	255	301	150	1	971	11.8
Joe Ellis	74	1054	199	487	.409	69	93	.742	282	88	143	2	467	6.3
Clyde Lee	66	1476	170	365	.464	74	131	.565	598	34	183	5	414	6.3
Ron Williams	73	1016	180	409	.440	75	83	.904	81	114	108	0	435	6.0
Charles Johnson	70	887	171	400	.428	33	46	.717	132	118	105	0	375	5.4
M. Abdul-Rahman***	55	763	107	256	.418	47	57	.825	88	129	110	1	261	4.7
M. Abdul-Rahman**	46	629	82	196	.418	44	51	.863	78	112	91	1	208	4.5
Bob Portman	32	176	32	70	.457	20	26	.769	51	7	16	0	84	2.6
George T. Johnson	56	349	41	100	.410	7	17	.412	138	8	40	0	89	1.6

HOUSTON

Player	G.	Min.	FGM	FGA	Pct.	FTM	FTA	Pct.	Reb.	Ast.	PF	Disq.	Tot. Pts.	Avg. Pts.
Rudy Tomjanovich	81	2972	655	1371	.478	205	335	.746	938	178	225	1	1560	19.3
Jack Marin	81	3019	624	1334	.468	248	292	.849	499	291	247	4	1496	18.5
Jimmy Walker	81	3079	605	1301	.465	244	276	.884	268	442	207	0	1454	18.0
Mike Newlin	82	2658	534	1206	.443	327	369	.886	340	409	301	5	1395	17.0
Calvin Murphy	77	1697	381	820	.465	239	269	.888	149	262	211	3	1001	13.0
Otto Moore	82	2712	418	859	.487	127	211	.602	868	167	239	4	963	11.7
Don Smith	48	900	149	375	.397	119	162	.735	304	53	108	2	417	8.7
Cliff Meely	82	1694	268	657	.408	92	137	.672	496	91	263	6	628	7.7
Paul McCracken	24	305	44	89	.494	23	39	.590	51	17	32	0	111	4.6
Stan McKenzie***	33	294	48	119	.403	30	37	.811	55	23	43	1	126	3.8
Stan McKenzie**	26	187	35	83	.422	16	21	.762	34	15	28	0	86	3.3
Greg Smith*	4	41	5	16	.313	0	0	.000	8	5	8	0	10	2.5
George E. Johnson	19	169	20	39	.513	3	4	.750	45	3	33	0	43	2.3
Eric McWilliams	44	245	34	98	.347	18	37	.486	60	5	46	0	86	2.0
Dick Gibbs*	1	2	0	1	.000	0	0	.000	0	1	1	0	0	0.0

KANSAS CITY-OMAHA

Player	G.	Min.	FGM	FGA	Pct.	FTM	FTA	Pct.	Reb.	Ast.	PF	Disq.	Tot. Pts.	Avg. Pts.
Nate Archibald	80	3681	1028	2106	.488	663	783	.847	223	910	207	2	2719	34.0
John Block***	73	2041	391	886	.441	300	378	.794	562	113	242	5	1082	14.8
John Block**	25	483	80	180	.444	64	76	.842	120	19	69	1	224	9.0
Sam Lacey	79	2930	471	994	.474	126	178	.708	933	189	283	6	1068	13.5
Tom Van Arsdale*	49	1282	250	547	.457	110	140	.786	173	90	123	1	610	12.4
Nate Williams	80	1079	417	874	.477	106	133	.797	339	128	272	9	940	11.8
Matt Guokas	79	2846	322	565	.570	74	90	.822	245	403	190	0	718	9.1
Don Kojis	77	1240	276	575	.480	106	137	.774	198	80	128	0	658	8.5
Ron Riley	74	1634	273	634	.431	79	116	.681	507	76	226	3	625	8.4
Johnny Green	66	1245	190	317	.599	89	131	.679	361	59	185	7	469	7.1
John Mengelt*	12	212	26	68	.382	11	19	.579	22	25	24	0	63	5.3
Mike Ratliff	58	681	98	235	.417	45	84	.536	194	38	111	1	241	4.2
Toby Kimball	67	743	96	220	.436	44	67	.657	191	27	86	2	236	3.5
Dick Gibbs***	67	735	80	222	.360	47	63	.746	94	62	114	1	207	3.1
Dick Gibbs**	66	733	80	221	.362	47	63	.746	94	61	113	1	207	3.1
Ken Durrett	8	65	8	21	.381	6	8	.750	14	3	16	0	22	2.8
Sam Sibert	5	26	4	13	.308	4	5	.800	4	0	4	0	12	2.4
Frank Schade	9	76	2	7	.286	6	6	1.000	6	10	12	0	10	1.1
Pete Cross*	3	24	0	4	.000	0	0	.000	4	0	5	0	0	0.0

LOS ANGELES

Player	G.	Min.	FGM	FGA	Pct.	FTM	FTA	Pct.	Reb.	Ast.	PF	Disq.	Tot. Pts.	Avg. Pts.
Gail Goodrich	76	2697	750	1615	.464	314	374	.840	263	332	193	1	1814	23.9
Jerry West	69	2460	618	1291	.479	339	421	.805	289	607	138	0	1575	22.8
Jim McMillian	81	2953	655	1431	.458	223	264	.845	447	221	176	0	1533	18.9
Harold Hairston	28	939	158	328	.482	140	178	.787	370	68	77	0	456	16.3
Wilt Chamberlain	82	3542	426	586	.727	232	455	.510	1526	365	191	0	1084	13.2
Bill Bridges***	82	2867	333	722	.461	179	255	.702	904	219	296	3	845	10.3
Bill Bridges**	72	2491	286	597	.479	133	190	.700	782	196	261	3	705	9.8
Keith Erickson	76	1920	299	696	.430	89	110	.809	337	242	190	3	687	9.0
Pat Riley	55	801	167	390	.428	65	82	.793	65	81	126	0	399	7.3
Jim Price	59	828	158	359	.440	60	73	.822	115	97	119	1	376	6.4
Flynn Robinson*	6	47	14	28	.500	6	8	.750	7	8	11	0	34	5.7
Mel Counts***	66	658	132	294	.449	39	58	.672	253	65	106	1	303	4.6
Mel Counts**	59	611	127	278	.457	39	58	.672	237	62	98	1	293	5.0
Travis Grant	33	153	51	116	.440	23	26	.885	52	7	19	0	125	3.8
Leroy Ellis*	10	156	11	40	.275	4	5	.800	33	3	13	0	26	2.6
John Q. Trapp*	5	35	3	12	.250	7	10	.700	14	2	10	0	13	2.6
Bill Turner***	21	125	19	58	.328	4	7	.571	27	11	16	0	42	2.0
Bill Turner**	19	117	17	52	.327	4	7	.571	25	11	13	0	38	2.0
Roger Brown	1	5	0	0	.000	1	3	.333	0	0	1	0	1	1.0

MILWAUKEE

Player	G.	Min.	FGM	FGA	Pct.	FTM	FTA	Pct.	Reb.	Ast.	PF	Disq.	Tot. Pts.	Avg. Pts.
Kareem Abdul-Jabbar	76	3254	982	1772	.554	328	460	.713	1224	379	208	0	2292	30.2
Bob Dandridge	73	2852	638	1353	.472	198	251	.789	600	207	279	2	1474	20.2
Lucius Allen	80	2693	547	1130	.484	143	200	.715	279	426	188	1	1237	15.5
Oscar Robertson	73	2737	446	983	.454	238	281	.847	360	551	167	0	1130	15.5
John McGlocklin	80	1951	351	699	.502	63	73	.863	158	236	119	0	765	9.6
Curtis Perry	67	2094	265	575	.461	83	126	.659	644	120	246	6	613	9.1
Terry Driscoll***	60	964	140	327	.428	43	62	.694	300	55	144	3	323	5.4
Terry Driscoll**	59	959	140	326	.429	43	62	.694	297	55	143	3	323	5.5
Mickey Davis	74	1046	152	347	.438	76	92	.826	226	72	119	0	380	5.1
Wali Jones	27	419	59	145	.407	16	18	.889	29	56	39	0	134	5.0
Gary Gregor	9	88	11	33	.333	5	7	.714	32	9	9	0	27	3.0
Russell Lee	46	277	49	127	.386	32	43	.744	43	38	36	0	130	2.8
Dick Cunningham	72	692	64	156	.410	29	50	.580	208	34	94	0	157	2.1
Chuck Terry	67	693	55	162	.340	17	24	.708	145	40	116	1	127	1.9

NEW YORK

Player	G.	Min.	FGM	FGA	Pct.	FTM	FTA	Pct.	Reb.	Ast.	PF	Disq.	Tot. Pts.	Avg. Pts.
Walt Frazier	78	3181	681	1389	.490	286	350	.817	570	461	186	0	1648	21.1
Dave DeBusschere	77	2827	532	1224	.435	194	260	.746	787	259	215	1	1258	16.3
Bill Bradley	82	2998	575	1252	.459	169	194	.871	301	367	273	5	1319	16.1
Earl Monroe	75	2370	496	1016	.488	171	208	.822	245	288	195	0	1163	15.5
Willis Reed	69	1876	334	705	.474	92	124	.742	590	126	205	0	760	11.0
Jerry Lucas	71	2001	312	608	.513	80	100	.800	510	317	157	0	704	9.9
Phil Jackson	80	1393	245	553	.443	154	195	.790	344	94	218	2	644	8.1
Dean Meminger	80	1453	188	365	.515	81	129	.628	229	133	109	1	457	5.7
Henry Bibby	55	475	78	205	.380	73	86	.849	82	64	67	0	229	4.2

NEW YORK—Continued

Player	G.	Min.	FGM	FGA	Pct.	FTM	FTA	Pct.	Reb.	Ast.	PF	Disq.	Tot. Pts.	Avg. Pts.
Dick Barnett	51	514	88	226	.389	16	30	.533	41	50	52	0	192	3.8
John Gianelli	52	516	79	175	.451	23	33	.697	150	25	72	0	181	3.5
Tom Riker	14	65	10	24	.417	15	24	.625	16	2	15	0	35	2.5
Harthorne Wingo	13	59	9	22	.409	2	6	.333	16	1	9	0	20	1.5
Luther Rackley	1	2	0	0	.000	0	0	.000	1	0	2	0	0	0.0

PHILADELPHIA

Player	G.	Min.	FGM	FGA	Pct.	FTM	FTA	Pct.	Reb.	Ast.	PF	Disq.	Tot. Pts.	Avg. Pts.
Fred Carter	81	2993	679	1614	.421	259	368	.704	485	349	252	8	1617	20.0
John Block*	48	1558	311	706	.441	236	302	.781	442	94	173	4	858	17.9
Tom Van Arsdale***	79	2311	445	1043	.427	250	308	.812	358	152	224	2	1140	14.4
Tom Van Arsdale**	30	1029	195	496	.393	140	168	.833	185	62	101	1	530	17.7
Bill Bridges*	10	376	47	125	.376	46	65	.708	122	23	35	0	140	14.0
Kevin Loughery	32	955	169	427	.396	107	130	.823	113	148	104	0	445	13.9
Leroy Ellis***	79	2600	421	969	.434	129	161	.801	777	139	199	2	971	12.3
Leroy Ellis**	69	2444	410	929	.441	125	156	.801	744	136	186	2	945	13.7
Manny Leaks	82	2530	377	933	.404	144	200	.720	677	95	191	5	898	11.0
Fred Boyd	82	2351	362	923	.392	136	200	.680	210	301	184	1	860	10.5
John Q. Trapp***	44	889	171	420	.407	90	122	.738	200	49	150	4	432	9.8
John Q. Trapp**	39	854	168	408	.412	83	112	.741	186	47	140	4	419	10.7
Don May*	58	919	189	424	.446	75	93	.806	210	64	135	1	453	7.8
Don May***	26	602	128	290	.441	53	62	.855	143	43	80	1	309	11.9
Jeff Halliburton	55	787	172	396	.434	71	88	.807	108	96	107	1	415	7.5
Jeff Halliburton**	31	549	122	280	.436	50	66	.758	82	68	78	1	294	9.5
Hal Greer	38	848	91	232	.392	32	39	.821	106	111	76	1	214	5.6
Dale Schlueter	78	1136	166	317	.524	86	123	.699	354	103	166	0	418	5.4
Dave Sorenson***	58	755	124	293	.423	64	90	.711	210	36	107	0	312	5.4
Dave Sorenson**	48	626	113	248	.456	59	79	.747	173	31	91	0	285	5.9
Mike Price	57	751	125	301	.415	38	47	.809	117	71	106	0	288	5.1
Dennis Awtrey*	3	37	3	7	.429	1	4	.250	14	2	8	0	7	2.3
Mel Counts*	7	47	5	16	.313	0	0	.000	16	3	8	0	10	1.4
Luther Green	5	32	0	11	.000	3	9	.333	3	0	3	0	3	0.6
Bob Rule*	3	12	0	1	.000	0	0	.000	2	1	2	0	0	0.0

PHOENIX

Player	G.	Min.	FGM	FGA	Pct.	FTM	FTA	Pct.	Reb.	Ast.	PF	Disq.	Tot. Pts.	Avg. Pts.
Charlie Scott	81	3062	806	1809	.446	436	556	.784	342	495	306	5	2048	25.3
Neal Walk	81	3114	678	1455	.466	279	355	.786	1006	287	323	11	1635	20.2
Dick Van Arsdale	81	2979	532	1118	.476	426	496	.859	326	268	221	2	1490	18.4
Connie Hawkins	75	2768	441	920	.479	322	404	.797	641	304	229	5	1204	16.1
Clem Haskins	77	1581	339	731	.464	130	156	.833	173	203	143	2	808	10.5
Gus Johnson	21	417	69	181	.381	25	36	.694	136	31	55	0	163	7.8
Dennis Layton	65	990	187	434	.431	90	119	.756	77	139	127	2	464	7.1
Lamar Green	80	2048	224	520	.431	89	118	.754	746	89	263	10	537	6.7
Corky Calhoun	82	2025	211	450	.469	71	96	.740	338	76	214	2	493	6.0
Walt Wesley***	57	474	77	202	.381	26	46	.565	141	31	77	1	180	3.2
Walt Wesley**	45	364	63	155	.406	18	34	.529	113	24	56	1	144	3.2
Scott English	29	196	36	93	.387	21	29	.724	44	15	38	0	93	3.2
Paul Stovall	25	211	26	76	.342	24	38	.632	61	13	37	0	76	3.0

PORTLAND

Player	G.	Min.	FGM	FGA	Pct.	FTM	FTA	Pct.	Reb.	Ast.	PF	Disq.	Tot. Pts.	Avg. Pts.
Geoff Petrie	79	3134	836	1801	.464	298	383	.778	273	350	163	2	1970	24.9
Sidney Wicks	80	3152	761	1684	.452	384	531	.723	870	440	253	3	1906	23.8
Lloyd Neal	82	2723	455	921	.494	187	293	.638	967	146	305	6	1097	13.4
Ollie Johnson	78	2138	308	620	.497	156	206	.757	417	200	166	0	772	9.9
Charlie Davis***	75	1419	263	631	.417	130	168	.774	116	185	194	7	656	8.7
Charlie Davis**	69	1333	243	590	.412	126	161	.783	111	175	174	6	612	8.9
Greg Smith***	76	1610	234	485	.482	75	128	.586	383	122	218	8	543	7.1
Greg Smith**	72	1569	229	469	.488	75	128	.586	375	117	210	8	533	7.4
Rick Adelman	76	1822	214	525	.408	73	102	.716	157	294	155	2	501	6.6
Terry Dischinger	63	970	161	338	.476	64	96	.667	190	103	125	1	386	6.1
Larry Steele	66	1301	159	329	.483	71	89	.798	154	156	181	4	389	5.9
Stan McKenzie*	7	107	13	36	.361	14	16	.875	21	8	15	1	40	5.7
Dave Wohl*	22	393	47	114	.412	24	33	.727	20	68	45	0	118	5.4
LaRue Martin	77	996	145	366	.396	50	77	.649	358	42	162	0	340	4.4
Bill Smith	8	43	9	15	.600	5	8	.625	8	1	8	0	23	2.9
Bill Turner*	2	8	2	6	.333	0	0	.000	2	0	3	0	4	2.0
Bob Davis	9	41	6	28	.214	4	6	.667	5	2	5	0	16	1.8

Walt Frazier's scoring and playmaking abilities were a big part of the New York Knicks' 1972-73 NBA championship drive.

SEATTLE

Player	G.	Min.	FGM	FGA	Pct.	FTM	FTA	Pct.	Reb.	Ast.	PF	Disq.	Tot. Pts.	Avg. Pts.
Spencer Haywood	77	3259	889	1868	.476	473	564	.839	995	196	213	2	2251	29.2
Dick Snyder	82	3060	473	1022	.463	186	216	.861	323	311	216	2	1132	13.8
Fred Brown	79	2320	471	1035	.455	121	148	.818	318	438	226	5	1063	13.5
John Brisker	70	1633	352	809	.435	194	236	.822	319	150	169	1	898	12.8
Jim Fox	74	2439	316	613	.515	214	265	.808	827	176	239	6	846	11.4
Butch Beard	73	1403	191	435	.439	100	140	.714	174	247	139	0	482	6.6
Lee Winfield	53	1061	143	332	.431	62	108	.574	126	186	92	3	348	6.6
Bud Stallworth	77	1225	198	522	.379	86	114	.754	225	58	138	0	482	6.3
Jim McDaniels	68	1095	154	386	.399	70	100	.700	345	78	140	4	378	5.6
Kennedy McIntosh***	59	1138	115	341	.337	40	67	.597	231	54	102	1	270	4.6
Kennedy McIntosh**	56	1105	107	328	.326	40	65	.615	222	53	98	1	254	4.5
Joby Wright	77	931	133	278	.478	37	89	.416	218	36	164	0	303	3.9
Garfield Heard*	3	17	4	9	.444	1	1	1.000	6	2	4	0	9	3.0
Charlie Dudley	12	99	10	23	.435	14	16	.875	6	16	15	0	34	2.8
Pete Cross***	29	157	6	25	.240	8	18	.444	61	11	29	0	20	0.7
Pete Cross**	26	133	6	21	.286	8	18	.444	57	11	24	0	20	0.8

*Finished season with another team.　　**Player total with this club only.　　***Player total with all clubs.

1972-73 PLAYOFF RESULTS

CONFERENCE SEMI-FINAL SERIES

EASTERN CONFERENCE

Boston Defeated Atlanta, 4-2

Apr. 1—Atlanta 109 at Boston 134
Apr. 4—Boston 126 at Atlanta 113
Apr. 6—Atlanta 118 at Boston 105
Apr. 8—Boston 94 at Atlanta 97
Apr. 11—Atlanta 101 at Boston 108
Apr. 13—Boston 121 at Atlanta 103

WESTERN CONFERENCE

Golden State Defeated Milwaukee, 4-2

Mar. 30—Golden State 90 at Milwaukee 110
Apr. 1—Golden State 95 at Milwaukee 92
Apr. 5—Milwaukee 113 at Golden State 93
Apr. 7—Milwaukee 97 at Golden State 102
Apr. 10—Golden State 100 at Milwaukee 97
Apr. 13—Milwaukee 86 at Golden State 100

New York Defeated Baltimore, 4-1

Mar. 30—Baltimore 83 at New York 95
Apr. 1—Baltimore 103 at New York 123
Apr. 4—New York 103 at Baltimore 96
Apr. 6—New York 89 at Baltimore 97
Apr. 8—Baltimore 99 at New York 109

Los Angeles Defeated Chicago, 4-3

Mar. 30—Chicago 104 at Los Angeles ....107 (ot)
Apr. 1—Chicago 93 at Los Angeles 108
Apr. 6—Los Angeles 86 at Chicago 96
Apr. 8—Los Angeles 94 at Chicago 98
Apr. 10—Chicago 102 at Los Angeles 123
Apr. 13—Los Angeles 93 at Chicago 101
Apr. 15—Chicago 92 at Los Angeles 95

CONFERENCE FINAL SERIES

EASTERN CONFERENCE FINALS
New York Defeated Boston, 4-3

Apr. 15—New York 108 at Boston 134
Apr. 18—Boston 96 at New York 129
Apr. 20—New York 98 at Boston 91
Apr. 22—Boston 110 at New York ....117 (2 ot)
Apr. 25—New York 97 at Boston 98
Apr. 27—Boston 110 at New York 100
Apr. 29—New York 94 at Boston 78

WESTERN CONFERENCE
Los Angeles Defeated Golden State, 4-1

Apr. 17—Golden State 99 at Los Angeles 101
Apr. 19—Golden State 93 at Los Angeles 104
Apr. 21—Los Angeles 126 at Golden State 70
Apr. 23—Los Angeles 109 at Golden State 117
Apr. 25—Golden State 118 at Los Angeles 128

CHAMPIONSHIP SERIES
New York Defeated Los Angeles, 4-1

May 1—New York 112 at Los Angeles 115
May 3—New York 99 at Los Angeles 95
May 6—Los Angeles 83 at New York 87
May 8—Los Angeles 98 at New York 103
May 10—New York 102 at Los Angeles 93

1971-72 STATISTICS

1971-72 WORLD CHAMPION LOS ANGELES LAKERS

Seated: Keith Erickson, Happy Hairston, Leroy Ellis, Coach Bill Sharman, Chairman of the Board and President Jack Kent Cooke, General Manager Fred Schaus, Wilt Chamberlain, John Q. Trapp and Elgin Baylor. Standing: Assistant Coach K. C. Jones, Gail Goodrich, Jim Cleamons, Pat Riley, Jim McMillian, Jerry West, Flynn Robinson and Trainer Frank O'Neill.

FINAL STANDINGS AND TEAM FIGURES

ATLANTIC DIVISION

Team	Atl.	Balt.	Bos.	Buf.	Chi.	Cin.	Clv.	Det.	G.S.	Hou.	L.A.	Mil.	N.Y.	Phil.	Pho.	Prt.	Sea.	W.	L.	Pct.	G.B.
Boston	4	2	..	6	3	4	5	5	2	5	1	2	3	6	3	4	3	56	26	.683	..
New York	1	4	3	5	2	2	5	4	3	5	1	3	..	3	1	3	3	48	34	.585	8
Philadelphia	3	0	0	3	1	2	4	4	1	1	0	1	3	..	1	2	4	30	52	.366	26
Buffalo	2	3	0	..	1	3	4	2	1	0	0	0	1	3	0	2	0	22	60	.268	34

CENTRAL DIVISION

Baltimore	4	..	2	3	1	4	1	3	1	3	1	0	2	4	4	3	2	38	44	.463	..
Atlanta	..	2	0	4	0	3	4	3	3	1	0	2	3	3	3	4	1	36	46	.439	2
Cincinnati	3	2	2	3	1	..	6	2	2	0	1	0	2	2	2	2	0	30	52	.366	8
Cleveland	2	5	1	2	0	2	..	1	0	2	1	0	1	2	0	4	0	23	59	.280	15

MIDWEST DIVISION

Milwaukee	3	5	3	4	4	5	4	5	2	5	1	..	2	4	4	6	6	63	19	.768	..
Chicago	5	4	2	3	..	3	4	5	3	5	1	2	3	4	5	6	2	57	25	.695	6
Phoenix	2	1	3	4	1	3	4	4	3	3	2	2	4	4	..	6	3	49	33	.598	14
Detroit	2	2	0	4	1	3	3	..	0	3	1	1	1	1	2	2	0	26	56	.317	37

PACIFIC DIVISION

Los Angeles	5	4	4	4	3	4	3	4	5	5	..	4	4	5	4	6	5	69	13	.841	..
Golden State	2	4	3	3	3	3	4	5	..	5	1	2	2	4	2	4	4	51	31	.622	18
Seattle	4	3	3	4	3	5	4	4	2	3	1	0	2	1	2	6	..	47	35	.573	22
Houston	4	2	0	4	1	4	2	3	1	..	1	0	0	4	1	4	3	34	48	.415	35
Portland	0	1	0	4	0	2	2	2	2	2	0	0	1	2	0	..	0	18	64	.220	51

1971-72 STATISTICS

TEAM STATISTICS—OFFENSE

	G.	FIELD GOALS Made	Att.	Pct.	FREE THROWS Made	Att.	Pct.	MISCELLANEOUS Rbds.	Ast.	PF.	Dis.*	SCORING Pts.	Avg.	Pt. Dif.
Los Angeles	82	3920	7998	.490	2080	2833	.734	4628	2232	1636	7	9920	121.0	+12.3
Phoenix	82	3599	7877	.457	2336	2999	.779	4301	1976	2026	20	9534	116.3	+ 5.5
Boston	82	3819	8431	.453	1839	2367	.777	4462	2230	2030	36	9477	115.6	+ 4.8
Milwaukee	82	3813	7653	.498	1774	2399	.739	4269	2160	1862	29	9400	114.6	+11.1
Philadelphia	82	3577	8057	.444	2049	2825	.725	4318	1920	2203	50	9203	112.2	− 3.7
Chicago	82	3539	7853	.451	2039	2700	.755	4371	2087	1964	24	9117	111.2	+ 8.3
Houston	82	3590	8277	.434	1813	2424	.748	4433	1777	1992	32	8993	109.7	− 1.5
Atlanta	82	3487	7570	.460	2018	2725	.741	4080	1897	1967	14	8982	109.5	− 1.8
Seattle	82	3461	7457	.464	2035	2659	.765	4123	1976	1738	18	8957	109.2	+ 0.4
Detroit	82	3482	7665	.454	1981	2653	.747	3970	1687	1954	26	8945	109.1	− 6.8
Golden State	82	3477	7923	.439	1917	2500	.767	4450	1854	1840	16	8871	108.2	+ 0.8
Cincinnati	82	3444	7496	.459	1948	2578	.756	3754	2020	2079	40	8836	107.8	− 4.0
New York	82	3521	7673	.459	1743	2303	.757	3909	1985	1899	15	8785	107.1	+ 2.4
Baltimore	82	3490	7748	.450	1804	2378	.759	4159	1816	1858	16	8784	107.1	− 1.2
Portland	82	3462	7840	.442	1835	2494	.736	3996	2090	1873	24	8759	106.8	− 9.7
Cleveland	82	3458	8074	.428	1758	2390	.736	4098	2060	1936	23	8674	105.8	− 7.6
Buffalo	82	3409	7560	.451	1549	2219	.698	3978	1759	2110	42	8367	102.0	− 9.3

TEAM STATISTICS—DEFENSE

Allowed By	G.	FIELD GOALS Made	Att.	Pct.	FREE THROWS Made	Att.	Pct.	MISCELLANEOUS Rbds.	Ast.	PF.	Dis.*	SCORING Pts.	Avg.
Chicago	82	3263	7189	.454	1914	2617	.731	3928	1853	2041	32	8440	102.9
Milwaukee	82	3370	8025	.420	1745	2358	.740	3922	1843	1788	10	8485	103.5
New York	82	3372	7513	.443	1920	2565	.749	4169	1626	1892	28	8584	104.7
Golden State	82	3560	8082	.440	1688	2265	.745	4381	1968	1912	25	8808	107.4
Baltimore	82	3332	7842	.452	1790	2412	.742	4244	1844	1869	28	8454	108.3
Los Angeles	82	3699	8553	.432	1515	1972	.768	4290	1994	1997	29	8913	108.7
Seattle	82	3619	8029	.451	1681	2248	.748	4183	2037	1975	29	8919	108.8
Phoenix	82	3568	7896	.452	1947	2658	.733	4009	1929	2182	45	9083	110.8
Boston	82	3498	7886	.444	2089	2766	.755	4179	1798	1842	16	9085	110.8
Houston	82	3542	7817	.453	2037	2737	.744	4298	1945	1944	19	9121	111.2
Buffalo	82	3479	7557	.460	2167	2842	.762	4187	1918	1728	9	9125	111.3
Atlanta	82	3601	7744	.465	1925	2530	.761	4004	1890	1996	25	9127	111.3
Cincinnati	82	3537	7588	.466	2093	2829	.740	4228	2028	1971	36	9167	111.8
Cleveland	82	3653	7537	.485	1994	2611	.764	4034	2322	1937	24	9300	113.4
Philadelphia	82	3614	7882	.459	2276	3063	.743	4427	2005	2059	33	9504	115.9
Detroit	82	3822	8106	.472	1862	2474	.753	4377	2214	1931	25	9506	115.9
Portland	82	3841	7906	.486	1875	2499	.750	4439	2312	1903	19	9557	116.5

INDIVIDUAL SCORING LEADERS
(Minimum 70 Games Played)

	G.	FG	FT	Pts.	Avg.		G.	FG	FT	Pts.	Avg.
Abdul-Jabbar, Mil.	81	1159	504	2822	34.8	Hudson, Atl.	77	775	349	1899	24.7
Archibald, Cin.	76	734	677	2145	28.2	Wicks, Port.	82	784	441	2009	24.5
Havlicek, Bos.	82	897	458	2252	27.5	Cunningham, Phila.	75	658	428	1744	23.3
Haywood, Sea.	73	717	480	1914	26.2	Frazier, N. Y.	77	669	450	1788	23.2
Goodrich, L. A.	82	826	475	2127	25.9	White, Bos.	79	770	285	1825	23.1
Love, Chi.	79	819	399	2037	25.8	Marin, Balt.	78	690	356	1736	22.3
West, L. A.	77	735	515	1985	25.8	Walker, Chi.	78	619	481	1719	22.0
Lanier, Det.	80	834	388	2056	25.7	Mullins, G. S.	80	685	350	1720	21.5
Clark, Balt.	77	712	514	1938	25.2	Thurmond, G. S.	78	628	417	1673	21.4
Hayes, Hou.	82	832	399	2063	25.2	Russell, G. S.	79	689	315	1693	21.4

FREE THROWS
(Minimum 350 Attempts)

	FTM	FTA	Pct.
Marin, Baltimore	356	398	.894
Murphy, Houston	349	392	.890
Goodrich, Los Angeles	475	559	.850
Walker, Chicago	481	568	.847
Van Arsdale, Phoenix	529	626	.845
Lantz, Houston	387	462	.838
Havlicek, Boston	458	549	.834
Russell, Golden State	315	378	.833
McKenzie, Portland	315	379	.831
Walker, Detroit	397	480	.827

FIELD GOALS
(Minimum 700 Attempts)

	FGM	FGA	Pct.
Chamberlain, Los Angeles	496	764	.649
Abdul-Jabbar, Milwaukee	1159	2019	.574
Bellamy, Atlanta	593	1089	.545
Snyder, Seattle	496	937	.529
Lucas, New York	543	1060	.512
Frazier, New York	669	1307	.512
McGlocklin, Milwaukee	374	733	.510
Walker, Chicago	619	1225	.505
Allen, Milwaukee	441	874	.505
Hudson, Atlanta	775	1540	.503

REBOUNDS
(Minimum 70 Games)

	G.	No.	Avg.
Chamberlain, Los Angeles	82	1572	19.2
Unseld, Baltimore	76	1336	17.6
Abdul-Jabbar, Milwaukee	81	1346	16.6
Thurmond, Golden State	78	1252	16.1
Cowens, Boston	79	1203	15.2
E. Smith, Buffalo	78	1184	15.2
Hayes, Houston	82	1197	14.6
Lee, Golden State	78	1132	14.5
Lanier, Detroit	80	1132	14.2
Bridges, Philadelphia	78	1051	13.5

ASSISTS
(Minimum 70 Games)

	G.	No.	Avg.
West, Los Angeles	77	747	9.7
Wilkens, Seattle	80	766	9.6
Archibald, Cincinnati	76	701	9.2
Clark, Baltimore	77	613	8.0
Havlicek, Boston	82	614	7.5
Van Lier, Chicago	79	542	6.9
Cunningham, Philadelphia	75	443	5.9
Mullins, Golden State	80	471	5.9
Frazier, New York	77	446	5.8
Hazzard, Buffalo	72	406	5.6

INTER-CLUB RECORDS—HOME, AWAY AND NEUTRAL COURT

	Home	Away	Neutral	Total		Home	Away	Neutral	Total
Atlanta	22-19	13-26	1-1	36-46	Houston	15-20	14-23	5-5	34-48
Baltimore	18-15	16-24	4-5	38-44	Los Angeles	36-5	31-7	2-1	69-13
Boston	32-9	21-16	3-1	56-26	Milwaukee	31-5	27-12	5-2	63-19
Buffalo	13-27	8-31	1-2	22-60	New York	27-14	20-19	1-1	48-34
Chicago	29-12	26-12	2-1	57-25	Philadelphia	14-23	14-26	2-3	30-52
Cincinnati	20-18	8-32	2-2	30-52	Phoenix	30-11	19-20	0-2	49-33
Cleveland	13-28	8-30	2-1	23-59	Portland	14-26	4-35	0-3	18-64
Detroit	16-25	9-30	1-1	26-56	Seattle	28-12	18-22	1-1	47-35
Golden State	27-8	21-20	3-3	51-31					

INDIVIDUAL STATISTICS

ATLANTA

Player	G.	Min.	FGM	FGA	Pct.	FTM	FTA	Pct.	Reb.	Ast.	PF	Disq.	Tot. Pts.	Avg. Pts.
Lou Hudson	77	3042	775	1540	.503	349	430	.812	385	309	225	0	1899	24.7
Pete Maravich	66	2302	460	1077	.427	355	438	.811	256	393	207	0	1275	19.3
Walt Bellamy	82	3187	593	1089	.545	340	581	.585	1049	262	255	2	1526	18.6
Jim Washington***	84	2961	393	885	.444	256	323	.793	736	146	276	3	1042	12.4
Jim Washington**	67	2416	325	729	.446	201	260	.785	601	121	217	0	851	12.7
Don Adams***	73	2071	313	798	.392	205	275	.745	502	140	266	6	831	11.4
Don Adams**	70	2030	307	779	.394	204	273	.747	494	137	259	5	818	11.7
Herm Gilliam	82	2337	345	774	.446	145	173	.838	335	377	232	3	835	10.2
Bill Bridges*	14	546	51	134	.381	31	44	.705	190	40	50	1	133	9.5
Don May	75	1285	234	476	.492	126	164	.768	217	55	133	0	594	7.9
Milt Williams	10	127	23	53	.434	21	29	.724	4	20	18	0	67	6.7
George Trapp	60	890	144	388	.371	105	139	.755	183	51	144	2	393	6.6
John Vallely*	9	110	20	43	.465	13	20	.650	11	9	13	0	53	5.9
Tom Payne	29	227	45	103	.437	29	46	.630	69	15	40	0	119	4.1
Jeff Halliburton	37	288	61	133	.459	25	30	.833	37	20	50	1	147	4.0
Larry Siegfried***	31	558	43	123	.350	32	37	.865	42	72	53	0	118	3.8
Larry Siegfried**	21	335	25	77	.325	20	23	.870	32	52	32	0	70	3.3
Bob Christian	56	485	66	142	.465	44	61	.721	181	28	77	0	176	3.1
Jim Davis*	11	119	8	33	.242	10	18	.556	36	6	8	0	26	2.4
Shaler Halimon	1	4	0	0	.000	0	0	.000	0	0	1	0	0	0.0

BALTIMORE

Player	G.	Min.	FGM	FGA	Pct.	FTM	FTA	Pct.	Reb.	Ast.	PF	Disq.	Tot. Pts.	Avg. Pts.
Archie Clark***	77	3285	712	1516	.470	514	667	.771	268	613	194	0	1938	25.2
Archie Clark**	76	3243	701	1500	.467	507	656	.773	265	606	191	0	1909	25.1
Jack Marin	78	2927	690	1444	.478	356	398	.894	528	169	240	2	1736	22.3
Earl Monroe*	3	103	26	64	.406	13	18	.722	8	10	9	0	65	21.7
Wes Unseld	76	3171	409	822	.498	171	272	.629	1336	278	218	1	989	13.0
Phil Chenier	81	2481	407	981	.415	182	247	.737	268	205	191	2	996	12.3
Dave Stallworth**	64	1815	303	690	.439	123	153	.804	398	133	186	3	729	11.4
Dave Stallworth***	78	2040	336	778	.432	152	188	.809	433	158	217	3	824	10.6
Mike Riordan**	54	1344	229	488	.469	84	123	.683	127	124	127	0	542	10.0
Mike Riordan***	58	1377	233	499	.467	84	124	.677	128	126	129	0	550	9.5
Stan Love	74 *	1327	242	536	.451	103	140	.736	338	52	202	0	587	7.9
Fred Carter*	2	68	6	27	.222	3	9	.333	19	12	7	0	15	7.5
John Tresvant	65	1227	162	360	.450	121	148	.818	323	83	175	6	445	6.8
Gary Zeller	28	471	83	229	.362	22	35	.629	65	30	62	0	188	6.7
Kevin Loughery*	2	42	4	17	.235	5	8	.625	5	8	5	0	13	6.5
Gus Johnson	39	668	103	269	.383	43	63	.683	226	51	91	0	249	6.4
Terry Driscoll	40	313	40	104	.385	27	39	.692	109	23	53	0	107	2.7
Dorie Murrey	51	421	43	113	.381	24	39	.615	126	17	76	2	110	2.2
Rich Rinaldi	39	159	42	104	.404	20	30	.667	18	15	25	0	104	2.7

1971-72 STATISTICS

BOSTON

Player	G.	Min.	FGM	FGA	Pct.	FTM	FTA	Pct.	Reb.	Ast.	PF	Disq.	Tot. Pts.	Avg. Pts.
John Havlicek	82	3698	897	1957	.458	458	549	.834	672	614	183	1	2252	27.5
Jo Jo White	79	3261	770	1788	.431	285	343	.831	446	416	227	1	1825	23.1
Dave Cowens	79	3186	657	1357	.484	175	243	.720	1203	245	314	10	1489	18.8
Don Nelson	82	2086	389	811	.480	356	452	.788	453	192	220	3	1134	13.8
Don Chaney	79	2275	373	786	.475	197	255	.773	395	202	295	7	943	11.9
Tom Sanders	82	1631	215	524	.410	111	136	.816	353	98	257	7	541	6.6
Steve Kuberski	71	1128	185	444	.417	80	102	.784	320	46	130	1	450	6.3
Art Williams	81	1326	161	339	.475	90	119	.756	256	327	204	2	412	5.1
Hank Finkel	78	736	103	254	.406	43	74	.581	251	61	118	4	249	3.2
Clarence Glover	25	119	25	55	.455	15	32	.469	46	4	26	0	65	2.6
Garfield Smith	26	134	28	66	.424	6	31	.194	37	8	22	0	62	2.4
Rex Morgan	28	150	16	50	.320	23	31	.742	30	17	34	0	55	2.0

BUFFALO

Player	G.	Min.	FGM	FGA	Pct.	FTM	FTA	Pct.	Reb.	Ast.	PF	Disq.	Tot. Pts.	Avg. Pts.
Bob Kauffman	77	3205	558	1123	.497	341	429	.795	787	297	273	7	1457	18.9
Elmore Smith	78	2886	579	1275	.454	194	363	.534	1184	111	306	10	1352	17.3
Walt Hazzard	72	2389	450	998	.451	237	303	.782	213	406	230	2	1137	15.8
Randy Smith	76	2094	432	896	.482	158	254	.622	368	189	202	2	1022	13.4
Fred Hilton	61	1349	309	795	.389	90	122	.738	156	116	145	0	708	11.6
Dick Garrett	73	1905	325	735	.442	136	157	.866	225	165	225	5	786	10.8
Mike Davis	62	1068	213	501	.425	138	180	.767	120	82	141	5	564	9.1
Jerry Chambers	26	369	78	180	.433	22	32	.688	67	23	39	0	178	6.8
Cornell Warner	62	1239	162	366	.443	58	78	.714	379	54	125	2	382	6.2
John Hummer	55	1186	113	290	.390	58	124	.468	229	72	178	4	284	5.2
Em Bryant	54	1223	101	220	.459	75	125	.600	127	206	167	5	277	5.1
Bill Hosket	44	592	89	181	.492	42	52	.808	123	38	79	0	220	5.0

CHICAGO

Player	G.	Min.	FGM	FGA	Pct.	FTM	FTA	Pct.	Reb.	Ast.	PF	Disq.	Tot. Pts.	Avg. Pts.
Bob Love	79	3108	819	1854	.442	399	509	.784	518	125	235	2	2037	25.8
Chet Walker	78	2588	619	1225	.505	481	568	.847	473	178	171	0	1719	22.0
Jerry Sloan	82	3035	535	1206	.444	258	391	.660	691	211	309	8	1328	16.2
Norm Van Lier***	79	2415	334	761	.439	237	300	.790	357	542	239	5	905	11.5
Norm Van Lier**	69	2140	306	671	.456	220	278	.791	299	491	207	4	832	12.1
Bob Weiss	82	2450	358	832	.430	212	254	.835	170	377	212	1	928	11.3
Clifford Ray	82	1872	222	445	.499	134	218	.615	869	254	296	5	578	7.0
Tom Boerwinkle	80	2022	219	500	.438	118	180	.656	897	281	253	4	556	7.0
Howard Porter	67	730	171	403	.424	59	77	.766	183	24	88	0	401	6.0
Jim Fox*	10	133	20	53	.377	20	28	.714	54	6	21	0	60	6.0
Jim King	73	1017	162	356	.455	89	113	.788	81	101	103	0	413	5.7
Jim Collins	19	134	26	71	.366	10	11	.909	12	10	11	0	62	3.3
Charlie Paulk	7	60	8	28	.286	7	9	.778	15	4	7	0	23	3.3
Kennedy McIntosh	43	405	57	168	.339	21	44	.477	89	18	41	0	135	3.1
Jackie Dinkins	18	89	17	41	.415	11	20	.550	20	7	10	0	45	2.5

CINCINNATI

Player	G.	Min.	FGM	FGA	Pct.	FTM	FTA	Pct.	Reb.	Ast.	PF	Disq.	Tot. Pts.	Avg. Pts.
Nate Archibald	76	3272	734	1511	.486	677	824	.822	222	701	198	3	2145	28.2
Tom Van Arsdale	73	2598	550	1205	.456	299	396	.755	350	198	241	1	1399	19.2
Nate Williams	81	2173	418	968	.432	127	172	.738	372	174	300	11	963	11.9
Sam Lacey	81	2832	410	972	.422	119	169	.704	968	173	284	6	939	11.6
Jim Fox***	81	2180	354	788	.449	227	297	.764	713	86	257	8	935	11.5
Jim Fox**	71	2047	334	735	.454	207	269	.770	659	80	236	8	875	12.3
John Mengelt	78	1438	287	605	.474	208	252	.825	148	146	163	0	782	10.0
Johnny Green	82	1914	331	582	.569	141	250	.564	560	120	238	5	803	9.8
Matt Guokas	61	1975	191	385	.496	64	83	.771	142	321	150	0	446	7.3
Norm Van Lier*	10	275	28	90	.311	17	22	.773	58	51	32	1	73	7.3
Jake Jones***	17	202	28	72	.389	20	31	.645	26	12	22	0	76	4.5
Jake Jones**	11	161	22	54	.407	13	21	.619	20	10	19	0	57	5.2
Ken Durrett	19	233	31	79	.392	21	28	.750	39	14	41	0	83	4.4
Gil McGregor	42	532	66	182	.363	39	56	.696	148	18	120	4	171	4.1
Fred Taylor***	34	283	36	117	.308	15	32	.469	54	18	40	0	87	2.6
Fred Taylor**	21	214	30	90	.333	11	19	.579	37	11	32	0	71	3.4
Darrall Imhoff*	9	76	10	29	.345	3	8	.375	27	2	22	1	23	2.6
Sid Catlett	9	40	2	9	.222	2	9	.222	4	1	3	0	6	0.7

1971-72 STATISTICS

CLEVELAND

Player	G.	Min.	FGM	FGA	Pct.	FTM	FTA	Pct.	Reb.	Ast.	PF	Disq.	Tot. Pts.	Avg. Pts.
Austin Carr	43	1539	381	894	.426	149	196	.760	150	148	99	0	911	21.2
John Johnson	82	3041	557	1286	.433	277	353	.785	631	415	268	2	1391	17.0
Butch Beard	68	2434	394	849	.464	260	342	.760	276	456	213	2	1048	15.4
Bobby Smith	82	2734	527	1190	.443	178	224	.795	502	247	222	3	1232	15.0
Rick Roberson	63	2207	304	688	.442	215	366	.587	801	109	251	7	823	13.1
Walt Wesley	82	2185	412	1006	.409	196	291	.674	711	76	245	4	1020	12.4
Charlie Davis	61	1144	229	569	.402	142	169	.840	92	123	143	3	600	9.8
Dave Sorenson	76	1162	213	475	.448	106	136	.779	301	81	120	1	532	7.0
Bobby Washington	69	967	123	309	.398	104	128	.813	129	223	135	0	350	5.1
John Warren	68	969	144	345	.417	49	58	.845	133	91	92	0	337	5.0
Steve Patterson	65	775	94	263	.357	23	46	.500	228	54	80	0	211	3.2
Greg Howard	48	426	50	131	.382	39	51	.765	108	27	50	0	139	2.9
Luther Rackley*	9	65	11	25	.440	1	4	.250	21	3	3	0	23	2.6
Jackie Ridge	32	107	19	44	.432	19	26	.731	15	7	15	0	57	1.8

DETROIT

Player	G.	Min.	FGM	FGA	Pct.	FTM	FTA	Pct.	Reb.	Ast.	PF	Disq.	Tot. Pts.	Avg. Pts.
Bob Lanier	80	3092	834	1690	.493	388	505	.768	1132	248	297	6	2056	25.7
Dave Bing	45	1936	369	891	.414	278	354	.785	186	317	138	3	1016	22.6
Jimmy Walker	78	3083	634	1386	.457	397	480	.827	231	315	198	2	1665	21.3
Curtis Rowe	82	2661	369	802	.460	192	287	.669	699	99	171	1	930	11.3
Terry Dischinger	79	2062	295	574	.514	156	200	.780	338	92	289	7	746	9.4
Howard Komives	79	2071	262	702	.373	164	203	.808	172	291	196	0	688	8.7
Willie Norwood	78	1272	222	440	.505	140	215	.651	316	43	229	4	584	7.5
Bob Quick	18	204	39	82	.476	34	45	.756	51	11	29	0	112	6.2
Jim Davis***	75	983	147	338	.435	100	154	.649	276	51	138	1	394	5.3
Jim Davis**	52	684	121	251	.428	64	98	.653	196	38	106	1	306	5.9
Harvey Marlatt	31	506	60	149	.403	36	42	.857	62	60	64	1	156	5.0
Steve Mix	8	104	15	47	.319	7	12	.583	23	4	7	0	37	4.6
Bill Hewitt	68	1203	131	277	.473	41	82	.500	370	71	134	1	303	4.5
Erwin Mueller	42	605	68	197	.345	43	74	.581	147	57	64	0	179	4.3
Isaiah Wilson	48	322	63	177	.356	41	56	.732	47	41	32	0	167	3.5

GOLDEN STATE

Player	G.	Min.	FGM	FGA	Pct.	FTM	FTA	Pct.	Reb.	Ast.	PF	Disq.	Tot. Pts.	Avg. Pts.
Jeff Mullins	80	3214	685	1466	.467	350	441	.794	444	471	260	5	1720	21.5
Cazzie Russell	79	2902	689	1514	.455	315	378	.833	428	248	176	0	1693	21.4
Nate Thurmond	78	3362	628	1454	.432	417	561	.743	1252	230	214	1	1673	21.4
Jim Barnett	80	2200	374	915	.409	244	292	.836	250	309	189	0	992	12.4
Ron Williams	80	1932	291	614	.474	195	234	.833	147	308	232	1	777	9.7
Joe Ellis	78	1462	280	681	.411	95	132	.720	389	97	224	4	655	8.4
Clyde Lee	78	2674	256	544	.471	120	222	.541	1132	85	244	4	632	8.1
Bob Portman	61	553	89	221	.403	53	60	.883	133	26	69	0	231	3.8
Nick Jones	65	478	82	196	.418	51	61	.836	39	45	109	0	215	3.3
Bill Turner	62	597	71	181	.392	40	53	.755	131	22	67	1	182	2.9
Odis Allison	36	166	17	78	.218	33	61	.541	45	10	34	0	67	1.9
Vic Bartolome	38	165	15	59	.254	4	5	.800	60	3	22	0	34	0.9

HOUSTON

Player	G.	Min.	FGM	FGA	Pct.	FTM	FTA	Pct.	Reb.	Ast.	PF	Disq.	Tot. Pts.	Avg. Pts.
Elvin Hayes	82	3461	832	1918	.434	399	615	.649	1197	270	233	1	2063	25.2
Stu Lantz	81	3097	557	1279	.435	387	462	.838	345	337	211	2	1501	18.5
Calvin Murphy	82	2538	571	1255	.455	349	392	.890	258	393	298	6	1491	18.2
Rudy Tomjanovich	78	2689	500	1010	.495	172	238	.723	923	117	193	2	1172	15.0
Cliff Meely	77	1815	315	776	.406	133	197	.675	507	119	254	9	763	9.9
Greg Smith***	82	2256	309	671	.461	111	168	.661	483	222	259	6	729	8.9
Greg Smith**	54	1519	212	473	.448	70	110	.636	322	159	167	3	494	9.1
Mike Newlin	82	1495	256	618	.414	108	144	.750	228	135	233	6	620	7.6
Larry Siegfried*	10	223	18	46	.391	12	14	.857	10	20	21	0	48	4.8
Don Adams*	3	41	6	19	.316	1	2	.500	8	3	7	1	13	4.3
Jim Davis*	12	180	18	54	.333	26	38	.684	44	5	18	0	62	5.2
Dick Gibbs	64	757	90	265	.340	55	66	.833	140	51	127	0	235	3.7
Curtis Perry*	25	355	38	115	.330	12	24	.500	122	22	47	1	88	3.5
John Vallely***	49	366	69	171	.404	30	45	.667	32	37	50	0	168	3.4
John Vallely**	40	256	49	128	.383	17	25	.680	21	28	37	0	115	2.9
John Egan	38	437	42	104	.404	26	32	.813	26	51	55	0	110	2.9
McCoy McLemore***	27	246	28	71	.394	20	24	.833	73	22	33	1	76	2.8
McCoy McLemore**	17	147	19	43	.442	9	12	.750	39	10	15	1	47	2.8
Dick Cunningham	63	720	67	174	.385	37	53	.698	243	57	76	0	171	2.7

1971-72 STATISTICS

LOS ANGELES

Player	G.	Min.	FGM	FGA	Pct.	FTM	FTA	Pct.	Reb.	Ast.	PF	Disq.	Tot. Pts.	Avg. Pts.
Gail Goodrich	82	3040	826	1695	.487	475	559	.850	295	365	210	0	2127	25.9
Jerry West	77	2973	735	1540	.477	515	633	.814	327	747	209	0	1985	25.8
Jim McMillian	80	3050	642	1331	.482	219	277	.791	522	209	209	0	1503	18.8
Wilt Chamberlain	82	3469	496	764	.649	221	524	.422	1572	329	196	0	1213	14.8
Happy Hairston	80	2748	368	798	.461	311	399	.779	1045	193	251	2	1047	13.1
Elgin Baylor	9	239	42	97	.433	22	27	.815	57	18	20	0	106	11.8
Flynn Robinson	64	1007	262	535	.490	111	129	.860	115	138	139	2	635	9.9
Pat Riley	67	926	197	441	.447	55	74	.743	127	75	110	0	449	6.7
John Trapp	58	759	139	314	.443	51	73	.699	180	42	130	3	329	5.7
Keith Erickson	15	262	40	83	.482	6	7	.857	39	35	26	0	86	5.7
Leroy Ellis	74	1081	138	300	.460	66	95	.674	310	46	115	0	342	4.6
Jim Cleamons	38	201	35	100	.350	28	36	.778	39	35	21	0	98	2.6

MILWAUKEE

Player	G.	Min.	FGM	FGA	Pct.	FTM	FTA	Pct.	Reb.	Ast.	PF	Disq.	Tot. Pts.	Avg. Pts.
Kareem Abdul-Jabbar	81	3583	1159	2019	.574	504	732	.689	1346	370	235	1	2822	34.8
Bob Dandridge	80	2957	630	1264	.498	215	291	.739	613	249	297	7	1475	18.4
Oscar Robertson	64	2390	419	887	.472	276	330	.836	323	491	116	0	1114	17.4
Lucius Allen	80	2316	441	874	.505	198	259	.764	254	333	214	2	1080	13.5
Jon McGlocklin	80	2213	374	733	.510	109	126	.865	181	231	146	0	857	10.7
John Block	79	1524	233	530	.440	206	275	.749	410	95	213	4	672	8.5
Greg Smith*	28	737	97	198	.490	41	58	.707	161	63	92	1	235	8.4
Wally Jones	48	1030	144	354	.407	74	90	.822	75	141	112	0	362	7.5
Curtis Perry***	75	1826	181	486	.372	76	119	.639	593	100	261	14	438	5.8
Curtis Perry**	50	1471	143	371	.385	64	95	.674	471	78	214	13	350	7.0
Toby Kimball	74	971	107	229	.467	44	81	.543	312	60	137	0	258	3.5
McCoy McLemore*	10	99	9	28	.321	11	12	.917	34	12	18	0	29	2.9
Charles Lowery	20	134	17	38	.447	11	18	.611	19	14	16	1	45	2.3
Bill Dinwiddie	23	144	16	57	.281	5	9	.556	32	9	23	0	37	1.6
Jeff Webb*	19	109	9	35	.257	11	13	.846	18	7	8	0	29	1.5
Barry Nelson	28	102	15	36	.417	5	10	.500	20	7	21	0	35	1.3

NEW YORK

Player	G.	Min.	FGM	FGA	Pct.	FTM	FTA	Pct.	Reb.	Ast.	PF	Disq.	Tot. Pts.	Avg. Pts.
Walt Frazier	77	3126	669	1307	.512	450	557	.808	513	446	185	0	1788	23.2
Jerry Lucas	77	2926	543	1060	.512	197	249	.791	1011	318	218	1	1283	16.7
Dave DeBusschere	80	3072	520	1218	.427	193	265	.728	901	291	219	1	1233	15.4
Bill Bradley	78	2780	504	1085	.465	169	199	.849	250	315	254	4	1177	15.1
Willis Reed	11	363	60	137	.438	27	39	.692	96	22	30	0	147	13.4
Dick Barnett	79	2256	401	918	.437	162	215	.753	153	198	229	4	964	12.2
Earl Monroe***	63	1337	287	662	.434	175	224	.781	100	142	139	1	749	11.9
Earl Monroe**	60	1234	261	598	.436	162	206	.786	92	132	130	1	684	11.4
Phil Jackson	80	1273	205	466	.440	167	228	.732	326	72	224	4	577	7.2
Dave Stallworth*	14	225	33	88	.375	29	35	.829	35	25	31	0	95	6.8
Dean Meminger	78	1173	139	293	.474	79	140	.564	185	103	137	0	357	4.6
Luther Rackley***	71	683	103	240	.429	50	88	.568	208	21	107	0	256	3.6
Luther Rackley**	62	618	92	215	.428	49	84	.583	187	18	104	0	233	3.8
Mike Price	6	40	5	14	.357	9	11	.818	6	6	10	0	19	3.2
Eddie Mast	40	270	39	112	.348	25	41	.610	73	10	39	0	103	2.6
Mike Riordan*	4	33	4	11	.364	0	1	.000	1	2	2	0	8	2.0
Charlie Paulk***	35	211	24	88	.273	15	21	.714	64	11	31	0	63	1.8
Charlie Paulk**	28	151	16	60	.267	8	12	.667	49	7	24	0	40	1.4
Eddie Miles	42	198	23	64	.359	16	18	.889	16	17	46	0	62	1.5
Greg Fillmore	10	67	7	27	.259	1	3	.333	15	3	17	0	15	1.5

PHILADELPHIA

Player	G.	Min.	FGM	FGA	Pct.	FTM	FTA	Pct.	Reb.	Ast.	PF	Disq.	Tot. Pts.	Avg. Pts.
Archie Clark*	1	42	11	16	.688	7	11	.636	3	7	3	0	29	29.0
Billy Cunningham	75	2900	658	1428	.461	428	601	.712	918	443	295	12	1744	23.3
Bob Rule***	76	2230	461	1058	.436	226	335	.675	534	116	189	4	1148	15.1
Bob Rule**	60	1987	416	934	.445	203	292	.695	479	110	162	4	1035	17.3
Fred Carter***	79	2215	446	1018	.438	182	293	.621	326	211	242	4	1073	13.6
Fred Carter**	77	2147	440	991	.444	179	284	.630	307	199	235	4	1059	13.8
Bill Bridges***	78	2756	379	779	.487	222	316	.703	1051	198	269	6	980	12.6
Bill Bridges**	64	2210	328	645	.509	191	272	.702	861	158	219	5	847	13.2
Kevin Loughery***	76	1771	341	809	.422	263	320	.822	183	196	213	3	945	12.4
Kevin Loughery**	74	1829	337	792	.426	258	312	.827	178	188	208	3	932	12.6
Fred Foster	74	1699	347	837	.415	185	243	.761	276	90	184	3	879	11.9
Hal Greer	78	2410	389	866	.449	181	234	.774	271	316	268	10	959	11.8
Jim Washington*	17	545	68	156	.436	55	67	.821	135	25	59	3	191	11.2
Dave Wohl	79	1628	243	567	.429	156	189	.825	99	315	178	2	642	8.1
Lucious Jackson	63	1083	137	346	.396	92	122	.754	309	88	141	1	366	5.8
Al Henry	43	421	68	156	.436	51	73	.699	137	8	42	0	187	4.3
Dennis Awtrey	58	794	98	222	.441	49	76	.645	248	51	141	3	245	4.2
Jake Jones*	6	41	6	18	.333	7	10	.700	6	2	6	0	19	3.2
Barry Yates	24	144	31	83	.373	7	11	.636	40	7	14	0	69	2.9

PHOENIX

Player	G.	Min.	FGM	FGA	Pct.	FTM	FTA	Pct.	Reb.	Ast.	PF	Disq.	Tot. Pts.	Avg. Pts.
Connie Hawkins	76	2798	571	1244	.459	456	565	.807	633	296	235	2	1598	21.0
Dick Van Arsdale	82	3096	545	1178	.463	529	626	.845	334	297	232	1	1619	19.7
Charlie Scott	6	177	48	113	.425	17	21	.810	23	26	19	0	113	18.8
Paul Silas	80	3082	485	1031	.470	433	560	.773	955	343	201	2	1403	17.5
Neal Walk	81	2142	506	1057	.479	256	344	.744	665	151	295	9	1268	15.7
Clem Haskins	79	2453	509	1054	.483	220	258	.853	270	290	194	1	1238	15.7
Dennis Layton	80	1849	304	717	.424	122	165	.739	164	247	219	0	730	9.1
Otto Moore	81	1624	260	597	.436	94	156	.603	540	88	212	2	614	7.6
Mel Counts	76	906	147	344	.427	101	140	.721	257	96	159	2	395	5.2
Lamar Green	67	991	133	298	.446	66	90	.733	348	45	134	1	332	5.0
Art Harris	21	145	23	70	.329	9	21	.429	13	18	26	0	55	2.6
Jeff Webb***	46	238	40	100	.400	16	23	.696	35	23	29	0	96	2.1
Jeff Webb**	27	129	31	65	.477	5	10	.500	17	16	21	0	67	2.5
John Wetzel	51	419	31	82	.378	24	30	.800	65	56	71	0	86	1.7
Fred Taylor*	13	69	6	27	.222	4	13	.308	17	7	8	0	16	1.2

PORTLAND

Player	G.	Min.	FGM	FGA	Pct.	FTM	FTA	Pct.	Reb.	Ast.	PF	Disq.	Tot. Pts.	Avg. Pts.
Sidney Wicks	82	3245	784	1837	.427	441	621	.710	943	350	186	1	2009	24.5
Geoff Petrie	60	2155	465	1115	.417	202	256	.789	133	248	108	0	1132	18.9
Stan McKenzie	82	2036	410	834	.492	315	379	.831	272	148	240	2	1135	13.8
Dale Schlueter	81	2693	353	672	.525	241	326	.739	860	285	277	3	947	11.7
Gary Gregor	82	2371	399	884	.451	114	151	.755	591	187	201	2	912	11.1
Rick Adelman	80	2445	329	753	.437	151	201	.751	229	413	209	2	809	10.1
Bill Smith	22	448	72	173	.416	38	64	.594	135	19	73	3	182	8.3
Charlie Yelverton	69	1227	206	530	.389	133	188	.707	201	81	145	2	545	7.9
Willie McCarter	39	612	103	257	.401	37	55	.673	43	45	58	0	243	6.2
Ron Knight	49	483	112	257	.436	31	62	.500	116	33	52	0	225	5.2
Larry Steele	72	1311	148	308	.481	70	97	.722	282	161	198	8	366	5.1
Jim Marsh	39	375	39	117	.333	41	59	.695	84	30	50	0	119	3.1
Darrall Imhoff***	49	480	52	132	.394	24	43	.558	134	52	98	2	128	2.6
Darrall Imhoff**	40	404	42	103	.408	21	35	.600	107	50	76	1	105	2.6

SEATTLE

Player	G.	Min.	FGM	FGA	Pct.	FTM	FTA	Pct.	Reb.	Ast.	PF	Disq.	Tot. Pts.	Avg. Pts.
Spencer Haywood	73	3167	717	1557	.461	480	586	.819	926	148	208	0	1914	26.2
Lenny Wilkens	80	2989	479	1027	.466	480	620	.774	338	766	209	4	1438	18.0
Dick Snyder	73	2534	496	937	.529	218	259	.842	228	283	200	3	1210	16.6
Don Smith	58	1780	322	751	.429	154	214	.720	654	124	178	1	798	13.8
Don Kojis	73	1857	322	687	.469	188	237	.793	335	82	168	2	832	11.4
Lee Winfield	81	2040	343	692	.496	175	262	.668	218	290	198	1	861	10.6
Jim McDaniels	12	235	51	123	.415	11	18	.611	82	9	26	0	113	9.4
Garfield Heard	58	1499	190	474	.401	79	128	.617	442	55	126	2	459	7.9
Barry Clemens	82	1447	252	484	.521	76	90	.844	288	64	198	4	580	7.1
Bob Rule*	16	243	45	124	.363	23	43	.535	55	6	27	0	113	7.1
Pete Cross	74	1424	152	355	.428	103	140	.736	509	63	135	2	407	5.5
Fred Brown	33	359	59	180	.328	22	29	.759	37	60	44	0	140	4.2
Jake Ford	26	181	33	66	.500	26	33	.788	11	26	21	0	92	3.5

*Finished season with another team.
**Player total with this club only.
***Player total with all clubs.

RECORDS OF TEAMS BY MONTHS

Team	Oct. W-L	Nov. W-L	Dec. W-L	Jan. W-L	Feb. W-L	Mar. W-L	Total W-L
Atlanta	3-6	2-11	8-8	7-8	7-8	9-5	36-46
Baltimore	3-6	7-7	5-9	9-5	5-12	9-5	38-44
Boston	6-2	8-7	13-3	10-6	10-5	9-3	56-26
Buffalo	5-7	5-7	4-10	3-11	3-14	4-11	22-60
Chicago	5-2	10-4	12-4	11-5	12-6	7-4	57-25
Cincinnati	1-6	7-6	2-14	6-9	6-12	8-5	30-52
Cleveland	2-8	6-6	7-10	1-13	4-12	3-10	23-59
Detroit	6-4	3-9	5-11	4-11	5-11	3-10	26-56
Golden State	6-3	10-6	9-4	13-1	10-6	8-5	51-31
Houston	2-8	4-10	8-7	5-9	8-6	7-8	34-48
Los Angeles	6-3	14-0	16-0	8-4	13-2	12-2	69-13
Milwaukee	8-1	13-3	11-3	11-4	12-4	8-4	63-19
New York	5-5	8-5	10-4	7-7	12-5	6-8	48-34
Philadelphia	7-2	4-10	4-12	7-7	4-10	4-11	30-52
Phoenix	3-4	8-7	11-5	9-8	11-5	7-4	49-33
Portland	1-5	2-14	5-13	4-11	3-14	3-7	18-64
Seattle	7-2	8-7	7-9	9-5	12-3	4-9	47-35

1971-72 CHAMPIONSHIP PLAYOFF RESULTS
CONFERENCE SEMI-FINAL SERIES

Boston Defeated Atlanta, 4-2
Mar. 29—Atlanta 108 at Boston 126
Mar. 31—Boston 104 at Atlanta 113
Apr. 2—Atlanta 113 at Boston 136
Apr. 4—Boston 110 at Atlanta 112
Apr. 7—Atlanta 114 at Boston 124
Apr. 9—Boston 127 at Atlanta 118

Los Angeles Defeated Chicago, 4-0
Mar. 28—Chicago 80 at Los Angeles 95
Mar. 30—Chicago 124 at Los Angeles 131
Apr. 2—Los Angeles 108 at Chicago 101
Apr. 4—Los Angeles 108 at Chicago 97

New York Defeated Baltimore, 4-2
Mar. 31—New York 105 at Baltimore ....108 (ot)
Apr. 2—Baltimore 88 at New York 110
Apr. 4—New York 103 at Baltimore 104
Apr. 6—Baltimore 98 at New York 104
Apr. 9—New York 106 at Baltimore 82
Apr. 11—Baltimore 101 at New York 107

Milwaukee Defeated Golden State, 4-1
Mar. 28—Golden State 117 at Milwaukee 106
Mar. 30—Golden State 93 at Milwaukee 118
Apr. 1—Milwaukee 122 at Golden State 94
Apr. 4—Milwaukee 106 at Golden State 99
Apr. 6—Golden State 100 at Milwaukee 108

CONFERENCE FINAL SERIES

EASTERN CONFERENCE FINALS
New York Defeated Boston, 4-1
Apr. 13—New York 116 at Boston 94
Apr. 16—Boston 105 at New York 106
Apr. 19—New York 109 at Boston 115
Apr. 21—Boston 98 at New York 116
Apr. 23—New York 111 at Boston 103

WESTERN CONFERENCE FINALS
Los Angeles Defeated Milwaukee, 4-2
Apr. 9—Milwaukee 93 at Los Angeles 72
Apr. 12—Milwaukee 134 at Los Angeles 135
Apr. 14—Los Angeles 108 at Milwaukee 105
Apr. 16—Los Angeles 88 at Milwaukee 114
Apr. 18—Milwaukee 90 at Los Angeles 115
Apr. 22—Los Angeles 104 at Milwaukee 100

CHAMPIONSHIP SERIES
Los Angeles Defeated New York, 4-1
Apr. 26—New York 114 at Los Angeles 92
Apr. 30—New York 92 at Los Angeles 106
May 3—Los Angeles 107 at New York 96
May 5—Los Angeles 116 at New York ....111(ot)
May 7—New York 100 at Los Angeles 114

ALL-TIME WINNINGEST NBA COACHES

Coach	W-L	Pct.
Red Auerbach	938-479	.662
RED HOLZMAN	663-555	.544
JACK RAMSAY	567-499	.532
GENE SHUE	565-563	.501
DICK MOTTA	556-510	.522
AL ATTLES	482-429	.529
Alex Hannum	471-412	.533
Larry Costello	430-300	.589
BILL FITCH	427-475	.473
Tom Heinsohn	427-263	.619
John Kundla	423-302	.583
COTTON FITZSIMMONS	399-413	.491
LENNY WILKENS	380-336	.531
JOHN MacLEOD	349-307	.532
Bill Sharman	333-240	.581
Richie Guerin	327-291	.529
Al Cervi	326-241	.575
Joe Lapchick	326-247	.569
Bill Russell	324-249	.565
Fred Schaus	315-245	.563
Les Harrison	295-181	.620
Paul Seymour	271-241	.529
Bill van Breda Kolff	266-256	.510
Eddie Gottlieb	263-318	.453
Jack McMahon	260-289	.474
BILLY CUNNINGHAM	221-101	.686
DON NELSON	218-174	.556
DOUG MOE	203-160	.559
Hubie Brown	199-208	.489
Dick McGuire	197-260	.431
TOM NISSALKE	189-266	.415
Bob Leonard	186-264	.413
Phil Johnson	155-185	.456
K. C. Jones	155- 91	.630
Dolph Schayes	151-172	.467
Ray Scott	147-134	.523
Jerry West	145-101	.589
Charles Wolf	143-187	.433
Bob Cousy	141-209	.403
Harry Gallatin	136-120	.531
Buddy Jeannette	136-173	.440
KEVIN LOUGHERY	134-260	.340
Johnny Egan	129-152	.459
LARRY BROWN	126- 91	.581
Charlie Eckman	123-118	.510
Paul Birch	120-147	.449
George Senesky	119- 97	.551
Fuzzy Levane	106-170	.384
Joe Mullaney	105- 88	.544
PAUL WESTHEAD	104- 46	.693

Active head coaches in capital letters.

1970-71 STATISTICS

1970-71 WORLD CHAMPION MILWAUKEE BUCKS
Seated: Bob Boozer, Greg Smith, Bob Dandridge, Oscar Robertson, Lew Alcindor, Jon McGlocklin, Lucius Allen, Coach Larry Costello; Standing: Trainer Arnie Garber, Jeff Webb, Marvin Winkler, Dick Cunningham, Bob Greacen, McCoy McLemore, Assistant Coach Tom Nissalke.

FINAL STANDINGS AND TEAM FIGURES

ATLANTIC DIVISION

Team	Atl.	Balt.	Bos.	Buf.	Chi.	Cin.	Clv.	Det.	L.A.	Mil.	N.Y.	Phil.	Pho.	Prt.	S.D.	S.F.	Sea.	W.	L.	Pct.	G.B.
New York	3	4	6	2	2	4	4	3	2	4	..	2	4	3	4	3	2	52	30	.634	....
Philadelphia	2	3	2	4	2	5	3	3	2	1	4	..	3	4	3	3	3	47	35	.573	5
Boston	4	3	..	4	4	4	3	2	3	0	0	4	2	2	3	3	3	44	38	.537	8
Buffalo	1	1	0	..	0	0	5	1	2	0	2	0	1	6	1	1	1	22	60	.268	30

CENTRAL DIVISION

Team	Atl.	Balt.	Bos.	Buf.	Chi.	Cin.	Clv.	Det.	L.A.	Mil.	N.Y.	Phil.	Pho.	Prt.	S.D.	S.F.	Sea.	W.	L.	Pct.	G.B.
Baltimore	3	..	3	3	2	3	4	2	2	1	2	3	3	2	4	2	3	42	40	.512	....
Atlanta	..	3	2	3	1	2	4	0	3	1	3	4	1	2	2	2	3	36	46	.439	6
Cincinnati	4	3	2	4	0	..	5	1	1	1	2	1	1	4	1	2	1	33	49	.402	9
Cleveland	0	0	1	7	0	1	..	2	0	0	0	1	0	2	0	1	0	15	67	.183	27

MIDWEST DIVISION

Team	Atl.	Balt.	Bos.	Buf.	Chi.	Cin.	Clv.	Det.	L.A.	Mil.	N.Y.	Phil.	Pho.	Prt.	S.D.	S.F.	Sea.	W.	L.	Pct.	G.B.
Milwaukee	4	4	5	4	5	4	4	5	4	..	1	4	4	3	4	6	5	66	16	.805	....
Chicago	3	3	1	4	..	4	4	3	2	1	3	3	3	6	4	3	4	51	31	.622	15
Phoenix	4	2	3	3	3	4	4	4	2	1	2	2	..	4	2	3	3	48	34	.585	18
Detroit	5	3	3	5	3	4	2	..	1	2	1	2	2	2	3	4	3	45	37	.549	21

PACIFIC DIVISION

Team	Atl.	Balt.	Bos.	Buf.	Chi.	Cin.	Clv.	Det.	L.A.	Mil.	N.Y.	Phil.	Pho.	Prt.	S.D.	S.F.	Sea.	W.	L.	Pct.	G.B.
Los Angeles	2	3	2	2	4	4	4	3	..	1	3	3	2	4	3	4	4	48	34	.585	....
San Francisco	3	3	2	3	2	3	3	4	2	0	2	2	3	4	..	3	3	41	41	.500	7
San Diego	3	1	2	3	0	3	4	2	3	1	1	2	4	4	..	2	5	40	42	.488	8
Seattle	2	2	2	3	2	4	4	1	2	1	3	2	2	4	1	3	..	38	44	.463	10
Portland	2	2	2	6	1	0	10	1	0	1	1	0	0	..	0	1	2	29	53	.354	19

1970-71 STATISTICS

TEAM STATISTICS (OFFENSE)

	G.	FIELD GOALS			FREE THROWS			MISCELLANEOUS				SCORING		Pt.
		Made	Att.	Pct.	Made	Att.	Pct.	Rbds.	Ast.	PF.	Dis.*	Pts.	Avg.	Dif.
Milwaukee	82	3972	7803	.509	1766	2379	.742	4344	2249	1847	15	9710	118.4	+12.2
Boston	82	3804	8616	.442	2000	2648	.755	4833	2052	2138	43	9608	117.2	+ 2.1
Cincinnati	82	3805	8374	.454	1901	2622	.725	4151	2022	2126	45	9511	116.0	− 3.2
Portland	82	3721	8562	.435	2025	2671	.758	4210	2227	2024	23	9467	115.5	− 4.5
Seattle	82	3664	8034	.456	2101	2790	.753	4456	2049	1917	20	9429	115.0	− 2.0
Philadelphia	82	3608	8026	.450	2199	2967	.741	4437	1976	2168	34	9415	114.8	+ 1.5
Los Angeles	82	3739	7857	.476	1933	2717	.711	4269	2205	1709	14	9411	114.8	+ 3.1
Atlanta	82	3614	7779	.465	2120	2975	.713	4472	1906	1958	23	9348	114.0	− 1.8
Phoenix	82	3503	8021	.437	2327	3078	.756	4442	1927	2132	30	9333	113.8	+ 1.9
San Diego	82	3547	8426	.421	2188	2921	.749	4686	1921	2128	39	9282	113.2	− 0.2
Baltimore	82	3684	8331	.442	1886	2500	.754	4550	1772	1966	20	9254	112.9	+ 0.6
Chicago	82	3460	7660	.452	2150	2721	.790	4325	2142	1797	12	9070	110.6	+ 5.2
Detroit	82	3468	7730	.449	2093	2808	.745	3923	1696	1969	18	9029	110.1	− 0.8
New York	82	3633	8076	.450	1760	2377	.740	4075	1779	1916	13	9026	110.1	+ 5.1
San Francisco	82	3454	7709	.448	1875	2468	.760	4643	1893	1833	25	8783	107.1	− 1.4
Buffalo	82	3424	7860	.436	1805	2504	.721	4261	1962	2232	55	8653	105.5	− 6.6
Cleveland	82	3299	7778	.424	1775	2380	.746	3982	2065	2114	37	8373	102.1	−11.2

TEAM STATISTICS (DEFENSE)

	G.	FIELD GOALS			FREE THROWS			MISCELLANEOUS				SCORING	
Allowed By		Made	Att.	Pct.	Made	Att.	Pct.	Rbds.	Ast.	PF.	Dis.*	Pts.	Avg.
New York	82	3343	7752	.431	1928	2565	.752	4591	1509	1889	22	8614	105.0
Chicago	82	3491	7709	.453	1658	2216	.748	4031	1914	2099	36	8640	105.4
Milwaukee	82	3489	8224	.424	1727	2322	.744	4004	1923	1770	11	8705	106.2
San Francisco	82	3583	8371	.428	1735	2318	.748	4305	1949	1882	16	8901	108.5
Detroit	82	3525	7713	.457	2040	2703	.755	4292	1912	2087	30	9090	110.9
Los Angeles	82	3796	8511	.446	1567	2107	.744	4552	2078	1951	23	9159	111.7
Phoenix	82	3506	7828	.448	2165	2923	.741	4173	2069	2202	42	9177	111.9
Buffalo	82	3486	7666	.455	2224	3018	.737	4447	1998	1956	25	9196	112.1
Baltimore	82	3640	8164	.446	1926	2584	.745	4435	1862	1897	20	9206	112.3
Philadelphia	82	3514	7806	.450	2260	3076	.735	4372	1970	2089	39	9288	113.3
Cleveland	82	3476	7480	.465	2337	3024	.773	4175	2307	1899	15	9289	113.3
San Diego	82	3639	8102	.449	2024	2745	.737	4345	2135	2141	41	9302	113.4
Boston	82	3612	8211	.440	2214	2982	.742	4342	1910	1962	27	9438	115.1
Atlanta	82	3801	8525	.446	1893	2515	.753	4279	1996	2074	30	9495	115.8
Seattle	82	3803	8117	.469	1985	2679	.741	4156	1994	2062	20	9591	117.0
Cincinnati	82	3795	8130	.467	2184	2991	.730	4675	2050	1979	37	9774	119.2
Portland	82	3900	8333	.468	2037	2758	.739	4885	2267	2035	32	9837	120.0

*–Individual player disqualified (fouled out of game).

INDIVIDUAL SCORING LEADERS
(Minimum of 70 Games Played)

	G.	FG	FT	Pts.	Avg.
Alcindor, Mil	82	1063	470	2596	31.7
Havlicek, Bos	81	892	554	2338	28.9
Hayes, S. D.	82	948	454	2350	28.7
Bing, Det	82	799	615	2213	27.0
Hudson, Atl	76	829	381	2039	26.8
Love, Chi	81	765	513	2043	25.2
Petrie, Port	82	784	463	2031	24.8
Maravich, Atl	81	738	404	1880	23.2
Cunningham, Phil	81	702	455	1859	23.0
Van Arsdale, Cin	82	749	377	1875	22.9
Walker, Chi	81	650	480	1780	22.0
Van Arsdale, Phoe	81	609	553	1771	21.9
Frazier, N. Y.	80	651	434	1736	21.7
Monroe, Balt	81	663	406	1732	21.4
Clark, Phil	82	662	422	1746	21.3
White, Bos	75	693	215	1601	21.3
Reed, N. Y.	73	614	299	1527	20.9
Hawkins, Phoe	71	512	457	1481	20.9
Mullins, S. F.	75	630	302	1562	20.8
Chamberlain, L. A.	82	668	360	1696	20.7

FIELD GOAL LEADERS
(Minimum 700 Attempts)

	FGM	FGA	Pct.
Johnny Green, Cincinnati	502	855	.587
Lew Alcindor, Milwaukee	1063	1843	.577
Wilt Chamberlain, Los Angeles	668	1226	.545
Jon McGlocklin, Milwaukee	574	1073	.535
Dick Snyder, Seattle	645	1215	.531
Greg Smith, Milwaukee	409	799	.512
Bob Dandridge, Milwaukee	594	1167	.509
Wes Unseld, Baltimore	424	846	.501
Jerry Lucas, San Francisco	623	1250	.498
Archie Clark, Philadelphia	662	1334	.496
Oscar Robertson, Milwaukee	592	1193	.496

FREE THROW LEADERS
(Minimum 350 Attempts)

	FTM	FTA	Pct.
Chet Walker, Chicago	480	559	.859
Oscar Robertson, Milwaukee	385	453	.850
Ron Williams, San Francisco	331	392	.844
Jeff Mullins, San Francisco	302	358	.844
Dick Snyder, Seattle	302	361	.837
Stan McKenzie, Portland	331	396	.836
Jerry West, Los Angeles	525	631	.832
Jimmy Walker, Detroit	344	414	.831
Bob Love, Chicago	513	619	.829
Calvin Murphy, San Diego	356	434	.820

1970-71 STATISTICS

REBOUND LEADERS
(Minimum 70 Games)

	G.	No.	Avg.
Wilt Chamberlain, Los Angeles	82	1493	18.2
Wes Unseld, Baltimore	74	1253	16.9
Elvin Hayes, San Diego	82	1362	16.6
Lew Alcindor, Milwaukee	82	1311	16.0
Jerry Lucas, San Francisco	80	1265	15.8
Bill Bridges, Atlanta	82	1233	15.0
Dave Cowens, Boston	81	1216	15.0
Tom Boerwinkle, Chicago	82	1133	13.8
Nate Thurmond, San Francisco	82	1128	13.8
Willis Reed, New York	73	1003	13.7

ASSISTS LEADERS
(Minimum 70 Games)

	G.	No.	Avg.
Norm Van Lier, Cincinnati	82	832	10.1
Len Wilkens, Seattle	71	654	9.2
Oscar Robertson, Milwaukee	81	668	8.2
John Havlicek, Boston	81	607	7.5
Walt Frazier, New York	80	536	6.7
Walt Hazzard, Atlanta	82	514	6.3
Ron Williams, San Francisco	82	480	5.9
Nate Archibald, Cincinnati	82	450	5.5
Archie Clark, Philadelphia	82	440	5.4
Dave Bing, Detroit	82	408	5.0

INTER-CLUB RECORDS—HOME, AWAY AND NEUTRAL COURT

	Home	Away	Neutral	Total
Atlanta	21-20	14-26	1-0	36-46
Baltimore	24-13	16-25	2-2	42-40
Boston	25-14	18-22	1-2	44-38
Buffalo	14-23	6-30	2-7	22-60
Chicago	30-11	17-19	4-1	51-31
Cincinnati	17-16	11-28	5-5	33-49
Cleveland	11-30	2-37	2-0	15-67
Detroit	24-17	20-19	1-1	45-37
Los Angeles	30-11	17-22	1-1	48-34
Milwaukee	34-2	28-13	4-1	66-16
New York	32-9	19-20	1-1	52-30
Philadelphia	24-15	21-18	2-2	47-35
Phoenix	27-14	19-20	2-0	48-34
Portland	18-21	9-26	2-6	29-53
San Diego	24-15	15-26	1-1	40-42
San Francisco	20-18	19-21	2-2	41-41
Seattle	27-13	11-30	0-1	38-44

INDIVIDUAL STATISTICS

ATLANTA

Player	G.	Min.	FGM	FGA	Pct.	FTM	FTA	Pct.	Reb.	Ast.	PF	Disq.	Pts.	Avg.
Lou Hudson	76	3113	829	1713	.484	381	502	.759	386	257	186	0	2039	26.8
Pete Maravich	81	2926	738	1613	.458	404	505	.800	298	355	238	1	1880	23.2
Walt Hazzard	82	2877	517	1126	.459	315	415	.759	300	514	276	2	1349	16.5
Walt Bellamy	82	2908	433	879	.493	336	556	.604	1060	223	240	1	1202	14.7
Bill Bridges	82	3140	382	834	.458	211	330	.639	1233	240	317	4	975	11.9
Jerry Chambers	65	1168	237	526	.451	106	134	.791	245	61	119	0	580	8.9
Jim Davis	82	1864	241	503	.479	195	288	.677	546	108	253	5	677	8.3
Len Chappell***	48	537	86	199	.432	71	88	.807	151	17	72	2	243	5.1
Len Chappell**	42	451	71	161	.441	60	74	.811	133	16	63	2	202	4.8
John Vallely	51	430	73	204	.358	45	59	.763	34	47	50	0	191	3.7
Bob Christian	54	524	55	127	.433	40	64	.625	177	30	118	0	150	2.8
Herb White	38	315	34	84	.405	22	39	.564	48	47	62	2	90	2.4
Bob Riley	7	39	4	9	.444	5	9	.556	12	1	5	0	13	1.9

BALTIMORE

Player	G.	Min.	FGM	FGA	Pct.	FTM	FTA	Pct.	Reb.	Ast.	PF	Disq.	Pts.	Avg.
Earl Monroe	81	2843	663	1501	.442	406	506	.802	213	354	220	3	1732	21.4
Jack Marin	82	2920	626	1360	.460	290	342	.848	513	217	261	3	1542	18.8
Gus Johnson	66	2538	494	1090	.453	214	290	.738	1128	192	227	4	1202	18.2
Kevin Loughery	82	2904	481	1193	.403	275	331	.831	219	301	246	2	1237	15.1
Wes Unseld	74	2904	424	846	.501	199	303	.657	1253	293	235	2	1047	14.1
Fred Carter	77	1707	340	815	.417	119	183	.650	251	165	165	0	799	10.4
Eddie Miles	63	1541	252	591	.426	118	147	.803	167	110	119	0	622	9.9
John Tresvant***	75	1577	202	436	.463	146	205	.712	382	86	196	1	550	7.3
John Tresvant**	67	1451	184	401	.459	139	195	.713	359	76	185	1	507	7.6
Al Tucker	31	276	52	115	.452	25	31	.806	73	7	33	0	129	4.2
George Johnson	24	337	41	100	.410	11	30	.367	114	10	63	1	93	3.9
Jim Barnes	11	100	15	28	.536	7	11	.636	16	8	23	0	37	3.4
Dorie Murrey***	70	716	78	178	.438	75	112	.670	221	32	149	4	231	3.3
Dorie Murrey**	77	172	77	172	.448	66	101	.653	214	31	146	4	220	3.2
Dennis Stewart	2	6	1	4	.240	2	2	1.000	3	1	0	0	4	2.0
Gary Zeller	50	226	34	115	.296	15	28	.536	27	7	43	0	83	1.7

BOSTON

Player	G.	Min.	FGM	FGA	Pct.	FTM	FTA	Pct.	Reb.	Ast.	PF	Disq.	Pts.	Avg.
John Havlicek	81	3678	892	1982	.450	554	677	.818	730	607	200	0	2338	28.9
Jo Jo White	75	2787	693	1494	.464	215	269	.799	376	361	255	5	1601	21.3
Dave Cowens	81	3076	550	1302	.422	273	373	.732	1216	228	350	15	1373	17.0
Don Nelson	82	2254	412	881	.468	317	426	.744	565	153	232	2	1141	13.9
Don Chaney	81	2289	348	766	.454	234	313	.748	463	235	288	11	930	11.5
Steve Kuberski	82	1867	313	745	.420	133	183	.727	538	78	198	1	759	9.3
Rich Johnson	1	13	4	5	.800	0	0	.000	5	0	3	0	8	8.0
Henry Finkel	80	1234	214	489	.438	93	127	.732	343	79	196	5	521	6.5
Art Williams	74	1141	150	330	.455	60	83	.723	205	233	182	1	360	4.9
Bill Dinwiddie	61	717	123	328	.375	54	74	.730	209	34	90	1	300	4.9
Rex Morgan	34	266	41	102	.402	24	56	.393	95	9	53	0	106	2.9
Garfield Smith	37	281	42	116	.362	22	96	.875	17	11	25	0	39	2.3
Tom Sanders	17	121	16	44	.364	7	8	.600	10	2	8	0	15	0.9
Willie Williams*	16	56	6	32	.188	3	5	.600						

1970-71 STATISTICS

BUFFALO

Player	G.	Min.	FGM	FGA	Pct.	FTM	FTA	Pct.	Reb.	Ast.	PF	Disq.	Pts.	Avg.
Bob Kauffman	78	2778	616	1309	.471	359	485	.740	837	354	263	8	1591	20.4
Don May	76	2666	629	1336	.471	277	350	.791	567	150	219	4	1535	20.2
Dick Garrett	75	2375	373	902	.414	218	251	.869	295	264	290	9	964	12.9
Mike Davis	73	1617	317	744	.410	199	262	.760	187	153	220	7	833	11.4
John Hummer	81	2637	339	764	.444	235	405	.580	717	163	284	10	913	11.3
Herm Gilliam	80	2082	378	896	.422	142	189	.751	334	291	246	4	898	11.2
Emmette Bryant	73	2137	288	684	.421	151	203	.744	262	352	266	7	727	10.0
Bill Hosket	13	217	47	90	.522	11	17	.647	75	20	27	1	105	8.1
Cornell Warner	65	1293	156	376	.415	79	143	.552	452	53	140	2	391	6.0
Fred Crawford*	15	203	36	106	.340	16	26	.615	35	24	18	0	88	5.9
George Wilson	46	713	92	269	.342	56	69	.812	230	48	99	1	240	5.2
Paul Long	30	213	57	120	.475	20	24	.833	31	25	23	0	134	4.5
Nate Bowman	44	483	58	148	.392	20	38	.526	173	41	91	2	136	3.1
Mike Silliman	36	366	36	79	.456	19	39	.487	62	23	37	0	91	2.5
Mike Lynn	5	25	2	7	.286	3	3	1.000	4	1	9	0	7	1.4

CHICAGO

Player	G.	Min.	FGM	FGA	Pct.	FTM	FTA	Pct.	Reb.	Ast.	PF	Disq.	Pts.	Avg.
Bob Love	81	3482	765	1710	.447	513	619	.829	690	185	259	0	2043	25.2
Chet Walker	81	2927	650	1398	.465	480	559	.859	588	179	187	2	1780	22.0
Jerry Sloan	80	3140	592	1342	.441	278	389	.715	701	281	289	5	1462	18.3
Tom Boerwinkle	82	2370	357	736	.485	168	232	.724	1133	397	275	3	882	10.8
Jim Fox	82	1628	280	611	.458	239	321	.745	598	196	213	0	799	9.7
Bob Weiss	82	2237	278	659	.422	226	269	.840	189	387	216	1	782	9.5
Matt Guokas***	79	2213	206	418	.493	101	138	.732	158	342	189	1	513	6.5
Matt Guokas**	78	2208	206	418	.493	101	138	.732	157	342	189	1	513	6.6
Jim King	55	645	100	228	.439	64	79	.810	68	78	55	0	264	4.8
John Baum	62	543	123	293	.420	40	58	.690	125	31	55	0	286	4.6
Jim Collins	55	478	92	214	.430	35	45	.778	54	60	43	0	219	4.0
Paul Ruffner	10	60	15	35	.429	4	8	.500	16	2	10	0	34	3.4
Shaler Halimon*	2	23	1	8	.125	0	1	.000	2	4	5	0	2	1.0
A. W. Holt	6	14	1	8	.125	2	3	.667	4	0	1	0	4	0.7

CINCINNATI

Player	G.	Min.	FGM	FGA	Pct.	FTM	FTA	Pct.	Reb.	Ast.	PF	Disq.	Pts.	Avg.
Tom Van Arsdale	82	3146	749	1642	.456	377	523	.721	499	181	294	3	1875	22.9
Johnny Green	75	2147	502	855	.587	248	402	.617	656	89	233	7	1252	16.7
Norm Van Lier	82	3324	478	1138	.420	359	440	.816	583	832	343	12	1315	16.0
Nate Archibald	82	2867	486	1095	.444	336	444	.757	242	450	218	2	1308	16.0
Sam Lacey	81	2648	467	1117	.418	156	227	.687	913	117	270	8	1090	13.5
Flynn Robinson	71	1368	374	817	.458	195	228	.855	143	138	161	0	943	13.3
Charlie Paulk	68	1213	274	637	.430	79	131	.603	320	27	186	6	627	9.2
Darrall Imhoff	34	826	119	258	.461	37	73	.507	233	79	120	5	275	8.1
Fred Foster*	1	21	3	8	.375	1	3	.333	4	0	2	0	7	7.0
Connie Dierking*	1	23	3	16	.188	0	0	.000	7	1	5	0	6	6.0
Bob Arnzen	55	594	128	277	.462	45	52	.865	152	24	54	0	301	5.5
Greg Hyder	77	1359	183	409	.477	51	71	.718	332	48	187	2	417	5.4
Tom Black***	71	873	121	301	.402	57	88	.648	259	44	136	1	299	4.2
Tom Black**	16	100	10	33	.303	6	15	.400	34	2	20	0	26	1.6
Moe Barr	31	145	25	62	.403	11	13	.846	20	28	27	0	61	2.0
Willie Williams***	25	105	10	42	.238	3	5	.600	23	8	14	0	23	0.9
Willie Williams**	9	49	4	10	.400	0	0	.000	13	6	6	0	8	0.9

CLEVELAND

Player	G.	Min.	FGM	FGA	Pct.	FTM	FTA	Pct.	Reb.	Ast.	PF	Disq.	Pts.	Avg.
Walt Wesley	82	2425	565	1241	.455	325	473	.687	713	83	295	5	1455	17.7
John Johnson	67	2310	435	1032	.422	240	298	.805	453	323	251	3	1110	16.6
Bob Smith	77	2332	495	1106	.448	178	234	.761	429	258	175	4	1168	15.2
McCoy McLemore*	58	1839	254	654	.388	170	220	.773	463	176	169	1	678	11.7
John Warren	82	2610	380	899	.423	180	217	.829	344	347	299	13	940	11.5
Dave Sorenson	79	1940	353	794	.445	184	229	.803	486	163	181	3	890	11.3
Luther Rackley	74	1434	219	470	.466	121	190	.637	394	66	186	3	559	7.6
Bob Washington	47	823	123	310	.397	104	140	.743	105	190	105	0	350	7.4
Len Chappell*	6	86	15	38	.395	11	14	.786	18	1	9	0	41	6.8
Bob Lewis	79	1852	179	484	.370	109	152	.717	206	244	176	1	467	5.9
Joe Cooke	73	725	134	341	.393	48	59	.814	114	93	135	2	316	4.3
Johnny Egan*	26	410	40	98	.408	25	28	.893	32	58	31	0	105	4.0
Cliff Anderson	23	171	19	59	.322	41	60	.683	37	16	22	1	79	3.4
Gary Freeman***	52	382	69	134	.515	29	40	.725	106	35	67	0	167	3.2
Gary Freeman**	11	47	7	12	.583	1	2	.500	8	4	4	0	15	1.4
Larry Mikan	53	536	62	186	.333	34	55	.618	139	41	56	1	158	3.0
Gary Suiter	30	140	19	54	.352	4	9	.444	41	2	20	0	42	1.4

1970-71 STATISTICS

DETROIT

Player	G.	Min.	FGM	FGA	Pct.	FTM	FTA	Pct.	Reb.	Ast.	PF	Disq.	Pts.	Avg.
Dave Bing	82	3065	799	1710	.467	615	772	.797	364	408	228	4	2213	27.0
Jimmy Walker	79	2765	524	1201	.436	344	414	.831	207	268	173	0	1392	17.6
Bob Lanier	82	2017	504	1108	.455	273	376	.726	665	146	272	4	1281	15.6
Terry Dischinger	65	1855	304	568	.535	161	211	.763	339	113	189	2	769	11.8
Otto Moore	82	1926	310	696	.445	121	219	.553	700	88	182	0	741	9.0
Steve Mix	35	731	111	249	.446	68	89	.764	164	34	72	0	290	8.3
Howard Komives	82	1932	275	715	.385	121	151	.801	152	262	184	0	671	8.2
Bob Quick	56	1146	155	341	.455	138	176	.784	230	56	142	1	448	8.0
Bill Hewitt	62	1725	203	435	.467	69	120	.575	454	124	189	5	475	7.7
Erwin Mueller	52	1224	126	309	.408	60	108	.556	223	113	99	0	312	6.0
Terry Driscoll	69	1255	132	318	.415	108	154	.701	402	54	212	2	372	5.4
Harvey Marlatt	23	214	25	80	.313	15	18	.833	23	30	27	0	65	2.8

LOS ANGELES

Player	G.	Min.	FGM	FGA	Pct.	FTM	FTA	Pct.	Reb.	Ast.	PF	Disq.	Pts.	Avg.
Jerry West	69	2845	667	1351	.494	525	631	.832	320	655	180	0	1859	26.9
Wilt Chamberlain	82	3630	668	1226	.545	360	669	.538	1493	352	174	0	1696	20.7
Harold Hairston	82	2921	574	1233	.466	437	431	.782	797	168	256	2	1485	18.6
Gail Goodrich	79	2808	558	1174	.475	264	343	.770	260	380	258	3	1380	17.5
Keith Erickson	73	2272	369	783	.471	85	112	.759	404	223	241	4	823	11.3
Elgin Baylor	2	57	8	19	.421	4	6	.667	11	2	6	0	20	10.0
Jim McMillian	81	1747	289	629	.459	100	130	.769	330	133	122	1	678	8.4
Willie McCarter	76	1369	247	592	.417	46	77	.597	122	126	152	0	540	7.1
John Tresvant*	8	66	18	35	.514	7	10	.700	23	10	11	0	43	5.4
Rick Roberson	65	909	125	301	.415	88	143	.615	304	47	125	1	338	5.2
Pat Riley	54	506	105	254	.413	56	87	.644	54	72	84	0	266	4.9
Fred Hetzel	59	613	111	256	.434	60	77	.779	149	37	99	3	282	4.8
Earnie Killum	4	12	0	4	.000	1	1	1.000	2	0	1	0	1	0.3

MILWAUKEE

Player	G.	Min.	FGM	FGA	Pct.	FTM	FTA	Pct.	Reb.	Ast.	PF	Disq.	Pts.	Avg.
Lew Alcindor	82	3288	1063	1843	.577	470	681	.690	1311	272	264	4	2596	31.7
Oscar Robertson	81	3194	592	1193	.496	385	453	.850	462	668	203	0	1569	19.4
Bob Dandridge	79	2862	594	1167	.509	264	376	.702	632	277	287	4	1452	18.4
Jon McGlocklin	82	2891	574	1073	.535	144	167	.862	223	305	189	0	1292	15.8
Greg Smith	82	2428	409	799	.512	141	213	.662	589	227	284	5	959	11.7
McCoy McLemore***	86	2294	303	787	.385	204	261	.782	568	206	235	2	810	9.4
McCoy McLemore**	28	415	49	133	.368	34	41	.829	105	30	66	1	132	4.7
Bob Boozer	80	1775	290	645	.450	148	181	.818	435	128	216	0	728	9.1
Lucius Allen	61	1162	178	398	.447	77	110	.700	152	161	108	0	433	7.1
Gary Freeman*	41	335	62	122	.508	28	38	.737	98	31	63	0	152	3.7
Marvin Winkler	3	14	3	10	.300	2	2	1.000	4	2	3	0	8	2.7
Dick Cunningham	76	675	81	195	.415	39	59	.661	257	43	90	1	201	2.6
Bob Greacen	2	43	1	12	.083	3	7	.429	6	13	7	0	5	2.5
Bill Zopf	53	398	49	135	.363	20	36	.556	46	73	34	0	118	2.2
Jeff Webb	29	300	27	78	.346	11	15	.733	24	19	33	0	65	2.2

NEW YORK

Player	G.	Min.	FGM	FGA	Pct.	FTM	FTA	Pct.	Reb.	Ast.	PF	Disq.	Pts.	Avg.
Walt Frazier	80	3455	651	1317	.494	434	557	.779	544	536	240	1	1736	21.7
Willis Reed	73	2855	614	1330	.462	299	381	.785	1003	148	228	1	1527	20.9
Dave DeBusschere	81	2891	523	1243	.421	217	312	.696	901	220	237	2	1263	15.6
Dick Barnett	82	2843	540	1184	.456	193	278	.694	238	225	232	1	1273	15.5
Bill Bradley	78	2300	413	912	.453	144	175	.823	260	280	245	3	970	12.4
Dave Stallworth	81	1565	295	685	.431	169	230	.735	352	106	175	1	759	9.4
Cazzie Russell	57	1056	216	504	.429	92	119	.773	192	77	74	0	524	9.2
Mike Riordan	82	1320	162	388	.418	67	108	.620	169	121	151	0	391	4.8
Phil Jackson	71	771	118	263	.449	95	133	.714	238	31	169	4	331	4.7
Greg Fillmore	39	271	45	102	.441	13	27	.481	93	17	80	0	103	2.6
Eddie Mast	30	164	25	66	.379	11	20	.550	56	4	25	0	61	2.0
Mike Price	56	251	30	81	.370	24	34	.706	29	12	57	0	84	1.5
Milt Williams	5	13	1	1	1.000	2	3	.667	0	2	3	0	4	0.8

PHILADELPHIA

Player	G.	Min.	FGM	FGA	Pct.	FTM	FTA	Pct.	Reb.	Ast.	PF	Disq.	Pts.	Avg.
Billy Cunningham	81	3090	702	1519	.462	455	620	.734	946	395	328	5	1859	23.0
Archie Clark	82	3245	662	1334	.496	422	536	.787	391	440	217	2	1746	21.3
Hal Greer	81	3060	591	1371	.431	326	405	.805	364	369	289	4	1508	18.6
Jim Washington	78	2501	395	829	.476	259	340	.762	747	97	258	6	1049	13.4
Bailey Howell	82	1589	324	686	.472	230	315	.730	441	115	234	2	878	10.7
Wally Jones	41	962	168	418	.402	79	101	.782	64	128	110	1	415	10.1
Dennis Awtrey	70	1292	200	421	.475	104	157	.662	430	89	211	7	504	7.2
Luke Jackson	79	1774	199	529	.376	131	189	.693	568	148	211	3	529	6.7
Connie Dierking***	54	737	125	322	.388	61	89	.685	234	60	114	1	311	5.8
Connie Dierking**	53	714	122	306	.399	61	89	.685	227	59	109	1	305	5.8
Fred Foster***	67	909	148	368	.402	73	106	.689	151	61	115	3	369	5.5
Fred Foster**	66	888	145	360	.403	72	103	.699	147	61	113	3	362	5.5
Fred Crawford***	51	652	110	281	.391	48	98	.490	144	78	77	0	268	5.3
Fred Crawford**	36	449	74	175	.423	32	72	.444	69	54	59	0	180	5.0
Cliff Anderson***	28	198	20	65	.308	46	67	.687	48	20	29	1	86	3.1
Cliff Anderson**	5	27	1	6	.167	5	7	.714	11	4	7	0	7	1.4
Bud Ogden	27	133	24	66	.364	18	26	.692	20	17	21	0	66	2.4
Al Henry	6	26	1	6	.167	5	7	.714	11	0	1	0	7	1.2
Matt Guokas*	1	5	0	0	.000	0	0	.000	1	0	0	0	0	0.0

PHOENIX

Player	G.	Min.	FGM	FGA	Pct.	FTM	FTA	Pct.	Reb.	Ast.	PF	Disq.	Pts.	Avg.
Dick Van Arsdale	81	3157	609	1346	.452	553	682	.811	316	329	246	1	1771	21.9
Connie Hawkins	71	2662	512	1181	.434	457	560	.816	643	322	197	2	1481	20.9
Clem Haskins	82	2764	562	1277	.440	338	431	.784	324	383	207	2	1462	17.8
Neal Walk	82	2033	426	945	.451	205	268	.765	674	117	282	8	1057	12.9
Paul Silas	81	2944	338	789	.428	285	416	.685	1015	247	227	3	961	11.9
Mel Counts	80	1669	365	799	.457	149	198	.753	503	136	279	8	879	11.0
Art Harris	56	952	199	484	.411	69	113	.611	100	132	137	0	467	8.3
Lamar Green	68	1326	167	369	.453	64	106	.604	466	53	202	5	398	5.9
Fred Taylor	54	552	110	284	.387	78	125	.624	86	51	113	0	298	5.5
John Wetzel	70	1091	124	288	.431	83	101	.822	153	114	156	1	331	4.7
Greg Howard	44	426	68	173	.393	37	58	.638	119	26	67	0	173	3.9
Joe Thomas	39	204	23	86	.267	9	20	.450	43	17	19	0	55	1.4

PORTLAND

Player	G.	Min.	FGM	FGA	Pct.	FTM	FTA	Pct.	Reb.	Ast.	PF	Disq.	Pts.	Avg.
Geoff Petrie	82	3032	784	1770	.443	463	600	.772	280	390	196	1	2031	24.8
Jim Barnett	78	2371	559	1283	.436	326	402	.811	376	323	190	1	1444	18.5
LeRoy Ellis	74	2581	485	1095	.443	209	261	.801	907	235	258	5	1179	15.9
Stan McKenzie	82	2290	398	902	.441	331	396	.836	309	235	238	2	1127	13.7
Rick Adelman	81	2303	378	895	.422	267	369	.724	282	380	214	2	1023	12.6
Gary Gregor	44	1153	181	421	.430	59	89	.663	334	81	120	2	421	9.6
Shaler Halimon***	81	1652	301	783	.384	107	162	.660	417	215	183	1	709	8.8
Shaler Halimon**	79	1629	300	775	.387	107	161	.665	415	211	178	1	707	8.9
Dale Schlueter	80	1823	257	527	.488	143	218	.656	629	192	265	4	657	8.2
Ed Manning	79	1558	243	559	.435	75	93	.806	411	111	198	3	561	7.1
Dorie Murrey*	2	20	1	6	.167	9	11	.818	7	1	3	0	11	5.5
Ron Knight	52	662	99	230	.430	19	38	.500	167	50	99	1	217	4.2
Bill Stricker	1	2	2	3	.667	0	0	.000	0	0	1	0	4	4.0
Walt Gilmore	27	261	23	54	.426	12	26	.462	73	12	49	1	58	2.1
Claude English	18	70	11	42	.262	5	7	.714	20	6	15	0	27	1.5

SAN DIEGO

Player	G.	Min.	FGM	FGA	Pct.	FTM	FTA	Pct.	Reb.	Ast.	PF	Disq.	Pts.	Avg.
Elvin Hayes	82	3633	948	2215	.428	454	676	.672	1362	186	225	1	2350	28.7
Stu Lantz	82	3102	585	1305	.448	519	644	.806	406	344	230	3	1689	20.6
Calvin Murphy	82	2020	471	1029	.458	356	434	.820	245	329	263	4	1298	15.8
Don Adams	82	2374	391	957	.409	155	212	.731	581	173	344	11	937	11.4
John Trapp	82	2080	322	766	.420	142	188	.755	150	138	337	16	786	9.6
John Block	73	1464	245	584	.420	212	270	.785	442	98	193	2	702	9.6
Larry Siegfried	53	1673	146	378	.386	130	153	.850	207	346	146	0	422	8.0
Rudy Tomjanovich	77	1062	168	439	.383	73	112	.652	381	73	124	0	409	5.3
Bernie Williams	56	708	112	338	.331	68	81	.840	85	113	76	1	292	5.2
Toby Kimball	80	1100	111	287	.387	51	108	.472	406	62	128	1	273	3.4
Curtis Perry	18	100	21	48	.438	11	20	.550	30	5	22	0	53	2.9
Johnny Egan***	62	824	67	178	.376	42	51	.824	63	112	71	0	176	2.8
Johnny Egan**	36	414	27	80	.338	17	23	.739	31	54	40	0	71	2.0

1970-71 STATISTICS

SAN FRANCISCO

Player	G.	Min.	FGM	FGA	Pct.	FTM	FTA	Pct.	Reb.	Ast.	PF	Disq.	Pts.	Avg.
Jeff Mullins	75	2909	630	1308	.482	302	358	.844	341	332	246	5	1562	20.8
Nate Thurmond	82	3351	623	1401	.445	395	541	.730	1128	257	192	1	1641	20.0
Jerry Lucas	80	3251	623	1250	.498	289	367	.787	1265	293	197	0	1535	19.2
Ron Williams	82	2809	426	977	.436	331	392	.844	244	480	301	9	1183	14.4
Joe Ellis	80	2275	356	898	.396	151	203	.744	511	161	287	6	863	10.8
Bob Portman	68	1395	221	483	.458	77	106	.726	321	67	130	0	519	7.6
Nick Jones	81	1183	225	523	.430	111	151	.735	110	113	192	2	561	6.9
Clyde Lee	82	1392	194	428	.453	111	199	.558	570	63	137	0	499	6.1
Adrian Smith	21	247	38	89	.427	35	41	.854	24	30	24	0	111	5.3
Levi Fontaine	35	210	53	145	.366	28	37	.757	15	22	27	0	134	3.8
Bill Turner	18	200	26	82	.317	13	20	.650	42	8	24	0	65	3.6
Al Attles	34	321	22	54	.407	24	41	.585	40	58	59	2	68	2.0
Ralph Ogden	32	162	17	71	.239	8	12	.667	32	9	17	0	42	1.3

SEATTLE

Player	G.	Min.	FGM	FGA	Pct.	FTM	FTA	Pct.	Reb.	Ast.	PF	Disq.	Pts.	Avg.
Bob Rule	4	142	47	98	.480	25	30	.833	46	7	14	0	119	29.8
Spencer Haywood	33	1162	260	579	.449	160	218	.733	396	48	84	1	680	20.6
Len Wilkens	71	2641	471	1125	.419	461	574	.803	319	654	201	3	1403	19.8
Dick Snyder	82	2824	645	1215	.531	302	361	.837	257	352	246	6	1592	19.4
Don Kojis	79	2143	454	1018	.446	249	320	.778	435	130	220	3	1157	14.6
Don Smith	61	1276	263	597	.441	139	188	.739	468	42	118	0	665	10.9
Lee Winfield	79	1605	334	716	.466	162	244	.664	193	225	135	1	830	10.5
Tom Meschery	79	1822	285	615	.463	162	216	.750	485	108	202	2	732	9.3
Pete Cross	79	2194	245	554	.442	140	203	.690	949	113	212	2	630	8.0
Barry Clemens	78	1286	247	526	.470	83	114	.728	243	92	169	1	577	7.4
Jake Ford	5	68	9	25	.360	16	22	.727	9	9	11	0	34	6.8
Garfield Heard	65	1027	152	399	.381	82	125	.656	328	45	126	0	386	5.9
Rod Thorn	63	767	141	299	.472	69	102	.676	103	182	60	0	351	5.6
Tom Black*	55	773	111	268	.414	51	73	.699	225	42	116	1	273	5.0

*Finished season with another team.
**Player total with this club only.
***Player total with all clubs.

1970-71 CHAMPIONSHIP PLAYOFF RESULTS

ATLANTIC DIVISION
New York Defeated Atlanta, 4-1

Mar. 25—Atlanta 101 at New York 112
Mar. 27—Atlanta 113 at New York 104
Mar. 28—New York 110 at Atlanta 95
Mar. 30—New York 113 at Atlanta 107
Apr. 1—Atlanta 107 at New York 111

MIDWEST DIVISION
Milwaukee Defeated San Francisco, 4-1

Mar. 27—Milwaukee 107 at San Francisco 96
Mar. 29—San Francisco 90 vs. Mil. at Madison 104
Mar. 30—San Francisco 102 vs. Mil. at Madison 114
Apr. 1—Milwaukee 104 at San Francisco 106
Apr. 4—San Francisco 86 vs. Mil. at Madison 136

EASTERN CONFERENCE FINALS
Baltimore Defeated New York, 4-3

Apr. 6—Baltimore 111 at New York 112
Apr. 9—Baltimore 88 at New York 107
Apr. 11—New York 88 at Baltimore 114
Apr. 14—New York 80 at Baltimore 101
Apr. 16—New York 84 at New York 89
Apr. 18—New York 96 at Baltimore 113
Apr. 19—Baltimore 93 at New York 91

CENTRAL DIVISION
Baltimore Defeated Philadelphia, 4-3

Mar. 24—Philadelphia 126 at Baltimore 112
Mar. 26—Baltimore 119 at Philadelphia 107
Mar. 28—Philadelphia 103 at Baltimore 111
Mar. 30—Baltimore 120 at Philadelphia 105
Apr. 1—Philadelphia 104 at Baltimore 103
Apr. 3—Baltimore 94 at Philadelphia 98
Apr. 4—Philadelphia 120 at Baltimore 128

PACIFIC DIVISION
Los Angeles Defeated Chicago, 4-3

Mar. 24—Chicago 99 at Los Angeles 100
Mar. 26—Chicago 95 at Los Angeles 105
Mar. 28—Los Angeles 98 at Chicago 106
Mar. 30—Los Angeles 102 at Chicago 112
Apr. 1—Chicago 86 at Los Angeles 115
Apr. 4—Los Angeles 99 at Chicago 113
Apr. 6—Chicago 98 at Los Angeles 109

WESTERN CONFERENCE FINALS
Milwaukee Defeated Los Angeles, 4-1

Apr. 9—Los Angeles 85 at Milwaukee 106
Apr. 11—Los Angeles 73 at Milwaukee 91
Apr. 14—Milwaukee 107 at Los Angeles 118
Apr. 16—Milwaukee 117 at Los Angeles 94
Apr. 18—Los Angeles 98 at Milwaukee 116

CHAMPIONSHIP SERIES
Milwaukee Defeated Baltimore, 4-0

Apr. 21—Baltimore 88 at Milwaukee 98
Apr. 25—Milwaukee 102 at Baltimore 83
Apr. 28—Baltimore 99 at Milwaukee 107
Apr. 30—Milwaukee 118 at Baltimore 106

1969-70 STATISTICS

WORLD CHAMPION 1969-70 NEW YORK KNICKERBOCKERS

Standing (left to right)—Coach William (Red) Holzman, Phil Jackson, Dave Stallworth, Dave DeBusschere, Capt. Willis Reed, Bill Hosket, Nate Bowman, Bill Bradley, Chief Scout Dick McGuire, and Trainer Dan Whelan. Seated (left to right)—John Warren, Don May, Walt Frazier, President Ned Irish, Chairman of the Board Irving Mitchell Felt, General Manager Ed Donovan, Dick Barnett, Mike Riordan, and Cazzie Russell.

FINAL STANDINGS AND TEAM FIGURES

EASTERN DIVISION

Team	N.Y.	Mil.	Balt.	Phil.	Cin.	Bos.	Det.	Atl.	L.A.	Chi.	Pho.	Sea.	S.F.	S.D.	W.	L.	Pct.	Scoring For	Scoring Agst.
New York	-	4	5	5	5	3	6	2	4	6	6	4	5	5	60	22	.732	9427	8682
Milwaukee	2	-	3	5	5	6	6	3	3	2	6	6	4	6	56	26	.683	9741	9363
Baltimore	1	3	-	3	4	5	5	4	4	5	3	2	5	6	50	32	.610	9900	9726
Philadelphia	2	2	4	-	3	4	5	3	2	3	4	-	6	4	42	40	.512	9998	9718
Cincinnati	2	2	3	4	-	3	4	3	2	3	3	1	2	4	36	46	.439	9616	9858
Boston	4	1	2	2	3	-	4	-	2	3	3	2	5	2	34	48	.415	9422	9574
Detroit	1	1	2	1	2	3	-	3	3	3	3	3	3	3	31	51	.378	9246	9518

WESTERN DIVISION

Atlanta	4	3	2	3	3	6	3	-	4	5	2	5	4	4	48	34	.585	9646	9612
Los Angeles	2	3	2	4	4	4	3	3	-	2	3	6	5	5	46	36	.561	9327	9164
Chicago	-	4	1	3	3	3	3	2	4	-	5	4	4	3	39	43	.476	9423	9567
Phoenix	-	-	3	2	3	4	3	4	4	2	-	4	3	7	39	43	.476	9786	9927
Seattle	2	1	4	6	5	1	3	2	-	3	3	-	4	2	36	46	.439	9589	9796
San Francisco	1	2	1	-	4	4	3	3	2	3	3	3	-	2	30	52	.366	9114	9476
San Diego	1	-	-	2	2	2	3	2	2	4	-	4	5	-	27	55	.329	9732	9986

TEAM STATISTICS

	G.	FGM	FGA	Pct.	FTM	FTA	Pct.	Reb.	Ast.	PF	Disq.	For	Agst.	Dif.
New York	82	3803	7975	.477	1821	2484	.733	4006	2135	2016	10	115.0	105.9	9.1
Milwaukee	82	3923	8041	.488	1895	2589	.732	4419	2168	1971	27	118.8	114.2	4.6
Philadelphia	82	3915	8345	.469	2168	2884	.752	4463	2127	2196	47	121.9	118.5	3.4
Baltimore	82	3925	8567	.458	2050	2652	.773	4679	1881	1896	21	120.7	118.6	2.1
Los Angeles	82	3668	7952	.461	1991	2641	.754	4154	2030	1896	41	113.7	111.8	1.9
Atlanta	82	3817	7907	.483	2012	2669	.754	4210	2142	2016	29	117.6	117.2	0.4
Phoenix	82	3676	7856	.468	2434	3270	.744	4183	2076	2183	33	119.3	121.1	-1.8
Chicago	82	3607	8133	.444	2209	2861	.772	4383	2133	1863	13	114.9	116.7	-1.8
Boston	82	3645	8235	.443	2132	2711	.786	4336	1875	2320	41	114.9	116.8	-1.9
Seattle	82	3709	8029	.462	2171	2851	.761	4312	2214	2175	42	116.9	119.5	-2.6
Cincinnati	82	3767	8271	.455	2082	2841	.733	4163	1992	2215	52	117.3	120.2	-2.9
San Deigo	82	3866	8867	.436	2000	2728	.733	4786	2036	2096	17	118.7	121.8	-3.1
Detroit	82	3565	7657	.466	2116	2881	.734	3831	1709	1930	22	112.8	116.1	-3.3
San Francisco	82	3555	8224	.432	2004	2646	.757	4772	1861	2050	32	111.1	115.6	-4.5

INDIVIDUAL SCORING LEADERS
(Minimum of 70 Games Played)

	G.	FG	FT	Pts.	Avg.
West, L.A.	74	831	647	2309	31.2
Alcindor, Mil.	82	938	485	2361	28.8
Hayes, S. D.	82	914	428	2256	27.5
Cunningham, Phil.	81	802	510	2114	26.1
Hudson, Atl.	80	830	371	2031	25.4
Hawkins, Phoe.	81	709	577	1995	24.6
Rule, Sea.	80	789	387	1965	24.6
Havlicek, Bos.	81	736	488	1960	24.2
Monroe, Balt.	82	695	532	1922	23.4
Bing, Det.	70	575	454	1604	22.9
VanArsdale, Cinc.	71	620	381	1621	22.8
Mullins, S. F.	74	656	320	1632	22.1
Greer, Phil.	80	705	352	1762	22.0
Robinson, Mil.	81	663	437	1765	21.8
Reed, N. Y.	81	702	351	1755	21.7
Walker, Chi.	78	596	483	1675	21.5
VanArsdale, Phoe.	77	592	459	1643	21.3
Caldwell, Atl.	82	674	379	1727	21.1
Love, Chi.	82	640	442	1722	21.0
Frazier, N. Y.	77	600	409	1609	20.9

FIELD GOAL PERCENTAGE LEADERS
(Minimum 700 or More Attempts in 70 Games)

	G.	FG	FGA	Pct.
Johnny Green, Cincinnati	78	481	860	.559
Darrall Imhoff, Phila.	79	430	796	.540
Lou Hudson, Atlanta	80	830	1564	.531
Jon McGlocklin, Milw.	82	639	1206	.530
Dick Snyder, Seattle	82	456	863	.528
Jim Fox, Phoenix	81	413	788	.524
Lew Alcindor, Milwaukee	82	938	1810	.518
Wes Unseld, Baltimore	82	526	1015	.518
Walt Frazier, New York	77	600	1158	.518
Dick Van Arsdale, Phoe.	77	592	1166	.508

LEADERS IN AVERAGE REBOUNDS
(Minimum 70 Games or More)

	G.	No.	Avg.
Elvin Hayes, San Diego	82	1386	16.9
Wes Unseld, Baltimore	82	1370	16.7
Lew Alcindor, Milwaukee	82	1190	14.5
Bill Bridges, Atlanta	82	1181	14.4
Gus Johnson, Baltimore	78	1086	13.9
Willis Reed, New York	81	1126	13.9
Billy Cunningham, Philadelphia	81	1101	13.6
Tom Boerwinkle, Chicago	81	1016	12.5
Paul Silas, Phoenix	78	916	11.7
Clyde Lee, San Francisco	82	929	11.3

FREE THROW PERCENTAGE LEADERS
(Minimun 350 or More Attempts in 70 Games)

	G.	FT	FTA	Pct.
Flynn Robinson, Milwaukee	81	439	489	.898
Chet Walker, Chicago	78	483	568	.850
Jeff Mullins, San Francisco	74	320	378	.847
John Havlicek, Boston	81	488	578	.844
Bob Love, Chicago	82	442	525	.842
Earl Monroe, Baltimore	82	532	641	.830
Lou Hudson, Atlanta	80	371	450	.824
Jerry West, Los Angeles	74	647	785	.824
Hal Greer, Philadelphia	80	352	432	.815
Jimmy Walker, Detroit	81	355	440	.807

LEADERS IN AVERAGE ASSISTS
(Minimum 70 Games or More)

	G.	No.	Avg.
Lenny Wilkens, Seattle	75	683	9.1
Walt Frazier, New York	77	629	8.2
Clem Haskins, Chicago	82	624	7.6
Jerry West, Los Angeles	74	554	7.5
Gail Goodrich, Phoenix	81	605	7.5
Walt Hazzard, Atlanta	82	561	6.8
John Havlicek, Boston	81	550	6.8
Art Williams, San Diego	80	503	6.3
Norm VanLier, Cincinnati	81	500	6.2
Dave Bing, Detroit	70	418	6.0

INTER-CLUB RECORDS—HOME, AWAY AND NEUTRAL COURT

	Home	Away	Neutral	Total
Atlanta	25-13	18-16	5-5	48-34
Baltimore	25-12	19-18	6-2	50-32
Boston	16-21	13-27	5-0	34-48
Chicago	23-10	9-25	7-8	39-43
Cincinnati	19-13	14-25	3-8	36-46
Detroit	18-20	10-25	3-6	31-51
Los Angeles	27-14	17-21	2-1	46-36
Milwaukee	27-11	24-14	5-1	56-26
New York	30-11	27-10	3-1	60-22
Philadelphia	22-16	16-22	4-2	42-40
Phoenix	22-15	12-25	5-3	39-43
San Diego	21-17	4-33	2-5	27-55
San Francisco	16-20	14-26	0-6	30-52
Seattle	22-14	10-26	4-6	36-46

1969-70 STATISTICS

INDIVIDUAL STATISTICS

ATLANTA

Player	G.	Min.	FGM	FGA	Pct.	FTM	FTA	Pct.	Reb.	Ast.	PF	Disq.	Pts.	Avg.
Lou Hudson	80	3091	830	1564	.531	371	450	.824	373	276	225	1	2031	25.4
Joe Caldwell	82	2857	674	1329	.507	379	551	.688	407	287	255	3	1727	21.1
Walt Hazzard	82	2757	493	1056	.467	267	330	.809	329	561	264	3	1253	15.3
Bill Bridges	82	3269	443	932	.475	331	451	.734	1181	345	292	6	1217	14.8
Jim Davis	82	2623	438	943	.464	240	318	.755	796	238	335	5	1116	13.6
Walt Bellamy***	79	2028	351	671	.523	215	373	.576	707	143	260	5	917	11.6
Walt Bellamy**	23	855	141	287	.491	75	124	.605	310	88	97	2	357	15.5
Gary Gregor	81	1603	286	661	.433	88	113	.779	397	63	159	5	660	8.1
Al Beard	72	941	183	392	.467	135	163	.828	140	121	124	0	501	7.0
Don Ohl	66	984	176	372	.473	58	72	.806	71	98	113	1	410	6.2
Dave Newmark	64	612	127	296	.429	59	77	.766	174	42	128	3	313	4.9
Grady O'Malley	24	113	21	60	.350	8	19	.421	26	10	12	0	50	2.1
Gene Tormohlen	2	11	2	4	.500	0	0	.000	4	1	3	0	4	2.0
Richie Guerin	8	64	3	11	.273	1	1	1.000	2	12	9	0	7	0.9

BALTIMORE

Player	G.	Min.	FGM	FGA	Pct.	FTM	FTA	Pct.	Reb.	Ast.	PF	Disq.	Pts.	Avg.
Earl Monroe	82	2865	695	1557	.446	532	641	.830	257	402	258	3	1922	23.4
Kevin Loughery	55	2037	477	1082	.441	253	298	.849	168	292	183	3	1207	21.9
Jack Marin	82	2947	666	1363	.489	286	339	.844	537	217	248	6	1618	19.7
Gus Johnson	78	2919	578	1282	.451	197	272	.724	1086	264	269	6	1353	17.3
Wes Unseld	82	3234	526	1015	.518	273	428	.638	1370	291	250	2	1325	16.2
Eddie Miles***	47	1295	238	541	.440	133	175	.760	177	86	107	0	609	13.0
Eddie Miles**	3	52	7	10	.700	3	5	.600	4	4	8	0	17	5.7
Mike Davis	56	1330	260	586	.444	149	192	.776	128	111	174	1	669	12.0
Ray Scott	73	1393	257	605	.425	139	173	.803	457	114	147	0	653	8.9
Leroy Ellis	72	1163	194	414	.469	86	116	.741	376	47	129	0	474	6.6
Al Tucker***	61	819	146	285	.512	70	87	.805	166	38	86	0	362	5.9
Al Tucker**	28	262	49	96	.510	33	42	.786	53	7	34	0	131	4.7
Fred Carter	76	1219	157	439	.358	80	116	.690	192	121	137	0	394	5.2
Bob Quick	15	67	14	28	.500	12	18	.667	12	3	9	0	40	2.7
Ed Manning	29	161	32	66	.485	5	8	.625	35	2	33	0	69	2.4
Brian Heaney	14	70	13	24	.542	2	4	.500	4	6	17	0	28	2.0

BOSTON

Player	G.	Min.	FGM	FGA	Pct.	FTM	FTA	Pct.	Reb.	Ast.	PF	Disq.	Pts.	Avg.
John Havlicek	81	3369	736	1585	.464	488	578	.844	635	550	211	1	1960	24.2
Don Nelson	82	2224	461	920	.501	337	435	.775	601	148	238	3	1259	15.4
Larry Siegfried	78	2081	382	902	.424	220	257	.856	212	299	187	2	984	12.6
Bailey Howell	82	2078	399	931	.429	235	308	.763	550	120	261	4	1033	12.6
Jo Jo White	60	1328	309	684	.452	111	135	.822	169	145	132	1	729	12.2
Tom Sanders	57	1616	246	555	.443	161	183	.880	314	92	199	5	653	11.5
Henry Finkel	80	1866	310	683	.454	156	233	.670	613	103	292	13	776	9.7
Emmette Bryant	71	1617	210	520	.404	135	181	.746	269	231	201	5	555	7.8
Steve Kuberski	51	797	130	335	.388	64	92	.696	257	29	87	0	324	6.4
Jim Barnes	77	1049	178	434	.410	95	128	.742	350	52	229	4	451	5.9
Rich Johnson	65	898	167	361	.411	46	70	.657	208	32	155	3	380	5.8
Don Chaney	63	839	115	320	.359	82	109	.752	152	72	118	0	312	5.0
Rich Nieman	6	18	2	5	.400	2	2	1.000	6	2	10	0	6	1.0

CHICAGO

Player	G.	Min.	FGM	FGA	Pct.	FTM	FTA	Pct.	Reb.	Ast.	PF	Disq.	Pts.	Avg.
Chet Walker	78	2726	596	1249	.477	483	568	.850	604	192	203	1	1675	21.5
Bob Love	82	3123	640	1373	.466	442	525	.842	712	148	260	2	1722	21.0
Clem Haskins	82	3214	668	1486	.450	332	424	.783	378	624	237	0	1668	20.3
Jerry Sloan	53	1822	310	737	.421	207	318	.651	372	165	179	3	827	15.6
Bob Weiss	82	2544	365	855	.427	213	253	.842	227	474	206	0	943	11.5
Tom Boerwinkle	81	2335	348	775	.449	150	226	.664	1016	229	255	4	846	10.4
Walt Wesley	72	1407	270	648	.417	145	219	.662	455	68	184	1	685	9.5
Al Tucker	33	557	97	189	.513	37	45	.822	113	31	52	0	231	7.0
Shaler Halimon	38	517	96	244	.393	49	73	.671	68	69	58	0	241	6.3
Bob Kauffman	64	775	94	221	.425	88	123	.715	211	76	117	1	276	4.3
Ed Manning***	67	777	119	321	.371	42	56	.750	232	36	122	1	280	4.2
Ed Manning**	39	616	87	255	.341	37	48	.771	197	34	89	1	211	5.4
Loy Petersen	31	231	33	90	.367	26	39	.667	26	23	22	0	92	3.0
John Baum	3	13	3	11	.273	0	0	.000	4	0	1	0	6	2.0

CINCINNATI

Player	G.	Min.	FGM	FGA	Pct.	FTM	FTA	Pct.	Reb.	Ast.	PF	Disq.	Pts.	Avg.
Oscar Robertson	69	2865	647	1267	.511	454	561	.809	422	558	175	1	1748	25.3
Tom VanArsdale	71	2544	620	1376	.451	381	492	.774	463	155	247	3	1621	22.8
Connie Dierking	76	2448	521	1243	.419	230	306	.752	624	169	275	7	1272	16.7
Johnny Green	78	2278	481	860	.559	254	429	.592	841	112	268	6	1216	15.6
Fred Foster	74	2077	461	1026	.449	176	243	.724	310	107	209	2	1098	14.8
Jerry Lucas	4	18	18	35	.514	5	7	.714	45	9	5	0	41	10.3
Norm VanLier	81	2895	302	749	.403	166	224	.741	409	500	329	18	770	9.5
Luther Rackley	66	1256	190	423	.449	124	195	.636	378	56	204	5	504	7.6
Herm Gilliam	57	1161	179	441	.406	68	91	.747	215	178	163	6	426	7.5
Bill Turner***	72	1170	197	468	.421	123	167	.737	304	43	193	3	517	7.2
Bill Turner**	69	1095	188	451	.417	118	157	.752	290	42	187	3	494	7.2
Adrian Smith	32	453	60	148	.405	52	60	.864	33	45	56	0	172	5.4
Jim King***	34	391	53	129	.411	33	41	.805	62	52	47	0	139	4.1
Jim King**	31	286	34	83	.410	22	27	.815	46	42	39	0	90	2.9
Wally Anderzunas	44	370	65	166	.392	29	46	.630	82	9	47	1	159	3.9
Bob Cousy	7	34	1	3	.333	3	3	1.000	5	10	11	0	5	0.7

DETROIT

Player	G.	Min.	FGM	FGA	Pct.	FTM	FTA	Pct.	Reb.	Ast.	PF	Disq.	Pts.	Avg.
Dave Bing	70	2334	575	1295	.440	454	580	.783	299	478	196	0	1604	22.9
Jimmy Walker	81	2869	666	1394	.478	355	440	.807	242	248	203	4	1687	21.0
Eddie Miles	44	1243	231	531	.435	130	170	.765	173	82	99	0	592	13.5
Otto Moore	81	2523	383	805	.476	194	305	.636	900	104	232	3	960	11.9
Terry Dischinger	75	1754	342	650	.526	174	241	.722	369	106	213	5	858	11.4
Howard Komives	82	2418	363	878	.413	190	234	.812	193	312	247	2	916	11.2
Harold Hairston	15	282	57	103	.553	45	63	.714	88	11	36	0	159	10.0
Erwin Mueller**	78	2353	300	646	.464	189	263	.719	483	205	192	1	789	10.1
Erwin Mueller**	74	2284	287	614	.467	185	254	.728	469	199	186	1	759	10.3
Walt Bellamy	56	1173	210	384	.547	140	249	.562	397	55	163	3	560	10.0
McCoy McLemore	73	1421	233	500	.466	119	145	.821	336	83	159	3	585	8.0
Steve Mix	18	276	48	100	.480	23	39	.590	64	15	31	0	119	6.6
Bob Quick***	34	364	63	139	.453	49	71	.690	75	14	50	0	175	5.1
Bob Quick**	19	297	49	111	.441	37	53	.698	63	11	41	0	135	7.1
Bill Hewitt***	65	1279	110	298	.369	54	94	.574	356	64	130	1	274	4.2
Bill Hewitt**	45	801	85	210	.405	38	63	.603	213	36	91	1	208	4.6
Paul Long	25	130	28	62	.452	27	38	.711	11	17	22	0	83	3.3
Geroge Reynolds	10	44	8	19	.421	5	7	.714	14	12	10	0	21	2.1
Tom Workman	2	6	0	1	.000	0	0	.000	0	0	1	0	0	0.0

LOS ANGELES

Player	G.	Min.	FGM	FGA	Pct.	FTM	FTA	Pct.	Reb.	Ast.	PF	Disq.	Pts.	Avg.
Jerry West	74	3106	831	1673	.497	647	785	.824	338	554	160	3	2309	31.2
Wilt Chamberlain	12	505	129	227	.568	70	157	.446	221	49	31	0	328	27.3
Elgin Baylor	54	2213	511	1051	.486	276	357	.773	559	292	132	1	1298	24.0
Harold Hairston***	70	2427	483	973	.496	326	413	.789	775	121	230	9	1292	18.5
Harold Hairston**	56	2145	426	870	.490	281	350	.803	687	110	194	9	1133	21.0
Mel Counts	81	2193	434	1017	.427	156	201	.776	683	160	304	7	1024	12.6
Dick Garrett	73	2318	354	816	.434	138	162	.852	235	180	236	5	846	11.6
John Tresvant***	69	1499	264	595	.444	206	284	.725	425	112	204	4	734	10.6
John Tresvant**	20	221	47	88	.534	23	35	.657	63	17	40	0	117	5.9
Keith Erickson	68	1755	258	563	.458	91	122	.746	304	209	175	3	607	8.9
Rick Roberson	74	2005	262	586	.447	120	212	.566	672	92	256	7	644	8.7
Willie McCarter	40	861	132	349	.378	43	60	.717	83	93	71	0	307	7.7
John Egan	72	1627	215	491	.438	99	121	.818	104	216	171	2	529	7.3
Bill Hewitt	20	478	25	88	.284	16	31	.516	141	28	39	0	66	3.3
Mike Lynn	44	403	44	133	.331	31	48	.646	64	30	87	4	119	2.7

MILWAUKEE

Player	G.	Min.	FGM	FGA	Pct.	FTM	FTA	Pct.	Reb.	Ast.	PF	Disq.	Pts.	Avg.
Lew Alcindor	82	3534	938	1810	.518	485	743	.653	1190	337	283	8	2361	28.8
Flynn Robinson	81	2762	663	1391	.477	439	489	.898	263	449	254	5	1765	21.8
Jon McGlocklin	82	2966	639	1206	.530	169	198	.854	252	303	164	0	1447	17.6
Bob Dandridge	81	2461	434	895	.485	199	264	.754	625	292	279	1	1067	13.2
Greg Smith	82	2368	339	664	.511	125	174	.718	712	156	304	8	803	9.8
Lennie Chappell	75	1134	243	523	.465	135	211	.640	276	56	127	1	621	8.3
Fred Crawford	77	1331	243	506	.480	101	148	.682	184	225	181	1	587	7.6
Don Smith	80	1637	237	546	.434	119	185	.643	603	62	167	2	593	7.4
John Arthurs	11	86	12	35	.343	11	15	.733	14	17	15	0	35	3.2
Guy Rodgers	64	749	68	191	.356	67	90	.744	74	213	73	1	203	3.2
Bob Greacen	41	292	44	109	.404	18	28	.643	59	27	49	0	106	2.6
Sam Williams	11	44	11	24	.454	5	11	.455	7	3	5	0	27	2.5
Dick Cunningham	60	416	52	141	.369	22	33	.667	160	28	70	0	126	2.1

1969-70 STATISTICS

NEW YORK

Player	G.	Min.	FGM	FGA	Pct.	FTM	FTA	Pct.	Reb.	Ast.	PF	Disq.	Pts.	Avg.
Willis Reed	81	3089	702	1385	.507	351	464	.556	1126	161	287	2	1755	21.7
Walt Frazier	77	3040	600	1158	.518	409	547	.748	465	629	203	1	1609	20.9
Dick Barnett	82	2772	494	1039	.475	232	325	.714	221	298	220	0	1220	14.9
Dave DeBusschere	79	2027	488	1082	.451	176	256	.688	790	194	244	2	1152	14.6
Bill Bradley	67	2098	413	897	.460	145	176	.824	239	268	219	0	971	14.5
Cazzie Russell	78	1563	385	773	.498	124	160	.775	236	135	137	0	894	11.5
Dave Stallworth	82	1375	239	557	.429	161	225	.716	323	139	194	2	639	7.8
Mike Riordan	81	1677	255	549	.464	114	165	.691	194	201	192	1	624	7.7
Bill Hosket	36	235	46	91	.505	26	33	.788	63	17	36	0	118	3.3
Nate Bowman	81	744	98	235	.417	41	79	.519	257	46	189	2	237	2.9
Don May	37	238	39	101	.386	18	19	.947	52	17	42	0	96	2.6
John Warren	44	272	44	108	.407	24	35	.686	40	30	53	0	112	2.5

PHILADELPHIA

Player	G.	Min.	FGM	FGA	Pct.	FTM	FTA	Pct.	Reb.	Ast.	PF	Disq.	Pts.	Avg.
Billy Cunningham	81	3194	802	1710	.469	510	700	.729	1101	352	331	15	2114	26.1
Hal Greer	80	3024	705	1551	.455	352	432	.815	376	405	300	8	1762	22.0
Archie Clark	76	2772	594	1198	.496	311	396	.785	301	380	201	2	1499	19.7
Darrall Imhoff	79	2474	430	796	.540	215	331	.650	754	211	294	7	1075	13.6
Jim Washington	79	2459	401	842	.476	204	273	.747	734	104	262	5	1006	12.7
Wally Jones	78	1740	366	851	.430	190	226	.841	173	276	210	2	922	11.8
Fred Hetzel	63	757	156	323	.483	71	85	.835	207	44	110	3	383	6.1
Matt Guokas	80	1558	189	416	.454	106	149	.711	216	222	201	0	484	6.1
Luke Jackson	37	583	71	181	.392	60	81	.741	198	50	80	0	202	5.5
George Wilson	67	836	118	304	.388	122	172	.709	317	52	145	3	358	5.3
Bud Ogden	47	357	82	172	.477	27	39	.692	86	31	62	2	191	4.1
Dave Scholz	1	1	1	1	1.000	0	0	.000	0	0	0	0	2	2.0

PHOENIX

Player	G.	Min.	FGM	FGA	Pct.	FTM	FTA	Pct.	Reb.	Ast.	PF	Disq.	Pts.	Avg.
Connie Hawkins	81	3312	709	1447	.490	577	741	.779	845	391	287	4	1995	24.6
Dick Van Arsdale	77	2966	592	1166	.508	459	575	.798	264	338	282	5	1643	21.3
Gail Goodrich	81	3234	568	1251	.454	488	604	.808	340	605	251	3	1624	20.0
Jim Fox	81	2041	413	788	.524	218	283	.770	570	93	261	7	1044	12.9
Paul Silas	78	2836	373	804	.464	250	412	.607	916	214	266	5	996	12.8
Dick Snyder	6	147	22	45	.489	7	8	.875	15	9	20	1	51	8.5
Jerry Chambers	79	1139	283	658	.430	91	125	.728	219	54	162	3	657	8.3
Neal Walk	82	1394	257	547	.470	155	242	.640	455	80	225	2	669	8.2
Art Harris***	81	1553	285	723	.394	86	134	.642	161	231	220	0	656	8.1
Art Harris**	76	1375	257	650	.395	82	125	.656	142	211	209	0	596	7.8
Lamar Green	58	700	101	234	.432	41	70	.586	276	17	115	2	243	4.2
Stan McKenzie	58	525	81	206	.393	58	73	.795	93	52	67	1	220	3.8
Neil Johnson	28	136	20	60	.333	8	12	.667	47	12	38	0	48	1.7

SAN DIEGO

Player	G.	Min.	FGM	FGA	Pct.	FTM	FTA	Pct.	Reb.	Ast.	PF	Disq.	Pts.	Avg.
Elvin Hayes	82	3665	914	2020	.452	428	622	.688	1386	162	270	5	2256	27.5
Don Kojis	56	1578	338	756	.447	181	241	.751	388	78	135	1	857	15.3
Jim Barnett	80	2105	450	998	.451	289	366	.790	305	287	222	3	1189	14.9
John Block	82	2152	453	1025	.442	287	367	.782	609	137	275	2	1193	14.5
Stu Lantz	82	2471	455	1027	.443	278	361	.770	255	287	238	2	1188	14.5
Bernie Williams	72	1228	251	641	.392	96	122	.787	155	165	124	0	598	8.3
Rick Adelman	35	717	96	247	.389	68	91	.747	81	113	90	0	260	7.4
Bobby Smith	75	1198	242	567	.427	66	96	.688	328	75	119	0	550	7.3
Toby Kimball	77	1622	218	508	.429	107	185	.578	621	95	187	1	543	7.1
John Trapp	70	1025	185	434	.426	72	104	.692	309	49	200	3	442	6.3
Art Williams	80	1545	189	464	.407	88	118	.746	292	503	168	0	466	5.8
Pat Riley	36	474	75	180	.417	40	55	.727	57	85	68	0	190	5.3

SAN FRANCISCO

Player	G.	Min.	FGM	FGA	Pct.	FTM	FTA	Pct.	Reb.	Ast.	PF	Disq.	Pts.	Avg.
Jeff Mullins	74	2861	656	1426	.460	320	378	.847	382	360	240	4	1632	22.1
Nate Thurmond	43	1919	341	824	.414	261	346	.754	762	150	110	1	943	21.9
Jim King	3	105	19	46	.413	11	14	.786	16	10	8	0	49	16.3
Joe Ellis	76	2380	501	1223	.410	200	270	.741	594	139	281	13	1202	15.8
Jerry Lucas***	67	2420	405	799	.507	200	255	.784	951	173	166	2	1010	15.1
Jerry Lucas**	63	2302	387	764	.507	195	248	.786	906	166	159	2	969	15.4
Ron Williams	80	2435	452	1046	.432	277	337	.822	190	424	287	7	1181	14.8
Clyde Lee	82	2641	362	822	.440	178	300	.593	922	80	263	5	902	11.0
Bill Turner	3	75	9	17	.529	5	10	.500	14	1	7	0	23	7.7
Dave Gambee	73	951	185	464	.399	156	186	.839	244	55	172	0	526	7.2
Bobby Lewis	73	1353	213	557	.382	100	152	.658	157	194	170	0	526	7.2
Bob Portman	60	813	177	398	.445	66	85	.776	224	28	77	0	420	7.0
Adrian Smith***	77	1087	153	416	.368	152	170	.894	82	133	122	0	458	5.9
Adrian Smith**	45	634	93	268	.347	100	110	.909	49	87	66	0	286	6.4
Al Attles	45	676	78	202	.386	75	113	.664	74	142	103	0	231	5.1
Dale Schlueter	63	685	82	167	.491	60	97	.619	231	25	108	0	224	3.6

SEATTLE

Player	G.	Min.	FGM	FGA	Pct.	FTM	FTA	Pct.	Reb.	Ast.	PF	Disq.	Pts.	Avg.
Bob Rule	80	2959	789	1705	.463	387	542	.714	825	144	278	6	1965	24.6
Len Wilkens	75	2802	448	1066	.420	438	556	.788	378	683	212	5	1334	17.8
Bob Boozer	82	2549	493	1005	.491	263	320	.822	717	110	237	2	1249	15.2
Dick Snyder***	82	2437	450	863	.528	169	208	.813	323	342	277	8	1081	13.2
Dick Snyder**	76	2290	434	818	.531	162	200	.810	308	333	257	7	1030	13.6
John Tresvant	49	1278	217	507	.428	183	249	.735	362	95	164	4	617	12.6
Tom Meschery	80	2294	394	818	.482	196	248	.790	666	157	317	13	984	12.3
Art Harris	5	178	28	73	.384	4	9	.444	19	20	11	0	60	12.0
Lucius Allen	81	1817	306	692	.442	182	249	.731	211	342	201	0	794	9.8
Barry Clemens	78	1487	270	595	.454	111	140	.793	316	116	188	1	651	8.3
Erwin Mueller	4	69	13	32	.406	4	9	.444	14	6	6	0	30	7.5
Lee Winfield	64	771	138	288	.479	87	116	.750	98	102	95	0	363	5.7
Dorie Murrey	81	1079	153	343	.446	136	186	.731	357	76	191	4	442	5.5
Rod Thorn	19	105	20	45	.444	15	24	.625	16	17	8	0	55	2.9
Al Hairston	3	20	3	8	.375	1	1	1.000	5	6	3	0	7	2.3
Joe Kennedy	14	82	3	34	.088	2	2	1.000	20	7	7	0	8	0.6

**Team Total.
***Combined Player Total.

1969-70 CHAMPIONSHIP PLAYOFF RESULTS

EASTERN DIVISION SEMI-FINALS

Milwaukee Defeated Philadelphia 4 Games to 1

- Mar. 25 – Philadelphia 118 at Milwaukee ... 125
- Mar. 27 – Philadelphia 112 at Milwaukee ... 105
- Mar. 30 – Milwaukee 156 at Philadelphia ... 120
- Apr. 1 – Milwaukee 118 at Philadelphia ... 111
- Apr. 3 – Philadelphia 106 at Milwaukee ... 115

New York Defeated Baltimore 4 Games to 3

- Mar. 26 – Baltimore 117 at New York 120 (2 OTs)
- Mar. 27 – New York 106 at Baltimore ... 99
- Mar. 29 – Baltimore 127 at New York ... 113
- Mar. 31 – New York 92 at Baltimore ... 102
- Apr. 2 – Baltimore 80 at New York ... 101
- Apr. 4 – New York 87 at Baltimore ... 96
- Apr. 6 – Baltimore 114 at New York ... 127

WESTERN DIVISION SEMI-FINALS

Atlanta Defeated Chicago 4 Games to 1

- Mar. 25 – Chicago 111 at Atlanta ... 129
- Mar. 28 – Chicago 104 at Atlanta ... 124
- Mar. 31 – Atlanta 106 at Chicago ... 101
- Apr. 3 – Atlanta 120 at Chicago ... 131
- Apr. 5 – Chicago 107 at Atlanta ... 113

Los Angeles Defeated Phoenix 4 Games to 3

- Mar. 25 – Phoenix 112 at Los Angeles ... 128
- Mar. 29 – Phoenix 114 at Los Angeles ... 101
- Apr. 2 – Los Angeles 98 at Phoenix ... 112
- Apr. 4 – Los Angeles 102 at Phoenix ... 112
- Apr. 5 – Phoenix 121 at Los Angeles ... 138
- Apr. 7 – Los Angeles 104 at Phoenix ... 93
- Apr. 9 – Phoenix 94 at Los Angeles ... 129

EASTERN DIVISION FINAL SERIES

New York Defeated Milwaukee 4 Games to 1

- Apr. 11 – Milwaukee 102 at New York ... 110
- Apr. 13 – Milwaukee 111 at New York ... 112
- Apr. 17 – New York 96 at Milwaukee ... 101
- Apr. 19 – New York 117 at Milwaukee ... 105
- Apr. 20 – Milwaukee 96 at New York ... 132

WESTERN DIVISION FINAL SERIES

Los Angeles Defeated Atlanta 4 Games to 0

- Apr. 12 – Los Angeles 119 at Atlanta ... 115
- Apr. 14 – Los Angeles 105 at Atlanta ... 94
- Apr. 16 – Atlanta 114 at Los Angeles 115 (OT)
- Apr. 19 – Atlanta 114 at Los Angeles ... 133

CHAMPIONSHIP SERIES

New York Defeated Los Angeles 4 Games to 3

- Apr. 24 – Los Angeles 112 at New York ... 124
- Apr. 27 – Los Angeles 105 at New York ... 103
- Apr. 29 – New York 111 at Los Angeles 108 (OT)
- May 1 – New York 115 at Los Angeles 121 (OT)
- May 4 – Los Angeles 100 at New York ... 107
- May 6 – New York 113 at Los Angeles ... 135
- May 8 – Los Angeles 99 at New York ... 113

TEAM PLAYOFF STATISTICS

Team	G.	W.	L.	FGM	FGA	Pct.	FTM	FTA	Pct.	Reb.	Ast.	PF	Disq.	Scoring Average For	Agst.	Diff.
Los Angeles	18	11	7	807	1671	.483	438	655	.669	981	506	396	7	114.0	110.1	3.9
New York	19	12	7	877	1919	.457	345	455	.758	950	450	446	2	110.5	106.8	3.7
Atlanta	9	4	5	418	928	.450	193	275	.702	496	211	231	5	114.3	114.0	0.3
Milwaukee	10	5	5	454	954	.476	226	308	.746	506	264	202	4	113.4	113.4	0.0
Baltimore	7	3	4	286	685	.418	163	212	.769	392	120	159	2	105.0	106.6	− 1.6
Phoenix	7	3	4	295	728	.405	168	218	.771	423	175	173	1	108.3	114.3	− 6.0
Chicago	5	1	4	224	520	.431	106	144	.736	275	118	113	0	110.8	118.4	− 7.6
Philadelphia	5	1	4	238	501	.475	91	134	.679	245	123	128	1	113.4	123.8	−10.4

1968-69 STATISTICS

1968-69 CHAMPION BOSTON CELTICS
Front row (left to right): Don Nelson, Sam Jones, Coach Bill Russell, President Jack Waldron, General Manager Red Auerbach, John Havlicek, Team Physician Dr. Thomas Silva, Larry Siegfired. Back row: Trainer Joe DeLauri, Emmette Bryant, Don Chaney, Tom Sanders, Rich Johnson, Jim Barnes, Bailey Howell, Mal Graham.

FINAL STANDINGS AND TEAM FIGURES

EASTERN DIVISION

Team	Bal.	Phil.	N.Y.	Bos.	Cin.	Det.	Mil.	L.A.	Atl.	S.F.	S.D.	Chi.	Sea.	Pho.	W.	L.	Pct.	For	Agst.
Baltimore	..	2	3	5	4	7	5	3	4	3	5	6	4	6	57	25	.695	9542	9193
Philadelphia	4	..	3	2	4	4	6	5	5	2	4	5	6	5	55	27	.671	9746	9332
New York	4	4	..	6	2	4	6	1	4	5	3	4	6	5	54	28	.659	9087	8626
Boston	2	5	1	..	5	5	5	2	3	3	4	4	3	6	48	34	.585	9102	8645
Cincinnati	3	3	4	2	..	3	5	2	2	3	2	5	3	4	41	41	.500	9392	9476
Detroit	-	3	3	1	4	..	2	3	-	2	3	3	4	4	32	50	.390	9356	9618
Milwaukee	1	-	-	1	1	4	..	1	2	3	4	1	3	6	27	55	.329	9040	9460

WESTERN DIVISION

Team	Bal.	Phil.	N.Y.	Bos.	Cin.	Det.	Mil.	L.A.	Atl.	S.F.	S.D.	Chi.	Sea.	Pho.	W.	L.	Pct.	For	Agst.
Los Angeles	3	1	5	4	4	3	5	..	4	4	7	4	5	6	55	27	.671	9204	8864
Atlanta	2	1	2	3	4	6	4	3	..	4	3	6	4	6	48	34	.585	9123	8942
San Francisco	3	4	1	3	3	4	3	3	3	..	3	3	4	4	41	41	.500	8947	9081
San Diego	1	2	3	2	4	3	2	-	4	3	..	3	3	7	37	45	.451	9456	9472
Chicago	-	1	2	2	1	3	5	3	1	4	3	..	4	4	33	49	.402	8587	8762
Seattle	2	-	-	3	3	2	5	1	2	3	3	3	..	3	30	52	.366	9191	9589
Phoenix	-	1	1	-	2	2	2	-	-	2	1	2	3	..	16	66	.195	9162	9878

1968-69 STATISTICS

TEAM STATISTICS

	G.	FGM	FGA	Pct.	FTM	FTA	Pct.	Reb.	Ast.	PF	Disq.	For	Agst.	Dif.
New York	82	3588	7813	.459	1911	2596	.736	4246	2071	2175	35	110.8	105.2	5.6
Boston	82	3583	8316	.431	1936	2657	.729	4840	1953	2073	27	111.0	105.4	5.6
Philadelphia	82	3754	8274	.454	2238	3087	.725	4513	1914	2145	44	118.9	113.8	5.1
Baltimore	82	3770	8567	.440	2002	2734	.732	4963	1682	2038	17	116.4	112.1	4.3
Los Angeles	82	3574	7620	.469	2056	3161	.650	4749	2068	1773	16	112.2	108.1	4.1
Atlanta	82	3605	7844	.460	1913	2785	.687	4599	2069	2082	28	111.3	109.4	1.9
San Diego	82	3691	8631	.428	2074	3039	.682	5026	1925	2110	19	115.3	115.5	-0.2
Cincinnati	82	3565	7742	.460	2262	3012	.751	4525	1983	2031	29	114.5	115.6	-1.1
San Francisco	82	3414	8218	.415	2119	2949	.719	5109	1822	2087	43	109.1	110.7	-1.6
Chicago	82	3355	8021	.418	1877	2577	.728	4550	1597	2064	29	104.7	106.9	-2.2
Detroit	82	3609	7997	.451	2141	3025	.707	4471	1757	2105	24	114.1	117.3	-3.2
Seattle	82	3543	8149	.435	2105	2979	.707	4498	1927	2281	54	112.1	116.6	-4.5
Milwaukee	82	3537	8258	.428	1966	2638	.745	4727	1882	2187	50	110.2	115.4	-5.2
Phoenix	82	3541	8242	.430	2080	2950	.705	4508	1918	2086	30	111.7	120.5	-8.8

INDIVIDUAL SCORING LEADERS

	G.	FG	FT	Pts.	Avg.
Hayes, San Diego	82	930	467	2327	28.4
Monroe, Baltimore	80	809	447	2065	25.8
Cunningham, Phil	82	739	556	2034	24.8
Rule, Seattle	82	776	413	1965	24.0
Robertson, Cin	79	656	643	1955	24.7
Goodrich, Phoenix	81	718	495	1931	23.8
Greer, Philadelphia	82	732	432	1896	23.1
Baylor, Los Angeles	76	730	421	1881	24.8
Wilkens, Seattle	82	644	547	1835	22.4
Kojis, San Diego	81	687	446	1820	22.5
Loughery, Balt	80	717	372	1806	22.6
Bing, Detroit	77	678	444	1800	23.4
Mullins, San Fran	78	697	381	1775	22.8
Havlicek, Boston	82	692	387	1771	21.6
Hudson, Atlanta	81	716	338	1770	21.9
Reed, New York	82	704	325	1733	21.1
Boozer, Chicago	79	661	394	1716	21.7
Van Arsdale, Pho	80	612	454	1678	21.0
Chamberlain, L.A.	81	641	382	1664	20.5
Robinson, Chi.-Mil	83	625	412	1662	20.0

FIELD GOAL PERCENTAGE LEADERS
(Minimum 230 FGM)

	FGM	FGA	Pct.
Wilt Chamberlain, Los Angeles	641	1099	.583
Jerry Lucas, Cincinnati	555	1007	.551
Willis Reed, New York	704	1351	.521
Terry Dischinger, Detroit	264	513	.515
Walt Bellamy, N.Y.-Det	563	1103	.510
Joe Caldwell, Atlanta	561	1106	.507
Walt Frazier, New York	531	1052	.505
Tom Hawkins, Los Angeles	230	461	.499
Lou Hudson, Atlanta	716	1455	.492
Jon McGlocklin, Milwaukee	662	1358	.487
Bailey Howell, Boston	612	1257	.487

FREE THROW PERCENTAGE LEADERS
(Minimum 230 FTM)

	FTM	FTA	Pct.
Larry Siegfried, Boston	336	389	.864
Jeff Mullins, San Francisco	381	452	.843
Jon McGlocklin, Milwaukee	246	292	.842
Flynn Robinson, Chi.-Mil	412	491	.839
Oscar Robertson, Cincinnati	643	767	.838
Fred Hetzel, Phi.-Cin	299	357	.838
Jack Marin, Baltimore	292	352	.830
Jerry West, Los Angeles	490	597	.821
Bob Boozer, Chicago	394	489	.806
Chet Walker, Philadelphia	369	459	.804

LEADERS IN REBOUNDS

	G.	No.	Avg.
Wilt Chamberlain, Los Angeles	81	1712	21.1
Wes Unseld, Baltimore	82	1491	18.2
Bill Russell, Boston	77	1484	19.3
Elvin Hayes, San Diego	82	1406	17.1
Nate Thurmond, San Francisco	71	1402	19.7
Jerry Lucas, Cincinnati	74	1360	18.4
Willis Reed, New York	82	1191	14.5
Bill Bridges, Atlanta	80	1132	14.2
Walt Bellamy, N.Y.-Det	88	1101	12.5
Bill Cunningham, Philadelphia	82	1050	12.8

LEADERS IN ASSISTS

	G.	No.	Avg.
Oscar Robertson, Cincinnati	79	772	9.8
Lennie Wilkens, Seattle	82	674	8.2
Walt Frazier, New York	80	635	7.9
Guy Rodgers, Milwaukee	81	561	6.9
Dave Bing, Detroit	77	546	7.1
Art Williams, San Diego	79	524	6.6
Gail Goodrich, Phoenix	81	518	6.4
Walt Hazzard, Atlanta	80	474	5.9
John Havlicek, Boston	82	441	5.4
Jerry West, Los Angeles	61	423	6.9

RECORD OF TEAMS BY MONTHS

Team	Oct. W-L	Nov. W-L	Dec. W-L	Jan. W-L	Feb. W-L	Mar. W-L	Total W-L
Atlanta	3-4	9-8	10-3	11-7	9-7	6-5	48-34
Baltimore	7-3	10-3	11-4	9-5	13-3	7-7	57-25
Boston	4-2	11-4	7-6	12-6	7-9	7-7	48-34
Chicago	3-4	7-11	7-8	6-9	5-9	5-8	33-49
Cincinnati	4-2	9-6	9-6	5-11	7-10	7-6	41-41
Detroit	3-4	7-8	4-10	9-9	4-12	5-7	32-50
Los Angeles	4-3	11-4	13-5	9-5	8-7	10-3	55-27
Milwaukee	1-5	5-10	4-15	5-9	8-7	4-9	27-55
New York	4-4	6-10	15-3	11-4	10-3	8-4	54-28
Philadelphia	3-2	9-4	14-4	9-7	12-5	8-5	55-27
Phoenix	4-3	1-12	3-15	3-12	3-14	2-10	16-66
San Diego	3-3	7-9	6-10	6-9	7-8	8-6	37-45
San Francisco	3-3	8-8	5-12	8-6	10-7	7-5	41-41
Seattle	2-6	8-11	4-11	5-9	6-8	5-7	30-52

1968-69 STATISTICS

INTER-CLUB RECORDS—HOME, AWAY AND NEUTRAL COURT

	Home W-L	Away W-L	Neutral W-L	Total W-L
Atlanta	28-12	18-21	2-1	48-34
Baltimore	29-9	24-15	4-1	57-25
Boston	24-12	21-19	3-3	48-34
Chicago	19-21	12-25	2-3	33-49
Cincinnati	15-13	16-21	10-7	41-41
Detroit	21-17	7-30	4-3	32-50
Los Angeles	32-9	21-18	2-0	55-27
Milwaukee	15-19	8-27	4-9	27-55
New York	30-7	19-20	5-1	54-28
Philadelphia	26-8	24-16	5-3	55-27
Phoenix	11-26	4-28	1-12	16-66
San Diego	25-16	8-25	4-4	37-45
San Francisco	22-19	18-21	1-1	41-41
Seattle	18-18	6-29	6-5	30-52

INDIVIDUAL STATISTICS

ATLANTA

Player	G.	Min.	FGM	FGA	Pct.	FTM	FTA	Pct.	Reb.	Ast.	PF	Disq.	Pts.	Avg.
Lou Hudson	81	2869	716	1455	.492	338	435	.777	533	216	248	0	1770	21.9
Zelmo Beaty	72	2578	588	1251	.470	370	506	.731	798	132	272	7	1546	21.5
Joe Caldwell	81	2720	561	1106	.507	159	296	.537	303	320	231	1	1281	15.8
Bill Bridges	80	2930	351	775	.453	239	353	.677	1132	298	290	3	941	11.8
Don Ohl	76	1995	385	901	.427	147	208	.707	170	221	232	5	917	12.1
Walt Hazzard	80	2420	345	869	.397	208	294	.707	266	474	264	6	898	11.2
Paul Silas	79	1853	241	575	.419	204	333	.613	745	140	166	0	686	8.7
Jim Davis	78	1367	265	568	.467	154	231	.667	529	97	239	6	684	8.8
Richie Guerin	27	472	47	111	.423	57	74	.770	59	99	66	0	151	5.6
Skip Harlicka	26	218	41	90	.456	24	31	.774	16	37	29	0	106	4.1
Dennis Hamilton	25	141	37	67	.552	2	5	.400	29	8	19	0	76	3.0
George Lehmann	11	138	26	67	.388	8	12	.667	9	27	18	0	60	5.5
Dwight Waller	11	29	2	9	.222	3	7	.429	10	1	8	0	7	0.6

BALTIMORE

Player	G.	Min.	FGM	FGA	Pct.	FTM	FTA	Pct.	Reb.	Ast.	PF	Disq.	Pts.	Avg.
Earl Monroe	80	3075	809	1837	.440	447	582	.768	280	392	261	1	2065	25.8
Kevin Loughery	80	3135	717	1636	.438	372	463	.803	266	384	299	3	1806	22.6
Jack Marin	82	2710	505	1109	.455	292	352	.830	608	231	275	4	1302	15.9
Wes Unseld	82	2970	427	897	.476	277	458	.605	1491	213	276	4	1131	13.8
Ray Scott	82	2168	386	929	.416	195	257	.759	722	133	212	1	967	11.8
Gus Johnson	49	1671	359	782	.459	160	223	.717	568	97	176	1	878	17.9
Leroy Ellis	80	1603	229	527	.435	117	155	.755	510	73	168	0	575	7.2
Ed Manning	63	727	129	288	.448	35	54	.648	246	21	120	0	293	4.7
John Barnhill	30	504	76	175	.434	39	65	.600	53	71	63	0	191	6.4
Barry Orms	64	916	76	246	.309	29	60	.483	158	49	155	3	181	2.8
Bob Quick	28	154	30	73	.411	27	44	.614	25	12	14	0	87	3.1
Tom Workman	21	86	22	54	.407	9	15	.600	27	2	16	0	53	2.5
Bob Ferry	7	36	5	14	.357	3	6	.500	9	4	3	0	13	1.9

BOSTON

Player	G.	Min.	FGM	FGA	Pct.	FTM	FTA	Pct.	Reb.	Ast.	PF	Disq.	Pts.	Avg.
John Havlicek	82	3174	692	1709	.405	387	496	.780	570	441	247	0	1771	21.6
Bailey Howell	78	2527	612	1257	.487	313	426	.735	685	137	285	3	1537	19.7
Sam Jones	70	1820	496	1103	.450	148	189	.783	265	182	121	0	1140	16.3
Larry Siegfried	79	2560	392	1031	.380	336	389	.864	282	370	222	0	1120	14.2
Don Nelson	82	1773	374	771	.485	201	259	.776	458	92	198	2	949	11.6
Tom Sanders	82	2184	364	847	.430	187	255	.733	574	110	293	9	915	11.2
Bill Russell	77	3291	279	645	.433	204	388	.526	1484	374	231	2	762	9.9
Em Bryant	80	1388	197	488	.404	65	100	.650	192	176	264	9	459	5.7
Jim Barnes***	59	606	115	261	.441	75	111	.676	224	28	122	2	305	5.2
Jim Barnes**	49	595	92	202	.455	65	92	.707	194	27	107	2	249	5.1
Don Chaney	20	209	36	113	.319	8	20	.400	46	19	32	0	80	4.0
Rich Johnson	31	163	29	76	.382	11	23	.478	52	7	40	0	69	2.2
Mal Graham	22	103	13	55	.236	11	14	.786	24	14	27	0	37	1.7
Bud Olsen*	7	43	7	19	.368	0	6	.000	14	4	6	0	14	2.0

CHICAGO

Player	G.	Min.	FGM	FGA	Pct.	FTM	FTA	Pct.	Reb.	Ast.	PF	Disq.	Pts.	Avg.
Bob Boozer	79	2872	661	1375	.481	394	489	.806	614	156	218	2	1716	21.7
Clem Haskins	79	2874	537	1275	.421	282	361	.781	359	306	230	0	1356	17.2
Jerry Sloan	78	2939	488	1170	.417	333	447	.745	619	276	313	6	1309	16.8
Jim Washington	80	2705	440	1023	.430	241	356	.677	847	104	226	0	1121	14.0
Tom Boerwinkle	80	2365	318	831	.383	145	222	.653	889	178	317	11	781	9.8
Barry Clemens	75	1444	235	628	.374	82	125	.656	318	125	163	1	552	7.4
Bob Weiss***	77	1478	189	499	.379	128	160	.800	162	199	174	1	506	6.6
Bob Weiss**	62	1236	153	385	.397	101	126	.802	135	172	150	0	407	6.6
Dave Newmark	81	1159	185	475	.389	86	139	.619	347	58	205	7	456	5.6
Flynn Robinson*	18	550	124	293	.423	95	114	.833	69	57	52	1	343	19.1
Bob Love***	49	542	108	272	.397	71	96	.740	150	17	59	0	287	5.9
Bob Love**	35	315	69	166	.416	42	58	.724	86	14	37	0	180	5.1
Erwin Mueller*	52	872	75	224	.335	46	90	.511	193	124	98	1	196	3.8
Loy Peterson	38	299	44	109	.404	19	27	.704	41	25	39	0	107	2.8
Jim Barnes*	10	111	23	59	.390	10	19	.526	30	1	15	0	56	5.6
Ken Wilburn	4	14	3	8	.375	1	4	.250	3	1	1	0	7	1.8

CINCINNATI

Player	G.	Min.	FGM	FGA	Pct.	FTM	FTA	Pct.	Reb.	Ast.	PF	Disq.	Pts.	Avg.
Oscar Robertson	79	3461	656	1351	.486	643	767	.838	502	772	231	2	1955	24.7
Tom Van Arsdale	77	3059	547	1233	.444	398	533	.747	356	208	300	6	1492	19.4
Jerry Lucas	74	3075	555	1007	.551	247	327	.755	1360	306	206	0	1357	18.3
Connie Dierking	82	2540	546	1232	.443	243	319	.762	739	222	305	9	1335	16.3
Fred Hetzel***	84	2276	456	1047	.436	299	357	.838	613	112	287	9	1211	14.4
Fred Hetzel**	31	685	140	287	.488	88	105	.838	140	29	94	3	368	11.9
Al Tucker***	84	1885	361	809	.446	158	244	.648	439	74	186	2	880	10.5
Al Tucker**	28	626	126	265	.475	49	73	.671	122	19	75	2	301	10.8
Adrian Smith	73	1336	243	562	.432	217	269	.807	105	127	166	1	703	9.6
Walt Wesley	82	1334	245	534	.459	134	207	.647	403	47	191	0	624	7.6
John Tresvant*	51	1681	239	531	.450	130	223	.583	419	103	193	5	608	11.9
Bill Dinwiddie	69	1028	124	352	.352	45	87	.517	242	55	146	0	293	4.2
Fred Foster	56	497	74	193	.383	43	66	.652	61	36	49	0	191	3.4
Pat Frink	48	363	50	147	.340	23	29	.793	41	55	54	1	123	2.6
Don Smith*	20	108	18	43	.419	2	7	.286	31	4	17	0	38	1.9
Doug Sims	4	12	2	5	.400	0	0	.000	4	0	4	0	4	1.0

DETROIT

Player	G.	Min.	FGM	FGA	Pct.	FTM	FTA	Pct.	Reb.	Ast.	PF	Disq.	Pts.	Avg.
Dave Bing	77	3039	678	1594	.425	444	623	.713	382	546	256	3	1800	23.4
Walt Bellamy***	88	3159	563	1103	.510	401	618	.649	1101	176	320	5	1527	17.4
Walt Bellamy**	53	2023	359	701	.512	276	416	.663	716	99	197	4	994	18.8
Harold Hairston	81	2889	530	1131	.469	404	553	.731	959	109	255	3	1464	18.1
Eddie Miles	80	2252	441	983	.449	182	273	.667	283	180	201	0	1064	13.3
Howard Komives***	85	2562	379	974	.389	211	264	.799	299	403	274	1	969	11.4
Howard Komives**	53	1726	272	665	.409	138	178	.775	204	266	178	1	682	12.9
Jim Walker	69	1639	312	670	.466	182	229	.795	157	221	172	1	806	11.7
McCoy McLemore***	81	1620	282	722	.391	169	214	.790	404	94	186	4	733	9.0
McCoy McLemore**	50	910	141	356	.396	84	104	.808	236	44	113	3	366	7.3
Terry Dischinger	75	1456	264	513	.515	130	178	.730	323	93	230	5	658	8.8
Dave Gambee***	59	926	210	465	.452	159	195	.815	257	47	159	4	579	9.8
Dave Gambee**	25	302	60	142	.423	49	62	.790	78	15	60	0	169	6.8
Otto Moore	74	1605	241	544	.443	88	168	.524	524	68	182	2	570	7.7
Dave DeBusschere*	29	1092	189	423	.447	94	130	.723	353	63	111	1	472	16.3
Jim Fox*	25	375	45	96	.469	34	53	.642	139	23	56	1	124	5.0
Sonny Dove	29	236	47	100	.470	24	36	.667	62	12	49	0	118	4.1
Rich Niemann*	16	123	20	47	.426	8	10	.800	41	9	30	0	48	3.0
Bud Olsen***	17	113	15	42	.357	4	18	.222	25	11	14	0	34	2.0
Bud Olsen**	10	70	8	23	.348	4	12	.333	11	7	8	0	20	2.0
Cliff Williams	3	18	2	9	.222	0	0	.000	3	2	7	0	4	1.3

LOS ANGELES

Player	G.	Min.	FGM	FGA	Pct.	FTM	FTA	Pct.	Reb.	Ast.	PF	Disq.	Pts.	Avg.
Elgin Baylor	76	3064	730	1632	.447	421	567	.743	805	408	204	0	1881	24.8
Wilt Chamberlain	81	3669	641	1099	.583	382	857	.446	1712	366	142	0	1664	20.5
Jerry West	61	2394	545	1156	.471	490	597	.821	262	423	156	1	1580	25.9
Mel Counts	77	1866	390	867	.450	178	221	.805	600	109	223	5	958	12.4
John Egan	82	1805	246	597	.412	204	240	.850	147	215	206	1	696	8.5
Keith Erickson	77	1974	264	629	.420	120	175	.686	308	194	222	6	648	8.4
Bill Hewitt	75	1455	239	528	.453	61	106	.575	332	76	139	1	539	7.2
Tom Hawkins	74	1507	230	461	.499	62	151	.411	266	81	168	1	522	7.1
Fred Crawford	81	1690	211	454	.465	83	154	.539	215	154	224	1	505	6.2
Cliff Anderson	35	289	44	108	.407	47	82	.573	44	31	58	0	135	3.9
Jay Carty	28	192	34	89	.382	8	11	.727	58	11	31	0	76	2.7

1968-69 STATISTICS

MILWAUKEE

Player	G.	Min.	FGM	FGA	Pct.	FTM	FTA	Pct.	Reb.	Ast.	PF	Disq.	Pts.	Avg.
Flynn Robinson***	83	2616	625	1442	.433	412	491	.839	306	377	261	7	1662	20.0
Flynn Robinson**	65	2066	501	1149	.436	317	377	.841	237	320	209	6	1319	20.3
Jon McGlocklin	80	2888	662	1358	.487	246	292	.842	343	312	186	1	1570	19.6
Lennie Chappell	80	2207	459	1011	.454	250	339	.737	637	95	247	3	1168	14.6
Wayne Embry	78	2353	382	894	.427	259	390	.664	672	149	302	8	1023	13.1
Fred Hetzel*	53	1591	316	760	.416	211	252	.837	473	83	193	6	843	15.9
Guy Rodgers	81	2157	325	862	.377	184	232	.793	226	561	207	2	834	10.3
Greg Smith	79	2207	276	613	.450	91	155	.587	804	137	264	12	643	8.1
Dave Gambee*	34	624	150	323	.464	110	133	.827	179	37	115	3	410	12.1
Don Smith***	49	945	144	390	.369	70	113	.619	409	37	115	3	358	7.3
Don Smith**	29	837	126	347	.363	68	106	.642	378	33	98	3	320	11.0
Dick Cunningham	77	1236	141	332	.425	69	106	.651	438	58	166	2	351	4.6
Sam Williams	55	628	78	228	.342	72	134	.537	109	61	106	1	228	4.1
Bob Love*	14	227	39	106	.368	29	38	.763	64	3	22	0	107	7.6
Rich Neimann***	34	272	44	106	.415	19	25	.760	100	16	61	1	107	3.1
Rich Neimann**	18	149	24	59	.407	11	15	.733	59	7	31	1	59	3.3
Bob Weiss*	15	242	36	114	.316	27	34	.794	47	27	24	1	99	6.6
Charlie Paulk	17	217	19	84	.226	13	23	.565	78	3	26	0	51	3.0
Jay Miller	3	27	2	10	.200	5	7	.714	2	0	4	0	9	3.0
Bob Warlick*	3	22	1	8	.125	4	5	.800	1	1	3	0	6	2.0

NEW YORK

Player	G.	Min.	FGM	FGA	Pct.	FTM	FTA	Pct.	Reb.	Ast.	PF	Disq.	Pts.	Avg.
Willis Reed	82	3108	704	1351	.521	325	435	.747	1191	190	314	5	1733	21.1
Dick Barnett	82	2953	565	1220	.463	312	403	.774	257	291	239	4	1442	17.6
Walt Frazier	80	2949	531	1052	.505	341	457	.746	499	635	245	2	1403	17.5
Dave DeBusschere**	76	2943	506	1140	.444	229	328	.698	888	191	290	6	1241	16.3
Dave DeBusschere**	47	1851	317	717	.442	135	198	.682	535	128	179	5	769	16.4
Bill Bradley	82	2413	407	948	.429	206	253	.814	350	302	295	4	1020	12.4
Cazzie Russell	50	1645	362	804	.450	191	240	.796	209	115	140	1	915	18.3
Walt Bellamy*	35	1136	204	402	.507	125	202	.619	385	77	123	1	533	15.2
Phil Jackson	47	924	126	294	.429	80	119	.672	246	43	168	6	332	7.1
Howard Komives*	32	836	107	309	.346	73	86	.849	95	137	96	0	287	9.0
Don May	48	560	81	223	.363	42	58	.724	114	35	64	0	204	4.3
Nate Bowman	67	607	82	226	.363	29	61	.475	220	53	142	4	193	2.9
Bill Hosket	50	351	53	123	.431	24	42	.571	94	19	77	0	130	2.6
Mike Riordan	54	397	49	144	.340	28	42	.667	57	46	93	1	126	2.3

PHILADELPHIA

Player	G.	Min.	FGM	FGA	Pct.	FTM	FTA	Pct.	Reb.	Ast.	PF	Disq.	Pts.	Avg.
Bill Cunningham	82	3345	739	1736	.426	556	754	.737	1050	287	329	10	2034	24.8
Hal Greer	82	3311	732	1595	.459	432	543	.796	435	414	294	8	1896	23.1
Chet Walker	82	2753	554	1145	.484	369	459	.804	640	144	244	0	1477	18.0
Archie Clark	82	2144	444	928	.478	219	314	.697	265	296	188	1	1107	13.5
Wally Jones	81	2340	432	1005	.430	207	256	.809	251	292	280	5	1071	13.2
Darrall Imhoff	82	2360	279	593	.470	194	325	.597	792	218	310	12	752	9.2
George Wilson***	79	1846	272	663	.410	153	235	.651	721	108	232	5	697	8.8
George Wilson**	38	552	81	182	.445	60	84	.714	216	32	87	1	222	5.8
Lucious Jackson	75	840	145	332	.437	69	97	.711	286	54	102	3	359	14.4
John Green	74	795	146	282	.518	57	125	.456	327	54	101	1	349	4.7
Matt Guokas	72	838	92	216	.426	54	81	.667	94	104	121	1	238	3.3
Shaler Halimon	50	350	88	196	.449	10	32	.313	86	18	34	0	186	3.7
Craig Raymond	27	177	22	64	.344	11	17	.647	68	8	46	2	55	2.0

PHOENIX

Player	G.	Min.	FGM	FGA	Pct.	FTM	FTA	Pct.	Reb.	Ast.	PF	Disq.	Pts.	Avg.
Gail Goodrich	81	3236	718	1746	.411	495	663	.747	437	518	253	3	1931	23.8
Dick Van Arsdale	80	3388	612	1386	.442	454	644	.705	548	385	245	2	1678	21.0
Dick Snyder	81	2108	399	846	.472	185	255	.725	328	211	213	2	983	12.1
Gary Gregor	80	2182	400	963	.415	85	131	.649	711	96	249	2	885	11.1
Jim Fox***	76	2354	398	847	.470	191	267	.715	818	166	266	6	827	10.9
Jim Fox**	51	1979	273	581	.470	157	214	.734	679	143	210	5	703	13.8
Stan McKenzie	80	1569	264	618	.427	219	287	.763	251	123	191	3	747	9.3
Bob Warlick***	66	997	213	509	.418	87	142	.613	152	132	122	0	513	7.8
Bob Warlick**	63	975	212	501	.423	83	137	.606	151	131	119	0	507	8.0
George Wilson*	41	1294	191	481	.397	93	151	.616	505	76	145	4	475	11.6
Neil Johnson	80	1319	177	368	.481	110	177	.621	396	134	214	3	464	5.8
Dave Lattin	88	987	150	366	.410	109	172	.634	323	48	163	5	409	6.2
McCoy McLemore*	31	710	141	366	.385	85	110	.773	168	50	73	1	367	11.8
Rodney Knowles	8	40	4	14	.286	1	3	.333	9	0	10	0	9	1.1
Ed Biedenbach	7	18	0	6	.000	4	6	.667	2	6	3	1	4	0.6

1968-69 STATISTICS

SAN DIEGO

Player	G.	Min.	FGM	FGA	Pct.	FTM	FTA	Pct.	Reb.	Ast.	PF	Disq.	Pts.	Avg.
Elvin Hayes	82	3695	930	2082	.447	467	746	.626	1406	113	266	2	2327	28.4
Don Kojis	81	3130	687	1582	.434	446	596	.748	776	214	303	6	1820	22.5
John Block	78	2489	448	1061	.422	299	400	.748	703	141	249	0	1195	15.3
Jim Barnett	80	2346	465	1093	.425	233	310	.752	362	339	240	2	1163	14.5
Toby Kimball	76	1680	239	537	.445	117	250	.468	669	90	216	6	595	7.8
Stuart Lautz	73	1378	220	482	.456	129	167	.772	236	99	178	0	569	7.8
Art Williams	79	1987	227	592	.383	105	149	.705	364	524	238	0	559	7.1
Pat Riley	56	1027	202	498	.406	90	134	.672	112	136	146	1	494	8.8
Rick Adelman	77	1448	177	449	.394	131	204	.642	216	238	158	1	485	6.3
Henry Finkel	35	332	49	111	.441	31	41	.756	107	21	53	1	129	3.7
John Trapp	25	142	29	80	.363	19	29	.655	49	5	38	0	77	3.1
Harry Barnes	22	126	18	64	.281	7	13	.538	26	5	25	0	43	2.0

SAN FRANCISCO

Player	G.	Min.	FGM	FGA	Pct.	FTM	FTA	Pct.	Reb.	Ast.	PF	Disq.	Pts.	Avg.
Jeff Mullins	78	2916	697	1517	.459	381	452	.843	460	339	251	4	1775	22.8
Rudy LaRusso	75	2782	553	1349	.410	444	559	.794	624	159	268	9	1550	20.7
Nate Thurmond	71	3208	571	1394	.410	382	621	.615	1402	253	171	0	1524	21.5
Joe Ellis	74	1731	371	939	.395	147	201	.731	481	130	258	13	889	12.0
Clyde Lee	65	2237	268	674	.398	160	256	.625	897	82	225	1	696	10.7
Bill Turner	79	1486	222	535	.415	175	230	.761	380	67	231	6	619	7.8
Ron Williams	75	1472	238	567	.420	109	142	.768	178	247	176	3	585	7.8
Al Attles	51	1516	162	359	.451	95	149	.638	181	306	183	3	419	8.2
Jim King	46	1010	137	394	.348	78	108	.722	120	123	99	1	352	7.7
Bob Lewis	62	756	113	290	.390	83	113	.735	114	76	117	0	309	5.0
Dale Schlueter	31	559	68	157	.433	45	82	.549	216	30	81	3	181	5.8
Bob Allen	27	232	14	43	.326	20	36	.556	56	10	27	0	48	1.8

SEATTLE

Player	G.	Min.	FGM	FGA	Pct.	FTM	FTA	Pct.	Reb.	Ast.	PF	Disq.	Pts.	Avg.
Bob Rule	82	3104	776	1655	.469	413	606	.682	941	141	322	8	1965	24.0
Lennie Wilkens	82	3463	644	1462	.440	547	710	.770	511	674	294	8	1835	22.4
Tom Meschery	82	2673	462	1019	.453	220	299	.736	822	194	304	7	1144	14.0
Art Harris	80	2556	416	1054	.395	161	251	.641	301	258	326	14	993	12.4
John Tresvant***	77	2482	380	820	.463	202	330	.612	686	166	300	9	962	12.5
John Tresvant**	26	801	141	289	.488	72	107	.673	267	63	107	4	354	13.6
Bob Kauffman	82	1660	219	496	.442	203	289	.702	484	83	252	8	641	7.8
Al Tucker*	56	1259	235	544	.432	109	171	.637	317	55	111	0	579	10.3
Joe Kennedy	72	1241	174	411	.395	98	124	.790	241	60	158	2	446	6.2
Tom Kron	76	1124	146	372	.392	96	137	.701	212	191	179	2	388	5.1
Erwin Mueller***	78	1355	144	384	.375	89	162	.549	297	186	143	1	377	4.8
Erwin Mueller**	26	246	69	160	.431	43	72	.597	104	62	45	0	181	7.0
Rod Thorn	29	567	131	283	.463	71	97	.732	83	80	58	0	333	11.5
Dorie Murrey	38	465	75	194	.387	62	97	.639	149	21	81	1	212	5.6
Al Hairston	39	274	38	114	.333	8	14	.571	36	38	35	0	84	2.2
Plummer Lott	23	160	17	66	.258	2	5	.400	30	7	9	0	36	1.6

*Finished season with another team.
**Player total with this club only.
***Player total with all clubs.

1968-69 CHAMPIONSHIP PLAYOFF RESULTS

EASTERN DIVISION SEMI-FINALS

New York Defeated Baltimore 4 Games to 0

Mar. 27 – New York 113 at Baltimore	101
Mar. 29 – Baltimore 91 at New York	107
Mar. 30 – New York 119 at Baltimore	116
Apr. 2 – Baltimore 108 at New York	115

Boston Defeated Philadelphia 4 Games to 1

Mar. 26 – Boston 114 at Philadelphia	100
Mar. 28 – Philadelphia 103 at Boston	134
Mar. 30 – Boston 125 at Philadelphia	118
Apr. 1 – Philadelphia 119 at Boston	116
Apr. 4 – Boston 93 at Philadelphia	90

WESTERN DIVISION SEMI-FINALS

Los Angeles Defeated San Francisco 4 Games to 2

Mar. 26 – San Francisco 99 at Los Angeles	94
Mar. 28 – San Francisco 107 at Los Angeles	101
Mar. 31 – Los Angeles 115 at San Francisco	98
Apr. 2 – Los Angeles 103 at San Francisco	88
Apr. 4 – San Francisco 98 at Los Angeles	103
Apr. 5 – Los Angeles 118 at San Francisco	78

Atlanta Defeated San Diego 4 Games to 2

Mar. 27 – San Diego 98 at Atlanta	107
Mar. 29 – San Diego 114 at Atlanta	116
Apr. 1 – Atlanta 97 at San Diego	104
Apr. 4 – Atlanta 112 at San Diego	114
Apr. 6 – San Diego 101 at Atlanta	112
Apr. 7 – Atlanta 108 at San Diego	106

EASTERN DIVISION FINAL SERIES
Boston Defeated New York 4 Games to 2
Apr. 6 – Boston 108 at New York 100
Apr. 9 – New York 97 at Boston 112
Apr. 10 – Boston 91 at New York 101
Apr. 13 – New York 96 at Boston 97
Apr. 14 – Boston 104 at New York 112
Apr. 18 – New York 105 at Boston 106

WESTERN DIVISION FINAL SERIES
Los Angeles Defeated Atlanta 4 Games to 1
Apr. 11 – Atlanta 93 at Los Angeles 95
Apr. 13 – Atlanta 102 at Los Angeles 104
Apr. 15 – Los Angeles 80 at Atlanta 99
Apr. 17 – Los Angeles 100 at Atlanta 85
Apr. 20 – Atlanta 96 at Los Angeles 104

CHAMPIONSHIP SERIES
Boston Defeated Los Angeles 4 Games to 3
Apr. 23 – Boston 118 at Los Angeles 120
Apr. 25 – Boston 112 at Los Angeles 118
Apr. 27 – Los Angeles 105 at Boston 111
Apr. 29 – Los Angeles 88 at Boston 89
May 1 – Boston 104 at Los Angeles 117
May 3 – Los Angeles 90 at Boston 99
May 5 – Boston 108 at Los Angeles 106

TEAM PLAYOFF STATISTICS

Team	G.	W.	L.	FGM	FGA	Pct.	FTM	FTA	Pct.	Reb.	Ast.	PF	Disq.	Scoring Average For	Agst.	Diff.
Los Angeles	18	11	7	712	1640	.434	443	679	.652	1078	419	430	4	103.7	99.1	4.6
Boston	18	12	6	755	1704	.443	431	570	.756	987	383	485	8	107.8	104.7	3.1
New York	10	6	4	422	964	.438	221	301	.734	555	227	240	2	106.5	103.4	3.1
Atlanta	11	5	6	446	1040	.429	235	363	.647	594	219	289	4	102.5	102.4	0.1
San Diego	6	2	4	246	531	.463	145	212	.684	296	113	154	1	106.2	108.7	- 2.5
Baltimore	4	0	4	168	393	.427	80	111	.721	209	62	94	0	104.0	113.5	- 8.5
Philadelphia	5	1	4	204	481	.424	122	171	.713	277	103	143	4	106.0	116.4	-10.4
San Francisco	6	2	4	218	601	.363	132	196	.673	385	129	156	0	94.7	105.7	-11.0

1967-68 STATISTICS

1967-68 CHAMPION BOSTON CELTICS

Front row (left to right): Sam Jones, Larry Siegfried, General Manager Red Auerbach, Chairman of Board Marvin Kratter, President Clarence Adams, Coach Bill Russell, John Havlicek. Back row: Trainer Joe DeLauri, Rick Weitzman, Tom Thacker, Tom Sanders, Bailey Howell, Wayne Embry, Don Nelson, John Jones, Mal Graham.

FINAL STANDINGS AND TEAM FIGURES

EASTERN DIVISION

Team	Phil.	Bos.	N.Y.	Det.	Cin.	Balt.	St.L.	L.A.	S.F.	Chi.	Sea.	S.D.	W.	L.	Pct.	For	Agst.
Philadelphia	..	4	5	7	5	8	5	4	5	4	6	7	62	20	.756	10051	9346
Boston	4	..	6	6	3	5	4	4	4	5	6	7	54	28	.659	9523	9186
New York	3	2	..	4	5	5	1	3	5	5	4	6	43	39	.524	9523	9374
Detroit	1	2	4	..	4	4	4	2	4	4	6	5	40	42	.488	9725	9889
Cincinnati	3	5	3	4	..	3	1	1	4	2	6	7	39	43	.476	9562	9631
Baltimore	0	3	3	4	5	..	2	3	2	2	5	7	36	46	.439	9627	9659

WESTERN DIVISION

Team	Phil.	Bos.	N.Y.	Det.	Cin.	Balt.	St.L.	L.A.	S.F.	Chi.	Sea.	S.D.	W.	L.	Pct.	For	Agst.
St. Louis	2	3	6	3	6	5	..	2	7	7	8	7	56	26	.683	9266	9042
Los Angeles	2	3	4	5	6	4	6	..	4	7	4	7	52	30	.634	9937	9477
San Francisco	3	3	2	3	3	5	1	4	..	6	7	6	43	39	.524	9598	9647
Chicago	1	2	2	3	5	5	1	1	2	..	3	4	29	53	.354	8982	9310
Seattle	0	1	3	1	1	2	0	4	1	5	..	5	23	59	.280	9732	10261
San Diego	1	0	1	2	0	0	1	1	2	4	3	..	15	67	.183	9215	9919

TEAM STATISTICS

Team	G.	FGM	FGA	Pct.	FTM	FTA	Pct.	Reb.	Ast.	PF	Disq.	For	Agst.	Dif.
Philadelphia	82	3965	8414	.471	2121	3338	.635	5914	2197	1851	23	122.6	114.0	8.6
Los Angeles	82	3827	8031	.477	2283	3143	.726	5225	1983	2152	30	121.2	115.6	5.6
Boston	82	3686	8371	.440	2151	2983	.721	5666	1798	2147	26	116.1	112.0	4.1
St. Louis	82	3504	7765	.451	2258	3111	.726	5325	1988	2046	36	113.0	110.3	2.7
New York	82	3682	8070	.456	2159	3042	.710	5122	1967	2364	25	116.1	114.3	1.8
Baltimore	82	3691	8428	.438	2245	2994	.750	5431	1534	2127	38	117.4	117.8	−0.4
San Francisco	82	3632	8587	.423	2334	3153	.740	6029	1901	2265	52	117.0	117.6	−0.6
Cincinnati	82	3679	7864	.468	2204	2892	.762	5129	2048	2016	29	116.6	117.4	−0.8
Detroit	82	3755	8386	.448	2215	3129	.708	5452	1700	2240	52	118.6	120.6	−2.0
Chicago	82	3488	8138	.429	2006	2718	.738	5117	1527	2130	42	109.5	113.5	−4.0
Seattle	82	3772	8593	.439	2188	3042	.719	5338	1998	2372	49	118.7	125.1	−6.4
San Diego	82	3466	8547	.417	2083	2929	.711	5418	1837	2188	27	112.4	121.0	−8.6

1967-68 STATISTICS

INDIVIDUAL SCORING LEADERS

	G.	FG	FT	Pts.	Avg.
Bing, Detroit	79	835	472	2142	27.1
Baylor, Los Angeles	77	757	488	2002	26.0
Chamberlain, Phila.	82	819	354	1992	24.3
Monroe, Baltimore	82	742	507	1991	24.3
Greer, Philadelphia	82	777	422	1976	24.1
Robertson, Cinn.	65	660	576	1896	29.2
Hazzard, Seattle	79	733	428	1894	23.9
Lucas, Cincinnati	82	707	346	1760	21.4
Beaty, St. Louis	82	639	455	1733	21.1
LaRusso, San Fran.	79	602	522	1726	21.8
Havlicek, Boston	82	666	368	1700	20.7
Reed, New York	81	659	367	1685	20.8
Boozer, Chicago	77	622	411	1655	21.5
Wilkens, St. Louis	82	546	546	1638	20.0
Howell, Boston	82	643	335	1621	19.8
Clark, Los Angeles	81	628	356	1612	19.9
S. Jones, Boston	73	621	311	1553	21.3
Mullins, San Fran.	79	610	273	1493	18.9
Rule, Seattle	82	568	348	1484	18.1
Walker, Phila.	82	539	387	1465	17.9

FIELD GOAL PERCENTAGE LEADERS
(Minimum 220 FGM)

	FGM	FGA	Pct.
Wilt Chamberlain, Phila.	819	1377	.595
Walt Bellamy, New York	511	944	.541
Jerry Lucas, Cincinnat	707	1361	.519
Jerry West, Los Angeles	476	926	.514
Len Chappell, Cin.-Det.	235	458	.513
Oscar Robertson, Cincinnati	660	1321	.500
Tom Hawkins, Los Angeles	389	779	.499
Terry Dischinger, Detroit	394	797	.494
Don Nelson, Boston	312	632	.494
Bob Boozer, Chicago	622	1265	.492
Henry Finkel, San Diego	242	492	.492

FREE THROW PERCENTAGE LEADERS
(Minimum 220 FTM)

	FTM	FTA	Pct.
Oscar Robertson, Cincinnati	576	660	.873
Larry Siegfried, Boston	236	272	.868
Dave Gambee, San Diego	321	379	.847
Fred Hetzel, San Francisco	395	474	.833
Adrian Smith, Cincinnati	320	386	.829
Sam Jones, Boston	311	376	.827
Flynn Robinson, Cin.-Chi.	288	352	.818
John Havlicek, Boston	368	453	.812
Jerry West, Los Angeles	391	482	.811
Cazzie Russell, New York	282	349	.808

LEADERS IN REBOUNDS

	G.	No.	Avg.
Wilt Chamberlain, Phila.	82	1952	23.8
Jerry Lucas, Cincinnati	82	1560	19.0
Bill Russell, Boston	78	1451	18.6
Clyde Lee, San Francisco	82	1141	13.9
Nate Thurmond, San Francisco	51	1121	22.0
Ray Scott, Baltimore	81	1111	13.7
Bill Bridges, St. Louis	82	1102	13.4
Dave DeBusschere, Detroit	80	1081	13.5
Willis Reed, New York	81	1073	13.2
Walt Bellamy, New York	82	961	11.7

LEADERS IN ASSISTS

	G.	No.	Avg.
Wilt Chamberlain, Phila.	82	702	8.6
Lenny Wilkens, St. Louis	82	679	8.3
Oscar Robertson, Cincinnati	65	633	9.7
Dave Bing, Detroit	79	509	6.4
Walt Hazzard, Seattle	79	493	6.2
Art Williams, San Diego	79	391	4.9
Al Attles, San Francisco	67	390	5.8
John Havlicek, Boston	82	384	4.7
Guy Rodgers, Chi.-Cinn.	78	380	4.9
Hal Greer, Philadelphia	82	372	4.5

RECORD OF TEAMS BY MONTHS

Team	Oct. W-L	Nov. W-L	Dec. W-L	Jan. W-L	Feb. W-L	Mar. W-L	Total W-L
Baltimore	3-4	5-7	6-9	8-11	9-8	5-7	36-46
Boston	5-0	10-5	10-5	10-7	12-5	7-6	54-28
Chicago	0-9	5-9	7-9	6-9	6-9	5-8	29-53
Cincinnati	5-3	4-8	7-9	9-7	7-12	7-4	39-43
Detroit	3-3	10-7	8-9	6-9	3-11	10-3	40-42
Los Angeles	5-2	7-8	10-7	7-7	13-3	10-3	52-30
New York	1-6	10-6	4-12	11-6	11-5	6-4	43-39
Philadelphia	5-1	10-6	15-2	8-6	14-2	10-3	62-20
St. Louis	9-1	10-5	8-5	13-5	10-7	6-3	56-26
San Diego	1-7	3-15	7-8	3-9	1-17	0-11	15-67
San Francisco	7-4	11-3	10-7	5-8	8-9	2-8	43-39
Seattle	2-6	5-11	4-14	5-7	4-10	3-11	23-59
Totals	46	90	96	91	98	71	492

INTER-CLUB RECORDS—HOME, AWAY AND NEUTRAL COURT

	Home W-L	Away W-L	Neutral W-L	Total W-L
Baltimore	17-19	12-23	7-4	36-46
Boston	28-9	20-16	6-3	54-28
Chicago	11-22	12-23	6-8	29-53
Cincinnati	18-12	13-23	8-8	39-43
Detroit	21-11	12-23	7-8	40-42
Los Angeles	30-11	18-19	4-0	52-30
New York	20-17	21-16	2-6	43-39
Philadelphia	27-8	25-12	10-0	62-20
St. Louis	25-7	22-13	9-6	56-26
San Diego	8-33	4-26	3-8	15-67
San Francisco	27-14	16-23	0-2	43-39
Seattle	9-19	7-24	7-16	23-59
Totals	241-182	182-241	69-69	492-492

INDIVIDUAL STATISTICS

BALTIMORE

Player	G.	Min.	FGM	FGA	Pct.	FTM	FTA	Pct.	Reb.	Ast.	PF	Disq.	Pts.	Avg.
Earl Monroe	82	3012	742	1637	.453	507	649	.781	465	349	282	3	1991	24.3
Ray Scott	81	2924	490	1189	.412	348	447	.779	1111	167	252	2	1328	16.4
Kevin Loughery	77	2297	458	1127	.406	305	392	.778	247	256	301	13	1221	15.9
Gus Johnson	60	2271	482	1033	.467	180	270	.667	782	159	223	7	1144	19.1
Jack Marin	82	2037	429	932	.460	250	314	.796	473	110	246	4	1108	13.5
Leroy Ellis	78	2719	380	800	.475	207	286	.724	862	158	256	5	967	12.4
Don Ohl*	39	1096	232	536	.433	114	148	.770	113	84	91	0	578	14.8
John Egan	67	930	163	415	.393	142	183	.776	112	134	127	0	468	7.0
Bob Ferry	59	841	128	311	.412	73	117	.624	186	61	92	0	329	5.6
Earl Manning	71	951	112	259	.432	60	99	.606	375	32	153	3	284	4.0
Stan McKenzie	50	653	73	182	.401	58	88	.659	121	24	98	1	204	4.1
Tom Workman***	20	95	19	40	.475	18	23	.783	25	3	17	0	56	2.8
Tom Workman**	1	9	1	2	.500	1	1	1.000	1	0	3	0	1	1.0
Tom Workman*	1	10	0	2	.000	0	0	.000	3	0	3	0	4	4.0
Roland West	4	14	2	5	.400	0	0	.000	5	0	4	0	4	1.0

BOSTON

Player	G.	Min.	FGM	FGA	Pct.	FTM	FTA	Pct.	Reb.	Ast.	PF	Disq.	Pts.	Avg.
John Havlicek	82	2921	666	1551	.429	368	453	.812	546	384	237	2	1700	20.7
Bailey Howell	82	2801	643	1336	.481	335	461	.727	805	133	285	4	1621	19.8
Sam Jones	73	2408	621	1348	.461	311	376	.827	357	216	181	0	1553	21.3
Bill Russell	78	2953	365	858	.425	247	460	.537	1451	357	242	2	977	12.5
Don Nelson	82	1981	312	632	.494	195	268	.728	431	103	178	1	819	10.0
Tom Sanders	78	1981	296	691	.428	200	255	.784	454	100	300	12	792	10.2
Larry Siegfried	62	1937	261	629	.415	236	272	.868	215	289	194	2	758	12.2
Wayne Embry	78	1088	193	483	.400	109	185	.589	321	52	174	1	495	6.3
Mal Graham	48	786	117	272	.430	56	88	.636	161	69	165	2	290	6.0
Tom Thacker	65	782	114	272	.419	43	84	.512	114	26	60	0	271	4.2
John ??s	51	475	86	253	.340	42	68	.618	10	8	8	0	214	4.2
Rick Weitzman	25	75	12	46	.261	9	13	.692	10	8	8	0	33	1.3

CHICAGO

Player	G.	Min.	FGM	FGA	Pct.	FTM	FTA	Pct.	Reb.	Ast.	PF	Disq.	Pts.	Avg.
Bob Boozer	77	2988	622	1265	.492	411	535	.768	756	121	229	1	1655	21.5
Flynn Robinson***	75	2046	444	1010	.440	288	351	.821	272	219	184	1	1176	15.7
Flynn Robinson**	73	2030	441	1000	.441	285	344	.828	268	214	180	1	1167	16.0
Jerry Sloan	77	2454	369	959	.385	289	386	.749	591	229	291	11	1027	13.3
Jim Washington	82	2525	418	915	.457	187	274	.682	825	113	233	1	1023	12.5
McCoy McLemore	76	2100	374	940	.398	215	276	.779	430	130	219	4	963	12.7
Keith Erickson	78	2257	377	940	.401	194	257	.755	423	267	276	15	948	12.2
Barry Clemens	78	1631	301	670	.449	123	170	.724	375	98	223	4	725	9.3
Clem Haskins	76	1477	273	650	.420	133	202	.658	227	165	175	1	679	8.9
Jim Barnes***	79	1425	221	499	.443	133	191	.696	415	55	262	7	575	7.3
Jim Barnes**	37	712	120	264	.455	74	103	.718	204	28	128	3	314	8.5
Dave Schellhase	42	301	47	138	.341	20	38	.526	47	37	43	0	114	2.7
Guy Rodgers*	4	129	16	54	.296	9	11	.818	14	28	11	0	41	10.3
Craig Spitzer	10	44	9	21	.381	2	3	.667	24	0	4	0	18	1.8
Ken Wilburn	3	26	5	9	.556	1	4	.250	10	2	4	0	11	3.3
Jim Burns	3	11	2	7	.286	0	0	.000	2	1	1	0	4	1.3
Erwin Mueller*	35	815	91	235	.387	46	82	.561	167	76	78	1	228	6.5
Reggie Harding	14	305	27	71	.338	17	33	.515	94	18	35	0	65	4.6

CINCINNATI

Player	G.	Min.	FGM	FGA	Pct.	FTM	FTA	Pct.	Reb.	Ast.	PF	Disq.	Pts.	Avg.
Oscar Robertson	65	2765	660	1321	.500	576	660	.873	391	633	199	2	1896	29.2
Jerry Lucas	82	3619	707	1361	.519	346	445	.778	1560	251	243	3	1760	21.4
Connie Dierking	81	2637	544	1164	.467	237	310	.765	766	191	315	6	1325	16.4
Adrian Smith	82	2783	480	1035	.464	320	386	.829	185	272	259	6	1280	15.6
John Tresvant***	85	2473	396	867	.457	250	384	.651	709	160	344	18	1042	12.3
John Tresvant**	30	802	121	270	.448	67	106	.632	169	46	105	3	309	10.3
Harold Hairston*	48	1625	317	630	.503	203	296	.686	355	58	127	1	837	17.4
Tom Van Arsdale***	77	1514	211	545	.387	188	252	.746	225	155	202	5	610	7.9
Tom Van Arsdale**	27	682	97	238	.408	87	116	.750	93	76	83	2	281	10.4
Bob Love	72	1068	193	455	.424	78	114	.684	209	55	141	1	464	6.4
Walt Wesley	66	918	188	404	.465	76	152	.500	281	34	168	2	452	6.8
Guy Rodgers***	79	1546	148	426	.347	107	133	.805	150	380	167	1	403	5.1
Guy Rodgers**	75	1417	132	372	.355	98	122	.803	136	352	156	1	362	4.8
Bill Dinwiddie	67	871	141	358	.394	62	102	.608	237	31	122	2	344	5.1
Gary Gray	44	276	49	134	.366	7	10	.700	23	26	48	0	105	2.4
Jim Fox*	31	244	32	79	.405	36	56	.643	95	12	34	0	100	3.2
Len Chappell*	10	65	15	30	.500	8	10	.800	15	5	6	0	38	3.8
Flynn Robinson*	2	16	3	10	.300	3	7	.429	4	5	4	0	9	4.5
Al Jackson	2	17	0	3	.000	0	0	.000	0	1	6	0	0	0.0

1967-68 STATISTICS

DETROIT

Player	G	Min.	FGM	FGA	Pct.	FTM	FTA	Pct.	Reb.	Ast.	PF	Disq.	Pts.	Avg.
Dave Bing	79	3209	835	1893	.441	472	668	.707	373	509	254	2	2142	27.1
Dave DeBusschere	80	3125	573	1295	.442	289	435	.664	1081	181	304	3	1435	17.9
Eddie Miles	76	2303	561	1180	.475	282	369	.764	264	215	200	3	1404	18.5
Harold Hairston***	74	2517	481	987	.487	365	522	.699	617	95	199	1	1327	17.9
Harold Hairston**	26	892	164	357	.459	162	226	.717	262	37	72	0	490	18.8
Terry Dischinger	78	1936	394	797	.494	237	311	.762	483	114	247	6	1025	13.1
John Tresvant*	55	1671	275	597	.461	183	278	.658	540	114	239	15	733	13.3
Jim Walker	81	1585	289	733	.394	134	175	.766	135	226	204	1	712	8.8
Len Chappell***	67	1064	235	458	.513	138	194	.711	361	53	119	1	608	9.1
Len Chappell**	57	999	220	428	.514	130	184	.707	346	48	113	1	570	10.0
Joe Strawder	73	2029	206	456	.452	139	215	.647	685	85	312	18	551	7.5
Tom Van Arsdale*	50	832	114	307	.371	101	136	.743	132	79	119	3	329	6.6
Jim Fox***	55	624	66	161	.410	66	108	.611	230	29	85	0	198	3.6
Jim Fox**	24	380	34	82	.415	30	52	.577	135	17	51	0	98	4.1
George Patterson	59	559	44	133	.331	32	38	.835	159	51	85	0	120	2.0
Paul Long	16	93	23	51	.451	11	15	.733	15	12	13	0	57	3.6
Sonny Dove	28	162	22	75	.293	12	26	.462	52	11	27	0	56	2.0
George Carter	1	5	1	2	.500	1	1	1.000	0	1	0	0	3	3.0

LOS ANGELES

Player	G.	Min.	FGM	FGA	Pct.	FTM	FTA	Pct.	Reb.	Ast.	PF	Disq.	Pts.	Avg.
Elgin Baylor	77	3029	757	1709	.443	488	621	.786	941	355	232	0	2002	26.0
Archie Clark	81	3039	628	1309	.480	356	481	.740	342	353	235	3	1612	19.9
Jerry West	51	1919	476	926	.514	391	482	.811	294	310	152	1	1343	26.3
Gail Goodrich	79	2057	395	812	.486	302	392	.770	199	205	228	2	1092	13.8
Mel Counts	82	1739	484	808	.475	190	254	.748	732	139	309	6	958	11.7
Tom Hawkins	78	2463	389	779	.499	125	229	.546	458	117	289	7	903	11.6
Darrall Imhoff	82	2271	293	613	.478	177	286	.619	893	206	264	3	763	9.3
Fred Crawford***	69	1182	224	507	.442	111	179	.620	195	141	171	1	559	8.1
Fred Crawford**	38	756	159	330	.482	74	120	.617	112	95	104	1	392	10.3
Erwin Mueller**	39	973	132	254	.520	61	103	.592	222	78	86	2	325	8.3
Erwin Mueller***	74	1788	223	489	.456	107	185	.578	389	154	164	3	553	7.5
Jim Barnes*	42	713	101	235	.430	59	88	.670	211	27	134	4	261	6.2
John Wetzel	38	434	52	119	.437	35	46	.761	84	51	55	0	139	3.7
Dennis Hamilton	44	378	54	108	.500	13	13	1.000	72	30	46	0	121	2.8
Cliff Anderson	18	94	7	29	.241	12	28	.429	11	17	18	1	26	1.4

NEW YORK

Player	G.	Min.	FGM	FGA	Pct.	FTM	FTA	Pct.	Reb.	Ast.	PF	Disq.	Pts.	Avg.
Willis Reed	81	2879	659	1346	.490	367	509	.721	1073	159	343	12	1685	20.8
Dick Barnett	81	2488	559	1159	.482	343	440	.780	238	242	222	0	1461	18.0
Cazzie Russell	82	2296	551	1192	.462	282	349	.808	374	195	223	2	1384	16.9
Walt Bellamy	82	2695	511	944	.541	350	529	.662	961	164	259	3	1372	16.7
Dick Van Arsdale	78	2348	316	725	.436	227	339	.670	424	230	225	0	859	11.0
Walt Frazier	74	1588	256	568	.451	154	235	.655	313	305	199	2	666	9.0
Howard Komives	78	1660	233	631	.369	132	161	.820	168	246	170	1	598	7.7
Phil Jackson	75	1093	182	455	.400	99	168	.589	338	55	212	3	463	6.2
Bill Bradley	45	874	142	341	.416	76	104	.731	113	137	138	2	360	8.0
Emmett Bryant	77	968	112	291	.385	59	86	.686	133	134	173	0	283	3.7
Fred Crawford*	31	426	65	177	.367	37	59	.627	83	46	67	0	167	5.4
Nate Bowman	42	272	52	134	.388	10	15	.667	113	20	69	0	114	2.7
Neil Johnson	43	286	44	106	.415	23	48	.479	75	33	63	0	111	2.6
Jim Caldwell	2	7	0	1	.000	0	0	.000	1	1	1	0	0	0.0

PHILADELPHIA

Player	G.	Min.	FGM	FGA	Pct.	FTM	FTA	Pct.	Reb.	Ast.	PF	Disq.	Pts.	Avg.
Wilt Chamberlain	82	3836	819	1377	.595	354	932	.380	1952	702	160	0	1992	24.3
Hal Greer	82	3263	777	1626	.478	422	549	.769	444	372	289	6	1976	24.1
Chet Walker	82	2623	539	1172	.460	387	533	.726	607	157	252	3	1465	17.9
Bill Cunningham	74	2076	516	1178	.438	368	509	.723	562	187	260	3	1400	18.9
Wally Jones	77	2058	413	1040	.397	159	202	.787	219	245	225	5	985	12.8
Lucious Jackson	82	2570	401	927	.433	166	231	.719	872	139	287	6	968	11.8
John Green***	77	1440	310	676	.459	139	295	.471	545	80	163	3	759	9.9
John Green**	35	367	69	150	.460	39	83	.470	122	21	51	0	177	5.1
Matt Guokas	82	1612	190	393	.483	118	152	.776	185	191	172	0	498	6.1
Bill Melchionni	71	758	146	336	.435	33	47	.702	104	105	75	0	325	4.6
Larry Costello	28	492	67	148	.453	67	81	.827	51	68	62	0	201	7.2
Ron Filipek	19	73	18	47	.383	7	14	.500	25	7	12	0	43	2.3
Jim Reid	6	52	10	20	.500	1	5	.200	11	3	6	0	21	3.5

1967-68 STATISTICS

ST. LOUIS

Player	G.	Min.	FGM	FGA	Pct.	FTM	FTA	Pct.	Reb.	Ast.	PF	Disq.	Pts.	Avg.
Zelmo Beaty	82	3068	639	1310	.488	455	573	.794	959	174	295	6	1733	21.1
Len Wilkens	82	3169	546	1246	.438	546	711	.768	438	679	255	3	1638	20.0
Joe Caldwell	79	2641	564	1219	.463	165	290	.569	338	240	208	1	1293	16.4
Bill Bridges	82	3197	466	1009	.462	347	484	.717	1102	253	366	12	1279	15.6
Paul Silas	82	2652	399	871	.458	299	424	.705	958	162	243	4	1097	13.4
Don Ohl**	70	1919	393	891	.441	197	254	.776	175	157	184	1	983	14.0
Don Ohl**	31	823	161	355	.454	83	106	.783	62	73	93	1	405	13.1
Dick Snyder	75	1622	257	613	.419	129	167	.772	194	164	215	5	643	8.6
Lou Hudson	46	966	227	500	.454	120	164	.732	193	65	113	2	574	12.5
Gene Tormohlen	77	714	98	262	.374	43	56	.589	226	68	94	0	229	3.0
George Lehman	55	497	59	172	.343	35	43	.814	44	93	54	0	153	2.8
Jim Davis	50	394	61	139	.439	25	64	.391	123	13	85	2	147	2.9
Tom Workman*	19	85	19	38	.500	17	22	.773	24	3	14	0	55	2.9
Jay Miller	8	52	8	31	.258	4	7	.571	7	1	11	0	20	2.5

SAN DIEGO

Player	G.	Min.	FGM	FGA	Pct.	FTM	FTA	Pct.	Reb.	Ast.	PF	Disq.	Pts.	Avg.
Don Kojis	69	2548	530	1189	.446	300	413	.726	710	176	259	5	1360	19.7
Dave Gambee	80	1755	389	853	.440	321	379	.847	464	93	253	5	1071	13.4
John Block	52	1805	386	865	.423	316	394	.802	571	71	189	3	1048	20.2
Toby Kimball	81	2519	354	894	.396	181	306	.592	947	147	273	3	889	11.0
Jon McGlocklin	65	1876	316	757	.417	156	180	.867	199	178	117	0	788	12.1
John Barnhill	75	1883	295	700	.421	154	234	.658	173	259	143	1	744	9.9
Art Williams	79	1739	265	718	.369	113	165	.685	286	391	204	0	643	8.1
Pat Riley	80	1263	250	660	.379	128	202	.634	177	138	205	1	628	7.9
Henry Finkel	53	1116	242	492	.492	131	191	.686	375	72	175	5	615	11.6
John Green*	42	1073	241	526	.458	100	212	.472	423	59	112	3	582	13.9
Jim Barnett	47	1068	179	456	.393	84	118	.712	155	134	101	0	442	9.4
Nick Jones	42	603	86	232	.371	55	69	.797	67	89	84	0	227	5.4
Charles Acton	23	195	29	74	.392	19	29	.655	47	1	35	0	77	3.3
Jim Ware	30	228	25	97	.258	23	34	.676	77	7	28	1	73	2.4
Tyrone Britt	11	84	13	34	.382	2	3	.667	15	12	10	0	28	2.5

SAN FRANCISCO

Player	G.	Min.	FGM	FGA	Pct.	FTM	FTA	Pct.	Reb.	Ast.	PF	Disq.	Pts.	Avg.
Rudy LaRusso	79	2819	602	1389	.433	522	661	.790	741	182	337	14	1726	21.8
Jeff Mullins	79	2805	610	1391	.439	273	344	.794	447	351	271	2	1493	18.9
Fred Hetzel	77	2394	533	1287	.414	395	474	.833	546	131	262	7	1461	19.0
Nate Thurmond	51	2222	382	929	.411	282	438	.644	1121	215	137	1	1046	20.5
Clyde Lee	82	2699	373	894	.417	229	335	.684	1141	135	331	10	975	11.9
Jim King	54	1743	340	800	.425	217	268	.810	243	226	172	1	897	16.6
Al Attles	67	1992	252	540	.467	150	216	.694	276	390	284	9	654	9.8
Bob Warlick	69	1320	257	610	.421	97	171	.567	264	159	164	1	611	8.9
Joe Ellis	51	624	111	302	.368	32	50	.640	195	37	83	2	254	5.0
Bob Lewis	41	342	59	151	.391	61	79	.772	56	41	40	0	179	4.4
Bill Turner	42	482	68	157	.433	36	60	.600	155	16	74	1	172	4.1
Dave Lattin	44	257	37	102	.363	23	33	.697	104	14	94	4	97	2.2
George Lee	10	106	8	35	.229	17	24	.708	27	4	16	0	33	3.3

SEATTLE

Player	G.	Min.	FGM	FGA	Pct.	FTM	FTA	Pct.	Reb.	Ast.	PF	Disq.	Pts.	Avg.
Walt Hazzard	79	2666	733	1662	.441	428	553	.774	332	493	246	3	1894	23.9
Bob Rule	82	2424	568	1162	.489	348	529	.658	776	99	316	10	1484	18.1
Tom Meschery	82	2857	473	1008	.469	244	345	.707	840	193	323	14	1190	14.5
Al Tucker	81	2368	437	989	.442	186	263	.707	605	111	262	6	1060	13.1
Rod Thorn	66	1668	377	835	.451	252	342	.737	265	230	117	1	1006	15.2
Bob Weiss	82	1614	295	686	.430	213	254	.839	150	342	137	0	803	9.8
Tom Kron	76	1794	277	699	.396	184	233	.790	355	281	231	4	738	9.7
Dorie Murrey	81	1494	211	484	.436	168	244	.689	600	68	273	7	590	7.3
George Wilson	77	1236	179	498	.359	109	155	.703	470	56	218	1	467	6.1
Bud Olsen	73	897	130	285	.456	17	62	.274	204	75	136	1	277	3.8
Henry Akin	36	259	46	137	.336	20	31	.645	57	14	48	1	112	3.1
Plummer Lott	44	478	46	148	.311	19	31	.613	93	36	65	1	111	2.5

*Finished season with another team. **Total with team. ***Season total.

1967-68 CHAMPIONSHIP PLAYOFF RESULTS

EASTERN DIVISION SEMI-FINAL
Philadelphia Defeated New York 4 Games to 2

Mar. 22—New York 110 at Philadelphia 118
Mar. 23—Philadelphia 117 at New York 128
Mar. 27—New York 132 at Philadelphia **138
Mar. 30—Philadelphia 98 at New York 107
Mar. 31—New York 107 at Philadelphia 123
Apr. 1—Philadelphia 113 at New York 97

Boston Defeated Detroit 4 Games to 2

Mar. 24—Detroit 116 at Boston 123
Mar. 25—Boston 116 at Detroit 126
Mar. 27—Detroit 109 at Boston 98
Mar. 28—Boston 135 at Detroit 110
Mar. 31—Detroit 96 at Boston 110
Apr. 1—Boston 111 at Detroit 103

EASTERN DIVISION FINAL
Boston Defeated Philadelphia 4 Games to 3

Apr. 5—Boston 127 at Philadelphia 118
Apr. 10—Philadelphia 115 at Boston 106
Apr. 11—Boston 114 at Philadelphia 122
Apr. 14—Philadelphia 110 at Boston 105
Apr. 15—Boston 122 at Philadelphia 104
Apr. 17—Philadelphia 106 at Boston 114
Apr. 19—Boston 100 at Philadelphia 96

WESTERN DIVISION SEMI-FINAL
San Francisco Defeated St. Louis 4 Games to 2

Mar. 22—San Francisco 111 at St. Louis 106
Mar. 23—San Francisco 103 at St. Louis 111
Mar. 26—St. Louis 109 at San Francisco 124
Mar. 29—St. Louis 107 at San Francisco 108
Mar. 31—San Francisco 103 at St. Louis 129
Apr. 2—St. Louis 106 at San Francisco 111

Los Angeles Defeated Chicago 4 Games to 1

Mar. 24—Chicago 101 at Los Angeles 109
Mar. 25—Chicago 106 at Los Angeles 111
Mar. 27—Los Angeles 98 at Chicago 104
Mar. 29—Los Angeles 93 at Chicago 87
Mar. 31—Chicago 99 at Los Angeles 122

WESTERN DIVISION FINAL
Los Angeles Defeated San Francisco 4 Games to 0

Apr. 5—San Francisco 105 at Los Angeles 133
Apr. 10—San Francisco 112 at Los Angeles 115
Apr. 11—Los Angeles 128 at San Francisco 124
Apr. 13—Los Angeles 106 at San Francisco 100

CHAMPIONSHIP SERIES
Boston Defeated Los Angeles 4 Games to 2

Apr. 21—Los Angeles 101 at Boston 107
Apr. 24—Los Angeles 123 at Boston 113
Apr. 26—Boston 127 at Los Angeles 119
Apr. 28—Boston 105 at Los Angeles 119
Apr. 30—Los Angeles 117 at Boston *120
May 2—Boston 124 at Los Angeles 109

TEAM PLAYOFF STATISTICS

Team	G.	W.	L.	FGM	FGA	Pct.	FTM	FTA	Pct.	Reb.	Ast.	PF	Disq.	Scoring Average For	Agst.	Diff.
Los Angeles	15	10	5	666	1406	.474	370	539	.686	962	323	374	3	113.5	108.9	4.6
Boston	19	12	7	836	1852	.451	505	691	.731	1301	429	523	15	114.6	111.5	3.1
St. Louis	6	2	4	242	542	.446	184	251	.733	397	158	150	3	111.3	110.0	1.3
Philadelphia	13	7	3	561	1282	.438	356	564	.631	890	277	307	8	113.7	112.8	0.9
New York	6	2	4	274	603	.454	131	182	.720	363	135	174	3	113.2	117.8	-4.6
San Francisco	10	4	6	430	970	.443	241	332	.726	585	236	298	12	110.1	115.0	-4.9
Detroit	6	2	4	260	636	.409	140	205	.683	405	96	160	4	110.0	115.5	-5.5
Chicago	5	1	4	192	469	.409	113	150	.753	307	77	122	1	99.4	106.6	-7.2

1966-67 STATISTICS

1966-67 CHAMPION PHILADELPHIA 76ERS

Front row (left to right): Matt Guokas, Luke Jackson, Billy Cunningham, Wilt Chamberlain, Dave Gambee, Chet Walker. Back row: Trainer Al Domenico, Coach Alex Hannum, Hal Greer, Billy Melchionni, Larry Costello, Wally Jones, Owner Irv Kosloff, General Manager Jack Ramsay.

FINAL STANDINGS AND TEAM FIGURES

EASTERN DIVISION

Team	Phil.	Bos.	Cin.	N.Y.	Balt.	S.F.	St.L.	L.A.	Chi.	Det.	W.	L.	Pct.	For	Agst.
Philadelphia	..	4	8	8	8	7	8	8	8	9	68	13	.840	10143	9378
Boston	5	..	8	9	8	6	5	5	8	6	60	21	.741	9664	9012
Cincinnati	1	1	..	6	6	5	6	3	4	7	39	42	.481	9487	9507
New York	1	0	3	..	7	5	4	5	6	5	36	45	.444	9425	9672
Baltimore	1	1	3	2	..	2	4	2	3	2	20	61	.247	9353	9881

WESTERN DIVISION

Team	Phil.	Bos.	Cin.	N.Y.	Balt.	S.F.	St.L.	L.A.	Chi.	Det.	W.	L.	Pct.	For	Agst.
San Francisco	2	3	4	4	7	..	5	6	6	7	44	37	.543	9911	9679
St. Louis	1	4	3	5	5	4	..	5	5	7	39	42	.481	9204	9334
Los Angeles	1	4	6	4	7	3	4	..	3	3	36	45	.444	9764	9736
Chicago	1	1	5	3	6	3	4	6	..	4	33	48	.407	9167	9407
Detroit	0	3	2	4	7	2	2	5	5	..	30	51	.370	9015	9163

TEAM STATISTICS

	G.	FGM	FGA	Pct.	FTM	FTA	Pct.	Reb.	Ast.	PF	Disq.	For	Agst.	Dif.
Philadelphia	81	3912	8103	.483	2319	3411	.680	5701	2138	1906	30	125.2	115.8	9.4
Boston	81	3724	8325	.447	2216	2963	.748	5703	1962	2138	23	119.3	111.3	8.0
San Francisco	81	3814	8818	.433	2283	3021	.758	5974	1876	2120	48	122.4	119.5	2.9
Los Angeles	81	3786	8466	.447	2192	2917	.751	5415	1906	2168	31	120.5	120.2	0.3
Cincinnati	81	3654	8137	.449	2179	2806	.777	5198	1858	2073	25	117.1	117.4	−0.3
St. Louis	81	3547	8004	.443	2110	2979	.708	5219	1708	2173	40	113.6	115.2	−1.6
New York	81	3637	8025	.453	2151	2980	.722	5178	1782	2110	29	116.4	119.4	−3.0
Chicago	81	3565	8505	.419	2037	2784	.732	5295	1827	2205	21	113.2	116.9	−3.7
Detroit	81	3523	8542	.412	1969	2725	.723	5511	1465	2198	49	111.3	116.8	−5.5
Baltimore	81	3664	8578	.427	2025	2771	.731	5342	1652	2153	51	115.5	122.0	7.5

1966-67 STATISTICS

TOP 25 SCORERS

Player–Team	G.	Min.	FGA	FGM	Pct	FTA	FTM	Pct.	Reb.	Ast.	PF	Disq.	Pts.	Avg.
Rick Barry, San Francisco	78	3175	2240	1011	.451	852	753	.884	714	282	258	1	2775	35.6
Oscar Robertson, Cincinnati	79	3468	1699	838	.493	843	736	.873	486	845	226	2	2412	30.5
Wilt Chamberlain, Phila.	81	3682	1150	785	.683	875	386	.441	1957	630	143	0	1956	24.1
Jerry West, Los Angeles	66	2670	1389	645	.464	686	602	.878	392	447	160	1	1892	28.7
Elgin Baylor, Los Angeles	70	2706	1658	711	.429	541	440	.813	898	215	211	1	1862	26.6
Hal Greer, Philadelphia	80	3086	1524	699	.459	466	367	.788	422	303	302	5	1765	22.1
John Havlicek, Boston	81	2602	1540	684	.444	441	365	.828	532	278	210	0	1733	21.4
Willis Reed, New York	78	2824	1298	635	.489	487	358	.735	1136	126	293	9	1628	20.9
Bailey Howell, Boston	81	2503	1242	636	.512	471	349	.741	677	103	296	4	1621	20.0
Dave Bing, Detroit	80	2762	1522	664	.436	370	273	.738	359	330	217	2	1601	20.0
Sam Jones, Boston	72	2325	1406	638	.454	371	318	.857	338	217	191	1	1594	22.1
Chet Walker, Philadelphia	81	2691	1150	561	.488	581	445	.766	660	188	232	4	1567	19.3
Gus Johnson, Baltimore	73	2626	1377	620	.450	383	271	.708	855	194	281	7	1511	20.7
Walt Bellamy, New York	79	3010	1084	565	.521	580	369	.637	1064	206	275	5	1499	19.0
Bill Cunningham, Phila.	80	2168	1211	556	.459	558	383	.686	589	205	260	2	1495	18.5
Lou Hudson, St. Louis	80	2446	1328	620	.467	327	231	.706	435	95	277	3	1471	18.4
Guy Rodgers, Chicago	81	3063	1377	538	.391	457	383	.806	346	908	243	1	1459	18.0
Jerry Lucas, Cincinnati	81	3558	1257	577	.459	359	284	.791	1547	268	280	2	1438	17.8
Bob Boozer, Chicago	80	2451	1104	538	.487	461	360	.781	679	90	212	0	1436	18.0
Eddie Miles, Detroit	81	2419	1363	582	.427	338	261	.772	298	181	216	2	1425	17.6
Dave DeBusschere, Detroit	78	2897	1278	531	.415	512	361	.705	924	216	297	7	1423	18.2
Jerry Sloan, Chicago	80	2942	1214	525	.432	427	340	.796	726	170	293	7	1390	17.4
Kevin Loughery, Baltimore	76	2577	1306	520	.398	412	340	.825	349	288	294	10	1380	18.2
Bill Bridges, St. Louis	79	3130	1106	503	.455	523	367	.702	1190	222	325	12	1373	17.4
Len Wilkens, St. Louis	78	2974	1036	448	.432	583	459	.787	412	442	280	6	1355	17.4

FIELD GOAL PERCENTAGE LEADERS
(Minimum 220 FGM)

	FGA	FGM	Pct.
Wilt Chamberlain, Phila.	1150	785	.683
Walt Bellamy, New York	1084	565	.521
Bailey Howell, Boston	1242	636	.512
Oscar Robertson, Cincinnati	1699	838	.493
Willis Reed, New York	1298	635	.490
Chet Walker, Philadelphia	1150	561	.488
Bob Boozer, Chicago	1104	538	.487
Tom Hawkins, Los Angeles	572	275	.481
Harold Hairston, Cincinnati	962	461	.479
Dick Barnett, New York	949	454	.478

FREE THROW PERCENTAGE LEADERS
(Minimum 220 FTM)

	FTA	FTM	Pct.
Adrian Smith, Cincinnati	380	343	.903
Rick Barry, San Francisco	852	753	.884
Jerry West, Los Angeles	686	602	.878
Oscar Robertson, Cincinnati	843	736	.873
Sam Jones, Boston	371	318	.857
Larry Siegfried, Boston	347	294	.847
Wally Jones, Philadelphia	266	223	.838
John Havlicek, Boston	441	365	.828
Kevin Loughery, Baltimore	412	340	.825
Elgin Baylor, Los Angeles	541	440	.813

LEADERS IN REBOUNDS

	G.	No.	Avg.
Wilt Chamberlain, Phila.	81	1957	24.2
Bill Russell, Boston	81	1700	21.0
Jerry Lucas, Cincinnati	81	1547	19.1
Nate Thurmond, San Francisco	65	1382	21.3
Bill Bridges, St. Louis	79	1190	15.1
Willis Reed, New York	78	1136	14.6
Darrall Imhoff, Los Angeles	81	1080	13.3
Walt Bellamy, New York	79	1064	13.5
Leroy Ellis, Baltimore	81	970	12.0
Dave DeBusschere, Detroit	78	924	11.8

LEADERS IN ASSISTS

	G.	No.	Avg.
Guy Rodgers, Chicago	81	908	11.2
Oscar Robertson, Cincinnati	79	845	10.7
Wilt Chamberlain, Phila.	81	630	7.8
Bill Russell, Boston	81	472	5.8
Jerry West, Los Angeles	66	447	6.8
Len Wilkens, St. Louis	78	442	5.7
Howard Komives, New York	65	401	6.2
K. C. Jones, Boston	78	389	5.0
Richie Guerin, St. Louis	79	345	4.4
Paul Neumann, San Francisco	78	342	4.4

RECORD OF TEAMS BY MONTHS

Team	Oct. W-L	Nov. W-L	Dec. W-L	Jan. W-L	Feb. W-L	Mar. W-L	Total W-L
Baltimore	1-7	3-13	4-11	4-13	6-9	2-8	20-61
Boston	4-1	11-3	12-4	13-4	10-5	10-4	60-21
Chicago	4-4	4-13	7-8	7-10	3-9	8-4	33-48
Cincinnati	2-4	7-7	4-11	10-5	8-12	8-3	39-42
Detroit	5-3	6-10	4-9	5-11	7-9	3-9	30-51
Los Angeles	2-6	6-8	5-9	8-9	10-6	5-7	36-45
New York	4-3	8-9	8-7	6-11	9-7	1-8	36-45
Philadelphia	5-0	15-2	15-1	12-3	11-4	10-3	68-13
St. Louis	3-3	6-7	6-9	9-11	8-8	7-4	39-42
San Francisco	4-3	11-5	9-5	10-7	6-9	4-8	44-37
Totals	34	77	74	84	78	58	

INTER-CLUB RECORDS—HOME, AWAY AND NEUTRAL COURT

	Home W-L	Away W-L	Neutral W-L	Total W-L
Baltimore	12-20	3-30	5-11	20-61
Boston	27-4	25-11	8-6	60-21
Chicago	17-19	9-17	7-12	33-48
Cincinnati	20-11	12-24	7-7	39-42
Detroit	12-18	9-19	9-14	30-51
Los Angeles	21-18	12-20	3-7	36-45
New York	20-15	9-24	7-6	36-45
Philadelphia	28-2	26-8	14-3	68-13
St. Louis	18-11	12-21	9-10	39-42
San Francisco	18-10	11-19	15-8	44-37
Totals	193-128	128-193	84-84	

INDIVIDUAL STATISTICS

BALTIMORE

Player	G.	Min.	FGA	FGM	Pct.	FTA	FTM	Pct.	Reb.	Ast.	PF	Disq.	Pts.	Avg.
Gus Johnson	73	2626	1377	620	.450	383	271	.708	855	194	281	7	1511	20.7
Kevin Loughery	76	2577	1306	520	.398	412	340	.825	349	288	294	10	1380	18.2
Leroy Ellis	81	2938	1166	496	.425	286	211	.738	970	170	258	3	1203	14.9
Don Ohl	58	2024	1002	452	.451	354	276	.780	189	168	153	1	1180	20.3
Ray Scott***	72	2446	1144	458	.400	366	256	.699	760	160	225	2	1172	16.3
Ray Scott**	27	969	463	206	.445	160	100	.625	356	76	83	1	512	19.0
John Egan	71	1743	624	267	.428	219	185	.845	180	275	190	3	719	10.1
Jack Marin	74	1323	632	283	.448	187	145	.775	313	75	199	6	711	9.6
John Green	61	948	437	203	.465	207	96	.464	394	57	139	7	502	8.2
John Barnhill	53	1214	447	187	.418	103	66	.641	157	136	80	0	440	8.3
Ben Warley	62	1037	312	125	.401	170	134	.788	325	51	176	6	384	6.2
Bob Ferry	51	991	315	132	.419	110	70	.636	258	92	97	0	334	6.5
Wayne Hightower	43	746	308	103	.334	124	89	.718	241	36	110	5	295	6.9
Mel Counts	25	343	167	65	.389	40	29	.725	155	30	81	2	159	6.4
John Austin	4	61	22	5	.227	16	13	.813	7	4	12	0	23	5.9

BOSTON

Player	G.	Min.	FGA	FGM	Pct.	FTA	FTM	Pct.	Reb.	Ast.	PF	Disq.	Pts.	Avg.
John Havlicek	81	2602	1540	684	.444	441	365	.828	532	278	210	0	1733	21.4
Bailey Howell	81	2503	1242	636	.512	471	349	.741	677	103	296	4	1621	20.0
Sam Jones	72	2325	1406	638	.454	371	318	.857	338	217	191	1	1594	22.1
Bill Russell	81	3297	870	395	.454	467	285	.610	1700	472	258	4	1075	13.4
Larry Siegfried	73	1891	833	368	.442	347	294	.847	228	250	207	1	1030	14.1
Tom Sanders	81	1926	755	323	.428	218	178	.817	439	91	304	6	824	10.2
Don Nelson	79	1202	509	227	.446	190	141	.742	295	65	143	0	595	7.5
K. C. Jones	78	2446	459	182	.397	189	119	.630	239	389	273	7	483	6.2
Wayne Embry	72	729	359	147	.409	144	82	.569	294	42	137	0	376	5.2
Jim Barnett	48	383	211	78	.370	62	42	.677	47	53	41	61	0	198	4.1
Toby Kimball	38	222	97	35	.361	40	27	.675	146	13	42	0	97	2.6
Ron Watts	27	89	44	11	.250	23	16	.696	38	1	16	0	38	1.4

CHICAGO

Player	G.	Min.	FGA	FGM	Pct.	FTA	FTM	Pct.	Reb.	Ast.	PF	Disq.	Pts.	Avg.
Guy Rodgers	81	3063	1377	538	.391	475	383	.806	346	908	243	1	1459	18.0
Bob Boozer	80	2451	1104	538	.487	461	360	.781	679	90	212	0	1436	18.0
Jerry Sloan	80	2942	1214	525	.432	427	340	.796	726	170	293	7	1390	17.4
Erwin Mueller	80	2136	957	422	.441	260	171	.658	497	131	223	2	1015	12.7
Don Kojis	78	1655	773	329	.426	222	134	.604	479	70	204	3	792	10.2
McCoy McLemore	79	1382	670	258	.385	272	210	.772	374	62	189	2	726	9.2
Jim Washington	77	1475	604	252	.417	159	88	.553	468	56	181	1	592	7.7
Keith Erickson	76	1454	641	235	.367	159	117	.736	339	119	199	2	587	7.7
Barry Clemens	60	986	444	186	.419	90	68	.756	201	39	143	1	440	7.3
Gerry Ward	76	1042	307	117	.381	138	87	.630	179	130	169	2	321	4.2
George Wilson***	55	573	234	85	.363	86	58	.674	206	15	92	0	228	4.1
George Wilson**	43	448	193	77	.399	70	45	.643	163	15	73	0	199	4.6
Len Chappell	19	179	89	40	.449	21	14	.667	38	12	31	0	94	4.9
Dave Schellhase	31	212	111	40	.360	22	14	.636	28	23	27	0	94	3.0
Nate Bowman	9	65	21	8	.381	8	6	.750	28	2	18	0	22	2.4

CINCINNATI

Player	G.	Min.	FGA	FGM	Pct.	FTA	FTM	Pct.	Reb.	Ast.	PF	Disq.	Pts.	Avg.
Oscar Robertson	79	3468	1699	838	.493	843	736	.873	486	845	226	2	2412	30.5
Jerry Lucas	81	3558	1257	577	.459	359	284	.791	1547	268	280	2	1438	17.8
Adrian Smith	81	2636	1147	502	.438	380	343	.903	205	187	272	0	1347	16.6
Harold Hairston	79	2442	962	461	.479	382	252	.660	603	153	251	7	1174	14.9
Connie Dierking	77	1905	729	291	.399	180	134	.744	603	133	251	7	716	9.3
Flynn Robinson	76	1140	599	274	.457	154	120	.779	133	110	197	3	668	8.8
Jon McGlocklin	60	1194	493	217	.440	104	74	.712	164	93	84	0	508	8.5
Bob Love	66	1074	403	173	.429	147	93	.633	257	49	153	3	439	6.7

1966-67 STATISTICS

Player	G.	Min.	FGA	FGM	Pct.	FTA	FTM	Pct	Reb.	Ast.	PF	Disq.	Pts.	Avg.
Len Chappell***	73	708	313	132	.422	47	33	.654	189	33	104	0	316	4.3
Len Chappell**	54	529	224	92	.411	60	39	.650	151	21	73	0	223	4.1
Walt Wesley	64	909	333	131	.393	123	52	.423	329	19	161	2	314	4.9
Fred Lewis	32	334	153	60	.392	41	29	.707	44	40	49	1	149	4.7
Jim Ware	33	201	97	30	.309	17	10	.588	69	6	35	0	70	2.1
George Wilson	12	125	41	8	.195	16	13	.813	43	0	19	0	29	2.4

DETROIT

Player	G.	Min.	FGA	FGM	Pct.	FTA	FTM	Pct.	Reb.	Ast.	PF	Disq.	Pts.	Avg.
Dave Bing	80	2762	1522	664	.436	370	273	.738	359	330	217	2	1601	20.0
Eddie Miles	81	2419	1363	582	.427	338	261	.772	298	181	216	2	1425	17.6
Dave DeBusschere	78	2897	1278	531	.415	512	361	.705	924	216	297	7	1423	18.2
Tom Van Arsdale	79	2134	887	347	.391	347	272	.784	341	193	241	3	966	12.2
Joe Strawder	79	2156	660	281	.426	262	188	.718	791	82	344	19	750	9.5
John Tresvant	68	1553	585	256	.438	234	164	.701	483	88	246	8	676	9.9
Ray Scott	45	1477	681	252	.370	206	156	.757	404	84	132	1	660	14.7
Wayne Hightower***	72	1310	567	195	.344	210	153	.729	405	64	190	6	543	7.5
Wayne Hightower**	29	564	259	92	.355	86	64	.744	164	28	80	1	248	8.6
Ron Reed	61	1248	600	223	.372	133	79	.594	423	81	145	2	525	8.6
Reggie Harding	74	1367	383	172	.449	103	63	.612	455	94	164	2	407	5.5
Charlie Vaughn	50	680	226	85	.376	74	50	.676	67	75	54	0	220	4.4
Dorrie Murrey	35	311	82	33	.402	54	32	.593	102	12	57	2	98	2.8
Bob Hogsett	7	22	16	5	.313	6	6	1.000	3	1	5	0	16	2.3

LOS ANGELES

Player	G.	Min.	FGA	FGM	Pct.	FTA	FTM	Pct.	Reb.	Ast.	PF	Disq.	Pts.	Avg.
Jerry West	66	2670	1389	645	.464	686	602	.878	392	447	160	1	1892	28.7
Elgin Baylor	70	2706	1658	711	.429	541	440	.813	898	215	211	1	1862	26.6
Gail Goodrich	77	1780	776	352	.454	337	253	.751	251	210	294	3	957	12.4
Darrall Imhoff	81	2725	780	370	.474	207	127	.614	1080	222	281	7	867	10.7
Archie Clark	76	1763	732	331	.452	192	136	.708	218	205	193	1	798	10.5
Walt Hazzard	79	1642	706	301	.426	177	129	.729	231	323	203	1	731	9.3
Tom Hawkins	79	1798	572	275	.481	173	82	.474	434	83	207	1	632	8.3
Rudy LaRusso	45	1292	509	211	.415	224	156	.696	351	78	149	6	578	12.8
Jim Barnes	80	1398	497	217	.437	187	128	.684	450	47	266	5	562	7.0
Jerry Chambers	68	1015	496	224	.452	93	68	.731	208	44	143	0	516	7.6
Mel Counts***	56	860	419	177	.422	94	69	.734	344	52	183	6	423	7.6
Mel Counts**	31	517	252	112	.444	54	40	.741	189	22	102	4	264	8.5
John Block**	22	118	52	20	.385	34	24	.706	45	5	20	0	64	2.9
Henry Finkel	27	141	47	17	.362	12	7	.583	64	5	39	1	41	1.5

NEW YORK

Player	G.	Min.	FGA	FGM	Pct.	FTA	FTM	Pct.	Reb.	Ast.	PF	Disq.	Pts.	Avg.
Willis Reed	78	2824	1298	635	.489	487	358	.735	1136	126	293	9	1628	20.9
Walt Bellamy	79	3010	1084	565	.521	580	369	.637	1064	206	275	5	1499	19.0
Dick Van Arsdale	79	2892	913	410	.449	509	371	.729	555	247	264	3	1191	15.1
Dick Barnett	67	1969	949	454	.478	295	231	.783	226	161	185	2	1139	17.0
Howard Komives	65	2282	995	402	.404	253	217	.858	183	401	213	1	1021	15.7
Dave Stallworth	76	1889	816	380	.466	320	229	.716	472	144	226	4	989	13.0
Cazzie Russell	77	1696	789	344	.436	228	179	.785	251	187	174	1	867	11.3
Emmette Bryant	63	1593	577	236	.409	114	74	.539	273	218	231	4	546	8.7
Henry Akin	50	453	230	83	.361	37	26	.703	120	25	82	0	192	3.8
Neil Johnson	51	522	171	59	.345	86	57	.663	167	38	102	0	175	3.4
Fred Crawford	19	192	116	44	.379	38	24	.632	48	12	39	0	112	5.9
Wayne Molis	13	75	51	19	.373	13	7	.538	22	2	9	0	45	3.5
Dave Deutsch	19	93	36	6	.167	20	9	.450	21	15	17	0	21	1.1

PHILADELPHIA

Player	G.	Min.	FGA	FGM	Pct.	FTA	FTM	Pct.	Reb.	Ast.	PF	Disq.	Pts.	Avg.
Wilt Chamberlain	81	3682	1150	785	.683	875	386	.441	1957	630	143	0	1956	24.1
Hal Greer	80	3086	1524	699	.459	466	367	.788	422	303	302	5	1765	22.1
Chet Walker	81	2691	1150	561	.488	581	445	.766	660	188	232	4	1567	19.3
Billy Cunningham	81	2168	1211	556	.459	558	383	.686	589	205	260	2	1495	18.5
Wally Jones	81	2429	982	423	.431	266	223	.838	265	303	240	6	1069	13.2
Lucious Jackson	81	2377	882	386	.438	261	198	.759	724	114	276	6	970	12.0
Dave Gambee	63	757	345	150	.435	125	107	.856	197	42	143	5	407	6.5
Larry Costello	49	976	293	130	.444	133	120	.902	103	140	141	2	380	7.8
Bill Melchionni	73	692	353	138	.391	40	39	.650	98	98	73	0	315	4.3
Matt Guokas	69	808	203	79	.389	81	49	.605	83	105	82	0	207	3.0
Bob Weiss	6	29	10	5	.500	5	2	.400	3	10	8	0	12	2.0

1966-67 STATISTICS

ST. LOUIS

Player	G.	Min.	FGA	FGM	Pct.	FTA	FTM	Pct.	Reb.	Ast.	PF	Disq.	Pts.	Avg.
Lou Hudson	80	2446	1328	620	.467	327	231	.706	435	95	277	3	1471	18.4
Bill Bridges	79	3130	1106	503	.455	523	367	.702	1190	222	325	12	1373	17.4
Len Wilkens	78	2974	1036	448	.432	583	459	.787	412	442	280	6	1355	17.4
Joe Caldwell	81	2256	1076	458	.426	308	200	.649	442	166	230	4	1116	13.8
Richie Guerin	80	2275	904	394	.436	416	304	.731	192	345	247	2	1092	13.7
Zelmo Beaty	48	1661	694	328	.473	260	197	.758	515	60	189	3	853	17.8
Rod Thorn	67	1166	524	233	.445	172	125	.727	160	118	88	0	591	8.8
Paul Silas	77	1570	482	207	.429	213	113	.531	669	74	208	4	527	6.8
Gene Tormohlen	63	1036	403	172	.427	84	50	.595	347	73	177	4	394	6.3
Dick Snyder	55	676	333	144	.432	61	46	.754	91	59	82	1	334	6.1
Tom Kron	32	221	87	27	.310	19	13	.684	36	46	35	0	67	2.1
Tom Hoover	17	129	31	13	.419	13	5	.385	36	8	35	1	31	1.8

SAN FRANCISCO

Player	G.	Min.	FGA	FGM	Pct.	FTA	FTM	Pct.	Reb.	Ast.	PF	Disq.	Pts.	Avg.
Rick Barry	78	3175	2240	1011	.451	852	753	.884	714	282	258	1	2775	35.6
Nate Thurmond	65	2755	1068	467	.437	445	280	.629	1382	166	183	3	1214	18.7
Paul Neumann	78	2421	911	386	.424	390	312	.800	272	342	266	4	1084	13.9
Jeff Mullins	77	1835	919	421	.458	214	150	.701	388	226	195	5	992	12.9
Fred Hetzel	77	2123	932	373	.400	237	192	.810	639	111	228	3	938	12.2
Tom Meschery	72	1846	706	293	.415	244	175	.717	549	94	264	8	761	10.6
Jim King	67	1667	685	286	.418	221	174	.787	319	240	193	5	746	11.1
Clyde Lee	74	1247	503	205	.408	166	105	.633	551	77	168	5	515	7.0
Al Attles	69	1764	467	212	.454	151	88	.583	321	269	265	13	512	7.4
Bud Olsen	40	348	167	75	.449	58	23	.397	103	32	51	1	173	4.3
Joe Ellis	41	333	164	67	.409	25	19	.760	112	27	45	0	153	3.7
Bob Warlick	12	65	52	15	.280	11	6	.545	20	10	4	0	36	3.0
George Lee	1	5	4	3	.750	7	6	.857	0	0	0	0	12	12.0

**—Team Total
***—Combined Player Total

1966-67 CHAMPIONSHIP PLAYOFF RESULTS

EASTERN DIVISION SEMI-FINALS
Boston defeated New York 3 to 1
Mar. 21—New York 110, at Boston 140
Mar. 25—Boston 115, at New York 108
Mar. 26—New York 123, at Boston 112
Mar. 28—Boston 118, at New York 109

Philadelphia defeated Cincinnati 3 to 1
Mar. 21—Cincinnati 120, at Philadelphia 116
Mar. 22—Philadelphia 123, at Cincinnati 102
Mar. 24—Cincinnati 106, at Philadelphia 121
Mar. 25—Philadelphia 112, at Cincinnati 94

EASTERN DIVISION FINAL SERIES
Philadelphia defeated Boston 4 to 1
Mar. 31—Boston 113, at Philadelphia 127
Apr. 2—Philadelphia 107, at Boston 102
Apr. 5—Boston 104, at Philadelphia 115
Apr. 9—Philadelphia 117, at Boston 121
Apr. 11—Boston 116, at Philadelphia 140

WESTERN DIVISION SEMI-FINALS
St. Louis defeated Chicago 3 to 0
Mar. 21—Chicago 100, at St. Louis 114
Mar. 23—St. Louis 113, at Chicago 107
Mar. 25—Chicago 106, at St. Louis 119

San Francisco defeated Los Angeles 3 to 0
Mar. 21—Los Angeles 108, at San Francisco 124
Mar. 23—San Francisco 113, at Los Angeles 102
Mar. 26—Los Angeles 115, at San Francisco 122

WESTERN DIVISION FINAL SERIES
San Francisco defeated St. Louis 4 to 2
Mar. 30—St. Louis 115, at San Francisco 117
Apr. 1—St. Louis 136, at San Francisco 143
Apr. 5—San Francisco 109, at St. Louis 115
Apr. 8—San Francisco 104, at St. Louis 109
Apr. 10—St. Louis 102, at San Francisco 123
Apr. 12—San Francisco 112, at St. Louis 107

CHAMPIONSHIP SERIES
Philadelphia defeated San Francisco 4 games to 2
Apr. 14—San Francisco 135, at Philadelphia *141
Apr. 16—San Francisco 95, at Philadelphia 126
Apr. 18—Philadelphia 124, at San Francisco 130
Apr. 20—Philadelphia 122, at San Francisco 108
Apr. 23—San Francisco 117, at Philadelphia 109
Apr. 24—Philadelphia 125, at San Francisco 122
*Overtime.

TEAM PLAYOFF STATISTICS

Team	G.	W.	L.	FGA	FGM	Pct.	FTA	FTM	Pct.	Reb.	Ast.	PF	Disq.	Scoring For	Agst.
Philadelphia	15	11	4	1563	704	.450	626	417	.666	1115	401	336	3	121.7	112.3
San Francisco	15	9	6	1680	704	.419	514	366	.712	1134	345	436	13	118.3	117.1
St. Louis	9	5	4	882	360	.408	409	310	.759	638	185	257	7	115.7	116.2
Boston	9	4	5	984	409	.416	302	223	.738	642	221	257	7	112.5	121.3
New York	4	1	3	441	174	.395	135	102	.756	288	91	123	4	104.3	115.3
Chicago	3	0	3	293	124	.423	89	65	.730	167	53	87	1	108.3	119.7
Los Angeles	3	0	3	310	127	.410	94	71	.755	185	68	73	2	108.3	118.0
Cincinnati	4	1	3	402	180	.448	80	62	.775	237	101	91	0	105.5	118.0

1965-66 STATISTICS

1965-66 CHAMPION BOSTON CELTICS

Seated (left to right): John Havlicek, K. C. Jones, Marvin Kratter, chairman of board; Coach Red Auerbach, President John J. Waldron, Bill Russell. Standing: Ron Bonham, Don Nelson, Tom Sanders, Mel Counts, John Thompson, Woody Sauldsberry, Willie Naulls, Sam Jones, Larry Siegfried, Trainer Buddy LeRoux.

FINAL STANDINGS AND TEAM FIGURES

EASTERN DIVISION

Team	Phil.	Bos.	Cin.	N.Y.	L.A.	Balt.	St.L.	S.F.	Det.	W.	L.	Pct.	For	Agst.
Philadelphia	..	6	6	8	8	5	7	8	7	55	25	.688	9387	9013
Boston	4	..	5	10	7	7	7	8	6	54	26	.675	9014	8623
Cincinnati	4	5	..	7	4	7	5	5	8	45	35	.563	9424	9331
New York	2	0	3	..	5	3	4	5	8	30	50	.375	9335	9543

WESTERN DIVISION

Team	Phil.	Bos.	Cin.	N.Y.	L.A.	Balt.	St.L.	S.F.	Det.	W.	L.	Pct.	For	Agst.
Los Angeles	2	3	6	5	..	6	8	7	8	45	35	.563	9557	9309
Baltimore	5	3	3	7	4	..	7	4	5	38	42	.475	9465	9560
St. Louis	3	3	5	6	2	3	..	6	8	36	44	.450	8913	8958
San Francisco	2	2	5	5	3	6	4	..	8	35	45	.438	9243	9455
Detroit	3	4	2	2	2	5	2	2	..	22	58	.275	8827	9373

TEAM STATISTICS

	G.	FGM	FGA	Pct.	FTM	FTA	Pct.	Reb.	Ast.	PF	Disq.	For	Agst.	Dif.
Boston	80	3488	8367	.417	2038	2758	.739	5591	1795	2012	39	112.7	107.8	4.9
Philadelphia	80	3650	8189	.446	2087	3141	.664	5652	1905	2095	39	117.3	112.7	4.6
Los Angeles	80	3597	8109	.444	2363	3057	.773	5334	2035	25	119.5	116.4	3.1
Cincinnati	80	3610	8123	.444	2204	2906	.758	5559	1818	2033	24	117.8	116.6	1.2
St. Louis	80	3379	7836	.431	2155	2870	.751	5167	1782	2179	47	111.4	112.0	-0.6
Baltimore	80	3599	8210	.438	2267	3186	.712	5542	1890	2199	52	118.3	119.5	-1.2
New York	80	3559	7910	.450	2217	3078	.720	5119	1896	2227	48	116.7	119.3	-2.6
San Francisco	80	3557	8512	.418	2129	2879	.730	5727	1872	2069	37	115.5	118.2	-2.7
Detroit	80	3475	8502	.409	1877	2734	.687	5427	1569	2016	27	110.3	117.2	-6.9

1965-66 STATISTICS
TOP 25 SCORERS

Player—Team	G.	Min.	FGA	FGM	Pct.	FTA	FTM	Pct.	Reb.	Ast.	PF	Disq.	Pts.	Avg.
Wilt Chamberlain, Phila.	79	3737	1990	1074	.540	976	501	.513	1943	414	171	0	2649	33.5
Jerry West, Los Angeles	79	3218	1731	818	.473	977	840	.860	562	480	243	1	2476	31.3
Oscar Robertson, Cinn.	76	3493	1723	818	.475	881	742	.842	586	847	227	1	2378	31.3
Rick Barry, San Fran.	80	2990	1698	745	.439	660	569	.862	850	173	297	2	2059	25.7
Walt Bellamy, Balt.-N.Y.	80	3352	1373	695	.506	689	430	.624	1254	235	294	9	1820	22.8
Hal Greer, Philadelphia	80	3326	1580	703	.445	514	413	.804	473	384	315	6	1819	22.7
Dick Barnett, New York	75	2589	1344	431	.469	605	467	.772	310	259	235	6	1729	23.1
Jerry Lucas, Cincinnati	79	3517	1523	690	.453	403	317	.787	1668	213	274	5	1697	21.5
Zelmo Beaty, St. Louis	80	3072	1301	616	.473	559	424	.758	1086	125	344	15	1656	20.7
Sam Jones, Boston	67	2155	1335	626	.469	407	325	.799	347	216	190	0	1577	23.5
Eddie Miles, Detroit	80	2788	1418	634	.447	402	298	.741	302	221	203	2	1566	19.6
Don Ohl, Baltimore	73	2645	1334	593	.445	430	316	.734	280	290	208	1	1502	20.6
Adrian Smith, Cincinnati	80	2982	1310	531	.405	480	408	.850	287	256	276	1	1470	18.4
Guy Rodgers, San Fran.	79	2902	1571	586	.373	407	296	.727	421	846	241	6	1468	18.6
Ray Scott, Detroit	79	2652	1309	544	.416	435	323	.743	755	238	209	1	1411	17.9
Bailey Howell, Baltimore	78	2328	986	481	.488	551	402	.730	773	155	306	12	1364	17.5
Kevin Loughery, Baltimore	74	2455	1264	526	.416	358	297	.830	227	356	273	8	1349	18.2
John Havlicek, Boston	71	2175	1328	530	.399	349	274	.785	423	210	158	1	1334	18.8
Dave DeBusschere, Detroit	79	2696	1284	524	.408	378	249	.659	916	209	252	5	1297	16.4
Len Wilkens, St. Louis	69	2692	954	411	.431	532	422	.793	322	429	248	4	1244	18.0
Chet Walker, Philadelphia	80	2603	982	443	.451	468	335	.716	636	201	238	3	1221	15.3
Richie Guerin, St. Louis	80	2363	998	414	.415	446	362	.812	314	388	256	4	1190	14.9
Nate Thurmond, San Fran.	73	2891	1119	454	.406	425	280	.654	1312	111	223	7	1188	16.3
Willis Reed, New York	76	2537	1009	438	.434	399	302	.757	883	91	323	13	1178	15.5
Rudy LaRusso, Los Angeles	76	2316	897	410	.457	445	350	.787	660	165	261	9	1170	15.4

FIELD GOAL PERCENTAGE LEADERS
(Minimum 210 FGM)

	FGA	FGM	Pct.
Wilt Chamberlain, Phila.	1990	1074	.540
John Green, N.Y.-Balt.	668	358	.536
Walt Bellamy, Balt.-N.Y.	1373	695	.506
Al Attles, San Francisco	724	364	.503
Happy Hairston, Cincinnati	814	398	.489
Bailey Howell, Baltimore	986	481	.488
Bob Boozer, Los Angeles	754	365	.484
Oscar Robertson, Cincinnati	1723	818	.475
Zelmo Beaty, St. Louis	1301	616	.473
Jerry West, Los Angeles	1731	818	.473

FREE THROW PERCENTAGE LEADERS
(Minimum 210 FTM)

	FTA	FTM	Pct.
Larry Siegfried, Boston	311	274	.881
Rick Barry, San Francisco	660	569	.862
Howard Komives, New York	280	241	.861
Jerry West, Los Angeles	977	840	.860
Adrian Smith, Cincinnati	480	408	.850
Oscar Robertson, Cincinnati	881	742	.842
Paul Neumann, San Francisco	317	265	.836
Kevin Loughery, Baltimore	358	297	.830
Richie Guerin, St. Louis	446	362	.812
Hal Greer, Philadelphia	514	413	.804

LEADERS IN REBOUNDS

	G.	No.	Avg.
Wilt Chamberlain, Philadelphia	79	1943	24.6
Bill Russell, Boston	78	1779	22.8
Jerry Lucas, Cincinnati	79	1668	21.1
Nate Thurmond, San Francisco	73	1312	18.0
Walt Bellamy, Balt.-N.Y.	80	1254	15.7
Zelmo Beaty, St. Louis	80	1086	13.6
Bill Bridges, St. Louis	78	951	12.2
Dave DeBusschere, Detroit	79	916	11.6
Willis Reed, New York	76	883	11.6
Rick Barry, San Francisco	80	850	10.6

LEADERS IN ASSISTS

	G.	No.	Avg.
Oscar Roberston, Cincinnati	76	847	11.1
Guy Rodgers, San Francisco	79	846	10.7
K. C. Jones, Boston	80	503	6.3
Jerry West, Los Angeles	79	480	6.1
Len Wilkens, St. Louis	69	429	6.2
Howard Komives, New York	80	425	5.3
Wilt Chamberlain, Philadelphia	79	414	5.2
Walt Hazzard, Los Angeles	80	393	4.9
Richie Guerin, St. Louis	80	388	4.9
Hal Greer, Philadelphia	80	384	4.8

INDIVIDUAL STATISTICS
BALTIMORE

Player	G.	Minutes	FG Att.	FG Made	FG Pct.	FT Att.	FT Made	FT Pct.	Re- b'nd	As- sist	Per. Fls.	Disq.	Tot. Pts.	Avg. Pts.
Don Ohl	73	2645	1334	593	.445	430	316	.734	280	290	208	1	1502	20.6
Bailey Howell	78	2328	986	481	.488	551	402	.730	773	155	306	12	1364	17.5
Kevin Loughery	74	2455	1264	526	.416	358	297	.830	227	356	273	8	1349	18.2
John Green***	79	1645	668	358	.536	388	202	.521	645	107	183	3	918	11.6
John Green**	72	1437	589	315	.535	357	187	.524	571	96	162	3	817	11.3
Jim Barnes***	73	2191	818	348	.425	310	212	.684	755	94	283	10	908	12.4
Jim Barnes**	66	1928	728	308	.423	268	182	.679	683	85	250	10	798	12.1
John Kerr	71	1770	692	286	.413	272	209	.768	586	225	148	0	781	11.0
John Egan***	73	1644	574	259	.451	227	173	.762	183	273	167	1	691	9.1
John Egan**	69	1586	558	254	.455	217	166	.765	181	259	163	1	674	9.8
Gus Johnson	41	1284	661	273	.413	178	131	.736	546	114	136	3	677	16.5
Bob Ferry	66	1229	457	188	.411	157	105	.669	334	111	134	1	481	7.3
Jerry Sloan	59	952	289	120	.415	139	98	.705	230	110	176	7	338	5.7
Ben Warley***	57	773	284	116	.408	97	64	.660	217	25	129	2	296	5.2
Ben Warley**	56	767	281	115	.409	97	64	.660	215	25	128	2	294	5.3
Wayne Hightower	24	460	186	63	.339	78	57	.731	131	35	61	2	183	7.6
Walt Bellamy	8	268	124	56	.452	67	40	.597	102	18	32	2	152	19.0
Willie Somerset	7	98	43	18	.419	11	9	.818	15	9	21	0	45	6.4
Gary Bradds	3	15	6	2	.333	4	3	.750	8	1	1	0	7	2.3
Thales McReynolds	5	28	12	1	.083	2	1	.500	6	1	10	0	3	0.6

1965-66 STATISTICS

BOSTON

Player	G.	Minutes	FG Att.	FG Made	FG Pct.	FT Att.	FT Made	FT Pct.	Re-b'nd	As-sist	Per. Fls.	Disq.	Tot. Pts.	Avg. Pts.
Sam Jones	67	2155	1335	626	.469	407	325	.799	347	216	170	0	1577	23.5
John Havlicek	71	2175	1328	530	.399	349	274	.785	423	210	158	1	1334	18.8
Bill Russell	78	3386	943	391	.415	405	223	.551	1779	371	221	4	1005	12.9
Larry Siegfried	71	1675	825	349	.423	311	274	.881	196	165	157	1	972	13.7
Tom Sanders	72	1896	816	349	.428	276	211	.764	508	90	317	19	909	12.6
Don Nelson	75	1765	618	271	.439	326	223	.684	403	79	187	1	765	10.2
Willie Naulls	71	1433	815	328	.402	131	104	.794	319	72	197	4	760	10.7
K. C. Jones	80	2710	619	240	.388	303	209	.690	304	503	243	4	689	8.6
Mel Counts	67	1021	549	221	.403	145	120	.828	432	50	207	5	562	8.4
Ron Bonham	39	312	207	76	.367	61	52	.852	35	11	29	0	204	5.2
Woody Sauldsberry	39	530	249	80	.321	22	11	.500	142	15	94	0	171	4.4
John Thompson	10	72	30	14	.467	6	4	.667	30	3	15	0	32	3.2
Sihugo Green	10	92	31	12	.387	16	8	.500	11	9	16	0	32	3.2
Ron Watts	1	3	2	1	.500	0	0	.000	1	1	1	0	2	2.0

CINCINNATI

Player	G.	Minutes	FG Att.	FG Made	FG Pct.	FT Att.	FT Made	FT Pct.	Re-b'nd	As-sist	Per. Fls.	Disq.	Tot. Pts.	Avg. Pts.
Oscar Robertson	76	3493	1723	818	.475	881	742	.842	586	847	227	1	2378	31.3
Jerry Lucas	79	3517	1523	690	.453	403	317	.787	1668	213	274	5	1697	21.5
Adrian Smith	80	2982	1310	531	.405	480	408	.850	287	256	276	1	1470	18.4
Harold Hairston	72	1794	814	398	.489	321	220	.685	546	44	216	3	1016	14.1
Tom Hawkins	79	2123	604	273	.452	209	116	.555	575	99	274	4	662	8.4
Wayne Embry	80	1882	564	232	.411	234	141	.603	525	81	287	9	605	7.6
Jack Twyman	73	943	498	224	.450	117	95	.812	168	60	122	1	543	7.4
Jon McGlocklin	72	852	363	153	.421	79	62	.785	133	88	77	0	368	5.1
Connie Dierking	57	782	322	134	.416	82	50	.610	245	43	113	0	318	5.6
Tom Thacker	50	478	207	84	.406	38	15	.395	119	61	85	0	183	3.7
George Wilson	47	276	138	54	.391	42	27	.643	98	17	56	0	135	2.9
Art Heyman	11	100	43	15	.349	17	10	.588	13	7	19	0	40	3.6
Enoch Olsen	4	36	8	3	.375	3	1	.333	13	2	4	0	7	1.8
Jay Arnette	3	14	6	1	.167	0	0	.000	0	0	3	0	2	0.7

DETROIT

Player	G.	Minutes	FG Att.	FG Made	FG Pct.	FT Att.	FT Made	FT Pct.	Re-b'nd	As-sist	Per. Fls.	Disq.	Tot. Pts.	Avg. Pts.
Eddie Miles	80	2788	1418	634	.447	402	298	.741	302	221	203	2	1566	19.6
Ray Scott	70	2652	1309	544	.416	435	323	.743	755	238	209	1	1411	17.9
Dave DeBusschere	79	2696	1284	524	.408	378	249	.659	916	209	252	5	1297	16.4
Tom VanArsdale	79	2041	834	312	.374	290	209	.721	309	205	251	1	833	10.5
Joe Strawder	79	2180	613	250	.408	256	176	.688	820	78	305	10	676	8.6
John Barnhill***	16	1617	606	243	.401	184	113	.614	203	196	134	0	599	7.9
John Barnhill**	45	926	363	139	.383	98	59	.602	112	113	76	0	337	7.5
John Tresvant***	61	969	400	171	.428	190	142	.747	364	72	179	2	484	7.9
John Tresvant**	46	756	322	134	.416	158	115	.736	279	62	136	2	383	8.3
Charles Vaughn***	56	1219	474	182	.384	144	106	.726	109	140	99	1	470	8.4
Charles Vaughn**	37	774	282	110	.390	82	60	.732	63	104	60	0	280	7.6
Don Kojis	60	783	439	182	.415	141	76	.539	260	42	94	0	440	7.3
Ron Reed	57	997	524	186	.355	100	54	.540	339	92	133	1	426	7.5
Rod Thorn	27	815	343	143	.417	123	90	.732	101	64	67	0	376	13.9
Joe Caldwell	33	716	338	143	.423	88	60	.682	190	65	63	0	346	10.5
Bill Buntin	42	713	299	118	.395	143	88	.615	252	36	119	4	324	7.7
Donnis Butcher	15	285	96	45	.469	34	18	.529	33	30	40	1	108	7.2
Bob Warlick	10	78	38	11	.289	6	2	.333	16	10	8	0	24	2.4

LOS ANGELES

Player	G.	Minutes	FG Att.	FG Made	FG Pct.	FT Att.	FT Made	FT Pct.	Re-b'nd	As-sist	Per. Fls.	Disq.	Tot. Pts.	Avg. Pts.
Jerry West	79	3218	1731	818	.473	977	840	.860	562	480	243	1	2476	31.3
Rudy LaRusso	76	2316	897	410	.457	445	350	.787	660	165	261	9	1170	15.4
Walt Hazzard	80	2198	1003	458	.457	257	182	.708	219	393	224	0	1098	13.7
Elgin Baylor	65	1975	1034	415	.401	337	249	.739	621	224	157	0	1079	16.6
LeRoy Ellis	80	2219	927	393	.424	256	186	.727	735	74	232	3	972	12.2
Bob Boozer	78	1847	754	365	.484	289	225	.779	548	87	196	0	955	12.2
Jim King	76	1499	545	238	.437	115	94	.817	204	223	181	1	570	7.5
Gail Goodrich	65	1008	503	203	.404	149	103	.691	130	103	103	1	509	7.8
Darrall Imhoff	77	1413	337	151	.448	136	77	.566	509	113	234	7	379	4.9
Gene Wiley	67	1386	289	123	.426	76	43	.566	490	63	171	3	289	4.3
John Fairchild	30	171	89	23	.258	20	14	.700	45	11	33	0	60	2.0

1965-66 STATISTICS

NEW YORK

Player	G.	Minutes	FG Att.	FG Made	FG Pct.	FT Att.	FT Made	FT Pct.	Re-b'nd	As-sist	Per. Fls.	Disq.	Tot. Pts.	Avg. Pts.
Walt Bellamy***	80	3352	1373	695	.506	689	430	.624	1254	294	9		1820	22.8
Walt Bellamy**	72	3084	1249	639	.512	622	390	.627	1152	262	217	7	1668	23.2
Dick Barnett	75	2589	1344	631	.469	605	467	.772	310	259	235	6	1729	23.1
Willis Reed	76	2537	1009	438	.434	399	302	.757	883	91	323	13	1178	15.5
Howard Komives	80	2612	1116	436	.391	280	241	.861	281	425	278	5	1113	13.9
Dave Stallworth	80	1893	820	373	.455	376	258	.686	492	186	237	4	1004	12.6
Dick VanArsdale	79	2289	838	359	.428	351	251	.715	376	184	235	5	969	12.3
Emmette Bryant	71	1193	449	212	.472	101	74	.733	170	216	215	4	498	7.0
Barry Clemens	70	877	391	161	.412	78	54	.692	183	67	113	0	376	5.4
Tom Gola	74	1127	271	122	.450	105	82	.781	289	191	207	3	326	4.4
Len Chappell	46	545	238	100	.420	78	46	.590	127	26	64	1	246	5.3
Jim Barnes	7	263	90	40	.444	42	30	.714	72	9	33	0	110	15.7
John Green	7	208	79	43	.544	31	15	.484	74	11	21	0	101	14.4
John Egan	7	58	16	5	.313	10	7	.700	2	14	4	0	17	2.4

PHILADELPHIA

Player	G.	Minutes	FG Att.	FG Made	FG Pct.	FT Att.	FT Made	FT Pct.	Re-b'nd	As-sist	Per. Fls.	Disq.	Tot. Pts.	Avg. Pts.
Wilt Chamberlain	79	3737	1990	1074	.540	976	501	.513	1943	414	171	0	2649	33.5
Hal Greer	80	3326	1580	703	.445	514	413	.804	473	384	315	6	1819	22.7
Chet Walker	80	2603	982	443	.451	468	335	.716	636	201	238	3	1221	15.3
Bill Cunningham	80	2134	1011	431	.426	443	281	.634	599	207	301	12	1143	14.3
Wally Jones	79	2196	799	296	.370	172	128	.744	169	273	250	6	720	9.0
Lucious Jackson	79	1966	614	246	.401	214	158	.738	676	132	216	2	650	8.2
Dave Gambee	72	1068	437	168	.384	187	159	.850	273	71	189	3	495	6.9
Al Bianchi	78	1312	560	214	.382	98	66	.673	134	134	232	4	494	6.3
Gerry Ward	65	838	189	67	.354	60	39	.650	89	80	163	3	173	2.7
Art Heyman***	17	120	52	18	.346	22	14	.636	17	11	23	0	50	2.9
Art Heyman**	6	20	3	3	.333	5	4	.800	4	4	4	0	10	1.7
Bob Weiss	7	30	9	3	.333	0	0	.000	4	2	10	0	6	0.9
Jesse Branson	5	14	6	1	.167	4	3	.750	9	1	4	0	5	1.0
Ben Warley	1	6	3	1	.333	0	0	.000	2	0	1	0	2	2.0

ST. LOUIS

Player	G.	Minutes	FG Att.	FG Made	FG Pct.	FT Att.	FT Made	FT Pct.	Re-b'nd	As-sist	Per. Fls.	Disq.	Tot. Pts.	Avg. Pts.
Zelmo Beaty	80	3072	1301	616	.473	559	424	.758	1086	125	344	15	1656	20.7
Len Wilkens	69	2692	954	411	.431	532	422	.793	322	429	248	4	1244	18.0
Richie Guerin	80	2363	998	414	.415	446	362	.812	314	388	256	4	1190	14.9
Cliff Hagan	74	1851	942	419	.445	206	176	.854	234	164	177	1	1014	13.7
Bill Bridges	78	2677	927	377	.407	364	257	.706	951	208	333	11	1011	13.0
Joe Caldwell***	79	1857	938	411	.438	254	179	.705	436	126	203	3	1001	12.7
Joe Caldwell**	46	1141	600	268	.447	166	119	.717	246	61	140	3	655	14.2
Joe Caldwell	46	1141	600	268	.447	166	119	.717	246	61	140	3	780	10.7
Rod Thorn***	74	1739	728	306	.420	236	168	.712	210	145	144	0	404	8.8
Rod Thorn**	46	924	385	163	.423	113	78	.690	109	81	77	0	384	5.9
Jim Washington	65	1104	393	158	.402	120	68	.567	353	43	176	4	384	5.9
Gene Tormohlen	77	775	324	144	.444	82	54	.659	314	60	138	3	342	4.8
John Barnhill	31	691	243	104	.428	86	54	.628	91	83	58	0	262	8.5
Jeff Mullins	44	587	296	113	.382	36	29	.806	69	66	68	1	255	5.8
Charles Vaughn	19	445	192	72	.375	62	46	.742	46	36	39	1	190	10.0
Paul Silas	46	586	173	70	.405	61	35	.574	236	22	72	0	185	3.8
John Tresvant	15	213	78	37	.474	32	27	.844	85	10	43	0	101	6.7
Mike Farmer	9	79	30	13	.433	5	4	.800	18	6	10	0	30	3.3

SAN FRANCISCO

Player	G.	Minutes	FG Att.	FG Made	FG Pct.	FT Att.	FT Made	FT Pct.	Re-b'nd	As-sist	Per. Fls.	Disq.	Tot. Pts.	Avg. Pts.
Rick Barry	80	2990	1698	745	.439	660	569	.862	850	173	297	2	2059	25.7
Guy Rodgers	79	2902	1571	586	.373	407	296	.727	421	846	241	6	1468	18.6
Nate Thurmond	73	2891	1119	454	.406	428	280	.654	1312	111	223	7	1188	16.3
Tom Meschery	79	2383	895	401	.448	293	224	.765	716	81	285	7	1026	12.8
Paul Neumann	66	1729	817	343	.420	317	265	.836	208	184	174	0	951	14.4
Al Attles	79	2053	724	364	.503	252	154	.611	209	342	225	5	882	11.2
McCoy McLemore	80	1467	528	225	.426	191	142	.743	488	55	197	4	592	7.4
Fred Hetzel	56	722	401	160	.399	92	63	.685	299	27	121	2	383	6.8
Gary Phillips	67	867	303	106	.350	87	54	.621	134	113	97	0	266	4.0
Keith Erickson	64	646	267	95	.356	65	43	.662	162	38	91	1	233	3.6
Enoch Olsen***	59	602	193	81	.420	88	39	.443	192	20	81	1	201	3.4
Enoch Olsen**	50	566	185	78	.422	85	38	.447	179	18	77	1	194	3.4
Wilbert Frazier	2	9	4	0	.000	2	1	.500	5	1	1	0	1	5.5

**—Team Total
***—Combined Player Total

1965-66 CHAMPIONSHIP PLAYOFF RESULTS

EASTERN DIVISION SEMI-FINALS
Boston defeated Cincinnati 3 to 2

Mar. 23—Cincinnati 107, at Boston 103
Mar. 26—Boston 132, at Cincinnati 125
Mar. 27—Cincinnati 113, at Boston 107
Mar. 30—Boston 120, at Cincinnati 103
Apr. 1—Cincinnati 103, at Boston 112

EASTERN DIVISION FINAL SERIES
Boston defeated Philadelphia 4 to 1

Apr. 3—Boston 115, at Philadelphia 96
Apr. 6—at Boston 114, Philadelphia 93
Apr. 7—at Philadelphia 111, Boston 105
Apr. 10—at Boston 114, Philadelphia *108
Apr. 12—Boston 120, at Philadelphia 112
*Overtime

WESTERN DIVISION SEMI-FINALS
St. Louis defeated Baltimore 3 to 0

Mar. 24—St. Louis 113, at Baltimore 111
Mar. 27—St. Louis 105 at Baltimore 100
Mar. 30—at St. Louis 121, Baltimore 112

WESTERN DIVISION FINAL SERIES
Los Angeles defeated St. Louis 4 to 3

Apr. 1—St. Louis 106, at Los Angeles 129
Apr. 3—St. Louis 116, at Los Angeles 125
Apr. 6—Los Angeles 113, at St. Louis 120
Apr. 9—Los Angeles 107, at St. Louis 95
Apr. 10—St. Louis 112, at Los Angeles 100
Apr. 13—Los Angeles 127, at St. Louis 131
Apr. 15—St. Louis 121, at Los Angeles 130

CHAMPIONSHIP SERIES
Boston defeated Los Angeles 4 to 3

Apr. 17—Los Angeles 133, at Boston *129
Apr. 19—Los Angeles 109, at Boston 129
Apr. 20—Boston 120, at Los Angeles 106
Apr. 22—Boston 122, at Los Angeles 117
Apr. 24—Los Angeles 121, at Boston 117
Apr. 26—Boston 115, at Los Angeles 123
Apr. 28—Los Angeles 93, at Boston 95

TEAM PLAYOFF STATISTICS

Team	G.	W.	L.	FGA	FGM	Pct.	FTA	FTM	Pct.	Reb.	Ast.	PF	Disq.	Scoring For	Scoring Agst.
Boston	17	11	6	1691	735	.435	651	499	.767	1153	368	484	5	115.8	110.2
Los Angeles	14	7	7	1363	633	.464	476	367	.771	768	311	358	3	116.6	116.3
St. Louis	10	6	4	966	432	.447	371	276	.744	597	251	247	3	114.0	115.4
Cincinnati	5	2	3	462	196	.424	199	159	.799	314	79	142	4	110.2	114.8
Baltimore	3	0	3	288	134	.465	90	55	.611	188	54	92	6	107.7	113.0
Philadelphia	5	1	4	502	191	.386	203	132	.650	361	96	143	3	104.0	113.6

1964-65 STATISTICS

1964-65 CHAMPION BOSTON CELTICS

Seated (left to right): K. C. Jones, Tom Heinsohn, President Louis Pieri, Coach Red Auerbach, Bill Russell, Sam Jones. Standing: Ron Bonham, Larry Siegfried, Willie Naulls, Mel Counts, John Thompson, Tom Sanders, John Havlicek, Trainer Buddy LeRoux.

FINAL STANDINGS AND TEAM FIGURES

EASTERN DIVISION

Team	Bos.	Cin.	Phil.	N.Y.	L.A.	St.L.	Balt.	Det.	S.F.	W.	L.	Pct.	Scoring For	Agst.
Boston	..	8	5	7	7	9	7	10	9	62	18	.775	9024	8351
Cincinnati	2	..	6	8	6	8	4	6	8	48	32	.600	9134	8952
Philadelphia	5	4	..	5	3	5	6	6	6	40	40	.500	9003	9015
New York	3	2	5	..	0	1	8	5	7	31	49	.388	8593	8886

WESTERN DIVISION

Los Angeles	3	4	7	10	..	6	7	7	8	49	31	.613	8948	8795
St. Louis	1	2	5	9	6	..	5	7	10	45	35	.563	8706	8464
Baltimore	3	6	4	2	4	5	..	6	7	37	43	.463	9087	9264
Detroit	0	4	4	5	3	3	4	..	8	31	49	.388	8681	8954
San Francisco	1	2	4	3	2	0	3	2	..	17	63	.213	8465	8960

TEAM STATISTICS

	G.	FGA	FGM	Pct.	FTA	FTM	Pct.	Reb.	Ast.	PF	Disq.	For	Agst.	Dif.
Boston	80	8609	3567	.414	2587	1890	.731	5748	2065	1772	36	112.8	104.5	8.3
St. Louis	80	7710	3269	.424	2947	2168	.736	5208	1691	2069	26	108.8	105.8	3.0
Cincinnati	80	7797	3482	.447	2866	2170	.757	5387	1843	1992	30	114.2	111.9	2.3
Los Angeles	80	7628	3336	.437	2984	2276	.763	5231	1601	1998	28	111.9	109.9	2.0
Philadelphia	80	8028	3391	.422	3011	2221	.738	5246	1692	2096	53	112.5	112.7	-0.2
Baltimore	80	7734	3421	.442	3144	2245	.714	5298	1676	2119	41	113.6	115.8	-2.2
Detroit	80	8297	3467	.418	2537	1747	.689	5394	1609	2058	35	108.5	111.9	-3.4
New York	80	7834	3339	.426	2684	1915	.713	5206	1550	2283	40	107.4	111.1	-3.7
San Francisco	80	8245	3323	.403	2844	1819	.640	5715	1653	2002	34	105.8	112.0	-6.2

TOP 25 SCORERS

Player–Team	G.	Min.	FGA	FGM	Pct.	FTA	FTM	Pct.	Reb.	Ast.	PF	Disq.	Pts.	Avg.
W. Chamberlain, SF-Phil.	73	3301	2083	1063	.510	880	408	.464	1673	250	146	0	2534	34.7
Jerry West, Los Angeles	74	3066	1653	822	.497	789	648	.821	447	364	221	2	2292	31.0
Oscar Robertson, Cincinnati	75	3421	1681	807	.480	793	665	.839	674	861	205	2	2279	30.4
Sam Jones, Boston	80	2885	1818	821	.452	522	428	.820	411	223	176	0	2070	25.9
Elgin Baylor, Los Angeles	74	3056	1903	763	.401	610	483	.792	950	280	235	0	2009	27.1
Walt Bellamy, Baltimore	80	3301	1441	733	.509	752	515	.685	1166	191	260	2	1981	24.8
Willis Reed, New York	80	3042	1459	629	.432	407	302	.742	1175	133	339	14	1560	19.5
Bailey Howell, Baltimore	80	2975	1040	515	.495	629	504	.801	869	208	345	10	1534	19.2
Terry Dischinger, Detroit	80	2698	1153	568	.493	424	320	.755	479	198	253	5	1456	18.2
Don Ohl, Baltimore	77	2821	1297	568	.438	388	284	.732	336	250	274	7	1420	18.4
Gus Johnson, Baltimore	76	2899	1379	577	.418	386	261	.676	988	270	258	4	1415	18.6
Jerry Lucas, Cincinnati	66	2864	1121	558	.498	366	298	.814	1321	157	214	1	1414	21.4
Hal Greer, Philadelphia	70	2600	1245	539	.433	413	335	.811	355	313	254	7	1413	20.2
John Havlicek, Boston	75	2169	1420	570	.401	316	235	.744	371	199	200	2	1375	18.3
Zelmo Beaty, St. Louis	80	2916	1047	505	.482	477	341	.715	966	111	328	11	1351	16.9
Dave DeBusschere, Detroit	79	2769	1196	508	.425	437	306	.700	874	253	242	5	1322	16.7
Len Wilkens, St. Louis	78	2854	1048	434	.414	558	416	.746	365	431	283	7	1284	16.5
Nate Thurmond, San Fran	77	3173	1240	519	.419	357	235	.658	1395	157	232	3	1273	16.5
Adrian Smith, Cincinnati	80	2745	1016	463	.456	342	284	.830	220	240	199	2	1210	15.1
Jim Barnes, New York	75	2586	1070	454	.424	379	251	.662	729	93	312	8	1159	15.5
Jack Twyman, Cincinnati	80	2236	1081	479	.443	239	198	.828	383	137	239	4	1156	14.5
Guy Rodgers, San Francisco	79	2699	1225	465	.380	325	223	.686	323	565	256	4	1153	14.6
Bob Boozer, New York	80	2139	963	424	.440	375	288	.768	604	108	183	0	1136	14.2
Lucious Jackson, Phila.	76	2590	1013	419	.414	404	288	.713	980	93	251	4	1126	14.8
Bob Pettit, St. Louis	50	1754	923	396	.429	405	332	.820	621	128	167	0	1124	22.5

FIELD GOAL PERCENTAGE LEADERS
(Minimum 220 FGM)

	FGA	FGM	Pct.
Wilt Chamberlain, SF-Phila	2083	1063	.510
Walt Bellamy, Baltimore	1441	733	.509
Jerry Lucas, Cincinnati	1121	558	.498
Jerry West, Los Angeles	1655	822	.497
Bailey Howell, Baltimore	1040	515	.495
Terry Dischinger, Detroit	1153	568	.493
John Egan, New York	529	258	.488
Zelmo Beaty, St. Louis	1047	505	.482
Oscar Robertson, Cincinnati	1681	807	.480
Paul Neumann, Phila-SF	772	365	.473

FREE THROW PERCENTAGE LEADERS
(Minimum 210 FTM)

	FTA	FTM	Pct.
Larry Costello, Philadelphia	277	243	.877
Oscar Robertson, Cincinnati	793	665	.839
Howard Komives, New York	254	212	.835
Adrian Smith, Cincinnati	342	284	.830
Jerry West, Los Angeles	789	648	.821
Sam Jones, Boston	522	428	.820
Bob Pettit, St. Louis	405	332	.820
Jerry Lucas, Cincinnati	366	298	.814
Dave Gambee, Philadelphia	368	299	.813
Hal Greer, Philadelphia	413	335	.811

LEADERS IN REBOUNDS

	G.	No.	Avg.
Bill Russell, Boston	78	1878	24.1
Wilt Chamberlain, SF-Phila.	73	1673	22.9
Nate Thurmond, San Fran.	77	1395	18.1
Jerry Lucas, Cincinnati	66	1321	20.0
Willis Reed, New York	80	1175	14.7
Walt Bellamy, Baltimore	80	1166	14.6
Gus Johnson, Baltimore	76	988	13.0
Lucious Jackson, Phila.	76	980	12.9
Zelmo Beaty, St. Louis	80	966	12.1
Elgin Baylor, Los Angeles	74	950	12.8

LEADERS IN ASSISTS

	G.	No.	Avg.
Oscar Robertson, Cincinnati	75	861	11.5
Guy Rodgers, San Francisco	77	565	7.3
K. C. Jones, Boston	78	437	5.6
Len Wilkens, St. Louis	78	431	5.5
Bill Russell, Boston	78	410	5.3
Jerry West, Los Angeles	74	364	4.9
Hal Greer, Philadelphia	70	313	4.5
Kevin Loughery, Baltimore	80	296	3.7
Elgin Baylor, Los Angeles	74	280	3.8
Larry Costello, Philadelphia	64	275	4.3

INTER-CLUB RECORDS—HOME, AWAY AND NEUTRAL COURT

	Home W-L	Away W-L	Neutral W-L	Total W-L
Baltimore	23-14	12-19	2-10	37-43
Boston	27-3	27-11	8-4	62-18
Cincinnati	25-7	17-21	6-4	48-32
Detroit	13-17	11-20	7-12	31-49
Los Angeles	25-13	21-16	3-2	49-31
New York	16-19	8-22	7-8	31-49
Philadelphia	13-12	9-21	18-7	40-40
St. Louis	26-14	15-17	4-4	45-35
San Francisco	10-26	5-31	2-6	17-63
Total	178-125	125-178	57-57	360

INDIVIDUAL STATISTICS

BALTIMORE

Player	G.	Min- utes	FG Att.	FG Made	FG Pct.	FT Att.	FT Made	FT Pct.	Re- b'nd	As- sist	Per. Fls.	Disq.	Tot. Pts.	Avg. Pts.
Walt Bellamy	80	3301	1441	733	.509	752	515	.685	1166	191	260	2	1981	24.8
Bailey Howell	80	2975	1040	515	.495	629	504	.801	869	208	345	10	1534	19.2
Don Ohl	77	2821	1297	568	.438	388	284	.732	336	250	274	7	1420	18.4
Gus Johnson	76	2899	1379	577	.418	386	261	.676	988	270	258	4	1415	18.6
Kevin Loughery	80	2417	957	406	.424	281	212	.754	235	296	320	13	1024	12.8
Wayne Hightower***	75	1547	570	196	.344	254	195	.768	420	54	204	2	587	7.8
Wayne Hightower**	27	510	174	60	.345	81	62	.765	173	16	61	1	182	6.7
Bob Ferry	77	1280	338	143	.423	199	122	.613	355	60	156	2	408	5.3
Wally Jones	77	1250	411	154	.375	136	99	.728	140	200	196	1	407	5.3
Sihugo Green	70	1086	368	152	.413	161	101	.627	169	140	134	0	405	5.8
Gary Bradds	41	335	111	46	.414	63	45	.714	84	19	36	0	137	3.3
Charles Hardnett	20	200	80	25	.313	39	23	.590	77	2	37	0	73	3.7
Al Butler	25	172	73	24	.329	15	11	.733	22	12	25	0	59	2.4
Les Hunter	24	114	64	18	.281	14	6	.429	50	11	16	0	42	1.8
Gary Hill***	12	103	36	10	.278	14	7	.500	16	7	11	0	27	2.3
Gary Hill**	3	15	1	0	.000	0	0	.000	1	1	1	0	0	0.0

BOSTON

Player	G.	Min- utes	FG Att.	FG Made	FG Pct.	FT Att.	FT Made	FT Pct.	Re- b'nd	As- sist	Per. Fls.	Disq.	Tot. Pts.	Avg. Pts.
Sam Jones	80	2885	1818	821	.452	522	428	.820	411	223	176	0	2070	25.9
John Havlicek	75	2169	1420	570	.401	316	235	.744	371	199	200	2	1375	18.3
Bill Russell	78	3466	980	429	.438	426	244	.573	1878	410	204	1	1102	14.1
Tom Sanders	80	2459	871	374	.429	259	193	.745	661	92	318	15	941	11.8
Tom Heinsohn	67	1706	954	365	.383	229	182	.795	399	157	252	5	912	13.6
Willie Naulls	71	1465	786	302	.384	176	143	.813	336	72	225	5	747	10.5
K. C. Jones	78	2434	639	253	.396	227	143	.630	318	437	263	5	649	8.3
Larry Siegfried	72	996	417	173	.415	140	109	.779	134	119	108	1	455	6.3
Ron Bonham	37	369	220	91	.414	112	92	.821	78	19	33	0	274	7.4
Mel Counts	54	572	272	100	.368	74	58	.784	265	19	134	1	258	4.8
John Thompson	64	699	209	84	.402	105	62	.590	230	16	141	1	230	3.6
Bob Nordmann	3	25	5	3	.600	0	0	.000	8	3	5	0	6	2.0
Gerry Ward	3	30	18	2	.111	1	1	1.000	5	6	6	0	5	1.7

CINCINNATI

Player	G.	Min- utes	FG Att.	FG Made	FG Pct.	FT Att.	FT Made	FT Pct.	Re- b'nd	As- sist	Per. Fls.	Disq.	Tot. Pts.	Avg. Pts.
Oscar Robertson	75	3421	1681	807	.480	793	665	.839	674	861	205	2	2279	30.4
Jerry Lucas	66	2864	1121	558	.498	366	298	.814	1321	157	214	1	1414	21.4
Adrian Smith	80	2745	1016	463	.456	342	284	.830	220	240	199	2	1210	15.1
Jack Twyman	80	2236	1081	479	.443	239	198	.828	383	137	239	4	1156	14.5
Wayne Embry	74	2243	772	352	.456	371	239	.644	741	92	297	10	943	12.7
Bud Olsen	79	1372	512	224	.438	195	144	.738	333	84	203	5	592	7.5
Tom Hawkins	79	1864	538	220	.409	204	116	.569	475	80	240	4	556	7.0
Harold Hairston	61	736	351	131	.373	165	110	.667	293	27	95	0	372	6.1
Jay Arnette	63	662	245	91	.371	75	56	.747	62	68	125	1	238	3.8
Arlen Bockhorn	19	424	157	60	.382	39	28	.718	55	45	52	1	148	7.8
Tom Thacker	55	470	168	56	.333	47	23	.489	127	41	64	0	135	2.5
George Wilson	39	288	155	41	.265	30	9	.300	102	11	59	0	91	2.3

DETROIT

Player	G.	Min- utes	FG Att.	FG Made	FG Pct.	FT Att.	FT Made	FT Pct.	Re- b'nd	As- sist	Per. Fls.	Disq.	Tot. Pts.	Avg. Pts.
Terry Dischinger	80	2698	1153	568	.493	424	320	.755	479	198	253	5	1456	18.2
Dave DeBusschere	79	2769	1196	508	.425	437	306	.700	874	253	242	5	1322	16.7
Eddie Miles	76	2074	994	439	.442	223	166	.744	258	157	201	1	1044	13.7
Ray Scott	66	2167	1092	402	.368	314	220	.701	634	239	209	5	1024	15.5
Reggie Harding	78	2699	987	405	.410	209	128	.612	906	179	258	5	938	12.0
Ron Thorn	74	1770	750	320	.427	243	176	.724	266	161	122	0	816	11.0
Joe Caldwell	66	1543	776	290	.374	210	129	.614	441	118	171	3	709	10.7
Don Kojis	65	836	416	180	.433	98	62	.633	243	63	115	1	422	6.5
Donnie Butcher	71	1157	353	143	.405	204	126	.618	200	122	183	4	412	5.8
Jack Moreland	54	732	296	103	.348	104	66	.635	183	69	151	4	272	5.0
Hub Reed	62	753	221	84	.380	58	40	.690	206	38	136	2	208	3.4
Willie Jones	12	101	52	21	.404	6	2	.333	10	7	13	0	44	3.7
Bob Duffy	4	26	11	4	.364	7	6	.857	4	5	4	0	14	3.5

**Team Total.
***Combined Player Total.

1964-65 STATISTICS

LOS ANGELES

Player	G.	Min-utes	FG Att.	FG Made	FG Pct.	FT Att.	FT Made	FT Pct.	Re-b'nd	As-sist	Per. Fls.	Disq.	Tot. Pts.	Avg. Pts.
Jerry West	74	3066	1655	822	.497	789	648	.821	447	364	221	2	2292	31.0
Elgin Baylor	74	3056	1903	763	.401	610	483	.792	950	280	235	0	2009	27.1
Rudy LaRusso	77	2588	827	381	.461	415	321	.773	725	198	258	3	1083	14.1
Dick Barnett	74	2026	908	375	.413	338	270	.799	200	159	209	1	1020	13.8
Leroy Ellis	80	2026	700	311	.444	284	198	.697	652	49	196	1	820	10.3
Jim King	77	1671	469	184	.392	151	118	.781	214	178	193	2	486	6.3
Gene Wiley	80	2002	376	175	.465	111	56	.505	690	105	235	11	406	5.1
Darrall Imhoff	76	1521	311	145	.466	154	88	.571	500	87	238	7	378	4.8
Walt Hazzard	66	919	306	117	.382	71	46	.648	111	140	132	0	280	4.2
Don Nelson	39	238	85	36	.424	26	20	.769	73	24	40	1	92	2.4
Bill McGill***	24	133	65	21	.323	17	13	.765	36	9	32	1	55	2.3
Bill McGill**	8	37	20	7	.350	1	1	1.000	12	3	6	0	15	1.9
Cotton Nash	25	167	57	14	.246	32	25	.781	35	10	30	0	53	2.1
Jerry Grote	11	33	11	6	.545	2	2	1.000	4	4	5	0	14	1.3

NEW YORK

Player	G.	Min-utes	FG Att.	FG Made	FG Pct.	FT Att.	FT Made	FT Pct.	Re-b'nd	As-sist	Per. Fls.	Disq.	Tot. Pts.	Avg. Pts.
Willis Reed	80	3042	1457	629	.432	407	302	.742	1175	133	339	14	1560	19.5
Jim Barnes	75	2886	1070	454	.424	379	251	.662	729	93	312	8	1159	15.5
Bob Boozer	80	2139	963	424	.440	375	288	.768	604	108	183	0	1136	14.2
Howard Komives	80	2376	1020	381	.374	254	212	.835	195	265	246	2	974	12.2
John Green	78	1720	737	346	.469	301	165	.548	545	129	194	3	857	11.0
John Egan	74	1664	529	258	.488	199	162	.814	143	252	139	0	678	9.2
Tom Gola	77	1727	455	204	.448	180	133	.739	319	220	269	8	541	7.0
Dave Budd	62	1188	407	196	.482	170	121	.712	310	62	147	1	513	8.3
Emmette Bryant	77	1332	436	145	.333	133	87	.654	167	167	212	3	377	4.9
Len Chappell	43	655	367	145	.395	100	68	.680	140	15	73	0	358	8.3
Art Heyman	55	663	267	114	.427	132	88	.667	99	79	96	0	316	5.7
Barry Kramer***	52	507	186	63	.339	84	60	.714	100	41	67	1	186	3.6
Barry Kramer**	19	231	86	27	.314	40	30	.750	41	15	31	1	81	4.4
Tom Hoover	24	153	32	13	.406	14	8	.571	58	12	37	0	34	1.4
John Rudometkin	1	22	8	3	.375	0	0	.000	7	0	5	0	6	6.0

PHILADELPHIA

Player	G.	Min-utes	FG Att.	FG Made	FG Pct.	FT Att.	FT Made	FT Pct.	Re-b'nd	As-sist	Per. Fls.	Disq.	Tot. Pts.	Avg. Pts.
Wilt Chamberlain***	73	3301	2083	1063	.510	880	408	.464	1673	250	146	0	2534	34.7
Wilt Chamberlain**	35	1558	808	427	.528	380	200	.526	780	133	70	0	1054	30.1
Hal Greer	70	2600	1245	539	.433	413	335	.811	355	313	254	7	1413	20.2
Lucious Jackson	76	2590	1013	419	.414	404	288	.713	980	93	251	4	1126	14.8
Chet Walker	79	2187	936	377	.403	388	288	.742	528	132	200	2	1042	13.2
Dave Gambee	80	1993	864	356	.412	368	299	.813	468	113	277	7	1011	12.6
Larry Costello	64	1967	695	309	.445	277	243	.877	169	275	242	10	861	13.5
John Kerr	80	1810	714	264	.370	181	126	.696	551	197	132	1	654	8.2
Paul Neumann**	40	1100	434	213	.491	184	148	.804	102	139	119	1	574	14.4
Al Bianchi	60	1116	486	175	.360	76	54	.711	95	140	178	10	404	6.7
Ben Warley	64	900	253	94	.372	176	124	.705	277	53	170	6	312	4.9
Connie Dierking**	38	729	311	121	.389	83	54	.651	239	42	101	3	296	7.8
Larry Jones	23	359	153	47	.307	52	37	.712	57	40	46	2	131	5.7
Steve Courtin	24	317	103	42	.408	21	17	.810	22	22	44	0	101	4.2
Jerry Greenspan	5	49	13	8	.615	8	8	1.000	11	0	12	0	24	4.8

ST. LOUIS

Player	G.	Min-utes	FG Att.	FG Made	FG Pct.	FT Att.	FT Made	FT Pct.	Re-b'nd	As-sist	Per. Fls.	Disq.	Tot. Pts.	Avg. Pts.
Zelmo Beaty	80	2916	1047	505	.482	477	341	.715	966	111	328	11	1351	16.9
Len Wilkens	78	2854	1048	434	.414	558	416	.746	365	431	283	7	1284	16.5
Bob Pettit	50	1754	923	396	.429	405	332	.820	621	128	167	0	1124	22.5
Cliff Hagan	77	1739	901	393	.436	268	214	.799	276	136	182	0	1000	13.0
Bill Bridges	79	2362	938	362	.386	275	186	.676	853	187	276	3	910	11.5
Charles Vaughn	75	1965	811	344	.424	242	182	.752	173	157	192	2	870	11.6
Richie Guerin	57	1678	662	295	.446	301	231	.767	149	271	193	1	821	14.4
Mike Farmer	60	1272	408	167	.409	94	75	.798	258	88	123	0	409	6.8
Paul Silas	79	1243	375	140	.373	164	83	.506	576	48	161	1	363	4.6
John Barnhill	41	777	312	121	.388	70	45	.643	91	76	56	0	287	7.0
Jeff Mullins	44	492	209	87	.416	61	41	.672	102	44	60	0	215	4.9
Bill McGill**	16	96	45	14	.311	16	12	.750	24	6	26	1	40	2.5
Ed Burton	7	42	20	7	.350	7	4	.571	13	2	13	0	18	2.6
John Tresvant	4	35	11	4	.364	9	6	.667	18	6	9	0	14	3.5

**Team Total.
***Combined Player Total

SAN FRANCISCO

Player	G.	Minutes	FG Att.	FG Made	FG Pct.	FT Att.	FT Made	FT Pct.	Rebnd	Assist	Per. Fls.	Disq.	Tot. Pts.	Avg. Pts.
Wilt Chamberlain**	38	1743	1275	636	.499	500	208	.416	893	117	76	0	1480	38.9
Nate Thurmond	77	3173	1240	519	.419	357	235	.658	1395	157	232	3	1273	16.5
Guy Rodgers	79	2699	1225	465	.380	325	223	.686	323	565	256	4	1153	14.6
Tom Meschery	79	2408	917	361	.394	370	278	.751	655	106	279	6	1000	12.7
Paul Neumann***	76	2034	772	365	.473	303	234	.772	198	233	218	3	964	12.7
Paul Neumann**	36	934	338	152	.450	119	86	.723	96	94	99	2	390	10.8
Al Attles	73	1733	662	254	.384	274	171	.624	239	205	242	7	679	9.3
McCoy McLemore	78	1731	725	244	.337	220	157	.714	488	81	224	6	645	8.3
Connie Dierking***	68	1294	538	218	.405	168	100	.595	435	72	165	4	536	7.9
Connie Dierking**	30	565	227	97	.427	85	46	.541	196	30	64	1	240	8.0
Gary Phillips	73	1541	553	198	.358	199	120	.603	189	148	184	3	516	7.1
Wayne Hightower**	48	1037	396	136	.343	173	133	.769	247	38	143	1	405	8.4
Bud Koper	54	631	241	106	.440	42	35	.833	61	43	59	1	247	4.6
John Rudometkin***	23	376	154	52	.338	50	34	.680	99	16	54	0	138	6.0
John Rudometkin**	22	354	146	49	.336	50	34	.680	92	16	49	0	132	6.0
Cotton Nash***	45	357	145	47	.324	52	43	.827	83	19	57	0	137	3.0
Cotton Nash**	20	190	88	33	.375	20	18	.900	48	9	27	0	84	4.2
Barry Kramer**	33	276	100	36	.360	44	30	.682	68	59	26	36	0	102	3.1
George Lee	19	247	77	27	.351	52	38	.731	55	12	22	0	92	4.8
Gary Hill**	9	88	35	10	.286	14	7	.500	15	6	10	0	27	3.0

**Team Total.
***Combined Player Total.

1964-65 CHAMPIONSHIP PLAYOFF RESULTS

EASTERN DIVISION SEMI-FINAL SERIES
Philadelphia defeated Cincinnati 3 to 1.
Mar. 24—Philadelphia 119 at Cincinnati.................117
Mar. 26—Cincinnati 121 at Philadelphia.................120
Mar. 28—Philadelphia 108 at Cincinnati....................94
Mar. 31—Cincinnati 112 at Philadelphia..................119

WESTERN DIVISION SEMI-FINAL
Baltimore defeated St. Louis 3 to 1.
Mar. 24—Baltimore 108 at St. Louis 105
Mar. 26—Baltimore 105 at St. Louis 129
Mar. 27—St. Louis 99 at Baltimore..........................131
Mar. 30—St. Louis 103 at Baltimore........................109

EASTERN DIVISION FINAL SERIES
Boston defeated Philadelphia 4 to 3.
Apr. 4—Philadelphia 98 at Boston..........................108
Apr. 6—Boston 103 at Philadelphia........................109
Apr. 8—Philadelphia 94 at Boston..........................112
Apr. 9—Boston 131 at Philadelphia......................*134
Apr. 11—Philadelphia 108 at Boston......................114
Apr. 13—Boston 106 at Philadelphia......................112
Apr. 15—Philadelphia 109 at Boston......................110

WESTERN DIVISION FINAL SERIES
Los Angeles defeated Baltimore 4 to 2.
Apr. 3—Baltimore 115 at Los Angeles 121
Apr. 5—Baltimore 115 at Los Angeles 118
Apr. 7—Los Angeles 115 at Baltimore 122
Apr. 9—Los Angeles 112 at Baltimore 114
Apr. 11—Baltimore 112 at Los Angeles 120
Apr. 13—Los Angeles 117 at Baltimore 115

CHAMPIONSHIP SERIES
Boston defeated Los Angeles 4 to 1.
Apr. 18—Los Angeles 110 at Boston........................142
Apr. 19—Los Angeles 123 at Boston........................129
Apr. 21—Boston 105 at Los Angeles........................126
Apr. 23—Boston 112 at Los Angeles..........................99
Apr. 25—Los Angeles 96 at Boston..........................129
*—Denotes overtime period.

TEAM PLAYOFF STATISTICS

Team	G.	W.	L.	FGA	FGM	Pct.	FTA	FTM	Pct.	Reb.	Ast.	PF	Disq.	Scoring For	Scoring Agst.
Boston	12	8	4	1339	555	.414	391	291	.744	867	283	344	10	116.8	109.8
Baltimore	10	5	5	978	432	.442	387	282	.729	648	195	272	6	114.6	113.9
Philadelphia	11	6	5	1056	463	.438	433	304	.702	707	232	288	7	111.8	111.7
St. Louis	4	1	3	418	165	.395	142	106	.746	265	75	114	2	109.0	113.3
Los Angeles	11	5	6	1050	462	.440	427	333	.780	724	239	305	6	114.3	119.1
Cincinnati	4	1	3	391	169	.432	122	106	.869	255	99	106	1	111.0	116.5

1963-64 STATISTICS

1963-64 CHAMPION BOSTON CELTICS

Seated (left to right): Sam Jones, Frank Ramsey, K. C. Jones, Coach Red Auerbach, President Walter A. Brown, Bill Russell, John Havlicek. Standing: Jack McCarthy, Tom Sanders, Tom Heinsohn, Clyde Lovellette, Willie Naulls, Jim Loscutoff, Larry Siegfried, Trainer Buddy LeRoux. Inset: Vice-President Lou Pieri.

FINAL STANDINGS AND TEAM FIGURES

EASTERN DIVISION

Team	W.	L.	FGA	FGM	Pct.	FTA	FTM	Pct.	Reb.	Ast.	PF	Disq.	Pts.	Avg.	Opp.
Boston	59	21	8770	3619	.413	2489	1804	.725	5736	1760	2125	19	9042	113.0	105.1
Cincinnati	55	25	7761	3516	.453	2828	2146	.759	5400	1916	2139	35	9178	114.7	109.7
Philadelphia	34	46	8116	3394	.418	2851	2184	.766	5132	1643	2251	29	8972	112.2	116.5
New York	22	58	7888	3512	.445	2852	1952	.684	5067	1563	2222	33	8976	112.2	119.6

WESTERN DIVISION

Team	W.	L.	FGA	FGM	Pct.	FTA	FTM	Pct.	Reb.	Ast.	PF	Disq.	Pts.	Avg.	Opp.
San Francisco	48	32	7779	3047	.438	2821	1800	.638	5499	1899	1978	33	8614	107.7	102.6
St. Louis	46	34	7776	3341	.430	2795	2115	.757	4959	1901	2266	39	8797	110.0	108.4
Los Angeles	42	38	7438	3272	.440	2910	2230	.766	5025	1676	1997	26	8774	109.7	108.7
Baltimore	31	49	7862	3456	.440	2958	2036	.688	5460	1423	2073	45	8948	111.9	113.6
Detroit	23	57	7943	3346	.421	2685	1928	.718	5145	1633	2235	50	8620	107.8	115.5

TOP 25 SCORERS

Player–Team	G.	Min.	FGA	FGM	Pct.	FTA	FTM	Pct.	Reb.	Ast.	PF	Disq.	Pts.	Avg.
Wilt Chamberlain, S. Fran.	80	3689	2298	1204	.524	1016	540	.531	1787	403	182	0	2948	36.9
Oscar Robertson, Cincinnati	79	3559	1740	840	.483	938	800	.843	783	868	280	3	2480	31.4
Bob Pettit, St. Louis	80	3296	1708	791	.463	771	608	.789	1224	259	300	3	2190	27.4
Walt Bellamy, Baltimore	80	3394	1582	811	.513	825	537	.651	1361	126	300	7	2159	27.0
Jerry West, Los Angeles	72	2906	1529	740	.484	702	584	.832	443	403	200	2	2064	28.7
Elgin Baylor, Los Angeles	78	3164	1778	756	.425	586	471	.804	936	347	235	1	1983	25.4
Hal Greer, Philadelphia	80	3157	1611	715	.444	525	435	.829	484	374	291	6	1865	23.3

1963-64 STATISTICS

Player—Team	G.	Min.	FGA	FGM	Pct.	FTA	FTM	Pct.	Reb.	Ast.	PF	Disq.	Pts.	Avg.
Bailey Howell, Detroit	77	2700	1267	598	.472	581	470	.809	776	205	290	0	1666	21.6
Terry Dischinger, Baltimore	80	2816	1217	604	.496	585	454	.776	667	157	321	10	1662	20.8
John Havlicek, Boston	80	2587	1535	640	.417	422	315	.746	428	238	227	1	1595	19.9
Sam Jones, Boston	76	2381	1359	612	.450	318	249	.783	349	202	192	1	1473	19.4
Dick Barnett, Los Angeles	78	2620	1197	541	.452	454	351	.773	250	238	233	3	1433	18.4
Cliff Hagan, St. Louis	77	2279	1280	572	.447	331	269	.813	377	193	273	4	1413	18.4
Ray Scott, Detroit	80	2964	1307	539	.412	456	328	.719	1078	244	296	7	1406	17.6
Jerry Lucas, Cincinnati	79	3273	1035	545	.527	398	310	.779	1375	204	300	6	1400	17.7
Wayne Embry, Cincinnati	80	2915	1213	556	.458	417	271	.650	925	113	320	7	1383	17.3
Gus Johnson, Baltimore	78	2847	1329	571	.430	319	210	.658	1064	169	321	11	1352	17.3
Len Chappell, Phila.-N.Y.	79	2505	1185	531	.448	403	288	.715	771	83	214	1	1350	17.1
John Kerr, Philadelphia	80	2938	1250	536	.429	357	268	.751	1017	275	187	2	1340	16.8
Chet Walker, Philadelphia	76	2775	1118	492	.440	464	330	.711	784	124	232	3	1314	17.3
Tom Heinsohn, Boston	76	2040	1223	487	.398	342	283	.827	460	183	268	3	1257	16.5
Don Ohl, Detroit	71	2366	1242	500	.408	331	225	.680	180	225	219	3	1225	17.3
Bob Boozer, Cin.-N.Y.	81	2379	1096	468	.427	376	272	.723	596	96	231	1	1208	14.9
Bill Russell, Boston	78	3482	1077	466	.433	429	236	.550	1930	370	190	0	1168	15.0
John Green, New York	80	2134	1026	482	.470	392	195	.497	799	157	246	4	1159	14.5

FIELD GOAL PERCENTAGE LEADERS
(Minimum 210 FGM)

	FGA	FGM	Pct.
Jerry Lucas, Cincinnati	1035	545	.527
Wilt Chamberlain, San Fran.	2298	1204	.524
Walt Bellamy, Baltimore	1582	811	.513
Terry Dischinger, Baltimore	1217	604	.496
Bill McGill, New York	936	456	.487
Jerry West, Los Angeles	1529	740	.484
Oscar Robertson, Cincinnati	1740	840	.483
Bailey Howell, Detroit	1267	598	.472
John Green, New York	1026	482	.470
Bob Pettit, St. Louis	1708	791	.463

FREE THROW PERCENTAGE LEADERS
(Minimum 210 FTM)

	FGA	FGM	Pct.
Oscar Robertson, Cincinnati	938	800	.853
Jerry West, Los Angeles	702	584	.832
Hal Greer, Philadelphia	525	435	.829
Tom Heinsohn, Boston	342	283	.827
Richie Guerin, N.Y.-St.L.	424	347	.818
Cliff Hagan, St. Louis	331	269	.813
Bailey Howell, Detroit	581	470	.809
Elgin Baylor, Los Angeles	586	471	.804
Wayne Hightower, San Francisco	329	260	.790
Paul Newman, Philadelphia	266	210	.789

LEADERS IN REBOUNDS

	G.	No.	Avg.
Bill Russell, Boston	78	1930	24.7
Wilt Chamberlain, San Fran.	80	1787	22.3
Jerry Lucas, Cincinnati	79	1375	17.4
Walt Bellamy, Baltimore	80	1361	17.0
Bob Pettit, St. Louis	80	1224	15.3
Ray Scott, Detroit	80	1078	13.5
Gus Johnson, Baltimore	78	1064	13.6
John Kerr, Philadelphia	80	1017	12.7
Elgin Baylor, Los Angeles	78	936	12.0
Wayne Embry, Cincinnati	80	925	11.6

LEADERS IN ASSISTS

	G.	No.	Avg.
Oscar Robertson, Cincinnati	79	868	11.0
Guy Rodgers, San Francisco	79	556	7.0
K. C. Jones, Boston	80	407	5.1
Jerry West, Los Angeles	72	403	5.6
Wilt Chamberlain, San Fran.	80	403	5.6
Richie Guerin, N.Y.-St.L.	80	375	4.7
Hal Greer, Philadelphia	80	374	4.7
Bill Russell, Boston	78	370	4.7
Len Wilkens, St. Louis	78	359	4.6
John Egan, New York	66	358	5.4

INTER-CLUB RECORDS—HOME, AWAY AND NEUTRAL COURT

EASTERN DIVISION

	Bos.	Cin.	Phil.	N.Y.	S.F.	S.L.	L.A.	Balt.	Det.	Home	Away	Neutral	W.	L.
Boston	..	5	10	10	5	7	6	9	7	26- 4	21- 17	12- 0	59- 21
Cincinnati	7	..	9	11	5	4	4	8	7	26- 7	18- 18	11- 0	55- 25
Philadelphia	2	3	..	8	4	3	4	5	5	18- 12	12- 22	4- 12	34- 46
New York	2	1	4	..	4	1	4	2	3	5	10- 25	8- 27	4- 6	22- 58

WESTERN DIVISION

	Bos.	Cin.	Phil.	N.Y.	S.F.	S.L.	L.A.	Balt.	Det.	Home	Away	Neutral	W.	L.
San Francisco	3	4	4	8	..	6	4	7	7	9	25- 14	21- 15	2- 3	48- 32
St. Louis	2	4	6	4	6	..	7	7	10	27- 12	17- 19	2- 3	46- 34
Los Angeles	3	4	5	6	5	5	..	7	7	24- 12	15- 21	3- 5	42- 38
Baltimore	1	2	5	7	3	3	3	..	7	20- 19	8- 21	3- 9	31- 49
Detroit	1	2	3	4	3	2	5	3	..	9- 21	6- 25	8- 11	23- 57
Total	21	25	46	58	32	34	38	49	57	185-126	126-185	49- 49	360-360

INDIVIDUAL STATISTICS

BALTIMORE

Player	G.	Minutes	FG Att.	FG Made	FG Pct.	FT Att.	FT Made	FT Pct.	Re-b'nd	As-sist	Per. Fls.	Disq.	Tot. Pts.	Avg. Pts.
Walt Bellamy	80	3394	1582	811	.513	825	537	.651	1361	126	300	7	2159	27.0
Terry Dischinger	80	2816	1217	604	.496	585	454	.776	667	157	321	10	1662	20.8
Gus Johnson	78	2847	1329	571	.430	319	210	.658	1064	169	321	11	1352	17.3
Rod Thorn	75	2594	1015	411	.405	353	258	.731	360	281	187	3	1080	14.4
Sihugo Green	75	2064	691	287	.415	290	198	.683	282	215	224	5	772	10.3

1963-64 STATISTICS

Player	G.	Minutes	FG Att.	FG Made	FG Pct.	FT Att.	FT Made	FT Pct.	Reb'nd	Assist	Per. Fls.	Disq.	Tot. Pts.	Avg. Pts.
Kevin Loughery*	66	1459	631	236	.374	177	126	.712	138	182	175	2	598	9.1
Don Kojis	78	1148	484	203	.419	146	82	.562	309	57	123	0	488	6.3
Charles Hardnett	66	617	260	107	.412	125	84	.672	251	27	114	1	298	4.5
Barney Cable	71	1125	290	116	.400	42	28	.667	301	47	166	3	260	3.7
Gene Shue	47	963	276	81	.293	61	36	.590	94	150	98	2	198	4.2
Paul Hogue**	15	147	30	12	.400	7	2	.286	31	6	35	1	26	1.7
Larry Comley	12	89	37	8	.216	16	9	.563	19	12	11	0	25	2.1
Mel Peterson	2	3	1	1	1.000	0	0	.000	1	0	2	0	2	1.0
Roger Strickland	1	4	3	1	.333	0	0	.000	0	0	1	0	2	2.0

*Played 1 game with Detroit—Played 65 games with Baltimore.

**Played 6 games with New York—Played 9 games with Baltimore.

BOSTON

Player	G.	Minutes	FG Att.	FG Made	FG Pct.	FT Att.	FT Made	FT Pct.	Reb'nd	Assist	Per. Fls.	Disq.	Tot. Pts.	Avg. Pts.
John Havlicek	80	2587	1535	640	.417	422	315	.746	428	238	227	1	1595	19.9
Sam Jones	76	2381	1359	612	.450	318	249	.783	349	202	192	1	1473	19.4
Tom Heinsohn	76	2040	1223	487	.398	342	283	.827	460	183	268	3	1257	16.5
Bill Russell	78	3482	1077	466	.433	429	236	.550	1930	370	190	0	1168	15.0
Tom Sanders	80	2370	836	349	.417	280	213	.761	667	102	277	6	911	11.4
Willie Naulls	74	1409	769	321	.417	157	125	.796	356	64	208	0	767	9.8
K. C. Jones	80	2424	722	283	.392	168	88	.524	372	407	253	0	654	8.2
Frank Ramsey	75	1227	604	226	.374	233	196	.841	223	81	245	7	648	8.6
Clyde Lovellette	45	437	305	128	.420	57	45	.789	126	24	100	0	301	6.7
Jim Loscutoff	53	451	182	56	.308	31	18	.581	131	25	90	1	130	2.5
Larry Siegfried	31	261	110	35	.318	39	31	.795	51	40	33	0	101	3.3
Jack McCarthy	28	206	48	16	.333	13	5	.385	35	24	42	0	37	1.3

CINCINNATI

Player	G.	Minutes	FG Att.	FG Made	FG Pct.	FT Att.	FT Made	FT Pct.	Reb'nd	Assist	Per. Fls.	Disq.	Tot. Pts.	Avg. Pts.
Oscar Robertson	79	3559	1740	840	.483	938	800	.853	783	868	280	3	2480	31.4
Jerry Lucas	79	3273	1035	545	.527	398	310	.779	1375	204	300	6	1400	17.7
Wayne Embry	80	2915	1213	556	.458	417	271	.650	925	113	325	7	1383	17.3
Jack Twyman	68	1996	993	447	.450	228	189	.829	364	137	267	0	1083	15.9
Tom Hawkins	73	1770	580	256	.441	188	113	.601	435	74	198	4	625	8.6
Adrian Smith	66	1524	576	234	.406	197	154	.782	147	145	164	1	622	9.4
Arlen Bockhorn	70	1670	587	242	.412	126	96	.762	205	173	227	4	580	8.3
Larry Staverman*	60	674	212	98	.462	90	69	.767	176	32	118	3	265	4.4
Bud Olsen	49	513	210	85	.405	57	32	.561	149	29	78	0	202	4.1
Jay Arnette	48	501	196	71	.362	54	42	.778	54	71	105	2	184	3.8
Tom Thacker	48	457	181	53	.293	53	26	.491	115	51	51	0	132	2.8

*Played 6 games with Baltimore, 20 games with Detroit and 34 games with Cincinnati.

DETROIT

Player	G.	Minutes	FG Att.	FG Made	FG Pct.	FT Att.	FT Made	FT Pct.	Reb'nd	Assist	Per. Fls.	Disq.	Tot. Pts.	Avg. Pts.
Bailey Howell	77	2700	1267	598	.472	581	470	.809	776	205	290	0	1666	21.6
Ray Scott	80	2964	1307	539	.412	456	328	.719	1078	244	296	7	1406	17.6
Don Ohl	71	2366	1224	500	.408	331	225	.680	180	225	219	3	1225	17.3
Bob Ferry	74	1522	670	298	.445	279	186	.667	428	94	174	2	782	10.6
Jack Moreland	78	1780	639	272	.426	210	164	.781	405	121	268	6	708	9.1
Willie Jones	77	1539	680	265	.390	141	100	.709	253	172	211	5	630	8.2
Don Butcher*	78	1971	507	202	.398	256	159	.621	329	244	249	4	563	7.2
Reggie Harding	39	1158	460	184	.400	98	61	.622	410	52	119	1	429	11.0
Eddie Miles	48	811	371	131	.353	87	62	.713	95	58	92	0	324	5.4
Darrall Imhoff	58	871	251	104	.414	114	69	.605	283	56	167	5	277	4.3
Bob Duffy**	48	662	229	94	.410	65	44	.677	61	79	48	0	232	4.8
Dave DeBusschere	15	304	133	52	.391	43	25	.581	105	23	32	1	129	8.6

*Played 26 games with New York—Played 52 games with Detroit.

**Played 2 games with St. Louis; 4 games with New York and 42 games with Detroit.

LOS ANGELES

Player	G.	Minutes	FG Att.	FG Made	FG Pct.	FT Att.	FT Made	FT Pct.	Reb'nd	Assist	Per. Fls.	Disq.	Tot. Pts.	Avg. Pts.
Jerry West	72	2906	1529	740	.484	702	584	.832	433	403	200	2	2064	28.7
Elgin Baylor	78	3164	1778	756	.425	586	471	.804	936	347	235	0	1983	25.4
Dick Barnett	78	2620	1197	541	.452	454	351	.773	250	238	233	3	1433	18.4
Rudy LaRusso	79	2746	776	337	.434	397	298	.751	800	190	268	5	972	12.3
LeRoy Ellis	78	1459	473	200	.423	170	112	.659	498	41	192	3	512	6.6
Don Nelson	80	1406	323	135	.418	201	149	.741	323	76	181	4	419	5.2

1963-64 STATISTICS

Player	G.	Minutes	FG Att.	FG Made	FG Pct.	FT Att.	FT Made	FT Pct.	Re-b'nd	As-sist	Per. Fls.	Disq.	Tot. Pts.	Avg. Pts.
Frank Selvy	73	1286	423	160	.378	122	78	.639	139	149	115	1	398	5.5
Gene Wiley	78	1510	273	146	.535	75	45	.600	510	44	225	4	337	4.3
Jim Krebs	68	975	357	134	.375	85	65	.765	283	49	166	6	333	4.9
Jim King	60	762	198	84	.424	101	66	.653	113	110	99	0	234	3.9
Hub Reed	46	386	91	33	.363	15	10	.667	107	23	73	0	76	1.7
Mel Gibson	8	53	20	6	.800	2	1	.500	4	6	10	0	13	1.4

NEW YORK

Player	G.	Minutes	FG Att.	FG Made	FG Pct.	FT Att.	FT Made	FT Pct.	Re-b'nd	As-sist	Per. Fls.	Disq.	Tot. Pts.	Avg. Pts.
Len Chappell*	79	2505	1185	531	.448	403	288	.715	771	83	214	1	1350	17.1
Bob Boozer**	81	2379	1096	468	.427	376	272	.723	596	96	231	1	1208	14.9
John Green	80	2134	1026	482	.470	392	195	.497	799	157	246	4	1159	14.5
Art Heyman	75	2236	1003	432	.431	422	289	.685	298	256	229	2	1153	15.4
Bill McGill***	74	1784	937	456	.487	282	204	.723	414	121	217	7	1116	15.1
John Egan****	66	2325	758	334	.441	243	193	.794	191	358	181	3	861	13.0
Tom Gola	74	2156	602	258	.429	212	154	.726	469	257	278	7	670	9.1
Al Butler	76	1379	616	260	.422	187	138	.738	168	157	167	3	658	8.7
John Rudometkin	52	696	326	154	.472	116	87	.750	164	26	86	0	395	4.6
Dave Budd	73	1031	297	128	.431	115	84	.730	276	57	130	1	340	4.7
Tom Hoover	59	988	247	102	.413	132	81	.614	331	36	185	4	285	4.8
Gene Conley	46	551	189	74	.392	65	44	.677	187	21	124	2	192	4.2
Jerry Harkness	5	59	30	13	.433	8	3	.375	6	6	4	0	29	5.8

*Played 1 game with Philadelphia—Played 78 games with New York.

**Played 32 games with Cincinnati—Played 49 games with New York.

***Played 6 games with Baltimore—Played 68 games with New York.

****Played 24 games with Detroit—Played 42 games with New York.

PHILADELPHIA

Player	G.	Minutes	FG Att.	FG Made	FG Pct.	FT Att.	FT Made	FT Pct.	Re-b'nd	As-sist	Per. Fls.	Disq.	Tot. Pts.	Avg. Pts.
Hal Greer	80	3157	1611	715	.444	525	435	.829	484	374	291	6	1865	23.3
John Kerr	80	2938	1250	536	.429	357	268	.751	1017	275	187	2	1340	16.8
Chet Walker	76	2775	1118	492	.440	464	330	.711	784	124	232	3	1314	17.3
Paul Neumann	74	1973	732	324	.443	266	210	.789	246	291	211	1	858	11.6
Ben Warley	79	1740	494	215	.435	305	220	.721	619	71	274	5	650	8.2
Al Bianchi	78	1437	684	257	.376	141	109	.773	147	149	248	6	623	8.0
Lee Shaffer	41	1013	587	217	.370	133	102	.767	205	36	116	1	536	13.1
Larry Costello	45	1137	408	191	.476	170	147	.865	105	167	150	3	529	11.8
Connie Dierking	76	1286	514	191	.372	169	114	.675	422	50	221	3	496	6.5
Dave Gambee	41	927	378	149	.394	185	151	.816	256	35	161	6	449	11.0
Dolph Schayes	24	350	143	44	.308	57	46	.807	110	48	76	3	134	5.6
Jerry Greenspan	20	280	90	32	.356	50	34	.680	72	11	54	0	98	4.9
Hubie White	23	196	105	31	.295	28	17	.607	42	12	28	0	79	3.4

ST. LOUIS

Player	G.	Minutes	FG Att.	FG Made	FG Pct.	FT Att.	FT Made	FT Pct.	Re-b'nd	As-sist	Per. Fls.	Disq.	Tot. Pts.	Avg. Pts.
Bob Pettit	80	3296	1708	791	.463	771	608	.789	1224	259	300	3	2190	27.4
Cliff Hagan	77	2279	1280	572	.447	331	269	.813	377	193	273	4	1413	18.4
Richie Guerin*	80	2366	846	351	.415	424	347	.818	256	375	276	4	1049	13.1
Len Wilkens	78	2526	808	334	.413	365	270	.740	335	359	287	7	938	12.0
Zelmo Beaty	59	1922	647	287	.444	270	200	.741	633	79	262	11	774	13.1
Bill Bridges	80	1949	675	268	.397	224	146	.652	680	181	269	6	682	8.5
Charlie Vaughn	68	1340	538	238	.442	148	107	.723	126	129	166	0	583	8.6
John Barnhill	74	1367	505	208	.412	115	70	.609	157	145	107	0	486	6.6
Mike Farmer	76	1361	438	178	.406	83	68	.819	225	109	140	0	424	5.6
Gene Tormohlen	54	640	250	94	.376	46	22	.478	216	50	128	3	210	4.1
Bob Nordmann**	19	259	66	27	.409	19	9	.474	65	5	51	1	63	3.3
Gerry Ward	24	139	53	16	.302	17	11	.647	21	21	26	0	43	1.8
Ken Rohloff	2	7	1	0	.000	0	0	.000	0	1	4	0	0	0.0

*Played 2 games with New York—Played 78 games with St. Louis.

**Played 7 games with New York—Played 12 games with St. Louis.

SAN FRANCISCO

Player	G.	Minutes	FG Att.	FG Made	FG Pct.	FT Att.	FT Made	FT Pct.	Re-b'nd	As-sist	Per. Fls.	Disq.	Tot. Pts.	Avg. Pts.
Wilt Chamberlain	80	3689	2298	1204	.524	1016	540	.531	1787	403	182	0	2948	36.9
Tom Meschery	80	2422	951	436	.458	295	207	.702	612	149	288	6	1079	13.5
Wayne Hightower	79	2536	1022	393	.385	329	260	.790	566	133	269	7	1046	13.2
Guy Rodgers	79	2695	923	337	.365	280	198	.707	328	556	245	4	872	11.0

Player	G.	Minutes	FG Att.	FG Made	FG Pct.	FT Att.	FT Made	FT Pct.	Rebnd	Assist	Per. Fls.	Disq.	Tot. Pts.	Avg. Pts.
Al Attles	70	1883	640	289	.452	275	185	.673	236	197	249	4	763	10.9
Gary Phillips	66	2010	691	256	.370	218	146	.670	248	203	245	8	658	10.0
Nate Thurmond	76	1966	554	219	.395	173	95	.549	790	86	184	2	533	7.0
Gary Hill	67	1015	384	146	.380	77	51	.662	114	103	165	2	343	5.1
George Lee	54	522	169	64	.379	71	47	.662	97	25	67	0	175	3.2
Ken Sears	51	519	120	53	.442	79	64	.810	94	42	71	0	170	3.3
John Windsor	11	68	27	10	.370	8	7	.875	26	2	13	0	27	2.5

1963-64 CHAMPIONSHIP PLAYOFF RESULTS

EASTERN DIVISION SEMI-FINAL
Cincinnati defeated Philadelphia 3 to 2

Mar. 22—Philadelphia 102 at Cincinnati.................127
Mar. 24—Cincinnati 114 at Philadelphia.................122
Mar. 25—Philadelphia 89 at Cincinnati..................101
Mar. 28—Cincinnati 120 at Philadelphia.................129
Mar. 29—Philadelphia 124 at Cincinnati.................130

WESTERN DIVISION SEMI-FINAL
St. Louis defeated Los Angeles 3 to 2

Mar. 21—Los Angeles 104 at St. Louis 115
Mar. 22—Los Angeles 90 at St. Louis 106
Mar. 25—St. Louis 105 at Los Angeles 107
Mar. 28—St. Louis 88 at Los Angeles 97
Mar. 30—Los Angeles 108 at St. Louis 121

EASTERN DIVISION FINAL SERIES
Boston defeated Cincinnati 4 to 1

Mar. 31—Cincinnati 87 at Boston 103
Apr. 2—Cincinnati 90 at Boston 101
Apr. 5—Boston 102 at Cincinnati 92
Apr. 7—Boston 93 at Cincinnati 102
Apr. 9—Cincinnati 95 at Boston 109

WESTERN DIVISION FINAL SERIES
San Francisco Defeated St. Louis 4 to 3

Apr. 1—St. Louis 116 at San Francisco 111
Apr. 3—St. Louis 85 at San Francisco 120
Apr. 5—San Francisco 109 at St. Louis 113
Apr. 8—San Francisco 111 at St. Louis 109
Apr. 10—St. Louis 97 at San Francisco 121
Apr. 12—San Francisco 95 at St. Louis 123
Apr. 16—St. Louis 95 at San Francisco 105

CHAMPIONSHIP SERIES
Boston defeated San Francisco 4 to 1

Apr. 18—San Francisco 96 at Boston 108
Apr. 20—San Francisco 101 at Boston 124
Apr. 22—Boston 91 at San Francisco 115
Apr. 24—Boston 98 at San Francisco 95
Apr. 26—San Francisco 99 at Boston 105

TEAM PLAYOFF STATISTICS

Team	G.	W.	L.	FGA.	FGM.	Pct.	FTA.	FTM.	Pct.	Reb.	Ast.	PF.	Disq.	Pts.	Avg.
Boston	10	8	2	918	400	.436	334	234	.701	736	221	275	6	1034	103.4
San Francisco	12	5	7	1171	503	.430	455	272	.598	736	245	320	9	1278	106.5
St. Louis	12	6	6	1098	480	.437	409	313	.765	709	281	334	2	1273	106.1
Cincinnati	10	4	6	954	399	.418	338	260	.769	684	227	283	9	1058	105.8
Philadelphia	5	2	3	495	204	.412	203	158	.778	289	109	134	3	566	113.2
Los Angeles	5	2	3	417	181	.434	180	144	.800	270	97	129	4	506	101.2
Totals	54	27	27	5053	2167	.429	1919	1381	.720	3424	1180	1475	33	5715	105.8

1962-63 STATISTICS

1962-63 CHAMPION BOSTON CELTICS

Seated (left to right): K. C. Jones, Bill Russell, President Walter A. Brown, Coach Red Auerbach, Treasurer Lou Pieri, Captain Bob Cousy, Sam Jones.
Standing: Frank Ramsey, Gene Guarilia, Tom Sanders, Tom Heinsohn, Clyde Lovellette, John Havlicek, Jim Loscutoff, Dan Swartz, Trainer Buddy LeRoux.

FINAL STANDINGS AND TEAM FIGURES

EASTERN DIVISION

Team	W.	L.	FGA	FGM	Pct.	FTA	FTM	Pct.	Reb.	Ast.	PF	Disq.	Pts.	Avg.	Opp.
Boston	58	22	8779	3746	.427	2777	2012	.725	5818	1960	2090	30	9504	118.8	8930
Syracuse	48	32	8290	3690	.445	3005	2350	.782	5516	1742	2277	33	9730	121.6	9427
Cincinnati	42	38	7998	3672	.459	2923	2183	.747	5561	1931	2203	39	9527	119.0	9426
New York	21	59	8007	3433	.429	2778	1971	.710	4952	1658	2144	49	8837	110.5	9417

WESTERN DIVISION

Team	W.	L.	FGA	FGM	Pct.	FTA	FTM	Pct.	Reb.	Ast.	PF	Disq.	Pts.	Avg.	Opp.
Los Angeles	53	27	7948	3506	.441	2931	2230	.761	5282	1739	1775	18	9242	115.5	8992
St. Louis	48	32	7780	3355	.431	2820	2056	.729	5096	1902	2077	35	8766	109.6	8624
Detroit	34	46	8188	3534	.432	2852	2044	.717	5315	1731	2181	40	9112	113.9	9408
San Francisco	31	49	8449	3805	.450	2797	1870	.669	5359	1906	1882	45	9480	118.5	9647
Chicago	25	55	7448	3371	.453	2944	2053	.697	5145	1773	2065	33	8795	109.9	9112

TOP 25 SCORERS

Player–Team	G.	Min.	FGA	FGM	Pct.	FTA	FTM	Pct.	Reb.	Ast.	PF	Disq.	Pts.	Avg.
Wilt Chamberlain, S. Fran.	80	3806	2770	1463	.528	1113	660	.593	1946	275	136	0	3586	44.8
Elgin Baylor, Los Angeles	80	3370	2273	1029	.453	790	661	.837	1146	386	226	1	2719	34.0
Oscar Robertson, Cinn.	80	3521	1593	825	.518	758	614	.810	835	758	293	1	2264	28.3

1962-63 STATISTICS

Player–Team	G.	Min.	FGA	FGM	Pct.	FTA	FTM	Pct.	Reb.	Ast	PF	Disq.	Pts.	Avg.
Bob Pettit, St. Louis	79	3090	1746	778	.446	885	685	.774	1191	245	282	8	2241	28.4
Walt Bellamy, Chicago	80	3306	1595	840	.527	821	553	.674	1309	233	283	7	2233	27.9
Bailey Howell, Detroit	79	2971	1235	637	.516	650	519	.798	910	232	300	9	1793	22.7
Richie Guerin, New York	79	2712	1380	596	.432	600	509	.848	831	348	228	2	1701	21.5
Jack Twyman, Cincinnati	80	2623	1335	641	.480	375	304	.811	598	214	286	7	1586	19.8
Hal Greer, Syracuse	80	2631	1293	600	.464	434	362	.834	457	275	286	4	1562	19.5
Don Ohl, Detroit	80	2961	1450	636	.439	380	275	.724	239	325	234	3	1547	19.3
Sam Jones, Boston	76	2323	1395	621	.476	324	257	.793	396	241	162	1	1499	19.7
Jerry West, Los Angeles	55	2163	1213	559	.461	477	371	.778	384	307	150	1	1489	27.1
Lee Shaffer, Syracuse	80	2392	1393	597	.429	375	294	.784	524	97	249	5	1488	18.6
Terry Dischinger, Chicago	57	2294	1026	525	.512	522	402	.770	458	175	188	2	1452	25.5
John Green, New York	80	2503	1261	582	.462	439	280	.638	964	152	243	5	1444	18.1
Tom Heinsohn, Boston	76	2004	1300	550	.423	407	340	.835	569	95	270	4	1440	18.9
Dick Barnett, Los Angeles	80	2544	1162	547	.471	421	343	.815	242	224	189	3	1437	18.0
Wayne Embry, Cincinnati	76	2511	1165	434	.458	514	343	.667	936	177	286	7	1411	18.6
Bill Russell, Boston	78	3500	1182	511	.432	517	287	.555	1843	348	189	1	1309	16.8
John Kerr, Syracuse	80	2561	1069	507	.474	320	241	.753	1039	214	208	3	1255	15.6
John Green, New York	80	2503	1261	582	.462	439	280	.638	964	152	243	5	1444	18.1
Ray Scott, Detroit	76	2538	1110	460	.414	457	308	.674	772	191	263	9	1228	16.2
Cliff Hagan, St. Louis	79	1716	1055	491	.465	305	244	.800	341	193	211	2	1226	15.5
John Havlicek, Boston	80	2200	1085	483	.445	239	174	.728	534	179	189	2	1140	14.5
Bob Boozer, Cincinnati	79	2488	992	440	.444	353	252	.714	878	102	299	8	1132	14.3
Guy Rodgers, San Francisco	79	3249	1149	445	.387	286	208	.727	394	825	296	7	1098	13.9

FIELD GOAL PERCENTAGE LEADERS
(Minimum 210 FGM)

	FGA	FGM	Pct.
Wilt Chamberlain, San. Fran.	2770	1463	.528
Walt Bellamy, Chicago	1595	840	.527
Oscar Robertson, Cincinnati	1593	825	.518
Bailey Howell, Detroit	1235	637	.516
Terry Dischinger, Chicago	1026	525	.512
Dave Budd, New York	596	294	.493
Jack Twyman, Cincinnati	1335	641	.480
Al Attles, San Francisco	630	301	.478
Sam Jones, Boston	1305	621	.476
John Kerr, Syracuse	1069	507	.474

LEADERS IN REBOUNDS

	G.	No.	Avg.
Wilt Chamberlain, San Francisco	80	1946	24.3
Bill Russell, Boston	78	1843	23.0
Walt Bellamy, Chicago	80	1309	16.4
Bob Pettit, St. Louis	79	1191	15.1
Elgin Baylor, Los Angeles	80	1146	14.3
John Kerr, Syracuse	80	1039	13.0
John Green, New York	80	964	12.1
Wayne Embry, Cincinnati	76	936	12.3
Bailey Howell, Detroit	79	910	11.5
Bob Boozer, Cincinnati	79	878	11.1

FREE THROW PERCENTAGE LEADERS
(Minimum 210 FTM)

	FGA	FGM	Pct.
Larry Costello, Syracuse	327	288	.881
Richie Guerin, New York	600	509	.848
Elgin Baylor, Los Angeles	790	661	.837
Tom Heinsohn, Boston	407	340	.835
Hal Greer, Syracuse	434	362	.834
Frank Ramsey, Boston	332	271	.816
Dick Barnett, Los Angeles	421	343	.815
Adrian Smith, Cincinnati	275	223	.811
Jack Twyman, Cincinnati	375	304	.811
Oscar Robertson, Cincinnati	758	614	.810

LEADERS IN ASSISTS

	G.	No.	Avg.
Guy Rodgers, San Francisco	79	825	10.4
Oscar Robertson, Cincinnati	80	758	9.5
Bob Cousy, Boston	76	515	6.8
Sihugo Green, Chicago	73	422	5.8
Elgin Baylor, Los Angeles	80	386	4.8
Len Wilkens, St. Louis	75	381	5.1
Bill Russell, Boston	78	348	4.5
Richie Guerin, New York	79	348	4.4
Larry Costello, Syracuse	78	334	4.3
John Barnhill, St. Louis	77	322	4.2

INDIVIDUAL STATISTICS
BOSTON

Player	G.	Minutes	FG Att.	FG Made	FG Pct.	FT Att.	FT Made	FT Pct.	Reb'nd	Assist	Per. Fls.	Disq.	Tot. Pts.	Avg. Pts.
Sam Jones	76	2323	1305	621	.476	324	257	.793	396	241	162	1	1499	19.7
Tom Heinsohn	76	2004	1300	550	.423	407	340	.835	569	95	270	4	1440	18.9
Bill Russell	78	3500	1182	511	.432	517	287	.555	1843	348	189	1	1309	16.8
John Havlicek	80	2200	1085	483	.445	239	174	.728	534	179	189	2	1140	14.3
Bob Cousy	76	1975	988	392	.397	298	219	.735	193	515	175	0	1003	13.2
Tom Sanders	79	2148	744	339	.456	252	186	.738	576	95	262	5	864	10.8
Frank Ramsey	77	1541	743	284	.382	332	271	.816	288	95	259	13	839	10.9
K. C. Jones	79	1945	591	230	.389	177	112	.633	263	317	221	3	572	7.2
Clyde Lovellette	61	568	376	161	.428	98	73	.745	177	95	137	0	395	6.5
Jim Luscutoff	63	607	251	94	.375	42	22	.524	157	25	126	1	210	3.3
Gene Guarilia	11	83	38	11	.289	11	4	.364	14	2	5	0	26	2.4
Dan Swartz	39	335	150	57	.380	72	61	.847	88	21	92	0	175	4.5

1962-63 STATISTICS

CHICAGO

Player	G.	Minutes	FG Att.	FG Made	FG Pct.	FT Att.	FT Made	FT Pct.	Re-b'nd	As-sist	Per. Fls.	Disq.	Tot. Pts.	Avg. Pts.
Walt Bellamy	80	3306	1595	840	.527	821	553	.674	1309	233	283	7	2233	27.9
Terry Dischinger	57	2294	1026	525	.512	522	402	.770	458	175	188	2	1452	25.5
Sihugo Green	73	2648	783	322	.411	306	209	.683	335	422	274	5	853	11.7
Charles Hardnett	78	1657	683	301	.441	349	225	.645	602	74	225	4	827	10.6
John Cox	73	1685	568	239	.412	135	95	.704	280	142	149	4	573	7.8
Bill McGill	60	590	353	181	.513	119	80	.672	161	38	118	1	442	7.4
Don Nelson	62	1071	293	129	.440	221	161	.729	279	72	136	3	419	6.8
Barney Cable*	61	1200	380	173	.455	96	62	.646	242	82	136	0	408	6.7
Larry Staverman	33	602	194	94	.485	62	49	.790	158	43	94	3	237	7.2
Mel Nowell	39	589	237	92	.388	66	48	.727	67	84	86	0	232	5.9
Bob Leonard	32	879	245	84	.343	85	59	.694	68	143	84	1	227	7.1
Maurice King	37	954	241	94	.390	34	28	.824	102	142	87	0	216	5.8
Nick Mantis*	32	684	244	94	.385	49	27	.551	85	83	94	0	215	5.1
Al Ferrari	18	138	37	12	.324	17	14	.824	12	14	21	0	38	2.1
Jeff Slade	3	20	5	2	.400	1	0	.000	7	0	3	0	4	1.3
Ralph Wells	3	48	7	1	.143	7	0	.000	6	7	6	0	2	0.7

*Cable—42 St. Louis, 19 Chicago; Mantis—9 St. Louis, 23 Chicago.

CINCINNATI

Player	G.	Minutes	FG Att.	FG Made	FG Pct.	FT Att.	FT Made	FT Pct.	Re-b'nd	As-sist	Per. Fls.	Disq.	Tot. Pts.	Avg. Pts.
Oscar Robertson	80	3521	1593	825	.518	758	614	.810	835	758	293	1	2264	28.3
Jack Twyman	80	2623	1335	641	.480	375	304	.811	598	214	286	7	1586	19.8
Wayne Embry	76	2511	1165	534	.458	514	343	.667	936	177	286	7	1411	18.6
Bob Boozer	79	2488	992	449	.414	353	252	.714	878	102	299	8	1152	14.3
Arlen Bockhorn	80	2612	954	375	.393	242	183	.756	322	261	260	6	933	11.7
Tom Hawkins	79	1721	635	299	.471	241	147	.610	543	100	197	2	745	9.4
Adrian Smith	79	1522	544	241	.443	275	223	.811	174	141	157	0	705	8.9
Hub Reed	80	1299	427	199	.466	98	74	.755	398	83	261	7	472	5.9
Dave Piontek	48	457	158	60	.380	16	10	.625	96	26	67	0	130	2.7
Bud Olsen	52	373	133	43	.323	39	27	.692	105	42	78	0	113	2.2
Dave Tieman	29	176	57	15	.263	10	4	.400	22	27	18	0	34	1.2
Joseph Buckhalter	2	12	5	0	.000	2	2	1.000	3	0	1	0	2	1.0

DETROIT

Player	G.	Minutes	FG Att.	FG Made	FG Pct.	FT Att.	FT Made	FT Pct.	Re-b'nd	As-sist	Per. Fls.	Disq.	Tot. Pts.	Avg. Pts.
Bailey Howell	79	2971	1235	637	.516	650	519	.798	910	232	300	9	1793	22.7
Don Ohl	80	2961	1450	636	.439	380	275	.724	239	325	234	3	1547	19.3
Ray Scott	76	2538	1110	460	.414	457	308	.674	772	191	263	9	1228	16.2
Bob Ferry	79	2479	984	426	.433	339	220	.649	537	170	246	1	1072	13.6
Dave DeBusschere	80	2352	946	406	.429	287	206	.718	694	207	247	2	1018	12.7
Willie Jones	79	1470	730	305	.418	164	118	.720	233	188	207	4	728	9.2
Jack Moreland	78	1516	622	271	.436	214	145	.678	449	114	226	5	687	8.8
Kevin Loughery	57	845	397	146	.368	100	71	.710	109	104	135	1	363	6.4
Jack Egan	46	752	296	110	.372	69	53	.768	59	114	70	0	273	5.9
Walt Dukes	62	913	255	83	.325	137	101	.737	360	55	183	5	267	4.3
Darrall Imhoff	45	468	153	48	.314	50	24	.480	155	28	66	1	120	2.7
Dan Doyle	4	25	12	6	.500	5	4	.800	8	3	4	0	16	4.0

LOS ANGELES

Player	G.	Minutes	FG Att.	FG Made	FG Pct.	FT Att.	FT Made	FT Pct.	Re-b'nd	As-sist	Per. Fls.	Disq.	Tot. Pts.	Avg. Pts.
Elgin Baylor	80	3370	2273	1029	.453	790	661	.837	1146	386	226	1	2719	34.0
Jerry West	55	2163	1213	559	.461	477	371	.778	384	307	150	1	1489	27.1
Dick Barnett	80	2544	1542	547	.471	421	343	.815	242	224	189	3	1437	18.0
Rudy LaRusso	75	2505	761	321	.422	393	282	.718	747	187	255	5	924	12.3
Frank Selvy	74	2369	747	317	.424	269	192	.714	289	281	149	0	826	10.3
Jim Krebs	79	1913	627	272	.434	154	115	.747	502	87	256	2	659	8.3
LeRoy Ellis	80	1628	530	222	.419	202	133	.658	518	46	194	1	577	7.2
Rod Hundley	65	785	262	88	.336	119	84	.706	106	151	81	0	260	4.0
Gene Wiley	75	1488	236	109	.462	68	23	.338	504	40	180	4	241	3.2
Ron Horn	28	289	82	27	.329	29	20	.690	71	10	46	0	74	2.6
Howie Joliff	28	293	55	15	.273	9	6	.667	62	20	49	1	36	1.3

1962-63 STATISTICS

NEW YORK

Player	G.	Minutes	FG Att.	FG Made	FG Pct.	FT Att.	FT Made	FT Pct.	Re-b'nd	As-sist	Per. Fls.	Disq.	Tot. Pts.	Avg. Pts.
Richie Guerin	79	2712	1380	596	.432	600	509	.848	331	348	228	2	1701	21.5
John Green	80	2553	1261	582	.462	439	280	.638	964	152	243	5	1444	18.1
Gene Shue	78	2288	894	354	.396	302	208	.689	191	259	171	0	916	11.7
Tom Gola*	73	2670	791	363	.459	219	170	.776	517	298	295	9	896	12.3
Dave Budd	78	1725	596	294	.493	202	151	.748	395	87	204	3	739	9.5
Al Butler	74	1488	676	297	.439	187	144	.770	170	156	145	3	738	10.0
Gene Conley	70	1544	651	254	.390	186	122	.656	469	70	263	10	630	9.0
Donnis Butcher	68	1193	424	172	.406	194	131	.675	180	138	164	1	475	7.0
Paul Hogue	50	1340	419	152	.363	174	79	.454	430	42	220	12	383	7.7
Bob Nordmann*	53	1000	319	156	.489	122	59	.484	316	47	156	6	371	7.0
John Rudometkin	56	572	307	108	.352	95	73	.768	149	30	58	0	289	5.2
Tom Stith	25	209	110	37	.336	10	3	.300	39	18	23	0	77	3.1
Jack Foley*	11	83	51	20	.392	15	13	.867	16	5	8	0	53	4.8
Cleveland Buckner	6	27	10	5	.500	4	2	.500	4	5	6	0	12	2.0

*Gola—21 San Francisco, 52 New York; Nordmann—27 St. Louis, 26 New York; Foley—5 Boston, 6 New York.

ST. LOUIS

Player	G.	Minutes	FG Att.	FG Made	FG Pct.	FT Att.	FT Made	FT Pct.	Re-b'nd	As-sist	Per. Fls.	Disq.	Tot. Pts.	Avg. Pts.
Bob Pettit	79	2840	1746	770	.446	885	685	.774	1191	245	282	8	2241	28.4
Cliff Hagan	79	1716	1055	491	.465	305	244	.800	341	193	211	2	1226	15.5
John Barnhill	77	2692	838	360	.430	255	181	.710	359	322	168	0	901	11.7
Len Wilkens	75	2569	834	333	.399	319	222	.696	403	381	256	6	888	11.8
Woody Sauldsberry*	77	2034	966	366	.379	163	107	.656	447	78	241	4	839	10.9
Zelmo Beaty	80	1918	677	297	.439	307	220	.717	665	85	312	12	814	10.2
Charles Vaughn	77	1845	708	295	.417	261	188	.720	258	252	201	3	778	10.1
Mike Farmer	80	1724	562	239	.425	139	117	.842	369	143	155	0	595	7.4
Phil Jordon	73	1420	527	211	.400	101	56	.554	319	103	172	3	478	6.5
Bill Bridges	27	374	160	66	.413	51	32	.627	144	23	58	0	164	6.1
Bob Duffy	42	435	174	66	.379	39	22	.564	39	83	42	0	154	3.7
Gene Tormohlen	7	47	10	5	.500	10	2	.200	15	5	11	0	12	1.7

*Sauldsberry—54 Chicago, 23 St. Louis.

SAN FRANCISCO

Player	G.	Minutes	FG Att.	FG Made	FG Pct.	FT Att.	FT Made	FT Pct.	Re-b'nd	As-sist	Per. Fls.	Disq.	Tot. Pts.	Avg. Pts.
Wilt Chamberlain	80	3806	2770	1463	.528	1113	660	.593	1946	275	136	0	3586	44.8
Guy Rodgers	79	3249	1150	445	.387	286	208	.727	394	825	296	7	1098	13.9
Tom Meschery	64	2245	935	397	.425	313	228	.728	624	104	249	11	1022	16.0
Willie Naulls*	70	1901	887	370	.417	207	166	.802	515	102	205	3	906	12.9
Al Attles	71	1876	630	301	.478	206	133	.646	205	184	253	7	735	10.4
Gary Phillips	75	1801	643	256	.398	152	97	.638	225	137	185	7	609	8.1
Wayne Hightower	66	1387	543	192	.354	157	105	.669	354	51	181	5	489	7.4
Ken Sears*	77	1141	304	161	.530	168	131	.780	206	95	128	0	453	5.9
George Lee	64	1192	394	149	.378	193	152	.788	217	64	113	0	450	7.0
Howard Montgomery	20	364	153	65	.455	23	14	.609	69	21	35	1	144	7.2
Hubie White	29	271	111	40	.360	18	12	.667	35	28	47	0	92	3.2
Fred LaCour	16	171	73	28	.384	16	9	.563	24	19	27	0	65	4.1
Tom Luckenbill	20	201	68	26	.382	20	9	.450	56	8	34	0	61	3.1
Dave Fedor	7	27	10	3	.300	0	0	.000	6	1	4	0	6	0.9
Dave Gunther	1	5	2	1	.500	0	0	.000	3	3	1	0	2	2.6

*Naulls—23 New York, 47 San Francisco; Sears—23 New York, 54 San Francisco.

SYRACUSE

Player	G.	Minutes	FG Att.	FG Made	FG Pct.	FT Att.	FT Made	FT Pct.	Re-b'nd	As-sist	Per. Fls.	Disq.	Tot. Pts.	Avg. Pts.
Hal Greer	80	2631	1293	600	.464	434	362	.834	457	275	286	4	1562	19.5
Lee Shaffer	80	2392	1393	597	.429	375	294	.784	524	97	249	5	1488	18.6
John Kerr	80	2561	1069	507	.474	320	241	.753	1039	214	208	3	1255	15.7
Chet Walker	78	1992	751	352	.469	362	253	.699	561	83	220	3	957	12.3
Larry Costello	78	2066	660	285	.432	327	288	.881	237	334	263	4	858	11.0
Len Chappell	80	1241	604	281	.465	238	148	.622	461	56	171	1	710	8.9
Dave Gambee	60	1234	537	235	.438	238	199	.836	289	48	190	2	669	11.2
Paul Neumann	80	1581	503	237	.471	222	181	.815	200	227	221	5	655	8.2
Dolph Schayes	66	1438	575	223	.388	206	181	.879	375	175	177	2	627	9.5
Al Bianchi	61	1159	476	202	.424	164	120	.732	134	170	165	2	524	8.6
Ben Warley	26	206	111	50	.450	35	25	.714	86	4	42	1	125	4.8
Joe Roberts	33	466	196	73	.372	51	35	.686	155	16	66	1	181	5.5
Porter Meriwether	31	268	122	48	.393	33	23	.697	29	43	19	0	119	3.8

INTER-CLUB RECORDS—HOME, AWAY AND NEUTRAL COURT

EASTERN DIVISION

	Bos.	Syr.	Cin.	N.Y.	L.A.	S.L.	Det.	S.F.	Chi.	Home	Away	Neutral	W.	L.
Boston	..	6	9	10	4	5	8	8	8	25- 5	21- 16	12- 1	58-	22
Syracuse	6	..	5	10	4	4	6	5	8	23- 5	13- 19	12- 8	48-	32
Cincinnati	3	7	..	10	3	3	4	6	6	23- 10	15- 19	4- 9	42-	38
New York	2	2	2	..	3	3	1	2	6	12- 22	5- 28	4- 9	21-	59

WESTERN DIVISION

	Bos.	Syr.	Cin.	N.Y.	L.A.	S.L.	Det.	S.F.	Chi.	Home	Away	Neutral	W.	L.
Los Angeles	5	4	6	5	..	7	11	8	7	27- 7	20- 17	6- 3	53-	27
St. Louis	3	5	5	6	5	..	8	9	7	30- 7	13- 18	5- 7	48-	32
Detroit	0	3	4	8	1	4	..	7	7	14- 16	8- 19	12- 11	34-	46
San Francisco	1	3	3	6	4	3	5	..	6	13- 20	11- 25	7- 4	31-	49
Chicago	2	2	4	4	3	3	3	4	..	17- 17	3- 23	5- 15	25-	55
Total	22	32	36	59	27	32	46	49	55	184-109	109-184	67- 67	360-360	

1962-63 CHAMPIONSHIP PLAYOFF RESULTS

EASTERN DIVISION SEMI-FINALS
Cincinnati 3, Syracuse 2

Mar. 19—Cincinnati 120 at Syracuse 123
Mar. 21—Syracuse 115 at Cincinnati 133
Mar. 23—Cincinnati 117 at Syracuse 121
Mar. 24—Syracuse 118 at Cincinnati 125
Mar. 26—Cincinnati 131 at Syracuse *127

WESTERN DIVISION SEMI-FINALS
St. Louis 3, Detroit 1

Mar. 20—Detroit 99 at St. Louis 118
Mar. 22—Detroit 108 at St. Louis 122
Mar. 24—St. Louis 103 at Detroit 107
Mar. 26—St. Louis 104 at Detroit 100

EASTERN DIVISION FINALS
Boston 4, Cincinnati 3

Mar. 28—Cincinnati 135 at Boston 132
Mar. 29—Boston 125 at Cincinnati 102
Mar. 31—Cincinnati 121 at Boston 116
Apr. 3—Boston 128 at Cincinnati 110
Apr. 6—Cincinnati 125 at Boston 125
Apr. 7—Boston 99 at Cincinnati 109
Apr. 10—Cincinnati 131 at Boston 142

WESTERN DIVISION FINALS
Los Angeles 4, St. Louis 3

Mar. 31—St. Louis 104 at Los Angeles 112
Apr. 2—St. Louis 99 at Los Angeles 101
Apr. 4—Los Angeles 112 at St. Louis 125
Apr. 6—Los Angeles 114 at St. Louis 124
Apr. 7—St. Louis 100 at Los Angeles 123
Apr. 9—Los Angeles 113 at St. Louis 121
Apr. 11—St. Louis 100 at Los Angeles 115

*—Denotes overtime period.

CHAMPIONSHIP SERIES
Boston 4, Los Angeles 2

Apr. 14—Los Angeles 114 at Boston 117
Apr. 16—Los Angeles 106 at Boston 113
Apr. 17—Boston 99 at Los Angeles 119
Apr. 19—Boston 108 at Los Angeles 105
Apr. 21—Los Angeles 126 at Boston 119
Apr. 24—Boston 112 at Los Angeles 109

TEAM PLAYOFF STATISTICS

Team	G.	FGA	FGM	Pct.	FTA	FTM	Pct.	Reb.	Ast.	PF	Disq.	Scoring Average For	Agst.	Diff.
Los Angeles	13	1191	536	.450	517	396	.766	833	239	338	7	113.0	110.5	2.5
Boston	13	1397	589	.422	480	357	.744	893	316	384	12	118.1	115.9	2.2
St. Louis	11	1081	466	.431	381	284	.745	692	263	325	11	110.5	109.5	1.0
Cincinnati	12	1180	527	.447	520	400	.769	815	276	344	6	121.2	122.6	-1.4
Syracuse	5	509	226	.444	192	152	.792	296	89	155	3	120.8	125.2	-4.4
Detroit	4	392	154	.393	152	106	.697	269	74	114	3	103.5	111.8	-8.3

1961-62 STATISTICS

1961-62 CHAMPION BOSTON CELTICS

Seated (left to right): K. C. Jones, Gary Phillips, President Walter A. Brown, Coach Red Auerbach, Treasurer Lou Pieri, Captain Bob Cousy, Sam Jones. Standing: Frank Ramsey, Tom Sanders, Tom Heinsohn, Bill Russell, Gene Guarilia, Jim Loscutoff, Carl Braun, Trainer Buddy LeRoux.

FINAL STANDINGS AND TEAM FIGURES

EASTERN DIVISION

Team	W.	L.	FGA	FGM	Pct.	FTA	FTM	Pct.	Reb.	Ast.	PF	Disq.	Pts.	Avg.	Opp.
Boston	60	20	9109	3855	.423	2715	1977	.728	6080	2049	1909	28	9687	121.1	8948
Philadelphia	49	31	8929	3917	.439	3207	2201	.686	5939	2073	2013	71	10035	125.4	9813
Syracuse	41	39	8875	3706	.418	2880	2246	.780	5764	1791	2344	53	9658	120.7	9473
New York	29	51	8696	3638	.418	2693	1911	.710	5440	1765	2056	39	9187	114.8	9574

WESTERN DIVISION

Team	W.	L.	FGA	FGM	Pct.	FTA	FTM	Pct.	Reb.	Ast.	PF	Disq.	Pts.	Avg.	Opp.
Los Angeles	54	26	8315	3552	.427	3240	2378	.734	5600	1878	2057	39	9482	118.5	9603
Cincinnati	43	37	8414	3806	.452	2969	2233	.752	5665	2154	2081	31	9845	123.1	9704
Detroit	37	43	8366	3472	.415	3142	2290	.729	5823	1723	2040	46	9324	115.4	9369
St. Louis	29	51	8461	3641	.430	2939	2226	.757	5557	1996	2166	51	9508	118.9	9770
Chicago	18	62	8405	3461	.412	2901	1952	.673	5547	1802	1954	30	8874	110.9	9553

TOP 25 SCORERS

Player–Team	G.	Min.	FGA	FGM	Pct.	FTA	FTM	Pct.	Reb.	Ast.	PF	Disq.	Pts.	Avg.
Wilt Chamberlain, Phila	80	3882	3159	1597	.506	1363	835	.613	2052	192	123	0	4029	50.4
Walt Bellamy, Chicago	79	3344	1875	973	.519	853	549	.644	1500	210	281	6	2495	31.6
Oscar Robertson, Cinn.	79	3503	1810	866	.478	872	700	.803	985	899	258	1	2432	30.3
Bob Pettit, St. Louis	78	3282	1928	867	.450	901	695	.711	1459	289	296	4	2429	31.1
Jerry West, Los Angeles	75	3087	1795	799	.445	926	712	.769	591	402	173	5	2310	30.8
Richie Guerin, New York	78	3348	1897	839	.442	762	625	.820	501	539	299	3	2303	29.5
Willie Naulls, New York	75	2978	1798	747	.415	455	383	.842	867	192	260	6	1877	25.0

1961-62 STATISTICS

Player–Team	G.	Min.	FGA	FGM	Pct.	FTA	FTM	Pct.	Reb.	Ast.	PF	Disq.	Pts.	Avg.
Elgin Baylor, Los Angeles	48	2129	1588	680	.428	631	476	.754	892	222	155	1	1836	38.3
Jack Twyman, Cincinnati	80	2991	1542	739	.478	433	353	.815	638	215	323	5	1831	22.9
Cliff Hagan, St. Louis	77	2786	1490	701	.470	439	362	.825	633	370	272	8	1764	22.9
Tom Heinsohn, Boston	79	2383	1613	692	.429	437	358	.819	747	165	280	2	1742	22.1
Paul Arizin, Philadelphia	78	2785	1490	611	.410	601	484	.805	527	201	307	18	1706	21.9
Hal Greer, Syracuse	71	2705	1442	644	.446	404	331	.819	526	313	252	2	1619	22.8
Bailey Howell, Detroit	79	2857	1193	553	.463	612	470	.768	996	186	317	10	1576	19.9
Gene Shue, Detroit	80	3143	1422	580	.408	447	362	.810	372	465	192	1	1522	19.0
Wayne Embry, Cincinnati	75	2623	1210	564	.466	516	356	.690	997	182	286	6	1484	19.8
Bill Russell, Boston	76	3433	1258	575	.457	481	286	.594	1790	341	207	3	1436	18.9
Sam Jones, Boston	78	2388	1284	596	.464	297	243	.818	458	232	149	0	1435	18.4
Rudy LaRusso, Los Angeles	80	2754	1108	516	.466	448	342	.763	828	179	255	5	1374	17.2
Dave Gambee, Syracuse	80	2301	1126	477	.424	470	384	.817	631	114	275	10	1338	16.7
Don Ohl, Detroit	77	2526	1250	555	.444	280	201	.718	267	244	173	2	1311	17.0
John Kerr, Syracuse	80	2768	1220	541	.443	302	222	.735	1176	243	282	7	1304	16.3
John Green, New York	80	2789	1164	507	.436	434	261	.601	1066	191	265	4	1275	15.9
Lee Shaffer, Syracuse	75	2093	1180	514	.436	310	239	.771	511	99	266	6	1267	16.9
Arlen Bockhorn, Cincinnati	80	3062	1234	531	.430	251	193	.789	376	366	280	5	1260	15.8

FIELD GOAL PERCENTAGE LEADERS
(Minimum 200 FGM)

	FGA	FGM	Pct.
Walt Bellamy, Chicago	1875	973	.519
Wilt Chamberlain, Philadelphia	3159	1597	.506
Jack Twyman, Cincinnati	1542	739	.479
Oscar Robertson, Cincinnati	1810	860	.478
Al Attles, Philadelphia	724	343	.474
Clyde Lovellette, St. Louis	724	341	.471
Larry Foust, St. Louis	433	204	.471
Cliff Hagan, St. Louis	1490	701	.470
Rudy LaRusso, Los Angeles	1108	516	.466
Wayne Embry, Cincinnati	1210	564	.466

FREE THROW PERCENTAGE LEADERS
(Minimum 200 FTM)

	FGA	FGM	Pct.
Dolph Schayes, Syracuse	319	286	.896
Willie Naulls, New York	455	383	.842
Larry Costello, Syracuse	295	247	.837
Frank Ramsey, Boston	405	334	.825
Cliff Hagan, St. Louis	439	362	.825
Tom Meschery, Philadelphia	262	216	.824
Richie Guerin, New York	762	625	.820
Tom Heinsohn, Boston	437	358	.819
Hal Greer, Syracuse	404	331	.819
Sam Jones, Boston	297	243	.818

LEADERS IN REBOUNDS

	G.	No.	Avg.
Wilt Chamberlain, Philadelphia	80	2052	25.7
Bill Russell, Boston	76	1790	23.6
Walt Bellamy, Chicago	79	1500	19.0
Bob Pettit, St. Louis	78	1459	18.7
John Kerr, Syracuse	80	1176	14.7
John Green, New York	80	1061	13.3
Bailey, Howell, Detroit	79	996	12.6
Oscar Robertson, Cincinnati	79	985	12.5
Wayne Embry, Cincinnati	75	977	13.0
Elgin Baylor, Los Angeles	48	892	18.6

LEADERS IN ASSISTS

	G.	No.	Avg.
Oscar Robertson, Cincinnati	79	899	11.4
Guy Rodgers, Philadelphia	80	663	7.9'
Bob Cousy, Boston	75	584	7.8
Richie Guerin, New York	78	539	6.9
Gene Shue, Detroit	80	465	5.8
Jerry West, Los Angeles	75	402	5.4
Frank Selvy, Los Angeles	79	381	4.8
Bob Leonard, Chicago	70	378	5.4
Cliff Hagan, St. Louis	77	370	4.8
Arlen Bockhorn, Cincinnati	80	366	4.6

INTER-CLUB RECORDS—HOME, AWAY AND NEUTRAL COURT

EASTERN DIVISION

	Bos.	Phil.	Syr.	N.Y.	L.A.	Cinn.	Det.	S.L.	Chi.	Home	Away	Neutral	W.	L.
Boston	..	8	10	8	6	7	5	7	9	23- 5	26- 12	11- 3	60-	20
Philadelphia	4	..	6	8	3	5	7	6	10	18- 11	18- 19	13- 1	49-	31
Syracuse	2	6	..	9	2	4	5	4	9	18- 10	11- 19	12-10	41-	39
New York	4	4	3	..	2	4	4	4	4	19- 14	2- 23	8-14	29-	51

WESTERN DIVISION

	Bos.	Phil.	Syr.	N.Y.	L.A.	Cinn.	Det.	S.L.	Chi.	Home	Away	Neutral	W.	L.
Los Angeles	3	6	6	6	..	7	8	10	8	26- 5	18- 13	10- 8	54-	26
Cincinnati	1	3	5	5	5	..	6	9	9	18- 13	14- 16	11- 8	43-	37
Detroit	3	1	4	5	4	6	..	7	7	16- 14	8- 17	13-12	37-	43
St. Louis	2	3	4	4	2	3	5	..	6	19- 16	7- 27	3- 8	29-	51
Chicago	1	0	1	6	2	1	3	4	..	9- 19	3- 20	6-23	18-	62
Total	20	31	39	51	26	37	43	51	62	166-107	107-166	87- 87	360-360	

INDIVIDUAL STATISTICS

BOSTON

Player	G.	Minutes	FG Att.	FG Made	FG Pct.	FT Att.	FT Made	FT Pct.	Re-b'nd	As-sist	Per. Fls.	Disq.	Tot. Pts.	Avg. Pts.
Tom Heinsohn	79	2383	1613	692	.429	437	358	.819	747	165	280	2	1742	22.1
Bill Russell	76	3433	1258	575	.457	481	286	.595	1790	341	207	3	1436	18.9
Sam Jones	78	2388	1284	596	.464	297	243	.818	458	232	149	0	1435	18.4
Frank Ramsey	79	1913	1019	436	.428	405	334	.825	387	109	245	10	1206	15.3
Bob Cousy	75	2114	1181	462	.391	333	251	.754	261	584	135	0	1175	15.7

1961-62 STATISTICS

Player	G.	Minutes	FG Att.	FG Made	FG Pct.	FT Att.	FT Made	FT Pct.	Re-b'nd	As-sist	Per. Fls.	Disq.	Tot. Pts.	Avg. Pts.
Tom Sanders	80	2325	804	350	.435	263	197	.749	762	74	279	9	897	11.2
K. C. Jones	80	2054	724	294	.406	232	147	.634	298	343	206	1	735	9.2
Jim Loscutoff	79	1146	519	188	.362	84	45	.536	329	51	185	3	421	5.3
Gary Phillips	67	713	310	110	.355	86	50	.581	107	64	109	0	270	4.0
Carl Braun	48	414	207	78	.377	27	20	.741	50	71	49	0	176	3.7
Gene Guarilia	45	367	161	61	.379	64	41	.641	124	11	56	0	163	3.6

CHICAGO

Player	G.	Minutes	FG Att.	FG Made	FG Pct.	FT Att.	FT Made	FT Pct.	Re-b'nd	As-sist	Per. Fls.	Disq.	Tot. Pts.	Avg. Pts.
Walt Bellamy	79	3344	1875	973	.519	853	549	.644	1500	210	281	6	2495	31.6
Bob Leonard	70	2464	1128	423	.375	371	279	.752	199	378	186	0	1125	16.1
Andy Johnson	71	2193	814	365	.448	452	284	.628	351	228	247	5	1014	14.3
Sihugo Green*	71	2388	905	341	.377	311	218	.701	399	318	226	0	900	12.7
Ralph Davis	77	1992	881	364	.413	103	71	.689	162	247	187	1	799	10.4
Woody Sauldsberry*	63	1765	869	298	.343	123	79	.642	536	90	179	5	675	10.7
Charlie Tyra	78	1606	534	193	.361	214	133	.621	610	86	210	7	519	6.7
Horace Walker	65	1331	439	149	.339	193	140	.725	466	69	194	2	438	6.7
Dave Piontek	45	614	225	83	.369	59	39	.661	155	31	89	1	205	4.6
Jack Turner	42	567	221	84	.380	42	32	.762	85	44	51	0	200	4.8
Howie Carl	31	382	201	67	.333	51	36	.706	39	57	41	1	170	5.5
George BonSalle	3	9	8	2	.250	0	0	.000	2	0	0	0	4	1.3

*Green—14 St. Louis, 57 Chicago. Sauldsberry—14 St. Louis, 49 Chicago.

CINCINNATI

Player	G.	Minutes	FG Att.	FG Made	FG Pct.	FT Att.	FT Made	FT Pct.	Re-b'nd	As-sist	Per. Fls.	Disq.	Tot. Pts.	Avg. Pts.
Oscar Robertson	79	3503	1810	866	.478	872	700	.803	985	899	258	1	2432	30.8
Jack Twyman	80	2991	1542	739	.479	435	353	.811	636	233	323	5	1831	22.9
Wayne Embry	75	2623	1210	564	.466	516	356	.690	977	182	286	6	1484	19.8
Arlen Bockhorn	80	3062	1234	531	.430	251	198	.789	376	366	280	5	1260	15.8
Bob Boozer	79	2488	936	410	.438	372	263	.707	804	130	275	3	1083	13.7
Adrian Smith	80	1462	499	202	.405	222	172	.775	151	167	101	0	576	7.2
Hub Reed	80	1446	460	203	.441	82	60	.732	440	53	267	9	466	5.8
Joe Buckhalter	63	728	334	153	.458	108	67	.620	262	43	123	1	373	5.9
Bob Nordmann	58	344	126	51	.405	57	29	.509	128	18	84	1	131	2.8
Bob Wieseharn	60	326	161	51	.317	30	17	.567	112	23	50	0	119	2.0
Dave Zeller	61	278	102	36	.353	24	18	.750	27	58	37	0	90	1.5

DETROIT

Player	G.	Minutes	FG Att.	FG Made	FG Pct.	FT Att.	FT Made	FT Pct.	Re-b'nd	As-sist	Per. Fls.	Disq.	Tot. Pts.	Avg. Pts.
Bailey Howell	79	2857	1193	553	.464	612	470	.768	996	186	317	10	1576	19.9
Gene Shue	80	3143	1422	580	.408	447	362	.810	372	465	192	1	1522	19.0
Don Ohl	77	2526	1250	555	.444	280	201	.718	267	244	173	0	1311	17.0
Bob Ferry	80	1918	939	411	.438	422	286	.678	503	145	199	2	1108	13.9
Ray Scott	75	2087	956	370	.387	388	255	.657	865	132	232	6	995	13.3
Walt Dukes	77	1896	647	256	.396	291	208	.715	803	125	327	20	720	9.4
George Lee	75	1351	500	179	.358	280	213	.761	349	64	128	1	571	7.6
Jack Moreland	74	1219	487	205	.421	186	139	.747	427	76	179	2	549	7.4
Willie Jones	69	1006	475	177	.373	101	64	.634	177	115	137	1	418	6.1
Jack Egan	58	696	301	128	.425	84	64	.762	86	102	64	0	320	5.5
Chuck Noble	26	361	113	32	.283	15	8	.533	43	63	55	1	72	2.8

LOS ANGELES

Player	G.	Minutes	FG Att.	FG Made	FG Pct.	FT Att.	FT Made	FT Pct.	Re-b'nd	As-sist	Per. Fls.	Disq.	Tot. Pts.	Avg. Pts.
Jerry West	75	3087	1795	799	.445	926	712	.769	591	402	173	4	2310	30.8
Elgin Baylor	48	2129	1588	680	.428	631	476	.754	892	222	155	1	1836	38.3
Rudy LaRusso	80	2754	1108	516	.466	448	342	.763	828	179	255	5	1374	17.2
Frank Selvy	79	2806	1032	433	.420	404	298	.738	412	381	232	0	1164	14.7
Jim Krebs	78	2012	701	312	.445	208	156	.750	616	110	290	9	780	10.0
Tom Hawkins	79	1903	704	289	.411	222	143	.644	514	95	244	7	721	9.1
Ray Felix	80	1478	398	171	.430	130	90	.692	473	55	266	6	432	5.4
Rod Hundley	78	1492	509	173	.340	127	83	.654	199	290	129	1	429	5.5
Howie Jolliff	64	1094	253	104	.411	78	41	.526	383	76	175	4	249	3.9
Bob McNeill*	50	441	136	56	.412	34	26	.765	56	89	56	0	138	2.8
Wayne Yates	37	263	105	31	.295	22	10	.455	94	16	72	1	72	1.9
Robert Smith	3	7	1	0	.000	0	0	.000	0	0	1	0	0	0.0

*McNeill—21 Philadelphia, 29 Los Angeles.

1961-62 STATISTICS

NEW YORK

Player	G.	Min-utes	FG Att.	FG Made	FG Pct.	FT Att.	FT Made	FT Pct.	Re-b'nd	As-sist	Per. Fls.	Disq.	Tot. Pts.	Avg. Pts.
Richie Guerin	78	3348	1897	839	.442	762	625	.820	501	539	299	3	2303	29.5
Willie Naulls	75	2978	1798	747	.415	455	383	.842	867	192	260	6	1877	25.0
John Green	80	2789	1164	507	.436	434	261	.601	1066	191	265	4	1275	15.9
Phil Jordon	76	2195	1028	403	.392	168	96	.571	482	156	258	7	902	11.9
Al Butler*	59	2016	754	349	.463	182	129	.709	337	205	156	0	827	14.0
Dave Budd	79	1370	431	188	.436	231	138	.597	470	82	230	10	514	6.5
Darrall Imhoff	76	1481	482	186	.386	139	80	.576	345	86	162	4	452	5.9
Cleveland Buckner	62	696	367	158	.431	133	83	.624	236	39	114	1	399	6.4
Whitey Martin	66	1018	292	95	.325	55	37	.673	158	115	158	4	227	3.4
Sam Stith	32	440	162	59	.364	38	23	.605	51	60	55	0	141	4.4
Donnis Butcher*	47	479	155	48	.310	69	42	.609	79	51	63	0	138	2.9
George Blaney	36	363	142	54	.380	17	9	.529	36	45	34	0	117	3.3
Bill Smith	9	83	33	8	.242	8	7	.875	16	7	6	0	23	2.6
Ed Burton	8	28	14	7	.500	4	1	.250	5	1	3	0	15	1.9
Doug Kistler	5	13	6	3	.500	4	2	.500	1	0	2	0	8	1.6

*Butler—5 Boston, 54 New York.

PHILADELPHIA

Player	G.	Min-utes	FG Att.	FG Made	FG Pct.	FT Att.	FT Made	FT Pct.	Re-b'nd	As-sist	Per. Fls.	Disq.	Tot. Pts.	Avg. Pts.
Wilt Chamberlain	80	3882	3159	1597	.506	1363	835	.613	2052	192	123	0	4029	50.4
Paul Arizin	78	2785	1490	611	.410	601	484	.805	527	201	307	18	1706	21.9
Tom Meschery	80	2509	929	375	.404	262	216	.824	729	145	330	15	966	12.1
Al Attles	75	2468	724	343	.474	267	158	.592	355	333	279	8	844	11.3
Tom Gola	60	2462	765	322	.421	230	176	.765	587	295	267	16	820	13.7
Guy Rodgers	80	2650	949	267	.356	182	121	.665	348	643	312	12	655	8.2
Ed Conlin	70	963	371	128	.345	89	66	.742	155	85	118	1	322	4.6
York Larese*	59	703	327	122	.373	72	58	.805	77	94	104	0	302	5.1
Ted Luckenbill	67	396	120	43	.358	76	49	.645	110	27	67	0	135	2.0
Joe Ruklick	46	302	147	48	.326	26	12	.461	87	14	56	1	108	2.3
Frank Radovich	37	175	93	37	.398	26	13	.500	51	4	27	0	87	2.3

*Larese—8 Chicago, 51 Philadelphia.

ST. LOUIS

Player	G.	Min-utes	FG Att.	FG Made	FG Pct.	FT Att.	FT Made	FT Pct.	Re-b'nd	As-sist	Per. Fls.	Disq.	Tot. Pts.	Avg. Pts.
Bob Pettit	78	3282	1928	867	.450	901	695	.771	1459	289	296	4	2429	31.1
Cliff Hagan	77	2786	1490	701	.470	439	362	.825	633	370	282	8	1764	22.9
Clyde Lovellette	40	1192	724	341	.471	187	155	.829	350	68	136	4	837	20.9
Barney Cable*	67	1861	749	305	.407	181	118	.652	563	115	211	4	728	10.9
Shellie McMillon*	62	1225	591	265	.448	182	108	.593	368	59	202	10	638	10.3
Al Ferrari	79	2046	582	208	.357	219	175	.799	213	313	278	9	591	7.5
Fred LaCour	73	1507	534	230	.429	130	106	.815	272	166	168	3	566	7.8
Larry Foust	57	1153	536	204	.471	178	145	.815	328	78	186	3	553	9.7
Bob Sims*	65	1345	433	193	.393	216	123	.549	183	154	187	4	509	7.8
Lennie Wilkens	20	870	491	140	.385	110	84	.764	131	116	63	0	364	18.2
Cleo Hill	58	1050	364	107	.346	137	106	.774	178	114	98	1	320	5.5
Vern Hatton*	40	898	309	112	.338	125	98	.784	102	99	63	0	322	8.1
Archie Dees*	21	288	331	51	.443	46	35	.761	77	16	33	0	137	6.5
Stacey Arceneaux	7	110	155	22	.393	13	6	.461	32	4	10	0	50	7.1
Jack McCarthy	15	333	56	18	.246	27	12	.444	56	70	50	1	48	3.2
Jim Darrow	5	34	73	3	.200	7	6	.857	7	6	9	0	12	2.4
Ron Horn	3	25	15	1	.083	2	1	.500	6	1	4	0	3	1.0
Richard Eichhorst	1	10	12	1	.500	0	0	.000	1	3	0	0	2	2.0

*Cable—15 Chicago, 52 St. Louis. Dees—13 Chicago, 8 St. Louis. Hatton—15 Chicago, 25 St. Louis. McMillon—14 Detroit, 48 St. Louis. Sims—19 Los Angeles, 46 St. Louis.

SYRACUSE

Player	G.	Min-utes	FG Att.	FG Made	FG Pct.	FT Att.	FT Made	FT Pct.	Re-b'nd	As-sist	Per. Fls.	Disq.	Tot. Pts.	Avg. Pts.
Hal Greer	71	2705	1442	644	.446	404	331	.819	524	313	252	2	1619	22.8
Dave Gambee	80	2301	1126	477	.424	470	384	.817	631	114	275	10	1338	16.7
John Kerr	80	2768	1220	541	.443	302	222	.735	1176	243	272	7	1304	16.3
Lee Shaffer	75	2083	1180	514	.436	310	239	.771	511	99	266	6	1267	16.9
Larry Costello	63	1854	726	310	.427	295	247	.837	245	359	220	5	867	13.7
Al Bianchi	80	1925	847	336	.397	221	154	.697	281	263	232	5	826	10.3

1961-62 STATISTICS

Player	G.	Minutes	FG Att.	FG Made	FG Pct.	FT Att.	FT Made	FT Pct.	Re-b'nd	As-sist	Per. Fls.	Disq.	Tot. Pts.	Avg. Pts.
Dolph Schayes	56	1480	751	268	.357	319	286	.896	439	120	167	4	822	14.7
Joe Roberts	80	1642	619	243	.393	194	129	.665	538	50	230	4	615	7.7
Paul Neumann	77	1265	401	172	.429	172	133	.773	194	176	203	3	477	6.2
Harvey Halbrook	64	908	422	152	.360	151	96	.636	399	33	179	7	400	6.3
Joe Graboski	38	468	221	77	.348	65	39	.600	154	28	62	0	193	5.1
Charles Osborne	4	21	8	1	.125	4	3	.750	9	1	3	0	5	1.2

*Graboski—3 St. Louis, 12 Chicago, 23 Syracuse.

1961-62 CHAMPIONSHIP PLAYOFF RESULTS

EASTERN DIVISION SEMI-FINALS
Philadelphia 3, Syracuse 2

Mar. 16—Syracuse 103 at Philadelphia 110
Mar. 18—Philadelphia 97 at Syracuse 82
Mar. 19—Syracuse 101 at Philadelphia 100
Mar. 20—Philadelphia 99 at Syracuse 106
Mar. 22—Syracuse 104 at Philadelphia 121

WESTERN DIVISION SEMI-FINALS
Detroit 3, Cincinnati 1

Mar. 16—Cincinnati 122 at Detroit 123
Mar. 17—Detroit 107 at Cincinnati 129
Mar. 18—Cincinnati 107 at Detroit 118
Mar. 20—Detroit 112 at Cincinnati 111

EASTERN DIVISION FINALS
Boston 4, Philadelphia 3

Mar. 24—Philadelphia 89 at Boston 117
Mar. 27—Boston 106 at Philadelphia 113
Mar. 28—Philadelphia 114 at Boston 129
Mar. 31—Boston 106 at Philadelphia 110
Apr. 1—Philadelphia 104 at Boston 119
Apr. 3—Boston 99 at Philadelphia 109
Apr. 5—Philadelphia 107 at Boston 109

WESTERN DIVISION FINALS
Los Angeles 4, Detroit 2

Mar. 24—Detroit 108 at Los Angeles 132
Mar. 25—Detroit 112 at Los Angeles 127
Mar. 27—Los Angeles 111 at Detroit 106
Mar. 29—Detroit 117 at Los Angeles 118
Mar. 31—Detroit 132 at Los Angeles 125
Apr. 3—Los Angeles 123 at Detroit 117

CHAMPIONSHIP SERIES
Boston 4, Los Angeles 3

Apr. 7—Los Angeles 108 at Boston 122
Apr. 8—Los Angeles 129 at Boston 122
Apr. 10—Boston 115 at Los Angeles 117
Apr. 11—Boston 115 at Los Angeles 103
Apr. 14—Los Angeles 126 at Boston 121
Apr. 16—Boston 119 at Los Angeles 105
Apr. 18—Los Angeles 107 at Boston *110

*—Denotes overtime period.

TEAM PLAYOFF STATISTICS

Team	G.	FGA	FGM	Pct.	FTA	FTM	Pct.	Reb.	Ast.	PF	Disq.	Scoring Average For	Agst.	Diff.
Boston	14	1536	625	.407	489	359	.734	934	360	407	17	114.9	110.1	4.8
Cincinnati	4	393	184	.468	124	101	.815	254	100	106	1	117.3	115.0	2.3
Los Angeles	13	1302	550	.422	560	430	.768	914	283	343	10	117.7	116.7	1.0
Philadelphia	12	1211	467	.386	473	339	.717	883	243	303	12	106.1	106.8	−0.7
Detroit	10	1043	446	.428	359	261	.727	635	232	273	12	115.3	120.4	−5.1
Syracuse	5	506	187	.370	151	122	.808	347	86	139	1	99.2	105.4	−6.2

1960-61 STATISTICS

1960-61 CHAMPION BOSTON CELTICS
Seated (left to right): K. C. Jones, Bob Cousy, Coach Red Auerbach, President Walter A. Brown, Bill Sharman, Frank Ramsey; standing, Trainer Buddy LeRoux, Tom Sanders, Tom Heinsohn, Gene Conley, Bill Russell, Gene Guarilia, Jim Loscutoff, Sam Jones. Inset: Treasurer Lou Pieri.

FINAL STANDINGS AND TEAM FIGURES

EASTERN DIVISION

Team	W.	L.	FGA	FGM	Pct.	FTA	FTM	Pct.	Reb.	Ast.	PF	Disq.	Pts.	Avg.	Opp.
Boston	57	22	9295	3699	.398	2804	2062	.735	6131	1872	2032	46	9460	119.7	9013
Philadelphia	46	33	8883	3768	.424	3108	2022	.651	5938	1959	1936	38	9558	121.0	9484
Syracuse	38	41	8746	3654	.418	2948	2278	.773	5726	1786	2280	43	9586	121.3	9416
New York	21	58	8347	3422	.410	2838	2135	.752	5315	1822	2223	37	8979	113.7	9486

WESTERN DIVISION

Team	W.	L.	FGA	FGM	Pct.	FTA	FTM	Pct.	Reb.	Ast.	PF	Disq.	Pts.	Avg.	Opp.
St. Louis	51	28	8795	3618	.411	2921	2147	.735	5994	2136	2135	36	9383	118.8	9201
Los Angeles	36	43	8430	3401	.403	2999	2204	.735	5816	1728	2043	32	9006	114.0	9010
Detroit	34	45	8357	3481	.417	3240	2408	.743	5813	1866	2157	47	9370	118.6	9558
Cincinnati	33	46	8281	3626	.438	2761	2060	.746	5581	2107	2159	40	9312	117.9	9585

TOP 25 SCORERS

Player–Team	G.	Min.	FGA	FGM	Pct.	FTA	FTM	Pct.	Reb.	Ast.	PF	Disq.	Pts.	Avg.
Wilt Chamberlain, Phila.	79	3773	2457	1251	.509	1054	531	.504	2149	148	130	0	3033	38.4
Elgin Baylor, Los Angeles	73	3133	2166	931	.430	863	676	.783	1447	371	279	3	2538	34.8
Oscar Robertson, Cincinnati	71	3032	1600	756	.473	794	653	.822	716	690	219	3	2165	30.5
Bob Pettit, St. Louis	76	3027	1720	769	.447	804	582	.724	1540	262	217	1	2120	27.9
Jack Twyman, Cincinnati	79	2920	1632	796	.488	554	405	.731	672	225	279	5	1997	25.3
Dolph Schayes, Syracuse	79	3007	1595	594	.372	783	680	.868	960	296	296	9	1868	23.6
Willie Naulls, New York	79	2976	1723	737	.428	456	372	.816	1055	191	268	5	1846	23.4

1960-61 STATISTICS

Player—Team	G.	Min.	FGA	FGM	Pct.	FTA	FTM	Pct.	Reb.	Ast.	PF	Disq.	Pts.	Avg.
Paul Arizin, Philadelphia	79	2935	1529	650	.425	639	532	.833	681	188	335	11	1832	23.2
Bailey Howell, Detroit	77	2952	1200	607	.469	798	601	.735	1111	196	297	10	1815	23.6
Gene Shue, Detroit	78	3361	1545	650	.421	543	465	.856	334	530	207	1	1765	22.6
Richie Guerin, New York	79	3023	1545	612	.396	626	496	.792	628	503	310	3	1720	21.8
Cliff Hagan, St. Louis	77	2701	1490	601	.444	467	283	.820	715	381	286	9	1705	22.1
Tom Heinsohn, Boston	74	2256	1566	627	.400	424	325	.767	732	141	260	7	1579	21.3
Hal Greer, Syracuse	79	2763	1381	623	.451	394	305	.774	455	302	242	0	1551	19.6
Clyde Lovellette, St. Louis	67	2111	1321	599	.453	329	273	.830	677	172	248	4	1471	22.0
Jerry West, Los Angeles	79	2797	1264	529	.418	497	331	.666	611	333	213	1	1389	17.6
Bob Cousy, Boston	76	2468	1382	513	.371	452	352	.779	331	587	196	0	1378	18.1
Bill Russell, Boston	78	3458	1250	532	.426	469	258	.550	1868	268	155	0	1322	16.9
Dick Barnett, Syracuse	78	2070	1194	540	.452	337	240	.712	283	218	169	0	1320	16.9
Frank Ramsey, Boston	79	2019	1100	448	.407	354	295	.833	431	146	284	14	1191	15.1
Sam Jones, Boston	78	2028	1069	480	.449	268	211	.787	421	217	148	1	1171	15.0
Rudy LaRusso, Los Angeles	79	2593	992	416	.419	409	323	.790	781	135	280	8	1155	14.6
Wayne Embry, Cincinnati	79	2233	1015	458	.451	331	221	.688	864	127	286	7	1137	14.4
Dick Garmaker, New York	71	2238	943	415	.440	358	275	.768	277	220	240	2	1105	15.6
Dave Gambee, Syracuse	79	2090	947	397	.419	352	291	.827	581	101	276	6	1085	13.7

FIELD GOAL PERCENTAGE LEADERS
(Minimum 200 FGM)

	FGA	FGM	Pct.
Wilt Chamberlain, Philadelphia	2457	1251	.509
Jack Twyman, Cincinnati	1632	796	.488
Larry Costello, Syracuse	844	407	.482
Oscar Robertson, Cincinnati	1600	756	.473
Barney Cable, Syracuse	564	266	.472
Bailey Howell, Detroit	1293	607	.469
Clyde Lovellette, St. Louis	1321	599	.453
Dick Barnett, Syracuse	1194	540	.452
Wayne Embry, Cincinnati	1015	458	.451
Hal Greer, Syracuse	1381	623	.451
Bob Ferry	776	350	.451

FREE THROW PERCENTAGE LEADERS
(Minimum 200 FTM)

	FTA	FTM	Pct.
Bill Sharman, Boston	228	210	.921
Dolph Schayes, Syracuse	783	680	.868
Gene Shue, Detroit	543	465	.856
Frank Ramsey, Boston	354	295	.833
Paul Arizin, Philadelphia	639	532	.833
Clyde Lovellette, St. Louis	329	273	.830
Dave Gambee, Syracuse	352	291	.827
Ken Sears, New York	325	268	.825
Oscar Robertson, Cincinnati	794	653	.822
Cliff Hagan, St. Louis	467	383	.820

LEADERS IN REBOUNDS

	G.	No.	Avg.
Wilt Chamberlain, Philadelphia	79	2149	27.2
Bill Russell, Boston	78	1868	23.9
Bob Pettit, St. Louis	76	1540	20.3
Elgin Baylor, Los Angeles	73	1447	19.8
Bailey Howell, Detroit	77	1111	14.4
Willie Naulls, New York	79	1055	13.4
Walter Dukes, Detroit	73	1028	14.1
Dolph Schayes, Syracuse	79	960	12.2
John Kerr, Syracuse	79	951	12.0
Wayne Embry, Cincinnati	79	864	10.9

LEADERS IN ASSISTS

	G.	No.	Avg.
Oscar Robertson, Cincinnati	71	690	9.7
Guy Rodgers, Philadelphia	78	677	8.7
Bob Cousy, Boston	76	587	7.7
Gene Shue, Detroit	78	530	6.8
Richie Guerin, New York	79	503	6.4
Jack McCarthy, St. Louis	79	430	5.4
Larry Costello, Syracuse	75	413	5.5
Cliff Hagan, St. Louis	78	381	4.9
Elgin Baylor, Los Angeles	73	371	5.1
Rod Hundley, Los Angeles	79	350	4.4

INTER-CLUB RECORDS—HOME, AWAY AND NEUTRAL COURT

EASTERN DIVISION

	Bos.	Phil.	Syr.	N.Y.	S.L.	L.A.	Det.	Cinn.	Home	Away	Neutral	W.	L.
Boston		8	10	10	8	8	7	8	21- 7	24- 11	12- 4	57- 22
Philadelphia	5		6	11	3	8	5	8	23- 6	12- 21	11- 6	46- 33
Syracuse	3	7		8	4	4	6	8	19- 9	8- 21	11- 11	38- 41
New York	3	2	5		1	3	5	2	10- 22	7- 25	4- 11	21- 58

WESTERN DIVISION

St. Louis	4	7	6	9		8	10	7	29- 5	15- 20	7- 3	51- 28
Los Angeles	2	2	6	7	5		9	5	16- 12	8- 20	12- 11	36- 43
Detroit	2	5	4	5	3	4		11	20- 11	3- 19	11- 15	34- 45
Cincinnati	3	2	4	8	6	8	2		18- 13	8- 19	7- 14	33- 46
Total	22	33	41	58	28	43	45	46	156- 85	85- 156	75- 75	316- 316

INDIVIDUAL STATISTICS

BOSTON

Player	G.	Minutes	FG Att.	FG Made	FG Pct.	FT Att.	FT Made	FT Pct.	Re- b'nd	As- sist	Per. Fls.	Disq.	Tot. Pts.	Avg. Pts.
Tom Heinsohn	74	2256	1566	627	.400	424	325	.767	732	141	260	7	1579	21.3
Bob Cousy	76	2468	1382	513	.371	452	352	.779	331	587	196	0	1378	18.1
Bill Russell	78	3458	1250	532	.426	469	258	.550	1868	268	155	0	1322	16.9
Frank Ramsey	79	2019	1100	448	.407	354	295	.833	431	146	284	14	1191	15.1
Sam Jones	78	2028	1069	480	.449	268	211	.787	421	217	148	1	1171	15.0
Bill Sharman	61	1538	908	383	.422	228	210	.921	223	146	127	0	976	16.0

1960-61 STATISTICS

Player	G.	Minutes	FG Att.	FG Made	FG Pct.	FT Att.	FT Made	FT Pct.	Re-b'nd	As-sist	Per. Fls.	Disq.	Tot. Pts.	Avg. Pts.
K. C. Jones	78	1605	601	203	.338	280	186	.664	279	253	190	3	592	7.6
Gene Conley	75	1242	495	183	.370	153	106	.693	550	40	275	15	472	6.3
Tom Sanders	68	1084	352	148	.420	100	67	.670	385	44	131	1	363	5.3
Jim Loscutoff	76	1153	478	144	.310	76	49	.645	291	25	238	5	337	4.4
Gene Guarilia	25	209	94	38	.404	10	3	.300	71	5	28	0	79	3.2

CINCINNATI

Player	G.	Minutes	FG Att.	FG Made	FG Pct.	FT Att.	FT Made	FT Pct.	Re-b'nd	As-sist	Per. Fls.	Disq.	Tot. Pts.	Avg. Pts.
Oscar Robertson	71	3032	1600	756	.473	794	653	.822	716	690	219	3	2165	30.5
Jack Twyman	79	2920	1632	796	.488	554	405	.731	672	225	279	5	1997	25.3
Wayne Embry	79	2233	1015	458	.451	331	221	.668	864	127	286	7	1137	14.4
Arlen Bockhorn	79	2669	1059	420	.397	208	152	.731	434	338	282	9	992	12.6
Bob Boozer	79	1573	603	250	.415	247	166	.672	488	109	193	1	666	8.4
Mike Farmer*	59	1301	461	180	.390	94	69	.734	380	81	130	1	429	7.3
Hub Reed	75	1216	364	156	.429	122	85	.697	367	69	199	7	397	5.3
Ralph Davis	73	1210	451	181	.401	52	34	.654	86	177	127	1	396	5.4
Larry Staverman	66	944	249	111	.446	93	79	.849	287	86	164	4	301	4.6
Win Wilfong	62	717	305	106	.348	89	72	.809	147	87	119	1	284	4.6

*Farmer-2 New York, 57 Cincinnati.

DETROIT

Player	G.	Minutes	FG Att.	FG Made	FG Pct.	FT Att.	FT Made	FT Pct.	Re-b'nd	As-sist	Per. Fls.	Disq.	Tot. Pts.	Avg. Pts.
Bailey Howell	77	2952	1293	607	.469	798	601	.753	1111	196	297	10	1815	23.6
Gene Shue	78	3361	1545	650	.421	543	465	.856	334	530	207	1	1765	22.6
Don Ohl	79	2172	1085	427	.394	278	200	.719	256	265	224	3	1054	13.3
George Lee	74	1735	776	310	.399	394	276	.701	490	89	158	1	896	12.1
Bob Ferry	79	1657	776	350	.451	255	189	.741	500	129	205	1	889	11.3
Walter Dukes	73	2044	706	286	.405	400	281	.703	1028	139	313	16	853	11.7
Shelly McMillon	78	1636	752	322	.428	201	140	.697	487	98	238	6	784	10.1
Chuck Noble	75	1655	566	196	.346	115	82	.713	180	287	195	4	474	6.3
Jack Moreland	64	1003	477	191	.400	132	86	.652	315	52	174	3	468	7.3
Willie Jones	35	452	216	78	.361	63	40	.635	94	63	90	2	196	5.6
Archie Dees	28	308	135	53	.393	47	39	.830	94	17	50	0	145	5.2

LOS ANGELES

Player	G.	Minutes	FG Att.	FG Made	FG Pct.	FT Att.	FT Made	FT Pct.	Re-b'nd	As-sist	Per. Fls.	Disq.	Tot. Pts.	Avg. Pts.
Elgin Baylor	73	3133	2166	931	.430	863	676	.783	1447	371	279	1	2538	34.8
Jerry West	79	2797	1264	529	.419	497	331	.666	611	333	213	1	1389	17.6
Rudy LaRusso	79	2593	992	416	.419	409	323	.790	781	135	280	8	1155	14.6
Rod Hundley	79	2179	921	323	.351	296	223	.753	289	350	144	0	869	11.0
Frank Selvy	77	2153	767	311	.405	279	210	.753	299	246	219	3	832	10.8
Tom Hawkins	78	1846	719	310	.431	235	140	.596	479	88	209	2	760	9.7
James Krebs	75	1655	692	271	.392	93	75	.806	456	68	223	2	617	8.2
Ray Felix	78	1510	508	189	.372	193	135	.699	539	37	302	12	513	6.6
Bob Leonard	55	600	207	61	.295	100	71	.710	70	81	70	0	193	3.5
Howard Jolliff	46	352	141	46	.326	23	11	.478	141	16	53	0	103	2.2
Ron Johnson*	14	92	43	13	.302	17	11	.647	29	2	10	0	37	2.6
Gary Alcorn	20	174	40	12	.300	8	7	.875	50	2	47	1	31	1.6

*Johnson-6 Detroit, 8 Los Angeles.

NEW YORK

Player	G.	Minutes	FG Att.	FG Made	FG Pct.	FT Att.	FT Made	FT Pct.	Re-b'nd	As-sist	Per. Fls.	Disq.	Tot. Pts.	Avg. Pts.
Willie Naulls	79	2976	1723	737	.428	456	372	.816	1055	191	268	5	1846	23.4
Richie Guerin	79	3023	1545	612	.396	626	496	.792	628	503	310	3	1720	21.8
Dick Garmaker	71	2238	943	415	.440	358	275	.768	277	220	240	2	1105	15.6
Phil Jordon*	72	2064	932	360	.386	297	208	.700	674	181	273	5	928	11.7
John Green	52	1784	758	326	.430	278	145	.522	828	97	194	3	797	10.2
Kenny Sears	52	1396	568	241	.424	325	268	.825	293	102	165	6	750	14.4
Charlie Tyra	59	1404	549	199	.362	173	120	.694	394	82	164	5	518	8.8
Bob McNeill	75	1387	427	166	.389	126	105	.833	123	238	148	2	437	5.8
David Budd	61	1075	361	136	.432	134	87	.649	297	45	171	2	399	6.5
Jim Palmer	55	688	310	125	.403	65	44	.677	179	30	128	0	294	5.3
Darrall Imhoff	62	994	310	122	.394	96	49	.510	296	51	143	2	293	4.7
Phil Rollins	61	816	293	109	.372	88	58	.659	97	123	121	1	276	4.5
Carl Braun	15	218	79	37	.468	14	11	.786	31	48	29	0	85	5.7
Jack George	16	268	93	31	.333	30	20	.667	32	39	37	0	82	5.1
Whitey Bell	5	45	18	7	.389	3	1	.333	7	1	7	0	15	3.0

*Jordan-48 Cincinnati, 31 New York. Rollins-7 St. Louis, 40 New York, 13 Cincinnati.

1960-61 STATISTICS

PHILADELPHIA

Player	G.	Minutes	FG Att.	FG Made	FG Pct.	FT Att.	FT Made	FT Pct.	Re-b'nd	As-sist	Per. Fls.	Disq.	Tot. Pts.	Avg. Pts.
Wilt Chamberlain	79	3773	2457	1251	.509	1054	531	.504	2149	148	130	0	3033	38.4
Paul Arizin	79	2935	1529	650	.425	639	532	.833	681	188	335	11	1832	23.2
Tom Gola	74	2712	940	420	.447	281	210	.747	692	292	321	13	1050	14.2
Guy Rodgers	78	2905	1029	397	.386	300	206	.687	509	677	262	9	1000	12.8
Andy Johnson	79	2000	834	299	.359	275	157	.571	345	205	249	3	755	9.6
Al Attles	77	1544	543	222	.409	162	97	.599	214	174	235	5	541	7.0
Ed Conlin	77	1294	599	216	.361	139	104	.748	262	122	123	1	536	7.0
Joe Graboski	68	1011	507	169	.333	183	127	.694	262	74	148	2	465	6.8
Vern Hatton	54	610	304	97	.319	56	46	.821	92	59	59	0	240	4.4
Joe Ruklick	29	223	120	43	.358	13	8	.615	62	10	38	0	94	3.2
Bill Kennedy	7	52	21	4	.190	6	4	.667	8	9	6	0	12	1.7

ST. LOUIS

Player	G.	Minutes	FG Att.	FG Made	FG Pct.	FT Att.	FT Made	FT Pct.	Re-b'nd	As-sist	Per. Fls.	Disq.	Tot. Pts.	Avg. Pts.
Bob Pettit	76	3027	1720	769	.447	804	582	.724	1540	262	217	1	2120	27.9
Cliff Hagan	77	2701	1490	661	.444	467	383	.820	715	381	286	9	1705	22.1
Clyde Lovellette	67	2111	1321	599	.453	329	273	.830	677	172	248	4	1471	22.0
Len Wilkens	75	1898	783	333	.425	300	214	.713	335	212	215	5	880	11.7
Sihugo Green	76	1968	718	263	.366	247	174	.704	380	258	234	2	700	9.2
John McCarthy	79	2519	746	266	.357	226	122	.540	325	430	272	8	654	8.3
Larry Foust	68	1208	489	194	.397	208	164	.788	389	77	185	0	552	8.1
Woody Sauldsberry	69	1491	768	230	.299	100	56	.560	491	74	197	3	516	7.5
Al Ferrari	63	1031	328	117	.357	116	95	.819	115	143	157	4	329	5.2
Fred LaCour	55	722	295	123	.417	84	63	.750	'178	84	73	0	309	5.6
Dave Piontek	29	254	96	47	.490	31	16	.516	68	19	31	0	110	3.8

SYRACUSE

Player	G.	Minutes	FG Att.	FG Made	FG Pct.	FT Att.	FT Made	FT Pct.	Re-b'nd	As-sist	Per. Fls.	Disq.	Tot. Pts.	Avg. Pts.
Dolph Schayes	79	3007	1595	594	.372	783	680	.868	960	296	296	9	1868	23.6
Hal Greer	79	2763	1381	623	.451	394	305	.774	455	302	242	0	1551	19.6
Dick Barnett	78	2070	1194	540	.452	337	240	.712	283	218	169	0	1320	16.9
Dave Gambee	79	2090	947	397	.419	352	291	.827	581	101	276	6	1085	13.7
Larry Costello	75	2167	844	407	.482	338	270	.799	292	413	286	9	1084	14.5
John Kerr	79	2676	1056	419	.397	299	218	.729	951	199	230	4	1056	13.4
Barney Cable	75	1642	574	266	.463	108	73	.676	469	85	246	1	605	8.1
Swede Halbrook	79	1131	463	155	.335	140	76	.543	550	31	262	9	386	4.9
Joe Roberts	68	800	351	130	.370	104	62	.596	243	43	125	0	322	4.7
Al Bianchi	52	667	342	118	.345	87	60	.690	105	93	137	5	296	5.7
Ernie Beck*	10	82	29	10	.345	7	6	.857	23	15	10	0	26	2.6
Cal Ramsey	2	27	11	2	.182	4	2	.500	7	3	7	0	6	3.0

*Beck–7 St. Louis. 3 Syracuse

1960-61 CHAMPIONSHIP PLAYOFF RESULTS

EASTERN DIVISION SEMI-FINALS
Syracuse 3, Philadelphia 0
Mar. 14–Syracuse 115 at Philadelphia 107
Mar. 16–Philadelphia 115 at Syracuse 115
Mar. 18–Syracuse 106 at Philadelphia 103

EASTERN DIVISION FINALS
Boston 4, Syracuse 1
Mar. 19–Syracuse 115 at Boston 128
Mar. 21–Boston 98 at Syracuse 115
Mar. 23–Syracuse 110 at Boston 133
Mar. 25–Boston 120 at Syracuse 107
Mar. 26–Syracuse 101 at Boston 123

WESTERN DIVISION SEMI-FINALS
Los Angeles 3, Detroit 2
Mar. 14–Detroit 102 at Los Angeles 120
Mar. 15–Detroit 118 at Los Angeles 120
Mar. 17–Los Angeles 113 at Detroit 124
Mar. 18–Los Angeles 114 at Detroit 123
Mar. 19–Detroit 120 at Los Angeles 137

WESTERN DIVISION FINALS
St. Louis 4, Los Angeles 3
Mar. 21–Los Angeles 122 at St. Louis 118
Mar. 22–Los Angeles 106 at St. Louis 121
Mar. 24–St. Louis 112 at Los Angeles 118
Mar. 25–St. Louis 118 at Los Angeles 117
Mar. 27–Los Angeles 121 at St. Louis 112
Mar. 29–St. Louis 114 at Los Angeles *113
Apr. 1–Los Angeles 103 at St. Louis 105
*–Denotes overtime period.

CHAMPIONSHIP SERIES
Boston 4, St. Louis 1
Apr. 2–St. Louis 95 at Boston 129
Apr. 5–St. Louis 108 at Boston 116
Apr. 8–Boston 120 at St. Louis 124
Apr. 9–Boston 119 at St. Louis 104
Apr. 11–St. Louis 112 at Boston 121

TEAM PLAYOFF STATISTICS

Team	G.	W.	L.	Pct.	FGA	FGM	Pct.	FTA	FTM	Pct.	Reb.	Ast.	PF	Disq.	Scoring Average For	Agst.	Diff.
Boston	10	8	2	.800	1092	451	.413	422	305	.723	821	247	290	4	120.7	109.1	11.6
Los Angeles	12	6	6	.500	1224	526	.430	481	359	.746	876	289	330	4	117.6	115.6	2.0
Syracuse	8	4	4	.500	855	317	.371	313	250	.799	604	160	257	9	110.5	118.2	–7.7
St. Louis	12	5	7	.417	1300	517	.398	427	309	.724	815	288	331	8	111.9	117.1	–6.2
Detroit	5	2	3	.400	536	218	.407	202	151	.748	327	131	144	6	117.4	122.2	–4.8
Philadelphia	3	0	3	.000	319	119	.373	139	86	.619	210	62	86	6	108.0	112.0	–4.0

1959-60 STATISTICS

1959-60 CHAMPION BOSTON CELTICS

Seated (left to right): Frank Ramsey, Bob Cousy, Coach Red Auerbach, President Walter Brown, Treasurer Lou Pieri, K. C. Jones, Bill Sharman; standing: Gene Guarilia, Tom Heinsohn, John Richter, Bill Russell, Gene Conley, Jim Loscutoff, Sam Jones, Trainer Buddy LeRoux.

FINAL STANDINGS AND TEAM FIGURES

EASTERN DIVISION

Team	W.	L.	FGA	FGM	Pct.	FTA	FTM	Pct.	Reb.	Ast.	PF	Disq.	Pts.	Avg.	Opp.
Boston	59	16	8971	3744	.417	2519	1849	.734	6014	1849	1856	42	9337	124.5	8713
Philadelphia	49	26	8678	3549	.409	2686	1797	.669	5916	1796	1715	21	8895	118.6	8730
Syracuse	45	30	8232	3406	.414	2662	2105	.791	5406	1676	1939	39	8917	118.9	8730
New York	27	48	8153	3429	.415	2539	1942	.765	5251	1667	1940	32	8800	117.3	8973

WESTERN DIVISION

Team	W.	L.	FGA	FGM	Pct.	FTA	FTM	Pct.	Reb.	Ast.	PF	Disq.	Pts.	Avg.	Opp.
St. Louis	46	29	7580	3179	.419	2885	2148	.745	5343	1881	1995	40	8506	113.4	8303
Detroit	30	45	7920	3146	.397	2847	2075	.729	5491	1472	1983	49	8367	111.6	8624
Minneapolis	25	50	7884	3040	.386	2691	1965	.730	5432	1444	1813	37	8045	107.3	8352
Cincinnati	19	56	7786	3210	.412	2672	1913	.716	5251	1747	2097	38	8333	111.1	8807

TOP 25 SCORERS

Player–Team	G.	Min.	FGA	FGM	Pct.	FTA	FTM	Pct.	Reb.	Ast.	PF	Disq.	Pts.	Avg.
Wilt Chamberlain, Phila.	72	3338	2311	1065	.461	991	577	.582	1941	168	150	0	2707	37.6
Jack Twyman, Cincinnati	75	3023	2063	870	.422	762	598	.785	664	260	275	10	2338	31.2
Elgin Baylor, Minneapolis	70	2873	1781	755	.424	770	564	.732	1150	243	234	2	2074	29.6
Bob Pettit, St. Louis	72	2896	1526	669	.438	722	544	.753	1221	257	204	0	1882	26.1
Cliff Hagan, St. Louis	75	2798	1549	719	.464	524	421	.803	803	299	270	4	1859	24.8
Gene Shue, Detroit	75	3338	1501	620	.413	541	472	.872	409	295	146	2	1712	22.8
Dolph Schayes, Syracuse	75	2741	1440	578	.401	597	533	.893	959	256	263	10	1689	22.5

1959-60 STATISTICS

Player—Team	G.	Min.	FGA	FGM	Pct.	FTA	FTM	Pct.	Reb.	Ast.	PF	Disq.	Pts.	Avg.
Tom Heinsohn, Boston	75	2420	1590	673	.423	386	283	.734	794	171	275	8	1629	21.7
Richie Guerin, New York	74	2429	1379	579	.420	591	457	.773	505	468	242	3	1615	21.8
Paul Arizin, Philadelphia	72	2618	1400	593	.424	526	420	.798	621	165	263	6	1606	22.3
George Yardley, Syracuse	73	2402	1205	546	.453	467	381	.816	579	122	227	3	1473	20.2
Bob Cousy, Boston	75	2588	1481	568	.384	403	319	.791	352	715	146	2	1455	19.4
Clyde Lovellette, St. Louis	68	1953	1174	550	.408	385	316	.821	721	127	248	6	1416	20.8
Willie Naulls, New York	65	2250	1286	551	.428	342	286	.836	921	138	214	4	1388	21.4
Bill Sharman, Boston	71	1916	1225	559	.456	291	252	.866	262	144	154	2	1370	19.3
Bill Russell, Boston	74	3146	1189	555	.467	392	240	.612	1778	277	210	0	1350	18.2
Bailey Howell, Detroit	72	2346	1119	510	.456	422	312	.739	790	63	282	13	1332	17.8
Kenny Sears, New York	64	2099	863	412	.477	418	363	.868	876	127	191	2	1187	18.5
Tom Gola, Philadelphia	75	2870	983	426	.433	340	270	.794	779	409	311	9	1122	15.0
Frank Ramsey, Boston	73	2009	1062	422	.397	347	273	.787	506	137	251	10	1117	15.3
John Kerr, Syracuse	75	2372	1111	436	.392	310	233	.752	913	167	207	4	1105	14.7
Phil Jordon, Cincinnati	75	2066	970	381	.393	338	242	.716	624	207	227	7	1004	13.4
Walter Dukes, Detroit	66	2140	871	314	.361	508	376	.740	883	80	310	20	1004	15.2
Larry Costello, Syracuse	71	2469	822	372	.453	289	249	.861	338	449	234	4	993	14.0
Rudy LaRusso, Minneapolis	71	2092	913	355	.389	357	265	.742	679	83	222	8	975	13.7

FIELD GOAL PERCENTAGE LEADERS
(Minimum 190 FGM)

	FGA	FGM	Pct.
Ken Sears, New York	863	412	.477
Hal Greer, Syracuse	815	388	.476
Clyde Lovellette, St. Louis	1174	550	.468
Bill Russell, Boston	1189	555	.467
Cliff Hagan, St. Louis	1549	719	.464
Wilt Chamberlain, Philadelphia	2311	1065	.461
Bill Sharman, Boston	1225	559	.456
Bailey Howell, Detroit	1119	510	.456
Sam Jones, Boston	782	355	.454
George Yardley, Syracuse	1205	546	.453

FREE THROW PERCENTAGE LEADERS
(Minimum 185 FTM)

	FTA	FTM	Pct.
Dolph Schayes, Syracuse	597	533	.893
Gene Shue, Detroit	541	472	.872
Ken Sears, New York	418	363	.868
Bill Sharman, Boston	291	252	.866
Larry Costello, Syracuse	290	249	.862
Willie Naulls, New York	342	286	.836
Clyde Lovellette, St. Louis	385	316	.821
George Yardley, Syracuse	467	381	.816
Cliff Hagan, St. Louis	524	421	.803
Paul Arizin, Philadelphia	526	420	.798

LEADERS IN REBOUNDS

	G.	No.	Avg.
Wilt Chamberlain, Philadelphia	72	1941	27.0
Bill Russell, Boston	74	1778	24.0
Bob Pettit, St. Louis	72	1221	17.0
Elgin Baylor, Minneapolis	70	1150	16.4
Dolph Schayes, Syracuse	75	959	12.8
Willie Naulls, New York	65	921	14.2
John Kerr, Syracuse	75	913	12.2
Walter Dukes, Detroit	66	883	13.4
Ken Sears, New York	64	876	13.7
Cliff Hagan, St. Louis	75	803	10.7

LEADERS IN ASSISTS

	G.	No.	Avg.
Bob Cousy, Boston	75	715	9.5
Guy Rodgers, Philadelphia	68	482	7.1
Richie Guerin, New York	74	468	6.3
Larry Costello, Syracuse	71	449	6.3
Tom Gola, Philadelphia	75	409	5.5
Dick McGuire, Detroit	68	358	5.3
Rod Hundley, Minneapolis	73	338	4.6
Slater Martin, St. Louis	64	330	5.2
Jack McCarthy, St. Louis	75	328	4.4
Cliff Hagan, St. Louis	75	299	4.0

INTER-CLUB RECORDS—HOME, AWAY AND NEUTRAL COURT

EASTERN DIVISION

	Bos.	Phil.	Syr.	N.Y.	St.L.	Det.	Minn.	Cin.	Home	Away	Neutral	W.	L.
Boston	..	8	8	12	6	9	8	8	25- 2	23- 9	11- 5	59- 16
Philadelphia	5	..	8	9	4	7	7	9	22- 6	12- 19	15- 1	49- 26
Syracuse	5	5	..	11	4	5	8	7	26- 4	11- 19	8- 7	45- 30
New York	1	4	2	..	3	5	5	7	13- 18	9- 19	5- 11	27- 48

WESTERN DIVISION

St. Louis	3	5	5	6	..	8	10	9	28- 5	12- 20	6- 4	46- 29
Detroit	0	2	4	4	5	..	7	8	17- 14	6- 21	7- 10	30- 45
Minneapolis	1	2	1	4	3	6	..	8	9- 13	9- 22	7- 15	25- 50
Cincinnati	1	0	2	2	4	5	5	..	9- 22	2- 20	8- 14	19- 56

INDIVIDUAL STATISTICS
BOSTON

Player	G.	Minutes	FG Att.	FG Made	FG Pct.	FT Att.	FT Made	FT Pct.	Re-b'nd	As-sist	Per. Fls.	Disq.	Tot. Pts.	Avg. Pts.
Tom Heinsohn	75	2420	1590	673	.423	386	283	.733	794	171	275	8	1629	21.7
Bob Cousy	75	2588	1481	568	.384	403	319	.792	352	715	146	2	1455	19.4
Bill Sharman	71	1916	1225	559	.456	291	252	.866	262	144	154	2	1370	19.3
Bill Russell	74	3146	1189	555	.467	392	240	.612	1778	277	210	0	1350	18.2
Frank Ramsey	73	2009	1062	422	.397	347	273	.787	506	137	251	10	1117	15.3
Sam Jones	74	1512	782	355	.454	220	168	.764	375	125	101	2	878	11.9
Maurice King	1	19	8	5	.625	1	0	.000	4	2	3	0	10	10.0

1959-60 STATISTICS

Player	G.	Minutes	FG Att.	FG Made	FG Pct.	FT Att.	FT Made	FT Pct.	Re-b'nd	As-sist	Per. Fls.	Disq.	Tot. Pts.	Avg. Pts.
Gene Conley	71	1330	539	201	.373	114	76	.667	590	32	270	10	478	6.7
K. C. Jones	74	1274	404	169	.408	170	128	.753	199	189	109	1	466	6.3
Jim Loscutoff	28	536	205	66	.322	36	22	.611	108	12	108	6	154	5.5
John Richter	66	808	332	113	.340	117	59	.504	312	27	158	1	285	4.3
Gene Guarilia	48	423	154	58	.377	41	29	.707	85	18	57	1	145	3.0

CINCINNATI

Player	G.	Minutes	FG Att.	FG Made	FG Pct.	FT Att.	FT Made	FT Pct.	Re-b'nd	As-sist	Per. Fls.	Disq.	Tot. Pts.	Avg. Pts.
Jack Twyman	75	3023	2063	870	.422	762	598	.785	664	260	275	10	2338	31.2
Phil Jordon	75	2066	970	381	.393	338	242	.716	624	207	227	7	1004	13.4
Wayne Embry	73	1594	690	303	.439	325	167	.514	692	83	226	1	773	10.6
Arlen Bockhorn	75	2103	812	323	.398	194	145	.747	382	256	249	8	791	10.5
Win Wilfong	72	1992	764	283	.370	207	161	.778	352	265	229	1	727	10.1
Hub Reed*	71	1820	601	270	.449	184	134	.728	614	69	230	6	674	9.5
Med Park	74	1849	582	226	.388	260	189	.727	301	214	180	2	641	8.7
Phil Rollins	72	1235	386	158	.409	127	77	.606	180	233	150	1	393	5.5
Dave Gambee*	61	656	291	117	.402	106	69	.651	229	38	83	1	303	5.0
Larry Staverman	49	479	149	70	.470	64	47	.734	180	36	98	0	187	3.8
Wayne Stevens	8	49	19	3	.158	10	7	.700	16	4	4	0	13	1.6

*Gambee—42 St. Louis, 19 Cincinnati; Reed—2 St. Louis, 69 Cincinnati.

DETROIT

Player	G.	Minutes	FG Att.	FG Made	FG Pct.	FT Att.	FT Made	FT Pct.	Re-b'nd	As-sist	Per. Fls.	Disq.	Tot. Pts.	Avg. Pts.
Gene Shue	75	3338	1501	620	.413	541	472	.872	409	295	146	2	1712	22.8
Bailey Howell	75	2346	1119	510	.456	422	312	.739	790	63	282	13	1332	17.8
Walter Dukes	66	2140	871	314	.361	508	376	.740	883	80	310	20	1004	15.2
Chuck Noble	58	1621	774	276	.357	138	101	.732	201	265	172	2	653	11.3
Ed Conlin	70	1636	831	300	.361	238	181	.761	346	126	158	2	781	11.2
Archie Dees	73	1244	617	271	.439	204	165	.809	397	43	188	3	707	9.7
Shellie McMillon	75	1416	627	267	.426	199	132	.663	431	49	198	3	666	8.9
Earl Lloyd	68	1610	665	237	.356	160	128	.800	322	89	226	1	602	8.9
Dick McGuire	68	1466	402	179	.445	201	124	.617	264	358	112	0	482	7.1
Billy Kenville	25	365	131	47	.359	41	33	.805	71	46	31	0	127	5.1
Tony Windis	9	193	60	16	.267	6	4	.667	47	32	20	0	36	4.0
Gary Alcorn	58	670	312	91	.292	84	48	.571	279	22	123	4	230	4.0

MINNEAPOLIS

Player	G.	Minutes	FG Att.	FG Made	FG Pct.	FT Att.	FT Made	FT Pct.	Re-b'nd	As-sist	Per. Fls.	Disq.	Tot. Pts.	Avg. Pts.
Elgin Baylor	70	2873	1781	755	.424	770	564	.732	1150	243	234	2	2074	29.6
Rudy LaRusso	71	2092	913	355	.389	357	265	.742	679	83	222	8	975	13.7
Rod Hundley	73	2279	1019	365	.358	273	203	.744	390	338	194	0	933	12.8
Frank Selvy*	62	1308	521	205	.393	208	153	.736	175	111	101	1	563	9.1
Bob Leonard	73	2074	717	231	.322	193	136	.705	245	252	171	3	598	8.2
Tom Hawkins	69	1467	579	220	.380	164	106	.646	428	54	188	3	546	7.9
Jim Krebs	75	1269	605	237	.392	136	98	.721	327	38	210	2	572	7.6
Ray Felix*	47	883	355	136	.383	112	70	.625	338	23	177	5	342	7.3
Ron Sobie*	16	234	108	37	.343	37	31	.838	48	21	32	0	105	6.6
Ed Fleming	27	413	141	59	.418	69	53	.768	87	38	46	0	171	6.3
Steve Hamilton	15	247	77	29	.377	23	18	.783	58	7	39	1	76	5.1
Charlie Share*	41	651	151	59	.391	80	53	.663	221	62	142	9	171	4.2
Boo Ellis	46	671	185	64	.346	76	51	.671	236	27	64	2	179	3.9
Bob Smith	10	130	54	13	.241	16	11	.688	33	14	10	0	37	3.7
Nick Mantis	10	71	39	10	.256	2	1	.500	6	9	8	0	21	2.1

*Felix—16 New York, 31 Minneapolis; Selvy—19 Syracuse, 43 Minneapolis; Share—38 St. Louis, 3 Minneapolis; Sobie—15 New York, 1 Minneapolis.

NEW YORK

Player	G.	Minutes	FG Att.	FG Made	FG Pct.	FT Att.	FT Made	FT Pct.	Re-b'nd	As-sist	Per. Fls.	Disq.	Tot. Pts.	Avg. Pts.
Richie Guerin	74	2420	1379	579	.420	591	457	.773	505	468	242	3	1615	21.8
Willie Naulls	65	2250	1286	551	.428	342	286	.836	921	138	214	4	1388	21.4
Kenny Sears	64	2099	863	412	.477	418	363	.868	876	127	191	2	1187	18.5
Carl Braun	74	1514	659	285	.432	154	129	.838	168	270	127	0	699	12.9
Charlie Tyra	70	2033	952	406	.426	189	133	.704	598	80	258	8	945	12.8
Dick Garmaker*	70	1932	815	323	.396	285	203	.772	313	206	186	4	849	12.1
Jack George	69	1604	620	250	.385	202	155	.767	197	240	148	1	655	9.5
Cal Ramsey	11	195	96	39	.406	33	19	.576	66	9	25	1	97	8.8
Jim Palmer*	74	1482	574	246	.429	174	119	.684	389	70	224	6	611	8.3
Mike Farmer	67	1536	568	212	.373	83	70	.843	385	57	130	1	494	7.4

1959-60 STATISTICS

Player	G.	Min-utes	FG Att.	FG Made	FG Pct.	FT Att.	FT Made	FT Pct.	Re-b'nd	As-sist	Per. Fls.	Disq.	Tot. Pts.	Avg. Pts.
Johnny Green	69	1232	468	209	.447	155	63	.406	539	52	195	3	481	7.0
Whitey Bell	31	449	185	70	.378	43	28	.651	57	35	59	0	168	5.4
Bob Anderegg	33	373	143	55	.385	42	23	.548	69	29	32	0	133	4.0
Brendan McCann	4	29	10	4	.100	3	3	1.000	4	10	2	0	5	1.3

*Garmaker—44 Minneapolis, 26 New York; Ramsey—4 St. Louis, 7 New York; Palmer—20 Cincinnati, 54 New York.

PHILADELPHIA

Player	G.	Min-utes	FG Att.	FG Made	FG Pct.	FT Att.	FT Made	FT Pct.	Re-b'nd	As-sist	Per. Fls.	Disq.	Tot. Pts.	Avg. Pts.
Wilt Chamberlain	72	3338	2311	1065	.461	991	577	.582	1941	168	150	0	2707	37.6
Paul Arizin	72	2618	1400	593	.423	526	420	.798	621	165	263	6	1606	22.3
Tom Gola	75	2870	983	426	.433	340	270	.794	779	409	311	9	1122	15.0
Guy Rodgers	68	2483	870	338	.389	181	111	.613	391	482	196	3	787	11.6
Woody Sauldsberry	71	1848	974	325	.334	103	55	.534	447	112	203	2	705	9.9
Andy Johnson	75	1421	648	245	.378	208	125	.601	282	152	196	5	615	8.2
Joe Graboski	73	1269	583	217	.372	174	131	.753	358	111	147	1	565	7.7
Joe Ruklick	39	384	214	85	.397	36	26	.722	137	24	70	0	196	5.0
Vern Hatton	67	1049	356	127	.357	87	53	.609	159	82	61	0	307	4.6
Ernie Beck	66	809	294	114	.388	32	27	.844	127	72	90	0	255	3.9
Guy Sparrow	11	80	45	14	.311	8	2	.250	23	6	20	0	30	2.7

ST. LOUIS

Player	G.	Min-utes	FG Att.	FG Made	FG Pct.	FT Att.	FT Made	FT Pct.	Re-b'nd	As-sist	Per. Fls.	Disq.	Tot. Pts.	Avg. Pts.
Bob Pettit	72	2896	1526	669	.438	722	544	.753	1221	257	204	0	1882	26.1
Cliff Hagan	75	2798	1549	719	.464	524	421	.803	803	299	270	4	1859	24.8
Clyde Lovellette	68	1953	1174	550	.468	385	316	.821	721	127	248	6	1416	20.8
Larry Foust*	71	1964	766	312	.407	320	253	.791	621	96	241	7	877	12.2
Dave Piontek*	77	1833	728	292	.401	202	129	.639	461	118	211	5	713	9.3
Al Ferrari	71	1567	523	216	.413	225	176	.782	162	188	205	7	608	8.6
John McCarthy	75	2383	730	240	.329	226	149	.659	301	328	233	3	629	8.4
Slater Martin	75	1756	383	142	.371	155	113	.729	187	330	174	2	397	6.2
Sihugo Green	70	1354	427	159	.372	175	111	.634	257	133	150	3	429	6.1
Bob Ferry	62	875	338	144	.426	119	76	.639	233	40	132	2	364	5.9
Jack McMahon	25	334	93	33	.355	29	16	.552	24	49	42	1	82	3.3

*Foust—47 Minneapolis, 25 St. Louis; Piontek—52 Cincinnati, 25 St. Louis.

SYRACUSE

Player	G.	Min-utes	FG Att.	FG Made	FG Pct.	FT Att.	FT Made	FT Pct.	Re-b'nd	As-sist	Per. Fls.	Disq.	Tot. Pts.	Avg. Pts.
Dolph Schayes	75	2741	1440	578	.401	597	533	.893	959	256	263	10	1689	22.5
George Yardley	73	2402	1205	546	.453	467	381	.816	579	122	227	3	1473	20.2
John Kerr	75	2372	1111	436	.392	310	233	.752	913	167	207	4	1105	14.7
Larry Costello	71	2469	822	372	.453	289	249	.862	388	449	234	4	993	14.0
Hal Greer	70	1979	815	388	.476	189	148	.783	303	188	208	4	924	13.2
Dick Barnett	57	1235	701	289	.412	180	128	.711	155	160	98	0	706	12.4
Bob Hopkins	75	1616	660	257	.389	174	136	.782	465	55	193	4	650	8.7
Al Bianchi	69	1256	576	211	.366	155	109	.703	179	169	231	5	531	7.7
Connie Dierking	71	1119	526	192	.365	188	108	.574	456	54	168	4	492	6.9
Barney Cable*	57	715	290	109	.376	67	44	.657	225	39	93	1	262	4.6
Togo Palazzi	7	70	41	13	.317	8	4	.500	14	3	7	0	30	4.3
Jim Ray	4	21	6	1	.167	0	0	.000	0	2	3	0	2	0.5
Paul Seymour	4	7	4	0	.000	0	0	.000	1	0	1	0	0	0.0

*Cable—7 Detroit, 50 Syracuse.

1959-60 CHAMPIONSHIP PLAYOFF RESULTS

EASTERN DIVISION SEMI-FINALS
Philadelphia 2, Syracuse 1

Mar. 11—Syracuse 92 at Philadelphia..............115
Mar. 13—Philadelphia 119 at Syracuse............125
Mar. 14—Syracuse 112 at Philadelphia............132

EASTERN DIVISION FINALS
Boston 4, Philadelphia 2

Mar. 16—Philadelphia 105 at Boston...............111
Mar. 18—Boston 110 at Philadelphia...............115
Mar. 19—Philadelphia 90 at Boston.................120
Mar. 20—Boston 112 at Philadelphia...............104
Mar. 22—Philadelphia 128 at Boston...............107
Mar. 24—Boston 119 at Philadelphia...............117

WESTERN DIVISION SEMI-FINALS
Minneapolis 2, Detroit 0

Mar. 12—Minneapolis 113 at Detroit................112
Mar. 13—Detroit 99 at Minneapolis..................114

WESTERN DIVISION FINALS
St. Louis 4, Minneapolis 3

Mar. 16—Minneapolis 99 at St. Louis...............112
Mar. 17—Minneapolis 120 at St. Louis.............113
Mar. 19—St. Louis 93 at Minneapolis................89
Mar. 20—St. Louis 101 at Minneapolis.............103
Mar. 22—Minneapolis 117 at St. Louis...........*110
Mar. 24—St. Louis 117 at Minneapolis..............96
Mar. 26—Minneapolis 86 at St. Louis................97

CHAMPIONSHIP SERIES
Boston 4, St. Louis 3

Mar. 27—St. Louis 122 at Boston....................140
Mar. 29—St. Louis 113 at Boston....................103
Apr. 2—Boston 102 at St. Louis......................86
Apr. 3—Boston 96 at St. Louis......................106
Apr. 5—St. Louis 102 at Boston....................127
Apr. 7—Boston 102 at St. Louis....................105
Apr. 9—St. Louis 103 at Boston....................122

*—Denotes overtime period.

1958-59 STATISTICS

1958-59 CHAMPION BOSTON CELTICS

Seated (left to right): Gene Conley, Bob Cousy, Coach Red Auerbach, President Walter A. Brown, Bill Sharman, Bill Russell; standing: Trainer Buddy LeRoux, K. C. Jones, Lou Tsioropoulos, Tommy Heinsohn, Ben Swain, Jim Loscutoff, Sam Jones, Frank Ramsey. Inset: Treasurer Lou Pieri.

FINAL STANDINGS AND TEAM FIGURES

EASTERN DIVISION

Team	W.	L.	FGA	FGM	Pct.	FTA	FTM	Pct.	Reb.	Ast.	PF	Disq.	Pts.	Avg.	Opp.
Boston	52	20	8116	3208	.395	2563	1963	.766	5601	1568	1769	46	8379	116.4	7912
New York	40	32	7170	2863	.399	2802	2217	.791	4091	1383	1899	34	7943	110.3	7925
Syracuse	35	37	7490	3050	.407	2642	2046	.775	4900	1340	1961	44	8146	113.1	7855
Philadelphia	32	40	7423	2826	.381	2425	1783	.735	4910	1375	1776	36	7435	103.3	7651

WESTERN DIVISION

Team	W.	L.	FGA	FGM	Pct.	FTA	FTM	Pct.	Reb.	Ast.	PF	Disq.	Pts.	Avg.	Opp.
St. Louis	49	23	7015	2879	.410	2757	2072	.752	5045	1567	1937	35	7830	108.8	7564
Minneapolis	33	39	7084	2779	.392	2718	2071	.762	5149	1373	1874	27	7629	106.0	7725
Detroit	28	44	7305	2811	.385	2627	1943	.740	4860	1317	1881	58	7656	105.1	7676
Cincinnati	19	53	7340	2854	.389	2375	1713	.721	4887	1369	1855	36	7421	103.1	8066

TOP 25 SCORERS

Player–Team	G.	Min.	FGA	FGM	Pct.	FTA	FTM	Pct.	Reb.	Ast.	PF	Disq.	Pts.	Avg.
Bob Pettit, St. Louis	72	2873	1640	719	.438	879	667	.758	1182	221	200	3	2105	29.2
Jack Twyman, Cincinnati	72	2713	1691	710	.420	558	437	.783	653	209	277	6	1857	25.8
Paul Arizin, Philadelphia	70	2799	1466	632	.431	722	587	.813	637	119	264	7	1851	26.4
Elgin Baylor, Minneapolis	70	2855	1482	605	.408	685	532	.777	1050	287	170	4	1742	24.9
Cliff Hagan, St. Louis	72	2702	1417	646	.456	536	415	.774	783	245	275	10	1707	23.7
Dolph Schayes, Syracuse	72	2645	1304	504	.387	609	526	.864	962	178	280	9	1534	21.3
Ken Sears, New York	71	2498	1002	491	.490	588	506	.861	658	136	237	6	1488	21.0

1958-59 STATISTICS

Player–Team	G.	Min.	FGA	FGM	Pct.	FTA	FTM	Pct.	Reb.	Ast.	PF	Disq.	Pts.	Avg.
Bill Sharman, Boston	72	2382	1377	562	.408	367	342	.932	292	179	173	1	1466	20.4
Bob Cousy, Boston	65	2403	1260	484	.384	385	329	.855	359	557	135	0	1297	20.0
Richie Guerin, New York	71	2558	1046	443	.424	505	405	.802	518	364	255	1	1291	18.2
John Kerr, Syracuse	72	2671	1139	502	.441	367	281	.706	1008	142	183	1	1285	17.8
Gene Shue, Detroit	72	2745	1197	464	.388	421	338	.803	335	231	129	1	1266	17.6
Tom Heinsohn, Boston	66	2089	1192	465	.390	391	312	.798	638	164	271	11	1242	18.8
George Yardley, Det.-Syr.	61	1839	1042	446	.428	407	317	.779	431	65	159	2	1209	19.8
Bill Russell, Boston	70	2979	997	456	.457	428	256	.598	1612	222	161	3	1168	16.7
Woody Sauldsberry, Phila.	72	2473	1380	501	.363	176	110	.625	826	71	276	12	1112	15.4
Larry Costello, Syracuse	70	2750	948	414	.437	349	280	.802	365	379	263	7	1108	15.8
Frank Ramsey, Boston	72	2013	1013	383	.378	436	341	.782	491	147	266	11	1107	15.4
Willie Naulls, New York	68	2061	1072	405	.378	311	258	.830	723	102	233	8	1068	15.7
Joe Graboski, Philadelphia	72	2482	1116	394	.353	300	270	.750	751	148	249	5	1058	14.7
Phil Jordon, Detroit	72	2058	967	399	.413	303	231	.762	594	83	193	1	1029	14.3
Vern Mikkelsen, Minneapolis	72	2139	904	353	.390	355	286	.806	570	159	246	8	992	13.8
Dick Garmaker, Minneapolis	72	2493	885	350	.395	368	284	.772	325	211	226	3	984	13.7
Walter Dukes, Detroit	72	2338	904	318	.352	452	297	.750	957	64	332	22	933	13.0
Tom Gola, Philadelphia	64	2333	773	310	.401	357	281	.787	710	269	243	1	901	14.1

FIELD GOAL PERCENTAGE LEADERS
(Minimum 230 FGM)

	FGA	FGM	Pct.
Ken Sears, New York	1002	491	.490
Bill Russell, Boston	997	456	.457
Cliff Hagan, St. Louis	1417	646	.456
Hal Greer, Syracuse	679	308	.454
Clyde Lovellette, St. Louis	885	402	.454
John Kerr, Syracuse	1139	502	.441
Bob Pettit, St. Louis	1640	719	.438
Larry Costello, Syracuse	948	414	.437
Sam Jones, Boston	703	305	.434
Paul Arizin, Philadelphia	1466	632	.431

FREE THROW PERCENTAGE LEADERS
(Minimum 190 FTM)

	FTA	FTM	Pct.
Bill Sharman, Boston	367	342	.932
Dolph Schayes, Syracuse	609	526	.864
Ken Sears, New York	588	506	.861
Bob Cousy, Boston	385	329	.855
Willie Naulls, New York	311	258	.830
Clyde Lovellette, St. Louis	250	205	.820
Paul Arizin, Philadelphia	722	587	.813
Vern Mikkelsen, Minneapolis	355	286	.806
Gene Shue, Detroit	421	338	.803
Richie Guerin, New York	505	405	.802
Larry Costello, Syracuse	349	280	.802

LEADERS IN REBOUNDS

	G.	No.	Avg.
Bill Russell, Boston	70	1612	23.0
Bob Pettit, St. Louis	72	1182	16.4
Elgin Baylor, Minneapolis	70	1050	15.0
John Kerr, Syracuse	72	1008	14.0
Dolph Schayes, Syracuse	72	962	13.4
Walter Dukes, Detroit	72	958	13.3
Woody Sauldsberry, Phila.	72	826	11.5
Cliff Hagan, St. Louis	72	783	10.9
Joe Graboski, Philadelphia	72	751	10.4
Willie Naulls, New York	68	723	10.6

LEADERS IN ASSISTS

	G.	No.	Avg.
Bob Cousy, Boston	65	557	8.6
Dick McGuire, Detroit	71	443	6.2
Larry Costello, Syracuse	70	379	5.4
Richie Guerin, New York	71	364	5.1
Carl Braun, New York	72	349	4.8
Slater Martin, St. Louis	71	336	4.7
Jack McMahon, St. Louis	72	298	4.1
Bill Sharman, Boston	72	292	4.1
Elgin Baylor, Minneapolis	70	287	4.1
Tom Gola, Philadelphia	64	269	4.2

INTER-CLUB RECORDS—HOME. AWAY AND NEUTRAL COURT

EASTERN DIVISION

	Bos.	N.Y.	Syr.	Phil.	St.L.	Mpls.	Det.	Cinn.	Home	Away	Neutral	W.	L.
Boston	..	7	7	9	4	9	8	8	26- 4	13- 15	13- 1	52- 20
New York	5	..	9	5	4	5	6	6	21- 9	15- 15	4- 8	40- 32
Syracuse	5	3	..	8	2	4	7	6	19-12	12- 17	4- 8	35- 37
Philadelphia	3	7	4	..	4	3	4	7	17- 9	7- 24	8- 7	32- 40

WESTERN DIVISION

	Bos.	N.Y.	Syr.	Phil.	St.L.	Mpls.	Det.	Cinn.	Home	Away	Neutral	W.	L.
St. Louis	5	5	7	5	..	8	8	11	28- 3	14- 15	7- 5	49- 23
Minneapolis	0	4	5	6	4	..	8	6	15- 7	9- 17	9-15	33- 39
Detroit	1	3	2	5	4	4	..	9	13-17	8- 20	7- 7	28- 44
Cincinnati	1	3	3	2	1	6	3	..	9-19	2- 25	8- 9	19- 53
Total	20	32	37	40	23	39	41	53	148-80	80-148	60-60	288-288

INDIVIDUAL STATISTICS

BOSTON

Player	G.	Minutes	FG Att.	FG Made	FG Pct.	FT Att.	FT Made	FT Pct.	Re-b'nd	As-sist	Per. Fls.	Disq.	Tot. Pts.	Avg. Pts.
Bill Sharman	72	2382	1377	562	.408	367	342	.932	292	179	173	1	1466	20.4
Bob Cousy	65	2403	1260	484	.384	385	329	.855	359	557	135	0	1297	20.0
Tom Heinsohn	66	2089	1192	465	.390	391	312	.798	638	164	271	11	1242	18.8
Bill Russell	70	2979	997	456	.457	428	256	.598	1612	222	161	3	1168	16.7
Frank Ramsey	72	2013	1013	383	.378	436	341	.782	491	147	266	11	1107	15.4
Sam Jones	71	1466	703	305	.434	196	151	.770	428	101	102	0	761	10.7
Jim Loscutoff	66	1680	686	242	.353	84	62	.738	460	60	285	15	546	8.3
Ben Swain	58	708	244	99	.400	110	67	.609	262	29	127	3	265	4.6

1958-59 STATISTICS

Player	G.	Minutes	FG Att.	FG Made	FG Pct.	FT Att.	FT Made	FT Pct.	Rebnd	Assist	Per. Fls.	Disq.	Tot. Pts.	Avg. Pts.
Gene Conley	50	663	262	86	.328	64	37	.578	276	19	117	2	209	4.2
K. C. Jones	49	609	192	65	.339	68	41	.603	127	70	58	0	171	3.5
Lou Tsioropoulos	35	488	190	60	.316	33	25	.758	110	20	74	0	145	4.1

CINCINNATI

Player	G.	Minutes	FG Att.	FG Made	FG Pct.	FT Att.	FT Made	FT Pct.	Rebnd	Assist	Per. Fls.	Disq.	Tot. Pts.	Avg. Pts.
Jack Twyman	72	2713	1691	710	.420	558	437	.783	653	209	277	6	1857	25.8
Dave Piontek	72	1974	813	305	.375	227	156	.687	385	124	162	3	766	10.6
Wayne Embry	66	1590	702	272	.387	314	206	.656	597	96	232	9	750	11.4
Arlen Bockhorn	71	2251	771	294	.381	196	138	.704	460	206	215	6	726	10.2
Jim Palmer	67	1624	633	256	.404	246	178	.724	472	65	211	7	690	10.3
Jack McCarthy	47	1827	657	245	.373	174	116	.667	227	225	158	4	606	12.9
Archie Dees	68	1252	562	200	.356	204	159	.779	339	56	114	0	559	8.2
Med Park	62	1126	361	145	.402	150	115	.767	188	108	93	0	405	6.5
(29 St. L.-33 Cin.)														
Jack Parr	66	1037	307	109	.355	73	44	.603	278	51	138	1	262	4.0
Larry Staverman	57	681	215	101	.470	59	45	.763	218	54	103	0	247	4.3
Phil Rollins	44	691	231	83	.359	90	63	.700	118	102	49	0	229	5.2
(23 Phila.-21 Cin.)														
Tom Marshall	18	272	79	23	.291	29	18	.621	52	27	22	0	64	3.6

DETROIT

Player	G.	Minutes	FG Att.	FG Made	FG Pct.	FT Att.	FT Made	FT Pct.	Rebnd	Assist	Per. Fls.	Disq.	Tot. Pts.	Avg. Pts.
Gene Shue	72	2745	1197	464	.388	421	338	.803	335	231	129	1	1266	17.6
Phil Jordon	72	2058	967	399	.413	303	231	.762	594	83	193	1	1029	14.3
Walter Dukes	72	2338	904	318	.352	452	297	.657	958	64	332	22	933	13.0
Ed Conlin	72	1955	891	329	.369	274	197	.719	394	132	188	6	855	11.9
(57 Syr.-15 Det.)														
Dick McGuire	71	2063	543	232	.427	258	191	.740	285	443	147	1	655	9.2
Earl Lloyd	72	1796	670	234	.349	182	137	.753	500	90	291	15	605	8.4
Joe Holup	68	1502	580	209	.360	200	152	.760	352	73	239	12	570	8.4
Dick Farley	70	1280	448	177	.395	186	137	.737	195	124	130	2	491	7.0
Chuck Noble	65	939	560	189	.338	113	83	.735	115	114	126	0	461	7.1
Shellie McMillon	48	700	289	127	.439	104	55	.529	285	26	110	2	309	6.4
Barney Cable	31	271	126	43	.341	29	23	.793	88	12	30	0	109	3.5

MINNEAPOLIS

Player	G.	Minutes	FG Att.	FG Made	FG Pct.	FT Att.	FT Made	FT Pct.	Rebnd	Assist	Per. Fls.	Disq.	Tot. Pts.	Avg. Pts.
Elgin Baylor	70	2855	1482	605	.408	685	532	.777	1050	287	270	4	1742	24.9
Vern Mikkelsen	72	2139	904	353	.390	355	286	.806	570	159	246	8	992	13.8
Dick Garmaker	72	2493	885	350	.395	368	284	.772	325	211	226	3	984	13.7
Larry Foust	72	1933	771	301	.390	366	280	.765	627	91	233	5	882	12.3
Rod Hundley	71	1664	719	259	.360	278	211	.759	248	200	205	1	729	10.3
Jim Krebs	72	1578	679	271	.399	123	92	.748	491	50	212	4	634	8.8
Bob Leonard	58	1598	552	206	.373	160	120	.750	178	186	119	0	532	9.2
Ed Fleming	71	1132	419	192	.387	190	137	.721	281	89	148	1	461	6.5
Boo Ellis	72	1202	379	163	.430	144	102	.708	380	59	137	0	428	5.9
Steve Hamilton	67	847	294	109	.371	109	74	.679	220	36	144	2	292	4.4

NEW YORK

Player	G.	Minutes	FG Att.	FG Made	FG Pct.	FT Att.	FT Made	FT Pct.	Rebnd	Assist	Per. Fls.	Disq.	Tot. Pts.	Avg. Pts.
Kenny Sears	71	2498	1002	491	.490	588	506	.861	658	136	237	6	1488	21.0
Richie Guerin	71	2558	1046	443	.424	505	405	.802	518	364	255	1	1291	18.2
Willie Naulls	68	2061	1072	405	.378	311	258	.830	723	102	233	8	1068	15.7
Carl Braun	72	1959	684	287	.420	218	180	.826	251	349	178	3	754	10.5
Ray Felix	72	1588	700	260	.371	321	229	.713	569	49	275	9	749	10.4
Frank Selvy	68	1448	605	233	.385	262	201	.767	248	96	113	1	667	9.8
Jack George	71	1881	674	233	.346	203	153	.754	293	221	149	0	619	8.7
(46 Phila.-25 N. Y.)														
Charlie Tyra	69	1586	606	240	.396	190	129	.679	485	33	180	2	609	8.8
Mike Farmer	72	1545	498	176	.353	99	83	.838	315	66	152	1	435	6.0
Ron Sobie	50	857	400	144	.360	133	112	.842	154	78	84	0	400	8.0
Pete Brennan	16	136	43	13	.302	25	14	.560	31	6	15	0	40	2.5
Jerry Bird	11	45	32	12	.375	1	1	1.000	12	1	7	0	25	2.3
Brendan McCann	1	7	3	0	.000	0	0	.000	1	1	1	0	0	0.0

PHILADELPHIA

Player	G.	Minutes	FG Att.	FG Made	FG Pct.	FT Att.	FT Made	FT Pct.	Rebnd	Assist	Per. Fls.	Disq.	Tot. Pts.	Avg. Pts.
Paul Arizin	70	2799	1466	632	.431	722	587	.813	637	119	264	7	1851	26.4
Woody Sauldsberry	72	2743	1380	501	.363	176	110	.625	826	71	276	12	1112	15.4

1958-59 STATISTICS

Player	G.	Min-utes	FG Att	FG Made	FG Pct.	FT Att.	FT Made	FT Pct.	Re-b'nd	As-sist	Per. Fls.	Disq.	Tot. Pts.	Avg. Pts.
Joe Graboski	72	2482	1116	394	.353	360	270	.750	751	148	249	5	1058	14.7
Tom Gola	64	2333	773	310	.401	357	281	.787	710	269	243	7	901	14.1
Guy Rodgers	45	1565	535	211	.394	112	61	.545	281	261	132	1	483	10.7
Andy Johnson	67	1158	466	174	.373	191	115	.602	212	90	176	4	463	6.9
Vern Hatton	64	1109	418	149	.356	105	77	.733	178	70	111	0	375	5.9
(24 Cin.-40 Phila.)														
Ernie Beck	70	1017	418	163	.390	65	43	.662	176	89	124	0	369	5.3
Guy Sparrow	67	842	406	129	.318	138	78	.565	244	67	158	3	336	5.0
(44 N.Y.-23 Phila.)														
Neil Johnston	28	393	164	54	.329	88	69	.784	139	21	50	0	177	6.3
Len Rosenbluth	29	205	145	43	.297	29	21	.724	54	6	20	0	107	3.7

ST. LOUIS

Player	G.	Min-utes	FG Att.	FG Made	FG Pct.	FT Att.	FT Made	FT Pct.	Re-b'nd	As-sist	Per. Fls.	Disq.	Tot. Pts.	Avg. Pts.
Bob Pettit	72	2873	1640	719	.438	879	667	.758	1182	221	200	3	2105	29.2
Cliff Hagan	72	2702	1417	646	.456	536	415	.774	783	245	275	10	1707	23.7
Clyde Lovellette	70	1599	885	402	.454	250	205	.820	605	91	216	1	1009	14.4
Slater Martin	71	2504	706	245	.347	254	197	.776	253	336	230	8	687	9.7
Jack McMahon	72	2235	692	248	.358	156	96	.615	164	298	221	2	592	8.2
Charlie Share	72	1713	381	147	.386	184	139	.755	657	103	261	6	433	6.0
Al Ferrari	72	1189	385	134	.348	199	145	.729	142	122	155	1	413	5.7
Sihugo Green	46	1109	415	146	.352	160	104	.650	252	113	127	1	396	8.6
(20 Cin.-26 St. L.)														
Hub Reed	65	950	317	136	.429	71	53	.746	317	32	171	2	325	5.0
Win Wilfong	63	741	285	99	.347	82	62	.756	121	50	102	0	260	4.1
Ed Macauley	14	196	75	22	.293	35	21	.600	40	13	20	1	65	4.6
Dave Gambee	2	7	1	1	1.000	0	0	.000	2	0	2	0	2	1.0

SYRACUSE

Player	G.	Min-utes	FG Att.	FG Made	FG Pct.	FT Att.	FT Made	FT Pct.	Re-b'nd	As-sist	Per. Fls.	Disq.	Tot. Pts.	Avg. Pts.
Dolph Schayes	72	2645	1304	504	.387	609	526	.864	962	178	280	9	1534	21.3
John Kerr	72	2671	1139	502	.441	367	281	.706	1008	142	183	1	1285	17.8
George Yardley	61	1839	1042	446	.428	407	317	.779	431	65	159	2	1209	19.8
(46 Det.-15 Syr.)														
Larry Costello	70	2750	948	414	.437	349	280	.802	365	379	263	7	1108	15.8
Hal Greer	68	1625	679	308	.454	176	137	.778	196	101	189	1	753	11.1
Al Bianchi	72	1779	756	285	.377	206	149	.723	199	159	260	8	719	10.0
Bob Hopkins	67	1518	611	246	.403	234	176	.752	436	67	181	5	688	10.0
Togo Palazzi	71	1053	612	240	.392	158	115	.728	266	67	174	5	595	8.4
Connie Dierking	64	726	260	105	.362	140	83	.593	233	34	148	2	293	4.6
George Dempsey	57	694	215	92	.428	106	81	.764	160	68	95	0	265	4.6
(23 Phila.-34 Syr.)														
Paul Seymour	21	266	98	32	.327	29	26	.897	39	36	25	0	90	4.3
Tom Kearns	1	7	1	1	1.000	0	0	.000	0	0	1	0	2	2.0

1958-59 CHAMPIONSHIP PLAYOFF RESULTS

EASTERN DIVISION SEMI-FINALS
Syracuse 2, New York 0

Mar. 13—Syracuse 129 at New York 123
Mar. 15—New York 115 at Syracuse 131

EASTERN DIVISION FINALS
Boston 4, Syracuse 3

Mar. 18—Syracuse 109 at Boston 131
Mar. 21—Boston 109 at Syracuse 120
Mar. 22—Syracuse 111 at Boston 133
Mar. 25—Boston 107 at Syracuse 119
Mar. 28—Syracuse 108 at Boston 129
Mar. 29—Boston 121 at Syracuse 133
Apr. 1—Syracuse 125 at Boston 130

WESTERN DIVISION SEMI-FINALS
Minneapolis 2, Detroit 1

Mar. 14—Detroit 89 at Minneapolis 92
Mar. 15—Minneapolis 103 at Detroit 117
Mar. 18—Detroit 102 at Minneapolis 129

WESTERN DIVISION FINALS
Minneapolis 4, St. Louis 2

Mar. 21—Minneapolis 90 at St. Louis 124
Mar. 22—St. Louis 98 at Minneapolis 106
Mar. 24—Minneapolis 97 at St. Louis 127
Mar. 26—St. Louis 98 at Minneapolis 108
Mar. 28—Minneapolis 98 at St. Louis *97
Mar. 29—St. Louis 104 at Minneapolis 106
*—Denotes overtime period.

CHAMPIONSHIP SERIES
Boston 4, Minneapolis 0

Apr. 4—Minneapolis 115 at Boston 118
Apr. 5—Minneapolis 108 at Boston 128
Apr. 7—Boston 123, Mpls. at St. Paul 110
Apr. 9—Boston 118 at Minneapolis 113
*—Denotes overtime period.

TEAM PLAYOFF STATISTICS

Team	G.	W.	L.	Pct.	FGA	FGM	Pct.	FTA	FTM	Pct.	Reb.	Ast.	PF	Disq.	For	Agst.	Scoring Average Diff.
Boston	11	8	3	.727	1298	516	.397	437	326	.746	907	299	287	8	123.3	115.5	7.8
Syracuse	9	5	4	.556	946	379	.401	386	327	.847	639	206	257	9	120.6	123.0	−2.4
Minneapolis	13	6	7	.462	1313	514	.391	442	347	.785	837	252	366	7	105.8	111.0	−5.2
St. Louis	6	2	4	.333	547	235	.430	241	178	.739	391	114	161	5	108.0	100.8	7.2
Detroit	3	1	2	.333	277	111	.401	107	86	.804	180	55	90	2	102.7	108.0	−5.3
New York	2	0	2	.000	248	90	.363	76	58	.763	155	43	70	4	119.0	130.0	−11.0

1957-58 STATISTICS

1957-58 CHAMPION ST. LOUIS HAWKS

Front Row (left to right): Coach Alex Hannum, Cliff Hagan, Jack Coleman, Captain Charley Share, Bob Pettit, Walt Davis, Ed Macauley. Rear row: Max Shapiro, ball boy; Slater Martin, Win Wilfong, Jack McMahon, Med Park, Frank Selvy, Trainer Bernie Ebert.

FINAL STANDINGS AND TEAM FIGURES

EASTERN DIVISION

Team	W.	L.	FGA	FGM	Pct.	FTA	FTM	Pct.	Reb.	Ast.	PF	Disq.	Pts.	Avg.	Opp.
Boston	49	23	7759	3006	.387	2585	1904	.737	5402	1508	1723	34	7916	109.9	7520
Syracuse	41	31	7336	2823	.385	2617	2075	.793	4895	1298	1820	28	7721	107.2	7564
Philadelphia	37	35	7276	2765	.380	2596	1977	.762	4836	1441	1763	31	7507	104.3	7516
New York	35	37	7307	2884	.395	3056	2300	.753	5385	1359	1865	41	8068	112.1	7981

WESTERN DIVISION

Team	W.	L.	FGA	FGM	Pct.	FTA	FTM	Pct.	Reb.	Ast.	PF	Disq.	Pts.	Avg.	Opp.
St. Louis	41	31	7162	2779	.388	3047	2180	.715	5445	1541	1875	40	7738	107.5	7643
Detroit	33	39	7295	2746	.376	2774	2093	.755	5168	1264	1807	32	7585	105.3	7754
Cincinnati	33	39	7339	2817	.384	2372	1688	.712	4959	1578	1835	30	7322	101.7	7420
Minneapolis	19	53	7192	2660	.370	3007	2246	.747	5189	1322	1982	60	7566	105.1	8025

*Detroit and Cincinnati tied for second place. Detroit won coin flip for home court advantage in playoff.

TOP 25 SCORERS

Player–Team	G.	Min.	FGA	FGM	Pct.	FTA	FTM	Pct.	Reb.	Ast.	PF	Disq.	Pts.	Avg.
George Yardley, Detroit	72	2843	1624	673	.414	808	655	.811	768	97	226	3	2001	27.8
Dolph Schayes, Syracuse	72	2918	1458	581	.398	696	629	.904	1022	224	244	6	1791	24.9
Bob Pettit, St. Louis	70	2528	1418	581	.410	744	557	.745	1216	157	222	6	1719	24.6
Clyde Lovellette, Cincinnati	71	2589	1540	679	.441	405	301	.743	862	134	236	3	1659	23.4
Paul Arizin, Philadelphia	68	2377	1229	483	.393	544	440	.809	503	165	167	156	1406	20.7
Bill Sharman, Boston	63	2214	1297	550	.424	338	302	.893	295	167	156	3	1402	22.3
Cliff Hagan, St. Louis	70	2190	1135	503	.443	501	386	.768	707	175	267	9	1391	19.9
Neil Johnston, Philadelphia	71	2408	1102	473	.429	540	442	.819	790	166	233	4	1388	19.5
Ken Sears, New York	72	2685	1014	445	.439	550	452	.822	785	126	251	7	1342	18.6
Vern Mikkelsen, Minn.	72	2390	1070	439	.410	471	370	.786	805	166	299	20	1248	17.3

1957-58 STATISTICS

Player–Team	G.	Min.	FGA	FGM	Pct.	FTA	FTM	Pct	Reb.	Ast.	PF	Disq.	Pts.	Avg.
Jack Twyman, Cincinnati	72	2178	1028	465	.452	396	307	.775	464	110	224	3	1237	17.2
Tom Heinsohn, Boston	69	2206	1226	468	.382	394	294	.746	705	125	274	6	1230	17.8
Willie Naulls, New York	68	2369	1189	472	.397	344	284	.826	799	97	220	4	1228	18.1
Larry Foust, Minneapolis	72	2200	982	391	.398	566	428	.756	876	108	299	11	1210	16.8
Carl Braun, New York	71	2475	1018	426	.418	378	321	.849	330	393	183	2	1173	16.5
Bob Cousy, Boston	65	2222	1262	445	.353	226	277	.850	322	463	136	1	1167	18.0
Bill Russell, Boston	69	2640	1032	456	.442	443	230	.519	1564	202	181	2	1142	16.6
Frank Ramsey, Boston	69	2047	900	377	.419	472	383	.811	504	167	245	8	1137	16.5
Dick Garmaker, Minnesota	68	2216	988	390	.395	411	314	.764	365	183	190	2	1094	16.1
John Kerr, Syracuse	72	2384	1020	407	.399	422	280	.664	963	88	197	4	1094	15.2
Larry Costello, Syracuse	72	2746	888	378	.426	378	320	.847	378	317	246	3	1076	14.9
Harry Gallatin, Detroit	72	1990	898	340	.379	498	392	.787	749	86	217	5	1072	14.9
Maurice Stokes, Cincinnati	63	2460	1181	414	.351	333	238	.715	1142	403	226	9	1066	16.9
Richie Guerin, New York	63	2368	973	344	.354	511	353	.691	489	317	202	3	1041	16.5
Ed Macauley, St. Louis	72	1908	879	376	.428	369	267	.723	478	143	156	2	1019	14.2

FIELD GOAL PERCENTAGE LEADERS
(Minimum 230 FGM)

	FGA	FGM	Pct.
Jack Twyman, Cincinnati	1028	465	.452
Cliff Hagan, St. Louis	1135	503	.443
Bill Russell, Boston	1032	456	.442
Ray Felix, New York	688	304	.442
Clyde Lovellette, Cincinnati	1540	679	.441
Ken Sears, New York	1014	445	.439
Neil Johnston, Philadelphia	1102	473	.429
Ed Macauley, St. Louis	879	376	.428
Larry Costello, Syracuse	888	378	.426
Bill Sharman, Boston	1297	550	.424

FREE THROW PERCENTAGE LEADERS
(Minimum 190 FTM)

	FTA	FTM	Pct.
Dolph Schayes, Syracuse	696	629	.904
Bill Sharman, Boston	338	302	.893
Bob Cousy, Boston	326	277	.850
Carl Braun, New York	378	321	.849
Dick Schnittker, Minneapolis	237	201	.848
Larry Costello, Syracuse	378	320	.847
Gene Shue, Detroit	327	276	.844
Willie Naulls, New York	344	284	.826
Ken Sears, New York	550	452	.822
Ron Sobie, New York	239	196	.820

LEADERS IN REBOUNDS

	G.	No.	Avg.
Bill Russell, Boston	69	1564	22.7
Bob Pettit, St. Louis	70	1216	17.4
Maurice Stokes, Cincinnati	63	1142	18.1
Dolph Schayes, Syracuse	72	1022	14.2
John Kerr, Syracuse	72	963	13.4
Walter Dukes, Detroit	72	954	13.3
Larry Foust, Minneapolis	72	876	12.2
Clyde Lovellette, Cincinnati	71	862	12.1
Vern Mikkelsen, Minneapolis	72	805	11.2
Willie Naulls, New York	68	799	11.8

LEADERS IN ASSISTS

	G.	No.	Avg.
Bob Cousy, Boston	65	463	7.1
Dick McGuire, Detroit	69	454	6.6
Maurice Stokes, Cincinnati	63	403	6.4
Carl Braun, New York	71	393	5.5
George King, Cincinnati	63	337	5.3
Jack McMahon, St. Louis	72	333	4.6
Tom Gola, Philadelphia	59	327	5.5
Richie Guerin, New York	63	317	5.0
Larry Costello, Syracuse	72	317	4.4
Dolph Schayes, Syracuse	72	234	3.3

INTER-CLUB RECORDS—HOME, AWAY AND NEUTRAL COURT

EASTERN DIVISION

	Bos.	Syr.	Phil.	N.Y.	St.L.	Det.	Cinn.	Mpls.	Home	Away	Neutral	W. L.
Boston	..	7	6	7	5	8	7	9	25- 4	17- 13	7- 6	49- 23
Syracuse	5	..	9	7	4	4	5	7	26- 5	9- 21	6- 5	41- 31
Philadelphia	6	3	..	8	7	4	3	6	16-12	12- 19	9- 4	37- 35
New York	5	5	4	..	3	5	5	8	16-13	11- 19	8- 5	35- 37

WESTERN DIVISION

	Bos.	Syr.	Phil.	N.Y.	St.L.	Det.	Cinn.	Mpls.	Home	Away	Neutral	W. L.
St. Louis	4	5	2	6	..	6	9		23- 8	9- 19	9- 4	41- 31
Detroit	1	5	5	4	6	..	6	6	14-14	13- 18	6- 7	33- 39
Cincinnati	2	4	6	4	3	6	..	8	17-12	10- 19	6- 8	33- 39
Minneapolis	0	2	3	1	3	6	4	..	13-17	4- 22	2-14	19- 53
Total	23	31	35	37	31	39	39	53	150-85	85-150	53-53	288-288

INDIVIDUAL STATISTICS

BOSTON

Player	G.	Minutes	FG Att.	FG Made	FG Pct.	FT Att.	FT Made	FT Pct.	Re-b'nd	As-sist	Per. Fls.	Disq.	Tot. Pts.	Avg. Pts.
Bill Sharman	63	2214	1297	550	.424	338	302	.893	295	167	156	3	1402	22.3
Tom Heinsohn	69	2206	1226	468	.382	394	294	.746	705	125	274	6	1230	17.8
Bob Cousy	65	2222	1262	445	.353	326	277	.850	322	463	136	1	1167	18.6
Bill Russell	69	2640	1032	456	.442	443	230	.519	1564	202	181	2	1142	16.6
Frank Ramsey	69	2047	900	377	.419	472	383	.811	504	167	245	8	1137	16.5
Lou Tsioropoulos	70	1819	624	198	.317	207	142	.686	434	112	242	8	538	7.7
Jack Nichols	69	1224	484	170	.351	80	59	.738	302	63	123	1	399	5.8
Arnie Risen	63	1119	397	134	.338	267	114	.683	360	59	195	5	382	6.1
Sam Jones	56	594	233	100	.429	84	60	.714	160	37	42	0	260	4.6
Andy Phillip	70	1164	273	97	.355	71	42	.592	158	121	121	0	236	3.4
Jim Loscutoff	5	56	31	11	.355	3	1	.333	20	1	8	0	23	4.6

1957-58 STATISTICS

CINCINNATI

Player	G.	Min-utes	FG Att.	FG Made	FG Pct.	FT Att.	FT Made	FT Pct.	Re-b'nd	As-sist	Per. Fls.	Disq.	Tot. Pts.	Avg. Pts.
Clyde Lovellette	71	2589	1540	679	.441	405	301	.743	862	134	236	3	1659	23.4
Jack Twyman	72	2178	1028	465	.452	396	306	.775	464	110	224	3	1237	17.2
Maurice Stokes	63	2460	1181	414	.351	423	238	.715	1142	403	226	9	1066	16.9
Jim Paxson	67	1795	639	225	.352	285	209	.733	350	139	183	2	659	9.8
George King	63	2272	645	235	.364	227	140	.617	306	337	124	0	610	9.7
Dick Ricketts	72	1620	664	215	.324	196	132	.673	410	114	277	8	562	7.8
Richie Regan	72	1648	569	202	.355	172	120	.698	175	185	174	0	524	7.3
Dave Piontek	71	1032	397	150	.378	151	95	.629	254	52	134	2	395	5.6
Don Meineke	67	792	351	125	.356	119	77	.647	226	38	155	3	327	4.9
Tom Marshall (9 Det., 29 Cinn.)	38	518	166	52	.313	63	48	.762	101	19	43	0	152	4.0
Dick Duckett	34	424	158	54	.342	27	24	.889	56	47	60	0	132	3.9
Gerald Paulson	6	68	23	8	.348	6	4	.667	10	4	5	0	20	3.3

DETROIT

Player	G.	Min-utes	FG Att.	FG Made	FG Pct.	FT Att.	FT Made	FT Pct.	Re-b'nd	As-sist	Per. Fls.	Disq.	Tot. Pts.	Avg. Pts.
George Yardley	72	2843	1624	673	.414	808	655	.811	768	97	226	3	2001	27.8
Harry Gallatin	72	1990	898	340	.379	498	392	.787	749	86	217	5	1072	14.9
Gene Shue	63	2333	919	353	.384	327	276	.844	333	172	150	1	982	15.6
Walt Dukes	72	2184	796	278	.349	366	247	.675	954	52	311	17	803	11.2
Dick McGuire	69	2311	544	203	.373	255	150	.667	291	454	178	0	556	8.1
Nat Clifton	68	1435	587	217	.363	146	91	.623	403	76	202	3	525	7.7
Chuck Noble	61	1363	601	199	.331	77	56	.727	140	153	166	0	454	7.4
Phil Jordon (12 N.Y., 46 Det.)	58	898	397	193	.413	93	64	.688	301	37	108	1	450	7.8
Bill Kenville	35	649	280	106	.379	75	46	.613	102	66	88	0	258	7.4
Joe Holup (16 Syr., 37 Det.)	53	740	278	91	.327	94	71	.755	221	36	99	2	253	4.8
Bob Houbregs	17	302	137	49	.358	43	30	.698	65	19	36	0	128	7.5
Bill Thieben	27	243	154	42	.294	27	16	.593	65	7	44	0	100	3.7
Dick Atha	18	160	47	17	.362	12	10	.833	24	19	24	0	44	2.4
Bill Ebben	8	50	28	6	.214	4	3	.750	8	4	5	0	15	1.9
Doug Bolstorff	3	21	5	2	.400	0	0	.000	0	0	1	0	4	1.3

MINNEAPOLIS

Player	G.	Min-utes	FG Att.	FG Made	FG Pct.	FT Att.	FT Made	FT Pct.	Re-b'nd	As-sist	Per. Fls.	Disq.	Tot. Pts.	Avg. Pts.
Vern Mikkelsen	72	2390	1070	439	.410	471	370	.786	805	166	299	20	1248	17.3
Larry Foust	72	2200	982	391	.398	566	428	.756	876	108	299	11	1210	16.8
Dick Garmaker	68	2216	988	390	.395	411	314	.764	365	183	190	2	1094	16.1
Bob Leonard	66	2074	794	266	.335	268	205	.765	237	218	145	0	737	11.2
Ed Fleming	72	1686	655	226	.345	255	181	.710	492	139	222	5	633	8.8
Jim Krebs	68	1259	527	199	.378	176	135	.767	502	27	182	4	533	7.8
Corky Devlin	70	1248	489	170	.348	172	133	.773	132	167	104	1	473	6.8
Dick Schnittker	50	979	357	128	.359	237	201	.848	211	71	126	5	457	9.1
Rod Hundley	65	1154	548	174	.318	162	104	.642	186	121	99	0	452	7.0
Bo Erias	18	401	170	59	.347	47	30	.638	83	26	52	1	148	8.2
Frank Selvy (26 St.L., 12 Minn.)	38	426	167	44	.263	77	47	.610	88	35	44	0	135	3.6
McCoy Ingram	24	267	103	27	.262	28	13	.464	116	20	44	1	67	2.8
Bob Burrow	14	171	70	22	.314	33	11	.333	64	6	15	0	55	3.9
George Brown	1	6	2	0	.000	2	1	.500	1	0	1	0	1	1.0

NEW YORK

Player	G.	Min-utes	FG Att.	FG Made	FG Pct.	FT Att.	FT Made	FT Pct.	Re-b'nd	As-sist	Per. Fls.	Disq.	Tot. Pts.	Avg. Pts.
Kenny Sears	72	2685	1014	445	.439	550	452	.822	785	126	251	7	1342	18.6
Willie Naulls	68	2369	1189	472	.397	344	284	.826	799	97	220	4	1228	18.1
Carl Braun	71	2475	1018	426	.418	378	321	.849	330	393	183	2	1173	16.5
Richie Guerin	63	2368	973	344	.354	511	353	.691	489	317	202	3	1041	16.5
Ray Felix	72	1709	688	304	.442	389	271	.697	747	52	283	12	879	12.2
Guy Sparrow	72	1661	838	318	.379	257	165	.642	461	69	232	6	801	11.1
Ron Sobie	55	1399	539	217	.403	239	196	.820	263	125	147	3	630	11.5
Charlie Tyra	68	1182	490	175	.357	224	150	.670	480	34	175	3	500	7.4
Art Spoelstra (50 Min., 17 N.Y.)	67	1305	419	161	.384	187	127	.679	332	57	225	11	449	6.7
Larry Friend	44	569	226	74	.327	41	27	.659	106	47	54	0	175	4.0
Mel Hutchins	18	384	131	51	.389	43	24	.558	86	34	31	0	126	7.0
Brendan McCann	36	295	100	22	.220	37	25	.676	45	54	34	0	69	1.9
Ron Shavlik	1	2	1	0	.000	0	0	.000	1	0	0	0	0	0.0

1957-58 STATISTICS

PHILADELPHIA

Player	G.	Minutes	FG Att.	FG Made	FG Pct.	FT Att.	FT Made	FT Pct.	Re-b'nd	As-sist	Per. Fls.	Disq.	Tot. Pts.	Avg. Pts.
Paul Arizin	68	2377	1229	483	.393	544	440	.809	503	135	235	7	1406	20.7
Neil Johnson	71	2408	1102	473	.429	540	442	.819	790	166	233	4	1388	19.5
Woody Sauldsberry	71	2377	1082	389	.360	218	134	.615	729	58	245	3	912	12.8
Joe Graboski	72	2077	1017	341	.335	303	227	.749	570	125	249	3	909	12.6
Tom Gola	59	2126	711	295	.415	299	223	.746	639	327	225	11	813	13.8
Ernie Beck	71	1974	683	272	.398	203	170	.837	307	190	173	2	714	10.1
Jack George	72	1910	627	232	.370	242	178	.736	288	234	140	1	642	8.9
George Dempsey	67	1048	311	112	.360	105	70	.667	214	128	113	0	294	4.4
Lennie Rosenbluth	53	373	265	91	.343	84	53	.631	91	23	39	0	235	4.4
Pat Dunn	28	206	90	28	.311	17	14	.824	31	28	20	0	70	2.5
Jim Walsh	10	72	27	5	.185	17	10	.588	15	8	9	0	20	2.0
Ray Radziszewski	1	6	3	0	.000	0	0	.000	2	1	1	0	0	0.0

ST. LOUIS

Player	G.	Minutes	FG Att.	FG Made	FG Pct.	FT Att.	FT Made	FT Pct.	Re-b'nd	As-sist	Per. Fls.	Disq.	Tot. Pts.	Avg. Pts.
Bob Pettit	70	2528	1418	581	.410	744	557	.745	1216	157	222	6	1719	24.6
Cliff Hagan	70	2190	1135	503	.443	501	385	.768	707	175	267	9	1391	19.9
Ed Macauley	72	1908	879	376	.428	369	267	.723	478	143	156	2	1019	14.2
Slater Martin	60	2098	768	258	.336	276	206	.746	228	218	187	0	722	12.0
Chuck Share	72	1824	545	216	.396	293	190	.648	749	130	279	15	622	8.6
Jack McMahon	72	2239	719	216	.300	221	134	.606	195	333	184	2	566	7.9
Win Wilfong	71	1360	543	196	.361	238	163	.685	290	163	199	3	555	7.8
Jack Coleman	72	1506	590	231	.413	131	84	.641	485	117	169	3	546	7.6
Med Park	71	1103	363	133	.366	162	118	.728	184	76	106	0	384	5.4
Walt Davis (35 Phil., 26 St. L.)	61	663	244	85	.348	82	61	.744	174	29	143	0	231	3.8
Red Morrison	13	79	26	9	.346	4	3	.750	26	0	12	0	21	1.6
Worthy Patterson	4	13	8	3	.375	2	1	.500	2	2	3	0	7	1.8

SYRACUSE

Player	G.	Minutes	FG Att.	FG Made	FG Pct.	FT Att.	FT Made	FT Pct.	Re-b'nd	As-sist	Per. Fls.	Disq.	Tot. Pts.	Avg. Pts.
Dolph Schayes	72	2918	1458	581	.398	696	629	.904	1022	224	244	6	1791	24.9
John Kerr	72	2384	1020	407	.399	422	280	.664	963	88	197	4	1094	15.2
Larry Costello	72	2746	888	378	.426	378	320	.847	378	317	246	3	1076	14.9
Ed Conlin	60	1871	877	343	.391	270	215	.796	436	133	168	2	901	15.0
Togo Palazzi	67	1001	579	228	.394	171	123	.719	243	42	125	0	579	8.6
Al Bianchi	69	1421	625	215	.344	205	140	.683	221	114	188	4	570	8.3
Bob Hopkins	69	1224	554	221	.399	161	123	.764	392	45	162	5	565	8.2
Bob Harrison	72	1799	604	210	.348	122	97	.795	166	169	200	1	517	7.2
Earl Lloyd	61	1045	359	119	.331	106	79	.745	287	60	179	3	317	5.2
Paul Seymour	64	763	315	107	.340	63	53	.841	107	93	88	0	267	4.2

1957-58 CHAMPIONSHIP PLAYOFF RESULTS

EASTERN DIVISION SEMI-FINALS
Philadelphia 2, Syracuse 1

Mar. 15—Philadelphia 82 at Syracuse	86
Mar. 16—Syracuse 93 at Philadelphia	95
Mar. 18—Philadelphia 101 at Syracuse	88

EASTERN DIVISION FINALS
Boston 4, Philadelphia 1

Mar. 19—Philadelphia 98 at Boston	107
Mar. 22—Boston 109 at Philadelphia	87
Mar. 23—Philadelphia 92 at Boston	106
Mar. 26—Boston 97 at Philadelphia	111
Mar. 27—Philadelphia 88 at Boston	93

WESTERN DIVISION SEMI-FINALS
Detroit 2, Cincinnati 0

Mar. 15—Cincinnati 93 at Detroit	100
Mar. 16—Detroit 124 at Cincinnati	104

WESTERN DIVISION FINALS
St. Louis 4, Detroit 1

Mar. 19—Detroit 111 at St. Louis	114
Mar. 22—St. Louis 99 at Detroit	96
Mar. 23—Detroit 109 at St. Louis	89
Mar. 25—St. Louis 145 at Detroit	101
Mar. 27—Detroit 96 at St. Louis	120

CHAMPIONSHIP SERIES
St. Louis 4, Boston 2

Mar. 29—St. Louis 104 at Boston	102
Mar. 30—St. Louis 112 at Boston	136
Apr. 2—Boston 108 at St. Louis	111
Apr. 5—Boston 109 at St. Louis	98
Apr. 9—St. Louis 102 at Boston	100
Apr. 12—Boston 109 at St. Louis	110

TEAM PLAYOFF STATISTICS

Team	G.	W.	L.	Pct.	FGA	FGM	Pct.	FTA	FTM	Pct.	Reb.	Ast.	PF	Disq.	Scoring Average For	Agst.	Diff.
St. Louis	11	8	3	.727	1055	426	.404	501	352	.703	787	236	335	9	109.5	107.0	2.5
Boston	11	6	5	.545	1164	422	.363	425	332	.781	855	207	294	12	106.9	101.3	5.6
Detroit	7	3	4	.429	683	255	.373	297	227	.764	505	125	186	4	105.3	107.7	-2.4
Philadelphia	8	3	5	.375	808	287	.355	243	181	.745	548	149	158	1	94.4	97.4	-3.0
Syracuse	3	1	2	.333	293	95	.324	101	77	.762	220	36	65	0	89.0	92.7	-3.7
Cincinnati	2	0	2	.000	215	69	.321	71	49	.690	151	24	55	1	93.5	112.0	-18.5

1956-57 STATISTICS

1956-57 CHAMPION BOSTON CELTICS
Front row (left to right): Lou Tsioropoulos, Andy Phillip, Frank Ramsey, Coach Red Auerbach, Captain Bob Cousy, Bill Sharman, Jim Loscutoff.
Standing: President Walter A. Brown, Dick Hemric, Jack Nichols, Bill Russell, Arnold Risen, Tom Heinsohn, Trainer Harvey Cohn, Treasurer Lou Pieri.

FINAL STANDINGS AND TEAM FIGURES

EASTERN DIVISION

Team	W.	L.	FGA	FGM	Pct.	FTA	FTM	Pct.	Reb.	Ast.	PF	Disq.	Pts.	Avg.	Opp.
Boston	44	28	7326	2808	.383	2644	1983	.750	4963	1464	1851	38	7599	105.5	7213
Syracuse	38	34	6915	2550	.369	2613	2075	.794	4350	1282	1809	34	7175	99.7	7277
Philadelphia	37	35	6533	2584	.396	2658	2062	.776	4305	1467	1732	36	7116	98.8	7116
New York	36	36	6645	2569	.387	2844	2117	.744	4723	1312	1824	20	7255	100.8	7265

WESTERN DIVISION

Team	W.	L.	FGA	FGM	Pct.	FTA	FTM	Pct.	Reb.	Ast.	PF	Disq.	Pts.	Avg.	Opp.
St. Louis	34	38	6669	2557	.383	2710	1977	.730	4566	1454	1848	36	7091	98.5	7097
Minneapolis	34	38	6965	2584	.371	2899	2195	.757	4581	1195	1887	49	7363	102.3	7421
Ft. Wayne	34	38	6612	2532	.383	2510	1874	.747	4289	1398	1643	17	6938	96.4	7104
Rochester	31	41	6807	2515	.369	2402	1698	.707	4171	1298	1866	38	6728	93.4	6886

St. Louis beat Minneapolis and Fort Wayne in special playoff games.

TOP 25 SCORERS

Player–Team	G.	Min.	FGA	FGM	Pct.	FTA	FTM	Pct.	Reb.	Ast.	PF	Disq.	Pts.	Avg.
Paul Arizin, Philadelphia	71	2767	1451	613	.422	713	591	.829	561	150	274	13	1817	25.6
Bob Pettit, St. Louis	71	2491	1477	613	.415	684	529	.773	1037	133	181	1	1755	24.7
Dolph Schayes, Syracuse	72	2851	1308	496	.379	691	625	.904	1008	229	219	5	1617	22.5
Neil Johnston, Philadelphia	69	2531	1163	520	.447	648	535	.826	855	203	231	2	1575	22.8
George Yardley, Ft. Wayne	72	2691	1273	522	.410	639	503	.787	755	147	231	2	1547	21.5
Clyde Lovellette, Minn.	69	2492	1348	574	.426	399	286	.717	932	139	251	4	1434	20.8
Bill Sharman, Boston	67	2403	1241	516	.416	421	381	.905	286	236	188	1	1413	21.1

1956-57 STATISTICS

Player—Team	G.	Min.	FGA	FGM	Pct.	FTA	FTM	Pct.	Reb.	Ast.	PF	Disq.	Pts.	Avg.
Bob Cousy, Boston	64	2364	1264	478	.378	442	363	.821	309	478	134	0	1319	20.6
Ed Macauley, St. Louis	72	2582	987	414	.419	479	359	.749	440	202	206	2	1187	16.5
Dick Garmaker, Minn.	72	2406	1015	406	.400	435	365	.839	336	190	199	1	1177	16.3
Jack Twyman, Rochester	72	2338	1023	449	.439	363	276	.760	354	123	251	4	1174	16.3
Tom Heinsohn, Boston	72	2150	1123	446	.397	343	271	.790	705	117	304	12	1163	16.2
Maurice Stokes, Rochester	72	2761	1249	434	.347	385	256	.665	1256	331	287	12	1124	15.6
Harry Gallatin, New York	72	1943	817	332	.406	519	415	.800	725	85	202	1	1079	15.0
Ken Sears, New York	72	2516	821	343	.418	485	383	.790	614	101	226	2	1069	14.3
Joe Graboski, Philadelphia	72	2501	1118	390	.349	322	252	.783	614	140	244	5	1032	14.3
Carl Braun, New York	72	2345	993	378	.381	303	245	.808	259	256	195	1	1001	13.9
Vern Mikkelsen, Minn.	72	2198	854	322	.377	424	342	.807	630	121	312	18	986	13.7
Ed Conlin, Syracuse	71	2250	896	335	.374	368	283	.769	430	205	170	0	953	13.4
John Kerr, Syracuse	72	2191	827	333	.403	313	225	.719	807	90	190	3	891	12.4
Mel Hutchins, Ft. Wayne	72	2647	953	369	.387	206	152	.738	571	210	182	0	890	12.4
Ray Felix, New York	72	1622	709	295	.416	371	277	.747	587	36	284	8	867	12.0
Dick Ricketts, Rochester	72	2114	869	299	.344	297	206	.694	437	127	307	12	804	11.2
Bob Leonard, Minn.	72	1943	867	303	.349	241	186	.772	220	169	140	0	792	11.0
Gene Shue, Ft. Wayne	72	2470	710	273	.385	316	241	.763	421	238	137	0	787	10.9

FIELD GOAL PERCENTAGE LEADERS
(Minimum 230 FGM)

	FGA	FGM	Pct.
Neil Johnston, Philadelphia	1163	520	.447
Charles Share, St. Louis	535	235	.439
Jack Twyman, Rochester	1023	449	.439
Bob Houbregs, Ft. Wayne	585	253	.432
Bill Russell, Boston	649	277	.427
Clyde Lovellette, Minneapolis	1348	574	.426
Paul Arizin, Philadelphia	1451	613	.422
Ed Macauley, St. Louis	987	414	.419
Ken Sears, New York	821	343	.418
Ray Felix, New York	709	295	.416

FREE THROW PERCENTAGE LEADERS
(Minimum 190 FTM)

	FTA	FTM	Pct.
Bill Sharman, Boston	421	381	.905
Dolph Schayes, Syracuse	691	625	.904
Dick Garmaker, Minneapolis	435	365	.839
Paul Arizin, Philadelphia	713	591	.829
Neil Johnston, Philadelphia	648	535	.826
Bob Cousy, Boston	442	363	.821
Carl Braun, New York	303	245	.808
Vern Mikkelsen, Minneapolis	424	342	.807
Joseph Holup, Syracuse	253	204	.806
Harry Gallatin, New York	519	415	.800

LEADERS IN REBOUNDS

	G.	No.	Avg.
Maurice Stokes, Rochester	72	1256	17.4
Bob Pettit, St. Louis	71	1037	14.6
Dolph Schayes, Syracuse	72	1008	14.0
Bill Russell, Boston	48	943	19.6
Clyde Lovellette, Minneapolis	69	932	13.5
Neil Johnston, Philadelphia	69	855	12.4
John Kerr, Syracuse	72	807	11.2
Walter Dukes, Minneapolis	71	794	11.2
George Yardley, Ft. Wayne	72	755	10.5
Jim Loscutoff, Boston	70	730	10.4

LEADERS IN ASSISTS

	G.	No.	Avg.
Bob Cousy, Boston	64	478	7.5
Jack McMahon, St. Louis	72	367	5.1
Maurice Stokes, Rochester	72	331	4.6
Jack George, Philadelphia	67	307	4.6
Slater Martin, N.Y.-St.L.	66	269	4.1
Carl Braun, New York	72	256	3.6
Gene Shue, Ft. Wayne	72	238	3.3
Bill Sharman, Boston	67	236	3.5
Larry Costello, Philadelphia	72	236	3.3
Dolph Schayes, Syracuse	72	229	3.2

INTER-CLUB RECORDS—HOME, AWAY AND NEUTRAL COURT

EASTERN DIVISION

	Bos.	Syr.	Phil.	N.Y.	St.L.	Minn.	Ft.W.	Roch.	Home	Away	Neutral	W.	L.
Boston	..	5	8	7	7	5	6	6	27- 4	12- 19	5- 5	44- 28
Syracuse	7	..	7	6	4	5	4	5	22- 9	12- 19	4- 6	38- 34
Philadelphia	4	5	..	8	7	4	5	4	26- 5	5- 26	6- 4	37- 35
New York	5	6	4	..	6	6	4	5	19- 12	11- 20	6- 4	36- 36

WESTERN DIVISION

	Bos.	Syr.	Phil.	N.Y.	St.L.	Minn.	Ft.W.	Roch.	Home	Away	Neutral	W.	L.
St. Louis	2	5	2	3	..	8	8	6	18- 13	11- 20	5- 5	34- 38
Minneapolis	4	4	5	3	4	..	5	9	18- 13	9- 22	7- 3	34- 38
Ft. Wayne	3	5	4	5	4	7	..	6	23- 8	7- 24	4- 6	34- 38
Rochester	3	4	5	4	6	3	6	..	19- 12	9- 22	3- 7	31- 41

1956-57 CHAMPIONSHIP PLAYOFF RESULTS

EASTERN DIVISION SEMI-FINALS
Syracuse 2, Philadelphia 0
Mar. 16—Syracuse 103 at Philadelphia 96
Mar. 18—Philadelphia 80 at Syracuse 91

EASTERN DIVISION FINALS
Boston 3, Syracuse 0
Mar. 21—Syracuse 90 at Boston 108
Mar. 23—Boston 120 at Syracuse 105
Mar. 24—Syracuse 80 at Boston 83

WESTERN DIVISION TIEBREAKERS
Mar. 14—Ft. Wayne 103 at St. Louis 115
Mar. 16—Minneapolis 111 at St. Louis 114

WESTERN DIVISION SEMI-FINALS
Minneapolis 2, Ft. Wayne 0
Mar. 17—Ft. Wayne 127 at Minneapolis 131
Mar. 19—Minneapolis 110 at Ft. Wayne 108

WESTERN DIVISION FINALS
St. Louis 3, Minneapolis 0
Mar. 21—Minneapolis 109 at St. Louis 118
Mar. 24—Minneapolis 104 at St. Louis 106
Mar. 25—St. Louis 143 at Minneapolis **135

CHAMPIONSHIP SERIES
Boston 4, St. Louis 3
Mar. 30—St. Louis 125 at Boston *123
Mar. 31—St. Louis 99 at Boston 119
Apr. 6—Boston 98 at St. Louis 100
Apr. 7—Boston 123 at St. Louis 118
Apr. 9—St. Louis 109 at Boston 124
Apr. 11—Boston 94 at St. Louis 96
Apr. 13—St. Louis 123 at Boston **125

1955-56 STATISTICS

1955-56 CHAMPION PHILADELPHIA WARRIORS

Front row (left to right): Coach George Senesky, Larry Hennessy, Paul Arizin, Jack George, George Dempsey, President Eddie Gottlieb. Standing: Ernie Beck, Neil Johnston, Joe Graboski, Walter Davis, Tom Gola, Jackie Moore.

FINAL STANDINGS AND TEAM FIGURES

EASTERN DIVISION

Team	W.	L.	FGA	FGM	Pct.	FTA	FTM	Pct.	Reb.	Ast.	PF	Disq.	Pts.	Avg.	Opp.
Philadelphia	45	27	6437	2641	.410	2829	2142	.757	4362	1886	1872	45	7424	103.1	7117
Boston	39	33	6913	2745	.397	2785	2142	.769	4583	1834	1874	44	7632	106.0	7585
New York	35	37	6395	2508	.392	2913	2196	.754	4562	1610	1923	43	7212	100.2	7242
Syracuse	35	37	6661	2466	.370	2703	2044	.756	4060	1710	1783	32	6976	96.9	6975

WESTERN DIVISION

Team	W.	L.	FGA	FGM	Pct.	FTA	FTM	Pct.	Reb.	Ast.	PF	Disq.	Pts.	Avg.	Opp.
Ft. Wayne	37	35	6174	2396	.388	2729	2002	.734	3974	1752	1789	20	6794	94.4	6743
Minneapolis	33	39	6543	2541	.388	2627	2066	.786	4133	1689	1978	43	7148	99.3	7212
St. Louis	33	39	6628	2506	.378	2761	1941	.703	4493	1748	1971	42	6953	96.6	7059
Rochester	31	41	6890	2551	.370	2567	1798	.700	4449	1747	1990	46	6900	95.8	7106

TOP 20 SCORERS

Player–Team	G.	Min.	FGA	FGM	Pct.	FTA	FTM	Pct.	Reb.	Ast.	PF	Disq.	Pts.	Avg.
Bob Pettit, St. Louis	72	2794	1507	646	.429	757	557	.736	1164	189	202	1	1849	25.7
Paul Arizin, Philadelphia	72	2724	1378	617	.448	620	507	.810	539	189	282	11	1741	24.2
Neil Johnston, Philadelphia	70	2594	1092	499	.457	685	549	.801	872	225	251	8	1547	22.1
Clyde Lovellette, Minneapolis	71	2518	1370	594	.434	469	338	.721	992	164	245	2	1526	21.5
Dolph Schayes, Syracuse	72	2517	1202	465	.387	632	542	.858	891	200	251	9	1472	20.4
Bill Sharman, Boston	72	2698	1229	538	.438	413	358	.867	259	339	197	1	1434	19.9
Bob Cousy, Boston	72	2767	1223	440	.360	564	476	.844	492	642	206	2	1356	18.8
Ed Macauley, Boston	71	2354	995	420	.422	504	400	.794	422	211	158	2	1240	17.5

1955-56 STATISTICS

Player—Team	G.	Min.	FGA	FGM	Pct.	FTA	FTM	Pct.	Reb.	Ast	PF	Disq.	Pts.	Avg.
George Yardley, Ft. Wayne	71	2353	1067	434	.407	492	365	.742	686	159	212	2	1233	17.4
Larry Foust, Ft. Wayne	72	2024	821	367	.447	555	432	.778	648	127	263	7	1166	16.2
Maurice Stokes, Rochester	67	2323	1137	403	.354	447	319	.714	1094	328	276	11	1125	16.8
Carl Braun, New York	72	2316	1064	396	.372	382	320	.838	259	298	215	3	1112	15.4
Jack Twyman, Rochester	72	2186	987	417	.422	298	204	.685	446	171	239	4	1038	14.4
Joe Graboski, Philadelphia	72	2375	1075	397	.269	340	240	.706	642	190	272	5	1034	14.4
Harry Gallatin, New York	72	2378	834	322	.386	455	358	.787	740	168	220	6	1002	13.9
Jack George, Philadelphia	72	2840	940	352	.374	391	296	.757	313	457	202	1	1000	13.9
Charles Share, St. Louis	72	1975	733	315	.430	498	346	.695	774	131	318	13	976	13.6
Vern Mikkelsen, Minnesota	72	2100	821	317	.386	408	328	.804	608	173	319	17	962	13.4
John Kerr, Syracuse	72	2114	935	377	.403	316	207	.655	607	84	168	3	961	13.3
Jack Coleman, Roch.-St.L.	75	2738	964	390	.412	249	177	.711	688	294	242	2	957	12.8

FIELD GOAL PERCENTAGE LEADERS
(Minimum 230 FGM)

	FGA	FGM	Pct.
Neil Johnston, Philadelphia	1092	499	.457
Paul Arizin, Philadelphia	1378	617	.448
Larry Foust, Ft. Wayne	821	367	.447
Ken Sears, New York	728	319	.438
Bill Sharman, Boston	1229	538	.438
Clyde Lovellette, Minneapolis	1370	594	.434
Charles Share, St. Louis	733	315	.430
Bob Houbregs, Ft. Wayne	575	247	.430
Bob Pettit, St. Louis	1507	646	.429
Mel Hutchins, Ft. Wayne	764	325	.425

FREE THROW PERCENTAGE LEADERS
(Minimum 190 FTM)

	FTA	FTM	Pct.
Bill Sharman, Boston	413	358	.867
Dolph Schayes, Syracuse	632	542	.858
Dick Schnittker, Minneapolis	355	304	.856
Bob Cousy, Boston	564	476	.844
Carl Braun, New York	382	320	.838
Slater Martin, Minneapolis	395	329	.833
Paul Arizin, Philadelphia	626	507	.810
Vern Mikkelsen, Minneapolis	408	328	.804
Neil Johnston, Philadelphia	685	549	.801
Jim Baechtold, New York	291	233	.801

LEADERS IN REBOUNDS

	G.	No.	Avg.
Bob Pettit, St. Louis	72	1164	16.2
Maurice Stokes, Rochester	67	1094	16.3
Clyde Lovellette, Minneapolis	71	992	14.0
Dolph Schayes, Syracuse	72	891	12.4
Neil Johnston, Philadelphia	70	872	12.5
Charles Share, St. Louis	72	774	10.8
Harry Gallatin, New York	72	740	10.3
Jack Coleman, Roch.-St.L.	75	688	9.2
George Yardley, Ft. Wayne	71	686	9.7
Larry Foust, Ft. Wayne	72	648	9.0

LEADERS IN ASSISTS

	G.	No.	Avg.
Bob Cousy, Boston	72	642	8.9
Jack George, Philadelphia	72	457	6.3
Slater Martin, Minneapolis	72	445	6.2
Andy Phillip, Ft. Wayne	70	410	5.9
George King, Syracuse	72	410	5.7
Dick McGuire, New York	62	362	5.8
Bill Sharman, Boston	72	339	4.7
Maurice Stokes, Rochester	67	328	4.9
Carl Braun, New York	72	298	4.1
Jack Coleman, Roch.-St.L.	75	294	3.9

INTER-CLUB RECORDS—HOME, AWAY AND NEUTRAL COURT

EASTERN DIVISION

	Phil.	Bos.	N.Y.	Syr.	Ft.W.	Minn.	St.L.	Roch.	Home	Away	Neutral	W.	L.
Philadelphia	..	7	6	9	5	6	6	6	21- 7	11- 17	13- 3	45- 27
Boston	5	..	5	8	4	7	5	5	20- 7	12- 15	7- 11	39- 33
New York	6	7	..	4	4	4	4	6	14-14	15- 14	6- 9	35- 37
Syracuse	3	4	8	..	5	5	6	4	23- 8	9- 19	3- 10	35- 37

WESTERN DIVISION

	Phil.	Bos.	N.Y.	Syr.	Ft.W.	Minn.	St.L.	Roch.	Home	Away	Neutral	W.	L.
Ft. Wayne	4	5	5	4	..	5	7	7	19- 8	10- 17	8- 10	37- 35
Minneapolis	3	2	5	4	7	..	5	7	13-12	6- 21	14- 6	33- 39
St. Louis	3	4	5	3	5	7	..	6	16-10	10- 17	7- 12	33- 39
Rochester	3	4	3	5	5	5	6	..	15- 14	7- 21	9- 6	31- 41

1955-56 CHAMPIONSHIP PLAYOFF RESULTS

Special Playoffs to Break Ties
Mar. 15—New York 77 at Syracuse 82
Mar. 16—Minneapolis 103 at St. Louis 97

EASTERN DIVISION SEMI-FINALS
Syracuse 2, Boston 1

Mar. 17—Syracuse 93 at Boston **110**
Mar. 19—Boston 98 at Syracuse 101
Mar. 21—Syracuse 102 at Boston 97

EASTERN DIVISION FINALS
Philadelphia 3, Syracuse 2

Mar. 23—Syracuse 87 at Philadelphia 109
Mar. 25—Philadelphia 118 at Syracuse 122
Mar. 27—Syracuse 96 at Philadelphia 119
Mar. 28—Philadelphia 104 at Syracuse 108
Mar. 29—Syracuse 104 at Philadelphia 109

WESTERN DIVISION SEMI-FINALS
St. Louis 2, Minneapolis 1

Mar. 19—Minneapolis 115 at St. Louis 116
Mar. 19—St. Louis 75 at Minneapolis 133
Mar. 21—St. Louis 116 at Minneapolis 115

WESTERN DIVISION FINALS
Ft. Wayne 3, St. Louis 2

Mar. 22—St. Louis 86 at Ft. Wayne 85
Mar. 24—Ft. Wayne 74 at St. Louis 84
Mar. 25—St. Louis 84 at Ft. Wayne 107
Mar. 27—Ft. Wayne 93 at St. Louis 84
Mar. 29—St. Louis 97 at Ft. Wayne 102

CHAMPIONSHIP SERIES
Philadelphia 4, Ft. Wayne 1

Mar. 31—Ft. Wayne 94 at Philadelphia 98
Apr. 1—Philadelphia 83 at Ft. Wayne 84
Apr. 3—Ft. Wayne 96 at Philadelphia 100
Apr. 5—Philadelphia 107 at Ft. Wayne 105
Apr. 7—Ft. Wayne 88 at Philadelphia 99

1954-55 STATISTICS

1954-55 CHAMPION SYRACUSE NATIONALS

Front row (left to right): Dick Farley, Billy Kenville. Center row: Earl Lloyd, Captain Paul Seymour, Coach Al Cervi, George King, Jim Tucker. Rear row: President Daniel Biasone, Wally Osterkorn, Business Manager Bob Sexton, Dolph Schayes, John Kerr, Billy Gabor, Red Rocha, Trainer Art Van Auken.

FINAL STANDINGS AND TEAM FIGURES

EASTERN DIVISION

Team	W.	L.	FGA	FGM	Pct.	FTA	FTM	Pct.	Reb.	Ast.	PF	Disq.	Pts.	Avg.	Opp.
Syracuse	43	29	6343	2360	.372	2450	1837	.750	3933	1778	1658	20	6557	91.1	6457
New York	38	34	6149	2392	.389	2593	1887	.728	4379	1744	1587	23	6671	92.7	6665
Boston	36	36	6533	2604	.399	2704	2097	.776	4293	1905	1859	48	7303	101.4	7309
Philadelphia	33	39	6234	2392	.384	2625	1928	.734	4238	1744	1716	29	6712	93.2	6732

WESTERN DIVISION

Team	W.	L.	FGA	FGM	Pct.	FTA	FTM	Pct.	Reb.	Ast.	PF	Disq.	Pts.	Avg.	Opp.
Ft. Wayne	43	29	5980	2333	.390	2710	1986	.733	3826	1737	1753	26	6652	92.4	6480
Minneapolis	40	32	6465	2506	.388	2517	1873	.744	3865	1468	1935	56	6885	95.6	6801
Rochester	29	43	6020	2399	.399	2420	1737	.718	3904	1695	1865	26	6535	90.8	6652
Milwaukee	26	46	6041	2187	.362	2672	1917	.717	3854	1544	1904	59	6291	87.4	6510

TOP 25 SCORERS

Player–Team	G.	Min.	FGA	FGM	Pct.	FTA	FTM	Pct.	Reb.	Ast.	PF	Disq.	Pts.	Avg.
Neil Johnston, Phila.	72	2917	1184	521	.440	769	589	.766	1085	215	255	4	1631	22.7
Paul Arizin, Philadelphia	72	2953	1325	529	.399	585	454	.776	675	210	270	5	1512	21.0
Bob Cousy, Boston	71	2747	1316	522	.397	570	460	.807	424	557	165	1	1504	21.2
Bob Pettit, Milwaukee	72	2659	1279	520	.407	567	426	.751	994	229	258	5	1466	20.4
Frank Selvy, Balt.-Mil.	71	2668	1195	452	.378	610	444	.728	394	245	230	3	1348	19.0
Dolph Schayes, Syracuse	72	2526	1103	422	.383	587	489	.833	887	213	247	6	1333	18.8
Vern Mikkelsen, Minn.	72	2559	1043	440	.422	598	447	.747	722	145	319	14	1327	18.4
Clyde Lovellette, Minn.	70	2361	1192	519	.435	398	273	.686	802	100	262	6	1311	18.7

1954-55 STATISTICS

Player—Team	G.	Min.	FGA	FGM	Pct.	FTA	FTM	Pct.	Reb.	Ast.	PF	Disq.	Pts.	Avg.
Bill Sharman, Boston	68	2453	1062	453	.427	387	347	.897	302	280	212	2	1253	18.4
Ed Macauley, Boston	71	2796	951	403	.424	558	442	.792	600	275	171	0	1248	17.6
Larry Foust, Ft. Wayne	70	2264	818	398	.487	513	393	.766	700	118	264	9	1189	17.0
Carl Braun, New York	71	2479	1032	400	.388	342	274	.801	295	274	208	3	1074	15.1
Harry Gallatin, New York	72	2548	859	330	.384	483	393	.814	995	176	206	5	1053	14.6
Paul Seymour, Syracuse	72	2950	1036	375	.362	370	300	.811	309	483	137	0	1050	14.6
Ray Felix, New York	72	2024	832	364	.438	498	310	.622	818	67	286	11	1038	14.4
George Yardley, Ft. W.	60	2150	869	363	.418	416	310	.745	594	126	205	7	1036	17.3
Jim Baechtold, New York	72	2536	898	362	.403	339	279	.823	307	218	202	0	1003	13.9
Slater Martin, Minn.	72	2784	919	350	.381	359	276	.769	260	427	221	7	976	13.6
Joe Graboski, Philadelphia	70	2515	1096	373	.340	303	208	.686	636	182	259	8	954	13.6
Nat Clifton, New York	72	2390	932	360	.386	328	224	.683	612	198	221	2	944	13.1
Bob Wanzer, Rochester	72	2376	820	324	.395	374	294	.786	374	247	163	2	942	13.1
Jack Coleman, Rochester	72	2482	866	400	.462	183	124	.678	729	323	201	1	924	12.8
Bob Davies, Rochester	72	1870	785	326	.415	293	220	.751	205	355	220	2	872	12.1
Mel Hutchins, Ft. Wayne	72	2860	903	341	.378	257	182	.708	665	247	282	0	864	12.0
Charles Share, Milwaukee	69	1685	577	235	.407	492	351	.713	684	84	273	17	821	11.0

FIELD GOAL PERCENTAGE LEADERS
(Minimum 210 FGM)

	FGA	FGM	Pct.
Larry Foust, Ft. Wayne	818	298	.487
Jack Coleman, Rochester	866	400	.462
Neil Johnston, Philadelphia	1184	521	.440
Ray Felix, New York	832	364	.438
Clyde Lovellette, Minneapolis	1192	519	.435
Bill Sharman, Boston	1062	453	.427
Ed Macauley, Boston	951	403	.424
Vern Mikkelsen, Minneapolis	1043	440	.422
John Kerr, Syracuse	718	301	.419
George Yardley, Ft. Wayne	869	363	.418

FREE THROW PERCENTAGE LEADERS
(Minimum 180 FTM)

	FTA	FTM	Pct.
Bill Sharman, Boston	387	347	.897
Frank Brian, Ft. Wayne	255	217	.851
Dolph Schayes, Syracuse	587	489	.833
Dick Schnittker, Minneapolis	362	298	.823
Jim Baechtold, New York	339	279	.823
Harry Gallatin, New York	483	393	.814
Odie Spears, Rochester	271	220	.812
Paul Seymour Syracuse	370	300	.811
Bob Cousy, Boston	560	460	.807
Carl Braun, New York	342	274	.801

LEADERS IN REBOUNDS

	G.	No.	Avg.
Neil Johnston, Philadelphia	72	1085	15.1
Harry Gallatin, New York	72	995	13.8
Bob Pettit, Milwaukee	72	994	13.8
Dolph Schayes, Syracuse	72	887	12.3
Ray Felix, New York	72	818	11.4
Clyde Lovellette, Minneapolis	70	802	11.5
Jack Coleman, Rochester	72	729	10.1
Vern Mikkelsen, Minneapolis	72	722	10.0
Arnie Risen, Rochester	69	703	10.2
Larry Foust, Ft. Wayne	70	700	10.0

LEADERS IN ASSISTS

	G.	No.	Avg.
Bob Cousy, Boston	71	557	7.8
Dick McGuire, New York	71	542	7.6
Andy Phillip, Ft. Wayne	64	491	7.7
Paul Seymour, Syracuse	72	483	6.7
Slater Martin, Minneapolis	72	427	5.9
Jack George, Philadelphia	68	359	5.3
Bob Davies, Rochester	72	355	4.9
George King, Syracuse	67	331	4.9
Jack Coleman, Rochester	72	323	4.5
Bill Sharman, Boston	68	280	4.1

INTER-CLUB RECORDS—HOME, AWAY AND NEUTRAL COURT

EASTERN DIVISION

	Syr.	N.Y.	Bos.	Phil.	Ft.W.	Minn.	Roch.	Mil.	Home	Away	Neutral	W.	L.
Syracuse		8	6	7	7	3	7	5	25- 7	10- 16	8- 6	43- 29
New York	4		6	5	7	5	5	6	17- 8	8- 19	13- 7	38- 34
Boston	6	6		7	4	3	4	6	20- 5	5- 22	11- 9	36- 36
Philadelphia	5	7	5		3	3	5	5	16- 5	4- 19	13- 15	33 39

WESTERN DIVISION

	Syr.	N.Y.	Bos.	Phil.	Ft.W.	Minn.	Roch.	Mil.	Home	Away	Neutral	W.	L.
Ft. Wayne	2	2	5	6		9	8	11	20- 6	9- 14	14- 9	43- 29
Minneapolis	6	4	6	6	3		8	7	18- 6	10- 14	12- 12	40- 32
Rochester	2	4	5	4	4	4		6	17- 11	4- 19	8- 13	29- 43
Milwaukee	4	3	3	4	1	5	6		6- 11	9- 16	11- 19	26- 46

1954-55 CHAMPIONSHIP PLAYOFF RESULTS

EASTERN DIVISION SEMI-FINALS
Boston 2, New York 1

Mar. 15—New York 101 at Boston	122
Mar. 16—Boston 95 at New York	102
Mar. 19—Boston 116 at New York	109

EASTERN DIVISION FINALS
Syracuse 3, Boston 1

Mar. 22—Boston 100 at Syracuse	110
Mar. 24—Boston 110 at Syracuse	116
Mar. 26—Syracuse 97 at Boston	*100
Mar. 27—Syracuse 110 at Boston	94

WESTERN DIVISION SEMI-FINALS
Minneapolis 2, Rochester 1

Mar. 16—Rochester 78, Minn. at St. Paul	82
Mar. 18—Minneapolis 92 at Rochester	94
Mar. 19—Rochester 110, Minn. at St. Paul	119

WESTERN DIVISION FINALS
Ft. Wayne 3, Minneapolis 1

Mar. 20—Minn. 79, Ft. W. at Elk'rt, Ind.	96
Mar. 22—Minn. 97, Ft. W. at Indianapolis	*98
Mar. 23—Ft. Wayne 91 at Minneapolis	*99
Mar. 27—Ft. Wayne 105 at Minneapolis	96

CHAMPIONSHIP SERIES
Syracuse 4, Ft. Wayne 3

Mar. 31—Ft. Wayne 82 at Syracuse	86
Apr. 2—Ft. Wayne 84 at Syracuse	87
Apr. 3—Syracuse 89, Ft. Wayne at Indpls.	96
Apr. 5—Syracuse 102, Ft. Wayne at Indpls.	109
Apr. 7—Syracuse 71, Ft. Wayne at Indpls.	74
Apr. 9—Ft. Wayne 104 at Syracuse	109
Apr. 10—Ft. Wayne 91 at Syracuse	92

*Denotes overtime period.

1953-54 STATISTICS

1953-54 CHAMPION MINNEAPOLIS LAKERS

Left to right: Slater Martin, Frank Saul, Jim Holstein, Jim Pollard, Clyde Lovellette, George Mikan, Vern Mikkelsen, Dick Schnittker, Whitey Skoog, Coach John Kundla.

FINAL STANDINGS AND TEAM FIGURES

EASTERN DIVISION

Team	W.	L.	FGA	FGM	Pct.	FTA	FTM	Pct.	Reb.	Ast.	PF	Disq.	Pts.	Avg.	Opp.
New York	44	28	5177	1934	.374	2525	1820	.721	3830	1469	1832	23	5688	79.0	5697
Boston	42	30	5580	2232	.400	2550	1851	.726	3867	1773	1969	46	6315	87.7	6147
Syracuse	42	30	5579	2054	.368	2650	1905	.719	3652	1541	1852	28	6013	83.5	5660
Philadelphia	29	43	5431	2023	.372	2272	1586	.698	3589	1468	1741	42	5632	78.2	5787
Baltimore	16	56	5539	2036	.368	2312	1566	.677	3816	1385	1777	24	5638	78.3	6127

WESTERN DIVISION

Team	W.	L.	FGA	FGM	Pct.	FTA	FTM	Pct.	Reb.	Ast.	PF	Disq.	Pts.	Avg.	Opp.
Minneapolis	46	26	5803	2184	.376	2067	1512	.731	3752	1323	1918	31	5880	81.7	5638
Rochester	44	28	5451	2010	.369	2518	1722	.684	3494	1454	1904	44	5742	79.8	5567
Ft. Wayne	40	32	5187	1952	.376	2315	1689	.730	3785	1474	1669	27	5593	77.7	5476
Milwaukee	21	51	5087	1757	.345	2202	1524	.692	3202	1298	1771	45	5038	70.0	5420

TOP 25 SCORERS

Player–Team	G.	Min.	FGA	FGM	Pct.	FTA	FTM	Pct.	Reb.	Ast.	PF	Disq.	Pts.	Avg.
Neil Johnston, Phila.	72	3296	1317	591	.449	772	577	.747	797	203	259	7	1759	24.4
Bob Cousy, Boston	72	2857	1262	486	.385	522	411	.787	394	518	201	3	1383	19.2
Ed Macauley, Boston	71	2792	950	462	.486	554	420	.758	571	271	168	1	1344	18.9
Geo. Mikan, Minneapolis	72	2362	1160	441	.380	546	424	.777	1028	174	268	4	1306	18.1
Ray Felix, Baltimore	72	2672	983	410	.417	704	449	.638	958	82	253	5	1269	17.6
Dolph Schayes, Syracuse	72	2655	973	370	.380	590	488	.827	870	214	232	4	1228	17.1
Bill Sharman, Boston	72	2467	915	412	.450	392	331	.844	255	229	211	4	1155	16.0
Larry Foust, Ft. Wayne	72	2693	919	376	.409	475	338	.712	967	161	258	4	1090	15.1
Carl Braun, New York	72	2373	884	354	.400	429	354	.825	246	209	259	6	1062	14.8
Bob Wanzer, Rochester	72	2538	335	322	.386	428	314	.734	392	254	171	2	958	13.3

1953-54 STATISTICS

Player—Team	G.	Min.	FGA	FGM	Pct.	FTA	FTM	Pct.	Reb.	Ast.	PF	Disq.	Pts.	Avg.
Harry Gallatin, New York	72	2690	639	258	.404	552	433	.784	1098	153	208	2	949	13.2
Arnie Risen, Rochester	72	2385	872	321	.368	430	307	.714	728	120	284	9	949	13.2
Joe Graboski, Philadelphia	71	2759	1000	354	.354	350	236	.674	670	163	223	4	944	13.3
Paul Seymour, Syracuse	72	2727	838	316	.377	368	299	.813	291	264	187	2	931	13.1
Bob Davies, Rochester	72	2137	777	288	.371	433	311	.718	194	323	224	4	887	12.3
Jim Pollard, Minn.	71	2483	882	326	.370	230	179	.778	500	214	161	0	831	11.7
George King, Syracuse	72	2370	744	280	.376	410	257	.627	268	272	179	2	817	11.3
Max Zaslofsky, Ft. Wayne	65	1881	756	278	.368	357	255	.714	160	154	142	1	811	12.5
Vern Mikkelsen, Minn.	72	2247	771	288	.374	298	221	.742	615	119	264	7	797	11.1
Don Sunderlage, Milw.	68	2232	748	254	.340	337	252	.748	225	187	263	8	760	11.2
Andy Phillip, Ft. Wayne	71	2705	680	255	.375	330	241	.730	265	449	204	4	751	10.6
Mel Hutchins, Ft. Wayne	72	2934	736	295	.401	223	151	.677	695	210	229	4	741	10.3
Paul Hoffman, Baltimore	72	2505	761	253	.332	303	217	.716	486	285	271	10	723	10.0
Ed Miller, Baltimore	72	1657	600	244	.407	317	231	.729	537	95	194	0	719	10.0
Connie Simmons, N. York	72	2006	713	255	.358	305	210	.689	484	128	234	1	720	10.0

FIELD GOAL PERCENTAGE LEADERS
(Minimum 210 FGM)

	FGA	FGM	Pct.
Ed Macauley, Boston	950	462	.486
Bill Sharman, Boston	915	412	.450
Neil Johnston, Philadelphia	1317	591	.449
Clyde Lovellette, Minneapolis	560	237	.423
Ray Felix, Baltimore	983	410	.417
Larry Foust, Ft. Wayne	919	376	.409
Eddie Miller, Baltimore	600	244	.407
Jack Coleman, Rochester	714	289	.405
Harry Gallatin, New York	639	258	.404
Mel Hutchins, Ft. Wayne	736	295	.401

FREE THROW PERCENTAGE LEADERS
(Minimum 180 FTM)

	FTA	FTM	Pct.
Bill Sharman, Boston	392	331	.844
Dolph Schayes, Syracuse	590	488	.827
Carl Braun, New York	429	354	.825
Paul Seymour, Syracuse	368	299	.813
Bob Zawoluk, Philadelphia	230	186	.809
Bob Cousy, Boston	522	411	.787
Harry Gallatin, New York	552	433	.784
George Mikan, Minneapolis	546	424	.777
Odie Spears, Rochester	238	183	.769
Ed Macauley, Boston	554	420	.758

LEADERS IN REBOUNDS

	G.	No.	Avg.
Harry Gallatin, New York	72	1098	15.3
George Mikan, Minneapolis	72	1028	14.3
Larry Foust, Ft. Wayne	72	967	13.4
Ray Felix, Baltimore	72	958	13.3
Dolph Schayes, Syracuse	72	870	12.1
Neil Johnston, Philadelphia	72	797	11.1
Arnie Risen, Rochester	72	728	10.1
Mel Hutchins, Ft. Wayne	72	695	9.7
Lew Hitch, Milwaukee	72	691	9.6
Joe Graboski, Philadelphia	71	670	9.4

LEADERS IN ASSISTS

	G.	No.	Avg.
Bob Cousy, Boston	72	518	7.2
Andy Phillip, Ft. Wayne	74	449	6.3
Paul Seymour, Syracuse	71	364	5.1
Dick McGuire, New York	68	354	5.2
Bob Davies, Rochester	72	323	4.5
Jack George, Philadelphia	71	312	4.4
Paul Hoffman, Baltimore	72	285	4.0
George King, Syracuse	72	272	3.8
Ed Macauley, Boston	71	271	3.8
Daniel Finn, Philadelphia	68	265	3.9

INTER-CLUB RECORDS—HOME, AWAY AND NEUTRAL COURT

EASTERN DIVISION

	N.Y.	Bos.	Syr.	Phil.	Balt.	Minn.	Roch.	Ft.W.	Mil.	Home	Away	Neutral	W.	L.
New York	..	5	5	7	3	7	5	3	5	18- 8	15- 13	11- 7	44- 28
Boston	5	..	5	6	9	3	4	4	6	16- 6	11- 19	15- 5	42- 30
Syracuse	5	5	..	4	7	3	5	6	7	27- 5	10- 19	5- 6	42- 30
Philadelphia	3	4	6	..	6	2	1	2	5	10- 9	6- 16	13- 18	29- 43
Baltimore	3	1	3	4	..	2	1	0	2	12- 20	0- 20	4- 16	16- 56

WESTERN DIVISION

	N.Y.	Bos.	Syr.	Phil.	Balt.	Minn.	Roch.	Ft.W.	Mil.	Home	Away	Neutral	W.	L.
Minneapolis	5	5	5	6	6	..	6	5	8	21- 4	13- 15	12- 7	46- 26
Rochester	1	4	3	7	7	5	..	8	9	18- 10	12- 15	14- 3	44- 28
Ft. Wayne	3	4	2	6	8	5	3	..	9	19- 8	11- 17	10- 7	40- 32
Milwaukee	3	2	1	3	6	3	1	2	..	10- 14	6- 17	5- 20	21- 51

1953-54 CHAMPIONSHIP PLAYOFF RESULTS

EASTERN DIVISION ROUND ROBIN

Mar. 16—Boston 93 at New York.............................71
Mar. 17—Syracuse 96 at Boston.............................*95
Mar. 18—New York 68 at Syracuse..........................75
Mar. 20—New York 78 at Boston.............................79
Mar. 21—Syracuse 103 at New York.........................99
Mar. 22—Boston 85 at Syracuse.............................98

EASTERN DIVISION FINALS
Syracuse 2, Boston 0

Mar. 25—Boston 94 at Syracuse............................109
Mar. 27—Syracuse 83 at Boston.............................76

WESTERN DIVISION ROUND ROBIN

Mar. 16—Ft. Wayne 75 at Rochester.........................82
Mar. 17—Rochester 88 at Minneapolis.....................109
Mar. 18—Minneapolis 90 at Ft. Wayne.......................85
Mar. 20—Ft. Wayne 73 at Minneapolis.......................78

Mar. 21—Rochester 89 at Ft. Wayne.........................71
Mar. 23—Minneapolis at Rochester (cancelled)

WESTERN DIVISION FINALS
Minneapolis 2, Rochester 1

Mar. 24—Rochester 76 at Minneapolis......................89
Mar. 27—Minneapolis 73 at Rochester......................74
Mar. 28—Rochester 72 at Minneapolis......................82

CHAMPIONSHIP SERIES
Minneapolis 4, Syracuse 3

Mar. 31—Syracuse 68 at Minneapolis.......................79
Apr. 3—Syracuse 62 at Minneapolis.......................60
Apr. 4—Minneapolis 81 at Syracuse.......................67
Apr. 8—Minneapolis 69 at Syracuse.......................80
Apr. 10—Minneapolis 84 at Syracuse.......................73
Apr. 11—Syracuse 65 at Minneapolis.......................63
Apr. 12—Syracuse 80 at Minneapolis.......................87

*—Denotes overtime period.

1952-53 STATISTICS

1952-53 CHAMPION MINNEAPOLIS LAKERS

Left to right: Coach John Kundla, Slater Martin, Frank Saul, Jim Holstein, Vern Mikkelsen, Lew Hitch, George Mikan, Jim Pollard, Bob Harrison, Whitey Skoog, Assistant Coach Dave McMillan.

FINAL STANDINGS AND TEAM FIGURES

EASTERN DIVISION

Team	W.	L.	FGA	FGM	Pct.	FTA	FTM	Pct.	Reb.	Ast.	PF	Disq.	Pts.	Avg.	Opp.
New York	47	23	5339	2059	.386	2652	1867	.704	4007	1575	2053	68	5985	85.5	5619
Syracuse	47	24	5329	1942	.364	2950	2197	.745	3472	1459	2132	49	6081	85.6	5775
Boston	46	25	5555	2177	.392	2617	1904	.728	3865	1666	1911	56	6258	88.1	6090
Baltimore	16	54	5615	2083	.371	2542	1745	.686	3727	1514	2141	93	5911	84.4	6360
Philadelphia	12	57	5546	1987	.358	2298	1560	.679	3763	1513	1860	70	5534	80.2	6137

WESTERN DIVISION

Team	W.	L.	FGA	FGM	Pct.	FTA	FTM	Pct.	Reb.	Ast.	PF	Disq.	Pts.	Avg.	Opp.
Minneapolis	48	22	5559	2166	.390	2221	1641	.739	3406	1351	1917	58	5973	85.3	5544
Rochester	44	26	5432	2019	.372	2747	2005	.730	3625	1520	2210	107	6043	86.3	5847
Ft. Wayne	36	33	5230	1876	.359	2491	1839	.738	3548	1438	2119	97	5591	81.0	5599
Indianapolis	28	43	5204	1829	.351	2277	1637	.719	3326	1281	1765	60	5295	74.6	5493
Milwaukee	27	44	5320	1873	.352	2400	1643	.685	3429	1427	2120	93	5389	75.9	5596

TOP 25 SCORERS

Player–Team	G.	Min.	FGA	FGM	Pct.	FTA	FTM	Pct.	Reb.	Ast.	PF	Disq.	Pts.	Avg.
Neil Johnston, Phila.	70	3166	1114	504	.452	794	556	.700	976	197	248	6	1564	22.3
Geo. Mikan, Minn.	70	2651	1252	500	.399	567	442	.780	1007	201	290	12	1442	20.6
Bob Cousy, Boston	71	2945	1320	464	.352	587	479	.816	449	547	227	4	1407	19.8
Ed Macauley, Boston	69	2902	997	451	.452	667	500	.750	629	280	188	0	1402	20.3
Dolph Schayes, Syracuse	71	2668	1022	375	.367	619	512	.827	920	227	271	9	1262	17.8
Bill Sharman, Boston	71	2333	925	403	.436	401	341	.850	288	191	240	7	1147	16.2
Jack Nichols, Milwaukee	69	2626	1170	425	.363	339	240	.708	533	196	237	9	1090	15.8
Vern Mikkelsen, Minn.	70	2465	868	378	.435	387	291	.752	654	148	289	14	1047	15.0
Bob Davies, Rochester	66	2216	880	339	.385	466	351	.753	195	280	261	7	1029	15.6
Bob Wanzer, Rochester	70	2577	866	318	.367	473	384	.812	351	252	206	7	1020	14.6
Carl Braun, New York	70	2316	807	323	.400	401	331	.825	233	243	287	14	977	14.0
Leo Barnhorst, India'lis	71	2871	1034	402	.389	259	163	.629	483	277	245	8	967	13.6
Larry Foust, Ft. Wayne	67	2303	865	311	.360	465	336	.723	769	151	267	16	958	14.3

1952-53 STATISTICS

Player—Team	G.	Min.	FGA	FGM	Pct.	FTA	FTM	Pct.	Reb.	Ast.	PF	Disq.	Pts.	Avg.
Paul Seymour, Syracuse	67	2684	798	306	.383	416	340	.817	246	294	210	3	952	14.2
Don Barksdale, Baltimore	65	2298	829	321	.387	401	257	.641	597	166	273	13	899	13.8
Joe Graboski, India'lis	69	2769	799	272	.340	513	350	.682	687	156	303	18	894	13.0
Arnie Risen, Rochester	68	2288	802	295	.368	429	294	.685	745	135	274	10	884	13.0
Harry Gallatin, New York	70	2333	635	282	.444	430	301	.700	916	126	224	6	865	12.4
Jim Pollard, Minn.	66	2403	933	333	.357	251	193	.769	452	231	194	3	859	13.0
Joe Fulks, Philadelphia	70	2085	960	332	.346	231	168	.727	387	138	319	20	832	11.9
Mel Hutchins, Milwaukee	71	2891	842	319	.379	295	193	.654	793	227	214	5	831	11.7
Fred Scolari, Ft. Wayne	62	2123	809	277	.342	327	276	.844	209	233	212	4	830	13.4
George King, Syracuse	71	2519	635	255	.402	442	284	.643	281	364	244	2	794	11.2
Red Rocha, Syracuse	69	2454	690	268	.388	310	234	.755	510	137	257	5	770	11.2
Jack Coleman, Rochester	70	2625	748	314	.420	208	135	.649	774	231	245	12	763	10.9

FIELD GOAL PERCENTAGE LEADERS
(Minimum 210 FGM)

	FGA	FGM	Pct.
Neil Johnston, Philadelphia	1114	504	.4524
Ed Macauley, Boston	997	451	.4523
Harry Gallatin, New York	635	282	.444
Bill Sharman, Boston	925	403	.436
Vern Mikkelsen, Minneapolis	868	378	.435
Ernie Vandeweghe, New York	625	272	.435
Jack Coleman, Rochester	748	314	.420
Slater Martin, Minneapolis	634	260	.410
George King, Syracuse	635	255	.402
Bob Lavoy, Indianapolis	560	225	.402

FREE THROW PERCENTAGE LEADERS
(Minimum 180 FTM)

	FTA	FTM	Pct.
Bill Sharman, Boston	401	341	.850
Fred Scolari, Fort Wayne	327	276	.844
Dolph Schayes, Syracuse	619	512	.827
Carl Braun, New York	401	331	.825
Fred Schaus, Fort Wayne	296	243	.821
Odie Spears, Rochester	243	199	.819
Paul Seymour, Syracuse	416	340	.817
Bob Cousy, Boston	587	479	.816
Bob Wanzer, Rochester	473	384	.812
Bill Tosheff, Indianapolis	314	253	.806

LEADERS IN REBOUNDS

	G.	No.	Avg.
George Mikan, Minneapolis	70	1007	14.4
Neil Johnston, Philadelphia	70	976	13.9
Dolph Schayes, Syracuse	71	920	13.0
Harry Gallatin, New York	70	916	13.1
Mel Hutchins, Milwaukee	71	793	11.2
Jack Coleman, Rochester	70	774	11.1
Larry Foust, Fort Wayne	67	769	11.5
Nat Clifton, New York	70	761	10.9
Arnie Risen, Rochester	68	745	11.0
Joe Graboski, Indianapolis	69	687	10.0

LEADERS IN ASSISTS

	G.	No.	Avg.
Bob Cousy, Boston	71	547	7.7
Andy Phillip, Phil.-Ft.W.	70	397	5.7
George King, Syracuse	71	364	5.1
Dick McGuire, New York	61	296	4.9
Paul Seymour, Syracuse	67	294	4.4
Ed Macauley, Boston	69	280	4.1
Bob Davis, Rochester	66	280	4.2
Leo Barnhorst, Indianapolis	71	277	3.9
George Senesky, Philadelphia	69	264	4.0
Bob Wanzer, Rochester	70	252	3.6

INTER-CLUB RECORDS—HOME, AWAY AND NEUTRAL COURT

EASTERN DIVISION

	N.Y.	Syr.	Bos.	Balt.	Phil.	Minn.	Roch.	Ft.W.	Mil.	Ind.	Home	Away	Neutral	W.	L.
New York	..	6	4	10	10	2	3	2	5	5	21- 4	15- 14	11- 5	47- 23
Syracuse	4	..	6	8	8	4	4	5	5	3	32- 2	10- 19	5- 3	47- 24
Boston	6	5	..	8	9	1	4	4	4	5	21- 8	11- 18	14- 4	46- 25
Baltimore	0	2	2	..	6	1	0	0	2	3	11- 20	1- 19	4- 15	16- 54
Philadelphia	0	2	1	4	..	0	2	0	1	2	4- 13	1- 28	7- 16	12- 57

WESTERN DIVISION

Minneapolis	4	2	5	5	6	..	4	9	6	7	24- 2	16- 15	8- 5	48- 22
Rochester	3	2	2	6	4	6	..	7	7	7	24- 8	13- 16	7- 2	44- 26
Ft. Wayne	4	1	2	6	5	1	3	..	7	7	25- 4	8- 19	3- 5	36- 33
Indianapolis	1	1	2	4	5	4	3	3	..	5	19- 14	4- 23	5- 6	28- 43
Milwaukee	1	3	1	3	4	3	3	3	6	..	14- 8	4- 24	9- 12	27- 44

1952-53 CHAMPIONSHIP PLAYOFF RESULTS

EASTERN DIVISION SEMI-FINALS
New York 2, Baltimore 0
Mar. 17—Baltimore 62 at New York 80
Mar. 20—New York 90 at Baltimore 81

boston 2, Syracuse 0
Mar. 19—Boston 87 at Syracuse 81
Mar. 21—Syracuse 105 at Boston ****111

EASTERN DIVISION FINALS
New York 3, Boston 1
Mar. 25—Boston 91 at New York 95
Mar. 26—New York 70 at Boston 86
Mar. 28—Boston 82 at New York 101
Mar. 29—New York 82 at Boston 75

WESTERN DIVISION SEMI-FINALS
Ft. Wayne 2, Rochester 1
Mar. 20—Ft. Wayne 84 at Rochester 77
Mar. 22—Rochester 83 at Ft. Wayne 71
Mar. 24—Ft. Wayne 67 at Rochester 65

Minneapolis 2, Indianapolis 0
Mar. 22—Indianapolis 69 at Minneapolis 85
Mar. 23—Minneapolis 81 at Indianapolis 79

WESTERN DIVISION FINALS
Minneapolis 3, Ft. Wayne 2
Mar. 26—Ft. Wayne 73 at Minneapolis 83
Mar. 28—Ft. Wayne 75 at Minneapolis 82
Mar. 30—Minneapolis 95 at Ft. Wayne 98
Apr. 1—Minneapolis 82 at Ft. Wayne 85
Apr. 2—Ft. Wayne 58 at Minneapolis 74

CHAMPIONSHIP SERIES
Minneapolis 4, New York 1
Apr. 4—New York 96 at Minneapolis 88
Apr. 5—New York 71 at Minneapolis 73
Apr. 7—Minneapolis 90 at New York 75
Apr. 8—Minneapolis 71 at New York 69
Apr. 10—Minneapolis 91 at New York 84

*—Denotes overtime period.

1951-52 STATISTICS

1951-52 CHAMPION MINNEAPOLIS LAKERS
Left to right: Slater Martin, Joe Hutton, Frank Saul, Bob Harrison, Jim Pollard, Howie Schultz, Vern Mikkelsen, Lew Hitch, George Mikan. (Coach John Kundla). Absent Whitey Skoog.

FINAL STANDINGS AND TEAM FIGURES

EASTERN DIVISION

Team	W.	L.	FGA	FGM	Pct.	FTA	FTM	Pct.	Reb.	Ast.	PF	Disq.	Pts.	Avg.	Opp.
Syracuse	40	26	5207	1894	.364	2589	1933	.747	3603	1373	1970	49	5721	86.7	5427
Boston	39	27	5510	2131	.387	2406	1765	.734	3750	1606	1734	47	6027	91.3	5759
New York	37	29	5282	2022	.383	2185	1565	.716	3834	1567	1770	16	5609	85.0	5560
Philadelphia	33	33	5367	2039	.380	2143	1634	.762	3647	1593	1806	57	5712	86.5	5795
Baltimore	20	46	5495	1882	.342	2211	1614	.730	3780	1417	1719	55	5378	81.5	5873

WESTERN DIVISION

Team	W.	L.	FGA	FGM	Pct.	FTA	FTM	Pct.	Reb.	Ast.	PF	Disq.	Pts.	Avg.	Opp.
Rochester	41	25	5172	2014	.389	2150	1661	.773	3373	1590	1804	62	5689	86.2	5469
Minneapolis	40	26	5733	2106	.367	1921	1436	.748	3543	1389	1763	60	5648	85.6	5250
Indianapolis	34	32	5513	2026	.367	1965	1422	.724	3288	1290	1586	37	5474	82.9	5466
Ft. Wayne	29	37	5013	1771	.353	2194	1609	.733	3619	1403	1751	70	5151	78.0	5286
Milwaukee	17	49	5055	1674	.331	2177	1485	.682	3540	1229	1848	68	4833	73.2	5357

TOP 25 SCORERS

Player–Team	G.	Min.	FGA	FGM	Pct.	FTA	FTM	Pct.	Reb.	Ast.	PF	Disq.	Pts.	Avg.
Paul Arizin, Phila.	66	2939	1222	548	.448	707	578	.818	745	170	250	5	1674	25.4
George Mikan, Minn.	64	2572	1414	545	.385	555	433	.780	866	194	286	14	1523	23.8
Bob Cousy, Boston	66	2681	1388	512	.369	506	409	.808	421	441	190	5	1433	21.7
Ed Macauley, Boston	66	2631	888	384	.432	621	496	.799	529	232	174	0	1264	19.2
Bob Davies, Rochester	65	2394	990	379	.383	379	294	.776	189	390	269	10	1052	16.2
Frank Brian, Ft. Wayne	66	2672	974	342	.351	433	367	.848	232	233	220	6	1051	15.9
Larry Foust, Ft. Wayne	66	2615	989	390	.394	394	267	.678	880	200	245	10	1047	15.9
Bob Wanzer, Rochester	66	2498	772	328	.425	417	377	.904	333	262	201	5	1033	15.7
Arnie Risen, Rochester	66	2396	926	365	.394	431	302	.701	841	150	258	3	1032	15.6
Vern Mikkelsen, Minn.	66	2345	866	363	.419	372	283	.761	681	180	282	16	1009	15.3
Jim Pollard, Minn.	65	2545	1155	411	.356	260	183	.704	593	234	199	4	1005	15.5
Fred Scolari, Baltimore	64	2242	867	290	.334	423	353	.835	214	303	213	6	933	14.6
Max Zaslofsky, New York	66	2113	958	322	.336	380	287	.755	194	156	183	5	931	14.1

1951-52 STATISTICS

Player—Team	G.	Min.	FGA	FGM	Pct.	FTA	FTM	Pct.	Reb.	Ast.	PF	Disq.	Pts.	Avg.
Joe Fulks, Philadelphia	61	1904	1078	336	.312	303	250	.825	368	123	255	13	922	15.1
Joe Graboski, Indianapolis	66	2439	827	320	.387	396	264	.667	655	130	254	10	904	13.7
Fred Schaus, Ft. Wayne	62	2581	778	281	.361	372	310	.833	434	247	221	7	872	14.1
Dolph Schayes, Syracuse	63	2004	740	263	.355	424	342	.807	773	182	213	5	868	13.8
Red Rocha, Syracuse	66	2543	749	300	.401	330	254	.770	549	128	249	4	854	12.9
Leo Barnhorst, India'lis	66	2344	897	349	.389	187	122	.652	430	255	196	3	820	12.4
Andy Phillip, Phila.	66	2933	762	279	.366	308	232	.753	434	539	218	6	790	12.0
Don Barksdale, Baltimore	62	2014	804	272	.338	343	237	.691	601	137	230	13	781	12.6
Stan Miasek, Baltimore	66	2174	707	258	.365	372	263	.707	639	140	257	12	779	11.8
Don Otten, Ft. W.-Milw.	64	1789	636	222	.349	418	323	.773	435	123	218	11	767	12.0
Harry Gallatin, N. York	66	1931	527	233	.442	341	275	.806	661	115	223	5	741	11.2
D. Eddleman, Mil.-Ft.W.	65	1893	809	269	.333	329	202	.614	267	134	249	9	740	11.4

FIELD GOAL PERCENTAGE LEADERS
(Minimum 210 FGM)

	FGA	FGM	Pct.
Paul Arizin, Philadelphia	1222	548	.448
Harry Gallatin, New York	527	233	.442
Ed Macauley, Boston	888	384	.432
Bob Wanzer, Rochester	772	328	.425
Vern Mikkelsen, Minneapolis	866	363	.419
Jack Coleman, Rochester	742	308	.415
George King, Syracuse	579	235	.406
Red Rocha, Syracuse	749	300	.401
Paul Walther, Indianapolis	549	220	.401
Bob Lavoy, Indianapolis	604	240	.397

FREE THROW PERCENTAGE LEADERS
(Minimum 180 FTM)

	FTA	FTM	Pct.
Bob Wanzer, Rochester	417	377	.904
Al Cervi, Syracuse	248	219	.883
Bill Sharman, Boston	213	183	.859
Frank Brian, Fort Wayne	433	367	.848
Fred Scolari, Baltimore	423	353	.835
Fred Schaus, Fort Wayne	272	310	.833
Joe Fulks, Philadelphia	303	250	.825
Bill Tosheff, Indianapolis	221	182	.824
Paul Arizin, Philadelphia	707	578	.818
Bob Cousy, Boston	506	409	.808

LEADERS IN REBOUNDS

	G.	No.	Avg.
Larry Foust, Ft. Wayne	66	880	13.3
Mel Hutchins, Milwaukee	66	880	13.3
George Mikan, Minneapolis	64	866	13.5
Arnie Risen, Rochester	66	841	12.7
Dolph Schayes, Syracuse	63	773	12.3
Paul Arizin, Philadelphia	66	745	11.3
Nat Clifton, New York	62	731	11.6
Jack Coleman, Rochester	66	692	10.5
Vern Mikkelsen, Minneapolis	66	681	10.3
Harry Gallatin, New York	66	661	10.0

LEADERS IN ASSISTS

	G.	No.	Avg.
Andy Phillip, Philadelphia	66	539	8.2
Bob Cousy, Boston	66	441	6.7
Bob Davies, Rochester	65	390	6.0
Dick McGuire, New York	64	388	6.1
Fred Scolari, Baltimore	64	303	4.7
George Senesky, Philadelphia	57	280	4.9
Bob Wanzer, Rochester	66	262	4.0
Leo Barnhorst, Indianapolis	66	255	3.9
Slater Martin, Minneapolis	66	249	3.8
Fred Schaus, Fort Wayne	62	247	4.0

INTER-CLUB RECORDS—HOME, AWAY AND NEUTRAL COURT

EASTERN DIVISION

	Syr.	Bos.	N.Y.	Phil.	Balt.	Roch.	Minn.	Ind.	Ft.W.	Mil.	Home	Away	Neutral	W.	L.
Syracuse		5	4	6	6	2	5	2	6	4	26- 7	12- 18	2- 1	40-	26
Boston	4	..	4	6	8	3	3	3	5	3	22- 7	10- 19	7- 1	39-	27
New York	5	5	..	6	7	2	2	3	3	4	21- 4	12- 22	4- 3	37-	29
Philadelphia	3	3	3	..	5	2	2	4	4	5	24- 7	6- 25	3- 1	33-	33
Baltimore	3	1	2	4	..	2	0	2	2	4	17- 15	2- 22	1- 9	20-	46

WESTERN DIVISION

	Syr.	Bos.	N.Y.	Phil.	Balt.	Roch.	Minn.	Ind.	Ft.W.	Mil.	Home	Away	Neutral	W.	L.
Rochester	4	3	4	4	4	..	2	6	6	8	28- 5	12- 18	1- 2	41- 25
Minneapolis	1	3	4	2	6	7	..	3	5	4	21- 8	5- 13- 19	6- 2	40- 26
Indianapolis	4	3	3	2	4	3	4	..	4	7	25- 6	4- 24	5- 2	34- 32
Ft. Wayne	0	3	3	2	4	3	5	5	..	4	22- 11	6- 24	1- 2	29- 37
Milwaukee	2	1	2	1	2	1	2	5	..		7- 13	3- 22	7- 14	17- 49

1951-52 CHAMPIONSHIP PLAYOFF RESULTS

EASTERN DIVISION SEMI-FINALS
Syracuse 2, Philadelphia 1

Mar. 20—Philadelphia 83 at Syracuse ... 102
Mar. 22—Syracuse 95 at Philadelphia ... 100
Mar. 23—Philadelphia 73 at Syracuse ... 84

New York 2, Boston 1

Mar. 19—New York 94 at Boston ... 105
Mar. 23—Boston 97 at New York ... 101
Mar. 26—New York 88 at Boston ... **87

EASTERN DIVISION FINALS
New York 3, Syracuse 1

Apr. 2—New York 87 at Syracuse ... 85
Apr. 3—New York 92 at Syracuse ... 102
Apr. 4—Syracuse 92 at New York ... 99
Apr. 8—Syracuse 93 at New York ... 100

WESTERN DIVISION SEMI-FINALS
Minneapolis 2, Indianapolis 0

Mar. 23—Indianapolis 70 at Minneapolis ... 78
Mar. 25—Minneapolis 94 at Indianapolis ... 87

Rochester 2, Ft. Wayne 0

Mar. 18—Ft. Wayne 78 at Rochester ... 95
Mar. 20—Rochester 92 at Ft. Wayne ... 86

WESTERN DIVISION FINALS
Minneapolis 3, Rochester 1

Mar. 29—Minneapolis 78 at Rochester ... 88
Mar. 30—Minneapolis 83 at Rochester ... 78
Apr. 5—Rochester 67 at Minneapolis ... 77
Apr. 6—Rochester 80 at Minneapolis ... 82

CHAMPIONSHIP SERIES
Minneapolis 4, New York 3

Apr. 12—New York 79, Minn. at St. Paul ... *83
Apr. 13—New York 80, Minn. at St. Paul ... 72
Apr. 16—Minneapolis 82 at New York ... 77
Apr. 18—Minneapolis 89 at New York ... *90
Apr. 20—New York 89, Minn. at St. Paul ... 102
Apr. 23—Minneapolis 68 at New York ... 76
Apr. 25—New York 65 at Minneapolis ... 82

*—Denotes overtime period.

1950-51 STATISTICS

1950-51 CHAMPION ROCHESTER ROYALS

Front row (left to right): Bob Davies, Bob Wanzer, William Holzman, Paul Noel, Frank Saul. Rear Row: Bill Calhoun, Joe McNamee, Arnold Risen, Jack Coleman, Arnold Johnson. Inset: Coach Les Harrison.

FINAL STANDINGS AND TEAM FIGURES

EASTERN DIVISION

Team	W.	L.	FGA	FGM	Pct.	FTA	FTM	Pct.	Reb.	Ast.	PF	Disq.	Pts.	Avg.	Opp.
Philadelphia	40	26	5665	1985	.350	2181	1664	.763	3586	1432	1710	61	5634	85.4	5386
Boston	39	30	5607	2056	.368	2415	1751	.725	3499	1579	1881	52	5881	85.2	5899
New York	36	30	5380	2037	.379	2231	1592	.714	3421	1551	1810	47	5666	85.8	5639
Syracuse	32	34	5365	1884	.351	2634	1912	.726	3259	1493	1995	64	5680	86.1	5644
Baltimore	24	42	5542	1955	.353	2020	1504	.745	3044	1345	1736	53	5414	82.0	5565
*Washington	10	25	2893	967	.334	1244	910	.731	1567	584	1050	26	2844	81.3	3011

*Disbanded January 9.

WESTERN DIVISION

Team	W.	L.	FGA	FGM	Pct.	FTA	FTM	Pct.	Reb.	Ast.	PF	Disq.	Pts.	Avg.	Opp.
Minneapolis	44	24	5590	2084	.373	1989	1464	.736	3409	1408	1801	49	5632	82.8	5264
Rochester	41	27	5377	2032	.378	2248	1692	.753	3015	1368	1534	35	5756	84.6	5553
Ft. Wayne	32	36	5927	2002	.338	2387	1718	.720	3725	1142	1961	79	5722	84.1	5849
Indianapolis	31	37	5779	2096	.363	1902	1363	.717	2779	1455	1569	35	5555	81.7	5716
Tri-Cities	25	43	6041	1988	.320	2425	1754	.728	3715	1476	2092	79	5730	84.3	5988

TOP 25 SCORERS

Player—Team	G.	FGA	FGM	Pct.	FTA	FTM	Pct.	Reb.	Ast.	PF	Disq.	Pts.	Avg.
George Mikan, Minneapolis	68	1584	678	.428	717	576	.803	958	298	308	14	1932	28.4
Alex Groza, Indianapolis	66	1046	492	.470	566	445	.786	709	156	237	8	1429	21.7
Ed Macauley, Boston	68	985	459	.466	614	466	.759	616	252	205	4	1384	20.4
Joe Fulks, Philadelphia	66	1358	429	.316	442	378	.855	523	117	247	8	1236	18.7

1950-51 STATISTICS

Player–Team	G.	FGA	FGM	Pct.	FTA	FTM	Pct.	Reb.	Ast.	PF	Disq.	Pts.	Avg.
Frank Brian, Tri-Cities	68	1127	363	.322	508	418	.823	244	266	215	4	1144	16.8
Paul Arizin, Philadelphia	65	864	352	.407	526	417	.793	640	138	284	18	1121	17.2
Dolph Schayes, Syracuse	66	930	332	.357	608	457	.752	1080	251	271	9	1121	17.0
Ralph Beard, Indianapolis	66	1110	409	.369	378	292	.775	251	318	96	0	1111	16.8
Bob Cousy, Boston	69	1138	401	.352	365	276	.756	474	341	185	2	1078	15.6
Arnie Risen, Rochester	66	940	377	.401	440	323	.734	795	158	278	9	1077	16.3
Dwight Eddleman, Tri-Cities	68	1120	398	.355	349	244	.699	410	170	231	5	1040	15.3
Fred Schaus, Ft. Wayne	68	918	312	.340	484	404	.835	495	184	240	11	1028	15.1
Vince Boryla, New York	66	867	352	.406	332	278	.837	249	182	244	6	982	14.2
Bob Davies, Rochester	63	877	326	.372	381	303	.795	197	287	208	7	955	13.5
Larry Foust, Ft. Wayne	68	944	327	.346	396	261	.659	681	90	247	6	915	13.5
Vern Mikkelsen, Minneapolis	64	893	359	.402	275	186	.676	655	181	260	13	904	14.1
Fred Scolari, Was.-Syra.	66	923	302	.327	331	279	.843	218	255	183	1	883	13.4
Ken Murray, Balt.-Ft. Wayne	66	887	301	.339	332	248	.747	355	202	164	7	850	12.9
Geo. Ratkovicz, Syracuse	66	636	264	.415	439	321	.731	547	193	256	11	849	12.9
Harry Gallatin, New York	66	705	293	.416	354	259	.732	800	180	244	4	845	12.3
Red Rocha, Baltimore	64	843	297	.352	299	242	.809	511	147	242	9	836	13.1
Max Zaslofsky, New York	66	853	302	.354	298	231	.775	228	136	150	3	835	12.7
Jack Coleman, Rochester	67	749	315	.421	172	134	.779	584	197	193	4	764	11.4
Andy Phillip, Philadelphia	66	690	275	.399	253	190	.751	446	414	221	8	740	11.2
Bob Wanzer, Rochester	68	628	252	.401	273	232	.850	232	181	129	0	736	10.8

FIELD GOAL PERCENTAGE LEADERS
(Minimum 200 FGM)

	FGA	FGM	Pct.
Alex Groza, Indianapolis	1046	492	.470
Ed Macauley, Boston	985	459	.466
George Mikan, Minneapolis	1584	678	.428
Jack Coleman, Rochester	749	315	.421
Harry Gallatin, New York	705	293	.416
Geo. Ratkovicz, Syracuse	636	264	.415
Paul Arizin, Philadelphia	864	352	.407
Vince Boryla, New York	867	352	.406
Jim Pollard, Minneapolis	893	359	.402
Vern Mikkelsen, Minneapolis	893	359	.402

FREE THROW PERCENTAGE LEADERS
(Minimum 170 FTM)

	FTA	FTM	Pct.
Joe Fulks, Philadelphia	442	378	.855
Bob Wanzer, Rochester	273	232	.850
Belus Smawley, Syr.-Balt.	267	227	.850
Fred Scolari, Wash.-Syr.	331	279	.843
Vince Boryla, New York	332	278	.837
Fred Schaus, Ft. Wayne	484	404	.835
Sonny Hertzberg, Boston	270	223	.826
Frank Brian, Tri-Cities	508	418	.823
Al Cervi, Syracuse	237	194	.819
Red Rocha, Baltimore	299	242	.809

LEADERS IN REBOUNDS

	G.	No.	Avg.
Dolph Schayes, Syracuse	66	1080	16.4
George Mikan, Minneapolis	68	958	14.1
Harry Gallatin, New York	66	800	12.1
Arnie Risen, Rochester	66	795	12.0
Alex Groza, Indianapolis	66	709	10.7
Larry Foust, Ft. Wayne	68	681	10.0
Vern Mikkelsen, Minneapolis	64	655	10.2
Paul Arizin, Philadelphia	65	640	9.8
Ed Macauley, Boston	68	616	9.1
Jack Coleman, Rochester	67	584	8.7

LEADERS IN ASSISTS

	G.	No.	Avg.
Andy Phillip, Philadelphia	66	414	6.3
Dick McGuire, New York	64	400	6.3
George Senesky, Philadelphia	65	342	5.3
Bob Cousy, Boston	69	341	4.9
Ralph Beard, Indianapolis	66	318	4.8
George Mikan, Minneapolis	68	298	4.4
Bob Davies, Rochester	63	287	4.6
Frank Brian, Tri-Cities	68	266	3.9
Fred Scolari, Wash.-Syr.	66	255	3.9
Dolph Schayes, Syracuse	66	251	3.8
Sonny Hertzberg, Boston	65	244	3.8

INTER-CLUB RECORDS—HOME, AWAY AND NEUTRAL COURT

EASTERN DIVISION

	Phil	Bos	NY	Syr	Balt	Wash	Mpls	Roch	FtW	Ind	T-C	Home	Away	Neutral	W-	L
Philadelphia	..	4	3	6	6	3	2	4	3	5	4	29- 3	10- 22	1- 1	40-	26
Boston	4	..	4	3	6	4	3	2	5	4	4	26- 6	9- 22	4- 2	39-	30
New York	5	4	..	5	5	2	3	3	4	1	4	22- 5	4- 0	0- 0	36-	30
Syracuse	2	5	5	..	5	2	2	2	4	3	3	24- 9	8- 25	0- 0	32-	39
Baltimore	3	3	2	3	..	1	2	1	4	2	3	21- 11	3- 25	0- 6	24-	42
Washington	0	3	1	0	2	..	0	0	1	2	1	6- 11	4- 13	0- 1	10-	25

WESTERN DIVISION

	Phil	Bos	NY	Syr	Balt	Wash	Mpls	Roch	FtW	Ind	T-C	Home	Away	Neutral	W-	L
Minneapolis	4	3	3	4	4	2	..	4	3	7	10	29- 3	12- 21	3- 0	44-	24
Rochester	2	4	3	4	5	5	4	..	5	4	5	29- 5	12- 22	0- 0	41-	27
Ft. Wayne	3	1	2	3	2	3	5	3	..	5	5	27- 7	5- 27	0- 2	32-	36
Indianapolis	1	1	5	3	4	2	3	5	3	..	4	19-12	10- 24	2- 1	31-	37
Tri-Cities	2	2	2	3	3	1	0	3	5	4	..	22-13	2- 28	1- 2	25-	43
Total	26	30	30	34	42	25	24	27	36	37	43	254- 85	85- 254	15- 15	354-	354

1950-51 CHAMPIONSHIP PLAYOFF RESULTS

EASTERN DIVISION SEMI-FINALS
New York 2, Boston 0
- Mar. 20—New York 83 at Boston 69
- Mar. 22—Boston 78 at New York 92

Syracuse 2, Philadelphia 0
- Mar. 20—Syracuse 91 at Philadelphia *89
- Mar. 22—Philadelphia 78 at Syracuse 90

EASTERN DIVISION FINALS
New York 3, Syracuse 2
- Mar. 28—Syracuse 92 at New York 103
- Mar. 29—New York 80 at Syracuse 102
- Mar. 31—Syracuse 75 at New York 97
- Apr. 1—New York 83 at Syracuse 90
- Apr. 4—Syracuse 81 at New York 83

WESTERN DIVISION SEMI-FINALS
Rochester 2, Fort Wayne 1
- Mar. 20—Fort Wayne 81 at Rochester 110
- Mar. 22—Rochester 78 at Fort Wayne 83
- Mar. 24—Fort Wayne 78 at Rochester 97

Minneapolis 2, Indianapolis 1
- Mar. 21—Indianapolis 81 at Minneapolis 95
- Mar. 23—Minneapolis 88 at Indianapolis 108
- Mar. 25—Indianapolis 80 at Minneapolis 85

WESTERN DIVISION FINALS
Rochester 3, Minneapolis 1
- Mar. 29—Rochester 73 at Minneapolis 76
- Mar. 31—Rochester 70 at Minneapolis 66
- Apr. 1—Minneapolis 70 at Rochester 83
- Apr. 3—Minneapolis 75 at Rochester 80

CHAMPIONSHIP SERIES
Rochester 4, New York 3
- Apr. 7—New York 65 at Rochester 92
- Apr. 8—New York 84 at Rochester 99
- Apr. 11—Rochester 78 at New York 71
- Apr. 13—Rochester 73 at New York 79
- Apr. 15—New York 92 at Rochester 89
- Apr. 18—Rochester 80 at New York 80
- Apr. 21—New York 75 at Rochester 79

*—Denotes overtime period.

LOWEST SCORING GAME IN NBA HISTORY

This low-scoring contest was played November 22, 1950 at Minneapolis. Larry Foust's basket with six seconds remaining enabled Fort Wayne to edge Minneapolis, 19-18, snapping the Lakers' 29-game homecourt winning streak.

FORT WAYNE PISTONS (19)

Player	Pos.	FGA	FGM	FTA	FTM	Reb.	Ast.	PF	Pts.
Fred Schaus	F	1	0	3	3	0	1	0	3
Jack Kerris	F	1	0	4	2	2	0	5	2
Larry Foust	C	2	1	1	1	1	0	3	3
Bob Harris		0	0	1	0	1	0	1	0
John Hargis	G	1	1	0	0	0	1	0	2
Ralph Johnson		1	0	0	0	0	1	1	0
John Oldham	G	5	1	4	3	4	0	2	5
Paul Armstrong		2	1	2	2	0	0	1	4
Totals		13	4	15	11	8	3	13	19

MINNEAPOLIS LAKERS (18)

Player	Pos.	FGA	FGM	FTA	FTM	Reb.	Ast.	PF	Pts.
Jim Pollard	F	1	0	1	1	1	1	2	1
Bud Grant		0	0	0	0	1	1	0	0
Vern Mikkelsen	F	2	0	0	0	3	0	2	0
Joe Hutton		0	0	0	0	0	0	0	0
George Mikan	C	11	4	11	7	4	0	1	15
Slater Martin	G	2	0	3	0	1	2	2	0
Bob Harrison	G	2	0	2	2	0	0	3	2
Arnie Ferrin		0	0	0	0	0	0	0	0
Totals		18	4	17	10	9	4	11	18

Score by Periods:	1st	2nd	3rd	4th	Totals
Fort Wayne Pistons	8	3	5	3	– 19
Minneapolis Lakers	7	6	4	1	– 18

Referees—Jocko Collins and Stan Stutz. Attendance—7,021.

1949-50 STATISTICS

1949-50 CHAMPION MINNEAPOLIS LAKERS

Left to right: Slater Martin, Billy Hassett, Don Carlson, Herm Schaefer, Bob Harrison, Tony Jaros, Coach John Kundla, Bud Grant, Arnie Ferrin, Jim Pollard, Vern Mikkelsen, George Mikan.

FINAL STANDINGS AND TEAM FIGURES

EASTERN DIVISION

Team	W	L	FGA	FGM	Pct.	FTA	FTM	Pct.	As't.	PF	Pts.	Avg	Oppo
Syracuse	51	13	5276	1869	.354	2396	1691	.706	1473	1833	5429	84.8	4907
New York	40	28	5351	1889	.353	2404	1710	.711	1308	1718	5488	80.7	5344
Washington	32	36	5493	1813	.330	2111	1575	.746	1057	1837	5201	76.5	5265
Philadelphia	26	42	5711	1779	.312	2037	1425	.700	1142	1768	4983	73.3	5194
Baltimore	25	43	5516	1712	.310	2123	1549	.730	1189	1792	4973	73.1	5353
Boston	22	46	5756	1945	.338	2163	1530	.707	1473	1644	5420	79.7	5590

CENTRAL DIVISION

Team	W	L	FGA	FGM	Pct.	FTA	FTM	Pct.	As't.	PF	Pts.	Avg	Oppo
Minneapolis	51	17	5832	2139	.367	1943	1439	.741	1406	1672	5717	84.1	5149
Rochester	51	17	5247	1956	.373	2319	1690	.729	1383	1585	5602	82.4	5074
Ft. Wayne	40	28	5901	1878	.318	2331	1634	.701	1364	2065	5390	79.3	5297
Chicago	40	28	5892	2003	.340	1934	1346	.696	1366	1977	5352	78.7	5243
St. Louis	26	42	5086	1741	.342	2149	1528	.711	1285	1596	5010	73.7	5202

WESTERN DIVISION

Team	W	L	FGA	FGM	Pct.	FTA	FTM	Pct.	As't.	PF	Pts.	Avg	Oppo
Indianapolis	39	25	5283	1982	.375	2145	1529	.713	1342	1676	5493	85.8	5256
Anderson	37	27	6254	1943	.311	2343	1703	.727	1240	1806	5589	87.3	5348
Tri-Cities	29	35	5515	1818	.330	2308	1677	.727	1330	2057	5313	83.0	5351
Sheboygan	22	40	5022	1727	.344	2338	1654	.707	1279	1766	5108	82.4	5443
Waterloo	19	43	4904	1746	.356	2002	1429	.714	1324	1780	4921	79.4	5264
Denver	11	51	5182	1731	.334	1999	1355	.678	1044	1692	4817	77.7	5526

25 TOP SCORERS

Player–Team	G.	FGA.	FGM.	Pct.	FTA.	FTM.	Pct.	As't.	PF.	Pts.	Avg.
George Mikan, Minneapolis	68	1595	649	.407	728	567	.779	197	297	1865	27.4
Alex Groza, Indianapolis	64	1090	521	.478	623	454	.729	159	221	1496	23.4
Frank Brian, Anderson	64	1156	368	.318	488	402	.824	189	192	1138	17.8
Max Zaslofsky, Chicago	68	1132	397	.351	381	321	.843	155	185	1115	16.4
Ed Macauley, St. Louis	67	882	351	.398	528	379	.718	200	221	1081	16.1
Dolph Schayes, Syracuse	64	903	348	.385	486	276	.774	259	225	1072	16.8
Carl Braun, New York	67	1024	373	.364	374	285	.762	247	188	1031	15.4
Ken Sailors, Denver	57	944	329	.349	456	329	.721	229	242	987	17.3
Jim Pollard, Minneapolis	66	1140	394	.346	242	185	.764	252	143	973	14.7
Fred Schaus, Ft. Wayne	68	996	351	.352	330	270	.818	176	232	972	14.3
Joe Fulks, Philadelphia	68	1209	336	.278	421	293	.696	56	240	965	14.2
Ralph Beard, Indianapolis	60	937	340	.363	282	215	.762	233	132	895	14.9
Bob Davis, Rochester	63	887	317	.357	347	261	.752	294	187	895	14.0
Dick Mehen, Waterloo	62	826	347	.420	281	198	.705	191	203	892	14.4
Jack Nichols, Wash.-Tri-Cities	67	848	310	.366	354	259	.753	142	179	879	13.1
Ed Sadowski, Phila.-Balt.	69	922	299	.324	373	274	.735	136	244	872	12.6
Paul Hoffman, Baltimore	60	914	312	.341	364	242	.665	161	234	866	14.4
Fred Scolari, Washington	66	910	312	.343	287	236	.822	175	181	860	13.0
Vern Gardner, Philadelphia	63	916	313	3.42	296	227	.767	119	236	853	13.5
Belus Smawley, St. Louis	61	832	287	.345	314	260	.828	215	160	834	13.7
Dike Eddleman, Tri-Cities	64	906	332	.366	260	162	.623	142	254	826	12.9
Don Otten, Tri-Cities-Wash.	64	648	242	.373	463	341	.737	91	246	825	12.9
Harry Gallatin, New York	68	664	263	.396	366	277	.757	56	215	803	11.8
Mike Todorovich, St.L.-Tri-Cities	65	852	263	.309	370	266	.719	207	230	792	12.2
Vern Mikkelsen, Minneapolis	68	722	288	.399	286	215	.752	123	222	791	11.6
Bob Wanzer, Rochester	67	614	254	.414	351	283	.806	214	102	791	11.8

FIELD GOAL PERCENTAGE LEADERS
(Minimum 200 FGM)

	FGA	FGM	Pct.
Alex Groza, Indianapolis	1090	521	.478
Dick Mehen, Waterloo	826	347	.420
Bob Wanzer, Rochester	614	254	.414
George Mikan, Minneapolis	1595	649	.407
Red Rocha, St. Louis	679	275	.405
John Hargis, Anderson	550	223	.405
Vern Mikkelsen, Minneapolis	722	288	.399
Ed Macauley, St. Louis	882	351	.398
Jack Toomay, Denver	514	204	.397
Harry Gallatin, New York	664	263	.396

FREE THROW PERCENTAGE LEADERS
(Minimum 170 FTM)

	FTA	FTM	Pct.
Max Zaslofsky, Chicago	381	321	.843
Chick Reiser, Washington	254	212	.835
Al Cervi, Syracuse	346	287	.829
Belus Smawley, St. Louis	214	260	.828
Frank Brian, Anderson	488	402	.824
Fred Scolari, Washington	287	236	.822
Fred Schaus, Ft. Wayne	330	270	.818
Leo Kubiak, Waterloo	236	192	.814
Bob Wanzer, Rochester	351	283	.806
John Logan, St. Louis	323	253	.783

LEADERS IN ASSISTS

	G.	No.	Avg.
Dick McGuire, New York	68	386	5.7
Andy Phillip, Chicago	65	377	5.8
Bob Davies, Rochester	64	294	4.6
George Senesky, Philadelphia	68	264	3.9
Al Cervi, Syracuse	56	264	4.7
Dolph Schayes, Syracuse	64	259	4.0
Jim Pollard, Minneapolis	66	252	3.8
Jim Seminoff, Boston	65	249	3.8
Carl Braun, New York	67	247	3.7
John Logan, St. Louis	62	240	3.9

CLUB VS. CLUB RECORDS

EASTERN DIVISION

	Syr	NY	Wash	Phil	Balt	Bos	Mpls	Roch	FtW	Chi	StL	Ind	And	TriC	Sheb	Wat	Den	Won
Syracuse		2	1	2	2	4	1	1	2	1	2	1	7	4	6	6	6	51
New York	0		5	5	5	5	1	1	2	4	1	1	1	1	2	2	2	40
Washington	0	1		4	3	3	2	1	2	2	2	0	1	1	2	2	2	32
Philadelphia	1	1	2		4	3	0	0	4	3	6	1	1	1	0	1	2	26
Baltimore	0	1	2	3		2	1	3	1	3	1	1	1	0	2	1	3	25
Boston	0	1	3	3	4		1	0	2	0	2	1	2	0	1	1	1	22

CENTRAL DIVISION

	Syr	NY	Wash	Phil	Balt	Bos	Mpls	Roch	FtW	Chi	StL	Ind	And	TriC	Sheb	Wat	Den	Won
Minneapolis	1	5	6	4	5	5		3	4	5	5	1	1	2	1	2	2	51
Rochester	1	5	6	5	3	6	3		3	4	3	1	1	2	2	1	2	40
Fort Wayne	0	4	2	4	3	4	2	3			5	1	1	2	1	2	2	40
Chicago	0	2	3	4	3	4	1	1	1		4	1	0	2	1	2	2	26
St. Louis	1	2	0	4	3	4	1	1	1	1		1	2	0	1	2	2	26

WESTERN DIVISION

	Syr	NY	Wash	Phil	Balt	Bos	Mpls	Roch	FtW	Chi	StL	Ind	And	TriC	Sheb	Wat	Den	Won
Indianapolis	2	1	1	2	1	1	1	1	1	1	1		5	4	5	5	7	39
Anderson	3	1	1	1	1	0	1	0	1	1	2	2		7	5	7	4	37
Tri-Cities	1	1	1	1	2	2	0	0	0	1	0	3	2		3	4	4	29
Sheboygan	1	1	2	0	0	1	1	0	0	0	1	2	0	2		3	5	19
Waterloo	1	0	1	0	1	1	0	1	0	0	0	1	1	0	3		3	13
Denver	1	0	0	0	1	1	0	0	0	0	0	0	3	0	3	2		11
Lost	13	28	36	42	43	46	17	17	28	28	42	25	27	35	40	43	51	561

INTER-CLUB RECORDS—HOME, AWAY AND NEUTRAL COURT

EASTERN DIVISION

	Home W-L	Away W-L	Neut. W-L
Syracuse	31- 1	15- 12	5- 0
New York	19-10	18- 16	3- 2
Wash'gton	21-13	10- 20	1- 3
Phila'phia	15-15	8- 23	3- 4
Baltimore	16-15	8- 25	1- 3
Boston	12-14	5- 28	5- 4
Totals	114-68	64-124	18-16

CENTRAL DIVISION

	Home W-L	Away W-L	Neut. W-L
Min'apolis	30- 1	18- 16	3- 0
Rochester	33- 1	17- 16	1- 0
Ft. Wayne	28- 6	12- 22	0- 0
Chicago	18- 6	14- 21	8- 1
St. Louis	17-14	7- 26	2- 2
Totals	126-28	68-101	14- 3

WESTERN DIVISION

	Home W-L	Away W-L	Neut. W-L
Ind'apolis	23- 5	13- 18	3- 2
Anderson	23- 9	11- 18	3- 0
Tri-Cities	22-13	4- 20	3- 2
Sheboygan	17-14	5- 22	0- 4
Waterloo	17-15	1- 22	1- 6
Denver	9-15	1- 26	1-10
Totals	111-71	35-126	11-24

Grand Totals—Home: 351-167. Away: 167-351. Neutral: 43-43.

1949-50 CHAMPIONSHIP PLAYOFF RESULTS

Central Division 1st place tie
Mar. 21—Minneapolis 78 at Rochester 76
Central Division 3rd place tie
Mar. 20—Chicago 69 at Ft. Wayne 86

EASTERN DIVISION SEMI-FINALS
Syracuse 2, Philadelphia 0

Mar. 22—Philadelphia 76 at Syracuse...............93
Mar. 23—Syracuse 59 at Philadelphia...............53

New York 2, Washington 0

Mar. 21—New York 90 at Washington 87
Mar. 22—Washington 83 at New York 103

EASTERN DIVISION FINALS
Syracuse 2, New York 1

Mar. 26—New York 83 at Syracuse *91
Mar. 30—Syracuse 76 at New York 80
Apr. 2—New York 80 at Syracuse 91

CENTRAL DIVISION SEMI-FINALS
Minneapolis 2, Chicago 0

Mar. 22—Chicago 75 at Minneapolis 85
Mar. 25—Minneapolis 75 at Chicago 67

Ft. Wayne 2, Rochester 0

Mar. 23—Ft. Wayne 90 at Rochester...............84
Mar. 25—Rochester 78 at Ft. Wayne *79

CENTRAL DIVISION FINALS
Minneapolis 2, Ft. Wayne 0

Mar. 27—Ft. Wayne 79 at Minneapolis 93
Mar. 28—Minneapolis 89 at Ft. Wayne...............82

WESTERN DIVISION SEMI-FINALS
Indianapolis 2, Sheboygan 1

Mar. 21—Sheboygan 85 at Indianapolis 86
Mar. 23—Indianapolis 85 at Sheboygan 95
Mar. 25—Sheboygan 84 at Indianapolis 91

Anderson 2, Tri-Cities 1

Mar. 21—Tri-Cities 77 at Anderson 89
Mar. 23—Anderson 75 at Tri-Cities 76
Mar. 24—Tri-Cities 71 at Anderson 94

WESTERN DIVISION FINAL
Anderson 2, Indianapolis 1

Mar. 28—Anderson 74 at Indianapolis 77
Mar. 30—Indianapolis 67 at Anderson 84
Apr. 1—Anderson 67 at Indianapolis 65

NBA SEMI-FINALS
Minneapolis 2, Anderson 0

Apr. 5—Anderson 50 at Minneapolis 75
Apr. 6—Minneapolis 90 at Anderson 71

CHAMPIONSHIP SERIES
Minneapolis 4, Syracuse 2

Apr. 8—Minneapolis 68 at Syracuse 66
Apr. 9—Minneapolis 85 at Syracuse 91
Apr. 14—Syracuse 77, Minn. at St. Paul 91
Apr. 16—Syracuse 69, Minn. at St. Paul 77
Apr. 20—Minneapolis 76 at Syracuse 83
Apr. 23—Syracuse 95 at Minneapolis 110

*—Denotes overtime period.

1948-49 STATISTICS

1948-49 CHAMPION MINNEAPOLIS LAKERS

Left to right: Don Forman, Herman Schaefer, Don Carlson, Don Smith, Tony Jaros, John Jorgensen, Earl Gardner, Arnie Ferrin, Jack Dwan, Jim Pollard, George Mikan. (Coach John Kundla.)

FINAL STANDINGS AND TEAM FIGURES

EASTERN DIVISION

Team	W	L	FGA	FGM	Pct.	FTA	FTM	Pct.	As't.	PF	Pts.	Avg	Oppo
Washington	38	22	5472	1751	.320	1914	1408	.736	972	1710	4910	81.8	4764
New York	32	28	5237	1688	.322	1959	1376	.702	1017	1559	4752	79.2	4663
Baltimore	29	31	5162	1736	.336	2053	1545	.753	1000	1730	5017	83.6	4934
Philadelphia	28	32	5695	1831	.322	1897	1360	.717	1043	1459	5022	83.7	5003
Boston	25	35	5483	1706	.311	1856	1181	.636	1135	1382	4593	76.6	4768
Providence	12	48	5427	1750	.322	1742	1207	.693	1026	1349	4707	78.5	5255

WESTERN DIVISION

Team	W	L	FGA	FGM	Pct.	FTA	FTM	Pct.	As't.	PF	Pts.	Avg	Oppo
Rochester	45	15	4869	1811	.372	2060	1420	.689	1259	1539	5042	84.0	4644
Minneapolis	44	16	5146	1885	.366	1759	1272	.723	1134	1386	5042	84.0	4599
Chicago	38	22	5750	1905	.331	1775	1228	.692	1220	1731	5038	84.0	4798
St. Louis	29	31	4858	1659	.341	1770	1229	.694	1269	1480	4547	75.8	4765
Ft. Wayne	22	38	5370	1536	.286	1979	1385	.700	1082	1722	4457	74.3	4651
Indianapolis	18	42	5367	1621	.302	1798	1240	.690	1225	1393	4482	74.7	4765

TOP 25 SCORERS

Player—Team	G.	FGA.	FGM.	Pct.	FTA.	FTM.	Pct.	As't.	PF.	Pts.	Avg.
George Mikan, Minneapolis	60	1403	583	.416	689	532	.772	218	260	1698	28.3
Joe Fulks, Philadelphia	60	1689	529	.313	638	502	.787	74	262	1560	26.0
Max Zaslofsky, Chicago	58	1216	425	.350	413	347	.840	149	156	1197	20.6
Arnie Risen, Rochester	60	816	345	.423	462	305	.660	100	216	995	16.6
Ed Sadowski, Philadelphia	60	839	340	.405	350	240	.686	160	273	920	15.3
Belus Smawley, St. Louis	59	946	352	.372	281	210	.747	183	145	914	15.5
Bob Davies, Rochester	60	871	317	.364	348	270	.776	321	197	904	15.1
Ken Sailors, Providence	57	906	309	.341	367	281	.766	209	239	899	15.8
Carl Braun, New York	57	906	299	.330	279	212	.760	173	144	810	14.2
John Logan, St. Louis	57	816	282	.346	302	239	.791	276	191	803	14.1

1948-49 STATISTICS

Player—Team	G.	FGA.	FGM.	Pct.	FTA.	FTM.	Pct.	As't.	PF.	Pts.	Avg.
Jim Pollard, Minneapolis	53	792	314	.396	227	156	.687	142	144	784	14.8
Connie Simmons, Baltimore	60	794	299	.377	265	181	.683	116	215	779	13.0
Ray Lumpp, Indianapolis-New York	61	800	279	.349	283	219	.774	158	173	777	12.7
Bob Feerick, Washington	58	708	248	.350	298	256	.859	188	171	752	13.0
Howie Shannon, Providence	55	802	292	.364	189	152	.804	125	154	736	13.4
Horace McKinney, Washington	57	801	263	.328	279	197	.706	114	216	723	12.7
Andy Phillip, Chicago	60	818	285	.348	219	148	.676	319	205	718	12.0
John Palmer, New York	58	685	240	.350	307	234	.762	108	206	714	12.3
Kleg Hermsen, Washington	60	794	248	.312	311	212	.682	99	257	708	11.8
Walter Budko, Baltimore	60	644	224	.348	309	244	.790	99	201	692	11.5
Fred Lewis, Indianapolis-Baltimore	61	834	272	.326	181	138	.762	107	167	682	11.2
John Reiser, Baltimore	57	653	219	.335	257	188	.732	132	202	626	11.0
Charles Halbert, Boston-Providence	60	647	202	.312	345	214	.620	113	175	618	10.3
Bob Wanzer, Rochester	60	533	202	.379	254	209	.823	186	132	612	10.2
Red Rocha, St. Louis	58	574	223	.389	211	162	.768	157	251	608	10.5

FIELD GOAL PERCENTAGE LEADERS
(Minimum 200 FGM)

	FGA	FGM	Pct.
Arnie Risen, Rochester	816	345	.423
George Mikan, Minneapolis	1403	583	.416
Ed Sadowski, Philadelphia	839	340	.405
Jim Pollard, Minneapolis	792	314	.396
Red Rocha, St. Louis	573	223	.389
Bob Wanzer, Rochester	533	202	.379
Connie Simmons, Baltimore	794	299	.377
Herm Schaefer, Minneapolis	572	214	.374
Belus Smawley, St. Louis	946	352	.372
Howie Shannon, Providence	802	292	.364
Bob Davies, Rochester	871	317	.364

FREE THROW PERCENTAGE LEADERS
(Minimum 150 FTM)

	FTA	FTM	Pct.
Bob Feerick, Washington	298	256	.859
Max Zaslofsky, Chicago	413	347	.840
Bob Wanzer, Rochester	254	209	.823
Herm Schaefer, Minneapolis	213	174	.817
Howie Shannon, Providence	189	152	.804
Harold Tidrick, Ind.-Balt.	205	164	.800
John Logan, St. Louis	302	239	.791
Walter Budko, Baltimore	309	244	.790
John Pelkington, Ft.W.-Balt.	267	211	.790
Joe Fulks, Philadelphia	638	502	.787

LEADERS IN ASSISTS

	G.	No.	Avg.
Bob Davies, Rochester	60	321	5.4
Andy Phillip, Chicago	60	319	5.3
John Logan, St. Louis	57	276	4.8
Ernie Calverley, Providence	59	251	4.3
George Senesky, Philadelphia	60	233	3.9
Jim Seminoff, Boston	58	229	3.9
George Mikan, Minneapolis	60	218	3.6
Ken Sailors, Providence	57	209	3.7
Bob Feerick, Washington	58	188	3.2
Bob Wanzer, Rochester	60	186	3.1

INTER-CLUB RECORDS—HOME, AWAY AND NEUTRAL COURT

EASTERN DIVISION

Team	Wash	NY	Balt	Phil	Bos	Prov	Roch	Mpls	Chi	StL	FtW	Ind	Home	Away	Neutral	W.
Washington		3	3	4	5	6	3	2	3	3	3	3	22- 7	15- 14	1- 1	38
New York	3		4	2	3	5	1	1	2	3	4	4	18- 11	12- 17	2- 0	32
Baltimore	3	2		4	4	2	1	1	1	2	4	5	17- 12	11- 17	1- 2	39
Philadelphia	2	4	2		3	6	0	1	3	3	0	4	19- 10	9- 21	0- 1	28
Boston	1	3	2	3		3	1	2	0	3	4	3	17- 12	7- 20	1- 3	25
Providence	0	1	4	0	3		2	0	0	0	1	1	7- 23	5- 23	0- 2	12

WESTERN DIVISION

Rochester	2	4	4	5	4		2	4	6	6	5	24- 5	20- 10	1- 0	45	
Minneapolis	2	4	4	4	3	5	4		4	4	4	6	26- 3	16- 13	2- 0	44
Chicago	3	3	4	2	5	5	2	2		3	4	5	16- 8	18- 14	4- 0	38
St. Louis	2	2	3	2	2	5	0	2	3		5	3	17- 12	10- 18	2- 1	29
Ft. Wayne	2	1	1	5	1	4	0	2	1	3		2	15- 14	5- 23	2- 1	22
Indianapolis	2	1	0	1	2	4	1	0	1	3	3		14- 15	4- 22	0- 5	18
Lost	22	28	31	32	35	48	15	16	22	31	38	42	212-132	132-212	16- 16	360

1948-49 CHAMPIONSHIP PLAYOFF RESULTS

EASTERN DIVISION SEMI-FINALS
Washington 2, Philadelphia 0

Mar. 23—Washington 92 at Philadelphia 70
Mar. 24—Philadelphia 78 at Washington 80

New York 2, Baltimore 1

Mar. 23—New York 81 at Baltimore 82
Mar. 24—Baltimore at New York 84
Mar. 26—Baltimore 99 at New York *103

WESTERN DIVISION SEMI-FINALS
Rochester 2, St. Louis 0

Mar. 22—St. Louis 64 at Rochester 93
Mar. 23—Rochester 66 at St. Louis 64

Minneapolis 2, Chicago 0

Mar. 23—Chicago 77 at Minneapolis 84
Mar. 24—Minneapolis 101 at Chicago 85

EASTERN DIVISION FINALS
Washington 2, New York 1

Mar. 29—New York 71 at Washington 77
Mar. 31—Washington 84 at New York *86
Apr. 2—New York 76 at Washington 84

WESTERN DIVISION FINALS
Minneapolis 2, Rochester 0

Mar. 27—Minneapolis 80 at Rochester 79
Mar. 29—Rochester 55, Minn. at St. Paul 67

CHAMPIONSHIP SERIES
Minneapolis 4, Washington 2

Apr. 4—Washington 84 at Minneapolis 88
Apr. 6—Washington 62 at Minneapolis 76
Apr. 8—Minneapolis 94 at Washington 74
Apr. 9—Minneapolis 71 at Washington 83
Apr. 11—Minneapolis 66 at Washington 74
Apr. 13—Washington 56, Minn. at St. Paul 77

*Denotes overtime period.

1947-48 STATISTICS

1947-48 CHAMPION BALTIMORE BULLETS
Left to right: Connie Simmons, Clarence Hermsen, Grady Lewis, Carl Meinhold, Paul Hoffman, Dick Schulz, Herman Feutsch, Chick Reiser, Herman Klotz, Player-Coach Buddy Jeannette.

FINAL STANDINGS AND TEAM FIGURES

EASTERN DIVISION

Team	W	L	FGA	FGM	Pct.	FTA	FTM	Pct.	As't.	PF	Pts.	Avg	Oppo
Philadelphia	27	21	4875	1279	.262	1349	963	.714	335	934	3521	73.4	3460
New York	26	22	4724	1355	.287	1291	868	.672	376	1076	3578	74.5	3427
Boston	20	28	4323	1241	.287	1246	821	.659	364	1065	3303	68.8	3491
Providence	6	42	4630	1268	.274	1275	782	.613	347	1105	3318	69.1	3873

WESTERN DIVISION

Team	W	L	FGA	FGM	Pct.	FTA	FTM	Pct.	As't.	PF	Pts.	Avg	Oppo
St. Louis	29	19	4551	1297	.285	1244	838	.674	218	1050	3432	71.5	3335
Baltimore	28	20	4283	1288	.301	1443	994	.689	320	1080	3570	74.4	3385
Chicago	28	20	4683	1390	.297	1305	860	.659	432	1138	3640	75.8	3513
Washington	28	20	4785	1336	.279	1203	865	.719	305	1084	3537	73.7	3415

TOP 25 SCORERS

Player—Team	G.	FGA.	FGM.	Pct.	FTA.	FTM.	Pct.	As't.	PF.	Pts.	Avg.
Max Zaslofsky, Chicago	48	1156	373	.323	333	261	.784	29	125	1007	21.0
Joe Fulks, Philadelphia	43	1258	326	.259	390	297	.762	26	162	949	22.1
Ed Sadowski, Boston	47	953	308	.323	422	294	.697	74	182	910	19.4
Bob Feerick, Washington	48	861	293	.340	240	189	.788	56	139	775	16.1
Stan Miasek, Chicago	48	867	263	.303	310	190	.613	31	192	716	14.9
Carl Braun, New York	47	854	276	.323	183	119	.650	61	102	671	14.3
John Logan, St. Louis	48	734	221	.301	272	202	.743	62	141	644	13.4
John Palmer, New York	48	710	224	.315	234	174	.744	45	149	622	13.0
Red Rocha, St. Louis	48	740	232	.314	213	147	.690	39	209	611	12.7

1947-48 STATISTICS

Player—Team	G.	FGA.	FGM.	Pct.	FTA.	FTM.	Pct.	As't.	PF.	Pts.	Avg.
Fred Scolari, Washington	47	780	229	.294	179	131	.732	58	153	589	12.5
Howard Dallmar, Philadelphia	48	781	215	.275	211	157	.744	120	141	587	12.2
Kleg Hermsen, Baltimore	48	765	212	.277	227	151	.665	48	154	575	12.0
Ernie Calverley, Providence	47	835	226	.271	161	107	.664	119	168	559	11.9
John Reiser, Baltimore	47	628	202	.322	185	137	.741	40	175	541	11.5
Belus Smawley, St. Louis	48	688	212	.308	150	111	.740	18	88	535	11.2
Ken Sailors, Providence	44	689	207	.300	159	110	.692	59	162	524	11.9
George Nostrand, Providence	45	660	196	.297	239	129	.540	30	148	521	11.6
Mike Bloom, Baltimore-Boston	48	640	174	.272	229	160	.699	38	116	508	10.6
Dick Holub, New York	48	662	195	.295	180	114	.633	37	159	504	10.5
Bud Jeannette, Baltimore	46	430	150	.349	252	191	.758	70	147	491	10.7
Mel Riebe, Boston	48	653	202	.309	137	85	.620	41	137	489	10.2
Horace McKinney, Washington	43	680	182	.268	188	121	.644	36	176	485	11.3
John Norlander, Washington	48	543	167	.308	182	135	.742	44	102	469	9.8
Charler Gilmur, Chicago	48	597	181	.303	148	97	.655	77	231	459	9.6
Charles Halbert, Chi.-Phil.	46	605	156	.258	220	140	.636	32	126	452	9.8

FIELD GOAL PERCENTAGE LEADERS
(Minimum 200 FGM)

	FGA	FGM	Pct.
Bob Feerick, Washington	861	293	.340
Ed Sadowski, Boston	953	308	.323
Max Zaslofsky, Chicago	1156	373	.323
Carl Braun, New York	854	276	.323
Chick Reiser, Baltimore	628	202	.322
John Palmer, New York	710	224	.315
Red Rocha, St. Louis	740	232	.314
Mel Riebe, Boston	653	202	.309
Belus Smawley, St. Louis	688	212	.308
Stan Miasek, Chicago	867	263	.303

FREE THROW PERCENTAGE LEADERS
(Minimum 125 FTM)

	FTA	FTM	Pct.
Bob Feerick, Washington	240	189	.788
Max Zaslofsky, Chicago	333	261	.784
Joe Fulks, Philadelphia	390	297	.762
Buddy Jeannette, Baltimore	252	191	.758
Howie Dallmar, Philadelphia	211	157	.744
John Palmer, New York	234	174	.744
John Logan, St. Louis	272	202	.743
John Norlander, Washington	182	135	.742
Chick Reiser, Baltimore	185	137	.741
Fred Scolari, Washington	179	131	.732

LEADERS IN ASSISTS

	G.	No.	Avg.
Howie Dallmar, Philadelphia	48	120	2.5
Ernie Calverley, Providence	47	119	2.5
Jim Seminoff, Chicago	48	89	1.8
Chuck Gilmur, Chicago	48	77	1.6
Ed Sadowski, Boston	47	74	1.6
Andy Philip, Chicago	32	74	2.3
Buddy Jeannette, Baltimore	46	70	1.5
John Logan, St. Louis	48	62	1.3
Carl Braun, New York	47	61	1.3
Saul Mariaschin, Boston	43	60	1.4

INTER-CLUB RECORDS—HOME AND AWAY

EASTERN DIVISION

Team	Phil.	N.Y.	Bos.	Prov.	St.L.	Balt.	Chi.	Wash.	Home	Away	W.	L.
Philadelphia	..	4	4	8	3	4	2	2	14- 10	13- 11	27- 21
New York	4	..	7	7	4	1	0	3	12- 12	14- 10	26- 22
Boston	4	1	..	6	2	1	3	3	11- 13	9- 15	20- 28
Providence	0	1	2	..	0	0	2	1	3- 21	3- 21	6- 42

WESTERN DIVISION

St. Louis	3	2	4	6	..	5	5	4	17- 7	12- 12	29- 19
Baltimore	2	5	5	6	3	..	5	2	17- 7	11- 13	28- 20
Chicago	4	6	3	4	3	3	..	5	14- 10	14- 10	28- 20
Washington	4	3	3	5	4	6	3	..	19- 5	9- 15	28- 20
Total	21	22	28	42	19	20	20	20	107- 85	85- 107	192- 192

1947-48 CHAMPIONSHIP PLAYOFF RESULTS

NBA SEMI-FINAL SERIES
Philadelphia 4, St. Louis 3

Mar. 23—Philadelphia 58 at St. Louis 60
Mar. 25—Philadelphia 65 at St. Louis 64
Mar. 27—St. Louis 56 at Philadelphia 84
Mar. 30—St. Louis 56 at Philadelphia 51
Apr. 1—Philadelphia 62 at St. Louis 69
Apr. 3—St. Louis 61 at Philadelphia 84
Apr. 6—Philadelphia 85 at St. Louis 46

NBA QUARTER-FINALS
Baltimore 2, New York 1

Mar. 27—New York 81 at Baltimore 85
Mar. 28—Baltimore 69 at New York 79
Apr. 1—New York 77 at Baltimore 84

Chicago 2, Boston 1

Mar. 28—Chicago 79 at Boston 72
Mar. 31—Chicago 77 at Boston 81
Apr. 2—Chicago 81 at Boston 74

NBA SEMI-FINAL SERIES
Baltimore 2, Chicago 0

Apr. 7—Baltimore 73 at Chicago 67
Apr. 8—Chicago 72 at Baltimore 89

CHAMPIONSHIP SERIES
Baltimore 4, Philadelphia 2

Apr. 10—Baltimore 60 at Philadelphia 71
Apr. 13—Baltimore 66 at Philadelphia 63
Apr. 15—Philadelphia 70 at Baltimore 72
Apr. 17—Philadelphia 75 at Baltimore 78
Apr. 20—Baltimore 82 at Philadelphia 91
Apr. 21—Philadelphia 73 at Baltimore 88

1946-47 STATISTICS

1946-47 CHAMPION PHILADELPHIA WARRIORS

Front row (left to right): Jerry Rullo, Angelo Musi, Peter A. Tyrell, General Manager; Pete Rosenberg, Jerry Fleishman. Back row: Assistant Coach Cy Kaselman, George Senesky, Ralph Kaplowitz, Howard Dallmar, Art Hillhouse, Joe Fulks, Matt Guokas, Coach Ed Gottlieb.

FINAL STANDINGS AND TEAM FIGURES

EASTERN DIVISION

Team	W	L	FGA	FGM	Pct.	FTA	FTM	Pct.	As't.	PF	Pts.	Avg	Oppo
Washington	49	11	5794	1723	.297	1391	982	.706	378	1144	4428	73.8	3835
Philadelphia	35	25	5384	1510	.280	1596	1098	.688	343	1082	4118	68.6	3909
New York	33	27	5255	1465	.279	1438	951	.661	457	1218	3881	64.7	3842
Providence	28	32	5582	1629	.292	1666	1092	.655	481	1215	4350	72.5	4450
Toronto	22	38	5672	1515	.267	1552	966	.622	463	1271	3996	66.6	4260
Boston	22	38	5133	1397	.272	1375	811	.590	470	1202	3605	60.1	3898

WESTERN DIVISION

Team	W	L	FGA	FGM	Pct.	FTA	FTM	Pct.	As't.	PF	Pts.	Avg	Oppo
Chicago	39	22	6309	1879	.297	1550	939	.606	436	1473	4697	77.0	4473
St. Louis	38	23	5877	1601	.272	1400	862	.616	292	1234	4064	66.6	3911
Cleveland	30	30	5699	1674	.294	1428	903	.632	494	1246	4251	70.9	4309
Detroit	20	40	5843	1437	.246	1494	923	.618	482	1351	3797	63.3	3917
Pittsburgh	15	45	4961	1345	.271	1507	984	.653	272	1360	3674	61.2	4057

TOP 25 SCORERS

Player—Team	G.	FGA.	FGM.	Pct.	FTA.	FTM.	Pct.	As't.	PF.	Pts.	Avg.
Joe Fulks, Philadelphia	60	1557	475	.305	601	439	.730	25	199	1389	23.2
Bob Feerick, Washington	55	908	364	.401	260	198	.762	69	142	926	16.3
Stan Miasek, Detroit	60	1154	331	.287	385	233	.605	93	208	895	14.9

1946-47 STATISTICS

Player—Team	G.	FGA.	FGM.	Pct.	FTA.	FTM.	Pct.	As't.	PF.	Pts.	Avg.
Ed Sadowski, Toronto-Cleveland	53	891	329	.369	328	219	.668	46	194	877	16.5
Max Zaslofsky, Chicago	61	1020	336	.329	278	205	.737	40	121	877	14.4
Ernie Calverley, Providence	59	1102	323	.293	283	199	.703	202	191	845	14.3
Charles Halbert, Chicago	61	915	280	.306	356	213	.598	46	161	773	12.7
John Logan, St. Louis	61	1043	290	.278	254	190	.748	78	136	770	12.6
Leo Mogus, Cleveland-Toronto	58	879	259	.295	325	235	.723	84	176	753	13.0
Coulby Gunther, Pittsburgh	52	756	254	.336	351	226	.644	32	117	734	14.1
Don Martin, Providence	60	1022	311	.304	168	111	.661	59	98	733	12.2
Fred Scolari, Washington	58	989	291	.294	180	146	.811	58	159	728	12.6
Henry Beenders, Providence	58	1016	266	.262	257	181	.704	37	196	713	12.3
John Janisch, Detroit	60	983	283	.288	198	131	.662	49	132	697	11.6
Horace McKinney, Washington	58	987	275	.279	210	145	.690	69	162	695	12.0
Earl Shannon, Providence	57	722	245	.339	348	197	.566	84	169	687	12.1
Mel Riebe, Cleveland	55	898	276	.307	173	111	.642	67	169	663	12.1
Mike McCarron, Toronto	60	838	236	.282	288	177	.615	59	184	649	10.8
Frank Baumholtz, Cleveland	45	856	255	.298	156	121	.776	54	93	631	14.0
Don Carlson, Chicago	59	845	272	.322	169	86	.541	59	182	630	10.7

FIELD GOAL PERCENTAGE LEADERS
(Minimum 200 FGM)

	FGA	FGM	Pct.
Bob Feerick, Washington	908	364	.401
Ed Sadowski, Tor.-Clev.	891	329	.369
Earl Shannon, Providence	722	245	.339
Coulby Gunther, Pittsburgh	756	254	.336
Max Zaslofsky, Chicago	1020	336	.329
Don Carlson, Chicago	845	272	.322
Connie Simmons, Boston	768	246	.320
John Norlander, Washington	698	223	.319
Ken Sailors, Cleveland	741	229	.309
Mel Riebe, Cleveland	898	276	.307

FREE THROW PERCENTAGE LEADERS
(Minimum 125 FTM)

	FTA	FTM	Pct.
Fred Scolari, Washington	180	146	.811
Tony Kapper, Pitt.-Bos.	161	128	.795
Stan Stutz, New York	170	133	.782
Bob Feerick, Washington	260	198	.762
John Logan, St. Louis	254	190	.748
Max Zaslofsky, Chicago	278	205	.737
Joe Fulks, Philadelphia	601	439	.730
Leo Mogus, Clev.-Tor.	325	235	.723
George Mearns, Providence	175	126	.720
Tony Jaros, Chicago	181	128	.707

LEADERS IN ASSISTS

	G.	No.	Avg.
Ernie Calverley, Providence	59	202	3.4
Ken Sailors, Cleveland	58	134	2.3
Ossie Schectman, New York	54	109	2.0
Howie Dallmar, Philadelphia	60	104	1.7
Marv Rottner, Chicago	56	93	1.7
Stan Miasek, Detroit	60	93	1.6
Earl Shannon, Providence	57	84	1.5
Leo Mogus, Toronto	58	84	1.4
John Logan, St. Louis	61	78	1.3
Bob Feerick, Washington	55	69	1.3
Bones McKinney, Washington	58	69	1.2

INTER-CLUB RECORDS—HOME AND AWAY

EASTERN DIVISION

Team	Wash.	Phil.	N.Y.	Prov.	Tor.	Bos.	Chi.	St.L.	Clev.	Det.	Pitt.	Home	Away	W- L
Washington	..	5	4	6	5	5	5	4	5	5	5	29- 1	20- 10	49- 11
Philadelphia	1	..	4	4	5	5	1	3	3	4	5	23- 7	12- 18	35- 25
New York	2	2	..	4	3	2	3	4	2	5	6	18- 12	15- 15	33- 27
Providence	0	2	2	..	3	5	3	2	4	4	3	19- 11	9- 21	28- 32
Toronto	1	1	3	3	..	2	2	4	0	3	3	15- 15	7- 23	22- 38
Boston	1	1	4	1	4	..	0	1	2	3	5	14- 16	8- 22	22- 38

WESTERN DIVISION

Team	Wash.	Phil.	N.Y.	Prov.	Tor.	Bos.	Chi.	St.L.	Clev.	Det.	Pitt.	Home	Away	W- L
Chicago	1	5	3	3	4	6	..	3	5	3	6	22- 9	17- 13	39- 22
St. Louis	2	3	2	4	2	5	4	..	5	6	5	22- 8	16- 15	38- 28
Cleveland	1	3	4	2	6	4	1	1	..	4	4	17- 13	13- 17	30- 30
Detroit	1	2	1	2	3	3	3	0	2	..	3	12- 18	8- 22	20- 40
Pittsburgh	1	1	0	3	3	1	0	1	2	3	..	11- 19	4- 26	15- 45
Total	11	25	27	32	38	38	22	23	30	40	45	202-129	129-202	331-331

1946-47 CHAMPIONSHIP PLAYOFF RESULTS

NBA SEMI-FINAL SERIES
Chicago 4, Washington 2

- Apr. 2—Chicago 81 at Washington 65
- Apr. 3—Chicago 69 at Washington 53
- Apr. 8—Washington 55 at Chicago 67
- Apr. 10—Chicago 69 at Washington 76
- Apr. 12—Washington 67 at Chicago 55
- Apr. 13—Washington 61 at Chicago 66

NBA QUARTER-FINALS
Philadelphia 2, St. Louis 1

- Apr. 2—St. Louis 68 at Philadelphia 73
- Apr. 5—Philadelphia 51 at St. Louis 73
- Apr. 6—Philadelphia 75 at St. Louis 59

New York 2, Cleveland 1

- Apr. 2—New York 51 at Cleveland 77
- Apr. 5—Cleveland 74 at New York 86
- Apr. 9—Cleveland 71 at New York 93

NBA SEMI-FINAL SERIES
Philadelphia 2, New York 0

- Apr. 12—New York 70 at Philadelphia 82
- Apr. 14—Philadelphia 72 at New York 53

CHAMPIONSHIP SERIES
Philadelphia 4, Chicago 1

- Apr. 16—Chicago 71 at Philadelphia 84
- Apr. 17—Chicago 75 at Philadelphia 85
- Apr. 19—Philadelphia 75 at Chicago 72
- Apr. 20—Philadelphia 73 at Chicago 74
- Apr. 22—Chicago 80 at Philadelphia 83

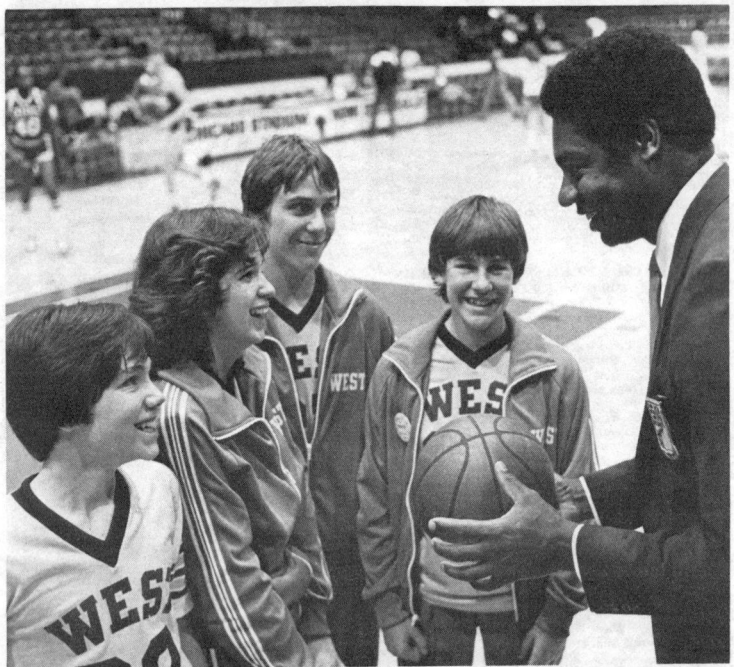

Oscar Robertson, Hall of Famer and national director of the Pepsi-Cola/NBA/Hotshot program, gives advice to national champions. The winners are (left to right) Phil Harwell, Brush Prairie, Wash.; Lisa Pech, Salem, Ore.; Brent Stehlik, Portland, Ore. and Kelly Cole, Milwaukie, Ore.

Pepsi-Cola/NBA Hotshot Program

The Pepsi-Cola/NBA Hotshot program, the largest youth skills recreation program of its kind, is in its sixth year with boys and girls throughout the nation participating through 1,500 local youth organizations.

The program is a one-minute competition in which youngsters 9-18 years old compete to score as many points as possible from different points on a basketball court. More than 2.8 million youths participated last year.

Competition begins during the summer and culminates with the national finals held during the NBA playoffs.

OFFICIAL RULES

OF THE

NATIONAL BASKETBALL

ASSOCIATION

1981-82

Published by The Sporting News, St. Louis, Missouri 63166
©1981 The National Basketball Association

NBA RULES COMMITTEE

Jerry Colangelo, Phoenix (Chairman)
Arnold Auerbach, Boston
Edward Donovan, New York
Cotton Fitzsimmons, Kansas City
Stu Inman, Portland
Frank Layden, Utah
Kevin Loughery, Atlanta
Don Nelson, Milwaukee
Carl Scheer, Denver
Scotty Stirling, Golden State
Rod Thorn, Chicago

ADVISORY

Joe Axelson, Vice President, Operations
Matt Winick, Operations Coordinator
Cecil Watkins, Referee Development Administrator
Darell Garretson, Chief of Staff

RULES INDEX

	RULE	SECTION	PAGE
BACK/FRONTCOURT			
Definition of	4	VI(a)	16
Foul rules (screening)	12B	III	35
Ten (10) second violation	4	VI(b)	17
Player position status	4	VI(a) Note(1)	17
BALL			
Control	7	II(d)	25
Dead ball	6	I(c)	23
	6	VI	24
Jump	6	III	23
Live	6	II	23
Other jump	6	IV	23
Putting in play	6	I	23
Restrictions	6	V	24
Tap rules	6	I(b)	23
Trapped	11	I,f,Note(3)	31
BASKET RING (HANGING)	12A	V	32
CAPTAIN, DUTIES	3	III	14
CLOCK (GAME)			
Expiration	2	VIII(d)	13
No time remaining	2	VIII Note(2)	13
Recording game time	2	VIII(e)	13
Starting—after missed free throw	5	VII(b)	21
Starting—throw-in	5	VII(c)	21
Stopping	5	V	20
CLOTHING, ADJUSTING	5	V Note(1)	20
COACH			
Bench	3	IV	14
Speaking to officials	3	IV(b)	14
Ejection	3	IV Note(2)	14
Conduct	12	VI	32
Suspension	Comments	G	41
Cursing	12A	VI Note(2)	33
CORRECTING ERRORS	2	VI	11
COURT			
Dimensions, markings	1	I	9
Diagram	—	—	8
DEFINITIONS			
Basket/Backboard	4	I	15
Blocking	4	II	15
Dribble	4	III	16
Fouls (all types)	4	IV	16
Free throw	4	V	16
Front/backcourt	4	VI	16
Held ball	4	VII	17
Legal goal	5	I	17
Personal foul	4	IV(a)	16
Pivot	4	VIII	17
Screen	4	X	18
Technical foul	4	IV(b)	16
Throw-in	4	XII	18
Traveling	4	IX	17
Try for goal	4	XI	18

	RULE	SECTION	PAGE
DELAY OF GAME	12	III	32
DRESS (PLAYER/TEAM)	Comments	J	42
DOUBLEHEADERS (NEUTRAL COURT)	3	VI(c)	15
END OF PERIOD	5	III	19
EQUIPMENT (GAME)	1	II	9
FAILURE TO REPORT	12A	VII(f)	34
FINES	12A	VII	33
FOULS (PERSONAL)			
Away from play	12B	VIII	37
Double	12B	IV	36
Elbow	12B	I(c)	34
Fighting	12B	VII	37
Flagrant	Comments	C	40
Loose ball	12B	VI	37
Offensive	12B	V	37
Punching	12B	VII	37
Team (5th)	12B	II(a)	36
FOULS (TECHNICAL/OTHERS)	12A		34
Elbow	12B	I(c)	34
Excessive time-out	12(A)	II	32
Fighting/punching fines	12A	VII	33
Hanging on rim	12A	V	32
Illegal defensive	12A	I	31
Unsportsmanlike	12A	VI(c)	33
FREE THROW			
Clock, start	5	VII	21
Ejection	9	II(a)	27
Injured player	9	II Note(1)	27
Line-up	9	I	27
Next play	9	IV	28
Penalty situation	12B	2	35
Time limit	9	II	27
Violations	10	I	28 & 29
GAME CANCELLATION	Comments	F	41
GOAL TENDING	11	I	30
HAND CHECKING	12B	I(c) Note(1)	34
HOME UNIFORM	3	VI	15
ILLEGAL DEFENSE	12	I	31, 32
Comments		D	40
JUMP BALLS			
Center circle	6	III	23
Double foul	6	IV	23
Held ball, others	6	IV	23
Illegal tap	6	V	24
Restrictions	6	IV	23
Violations	10	I	28 to 31
KICKING BALL	10	I(d) Note(3)	29
LIVE BALL	6	II	23
OFFENSIVE FOUL	4	IV(d)	16
OFFICIALS			
Correcting errors	2	VI	11
	5	V(8)	20
Different decisions	2	IV	10 & 11
Disagreement	8	II(c)	26

	RULE	SECTION	PAGE
Discussion, coaches	2	II Note(2)	10
Duties	2	I & VI	10
Elastic power	2	III	10
In charge	2	II(f)	10
Inspection	2	II(a)	10
Pre-game meeting	2	II(i)	10
Reporting on floor	2	II(h)	10
Safety	2	II(b)	10
OVERTIMES (TIE SCORE)	5	IV	20
OUT-OF-BOUNDS (THROW-IN)			
Player	8	I	26
Ball	8	II	26
Designated thrower	8	II(d)	26
Throw-in position	8	II(e)	26
Violation penalty	8	III(d)	27
PERSONAL FOUL			
Types	12B	I	34
Dribbler	12B	II	34 & 35
Screening	12B	III	35
Penalties	12B	III(1)	35
PLAYER			
Conduct	12A	VI	32
Conduct (halftime and end of game)	12A	VII(g)	34
Cursing	12A	VI Note(2)	33
Disconcerting	10	I(4)	28
Ejected	12A	VII(a) Note(1)	33 & 34
Equipment	2	II(b,c,d)	10
Fighting	12A	VII(b)	34
Hanging on rim (game)	12A	V	32
Hanging on rim (warm-up)	12A	VII(i)	34
Numbering	3	VI(a)	15
Substitution	12A	IV	32
Suspension	Comments	G	41
Time-out	5	V	20
Use of stickum	12A	VII(e)	34
Wearing Jewelry	2	II(c)	10
PLAY SITUATIONS			
Additional time-outs	5	VIII Note(1)	22
Dribble out-of-bounds	10	I	28
Excessive time-out (position)	12A	II	32
Foul attempt (no time on clock)	9	I Note(1)	27
Free throw opponents basket	5	I	18
Game clock 0:00	5	III	19
Field Goal—opponents basket	5	I Note(2)	19
Illegal tap	2	VIII Note(1)	13
	6	V	24
Injury—defensive player	5	V	20
Injury—jumper 1	5	V	20
Injury—foul shooter	5	V	20
Putting ball in play	10	I(c)	29
	6	I	23
Points allowed—one play	12B	II Note(1)	36
Time-out (backcourt)	5	VIII(d)	22

	RULE	SECTION	PAGE
PROTEST	3	III(c)	14
	Comments	H	41
SCORERS, DUTIES OF	2	VII	12
SCORING			
Discrepancy (running score)	5	I Note(3)	19
Legal goal	5	I(a)	19
Tap in of foul	5	I Note(1)	19
Three-point play	5	I(b)	19
Wrong basket	5	I Note(1)	19
STARTING LINE-UPS	3	II	14
SUBSTITUTES	3	V	15
SUBSTITUTIONS	12A	IV	32
TEAM CONTROL	7	II(d)	25
TEAM RULES	3	I	13
Line-ups	3	II	14
TECHNICAL FOULS	12B	VI	32
TEN SECOND RULE (FOULS)	10	I	28
TIME-OUT RULES			
After a score	5	VIII(e)	22
Backcourt	5	VIII(d)	22
Excessive	12	II	32
Mandatory	5	VIII(c)	22
Number	5	VIII(a)	21
Options	5	VIII(d)	22
Regular	5	VIII	21
Two (2) minutes remaining	5	VIII(f)	22
Twenty seconds	5	VI	21
TIMERS, DUTIES OF	2	VIII	13
TIMING (LENGTH)			
Between halves	5	II(c)	19
Disqualification	5	II(d)	19
Overtime	5	II(b)	19
Periods	5	II(a)	19
Time-outs	5	II(d)	19
TIMING REGULATIONS			
End of period	5	III	19
Illegal tap	6	V(c)	24
Public address announcement	5	II Note(2)	19
Replacing–disqualified player	5	V(a) (9)	20
Tie score	5	IV	20
Time-in	5	VII	21
Time-out (regular)	5	V	21
Time-out (last two minutes)	5	VIII	21
TWENTY-FOUR (24) SECOND CLOCK			
Expiration	7	II(h)	25
Inadvertent whistle	7	II(g) Note(2)	25
Resetting	7	II(k)	25
	7	IV	26
Starting and stopping	7	II	25
	7	II(f)	25
Team control	7	II(d)	25
Team possession	7	II(c)	25
Technical foul	7	II(k)	25

	RULE	SECTION	PAGE
UNIFORMS	3	VI(b)	15
VIOLATIONS			
Backcourt	10	I(h)	30
Boundary line	10	I	30
Designated player	10	I(c) (3)	29
Double dribble	10	I(e)	29
Free throw (time limit)	9	III	28
Jump ball	10	I(f) (1) (2)	29
Out-of-bounds	10	I(b)	29
Putting ball in play	10	I(c)	29
Run, kick and fist	10	I(d)	29
Three (3) seconds	10	I(g)	29
Ten (10) seconds	10	H	30
Throw-in	8	III	27

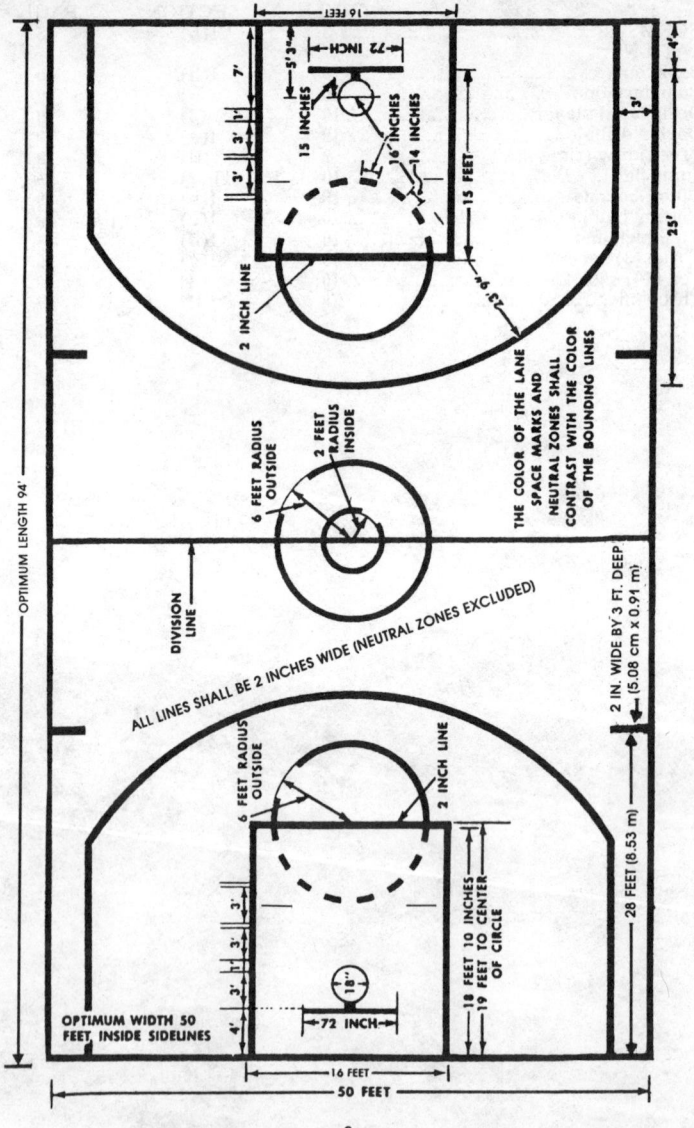

Official Rules
RULE NO. 1—COURT DIMENSIONS—EQUIPMENT

Section I—Court and Dimensions

a. The playing court shall be measured and marked as shown in court diagram. (See page 8)

b. A free throw lane shall be marked at each end of the court with dimensions and markings as shown on court diagram. All boundary lines are part of the lane; lane space marks and neutral zone marks are **not**. The color of the lane space marks and neutral zones shall contrast with the color of the boundary lines. The areas identified by the lane space markings are two inches by thirty-six and the neutral zone marks are twelve inches by thirty-six inches.

c. A free throw line, 2 inches wide, shall be drawn across each of the circles indicated in court diagram. It shall be parallel to the end line and shall be 15 feet from the plane of the face of the backboard.

d. Three-point field goal area which has parallel lines three feet from the sidelines, extending from the baseline, and an arc of 23 feet-nine inches from the middle of the basket which intersects the parallel lines.

e. Four hash marks shall be drawn (two inches wide) perpendicular to the side line on each side of the court and 28 feet from the base line. The hash mark shall extend three feet onto the court.

Section II—Equipment

a. The backboard shall be a rectangle measuring 6 feet horizontally and 4 feet vertically. The front surface shall be flat and transparent.

b. A transparent backboard shall be marked as follows: a rectangle marked by a 2" white line shall be centered behind the ring. This rectangle shall have outside dimensions of 24" horizontally and 18" vertically.

NOTE: (1) Home management is required to have a spare board with supporting unit on hand for emergencies, and a steel tape or extension ruler and a level for use if necessary.

c. Each basket shall consist of a pressure-release NBA approved metal safety ring 18" in inside diameter with white cord net 15 to 18 inches in length. The cord of the net shall not be less than 30 thread nor more than 120 thread and shall be constructed as to check the ball momentarily as it passes through the basket.

d. Each basket ring shall be securely attached to the backboard with its upper edge 10 feet above and parallel to the floor and equidistant from the vertical edges of the board. The nearest point of the inside edge of the ring shall be 6" from the plane of the face of the board. The ring shall be painted orange.

e. (1) The ball shall be an officially approved NBA ball between 7½ and 8½ lbs. pressure.

   (2) Six balls must be made available to each team for pre-game warmup.

f. At least one electric light is to be placed behind the backboard, obvious to officials and synchronized to light up when the horn sounds at the expiration of time for each period. The electric light is to be "red."

RULE NO. 2–OFFICIALS AND THEIR DUTIES

Section I–The Game Officials

a. The game officials shall be a lead official and a referee. They will be assisted by table officials including two trained timers, one to operate the game clock, the other to operate the 24 second timer and by a scorer who will compile the statistics of the game. All officials shall be approved by the Commissioner.

b. The officials shall wear the uniform prescribed by the NBA.

Section II–Duties of the Officials

a. The officials shall, prior to start of game, inspect and approve all equipment, including court, baskets, balls, backboards, timers and scorer's equipment.

b. The officials shall not permit players to play with any type of hand, arm, face, nose, ear, head or neck jewelry.

c. The official shall not permit any player to wear equipment which, in his judgment is dangerous to other players. Any equipment which is of hard substance (casts, splints, guards and braces) must be padded or foam covered and have no exposed sharp or cutting edge. All face masks and eye or nose protectors must conform to the contour of the face and have no sharp or protruding edges. Approval is on a game to game basis.

d. All equipment used must be appropriate for basketball and equipment that is unnatural and designed to increase a players height or reach, or to gain an advantage shall not be used.

e. The officials must check the three game balls to see they are properly inflated. The recommended ball pressure should be between $7\frac{1}{2}$ and $8\frac{1}{2}$ pounds.

f. The senior official shall be the referee in charge.

NOTE: (1) If a coach desires to discuss a rule or interpretation of a rule prior to the start of a game, it will be mandatory for the officials to ask the other coach to be present during the discussion. The same procedure shall be followed for requests made at the start of a period.

g. The designated official shall toss the ball at the start of the game; the lead official shall decide whether or not a goal shall count if the officials disagree; he shall decide matters upon which scorers and timers disagree.

h. All officials shall be present during the 20-minute pre-game warm-up period to observe and report to the Commissioner any infractions of Rule 12-VII i–hanging on the rim and to review scoring and timing procedures with table personnel if necessary.

i. Officials must meet with team captains to discuss rules & interpretations, prior to start of game.

j. Officials must report by Telex to the Commissioner of any atypical or unique incident, flagrant foul, punching foul, fighting or team beginning game with less than 8 players.

Section III–Elastic Power

The officials shall have power to make decisions on any point not specifically covered in the rules. The Commissioner will be advised of all such decisions at the earliest possible moment.

Section IV—Different Decisions By Officials

The lead official shall have the authority to set aside or question decisions made by the other within the limits of his respective outlined duties.

Question (1)—A violation and personal contact occur at same time. Both are observed by the same official, or the violation by one and foul by the other. What is the proper procedure?

Answer—The foul takes precedence over any violation.

Question (2)—Ball in flight on try for field goal by A1, A2 pushes B1. After personal foul while ball is rolling around the ring B2 bats ball away from ring. Which infraction of the rules shall be penalized?

Answer—Both. Two points to Team A, the penalty for personal foul.

NOTE: (1) It is the primary duty of the trail official to signal if goals count. If for any reason he does not know if goal is made he should ask the other official. If neither saw the goal made they should refer to the timer. If the timer saw the goal scored it shall count. Exception: The drive-in or quick down court shot shall be the responsibility of the lead official.

Section V—Time and Place for Decisions

a. The officials shall have power to have decisions for infractions of rules committed either within or outside the boundary lines. This includes periods when the game may be stopped for any reason.

b. When a foul occurs, an official shall signal the timer to stop his watch and if it is a personal foul, he shall also designate the number of the offender to the scorer and indicate with his fingers the number of free throws to be attempted.

c. When a team is entitled to a throw-in, an official shall clearly signal the act which caused the ball to become dead, the throw-in spot and the team entitled to the throw-in; unless it follows a successful goal or an awarded goal.

Section VI—Correcting Errors

a. Officials may correct an error if a rule is inadvertently set aside and results in:

    (1) A team not shooting a merited penalty shot.

    (2) A team shooting an unmerited penalty shot.

    (3) Permitting the wrong player to attempt a free throw.

NOTE: (1) Officials should be notified of error at first dead ball. All errors must be rectified before the start of the next quarter. Ball is not in play on corrected foul and whether foul shot is made or missed, play shall be resumed at the same spot where referee declared the ball dead and under the same conditions as would have prevailed had play not been stopped to correct error. If the officials are notified of error within 24 seconds, any play action that occurs during that time period is to be nullified. This nullifies scoring and fouls committed by either team. However, if a player or coach is ejected during this period he is not permitted to return to the game. The official shall also reset the game clock so that the time left to play shall be the same as it was when the error occurred. However, any acts of unsportsmanlike conduct or points scored there from are not nullified.

NOTE: (2) Errors in the fourth quarter and over-times, in order to be rectified, must be discovered before the end of the period.

NOTE: (3) If any period begins with teams lined up improperly and scores result from this error all points will be deleted and the period re-started unless 24 seconds have elapsed from the game clock. If 24 seconds have elapsed, all points count and teams shoot for the same baskets. Example: 12:00 to 11:36—do not restart.

Section VII—Duties of Scorers

a. The scorers shall record the field goals made, the free throws made and missed, and shall keep a running summary of the points scored. They shall record the personal and technical fouls called on each player and shall notify the official immediately when a sixth personal foul is called on any player. They shall record the time-outs charged to each team, shall notify a team and its coach through an official whenever that team takes a sixth and seventh charged time-out and shall notify the nearest official each time a team is granted a charged time-out in excess of the legal number. In case there is a question about an error in the scoring, the scorer shall check with the official at once to find the discrepancy. If the error cannot be found, the official shall accept the record of the official scorer, unless he has knowledge that forces him to decide otherwise.

b. The scorers shall keep a record of the names, numbers and positions of players who are to start the game and of all substitutes who enter the game. When there is an infraction of the rules pertaining to submission of line-up, substitutions or numbers of players, they shall notify the nearer official immediately if the ball is dead, or as soon as it becomes dead if it is in play when the infraction is discovered. Scorer shall mark the time at which players are disqualified by reason of receiving six personal fouls so that it may be easy to ascertain the order in which the players are eligible to go back in the game in accordance with Rule 3-1.

c. The scorers shall use a horn or other device unlike that used by the officials or timers to signal the officials. This may be used when the ball is dead or in certain specified situations when the ball is in control of a given team. Scorer shall signal coach on the bench on every personal foul, designating number of personal fouls a player has, and number of team. NOTE: White paddles—team fouls; Red paddles—personal fouls.

d. When a player is disqualified from the game, or whenever a penalty shot is being awarded, a buzzer, a siren or some other clear audible sound must be used by the scorer or timer to notify the game officials. It is the duty of the scorekeeper to be certain the officials have acknowledged the 6th personal foul buzzer and the penalty shot buzzer.

Question (1)—The scorers fail to notify the official that a player has committed his 6th personal foul and he remains in the game. What should be done?

Answer—Playing time consumed, if any, and points scored count. The offending player must be removed as soon as the official discovers the error. Scorers should notify an official as soon as a player commits his 6th personal foul, but if play is resumed before such notification, they should signal when the ball is next dead or is in control of the offending team.

Question (2)—What should be done if the scorer's horn sounds, while the ball is in play?

Answer—Players should ignore the horn since it does not make the ball dead. The scorers should not signal while the ball is in play except in certain cases such as are noted in the first question above. The officials must use their judgment in blowing the ball dead to consult the scorers.

Question (3)—If the scorers fail to notify a team or its coach when it takes its 7th charged time-out, should the team be penalized if it takes an 8th time-out?

Answer—Yes.

e. Scorers shall record on scoreboard the number of team fouls to a total of five—which will indicate that the team is in a penalty situation.

Section VIII—Duties of Timers

a. The timers shall note when each half is to start and shall notify the referee and coach five minutes before this time, or cause them to be notified at least five minutes before the half is to start. They shall signal the scorers two minutes before starting time. They shall record playing time and time of stoppages as provided in the rules. The timer shall be provided with an extra stop watch to be used in time outs, etc., other than the official game clock or watch. Official clock or scoreboard should show 12 minute quarters.

b. At the beginning of each quarter or extra period or whenever play is resumed by a jump ball the game clock shall be started when the ball has been legally tapped by either of the jumpers. If, after time has been out, the ball is put in play by a throw-in from out of bounds or by a free throw, the game watch shall be started when the official gives the time-in signal as the ball is touched by a player in the court.

NOTE: (1) During a jump ball time may not be reduced from the 24 second clock or game clock if there is an illegal tap.

c. The game clock shall be stopped: at the expiration of time for each period and when an official signals time-out. For a charged time-out, the timer shall start a time-out watch and shall signal the official when it is time to resume play.

d. The timers shall indicate with a controlled game horn the expiration of playing time. If the timer's signal fails to sound, or not heard, the timer shall use other means to notify the official immediately. If, in the meantime, a goal has been made or a foul has occurred, the official shall consult the timer. If the timer agrees that time expired before the ball was in flight, the goal shall not count. If they agree that the period ended before the foul occurred, the foul shall be disregarded unless it was unsportsmanlike. If there is disagreement the goal shall count or the foul shall be penalized unless the official has other knowledge.

NOTE: (2) However, in a dead ball situation, if the clock shows :00 the period or game is considered to have ended although the buzzer may not have sounded.

e. Record only actual playing time in the last two minutes of the fourth period and the last two minutes of any overtime period or periods.

NOTE: (3) Clock will be stopped immediately without signal from official, on all violations.

RULE NO. 3—PLAYERS, SUBSTITUTES AND COACHES
Section I—Team

Each team shall consist of five players, one of whom shall be designated as the captain. No team may be reduced to less than five players. If and when a player in the game receives his sixth personal foul and all substitutes have already been disqualified, said player remains in the game and is charged with a personal and team foul. A technical foul also is assessed against his team. All subsequent personal fouls, including offensive fouls, shall be treated similarly. All players who have six or more personal fouls and remain in game shall be treated similarly.

In the event a player is injured and must leave the game, he must be replaced by the last player who was disqualified by reason of receiving six personal fouls. Each subsequent requirement to replace an injured player will be treated in this inverse order. Any such re-entry in a game by a disqualified player shall be penalized by a technical foul.

Section II—Starting Line-Ups

At least ten minutes before the game is scheduled to begin the scorers shall be supplied with the name and number of each player who may participate in the game. Starting line-ups will be indicated. Failure to comply with this provision should be reported to the Commissioner.

Section III—The Captain

a. Only the designated captain may talk to an official during a time out charged to his team.

b. He may discuss a rule interpretation but not a judgment play.

c. If the captain and the official are not in agreement, the coach may then enter an official protest and the game continues to completion. The official will then inform the official scorer and have it entered into the official score-book with time, score and rule quoted. The public address announcer will be instructed to inform the spectators that the game is being played under protest.

Section IV—The Coach and Others

a. The coach position may be on or off the bench from the 28' hash mark to the base line. All assistants and trainers must remain on the bench. Coaches and trainers may not leave this restricted 28 foot area unless specifically requested to do so by the referees. Coaches and trainers are not permitted to go to the scorers tables, for any reason, except during time-out or between periods and only to check statistical information. The penalty for violation of this rule is a technical foul.

b. Coaches are not permitted to talk to an official during any time-out. (See Sec. 3(a) for captain's rights.)

c. A playing coach will have no special privileges. He is to conduct himself in the same manner as any other player.

d. Any club personnel not seated on the bench must conduct themselves so as not to reflect unfavorably on the dignity of the game or that of the officials. Violations by any of the personnel indicated shall require a written report to the Commissioner for subsequent action.

e. The bench shall be occupied only by league-approved coach, assistant coaches, players and trainer.

NOTE: (2) If a player, coach or assistant coach is ejected from a game or games, he shall not at any time before, during or after such game or games appear in any part of the auditorium or stands where his team is playing, during such ejection. A player, coach or assistant coach may only remain in the dressing room of his team during such suspension.

A violation of this rule shall call for an automatic fine of $500.

Section V—Substitutes

a. A substitute shall report to the scorer and be in the 8 ft. box area in front of the scorers table and give his name, number and who he is to replace. The scorer shall sound the horn as soon as the ball is dead to indicate a substitution. The horn does not have to be sounded between quarters and halves. No substitute may enter a game after a field goal by either team, unless the ball is dead due to a technical foul. He may enter after the 1st of 2 or more free throws, whether made or missed.

b. The substitute shall remain outside the boundary lines, in the box area, until he is beckoned on by an official. If the ball is about to become alive, the beckoning signal shall be withheld.

NOTE: (1) A substitute must be ready to enter when beckoned. He must have discarded any articles of clothing he will not wear on the playing floor. No delays for removal of sweat clothes will be permitted.

c. The substitute shall not replace a free throw shooter or a player involved in a jump ball.

d. Once the substitute has been beckoned onto court, he must enter the game and cannot be removed until the next dead ball.

NOTE: (2) A substitute **can be** recalled from the scorer's table prior to being beckoned in the game.

e. Any player who fails to properly report to the scorer as shown in (a) above shall not be permitted to enter the game until the next dead ball. Any player who doesn't wait until he is properly beckoned on the floor by the referee as in (b) above shall be charged with a technical foul.

NOTE: (3) Notification of all above infractions and ensuing procedures shall be in accordance with Rule II, Section 7.

Question: May a substitution be made during an official's time-out?

Answer: No.

Section VI—Uniforms (Players Jerseys)

a. Each player shall be numbered on the front and back of his jersey with a number of solid color contrasting with the color of the shirt.

b. Each number must be not less than ¾" in width and not less than 6" in height on both front and back. Each player shall have his surname affixed to the back of his game jersey in letters at least 2" in height.

c. The home team shall wear light color jerseys with the visitors dressed in dark jerseys. For neutral court games and doubleheaders the 2nd team named in the official schedule shall be regarded as the home team and shall wear the light colored jerseys.

RULE NO. 4—DEFINITIONS
Section I—Basket/Backboard

A team's own basket is the ring and net through which its players try to throw the ball. The visiting team has the choice of basket for the first half.

The teams change baskets for the second half. All overtime periods are considered extensions of the 2nd half.

All parts of the backboard (front, sides, bottom and top) are considered in play when struck by the basketball except the back of the backboard which is not in play.

NOTE: (1) The basket selected by the visiting team when **first entering upon the court** shall be their basket for the first half.

Section II—Blocking

Blocking is personal contact which impedes the progress of an opponent.

Section III—Dribble

A dribble is ball movement caused by a player IN CONTROL who throws or taps the ball in the air or to the floor and then touches it once before the dribble ends. The dribble ends when the dribbler: (a) touches the ball with both hands simultaneously, or (b) permits it to come to rest while he is in contact with it, or (c) tries for goal, or (d) otherwise loses control, or when ball becomes dead.

Question (1)—Is a player dribbling while tapping the ball during a jump, or when a pass rebounds from his hand or when he fumbles or when he taps a rebound or a pass away from other players who are attempting to get it?

Answer—No, the player is not in control under these conditions.

Question (2)—Is it a dribble when a player stands still and: (a) bounces the ball; or (b) holds the ball and touches it to the floor once or more?

Answer—(a) Yes; (b) No.

Question (3)—May a dribbler alternate hands?

Answer—Yes.

Question (4)—May a player touch the ball more than once while dribbling before it touches the floor?

Answer—No.

Question (5)—May a dribbler in control step out of bounds then return to the court to continue his dribble?

Answer—No. He may not be the first to touch the ball upon returning to the court.

Section IV—Fouls

a. A personal foul is a foul which involves contact with an opponent.

b. A technical foul is a foul which does not involve contact with an opponent and can be assessed against player and against non-player who is on the bench.

c. A double foul is a situation in which two opponents commit personal or technical fouls against each other at approximately the same time.

d. Offensive foul is a foul committed by a player while he, his team or a teammate is in control of the ball.

e. A fighting or punching foul may be called during a live or dead ball situation.

f. An elbow foul may be called only if contact is made.

g. A flagrant foul requires the ejection of the fouler.

Section V—Free Throw

A free throw is the privilege given a player to score one point by an unhindered throw for goal from a position directly behind the free throw line.

Section VI—Front/Back Court

a. A team's front court consists of that part of the court between its end line and the nearer edge of the center line, including its basket and inbounds part of backboard. A team's back court consists of the entire division line and the rest of the court to include opponent's basket and inbounds part of backboard.

NOTE: (1) A ball which is in contact with a player or with the court is in the back court if either the ball or the player is touching the back court. It is in the front court if neither the ball nor the player is touching the back court.

A ball which is not in contact with a player or the court retains the same status as when it was last in contact with a player or the court.

Question—From the front court, a player passes the ball across the division line, it touches a teammate who is in the air after leaping from the back court or it touches an official in the back court. Is the ball in the back court?

Answer—Yes. The location of a player is determined by the point where his foot is touching the floor. When he is in the air from a leap, he retains the same status as when he last touched the floor as far as the boundary or the division line or the free throw line is concerned. The location of an official is determined in the same manner as that of a player. Hence, if the official is touching the back court of the team in control, he is in the back court. When the ball touches an official it is the same as touching the floor at the official's location.

b. The team on the offense must bring the ball across the center or division line within 10 seconds. No additional 10 second count is permitted in the backcourt. Exception: Kicked ball violation or punched ball violation.

NOTE: (2) Ball is considered in frontcourt once it has broken the plane of the mid-court line.

Section VII—Held Ball

Held ball occurs when two opponents have one or both hands firmly on the ball.

NOTE: (1) Held ball should not be called until both players have both hands so firmly on the ball that neither can gain sole possession without undue roughness. If a player is lying or sitting on the floor while in possession, he should have opportunity to throw the ball, but held ball should be called if there is danger of injury.

Section VIII—Pivot

A pivot takes place when a player who is holding the ball steps once or more than once in any direction with the same foot, the other foot, called the pivot foot, being kept at its point of contact with the floor.

Section IX—Traveling

Running with ball is progressing in any direction in excess of prescribed limits while holding the ball. The limits follow: (a.) A player who receives the ball while standing still may pivot, using either foot as the pivot foot. (b.)

A player who receives the ball while he is progressing or upon completion of a dribble may use a two-count rhythm in coming to a stop or in getting rid of the ball. The first count occurs:

    (1) As he receives the ball if either foot is touching the floor at the time he receives it;

    (2) As the foot touches the floor or as both feet touch the floor simultaneously after he receives the ball if both feet are off the floor when he receives it.

The second count occurs when, after the count of one, either foot touches the floor or both feet touch the floor simultaneously.

When a player comes to a stop on the count of one he may pivot and may use either foot as the pivot foot.

When a player comes to a stop on the count of two, if one foot is in advance of the other he may pivot but the rear foot only may be used as the pivot foot; however, if neither foot is in advance of the other he may use either foot as the pivot foot.

    (1) A player who receives the ball while standing still, or who comes to a legal stop while holding the ball, may lift the pivot foot or jump when he throws for goal or passes, but the ball must leave his hands before the pivot foot again touches the floor, or before either foot again-touches the floor if the player has jumped;

    (2) In starting a dribble after receiving the ball while standing still, or after coming to a legal stop, a player may not jump before the ball leaves his hands, nor may he lift the pivot from the floor before the ball leaves his hands.

    (3) A player who leaves the floor with the ball must pass or shoot before he returns to the floor. If he drops the ball while in the air he may not be the first to touch the ball.

Question (1)—Is it traveling if a player falls to the floor while holding the ball?

Answer—No. Unless he makes progress by sliding.

Question (2)—A1 jumps to throw the ball. B1 prevents the throw by placing one or both hands firmly on the ball so that (a) A1; or (b) A1 and B1 both return to the floor holding it.

Answer—Held ball. However, if A1 voluntarily drops the ball before he returns to the floor and he then touches the ball before it is touched by another player, A1 has committed a traveling violation.

Section X—Screen

A screen is legal action of a player who, without causing undue contact, delays or prevents an opponent from reaching a desired position.

Section XI—Try for Goal

A try for field goal is a player's attempt to throw the ball into his basket for a field goal. The try starts when the player begins the motion which habitually precedes the actual throw. It continues until the throwing effort ceases and he returns to a normal floor position. The term is also used to include the movement of the ball in flight until it has become dead or has been touched by a player.

Section XII—Throw-In

A throw-in is a method of putting ball in play from out of bounds in accordance with Rule No. 6. The throw-in begins when the ball is at the disposal of the team or player entitled to it and ends when the passed ball touches or is touched by an inbounds player other than the thrower in.

RULE NO. 5—SCORING AND TIMING

Section I—Scoring

a. A legal goal is made when a live ball enters the basket from above and remains in or passes through.

b. A goal from the field counts 2 points unless attempted from beyond the 3 pt. line which counts 3 points.

c. A goal from the free throw line counts one point for the thrower's team.

NOTE: (1) If a free throw attempt is unsuccessful and while the ball is in the air it is tapped into the basket by a player who has not obtained complete control of the ball with both feet touching the floor, the basket, if scored, shall count two points and shall be credited to the player tapping the ball in.

Question—A player makes a free throw in his opponent's basket. Does the point count for his opponent?

Answer—No. If the mistake is discovered before time is in, the error should be corrected and player required to make attempt at his own basket.

NOTE: (2) Goals from the field, thrown in an opponent's basket shall be credited to the opponent's score and mentioned in a footnote. Basket is credited to opponent nearest the shooter. Any field goal that, in the opinion of the officials, is intentionally scored in the wrong basket shall be disallowed.

NOTE: (3) If a discrepancy in the score cannot be resolved, the running score shall be official.

NOTE: (4) For successful 3 point field goal player must have one or both feet on the floor and be beyond 3 point line when he attempts shot. After release of ball he may land on line or in 2 point area.

NOTE: (5) A player may not assist himself to score by using the ring or backboard to lift, hold or raise himself.

Section II—Timing

a. All periods of regulation play in the NBA will be twelve minutes.

b. All overtime periods of play will be five minutes.

c. Fifteen minutes will be permitted between halves of all games.

d. Ninety seconds will be permitted between all periods and for time-outs except one 20-second time-out per half.

e. A team is permitted 30 seconds to replace a disqualified player.

NOTE: (1) The game is considered to be in the 2:00 minute part when the game clock shows 2:00 or less time remaining in the period.

NOTE: (2) The public address operator is required to announce the fact that there are two minutes remaining in regulation or overtime periods.

Section III—End of Period

a. Each period ends when time expires.

Exceptions:

(1) If a live ball is in flight, the period ends when the goal is made or missed.

(2) If a foul occurs at approximately the instant time expires for a period, the period officially ends after the free throw or throws are attempted.

NOTE: (1) No line-up of players will be permitted in conditions outlined in (2) above.

(3) If the ball is in the air when the buzzer sounds ending a period and it subsequently is touched by a defensive player, the goal, if succssful, shall count.

(4) If a time-out request is made at approximately the instant time expires for a period, the period ends and the time-out shall not be granted.

NOTE: (2) If the ball is dead and the game clock shows :00, the period has ended even though the buzzer may not have sounded.

Section IV—Tie Score—Overtime

If the score is tied at the end of the 4th period, play shall resume in 90 seconds without change of baskets for one or more periods whichever is needed to determine a winner. (See Rule 5, Sec II (d) for amount of time between overtime periods.)

Question—With score tied, a foul is committed near the expiration of time in the fourth period. If free throw is successful, should an extra period be played?

Answer—If the foul occurs before the ball becomes dead and the fourth period is ended, no extra period is played. However, if the foul occurs after the fourth period has ended, the extra period must be played whether the foul shot is made or not.

Section V—Time-Out

a. Time-out occurs and the timing instruments shall be stopped when:

(1) A foul is called.

(2) A jump ball is called.

(3) Granting of a player's request for a time-out, such request being granted only when the ball is dead or in control of the requesting player's team. The scoring team cannot stop play immediately after scoring, by calling a time-out or making a substitution. The team scored upon shall have the opportunity to put the ball in play.

(4) An unusual delay in getting the ball into play after a field goal.

(5) On all floor violations (whenever official's whistle sounds, goal tending included).

(6) Time-out for any other emergency. (Official's time.)

NOTE: (1) Officials may not use official time to permit a player to change or repair equipment.

NOTE: (2) If on a jump ball or foul shot situation a player is injured or ejected and must be removed from the game, the opposing coach selects his replacement. The injured player cannot return to the game. Exception: If the player is injured due to a flagrant foul he may reenter the game at any time and the offended player's coach may choose any player on his squad to attempt the free throw(s).

(7) During the last two minutes of the regulation game or any overtime period, a field goal is scored.

NOTE: (3) Whenever a team is granted a time-out, play shall not resume until the full 90 seconds have elapsed. Unless it is a 20-second time-out.

(8) No time-out will be charged if it is called to correct a wrong interpretation of a call and correction is sustained.

b. Time-out shall not be granted:

(1) After a score of any kind to the team that has scored.

(2) Unless the team has possession of the ball.

(3) When a player of the team not in possession is injured, until a goal is scored or the ball becomes dead or his team gains possession.

NOTE: (4) If a request for time-out is made it should be ignored. However, if an official upon receiving a time-out request, inadvertently blows his whistle, play shall be suspended and the team in possession shall put the ball into play immediately at the sideline nearest where the ball was when the time-out was called. The team in possession shall have only the time remaining of the original ten seconds in which to move the ball to front court. The 24 second clock shall remain the same.

Section VI—Twenty (20) Second Time-Out

a. Each team is entitled to one (1) 20-second time-out per half for a total of two (2) per game, including overtimes.

b. During a 20-second time-out a team may only substitute for one player. If the team calling the 20-second time-out replaces a player the opposing team may also replace one player.

c. Only one player per team may be replaced during a 20-second time-out. If two players on the same team are injured at the same time and must be replaced the coach must call a regular (90-second) time-out.

d. If a second 20-second time-out is called during a half, it automatically becomes a regular charged time-out. An overtime is considered to be an extension of the second half.

e. The official shall instruct the timer to record the 20 seconds and to inform him when the time has expired.

f. This rule may be used for any reason.

g. Players should say "20-second time-out" when requesting this time.

h. A team is not entitled to any options during the last 2 minutes of game or overtime when a 20 second time out is called.

Section VII—Time-In

a. After time has been out, the game clock shall be started when the official signals time-in; the timer is authorized to start game clock if officials neglect to signal.

b. On a free throw that is unsuccessful and the ball is to continue in play, the clock shall be started when the missed free throw is touched by any player.

c. If play is resumed by a throw-in from out of bounds, the clock shall be started when the ball touches any player within the playing area of the court.

d. Time-out during the last two minutes of regulation play or overtimes (See 5, VIII-d.). The last two minutes begin when the clock shows 2:00 minutes to play.

Section VIII—Regular Time-Outs—90 Seconds

Time-outs are considered regular unless called, "20-second time-out."

a. Each team is entitled to seven (7) charged time-outs during regulation play. Each team is limited to no more than four (4) time-outs in the fourth period and no more than three (3) time-outs in the last two minutes of regulation play. (This is in addition to one 20-second time-out per half.)

b. In overtime periods each team shall be allowed two (2) time-outs regardless of the number of time-outs called or remaining during the regulation play or previous overtimes. There is no restriction as to when a team must call its time-outs during any overtime period.

NOTE: (1) Additional time-outs may be granted at the expense of a technical foul and all privileges apply. (Exception: see Rule 12A, II)

c. Each team must take at least one time-out per period. If neither team has taken a time-out during the first five minutes of each of the four regulation periods, it shall be mandatory for the official scorer to take a time-out before the sixth minute of play is completed. Time-out is charged to the home team. If neither team has taken a second time-out before the ninth minute of play, it shall be mandatory for the official scorer to take a time-out before the tenth minute of play has elapsed. Time-out is charged to the visiting team. If one team takes two time-outs during any single period, it is not mandatory for the official scorer to take a time-out.

d. Time-out in back court: during the last two minutes of regulation play or overtimes, if a team requests a time-out after the ball is out-of-bounds or after getting the ball from a rebound or change of possession, time-out shall be granted, and upon resumption of play, they shall have the option of putting the ball into play at midcourt or at the out of bounds spot.

However, once the ball is thrown in from out-of-bounds or the ball is dribbled or passed after receiving it from a rebound or change of possession and a time-out request is granted—upon resumption of play, the ball shall be put into play at the spot nearest where the ball was when time-out was called, and the time shall remain as it was when the time-out was called.

Question—During the last two minutes of regulation play, team A attempts a field goal. The ball rebounds to the corner of team B's backcourt where B secures possession and immediately requests a timeout. Where is the ball put into play?

Answer—The team calling the time-out, upon resumption of play, shall have the **option** of putting the ball into play on that side of the court where the ball was when time-out was called or moving the ball to midcourt on that side of the court. However, if the time-out request was made immediately after a score, the team scored upon would have the **option** of putting the ball into play at the division line on either side of the court or at the endline.

NOTE: (2) In both situations, time-out is granted.

Question—A player receives the ball from a throw-in in the backcourt or from a rebound or change of possession and a time-out request is granted, where is the ball put into play after the resumption of time?

Answer—Ball is put into play, after the time-out, at the spot nearest where the ball was when time-out was called.

In the case where possession may change, with the ball still in play, the team now in possession may call a time-out without penalty.

If a regular time-out is called in the backcourt in the last two minutes of regulation play or overtimes, the team shall have the option of moving the ball to mid-court. At all other times, the ball shall be passed in from a point out-of-bounds nearest to where the ball was when the time-out was called.

NOTE: (3) The official scorer shall notify a team when it has been charged with a time-out.

e. A time-out shall not be called by the official scorer after a score of any kind, except after a free throw that is to be followed by another free throw attempt.

f. When the clock shows 2:00 remaining in regulation play or overtimes, the game is considered to be in the 2:00 minute period.

RULE NO. 6—PUTTING BALL IN PLAY—LIVE/DEAD BALL

Section I—Start of Games/Quarters and Others

a. The game and overtimes shall be started with a jump ball in the center circle.

b. The team which gains possession after the opening tap will put the ball into play at their opponent's end line to begin the fourth period. The team losing the opening tap will put the ball into play at their opponent's end line at the beginning of the second and third quarters.

NOTE: (1) In putting the ball into play, the thrower-in may run along the end line or pass it to a teammate who is also out-of-bounds at the end line—as after a score.

c. After any dead ball, play shall be resumed by a jump, a throw-in or by placing ball at the disposal of a free-thrower.

d. On any floor violation except where the ball goes out-of-bounds at the endline or when defensive goal-tending is called, the ball shall be put into play at the sideline.

e. On a violation which requires putting the ball in play in the backcourt, the official will give the ball to the offensive player as soon as he is in a position out-of-bounds and ready to accept the ball.

Section II—Live Ball

a. The ball becomes alive when:

(1) Tossed by an official on any jump ball.

NOTE: (1) Clock starts only when legally tapped. (See Rule 5)

(2) Ball is placed at the disposal of designated player for throw-in.

(3) Ball is placed at the disposal of a free-throw shooter.

Section III—Jump Balls in Center Circle

a. The ball shall be put in play in the center circle by a jump between two opponents:

(1) at the start of the game.

(2) at the start of each overtime period.

(3) double foul on ball by both involved players.

Section IV—Other Jump Balls

a. The ball shall be put in play by a jump ball at the circle which is closest to the spot where:

    (1) a held ball occurs.

    (2) a ball out of bounds caused by both teams.

    (3) a double free-throw violation occurs.

    (4) the ball lodges in a basket support.

    (5) the ball becomes dead when neither team is in control and no goal or infraction is involved.

    (6) unless both officials have conflicting possession decisions.

NOTE: (1) In (1) or (2) the jump ball shall be between the two involved players unless injury or ejection precludes one of the jumpers from participation. If injured player must leave the game, the coach of the opposing team shall select from his opponent's bench a player who will replace the injured player. The injured player will not be permitted to re-enter the game.

Section V—Restrictions Governing Jump Balls

a. Each jumper must have one, but may have both feet on or inside that half of the jumping circle which is farthest from his own basket.

b. The ball must be tapped by one or both of the players participating in jump ball after it reaches its highest point. If ball falls to floor without being tapped by at least one of the jumpers, the official off the ball shall whistle the ball dead and signal another toss.

c. Neither jumper may tap the tossed ball before it reaches its highest point.

d. Neither jumper may leave the circle until the ball has been tapped.

e. Neither jumper may catch the tossed ball nor tapped ball until such time as it has been touched by one of the eight non-jumpers, the floor, the basket or the backboard.

f. Neither jumper is permitted to tap ball more than twice on any jump ball.

g. The eight non-jumpers will remain outside the restraining circle until the ball has been tapped. Teammates may not occupy adjacent positions around the restraining circle if an opponent desires one of the positions.

Penalty for c., d., e., f., g.: Ball awarded out of bounds to opponent.

Question—During a jump ball is a jumper required to (a) face his own basket; (b) jump and attempt to tap ball?

Answer—(a) No specific facing is required, (b) No. But if neither jumper taps the ball, it must be tossed again with both jumpers being ordered to jump.

NOTE: (1) During any jump ball situation officials shall sound whistle only if an infraction that occurs benefits offending team.

Section VI—Dead Ball

a. The ball becomes dead or remains dead when:

    (1) held ball occurs or ball lodges between the basket and backboard.

    (2) time expires for a period, half or extra period.

(3) there is an unsuccessful attempt: (a) on a free throw for technical foul or (b) a free throw which is to be followed by another throw.

(4) a foul occurs.

(5) a floor violation (traveling, 3 secs, 24 secs, 10 secs, etc.) occurs or there is basket interference or a free throw violation by the thrower's team.

(6) Any goal is made in the last two minutes of the fourth quarter.

EXCEPTION: The ball does not become dead when (2), occurs after a live ball is in flight.

Question—If the ball is in flight and on its downward path on a field goal try by Team A and the period expires, does the goal count if the ball is touched by: Team A or Team B?

Answer—It is basket interference when touched by Team B. No points scored if touched by Team A.

RULE NO. 7—24-SECOND CLOCK

Section I—Definition

For the purpose of clarification the 24-second device shall be referred to as "the 24-second clock."

Section II—Starting and Stopping of 24-Second Clock

a. The 24-second clock will start when a team gains possession of the ball.

b. A team in possession of the ball must attempt a field goal within 24 seconds after gaining possession of the ball. To constitute a legal field goal attempt, the following conditions must be complied with:

(1) The ball must leave the player's hand prior to the expiration of 24 seconds.

(2) After leaving the player's hand the ball must hit the rim or a legal surface of the backboard. If it does not and the 24 seconds expires there has been a violation committed.

c. A team is considered in possession of the ball when holding, passing or dribbling.

NOTE: (1) In the case of passing or dribbling, the team is considered in possession of the ball even though the ball has been batted away but the opponent has not gained possession. No three second violation can occur under these conditions.

d. Team control ends when:

(1) there is a try for field goal.

(2) opponent gains possession.

(3) ball becomes dead.

e. If a ball is touched by a defensive player who does not gain possession of the ball, the 24-second clock shall continue to run.

f. If a defensive player causes the ball to go out of bounds, the 24-second clock is stopped and the offensive team shall, on regaining the ball for throw-in, have the unexpired time or 5 seconds, whichever is longer, to attempt a shot.

g. If during any period there are 24 seconds OR LESS left to play in the period, the 24-second clock shall not function.

NOTE: (2) If an official inadvertently blows his whistle and the 24-second clock buzzer sounds while the ball is in air, play shall be suspended and play resumed by a jump ball between any two opponents in the nearest free throw circle if shot is unsuccessful. If the shot is successful, the goal shall count and the whistle is ignored. It should be noted that even though the official blows his whistle, all provisions of the above rule apply.

h. If there is a question whether or not an attempt to score has been made within the 24 seconds allowed the final decision shall be made by the officials.

i. On a throw-in, the 24-second clock shall start when the ball touches any player on the court.

j. Any time a personal foul is called the clock is to be re-set to 24 seconds.

k. Any time a technical foul is called on the defensive team, the clock shall remain as is or be re-set to 10 seconds, whichever is greater. If the technical is called on the offensive team the 24-second clock is never re-set.

l. Whenever the 24-second clock shows 0, and the ball is dead, 24-second time is considered expired even though the horn may not have sounded.

m. On any deliberate kicked ball or punching the ball with the fist violation the 24-second clock will be re-set to 24 seconds.

Section III—Putting Ball In Play After Violation

If a team fails to attempt a shot within the time allotted, the ball shall be taken out of bounds on the side of the court nearest to the spot where the play was suspended and handed to the thrower-in.

Section IV—Resetting 24-Second Clock

An official shall have the power to reset the 24-second clock to cover any special situation that he thinks warrants such action. On all technical fouls, on the defensive team, the 24-second clock shall remain the same as when play was stopped or re-set to 10 seconds, whichever is greater. On technical fouls on the offensive team the clock is never reset.

On all violations where there is a loss of possession the clock is reset.

RULE NO. 8—OUT OF BOUNDS AND THROW-IN

Section I—Player

a. The player is out of bounds when he touches the floor or any object on or outside a boundary. For location of a player in the air his position is that from which he last touched the floor.

Section II—Ball

a. The ball is out of bounds when it touches a player who is out of bounds or any other person, the floor, or any object on, above or outside of a boundary or the supports or back of the backboard.

NOTE: (1) Any ball that rebounds or passes behind or over the backboard from any point is considered out of bounds.

Question—Ball glances off face of backboard and across boundary line, but before it touches the floor or any obstruction out of bounds it is caught by a player who is inbounds. Is the ball inbounds or out of bounds?

Answer—Inbounds.

b. The ball is caused to go out of bounds by the last player to touch it before it goes out, provided it is out of bounds because of touching something other than a player. If the ball is out of bounds because of touching a player who is on or outside a boundary, such player caused it to go out.

c. If the ball goes out of bounds and was last touched simultaneously by two opponents, both of whom are inbounds or out of bounds, or if the official is in doubt as to who last touched the ball, or if the officials disagree, play shall be resumed by a jump ball between the two involved players in the nearest restraining circle.

d. After the ball is out of bounds the official shall designate a **nearby opponent of the player who committed the violation** and he shall make the throw-in at the spot out of bounds nearest where the ball crossed the boundary.

e. After any playing court violation, the ball is to be put into play at the sideline.

Section III—The Throw-In

a. The throw-in starts when the ball is at the disposal of a player entitled to the throw-in. He shall pass it inbounds within 5 seconds from the time the throw-in starts. Until the passed ball has crossed the plane of the boundary no player shall have any part of his person over the boundary line and teammates shall not occupy adjacent positions near the boundary if an opponent desires one of the positions.

b. On out of bound plays the ball shall be put in play at the point where the ball crossed a boundary line and not from original throw-in spot.

c. After a score, field goal or free throw, the latter coming as the result of a personal foul, any player of the team not credited with the score shall put the ball into play from any point out of bounds at the end line of the court where the goal was made. He may pass the ball to a teammate behind the end line, however, the 5 second pass-in rule applies.

d. After a free throw violation by the throwing team, the throw-in is made from out of bounds at either end of the free throw line extended.

e. Any ball out of bounds in a team's front court cannot be passed into the back court. On all back-court rule violations, the ball shall be given to opposing team at center court and must be passed into the front court.

NOTE: (1) Penalty for violating this rule is loss of ball to opposing team at point of infraction.

RULE NO. 9—FREE THROW

Section I—Positions

When a free throw is awarded, an official shall take the ball to the free throw line of the offended team. After allowing reasonable time for the players to take their positions, he shall put the ball in play by placing it at the disposal of the free throw shooter. The same procedure shall be followed for each free throw of a multiple throw. During a free throw for personal foul, each of the spaces perpendicular to the end line must be occupied by an opponent of the free thrower. Teammates of the free thrower must occupy the next adjacent spaces on each side. It is not mandatory for the defensive team to occupy the third adjacent space. However, no teammates of the free thrower are permitted in these spaces. No more than three defensive team players are allowed on the free throw lanes. All other players not stationed on the free throw lanes must be at least six feet from the foul shooter and/or the free throw lanes or foul circle.

NOTE: (1) If the ball is to become dead after the last free throw, players shall not take positions along the free-throw lane.

EXAMPLE: All technical foul attempts and any fouls which will be attempted with game clock showing :00.

Section II—Shooting of Free Throw

a. The free throw or throws awarded because of a personal foul shall be attempted by the offended player. Exception: If a player is fouled and is subsequently ejected from the game, before shooting the awarded free throw(s), he must immediately leave the court and another of the four players on the court will be designated by the opposing coach to shoot such free throw(s).

NOTE: (1) If a player is fouled and injured on the same play and cannot shoot the awarded shots, the opposing coach shall select from his opponent's bench the player who will replace the injured player and this player will attempt the shot(s). The injured player will not be permitted to re-enter the game, unless such injury is a result of a flagrant foul by an opponent. If a flagrant foul is called and the offended player is unable to attempt the free throws his coach may designate any member of the squad to attempt the free throw(s).

b. A foul try, personal or technical, shall neither be legal nor count unless an official handles the ball and is also in the free throw area when foul try is attempted.

c. A player awarded 2 free throws must attempt both even though the first attempt is nullified by a violation.

Section III—Time Limit

The try for goal shall be made within 10 seconds after the ball has been placed at the disposal of the free thrower at the free throw line; this applies to each free throw.

Section IV—Next Play

After a successful free throw which is not followed by another free throw, the ball shall be put in play by a throw-in: as after a field goal if the try is successful.

EXCEPTION: After a free throw for a foul which occurs during a dead ball which immediately precedes any period, the ball shall be put into play by the team entitled to the throw-in in the period which follows. (See Rule 6, Section I (b)).

RULE NO. 10—VIOLATIONS AND PENALTIES
Section I—A Player Shall Not:

A. Violate the free throw provisions:

(1) After the ball is placed at the disposal of a free thrower, he shall throw within 10 seconds in such a way that the ball enters the basket or touches the ring before it is touched by a player.

(2) Touch the ball or basket while the ball is on or within the basket.

(3) Touch the floor on or across the free throw line or lanes.

NOTE: (1) The restriction in (3) above applies until the ball leaves the free thrower's hands, except for the free thrower who may not cross the free throw line until the ball touches the ring or backboard or the free throw ends.

(4) Disconcert the free thrower in any way once the ball has been placed at the disposal of the free-throw shooter.

(5) Deflect or catch ball before it reaches the basket or backboard.

PENALTY:

a. In (1), (2), (3), (4), (5), if violation by offense, no point can be scored. Ball is awarded out of bounds to opponents opposite free throw line extended.

b. In (1), (2), (3), (4), if violation is by defense and throw is successful, disregard violation; if throw is unsuccessful, substitute throw shall be attempted.

c. In (5), if the violation is by the defensive team the point is scored and the same player receives another free throw attempt. The additional free throw is considered a new play. This can only occur when the ball will be in play after the free throw. If it occurs on the first attempt of multiple free throws only the 1 point is awarded.

NOTE: (2)

a. If there is a violation by each team, ball becomes dead, no point can be scored, play shall be resumed by a jump ball between any two opponents in nearest free throw circle.

b. The out of bounds in "a" under Penalty and the jump ball provision in "a" above do not apply if the free throw is to be followed by another free throw or if there are free throws by both teams.

B. Cause the ball to go out of bounds.

Question—Dribbler in control steps on or outside a boundary, but does not touch the ball while he is out of bounds, returns in-bounds and continues dribbling. Is this a violation?

Answer—Yes.

C. Violate provisions of putting ball in play from out of bounds.

(1) Thrower-in shall not carry ball into the court nor fail to pass it within 5 seconds, nor touch it in the court before it has touched another player.

(2) No player shall have any part of his person over the boundary line before the ball has been passed across the line.

(3) After an official has designated a player to throw ball in, there shall be no change of player unless a time-out by either team has subsequently been called.

(4) A player shall not step or run over any boundary line while putting ball in play.

(5) If the ball enters the basket from an out of bounds throw in, a violation has occurred.

PENALTY: Loss of ball (The ball is put into play at the point of infraction).

D. Run with ball, kick it, or strike it with the fist.

NOTE: (3) Kicking the ball or blocking it with any part of a players' leg is a violation when it is a positive act; accidentally striking the ball with the foot or leg is not a violation.

E. Dribble a second time after his first dribble has ended, unless it is after he has lost control: (a) through a try for field goal at his own basket; or (b) through a bat by an opponent; or (c) through a pass or fumble which has then touched another player.

F. Violate provisions governing jump ball situations:

(1) If both teams violate the jumping rule, or if the official makes a bad toss, the toss should be repeated;

(2) If a foul is committed on any jump ball, it shall result in the loss of the ball for the offending team and the offended team shall be awarded the ball at the sideline nearest the jumping circle.

NOTE: (4) To be treated as a loose ball foul.

G. Remain for more than 3 seconds in that part of his free throw lane between the end line and extended 4 ft. (imaginary) off the court and the farther edge of the free throw line while the ball is in control of his team.

NOTE: (5) Allowance may be made for a player who, having been in the restricted area for less than 3 seconds is in the act of shooting at the end of the third second.

NOTE: (6) Three second count shall not begin until the ball is in control in the offensive team's front court.

Question—Does the 3-second restriction apply: (a) to a player who has only one foot touching the lane boundary; or (b) while the ball is dead or is in flight on a try or while the ball is loose?

Answer—(a) Yes, the line is part of the lane. (b) No, the team is not in control.

H. Be in continuous control of a ball which is in his back court for more than 10 consecutive seconds.

I. Be the first to touch a ball which he or a teammate caused to go from front court to back court while his team was in control of the ball.

EXCEPTION: This restriction does not apply if, after a jump ball in the center circle, the player who first secures control of the tapped ball is in his front court at the time he secures such control and causes the ball to go to his back court, not later than the first loss of control by him and provided it is the first time the ball is in his back court following the jump ball. Once said player establishes a positive offensive position this exception does not apply.

NOTE: (7) During a jump ball, a try for goal or a situation in which a player taps the ball away from congested area, as during rebounding, in an attempt to get the ball out where player control may be secured, the ball is not in control of either team. Hence the restriction on first touching does not apply.

Question—Player A receives pass in his front court and throws ball to his back court where ball: (a) is touched by a teammate; or (b) goes directly out of bounds; or (c) lies or bounces with all players hesitating to touch it.

Answer—Violation when touched in (a). In (b) it is a violation for going out of bounds. In (c) ball is alive so that B may secure control. If A touches ball first, it is a violation. In either case, 24 second clock continues to run and rules apply.

PENALTY: Items D. thru G. Ball becomes dead when violation occurs. Ball is awarded to opponent at out of bounds spot nearest violation.

J. Use "STICK-UM" or any similar substance.

PENALTY: Fine of $25 for first violation, doubled for each subsequent violation upon notification to Commissioner by either official.

K. Excessive and/or vigorous swinging of the elbows in a swinging motion (no contact necessary) and when a defensive player is nearby and the offensive player has the ball—is considered a violation (loss of ball).

L. If the ball enters the basket from below, a violation has occurred.

RULE NO. 11—BASKETBALL INTERFERENCE—GOAL-TENDING
Section I—A Player Shall Not:

a. Touch the ball or basket when the ball is on or within either basket.

b. Touch the ball when it is touching the cylinder having the ring as its lower base.

EXCEPTION: In a or b if a player near his own basket has his hand legally in contact with the ball, it is not a violation if his contact with the ball continues after the ball enters the cylinder, or if, in such action, he touches the basket.

NOTE: (1) Impetus factor by offensive player!

c. Touch the ball when it is not touching the cylinder but is in downward flight during a try for field goal while the entire ball is above the basket ring level and before the ball has touched the ring or the try has ended.

NOTE: (2) For goal-tending to occur, the ball, in the judgment of the official, must have a chance to score. This section is not intended to conflict with paragraph (d) or (e) of Rule 11, Section I.

d. During a field goal attempt, touch a ball after it has touched any part of the backboard above ring level whether ball is considered on its upward or downward flight.

e. During a field goal attempt, touch a ball after it has touched the backboard below ring level and while ball is on its upward flight.

f. Trap ball against face of backboard.

NOTE: (3) To be a trapped ball three elements must exist simultaneously. The hand, the ball and the backboard must all occur at the same time. A batted ball against the backboard is not a trapped ball.

NOTE: (4) Any live ball from within the playing area that is in flight is considered to be a "field goal attempt" or trying for a goal except a "tap" from a jump ball situation.

PENALTY FOR ABOVE. If violation is at the opponent's basket, offended team is awarded two points, if attempt is from the two point zone and three points if from the three point zone. The crediting of the score and subsequent procedure is the same as if the awarded score has resulted from the ball having gone through the basket except that the official shall hand the ball to a player of the team entitled to the throw-in. If violation is at a team's own basket, no points can be scored and the ball is awarded to the offended team at the out of bounds spot on the side at either end of the free throw line extended. If there is a violation by both teams, play shall be resumed by a jump ball between any two opponents in the nearest circle.

RULE NO. 12—FOULS AND PENALTIES
A. Technical Foul
Section I—Illegal Defenses

a. Illegal defenses which violate the rules and accepted guidelines set forth are not permitted in the NBA.

b. When the offensive team is in its frontcourt with the ball, no defensive player may guard an area of the court instead of guarding an opponent, unless so permitted in the guidelines.

c. When the offensive team is in the front court with the ball, a defensive player may not station himself in the 12-foot key area (inside lane) for three seconds if he is not playing an opponent adjacent to the lane and within the guidelines set forth. The three-second count starts when the offensive team is in clear control of the ball in its frontcourt.

1. Penalties for Illegal Defenses and 3 Second Defensive Lane Violation.

On the first violation, the 24-second clock is reset to 24. On the second and succeeding violations, the clock is reset to 24 and one free throw (technical) is attempted. When a violation occurs during the last 24 seconds of any period (including overtime) regardless of the number of prior offenses, one free throw is awarded for the violation. (On all violations, the ball is awarded to offended team out of bounds at the free throw line extended on either side of the court).

2. Guidelines for Defensive Coverage

a. Weak side defenders may be in a defensive position within the "outside lane" with no time limit and inside the "inside lane" for 2.9 seconds. They may enter and re-enter the "inside lane" as often as they wish.

b. When a defensive player is guarding a player who is positioned adjacent to the three-second lane, the defensive player may be in the "inside lane" area, so long as he maintains a closely guarded position. (Closely guarding is considered to be within extended arms reach).

c. An offensive player without the ball may not be double-teamed from the weak side. Only the player with the ball may be double-teamed.

d. An offensive player with or without the ball may be double-teamed on the strong side.

e. When an offensive player takes a position above the foul line, the defensive player may be positioned no further (toward the baseline) than the broken circle. Defensive player may enter and re-enter this "inside lane" as many times as he desires (2.9 seconds).

f. When an offensive player takes a position above the top of the circle, the defensive player may be no further (toward the baseline) from him than the foul line. The defensive player may enter and re-enter the "inside lane" as many times as he desires (2.9 seconds). The defensive player may station himself in either "outside lane" for as long as he desires.

g. A defensive player must follow his offensive man, switch to another man at the point where the two offensive players cross, or double-team the ball. The 2.9-second time limit on this play shall begin when the defensive player is no longer "closely guarding" a man within the guidelines as set forth.

(Failure to comply with paragraphs 1 through 7 will be adjudged an Illegal Defense).

Section II—Excessive Time-Outs

a. Requests for time out in excess of authorized number shall be granted. However, a technical foul penalty shall be assessed. A team is entitled to all regular time out privileges.

EXCEPTION: During the last two minutes of play and/or overtimes, if a team calls an excessive time out, the ball shall remain at the out-of-bounds spot where the ball was when the excessive time out was called.

Section III—Delay of Game

a. A player shall not delay the game by preventing ball from being promptly put into play such as:

(1) attempt to gain an advantage by interfering with ball after a goal.

(2) failing to immediately pass ball to the nearest official when a violation is called.

(3) bat ball away from an opponent before the player has the opportunity to in-bounds the ball.

Section IV—Substitutions

a. A substitute shall not enter the court without reporting to the scorer (standing in the 8 ft. box) and being beckoned by an official.

b. A substitute shall not enter after having been disqualified.

c. It is the responsibility of each team to have the proper number of players on the court at all times.

NOTE: (1) Penalty for failure to report to the scorer is $25 fine. No technical foul.

Section V—Basket Ring

a. Any player, who in the opinion of the officials, has deliberately hung on the basket ring shall be assessed a technical foul and a $100 fine.

Section VI—Conduct

An official may assess a technical foul without prior warning at any time.

a. Officials may penalize, without prior warning, any act of unsportsmanlike conduct by anyone seated on the bench which, in the opinion of the officials, is detrimental to the game.

b. The first infraction shall be penalized by a technical foul and a $100 fine. The second infraction shall be penalized by a technical foul with violator expelled from the game and an additional $150 fine.

NOTE: (1) Technical foul called for: delay of game, or illegal defensive alignments are not considered acts of unsportsmanlike conduct.

c. A technical foul shall be assessed for unsportsmanlike tactics such as:

(1) disrespectfully addressing an official.

(2) physically contacting an official.

(3) overt actions indicating resentment to a call.

(4) use of profanity.

(5) a coach entering onto the court without permission of an official.

NOTE: (2) Cursing or blaspheming an official shall not be considered the only cause for imposing technical fouls. Running tirade, continuous criticism or griping may be sufficient cause to assess a technical. Flagrant misconduct shall result in ejection from the game.

NOTE: (3) Assessment of technical foul shall be avoided whenever and wherever possible, but when necessary they are to be applied without delay or procrastination. Once the game is over technicals may not be called for unsportsmanlike behavior. Written report shall be submitted.

NOTE: (4) If a personal foul and a technical foul are called against the same team at the same time, the technical foul shall be attempted first.

NOTE: (5) On technical foul attempts, whether the attempt has been successful or not, the ball shall be returned to the team having possession at the time the foul was called and play shall be resumed from a point out of bounds where play ended.

NOTE: (6) A foul which occurs when the ball is dead is a technical foul and must be unsportsmanlike in order to be penalized. Exception: fighting foul.

NOTE: (7) The shooter of a technical must be in the game when the technical is called. If substitute is beckoned into game prior to the calling of a technical he is permitted to attempt the technical. If technical is called before start of game anyone noted in the scorebook as a starter may attempt the technical.

NOTE: (8) A referee may eject a player or a coach with only one technical.

Question—May a player or a coach be ejected without the assessment of a technical foul?

Answer—No, ejection calls for the assessment of a technical foul. Exception: A player may be ejected after a flagrant foul.

NOTE: (9) Only 2 technicals for unsportsmanlike conduct may be called on a player, coach, trainer. Additional unsportsmanlike behavior is to be reported by Telex immediately to the commissioner.

NOTE: (10) Eye guarding (placing hand in front of opponents eyes when guarding from the rear) is unsportsmanlike and is a technical foul.

NOTE: (11) Fighting or punching fouls (technicals) may be called on opponents. Foul tries are not attempted. All other technicals are attempted.

NOTE: (12) The deliberate act of throwing the ball or any object at an official by player, coach or trainer is a technical foul and ejection from the game.

Section VII—Fines

a. Technical foul for unsportsmanlike conduct, violators are assessed a $100 fine for the first offense, and an additional $150 for the second offense in any one given game, for a total of $250 in fines. For ejection after the first technical foul, violators are assessed a $250 fine. If a player is ejected for a punching or fighting foul he shall be fined $250.

NOTE: (1) Whether or not said player(s) are ejected, a fine not exceeding $10,000 and/or suspension may be imposed upon such player(s) by the Commissioner at his sole discretion.

b. During a fight all players not involved must remain in vicinity of their bench. Violators will be assessed a $150 fine.

c. A player, coach or assistant coach, upon being notified by an official that he has been ejected from the game, must leave the playing area IMMEDIATELY and remain in the dressing room of his team during such suspension until completion of the game. Violation of this rule shall call for an automatic fine of $500. A fine not to exceed $10,000 and possible forfeiture of the game may be imposed for any violation of this rule.

d. Any player who in the opinion of the officials has deliberately hung on the basket shall be assessed a technical foul and a fine of $100.

e. Penalty for the use of "stickum" is a fine of $25 for the first violation, doubled for each subsequent violation.

f. Any player who fails to properly report to the scorer (Rule 3, V a.) shall be subject to a $25 fine on recommendation of the official scorer.

g. At half-time and the end of each game, the coach and his players are to leave the court and go directly to their dressing room, without pause or delay. There is to be **absolutely** no talking to game officials.

PENALTY—$100 fine to be doubled for any additional violation.

h. Each player, when introduced prior to the start of the game, must be uniformly dressed.

PENALTY—$100 fine.

i. A $250 fine shall be assessed to any player(s) hanging on the rim during pre-game warm-up. Officials shall be present during warm-up to observe violations.

j. Any player who is guilty of contact with the rim or backboard which causes the backboard to shatter is ejected from the game. (See Comment on Rules—I Guides for Administration and Application of the Rules.)

k. If a flagrant foul is called it must be reported to the commissioner by Telex.

B. PERSONAL FOUL

Section I—Types

a. A player shall not hold, push, charge into, impede the progress of an opponent by extended arm, knee or by bending the body into a position that is not normal.

b. Contact caused by a defensive player approaching the ball holder from the rear is a form of pushing or holding.

c. Excessive use of elbows (2 shots if contact is made by elbows).

NOTE: (1) A defensive player is not permitted to retain hand contact with an offensive player when the player is in his "sights."

Hand checking will be eliminated by rigid enforcement of this rule by both officials. The illegal use of hands will not be permitted.

NOTE (2) A player who pushes or shoves another player into a third player is considered to be the fouler and is penalized accordingly.

Section II—By Dribbler

A dribbler shall not charge into nor contact an opponent in his path nor attempt to dribble between two opponents or between an opponent and a boundary, unless the space is such as to provide a reasonable chance for him to go through without contact. If a dribbler, without contact, passes an opponent sufficiently to have head and shoulders in advance of him, the greater responsibility for subsequent contact is on the opponent. If a dribbler in his progress has established a straight line path, he may not be crowded out of that path but, if an opponent is able legally to establish a defensive position in that path, the dribbler must avoid contact by changing direction or ending his dribble. After an official blows his whistle, for a foul, a player may not legally dribble again.

Section III—By Screening

a. A player who screens shall not: (1) when he is behind a stationary opponent, take a position closer than a normal step from him; (2) when he assumes a position at the side or in front of a stationary opponent, make contact with him; (3) take a position so close to a moving opponent that this opponent cannot avoid contact by stopping or changing direction. In (3) the speed of the player to be screened will determine where the screener may take his stationary position. This position will vary and may be one to two normal steps or strides from his opponent. (4) **Move after assuming his screening position, except in the same direction and path of his opponent.**

b. If the screener violates any of these provisions and contact results, he has committed a personal foul.

1. Penalties for Sections I, II, III

Offender is charged with one foul and if it is his sixth personal foul he is disqualified. Offended player is awarded one free throw providing it is not an offensive foul. A second free throw shall be awarded if the foul is:

a. Flagrant (fouls are to be attempted whether the ball is dead, in possession or loose).

b. Against a field goal shooter whose attempt was not successful.

c. Swinging of elbows (contact must be made. Fouls are to be attempted whether the ball is dead, in possession or loose).

d. Committed by a player whose team has exceeded the limit for team fouls per quarter. (See 2 below.)

e. Committed by a defensive player before ball is thrown in from out of bounds.

f. Against any offensive player who has a clear path to the basket thereby being deprived of the opportunity of scoring.

g. Undercutting an opponent.

NOTE: (1) If a player is fouled and is subsequently ejected from the game before shooting the awarded free throw(s), he must immediately leave the court and another of the four players on the floor will be designated by the opposing coach to shoot such free throw(s).

NOTE: (2) When a foul is committed by an opponent of a player who as part of a continuous motion which started before the foul occurred, succeeds in making a goal, the goal shall count even if the ball leaves the player's hands after the whistle blows. The player must, in the opinion of the officials be throwing for a goal or starting an effort at the time the foul occurs. The goal does not count if the time expires before the ball leaves the player's hand.

h. When ball is being inbounded, in the front court, any defensive team foul is 2 shots if foul occurs before ball is released.

2. Free Throw Penalty Situations

a. Each team shall be limited to four team fouls per quarter. Team fouls charged to a team in excess of four will be penalized by an additional free throw except as hereinafter provided.

(1) The first four team fouls committed by a team in each quarter—no shots will be taken—the opponents shall put the ball into play at the sideline nearest where the foul occurred. (Not closer to end-line than foul line extended.) The first three team fouls committed each over-time period—the ball shall be put into play in the same manner as in the first four quarters. Shooting, elbowing, flagrant and fighting (punching) fouls will carry their own penalties and are included in the team totals.

(2) During each over-time period the limitation shall be three personal fouls per team with an additional free throw for each foul in excess of three.

(3) If a team has not committed its quota of four team fouls during the first ten minutes of each quarter or its three team fouls in the first three minutes of any overtime period it shall be permitted to incur one team foul during the last two minutes of each regular quarter and the last two minutes of any overtime period without penalty.

(4) On all 2 shot foul attempts no additional free throws are awarded in the penalty stage for fouls such as: flagrant swinging elbow, unsuccessful field goal or common foul prior to ball being passed in to front court.

(5) If the foul committed by a player calls for a single free throw after a successful field goal, no additional free throw is allowed if first foul attempt is missed.

NOTE: (1) The highest number of points that may be scored by the same team in one play is three. Exception: On a successful 3 point field goal 4 points may be scored.

NOTE: (2) Penalty free throws must be attempted by the player who attempted the original free throws.

Section IV—Double Fouls

a. On all double fouls, personal or technical, no free throws are attempted. Where double fouls are personal fouls a personal foul is charged to each player but not to team totals.

NOTE: (1) If the double foul is "on" the ball, play resumes with a jump ball between the involved players at the center jump ball circle. There can be no scoring in this situation.

NOTE: (2) If the double foul is "off" the ball, the team that had possession of the ball at the time of the call retains possession. Play is resumed at a point out of bounds nearest where the play was interrupted and the 24-second clock is reset to 24 seconds.

NOTE: (3) If the ball is in the air when a double off the ball foul occurs and the field goal is unsuccessful, there will be a jump ball at the nearest free throw circle between the two players involved. If the goal is successful, the team that has been scored upon will put the ball into play at the end line, as after any score.

Section V—Offensive Fouls

All personal fouls by players of the offensive team shall be penalized as follows: Personal foul charged against the offensive player, ball awarded to the opponent out of bounds at a point nearest to where foul occurred. Official must handle ball. No charge is made to team total.

Exception: If player is playing with 6 personal fouls, because all other players have fouled out, all fouls including offensive fouls will be considered team fouls.

Section VI—Loose Ball Fouls

A personal foul committed while the ball is in the air for a shot or during rebounding and where there is no ball possession will be treated in the following manner: The offending team will be charged with a team foul, the offending player with a personal foul, no shot will be taken and the team fouled will retain possession. All other loose balls will be treated in a similar manner. If such foul occurs during a penalty situation all shots that apply on the personal will be attempted.

NOTE: (1) When a "loose ball" foul is called against the defensive team that is then followed by a successful field goal (or successful foul try), the foul shot will be attempted, allowing for the 3 point or 4 point play. This applies regardless which offensive player is fouled. If a foul is called against the offensive team during this type of situation, the original rule applies (no shot and possession).

Section VII—Fighting Fouls

A foul called against a player for punching or fighting is to be charged as a team foul and a personal foul where only one player is involved. However, the penalty situation does not apply and whether the foul try is made or missed, the ball shall be given to the team shooting the attempt at mid-court. If **two players** are involved the fouls are technical and no shots will be attempted as in any other double foul situation. It is the official's decision whether or not the offending player or players shall be ejected. Whether or not said player or players are ejected, a fine not exceeding $10,000 and/or suspension may be imposed upon such player(s) by the Commissioner at his sole discretion. (See Rule 12A—Section VII—page 33.)

NOTE: (1) This rule applies whether the play is in progress or ball is dead.

NOTE: (2) In the case where one punching foul is followed by another, all aspects of the rule are applied in both cases, and the team last offended is awarded possession.

Section VIII—Away From Play Foul

During the last two minutes of the game, when ball is in play, and any overtime period, all deliberate defensive fouls away from the play, except loose ball fouls will be treated as follows:

The foul is charged to the player and the team but is treated as a technical, with no fine. Anyone in the game may attempt the free throw and the ball remains in the possession of the offended team.

Question—During the last two minutes of the fourth period, player A1 is out of bounds and attempting to inbounds the ball. Player B1 reaches across the out-of-bounds line and fouls player A1. How is this treated?

Answer—This is considered a deliberate away-from-the-play foul, and is a one (1) shot foul attempt, which is treated as a technical. (If this occurred during the game, at a time other than the last two minutes of the fourth period or overtime, it would be a two-shot foul attempt.)

COMMENTS ON THE RULES
I. GUIDES FOR ADMINISTRATION AND APPLICATION OF THE RULES

Each official should have a definite and clear conception of his overall responsibility to include the intent and purpose of each rule. If all officials possess the same conception there will be a guaranteed uniformity in the administration of all contests.

The restrictions placed upon the player by the rules are intended to create a balance of play; equal opportunity for the defense and the offense; to provide reasonable safety and protection; and to emphasize cleverness and skill without unduly limiting freedom of action of player or team.

The primary purpose of penalties is to compensate a player who has been placed at a disadvantage through an illegal act of an opponent. A secondary purpose is to restrain players from committing acts which, if ignored, might lead to roughness even though they do not affect the immediate play. To implement this philosophy, many of the rules are written in general terms while the need for the rule may have been created by specific play situations. This practice eliminates the necessity for many additional rules and provides the officials the latitude and authority to adapt application of the rules to fit conditions of play in any particular game.

II. BASIC PRINCIPLES

A. CONTACT SITUATIONS

1. Incidental Contact:

a. The mere fact that contact occurs does not necessarily constitute a foul. Contact which is incidental to an effort by a player to play an opponent, reach a loose ball, or perform normal defensive or offensive movements, should not be considered illegal. If, however, a player attempts to play an opponent from a position where he has no reasonable chance to perform without making contact with his opponent, the responsibility is on the player in this position.

2. Guarding an Opponent.

In all guarding situations, a player is entitled to any spot on the court which he desires provided he gets to that spot first and without contact with an opponent.

a. In most guarding situations, the guard must be facing his opponent at the moment he assumes a guarding position after which no particular facing is required.

b. A player may continue to move after gaining a guarding position in the path of an opponent provided he is not moving directly or obliquely toward his opponent when contact occurs. A player is never permitted to move into the path of an opponent after the opponent has jumped into the air.

c. A player who extends an arm, shoulder, hip or leg into the path of an opponent and thereby causes contact is not considered to have a legal position in the path of an opponent.

d. A player is entitled to an erect (vertical) position even to the extent of holding his arms above his shoulders, as in post play or when double teaming in pressing tactics.

e. A player is not required to maintain any specific distance from an opponent.

f. Any player who conforms to the above is absolved from responsibility for any contact by an opponent which may dislodge or tend to dislodge such player from the position which he has attained and is maintaining legally. If contact occurs, the official must decide whether the contact is incidental or a foul has been committed.

The following are the usual situations to which the foregoing principles apply:

a. Guarding a player with the ball.
b. Guarding a player who is trying for goal.
c. Switching to a player with the ball.
d. Guarding a dribbler.
e. Guarding a player without the ball.
f. Guarding a post player with or without the ball.
g. Guarding a rebounder.

3. Screening.

When a player screens in front or at the side of a stationary opponent, he may be as close as he desires providing he does not make contact. His opponent can see him and, therefore, is expected to detour around the screen.

If he screens behind a stationary opponent, the opponent must be able to take a normal step backward without contact. Because the opponent is not expected to see a screener behind him, the player screened is given latitude of movement.

To screen a moving opponent, the player must stop soon enough to permit his opponent to stop or change direction. The distance between the player screening and his opponent will depend upon the speed at which the players are moving.

If two opponents are moving in the same direction and path, the player who is behind is responsible for contact. The player in front may stop or slow his pace, but he may not move backward or sidewards into his opponent. The player in front may or may not have the ball. This situation assumes the two players have been moving in identically the same direction and path before contact.

4. The Dribble.

If the dribbler's path is blocked, he is expected to pass or shoot; that is, he should not try to dribble by an opponent unless there is a reasonable chance of getting by without contact.

B. THE ACT OF TRYING FOR GOAL

A player is trying for goal when he has the ball and (in the judgment of the official) is throwing, or attempting to throw for goal. It is not essential that the ball leave the player's hand. His arm might be held so that he cannot throw yet he may be making an attempt. He is thus deprived of his opportunity to score, and is entitled to two free throws.

If a player is fouled when tapping a tossed ball or a rebound toward or into the basket, he is not considered to be "trying for goal." If a live ball is in flight when time expires, the goal, if made, shall count.

C. FOULS: FLAGRANT–UNSPORTSMANLIKE

To be unsportsmanlike is to act in a manner unbecoming to the image of professional basketball. It consists of acts of deceit, such as accepting a personal foul charge which should be credited to a teammate or willfully accepting a free throw which belongs to a teammate, disrespect of officials, vulgarity such as the use of profanity. The penalty for acts of unsportsmanlike conduct is a technical foul. Repeated unsportsmanlike acts shall result in expulsion from the game and a total of $250 in fines.

A flagrant foul is defined as attempting to hurt an opponent and involves violent or savage contact such as kicking, kneeing or running under a player while this player is in the air as the result of attempting a shot or otherwise. A flagrant foul always carries a penalty of two free throws, is charged as a personal foul and a team foul. The shots are attempted whether the ball is in possession or loose. The player is ejected. A fine not exceeding $10,000 and/or suspension may be imposed upon such player(s) by the Commissioner at his sole discretion.

If the offended player is unable to shoot the foul (flagrant) his coach may choose any player on or off the floor to attempt the foul shots.

D. ILLEGAL DEFENSIVE ALIGNMENTS

The term Illegal Defense has replaced Zone Defense in NBA usage. The rule now in place, supported by guidelines, defines approved coverage by defensive players and teams. Violations of these rules and guidelines will be noted as illegal defense.

E. CHARGING-BLOCKING

A player is never permitted to move into the path of an opponent who has become airborne.

If contact occurs on this play, and it is anything but negligible and/or incidental, the personal is charged to the player who moved into the airborne player's path.

The opposite is also true. If an airborne player causes contact with a **stationary** opponent, and it be anything but negligible and/or incidental, the personal is charged to the airborne player.

On a drive-in shot, if the defensive player has established his defending position **legally** and the offensive player (the shooter) causes contact either prior to the release of the ball or immediately after release of the ball, the personal is on the shooter–an offensive foul.

In this type of play situation–where the shooter is responsible for contact –no points can be scored and the goal, if successful, is wiped out. This interpretation is consistent with the one that protects the shooter prior to his release of the ball while in a "shooting motion" as well as protecting him after release–until he "regains a normal playing position."

With this interpretation, not only is the defensive player held responsible for his position and movement before and after release of the ball on an attempted shot—but the offensive player is held responsible for his position and movement as well. Consistency on this play places neither player at a disadvantage nor accords him an undue advantage. Both are equally responsible for their position and movement that precedes and follows release of the ball on an attempted shot. Of course, if the personal is on the defensive player, it is a "shooting" foul and if on the offensive player, it is an offensive foul, and again—the goal, if successful, is wiped out.

In summary, the mere fact that contact occurs on this play or any other similar play, does not mean that a personal foul has been committed. The officials must decide whether the contact is negligible and/or incidental, judging each situation separately. In judging this play, the officials must be aware that if either player has been placed at a disadvantage by the contact that has occurred, then a personal foul should be called on the responsible player. A defensive player may not submarine an offensive player at any time. A player taking a charge may protect himself but may not submarine an opponent.

NOTE: (1) When an offensive player is driving to the basket a defensive player will not benefit for the setting of a block directly under the basket with no intent to play defense. The official will permit the play to continue unless it is a blocking foul.

F. GAME CANCELLATION

For the purpose of game cancellation, the officials' jurisdiction begins with the opening tipoff. Prior to this, it shall be the decision of the home management whether or not playing conditions are such to warrant postponement.

However, once the game begins, if because of extremely hazardous playing conditions the question arises whether or not the game should be cancelled, the lead official shall see that EVERY effort is made to continue the game before making the decision to terminate it.

G. PHYSICAL CONTACT—SUSPENSION

"Any player or coach guilty of intentional physical contact with an official, shall automatically be suspended without pay for one game. A fine and/or longer period of suspension will result if circumstances so dictate."

H. PROTEST

In order to protest against or appeal from the result of a game, notice thereof must be given to the Commissioner within forty-eight (48) hours after the conclusion of said game, by telegram, stating therein the grounds for such protest. No protest may be filed in connection with any game played during the regular season after midnight of the day of the last game of the regular schedule. A protest in connection with a playoff game must be filed not later than midnight of the day of the game protested. A game may be protested only by a Governor, Alternate Governor or Head Coach. The right of protest shall inure not only to the immediately allegedly aggrieved contestants, but to any other member who can show an interest in the grounds of protest and the results that might be attained if the protest were allowed. Each telegram of protest shall be immediately confirmed by letter and no protest shall be valid unless the letter of confirmation is accompanied by a check in the sum of $1,500 payable to the Association. If the member filing the protest prevails, the $1,500 is to be refunded. If the member does not prevail, the $1,500 is to be forfeited and retained in the Association treasury.

If during the course of a game, a Governor, Alternate Governor, Head Coach or other representative of a member states to an official, the scorer's table or the press or broadcast announcers that the result of such game is, will, or may be protested, then such member shall immediately become obligated to forward to the Commissioner $500 of the Protest Fee. If a notice of protest is thereafter filed, the letter of confirmation shall be accompanied by a check in the sum of the remaining $1,000 of the Protest Fee. If no notice of protest and confirming letter are subsequently filed within the applicable period stated above, such $500 shall not be refunded to such member.

Upon receipt of a protest, the Commissioner shall at once notify the member operating the opposing team in the game protested and require both of said members within five (5) days to file with him such evidence as he may desire bearing upon the issue. The Commissioner shall decide the question raised within five (5) days after receipt of such evidence.

I. SHATTERING BACKBOARDS

Any player whose contact with the rim or backboard causes the backboard to shatter will be penalized in the following manner:

Pre-game warm-up: $250 fine and suspended from game.

During game: $100 fine, technical foul and suspension for the remainder of the game and next regularly-scheduled game.

Halftime warm-up: $250 fine and suspension for the remainder of the game and next regularly-scheduled game.

The Commissioner will review all actions and plays involved in shattering backboards.

J. PLAYER/TEAM CONDUCT AND DRESS

1. Each player when introduced, prior to the game, must be uniformly dressed.

2. Players, coaches and trainers are to stand and line up in a dignified posture along the sidelines or on the foul line during the playing of the National Anthem.

3. Coaches and assistant coaches must wear a sport coat or suit coat.

4. While playing, players must keep their shirts tucked into their uniform pants.

MAJOR 1981-82 RULE CHANGES—CLARIFICATIONS

1. Rule 1, Section II, Equipment, page 9 (adoption of a moveable basketball ring—type approved by NBA).

2. Rule 3, Section V, Substitutes, page 5 (substitutes must report to area in front of scorer (8 ft. box) in order to be beckoned into game).

3. Rule 12, A, Section I, Illegal Defense, page 31 (new rules and guidelines for Illegal Defensive Alignments).

4. Rule 12, B, 1, Penalties, page 34 (Elimination of back court foul as a 2 shot foul).

5. Rule 12, B, 1, Penalties, page 35 (Elimination of penalty free throws on unsuccessful field goal, in penalty stage).

6. Rule 12, B, 2(5), page 36 (Elimination of penalty free throws on successful field goal, in penalty stage).

7. Rule 6, Section I, e, page 23—Putting the ball in play (on violation which requires putting ball in play in the backcourt only, the techniques will be: "The official will give the ball to the offensive player as soon as he is in a position out of bounds and ready to accept the ball").

Official Signals

TECHNICAL FOUL	CANCEL SCORE CANCEL PLAY	3 SECOND RULE INFRACTION	24-SECOND VIOLATION

Form T	Shift arms across body	Fingers sidewards	Tap head

TRAVELLING	JUMP BALL	BASKET INTERFERENCE	GOAL TENDING TWO POINTS
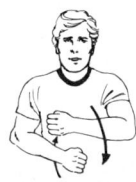			
Rotate fists	Thumbs up	Rotate finger	"Flag" from wrist

FOR 3 PT. FIELD GOAL		ILLEGAL DRIBBLE	DIRECTION OF PLAY
	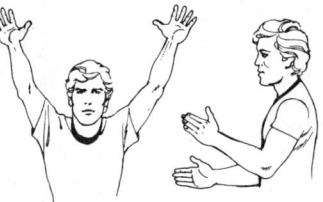		
Official will raise one arm on attempt	If goal is successful raise the other arm.	Patting motion	Point-Direction call team color

Official Signals

TIME IN — Chop with hand or finger

TIME-OUT — Open palm

PERSONAL FOUL — Clenched fist

TO DESIGNATE OFFENDER — Hold up number of player

LOOSE BALL FOUL — Extend arms to shoulder level

ILLEGAL USE OF HANDS — Signal foul: strike wrist

HOLDING — Signal foul: grasp wrist

PUSHING — Signal foul: imitate push

CHARGING — Clenched fist striking

DOUBLE FOUL — Waving clenched fists

BLOCKING — Hands on hips

NOTES

NOTES

NOTES

NOTES

NOTES

NOTES